AF512977

Expert Computer Course (ECC)

made simple

by

Satish Jain

B.Sc., B.E.(IISc), M.E.(IISc), M.Tech.(IIT Kanpur),
Ex Professor of Information Technology,
Institute of Information Technology & Management
GGS Indraprastha University, Delhi.

M. Geetha

B. Com., Dipl. Computer Science

bpb

www.bpbonline.com

FIRST EDITION 2017

REPRINT 2026

ISBN: 978-81-8333-507-2

Distributors:

BPB PUBLICATIONS
20, Ansari Road, Darya Ganj
New Delhi-110002
Ph: 23254990/23254991

MICRO MEDIA
Shop No. 5, Mahendra Chambers,
150 DN Rd. Next to Capital Cinema,
V.T. (C.S.T.) Station, MUMBAI-400 001
Ph: 22078296/22078297

DECCAN AGENCIES
4-3-329, Bank Street,
Hyderabad-500195
Ph: 24756967/24756400

BPB BOOK CENTRE
376 Old Lajpat Rai Market,
Delhi-110006
Ph: 23861747

Published by Manish Jain for BPB Publications, 20 Ansari Road, Darya Ganj, New Delhi-110002 and Printed by him at Manipal Technologies Limited, Manipal

www.bpbonline.com

Dedicated to

Lord Ganesha, Lord Murgan, Sri Raja Rajeshwari and *Sri Sai Baba*

whose blessings overcome all hurdles in life

PREFACE

The objective of writing this book is to cover the entire syllabus of the "Expert Computer Course (ECC)" designed by NIELIT (DOEACC), in simple English and user friendly style.

The book is divided into Sixteen chapters. Each chapter covers specific topic as per the syllabus outlined by NIELIT (DOEACC). Each chapters contains diagrams and screens are used to explain each concept clearly. It is hoped, that a person with some understanding of elementary English language would be able to use this book and become an expert in the IT field.

The book begins with the concepts of Computer and its Components. After understanding the basic concepts of computers in the first chapter, the next Chapter explains the Operating system and Linux Operating systems. It also helps the users to understand the concept of files and directory management.

Chapter Three will help the reader to understand the basic computer hardware such as Electricity and power systems of CPUs and motherboards.

Chapter Four will help the reader to understand the elements of MS Word along the various tools and ample number of screens.

Chapter Five explains the concept of Spreadsheet (MS Excel).

Chapter Six will help the reader to use PowerPoint in creating Presentations.

Chapter Seven will help the reader to understand the concept of DBMS (MS Access). This chapter explains DMBS in such a manner that students of all streams can understand the subject matter very easily.

Chapter Eight deals with the basic concepts of Cyber Security. It discusses how to protect networks, programs and data from Internet attack and damage from unauthorized access.

Chapter Nine contains PC Maintenance, Security & Troubleshooting.

Chapter Ten discusses with Networking & Troubleshooting. It will help the reader to make tech-savvy through LAN, WAN and concept of Internet.

Chapter Eleven discusses the Latest Trends in IECT & e-governance.

Chapter Twelve will help the reader to understand the applications of digital financial services in India along with various schemes.

Chapter Thirteen will help the reader to understand the E-Mail concepts and their applications.

Chapter Fourteen discusses the basic components of Multimedia.

Chapter Fifteen discusses the basic of HTML Programming.

Chapter Sixteen will help the reader to understand the varieties of Skills such as 'people skills', 'inter-personal skills', 'social skills' or 'transferable skills'.

A set of questions papers solved and unsolved are also given.

We shall feel obliged to the readers if they send us their critical opinion regarding the presentation, readability and coverage in this book and request them to mail their suggestions, if any, to improve the subject matter. The suggestions may be e-mailed to *bpbpublications@gmail.com*.

1st March, 2017

Authors

Creativity is thinking up new things,
Innovation is doing new things.

—THEODORE LEVITT

Expert Computer Course (ECC)

Detailed Syllabus

Module 1 – Introduction to Computer & Basic Concepts:

- **What is Computer:** Characteristics of Computer System, Basic Applications of Computer; Processing Unit, Keyboard, mouse and VDU, Other Input devices, Other Output devices, Computer Memory;
- **Concept of Hardware and Software:** Hardware, Software, Application Software, Systems software, Programming Languages; Representation of Data/Information; Concept of Data processing;

Module 2 – Operating System:

- **Basics of Operating System:** Operating system, Basics of popular operating system (LINUX, WINDOWS);
- **The User Interface:** Task Bar, Icons, Start Menu, Running an Application-notepad, paint etc..,
- **Operating System Simple Setting:** Changing System Date And Time, Changing Display Properties, To Add Or Remove A Windows Component, Changing Mouse Properties, Adding and removing Printers;
- **File and Directory Management:** Types of files, What is a file, Naming conventions, File Extensions, File Pathway, Windows Explorer window, Viewing files, File property dialogue box, Explain file size (bytes, kilo, mega, giga,tera) and abbreviations used, Create a Folder, Move a file (multiple files) into a folder, Delete files and folders, Recovering deleted files, Renaming files, Searching for files, Creating and deleting shortcuts on desktop, How programs may save files in specific location by default. How to find where file is being saved;
- **Desktop:** exploring the desktop, cleaning the desktop;
- **Keep Software updated:** how to set automatic updates for windows operating system.

Module 3 – Basic Computer Hardware:

- Introduction,
- Getting started with PC hardware support, Electricity and power systems, CPU and motherboards,
- Basic Input/Output System, Memory systems, Bus structures, color combination of network cable Expansion cards, Ports, connectors, and cables,
- Data storage devices,
- Video and multimedia input/out devices,
- Printers, Portable computers and devices, connecting computers,

Module 4 – Word Processing:

- **Word Processing Basics:** Opening Word Processing Package, Menu Bar, Using The Help, Using The Icons Below Menu Bar;
- **Opening and Closing Documents:** Opening Documents, Save and Save as, Page Setup, Print Preview, Printing of Documents;
- **Text Creation and Manipulation:** Document Creation, Editing Text, Text Selection, Cut, Copy and Paste, Spell check, Thesaurus;
- **Formatting the Text:** Font and Size selection, Alignment of Text, Paragraph Indenting, Bullets and Numbering, Changing case;
- **Formatting a Document:** Set page margin, paragraphs and sections within a document, Adjust indents and hanging indents;
- **Table Manipulation:** Draw Table, Changing cell width and height, Alignment of Text in cell, Delete / Insertion of row and column Border and shading, Table Formula;
- **Inserting Graphic Elements:** Insert a clip art picture, insert symbols and special characters, adding a watermark; Using word art; adding a drop cap;
- **Mail Merge:** Using mail merge; printing mailing labels; merging for sending e-mails using outlook.
- Use of local language
- Macros

Module 5 – Spreadsheet:

- **Elements of Electronic Spread Sheet:** Opening of Spread Sheet, Addressing of Cells, Printing of Spread Sheet, Saving Workbooks;
- **Manipulation of Cells:** Entering Text, Numbers and Dates, Creating Text, Number and Date Series, Editing Worksheet Data, Inserting and Deleting Rows, Column, Changing Cell Height and Width;
- **Formulas and Function:** Using Formulas, Function, basic mathematical operators, using AutoSum etc., using formulas with multiple cell references, finding the right function, relative and absolute cell references, fixing formula errors; Charts: learning about charts, creating charts; Working with graphics; Clip Art; SmartArt.
- Use of Pivot Table and Pivot Chart.

Module 6 – Presentation:

- **Basic Concepts of presentation:** Using PowerPoint, Opening A Power Point Presentation, Saving A Presentation;
- **Creation of Presentation:** Creating a Presentation Using a Template, Creating a Blank Presentation, Entering and Editing Text, Inserting And Deleting Slides in a Presentation;
- **Preparation of Slides:** Inserting Word Table or An Excel Worksheet, Adding Clip Art Pictures, Inserting Other Objects, Resizing and Scaling an Object;
- **Presentation of Slides:** Viewing A Presentation, Choosing a Set Up for Presentation, Printing Slides And Handouts;
- **Slide Show:** Running a Slide Show, Transition and Slide Timings, Automating a Slide Show.

Module 7 – Database Management System:

- Introduction to the concepts of database management system; Creating a database;
- **Creating a Table:** Concepts of field, field types; entering data in a table, preview and print a table, changing row and column height; closing and opening of table, sorting of table, finding and replacing texts; using queries wizard; creating report from tables / queries from report wizard, modifying a report, printing of report; creating a form using wizard, entry in the forms; basic of formatting of forms and reports.

Module 8 – Cyber Security:

- **Cyber Security:** Basic concepts of threats, vulnerabilities, controls; risk; confidentiality, integrity, availability; security policies; security mechanisms; Data Security and protection: concept, creating strong passwords; how to stay safe when surfing on Internet: "In private Browsing", identifying secure website, clear cookies;
- **Know how to identify a secure web site:** https, lock symbol; Security Considerations: Know about security threats from web sites like: viruses, worms, Trojan horses, spyware. Understand the term malware; Netiquettes, DOS, DDOS;
- **Netiquettes; Security Considerations:** Be aware of the possibility of receiving fraudulent and unsolicited e-mail; phishing, Recognize attempted phishing;
- Basics of Software Licensing
- Overview and understanding of IT Act 2000.

Module 9 – PC Maintenance, Security and Troubleshooting:

- **Computer Maintenance and Security:** Overview of Computer Maintenance and Security, Inbuilt PC Security, tools, Securing documents, Antivirus, Upgrading Operating System and Application software. security; Cleaning the monitor, keyboard, CPU;
- **Deleting unnecessary programs and files:** Disk cleanup, deleting toolbars; defrag hard drive;
- **Computer Maintenance Programs:** Ccleaner, myDefrag, Spinrite etc.;
- **Basic troubleshooting:** restart computer, checking cables, uninstalling a software, start windows in safe mode etc.
- Windows installation and upgrades, CPUs and motherboards, Memory systems, Expansion cards, Data storage devices, Ports, connectors, and cables, Printers and scanners, Display devices, Portable computers and devices, Networking, Security, Maintaining the PC environment.

Module 10 – Networking & Troubleshooting:

- **Basic of Computer Networks:** LAN, WAN, Wi-Fi, Broadband, Bluetooth;
- **Internet:** Concept of Internet, Applications of Internet, Connecting to the Internet, Troubleshooting; WWW, TCP/IP, DNS, Search Engine; Key web browser features, Brief about switch, router, gateway;
- **Various applications of Internet:** e-mail, information gathering, retailing etc.;
- **Methods of connecting to the Internet:** Dial up, ISDN and broadband; Brief introduction to Internet addressing, Internet protocols (TCP/IP, FTP and HTTP);
- **Define and understand the terms:** Internet Service Provider (ISP), Uniform Resource Locator (URL), hyperlink;
- Know how to identify a secure web site: https, lock symbol; Security Considerations: Know about security threats from web sites like: viruses, worms, Trojan horses, spyware.
- Using Favorites Folder, Downloading Web Pages, Printing Web Pages, Understanding URL, Set the web browser Home Page/Start Page; Bookmark a web page, Delete a bookmark, Publishing on the Web, Downloading Web Pages, Printing Web Pages; Complete a web-based from using: text boxes, drop-down menu, list boxes, check boxes, radio buttons; Understanding benefits of Search Engines and Popular Search Engines (Google, Alta Vista, Excite);
- Commerce on Internet, Impact of Internet on Society.
- Overview of use of search engines and e-mail messages;
- **Instant Messaging and Collaboration:** Using Instant messaging, Instant messaging providers, Use of Social Networking Sites viz. Facebook, Twitter etc.; Introduction to the concepts of IPv4 and IPv6 networks;
- Network troubleshooting

Module 11 – Latest Trends in IECT & e-Governance:

- **Applications of IECT:** e-governance, Multimedia and Entertainment; Project Management using IT tools & related applications
- **Introduction to Cloud Computing:** What is cloud computing, Properties & Characteristics, Service models, Deployment models; Concepts of: IaaS (Infrastructure as a Service), PaaS (Platform as a Service), SaaS (Software as a service), DaaS (Desktop as a Service).
- Introduction to Mobile Computing, its components and characteristics.
- **Digital Signature:** Definition as per ITA 2000, how digital signature works; role of certifying authorities: Digital Certificates and their uses, Certifying Authority regulation in India, Obtaining a trial version of a Digital Certificate; legal aspect covering digital signatures in India; how to use digital signatures on electronic documents.
- **e-Governance:** Definition of e-Governance, Pillars of e-Governance, Infrastructure for e-Governance, Mission Mode Projects (At least 5), Familiarization with terminology like change management, processing engineering, Govt. Processing engineering and Governance, e-Governance project life cycle, electronically delivery of services, messaging system and case study of any 5 public utility portal related with the Department (especially, public grievance redressal system, RTI, Vigilance, Department working and financial inclusion, linkage with Aadhar etc.)

Module 12 – Application of Digital Financial Services

- Why savings are needed, Why save in a bank, Banking products-ATM card, Rupay Card, Banking Instruments-Cheque, Demand Draft (DD), Currency Notes, Banking Services Delivery Channels, Know Your Customer (KYC), Opening of bank account and documents required, Types of bank accounts, Bank's services including remittances, loan, mobile banking, Overdraft, Pension etc., Types of Insurance, Pradhan Mantri Jan Dhan Yojana (PMJDY), password security and ATM withdrawal, Insurance, Social Security Schemes-Atal Pension Yojana (APY), Pradhan Mantri Suraksha Bima Yojana (PMSBY), Pradhan Mantri Jeevan Jyoti Bima Yojana (PMJJBY), Pradhan Mantri Mudra Yojana (PMMY).

Module 13 – Electronic Mail – A detailed view:

- Basics of E-mail: What is an Electronic Mail,
- Mailbox: Inbox and Outbox, Creating and Sending a new E-mail, Forwarding an E-mail message, Sorting and Searching emails, Document collaboration; instant Messaging and Collaboration: Using Instant messaging, Instant messaging providers, Netiquettes;
- Configuring mail on mobiles, creating groups, message formations, do's & don't using mobile, attachment, different between Bcc & Cc.
- **Email Protocols:** SMTP, POP3, IMAP4, MIME5; Email Clients: Netscape mail clients, Outlook Express, Web based E-mail; Email encryption.

Module 14 – Introduction to Multimedia:

- Basic concepts, Hardware requirement for multimedia computer; Textural information;
- **Components of Multimedia:** Images and their types, Animation, Digital audio, Digital Video Software for Multimedia, introduction to MS-Publisher and Photo-draw, Developing simple application and presentations using MS-Publisher.

Module 15 – HTML Programming Basics:

- Concepts of HTML page structure,
- FrontPage / Interdev
- HTML text, HTML Links, Using CSS, Using tables,
- HTML document tables,
- HTML frames,
- HTML images,

Module 16 – Soft Skills:

- **Effective communication:** features of effective communication; Communication Skills & Call Handling Skills
- **Listening skills:** Types of Listening; Tips for Effective/ Listening: Academic Listening- (lecturing), Listening to talks and Presentations, Listening to Announcements.
- Corporate culture
- CRM Concepts
- Selling Skills
- Behavioral Skills
- Vocabulary Development
- Pronunciation
- Reading
- Listening And Speaking
- Writing
- Integrated Skills
- Non-Verbal Communication

Contents

Expert Computer Course (ECC)

CHAPTER 1

Introduction to Computer & Basic Concepts

1.1 INTRODUCTION

Computer is general purpose machine designed to automatically accept and store data, manipulate them, and produce output results under the direction of a detailed step-by-step stored program of instructions. It is actually a combination of both hardware and software that transforms data into information and performs calculation. It is an electronic device used for storing and processing data, information.

1.2 WHAT IS A COMPUTER?

A computer is a digital electronic device that can perform a variety of operations according to a set of instructions called *program*. It then displays or prints the result. A computer (See Figure 1.1) is a general purpose machine that manipulates raw facts according to a set of instructions that are fed into it. A computer performs five major operations or functions irrespective of its size and make. These are:

- it accepts data or instructions as input,
- it stores data and instruction
- it processes data as per the instructions,
- it controls all operations inside a computer, and
- it gives results in the form of output.

Figure 1.1 Parts of computer system

Computers work through an interaction of hardware and software.

Now before proceeding further there are few terms that need to understood:

- **Data:** Raw facts or figure that need to be processed.
- **Information:** Meaningful data which is processed, organized and presented in an understandable form.
- **Instruction:** Command that tells computer what to do.
- **Processing:** Sequence of action taken on data to convert it into information.
- **Hardware:** The physical components of computer.
- **Program:** The instructions that tell the computer what to do, either in sequential or non-sequential manner.
- **Software:** A sequence of instructions given to computer to perform a particular task.

1.3 CLASSIFICATION OF COMPUTER

Computers are classified according to their size, basis of work and the purpose of work, which are described as follows:

On the Basis of Si e

- **Microcomputer/Microprocessor/Portable Computer:** These types of computer are widely used by single user and are small in size and cheaper (see figure 1.2).

Figure 1.2 Classification of computer on the basis of size

Types of microcomputer:

- *Desktop Computer/Personal Computer:* Input, processing, memory and output unit are self-contained, and are housed within a horizontal or vertical case called the system unit.
- *Notebook/Ultra Book/Laptop:* An extremely lightweight computer having integrated screen or keyboard, which uses flat panel technology, and can be moved from place to place. These types of computer consume less battery.
- *Handheld Computers/Palmtops:* Extremely small computer, having smaller screen and stores programs and data within the unit or on a memory card. They have no keyboard and the screen serves both an Input device and Output device.
- *Tablet Computers:* These are lighter notebook computer having a smaller screen, in which input is given either by touch screen or by pen called stylus. For example, Ipad.

- *Smart atch:* A smartwatch or Watch phone is a computerized wristwatch or a wearable computer, which offers full mobile phone feature capability thus allowing a user to make or answer phone calls, Send or receive text/Wats app messages. It is used to perform some basic tasks, such as calculations, translations, game-playing. By using a mobile operating system one can also run mobile apps on it. Smart watches can be customized according to one's need.
  Smart watches function as portable media players, thus offering a playback of FM radio, audio, and video files to the user via a Bluetooth headset. It also supports wireless technologies like Bluetooth, Wi-Fi, and GPS.
  Smart watches are used to upload data onto a computer or online to create a log of activities for analysis or sharing. It serves as full GPS watches, which displays maps, current location, and record tracks. It is also called as Fitness tracker as it tracks the daily activity of the user, including Lap times, speed display, Route tracking, Monitor heart beat rate.
  Some of the widely used smart watches are:
  - *Motorola:* Motorola Motoactv, Moto 360
  - *Samsung:* Samsung Galaxy Gear, Gear 2, Gear 2 Neo and Gear Fit, Gear Live, Gear S
  - *Apple:* Apple Watch
- *Workstation:* It is mainly used by an individual as it is faster and more capable than a personal computer. It is used by small engineering companies, architects, graphic designer who requires a faster micro-processor and a large amount of Random access memory.
- *Minicomputer:* These types of computer are smaller in size and are faster than micro computers, and it is a multi-user (multi-processing) device, supporting from 4 to about 200 users simultaneously, and are used to carry out some specific task in engineering and Computer Aided Design (CAD). Examples Digital Alpha, Sun Ultra.
- *Mainframe:* These are large, powerful, expensive computers used by organizations to connect thousands of users simultaneously. Mainframe are just below supercomputer in computer hierarchy and in some ways are more powerful than supercomputer as it supports simultaneous programs. This computer contains specialized hardware and software, for processing millions of transactions. Examples IBM 370, S/390.
- *Super Computer:* It is the fastest, powerful and the most expensive machine available today and used to carry immense amount of mathematical calculations. Super computer is used in weather forecasting, scientific simulation, nuclear research and petroleum exploration, etc.

☞ *Supercomputer channels all its po er into e ecuting a fe programs as fast as possible hereas a mainframe uses its po er to e ecute man program concurrentl .*

On the Basis of Work

- *Analog Computers:* These types of computer use continuous physical phenomena having specific magnitude such as electrical and mechanical quantities to model the problem being solved. Operations are performed on it by manipulating and processing the data. Examples: Thermometer, Speedometer etc.
- *Digital Computers:* Digital computers process information which is in a binary or two-state form, namely zero and one. Digital computers fall into ranges called microcomputers, minicomputers, mainframes and supercomputers. It can produce desired graphics, sound.
- *H brid computer Analog Digital* : This type of computer is capable of inputting and outputting data in both analog and digital form. It is basically a digital computer that accepts analog signal and convert them into digital form for processing. It offers a cost effective method of performing complex simulations.

On the Basis of area of applications

Computer are either general purpose or specific purpose.

- *General purpose computer:* These are designed to perform a wide range of tasks. They can store numerous programs, but are lack in speed and efficiency. Example: Microcomputer
- *Specific purpose computer:* These are designed to handle a specific problem or to perform a specific task. Instructions which are needed to perform the given task are permanently stored into the internal memory, so that it can perform the task on single computer.

1.3.1 Limitations of Computer

The four main limitation of computer are:

- *No IQ:* It has to be instructed each and every step, and its sequence of execution.
- *Lack of decision making po er:* It does not possess power of taking decision on its own.
- *No Heuristics:* It cannot learn from its mistakes.
- *Emotionless:* It works on the instructions given by human.

1.3.2 Characteristics of Computers

The five major characteristics of computers which have made them very useful are:

Speed

A computer is a very fast device. It can perform, in a few seconds, the amount of work that a human being can do in an entire year working round the clock. The speed of a computer is usually 2 to 4 GHz. A powerful computer is capable of performing about 10 to 40 million arithmetic calculations in a second.

Accuracy

The *accurac* of a computer is consistently high and the degree of accuracy of a particular computer depends upon its design. But for a particular computer, each and every calculation is performed with the same accuracy. For example, the computer accurately give the result of division of any number up to 10 decimal points.

Versatility

Versatility is one of the most wonderful things about computer. Multi-processing features of computer makes it quiet versatile in nature. One moment, it is preparing the results of particular examination, the next moment it is busy preparing electricity bills, and in between it may be helping an office secretary to trace an important letter in seconds.

Reliability

Computer provide very high speed accompanied by an equality high level for reliability. Thus computers never make mistakes of their own accord.

Power of Remembering

A computer can store and recall any amount of information because of its secondary storage capability. Even after several years, the information recalled will be as accurate as on the day when it was fed to the computer.

Diligence

The computer is a machine, does not suffer from the human traits of tiredness. Nor does it loses concentration even after working continuously for a long time. This characteristics is especially useful for those jobs where same tasks is done again and again. It can perform long and complex calculations with same speed and accuracy from the start till the end.

Storage Capacity

The computers have a lot of a storage devices which can store a tremendous amount of data. Data storage is essential function of the computer. Second storage devices like floppy disk can store a large amount of data permanently.

Automatic

Job can be performed without human invention.

Plug and Play

It can automatically configure new hardware and software components.

1.3.3 Basic Applications of Computer

A computer is a general purpose tool, which can do a variety of jobs. You can use a computer for different application by changing various kind of software packages.

Some common uses of a computer are shown in Figure 1.3 which are discussed below.

- **Scientific Research:** Computer was first used in scientific research. The speed and the accuracy of a computer enabled scientific analysis carried out very fast. Computers are now an integral part of teaching techniques in Universities, and research institutes. Without computers, researchers find themselves in a very difficult situation to carry out their studies.
- **Office Management:** Almost every organisation (business or non-business) are moving towards making paper-less office so that computers are widely used today.
- **Internet:** It is a network of computers in the world. You can browse through much more information than you could do in a library. That is because computers can store enormous amounts of information. You also have very fast and convenient access to information. Through E-Mail you can communicate with a person sitting thousands of miles away in seconds.
- **Books Publishing:** With desktop publishing, you can create page layout for entire books on your personal computer. Nowadays, newspapers, magazines/books are designed using DTP and printed at one place and distributed so that we can get them every morning.
- **Computers in Medicine:** You can diagnose diseases. You can learn the cures. Software is used in magnetic resonance imaging to examine the internal organs of the human body. Software is used for performing surgery. Computers are used to store patient data.
- **Mathematical Calculations:** Thanks to computers, which have computing speeds of over a million calculations per second we can perform the biggest of mathematical calculations.
- **Banks:** All financial transactions are done by computer software. They provide security, speed and convenience. The use of a computer has allowed the banks to improve many of the facilities offered by them. One can use the **ATM Automated Teller Machines** to deposit and withdraw cash 24 hours a day throughout the year.
- **Travel:** One can book air tickets or railway tickets and make hotel reservations online. It reduces the time wastage and travel time for everyone.
- **Telecommunications:** All mobile phones have software embedded in them for maintaining customer details and also sending message, audio and video through the mobile software. Now a day's Internet is available in the mobile phone itself.
- **Defence:** There is software embedded in almost every weapon. Software is used for controlling the flight and targeting in ballistic missiles. Software is used to control access to atomic bombs.
- **E-Learning:** Instead of a book it is easier to learn from E-learning software. It not only contains text but contains image and animation so it is very easy to understand every thing.
- **Examinations:** We can give online exams and get instant results. You can check your examination results online.
- **Computers in Business:** Shops and supermarkets use software, which calculate the bills. Taxes can be calculated and paid online. Accounting is done by Software is used in major stock markets. One can do trading online.
- **Entertainment:** Movies, animation films, advertisement in newspapers and TVs, etc., use computers extensively. The entertainment industry uses computer even to plan the production of movies, as well as to create various special effects.
- **Communication:** Use of **email** or **Electronic-mail**, where one can use a computer to pass long messages, reports, etc., to many persons all over the world for a very low price.

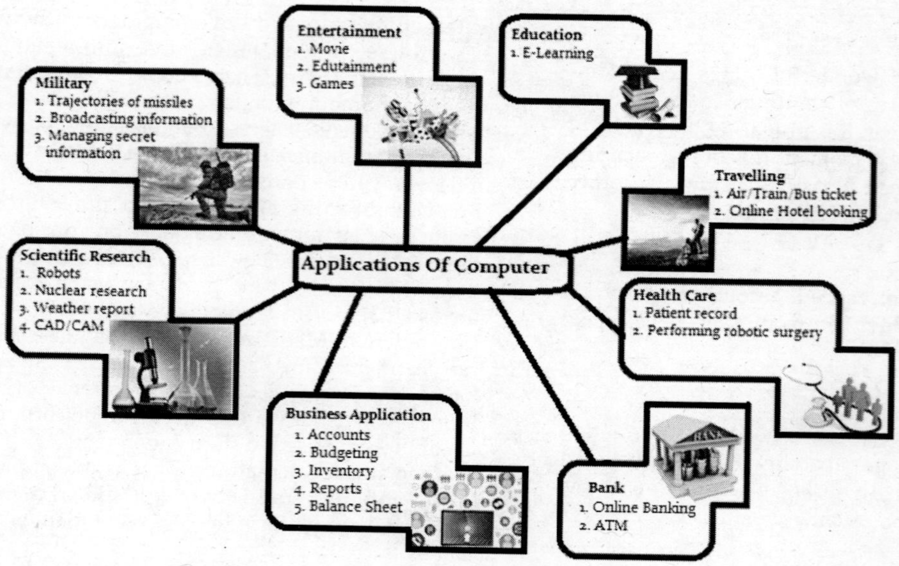

Figure 1.3 Picture showing different jobs where computer can be employed

- **Accounting:** Specialized programs, such as Tally.ERP 9, are available to handle company financial accounts and inventory management.

1.4 COMPONENTS OF A COMPUTER SYSTEM

The five major functional units of a digital computer (See Figure 1.4) are:

(a) Central Processing Unit (CPU)
(b) Input Device (Visual Display Unit(VDU), Keyboard and Mouse)
(c) Output Devices
(d) Computer Memory

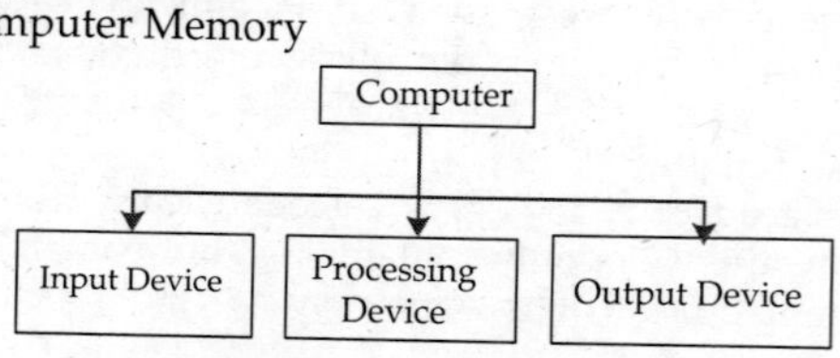

Figure 1.4 Components of Computer

1.4.1 Central Processing Unit (CPU)

The CPU is the brain of a computer. Its primary job is to run program and control the operation of all other components, such as memory, keyboard and printer.

A block diagram of the basic computer organization is shown in Figure 1.5.

The Figure shows the basic arrangement of different units of a computer. It depicts the five major building blocks or functional units of a digital computer system. These five units correspond to the five basic operations, namely inputting, storing, processing, outputting and controlling data, carried out by all computer systems. The five units are:

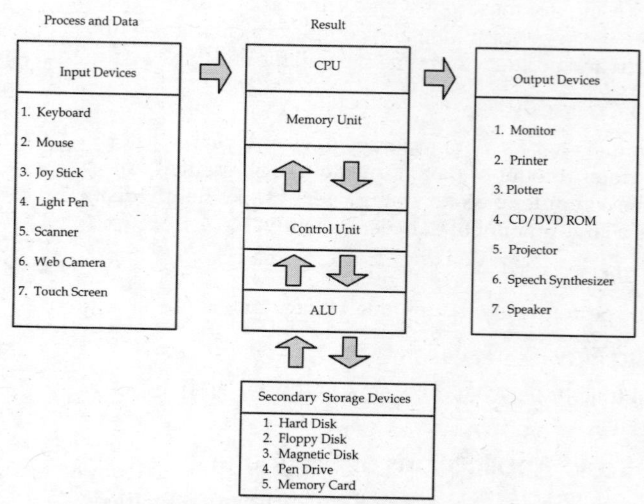

Figure 1.5 Block diagram of the computer

Inputting: Refers to the process of entering data into the computer, by the user using an input device, such as keyboard.

Storing: Refers to the holding of data and instructions in the computer's main memory, for manipulations (See Figure 1.6).

Processing: Refers to performing operations (both arithmetic and logical) or manipulation of data entered into the computer so that useful information may be taken out of the entered data.

Outputting: Refers to the process of showing the information or result to the user either on screen (monitor) or on paper (through printer).

Controlling: Refers to directing all the above processes, in coordination. This controlling is done by the Control Unit (CU) in a CPU.

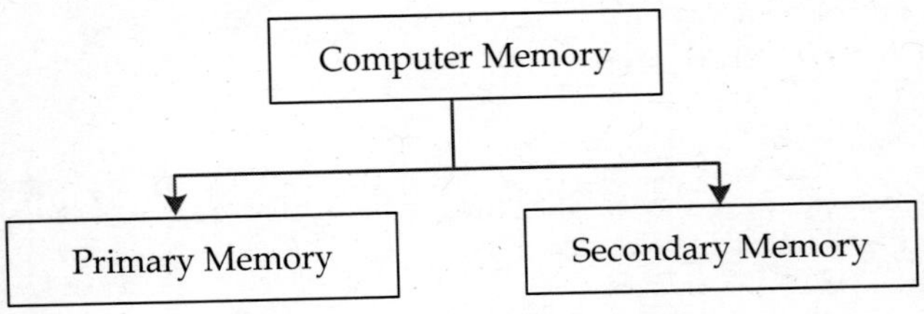

Figure 1.6 Computer Memory

The CPU of a small computer has a single microprocessor. The CPU of a large computer may contain a number of microprocessors and every microprocessor does one specific job.

A microprocessor contains a control unit and an Arithmetic and Logic Unit (ALU). When main memory is added to a microprocessor, it becomes a CPU.

The major sections of a CPU are:

(a) Primary Memory

(b) ALU

(c) Control Unit

Primary Memory

Primary memory or the Main memory unit is one of the major parts of a computer. It holds data which is currently manipulated by the CPU. It also keeps the necessary operating system, such as MS Disk Operating System (MS-DOS) or Windows. Since Primary memory is present within the CPU itself, it is also known as *internal memor* or RAM.

Arithmetic Logic Unit

ALU of a computer system is the place where the actual execution of instructions takes place. To be more precise, all calculations are performed and all comparisons (decisions) are made in the ALU.

Intermediate results generated in the ALU are temporarily stored in the memory unit until needed again at a later time. The data and instructions, stored in the main memory prior to processing, are transferred, as and when needed, to the ALU, where processing takes place. No processing is done in the memory unit.

Data may move from primary memory to ALU and back again to memory many times during the processing operation. After completion of processing, the final results which are stored in memory unit or RAMs are sent to an output device, such as monitor or printer.

All ALUs are designed to perform the four basic arithmetic operations–add, subtract, multiply, divide–and logic operations, such as less than, equal to or greater than.

Control Unit (CU)

This unit is responsible for controlling the entire working of the computer. The timing and control signals are generated by this unit and sent to other units for execution of the program for proper control. It also controls the transfer of data between memory and input/output devices.

1.4.2 VDU or Monitor, Keyboard and Mouse

Input/Output I/O de ices are those devices which are used to enter information into a computer or display results of data processing devices. These devices are discussed below.

Visual Display Unit (VDU) or Monitor

A computer monitor, technically termed as a VDU, can be described as an electronic device that transmits information from the computer onto a screen, thereby acting as an interface and connecting the viewer with the computer.

At present, computer monitors are available in a variety of shapes, designs, and colors. However, based on the technology used to make computer monitors, they can be broadly categorized into three types. (See Figure 1.7)

Figure 1.7 Types of monitor

Cathode Ray Tube CRT : These monitors employ the CRT technology which is most commonly used in the manufacturing of television screens. A cathode ray tube is basically a vacuum tube containing an electron gun at one end and a fluorescent screen at another end. From this electron gun, a process called thermionic emission generates a strong beam of electrons.

There are several advantages of using CRT monitors. These are:

- These monitors are highly reliable and efficient, and are capable of generating a resolution of up to 2048 x 1536 pixels, thereby providing a clear picture quality. Also, CRT monitors that are now available are capable of producing thousands of different colors.
- CRT monitors are affordable and cost effective.
- In modern technological advancements have resulted in the development of flat screen CRT monitors that reduce the glare and are good for the eyes.

Liquid Crystal Display LCD : It is also known as liquid crystal diode, is one of the most advanced technologies available at present. Typically, LCD monitor consists of a layer of color or monochrome pixels arranged schematically between a couple of transparent electrodes and two polarizing filters.

At present, there are two types of LCD technology available. These include the active matrix or TFT and a passive matrix technology. Among these, TFT technology is more secure and reliable, and generates better picture quality.

Some major advantages of using an LCD monitor include:

- These monitors are compact, lightweight, and do not consume much desk space.
- These monitors do not consume much electricity and can even be operated by using batteries.

However, LCD monitors have certain disadvantages. These monitors are very expensive. Image quality is not constant when viewed from different angles. LCD monitor's resolution is always constant.

Light-Emitting Diodes LED : LED monitors are the latest types of monitors available in the market today. Like LCD, it has a flat panel display making use of light-emitting diodes for back-lightning instead of Cold Cathode Fluorescent (CCFL) back-lightning used in LCDs. Primarily, the display is of LCD only but the back-lightning is done by LEDs. LED monitors use much lesser power than CRT and LCD.

Some advantages of LED monitors are:

- They produce images with higher contrast
- Lifespan and durability of LED monitors is more than CRT or LCD monitors
  Because of the technology, the monitor panels can be made very thin.
- Do not produce much heat while running.

Keyboard

Programs and data are entered into a computer through a keyboard which is attached to a computer. A keyboard is similar to the keyboard of a typewriter. It contains alphabets, digits, special characters, function keys and some control keys. When a key is pressed, an electronic signal is produced which is detected by an electronic circuit called *ke board encoder* (See Figure 1.8).

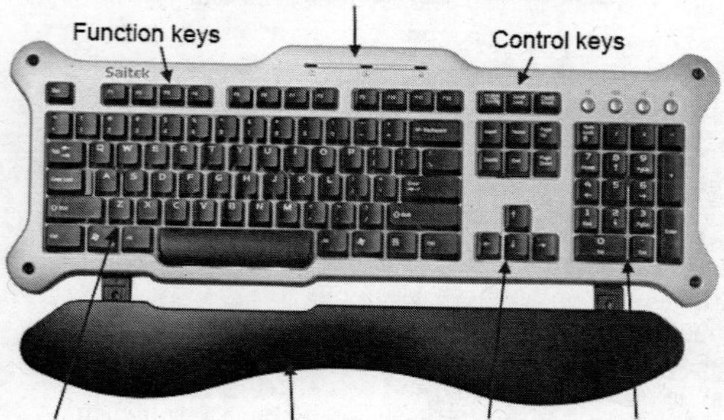

Figure 1.8 Keyboard depicting different keys' functions

Types of keys on keyboard

- *Alphanumeric ke s:* It includes all the numbers and letters on the keyboard. e.g., A-Z and 0-9.
- *Functions ke :* Keys from F1 to F12.
- *Punctuation ke s:* These include comma, semicolon and brackets.
- *Special ke s:* These includes controls keys, Arrows key, Caps lock key, Delete key.

☞ *At the top of the ke board are function ke s* F1 *to* F12 . *Their functions depend upon the program being run.* F1 *ke is used to get help from the program.*

Mouse

A mouse is a pointing device. It is held in one hand and is moved across a flat surface Figure 1.9.

Figure 1.9 Mouse

The mouse can also be used to draw sketches, diagrams, etc., on the monitor screen. It is also moved on the graphic tablet for drawing work. The mouse is also used to edit text. For editing a text on the screen, the cursor can be quickly placed close to the desired point of the screen by moving the mouse.

Types of keys on Mouse

- *Mechanical mouse:* Movement of cursor is relative to the movement of ball present at the bottom of mouse.
- *Optical mouse:* It uses light emitting diode for detecting movement.
- *Wireless mouse:* It relay signal to base station, which is wired to computer's mouse port.
- *Laser mouse:* It uses infrared light emitting diode.

One type of mouse uses a rolling ball; others use optical sensing techniques. They are linked to the PC by using a cable or by using infrared light. A typical mouse has two or three buttons. What the mouse buttons do depend on the application program running in your PC. In some systems, it is also possible to specify independent functions to the buttons.

1.4.3 Other Input Devices

Input de ices are those devices which are used to enter information into a computer or other data processing devices. These devices are:

Joystick

A joystick is also a pointing device. It is used to move the cursor position on a monitor screen. Its function is similar to that of a mouse and is used for playing games. A joystick is a stick which has a spherical ball at its lower end as well as at its upper end (See Figure 1.10). The lower spherical ball moves in a socket. The joystick can be moved right or left, forward or backward direction. The electronic circuitry inside the joystick detects and measures the displacement of the joystick from its central position. This information is sent to the processor.

Figure 1.10 Joystick

Light Pen

A light pen is a pointing device. It is used to select a displayed menu option on the monitor. It is a photosensitive pen-like device. It is capable of sensing a position on the monitor screen when its tip touches the screen (See Figure 1.11).

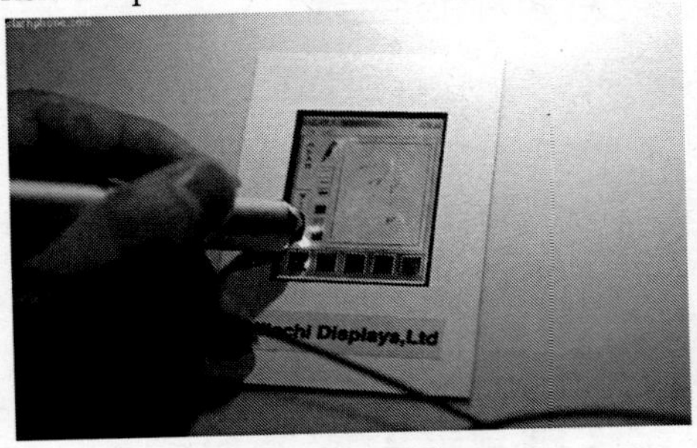

Figure 1.11 Light pen

Touch Screen

A *touch screen* is a computer display screen that is sensitive to human touch, allowing a user to interact with the computer by touching pictures or words on the screen. Touch screens are used with information kiosks, computer based training devices and systems designed to help individuals who have difficulty in manipulating a mouse or keyboard. Some tablets on Smartphone comes with a small object which looks like a pen, called as stylus. By using which you can select something or draw on your screen with it. Some touch screen use transparent plastic protector to protect them from scratch. (See Figure 1.12).

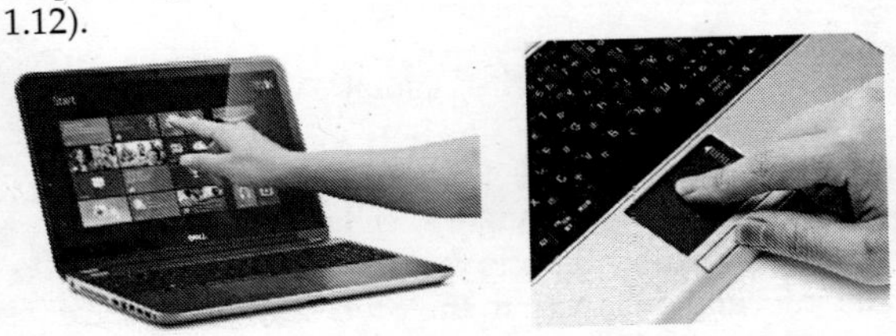

Figure 1.12 Touch Screen and Touch pad

Touch Pad/Track Pad

It has a special surface which understands the position of your fingers as the position of the cursor on the screen. It mainly translates the motion and position of user's fingertip to the relative position on the screen. It is widely used in laptops, notebooks, mobile devices. Some of the new touchpads can understand more than one finger and you can give commands like zoom in and out with just a gesture.

Graphics Tablet/Digitizer

A *graphics tablet* is a graphic input device that functions like a drawing tablet. The user makes contact with the graphic tablet with a device called a cursor, which is a pen-like instrument that is connected to the tablet by a wire or without wires (See Figure 1.13). For sketching, the user draws with the tablet cursor and the screen cursor "draws" a corresponding image. For tracing an existing image, the screen cursor is often not required.

Figure 1.13 Graphics Tablets

Microphone

A microphone, is a sound capture device which allows you to record voices or sounds convert them into digital form and then place them onto computers, generally as a wav file. Microphones can also be used with other applications such as a voice dictation program or a voice conference program and it is used in smart phone, video recorder, movie production etc. (See Figure 1.14) When connecting the microphone to the back of the computer, the microphone will be placed in the hole which generally has Mic or Microphone written next to it. While chatting you use microphone to speak and headphone to listen.

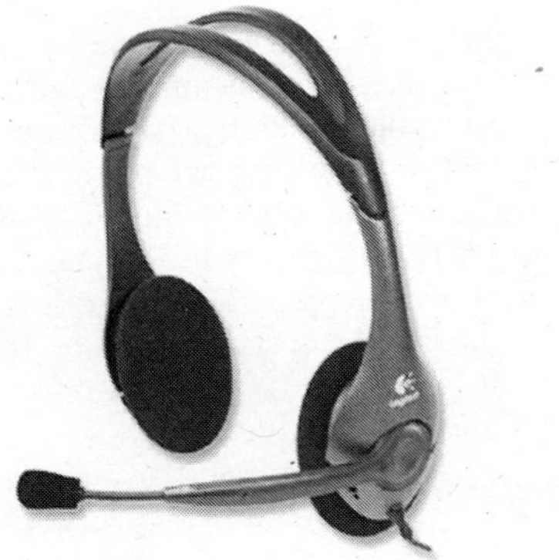

Figure 1.14 Microphone with earphone

Scanner

Scanners are a kind of input devices which can captures an image or document and then import it to your computer. They are capable of entering information directly into the computer. The main advantage of direct entry of information is that users do not have to type the information. This provides faster and more accurate data entry (See Figure 1.15). Scanners are of three types. They are:

Figure 1.15 Scanner

Type of Scanner

Scanner	Handheld Scanners	Flatbed Scanners	Drum Scanners
Size	Small in size and can be held in hand	Large, create high quality images	Medium size, and has rolling drum
Cost	Less expensive	More expensive	Expensive
Passes	Multiple passes are required to scan single page	Can scan page in a single pass	Scan in a single pass
Surface	They can be held in a hand	It has flat surface on which the image to be scanned is placed	Drum rolls over which the entire sheet to be scanned is placed

Voice Input and Recognition System

Voice input and recognition system is an input device, consisting of a microphone or telephone that converts human speech into an electrical signals. A signal pattern obtained in this manner is sent to the computer where it is matched against pre-stored patterns to identify the input. When a close match is found, a word is recognized by the system. The set of pre-stored patterns is known as the vocabulary of the system. To build up this vocabulary, the system has to be trained to recognize the words and phrases that are to be present in the vocabulary.

Optical Mark Reader (OMR)

Optical mark readers are special scanners used for recognizing a pre-specified type of mark made by pencil or pen. For example, in the objective test paper of competitive examinations, you mark your answers on a special sheet by darkening a small square, using a pen or pencil. These answer sheets are fed into the computer using the optical mark reader. The computer can then evaluate the answer sheets. The use of OMR is not limited to the grading of objective type tests. In fact, any input data that is in the nature of a choice or selection can be recorded for OMR input.

OMR focuses light on the page being examined and the light pattern reflected from the dark marks is then detected. Figure 1.16 shows the OMR characters.

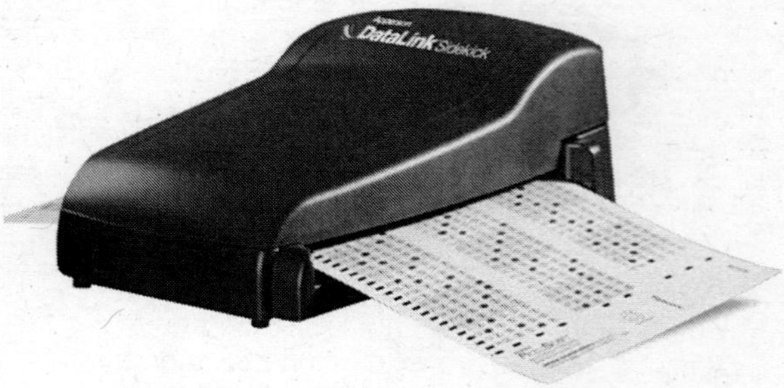

Figure 1.16 Optical marks in an answer sheet

Bar-code Reader

Bar-code readers are special devices used to read bar coded data. Bar code is a specialized code used for fast identification of items. It consists of a series of small lines, known as bars. The actual coding of the bars is the width of the bar, not the height. These are primarily used for identification of goods, such as books, postal packages, badges, etc., (See Figure 1.17).

Figure 1.17 Bar codes

Magnetic Ink Character Recognition (MICR)

MICR detects the special encoded characters on bank cheques and deposit slips. After detecting the encoded characters, the MICR converts them into digital data for the computer. Figure 1.18 shows a bank cheque which will be processed using a MICR device.

Trackball

A trackball is also a pointing device, contains a ball in the middle, which can rotate in any direction. It looks like an upside down mouse. The user spins the ball in different directions to move the cursor on the monitor (See Figure 1.19). The associated electronic circuitry detects the direction and speed of the spin. The information is sent to the processor. This type of pointing device is normally used in a CAD (Computer Aided Design).

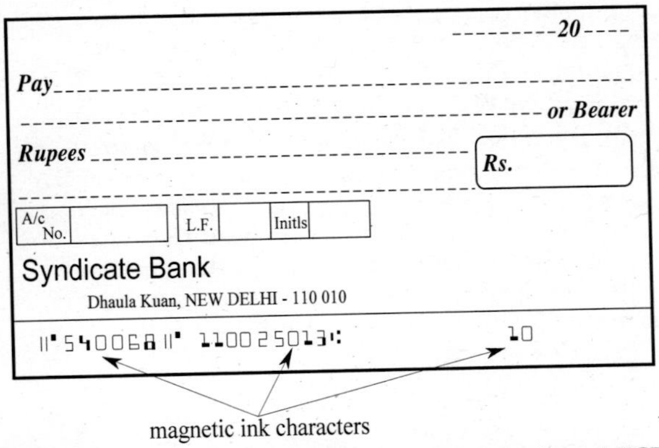

Figure 1.18 A bank cheque that is processed using a MICR device

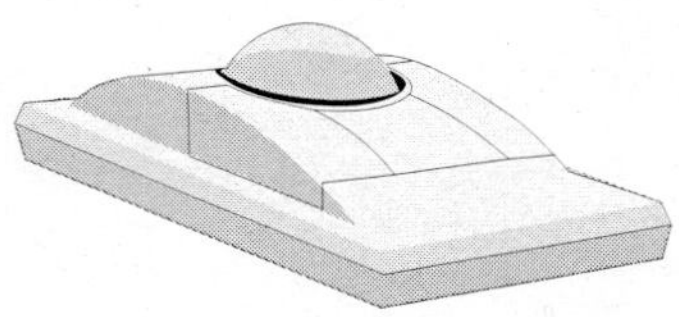

Figure 1.19 Trackball

Web Cameras

A web camera is a video capture device which, allows a computer to accept input just by focussing on an object in real time. The camera is focussed on the input object to take a picture of the object. Image can be saved and transferred over network to a distant place by email or uploading them to the Internet.

The image of the object can be seen on the monitor of the distant computer connected through a network or through Internet. Voice can also be transmitted over the network. Thus, two or more persons can talk and see each another in this way. This method is used in video conferencing. By using web camera one can make video call by using Skype or any other video calling program. (See Figure 1.20)

Figure 1.20 Web Camera

Digital Camera/Digicam

It is an image capturing device which is used to take high definition photos. It does not use film and displays photos/ videos on LCD screen and saves them on memory card. From memory card images/ videos can be transfer to your computer and you can store them safely over there. You can also use a photo editing software e.g. Photo editor to edit photos on computer. Digital cameras, nowadays are integrated into mobile devices such as tablets and smartphones (See Figure 1.21).

Figure 1.21 Digital Camera

Video Camera

It is a recording device which capture continuous motion picture and generate a signal for displaying on a monitor. Nowadays, memory cards are used to store images and make it very easy to transfer and save videos on a computer. Hours of video can be stored on a tiny memory card.

Video cameras are used to capture daily moments, celebrations. It is also used by scientist to examine a scientific event and by astronauts to equip a spacecraft.

Biometric Sensor

Biometric Sensor is the device that is used to identifies finger prints, DNA identification, eye retinas and voice patterns, facial patterns, hand measurements, face shape and signature verification (See Figure 1.22). They are used for security purposes to identify the persons who are permitted to enter the organization.

1.4.4 Other Output Devices

Output devices are those devices of computer system that supplies information or results either in the form of hardcopy (printer) or softcopy (monitor). Some of the common output devices are as follows:

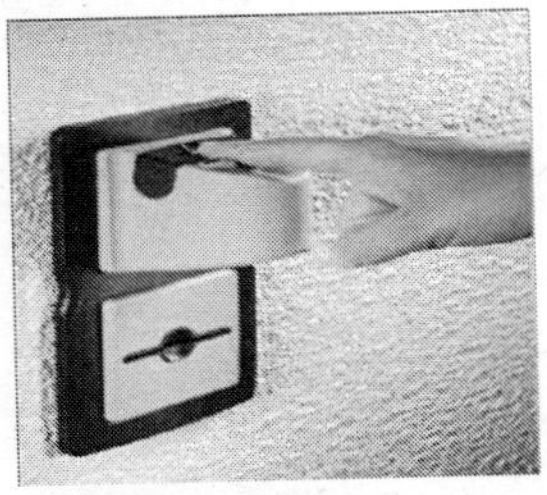

Figure 1.22 Biometric Sensor

(a) Printers
(b) Plotters
(c) Multimedia Projector
(d) Speech Synthesizer

Printers

Printers provide information in a permanent readable form. They produce printed outputs of results, programs and data. You can print text, numbers, images and photos. The printer is usually connected to the computer through a USB cable. Before printing you must check your computer is connected to the printer and the printer is on. Apart from printing on plain paper you can also print on envelopes, stickers.

The printers can be classified as:

(a) Impact Printers

(b) Non-impact Printers

Impact printers use an electro-mechanical mechanism that causes hammers or pins to strike against a ribbon and paper to print the text. The impact printers are further classified into the following categories:

(a) Line Printers

(b) Character Printers

Line Printers: A line printer prints one line of the text at a time. Printing speeds may vary from 300–3000 lines per minute. Different types of line printers are–*Drum printer* and *Chain printer*.

- **Drum Printer:** A drum printer consists of a cylindrical drum on which the characters are embossed. The printer receives all characters to be printed in one line of the text from the processor. The hammers hit the ribbon and paper against the desired character on the drum when it comes in the printing position. Its noise level is high and speed varies from 200 to 2000 lines per minute. They are expensive also.
- **Chain Printer:** A chain printer uses a rapidly, rotating chain which is called print chain. To print a line, the characters in the line are transmitted from the memory to printer buffer. The band is rotated at a high-speed. The noise level of the printer is high and its speed lies in the range of 400-2400 lines per minute.

Character Printers Serial Printer : A character printer prints one character of the text at a time. They are low-speed printers. Their printing speed lies in the range of 30-600 characters per second. Different types of character printers are–*Dot matri printers* and *Letter qualit printers*.

- **Dot Matrix Printer:** A dot matrix printer is the oldest and the most popular serial printer (See Figure 1.23). The printhead contains a vertical array of pins. As the printhead moves across the paper, selected pins fire against the ribbon to form a pattern of dots on the paper.

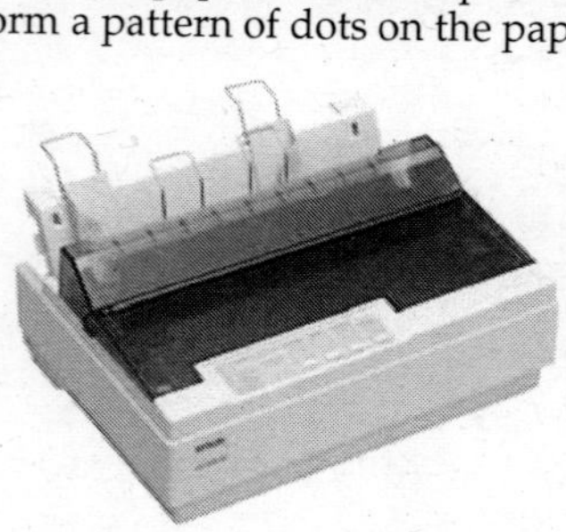

Figure 1.23 Dot matrix printer

A dot matrix printer is faster and can print many copies than a letter quality printer. These printers operate at two or three speeds. The lower the speed the better is the printing quality. Higher speed is for draft printing and lower speed is for Near-Letter Quality (NLQ) printing.

- **Letter Quality printers:** These printers print full characters, which means that a character is not made up of dots. The most popular printer of this type is daisy-wheel printer. In a daisy-wheel printer, the printhead resembles a daisy flower, with its print arms appearing like the petals of the flower. The daisy-wheel printer has a speed up to 90 characters per second. These are no more in use today.

Non impact printers use thermal, chemical, electrostatic, laser beam or inkjet technology for printing the text. Usually a non-impact type printer is faster than an impact type. These printers are categorized as:

(a) Electromagnetic Printer

(b) Thermal Printer

(c) Inkjet Printer

(d) Laser Printer

Electromagnetic Printer: This printer uses magnetic recording techniques. By using this technique, the required output is written on a drum surface. Then this surface is passed through magnetic powder which adheres to the charged areas. The powder is then pressed onto the paper.

Thermal Printer: This type of printer uses special heat-sensitive paper. These papers have a special heat-sensitive coating. When a spot on the paper is heated, it becomes dark. A character is printed with a matrix of dots. These printers have a speed of 200 characters per second.

Inkjet Printers: Inkjet printers are more efficient than dot matrix printers. The print quality is good because the character is formed by the dozens of tiny ink dots. These printers produce better quality of text and graphics and are faster. Almost all inkjets offer a colour option (cyan, yellow, magenta and black) as standard, in varying degrees of resolution. Inkjet printers are capable of producing high quality print which almost matches the quality of a laser printer. A standard ink jet printer has a resolution of 300 dots per inch, although newer models have improved on that (See Figure 1.24).

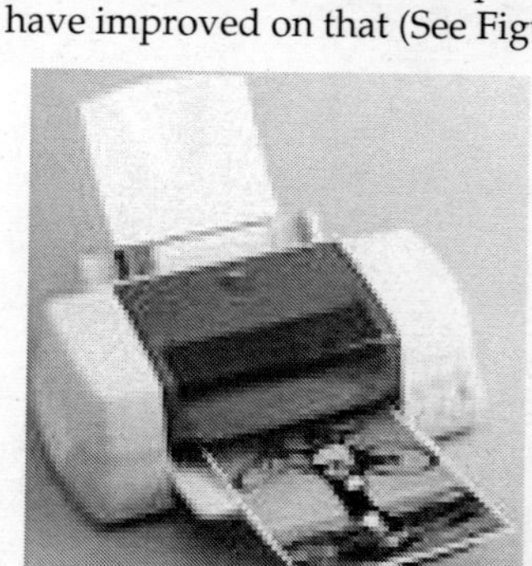

Figure 1.24 Inkjet printer

Laser Printers

Laser printers are non-impact type printers. These printers are expensive and require periodic maintenance. Low-speed laser printers produce 10 pages or more per minute and are used with microcomputers. High-speed laser printers produces upto 300 pages per minute and they are used with mini and large computers. Laser printers have become popular for voluminous printing work. They are mainly used for desktop publishing work. Figure 1.24 illustrates a laser printer.

3D Printers

3D printing is a form of additive manufacturing technology where a three dimensional object is created by laying down successive layers of material. It is also known as rapid prototyping, is a mechanized method whereby 3D objects are quickly made on a reasonably sized machine connected to a computer containing blueprints for the object. This method for creating 3D models with the use of inkjet technology saves time and cost by eliminating the need to design; print and glue together separate model parts. Now, you can create a complete model in a single process using 3D printing. The basic principles include materials cartridges, flexibility of output, and translation of code into a visible pattern.

Figure 1.25 Laser printer

3D Printers are machines that produce physical 3D models from digital data by printing layer by layer. It can make physical models of objects either designed with a CAD program or scanned with a 3D Scanner. It is used in a variety of industries including jewellery, footwear, industrial design, architecture, engineering and construction, automotive, aerospace, dental and medical industries, education and consumer products.

Plotters

Plotters are output devices. They are used to produce precise and good quality graphics and drawings under the control of the computer. They use ink pen or inkjet to draw graphics or drawings. Either single colour or multicoloured pens can be employed. It is used for architectural plan and large advertising banners. Figure 1.26 shows a plotter.

Figure 1.26 Plotter

Multimedia Projector

Multimedia Projector is an output device connected to a PC and used to project information from a computer on to a large screen (a cloth screen or wall). The information is thus viewed by a large number of people. It is widely used for giving presentations. The presenter can directly point to, mark or edit the displayed information to make it more understandable. Audio, video, image and animation can be prepared on a PC and by using a multimedia projector the presentation can be made more lively and interesting (See Figure 1.27).

Figure 1.27 Projector

Speech Synthesizer

Speech Synthesizer is an output device that converts textual data into spoken sentences. To produce the speech, basic sound units called *phonemes* are combined. The sequence of words in a text is combined into phonemes, amplified and outputted through a speaker attached to a computer (See Figure 1.28).

Figure 1.28 Speech Synthesizer

Speakers

Speakers are the hardware devices connected to a computer's sound card that outputs sounds generated by the card. A speaker makes sound by being fed on electrical signals which is changed or modulated, corresponding to the sound that is to be made. The speaker converts the changes or waves in the electrical signal to matching sound waves, which we hear.

Figure 1.29 Speakers

There is no volume control in the PC, since it was not intended to produce sophisticated sounds. Speakers are further attached to the system to enhance the sound quality. (See Figure 1.29)

Figure 1.30 Head Phones

Head phones/stereo phones/headsets: These are the small pair of loudspeakers, which are placed closer to user's ear so that only one person can hear the output at a time (See Figure 1.30).

1.4.5 Computer Memory

A computer needs memory to store data. It also needs memory to perform arithmatical operations and storing programs and pictures. Computer memory is of two types (Figure 1.6):

(a) Primary Memory

(b) Secondary Memory

Primary memory is a part of the CPU whereas the secondary memory is external to the CPU. The secondary memory stores the data and keep it even when the electricity to the PC is cut off whereas the primary memory looses its contents immediately.

Primary memory is made up of electronic circuits and keeps data as long as voltage supply is on. When power supply to a PC is switched off, the data is lost.

Primary memory can be divided into the following two types:

(a) RAM
(b) ROM

Random Access Memory (RAM)

RAM stands for Random Access Memory and it is a read/write memory. Information can be written into and read from a RAM. It is a volatile memory. It retains the stored information as long as it is supplied with power. Types of RAM is shown in Table 1.1.

Read Only Memory (ROM)

ROM stands for Read Only Memory and it is a permanent type memory. Its contents are not lost when power supply is switched off. The user cannot write into a ROM. Its contents are written at the time of manufacturing. ROMs store permanent programs and other types of information which are needed by the computer to execute the programs. ROMs store functions, such as sine, cosine, logarithm, square root, exponential and code conversion tables, etc. Types of ROM is shown in Table 1.2.

Table 1.1 Types of RAM

Static RAM/SRAM	Dynamic RAM/DRAM	Enhanced version of RAM
Requires constant power flow to hold information	It stores its information in cell called capacitor and transistor	EDORAM Extended data output random access memory.
Expensive and faster	Less expensive and slower	SDRAM: Synchronous dynamic random access memory.
More power is required	Less power is required	DDR SDRAM: Double data rate synchronous dynamic random access memory.

Table 1.2 Types of ROM

Static RAM/SRAM	Dynamic RAM/DRAM	Enhanced version of RAM
Programmable read only memory	Erasable programmable read only memory	Electrically erasable programmable read only memory
Information cannot be altered once written	Information can be changed by exposing to ultraviolet light	Information can be erased and reprogrammed by using electric charge.

Secondary Memory/Auxilary Memory

Secondary memory is employed for bulk storage (mass storage) of programs, data and other information. It has much larger capacity than the main memory. It stores system software, assemblers, compilers, useful packages, large data files, etc. The secondary memory is non-volatile in nature. The magnetic memories, such as hard disks and floppy disks are the most common secondary memories used in computers.

Random access devices are direct access devices. In such devices the information is available at random, i.e., it is available in any order.

☞ *A random access storage de ice is one in hich an location in the de ice ma be accessed at random and retrie al of infor mation stored is direct.*

Magnetic disks and magnetic drums are typical direct access storage devices.

Magnetic Tape

Magnetic tape was one of the most popular storage medium for storing large volumes of data that are needed to be serially accessed and processed. The tape is a plastic ribbon usually 1/2 inch wide that is coated on one side with an iron-oxide material which can be magnetized. The tape ribbon itself is stored in reels of 50 to 2400 feet. It is similar to the tape used on a tape-recorder except that it is of higher quality and more durable. The magnetic tape can be erased and reused again and again (See Figure 1.31).

Figure 1.31 Magnetic tape

1.5 CONCEPT OF HARDWARE AND SOFTWARE

Let us discuss the concept of hardware and software in brief.

1.5.1 Hardware

The physical components of a computer are called hardware. Such items may be electronic, electrical, magnetic, mechanical or optical components. Examples of components are microprocessors, ICs, hard disks, floppy disks, optical disks, monitors, keyboard, printer, plotter, etc.

1.5.2 Software

It is the set of computer programs, procedures, and associated documentation related to the effective operation of a computer system.

Role of Software in Computers

A set of instructions that perform a particular task is called the program or software program. The instructions in the program direct the computer to perform input operations, process the data and output the results.

Types of Software

The software are classified into the following categories (See Figure 1.32).

1. System Software/System Packages
2. Application Software /Application packages

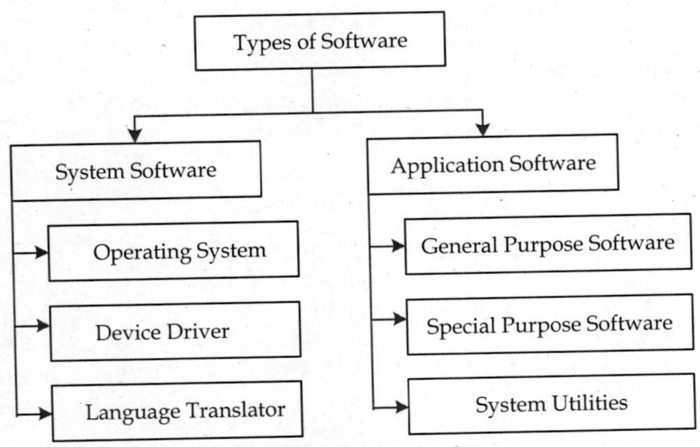

Figure 1.32 Types of software

- *S stem Soft are/S stem Packages:* It is the sets of one or more general purpose programs designed to control the operation of a computer system. These programs are written to assist the users of the computer system by performing tasks, such as controlling all the operations, moving data in and out of a computer and all the other steps in executing the application program.

Types of System Software:

- *Operating S stems:* An operating system is a master control program that runs the computer and acts as a scheduler. It controls the flow of signals from CPU to various parts of the computer. It is the first program which is loaded (copied) into the computer's memory after the computer is switched on. Popular operating systems include MS-DOS, Linux, Windows and UNIX.
- *De ice Dri ers:* A device driver controls a particular type of device that is attached, such as keyboard or a mouse.
- *Language Translators:* Translates programming language into machine language, translated programs are called as Object code.

The types of language translators are shown in Table 1.3.

Table 1.3 Types of Language Translators

Assembler	Compiler	Interpreter
Convert assembly language to machine language Code consist of mnemonic code Reads the whole page in single go	Convert source code written in high level language into machine language. Code consist of high level language Reads the whole source code in single run and traps the error	Convert high level language into machine language Cose consist of high level language Reads or convert the source code line by line.

- *Application Soft are /Application packages:* These are the sets of one or more programs designed to carry out operations for a specified application. For example, every month a payroll package produces the pay-slips for the workers of a company. Similarly, an inventory package may produce the list of different parts/equipment available in an organization.

  Typical software applications that you might use are:
- **Word processors**–MS Word.
- **Spreadsheet software**–MS Excel
- **Graphics and Web Designing software**–Corel Draw, Photoshop, Picasa, Dreamweaver, FrontPage.

  Types of application software
- *General purpose soft are:* Used to perform simple task, e.g., Word processing, multimedia software.
- *Special Purpose Soft are:* Used to perform specific task, as they target on a very narrow solution to a problem. e.g., Inventory management, Payroll system.
- *S stem Utilities:* These are used to support, enhance and secure the existing data in computer system. System utilities consist of:
  - *Disk Fragmenter:* It is used to arrange unused space on hard disk.
  - *Disk Compression:* It is used to compress the information stored on hard disk, so that more information can be stored on it.
  - *Backup Utilities:* It makes the copy of all information stored on disk.
  - *Disk Cleaners:* It is used to find files that have not been used for a long time and delete them the speed of slow computer can be increased.
  - *Anti irus:* Program which scans the system and prevent the files of computer system from getting corrupted. e.g., Norton.
  - *Clipboard Manager:* It is used to increase the clipboard capability of operating system.

1.5.3 Programming Computer Language

Languages are a means of communication. Normally people interact with each other through a language. On the same pattern, communication with computers is carried out through a language. This language is understood both by user and the machine. Computer languages are broadly classified as:

(a) Machine Language

(b) Assembly Language

(c) High-level Language

Machine Language

The set of instruction codes, whether in binary or in decimal notation, which can be directly understood by the computer without the help of a translating program is called a *machine code* or *machine language program*.

A computer understands information composed of only zeros and ones. This means that a computer uses binary digits for its operation. The computer's instructions are therefore coded and stored in the memory in the form of 0s and 1s. A program written in the form of 0s and 1s is called a *machine language program*. There is a specific binary code for each instruction.

Advantages and Limitations of Machine Language

Programs written in machine language can be executed very fast by the computer. This is mainly because machine instructions are directly understood by the CPU and no translation of the program is required. However, writing a program in machine language has several disadvantages which are discussed below.

Machine Dependent

Because the internal design of computers is different from one another and needs different electrical signals to operate, the machine language is also different from one type of computer to another.

Difficult to Program

Although machine language is easily used by the computer, it is very difficult to write a program in this language. It is necessary for the programmer either to memorize dozens of code numbers for the commands in the machine's instruction set or to constantly refer to a reference card.

Error Prone

For writing a program in machine language, the programmer not only has to remember the *opcodes*, but also has to keep a track of the storage locations of data and instructions. It is therefore becomes very difficult for him to concentrate fully on the logic of the problem. This frequently causes errors in programming.

Difficult to Modify

It is very difficult to correct or modify machine language programs. Checking machine instructions to locate errors is as tedious as writing them initially.

Assembly Language

The instruction words which direct the computer are stored in the machine in numerical form. The programmer, however, rarely writes his instructions in numerical form, instead, each instruction to the computer is written using a letter code to designate the operation to be performed, plus the address in memory of the number to be used in this step of the calculation. Later, the alphabetical section of the instruction word is converted to numerical form using an assembler.

Advantages of Assembly Language Programs

(a) Assembly language program take less computation time and memory as compared to high level language programs.

(b) An assembly language program needs less processing power of a CPU and thus runs faster than high level language program.

Disadvantages of Assembly Language Programs

(a) Programming is difficult and debugging is time consuming.

(b) In order to write an assembly program, a programmer must have detailed knowledge of the structure of the computer he is using, including the knowledge of registers, instruction set of the computer, connection of ports to the peripherals, etc.

(c) The program written for one computer cannot be used for another computer of a different make.

(d) Number of instructions in an assembly language program may be very large, because we need one instruction for each operation.

High-Level Language

To overcome the difficulties associated with *assembl lan guages, high-le el* or *procedure-oriented* languages were developed. High-level languages permit programmers to describe tasks in a form which is problem oriented rather than computer oriented. A programmer can formulate problems more efficiently in a high-level language. Besides, he need not to have a precise knowledge of the architecture of the computer he is using.

The instructions written in a high-level language are called *statements*. The statements resemble more closely English and mathematics as compared to mnemonics in assembly languages. Examples of high-level languages are Beginner's All-Purpose Symbolic Instruction Code (BASIC), PASCAL (Programming Language named for Blaise Pascal), Formula Translation (FORTRAN), COmmon Business-Oriented Language (COBOL), etc.

1.6 REPRESENTATION OF DATA/INFORMATION

1.6.1 Definition of Information and Data

Data is a general term used to denote any or all facts, numbers, letters, symbols, etc., that can be processed or manipulated or produced by a computer. However, all types of information stored in a computer are stored internally in the simple format: a sequence of 0's and 1's.

Technically, data are raw facts and figures, such as order and payments, which are processed into information, such as balance due and quantity on hand. However, in common usage, both data and information are used synonymously.

1.6.2 Basic Data Types

There are two types of data, namely, *integer* and *floating point.* From these two data types we can further derive two others — *character* and *double precision* (precision means how many digits can be used in the number). If you attempt to store a number with many digits, such as 2.1234543, (as a floating point variable, only 6 digit 2.123454) will be retained.

The bytes occupied by each of these types of data in memory of a computer as well as the names given to them are shown in Table 1.4.

Table 1.4 Typical Range and Size of Basic Data Types

Type	Range		Bytes	Represents
	From	*To*		
char/short	ASCII –128	127	1	characters
unsigned char	ASCII 0	255	1	characters
int	–32,768	32,767	2	whole numbers
unsigned int	0	65,535	2	whole numbers
long	–2,147,438,648	2,147,438,647	4	whole numbers
unsigned long	0	4,294,967,295	4	whole numbers
float	3.4×10^{-38}	3.4×10^{38}	4	fractional numbers
double	1.7×10^{-308}	1.7×10^{308}	8	fractional numbers
long double	3.4×10^{-4932}	3.4×10^{4932}	10	fractional numbers

If we need to store integer values less than −32,768 or greater than 32,767, then we should use long int. If we need to store integer values in the range −32767 and 32767, then we can use *short int*.

There are a number of cases where a variable will have to hold only non-negative values. For instance, variables that are used to count things are often restricted to non-negative numbers. C++ language allows us to declare the variable that take non-negative values or numbers only (or unsigned). This doubles the range of values a variable can take. Thus, a *signed short int* has a range from −32,767 to 32,767, whereas an *unsigned short int* has a range from 0 to 65,535.

The data type *char* can be used to hold either characters or numbers. For instance, after making the declaration

```
char c;
```

we can make either of the following assignments;

```
c = 'A'; or c = 65;
```

Note that characters having constant values are enclosed in single quotes. The quotes tell the compiler to get the numeric code (ASCII code value) of the character.

☞ *In the ASCII character set character codes are ordered alpha beticall . For e ample ASCII code alue of an upper case A is 65 B is 66 ... Z is 90. ASCII code alue of lo er case letters i.e. a starts at 97 and runs through 122.*

int: Int is the basic integer data type. It is treated as an integer in that it cannot hold fractional values.

float: Integers are not adequate for representing numbers that have very large value as well as that have fractional values. For this, we need floating-point types of data representation. The simplest method is to place a decimal point in the number as seen below:

```
0.356
0.000001
```

In order to declare a variable capable of holding one of these values we use the keyword *float* or *double*.

double: The keyword double stands for double precision. It is capable of representing a real number ranging from 1.7×10^{-308} to 1.7×10308 which gives twice as much precision as represented by a float.

☞ *The precision refers to the number of decimal places that a number can be represented in.*

void: The data type void has two important purposes. The first is to indicate that a function does not return a value and the other is to declare a generic pointer.

Number system

A number system of base, or radix, r is a system that uses distinct symbols for r digits. Numbers are represented by a string of digit symbols. For example, Binary 0, 1 and base is 2. Decimal 0, 1,2-9 and base is 10. Octal 0, 1,2-7 and base is 8. Hexadecimal 0,1,2-9,A,B,C,D,E,F and base is 10.

1.6.3 Storage of Data

Data now a days are stored in hard disk, CD-ROM (Compact Disk Read Only Memory), Digital Video/Versatile Disk (DVD), pendrive and portable hard drive.

Data stored on hard disk and CD-ROM, etc., can be accessed directly. Thus, these storage devices are faster, and can also be used to transfer data from one computer to another or between a computer and a smartphone.

Hard Disk

A hard disk is a device used for mass storage of data needed for direct access. It is more stable, rigid and also it is contained in a dust-free environment. It stores more information.

The data and instructions that are entered into the computer system through input units must be stored inside the computer before the actual processing can start. Similarly, the results produced by the computer after processing must also be kept somewhere inside the computer system before those can be passed on to the output units. Moreover, the intermediate results produced by the computer must also be preserved for ongoing processing (See Figure 1.33).

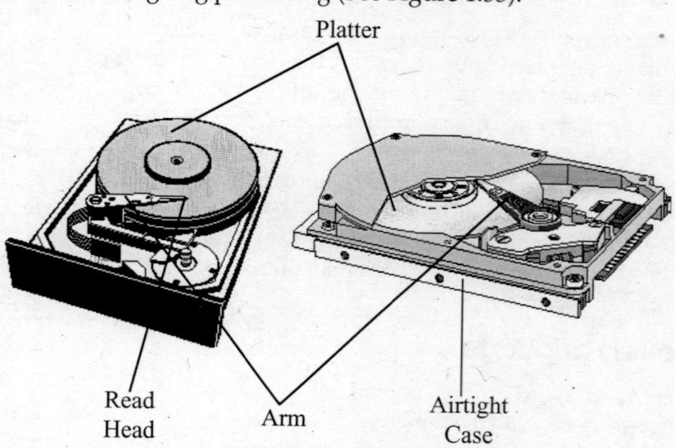

Figure 1.33 Hard disk

The specific functions of the storage unit are to store the following:

(a) All data and instructions to be processed,
(b) Intermediate results of processing, and
(c) Final results before sending them to output devices.

Never scratch CD/DVD surface as your data will be lost.

☞ *Computers also pro ide the facilit of di iding the main memor into ords or b tes. A b te usuall consists of 8 bits of information.*

Compact Disk (CD)

It is an optical read (CD-R) and write (CD-RW) memory. The disk is made up of a resin, such as polycarbonate. It is coated with a material which will change its reflecting property when a high intensity laser beam is focused on it. The coating material is highly reflective, usually aluminium. The high intensity laser beam forms a tiny pit along a trace to represent '1' and the surface without a pit known as 'land' represents '0'. Figure 1.34 shows a compact disk.

Figure 1.34 Compact disk

For reading data, a laser beam is employed. In some cases, separate laser beams are employed: one for writing and the other for reading. The reflected laser light is sensed by a photodiode to read data. The intensity of the reflected light of laser changes as it encounters a pit. A pit spreads the light so that the photodiode receives less reflected light. But land reflects sufficient light to the photodiode. Thus, this change in reflected light is sensed and converted into electrical signals for data reading purposes.

Optical disks are of two types, namely compact disks or CD-ROMs and WORM (Write Once and Read Many) disks.

CD-ROM can store about 700 MB of data, making it an excellent medium for storing massive amount of data, higher capacity software, such as electronic reference books, business and entertainment software.

Digital Video Disk/Digital Versatile Discs (DVD)

Digital Video Disk (DVD) is introduced by Philips and Sony in 1995. It is an optical storage device that looks the same as a CD. A DVD has the same dimensions as a standard CD but cannot be read by a CD player, although a DVD player can read standard CDs. A DVD can store up to 4.7 GB of data.

Pen Drive/USB Flash Drive

A thumb drive, also known as flash drive, pen drive, memory stick or USB drive is a small portable device in the shape of the thumb, which can be connected to the USB port of a computer, which stores, transfer data quickly and easily. The main components of a thumb drives is flash memory. Flash memory is a special type of memory which can retain data even when there is no current passing through it. It is somewhat like an external hard drive. They are cheap resistant and came in different size. (See Figure 1.35)

Memory Cards

A memory card is a device offering an easy, fast and reliable way for storing and transferring digital files. It works like a portable hard disk drive but comes with some superior advantages, since almost every memory card is based on flash memory technology, of having much smaller form factor and being non-volatile and solid state. Making flash memory cards much more durable and reliable than hard disk drives.

Figure 1.35 Pen drive

Memory cards are made by a variety of manufacturers and can be found in different storage capacities and transfer speeds.

MicroSD Memory Card The microSD card is even smaller than the miniSD card. The microSD card is designed for use in cellular phones and small mobile devices. The microSD card can accessed in a SD card slot via an adapter (See Figure 1.36).

Portable Hard Drive Portable hard disk drive that is plugged into an external port on a computer, such as USB or FireWire are used for backup. For laptops, the PC Card slot may be used to connect a cable to a full-size drive, or the hard disk that may be contained entirely inside the PC Card (See Figure 1.37). The portable size available in the market are 320 GB, 500 GB and 1 and 2 Tetra GB.

Figure 1.36 SD card

Figure 1.37 Portable hard drive

It allows the user to back up or store important information separate from the main internal hard drive, which could become compromised by online or offline activities. Documents such as music files, DVD images, movies, disk images, and even a backup of the contents of your main internal hard drive, can all be kept securely and safely on an external hard drive.

Comparison among Floppy CD and DVD

Storage Device	Floppy Disk	CD	DVD
Storage Capacity	1.44 MB	700 MB	4700 MB

By comparing the storage capacity of floppy disk, CD and DVD, one can say that 1 DVD can store data of approximately of 7 CD and 1 CD can store data of approximately 466 Floppy disk.

i.e. 1 DVD = 7CD
1 CD = 486 Floppy Disk

1.7 CONCEPT OF DATA PROCESSING

Data is a collection of facts that are to be organized and manipulated to become useful information. A collection of sales order, class attendance cards are a few examples. But, *processing* is a series of actions or operations that converts input data items into useful output information. Hence, *data processing* is defined as a series of actions or operations that converts data into information. *Data processing* comprises of the following steps:

(a) Capturing data
(b) Storing data
(c) Updating and retrieving data and other useful information

☞ *Manipulation of ra facts into useful information is called* ***data processing****. Data processing ma be carried out b using manual or electronic methods.*

1.7.1 Basic Tasks in Business Data Processing

Business data processing is the manipulation of raw facts using electronic machines. The main purpose of Electronic Data Processing (EDP) is to do complex jobs of processing at an incredible speed.

Sometimes, a part of the data processing job may be done by using manual methods. As an example, a class teacher may prepare the list of marks manually for further processing by a computer to award students the grades and merit position in the class. The latter part is faster and more accurate when done on an electronic machine such as a digital computer.

Since electronic machines are accurate and fast in operations as well as cheaper in price, one may prefer them over manual methods. A business data processing cycle consists of three basic steps (See Figure 1.38). These are:

(a) Input cycle,
(b) Processing cycle, and
(c) Output cycle

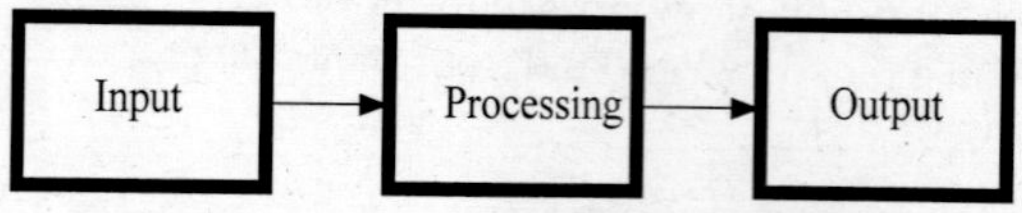

Figure 1.38 Block diagram of a basic data processing cycle

Input Cycle

In this phase, data are prepared in some convenient form and on a storage medium most suitable for entry into a processing machine. For example, in a manual system, we may prefer to write data in a tabular form or on a sheet of paper such as the marks sheet of students of a class. We do so, because it is very convenient to read the marks written in tabular form. In case of an electronic data processing machines, we may store data on a floppy disk or a zip disk or a compact disk.

Processing Cycle

In this cycle, we manipulate or combine the input data with other data as per the instructions. For example, in a manual processing cycle, a class teacher adds the marks secured by each student in different subjects. The teacher divides this addition by the maximum marks and calculates the percentage of marks. The teacher can also award a grade, based on the percentage of marks. In an electronic data processing system, these actions are performed automatically in accordance with a series of instructions called a *program*, which is stored in the computer. The computer will do exactly the same job as is told to it by the set of instructions or program.

Output Cycle or Managing Output

Once data are processed, the results are to be brought out in a most suitable form for the user. This is called the *output c cle*. For example, in the marks processing case, the marks of each student for each subject are transferred to print report cards. Remarks about pass/fail are also recorded on this report along with the merit and the grades. This job is done by a class teacher in a manual data processing system and by a computer using printer in an electronic data processing system.

MODEL QUESTIONS AND ANSWERS

A. Multiple Choice

1.1 Which of the following device can store large amounts of data?

a. Floppy disk b. Hard disk
c. CD-ROM d. Zip disk

1.2 Which of the following holds the ROM, CPU, RAM and expansion cards?

a. Hard disk b. Floppy disk
c. Mother board d. None of the above

1.3 The language that the computer can understand and execute is called:

a. Machine or binary language b. Application software
c. System program d. None of the above

1.4 Main memory stores
a. Data only
b. Program only
c. Data, program and results or any other kind of information
d. None of these

1.5 CD-ROM is a
a. Temporary memory b. Permanent storage
c. Magnetic memory d. None of the above

1.6 Information retrieval is fastest from
a. Pen drive b. CD
c. Hard disk d. All of the above

1.7 RAM means
a. Random Access memory b. Read also memory
c. Read Access memory d. Random also memory

1.8 Which one of the following is a secondary storage device?
a. CD-ROM b. RAM
c. Both (a) and (b) d. None of the above

1.9 Indicate which, of the following best describes the term software
a. Operating system programs
b. Application programs
c. Both (a) and (b)
d. None of the above

1.10 Which one of the following is not an input device?
a. Microphone b. Mouse
c. Scanner d. None of the above

1.11 What is the control unit's function in the CPU?
a. To transfer data to primary storage
b. To store program instructions
c. To perform logic functions
d. To decode program instruction

1.12 CPU consists of
a. ALU b. ALU and control unit
c. ALU, control unit and registers d. None of these

1.13 ________ transforms one interface into another interface
a. Program b. Software
c. Data d. None

1.14 In latest generation computers, the instructions are executed
a. Parallel only b. Sequentially only
c. Both sequentially and parallel d. All of above

1.15 Give the correct abbreviation of CD:
a. Command Description b. Change Data
c. Copy Density d. Compact Disk

1.16 VGA is
a. Video Graphics Array b. Visual Graphics Array
c. Volatile Graphics Array d. Video Graphics Adapter

1.17 MICR stands for
a. Magnetic Ink Code Reader
b. Magnetic Ink Character Reader
c. Magnetic Ink Cases Reader
d. None of the above

1.18 VDU stands for
a. Video Display Unit b. Visible Display Unit
c. Visual Display Unit d. Video Diode Unit

1.19 What is the full form of CRT?
a. Current ray tube b. Current ray technology
c. Cathode Ray tube d. Cathode Ray technology

1.20 Which of the following is input device?
a. Scanner b. Speaker
c. Monitor d. Projector

B. State whether the following are True or False

2.1 Computers cannot help in decision making process.
2.2 ALU is a part of CPU.
2.3 The floppy disk having program in it, is not a magnetic storage device.
2.4 The main advantage of computer graphics is that it substantially increases productivity.
2.5 OCR is a device that scans written or typed text and transforms it into computer readable form.
2.6 The processing of one program after the other without user intervention is an example of batch processing.
2.7 Access to data stored on magnetic tape is random.
2.8 Computer software is normally classified as system software and application software.
2.9 The group of 8 bits is used to represent a byte.
2.10 Logical errors in a program can be identified by the computer.

Answers

A.	1.1	a	1.2	c	1.3	a	1.4	c	1.5	b
	1.6	c	1.7	a	1.8	a	1.9	b	1.10	d
	1.11	c	1.12	b	1.13	b	1.14	c	1.15	d
	1.16	a	1.17	b	1.18	c	1.19	c	1.20	a
B.	2.1	F	2.2	T	2.3	F	2.4	T	2.5	T
	2.6	T	2.7	F	2.8	T	2.9	T	2.10	T

CHAPTER 2

Operating System

2.1 BASICS OF OPERATING SYSTEM

An Operating System (OS) is a set of system software programs in a computer that regulates the ways an application software programs use the computer hardware and the ways that users control the computer. For hardware functions, such as input/output and memory space allocation, operating system programs act as an intermediary between an application programs and the computer hardware. Although application programs are usually executed directly by the hardware. Operating System is also a field of study within Applied Computer Science.

The job of an operating system for a computer is to manage the hardware and software resources of the system. In desktops or laptops, the hardware resources include processes, hard disk, memory, disk space, mouse, printers, other peripherals, etc., whereas the software resources are the various software applications used on that desktop/laptop. Operating systems also play a very important role in providing a consistent interface for the applications irrespective of the hardware or peripherals used. There may be different drivers used along with the operating systems for this purpose.

2.1.1 The Operating System

Operating system works as an interface between the user and the computer and all other programs need an OS to start them. It is software that controls the internal activities of the computer hardware and provides user interface. It is the first program loaded into the computer's memory and states the computer authentically when the power is turned on. Popular operating systems are Windows XP, Windows 10, LINUX and UNIX.

Operating systems

- Controls and coordinates the operation of computer.
- Controls input and output devices.
- Controls execution of computer programs.
- Does all the interaction between user and the computer.
- Helps you to manage and manipulate files and the use of main memory of computer.

An operating system performs the functions:

- Processor Management: It assigns processors (if a computer has more than one processor) to the different tasks that must be performed by the computer system.
- Memory Management: It allocates the main memory and secondary memory to the system programs, user programs and data.

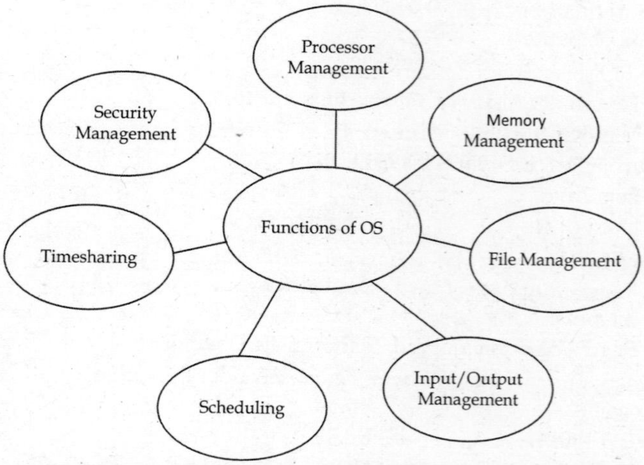

- Input/output Management: It carries out the input/output management, co-ordinates and assigns different input and output devices.
- File Management: It manages files on various storage devices and transfer these files from one storage device to another.
- Scheduling: It establishes and enforces the job priority.
- Timesharing: It co-ordinates and assigns compilers, assemblers, utility programs, and other software packages to various users working on the computer system.
- Security Management: It establishes data security and integrity.

All operating systems can be classified into following categories:

- Single User Operating System: It allows only one user to work on a computer at a time, e.g., Windows XP.
- Multiuser Operating System: It allows a number of users to work together on a single computer by providing a terminal connected to a single computer, e.g., Unix.
- Single Tasking Operating System: It executes a single job/program at a time, e.g., MS-DOS.
- Multitasking Operating System: It supports the execution of more than one job at a time, e.g., Windows 2012.
- Multiprogramming Operating System: In this several programs can be run at a same time via time sharing mechanism, e.g., Linux.
- Real Time Operating System: It responds to an event within a predetermined time, e.g., Windows CE.
- Batch Processing Operating System: Similar types of job are grouped under batch and then jobs are executed without any user interruption, e.g., MS-DOS.

- Multiprocessing Operating System: It uses more than two CPUs within a single computer system, e.g., LINUX, UNIX.

Windows 8 and 10 are the later versions of Windows desktop operating system for the PC. Windows 7 brings a new, more personalized look to the desktop that will also make it easier for users to scan or import images. It is meant to acquire music files on the Web and transfer them to portable devices. Windows 7 will allow different family members to use their own desktop and personal set of files.

Windows 8

Windows 8 is the eighth version of MS Windows, released on October 26, 2012. It includes several improvements to Windows 8, but the most notable feature is an updated user interface, which displays a grid of tiles on the home screen. These tiles provide one-click access to programs, games, and utilities. For example, it includes Photos, Videos, Music, Internet Explorer, Maps, Weather. Several of the tiles, such as the Maps, Weather, and custom social networking tiles, display information that is updated dynamically.

The tile-based interface (called "Metro") optimized for touchscreens as well as mice makes Windows 8 a suitable operating system for both traditional PCs and tablets. It also functions on hybrid systems that include a touchscreen but also support traditional input devices. While the tile-based interface is a major part of Windows 8, but did not get rid of the standard Windows desktop interface.

Windows 10

Windows 10 is a personal computer operating system released by MS as part of the Windows NT family of operating systems. On June 1, 2015, MS first announced that Windows 10 would be released on July 29, 2015. Windows 10 expanding on Metro-style apps and these apps can be designed to run across multiple MS product families including PCs, tablets, smartphones, embedded systems, Xbox One, Surface Hub and HoloLens. The Windows user interface was revised to handle transitions between a mouse-oriented interface and a touchscreen-optimized interface based on available input devices – particularly on 2-in-1 PCs; both interfaces include an updated Start menu that blends the elements of Windows 7's traditional Start menu with the tiles of Windows 8. The first release of Windows 10 also introduces a virtual desktop system, a window and desktop management feature called Task View, the MS Edge web browser, support for fingerprint and face recognition login, new security features for enterprise environments, and DirectX 12 and WDDM 2.0 to improve the operating system's graphics capabilities for games.

2.1.2 Basics of Popular Operating Systems (Linux, Windows)

Windows

One of today's most common operating system is MS Windows. It is the world's largest selling operating system for PCs.

Windows belongs to the category of software called a GUI (Graphical User Interface). The user interface determines how you interact with your computer. The hardware part of the interface consists of your screen monitor, the keyboard and the mouse. The software part of the interface determines what things look like on the screen and how you give commands to your PC to get your work done. With the advent of Windows environment, many of day-to-day computer tasks, such as running programs, opening files, choosing commands, etc. are done by using a graphical approach that is very intuitive to new users of computers. Further, Windows programs use the same command structure and graphical items on the screen, so if you have mastered one Windows program, learning other programs becomes very easy.

As soon as you switch on the power supply, Windows operating system program gets loaded in PC after initial checks and takes the PC's control. It provides the communication link between your computer hardware and the software that you use. For example, when you tell your spreadsheet software to save a file, the operating system tells the computer system how and where to save it.

However, Windows is more than an operating system. It provides functions that let you manage many programs simultaneously, customize PC, and do many of the maintenance tasks associated with a PC. It also comes with many accessories, software programs, such as utilities and media player, etc.

Windows takes care of PC and does many things in the background that are not visible to you. It keeps busy behind the scenes managing your software packages and hardware working. Windows does the following jobs:

- Provides ways for you to start application programs.
- Runs more than one program at a time. This is called multitasking. It means that you can have both a word processing program and spreadsheet program opened at the same time can easily and switch between them.
- Provides a way for you to manage files. Files are documents that you create, namely, letters, memos, and worksheets. Use Windows Explorer, the file management program that comes with Windows, to copy, move, organize, delete, and otherwise work with the files.
- Helps you to set up the Internet access.
- Windows comes with Outlook Express which is an e-mail program. Use this program to send and receive electronic mail, via Internet.
- Windows comes with a number of useful accessory programs, such as WordPad a word processing program. It has a text editor called Notepad for typing notes, etc.
- It provides a way for you to customize the desktop and other screen areas of the monitor.

Linux Operating System

Overview of Linux Linux is a multiuser, multitasking operating system first developed by Linus Benedict Torvalds. Linux is a 32-bit operating system. It runs on a wide variety of platforms, such as Intel, Sparc, Alpha etc. It can be considered in every sense as a full-blown implementation of UNIX. But it cannot be called as UNIX because UNIX is a registered trademark product owned by American Telephone & Telegraph company (AT&T). Linux is distributed as a free software under a free software licence called the GNU General Public License (GNU/GPL).

Advantages of Linux over Windows The advantage of Linux operating systems are:

1. Low Cost: The majority of Linux variants are available for free at a much lower price than MS Windows.
2. Stability: Linux does not need to be rebooted periodically to maintain performance levels. It does not freeze up or slow down over time due to memory leaks .
3. Performance: Linux provides persistent high performance on workstations and on networks. It can handle unusually large numbers of users simultaneously.
4. Network friendliness: Linux was developed by a group of programmers over the Internet and has therefore strong support for network functionality; client and server systems can be easily set up on any computer running Linux. It can perform tasks, such as network backups faster and more reliably than alternative systems.
5. Flexibility: Linux can be used for high performance server applications, desktop applications, and embedded systems. You can save disk space by installing the components needed for a particular use.
6. Compatibility: It runs all common UNIX software packages and can process all common file formats.
7. Fast and easy installation: Most Linux distributions come with user-friendly installation and setup programs. Popular Linux distributions come with tools that make installation of additional software user friendly.
8. Full use of hard disk: Linux continues work well even when the hard disk is almost full.
9. Multitasking: Linux is designed to do many things at the same time; e.g., a large printing job in the background would not slow down other work.

Disadvantages of Linux over Windows

1. Linux has more then three hundred version and all version can not be installed on a single computer system.
2. There are so many distributions of Linux that new users may get confused.
3. Some hardware devices and software may not be compatible with a particular version of Linux.

Basic Linux Elements The basic elements of Linux are discussed in the following sub-sections:

Kernel The kernel is at the core of Linux system and is loaded into the memory as soon as the system starts up. It manages main memory, files and peripheral devices. Maintaining the time and date, launching applications, and allocating system resources are the functions of this part of the operating system.

Shell Shell is a program which interprets commands given by the user. The command can be either typed in through the command line or contained in a file called 'shell script'. Commands in 'shell script' files are interpreted by the shell.

File System Linux treats everything as file. Even a directory is treated as a file that contains entries for several other files. All the hardware devices, such as I/O devices, storage devices etc., are treated as files.

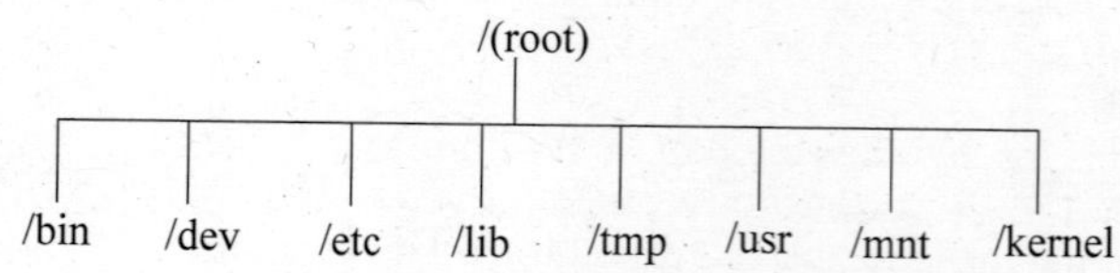

Figure 2.1 Linux file system

The Linux file system is organized in an hierarchy which starts with the root directory. The root is represented by a forward slash (/). Under the root directory several system directories and the home directory are there. Figure 2.1 lists the standard system directories in Linux.

Linux uses forward slash (/) as a separator (Windows or DOS uses backslash (\) as a separator). For example, a subdirectory mydir of the directory usr, will be shown as /usr/mydir. The slash (/) before the usr represents the root directory.

/bin This directory contains executable program files (binary files). In this directory, one can find the files for the Linux commands. (Similar to command.com file in DOS).

/dev This directory contains the special device files. For example, the printer may be a file known as prn in this directory, the hard disk may be hda file and its first partition would be hda0.

/etc This directory contains all the system-wide configuration information as text files.

/lib This directory contains the library files. Library files contain the reusable functions and routines for the programmer to use.

/tmp This directory contains all the temporary files, which will eventually be deleted from the system. This is similar to the C:\windows\temp directory in Windows 98.

/usr This directory contains the home directories of the users, source text for the online manual (man) pages, games and other directories. There is one home directory for each user. For example, for a user called "mini", there will be a directory with the same name in usr directory. The directory mini will contain, all the files and sub-directories created by the user "mini".

/kernel This directory contains all the kernel specific code. Kernel is the heart of the Linux system. It is responsible for resource allocation, security and low-level hardware interfaces.

/mnt This is the directory where the storage devices other than hard disks (floppy disks and CD disks) are mounted. This directory contains the sub-directories "floppy" and "cdrom" which when mounted show the contents of the CD-ROM or floppy disk respectively.

Commands

A Linux command is a series of characters that you type. These characters consist of words separated by white spaces. The first word is the command itself and the rest are the command's arguments. The arguments provide information that the command may need for its execution. Linux commands are case-sensitive. That is, cp is different from CP and cP.

☞ You must type all Linux commands in lowercase letters.

Commands are issued to the shell at the command line. A command line comprises of commands, the line of instructions, options and any command line arguments that you may provide. For example, the following is a command line:

$ man cp

Commands are entered at the shell prompt ($, #). Prompt is merely a symbol that appears at the start of a command line. This lets you know that Linux is ready and waiting for your command.

Device Drivers Device drivers are software packages that form a major part of the kernel. They control the interaction between the hardware devices and the operating system.

Utilities Utilities are software tools included with the Linux operating system that lets you do miscellaneous jobs, such as text editing, programming and communications.

File Handling in Linux

Each directory or file in Linux is referred to, by using its pathname beginning from the root directory. For example, the directory usr is referred to as /usr (/ or root is its parent directory); mini is referred to as /usr/mini, where usr is the parent directory of mini directory.

There are two types of pathnames. These are:

(a) Absolute Pathname
(b) Relative Pathname

An absolute pathname tells you the complete path of a directory starting from the root, as explained above. Root is represented by a forward slash (/). For example, absolute pathname of "Delhi" directory is /usr/mini/sales/north/Delhi.

Relative pathname gives location of a directory, relative to the current working directory. For example, suppose your current working directory is /usr/mini/sales/north. Then the relative pathname to the "Delhi" directory is Delhi. Relative pathnames do not start with a "/".

☞ If you do not start a pathname with "/", Linux assumes that you are using relative pathname.

Identifying the Current Working Directory

To find out which directory you are currently working in, type the following command.

$ pwd Enter

The pwd command prints the absolute pathname of your current working directory. It takes no arguments. For example, in Figure 2.2, the user "mini" got the result as /usr/mini.

Making New Directories (mkdir) To create a new directory, use the mkdir command followed by the directory name. For example, suppose user mini (who is currently in the home directory /usr/mini) wants to create a directory named "sales", user need to give the following command (See Figure 2.2).

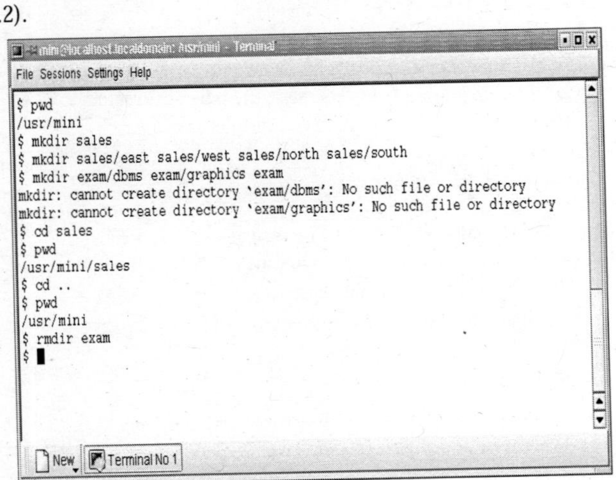

Figure 2.2 A sample Linux session using various commands

$ mkdir sales Enter

The sub-directory "sales" is created under the current directory (i.e. /usr/mini).

To create a number of directories with one mkdir command, separate the directory names with spaces. For example, the following command creates various directories (See Figure 2.2).

$ mkdir sales/east sales/west sales/north sales/south Enter

The above command will create four directories under the sales directory.

☞ The order of specifying the arguments is important. Note that we cannot create a sub-directory before creating its parent directory.

If we enter the command as:

$ mkdir exam/dbms exam/graphics exam Enter

In this case, the system will fail to create the two subdirectories dbms and graphics, but it will create the exam directory.

Moving to a Different Directory (cd) You can change your working directory by using the cd command followed by the pathname (absolute or relative) to which you want to move.

For example, to move to the sales directory, type the following command:

```
$ cd sales[Enter]
```

Note that in the above command, we have made use of the relative pathname. After giving the above command, if you give the pwd command, you will see the result as /usr/mini/sales (See Figure 2.2).

☞ The cd command without any following pathname always takes the user back to the user's HOME directory.

☞ Linux uses a single dot (.) to represent the current working directory and double dots (..) to represent the parent directory of the current working directory. For example, typing `cd..` will take user "mini" to her HOME directory (/usr/mini), since that is the parent directory of sales.

Removing a Directory (rmdir) The command rmdir is used for deleting a directory. The directory to be deleted must be empty for this command to work. For example, to remove the "exam" directory, type the following command (See Figure 2.2):

```
$ rmdir exam[Enter]
```

☞ We can also delete more than one directory by separating the multiple directory names with spaces.

☞ You cannot remove a directory if you are placed in one of its sub-directories.

Listing the Contents of Directories (ls)

To list the files and sub-directories of the current directory, ls command is used. Its function is equivalent to the DIR command of DOS. For example, to list the contents of current directory, user "mini" should type the following:

```
$ ls
```

following result will get displayed:

east
north
south
west

The order of display is numerals→uppercase characters→lowercase characters. That is, the list is displayed with numerals having precedence over alphabets and in alphabets, uppercase has precedence over lower case.

If the names of files and directories under a specified directory (say north) are to be listed out, then we need to specify the directory name with ls command, as follows:

```
$ ls north
```

The above command will give the result as shown in Figure 2.3.

Usually, a directory contain many files, and user may be interested in knowing whether a particular file is available or not. In that case, he/she just has to use ls with the filename, as follows:

```
$ ls March
```

The above command will prompt–File Not Found error, since there is no file called "March" in our current directory. Had the file existed, ls would have displayed the filename.

The command ls can be used along with a number of options. Options are nothing but predetermined arguments used along with a minus sign (-). The different options forces the command to work differently.

For example, the following command will display file and directory names in multiple columns.

```
$ ls -x
```

The result is:

```
east     north     south     west
```

Table 2.1 lists the different options of ls and their uses.

Table 2.1 Options of the command ls

Option	Used to
-x	get multi-columnar output.
-r	list files and sub-directories in reverse order.
-t	list files and sub-directories with time order.
-a	list all files, including the normally hidden files.
-A	list all files excluding . and .. .
-c	list files by inode modification time.
	list the inode for each file.
-i	display permissions, owner, size, modification time etc., along with file and directory names.

```
$ ls -1
```

To list the names of files and sub-directories of the current directory, Is command is used. Its function is equivalent to the DIR command in MS-DOS. For example, to list the contents of current directory, user "mini" should type the following:
The purpose of -1 is that along with file and directory names. It will display names of hidden files also.

```
$ ps
```

It will display information about a selection of active process.

```
$ kill all
```

It sends a signal to all processes running any of the specified commands.

Creating Files (using cat) To create a file, type the command cat at the shell prompt, followed by > character and the filename. For example, to create a file called January, enter the following command.

```
$ cat > January[Enter]
```

After you press Enter key, you will be prompted to enter the contents of the file. Type the data and press [Ctrl] + [D] keys together to terminate the command line (See Figure 2.3).

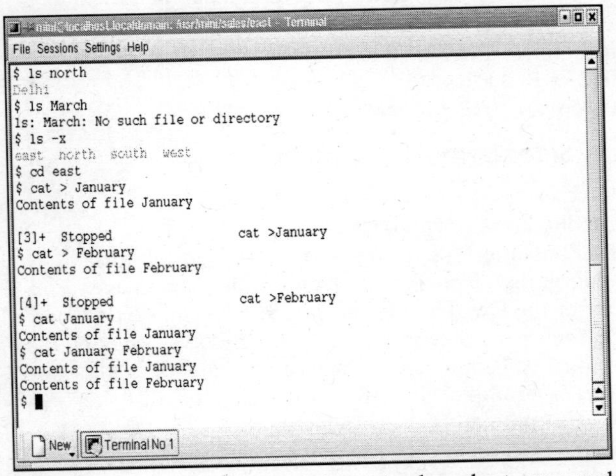

Figure 2.3 A sample Linux session using ls and cat commands

Listing the Contents of Files (cat) To list the contents of a file, use the command cat followed by the filename. DOS has TYPE command for this.

For example, to list the contents of file January type the following:

$ cat January Enter

Absolute pathname can be given to display a file in another directory. The cat command can also display more than one file by separating different filenames with spaces, as seen in the following command:

$ cat January February Enter

The above command will display the contents of the two files in different rows. Use of cat command to create and display the contents of files is shown in Figure 2.3.

Copying Files (cp) The command cp is used to copy a file into another. DOS equivalent for cp is the COPY command. Like in DOS, the cp command requires two arguments – a source filename, the contents of which are to be copied and a target filename, to which the contents are to be copied.

For example, to copy the file January into another file, say March, type the following (See Figure 2.4):

$ cp January March Enter

Note that the ls command will now show three files, namely January, February and March.

☞ Use cp with -i option if you want the system to ask for confirmation before copying the files.

Here, the file January is copied to a new file called March.

☞ If March file already exists, its contents will be destroyed and re-placed by contents of January file.

If you want to give more than one options along with command, you can use either of the following:

$ ls -l -a -t

$ ls -lat

Both the above methods will work.

Deleting Files (rm) To delete or remove a file, the rm command is used. This is equivalent to the DEL command in DOS.

For example, to remove the file March, type the following command:

$ rm March Enter

This is shown in Figure 2.4.

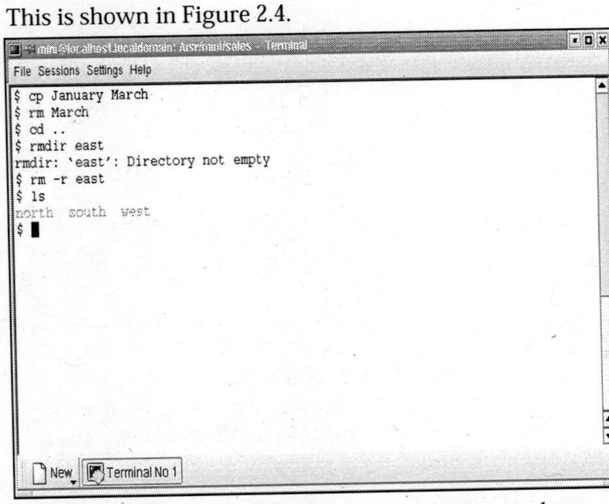

Figure 2.4 A sample Linux session using cp and rm commands

☞ Use rm with -i option if you want the system to ask for confirmation, like in cp.

To remove a directory, use rm with -r option. Here -r stands for recursive deletion. For example, the following command will remove the directory accounts.

$ rm -r accounts Enter

☞ Unlike rmdir, rm -r will remove directories even if they are not empty.

In Figure 2.4, the system did not delete the directory "east" when rmdir command was given, but did so with the rm -r command.

Moving Files (mv) A file can be moved, using the mv command. Equivalent command in DOS is MOVE. The following command will displace the directory north from "sales" directory to the directory "/usr/mini".

$ mv north /usr/mini/north Enter

The above command does not create a copy of "north" but displaces it.

Now if you type the ls command, you will only see two directories, south and west (See Figure 2.5). The directory "east" was removed using rm -r command and "north" is moved to a different directory. The directory "/usr/mini" now contains the north directory and all its sub-directories and files as shown by the ls command in Figure 2.5.

Perform mv operation again to bring back the directory.

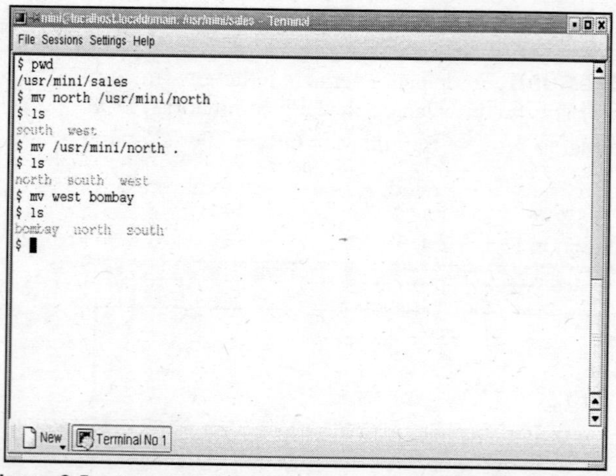

Figure 2.5 A sample Linux session using commands discussed till now

$ mv /usr/mini/north.

Note that the dot (.) represents current directory.

Files and directory can also be renamed by using the mv command. For example, the following command will rename the directory "west" as "bombay" (See Figure 2.5):

$ mv west bombay Enter

Files can also be renamed in the same way. If the destination exists, it will be overwritten and if it does not exist, it will be created.

☞ mv also has the -i option like cp and rm commands and works in the same way.

Installation of Linux

We will be discussing about the installation of popular Red Hat Linux 7.2 in this section. Before listing the procedures to follow for installing the Linux operating system, let us see what are the hardware and software requirements of Linux.

Hardware Requirements Red Hat Linux can be installed if the following basic hardware requirements are met:

(a) x86 platform namely 80386, 80486 etc.
(b) Intel, Sparc, Alpha or Advanced Micro Devices (AMD)
(c) processor
(d) x386 CPU family or above
(e) Minimum 128 MB RAM
(f) Minimum 2 GB free hard disk space
(g) Input devices, such as keyboard, mouse etc.
(h) Controller cards, such as Small Computer System Interface (SCSI), Integrated Development Environment (IDE), Firewire, etc.
(i) A Network card such as ISA, PCI or USB, etc.
(j) Sound card compatible to Linux

Software Requirements Software requirements for Linux installation are listed as follows:

(a) A partitioning program such as fdisk or disk druid supplied by Red Hat.
(b) Linux Software package.

Preliminary Steps before Installation

The first step is to create an installation disk.

➡ **To create the installation disk:**

1. Copy the "boot.img" file from the Red Hat CD-ROM disk into a floppy disk. This file can be found in the /images directory of the CD. The file can be created using either the DOS rewrite command (in a DOS/WIindows system) or the Linux dd command (in an existing Linux or UNIX system). For example, to create an installation diskette using the dd command, do the following:
   (a) Insert and mount the CD-ROM and then insert a blank floppy into the floppy drive of your computer.
   (b) Now give the following command
   # dd if=mnt/cdrom/images/boot.img of=/dev/fd0 bs=1440k Enter
   The above command will copy from the input file ("if") mnt/cdrom/boot.img onto the output file ("of") /dev/fd0. It is assumed that floppy drive is accessible from /dev/fd0.

   To create an installation diskette using the rawrite program, give the following command (it is assumed that CD-ROM is accessible as drive D):
   D:>cd images dosutils\rawrite Enter
   For the source file enter "D:\boot.img" and for destination enter "A:".
   The bootable installation disk is now ready and you can use it to install your Linux system.
   Red Hat Linux can also be installed by booting using any of the following methods:
   (a) Booting using a floppy diskette (created as explained above)
   (b) Booting directly from the CD-ROM (your Basic Input Output System (BIOS) should support this)
   (c) Using a hard drive partition to hold the installation software
   (d) Booting from a DOS command line
   (d) Booting from across a network using Hypertext Transfer Protocol (HTTP) or File Transfer Protocol (FTP) protocols.
   (e) Booting from an NFS (Network File System) mounted hard drive.
2. The next step is to plan a partitioning strategy. This step is based on the knowledge of existing hardware. The planning process should also take into consideration the future expansion of the system. Knowing how to allocate the hard disk space for each of the Linux software is a real big challenge which every Linux system administrator has to take. He should find answers to the following questions:

(a) How much of the disk is required presently and in future?
(b) Is any other operating system also required?
(c) How many application software packages are expected to be installed in future?
(d) How much data needs to be backed up?
(e) How many users will the system have?

3. If you require that the system should boot any other operating system also along with Linux, the next step is to choose a boot loader. Boot loader is a software that is responsible for booting Linux along with any other operating system. Examples include LILO (LInux LOader) and GRUB (GRand Unified Bootloader).
4. Now insert the floppy disk (the installation diskette you have created if you are using floppy to boot your system) into a floppy drive and power-on your system. After a few moments, the Red Hat installation program screen will appear.

Hard Drive Partitioning

A hard disk must be partitioned taking into consideration the present and future requirements. For example, let us consider that we have a given hard disk of 40 GB capacity. The different partitions can be as follows:

/swap directory	About double the main memory size. For example, a system having 128 MB memory should get 256 MB swap space.
/directory (root)	About 60% of the available space.
/bin directory	About 20% of the available space.
/usr directory	Remaining space.

The size of /usr should be the largest one. This is because all the users' directories and files, installed application softwares, Web pages, log files, etc., will be stored here only.

Booting a Linux system

The general booting procedure involves checking of the basic subsystems of your computer, such as amount and validity of RAM, CPU time and speed, presence of floppy, CD-ROM or hard drive, keyboard and other attributes. The Linux may fail to boot if it detects a hardware failure, missing hardware or hardware mis-configuration.

Next the BIOS will look for the bootable disk, in the order given in the settings (such as search floppy first, then CD-ROM and then the hard drive). Following this, it will look for the boot code in the Master Boot Record (MBR) of the first hard disk. This area of the disk (MBR) contains the boot sector which loads the boot loader (viz. LILO, GRUB or BootMagic).

When the Linux kernel is loaded, the kernel will carry out the following:

(a) Initialize and load a RAM disk image.
(b) Perform timing tests.
(c) Parse for any boot time kernel arguments.
(d) Recognize, set-up and initialize the CPU.
(e) Set up kernel memory and process handling.
(f) Open a console for displaying kernel boot messages.
(g) Initialize configured system devices.
(h) Start memory handling (paging, etc.)
(i) Set up and mount the file system.
(j) Start the init command.

The entire sequence of events that take place when the Linux kernel is loaded can be found in the file usr/src/linux/init/main.c.

☞ If all goes well, you will see a "login" prompt. You can now login using your username and password.

2.2 THE USER INTERFACE IN WINDOWS XP

Windows XP automatically starts when you turn on your computer. Windows XP lets many users to create their own accounts, with optional passwords. Each account contains all the settings that the account's user likes, such as screen colours, Start menu options, and other preferences. When some one first starts the computer, a Welcome screen appears with each user's account name and an associated icon (See Figure 2.6). From the list of available users, click the user account with which you want to log on. For example, click first name icon for Satish Jain.

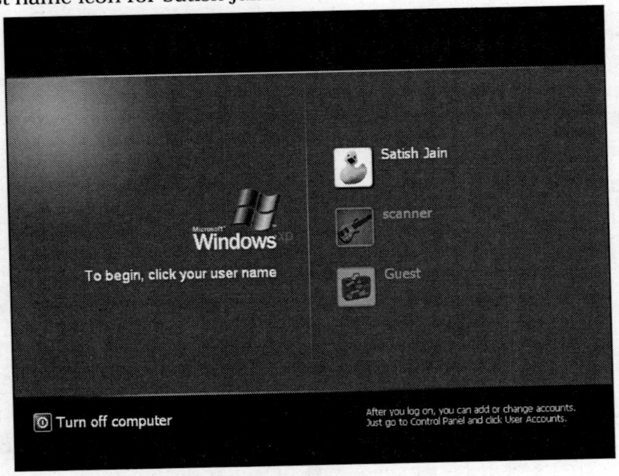

Figure 2.6 Select the User Account

Windows Terminology

Windows terminology has very specific meaning. Various terms used are given below. Whenever indoubt, you should refer to the help for meaning of each term.

Choose: Executes a command.

Select: Selects an item to activate it so that it can be changed. Selecting a command or option turns it on but does not complete it. Selected text or menu names/items appear in reverse type or a different colour. Selected options show a dot (•) or an (×). Also the selected graphics appear enclosed by a dashed line or enclosed in boxes known as handles.

Point: Move the mouse so that the arrow pointer is on the desired menu name, command name, or graphic object.

Pointer: Pointer is the on its screen symbol controlled by the mouse. The pointer changes its shape to indicate the current status and the type of functions and selections available.

I-beam: When the mouse pointer is in a text area that you can edit, the pointer appears as a vertical I-beam.

Mouse Buttons: MS mouse has two buttons and other makes may have three. Clicking the left button completes an action and clicking the right most button changes to shortcut menu.

Using the Mouse

The mouse is a very convenient hand-held pointing device which is used to control the position of the on-screen pointer. As you move the mouse on your desk or mouse pad, the pointer moves on the screen corresponding to the mouse movement. Using the mouse, you can select menus, commands, text, graphic objects, or window.

☞ You must make sure that the surface must be smooth and clean on which you move the mouse. You must avoid using the mouse on paper or cardboard surfaces.

The main mouse actions are:

Click: Press and release the left mouse button quickly as you point to an item. Clicking is used to reposition the insertion point in text, select a menu, choose a command from a menu, or select an option from a dialog box.

Double-click: As you point to the pointed item on the screen; press and release the left mouse button twice quickly. By double-clicking an icon or file name, you can open an application or window related to that icon or file name.

Right click: Position the tip of the mouse pointer in the desired location on a document or toolbar and then click the right mouse button.

Shift+click: Press and hold down the Shift key as you click. You use this method to select many consecutive file names, or to select text between the current insertion point and the location where you press Shift+click keys together.

Ctrl+click: Press and hold down the Ctrl key as you click. This is used to select many nonconsecutive file names or item of choices.

Dragging: Dragging is moving objects on the monitor's screen. It is similar to moving objects on a desk. For example, clicking and dragging an icon is like physically picking up a pencil with your hand on a desk and putting the pencil in a new location. Similarly, to move object on your monitor's screen, you first position the mouse pointer on the object. Next, you "pick up" the object by pressing and holding down the left mouse button. While you are still holding down the mouse button, move the mouse pointer to where you want to "drop" the object, and then release the mouse button.

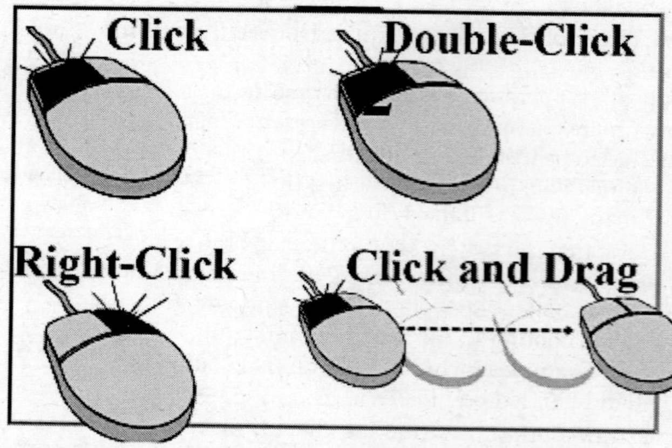

➡ **To select an object or menu item using the mouse:**

1. Move the mouse so that the tip of the pointer on the screen is on the command, graphic object, or text that you want to select.
2. Now without moving the mouse, press and release the left mouse button quickly.

➡ **To *drag* with the mouse:**

1. Move the mouse so that the tip of the pointer is on the object or at the beginning of the text to be selected. (Note that over text, the pointer appears as an I-beam).
2. Press and hold down the mouse left button.
3. Holding down the mouse button, move the mouse slowly to the right or left and up or down. This is called dragging (See Figure 2.7). Notice that while dragging a graphic, the object moves as you move the mouse. However, when you are selecting text, the highlighted text area expands as you move the mouse.
4. Release the mouse button.

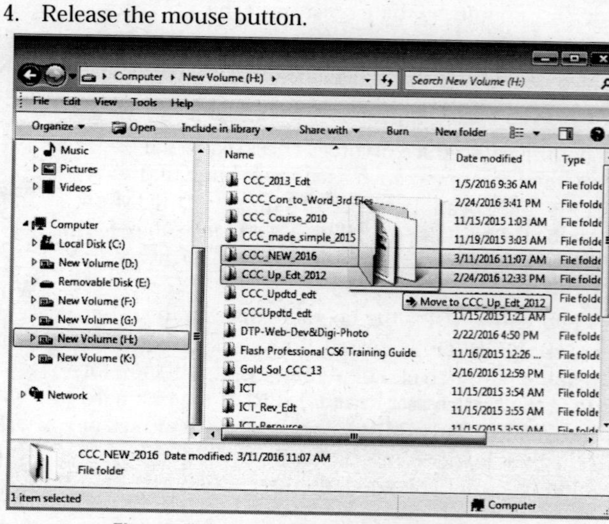

Figure 2.7 Moving an Icon by dragging

Using the Keyboard

The mouse and the keyboard need to work as a team for controlling the Windows operations. Some tasks can be performed more easily with the mouse and some with the keyboard.

Keyboard Terminology

The following conventions are followed throughout the book while using the keyboard. A comma (,) sign between keystrokes indicates that you release the first key before pressing the second key say for example — Alt, Space bar means press and release the Alt key and then press Space bar.

A plus (+) sign between keystrokes indicates that you press and hold down the first key and then press the second key say for example — Alt+Esc means press and hold down the Alt key and press the Esc key.

Alt *letter ke* Press and release the Alt key and then press the corresponding letter key. This action opens a menu without choosing a command.

Alt *letter ke* Press and hold down the Alt key and press the underlined letter key. This action opens a menu or selects an option in a dialog box.

etter ke Press the letter in the command that is underlined in the menu on-screen to choose a command in a menu (this book shows the letter you are to press in bold and underlined). Press C, for example, to choose the Copy command.

rro ke Press the appropriate directional arrow key say for example, ↑ ← ↓ → arrow keys.

Keystrokes to Control the Menus

The following table describes the use of the keyboard for working with menus.

Keystroke	Action
Alt	To activate the menu bar.
Alt+letter key	To select the menu indicated by the letter (letter is underlined in the menu on-screen; and shown in bold and underlined in this book).
Letter key	To execute the command in the menu indicated by the letter.
Arrow keys	To select but not to choose the next menu (use the right or left arrows) or the next command (use the up or down arrows as the case may be).
Enter	To execute the selected command in the menu.
Esc	To close the current menu without making a choice. Press Esc a second time to deactivate the menu bar and return to the document.

Keystrokes to Control Dialog Boxes

The following table describes the use of the keyboard for working with dialog boxes.

Keystroke	Action
Arrow keys	To select or to scroll file names in a list box.
Tab	To select the next text box, list box, group of options, or button.
Shift+Tab	To select the previous text box, list box, group of options, or button.
Alt+letter	This option selects the option, text box, or list box specified by the letter (letter is underlined on-screen and shown in bold and underlined in this book.)
Space bar	To select or deselect the active check box or button.
Enter	To choose the bold or outlined button (usually the OK button). Pressing this key completes the command or opens another dialog box.
Esc	Closes an open dialog box without making any changes.

2.2.1 Desktop

The Desktop is the work area on a Windows screen where you are made to work. It is the main screen that you can see after you switch ON your computer and log on to Windows. It is called the Desktop because Windows uses your whole screen in a way that is similar to the way you use the top of your desk. As you work in Windows XP, you move items on the Desktop, retrieve and put away items and perform many other day-to-day tasks.

Exploring the Desktop

The different icons of the Windows XP opening screen are as shown in Figure 2.8 and discussed in the following paragraphs.

2.2.2 The Taskbar

Along the bottom of the screen as seen in Figure 2.9 is the Taskbar. The Taskbar can also be displayed along the side or the top of the screen.

The different parts of the Taskbar (as seen in Figure 2.9) are explained in the following Table 2.2.

Table 2.2 Desktop icons

Taskbar Elements	Function
Start button	It is located at the left end of the Taskbar. Clicking the start button brings up the start menu as seen in Figure 2.8.
Toolbars	Toolbars represent a set of related icons for an easy access of mouse. For example, the Quick launch toolbar provides icons for launching Internet Explorer and Outlook Express. Windows provides several toolbars which you can use as per your convenience.

(Contd...)

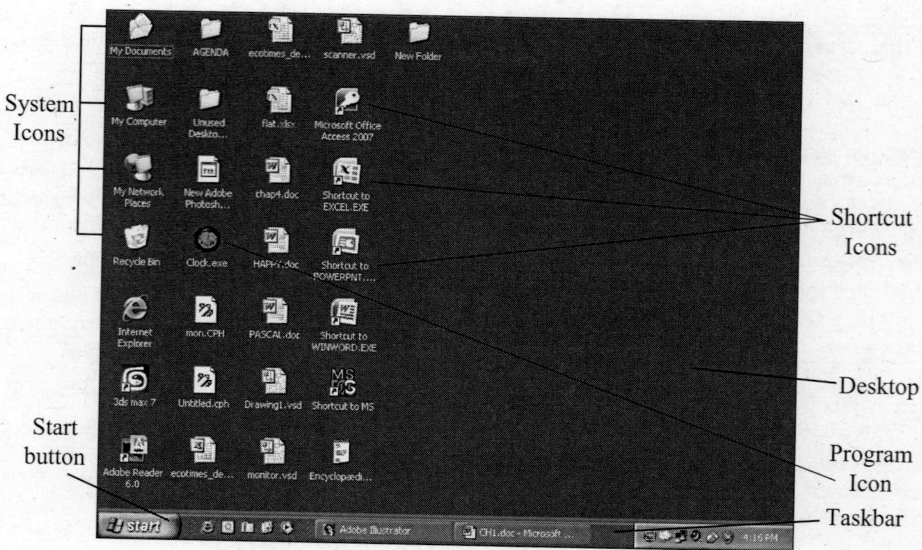

Figure 2.8 Different parts of the Windows XP screen

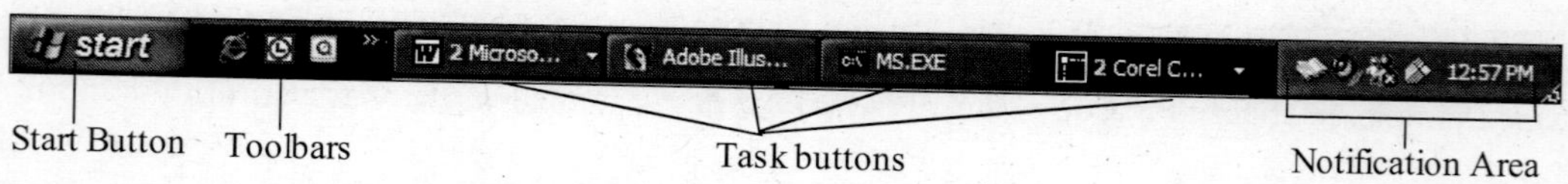

Figure 2.9 Different Parts of the Taskbar

Taskbar Elements	Function
Task buttons	Task buttons are displayed in the center portion of the Taskbar. A button appears for each program you have started or each document you have opened. You can click these buttons to move from one open Program or Folder to another.
Notification area	The right corner of the Taskbar has the Notification area in which Windows provides information about the status of your system. To see the description of the icon appearing in the notification area, position the mouse pointer on the icon.

Customization of Taskbar

There is no reason to customize the Taskbar. But if you really want to customize the Taskbar and change its properties then follow the undermentioned steps.

➡ **To customize the Taskbar:**

1. Right Click on unoccupied area of the Taskbar and then choose Properties. The Taskbar and Start Menu properties dialog box appears as shown in Figure 2.10.
2. In this dialog box, click on Taskbar Options Tab to change the settings ON or OFF. If check mark appears, it means option is ON otherwise option is OFF.
   Select _ock the taskbar check box, if you want the Taskbar to fix in a position from where it cannot be moved to a

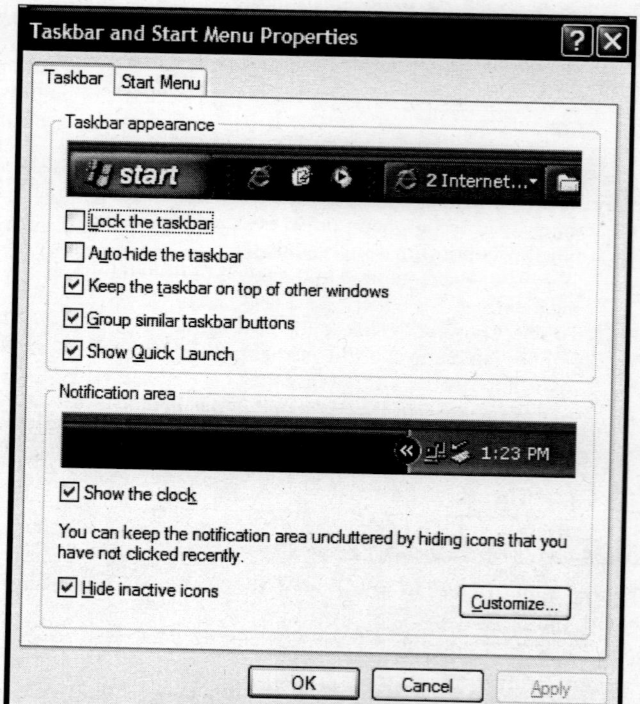

Figure 2.10 Taskbar Properties dialog box with Taskbar Options Tab

new location on the desktop. It also locks the size and position of the toolbars so that it cannot be changed.
Select A_to-hide the taskbar check box, if you want to hide the Taskbar. When you want it to reappear then move the mouse pointer over the Taskbar location.
Select Keep the taskbar on top of other windows check box, if you want taskbar to appear always on top whether any program is open or not.
Select _roup similar taskbar buttons check box, if you want the different buttons of the same program into one button.
Select Show _uick Launch check box, if you want to display the Quick Launch bar on the Taskbar.
Select Show the clock check box to show the system clock on the Taskbar.
Select _ide inactive icons check box when you want to hide the unused icons from the notification area of the taskbar.

3. After changing the setting according to you need, click on the Apply button and then OK button to save the settings.

Cleaning the Desktop

This feature is new in Windows XP. With the help of Desktop Cleanup Wizard you can remove shortcuts that you do not use from your desktop. The wizard automatically runs every 60 days, or you can start it yourself whenever you want.

➡ **To Remove unused desktop icons:**

1. In Display Properties dialog box, select Desktop Tab (See Figure 2.11).
2. In this dialog box, click Customize Desktop... button.
3. A dialog box Desktop Items appears as seen in Figure 2.11.

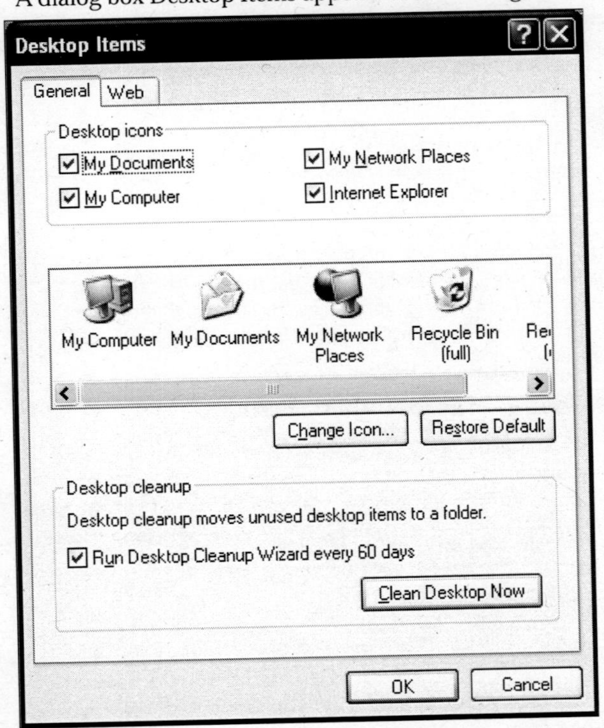

Figure 2.11 Display properties with Desktop Items dialog box

4. Under Desktop cleanup group, click Clean Desktop Now. Follow the directions in the Desktop Cleanup Wizard. The Desktop Cleanup Wizard displays a list of desktop icons that have not been used for 60 days or more, enabling you to remove those icons that you do not want on your desktop.

2.2.3 Start Menu

Start menu appears when you click on the Start button on the Taskbar as seen in Figure 2.12. The Start menu provides you with more customization options. It shows you who is logged on. It automatically adds the most frequently used programs to the top-level menu. It enables you to move any programs you want to the Start menu Items, such as My Pictures and My Documents folders and Control Panel are also now available from the top level.

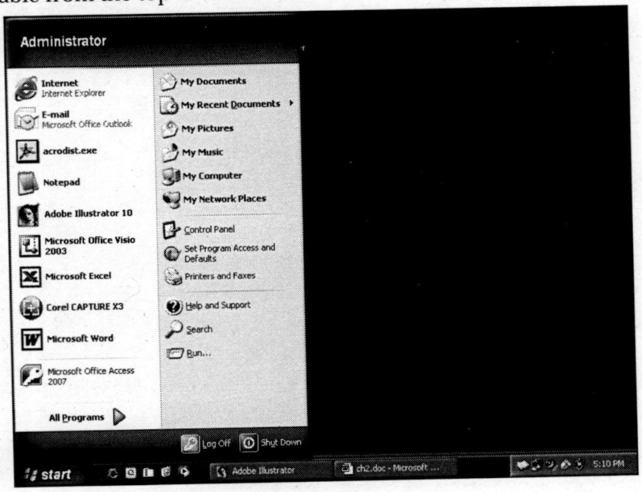

Figure 2.12 Start menu

All Programs

It displays the Programs menu which contain many application programs you can run.

My Recent Documents

It displays the Document menu that contains the list of the documents you have recently opened. To open the recently used documents, choose it from the list of this menu.

Control Panel

It allows you to install software and change different settings of Windows, such as Date, Time, Keyboard, Mouse, Password, Display, Sound settings.

Printers and Faxes

It allows you to see the current status of the printers and Faxes.

Help and Support

It displays online help which is a set of screens of information about Windows itself and the accessories that comes with it.

Search

It displays a window by which you can find files, folders, computers, people, pictures, etc.

Run

It allows you to run any program by typing name and location of that program.

Log Off

If your computer is on a local area network, this command closes all the programs, disconnects your computer from the network, and prepares your computer to be used by someone else for logging on.

Turn off Computer

It displays the Turn off Computer dialog box. Choose Turn off if you are ready to switch off computer. Choose Restart to restart your computer. Choose Stand by if you want to put your computer to low power state.

Customization of Start Menu

➡ **To customize the Start menu:**

1. Right Click on unoccupied area of the task bar and then choose Properties. The Taskbar and Start Menu properties dialog box appears as shown in Figure 2.10. In this dialog box, click Start Menu Tab to customize the start menu (See Figure 2.13).

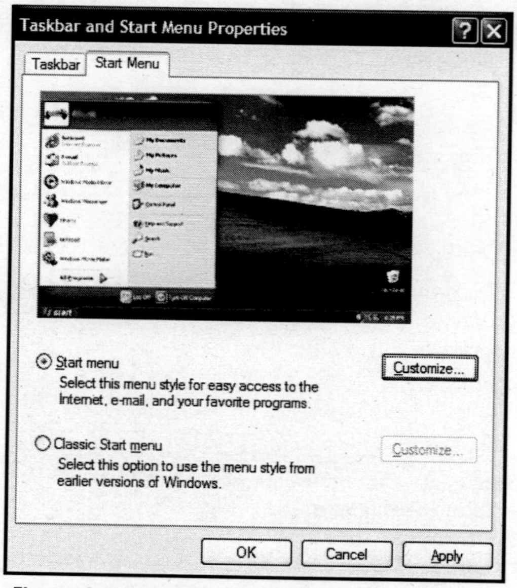

Figure 2.13 Taskbar Properties dialog box with Start Menu Programs Tab

2. In this Tab, Select _tart menu option to select the default Start menu.
   Select the Classic Start menu option to select the style from an earlier version of Windows.
   If you want to make additional selections for the Start menu style, click Customize... . It includes specifying the items you want to display on the Start menu, clearing your list of recently used programs, documents, and Web sites, etc.
3. After that, click on the Apply button and then click OK button to save the changes.

2.2.4 Icons and their Types

An icon is a graphic object that shows a program or a file on your desktop or monitor. The different types of icons are described in the successive sub-sections (See Figure 2.8).

System Icons

System icons are displayed along left edge of the screen. These objects are created automatically by Windows during its installation. The five system icons are explained in the following Table 2.3.

Table 2.3 System Icon

System Icon	Function
My Computer	This icon lets you browse through the resources connected to your computer.
My Documents	This icon represents a folder that is used by many programs as a default location for starting the documents.
Internet Explorer	This icon starts Internet Explorer.
Network Neighborhood	This icon opens a Windows Explorer window displaying the names of each server or computer in your own work group.
Recycle Bin	This icon provides temporary storage for files and folders that you delete.

Shortcut Icons

These are the icons with small arrows in the lower left corner. A shortcut icon provides easy access to some objects on your system, such as a program, a document, or a printer, etc. The shortcut icon only contains information about the location of the object but not the object itself.

Program, Folder and Document Icons

These are non–system icons without arrows and they represent the actual objects they describe.

☞ Thus, if you delete such an icon you are deleting the object itself, from the hard disk. So be very careful!

My Computer Icon

My Computer icon lets you browse through all the resources attached to your PC. When you click on My Computer icon, a Windows Explorer window similar to the one shown in Figure 2.14 appears.

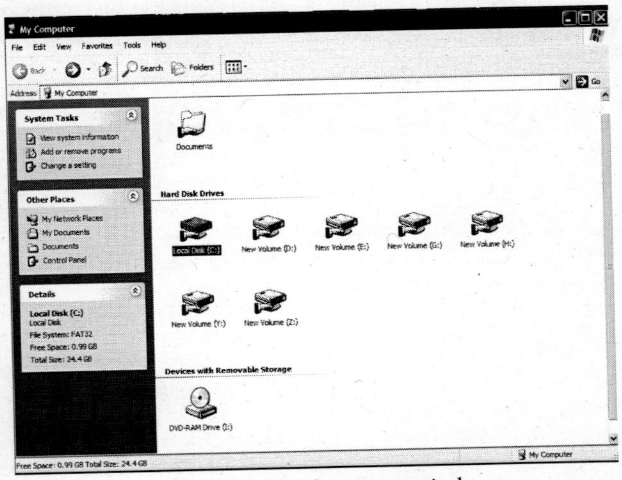

Figure 2.14 My Computer window

Windows Explorer is a program that Windows uses to display the folder contents. This window includes icons for each of the computer's disk drives (floppy disk, hard disk, CD-ROM, zip drive, etc.) and network directories if you have connected your PC to a network. It also shows additional system folders, providing access to the Windows Control Panel, printers, Dial-Up Networking, and a folder that manages scheduled tasks.

> ☞ To change the name of My Computer Icon, right-click the icon. Choose Rename from the context menu. Type the name you want to use and then press Enter key.

Recycle Bin

Files and folders deleted from your hard drives are not actually deleted but transferred to the Recycle Bin. The Recycle Bin icon appears on the desktop and looks like a waste paper basket. When you open the icon, a Folder window opens, displaying the files and folders that have been deleted since the Recycle Bin was last emptied. In effect, the Recycle Bin works like a folder.

> ☞ Unlike a folder, the Recycle Bin is not contained on a single drive. Each of your computer's hard drives maintains its own Recycle Bin folder, and the contents of all the Recycle folders are visible whenever you open the Recycle Bin (See Figure 2.15).

2.2.5 Running an Application Window

Application window contains a program which you are running and working with, namely, the Window that shows MS Word, Excel, PowerPoint, etc. Most of the work that you do will be in application window.

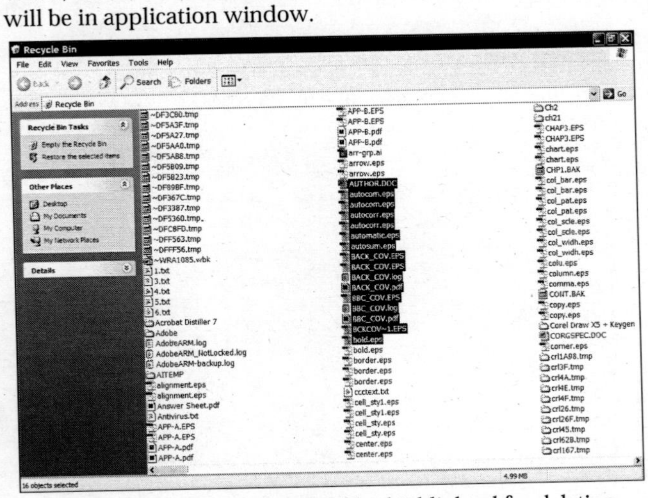

Figure 2.15 Recycle Bin with files highlighted for deletion

➡ **To open an application window:**

1. Click the Start button. The Start menu appears.
2. Highlight the All programs menu item that displays the list of programs comes up. Select item that has a pointer to the right of its name is a Program group. A Program group is a collection of Programs and related document files. When you choose a Program group, it opens a menu listing the items in the program group.
3. From the All Program menu item list, click the desired application, such as Word, Access, PowerPoint etc. For example, an application window (MS Word) open (See Figure 2.16).

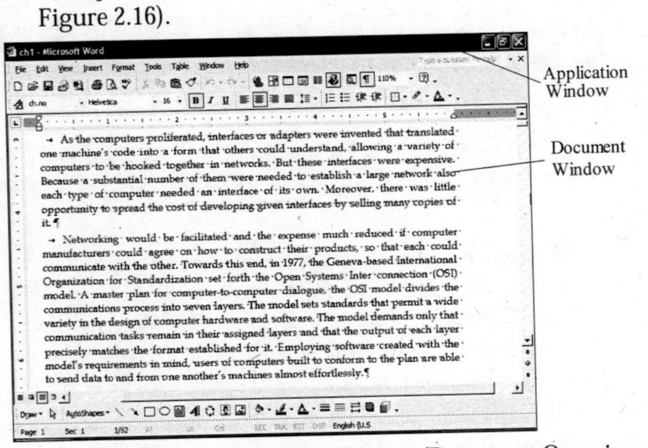

Figure 2.16 Application Window (Document Open in MS Word)

Notepad

The Notepad is also one of the products in Accessories group of Windows 7. It can be used for writing notes and e-mail messages. It is useful for editing and storing all textual data.

Starting Notepad

➡ **To start Notepad, do this:**

1. Click Start button, choose All Programs, highlight Accessories, and then choose Notepad. The Notepad window appears as shown in Figure 2.17.

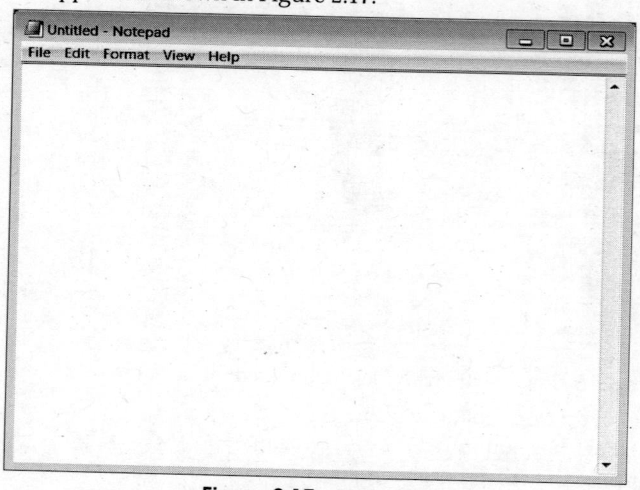

Figure 2.17 Notepad

➡ **To open a new file in the Notepad, do this:**

1. Click the File menu and choose New.

➡ **To open an existing file, do this:**

1. Click the File menu and choose Open... .
2. In the Open dialog box, that appears, specify the name and location of the file you want to open.
3. Then click Open button.

☞ Notepad can open files with the extensions .BAT, .SYS, .INI, and .TXT as these files are all in ASCII code.

➡ **To close a Notepad file do this:**

1. Click the File menu and choose Exit or press Alt + F4 keys together.

WordPad

WordPad is a basic word processing program inbuilt with Windows 7 that you can use to create and edit documents. It does not have word processing facilities as much as MS Word. But, Word Pad documents can include rich formatting and graphics, and you can link to or embed objects, such as pictures or other documents.

➡ **To start WordPad do this:**

1. Click Start button, choose All Programs, highlight Accessories, and then choose WordPad.
2. The WordPad window will appear as shown in Figure 2.18. Various elements of the WordPad screen are marked in this Figure. With WordPad, you can open and edit a document.

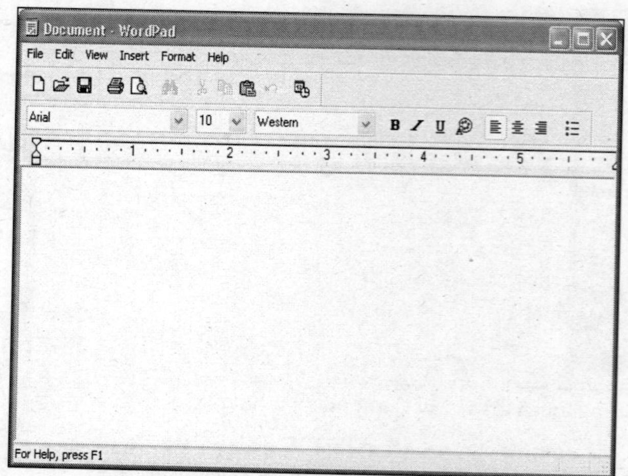

Figure 2.18 WordPad's Opening Screen

☞ WordPad does not offer many of the advanced features that you get in MS Word. But all the same it does offer many of the formatting tools that you need to create a letter, memo, etc.

Opening and Saving Files in WordPad

In WordPad, you can open and edit a document.

➡ **To Open a document in WordPad do this:**

1. Click WordPad button and choose Open. The Open dialog box appears as in Figure 2.19. Or
   In the Recent Documents pane, WordPad program keeps track of the last files you opened. If you want to open file once again, you can just click that filename.

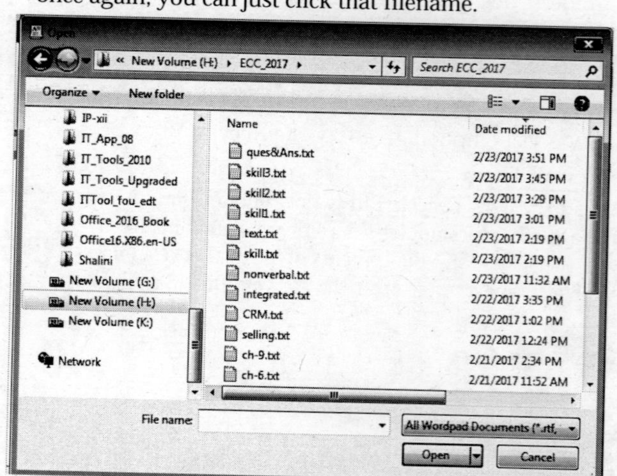

Figure 2.19 WordPad's Open Dialog Box

2. In the Open dialog box, from the left pane double click the drive and then double click the folder in which your file exists, then from the right pane, select the file which you want to open.
3. Then click the Open button.

➡ **To save a document do this:**

1. To name a document or when saving it for the first time, click WordPad button and choose Save as. The Save As dialog box appears as in Figure 2.20. In Save As dialog box, specify the name and location of the file.

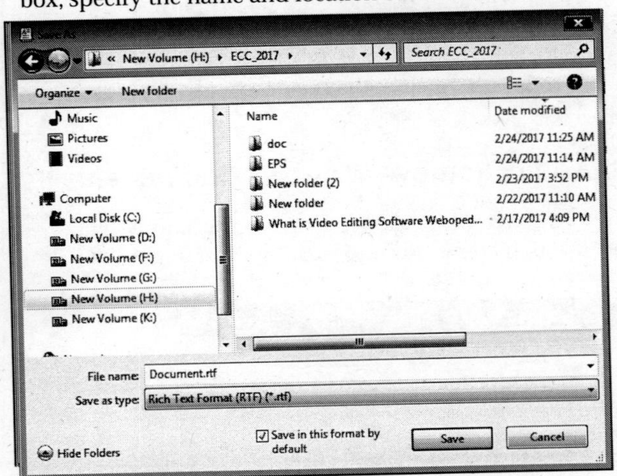

Figure 2.20 WordPad's Save As dialog box

2. To Save an existing document, click WordPad button and choose Save.

☞ WordPad supports text documents (.txt), rich text files (.rtf), Word documents (.docx), and OpenDocument Text (.odt) file formats in which you can open and save documents.

Previewing and Printing the WordPad Document

Before you print a document, it is necessary to preview it to check the overall appearance of the document.

➡ **To preview your document, do this:**

1. Click the Print Preview button, on the toolbar, or open the File menu and choose Print Preview.

➡ **To preview a WordPad document, do this:**

1. Click the WordPad button and choose Print. A sub menu appears, in the right side pane, choose Print preview options.
2. The WordPad window shows approximately how the printed page will appear.
3. Click Print button to begin printing, or click Close print preview button to return to the regular view of your document.

➡ **To print a WordPad document, do this:**

1. When you are ready to print, choose Office button. A drop-down menu appears. Choose Print. The Print dialog box appears as in Figure 2.21.

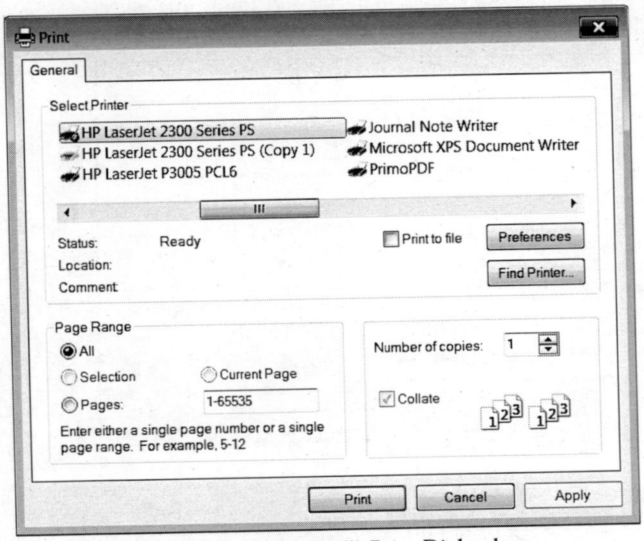

Figure 2.21 WordPad's Print Dialog box

2. Complete the dialog box by selecting the printer, the pages you want to print, and the number of copies.
3. Click OK button. Make sure that the printer is On-line and switched ON.

2.3 OPERATING SYSTEM SIMPLE SETTING

Most of the changes you will make take place by using the Widows Control Panel, which is a special folder that contains many small programs called applets. Each applet is designed to let you adjust setting for a particular part of your system.

To use Windows XP effectively, you have to configure or reshape Windows and the other programs that you run to work with your computer's hardware. You do this using the following features:

Feature	**Function**
Properties	These are the settings for many different objects in your computer's hardware and software.
Control Panel	This lets you to see and change many properties and other settings.
Wizards	These are the programs that help in automating the process of installing hardware, software and configuring software.

Properties

Every object in Windows XP–the hardware components of your computer, software programs, files, and icons–has properties. These properties are settings that determine how that object works. For example, a file has properties, such as filename, size and the date the file was last modified.

➡ **To change the properties of an object:**

1. Right click the object, the shortcut menu is displayed as seen in Figure 2.22.
2. From the shortcut menu click Properties. The Properties dialog box appears.

The properties that you can change depend upon this object you have selected.

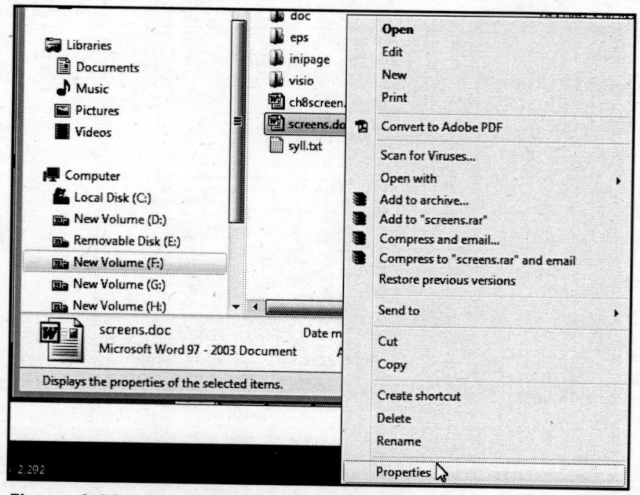

Figure 2.22 Shortcut Menu to change the property of an object

2.3.1 Changing System Date and Time

You can change your computer's date and Time by double-clicking on your notification area's clock.

➡ **To change the Date and Time:**

1. Double-click the notification area's clock. The Date and Time Properties dialog box appears as shown in Figure 2.23.

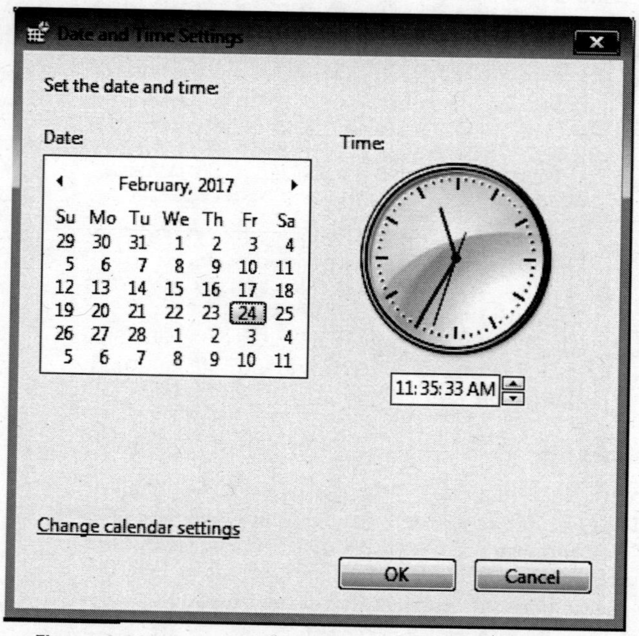

Figure 2.23 Shortcut Menu to change the Date and Time

2. To change the month, click the arrow in the month list, and then click the correct month.
3. To change the year, click the arrows in the year list.
4. To change the day, click the correct day on the calender.

2.3.2 Display Properties

The settings which are related with computer or desktop is the display properties. The display properties include wallpaper, screen saver, colour, font, etc. The display properties can be set through Display Properties dialog box.

➡ **To show the display properties dialog box:**

1. Click on the Start button then click on Control Panel. In Control Panel window, double click on Display icon to open it. Alternatively, right click at an empty space on the desktop and then choose Properties. This will show the Display Properties dialog box on the screen (See Figure 2.24).

2.3.3 To Add or Remove Windows Component

A Windows XP Wizard is a step-by-step procedure that guides you through some process, such as installing a program.

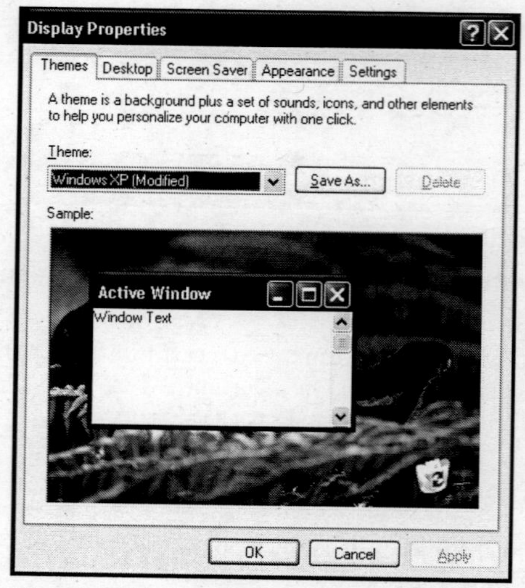

Figure 2.24 Display Properties dialog box

➡ **To add or remove Windows Component:**

1. Click the Start button and then choose Control Panel. The Control Panel window opens.
2. Click Add/Remove Windows Programs dialog box appears as shown in Figure 2.25.
3. Click the Add/Remove Windows Components button. Windows searches your computer for installed Windows components and then displays the Windows Components Wizard as shown in Figure 2.26.
4. Select a component from the list of available components by enabling the check box next to it. Some components have subcomponents that you can choose from. If so, the Details button become active, and you can click it to see a list of subcomponents to choose from.

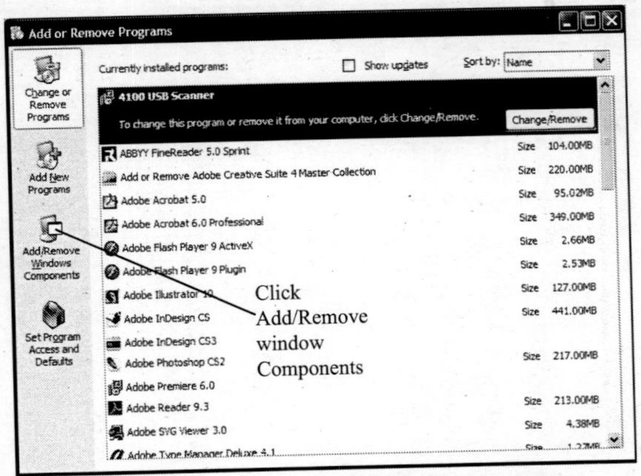

Figure 2.25 Add/Remove Programs dialog box

5. Once you select all the components that you want to install, click the Next button. Windows OS builds a list of files that must be installed and copies them to your drive. Windows might prompt you to insert your Windows CD-ROM during this process.

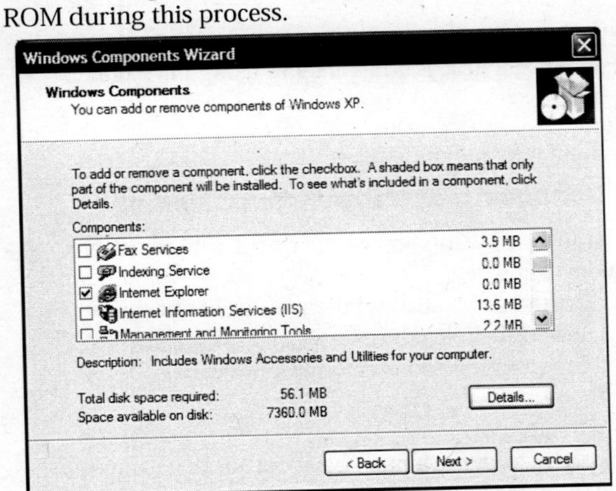

Figure 2.26 Windows Components Wizard dialog box

6. After Windows has installed the components, it lets you to know that the process has been completed successfully. Click the Finish button to finish. Depending on the components you added. Windows might need to restart your computer.

2.3.4 Changing Mouse Properties

Use the mouse to interact with items on your screen as you would use your hands to interact with the objects.

While your mouse should just work when you start up your computer, you can make some changes to its functionality and to the look and behavior of your mouse pointer on the screen. For example, you can switch the role of the buttons on your mouse, or adjust the speed of double-clicking. For the mouse pointer, you can change its appearance, improve its visibility, or set it to be hidden when you are typing.

Button Tab of the Mouse

Make changes to the mouse and mouse pointers in the Mouse Control Panel. To open Mouse properties dialog box, click Start, click Control Panel, and then double-click Mouse. The Mouse Properties dialog box appears as in Figure 2.27.

1. To Configure the behaviour of the mouse, click the Buttons tab in the Mouse properties dialog box.

Pointers tab of the Mouse

2. To Configure the behaviour of the mouse, click the Pointers tab in the Mouse properties dialog box (See Figure 2.28).

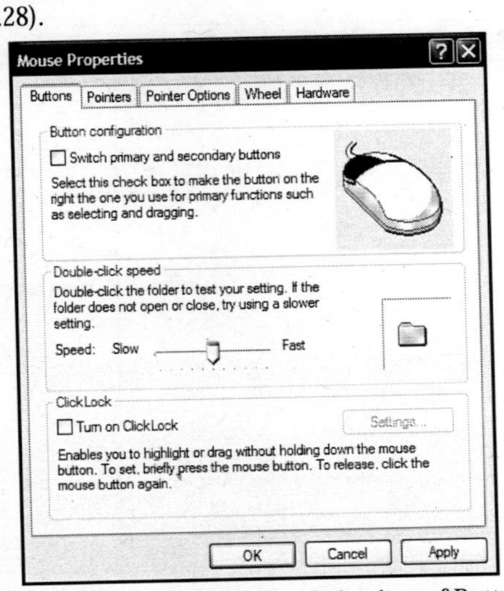

Figure 2.27 Mouse Properties dialog box of Button tab

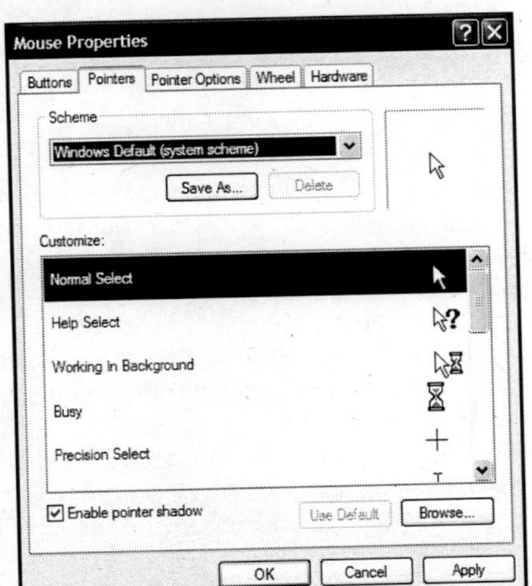

Figure 2.28 Mouse Properties dialog box of Pointers tab

To change the appearance of your mouse pointer, select pointers tab and do one of the following options.

- To change all of your pointers at one time, select a new scheme, under Schema.

- To change a particular pointer, select it in the Customize list. Click Browse... button. A list of selected cursor files appear. Select the name of the new pointer file you want to use for that task.

Pointer Options Tab of the Mouse

3. To Configure the behaviour of the mouse. Click the Pointer Options tab in the Mouse properties dialog box (See Figure 2.29).
   In the Motion section area, drag the slider to adjust the speed of your mouse. It causes the pointer to respond more quickly or slowly to the movements of the mouse. Or

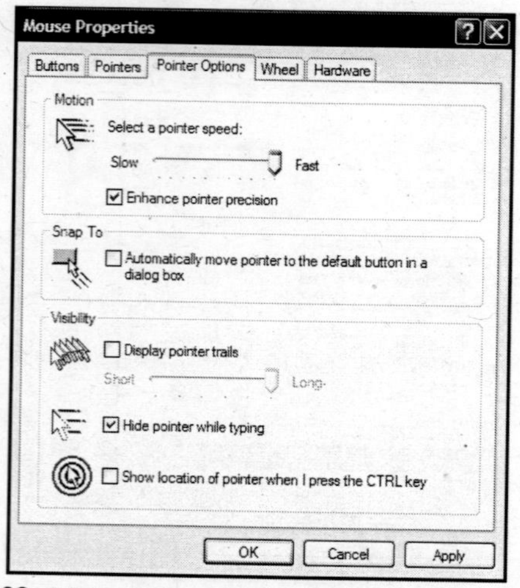

Figure 2.29 Mouse Properties dialog box of Pointers Options tab

Select the Enhance pointer precision check box to provide finer control of your pointer at short distances without closing the ability to move the point quickly across the screen. Clear the check box to turn off this feature.

In the Snap To section area, you can get the mouse snap to default buttons (such as OK or Apply) in dialog boxes by selecting Automatically move pointer to the default button in a dialog box under Snap To.

In the Visibility Section Area

- If you select the Display pointer trails check box, you can adjust the length of the pointer trail by moving the slider below the check box.
- To make the pointer invisible while typing, select the Hide pointer while typing check box. The pointer disappears when you are typing and reappears when you move the mouse.
- Select the Show location of pointer when I press the Ctrl key check box to find the pointer more easily when it is not in motion.

Wheel Option Tab of the Mouse

- To Configure the behaviour of the mouse, click the Wheel tab in the Mouse properties dialog box (See Figure 2.30).

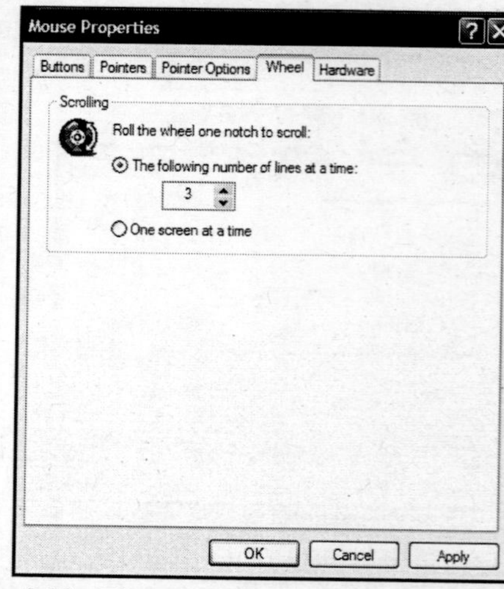

Figure 2.30 Mouse Properties dialog box of Wheel tab

In the Scrolling Section Area

- Select the number of lines to scroll with each notch on the wheel.
- Or click scroll one screen at a time. It means (scrolling one screen at a time is equivalent to using the page up or page down keys on your keyboard).
- If your mouse does not have a mouse wheel, the wheel tab may not appear.

Managing Documents with Right Mouse Button

Using the right mouse button you can perform several actions on the document. These are:

- Selecting documents by clicking them to highlight them.
- Copying selected files to a disk.
- Cutting or copying selected text to the Clipboard.
- Deleting documents.
- Renaming documents.

On right-clicking a folder's name it will produces a menu, which enable you to perform all these actions.

2.3.5 Adding and Removing Printers

Windows XP provides the Add a Printer Wizard to simplify installing printers. The Printer folder is used for running the wizard and for managing printing processes. You can open the Printers folder in the following ways.

➡ **To add printer:**

1. Click Start menu, or click Control Panel and choose Printers and Faxes. The Printers and Faxes dialog box appears.
2. Under Printer Tasks click Add a printer to open the Add printer wizard, and then click Next.
3. Select the option that describes the printer you want to use.
   - Click Local printer.
   - Automatically detect and install my plug and play printer check box. Or
   - A network printer.

4. Select the port you want your printer to use.
   - Create a new port.
   - Click Local port and then click Next.
5. Follow the instructions on the screen to finish adding a printer with the Add Printer Wizard.

☞ The only difference between installing a network printer and a local printer with the Add Printer Wizard is that you must specify the path to the network printer or browse to find its network location.

➡ **To remove printer:**

1. Select the printer you want to remove from the printers and Faxes list.
2. Right click the mouse and click Delete this printer from the Printer Task pane.
3. The selected printer options remove from the list.

2.4 FILE AND DIRECTORY MANAGEMENT IN WINDOWS XP

The main function of computer is to manage data and information. The stored data and information on your computer, can be considered as file. File includes text, photos, and video. Each type of file has its specific icon, that makes you understand the type of file.

2.4.1 Types of Files

Everything on your computer is made up of files on your hard disk. Windows itself is just thousands of different files that interact with one another. The applications you use from day to day are also collections of many files that interact with one another and with Windows files. All the documents you create are themselves files that are loaded by the applications you use to create them. For example, when you save a document in MS Word, that document is saved as file on your disk.

What is a File?

A collection of data or information that has a name, called the filename, Almost all information stored in a computer must be in a file. There are many different types of files: data files, text files, program files, directory files, and so on. Different types of files store different types of information. For example, program files store programs, whereas text files store text.

In any computer system, especially in personal computers, a file is an entity of data available to system users (including the system itself and its application programs) that is capable of being manipulated as an entity (for example, moving file from one file directory to another). The file must have a unique name within its own directory. Some operating systems and applications describe files with given formats by giving them a particular file name suffix. (The file name suffix is also known as a file name extension.) For example, a program or executable file is sometimes given or required to have an ".exe" suffix.

Naming Conventions

A number of TSD (time sequence data) naming conventions are in use today. These formats are organized in three classes. The classes are called associated, coded, and sequenced. The filename extension defines the type of data storage format. For example, the extensions "HDR", "CFG", "DAT", and "INF" are used to indicate that the file contents are compatible with the IEEE COMTRADE standard. The non-extension part of an associated filename or the name is left at the discretion of the user and could be assigned in a coded or sequenced way.

The following fundamental rules enable applications to create and process valid names for files and directories, regardless of the file system:

- Use a period to separate the base file name from the extension in the name of a directory or file.
- Use a backslash (\) to separate the components of a path. The backslash divides the file name from the path to it, and one directory name from another directory name in a path. You cannot use a backslash in the name for the actual file or directory because it is a reserved character that separates the names into components.
- Use a backslash as required as part of volume names, for example, the "C:\" in "C:\path\file" or the "\\server\share" in "\\server\share\path\file" for Universal Naming Convention (UNC) names.
- Volume designators (drive letters) are similarly case-insensitive. For example, "D:\" and "d:\" refer to the same volume.
- Use any character in the current page for a name, including Unicode characters and characters in the extended character set (128–255), except for the following:

  The following reserved characters:
  - < (less than)
  - > (greater than)
  - : (colon)
  - " (double quote)
  - / (forward slash)
  - \ (backslash)
  - | (vertical bar or pipe)
  - ? (question mark)
- Integer value zero, sometimes referred to as the ASCII NUL character.
- Any other character that the target file system does not allow.

File Extensions

A file extension (or simply "extension") is the suffix at the end of a filename that indicates what type of file it is. For example, in the filename "BPB.docx," the .docx is the file extension. It indicates the file is a document. Some other examples include .txt, which is used for Notepad files, notepad and .PSD, which is the standard file extension for Photoshop documents.

By having file extensions you can quickly identify the type of file and have a better idea of how that file may be opened.

File Pathway

A pathname gives the exact computer system location of a file. The document and folder concept in Windows makes working with paths much easier than Windows. The folders in Windows used to be called directories. A directory is just a collection of files and other directories. In file listings, Windows OS displays a folder icon with a name to represent a directory that holds other files. Folders can hold subfolders, so the location of a file, the file's path, might be deep within several nested folder on a disk drive.

A full pathname begins with a disk drive name followed by a colon (:) followed by a backslash (\). If file resides in the disk drive's top folder (called the root directory), you then type the filename. However, the file resides in another folder, you must list the folder after the backslash. If the file resides in several nested folder, you must list each folder in order, from the outermost to the innermost, and separate each folder name with a backslash.

The following full pathnames to specific files:

```
c:\autoexec.bat
d:\Sherry\WordProc\Home\Insure\Fire and Casualty
```

The first filename is autoexec.bat located in the root directory. The second filename is Fire and Casualty located within a series of nested directories.

Windows Explorer program, displays entire computer system graphically including all its files, in a tree structure form. With Explorer, you can access every data inside computer hard disk.

2.4.2 Windows Explorer

You can start Windows Explorer in one of the two ways depending upon how you start it.

- To use My Computer window to browse through the folders and files on a disk drive. Or

➡ **To start Windows Explorer in Explorer View do the following:**

1. Open the View menu. Select Explorer. A sub menu appears. Click the Folders. Alternatively, Click the Start button, highlight All programs, highlight Accessories, a sub menu appears. Click Windows Explorer (See Figure 2.31).

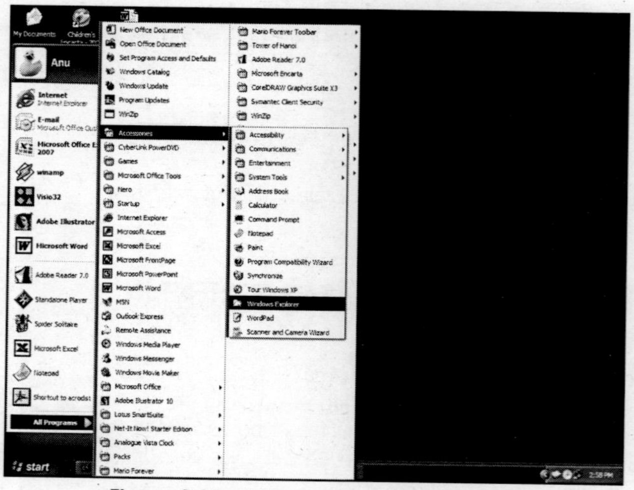

Figure 2.31 Selecting Windows Explorer

2. Browsing Folders: The left pane of the Explorer window shows all the drives, folders, and desktop items on your PC. A drive or folder that contains other folders has a plus sign to the left of the icon. Click the plus sign to expand it and see the folders inside (See Figure 2.32).

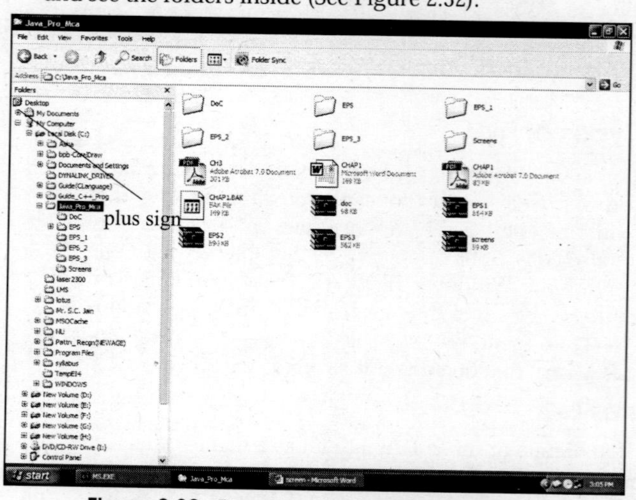

Figure 2.32 Browsing Folders in the left pane

3. Opening a Folder: Click a folder in the list which appears in the left pane. All the files and folders in that folder are seen in the right pane (See Figure 2.33).
4. Opening a File: The right pane works the same way as My Computer window. You will double-click a file or folder in this pane to open it (See Figure 2.34).

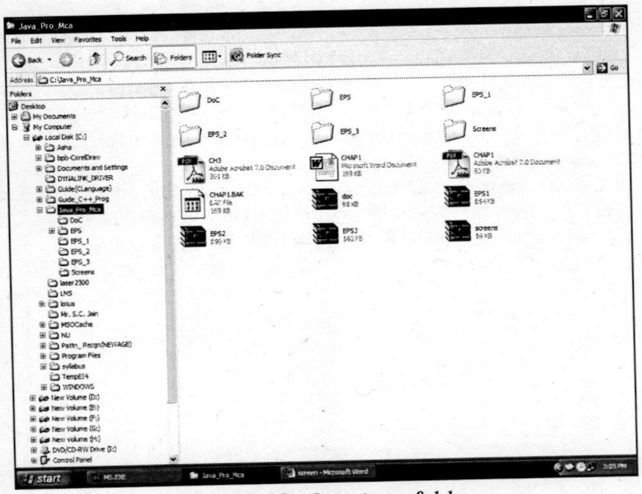

Figure 2.33 Opening a folder

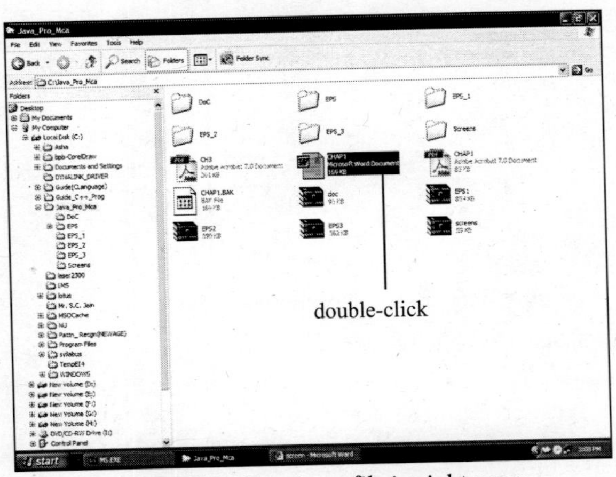

Figure 2.34 Opening a file in right pane

5. Copying a File to another drive: Copying a file to another drive is easy. Just drag a file from the right pane to another disk drive (or a folder on another drive) to copy it there. Observe that the icon you are dragging also takes on a small plus sign to let you know that the file will be copied, but it is not moved (See Figure 2.35).

Customizing Windows Explorer

You can customize many features of the Windows Explorer as per your needs and working habits. The properties that can be customized are as follows:

- The size of the icons used to represent files and folders.
- Displaying the files and folders as a list or as icons.
- The information displayed for each file and folder.
- The order in which files and folders are shown.

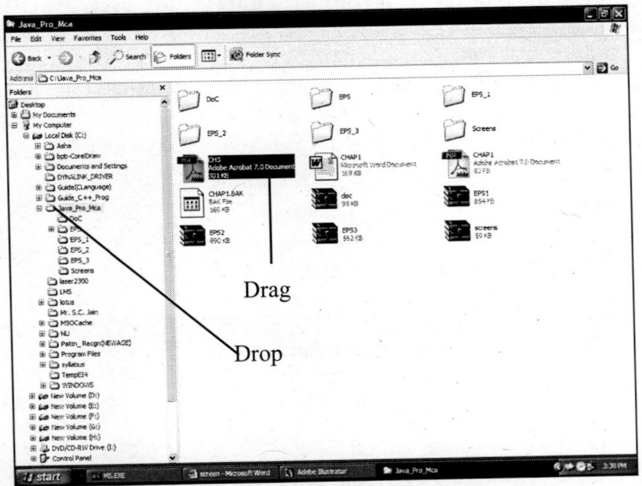

Figure 2.35 Copy a file to another drive in the left pane

Changing Views

➡ **To change the view:**

1. Click the View menu and choose the desired view (See Figure 2.36). Alternatively, click the arrow next to the view button on the toolbar or, click the view button on the toolbar to scroll through the different views. Select the desired view and press Enter key.

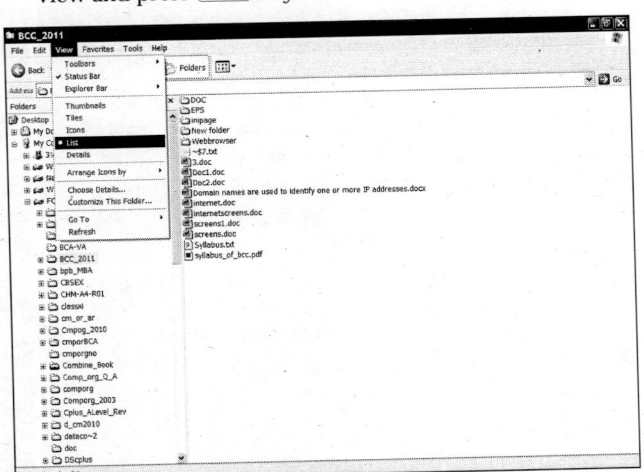

Figure 2.36 Choose the desired View from the list

File Property dialogue box

When you create a file, Windows automatically adds properties to the files, such as name, creation date, modified date, and size. These properties are important to Windows, however, they may not be useful when you are searching for a file. You can add or modify common file properties and create or modify custom tag properties to locate files faster and easier. You can add or modify properties for most files. If you want to remove some or all of the property information in a file, you can quickly remove it by using the Properties dialog box.

➡ **To add or change common properties in the details pane:**

1. Open the folder that contains the file you want to change, and then click the file.
2. In the details pane at the bottom of the window, click next to the property that you want to add or change, type the new property (or change the property), and then click Save (See Figure 2.37).

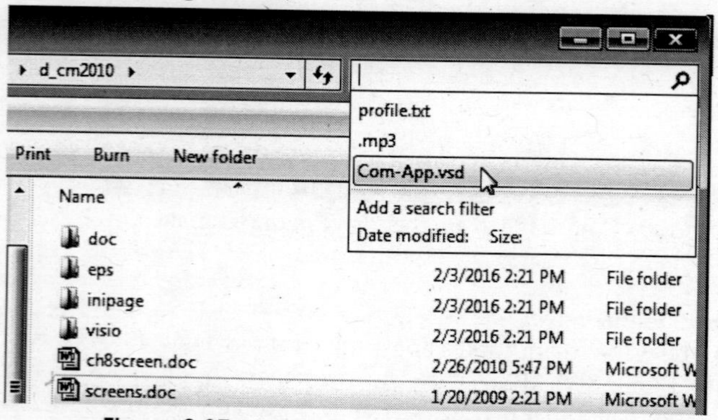

Figure 2.37 Adding a tag in the Details pane

3. To add more than one property, separate each entry with a semicolon. To rate a file by using the ratings property, click the star that represents the rating you want to apply.

➡ **To remove properties from a file:**

1. If you plan to share a file with someone, you might want to remove some of the file's properties, especially if they contain personal information. For example, the Author property might include the names of people who collaborated on a file, and tags might have words or phrases that you don't want other people to see.
2. Right-click the file, and then click Properties as shown in Figure 2.38.

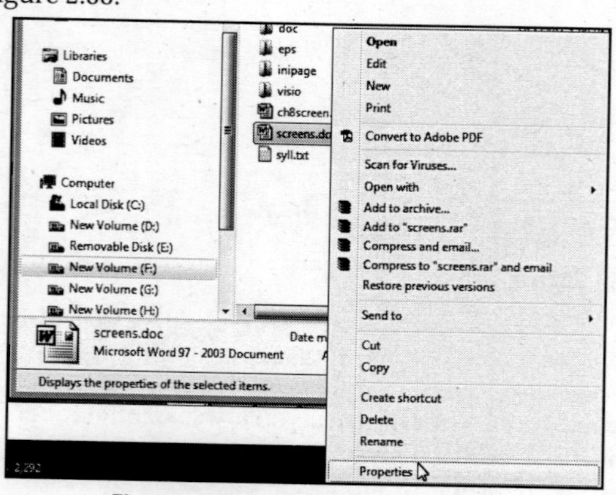

Figure 2.38 Selecting Properties

3. In the Properties dialog box, click the Details tab.
4. In the Remove Properties dialog box, do one of the following:
   - Click Create a copy with all possible properties removed, and then click OK. This keeps the original version of the file with all of its properties, and makes a copy with all of the properties removed that's suitable for sharing.
   - Click Remove the following properties from this file, select the check box for each property that you want to remove, and then click OK. This permanently removes the selected properties from the file without making a copy (See Figure 2.39).

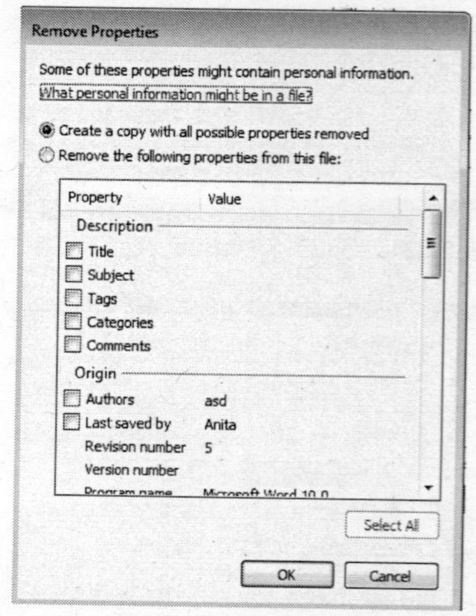

Figure 2.39 Remove Properties

File Size and abbreviations used

File size measures the size of a computer file. Typically it is measured in bytes or bits. The actual amount of disk space consumed by the file depends on the file system. The maximum file size which a file system supports depends on the number of bits reserved to store size information and the total size of the file.

A byte is a sequence of 8 bits (enough to represent one alphanumeric character) processed as a single unit of information. A single letter or character would use one byte of memory (8 bits), two characters would use two bytes (16 bits).

In another way, a bit is either an 'on' or an 'off' which is processed by a computer processor, we represent 'on' as '1' and 'off' as '0'. 8 bits are known as a byte, and it is bytes which are used to pass our information in it's basic form - characters. Byte–A byte is a unit of data which is eight binary digits (0 and 1) long (1 byte = 8 bits). A byte is the unit which most computer use to represent a character such as a letter, numeral or typographic symbol. For example, g, 5, #. A byte can also hold a string of bits that need to be used in some larger unit for application purposes.

☞ To check the size of a file, point a mouse cursor over a file and check the size in the box that appears.

Kilobyte (KB)
A kilobyte (KB) is actually $2^{10} = 1024$ bytes. or

1 KB = 1,024 bytes (1,000 bytes and hence the name)
Megabyte (MB)
A megabyte (MB) is 2^{20} byte or 1,048,576 bytes in decimal notation. or

1 MB = 1,024 KB (1,000 KB)
Gigabyte (GB)
A gigabyte (GB) is 2^{30} byte or 1,073,741,824 bytes in decimal notation. or

1 GB = 1,024 MB (1,000 MB)
Terabyte (TB)
A terabyte is a measure of computer storage capacity and it is equal to the 2^{40} bytes. or
1 TB = 1,024 GB (1,000 GB)

Working with Files and Folders

Files and folders are two fundamental concepts of the Windows operating system. You create and organize files and folders as soon as you save your work in a PC.

File

A file is any collection of related information that is given a name and stored on a disk so that it can be read and manipulated whenever required.

Folder

As you work in Windows, you would see that a hard disk contains hundreds of files even before you start creating your own file. It would be impossible to keep track of all these files if they are not arranged properly. In Windows, the fundamental device for managing files is a folder.

A folder can either be open or closed. When it is closed, all you see is its name and the folder icon. When a folder is open, it has its own window, and the files contained in the folder are shown in the window. So, folder is a location on hard disk of your computer where you can save and organise your files and programs.

Sometimes, you may have a lot of files in one folder. To organize your files for finding them easily, you can create subfolder. Subfolder is a folder inside a folder.

The Folder Tree

The arranging power of the folder system lies in the fact that it is hierarchical.

☞ Hierarchical means that folders can contain other folders. This feature allows you to organize and keep track of a large number of folders.

If Folder A is inside Folder B, then Folder A is a subfolder of B. Any folder can contain as many subfolders as you want, but each subfolder (like each file) is contained in only one folder. And so, a diagram showing which folders are contained in which other folders looks something like a family tree. This diagram is called the folder tree, the folder hierarchy or folder list.

At the top of the folder tree is the founder of the Folder family, namely the desktop. Next to the desktop are My Computer, etc., and additional files and folders that you might have copied to the desktop.

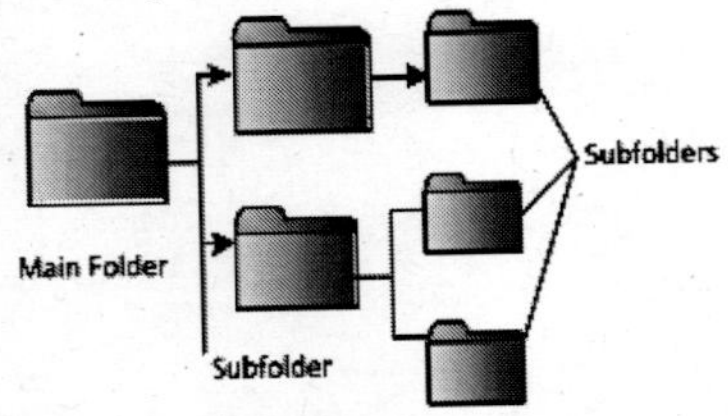

Underneath My Computer are icons representing all of your system's storage media namely, hard disk drives, floppy disk drives, CD-ROMs, etc.

Basic file and folder operations are the following:

- Creating
- Naming
- Opening
- Closing

Selecting Files and Folders

Windows works on the rule, select and do. It means, you first have to select the file or folder you want to use. Files and folders are represented in Folder and Windows Explorer windows by icons, with the name of the file or folder printed underneath its icon.

➡ **To select and open a file or folder do this:**

- In Web style view, to select a file or folder, move the cursor over its icon. When the icon appears highlighted, the object is selected. To open the file or folder, click the icon once.
- In Classic style, to select an object single click the object that you want and to open a file or folder double-click on it.

To select more than one object, select the first object, and then press the Ctrl key while selecting other objects.

➡ **To select all the items in a folder:**

- Open a Folder or Windows Explorer window.
- Click the Edit menu and choose Select All. Or press Ctrl+A keys together on the keyboard.

Creating Files and Folders

➡ **To create a new File/Folder:**

1. In the Folder window click the File menu and choose New. Alternatively, right click on the empty area of the Desktop and choose New.
2. In both the cases, a submenu lists the new objects you can create: folders, shortcuts, and a variety of types of files (See Figure 2.40).
3. Select an element of the list. Windows creates the selected object.

☞ Don't use filename like File1, File 2 etc., but choose names that describes the file's content.

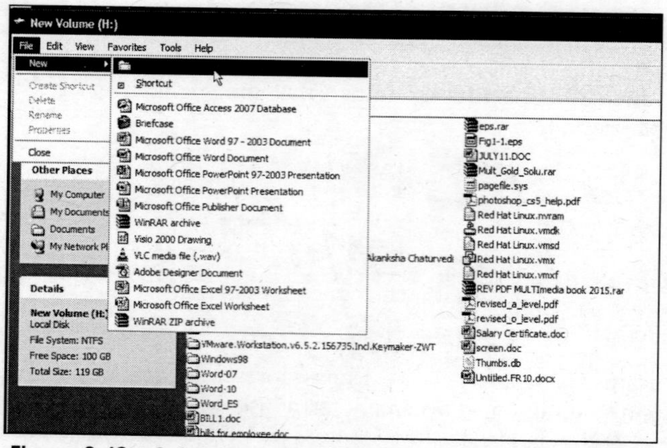

Figure 2.40 Submenu Indicating the New Objects that can be created

Naming and Renaming Files and Folders

Name of each folder should describe the content of its file.

➡ **To rename a file or folder:**

1. Select the file/folder you want to rename. Click the File menu and choose Rename. Alternatively, right click the file/folder and choose Rename from the context menu or press F2 key. Alternatively, in the left task pane click Rename this file/folder.
2. A box appears around the current name, and the entire name is selected. Type the new name in the box and press Enter key (See Figure 2.41).

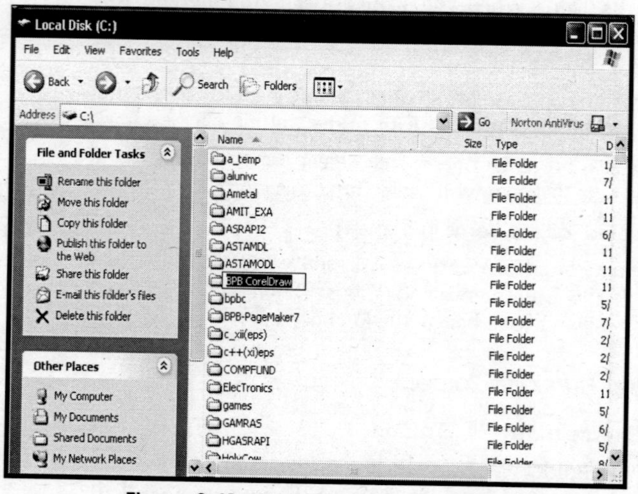

Figure 2.41 Renaming a file or folder

To edit the old name instead of typing the new one, Click inside the name-box at the place where you want to begin typing or deleting.

Opening Files and Folders

Any object in a Windows Explorer or Folder window can be opened by single-clicking (in Web style) or double-clicking its icon (in Classic style).

Moving or Copying Folders and Files

To move or copy an object, select the object and drag it from its current position to its new position. When you release the mouse button, the shortcut menu appears as shown in Figure 2.42. From this Shortcut menu, choose Copy Here, Move Here, or Create Shortcut(s) Here. Select the option as per requirement.

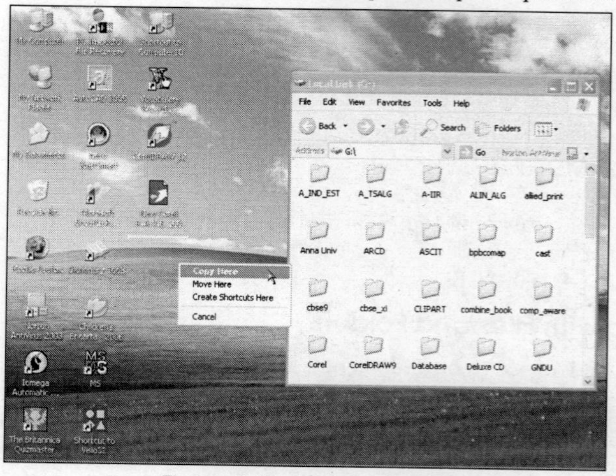

Figure 2.42 Shortcut menu

☞ If you drag a folder or file to a new location on your computer, the object will be moved. But if you drag it from computer to other device it will be copied.

Deleting Files and Folders

➡ **To delete file(s) and folder(s), do this:**

1. Select the file or folder to be deleted.
2. Click the Delete button on the toolbar.
3. Click Yes in the dialog box.

Alternatively, you can right click the objects and then choose Delete from the context menu. The selected file(s) and folder(s) are deleted.

☞ Objects deleted from your computer go to the Recycle Bin folder. You can recover them by double-clicking the Recycle Bin folder, if desired.

Closing Files and Folders

To close a windows explorer, click × button present in the upper-right corner of the window.

Opening and Closing Different Window

There are three types of window openings namely, application window, document window and folder window. Document window contains a document you are working on within an application window. Most of the applications allow you to have multiple documents window open at a time. The document window is also referred to as child window.

➡ **To open a document window:**

1. Click File menu and choose Open. The Open dialog box appears, click the file in the look in: drop-down list box and choose the file you want to open.

➡ **To close a document window:**

1. Click File menu and choose Close. Alternatively, click the × close button in the upper right corner of the window. Or
2. Right click the document in the taskbar and choose Close or press Alt + F4 keys together (See Figure 2.43).

☞ Many of the features of Windows XP are also included in Windows 7.

Searching for Files

With the help of Search Companion of Windows XP, you can search for all types of objects, from pictures, music, and documents, to printers, computers, and people. You can search in your own computer, other computers that are connected to your computer using network, and the Internet by using windows button or windows explorer.

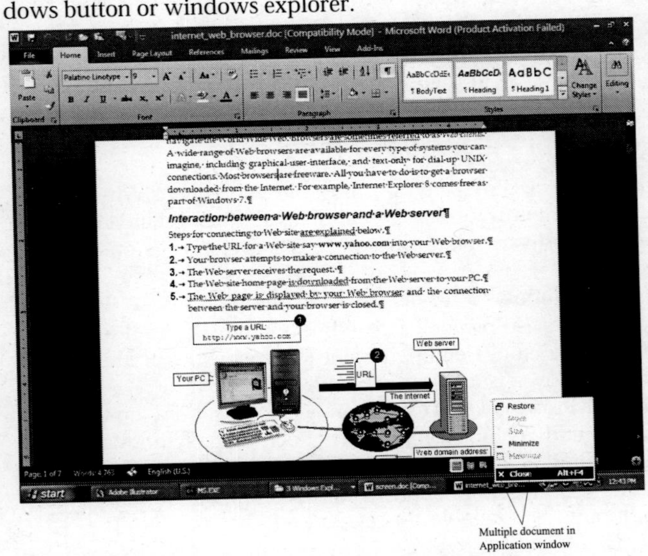

Figure 2.43 Closing a document window in the task bar

In Search Companion, you can specify several search criteria. For example, you can search files and folders by name, type, and size, file based on when you last worked on it or files containing specific text.

➡ **To use the Search Feature:**

1. Click the Start button and then click on Search.
2. The Search Result dialog box appears, as in Figure 2.44. In the left pane of the window, click All files and folders link. Left pane will change and appears as seen in Figure 2.45.

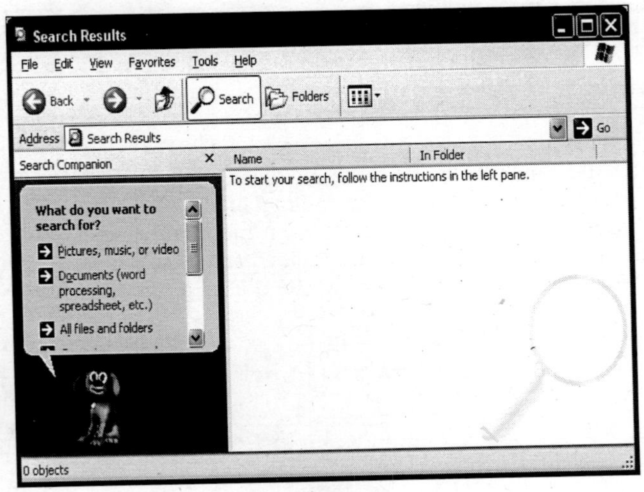

Figure 2.44 The Search Result Dialog Box

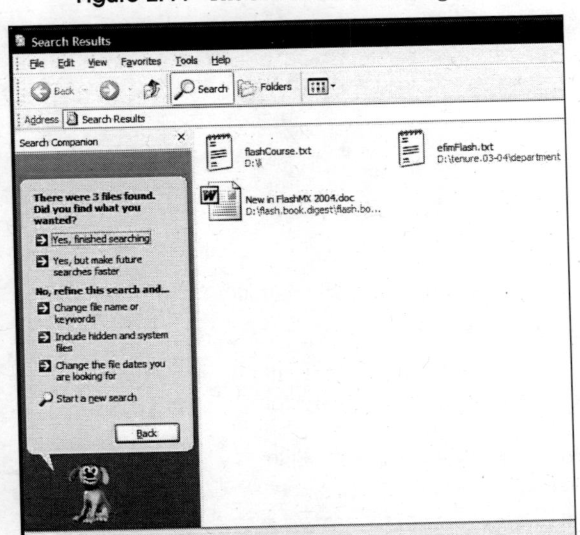

Figure 2.45 Searching Files

3. Type the full file name or a part of it in All or part of the file name box of the file or folder, or type a word or phrase that is in the file.
   In Look in: drop down list, click the drive, folder, or network you want to search.
   Click When was it modified? if you want to give.
   Click What size is it? if you know.
   Click More advanced options to specify additional search criteria.
4. Finally click on Search button to search.

How to find where file is being saved

Fortunately, there are a few ways to find those missing files, even if your computer does not keep track of recently accessed documents.

How can you find the file being saved?

Using Windows search utility, you can search for the file and specify the date it was modified.

When a file is created on Windows, it's modified date attribute is set with the date and time... it was last changed (even if it's a new file...since that was the last time it was changed).

1. In XP, Click on Start\Search and make sure you select All files and folders.
2. In the "All or part of the file name" field, enter the wildcard parameter *.* which will search for all files.
3. Click on the arrow next to "When was it modified", and select the Specify dates radio button, then enter the date when you saved the file (See Figure 2.46).

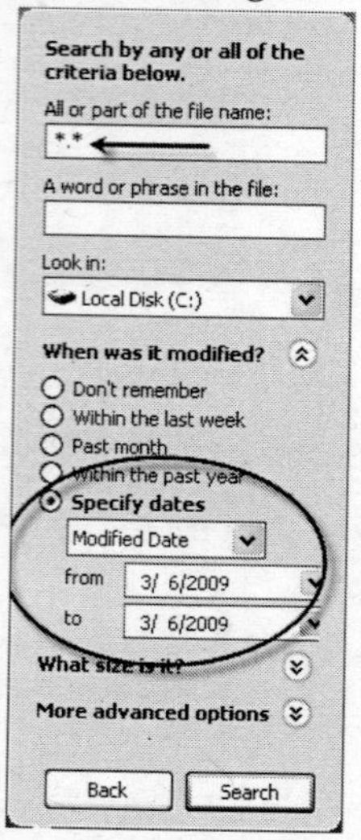

Figure 2.46 Using Search utility

Recovering Deleted Files

If you can not find a file on your computer or you accidently modified or deleted a file, you can restore it from a Recycle bin.

➡ **To recover a file from the Recycle Bin:**

1. Open the Recycle Bin.
2. Select the file(s) you want to recover.
3. Click the File menu and choose Restore. Alternatively, click Restore the selected items from the left task pane.

The file returns to the folder it was deleted from—the address given in the Original Location column of the Details view. If the object is a folder, all of its contents will return with it.

If your files are not found in the Recycle Bin, don't save or delete anything from your computer. Your chances of recovering the file are much higher if you don't save anything new. This is because when a file is deleted, it is actually just set to be overwritten. If no new data has overwritten the original file, then it can usually be recovered.

Download a data recovery program on a different drive. Make sure that you don't save it to the drive that you need to recover a file from, or you may overwrite the file you need to recover. Some of the more popular free programs include:

- Recuva
- Restoration
- Glary Undelete

Download a portable version of the recovery program if possible, so that you can run it directly from a USB drive without need to install it.

Run the recovery program–While every program is different, they all follow the same basic steps. Make sure that you don't install the program to the same drive that you are trying to recover from.

Specify what you are looking for–Point the recovery program at the disk that the file was on when it was deleted. You can also recover files from a USB drive. Most recovery programs will ask what type of file you are searching for. You can also specify the file name, or get a list of all recoverable files to browse through.

Browse for the file you want–Once the scan has returned results, look through the list to see if your file was recovered. Different programs will have different methods for recovery, but in general you just need to select your file and click the Restore button.

2.5 WINDOWS 7 OPERATING SYSTEM

There are various types of Windows. A type of Windows is referred to as a version. Windows 7 is the version of Windows desktop operating system for the PC. It is more advanced and robust operating system than any other operating system of MS Corporation.

2.5.1 Different Versions of Windows 7

MS Corporation of USA provides multiple versions of Windows 7 with a mixture of features and capabilities intended for different hardware platforms, personal preferences and business needs.

Versions of Windows 7 are discussed as follows:

- Windows 7 Home Premium: This edition is mostly used in new PCs. It includes entertainment features as its predecessor, Window Vista Home Premium.
- Windows 7 Professional: This edition is a superset of Home Premium and includes all features including Windows Media Center.
- Windows 7 Ultimate / Enterprise: These editions are identical. Ultimate is available on retails and Original Equipment Manufacturer (OEM) editions. But, Enterprise is distributed only to large-sized customers. This edition contains all features found in the Home Premium and Professional editions with some advance networking features, BitLocker encryption and support for multiple languages.

All of these editions are available in 32-bit and 64-bit options. Today Windows 7 64-bit is commonly installed on new computers, especially on systems with 4 GB or more RAM.

☞ Windows 7 has a good antivirus program. You can download a free antivirus program called MS Security Essentials that works well with any editions of Windows 7.

Features of Windows 7 Operating System

Windows 7 offers many new features over Windows XP. Some vital features of Windows 7 are as follows:

- Libraries: Libraries make it simple to pull documents, music, pictures, etc., from various places (folders) and have them shown up together. Note that while the files are displayed together, they are actually stored in their original folders, so the same file may be in multiple libraries.
- Windows Aero: 3D Graphical User Interface (GUI) with translucent "glass-like" window to view a thumbnail of programs when pointed on the taskbar.
- Instant Search: It is much faster and more diligent than other Windows OS. Search is integrated into every folder, making it simple to find a file from anywhere without having to use the Start Menu.
- Windows Defender and Firewall: Advanced anti-spyware and two-way firewall have been incorporated within the Windows 7 operating system to protect the OS, services, programs, Internet Explorer, and other parts of the computer from spyware.
- Internet Explorer 8: It is an improved Web browser, which is more secure and comes with a tabbed interface.
- Windows Media Player 12: Big work is done here with a new interface for the media library, photo display and organization, search-as-you-type capabilities, and music sharing.
- Windows Live Mail: A replacement for Outlook Express, this offers better stability, real time search, junk mail filtering and anti-phishing.
- Ease of Access Center: Ease of Access Center is same as Accessibility Options available in earlier versions of Windows. It now comes with several improvements and new features that you can use to get suggestions for accessibility features.
- Taskbar Improvements: Taskbar in Windows 7 makes it simple to rearrange icons on the taskbar and have them to stay where they are placed. It is also easy to review recent documents visited, Web sites, playlist, etc.
- Jump Lists: With Jump Lists, you can quickly find files that you have recently worked with. With this feature, you can right click the icon and select it from the list.
- Parental Controls: Parental Controls option makes it easy for parents to select games for their children to play. Parents can restrict specific game titles, control their children to play the games that are below a certain age level, or block games with certain types of content that they may not want their children to see or hear.
- BitLocker Drive Encryption: It encrypts the contents of the computer's system drive (C: drive) or any other internal hard disk or removable hard drive or (USB) flash drive to make it unreadable. Security can further be enhanced by requiring a USB key to be inserted with decryption key.
- User Account Control: It asks for permission whenever administrative tasks are requested to make sure that you asked for them, rather than a virus or spy-ware application. This is true even if you log on with a user name that has administrative rights. It can be customized to be as obtrusive or secure as desired.
- Home Group: Home group make it easier to setup a home network and share files, videos, photos, etc., with other using network. A wizard is used to set up the feature and a password is used by other computers wishing to join the group. Home groups are only accessible when the network location is set to "Home" and does not interfere with a domain that the computer may belong to at work.
- Other Features: Windows XP mode in Windows 7 provides the ability to run applications with compatibility issues with Windows 7 via a Virtual Machine (VM) running XP SP 3. Application installed in the VM appear in the Windows 7 Start Menu and runs like any other application. It is available as a free download from MS Web site. It requires AMD-V or Intel-VT enabled in the Basic Input Output System (BIOS).

  Battery life has been extended on laptops due to updated drivers, allowing more sleep features for devices and providing Adaptive Display Brightness, which automatically dims the display if the computer has not been used in a while.

  Touch screen support is available via Windows Touch if display supports it, allowing menu selections, scrolling media playing, etc., all possible without using a keyboard or mouse.

2.6 BASIC ELEMENTS OF OPENING SCREEN OF WINDOWS 7

Different parts of the Windows 7 opening screen are as marked in Figure 2.47 and discussed in the following sections.

2.6.1 Exploring the Desktop

As you work in Windows 7, you move items on the Desktop, retrieve and put away items and perform many other day-to-day tasks. By default, the only item on the Desktop is the Recycle Bin. Functions of the Desktop icons are explained in the following Table.

System Icon	Function
Computer	This icon lets you to browse through the resources connected to your computer.
User's Files	This icon represents the name of the (personal user who logs on to the computer). Its folder contents are unique for every user on the computer. This folder contains files that belong to the user.
Recycle Bin	This icon provides temporary storage for files and folders that you want to delete.
Network	This icon opens a Window displaying the names of each server or computer in your own work group.
Control Panel	This icon opens a window containing system configuration and management tools.

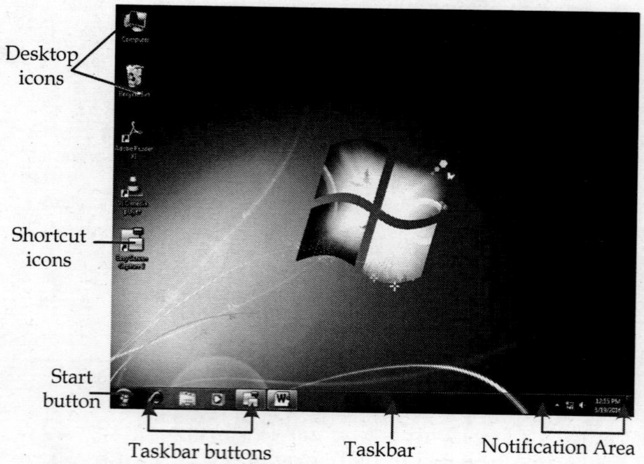

Figure 2.47 Different parts of the Windows 7 screen

Computer Icon

Computer is the gateway to resources stored on your own system. Computer icon on desktop allows you to browse through all the resources attached to your PC. When you click on Computer icon, a window appears as shown in Figure 2.48. The computer's information is divided into three parts:

(a) Hard Disk Drives: Display the hard disk drives of the computer.

(b) Devices with Removable Storage: Display floppy disk, CD-ROM, Zip drive, etc.

(c) Network Location: In the left pane of the Computer window, it displays the location of any disk drive or folder which is connected to the computer.

Rest of the features, such as shortcut icons and Recycle Bin will be explained later.

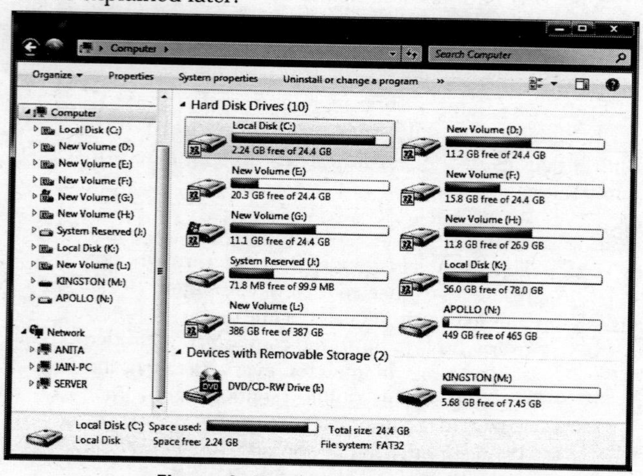

Figure 2.48 Computer window

The Taskbar

Taskbar is the horizontal bar at the bottom of the screen (See Figure 2.47).

Taskbar Elements	Function
Start button	It is located at the left end of the taskbar. Clicking the start button brings up the Start menu as seen in Figure 2.49.
Taskbar Icons	Taskbar Icons represents a set of icons. It lets you to launch programs with single click. When clicked, these buttons or icons activate certain functions or tasks. For example, the Taskbar Icons includes icons for launching Internet Explorer, Windows Media Player, Windows Explorer. You can also add your favourite programs in Taskbar. Right click the program that you want to add and then click this program to Taskbar.
Show Desktop button	Show Desktop button is used to temporary hide all the open windows to show the desktop.
Task buttons	Task buttons are displayed in the center portion of the Taskbar. A button appears for each program you have started or each document you have opened. You can click these buttons to move from one open Program or Folder to another (See Figure 2.47).

2.6.2 Elements of a Window

When you start a program, it appears on the Windows 7 desktop. You work with a program by manipulating the various elements of its window. These elements of a program window are shown in Figure 2.50.

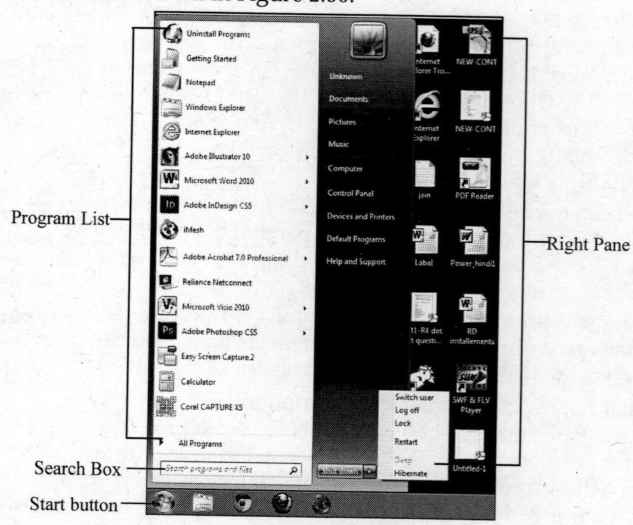

Figure 2.49 Start menu

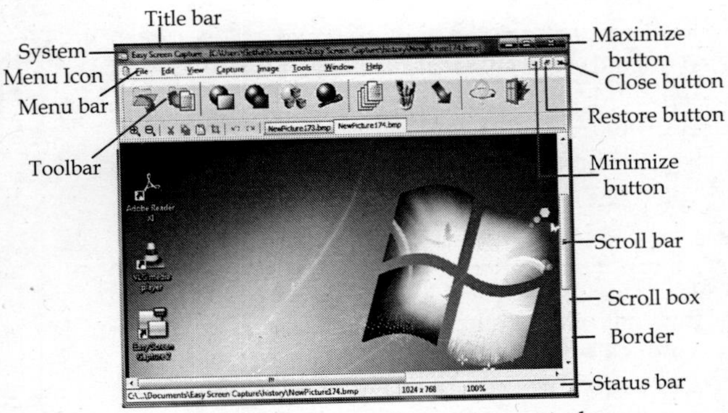

Figure 2.50 Elements of a program window

Borders

The four edges that define the perimeter of a window are known as borders. Borders also give a way to change the size of the window.

Title Bar

Just below the top border of the window is the Title bar. It displays the name of the program or the document. It is also used for moving the window.

System Menu Icon

System menu icon is the small icon located on the left side of the Title bar. The System menu icon performs two functions (See Figure 2.50). These are:

- It opens the menu whenever you click this icon. In most of the programs, the command on a System menu lets you control the size of the window. But some programs may have special items on their menus.
- System menu icon for a program or document will close the window that terminates the program or closes the document when you double-click it.

Close Button

At the right edge of the Title bar is a square containing an × called the Close button. Clicking the Close button closes a document or folder, or terminates a program (See Figure 2.50).

Minimize, Maximize and Restore Buttons

The three small buttons at the right end of the Title bar as shown in Figure 2.50 with small graphics are Minimize button, Maximize or Restore button, and the Close buttons. These are control buttons with which you can quickly change the size of a window or close it.

- Clicking the minimize button reduces the window to a button on the Task bar. Once minimized, the window no longer takes space on the desktop but the program in it continues to run.
- Clicking the maximize button enlarges the window to occupy the whole desktop. When the window is maximized, the minimizes and restore buttons appear.

Scroll Bars, Scroll Boxes and Scroll Buttons

If a window is not long enough to display its contents completely, you can scroll the vertical scroll bar which appears along the right edge. Similarly, if the window is not wide enough, a horizontal scroll bar appears along the bottom of the window.

☞ Scroll bars offer an easy way to navigate through a window with the mouse. They also provide useful information about the contents of the window.

Scroll bars have small rectangular boxes called scroll box (See Figure 2.50). The position of this box within the scroll bar tells you where you are within the window itself. If the scroll box is at the top of the scroll bar, it means you are at the top of the document.

Scroll buttons appear along the top and bottom edges of the vertical scroll bar, and along the left and right edges of the horizontal scroll bar.

Menu Bar

The row of words just below the Title bar constitute the Menu bar (See Figure 2.50). Menu bar appears only in an application window and not in a document window. Each word on the Menu bar represents a menu which opens up when you click it (See Figure 2.51). The names of the menus may vary from program to program but they have some common headings, such as File, Edit, Window and Help.

☞ In Windows 7, Menu bar is hidden by default, such as in Control Panel. To display the menu bar, you have to press Alt key. Menu bar is displayed above the toolbar. If you want to permanently display the Menu bar, Select Layout from the Organize tab of that window and then select Menu bar. Menu bar appears on the screen.

Choosing Menu Commands

Choosing a menu command involves two steps:

- Click to open it.
- Selecting the required command from the menu.

➡ **To open a menu:**

1. Use the mouse click on the menu name. Or use the keyboard, press Alt+(underlined letter in the menu name). For example, to open the Edit menu press Alt+E keys together (See Figure 2.51).

After a menu is opened, you can select a menu command either one of the following ways:

- By typing the underlined letter in the command name (e.g. P for Paste in Figure 2.51). Or
- By clicking on a command's name.
- By pressing the ↓ arrow or ↑ arrow keys to highlight the desired command name and then pressing Enter key.

To close a menu without selecting any command, press the Esc key or click anywhere outside the menu.

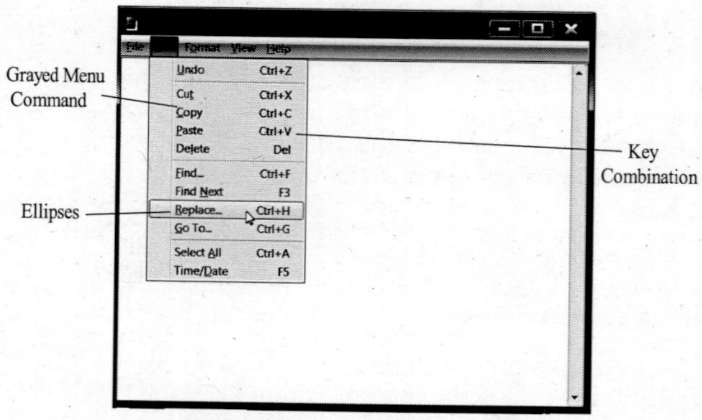

Figure 2.51 Edit menu open

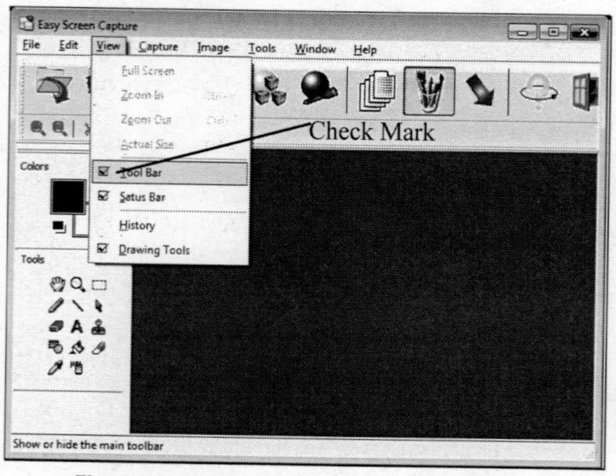

Figure 2.52 Special Indicators in Menu

Special Indicators in Menus

When you open a menu you would notice that many of the commands have additional words or symbols next to the command name (See Figure 2.52).

These additional words or symbols next to the command name indicate the following:

Grayed (Dimmed) Command Name

When a command is displayed as grayed, or dimmed as shown in Figure 2.51, it means that this choice is not currently available for selection. A command can be dimmed for many reasons. For example, if a window is already Maximized, the Maximize command on the System menu will be dimmed because this choice does not make sense.

Ellipses(...)

Ellipses as shown in Figure 2.51 next to a command means that you will be asked for additional information before it is executed on selecting such command. A dialog box appears on the screen, asking you to provide additional information.

Check Mark (✔

A check mark preceding a command as shown in Figure 2.52 means the command is a toggle that is activated (turned on). A toggle is a command that is alternately turned Off and On each time you select it. Each time you select one of these commands, it switches from On to Off or Off to On. If there is no check mark, then the command or setting is Off.

Triangle

A triangle to the right of a menu command as shown in Figure 2.52 means that the command has additional choices to choose from. This is also called a cascading menu. You can make selections from a cascaded menu in the same way as you would select from a normal menu.

A Key Combination

Some menu commands list keystrokes that can be used for opening the menu and choosing that command (See Figure 2.51). These are also called shortcut keys.

Shortcut Menus

Pressing the right mouse button brings up a small menu related to the currently selected object or the one the mouse is pointing to. This menu is also referred to as popup menu. For example, if you right click the Taskbar, you will get a menu of commands releated only to the Taskbar (See Figure 2.53).

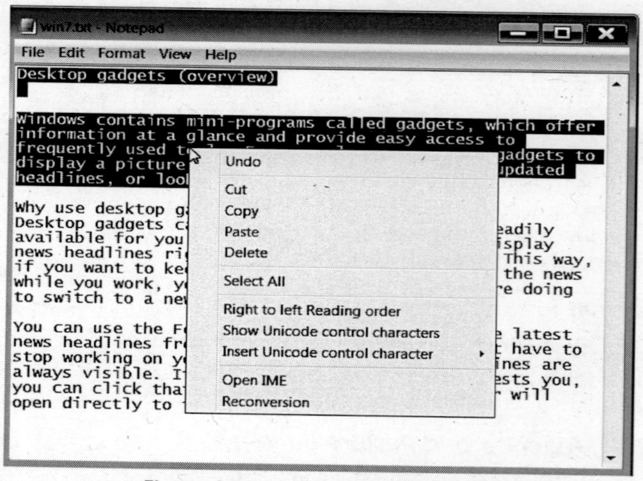

Figure 2.53 Shortcut/Popup menu

Dialog Boxes

A dialog box as shown in Figure 2.54 is a special type of window that asks you a question, allows you to select options to perform a task, or provides information. A dialog box will appear when you select a command with ellipsis(...) after it. Dialog boxes appear when Windows or its application program needs more information to execute the command. The various dialog box elements are as follows:

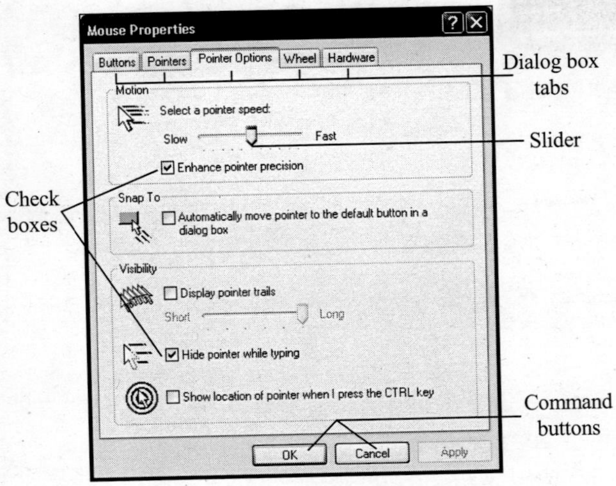

Figure 2.54 Dialog box Tabs

Dialog Box Tabs

Some of the dialog boxes have multiple option pages (See Figure 2.54). You need to select the page of your choice by clicking its icon at the top of the dialog box. Using the keyboard, press Ctrl + tab to flip through the option pages.

Moving between Dialog Box Elements

Dialog boxes often have several sections in them as seen in Figure 2.54. You can move between the sections in two ways:

- By clicking on the section that you want to change.
- Using the keyboard, you can press the Tab key to move between sections and press the Spacebar to select them.

Entering Information in a Dialog Box

The dialog boxes have following eight different types of sections where you need to enter information (See Figures 2.54 and 2.55).

- Text boxes
- Check boxes
- Option buttons
- Command buttons
- List boxes
- Sliders
- Spinners

Text Boxes Text box is also called an Edit box and it is where you type in the information (See Figure 2.55). To enter information on the text box, click the text box. The insertion point appears in the text box. The insertion point indicates the place where the character you type will appear.

- If the text box is empty, the insertion point appears at the left side of the box.
- If the box already contains text, the insertion point appears at the point where you clicked the mouse.

Check Boxes Check boxes are small square boxes (See Figure 2.54). Each check box is independent of all other check boxes in the dialog box. To select a check box item, click the box or anywhere in the text next to the box and similarly, to deselect repeat the same procedure. A check box when selected displays an (×) or (✔) within the box. Some check boxes have three states — checked, unchecked, and partly checked. A gray (in place of a black) check mark means that certain condition applies to it and some of the selections do not apply.

Option Buttons Option buttons are also called radio buttons and present a set of mutually exclusive options (See Figure 2.55). Option buttons are always presented in groups of two or more and may either be round or diamond shaped. You may select any one option from the group, but not more than one. To select the option click the button or any where in the text next to the button.

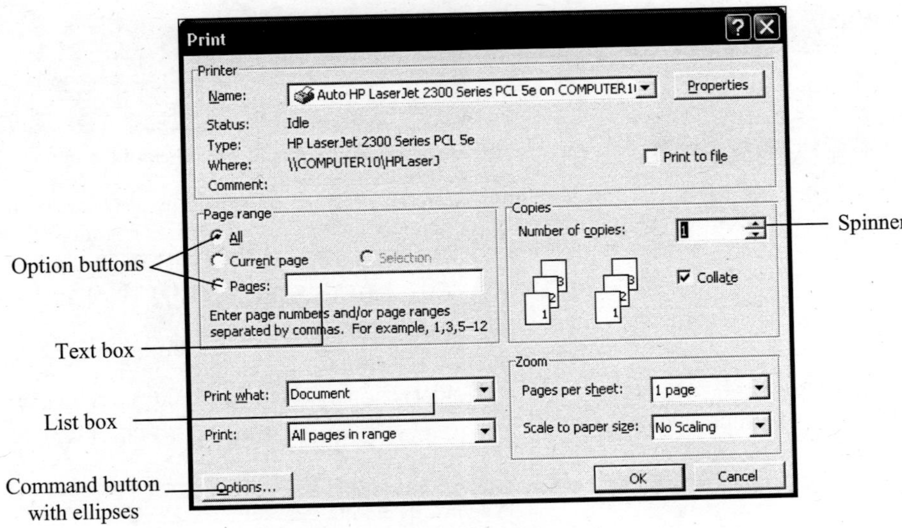

Figure 2.55 Dialog box elements

Command Buttons Command buttons are like option buttons and are used to execute a command immediately. They are rectangular and not square or circular in shape. An example of a command button is the OK button which is found on almost every dialog box (See Figure 2.54).

Drop-Down List Boxes A Drop-down List box presents a list of options or items from which you can select. To make a selection from a list box, using the mouse, click on it or using the keyboard highlight the desired option and then press Enter to choose it (See Figure 2.55).

Sliders A slider works like a sliding control. Moving it in one direction increases some value, moving it in the other direction decreases the same value (See Figure 2.54).

Spinners A spinner is a pair of arrows used to increase or decrease the value in a text box (See Figure 2.55). To increase the value in the text box, click up arrow and to decrease the value click down arrow.

2.6.3 Switching between two Windows

You may have different Application windows open at the same time. In such a case, the window on the top is called the active window i.e., window in which you are working and it is also called the foreground window. Active window's title bar is normally displayed in one colour, while the title bars of all inactive windows are displayed in another colour. In addition, Taskbar button for the active window appears to be pressed in the taskbar.

➡ **To change the active window, use any one of the following methods:**

1. Click the Taskbar button for the window you want to switch to. Or
2. Press and hold the Alt key. Then press Tab key to bring up the Taskbar Switcher window (See Figure 2.56).

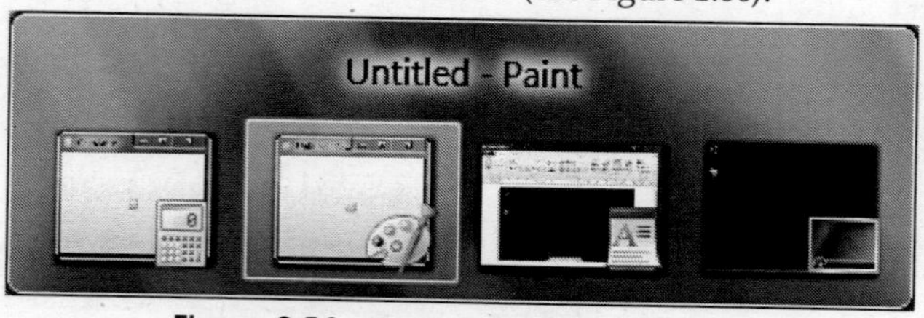

Figure 2.56 Taskbar Switcher window

3. The Task Switcher window displays an icon for each running program and draws a box around the icon of the active window. Continue holding Alt key and pressing Tab key until the window that you want to keep active.
4. Windows 7 brings the program's window to the foreground.

➡ **To see the thumbnail preview of the open window:**

1. Move the mouse pointer to the Taskbar button of the window you want to see the preview.
2. A small picture of the window called thumbnail appears as seen in Figure 2.57.

Figure 2.57 Thumbnail preview of window

➡ **To see the Windows Aero 3D Flip view of the open windows:**

1. Press the Windows logo key + Tab key to open Aero Flip 3D (See Figure 2.58).
2. While holding down the Windows logo key, press Tab key repeatedly or rotate the mouse wheel to cycle through open windows.

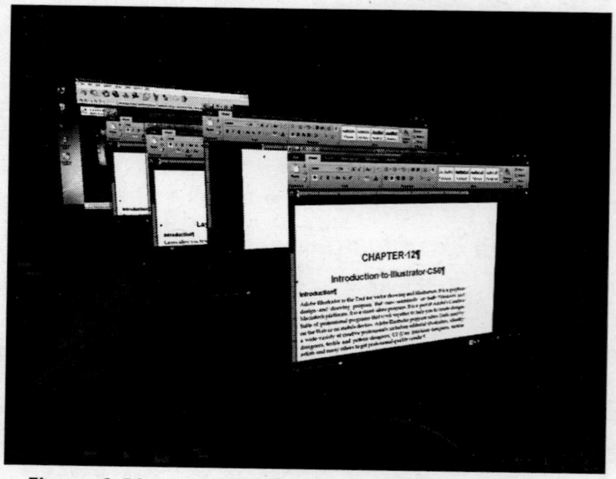

Figure 2.58 Aero 3D Flip view of the open windows

☞ Aero Flip 3D and thumbnail preview would not work in the computer unless your computer is running Windows Aero.

2.7 FILE MANAGEMENT IN WINDOWS 7

Files and folders are two of the most fundamental concepts of Windows operating system. You can create and organize files and folders as soon as you save your work in a PC.

2.7.1 Elements of Folder or Library Window

When you open a folder or library, you see it in a window. The various elements of this window are designed to help you to navigate around Windows or work with files, folders, and libraries more easily. Elements of folder or library window are marked in Figure 2.59 which are explained below.

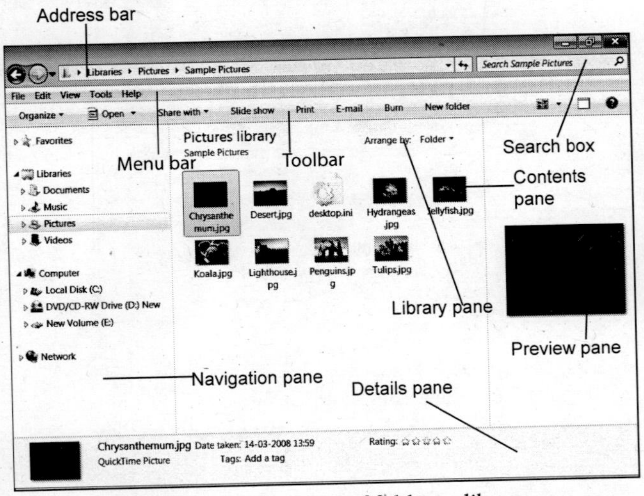

Figure 2.59 Elements of folder or library window in Windows 7

Navigation Pane

Navigation pane appears at the left side of window. It shows four or five nodes, such as Favorites, Libraries, Computer, Network and HomeGroup (visible only if the network location is set to Home). You can hide the navigation pane, adjust its width, or change its content to include only the Favorites node and hierarchical folders list. You can also use the navigation pane to access libraries, folders, saved searches, and even entire hard disks.

Address Bar

Address bar is used to navigate to a different folder or library or to go back to a previous one (See Figure 2.59). It also shows you where you are and helps you get where you want to go.

Back and Forward buttons are used to navigate to other folders or libraries you have already opened without closing the current window.

History drop-down list lets you to revisit the addresses you entered in previous sessions.

The new breadcrumb trail feature is used to help you in navigating to the address bar. To use this feature, click any folder name to move straight to that location or click down arrow next to the folder to display other subfolders at the same level (See Figure 2.60).

Toolbar

Toolbar is used to perform common tasks, such as changing the appearance of your files and folders, burning files to a CD, or starting a digital picture slide show. A few elements on the toolbar are always available, including the Organize menu on left and three buttons on the far right, which change views, show or hide the preview pane, and open a Help window (See Figure 2.59). But, the other buttons on the toolbar vary depending on the current selection.

Library Pane

Library pane appears only when you are in a library, such as Pictures library (See Figure 2.59). It is used to customize the library or arrange the files by different properties.

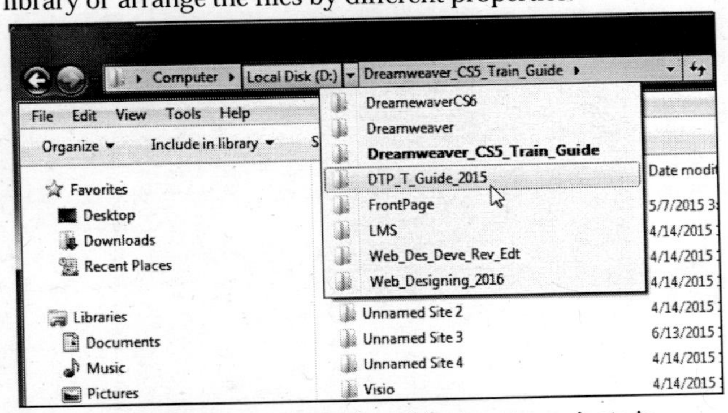

Figure 2.60 Breadcrumb trail feature to navigate in the address bar

Search Box

Type a word or phrase in the search box to look for an item in the current folder or library (See Figure 2.59). The scope of search is restricted to the current location and displays search results immediately in the contents pane. The width of the search box can be adjusted by dragging its left edge in either direction.

Details Pane

Details pane displays the properties associated with the selected file (See Figure 2.59). File properties provides information about a file, such as author, date you last changed the file, and any descriptive tags you might have added to the file. You can adjust the height of Details pane by dragging the top border up or down.

Preview Pane

Use the preview pane to see the contents of most files. If you select an e-mail message, text file, or picture, for example you can see its contents without opening it in a program (See Figure 2.59). If you do not see the Preview pane, click the Preview pane button in the toolbar to turn it on.

Menu Bar

By default, Menu bar is hidden. If it is seen, it is placed above the toolbar shown in Figure 2.59. If the menu bar is not displayed, you can make it appear temporarily.

➡ **To display menu bar:**

1. Click the Organize menu, choose Layout and then select Menu bar. Or alternatively, press Alt or F10 keys.

Selecting Files and Folders in Windows 7

➡ **To select a single file:**

1. Open the folder or Windows Explorer window containing the file.
2. Click the file.

➡ **To select multiple files:**

1. Open the folder or Windows Explorer window containing the file.
2. Click the first file.
3. Then press and hold down Ctrl key and then click the other files you want to select (See Figure 2.61).

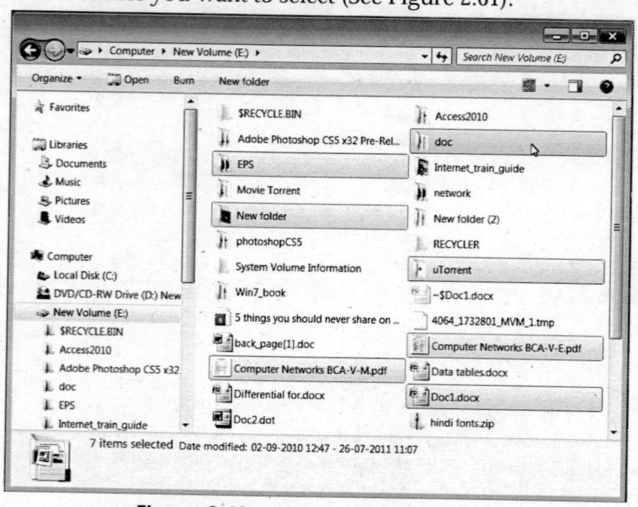

Figure 2.61 Selecting multiple files

➡ **To select a group of files:**

1. Open the folder or Windows Explorer window containing the file.
2. Move and position the mouse to the left of the first file you want to select.
3. Then click and drag mouse to the right until all the files you want are selected. (See Figure 2.62).

➡ **To select all the items in a folder:**

1. Open the folder or Windows Explorer window containing file.
2. Click the Organize menu and choose Select all. Or press Ctrl + A keys together.
3. Windows Explorer selects all the files in the folder.

Creating Files and Folders in Windows 7

➡ **To create a new File/Folder:**

1. In the Folder window, click the File menu and choose New or right click an empty area of folder window and choose New.
2. In both cases, a submenu lists the new objects you can create: folders, shortcuts, and a variety of types of files (See Figure 2.63).

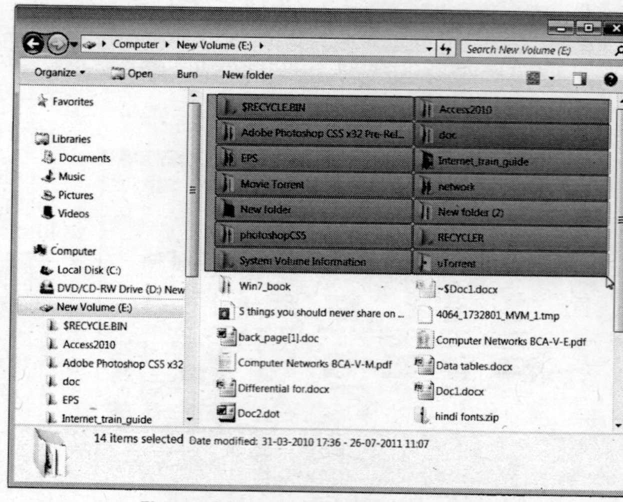

Figure 2.62 Selecting group of files

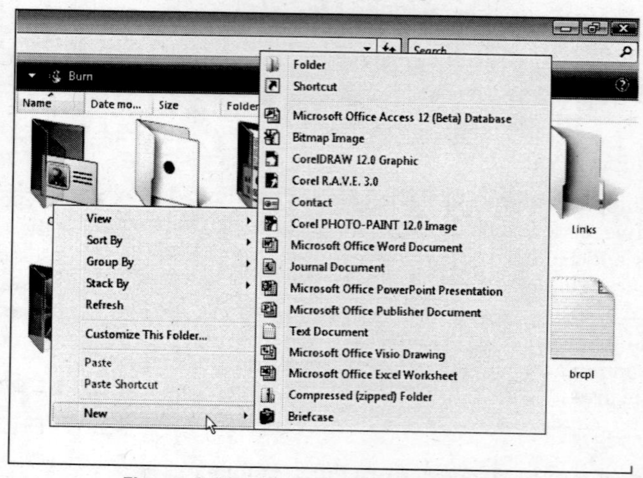

Figure 2.63 Creating new file or folder

3. Select an element out of the list. Windows 7 creates the selected object.

☞ If you click *older b tton* from the *oolbar*, Windows 7 creates a new folder.

Naming and Renaming Files and Folders in Windows 7

➡ **To rename a file or folder:**

1. Select the file/folder you want to rename.
2. Click the Organize menu and choose Rename. Or press F2 key (See Figure 2.64). Or alternatively, right click the file/folder and choose Rename from the context menu.
3. A box appears around current name, with its details selected. Type the new name in the box and press Enter key (See Figure 2.64).

Figure 2.64 Renaming a folder

Opening File and Folder in Windows 7

1. You have to double-click a file or folder in this pane to open it (Figure 2.65).

Moving or Copying Folder and File

Moving/copying a file or folder to another drive or folder is easy. Just drag a file/folder from the right pane to another disk drive (or a folder on another drive) to copy/move it there.

➡ **To move a file or folder to another drive or folder:**

1. Select the file or folder you want to move.
2. Point to the selected file or folder, and then press and hold down the left mouse button.

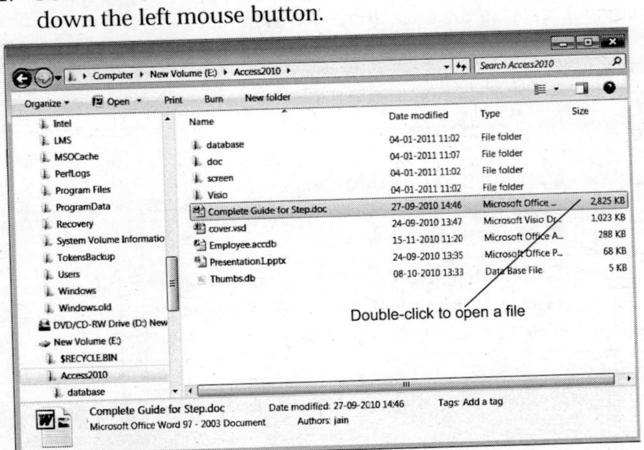

Figure 2.65 Opening a file

3. Drag the file/folder from the right pane to the left pane and drop it into the selected folder or drive where you want (See Figure 2.66).
4. A Move button as shown in Figure 2.66 indicates where the file or folder will be moved.

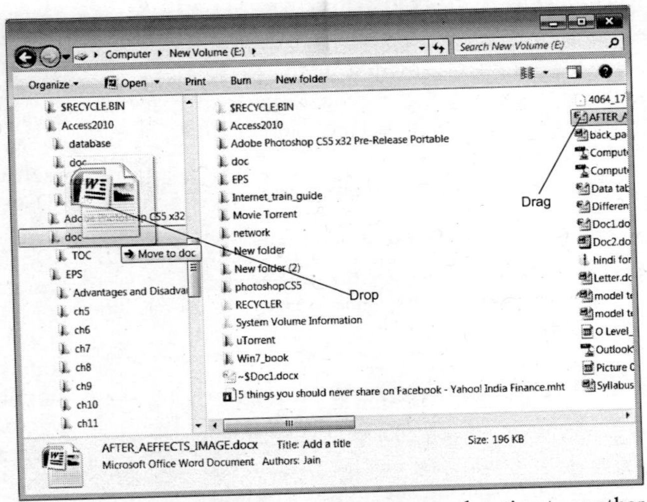

Figure 2.66 Moving a file or folder from one location to another

5. Release the mouse button to move the file/folder into desired place.

➡ **To copy a file or folder to another drive or folder:**

1. Select the file or folder which you want to copy.
2. Point to the selected file or folder, and then press and hold down the left mouse button.
3. Press Ctrl key while dragging the file/folder from the right pane to the left pane and drop it into the selected folder or drive where you want (Figure 2.67).
4. A Copy button as shown in the Figure 2.67 indicates where the file or folder will be copied.
5. Release the mouse button to copy the file/folder into desired place.

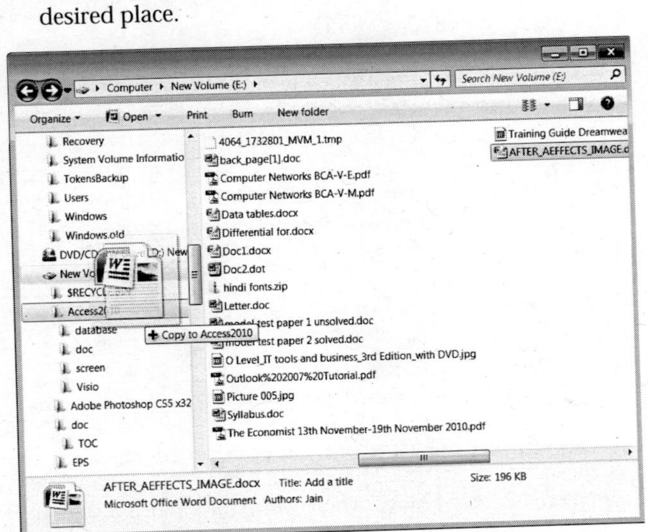

Figure 2.67 Copy a file or folder

Deleting Files and Folders in Windows 7

➡ **To delete file(s) and folder(s):**

1. Select the file or folder that you want to delete.
2. Click the Organize menu and choose Delete . Or alternatively, right click the file/folder and choose Delete from the context menu.
3. The Delete File dialog box appears. Click Yes in this dialog box.
4. The selected file get deleted from the folder.

☞ Objects deleted from your computer are sent to the Recycle Bin. You can recover them by double-clicking the Recycle Bin folder, if desired.

2.8 START MENU IN WINDOWS 7

Start menu appears when you click on the Start button on the Taskbar as seen in Figure 2.49. The Start menu provides you more customization options. It shows you who is logged on. It automatically adds the most frequently used programs to the top-level menu. It enables you to move any programs which you want to be in the Start menu. Start menu is divided into three basic parts. These are;

(a) Program List
(b) Search Box
(c) Right Pane

2.8.1 Program List (Left Pane)

Left pane of the Start menu shows recently used programs and those programs that have been pinned to Start menu. Program list shows up to eight recently used programs. If you want to see the complete list of programs installed in your computer, then click on the All Programs (See Figure 2.49).

2.8.2 Search Box (Lower Left Pane)

Lower left pane of the Start menu is the search box which allows computer to search files, folders, programs or computer that are connected to your computer (See Figure 2.49). To search any files or folder, type the name of the file or folder in search box and then press Enter key. To clear the search result, click on the Clear button [X].

2.8.3 Right Pane

Right Pane of the start menu gives access to commonly used folders. These are shown in Figure 2.49 which are discussed below.

Current User–It opens the folder of the user who is currently logged on to Windows. This folder contains files, such as Documents, Pictures, etc.

Documents–It opens the Document Folder where you can store files.

Pictures–It opens Picture Folder where you can store pictures and graphic files.

Music–It opens the Music Folder where you store and play the music files.

Games–It opens the Game Folder from where you can access the games which are installed in your computer.

Computer–It opens a computer from where you can access hard disk drives, printers, scanner, CD drive and other hardware connected to your computer.

Control Panel–It opens window that allows you to install software and change different setting of Windows, such as Date, Time, Keyboard, Mouse, Password, Display, Sound settings, etc.

Devices and Printers–It opens a window where you can see information about the printer, mouse, and other devices installed on your computer.

Default Programs–It opens a window where you can see information about the printer, mouse, and other devices installed in your computer.

Help and Support–It displays help which is a set of screens of information about Windows itself where you can browse and search Help topics using Windows and your computer.

At the bottom of the right pane is the Shut down button. Click the Shut down button to turn off your computer. Clicking the arrow next to Shut down button displays a menu with additional options for switching users, logging off, restarting, Sleep, or shutting down as seen in Figure 2.49.

☞ If you want Windows 7 to automatically reopen all the programs and documents currently on your screen, click the power button arrow from the Start menu and then click Sleep.

2.9 SHORTCUTS

A shortcut is a small file that is linked to a program, document, folder or an Internet address. The file is represented by an icon with an arrow in its lower left corner.

Shortcut is linked to a file or folder, which can be located anywhere–on a local hard disk or CD-ROM drive or on a floppy disk.

2.9.1 Creating a Shortcut

A shortcut can be created in the following two ways:

- By using cut and paste or
- By using the Create Shortcut wizard.

☞ A shortcut is a pointer to an object, and not the object itself. This means that you can create and delete shortcuts without affecting the object which is linked to a file.

➡ **To create a shortcut using copy and paste:**

1. Right click the items for which you want to create a shortcut.
2. From the context menu, choose Copy.
3. Now right click on the desktop and choose Paste from the context menu.

➡ **To create a shortcut using the create shortcut wizard:**

1. Right-click the desktop, from the Context menu choose New, and then choose Shortcut as seen in Figure 2.68.

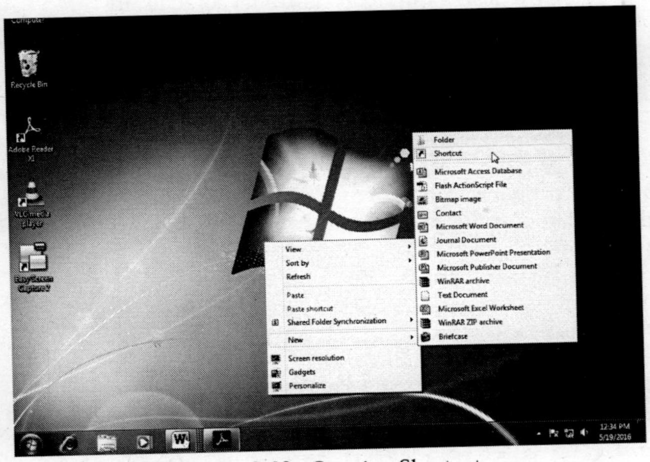

Figure 2.68 Creating Shortcut

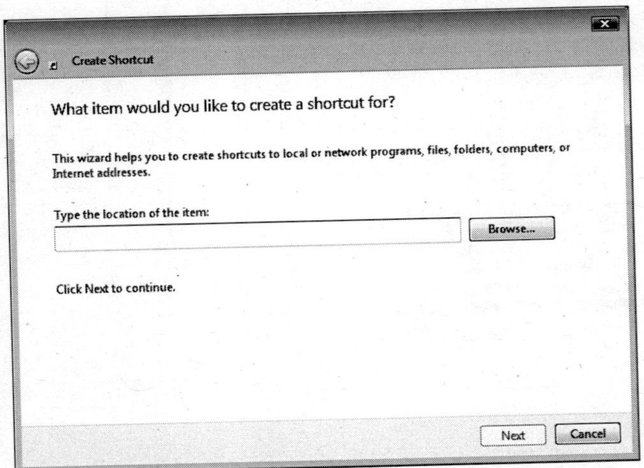

Figure 2.69 Creating Shortcut wizard

2. The wizard for Create Shortcut appears as shown in Figure 2.69.
3. Click the Browse... button. In the Browse for Folder dialog box, locate the item for which you want to create a shortcut.
4. Click Next → type a name for your shortcut, click Finish, and your shortcut will appear on the desktop.

2.9.2 Renaming a Shortcut

When you create a shortcut, Windows gives it a default name based on the underlying object.

➡ **To change the shortcut name:**

1. Right-click the shortcut.
2. From the context menu, choose Rename.
3. Type the name that you want to use.

2.9.3 Deleting a Shortcut

➡ **To delete a shortcut:**

1. Select the icon and press the Del key. Alternatively, right click the shortcut which you want to be deleted and choose Delete from the context menu.
2. Windows prompt you for conformation before deletion.

2.9.4 The Search Feature in Windows 7

With the help of Search feature of Windows 7, you can search not only documents but also e-mail messages, contacts, Internet Explorer Favorites, applications and much more. You can search in your own computer and other computers that are connected to your computer by using network. You can also use search filters to specify the property in your search. Windows 7 provides several ways to find files and folders or programs. These are:

1. One way is to type in the Search box at the top of any open window.
2. Second method is to type in the Search box on the Start menu. When you start typing, the search begins automatically.

☞ You can use the Search box on the Start menu to find files, folders, programs, and e-mail messages stored on your computer.

How to find where file is being saved

➡ **To find a program or file using Start menu:**

1. Click the Start button.
2. Click the Search box and type a word or part of a word in this box (Figure 2.70).
3. As you type, Windows 7 displays the programs, documents and other data items that match your text on the Start menu.
4. If you see a program or document you want, click on it to open it (Figure 2.70).

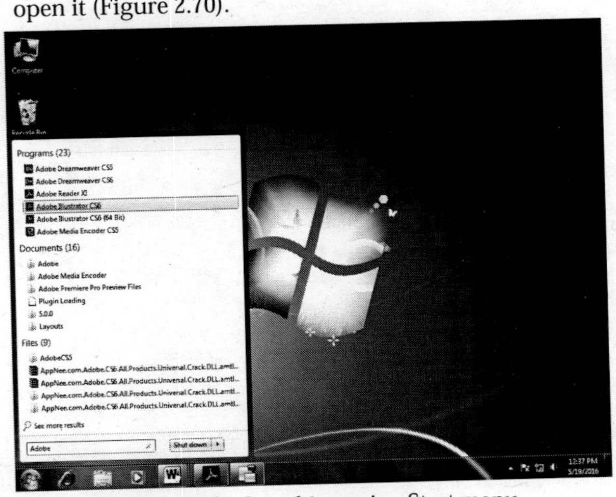

Figure 2.70 Searching using Start menu

➡ **To find a file or folder using the search box in a folder:**

1. Open the folder in which you want to search.

2. Click the Search box and type a word or part of a word in this box (Figure 2.71).
3. As you type, the contents of the folder are filtered to reflect each successive character you type. When you see the file that you want, stop typing.
4. Double-click to open it.

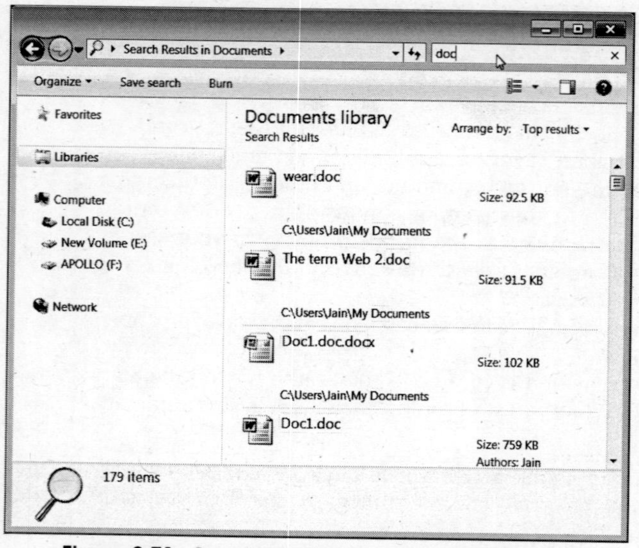

Figure 2.71 Searching using Search box in a Folder

If you are searching for a file based on one or more of its properties such as a tag or the date the file was last modified, you can use search filters to specify the property in your search.

➡ **To find a file or folder using search filter in a folder:**

1. Open the folder in which you want to search.
2. Click the Search box and then click the appropriate search filter such as Authors, type and date modified (Figure 2.72).

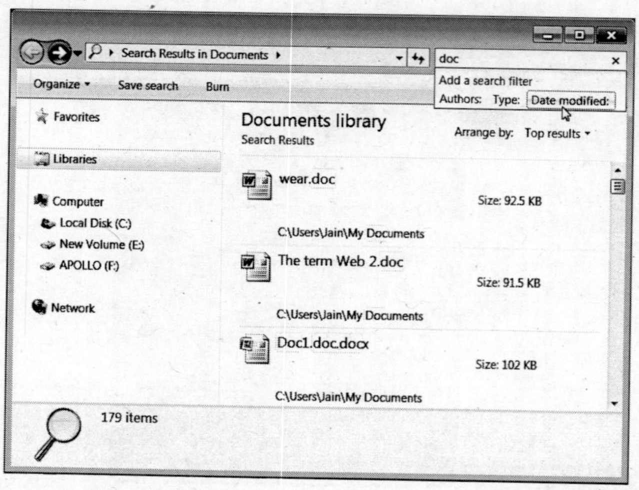

Figure 2.72 Searching using Search filter in a Folder

3. Depending on the search filter you click. The contents are filtered.
4. Double-click to open the file.

How Programs may save files in specific location by default

When you save a file in a program and you don't manually change the folder, the file ends up in My Documents by default.

1. The first method is to open Windows Explorer, right-click on any one of the libraries, and select Properties from the popup menu. For this example, we will use the Documents library as shown in Figure 2.73.

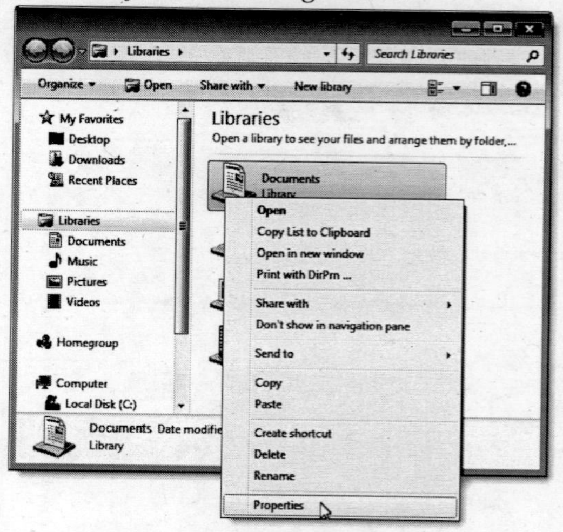

Figure 2.73 Document libarary Menu

Or

Open the start menu and click on your users name in the top right corner.

Next right click on the Documents folder listed in the left hand pane under libraries.

2. The Documents Properties dialog box displays. Each of the four default libraries has two folder locations: one from your user folder (e.g., C:\Users\Jain) and one from the Public profile folder (e.g., C:\Users\Public). To add a custom folder to the selected library, click Include a folder as shown in Figure 2.74.
3. The Include Folder in Documents dialog box displays. Navigate to the custom folder you want to use as the default save location, select it, and click Include Folder as shown in Figure 2.75.
4. The custom folder is added to the list of Library locations. Select the custom folder and click Set save location.
5. The check marks moves to the custom folder indicating it is now the default save location as shown in Figure 2.76.
6. Click OK to save your changes and close the dialog box.

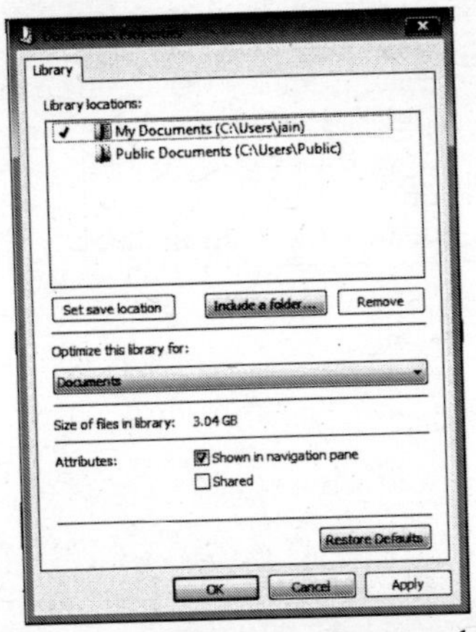

Figure 2.74 Document Property box

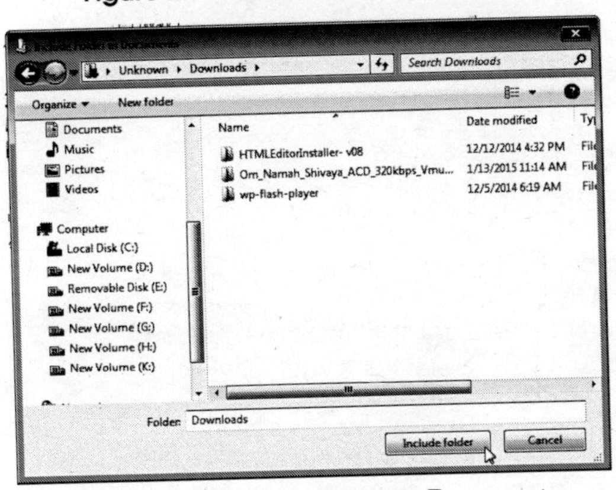

Figure 2.75 Include Folder in Documents

2.9.5 Keep Software Updated

There is an easy, free way to help to keep your PC safer and running smoothly. It is called Windows Update. All you have to do is turn it on, and you'll get the latest security and other important updates from MS automatically.

Setting up Windows Update is simple. If you have already got automatic updating turned on, Windows Update in Control Panel will open and show your update status. If it is not yet turned on, you'll be guided through the steps to do so. After that, all the latest security and performance improvements will be installed on your PC quickly and reliably.

➡ **To keep software updated:**

1. Open Control Panel and select Windows Updated.
2. In the left pane, click Change settings.
3. Under Important updates, choose the option that you want.
4. Under Recommended updates, select the Give me recommended updates the same way I receive important updates check box, and then click OK. Administrator permission required If you're prompted for an administrator password or confirmation, type the password or provide confirmation.

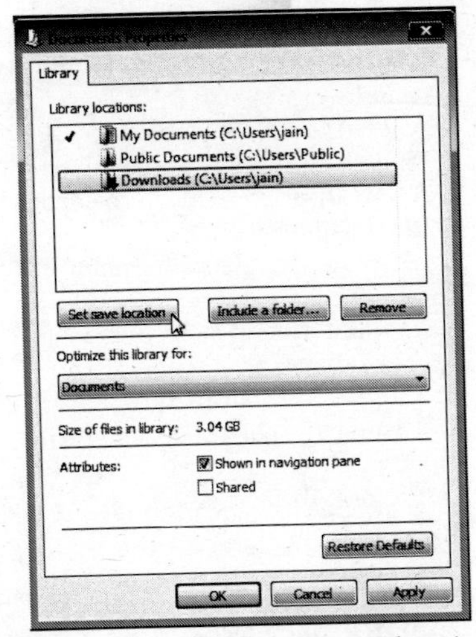

Figure 2.76 Selecting Set save location

You can also choose if you want to allow anyone to install updates by selecting the Allow all users to install updates on this computer check box. This applies only to updates and software that are installed manually; automatic updates will be installed regardless of the user.

Windows Shortcut Keys

General Shortcuts

Shortcut	Action
CTRL+A	Select All
CTRL+C	Copy
CTRL+X	Cut
CTRL+V	Paste
CTRL+Z	Undo
DELETE	To move to Recycle Bin
SHIFT+DELETE	Delete item permanently without moving to Recycle Bin
F2	Rename the selected item
F3	Search for a file or a folder
F4	Display the Address Bar list in My Computer or Windows Explorer
F5	Refresh the contents of the active window
F6	Cycle through the screen elements in a window or the desktop
F10	Activate the menu bar in the active program
CTRL while dragging an item	Copy the selected item
ALT+ENTER	View the properties for the selected item
ALT+F4	Close the active item, or quit the active program
ALT+ENTER	Display the properties of the selected object

(Contd...)

Shortcut	Action
ALT+SPACEBAR	Open the shortcut menu for the active window.
CTRL+F4	Close the active window
ALT+TAB	Switch between the open items
ALT+ESC	Cycle through items in the order that they had been opened
SHIFT+F10	Display the shortcut menu for the selected item
ALT+SPACEBAR	Display the System menu for the active window
CTRL+ESC	Display the Start menu
ALT+ Underlined letter in a menu name	Display the corresponding menu
Underlined letter in a command name on an open menu	Perform the corresponding command
RIGHT ARROW	Open the next menu to the right, or open a submenu
LEFT ARROW	Open the next menu to the left, or close a submenu
BACKSPACE	View the folder one level up in My Computer or Windows Explorer
SHIFT when you insert a CD-ROM into the CD-ROM drive	Prevent the CD-ROM from automatically playing
CTRL+SHIFT+ESC	Open Task Manager

Windows Explorer Shortcuts

Shortcut	Action
HOME	Display the top of the active window.
END	Display the bottom of the active window.
LEFT ARROW	Collapse the current selection if it is expanded, or select the parent folder.
RIGHT ARROW	Display the current selection if it is collapsed, or select the first subfolder.
NUM LOCK + *	Display all of the subfolders that are under the selected folder.
NUM LOCK + +	Display the contents of the selected folder.
NUM LOCK+ -	Collapse the selected folder.

Dialog box Shortcuts

Shortcut	Action
CTRL+TAB	Move forward through the tabs.
CTRL+SHIFT+TAB	Move backward through the tabs.
TAB	Move forward through the options.
SHIFT+TAB	Move backward through the options.
ALT+Underlined letter	Perform the corresponding command or select the corresponding option.
ENTER	Perform the command for the active option or button.
SPACEBAR	Select or clear the check box if the active option is a check box.
Arrow keys	Select a button if the active option is a group of option buttons
BACKSPACE	Open a folder one level up when a folder is selected in the Save As or Open dialog box
F1	Display Help
F4	Display the items in the active list

Accessibility Shortcuts

Shortcut	Action
Right SHIFT for eight seconds	Switch Filter Keys on or off
Left ALT+ left SHIFT + PRINT SCREEN	Switch High Contrast on or off
Left ALT + left SHIFT + NUM LOCK	Switch the MouseKeys on or off
SHIFT five times	Switch the Sticky Keys on or off
NUM LOCK for five seconds	Switch the Toggle Keys on or off

Natural keyboard shortcuts

Shortcut	Action
Windows Logo	Display or hide the Start menu
Windows Logo+BREAK	Display the System Properties dialog box
Windows Logo+D	Display the desktop
Windows Logo+M	Minimize all open windows
Windows Logo+SHIFT+M	Restore minimized windows
Windows Logo+F	Search for a file or a folder
CTRL+Windows Logo+F	Search for computers
Windows Logo+F1	Display Windows Help
Windows Logo+L	Lock the keyboard
Windows Logo+R	Open the Run dialog box
Windows Logo+U	Open Utility Manager

Text Editing

Shortcut	Action
CTRL+A	Select All
CTRL+C	Copy
CTRL+X	Cut
CTRL+V	Paste
CTRL+Z	Undo
CTRL+RIGHT ARROW	Move the insertion point to the beginning of the next word
CTRL+LEFT ARROW	Move the insertion point to the beginning of the previous word
CTRL+DOWN ARROW	Move the insertion point to the beginning of the next paragraph
CTRL+UP ARROW	Move the insertion point to the beginning of the previous paragraph
CTRL+SHIFT with any of the arrow keys	Highlight a block of text

(Contd...)

MODEL QUESTIONS AND ANSWERS

A. Multiple Choice

1.1 A file deleted from disk drive A: in Windows goes to ________.

a. Recycle Bin b. My Computer
c. Windows Explorer d. Permanently deleted.

1.2 The term Operating System means ________

a. A set of programs which controls computer working
b. The way a computer operator works
c. Conversion of high-level language in to machine level language
d. The way a floppy disk drive operates

1.3 The operating system of a computer serves as a software interface between the user and the ________.

a. Memory b. Peripheral
c. Hardware d. Screen

1.4 Software is a program that directs the overall operation of the computer, facilitates its use and interacts with the user. What are the different types of this software?

a. Operating system b. Language Compiler
c. Utilities d. All of the above

1.5 ________ is the screen background and main area of window where you can open and manage files and programs.

a. Icons b. Desktop
c. Application window d. Screen Saver

1.6 An application can be opened through shortcut on desktop by

a. Double clicking on its shortcut
b. Right clicking and choosing "Open" option
c. Selecting the icon and pressing Enter key
d. All of the above

1.7 Which of the following statements is incorrect in context of shortcut icons.

a. Shortcuts can be created by dragging and dropping.
b. Shortcuts can be created by using cut and paste methods.
c. Shortcuts can be created by using the Shortcut wizard.
d. None of the above.

1.8 A new printer can be added by Printer and Faxes option in

a. Control Panel b. File Manager
c. Dynamic Data Exchange d. None of these

1.9 GUI is used as an interface between

a. Hardware and software b. Man and machine
c. Software and user d. None of the above

1.10 Exchange of images or data from one application to another is done by using

a. Icons b. Control Panel
c. Clipboard d. None of these

1.11 Which of the following file format supports in Windows 7?

a. NTFS b. BSD
c. EXT d. All of the above

1.12 What is the meaning of "Hibernate" in Windows XP/Windows 7?

a. Restart the computer in safe mode
b. Restart the computer in hibernate mode
c. Shutdown the computer terminating all the running applications
d. Shutdown the computer without closing the running applications

1.13 Windows ____ is the newest version of the Windows operating system.

a. 5 b. 6
c. 8 d. 10

1.14 When you point to a button, its function will display in a ________.

a. ScreenAlert b. ScreenTip
c. ScreenBar d. ScreenList

1.15 The ____ list contains programs that accomplish a variety of tasks commonly required on a computer. Most of these programs are installed with the Windows 7 operating system, such as Calculator, Snipping Tool, and WordPad.

a. Helper Programs b. Necessities
c. Utilities d. Accessories

1.16 What is the function of an operating system?

a. Manages computer's resources very efficiently
b. Takes care of scheduling jobs for execution
c. Manages the flow of data and instructions
d. All of the above

1.17 The opening screen consists of four main components these are

a. Windows desktop b. Start button
c. Notification area d. All of the above

1.18 How many scroll bars can be visible on the text area if your document is over 100%?

a. Two b. One
c. Three d. Four

1.19 Which button appears immediately after a window has been maximized?

a. The Close button b. The Minimize button
c. The Maximize button d. The Restore button

1.20 Which windows program do you use to manage folders and files?

a. Accessories b. Control Panel
c. Explorer d. Office

1.21 The ________ provides access to all active application by maintaining a row of open application title boxes.

a. Title bar b. Task bar
c. Start menu d. None

1.22 An operating system is:
a. Integrated software b. Application software
c. CD-ROM software d. System software

1.23 Which components appear in the initial windows start up display?
a. Dialog box b. Taskbar
c. Start menu d. All of the above

1.24 It is the default folder for many Windows applications to save your file.
a. My Document b. My Pictures
c. Document and Settings d. My Computer

1.25 Taskbar is used for
a. Navigation program b. Switching between program
c. Start a program d. All of above

B. State whether the following are True or False

2.1 Uninstalling a program means that you delete all of the program's files from your computer and remove the program's icons from the start menu and desktop.
2.2 The Windows 7 Enterprise and Ultimate editions both contain the same features.
2.3 The System menu contains commands associated with the My Computer window.
2.4 Title bar is present at the top most line of a window bar.
2.5 A folder can not contain files as well as sub folders.
2.6 Recycle Bin does not allow you to easily recover deleted files and folders in Windows.
2.7 My Documents usually includes the All Program, My Recent Documents, Printers and Faxes are all computer commands.
2.8 Icon is a picture or image that you can display on your desktop.
2.9 When you select Computer icon and press Alt + Enter to open system properties dialog box.
2.10 Linux is one of the open source operating systems.
2.11 Windows Control Panel gives you access to all of your computer'settings and enables you to install and remove programs.
2.12 Just above the Start button is a search box.
2.13 The left side of the Start menu contains a list of frequently used folders including documents, pictures, music and games.
2.14 The Taskbar contains start button, Quick Launch and Notification area.
2.15 Right click press and release the right mouse button once, typically open a dialog box.
2.16 A folder is a set of files and folders.
2.17 You cannot create a new folder on the desktop.
2.18 Linux is a proprietary software.
2.19 When a folder is copied to another place, the subfolders in the folder also get copied.
2.20 To use computer, you need an operating system.

Answers

A. 1.1 d 1.2 a 1.3 c 1.4 d 1.5 b
1.6 d 1.7 d 1.8 a 1.9 c 1.10 c
1.11 a 1.12 d 1.13 d 1.14 b 1.15 d
1.16 d 1.17 d 1.18 a 1.19 d 1.20. c
1.21 b 1.22 d 1.23 b 1.24 a 1.25 d

B. 2.1 T 2.2 F 2.3 T 2.4 T 2.5 F
2.6 F 2.7 F 2.8 T 2.9 F 2.10 T
2.11 T 2.12 T 2.13 F 2.14 T 2.15 F
2.16 T 2.17 F 2.18 F 2.19 T 2.20 T

CHAPTER 3

Basic Computer Hardware

3.1 INTRODUCTION

In comupter hardware refers to the physical components that make up a computer system. There are many different kinds of hardware that can be installed inside, and connected to the outside, of a computer. Sometimes be seen abbreviated as computer hw.

Hardware is divided into two categories: main hardware and peripherals. Peripherals are then subdivided into input, output and storage devices. Main hardware includes the pieces a computer needs to run, namely a central processing unit, or CPU, random access memory (RAM), and read-only memory (ROM). These components are at the core of any computer. Output peripherals are those that show data to a user, such as a monitor and a printer. Input peripherals are those that receive data from the user, such as a keyboard and a touchpad or mouse. Storage devices include hard drives and CD/DVD/BluRay drives.

3.2 GETTING STARTED WITH PC HARDWARE SUPPPORT

PC hardware support various components in the front part of a System Unit and their functions as shown in Figure 3.1.

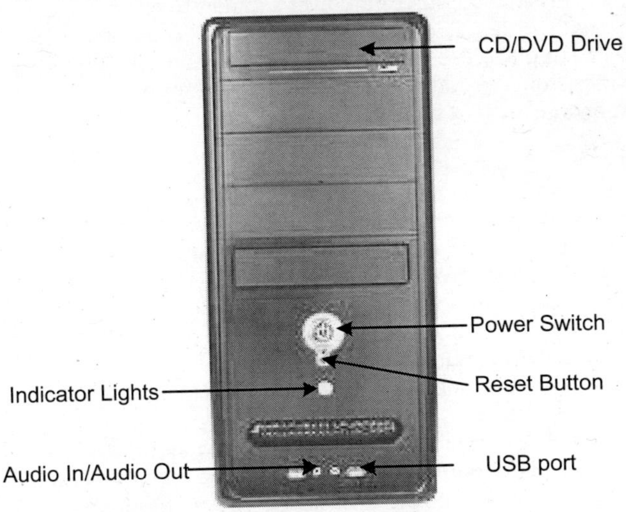

Figure 3.1 Parts of front panel of system

3.2.1 Front Panel

Power Switch–Depending on the model, this switch is located either in the front or at the rear of the system unit. It is used to switch the system ON or OFF.

Reset Button–This is a press switch which can be used to restart the PC without switching off the mains power supply. However, use this switch as a last resort when the PC hangs and does not accept a command from the keyboard. When you restart the PC, it will lose all the information currently stored in its memory.

Power Light (Power LED)–Most computers have both 'power lights' and 'hard drive lights'. The power light (power LED) lets you know when the computer is on. If it's on constantly, the computer is operating normally. If it's blinking, it's likely that the computer has gone into either hibernation or suspend mode. The hard drive LED lights up when the hard drive is being accessed or is otherwise active.

CD-ROM/DVD Drive–It is called optical Disc Drive. It is used for CD, DVD and Blue-ray drives that read and write CDs and DVDs.

Audio In/Audio Out–Many computers include audio ports on the front of the computer case that allow you to easily connect speakers, microphones, and headsets without fumbling with the back of the computer.

USB Port–Most desktop computers have several USB ports. These can be used to connect almost any type of device, including mice, keyboards, printers, and digital cameras. They will often appear on the front and back of the computer.

3.2.2 Rear Panel

If you look at the rear panel of the system unit of your PC, you will see certain holes and slots fitted with different cables. Details of such parts are explained in Figure 3.2.

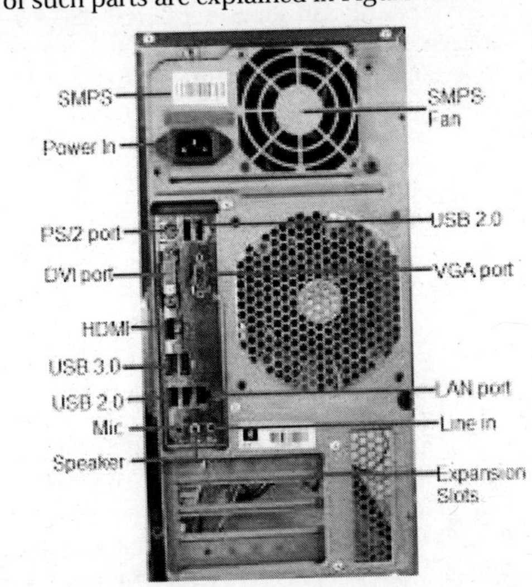

Figure 3.2 Parts of the rear panel of system

Power Socket– This is where you will connect the power cord to the computer. Cables plugged into the these sockets carry electric power supply from the electrical outlet to your system unit and from the system unit to the monitor.

Video port for Monitor–This connector is used to attached a computer display monitor to a computer's video card. The connector has 15 holes and it is a female port. It look like a serial port connector, however that port has pins not holes in it.

PS/2 Ports–It is used for old computer to connect the keyboard and mouse with the system. Typically with an icon for a mouse (cyan) or for a keyboard (magenta). The data transfer rate about 7,000 to 12,000 bps.

Serial Port–A serial port used to connect external modems or old computer mouse. It comes in two versions a 9-pin version or a 25-pin model. The 9-pin is found in new computers. Data travels over a serial port at 115 kilobits per second.

Parallel Port–A parallel port is used to connect external devices such as scanners and printers. The 25-pin port is sometimes it is called a printer port. It is also known by IEEE 1284-compliant Centronics port.

The port is sometimes also called more simply a "printer" port. There are two variants for this type of interface. The ports look exactly like the traditional parallel port but are called ECP (Extend Capabilities Port) and EPP (Enhanced Parallel Port). These interfaces are ten times faster than the older printer port. The Data Transfer rate 360 Bps (bytes per second) for Centronics or standard mode; about 2 MBps for EPP (Enhanced Parallel Port) mode;

Fan Housing–The power supply fitted inside the system unit has a small fan to release the heat out of the machine. You should make sure that the system unit is placed away from the wall so that the hot air released by the fan can be thrown out.

USB Port–It can connect all kinds of external USB devices such as external hard disk, printer, scanner, mouse, video camera, PDA and keyboard etc. It was introduced in 1997. There are four different types of USB computer ports. USB 1.0 and 1.1 released between 1996 and 1998 with a speed range starting from 1.5 Mb/sec up to 12 Mb/sec (megabits per seconds). Then USB 2.0 was released in 2000 with a maximum speed of 480 Mb/sec. Finally USB 3.0 was released in 2008 with a maximum speed of 5 Gb/sec.

Sound Connectors–Some PCs have in-built sound connectors but, in some systems they are on a separate expansion slots. There are three identical round rings i.e. output for speakers, input for microphone, and Line input for other devices such as audio CD player, audio/video system.

Game Port and Joystick Connector–A joystick connector is a 15-pin female D-sub connector with two rows: One with 8 holes and the other with 7. The connector is also known as a game port and is used as a Music Instrument Digital Interface (MIDI) port for connecting computer peripherals such as a synthesizer and is located on the sound card.

Modem–It connects a PC's modem to the telephone network. The Data transfer rate 300 bps to about 56 Kbps for standard modems that use the voice band of a phone line; up to about 8 Mbps for broadband Asymmetric Digital Subscriber Line (ADSL) Modem. RJ11 connector with 2 to 6 pins is smaller then Ethernet's RJ45 connector with 8 pins.

Ethernet Port (RJ-45)–For fast Internet connections and for networking, an Ethernet or network port is used. The port is used to connect network cabling to a computer. Data moves through them at speeds of either 10 megabits or 100 megabits or 1 gigabit (1,000 megabits) depending on what speed the network card in the computer. The "ACT" light flickers when data is moving through the network to or from the port. The 10 or 100 lights relate to data speed. "10" means data is moving across the network at 10 Megabits per second. "100" means the network is moving data at 100 megbits per second.

IEEE 1394 or Firewire port–This port is used to transfer large amounts of data very quickly. Usually camcorders and other video equipment use this port to get data onto a computer. Data can move across the port at up to 400 megabits per second.

3.3 ELECTRICITY AND POWER SYSTEM

The power supply as its name might suggest is the device that supplies power to all the components in the computer. Its case holds a transformer, voltage control, and cooling fan. The electricity you get in the form of alternating current (AC), while the electricity your PC requires is direct current (DC), Therefore,the primary function of your power supply is to convert the AC power into a DC form that your PC can use. It converts about 100-120 volts of AC power to low-voltage DC power for the internal components to use. The most common computer power supplies are built to conform with the ATX form factor. This enables different power supplies to be interchangable with different components inside the computer. ATX power supplies also are designed to turn on and off using a signal from the motherboard, and provide support for modern functions such as standby mode.

3.4 CPUs

The Central Processing Unit (CPU; sometimes just called processor) is a machine that can execute computer programs. It is sometimes referred to as the brain of the computer. It also interprets and execute most of the commands from the computer's other hardware and software. All sorts of devices use a CPU, including desktop, laptop, and tablet computers, smartphones and also your flat screen television set. Intel and AMD are the two most popular CPU manufacturers for desktops, laptops, and servers.

There are four steps that nearly all CPUs use in their operation: fetch, decode, execute, and writeback. The first step, fetch, involves retrieving an instruction from program memory. In the decode step, the instruction is broken up into parts that have significance to other portions of the CPU. During the execute step various portions of the CPU, such as the arithmetic logic unit (ALU) and the floating point unit (FPU) are connected so they can perform the desired operation. The final step, writeback, simply writes back the results of the execute step to some form of memory. The clock speed of a processor is the number of instructions it can process in any given second, measured in Gigahertz (GHz) (See Figure 3.3).

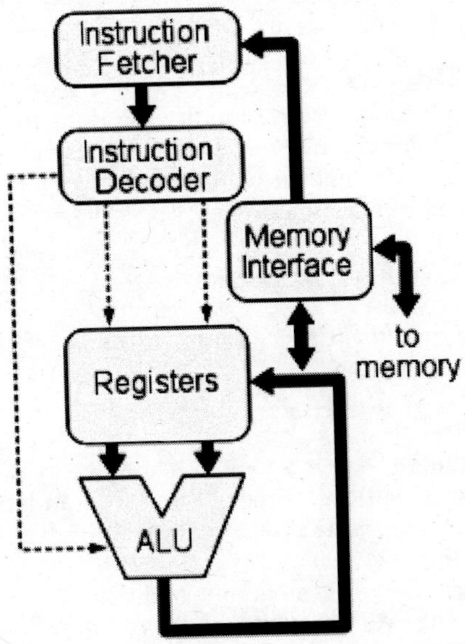

Figure 3.3 CPU

3.5 MOTHERBOARD

The motherboard is the main circuit board of a computer. It contains the central processing unit (CPU), the Basic Input/Output System (BIOS), memory, mass storage interfaces, serial and parallel ports, expansion slots, and all the controllers for standard peripheral devices like the keyboard, disk drive and display screen (See Figure 3.4).

Figure 3.4 Motherboard

The chipset and other motherboard circuitry are the "smarts" of the motherboard. Their job is to direct traffic and control the flow of information inside the computer. The chipset is a critical part of any computer, because it plays a big role in determining what sorts of features the computer can support.

The motherboard plays an important role in the following important aspects of the computer system:

1. Organization: In one-way or another, everything is connected to the motherboard. The way that the motherboard is designed and laid out dictates how the entire computer is going to work.
2. Control: The motherboard contains the chipset and BIOS (Basic Input Output System) program ROM, and they control most of the data flow within the computer.
3. Communication: All communications between PC and its peripherals, goes through the motherboard.
4. Processor Support: The motherboard dictates directly your choice of processor for use in the system.
5. Peripheral Support: The motherboard determines, in large part, what types of peripherals you can use in your PC. For example, the type of video card your system will use (ISA or (Industry Standard Architecture), VLB or (Video Electronics Standards Association Local Bus), PCI or Peripheral Component Interconnect) is dependent on what system buses your motherboard uses.
6. Performance: The motherboard is a major determining factor in PC s performance for two main reasons. First, the motherboard determines what types of processors, memory, system buses, and hard disk interface speed your system can have, and these components dictate directly PC s performance. Second, the qualities of the motherboard circuitry and chipset have an impact on performance.
7. Upgradability: The capabilities of the motherboard dictate to what extent you will be able to upgrade the machine. For example, there are some motherboards that will accept regular Pentiums of up to 133 MHz speed only, while others will go to 200 MHz. Hence, the second type will give more room to upgrade the PC.

3.6 BASIC INPUT/OUTPUT SYSTEM

BIOS is an essential set of solutions stored in a chip that provides an interface between the operating system and the hardware of a PC.

☞ BIOS is a set of instructions built into your computer to control how information and data flow in and out of your computer.

The BIOS software has a number of different roles, but its most important role is to load the operating system. When you turn on your computer, the microprocessor tries to execute its first instruction; it has to get that instruction from somewhere. The BIOS provides those instructions. Some of the other common tasks that the BIOS performs include:

- A power-on self-test (POST) for all of the different hardware components in the system to make sure everything is working properly.
- Activating other BIOS chips on different cards installed in the computer. For example, SCSI and graphics cards often have their own BIOS chips.
- Providing a set of low-level routines that the operating system uses to interface to different hardware devices-it is these routines that give the BIOS its name. They manage things like the keyboard, the screen, and the serial and parallel ports especially when the computer is booting.
- Managing a collection of settings for the hard disks, clock, etc.

☞ The BIOS is a special software that interfaces the major hardware components of your computer with the operating system. It is usually stored on a flash memory chip on the motherboard, but sometimes the chip is another type of ROM.

The BIOS supports all peripheral technologies including hard disk drive as well as internal services such as the real time clock. The CMOS is the memory located on the motherboards that stores the BIOS setting. When the system starts, the BIOS loads the setting from the CMOS.

3.6.1 BIOS-Power On Self Test (Post)

The Power-On Self Test (POST) is a built-in diagnostic program that checks PC hardware to ensure that everything is present and functioning properly, before the actual booting begins. The most important job of the BIOS is to give the microprocessor its first instructions and to load the operating system when the computer is switched on. It then performs a POST. This is an inspection to check that everything in the PC is working properly.

If everything is found to be working properly, the BIOS will then try to boot the computer from the hard disk drive. This is the process of launching the operating system.

☞ Sometimes, errors occur during the booting sequence. For instance, if there is a floppy disk left in the drive when you switch your computer on, you might get an error asking you to remove the disk.

The booting sequence for PC is as follows:

1. The first thing is BIOS working, as soon as PC is switched on.
2. The BIOS checks the CMOS for the settings that you have specified for operating system (such as background, font, etc.). It is a ROM chip that stores basic information about the PC and configurations. The BIOS will check this to find out the type of hard drive, CD drive, floppy disk drive, etc. in the computer and how much memory is there.
3. The BIOS loads in the main memory, interrupt handlers, which are the programmes that act like translators. It loads the device drivers, which are software-identifying hardware components like a keyboard, mouse, hard disk and floppy disk. It will check the motherboard ports to make sure that all these devices are working properly.
4. The BIOS also performs the POST to make sure that everything is working properly.
5. It will finally display the system settings.

3.6.2 BIOS Setup Utility

BIOS setup utility enables the user to modify the PC settings and store them in the CMOS. This utility also enables to control the booting sequence. It can be used to change the BIOS to correct any hardware problem such as floppy disk drive error, etc.

To enter the BIOS setup utility, do the following:

- Start the system.

To enter or to modify the CMOS setup, press a key or combination of keys during the initial startup sequence. Most PC systems use "Esc", "Del", "F1", "F2", "Ctrl-Esc" or Ctrl-Alt-Esc keys" to enter setup.

Once you have entered setup, you will see a set of text screens with a number of options. Some of these are standard, while others vary according to the BIOS manufacturer. Common options include the following:

- System Time/Date - Set the system time and date.
- Boot Sequence - The order in which BIOS will try to load the operating system.
- Plug and Play - A standard for auto-detecting connected devices. You should set it to "Yes" if your PC and operating system both support it.
- Mouse/Keyboard - " Enable Num Lock, " "Enable the Keyboard, " "Auto-Detect Mouse".
- Drive Configuration - Configure hard drives, CD-ROM and floppy disk drives.
- Memory - Direct the BIOS to shadow to a specific memory address.
- Security - Set a password for accessing the computer if need be.
- Power Management - Select whether to use power management, as well as set the amount of time for standby and suspend.
- Exit - Save your changes, discard your changes or restore default settings.

After you have finished with the changes, choose "Save Changes" and exit. The BIOS will then restart the PC so that the new settings take effect.

☞ Press ESC key to exit without saving the new changes. A dialog box appears confirming if you want to exit without saving. Enter "Y" and press the enter key to exit without saving.

3.6.3 Setting the BIOS Password

The BIOS password is used to protect the settings stored in the CMOS. You should enable the password option from the Advanced Setup page. When enabled, the system prompts the user to enter the password before accessing the Setup Utility.

You should remember the following points when changing the BIOS password:

1. Make it a habit to change password regularly.
2. The password can have a maximum of six alphabets or numerals.
3. Use a password that you find easy to remember but difficult for others to guess.

3.6.4 Upgrading the BIOS

By updating the BIOS, you can add additional functions and fix all errors and bugs. You must also upgrade the BIOS if the software or hardware that you installed needs an updated version of the BIOS. You can get updated BIOS by removing the old motherboard and installing a new one. However, if the BIOS is not permanently soldered on the motherboard, you can remove the BIOS chip and install a newer version of the chip on the PC motherboard.

You can also update the BIOS if your system has an Electronically Erasable Programmable Read Only Memory (EEPROM) for the BIOS. This enables you to change the BIOS using software. You can download the BIOS from the motherboard company's website. Some motherboards have a flash recovery jumper that you can use to restore the system if BIOS upgrade does not work properly.

3.6.5 BIOS Error Codes

When a computer is first switched on, the hardware runs a Power-On Self Test (POST). If errors are encountered during this POST test, they are displayed via an audio beep or in the form of a code number flashed across the screen. With this audio code in hand, you can determine what part of the system is having problems and accordingly find a solution. The pattern of beeps, whether it is the number of beeps or the length of those beeps, will give you an indication of the actual problem. Beep sound is a distress signal from the PC in a morse-code like pattern.

S.No	Number of Beeps	Solving Problem
1	Short Beep	System OK. If system does not start, check that the power and data cables are properly connected.
2/3/4	Short Beeps	Check that the RAM and video adapter cards are properly connected.
5	Short Beeps	Check that the RAM and microprocessor properly installed. Replace the microprocessor or the motherboard.
6	Short Beeps	Try attaching a different keyboard. Change the keyboard card.
7	Short Beeps	Replace the CPU or the motherboard.
8	Short Beeps	Check that the video card is properly installed. Replace the video card.
9	Short Beeps	Check that the BIOS chip is properly connected. Replace the BIOS chip.
10	Short Beeps	Replace the CMOS chips. Replace the motherboard.
11	Short Beeps	Check that the cache memory chip is properly connected. Replace the cache memory chip.
12	1 Long, 3 Short Beeps	Check that the RAM is properly connected.
13	1 Long, 8 Short Beeps	Check that the video card is properly installed. Replace the video card.

3.7 MEMORY SYSTEMS

Memory is an electronic circuitry that allows data to be stored and retrieved. The secondary memory stores the data and keeps it even when the electricity to the PC is cut off whereas the primary memory loses its contents on switching off power ssupply.

3.7.1 Main Memory or Primary Memory

Primary Memory, also known as Main Memory, is one of the important parts of the computer, because memory's size determines the length and number of programs that can be stored at a time. Its size also indicates the amount of data that can be processed quickly.

Primary memory is a fast Random Access Memory (RAM) made up of ICs called SIMS. The main memory is directly addressed by the CPU.

☞ Main Memory is a small and relatively fast storage unit that stores data and instructions which are being currently used by the CPU.

Main memory is divided into the following two types.

(a) RAM (Random Access Memory)
(b) ROM (Read Only Memory)

3.7.2 Random Access Memory (RAM)

RAM stands for Random Access Memory and it is a read/write memory. Information can be written to as well read from RAM. It is a volatile memory. It retains the stored information as long as it is supplied with power. When power supply is switched off or interrupted, the stored information in the RAM is lost. RAMs of various capacities are available, for example, 64, 128 and 256 MB simms are now available at affordable price. These are made up of very large sized integrated circuits called VLSI chips.

Static and Dynamic RAM

There are two important types of RAMs: static RAM and dynamic RAM. Static RAMs retain stored information only as long as the power supply is on. But a dynamic RAM loses its stored information in a very short time (a few milliseconds) even though the power supply is on. Therefore, dynamic RAMs have to be refreshed periodically, generally every 2 milliseconds. The dynamic RAMs are cheaper and have high packing density and moderate speed. They consume less power. They are used where large capacity of main memory is needed. Static RAMs are costlier and consume more power. They do not need refreshing circuitry. They have higher speeds than dynamic RAMs. Static RAM and dynamic RAM are also written as SRAM and DRAM respectively.

Volatility of Memory

Volatile memory is the memory whose contents are lost when power is switched off. A computer's main memory, made up of dynamic RAM or static RAM chips, loses its contents immediately upon interruption of power supply. A random access memory (RAM) is volatile but secondary memory containing magnetic elements is non-volatile, because they retain stored data when power supply is switched off.

3.7.3 Read Only Memory (ROM)

ROM stands for Read Only Memory and it is a permanent type memory. Its contents are not lost when power supply is switched off. The user cannot write into a ROM. Its contents are written at the time of manufacturing. ROMs store permanent programs and other types of information which are needed by the computer to execute the programs. ROMs store functions, such as sine, cosine, logarithm, square root, exponential and code conversion tables, etc.

☞ ROM is a semiconductor-based memory that contains instructions or data which can be read but not modified. To create a ROM chip, the designer supplies a semiconductor manufacturer with the instructions or data to be stored.

What ROMs can do?

(a) The stored information in ROM can only be read at the time of operation.
(b) Information can not be written into a ROM by user/programmer as in the case of Random Access Memory (RAM)
(c) The contents of ROMs are decided by the manufacturers and they are permanently stored in a ROM at the time of manufacture.
(d) ROMs store function tables such as square root table, etc. in many digital devices.
(e) Small sized ROMs are used for implementing truth tables.

Types of ROMs

ROMs are further classified as:
(a) PROMs (Programmable ROMs)
(b) EPROM (Erasable PROM)
(c) EEPROM (Electrically erasable PROM)

PROMs

PROM stands for Programmable Read Only Memory. Instructions can be stored in PROM only once. Then it becomes ROM and we cannot change instructions in it. Initially PROM is a blank chip. Once instructions are written on it, then it become ROM. Now we cannot change or delete the instructions. If there is any error in writing instructions then PROM chip becomes unusable.

EPROM (Erasable PROM)

EPROM is a special type of memory that retains its contents until it is exposed to ultraviolet light. The ultraviolet light clears its contents, making it possible to reprogram the memory. To write to and erase an EPROM, you need a special device called a PROM programmer or PROM burner.

EEPROM (E^2 PROM)

This is an electrically erasable PROM. The chip can be erased and reprogrammed on the board on a byte to byte basis. It requires much shorter time, a few seconds as compared to 10-20 minutes for EPROM. Like other types of PROM, EEPROM retains its contents even when the power is turned off. Also like other types of ROM, EEPROM is not as fast as RAM.

☞ E^2 PROM requires 21 Volts pulses for writing or erasing and 5V for read operation.

Extended Memory

Extended memory is the memory beyond the 1MB limit. Any memory available after the 1MB memory is called extended memory (XMS). For Windows user this memory is very useful. Windows operating system can use this extended memory and any program specifically written for these environment can use the extended memory available in the computer system.

Expanded Memory

Expanded memory specification is a specification which defines a method to access system memory above 1MB of RAM on primarily PC-XT and AT compatible computers. This specification is called with many different names such as EMS Memory, LIM Memory and Expanded memory.

Cache Memory

A CPU cache is a cache memory used by the CPU of a computer to reduce the average time to access main memory. The Cache is a smaller, faster memory as the memory which stores copies of the data from the most frequently used main memory location.

The high-speed memory used for the Cache purpose is very costly that is the reason it is not used as the main memory of the computer. The information frequently required by the processor is kept in the Cache memory by the Cache controller. This Cache controller always tries to make sure that the data required by the processor in the next memory access is available in the Cache memory. This improves the speed of the computer very much because if the required data is in the cache memory it is made available to the CPU without any wait state. When the required data is available in the cache it is called a hit. In case of a cache hit the processor immediately reads or writes the data in the data cache line. The proportion of accesses that result in a cache hit is known as the hit rate, and is a measure of the effectiveness of the cache.

☞ Cache memory is a very high speed memory built in the processor and it is used between main memory (RAM) and the processor.

The performance of the cache depends on the following:

- Speed and size of the Cache memory
- The logic used to read data around the memory area read by the CPU.
- The logic used to guess next required data by the processor.

Most of the new micro processors have the Cache memory added in the CPU chip itself to speed up the process even further. Even on these CPUs with built in internal Cache, you can add external Cache.

Levels of Cache

In standard PC's we find processor with Level 1 (L1) and Level 2 (L2) cache. Some processors like the Intel Itanium have three levels of built-in cache, but these processors are used for very special server applications only.

Level 1 (L1) Cache

Level 1 cache is built into the actual processor core. It is a piece of RAM, typically 8, 16, 20, 32, 64 or 128 Kbytes size, which operate at the same clock frequency as the rest of the CPU. Thus you could say the L1 cache is part of the processor.

L1 cache is normally divided into two sections, one for data and one for instructions. For example, an Athlon processor may have a 32 KB data cache and a 32 KB instruction cache. If the cache is common for both data and instructions, it is called a unified cache.

Level 2 (L2) Cache

The level 2 cache is normally much larger (and unified), such as 256, 512 or 1024 KB. The purpose of the L2 cache is to constantly read in slightly larger quantities of data from RAM, so that these are available to the L1 cache.

Traditionally, the L2 cache is connected to the front side bus. Through it, it connects to the chipset's north bridge and RAM.

3.8 BUS STRUCTURES

A group of lines that serves as a connecting path for several devices is called bus.In addition to the lines that carry the data, the bus must have lines for address and control purposes. In computer architecture, a bus is a subsystem that transfers data between computer components inside a computer or between computers.

3.8.1 Concept of System Bus

In order to transfer data, each register (temporary storage device for data) should be connected to other registers through wires. If we provide exclusive connections between any one register to any other register, the number of wires required will be very large. Instead, an electronic bus system can be designed for the exchange of data among all such registers.

☞ A bus is a communication pathway connecting two or more registers or electronic devices. Control signals produced by the control unit control the communication among all such electronic units that are connected by the bus.

You can correlate an electronic bus with the passenger bus that runs on road. A single bus carries multiple passengers. When the bus reaches the destination, passengers get down from the bus, and reach the place of choice. Similarly, in an electronic bus, signals or data bits are carried from many registers, (though not all at the same time). These data bits are then accepted by the register for which it was meant. Different kinds of system bus are given in details in the following subsections.

Data Bus

Data bus is used to transfer data among the registers of a CPU and the main memory of a PC. The bus width of the data bus is an important parameter that affects the overall speed of a PC system. This is because each wire of a bus can transfer one bit at a time. Hence 8-bit bus (one having 8 parallel wires) can move 8 bits (one byte) at a time, a 16-bit bus can transfer two bytes, and a 32-bit bus can transfer four bytes at a time. This is similar to a multi-lane highway. The wider the highway, the more traffic can flow simultaneously. Similarly, a wider data bus enables more bits of data to travel simultaneously resulting in faster exchange of data.

Address Bus

We know that every storage location where data or program is kept in the main memory has a unique address. In order to retrieve data from memory, it is necessary to specify the address of the location where the data is available. The address bus is used to carry the address of the main memory location whenever data is to be transferred from or to the main memory.

The width of the address bus must be equal to the number of bits in the memory address register (MAR) of the system. The width of the address bus is an important parameter for a computer system because it determines the maximum number of memory locations that the computer system can address. For example, if the address bus was only 8 bits wide, the CPU could address only 2^8 i.e. 256 byes of memory. Today, most systems have 32-bit wide address buses that can address 2^{32} bytes (over 4 billion bytes), or 4 GB of main memory.

Control Bus

In addition to sending addresses and exchanging data with the main memory, a CPU also needs to send control signals to the memory to specify whether the data is to be read from or written to the specified address location. Such signals, which are in the form of READ/WRITE commands, are carried by the control bus.

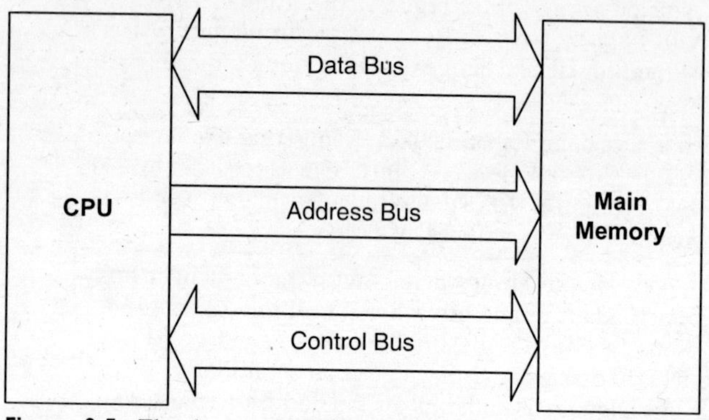

Figure 3.5 The three types of buses used between the CPU and main memory

Figure 3.5 shows the three different types of buses used for interconnecting the CPU and main memory. The Data bus transfers data bothways i.e. from CPU to main memory and vice versa. The control bus will send control pulses to main memory and receive acknowledgements on the completion of an action. The address bus is used to select the location of the memory for reading or writing data into it. Thus, it is only one way transfer of address.

Although a CPU can have its own distinctive set of control signals, some controls are common to all CPUs:

- Interrupt Request (IRQ) Lines: Hardware line used by devices to interrupt signals to the CPU. It allows the CPU to interrupt its current job to process the present request.
- System Clock Control Line: Delivers the internal timing for various devices on the motherboard and CPU.

Types of Bus Organization

Single Bus Architecture

Three units share the single bus. At any given point of time, information can be transferred between any two units. Here, I/O units use the same memory address space (Memory mapped I/O). So no special instructions are required to address the I/O, it can be accessed like a memory location. Since all the devices do not operate at the same speed, it is necessary to smooth out the differences in timings among all the devices A common approach used is to include buffer registers with the devices to hold the information during transfers (See Figure 3.6).

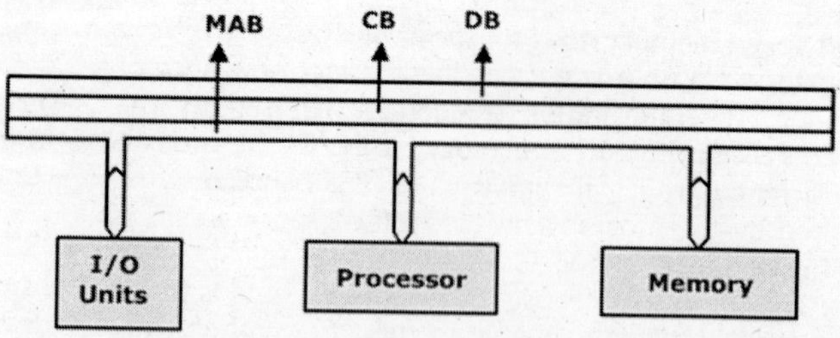

Figure 3.6 Single Bus Architecture

Two Bus Architecture

Various units are connected through two independent buses. I/O units are connected to the processor though an I/O bus and Memory is connected to the processor through the memory bus. I/O bus consists of address, data and control bus Memory bus also consists of address, data and control bus In this type of arrangements processor completely supervises the transfer of information to and from I/O units. All the information is first taken to processor and from there to the memory. Such kind of transfers are called as program controlled transfer (See Figure 3.7)

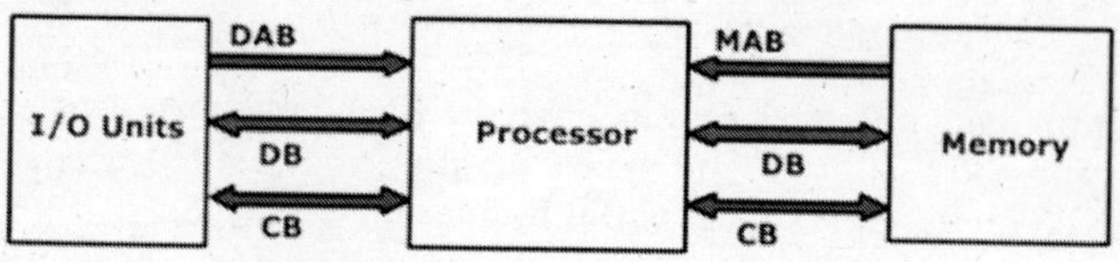

Figure 3.7 Two Bus Architecture

Various Bus Standards

There are some of the common expansion various bus types. These are:

ISA (Industry Standard Architecture)

The Industry Standard Architecture, or ISA, bus introduced in the early 1981 with original IBM PC (International Business Machine Personal Computer) included the 8-bit subset of the ISA bus. In 1984, IBM introduced the PC-AT which was the first full 16-bit implementation of the ISA bus.

8-Bit ISA Bus

In 8-bit ISA bus, only the first portion of the slot (closest to the back of the card) is used. It is used in 8088 processor s system bus and it runs at 4.77 MHz.

16-Bit ISA Bus

In 16-bit ISA bus, both sections of the card are being utilized. It is used in Intel 80286 and its speed increased to 8 MHz. It runs at a maximum of 8 MHz. However, it requires 2-3 clock ticks to move 16 bits of data. The ISA bus works synchronous with the CPU. If the system bus is faster than 10 MHz, many expansion boards become flaky and the ISA clock frequency is reduced to a fraction of the system bus clock frequency.

ISA bus has two sides in the modern PC. These are:

(a) Internal ISA bus, which is used on the simple ports, like keyboard, diskette drive, serial and parallel ports.
(b) External expansion bus, which can be connected with 16-bit ISA adapters.

There are some problems which is associated with ISA bus. These are:

(a) Narrow and Slow: The ISA bus cannot transfer enough data bits at a time. It has a very limited bandwidth.
(b) Lack of Intelligence: It means that the CPU has to control the data transfer across the bus. The CPU cannot start a new assignment until the transfer is completed.

EISA (Extended Industry Standard Architecture)

EISA is a computer bus which provide 32-bit slots at an 8.33 MHz cycle rate for the use with 386DX or higher processors. In addition, the EISA can accommodate a 16-bit ISA card in the first row.

EISA incorporates many of the benefits of the Micro Channel bus while maintaining compatibility with legacy ISA expansion boards. EISA connectors are a superset of the 16-bit connectors used on ISA system boards. ISA 8-bit and 16-bit expansion boards can be installed into the ISA compatible portion of the EISA slot. EISA expansion boards use the signals on the ISA compatible portion of the connector as well as additional signals that provide enhanced function and performance.

Following are the enhancements which are introduced in EISA over ISA:

(a) 32-bit memory addressing for CPU, DMA (Direct Memory Access), and bus master devices.
(b) A synchronous data transfer protocol for high-speed burst transfers.
(c) Automatic translation of bus cycles between EISA and ISA masters and slaves.
(d) Support of intelligent bus master peripheral controllers.
(e) Enhanced DMA arbitration and transfer rates.
(f) 33 MB/sec transfer rate for bus masters and DMA devices.
(g) Shareable interrupts, programmable for edge or level triggering.
(h) Automatic configuration of system and expansion boards.

Some of the key features of the EISA bus are as follows:

(a) ISA Compatibility: ISA cards will work in EISA slots.
(b) 32-Bit Bus Width: Bus was expanded to 32 bits.
(c) Bus Mastering: The EISA bus supports bus mastering adapters for greater efficiency, including proper bus arbitration.
(d) Plug and Play: EISA automatically configures adapter cards, similar to the Plug and Play standards of modern systems.

VL (VESA Local) Bus

The VLB is older local bus architecture popular on 486 computer systems in 1993 and 1994. It is a 32-bit bus that supports bus mastering and runs at speed up to 40 MHz. VLB 2.0 was later released in 1994 and had a 64-bit bus and a bus speed of 50 MHz.

The VLB provides a high-speed data path between the CPU and peripherals (video, disk, network, etc.) running at the speed of the processor. The VLB generally provides up to three slots on the motherboard, each slot using one 32-bit connector placed adjacent to the standard ISA, EISA, PCI (Peripheral Component Interconnect), or Micro Channel connector. It is an inexpensive and simple technology. Because VLB runs directly with the system bus. Therefore, data transfer is done at CPU speed, synchronous and in width. The problem with VLB was compatibility. Adapters and system boards would not always work together. PCI and AGP bus architectures have completely replaced the VLB.

Peripheral Component Interconnect

Peripheral Component Interconnect (PCI) is one of the latest developments in bus architecture and is the current standard for PC expansion cards. Intel developed and launched it as the expansion bus for the Pentium processor in 1993. It is a local bus like VESA, that is, it connects the CPU, memory and peripherals to wider, faster data pathway.

PCI supports both 32-bit and 64-bit data width; it is compatible with 486s and Pentiums. The bus data width is equal to the processor, such as, a 32 bit processor would have a 32 bit PCI bus, and operates at 33MHz.

PCI was used in developing Plug and Play (PnP) and all PCI cards support PnP. This means a user can plug a new card into the computer, power it on and it will "self-identify" and "self-specify" and start working without manual configuration using jumpers.

AGP (Accelerated Graphics Port)

Accelerated Graphics Port (also called Advanced Graphics Port) is a high-speed point-topoint channel for attaching a graphics card to a computer's motherboard to convey 3D graphics much more quickly and smoothly on ordinary personal computers. It is especially useful in the following areas:

(a) Conjuction with gaming,
(b) Three-Dimensional (3D) video,
(c) Sophisticated scientific/engineering graphics programs.

AGP interface uses computer's Random Access Memory (RAM) to refresh the monitor image and to support the texture mapping, z-buffering, and alpha blending required for 3-D image display. AGP offers high-speed data transfer to and from RAM, optimizing the use of memory and minimizing the amount of memory necessary for high-performance graphics.

3.9 PORTS

A port is a means by which data is transferred between an input device to output device or vice versa. The CPU receives or transfers data from main memory and thus uses the memory addresses to send or receive data. Specialized hardware are used to place data from the devices in the memory addresses and to send data from the memory addresses to the devices. All computer systems have ports for connecting peripheral devices such as printers, keyboard, mouse and modems.

3.9.1 PS/2 PORT

The PS/2 (Personal System/2) standard was introduced by IBM in 1987. It is an electronic plug which connects mouse or keyboard. Most PCs come with two PS/2 ports. It accepts a PS/2 cable with a mini-DIN connector, and is most often used to plug in a keyboard or mouse. The PS/2 port is female while the mini-DIN cable is male. The connector is small with a diameter of about 1/3 inch (9.5mm). The PS/2 port was initially a large DIN plug used for a keyboard, while the mouse was commonly plugged into a serial port.

The PS/2 mouse connector has replaced the older DE-9 RS-232 "serial mouse" connector, while the keyboard connector has replaced the larger 5-pin DIN used in the IBM PC/AT design. The keyboard and mouse interfaces are electrically similar. But, the main difference between the two is that open collector outputs are required on both ends of the keyboard interface to allow bidirectional communication. Normal desktop motherboards will not identify the keyboard and mouse if they are placed on each other's sockets. Female pin connection of the PS/2 from the front is shown in Figure 3.8 and the details of these pins are shown in Table 3.1.

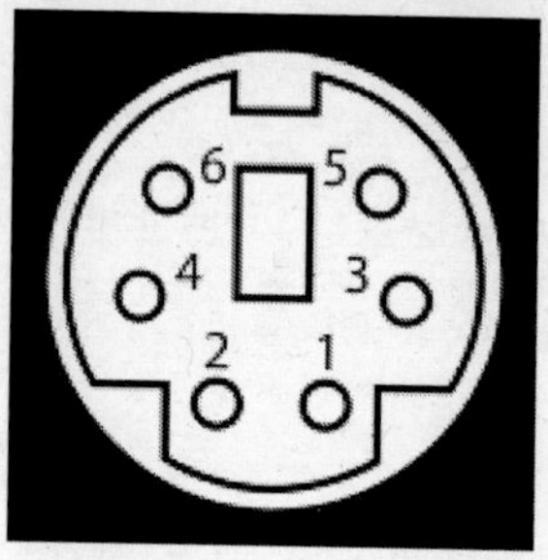

Figure 3.8 PS/2 Port

Table 3.1 Female Connector from the front

Pin 1	+DATA	Data
Pin 2	Not connected	Not connected
Pin 3	GND	Ground
Pin 4	Vcc	+5 V DC at 100 mA
Pin 5	+CLK	Clock
Pin 6	Not connected	Not connected

3.9.2 COM Port/Serial Port

COM/serial port is an asynchronous port through which information transfers in or out one bit at a time. Usually referred to as a DB9 or DB25 connection. Where D represents the shape of the connector. The number 9/25 indicating the number of pins found on the connector. DB9 Serial connections are now commonly found on modern PCs and DB9 serial connection is identified first by its 9 pins. The DB9 is shaped like a D. (See Figure 3.9) It will generally be a male connector on the back of the computer whereas DB25 is commonly found on older computers.

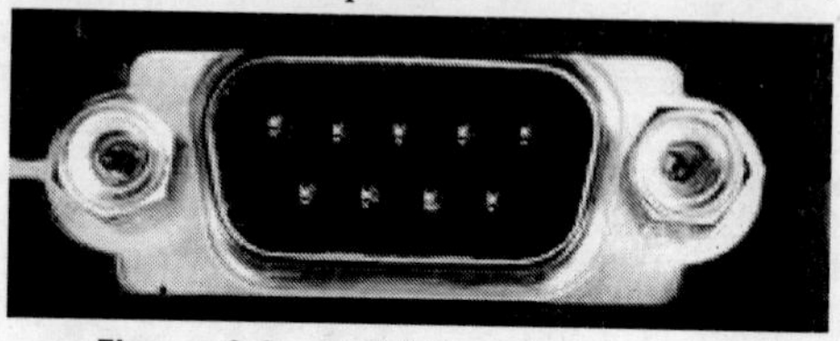

Figure 3.9 COM Port or Serial Port

Following is the list of component that is used with Serial port in computer:

(a) Mouse
(b) Keyboard
(c) Modem
(d) Network

☞ In present day PCs, USB interface is used to replace the serial port.

3.9.3 LPT Port/Parallel Port

LPT (Line Printing Terminal) is the original name of the parallel port interface on IBM PC compatible computers. It was designed to operate a text printer that used IBM's 8-bit extended ASCII character set. A parallel port is a type of socket found on personal computers for interfacing with various peripherals. It is also known as a printer port. LPT port which you might have seen on the back of the PC is shown in Figure 3.10.

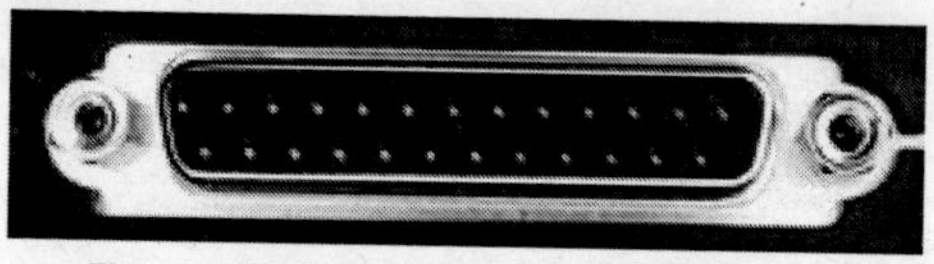

Figure 3.10 LPT Port or Parallel Port

Usually, a PC will have 2 LPT ports. You may also find some PCs with 3 LPT ports. These ports are each with their own name LPT1, LPT2 and LPT3. They were designed primarily for printers. However, there is a variety of peripherals that can be connected to these ports.

☞ Modern printers are connected through USB connection. On many high-end PCs, the parallel port is omitted for cost savings. Printers print at much higher speed when connected with USB port.

Uses of LPT Port

LPT port is also used to connect various peripherals of the computer system. Some of the peripherals in which LPT port is used are as under:

(a) Printers
(b) Zip drive
(c) Old type of scanners
(d) Old sound cards
(e) Old Webcams
(f) Old gamepads and joysticks

☞ LPT port has an 8-bit parallel databus, plus 4 pins for controlling output i.e. Strobe, Linefeed, Initialize, and Select In, and 5 more pins to control input i.e. ACK, Busy, Select, Error, and Paper Out. Data transfer speed of LPT port is about 12, 000 kbit/s.

Usb Port

Universal Serial Bus (USB) is standardized by the USB Implementers Forum (USB-IF), an industry standards body incorporating leading companies from the computer and electronics industries. USB is a serial bus standard which was designed to allow peripherals to be connected using a single standardized interface socket, to improve plug-and-play capabilities by allowing devices to be connected and disconnected without rebooting the computer. (See Figure 3.11) Other convenient features include powering low-consumption devices without the need for an external power supply and allowing some devices to be used without requiring individual device drivers to be installed.

Figure 3.11 Commonly used USB Plug

☞ The Universal Serial Bus is a single, standardized, easy-to-use way to connect up to 127 devices to a computer.

A sample list of USB devices that you can buy today includes:
(a) Printers
(b) Scanners
(c) Mice
(d) Joysticks
(e) Flight yokes
(f) Digital cameras
(g) Webcams
(h) Modems
(i) Speakers
(j) Network connections

Infrared (Irda) Port

The Infrared port commonly referred to as the IRDA (Infrared Data Association). It is a port much like what you would find on your TV/VCR remote. This port allows two computers or a computer and a device to communicate amongst each other without the uses of wires. For example, if both your laptop computer and printer have IrDA ports, you can simply put your computer in front of the printer and output a document, without needing to connect the two with a cable.

☞ The Infrared Data Association (IrDA) defines physical specifications communications protocol standards for the short-range exchange of data over infrared light.

IrDA ports support same transmission rates as parallel ports. The only restriction is that the two devices must be within a few feet of each other and there must be a clear line of sight between them.

Bluetooth

Bluetooth technology has changed the market for wireless devices because it is cheap, consumes lower energy, and has been implemented in various aspects of lives including cars, audio devices, and most commonly in mobile phones.

☞ *l etooth* uses short-range radio frequencies to transmit information from fixed and mobile devices. These devices must be within the range of 32 feet, or 10 meters for Bluetooth to effectively work.

A Bluetooth port enables connections for Bluetooth-enabled devices for synchronizing. Typically there are two types of ports:
(a) Incoming port: The incoming port enables the device to receive connections from Bluetooth devices
(b) Outgoing port: The outgoing port makes connections to Bluetooth devices.

Firewire Port

Firewire ports are forms of a serial port that make use of FireWire technology to transfer data rapidly from one electronic device to another. Usually camcorders and other video equipment use this port to get data onto a computer. Data can move across the port at up to 400 megabits per second. Apple Corporation of USA invented this technology and had branded it as Firewire. (See Figure 3.12)

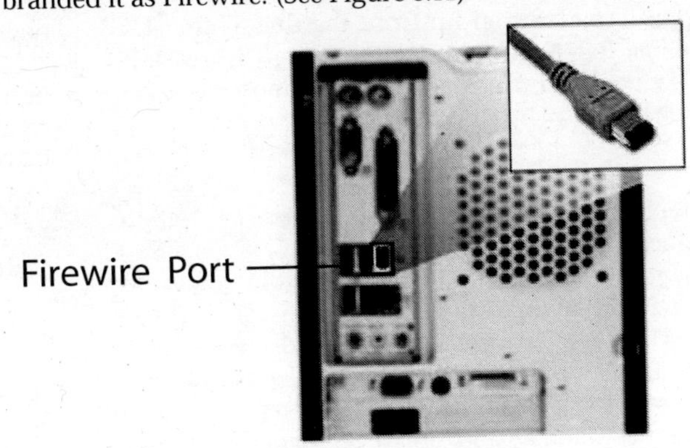

Figure 3.12 Firewire Port

Firewire port has the ability to interact with a number of different devices. For example, a Firewire connection can provide an ideal way to connect a scanner to a computer system. Because the transfer rate of a Firewire port can reach up to 400 Mbps. The data transfer is relatively fast and also results in excellent quality.
Following types of cables of Firewire port are available. These are: (See Figure 3.13)
(a) 4-Pin: Typically found on Windows laptops. Four-pin cables carry data only.

(b) 6-Pin: Commonly found on desktop systems and all Apple make computers. It can carry power and data from one device to another.

(c) 9-Pin: It can carry power and data from one device to another.

Figure 3.13 Two types of Firewire cables

☞ Firewire is used to connect peripherals to computer system. While it is much faster than USB, Firewire can connect lesser number of devices as compared to USB.

DVI Port

DVI is a new form of video interface technology made to maximize the quality of flat panel LCD monitors and high-end video graphics cards. It is a replacement for the P&D Plug & Display standard, and a step up from the digital-only DFP format for older flat panels. DVI is becoming increasingly popular with video card manufacturers, and most cards purchased include both a VGA and a DVI output port.

SCSI Port

SCSI (pronounced as "scuzzy"), stands for Small Computer System Interface. It is a set of ANSI (American National Standard Institute) standard electronic interfaces that allow personal computers to communicate with peripheral hardware, such as disk drives, tape drives, CD-ROM drives, printers, and scanners faster and more flexibly than previous interfaces. The present set of SCSIs are parallel interfaces in many personal computers today and are supported by all major operating systems.

The latest SCSI standard is Ultra-3 (sometimes spelled "Ultra3") which increases the maximum burst rate from 80 Mbps to 160 Mbps by being able to operate at the full clock rate rather than the half-clock rate of Ultra-2. The standard is also sometimes referred to as Ultra160/m. New disk drives supporting Ultra160/m will offer much faster data transfer rates. Ultra160/m also includes Cyclical Redundancy Checking (CRC) for ensuring the integrity of transferred data and domain validation for testing the SCSI network.

3.10 EXPANSION CARDS

The expansion card also known as expansion board or adapter card in circuit board that can provides additional capabilities to the computer system. The cards are plugged into the expansion sockets present on the computer's motherbord to provide the computer an added functionality. However, now-a-days most of the adapters come in-built on the motherboard and no expansion card is required, unless the need for high performance is required.

3.10.1 Sound Card

Sound card is applied to external audio interfaces that use software to generate sound. The use of sound cards include providing the audio component for multimedia applications, such as music composition, editing video or audio, presentation, education and entertainment (games) and video projection. Most sounds cards use a Digital-to-Analog Converter (DAC), which converts digital data into an analog format. The output signal is connected to an amplifier or headphones.

3.10.2 Video Card

A video card also called a video adapter, display card, graphics card. It is an expansion card which generates a feed of output images to a display (such as a computer monitor).

3.10.3 Network Interface Card

A Network Interface Card (NIC) is a circuit board or card that is installed in a computer so that it can be connected to a nework. A network interface card provides the computer with a dedicated, full-time connection to a network. Personal computers and workstations on a local area network typically contain a network interface card specifically designed for the LAN (Local Area Network) transmission technology.

3.10.4 Modem

Modem is an expansion card that allows two computers to communicate over ordinary phone lines. It converts digital data into analog data, transmits over the telephone lines and also converts incoming analog signals back to digital signals for the receiving computer.

3.10.5 PC Card

A PC Card (known as a PCMCIA or Personal Computer Memory Card International Association card) is a credit card-size memory or I/O device that fits into a personal computer. The most common use of a PC Card is the telecommunications modem for notebook computers. There are 16-binary digit and 32-bit (CardBus). The PC Card is based on standards published by the PCMCIA, an industry group organized in 1989 to promote standards for both memory and I/O integrated circuit card.

3.10.6 Storage Card

A storage card, often also called a flash memory card or simply a memory card that is connected to a computer in order to provide users with extra space to store their data on. This can include data such as music, pictures, text or video and is transferable to other devices such as digital cameras and mobile phones. Some of the most common on the market today include the Secure Digital (SD) Card, the Mini/Micro SD Card, and the MultiMediaCard (MMC).

3.10.7 Wireless/cellular Card

A wireless card is used to provide a computer with the capability of connecting to a radio-based computer network rather that one which is connected using wires. These can come preinstalled inside of a computer or laptop or be external, come separately, although almost all modern devices come with this already included inside of the computer. The most common use of this card is to allow a device to connect to WiFi, using a wireless router or access point. The WiFi point receives data through wires and transmits it using radio waves, for a wireless card inside of a device to pick up and decode, as well as receiving the signals in the opposite direction.

3.10.8 TV Tuner Card

A Television Tuner card is a card which is inserted into a computer to allow a device to receive television signals that would not otherwise be suited to picking them up. Cards are usually either PCI, mini PCI or PCIe, or sometimes as an external USB device. Most cards have an inbuilt processor to free up space from the system s CPU and ease the pressure on the computer. Cards can be either analog or digital depending on which type of television the user wishes to view, and many hybrid tuners exist which are able to switch between the two types. High-end tuner cards often include a special chip to encode and decode the data being transmitted, however smaller and cheaper cards are less likely to have this capability due to the high power it takes to run them.

3.10.9 Video capture card

A video capture card is used to allow a computer to convert an analog video signal into a digital video data form. Many TV tuner cards double up as video capture cards, allowing the user to record TV transmissions as they are being broadcast and viewed.

3.11 CONNECTORS

The part of a cable that plugs into a port or interface to connect one device to another. Most connectors are either male (containing one or more pins) or female (containing holes in which the male connector can be inserted).

3.11.1 DIN Connector

DIN is short for Deutsches Institute for Normung. A DIN connector is an electrical connector that was originally standardized by German national standards organization. DIN connectors are used in personal computers. For example, the keyboard connector is a DIN connector (See Figure 3.14).
A DIN (or DIN5) connectors is a plug with 5 pins, formerly used to connect keyboards to computers.

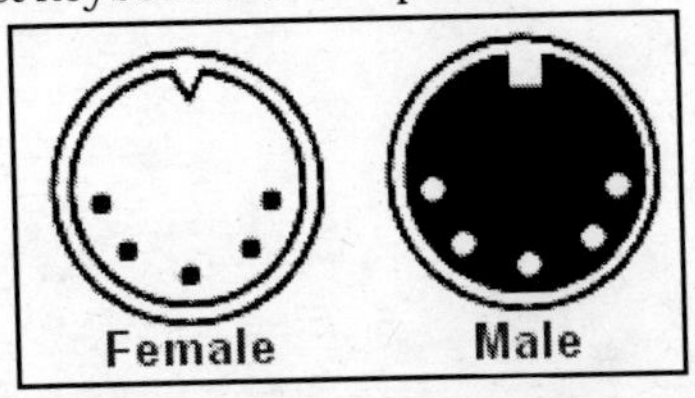

Figure 3.14 DIN connector

The DIN 5 connector has been made by PS/2 and USB connectors.

Pin number	Function
1	Reset (_RST)
2	+ 5 V (power)
3	Data
4	Ground
5	Clock

3.11.2 Mini-DIN connector

Mini-DIN connectors are cylindrical in shape and feature between three and nine pins, each compatible with various audio and/or visual devices. Four-pin mini-DIN connectors are used to carry a separate video (commonly called S-video) signal.
Some examples of standard mini-DIN connectors include:

- Mini-DIN-3 connectors were used in early implementations of Apple LocalTalk.
- Mini-DIN-4 connectors are used for S-video, and were used for Apple Desktop Bus.
- Mini-DIN-6 connectors were used for IBM PC compatible PS/2 keyboard and mouse ports.
- Mini-DIN-8 connectors were used for Apple and Sun Microsystems keyboard and mouse ports, as well as for serial printer, modem, and Apple LocalTalk connections.
- Mini-DIN-7 and Mini-DIN-9 connectors have been used for a variety of audio and video applications.
- Mini-DIN-6 and Mini-DIN-8 connectors are frequently used in ham radio applications to interface with computers for data packet communications and radio programming.

3.11.3 RCA Connector

An RCA (Radio Corporation of America) connector, sometimes called a phono connector or cinch connector, is a type of electrical connector commonly used to carry audio and video signals. The RCA plug is used to send video and audio signals (in mono or stereo) through a two-wire cable, with either an analog or digital transmission method.

The connector's colour indicates how it is meant to be used. For stereo analog audio transmissions, the connectors are red and white as shown in Figure 3.15.

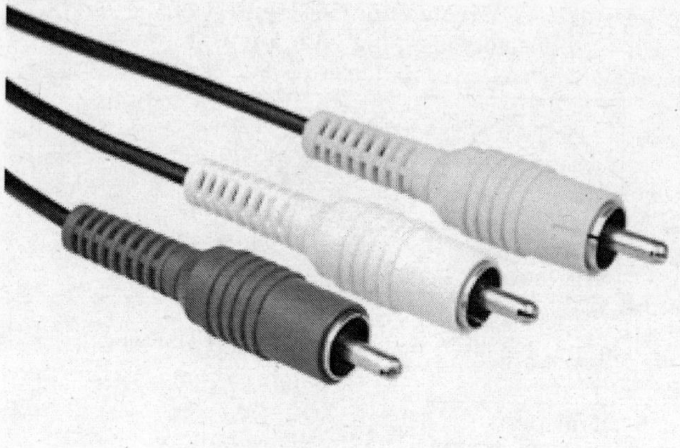

Figure 3.15 RCA connector

For a composite video signal, the connector is yellow (See Figure 3.16).

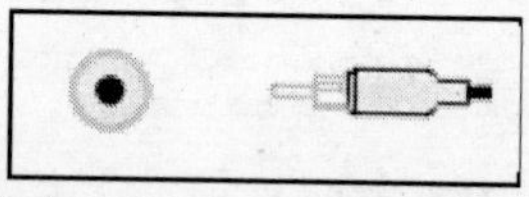

Figure 3.16 RCA cable in yellow colour

The RCA connector is also used for sending component video, also called YUV or YCrCb, is a color representation model in which Y represents luminance (black and white), and U and V represent the chrominance (information regarding the color). In YUV representation, U is sometimes written as Cr and V is sometimes written as Cb therefore YCrCb notation is also used in color representation. For such a video signal, 3 connectors, colored red, green, and blue, are used (See Figure 3.17).

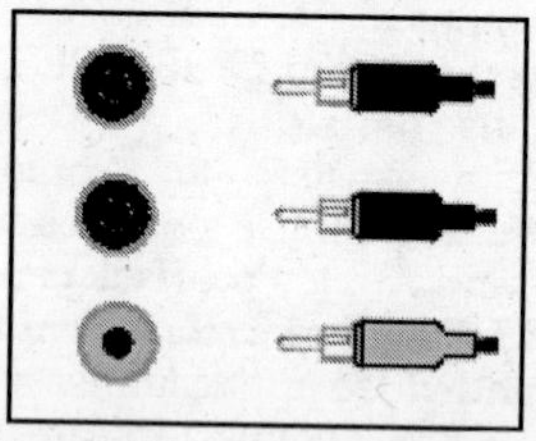

Figure 3.17 Three RCA cables: 1 green, 1 blue and 1 red

3.11.4 AV (Audio Video) Connector

Audio connectors and video connectors are electrical connectors (or optical connectors) for carrying audio signal and video signal. Either analog or digital format. Analog A/V connectors often use shielded cables to inhibit Radio Frequency Interference (RFI) and noise. The most common types of connectors used between your new A/V receiver, video display (with an emphasis on HDTV), DVD/CD player, loudspeakers, and subwoofer.

Audio connectors are electrical connectors designed and used for audio frequencies. They can be analog or digital. Common audio connectors include:

- Banana Connector: A banana connector (commonly banana plug for the male, banana socket or banana jack for the female) is a single-wire (one conductor) electrical connector used for joining wires to equipment. The term 4 mm connector is also used in Europe. Although not all banana connectors will mate with 4 mm parts. The plug is a four-leafed spring tip that snaps into the jack. The plugs are frequently used to terminate patch cords for electronic test equipment. They are also often used as the plugs on the cables connecting the amplifier to the loudspeakers in hi-fi (high fidelity) sound systems (See Figure 3.18).

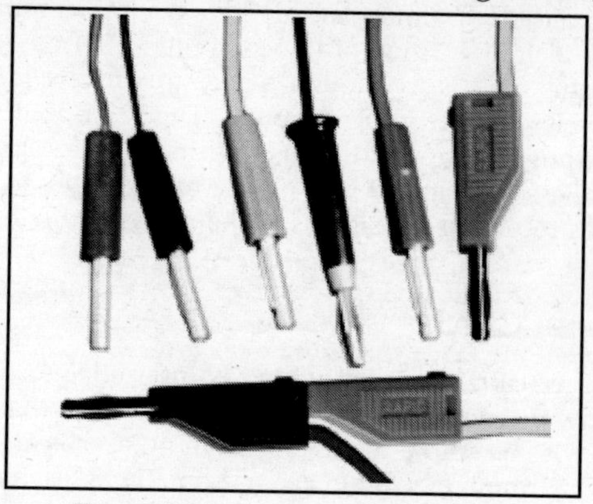

Figure 3.18 Various banana plugs

- Five-way Binding Posts: A type of speaker cable input and receiver/amplifier output connector that accepts bare speaker wire when you unscrew the top and push the wire through the hole. It is also used for high-level connections for amplified audio signals from an A/V receiver's speaker outputs to the speakers. Stereo systems with amplifiers or preamps lacking a subwoofer output would also use the amplifier's high-level outputs and the subwoofers hi-level inputs. Signals may be routed through the subwoofer and then to the main speakers, or separately from the amplifier to the main speakers with a second set to the subwoofer (See Figure 3.19).

Video connectors carry only video signals. Common video-only connectors include:

- Component Video: The most common type of connector used for both standard-quality video and HD video, it uses three coaxial RCA cables and plugs color-coded red, green and blue (the three cables may be wrapped together for convenience) to carry analog standard or high definition video between a set top satellite or cable-TV box to the A/V receiver and TV display or projector (See Figure 3.20).

Figure 3.19 Five-way binding posts

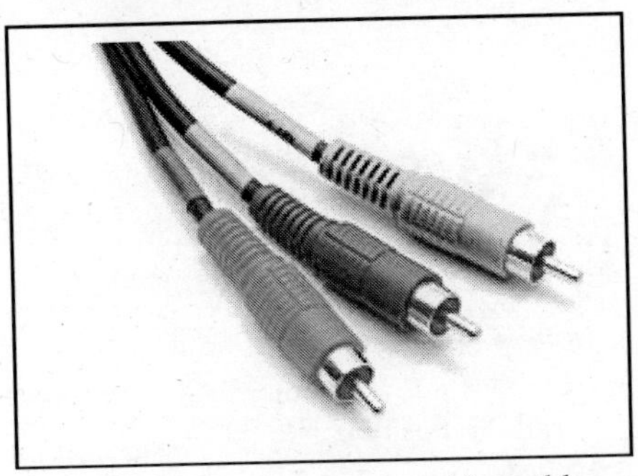

Figure 3.20 Component video cable

- Composite Video: A single video connector that combines all the color, brightness, and sync signals into one cable using a single RCA connector. It is the most common type of analog video connection between older VCRs and TVs (except for RF (Radio Frequency) connectors). Use composite video only if your TV, VCR or DVD player lacks S-video or component-video connectors. Composite video will not carry High Def or progressive-scan video signals (See Figure 3.21).

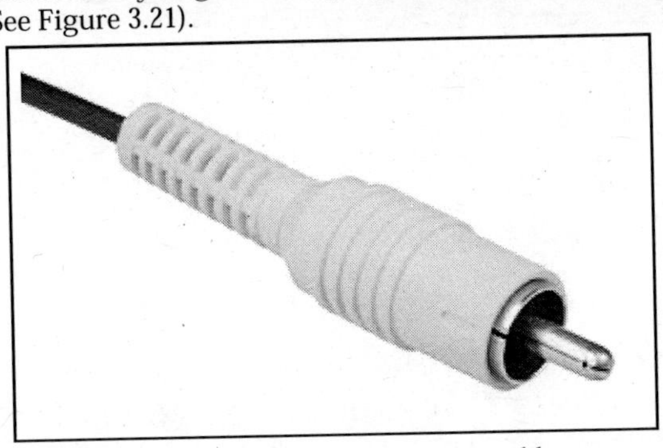

Figure 3.21 Composite video cable

3.11.5 USB Connectors

Most computer users are familiar with USB, which has become the most commonly used way to connect peripheral devices to a computer. For example, mouse, printer, digital camera, scanner, and other devices probably all connect to your computer via a USB port. Many memory storage devices, such as portable hard drives, flash drives, and memory card readers, also connect to a computer via USB.

USB connectors make it possible to connect a device to your computer using USB. A long cable is used to connect the device to your computer. Usually, the connectors on each end of the cable are quite different, making it necessary to know which of them goes to your computer and which gets plugged into the device.

Different types of USB Connectors

There are many types of UBS connector cards you may use depending on the device you are connecting.

Type-A

These types of USB connectors are identified by their rectangular shaped plug. The plug is always found in the cable and the receptacle is found in the device. They are commonly used with keyboard, mouse, data cards etc. The image of a type A connector and the pin position are shown in Figures 3.22 and 3.23, respectively.

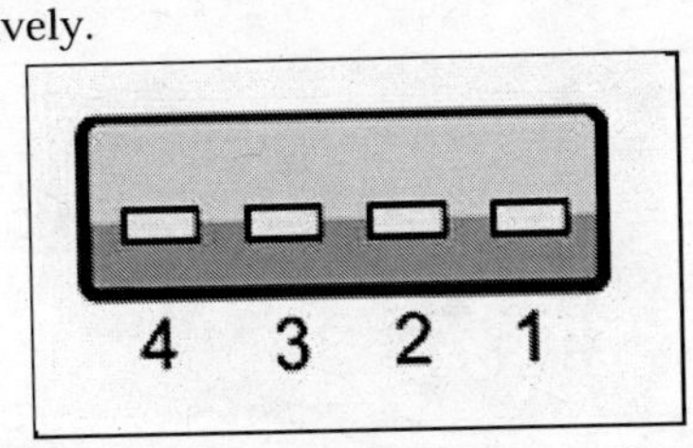

Figure 3.22 The pin-position of Type A USB connector

Figure 3.23 The image of Type A male and female USB connector

The pin-out of the Type A USB Connector.

Pin 1	VBus
Pin 2	D-
Pin 3	D+
Pin 4	Ground

Type-B

The Type-B connectors are designed to be used with devices which are meant to be connected with the device having Type-A receptacle. These connectors are square shaped with beveled exterior corners. They are found in USB devices like printers, USB to serial converters, simple USB powered devices like battery chargers, etc. The image of a type B connector and the pin position are shown in Figures 3.24 and 3.25, respectively.

Figure 3.24 Female Type B connector

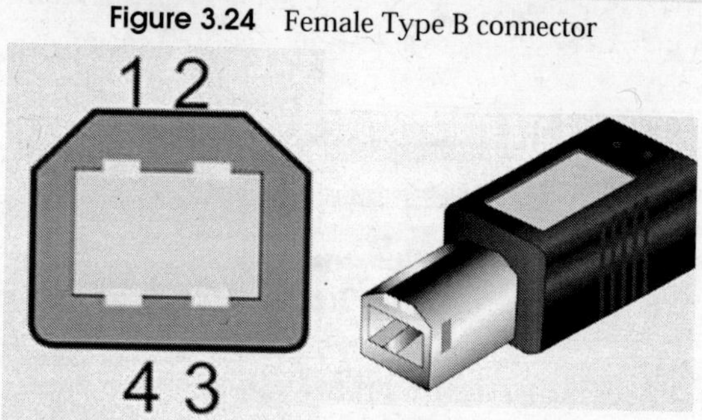

Figure 3.25 Male Type B connector and pin position

Mini-A and Mini-B

The Mini-A and Mini-B connectors are used with USB devices which are meant to be connected to Type A receptacles. But these connectors are smaller than the Type B connector. They are designed to be connected with small sized USB devices like camera, mobile phones, etc. (See Figure 3.26).

The pin-out of the Mini USB Connector

Pin 1	VBus
Pin 2	D-
Pin 3	D+
Pin 4	ID
Pin 5	Ground

Micro-A and Micro-B

The Micro-A and B connectors are introduced to replace the Mini-A and Mini-AB connectors. They are smaller in size than the Mini connectors. They have up to 10, 000 mating cycles. The Micro connectors are used with small devices like mobiles, smart phones, PDAs (Personal Digital Assistants), etc. (See Figure 3.27).

Figure 3.26 The image of Mini A and B male USB connector and Pin position

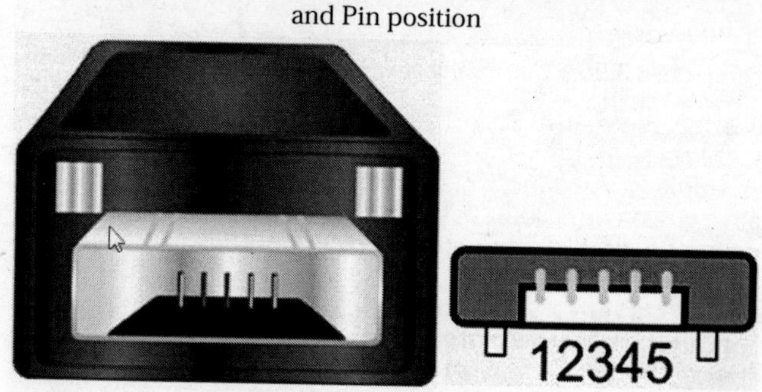

Figure 3.27 The image of Micro B and A male connector and pin position

The pin-out of the Micro USB connector

Pin 1	VBus
Pin 2	D-
Pin 3	D+
Pin 4	ID
Pin 5	Ground

3.11.6 FireWire (IEEE 1394)

IEEE (Institute of Electrical and Electronics Engineers) 1394, also named "FireWire" by Apple, and "i.Link" by Sony, and it was developed by Apple in 1986. It is a standard I/O interface designed to service the demands of the emerging multimedia bus requirements. It includes a plug-and-socket connection with a serial bus interface. Up to 63 devices may be connected at the same time with (relatively) high data transfer speeds.

The IEEE 1394 standard has proved very popular for communication between computers and peripheral devices. IEEE 1394 interface has the following features:

- Real-time data transferring for multimedia applications
- 100-800 Mb/s data transfer rate
- Hot plugging is allowed (at a minimum ratio)
- Line terminators are not required
- Plug-and-play
- Auto-configuration for many peripheral devices
- Same connectors for multiple devices and components

The FireWire system is commonly used to connect digital cameras and other storage devices. FireWire has an edge over USB in terms of power distribution, reliability and data transfer speed. Moreover, FireWire system has adopted the functionalities and characteristics of SCSI.

3.11.7 HDMI

It stands for "High-Definition Multimedia Interface." HDMI is a digital interface for transmitting audio and video data in a single cable. It is supported by most HDTVs and related components, such as DVD and Blu-ray players, cable boxes, and video game systems.

While other types of A/V connections require separate cables for audio and video data, HDMI carries the audio and video streams together, greatly eliminating cable clutter. For example, a component cable connection requires three cables for video and two for audio, totaling five cables in all. The same information can be transmitted using one HDMI cable.

Because HDMI is a digital connection, HDMI cables are less prone to interference and signal noise than analog cables. Also, since most components, such as DVD players and digital cable boxes process information digitally, using HDMI eliminates the analog to digital conversion other interfaces require. Therefore, HDMI often produces the best quality picture and sound compared to other types of connections.

HDMI connectors come in 4 types:

- Type A is the most popular. This connector can be identified by its 19 pins on the male head. Type A is compatible with single-link DVI-D connections.
- Type B is larger than Type A, coming in at 29 pins on the male head. Type B is compatible with dual-link DVI-D connections.
- Type C is a 19-pin connector that is most often used with portable devices, like camcorders and digital cameras.
- Type D looks similar to a micro-USB cord. It also has 19 pins.

3.11.8 VGA Connector

A Video Graphics Array (VGA) connector is a three-row 15-pin DE-15 connector. The 15-pin VGA connector is found on many video cards, computer monitors, and high definition television sets. On laptop computers or other small devices, a mini-VGA port is sometimes used in place of the full-sized VGA connector.

3.11.9 DVI (Digital Visual Interface)

A large computer-like 18-pin connector that carries digital video signals, including High Definition signals, between a set-top HD cable or satellite box or DVD player and an HDTV set. DVI digital video signals are protected by HDCP (High-bandwidth Digital Content Protection) protocol, which prevents you from copying high-quality digital video.

DVI connectors come in 3 varieties.

- DVI-A can transmit analog signals, allowing it to be backwards compatible with VGA (useful for CRT monitors and LCDs of lower quality).
- DVI-D can transmit the newer digital signals.
- DVI-I is capable of both analog and digital.
- In certain cases, you may need a VGA-to-DVI or DVI-to-VGA converter cable.

3.12 CABLES CONCEPTS

Networking cables are used to connect one network device to other network devices or to connect two or more computers to share printer. There are several types of cable which are commonly used with LANs. The type of network cable is related to the network's topology, protocol and size.

There are various types of cables used in networks. These are:

a) Twisted pair cable
b) Coaxial Cable
c) Fiber optic cable

3.12.1 Twisted Pair Cable

A twisted pair consists of two insulated copper wires, typically about 1 mm thickness. The wires are twisted together in a helical shape. It is a type of cable wiring in which two conductors of a single circuit are twisted together for the purposes of canceling out electromagnetic interference (EMI). This type of cable is used for home and corporate Ethernet networks. It is commonly used in local telephone communication and for digital data transmission over short distances up to 1 km. There are two varieties of twisted pair cable. One is Unshielded Twisted Pair (UTP) and Shielded Twisted Pair (STP) (See Figure 3.28).

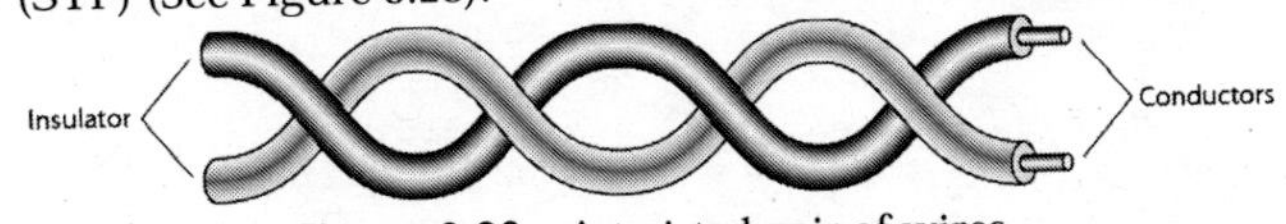

Figure 3.28 A twisted pair of wires

Twisted pair cabling comes in several varieties. In computer networks, two of these are important. Category 3 twisted pair's cable consists of two insulated wires gently twisted together. Four such pairs are typically grouped together in a plastic sheath for protection and to keep the eight wires together. Another more advanced category, 5 twisted pairs were introduced. They are similar to category 3 pairs, but with more twist per centimeter and Teflon insulation, which results in less crosstalk and better quality signal over longer distances, making them more suitable for high-speed computer communication.

UTP: Unshielded twisted pair cable is more commonly used for LAN media. The twisted pair version of Ethernet is designated as 10BASE-T, in which 10 refers to the Ethernet rate of 10 Mbps (See Figure 3.29)

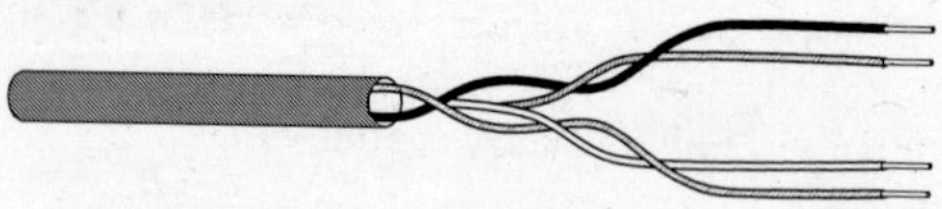

Figure 3.29 Unshielded twisted-pair (UTP) cable

RJ-45 is the standard for Unshielded Twisted pair for cabling connector. This is a plastic connector that looks like a large telephone-style connector. A slot allows the RJ-45 to be inserted in one way. This standard designates which wire goes with each pin inside the connector. RJ stands for Registered Jack See Figure 3.30.

Figure 3.30 Unshielded twisted-pair (UTP) cable

STP: Shielded Twised Pair is used with the traditional Token Ring cabling. It requires a custom connector. STP has a characteristic impedance of 150 ohms. Shielded wire (Figure 3.31) is used in an electrically noisy environment to limit the effects of noise absorption.

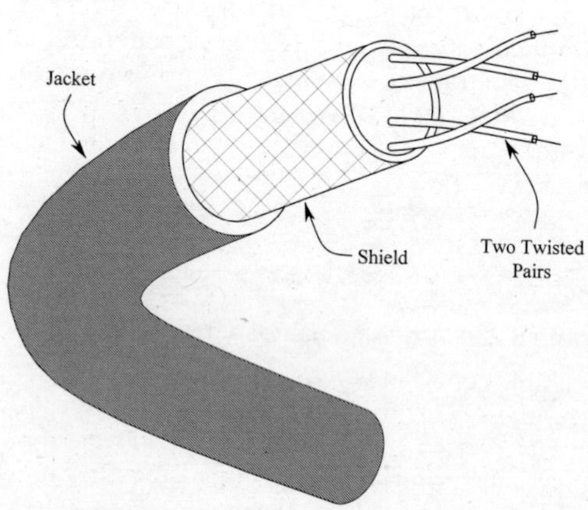

Figure 3.31 Shielded two pair cable

Advantages

(a) Being the oldest method of data transmission, trained manpower to repair and service this media of communications are easily available.

(b) In a telephone system, signals can travel several kilometres without amplification when twisted pair wires are used

(c) This media can be used for both analog and digital data transmission. The bandwidth depends on the thickness of the wire and the distance traveled, but several megabits per second can be achieved for a few kilometres in many cases.

(d) It is the least expensive media of transmission for short distances.

(e) If portion of a twisted-pair cable is damaged, the entire network is not shut down as it may be the case with coaxial cable.

Disadvantages

(a) Easily picks up noise signals which results in higher error rates when the line length exceeds 100 metres.

(b) Being thin in size, it is likely to break easily.

(c) It can support 19,200 bps up to 50 feet on RS-232 port. On a 10BaseT, which supports 10 Mbps, twisted pair wires can be used up to 100 metres.

☞ Unshielded twisted pair, commonly referred to as UTP is by far the more common of the two configurations.

3.12.2 Coaxial Cable

Coaxial cables are groups of specially wrapped and insulated wire lines that are able to transmit data at high rates. As shown in Figure 4.4, they consist of a central copper wire surrounded by a PVC (Polyvinyl Chloride) insulation over which a sleeve of copper mesh is placed. The metal sleeve is again shielded by an outer shield of thick PVC material. The signal is transmitted by the inner copper wire and is electrically shielded by the outer metal sleeve (See Figure 3.32).

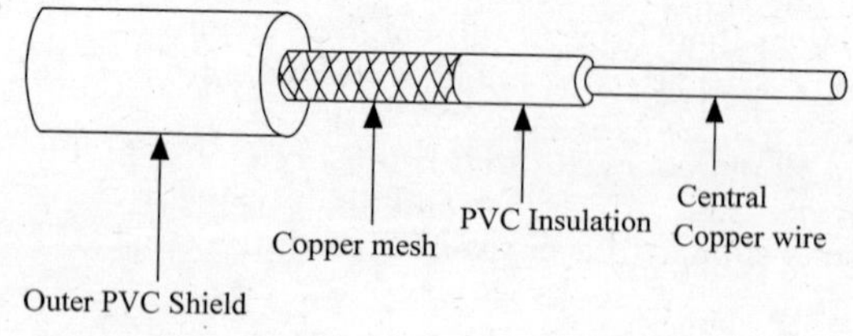

Figure 3.32 A coaxial cable

There are two types of Coaxial cable:

Thinnet cable (10Base2)–Thinnet coaxial cable is connected using special connectors and requires to be terminated at each end using a 50ohm resistor.

Thicknet cable (10Base5)–Thicknet cable is connected to a network using a device called a transceiver. This device includes a piece of equipment that actually pierces the cable to connect to it. This connector is known as a vampire tap or a piercing tap. A computer's NIC can then be connected to the transceiver using a special transceiver cable.

Advantages Coaxial Cable

(a) Coaxial cable can support greater cable lengths between network devices than twisted pair cable.
(b) Thick coaxial cable has an extra protective plastic cover that help keep moisture away.
(c) It can be used for both analog and digital data transmissions. For analog data transmission, 75-ohm broadband coaxial is used and for digital transmission, 50 ohm baseband cable is used.
(d) It is inexpensive as compared to twisted pair wires and UTP cables but easy to handle.

Disadvantages

(a) Thick coaxial is that it does not bend easily and is difficult to install.
(b) More expensive to install compare to twisted pair cable.

3.12.3 Fiber Optic Cable

A fiber-optic cable is transparent thin fibers, usually made of glass or plastic and transmits signals in the form of light. An optical transmission system works on three key components:
(a) Light source
(b) Transmission medium
(c) Detector
A pulse of light indicates 1-bit whereas absence of light indicates 0 bit. Transmission medium is an ultra-thin fiber of glass. The function of detector generates an electrical pulse when light falls on it. Fiber-optic cables are similar to coaxial except without the braid (See Figure 3.33).

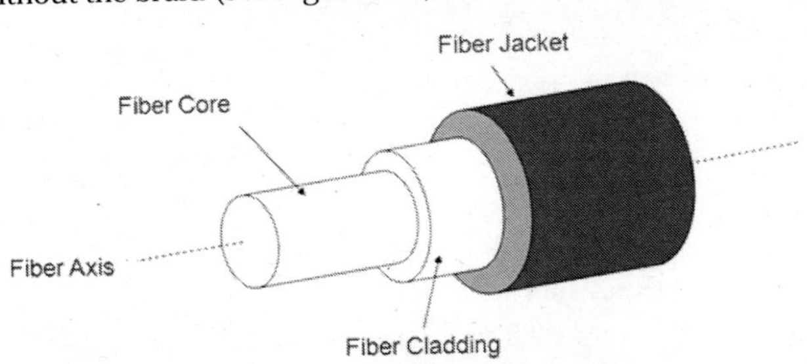

Figure 3.33 A Fiber optic cable

The fiber core is surrounded by a glass cladding with a lower index of refraction than the core, to keep all the light in the core. The function of thin fiber jacket is to protect the cladding. Types of fiber-optic cable are as follows:
(a) Single-mode: In single-mode fibers, the core is 8 to 10 microns. It uses a specific light wavelength. It is often used for intercity telephone trunks and video applications.
(b) Multi-mode: In multi-mode fibers, the core is typically 50 microns in diameter (about the thickness of a human hair). It uses a large number of frequencies or modes. Multi-mode fiber type is usually specified for LANs and WANs.

Advantages of Fiber Optic cable

(a) Very high data rate, low error rate. 1000 Mbps (1 Gbps) over distances of kilometers common. Error rates are so low they are almost negligible.
(b) Difficult to tap, which makes it hard for unauthorized taps as well. This is responsible for higher reliability of this medium.
(c) Much thinner (per logical phone line) than existing copper circuits. Because of its thinness, phone companies can replace thick copper wiring with fibers having much more capacity for same volume. This is important because it means that aggregate phone capacity can be upgraded without the need for finding more physical space to hire the new cables.
(d) Not susceptible to electrical interference (lightning) or corrosion (rust).
(e) Greater repeater distance than coax.

Disadvantages

(a) Difficult to tap. It really is point-to-point technology. In contrast, tapping into coax is trivial. No special training or expensive tools or parts are required.
(b) One-way channel. Two fibers needed to get full duplex (both ways) communication.

3.12.4 Color Combination of Network Cable

There are several color combination of cable used for twisted-pair networks. These cable can be categorized as Cat 5, Cat 5e, and Cat 6 UTP cable. Cat 5 UTP cable can support 10/100 Mbps Ethernet network, whereas Cat 5e and Cat 6 UTP cable can support Ethernet network running at 10/100/1000 Mbps. You might hear about Cat 3 UTP cable, it's not popular anymore since it can only support 10 Mbps Ethernet network.

Straight and crossover cable can be Cat3, Cat 5, Cat 5e or Cat 6 UTP cable, the only difference is each type will have different wire arrangement in the cable for serving different purposes.

Ethernet network cables are straight and crossover cable. This Ethernet network cable is made of 4 pair high performance cable that consists of twisted pair conductors that used for data transmission. Both end of cable is called RJ45 connector.

There are three types of network cables commonly used in PC networks - Straight-through and cross-over.

Straight-through Cable

You usually use straight cable to connect different type of devices. This type of cable will be used most of the time and can be used to:

1. Connect a computer to a switch/hub's normal port.

2. Connect a computer to a cable/DSL modem's LAN port.
3. Connect a router's WAN port to a cable/DSL modem's LAN port.
4. Connect a router's LAN port to a switch/hub's uplink port. (normally used for expanding network)
5. Connect 2 switches/hubs with one of the switch/hub using an uplink port and the other one using normal port.

If you need to check how straight cable looks like, it is easy. Both side (side A and side B) of cable have wire arrangement with same color.

Pin ID	side A	side B
1	Orange-white	green-white
2	Orange	green
3	green-white	orange-white
4	blue	brown-white
5	blue-white	Brown
6	green	orange
7	brown-white	Blue
8	brown	blue-white

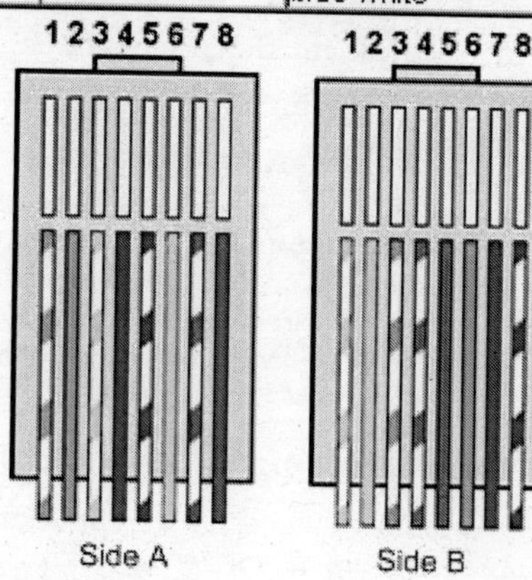

Crossover Cable

Sometimes you will use crossover cable, it is usually used to connect same type of devices. A crossover cable can be used to:

1. Connect two computers directly.
2. Connect a router's LAN port to a switch/hub's normal port,
3. Connect two switches/hubs by using normal port in both switches/hub.

If you need to check how crossover cable looks like, both side (side A and side B) of cable have wire arrangement with following different color.

Purpose of this cross cable is RX (receiving terminal) to TX (transmitting) of one PC to another PC and vice versa.

As we use two PCs (same devices), straight cable will connect TX to TX and RX to RX of two computers, so cross cable is required. If you use HUB or switch, then straight cable will work because it has terminal arrangement like cross cable.

Pin ID	side A	side B
1	Orange-white	green-white
2	Orange	green
3	green-white	orange-white
4	blue	brown-white
5	blue-white	Brown
6	green	orange
7	brown-white	Blue
8	brown	blue-white

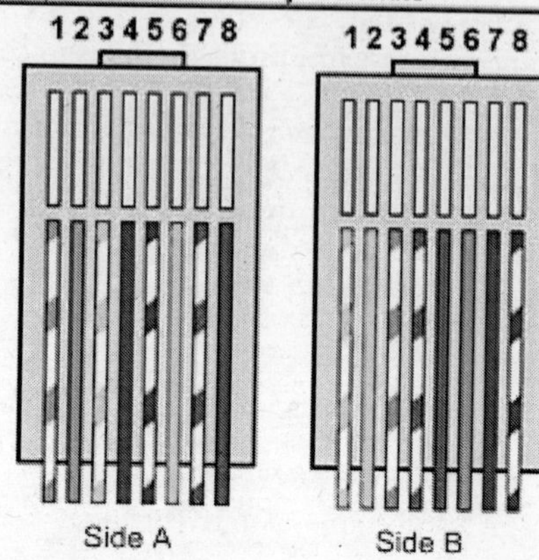

If we apply the 568A color code and show all eight wires, out pin-out looks like this:

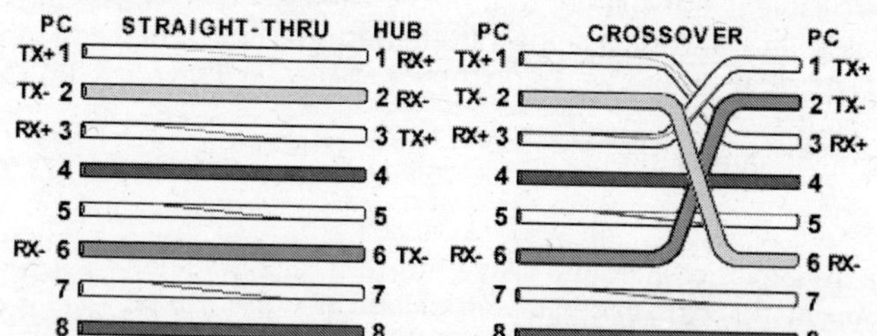

Both the T-568A and the T-568B standard By looking at a T-568A UTP Ethernet straight-thru cable and an Ethernet crossover cable with a T-568B end, we see that the TX (transmitter) pins are connected to the corresponding RX (receiver) pins, plus to plus and minus to minus. You can also see that both the blue and brown wire pairs on pins 4, 5, 7, and 8 are not used. These same pins 4, 5, 7, and 8 are not used or required in 100BASE-TX as well. So using these wires, it is simply easier to make a connection with all the wires grouped together. Otherwise you will be spending time trying to fit those tiny little wires into each of the corresponding holes in the RJ-45 connector.

Rollover Wired Cables

Rollover wired cables most commonly called rollover cables, have opposite Pin assignments on each end of the cable or in other words it is "rolled over". Pin 1 of connector A would be connected to Pin 8 of connector B. Pin 2 of connector A would be connected to Pin 7 of connector B and so on. Rollover cables, sometimes referred to as Yost cables are most commonly used to connect to a devices console port to make programming changes to the device. Unlike crossover and straight-wired cables, rollover cables are not intended to carry data but instead create an interface with the device.

Connector A	Connector B
Pin 1	Pin 8
Pin 2	Pin 7
Pin 3	Pin 6
Pin 4	Pin 5
Pin 5	Pin 4
Pin 6	Pin 3
Pin 7	Pin 2
Pin 8	Pin 1

Rollover Wiring Guide
568-B

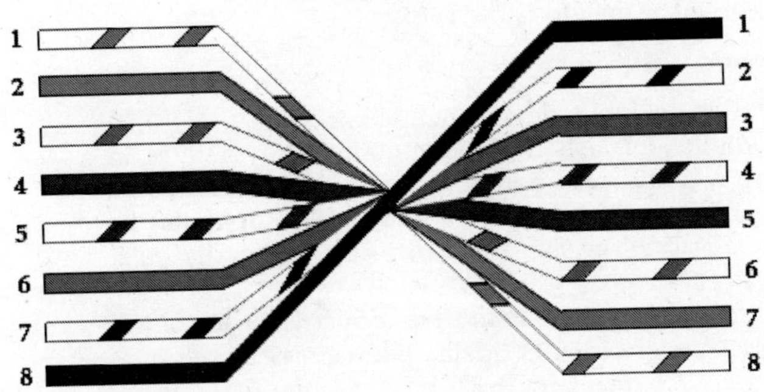

3.13 DATA STORAGE DEVICES

Storage devices are one of the components of computer device. They store virtually all the data and applications on a computer except hardware firmware. They are available in different form factors depending on the type of underlying device.
There are two different types of storage devices. These are:
Primary Storage Devices–It is small in size. It hold data temporarily and are internal to the computer such as RAM.
Secondary Storage Devices–These have large storage capacity, and they store data permanently. They can be both internal and external to the computer, such as hard disk, compact disk drive and USB storage device.

Hard Disk

A hard disk is a device used for mass storage of data needed for direct access. It is more stable, rigid and also it is contained in a dust-free environment. It stores more information.

The data and instructions that are entered into the computer system through input units must be stored inside the computer before the actual processing can start. Similarly, the results produced by the computer after processing must also be kept somewhere inside the computer system before those can be passed on to the output units. Moreover, the intermediate results produced by the computer must also be preserved for ongoing processing (See Figure 3.34).

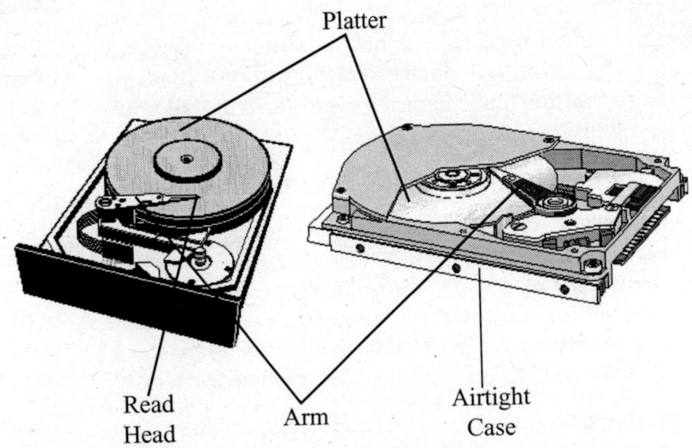

Figure 3.34 Hard disk

The specific functions of the storage unit are to store the following:

(a) All data and instructions to be processed,

(b) Intermediate results of processing, and

(c) Final results before sending them to output devices.

Floppy Drive

The smallest and most portable of all the storage devices usually holds about 1.44 MB of storage. Use a floppy disk media.

Super Drive

The SuperDisk is a drive which supports a special floppy diskette which can store up to 120MB or 240MB of information.

Zip Drive

New generation similar to the floppy disk drive created by Iomega The Iomega Zip Drive was first released 1994 and today is becoming a popular solution for PC and Macintosh computers as a removable solution. Zip Drives Disks come in 100MB, 250MB and 750MB

Flash Drive

A compact and portable device use for storing data anywhere from 128MB up to 4GB.

Portable hard drives

Small, lightweight and easy to carry with you throughout the day, portable hard drives do not need plugging into the mains as they are powered by USB, which is ideal for saving important documents when you are away or using your laptop on its battery away from a plug socket.

Wireless Hard Drives

Wireless hard drives connect to your devices without any cables. They are small and portable, so you can expand the storage of your laptop, tablet, and smartphone from a single convenient hard drive.

Cloud storage

Cloud storage is ideal for students and business as you can access all your data from any device. Your important files are encrypted, stored online and can be accessed from any of your online devices, anywhere in the world.

Network attached storage (NAS drives)

Whether you are using a laptop, tablet, or smartphone, a NAS drive lets you access your files from a single place - it is just like having your own personal Cloud. They are ideal for families as everyone can have their own accounts and secure folders. You can even save and download your files from anywhere in the world; all you need is an internet connection.

USB Flash Drives

USB sticks, which are also known as flash drives, are simple storage devices that can easily be slipped into a pocket, bag, or even wallet. They are ideal for quickly sharing files between friends, colleagues, and other devices..

3.14 VIDEO AND MULTIMEDIA INPUT/OUTPUT DEVICES

To develop the system of multimedia we use the various hardware/software components are:

3.14.1 Input and Output Devices

Before a computer can process your data, you need some method to input the data into the machine. The device you use will depend on what form this data takes (be it text, sound, artwork, etc.).

Similarly, after the computer has processed your data, you often need to produce output of the results. This output could be a display on the computer screen, hardcopy on printed pages, or even the audio playback of music you composed on the computer.

The terms "input" and "output" are used to describe the process of entering or displaying the data by the computer.

Keyboard

A keyboard is a human interface device which is represented as a layout of buttons. Each button or key to call upon a particular function of the computer.

Optical Character Recognition Device

OCR is the mechanical or electronic conversion of images of typewritten or printed text into machine-encoded text.

ointing e ices

The graphical user interfaces (GUIs) in use today require some kind of device for positioning the on-screen cursor. Typical pointing devices are: mouse, trackball, touch pad, trackpoint, graphics tablet, joystick, and touch screen.

Mouse

Mouse is a pointing device sits on the flat surface and is moved with your hand. It also detects two-dimensional motion relative to a surface. It is also used to enter positional information as 2D or 3D data from a standard reference point. Movement of mouse is tracked by software, which can also set the tracking speed.

The trackball is sort of like an upside down mouse, with the ball located on the top. You use your fingers to roll the trackball, and internal rollers sense the motion which is transmitted to the computer.

Joystick is also a pointing device which is used to move cursor position on a monitor screen.

Touch screen

The use can make choices and press button images on the screen. You also use stylus, which you hold like a pen, to write on the surface of a small touch screen.

Microphone

Microphone is an input device to input sound that is then stored in digital form. It has a diaphragm that vibrates in response to sound waves. Vibrations modulate a continuous electric current to sound waves. Modulated current can be digitized and stored as standardized format for audio data, such as .wav file.

Microphone plugs into a sound input board. It can control the sampling rate gives better fidelity but requires more space. Sampling rate for music is 20,000 Hz and Sampling rate for speech is 10,000 Hz.

MIDI Devices

A MIDI is a musical keyboard can be attached to a computer and allow to play music that is captured by the computer system.

MIDI consists of two parts:

1. Hardware standard–It specifies cables, circuits, connectors, and electrical signals to be used.
2. Message standard–Types and formats of messages to be transmitted to/from synthesizers, control units (keyboards), and computers.

   Messages consist of a device number, a control segment to tell the device the function to be performed (turn on/off a specified circuit), and a data segment to provide the information necessary for the action (volume of sound, or frequency of basic sound). An entire piece of music can be described by a sequence of MIDI messages.

Digital Camers and Scanners

Digital camera capture the still image or video of a given number of pixels (resoultion) and the images are strored in the camera's memory to be uploaded to a computer.

Digital image caputre, light is focused on photosensitive cells to produce electric current in response to intensity and wave-length of light. Electric current is scanned for each point on the image and translated to binary code. Codes correspond to pixel values can can be used to rebuild the original picture.
Scanner is the most useful equipment in a multimedia. The most commonly used scanner for multimedia application is colour flatbed scanners that provide resolute of 600 dot per inch.
Scanning mechanism shines bright light on the image and codes and records the reflected light for each point. Scanner does not store data sends it to the computer, possibly after compression of the same the quality of images are:

- Depends on the quality of optics and sharpness of focus
- Perceived by sharpness of resulting image
- Accuracy of encoding for each pixel depends on the precision of photosensitive cells
- Resolution of scanner/camera

Video Camera

Video camera is a camera capable of recording live motion video with audio. Standard video camera contains photosensitive cells, scanning one frame after another. Output of the cells gets recorded as analog stream of colors, or sent to digiting circuitary to generate a stream of digital codes.

Output Devices

Following is a brief description of output devices used in multimedia.

Monitor

The monitors for a multimedia application must be high-end, large screen graphics and liquid crystal display. Pictures on monitor are formed with picture elements called pixel. Montiors may be monochrome that will display results in black and white. The detailed description about monitor are discussed in Chapter 1.

Speakers

Speaker produces sound output. We can listen recorded voices, sounds or music with the help of speaker. Speaker produces sound output with the help of sound card.

Printers

Printers are the most popular output device. It provides information in a permanent readable form. It produces printed output of results, programs, and data. Printers can be divided into two categories:

- Impact printers
- Non-impact printers

The detailed explanation about printers are discussed in the Chapter 1.

3.14.2 Classification of Printers

Printers are also classified by the following characteristics:

Quality of Type

The output produced by printers is said to be either letter quality (as good as a typewriter), near letter quality, or draft quality. Only daisy-wheel, inkjet and laser printers produce letter-quality type. Some dotmatrix printers also claim letter-quality print.

Speed

Measured in characters per second or pages per minute. The speed of printers varies widely. Daisy-wheel printers tend to be the slowest, printing about 30 Cps. Line printers are fastest (up to 3,000 lines per minute). Dotmatrix printers can print up to 500 Cps, and laser printers range from about 4 to 20 text pages per minute.

Impact or Non-impact

Impact printers include all printers that work by striking an ink ribbon. Daisy-wheel, dotmatrix and line printers are impact printers. Non-impact printers include laser printers and inkjet printers. Impact printers are much noiser.

Graphics

Some printers (daisy-wheel and line printers) can print only text. Other printers can print both text and graphics.

Fonts

Some printers, like dotmatrix printers, are limited to one or a few fonts. In contrast, laser and ink-jet printers are capable of printing and almost unlimited variety of fonts. Daisy-wheel printers can also print different fonts, but you need to change the daisy-wheel.
While buying a printer, the four main aspects to look at are as follows:

Resolution

The printers resolution is the sharpness at which the graphics or text appear on the paper when the print is removed. This resolution is generally measured in dots per inch. General printers will give you a resolution of about six hundred dots per inch. This resolution would be adequate enough for normal everyday print jobs.

Speed

In a workplace or if a person requires many print outs day in and day out the speed at which the printer functions becomes a crucial aspect. The normal everyday printers are capable of removing about three to six printed sheets of paper every sixty seconds. However, this number reduces if you are removing colour print outs. The printer that cost more are capable of removing print outs, both colour and black and white, at a faster rate.

Colour

You would need a colour printer if your work demands that coloured images be part of the print outs. With colour printers, you have the best of both worlds, because they can also be programmed to give print outs in only black and white.

☞ Depending on the manufacturer and model of the printer, ink cartridge comes in various combinations, such as separate black and colour cartridges. Colour and black in a single cartridges or even a cartridge for each ink colour.

Memory

Printers have a small quantity of memory storage space. However the user can make this bigger. Increasing the memory is beneficial and also makes the printer quicker when it has to give printouts of large number of graphics.

Printer Port

A Printer port is used to connect the system and a device together, using a connecting cable, so that they can communicate together. Different ports available are located at the back of the system case.

The parallel port connector has 25 pins to connect devices, such as printer. So parallel port is also called printer port. Newer systems feature on Enhanced Capabilities Port (ECP) able to provide duplex operation and higher data rates.

Printer Driver

A driver is a program that controls the behaviour of device connected to a computer. It provides a connection between peripheral devices and the operating system. All devices, such as monitors, modems and printers require drivers for their functioning. Drivers for certain devices, such as the keyboard form a part of the operating system. Other devices like printers need to have their drivers installed separately.

3.14.3 Portable Computers and Devices

A portable computer is a computer that comes with a keyboard and display and one which can be easily moved. Portable computers generally take up less space than desktop systems. Compared to other mobile computing device or laptop, portable computer makes use of standard motherboards and also provide plug in slots for add in cards. Compared to a desktop computer, the power consumed is less in case of portable computer and can help in power and cost savings.

A portable device is any device that can easily be carried. It have battery powered devices with base computing resources in the form of a processor, memory, and storage and network access. It is a small form factor of a computing device that is designed to be held and used in the hands.

Portable devices are becoming an increasingly important part of personal computing as the capabilities of devices like laptops, tablets and smartphones. The latest devices are thin and lightweight, making them easy to carry and hold. Small plug-and-play devices such as USB drives, external hard disks and webcams can also be called portable devices.

Notebook computers and portable devices are examples of portable computers. There are several different types of mobile computing devices. A notebook (or laptop) is a portable version of a desktop system. It often has similar hardware and runs similar software.

The following are some types of portable comptuer:

(a) Laptops and Notebooks
(b) PDAs (Personal Digital Assistants)
(c) Tablet Personal Computer (PC)

Laptops and Notebooks

A laptop PC is a small, compact and portable machine which runs on battery power. You can unfold it and work with it on your lap and hence the name is given to it. It can be carried in your suitcase easily. It is comparatively costly and is mainly used by senior executives or correspondents who mostly remain on tour. Figure 3.35 depicts a laptop model.

Figure 3.35 A laptop model

A Notebook is a smaller and lighter version of the laptop model.

PDAs (Personal Digital Assistants)

Personal Digital Assistant (PDA) is a handheld computer and popularly known as a palmtop. It has a touch screen and a memory card for storage of data (See Figure 3.36). PDAs can also be effectively used as portable audio players, web browsers and smart phones. Most of them can access the Internet by means of Bluetooth or Wireless Fidelity (Wi-Fi) communication.

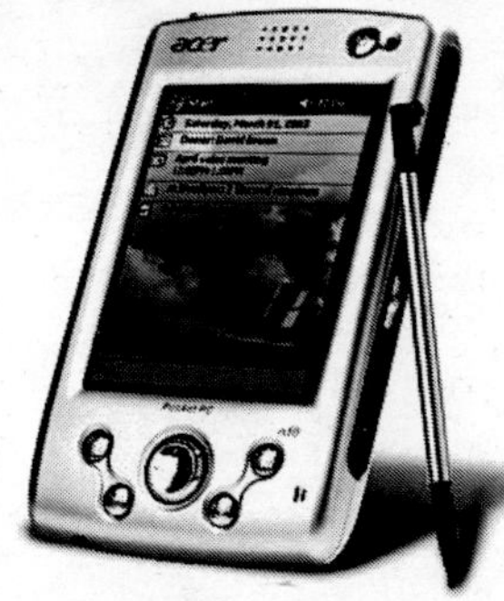

Figure 3.36 PDA

Tablet PC

A tablet PC or simply tablet, is a medium-sized mobile computer integrated into a flat touch screen and primarily using stylus, digital pen or fingertip input along with a virtual onscreen keyboard in lieu of a physical keyboard. It is a touch-pad device that combines the features and qualities of a smart phone and a laptop. Figure 3.37 depicts a Tablet PC.

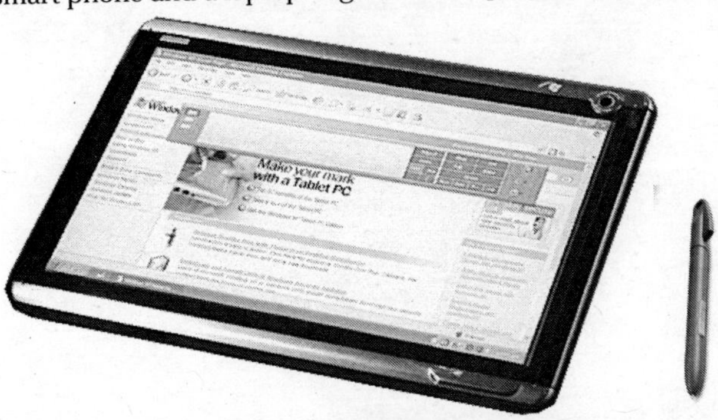

Figure 3.37 A Tablet PC

Tablet PCs have a wireless adapter for Internet and local network connection. Software applications for tablet PCs include Office Suites, Web browsers, games and a variety of applications. However, since portable computer hardware components are low powered, demanding PC applications may not provide an ideal experience to the user.

Apple computers has come out with a refined second-generation tablet ipad2 that squeezes more power into a thinner shell. Its new features include:

(a) Design: iPad 2 is 33% thinner and 15% lighter than previous model.

(b) Processor: Dual-core A5 - promises to be twice as fast, with graphics performance up to nine times better than original iPod.

(c) Cameras: Front-facing Video Graphics Array or VGA camera for video chat. Rear-facing camera for taking pictures and HD video.

(d) Cover: Attached magnetically, doubles as stand to hold iPad upright for viewing or typing.

(e) HDMI port: Allows user to mirror iPad on High Definition Television (HDTV) screen.

Latest 10" inches tablet PC made by Dixons Retail plc running Android 2.2, having a 1 GHz NVIDIA Tegra chipset, 512 MB of Random Access Memory (RAM) and Read Only Memory (ROM), 1.3 MB camera, Wi-Fi b/g connectivity, Bluetooth 2.1, a micro SD card slot, a Universal Serial Bus (USB) port and a 16h battery life for audio playback and 6.5h for 1080p video and Motorola announces Xoom Tablet, a 10 inch tablet powered by the upcoming Android 3.0 Honeycomb, Samsung announces Galaxy Tab 10.1 and 1280 × 800 resolution, powered by google Android 3.0 and Blackberry's PlayBook 7-inch, 1024 × 600 screen running on Blackberry Tablet OS.

Connecting the Computers together

There are several different ways to connect your computers together. These are:

To connect two computers with a USB Cable

If you have two PCs with USB ports, you can connect them to one another using a special type of USB cable called a "bridging cable". Once the computers are connected to one another, you can quickly transfer files from one computer to another. For high-speed use, use a USB 2.0 cable, which has a better transfer rate than a standard network connection.

Eqiupment needed

In order to do the transfer, you will need three main pieces of equipment: an Ethernet crossover cable, a null modem serial cable or a special purpose USB cable.

Creating an ethernet network will allow you to transfer data between more than two computers. Note that at least one of the computers must have an Ethernet daptor – as long as the other computers have at least a USB port, you can perform the connection using a crossover cable.

➡ Connecting two PCs using USB cable:

1. Connect a USB-to-USB cable bridging cable. Both computers should be switched on and logged into the "Administrator" account. On the USB port computer, plug the USB bridge into the USB slot and the end bridge into the other computer.
2. You must install the USB bridge cable driver software as a link adapter or a network adapter.
3. If you choose to install a link adapter, you will be allowed to transfer files from one PC to another, but if you choose to install a network adapter, you will be able to access the whole network's PCs.
4. Once installation is complete, you should be able to start the data transfers between the computers.

To Connect Two Computers Together with an Ethernet Cable

If you access to a network, and need to transfer files or establish a connection between two computers, you can connect the computers to one another using a crossover Ethernet cable. After connecting your computers together with an Ethernet cable, you will be required to modify the network settings on one of the computers to establish the cable connection. You will then have the ability to transfer or share files, and play network games between both computers.

Verify Network configuration

Before trying to join the domain, it is better to take a look at the Network Connections in the Control Panel to ensure that the network card is detected and the appropriate software has been loaded. To verify your network connection, log on to the system as a user with administrative rights. If the network software has loaded properly, you will see an icon named Local Area Connection (as shown in Figure 3.38). If you have more than one NIC installed, you will see more than one Local Area Connection icon.

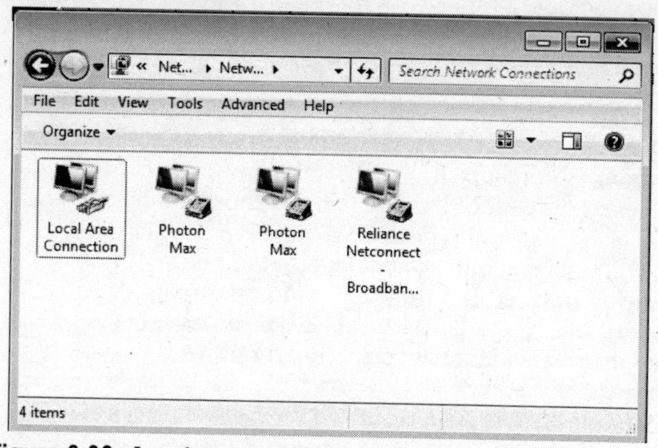

Figure 3.38 Local area connection icon in network connections

If you do not see a Local Area Connection icon, your NIC may not have been properly detected. Use the Device Manager to isolate the problem, or try to add the network adapter manually using the Add New Hardware Wizard in the Control Panel and your OEM-provided disk or CD-ROM.

➡ To connect two computers together with an Ethernet cable:

1. Verify that you have a crossover Ethernet cable. A crossover Ethernet cable is required to connect computers.
2. Plug each end of the Ethernet cable into an Ethernet network port on each computer to connect the computers together with the cable.
3. Click the Start menu and choose choose Control panel.
4. Select "Network and Sharing Center" from the options displayed in the window as shown in Figure 3.39.
5. Select and open the icon labeled "Unidentified network" from the network map at the top of the Network and Sharing Center window. This icon may display as "Multiple networks" if you have more than one network as shown in Figure 3.40.
6. By double clicking on the icon, you can check whether the connection is enabled or not, and if you highlight the connection and expand the details, you should also see the IP address that was assigned by DHCP (See Figure 3.41).

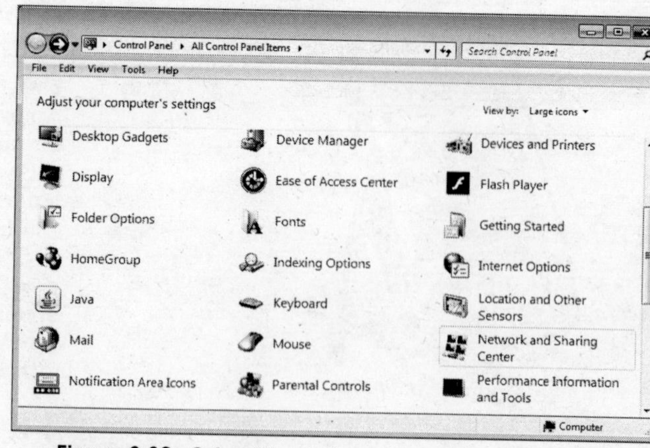

Figure 3.39 Select Network and sharing center option

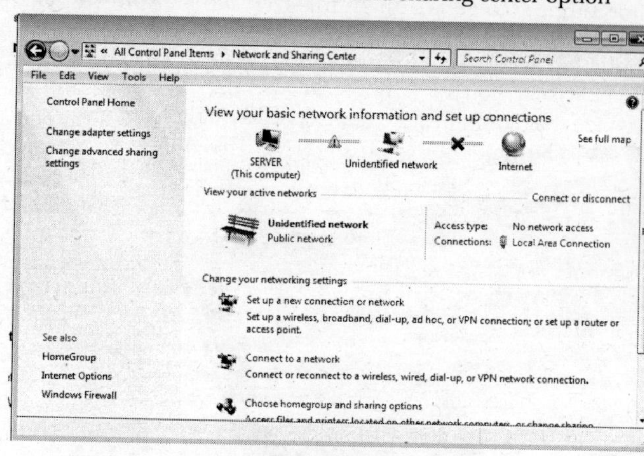

Figure 3.40

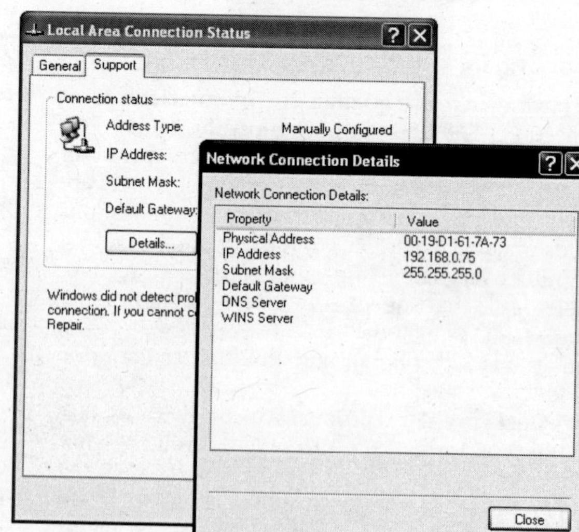

Figure 3.41 IP address Information

7. To view your network configuration information, right click the Local Area Connection icon and click Properties. The properties page, shown in Figure 3.42, lists the installed components.

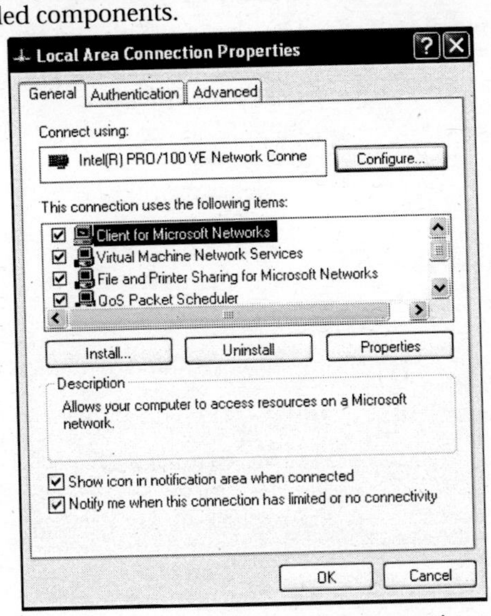

Figure 3.42 Local area connection properties page

- Network card type
- Protocol
- Client software.

TCP/IP is automatically configured to use DHCP. To statically assign IP information, select TCP/IP and click Properties. Figure 3.43 shows the Internet Protocol (TCP/IP) properties page.

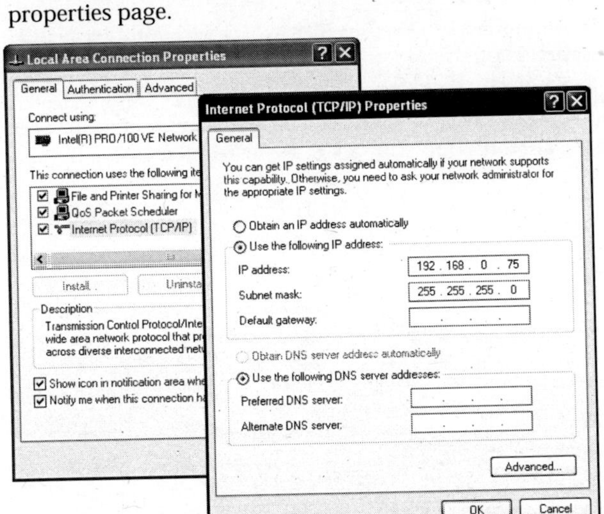

Figure 3.43 Internet protocol properties page

8. After entering the IP Address in both of your computers, now you will need the change the sharing setting of your computers to permit access rights for another computer.

9. Click change advanced sharing setting on the left side. Now you will need to change your network setting to those options as shown listed below:
   - Turn on network discovery
   - Turn on file and printer sharing
   - Allow windows to manage homegroup connection (recommended).
   - Trun on sharing so anyone with network access can read and write files in the public folders.
   - Use 128 bit encryption to help protect files sharing connections (recommended).
   - Turn off password protected sharing.
10. After that click on Finish and restart both of your computers.
11. Turn On Drive Sharing
    Now you will able to see your both computer in your windows network place location and to share your drive via network you will just need to Turn On the drive sharing by making some changes in that drive's properties (See Figure 3.44).

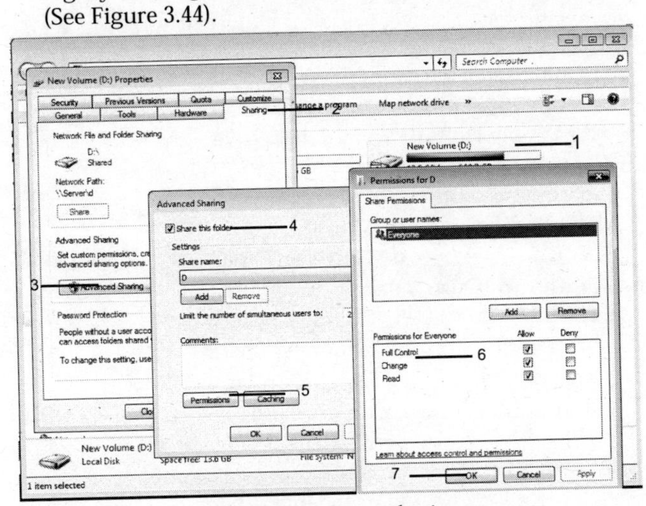

Figure 3.44 Drive sharing

Here is the list of some steps what you can follow to turn on the drive sharing in your computer or laptop:

1. Right click on your drive and select Properties.
2. Then, select "Sharing".
3. Then, click on "Advanced Sharing".
4. Then, tick the "Share this folder".
5. Then, click on "Permissions".
6. Then, tick on "Full control".
7. Then, click on "OK".
8. Again click OK and close the window.

MODEL QUESTIONS AND ANSWERS

A. Multiple Choice

1.1 A place on the system unit that allows the transfer of data between a variety of devices and the computer is a:

a. Port b. ROM

c. Drive d. Keyboard

1.2 Which of the following is TRUE about USB ports?
a. USB 2.0 is faster than FireWire
b. They have speed up to 480 megabits per second
c. They are being phased out by parallel ports
d. They transfer information wirelessly

1.3 The port most often used to connect a keyboard to a computer is a(n):
a. Ethernet port b. WiFi port
c. FireWire port d. USB port

1.4 If you want to connect a flat-panel monitor to your computer, you need to use the:
a. DVI port b. S-Video port
c. Video port d. Ethernet port

1.5 Which one of the following is not found on motherboard?
a. RAM b. CPU
c. HDD d. BIOS

1.6 Power connectors receive electrical power from the ________ and distribute it to the CPU, chipset, main memory and expansion cards.
a. Motherboard b. Universal Serial Bus
c. Power Supply Unit d. Hard disk drive

1.7 Additional peripherals such as __________ were provided as expansion cards.
a. USB Flash drive b. Mouse
c. Serial port d. Universal Serial Bus

1.8 The Motheboard is also called
a. Board b. Component Board
c. System Board d. Computer Board

1.9 The high speed mode of operation of the USB was introduced by _______.
a. ISA b. USB 3.0
c. USB 2.0 d. ANSI

1.10 Which of the following retains the information it's storing when the power to the system is turned off?
a. CPU b. ROM
c. DRAM d. DIMM

1.11 Which allows faster access:
a. RAM b. ROM
c. virtual memory d. Access memory

1.12 A teletypewriter terminal is an example of
a. input devices b. output devices
c. input/output devices d. storage devices

1.13 Devices that accept data from outside computer and transfer into CPU are called.
a. Input devices b. Digital devices
c. Analogue devices d. Truth table peripherals

1.14 Devices that are used to receive data from central processing unit are classified as
a. Input devices b. Digital devices
c. Analogue devices d. Truth table peripherals

1.15 From what location are the 1st computer instructions available on boot up?
a. ROM BIOS b. CPU
c. boot.ini d. CONFIG.SYS

1.16 Which peripheral port provides the fastest throughput to laser printers?
a. RS-232 b. Parallel
c. Serial d. None of the above

1.17 Which device uses a DMA channel?
a. Modem b. Network Card
c. Sound Card d. All of the above

1.18 How many pins on a VGA?
a. 15 b. 9
c. 25 d. 32

1.19 How does a parallel port communicate information to a peripheral device?
a. one bit at a time b. one byte at a time
c. 8 bytes at a time d. 16,555 bytes at a time

1.20 Which of the following stores more data?
a. DVD b. CD ROM
c. Floppy Disk d. CD RW

1.21 Which of the following is NOT an item of computer hardware?
a. keyboard b. System base unit
c. Speaker d. Icon

1.22 Information stored in Random Access Memory (RAM) is volatile. This means that it:
a. Is kept in memory even when the computer is powered off.
b. It lost when the computer is switched off.
c. Is automatically saved to disk when the computer is switched off.
d. Can burn if exposed to air.

1.23 Which standard body created the cables and connector specification used to support Ethernet implementation?
a. ISO b. NSI
c. EIA/TIA d. IETF

1.24 Which type of cable has glass center core?
a. UTP b. Fiber-Optic
c. STP d. Coaxial

1.25 Crossover cable connect the following devices:
a. Workstation to Workstation b. Switch to hub
c. Router to PC d. All of the above

B. State whether the following are True or False

2.1 The various cards in a PC requires DC voltage to function.

2.2 100 transceivers can be integrated onto a Thicknet backbone.

2.3 Parallel port communicates information to a peripheral device one bit at a time.

2.4 Using a portion of hard disk space to serve as RAM is called Access memory.

2.5 The function of power supply converts AC current into DC current.

2.6 10baseT is the name for twisted pair cable.

2.7 USB is a parallel mode of transmission of data and this enables for the fast speeds of data transfers.

2.8 In USB the devices can communicate with each other.

2.9 The USB address space can be shared by the user's memory space.

2.10 BIOS is a type of hardware.

2.11 To connect two computers directly, a straight through cable is used.

2.12 Crossover cable can be used to connect two computers directly.

2.13 RJ-11 is used for telephone, modem or ADSL connections.

Answers

A.	1.1 a	1.2 b	1.3 d	1.4 a	1.5 c
	1.6 c	1.7 d	1.8 c	1.9 c	1.10 b
	1.11 a	1.12 c	1.13 a	1.14 a	1.15 a
	1.16 b	1.17 c	1.18 a	1.19 b	1.20 a
	1.21 d	1.22 b	1.23 c	1.24 b	1.25 d
B.	2.1 T	2.2 T	2.3 F	2.4 F	2.5 T
	2.6 T	2.7 F	2.8 F	2.9 F	2.10 T
	2.11 F	2.12 T	2.13 T		

CHAPTER 4

Word Processing

4.1 INTRODUCTION

Word processing is the most common application package to create, edit, and print documents using a computer. To perform word processing, you need a computer, a special program called a word processor, and a printer. A word processor enables you to create a document, store it electronically on a disk, display it on a screen, modify it by entering commands and characters from the keyboard, and print it on a printer.

The great advantage of word processing over using a typewriter is that you can make changes without retyping the entire document. If you make a typing mistake, you simply back up the cursor and correct your mistake. If you want to delete a paragraph, you simply remove it, without leaving a trace. It is equally easy to insert a word, sentence, or paragraph in the middle of a document. Word processor also makes it easy to move sections of text from one place to another within a document, or between documents. When you have made all the changes you want, you can send the file to a printer to get a hardcopy. You can also mail it electronically to the addressee.

4.2 WORD PROCESSING BASICS

Word processing package, such as Word 2010 helps to enter text and manipulate words and phrases. You can change typed letter, document and report easily and store them for future use. You can even print these documents as and when desired.

☞ A word processor allows you to function more effectively and efficiently with minimum effort.

Word 2010 is a Word Processor that operates under Windows Operating System. When you use a computer program to create, and edit text documents, you are using word processor. Word 2010 is one of the most sophisticated word processing programs available to day. With Word 2010, it is easier than ever to efficiently create a wide range of business and personal documents, from a simples letter to the most complex project report. Word 2010 includes many desktop features that you can use to enhance the appearance of documents so that they are easy to read.

4.2.1 Opening Word Processing Package (MS Word 2010)

➡ **To start Word 2010, do this:**

1. Click Start button, highlight All Programs and click MS Office. Select MS Office Word 2010 (See Figure 4.1).

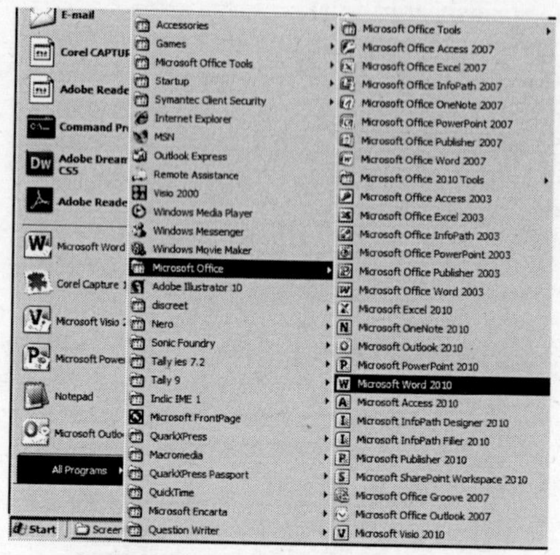

Figure 4.1 Starting MS Word 2010

4.2.2 Using Word 2010 Interface

User interfaces of MS Word 2010 is similar to MS Word 2007. MS Word 2010 has introduced several new features, such as improved WordArt, improved themes, background removal, and other image editing features. The new user interface that replaces menus, toolbars, and most of the task panes from previous versions of MS Word have been replaced by the File tab and Ribbon. It is designed to help you to be more productive. You can find the right features of various tasks more easily, discover new functionality and be more efficient. Figure 4.2 shows the elements of Word 2010 application window and an open Word 2010 document in detail.

4.2.3 File Tab

File tab is the colored tab which is located in the upper-left corner of MS Office 2010 programs and below the Quick Access Toolbar (See Figure 4.2). When you click the File tab, you can see the Backstage view. File Tab replaces the office button in Word 2007. It contains commands like New, Open, Save, Save As, Print, etc.

4.2.4 Quick Access Toolbar

This toolbar is located by default at the top of Word 2010 window. By default, this toolbar displays the Save, Undo and Repeat buttons.

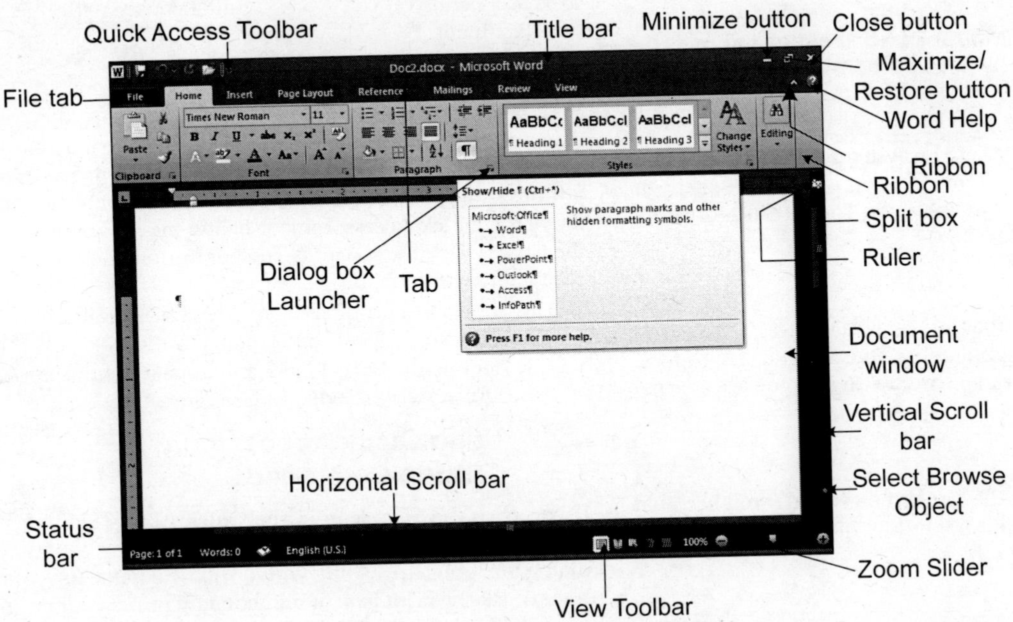

Figure 4.2 Elements of Word 2010 window

4.2.5 Dialog Box Launcher

Dialog box launchers are small icons that appear in some groups. Clicking a Dialog Box Launcher opens a related dialog box or task pane, providing more options related to that group.

4.2.6 Terminology

Following terminology for Word 2010 is used in this book.

elect–Highlight or mark a section of text, menu name, command, dialog box option, or graphical object with the keyboard or with mouse actions.

hoose–Execute and complete a command. You may execute some commands when you select the command on the Ribbon tabs. Other commands are executed when you choose OK from a dialog box.

cti e–Bring an application or document window to the foreground. When you are working with more than one application or more than one document within Word 2010, the active window is the window in which you are currently working.

4.2.7 Word 2010 Document Window

Title Bar

It is at the top of an open window and is called Title bar (See Figure 4.2).

Minimize button

An underscore(_) at the right of a title bar which stores an application programme at the bottom of the screen.

Maximize button

A box at the right of a title bar that fills available space with the document or application.

Close button

A box at the right of a title bar marked as (X) that closes the window or dialog box, when you click it with a mouse pointer.

Restore button

A double box at the right of a title bar that restores an application or document into a sizable window.

Help button

It appears at the right end of the Ribbon. When the mouse pointer is over any button for a few seconds (called hovering), it displays a ScreenTip with not only the button's name but also its function.

Status bar

It is present at the bottom of the window, and gives you information about the current document. You can turn off the display of an item of information by right-clicking the status bar and then on clicking that item.

View toolbar

At the right end of the status bar is the view toolbar. It provides tools for adjusting the view of document.

Mouse pointer

The on-screen arrow, I-beam, or drawing button indicates the current location affected by mouse actions.

Select Browse Object

The toolbar that enables you to browse through an active document by field, endnote, footnote, comment, section, page, edits, heading, graphic, or by table. Go To and Find functions are also part of this toolbar.

Ruler

A bar containing a scale that indicates tabs, paragraph indents, and margins in the paragraph where the insertion point (cursor) is located. The ruler can be used with the mouse to format paragraphs quickly.

Split box

Light gray bar present at the top of the vertical scroll bar, that you can drag down to split a window into two views of the same document.

ScreenTips

Screentips show the name of the command button shown in ribbon. Screentips appear as soon as you position the mouse pointer on the selected tabs command.

4.2.8 Ribbon Command

Ribbon is displayed just below the title bar. In Ribbon, Commands are organized in logical groups, which are collected together under tabs (See Figure 4.2). You can hide the Ribbon by double-clicking the active tab. Different types of Tabs are available in Word 2010.

- Home Tab: This button is related to working with document, such as clipboard, font, paragraph, styles, and editing.
- Insert Tab: This button is used to insert tables, header and footer, and symbols.
- Page Layout Tab: This button is related to page-formatting options. You can format your themes, set margins, insert page and section breaks, add line numbers, add background colors and water marks and adjust the entire document's indentation and spacing.
- Reference Tab: By using this button you can add Tables of Contents, Footnotes, Bibliography, Captions, Index and Table of Authorities.
- Mailing Tab: This button contains commands related to creating mass mailings. It contains create, start mail merge, write & insert fields, preview results and finish.
- Review Tab: This button is related to proofing, language comments, tracking, changes, compare and protect.
- View Tab: This button contain commands related to changing the view or the display of documents.

Scroll Bar

The scroll bar appears at the left for vertical scrolling and at the bottom for horizontal scrolling as seen in Figure 4.2.

In Word 2010, you can work simultaneously with more than one document.

Using Quick Access Toolbar

You can add buttons to the Quick Access Toolbar which expands to accommodate them. If you add many buttons, it might become difficult to view the text in the title bar or all the buttons might not be visible. To resolve this problem, you can move the Quick Access Toolbar below the Ribbon by clicking the Customize Quick Access Toolbar button and then clicking Show Below the Ribbon.

1. At the right end of the Quick Access Toolbar, click the Customize Quick Access Toolbar button.
   By default, the Save, Undo, and Repeat buttons appear on the Quick Access Toolbar (See Figure 4.2).

4.2.9 Using Quick Access Icons by Ribbon Command

If you click the Save icon in the Quick Access toolbar, Word 2010 saves your current file. If you are saving a new file, a dialog box pops up, asking you to choose a name for your file. If you click the Print icon, it immediately prints your entire file through the default printer.

The Redo icon reverses the last Undo command you choose. For example, if you delete a paragraph, it disappears. Then if you immediately click the Undo icon, the paragraph reappears. If you immediately click the Redo icon, the Redo command reverses the Undo command and deletes the paragraph once more.

The Undo icon is unique. It offers two ways to use it. First, you can click the Undo icon to undo the last action you chose. Second, you can click the downward-pointing arrow that appears to the right of the Undo icon to display a list of one or more of your previous actions as shown in Figure 4.3.

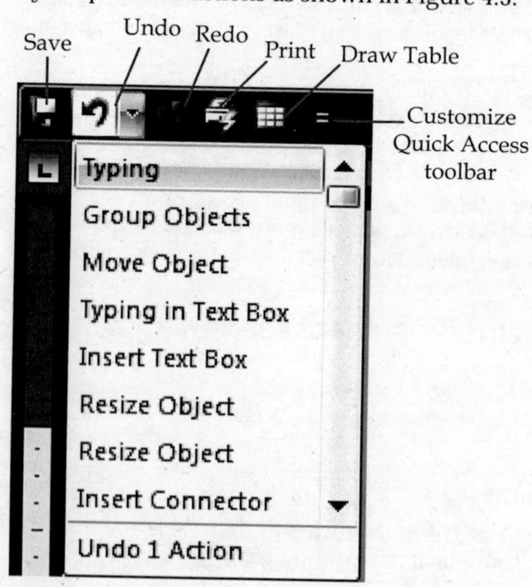

Figure 4.3 The Undo icon displays a list of actions

Rulers

The ruler helps you to control the margins, paragraph indentation, and tab settings for a document.

☞ The horizontal ruler is always displayed at the top of the document window. The vertical ruler is displayed only in the Page Layout view or in Print Preview.

Displaying or Hiding Rulers

Word 2010 gives you the flexibility to hide or display ruler according to your working needs.

➡ **To display the ruler, do this:**

1. On the View tab, in the Show group, select the Ruler check box (See Figure 4.4).
2. Horizontal and vertical rulers appear above and to the left of the page.

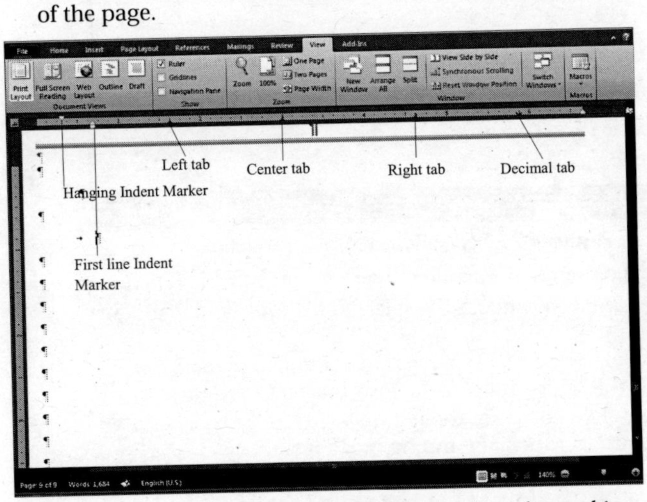

Figure 4.4 Word 2010 horizontal ruler including tabs marking

Reading the Horizontal Ruler

Margin settings are managed by the upward facing pointers at the bottom edge of the ruler. Dragging these pointers adjust the position of the right or left margin. However, if you drag these pointers, Word 2010 displays a vertical line showing the position of the margin in the document.

The paragraph indentation setting is managed by the downward-facing pointer at the top edge of the ruler. Dragging this pointer adjusts the indentation of the first line of a paragraph. However, if you drag the pointer, Word 2010 shows a vertical line so that you can see the exact position of the new indentation setting.

Note that you can adjust tab settings by double-clicking on the ruler. There are four types of tab with details given in Table 4.1.

Table 4.1 Different types of tab

Tab	Function
Left-aligned	Characters appear to the right of the tab as you type; indicated by an L-shaped angle in the box.
Centre-aligned	Characters are centred at the tab position; indicated by an angle with the vertical bar centred over the base line.
Right-aligned	Characters extend to the left of the tab as you type; indicated by a reverse L-shaped angle.
Decimal	The decimal point aligns with the tab position; indicated by the symbol for a centre-aligned tab with a decimal point to the right of the vertical member.

The Status Bar

The Status bar, seen at the bottom of Word 2010 Window shows information about the active document or the work you are processing.

Displaying Status Bar

The location of the insertion point is displayed on the status bar. By default, status bar tells you, which page the insertion point is on, but you can also display its location by section, line, and column and in inches from the top of the page. Simply right-click the status bar, and then click the option you want to display. After selecting the options, the screen appears as seen in Figure 4.5.

➡ **To hide the items on the status bar, do this:**

Right click the mouse on the Status Bar, Customize Status Bar pop-up menus appears. Select the options you want to hide the items in the Status bar.

Reading the Status Bar

The status bar shows the information about the text visible on the screen. Table 4.2 explains the message appearing in the status bar (See Figure 4.5).

Table 4.2 Message in the Status Bar

Message	Explanation
Page 6	You are in page 6 of the document.
Sec 1	In section 1 of the document.
Page 6 of 6	On page 6 of 6 pages in the document. This page number is based on the actual number of pages in the document, not on the printed page number.

(Contd...)

Figure 4.5 Word 2010 Status Bar elements

	If you have started numbering pages from a number other than 1, this will not match the printed page number.
At 8.4"	A line of text that is vertical position from the top of the page.
Line 6	The six line of the text on this page.
Word count	Number of words in the document.
Col 1	Beginning of the line character position within the line of the text.
Over/Insert	Indicates, overtype mode is on or off.
View tabs	Different view of the document.
Zoom	Click the Zoom slider. If you move Zoom In (i.e.+ icon) it moves to increases. If you move Zoom Out (i.e - icon) it moves to decrease.

4.2.10 Getting Help

You can use the Word Help system to get assistance on any Word topic or task. This system is a combination of tools and files that were stored on your computer when Word 2010 was installed. If your computer is connected to the Internet, you can also access resources from Office.com.

➡ **To get help, do this:**

1. Click the Word Help button located at the right end of the Ribbon. Or, press the F1 key. The Word Help window opens displaying a list of general help topics as shown in Figure 4.6.
2. Click any topic to display the corresponding information (See Figure 4.6).
3. To find help on a specific topic, type a word or phrase related to the topic in the Search box, and then press the Enter key. For example, we have type the word, such as SmartArt graphics in the Search box (See Figure 4.7).

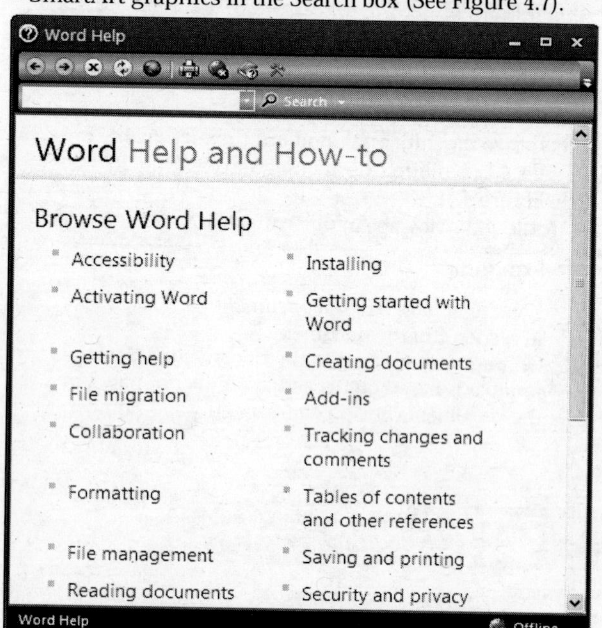

Figure 4.6 Word Help dialog box

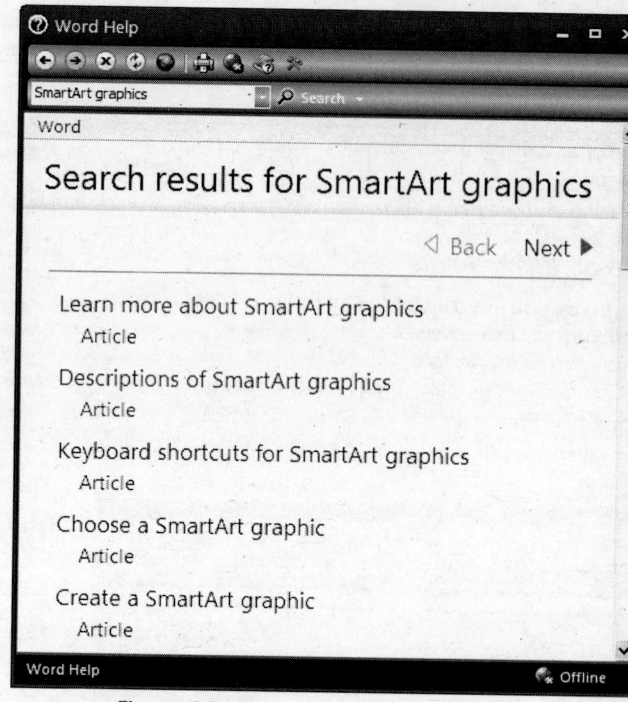

Figure 4.7 Type a word in the search box

4. The Help window displays a list of topics, i.e. searched for Alignment text. Choose the selected list topic you want (See Figure 4.7).
5. The Help window displays step-by-step explanations.
6. Click the Close button to close the Help window in the upper-right corner of the window.

➡ **To resize or reposition the help, do this:**

1. To resize the Help Window, move the pointer over a corner of the Help window until you see the double-headed arrow and then drag the corner until the window is of the size that you want it to be.
2. To move the Help window, move the pointer to the title bar and drag the window as you want to keep it.

4.3 OPENING AND CLOSING DOCUMENTS

4.3.1 Opening an Existing Documents

You can open Word document, can make modifications and save it with another name in different location.

➡ **To open an existing document, do this:**

1. Click the File tab, the Backstage view appears.
2. Click the Open tab. The Open dialog box appears as shown in Figure 4.8.
3. In the Look in: drop-down list choose the location of the file you want to open.
4. Click the drop-down triangle views button to change the way the folder and file list is displayed in the Table 4.3 below.

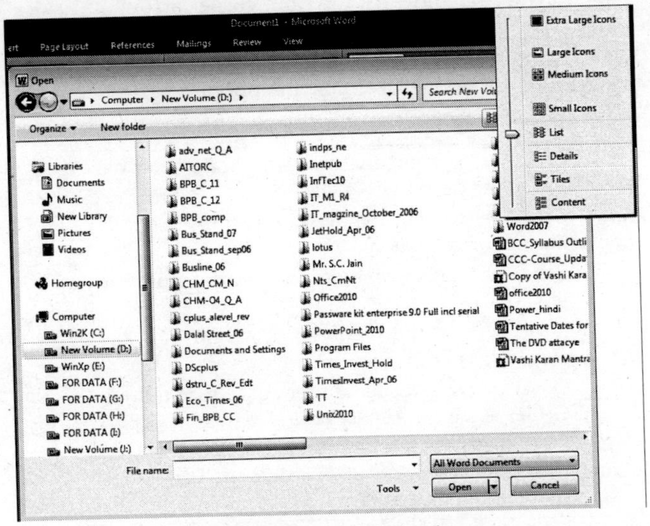

Figure 4.8 Open dialog box

Table 4.3 List Options of open dialog box

Button	Function
Thumbnails	It displays icons in Thumbnails. When you click a folder name, a thick highlighted border appear.
Tiles	It displays icons in medium size.
Icons	It displays icons in smaller size.
List	Displays a list of commands.
Details	Displays the details the size type, last modified, etc.
Properties	Displays the properties of the file.
Preview	Displays a preview of the file.

5. Select the document from the list, and then click the Open button.
6. The selected Word 2010 document is opened.

Moving around in a Document

Scroll through a document

You can scroll through a document by using the mouse or the keyboard. If you split the document window, you can see two different parts of a document.

Scrolling through a document by using the mouse

To	Do this
Scroll up one line	Click the up scroll arrow
Scroll down one line	Click the down scroll arrow
Scroll up one screen	Click above the scroll box
Scroll down one screen	Click below the scroll box
Scroll to a specific page	Drag the scroll box
Scroll left	Click the left scroll arrow
Scroll right	Click the right scroll arrow
Scroll left, beyond the margin, in normal view	Hold down Shift key and click the left scroll arrow

For a quick way to scroll up or down one page, click Select Browse Object on the vertical scroll bar, and then click the desired option (See Figure 4.2).

Typing and Editing a Document

You can start typing in a document without worrying about the end of the right margin. The words at the end of the line will automatically wrap text to the next line. You may correct the text by pressing Backspace key. The editing of documents is based on the windows principle, that is select and do.

4.3.2 Save and Save As

The first time you save a file, you need to specify three items:

1. The drive and folder in which you want to store your file.
2. The name of the file.
3. The format to save the file.

➡ **To save a document, do this:**

1. Click File tab and then select Save tab. Alternatively, choose the save button on the Quick Access toolbar.
2. When you save a document for the first time, Word 2010 displays the Save As... dialog box, so that you can type a name for the document (See Figure 4.9).
3. Click Save in: drop-down, to specify a drive and folder to save your file.
4. Click in the File name: text box and type a name of the file.
5. Click Save button.

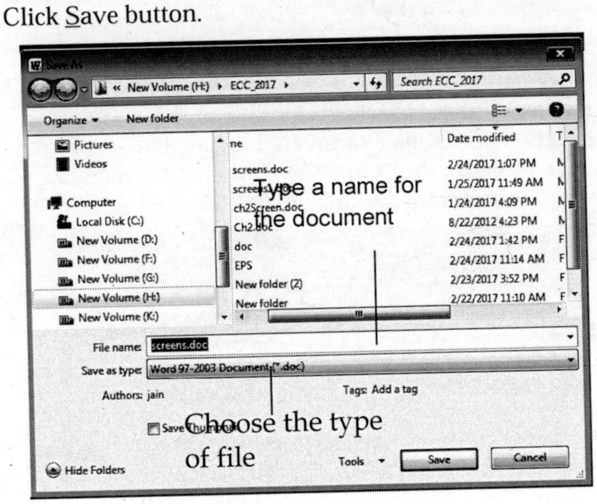

Figure 4.9 Save As dialog box

Naming a Document

In Windows, a filename can be from one to 255 characters along, followed by a period and upto three character filename extension. (In most cases, it is best to let Word supply the default extension for Word documents, which is .docx). You can use any characters except the following characters for naming the files:

* ? : [] + = \ / : / <>

You cannot use a period except to separate the filename from the extension.

4.3.3 Page Setup Options

Word 2010 default margins are 1 inch at the top and bottom each and 1 inch on the left and right. You can change the margins for the entire document or for different parts of the document (if you divide the document into sections).

Note that in Draft and Outline view, you do not see the margins. However, you can see the space between them in Print Layout view, and you can see the page as it will print. Always select the Print Layout view if you want to see headers, footers, page numbers, footnotes, etc.

You can also select one of the two types of page orientations namely, portrait (vertical) and landscape (horizontal). You can change the paper size and page orientation for a section or for the entire document.

☞ Indents are added to margin settings. That is, if you specify a 1.0" left margin and a 1/2" left indent, your text will print 1 1/2 from the left margin. If you set a 1.0" right margin and indent the right edge of a paragraph 1.0", the text will stop 2.0" from the right edge of the page (See Figure 4.10).

A page can have only one user-defined left margins setting and only one user-defined right margin setting, but each paragraph on the page can have different left and right indentation.

Setting Document Margins

There are two methods to set margins. These are:

- Page Setup command in the Page Layout tab.
- Adjust the margin using the rulers in the Print Layout View.

➡ **To set margins with the page setup command, do this:**

1. Select the sections for which you want to change margins. Alternatively, position the insertion point in the section whose margins you want to change.

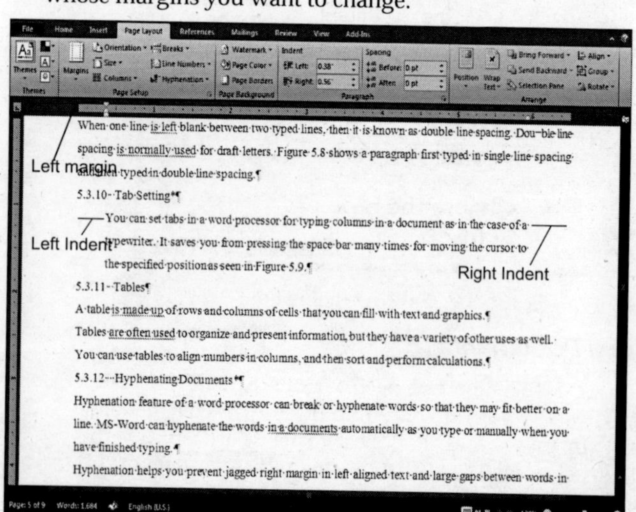

Figure 4.10 Page margins and indents

2. Click Page Layout tab and click the right corner arrow of Page setup. The Page Setup dialog box appears. Click the Margins tab property sheet as seen in Figure 4.11 appears.
3. Margins Property sheet has the following options:

Option	Description
Top:	Select or type out the desired margin from the top of the page.
Bottom:	Select or type out the desired margins from the bottom of the page.
Left:	Select or type out the desired margin from the left edge of the page.
Right:	Select or type out the desired margin from the right edge of the page.
Gutter:	Select or type out the gutter space as required. Gutter is the extra space added to the margins to leave the space for binding the documents.
Orientation	Select between Portrait (vertical) or Landscape (horizontal) page setting.

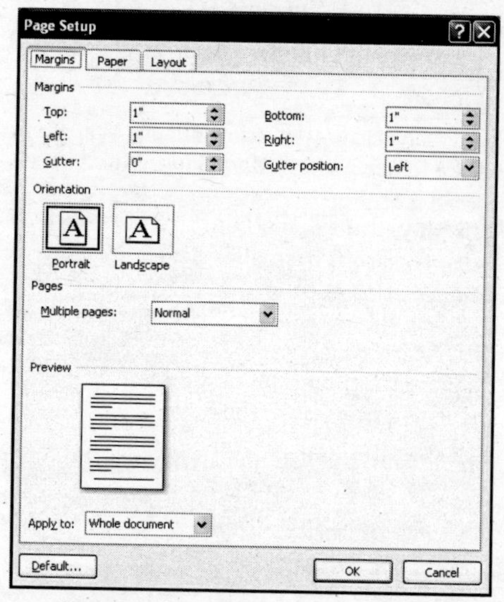

Figure 4.11 Page Setup dialog box

4. In the Pages area, select the Multiple pages: list.
   Mirror margins—This option adjusts left and right margins so that when you print on both sides of the page the inside and outside margins of the facing pages are of the same width.
   The Preview box displays the effect of the settings you select.
5. In the Apply to: choose the portion of the document from where you want to apply the new settings.
6. Click OK.

➡ **To set the margins using the ruler, do this:**

1. Switch to Print Layout view.
2. If the ruler is not displayed, click View tab. In the Show group, click the Ruler check box.

3. Point to the transition area on the ruler that is where gray becomes white.
4. The mouse pointer will become a two-headed arrow.
5. Drag the margin to the desired position with a mouse. The ruler's dimensions change as you drag (See Figure 4.12).

Paper Size

Page margins are usually set in according to paper size you use.

➡ **To select paper size, do this:**

1. Select the text, in the section you want to change.
2. In the Page Setup dialog box click Paper tab. The property sheet shown in Figure 4.13 appears.

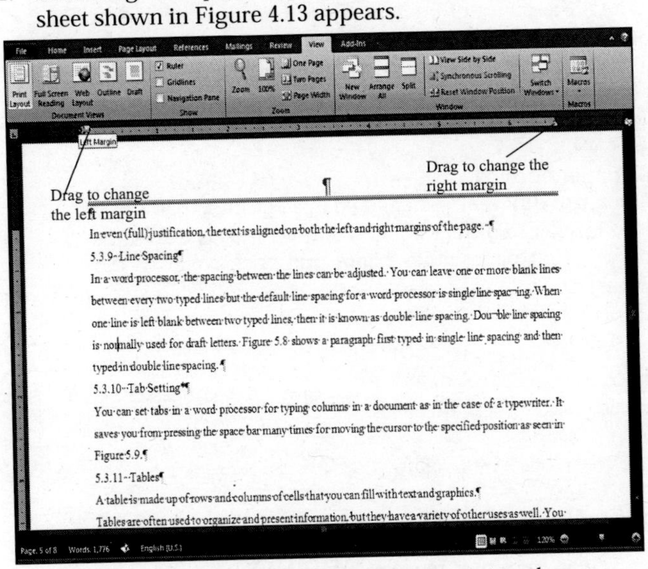

Figure 4.12 Drag ruler ends in print Layout to change the margins

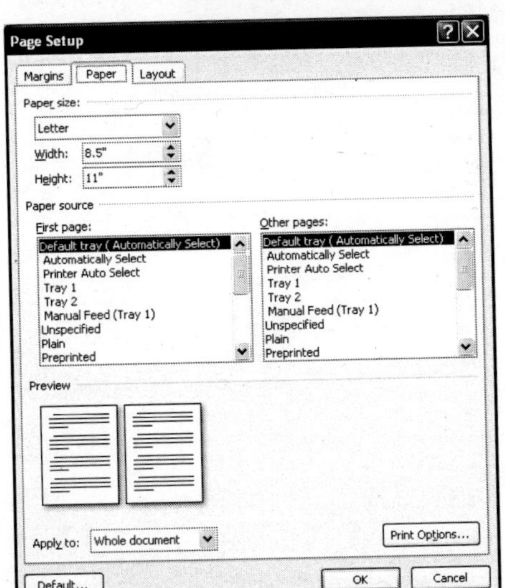

Figure 4.13 Paper size property sheet tab

3. The Page Setup dialog box has the following options:

Option	Function
Paper size:	The list in the form of drop-down offers different standard paper size. Select from the standard sizes or specify the width and height as the case may be. The commonly used paper size is A4 and legal.
Width:	Type or select the width of the paper you are using.
Height:	Type or select the height of the paper you are using.

4. In the Apply to: select the portion of the document you want to print on the selected paper size.
5. Click the Default... buttons if you want to save these settings as default settings, so that they can apply to all pages printed hereafter.
6. Click OK.

4.3.4 Previewing and Printing a Document

When you are ready to print a document, you can click the File tab, point to print. The Backstage view appears then click Print icon. Word then uses your computer's default printer and the settings specified in the Print Backstage view. You can also to use a different printer or change the printer settings on the File tab Backstage view. You can then specify which printer to use, what to print, and how many copies. You can also make other changes to the settings.

☞ Before you print a document, you may want to check how it will look on paper by previewing it. Previewing is essential for multi-page documents but is helpful even for one-page documents also.

Setting Printer Properties Options

Windows manages details of setting up a printer. However, Windows leaves three tasks for you:

- Selecting the printer you want to use in Word 2010.
- Installing the printers if not available in the list of Windows printers.
- Changing the printer setup for special printing needs.

☞ Most of the printer options are set by Word 2010 depends upon the printer selected by you. In this, many options are available to you so that you can customize the printing options as per your requirement.

➡ **To set printer specific options, do this:**

1. Click the File tab, the Backstage view appears as shown in Figure 4.14.
2. Under the Printer drop-down list select the printer.
3. Click the Printer Properties in the File Backstage view as shown in Figure 4.14.
4. The Printer Properties dialog box appears as shown in Figure 4.15.

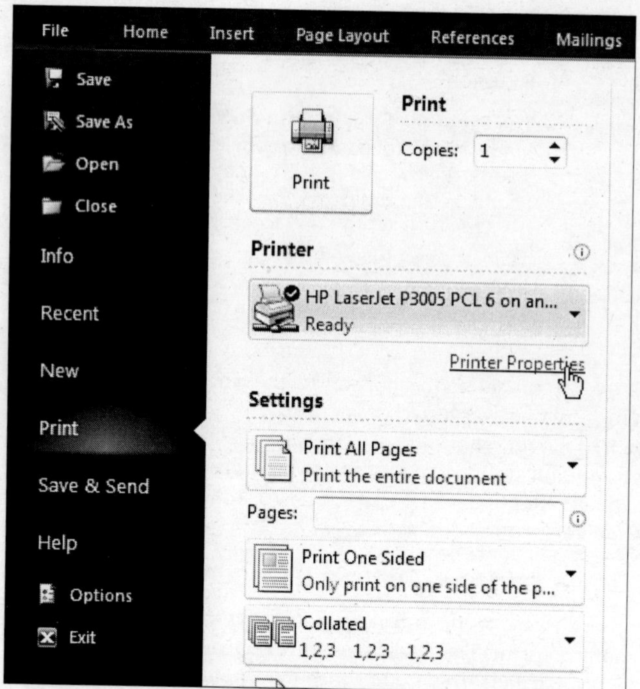

Figure 4.14 Selecting Printer Properties in the File tab

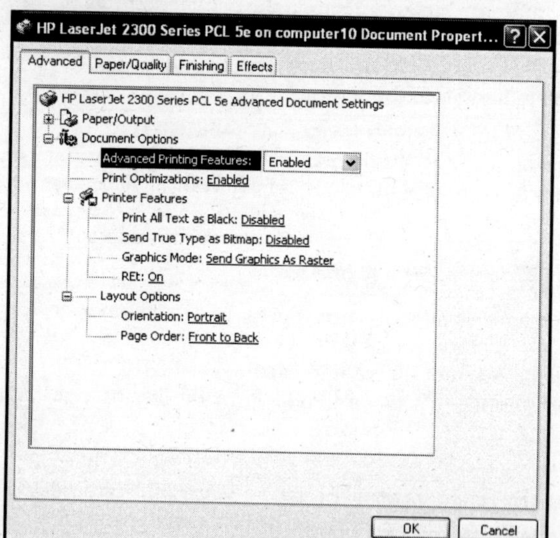

Figure 4.15 Selecting Printer Properties dialog box

5. The Properties dialog box generally has the following tabs.

Tab	Options
Advanced	Additional features, such as page protection, copies, paper size and postscript options may be found on the Advanced tab.

(Contd...)

Tab	Options
Paper/ Quality	Sets the option for the paper and the quality of printing.
Finishing	Select the quality of printing that you desire. This options can vary from printer to printer.
Effects	It shows prints of your document on a paper size that is different from the one for which it is formatted. It also specifies the percentage of normal size.

6. Click the Advanced tab. The options are:
   In the page order section
   - If you choose Front to Back, it specifies the order in which the pages of your document will be printed. It starts printing from page 1 to end.
   - If you choose Back to Front, it prints the document from end to first page.
7. Click the Paper/Quality tab as shown in Figure 4.16 the options are:
   In the paper options
   - Click use different paper to enable settings that allow you to select a different paper source and type settings for the first page, other pages and back cover in the print job.
   - Source is: click the drop-down list and choose the desired option where the paper is located in the printer.
   - Type is: select the kind of paper you want to use.
8. Click OK.
9. In the Print dialog box, again click OK.

Printing the Current Document

The simplest way to print is to open a document, click File tab,

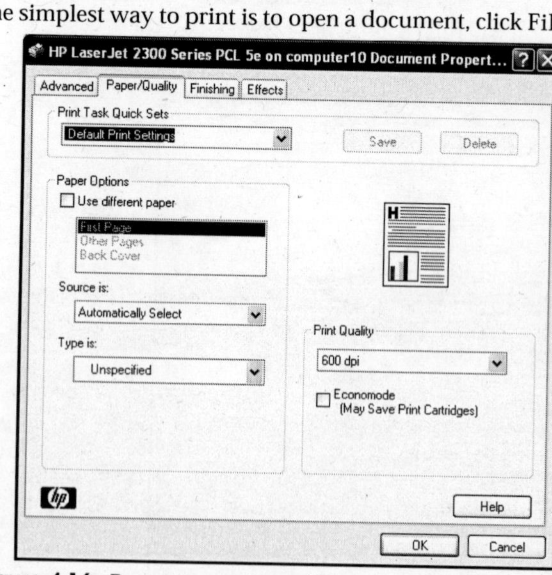

Figure 4.16 Properties options of Paper/Quality tab property sheet

choose Print tab. The Backstage view appears choose Print icon. Alternately, click the Print button on the Quick Access toolbar. By default, Word 2010 prints one copy of all pages of the currently open document on the selected printer without printing hidden text.

➡ **To print a copy of the document, do this:**

1. Open the document you want to print.
2. Click the File tab and then choose Print command. The Print backstage view appears then click Print icon or press Ctrl + Shift + F12 keys together (See Figure 4.17).
3. The Print Backstage view closes and in the status bar displays the process of the print job (Figure 4.18).

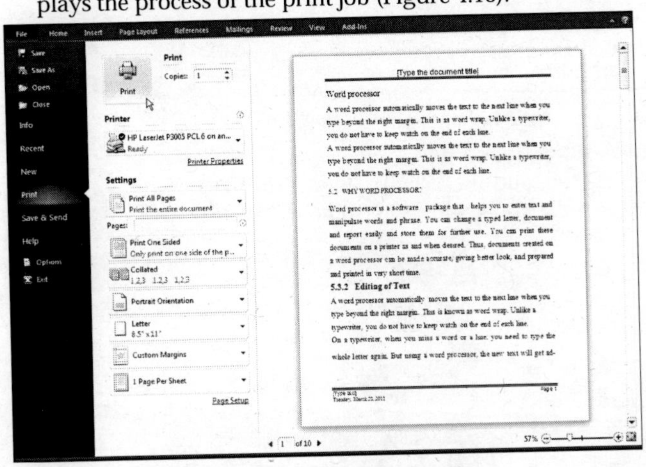

Figure 4.17 Print Backstage view

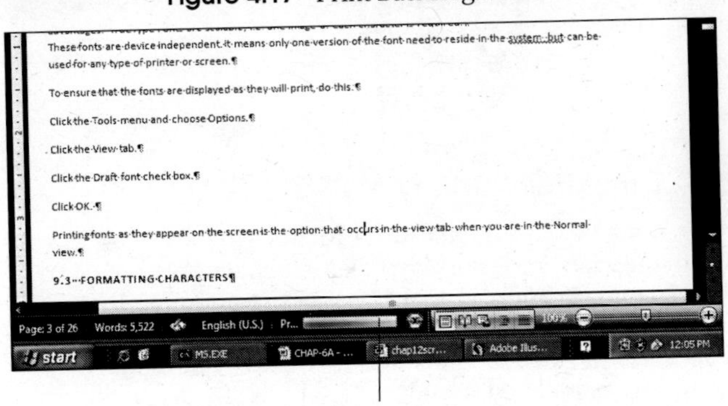

The process of print job in the status bar

Figure 4.18 Displaying the print process in the status bar

Page Range Options

- To print the entire document, click All button.
- To print just the page in your document currently containing the insertion point, click on the Print Current Page button.
- To print the selected text, first select it, then in the Print dialog box, use the Selection button in the Page Range area. This choice will be dimmed unless you have selected something in your document.
- To print a range of pages, say, pages 6-10 in a 50 page document, type the first page number and the last desired page number in the Pages: text box. Separate the numbers with hyphens (like 6-10).
- You can also print pages in a certain section. To print the second section in your document, type s2 in the Pages box. If you want to print from page 7 in the second section to page 10 in the third section, type p7s2-p10s3 in the Pages box.
- The Print: drop-down list has the following option which allows you to select the pages you want to print.

Option	Description
All pages	This is the default option and Word 2010 prints all pages in the range.
Odd pages	This option when selected prints the odd numbered pages in the range.
Even pages	This option when selected prints the even numbered pages in the range.

Odd and Even pages option is very useful when you want to do double-sided printing.

Copies: In the number of Copies: box, specify the number of copies of the document you want to print.

Collate: This option determines how multiple copies are printed. Say, you print five copies of a 10-page document without the Collate option, Word 2010 will first print all five copies of page 1 then all five copies of page 2 and so on. You will need to arrange them manually to make the sets. With the Collate option Word 2010 prints five sets, each one complete and in order.

➡ **To cancel printing, do this:**

1. Click the Start button and then click Printers and Faxes.

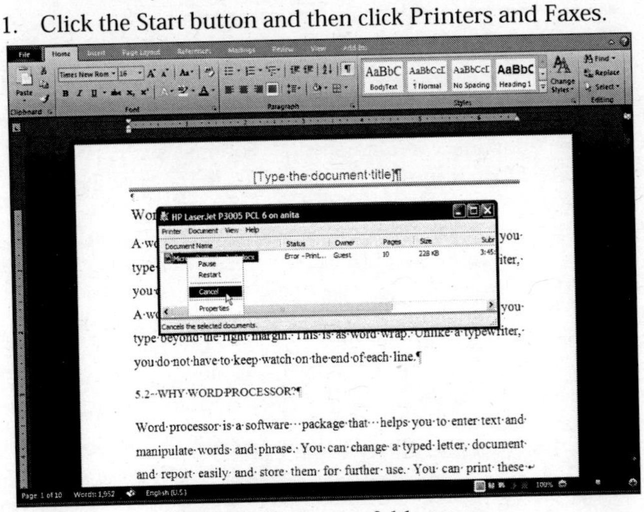

Figure 4.19 Printer folder open

2. In the Printers and Faxes dialog box, open the printer that you are using by double-clicking the printer's icon (See Figure 4.19).

3. Select the document of which you want to cancel printing, and then choose Document Name, right click and choose Cancel Printing.

Previewing a Document

Previewing a document allows you to visualize the document in its printable format before actually executing the Print command. The preview of a document displays the document in a printable format and shows how the document will appear after taking a printout.

➡ **To preview the document, do this:**

1. Open the document whose print preview you want to view.
2. Click the File tab and then choose Print option from the File tab. The Print options are visible in the Backstage view as shown in Figure 4.20.

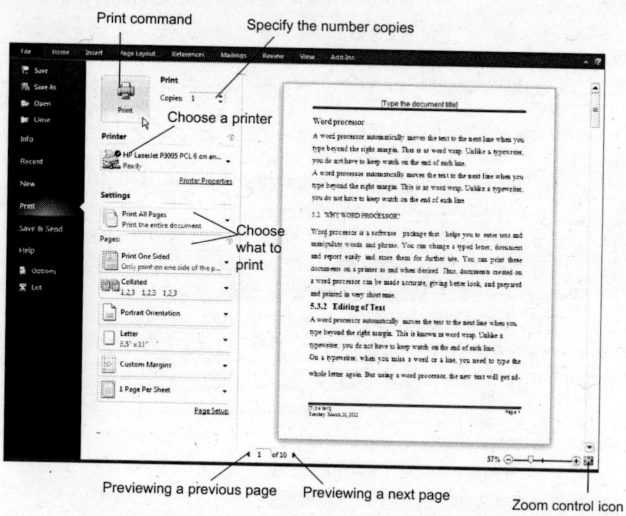

Figure 4.20 Print preview in the Backstage view

3. The Backstage view (See Figure 4.20) consists of three panes. The left pane contains several options, such as Save, Save As, Open, Close, Info, Recent, etc. In the middle pane, print options and its related printer settings are shown. In the right pane, the preview document is seen. In the bottom of the right pane, the Zoom control button is available. The + (plus) button is used to increase the document and the – (minus) button is used to decrease the preview document. The Next button goes to next page of document and the previous button to move to the previous page of document.

4.3.5 Closing and Quitting Word 2010

After finishing a document, you should close the window to remove it from the screen and to free computer's main memory.

➡ **To close a document and exit Word 2010, do this:**

1. Click the File tab, and then choose Close tab.
2. The window closes if no changes have been made to the document since the last save. However, if you made changes since the last time you saved the document, Word 2010 displays an Alert dialog box, asking whether you want to save your work before closing (See Figure 4.21).
3. After you have saved the contents of the document, the window is closed.

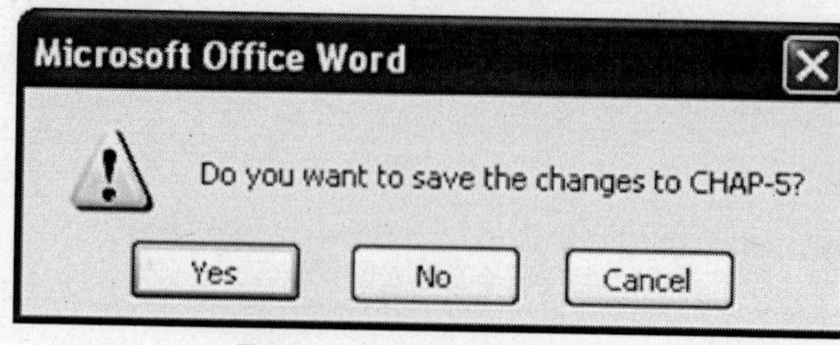

Figure 4.21 Alert dialog box

➡ **To quit Word 2010, do this:**

1. Click File tab, and then choose Exit. Word 2010 window closes, and the application is terminated (See Figure 4.22).

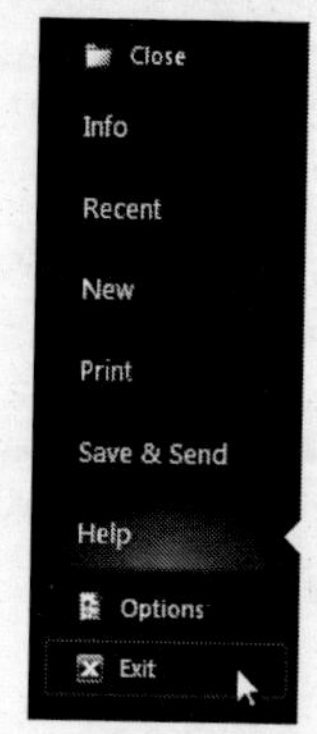

Figure 4.22 Selecting Exit from the File tab

4.4 TEXT CREATION and MANIPULATION

When you open a new document in Word 2010, the insertion point is at the top left corner of the screen. You can start typing in this document. You can make changes at any time by editing the document.

You can click the Show/Hide button on the Paragraph group to display or hide all non-printing characters, such as paragraph marks, tab characters, and spaces. These characters are not printed, even if they are shown on the screen (See Figure 4.23).

4.4.1 Creating a Blank Document

If you are creating a document, such as memo, letter, report, or resume, Brochures, Calendars, Card, etc., you can save time by using one of the wizards or templates that come with Word 2010.

You can also create a blank document which is based on the blank template of Word 2010. The blank template offers you the flexibility to create and edit documents according to your requirements.

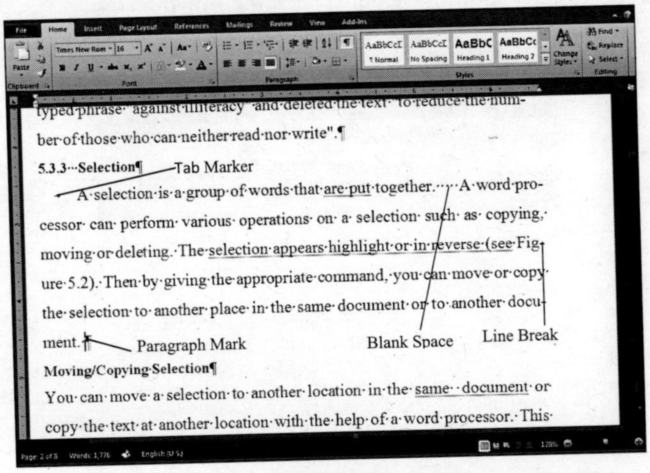

Figure 4.23 A screen displaying non-printing characters

➡ **To create a new document, do this:**

1. Click File tab, a Backstage view appears, click the New tab in the Backstage view as shown in Figure 4.24.
2. Select the Blank document option under Available templates as shown in Figure 4.24.
3. Click the Create button as seen in Figure 4.24. The new blank document is created as seen in Figure 4.25.

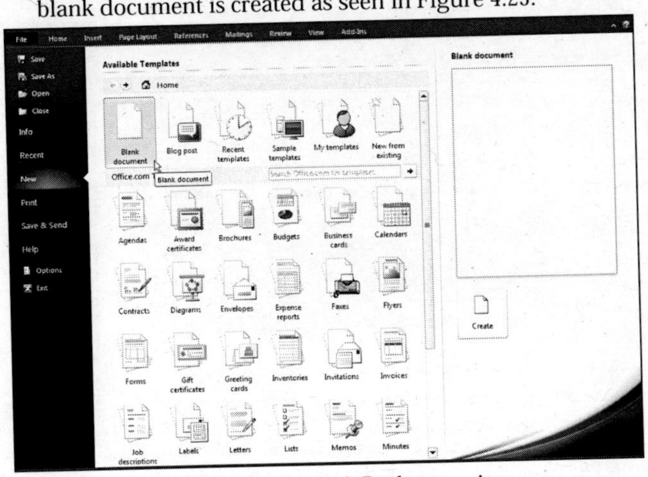

Figure 4.24 New tab Backstage view

Starting a New Paragraph

In Word 2010, a paragraph is any amount of text or graphics followed by a paragraph mark. A paragraph ends whenever you press the Enter key. Even if you have not typed any text but press Enter key, Word 2010 inserts a paragraph mark ( ). In Word 2010, many types of formatting (for example, justification and line spacing) are applied to paragraphs as a whole.

➡ **To start a new paragraph, do this:**

1. Place the insertion point where you want to start the new paragraph, and press the Enter key.

When you press Enter key, Word 2010 inserts a paragraph mark and moves the insertion point to the first line of the new paragraph.

Figure 4.25 Word blank document

Starting a New Line

Word 2010 automatically wraps text to the next line when the typed text reaches the end of the right margin.

➡ **To start a new line within the same paragraph, do this:**

1. Position the insertion point where you want to start the new line, and then press Shift + Enter keys together.
2. Word inserts a line break character and moves the insertion point to the beginning of the next line.
3. To see the line breaks, click the Show/Hide command on the paragraph group of Home tab.

4.4.2 Editing Text

On a typewriter, when you miss a word or a line, you need to type the whole letter again. But using a Word 2010, you can insert new words, new sentences or paragraphs anywhere in the text typed earlier. The new text will get adjusted automatically.

Similarly, you can delete any portion of the text and the remaining part of the matter will get adjusted automatically.

In Figure 4.26, you can see the highlighted text is newly inserted and rest of the text gets deleted.

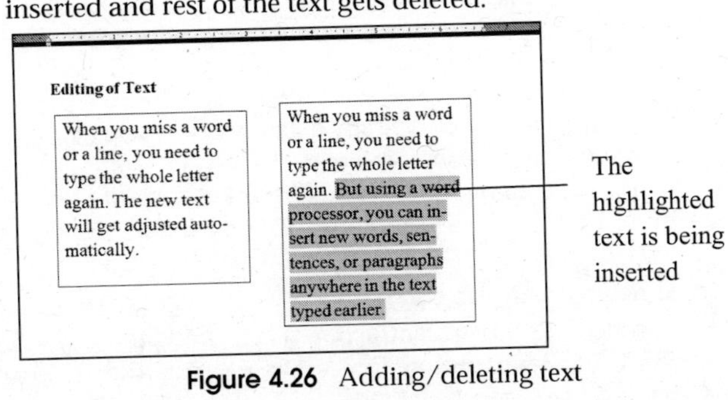

Figure 4.26 Adding/deleting text

Inserting Text

If you notice that some text has been left out of the document, you can move the Insertion pointer to that position and type it in. This method is called Inserting.

Typing over the Existing Text

By default, Word moves the existing text to the right as you insert new characters. If you want the new text to replace the existing text, character by character, switch to overtype mode. Again clicking the overtype mode in the status bar will automatically replace the insert mode.

➡ **To type over the existing text, do this:**

1. Click the File tab and then choose Options.
2. The Word Options dialog box, click Advanced tab in the left pane and then under Editing options, select use the Insert key to control overtype mode check box.
3. Click OK.

Applying Corrections in the Typed Text

To correct simple typing mistakes, press Backspace or Del keys. To delete more characters, first select the text you want to delete and then press the Backspace or Del key. Table 4.4 lists different methods for deleting texts and graphics.

Table 4.4 Key Combinations for deleting Text or Graphics

To delete	Key combination
Selected text	Press Backspace or Del
Characters before the insertion point	Press Backspace key
Characters after the insertion point	Press Del key
A word before the insertion point	Ctrl + Backspace
A word after the insertion point	Ctrl + Del

➡ **To restore the deleted text, do this:**

1. On the Quick Access toolbar, click the Undo button. Alternatively, click the Ctrl + Z keys together.

➡ **To replace a selection with a new text, do this:**

1. Select the text you want to replace.
2. Type the new text.

The text you type replaces the entire selection.

Undoing Mistakes

If you make a mistake in Word 2010, you can apply "Undo" command. For example, if you accidentally delete a word, you can bring it back with the Undo command. To reverse the action of undo use the "Redo" command. There are certain actions you cannot undo, such as saving or printing a document.

➡ **To undo or redo changes do this:**

1. To undo or redo the most recent action, click the Undo (press Ctrl + Z) or Redo button (press Ctrl + Y) on the Quick Access toolbar.
2. To undo or redo multiple actions, click the down arrow next to either the Undo or the Redo button, and then select the actions you want to undo or redo (See Figure 4.27).

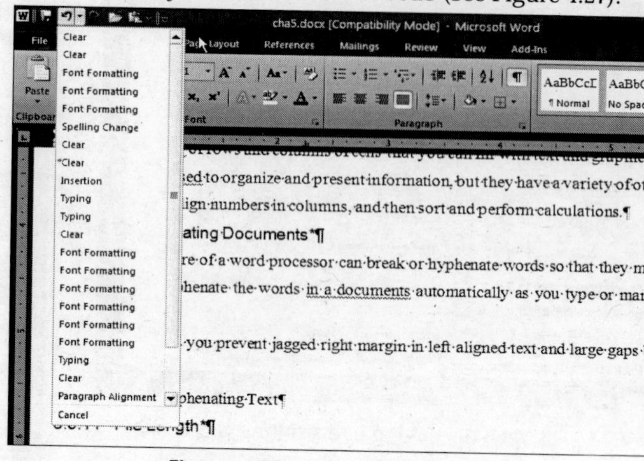

Figure 4.27 Selecting undo list

Select the Text with the Pop-up Toolbar

Word 2010 displays a pop-up toolbar. For example, select the text on which you want to apply formatting, such as bold, font size, etc., a pop-up toolbar appears to the upper right of the selected text as a faint image. The closer you move the mouse towards this pop-up toolbar, the darker and sharper the toolbar appears as seen in Figure 4.28.

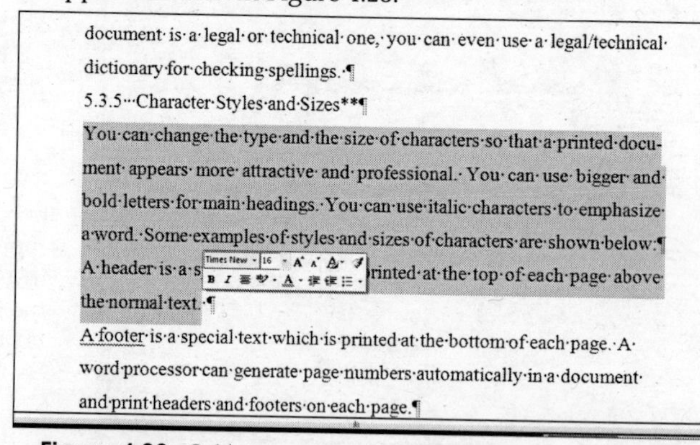

Figure 4.28 Selecting text and displaying pop-up toolbar

Displaying Different Views of a Document

The type of work that you do will help you to determine the best screen view as per your needs. There are different views available in Word 2010. These are:

- Print Layout View
- Full screen Reading View
- Web Layout View
- Outline View
- Draft View

There are two ways so that you can change the view. These are:

- Click the View tab, in the Document views group, and switch to any view you wish to see the document.
- Click view buttons that are found on the right side of the status bar (See Figure 4.29).

Editing text in Print Layout View

This is the default view. Print Layout view is used to see how text, graphics and other elements, such as header, footer, etc., will look on the printed output. This view is useful for editing headers and footers, for adjusting margins and for working with columns and drawing objects.

➡ **To work in Print Layout view, do this:**

1. Click the View tab, in the Document views group and click Print Layout command. Alternatively click from the status bar icons (Figure 4.29).

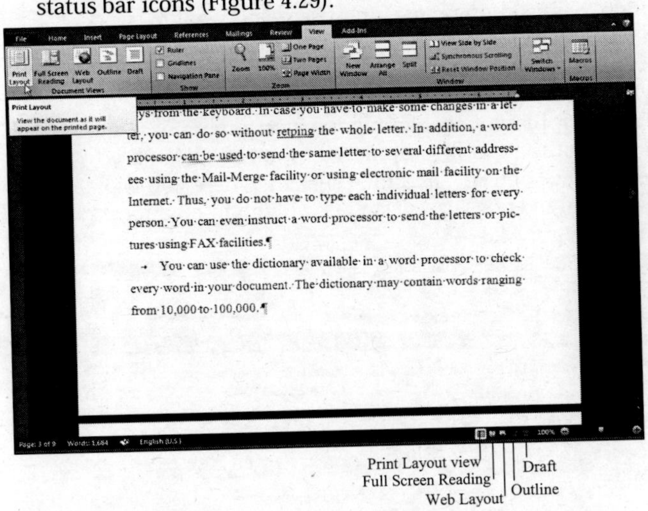

Figure 4.29 Editing a document in Print Layout view

Editing text in Full Screen Reading View

Full screen view displays as much of the typing area of the document as will fit on the screen at a size which is comfortable for reading. In this view, the Ribbon is replaced by a single toolbar at the top of the screen. You can print the document, highlight text and write comments. You can also move from page to page and adjust the view.

➡ **To switch to full screen view, do this:**

1. Click the View tab, in the Document Views group and click Full Screen Reading command as in Figure 4.29. Alternatively, click Full Screen reading from the status bar icons.
2. In Full reading screen, click the View Options, a drop-down menu appears. You can make the text larger or smaller for reading by clicking Increase Text Size or Decrease Text Size. This will temporarily change as to fits text on a page. It does not affect the original document.
3. You can read one page at a time by clicking Show one page, or you can read two pages at a time by clicking Show Two pages.
4. While reading in full screen view, you can edit document by clicking Allow Typing.
5. To go to the previous screen or to the next screen, click jump to a screen at the top of the title bar in the full screen view (See Figure 4.30).
6. To exit Full Screen Reading view, click Esc button or click Print Layout button.

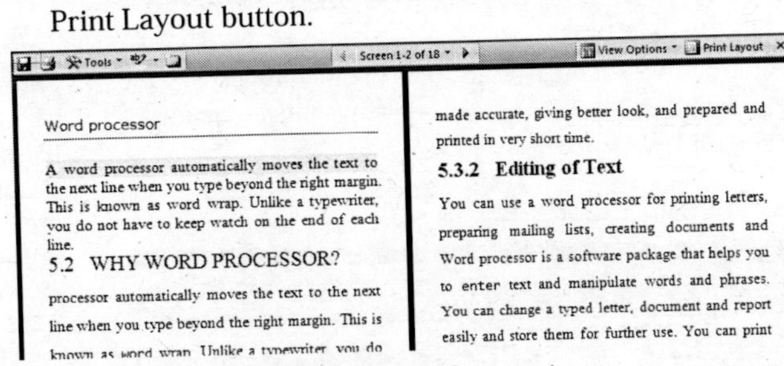

Figure 4.30 Full Screen view

Editing in Web Layout View

While creating a Web page in Word 2010, you should work in Web Layout view. In Web Layout view, you can see that background text is wrapped to fit the window. Graphics are positioned at proper places, so that the page will look just as it would look in a Web browser (See Figure 4.31).

➡ **To switch to Web Layout view, do this:**

Click the View tab, in the Document views group and click Web Layout view command as in Figure 4.31. Alternatively, click Web layout from the status bar icons.

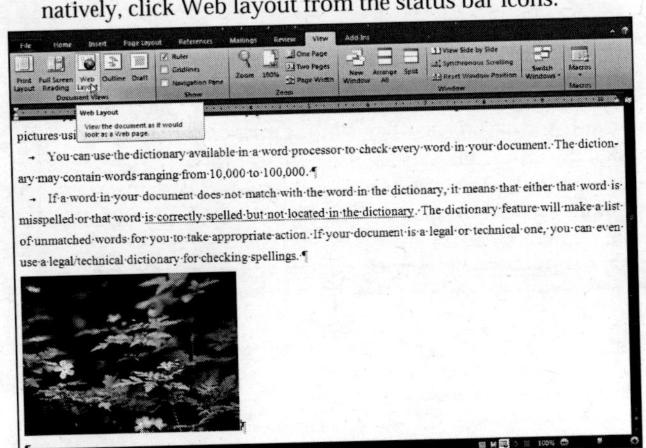

Figure 4.31 Document seen in Web layout view

Editing text in Outline View

In the Outline View, you can collapse a document to see only the main headings or expand it to see the entire document. In this view it is easy to scroll or move text to a longer distance or to change the hierarchy of topics (See Figure 4.32).

➡ **To switch to Outline View, do this:**

1. Click the View tab, in the Document views group and click Outline view command as in Figure 4.31. Alternatively, click Outline view from the status bar icons.

In the outline view, the outline toolbar appears as seen in Figure 4.32. Word 2010 indents the formatting headings and body text paragraphs to different levels. Note that (+) or (–) sign appears to the left of each heading.

- A plus sign (+) indicates that sub-heading or paragraphs of the body text are associated with the heading.
- A minus sign (–) indicates that no headings or paragraphs are beneath the heading.

☞ In the outline view you will also get the options of viewing headings at different levels or of viewing entire document, including the body text.

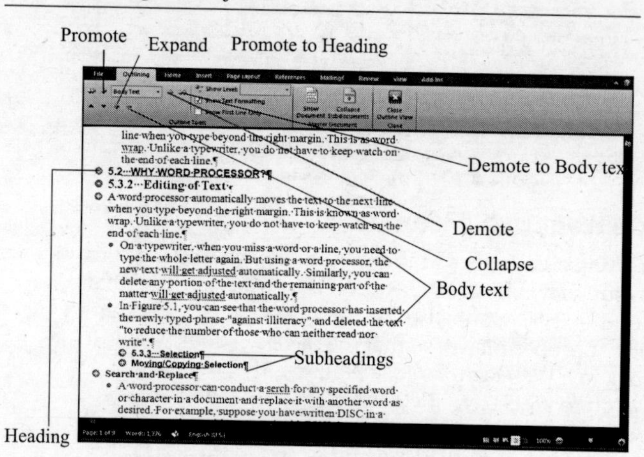

Figure 4.32 Document in Outline view

Editing in Draft View

Draft view is the best view as most of your typing and editing as can be seen (Figure 4.33). In this view, you can see character and paragraph formatting as they will be printed. Line and page breaks, tab stops and alignments are accurate. The area outside the text body–the area containing headers, footers, footnotes, page numbers, margin spacing, etc., do not appear. Images are also not shown in Draft view.

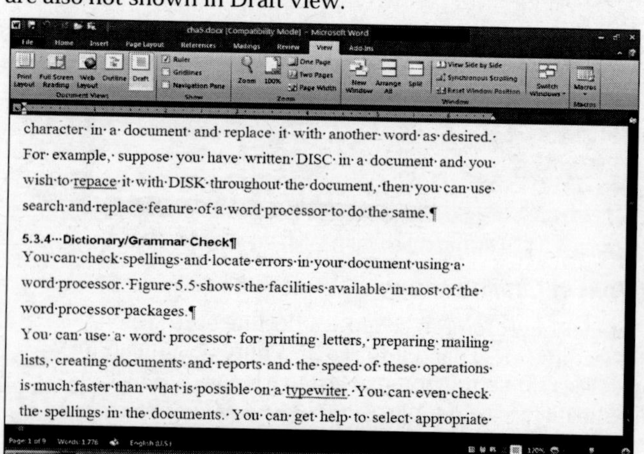

Figure 4.33 Document in Draft view

➡ **To switch to Draft view, do this:**

1. Click the View tab, in the Document views group and click Draft view command as in Figure 4.33. Alternatively, click Draft view from the status bar icons.

☞ Note that the cursor movement is very fast in Draft view.

4.4.3 Text Selection

Before you can move, format, delete, or change text or a graphic picture, you must select the items. You can select the item using a mouse or keyboard. Note that the selected text or graphics are highlighted. To cancel the selection, click outside the selection, or use the arrow keys to move the insertion point.

➡ **To select text, do this:**

1. Position the insertion point from where you want to select the text.
2. Now press the left mouse button and select the text by moving mouse pointer. Alternatively, you can also select text and graphics by positioning the insertion point at the beginning of the text or graphic you want to select, holding down the Shift key, and then clicking where you want the selection to end. The selected text highlighted appears as seen in Figure 4.34.

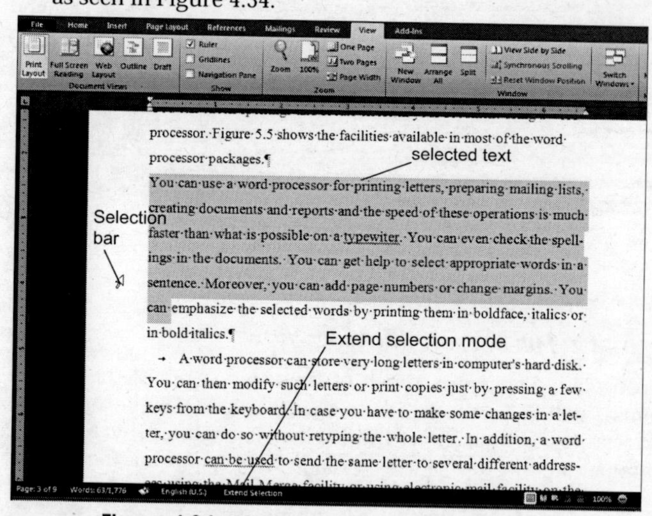

Figure 4.34 Using selection bar to select text

☞ Always select the text first which you want to modify before doing any font format.

Selecting Text with a Mouse

You can select a piece of text, or a single character or an entire document. You can also combine mouse and keyboard selection techniques.

➡ **To select a small amount of text with the mouse, do this:**

1. Click and hold the mouse button at the beginning of the text you want to select.

2. Drag the pointer in any direction across the text you want to select.

☞ If the pointer touches the edge of the window as you are dragging, the window scrolls in that direction if more text exists.

You can select text by using one of the methods given in Table 4.5.

Table 4.5 Method for Selecting Text

Text to select	Mouse Action
A word	Double-click the word.
A line	Click selection bar (blank margin to left of a line of text).
Multiple lines	Click selection bar and drag up or down till the end of lines.
A paragraph	Double-click selection bar.
Document	Press Ctrl key and click in selection bar.
Rectangular block or column (not within a table)	Click the top left of the column to be selected and then hold Alt key while you drag to select the text.

Selecting Text with a Keyboard

The method for selecting text is to hold down the Shift key as you move the insertion point. You can select text by using Shift key in combination with any move key. Some of these key combinations are listed in Table 4.6.

Table 4.6 Key Combination for Selecting Text

To Select	Press
A word	Shift + Ctrl + ← or → arrow key
To the beginning of a line	Shift + Home
To the end of a line	Shift + End
To the end of a paragraph	Ctrl + Shift + ↓
To the beginning of a paragraph	Ctrl + Shift + ↑
One line at a time	Shift + ↑ or Shift + ↓
To the beginning of a document	Shift + Ctrl + Home
To the end of a document	Shift + Ctrl + End

➡ **To select from the insertion point to a distant location, do this:**

1. Move the insertion point to the beginning of the text you want to select.
2. Press F8 (Extend Selection).

☞ While you are in Extend Selection mode, the word appears on the status bar at the bottom of the screen.

3. Press one of the keys listed in the Table 4.7. And finally press Esc key.

Table 4.7 Selecting Text from the Insertion Point

To Select	Press
Next or previous character	← or → arrow key
The end of a line	End key
The beginning of a line	Home key
The top of the previous screen	PgUp key
The bottom of the next screen	PgDn key
The beginning of a document	Ctrl + Home keys
The end of a document	Ctrl + End keys

4.4.4 Cut, Copy and Paste

"Copying" means to make a copy of the selected text or graphic and insert it in another location, leaving the original document unchanged.

➡ **To copy text from one location to another in the same document, do this:**

1. Select the text you want to copy.
2. Click Copy option from the Clipboard group. The selected text will be placed on the Clipboard which is an accessory in Word (see Figure 4.35).
3. Now position the insertion point at the location you want to place the text.

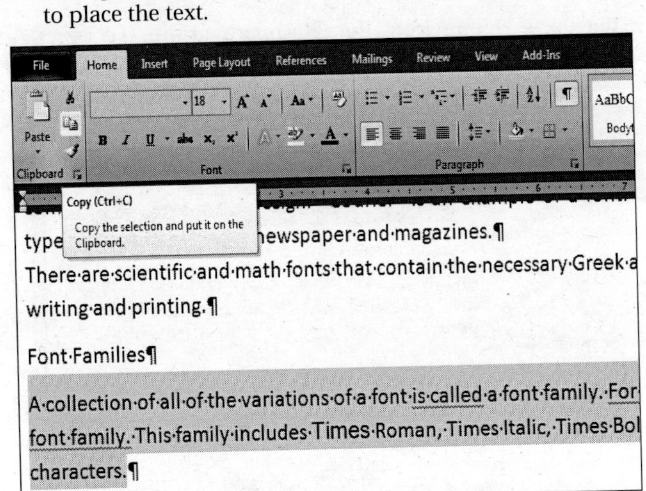

Figure 4.35 Select the text to be copied

4. Click the Paste option from the Clipboard group as shown in Figure 4.36. The selected text will be pasted.

Moving Text

"Moving" means to remove (cut) the selected text or graphic from one location and insert it in another location in the same document in another document.

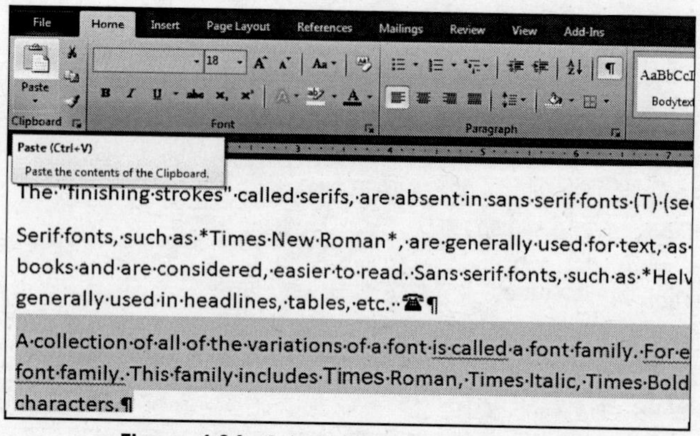

Figure 4.36 Selected text has been pasted

➡ **To move text from one location to another in the same document, do this:**

1. Select the text you want to move (See Figure 4.37).
2. Click the Cut option from the Clipboard group. The selected text will disappear from the screen and will be placed on the Clipboard.
3. Now position the insertion point at the location you want to paste the text.
4. Click the Paste option from the Clipboard group. The selected text will be moved (See Figure 4.38).

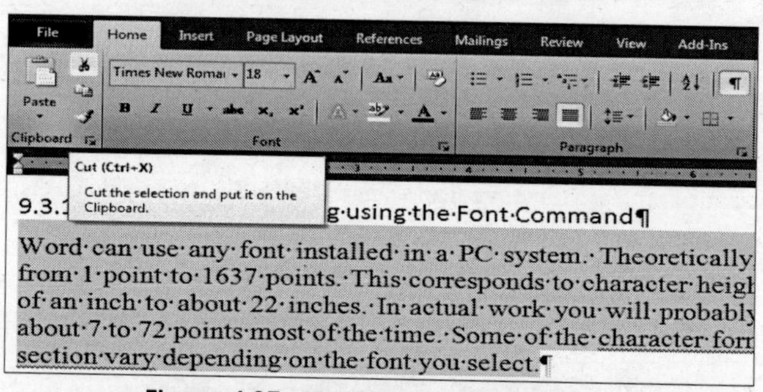

Figure 4.37 Highlight the text to move

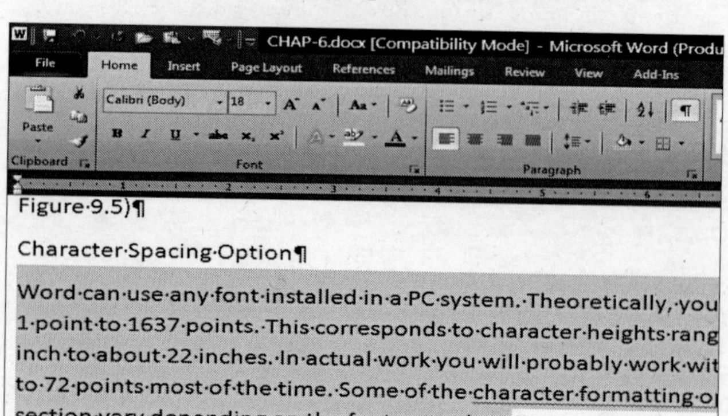

Figure 4.38 Highlighted text pasted in the new location

Moving and Copying using Drag and Drop Technique

Drag-and-drop editing is an easy way to move or copy a selection with in a short distance of a document. You can drag and drop items between documents. However, to move or copy a selection to a longer distance in a document or to a different document, you should use the Cut (Ctrl+X) Copy (Ctrl+C), and Paste (Ctrl+V) commands.

➡ **To move text using drag-and-drop editing, do this:**

1. Select the text or the graphics you want to move.
2. Point to the selected text or graphics, and then press and hold down the left mouse button. When the drag-and-drop pointer appears as in Figure 4.39, drag the dotted insertion point to the new location.
3. Release the mouse button to drop the text into desired place.

➡ **To copy text/graphics using drag-and-drop editing, do this:**

1. Select the text or the graphics you want to copy.
2. Press and hold down Ctrl key, point to the selected text or the graphics, and then press and hold down the left mouse button while you drag the dotted insertion point to the new location.

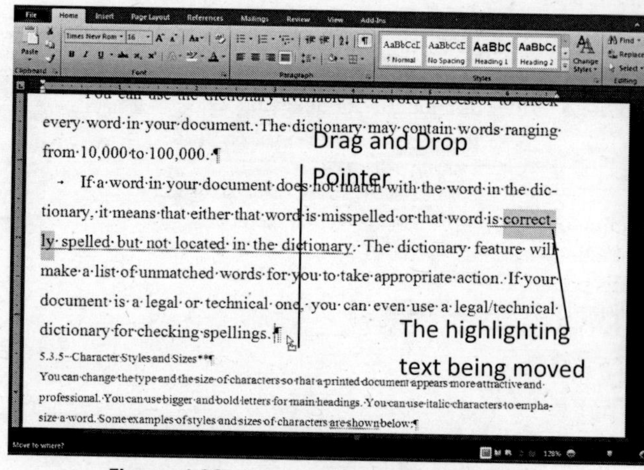

Figure 4.39 Drag and Drop mouse pointer

➡ **To move or copy the text/graphics using the toolbar, do this:**

1. Select the text or the graphics you want to move or copy.
2. Do one of the following:
   - To move the selection, click the Cut button on the Home tab of Clipboard group.
   - To copy the selection, click the Copy button on the Home tab of Clipboard group.

   Word places the selected text to the Clipboard.
3. Place the insertion point in the new location, where you want to insert the new text or the graphics. Now click the paste command on the Home tab of Clipboard group. Selected text/graphic will be pasted.

Using Keyboard Shortcuts for Moving and Copying

Word 2010 has many keyboard shortcuts, i.e., combination of keys for moving and copying text and graphics. Table 4.8 lists different methods for cutting, copying and moving text or graphics using the keyboard shortcuts.

Table 4.8 Keyboard Shortcuts for Moving and Copying Text or Graphics

Action	Key combination
Copy the selected text or the graphics to the Clipboard	Ctrl+C keys pressed together.
Move the selected text or the graphics to the Clipboard	Ctrl+X or Shift+Del keys pressed together.
Paste Clipboard contents into a document	Ctrl+V or Shift+Ins keys pressed together.
Move a paragraph up	Alt+Shift + ↑ arrow keys pressed together.
Move a paragraph down	Alt+Shift + ↓ arrow keys pressed together.

Deleting Text

To Delete characters to the right of insertion point press Del key but to delete characters to left of insertion point use Backspace key. However, when you have to delete number of lines, deleting one letter at a time becomes a lengthy process. It would be better if you select or highlight all the lines to be deleted as a block.

➡ **To delete text do this:**

1. Select the text to be deleted by pressing the left mouse button, and dragging to text, you want to select.
2. Now press Del key from the keyboard.

4.4.5 Using Spelling Checker

Spelling checker is a flexible and powerful tool that will automatically check spelling in a paragraph or in the entire document. It finds and corrects the spelling errors but does not consider the context of words. For example, it cannot check the improper usage of various words, namely farm in place of form or no in place of know.

The spelling checker compares each word in the document with the correct spelling stored in its electronic dictionary. If it does not find a word, then it asks you to verify the spelling of that word.

When automatic spell checking is on, Word 2010 uses a red wavy line to underline words it thinks are not spelled correctly, so that you can spot them on the screen. An icon of an open book with a red cross also appears at the right in the status bar to indicate that the current document has spelling mistakes.

Spell checking begins at the insertion point in your document and works throughout your document, checking its entire contents.

Writing Rules:

1. After ever word type, press spacebar once, i.e. to separate word with a space e.g. BPB Publications.
2. While using punctuation after a word, don't use space between the word and symbol. e.g. Oh!

☞ You can check spelling in a smaller selection of text by first selecting that area of text and then checking the spelling.

Checking a Document's Spelling Automatically

Spell checking and underlining occur as you type the text in Word 2010 document. However, automatic spell checking works only when this feature is enabled.

➡ **To switch on automatic spelling check, do this:**

1. Click the File tab on the ribbon. The backstage view appears select Options.
2. The Word Options dialog box appears. In the left side pane options, select Proofing as seen in Figure 4.40.

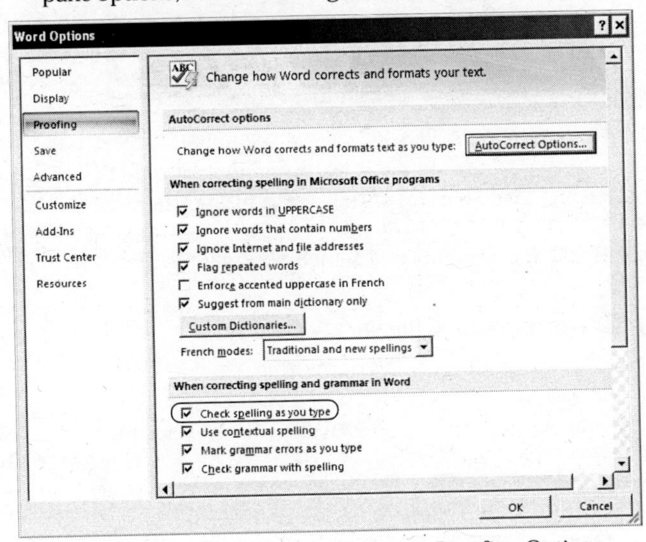

Figure 4.40 Word Options displaying Proofing Options

3. In Proofing page options, right side pane, under When correcting spelling and grammar in Word, select Check spelling as you type check box. Then click OK.

➡ **To check spelling of words with a wavy underline, do this:**

1. Right-click an underlined word. A popup menu appears (Figure 4.41). It displays a list of suggested words and additional options.
2. You have five choices for correcting the misspelled word. These are:
   - Select a word from the list shown in the pop-up menu.
   - Select Ignore to leave the word as it is.
   - Select Ignore All to ignore all occurrences of the word in your document.

- Select Add to Dictionary to add the word to the selected dictionary displayed in the Custom Dictionary in the Spelling dialog box.
- Select AutoCorrect and choose the correct spelling to automatically correct the misspelled word.

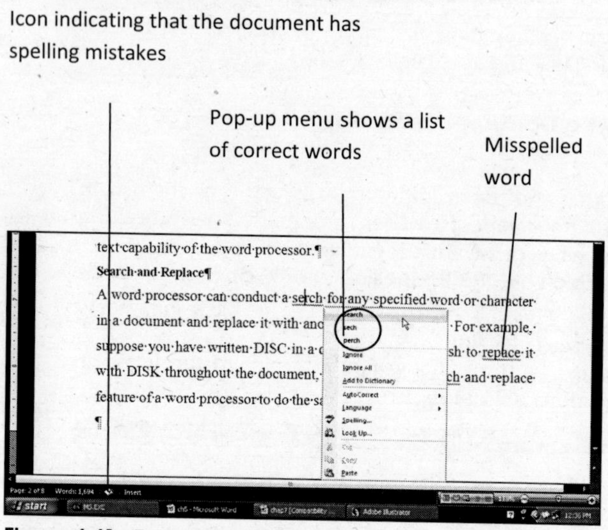

Figure 4.41 Popup Menu showing a list of suggested words

To go to the next word, double-click the open book icon in the Status bar at the bottom of the screen to find the next underlined word in the document.

3. Repeat step 2 for each word of which you want to check spelling.

Spelling Command for Checking Spelling

➡ **To check spelling with spelling command, do this:**

1. Select the word or a document that you want to check for spelling. If you select nothing, Word 2010 checks the entire document.
2. Click the Review tab. Click Spelling Grammar icon or press F7 key in the Proofing group. Word 2010 scrolls through your document and selects words that it does not recognize. The misspelled word is highlighted in the text and displayed in the Not in Dictionary: box (Figure 4.42).
3. Select the correct word from the Suggestions: list and then choose any one from the following list:
   - Click Ignore Once, to leave the word as it is.
   - Click Ignore All, to ignore all occurrences of the word in the document.
   - Click the Add to Dictionary, button to add this word to the Word 2010 dictionary. The selected word will be added to the dictionary.
   - Click the Change button to change the word.
   - Click Change All to change all occurrences of the misspelled word in the document.

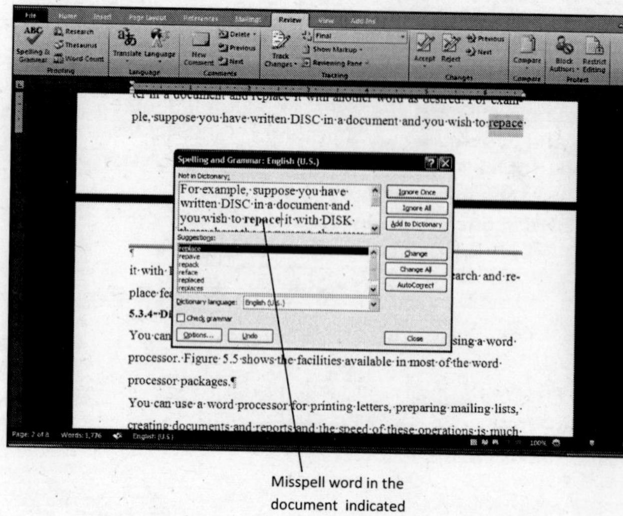

Figure 4.42 Spelling and Grammar dialog box

4. If none of the words in the Suggestions: list are correct, you can edit the word from within the Not in Dictionary: box.
5. After editing the word do one of the following:
   - Click the Change button to update the document window.
   - Click the Undo Edit button to undo the spelling change.
6. Word will now continue search the misspelled word. Click Cancel to stop the spell checking if so desired.
7. If you are checking a selected portion of a document, then after reaching the end of the selection, a dialog box asks whether you want to check the remaining portion of the document. Click Yes to check the remaining document or No to exit the spell checker.

➡ **To edit your document without closing the spelling and grammar dialog box, do this:**

1. Drag the Spelling and Grammar dialog box away from the area that you want to edit.
2. Click in the document or press Ctrl+Tab keys to activate the document window.
3. After editing the document, click the Resume button in the Spelling and Grammar dialog box or press Ctrl+Tab keys to resume checking spelling, from where you had stopped.

Double Words Correction

When Word spelling checker detects double words, (say the the) then the Not in Dictionary: box changes to the Repeated Word: box, (Figure 4.43) and the repeated word get highlighted in red.

To delete the repeated word, click the Delete button.

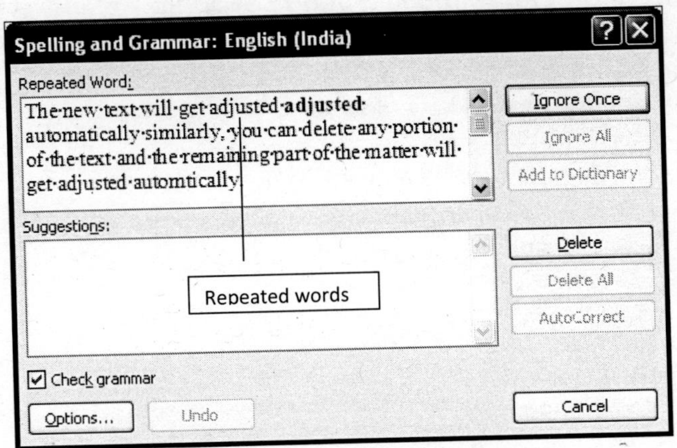

Figure 4.43 Repeated word indicated

Setting Options for Checking Spelling

The Spelling and Grammar dialog box has the Options... button. Clicking this button, will opens up the Word Options and Proofing page options dialog box appears. In this page, you can select different options to customize the spell checking operations.

➡ **To set spelling check options, do this:**

1. In the Spelling and Grammar dialog box click Options... button. Word Options dialog box appears. (Figure 4.40)
2. Various options of Proofing in Word option are as follows:

Option	Function
When correcting spelling in MS Office programs	
Ignore words in UPPERCASE	Ignores words in all uppercase letters namely proper nouns.
Ignore words that contain numbers	Ignores words that include numbers.
Ignore Internet and file addresses	Ignores Internet addresses and file names.
Flag repeated words	Ignores the repeated words in the document.
Suggest from main dictionary only	Suggestions will come from the Main dictionary only, not from any open custom dictionaries.
When correcting spelling and grammar in Word 2010	
Check spelling as you type	Automatically identifies words not found in the dictionary by placing a red wavy line under each word.
Use Contextual spelling	It suggests related spelling.
Mark Grammar Errors as you type	Turn this off to stop Word from checking grammar (green underlining words and phrases)
Check grammar with spelling	Turn this off to stop word from checking grammar when using the spelling and Grammar dialog box

3. Click OK.

4.4.6 Using Thesaurus

Thesaurus is a Word 2010 electronic database, that contains English words with similar meaning. It defines selected words and offers alternative terms. When you are not sure of a particular word's meaning, or you think you are using a particular word too often, or when you cannot come up with the right word, use thesaurus. The Thesaurus is one of a set of Research services provided by Word 2010.

➡ **To use the thesaurus, do this:**

1. Select the word for which you want to locate a synonym (similar meaning word).
2. Click the Review tab on the ribbon in the Proofing group. Click the Thesaurus button or press Shift+F7 keys together.
3. The Research task pane opens. For example, type the word appropriate in the Search for: box. Click the arrow to the right of the box. A listing of synonyms for the word appropriate appears. (Figure 4.44)

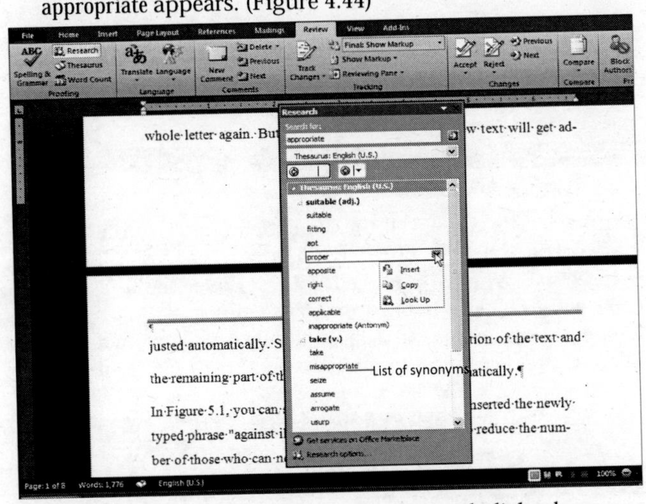

Figure 4.44 List of synonyms in Research dialog box

4. Synonyms for appropriate are now listed in the task pane.
5. For example, select the word proper. Click the arrow next to accurate and then click Insert.
6. The word proper replaces appropriate in the document.
7. Close the Research task pane.

4.5 FORMATTING THE TEXT DOCUMENT

Formatting is the process of specifying how a document should appear when printed. Formatting refers to the appearance and arrangement of the text in the document. You can apply formatting to a single character, a word, a line or an entire paragraph. The basic formatting involves changing the font and font size of text and alignment of text.

The Paragraph formatting involves controlling the appearance of text in a paragraph as a whole. The Paragraph formatting options are: text alignment, paragraph indentation, line spacing, spacing before and after the paragraph, and border and shading, etc.

4.5.1 Font and Size Selection

To modify character appearance, you can also use the commands in Ribbon or when you select the text, a mini toolbar appears.

➡ **To change the font using Ribbon, do this:**

1. Select the text of which you want to change the font. Click the down arrow to the right of the font list box (See Figure 4.45).

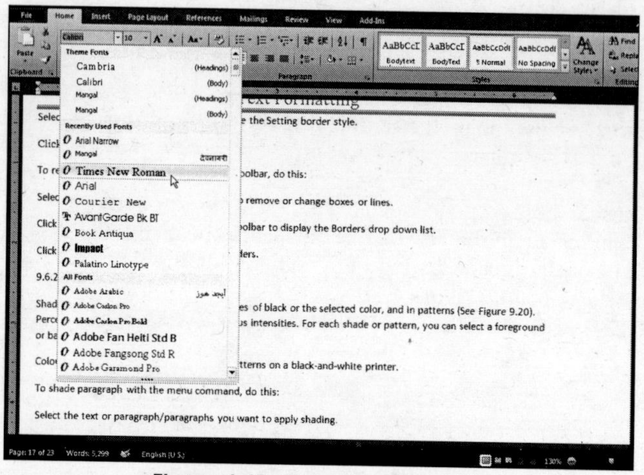

Figure 4.45 Font drop-down list

2. The drop-down list shows all the available fonts. Use the scroll arrow on the right of the drop-down list to scroll through the list. When you move the cursor over the font you can see the changes in the appearance of text.
3. To change the size, enter the desired font size in Font size list box and press Enter. Or you can select from the mini toolbar (See Figure 4.46).

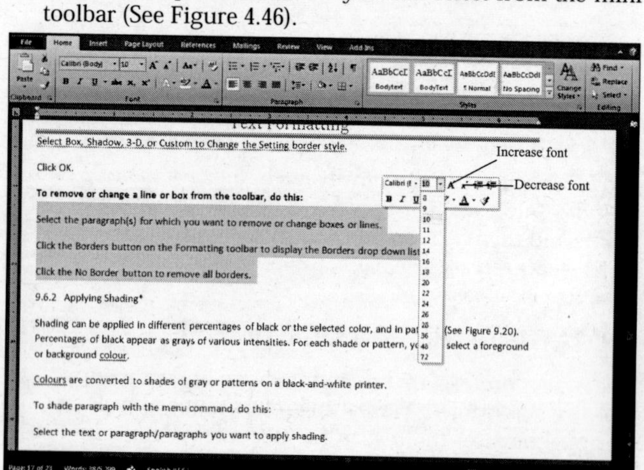

Figure 4.46 Font size drop-down list on the mini toolbar

4. To make a character Regular, Bold, Italic click the corresponding button on the mini toolbar (See Figure 4.46). These are toggle buttons clicking them once switches on the option and clicking them the second time switches off the option.

Applying Character Formatting using Keyboard

Most of the character formatting can also be applied using the keyboard shortcut as discussed in the following sections:

➡ **To format using shortcut keys, do this:**

1. Select the text you want to format and use the shortcut key combinations for the desired formatting effect.

Format	Shortcut
Bold	Ctrl + B
Italic	Ctrl + I
Single underline	Ctrl + U
Word underline	Ctrl + Shift + W
Double underline	Ctrl + Shift + D
SMALL CPAS	Ctrl + Shift + K
ALL CAPS	Ctrl + Shift + A
Hidden text	Ctrl + Shift + H
Superscript	Ctrl + Shift + =
Subscript	Ctrl + =
Copy formatting	Ctrl + Shift + C
Paste formatting	Ctrl + Shift + V
Remove formatting	Ctrl + Spacebar
Change case of letter	Shift + F3
Font	Ctrl + Shift + F. This command activates the Font dialog box. Type a new font name or use the arrow keys to highlight the desired font.
Symbol font	Ctrl + Shift + Q
Next larger point size available for selected fonts	Ctrl + Shift + >
Next smaller point size available for selected fonts	Ctrl + Shift + <
Up one point size	Ctrl +]
Down one point size	Ctrl + [

4.5.2 Alignment of Text

The attribute Alignment of a paragraph refers to the position of the main document text on the page. Different alignment options in Word 2010 are given in Table 4.9 and shown in Figure 4.47.

Table 4.9 Different Alignment Options for a Paragraph

Left Alignment	Aligns the text at the left margin and makes a zig-zag right margin.
Right Alignment	Aligns the text to the right margin and makes a zig-zag left margin.
Centre Alignment	Centres text between the left and right margins on the centre line. In this case both the margins are zig-zag.
Justify	Aligns the text at both the margins by increasing the spacing between the words.

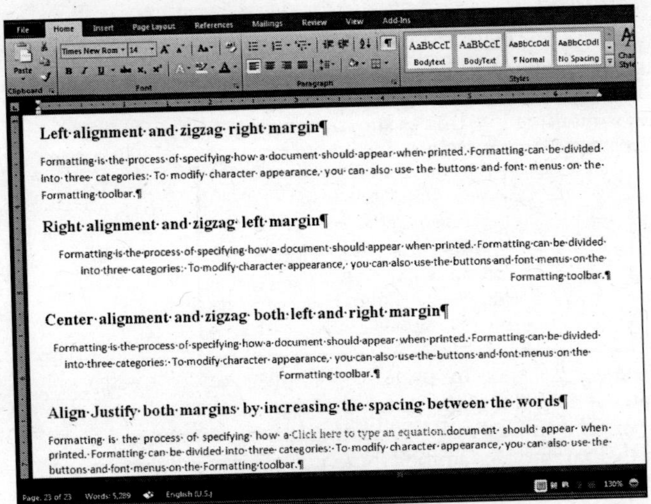

Figure 4.47 Paragraph alignment options

4.5.3 Paragraph Indenting

Indents are the white space added to the margins, and thus decreasing the text area for paragraphs. So, when you have a "right margin and you want to add a right indent of 1.0", your text will be printed 2.0" from the right edge of the paper.

> ☞ The first line of each paragraph can be indented differently from other lines in the paragraph. The first line can be shorter than the others, creating a regular indent, or longer than the others creating a hanging indent.

Once you change the indent, each new paragraph you start by pressing the Enter key will maintain the same indentation setting until you change it.

Line Spacing

Line spacing in a paragraph means the amount of space between the lines. Word 2010 offers the line spacing options as given in Table 4.10.

Table 4.10 Different Options of Line Spacing

Option	Description
Single spacing	No blank line space appears between the lines of text.
Double spacing	A blank line space appears between the lines of text.
1 1/2 spacing	Half the height of one line space of text appears between the lines of text.
Exact line height	Specify the space you want between the lines.

Space before and after Paragraphs

There is a spacing box in the Paragraph dialog box which lets you to define the amount of white space that Word 2010 must place before and after paragraphs. Space settings can be entered in points (pts), inches (in), centimetres (cm), or lines (li). Thus, 12 points would be entered as 12 pt.

Formatting Paragraphs using Dialog Box Launcher

➡ **To format paragraphs, do this:**

1. Position the insertion point anywhere in the paragraph to be formatted or select multiple paragraphs.
2. Click the Home tab of Paragraph group. Click Paragraph launcher dialog box. The Paragraph dialog box as in Figure 4.48 appears.

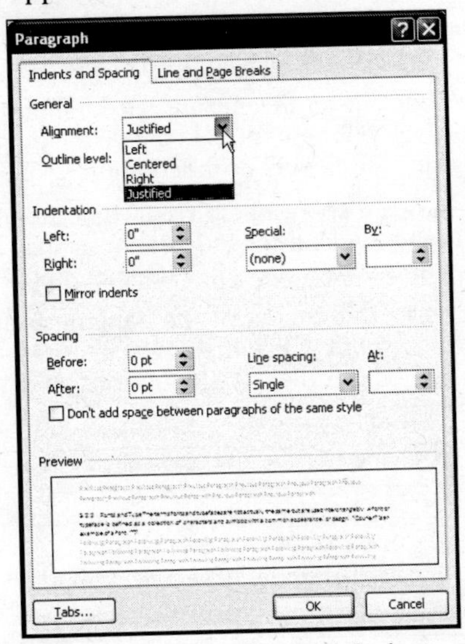

Figure 4.48 Paragraph dialog box with Indents and Spacing Property sheet

3. Click the Indents and Spacing tab, the property sheet as in Figure 4.48 appears.

   Various options in Indents and Spacing tab are:

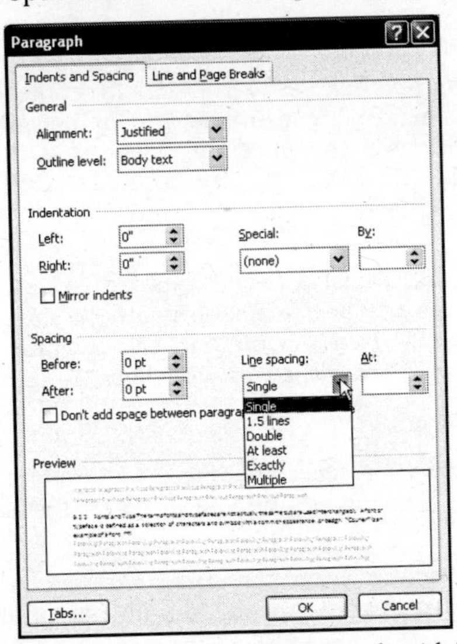

Figure 4.49 Indents and Spacing tab with line spacing options

General Options:

- The Alignment list box show the current alignment.
- Change the current alignment, if need be. For this, click the down arrow next to the list box. Open it to show the list. From the list, click alignment option as required.

Paragraph Indent Options:

- The Indents and Spacing tab to displays line spacing/indentation options (See Figure 4.49).
- The Left text box shows the current left indentation. Enter the new value for indentation or use the up and down arrow keys to change the indentation.
- The Right text box displays the current right indentation. Enter the new value for indentation or use the up and down arrow keys to change the indentation.
- To apply the first line indent or the hanging indent use the Special: list box. Click the down arrow key of the Special: list box to display the options as given below:

Option	Effect
First line	This indents only the first line of the paragraph.
Hanging indent	This indents all except the first line of the paragraph.

Click the option as needed to select it.

- In the By: text box, enter the indention or use the up and down arrow to give the required indentation. The Preview box displays the effect of the selected indentation.

Line Spacing Options:

- Line spacing text box has the options for controlling the line spacing. Click the down arrow in the spacing box. The options are given below:

Option	Explanation
Single	Default value.
Double	Places a blank line between successive lines.
1.5 Lines	Leaves half the line space between the lines.
At Least	Indicates the minimum space between lines.
Exactly	Gives the exact space between lines.

Space Before/After Paragraphs Options:

- Type the space or select the space required in the Before: text box for adding space before the paragraph.
- Type the space or select the space required in the After: text box for adding space after the paragraph.

4. Click OK or press the Enter key to close the paragraph dialog box.

Hanging Indent

A hanging indent refers to a paragraph that has all lines except the first one indented. It is called a hanging indent, because the first line hangs out over the rest of the paragraph. They look something like this as shown below:

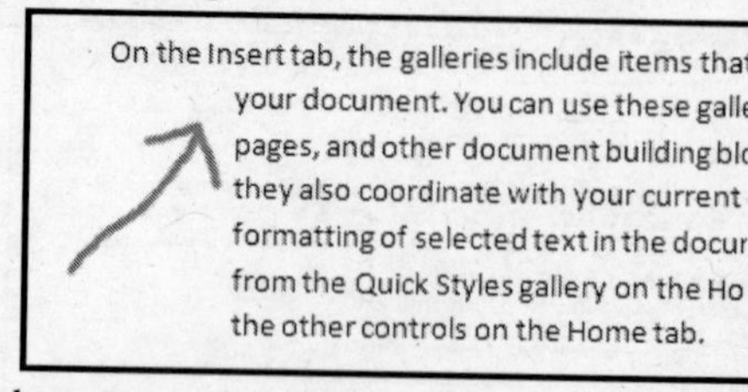

Create a hanging indent by pressing the space key to create spaces, or even by tabbing across the page. Better way to create a hanging indent in Word, is to place the cursor anywhere in the paragraph. On the Home tab, click the dialogue launcher for the Paragraph group.

When the Paragraph window opens, go down to the Special selector and choose hanging. You can either keep the default setting for the size of the indent, or you can adjust it by typing a new number into the box or by clicking on the up and down arrows to the right as shown in Figure 4.50.

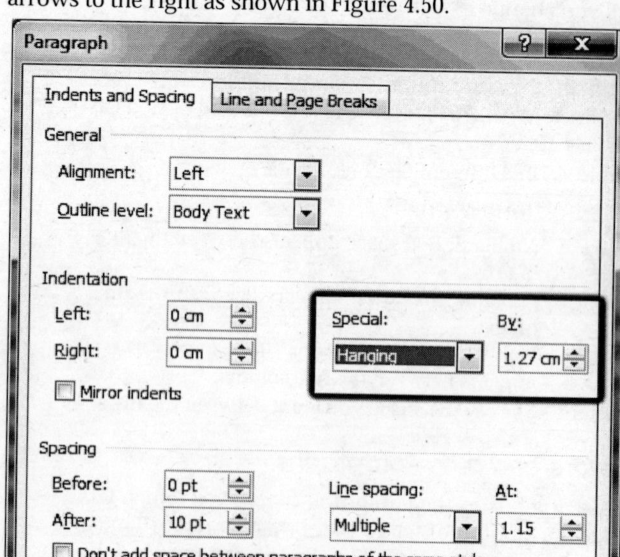

Figure 4.50 Selecting Special selector in paragraph dialog box

To adjust or remove a hanging indent that is already there, just repeat the steps above: click the Paragraph dialogue launcher and then change the Special selector or adjust the indent size.

☞ The hanging indent is only applied to the current paragraph i.e. the paragraph in which the cursor is placed. All other paragraphs remains unaffected.

Formatting Paragraphs using Ruler

➡ **To format paragraphs using ruler, do this:**

1. Position the insertion point anywhere in the paragraph you want to format or select multiple paragraphs to align.
2. Click the appropriate alignment button, e.g., left, centre, right, justified alignment on the Home tab of paragraph group.

➡ **To indent paragraphs using mouse, do this:**

1. Position the insertion point in the paragraph to be indented or select as many paragraphs, as you want to indent.
2. On the Home tab of paragraph group click the indentation button.
3. The increase Indent button moves the indent marker to the right by one tab stop and the decrease indent moves it back by one tab stop.

➡ **To indent paragraphs using the ruler, do this:**

1. Position the insertion point in a paragraph or select multiple paragraphs, that you want to indent.
2. Indent markers appear on the ruler.
3. Drag the appropriate triangular indent markers to the desired location.
4. As you drag the marker, the rulers scale shows the position of the indent mark in relation to its respective margin (See Figure 4.51).

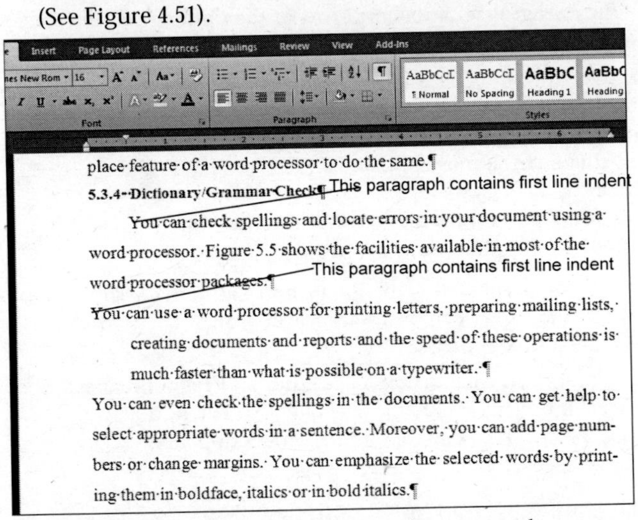

Figure 4.51 Indentation buttons on the paragraph group

5. When you release the mouse button after positioning it, the text in selected paragraphs moves accordingly.

Formatting Paragraphs using Shortcut Keys

➡ **To format paragraphs using the shortcut keys, do this:**

1. Position the insertion point anywhere in the paragraph to be aligned or select multiple paragraphs.
2. Use one of the keyboard shortcuts given below:

Alignment	Key combinations
Left	Ctrl+L keys together.
Right	Ctrl+R keys together.
Centre	Ctrl+E keys together.
Justify	Ctrl+J keys together.

➡ **To indent paragraphs using the keyboard shortcuts, do this:**

1. Position the insertion point in a paragraph or select multiple paragraphs to be indented.
2. Use the shortcut key combination as explained below:

Key combination	Effect
Ctrl+M	Left indent.
Ctrl+Shift+M	Remove left indent.
Ctrl+T	Create hanging indent.
Ctrl+Shift+T	Reduce hanging indent.
Ctrl+Q	Remove paragraphs formatting.

➡ **To change the line spacing using the keyboard shortcuts, do this:**

1. Position the insertion point in a paragraph or select the paragraphs for which you want to change the line spacing.
2. Use one of the keyboard shortcuts given below:

Key combination	Effect
Ctrl+1	Creates single spaced lines.
Ctrl+2	Creates double spaced lines.
Ctrl+5	Creates one and half spaced lines.
Ctrl+0 (zero)	Add or remove one line space preceding a paragraph

➡ **To add a single line of space before a paragraph, do this:**

1. Position the insertion point in a paragraph or select the paragraph before which you want to add single line of space.
2. Press Ctrl+0 (zero) keys together.
3. To remove the single line of space added before the paragraph, add Ctrl+0 (zero) a second time.

Paragraphs and Sections within a document

By default, a document contains a single section. Section breaks divide the document into sections. The breaks appear as double-dotted lines. You will see section breaks in Normal view if all non-printing characters are displayed. You can use section break to change the formatting of pages in a document. You can also create a different header or footer for a section of your document.

➡ **To display non-printing characters, do this:**

1. Click File tab on the ribbon. The backstage view appears. Click Options.
2. Select the Display option in the left pane, under Always show these formatting marks on the screen and then click All in Formatting marks area.

➡ **To insert a section break, do this:**

1. Position the insertion point where you want the section break to occur.
2. In the Page Layout tab, choose Page Setup group, at the top right corner, click Breaks drop-down arrow. The list of options appear as shown in Figure 4.52.
3. Choose an option from the following:

Option	Description
Next page	This selection would start the new section on a new page.
Continuous	This selection would Insert a section break without starting it on a new page.
Even page	This selection would start a section on an even numbered page (i.e., left hand page).
Odd page	This selection would start a section on an odd numbered page (i.e., on the right hand page).

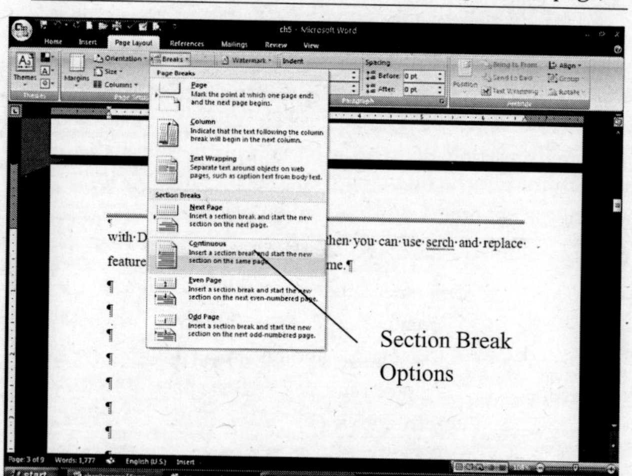

Figure 4.52 Section breaks group dialog box

A section insertion places a double-dotted, non-printing line containing the words End of Section at the insertion point on your screen (See Figure 4.53).

Section-formatting information is stored with section breaks. You can copy section information by copying and pasting section breaks, to the chapters where you wish to apply the new document formatting.

☞ Section breaks differ from paragraph marks ( ), in that a section break controls the information below it, while a paragraph mark controls the information that precedes it.

Click section break to select it. Selected section break appears as in Figure 4.53. Now use the Cut/Copy and Paste command to copy the section breaks.

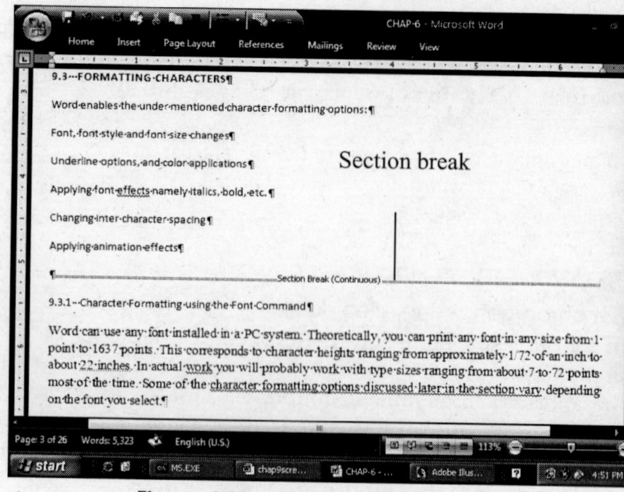

Figure 4.53 Selected section break

Deleting Section Breaks

Select a section break and press the Backspace or Del key. Text after the removed section break will take on the characteristics of the preceding text. It may take a moment for Word 2010 to reformat and re-paginate the document.

Keeping Two Or More Paragraphs Together

Automatic page breaks may occur where it should not be, namely, just after paragraph headings or in the middle of a table. Word 2010 offers methods to keep such paragraphs/lines together. These are explained in the following paragraphs.

➡ **To keep lines together, do this:**

1. Select the lines you wish to keep together.
2. Click the Page Layout tab.
3. Click the Paragraph Launcher arrow at the right corner of Paragraph group. The Paragraph dialog box appears.
4. Click the Line and Page Breaks tab property sheet as in Figure 4.54 appears.
5. Enable the Keep lines together option by clicking the check box so that a check mark appears.
6. Click OK.

➡ **To use keep with next option command, do this:**

1. Select the paragraphs you wish to keep together.
2. Click the Home tab. Click the Paragraph Launcher arrow present at the right corner of Paragraph group. The Paragraph dialog box appears.
3. In the Paragraph dialog box, click Line and Page breaks tab (See Figure 4.54). Enable Keep with next option by clicking the check box so that a check mark appears.
4. Click OK.

➡ **To remove special paragraph and line options, do this:**

1. Select the Paragraph(s)/Lines you wish to change.
2. Click the Page Layout tab and choose Paragraph group.

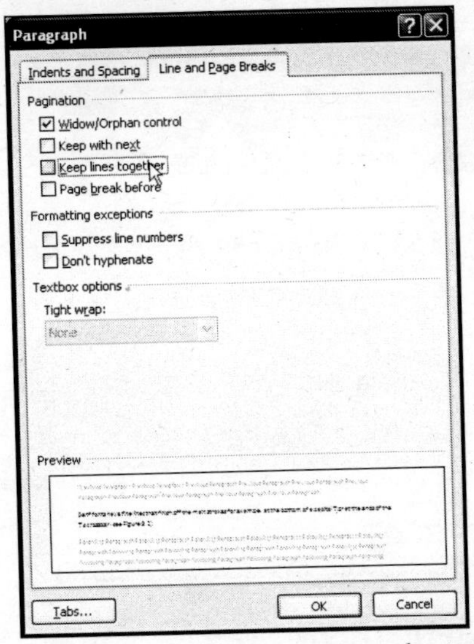

Figure 4.54 Line and Page breaks property sheet of paragraph dialog Box

3. In Paragraph dialog box, click the Line and Page breaks tab as shown in Figure 4.54. Click the check boxes to remove the check marks.
4. Click the unwanted options from keep together option.
5. Click OK.

4.5.4 Bullets and Numbering

Word 2010 provides the ability to create bulleted, numbered and multilevel lists. A bulleted list is a list with a graphic character, a very small picture or a bullet at the beginning of each paragraph in the list. A numbered list is similar to bulleted list, except each paragraph is numbered or lettered. The style of each list type can be changed and different bullets can be used.

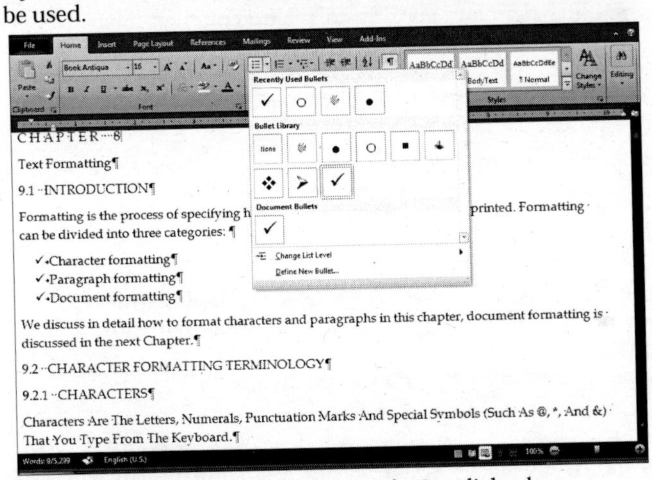

Figure 4.55 Bullets and numbering dialog box

➡ **To create a bulleted list, do this:**

1. Select the text to be bulleted or the location of the new list to be created.
2. To use the last style of bullets for the list, press the Bullets or Numbering button as shown in Figure 4.55. Press it again to end the list. Or

   Right-click in the selected text and select Bullets or Numbering from the shortcut menu to view a gallery of available styles.

☞ The bullet or number appears at the beginning of a line of text when the Enter key is pressed at the end of the preceding line of text.

Use of Tab and Tab Setting

Tabs are used for creating relatively simple lists of items. Each paragraph in a Word 2010 document can take several different tab settings. It offers four types of tab settings (See Figure 4.56). Each tab is meant to align text. Tabs are particularly useful for making columnar lists. The different tabs and their functions are as given below:

Tab	Function
Left Tab	Text typed at these tabs aligns against the left edge of the stop.
Centre Tab	A centre tab stop, centres your text around the tab stop.
Right Tab	Right tab stop, positions whatever you type to the left of the tab.
Decimal Tab	Decimal tab stops, align columns of numbers on the decimal point. This is mainly used for financial reports.

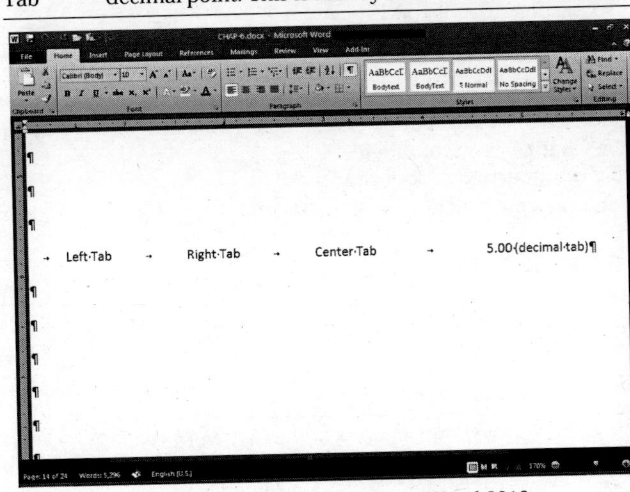

Figure 4.56 Tabs available in Word 2010

Setting Tab Stops with the Tabs Dialog Box

➡ **To set tabs using the tabs dialog box, do this:**

1. Position the insertion point in paragraph in which you want to insert tab.
2. Click the Home tab. Click Paragraph Launcher dialog box.

3. The Paragraph dialog box appears, click Tabs... button. Tabs dialog box appears as shown in Figure 4.57.
4. In the Tab stop position box, enter the position where you want to insert the tab stop.
5. In the alignment area, select the type of tab you want to insert.

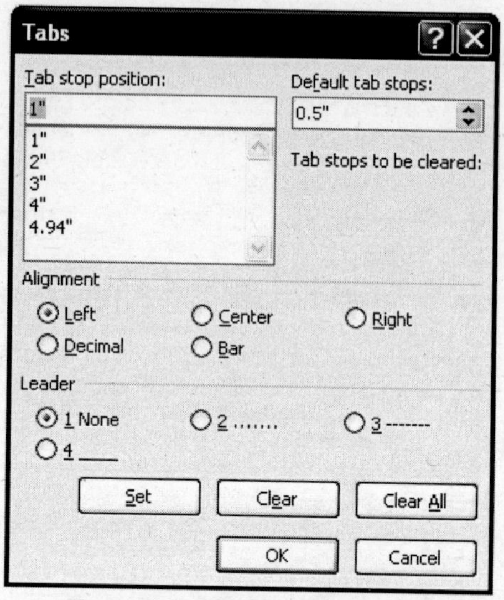

Figure 4.57 The Tabs dialog box

☞ Measurements in the Tabs dialog box are in inches as default, unless you type another one (cm for centimeter, pt for point, or pi for pica). As an example, 5 cm would position the left tab stop five centimetres from the left margin.

4.5.5 Using the Change Case Command

Word provides facilities to change to capital letters of any text by using the Change Case command.

➡ **To apply capitalization, do this:**

1. Select the text for which you want to change capitalization.
2. Click the Home tab of Font group. Click Change Case command (Figure 4.58).
3. The options offered by the Change case dialog box are as follows:

Option	Description
Sentence case	The first character of the first word is capitalized.
lower case	All the characters are in lowercase.
UPPER CASE	All the characters are in uppercase.
Capitalize Each Word	The first letter of each word is capitalized.
tOGGLE cASE	The first letter of each selected word is in lowercase, the rest are in uppercase.

4. The above options are applied in the text and shown in Figure 4.58.

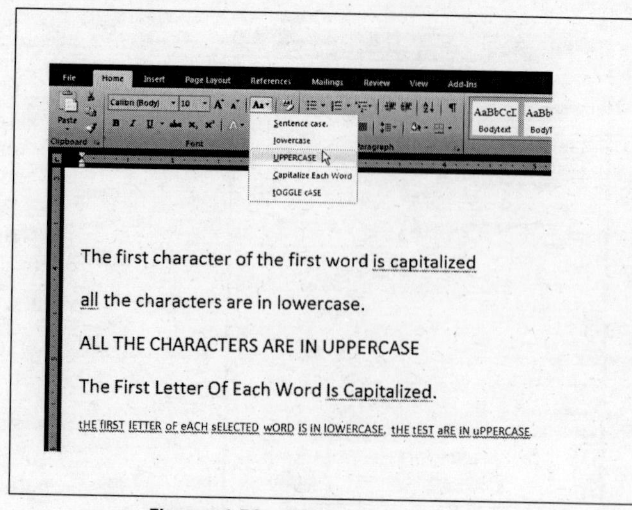

Figure 4.58 Changed case options

4.6 TABLE MANIPULATION

You should use tables to create documents, such as forms, financial reports, catalogs and biodata. Word tables consist of horizontal rows and vertical columns. You type in the areas called cells which is formed by the intersection of rows and columns. Cells can contain text, numbers, or graphics.

You can even control the size, shape, and appearance of the cells, and use border and shading features. You can insert and delete rows and columns in a table.

☞ A new feature called the Table Wizard helps you to automate table creation.

4.6.1 Concept of Table

A table is made of rows and columns of cells that you can fill with text and graphics. You can use tables to align numbers in columns, and then sort and perform calculation on them. You can also use tables to create page layouts and arrange text and graphics.

Rows–A row is a horizontal block of cells that runs through the entire width of the table.

Column–A columns is a vertical block of cells that runs through the table.

Cell–A cell is the intersection of a row and a column.

4.6.2 Draw Table

Word 2010 allows you to draw a table by selecting the Insert Table grid on the insert tab or Insert table... using the Table options in the Table groups.

➡ **To draw a table using the mouse, do this:**

1. Position the insertion point where you want to insert a table.
2. Click the Insert tab of Tables group. Click down arrow and choose the Insert table grid as shown in Figure 4.59 appears. Drag the mouse button to highlight the desired number of rows and columns.

3. The displayed grid represents the required number of rows and columns. Click the mouse button after getting the right number in the grid.

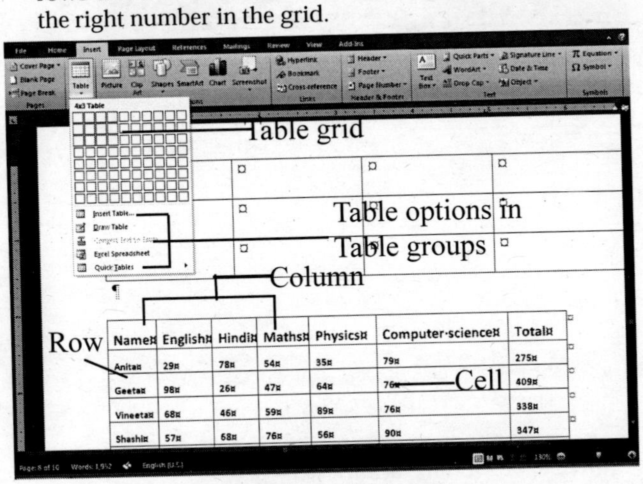

Figure 4.59 Table grid

4. Word inserts an empty table when you release the mouse button (See Figure 4.59).

➡ **To create a table using the table option, do this:**

1. Position the insertion point where you want to insert the table.
2. In Insert tab of Tables group, click the Table down arrow highlight Insert Table... options. The Insert Table dialog box as shown in Figure 4.60.
3. Enter the desired number of rows and columns as required in the table.
4. Click OK.

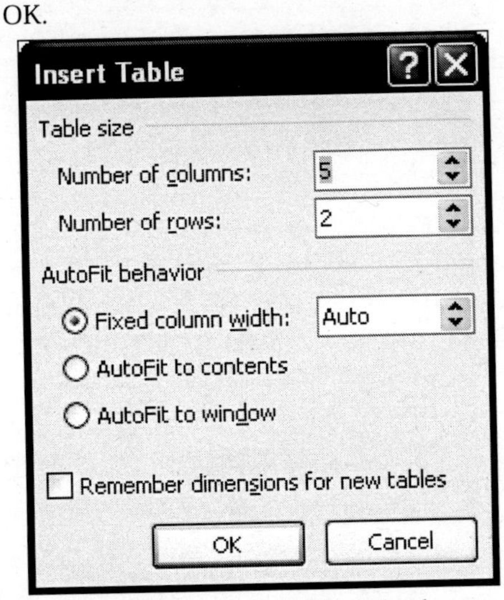

Figure 4.60 Insert Table dialog box

Entering and Editing Text in a Table

You can move, enter and edit text in a table just as you do with other types of text matter. Use mouse or arrow keys to position the insertion point, then type the text. The cell borders work as margins. Word 2010 automatically wraps text within the cell as you reach the right edge.

➡ **To move within a table using the mouse, do this:**

1. Position the pointer in the cell you want to move and click.

➡ **To move within a table using the keyboard, do this:**

1. The insertion point will move left and down to the next row when you press Tab key in the last column on the right side of a table.
2. It will move right and up one row when you press Shift+Tab past the last column on the left.

You can apply all of Word 2010 paragraph and character formats to the text in cells. Cells can contain multiple paragraphs as well as multiple paragraph formats.

4.6.3 Changing Cell Width and Height

Changing Row Heights

Word 2010 sets the height of each row automatically in order to accommodate the cell containing the tallest entry. For example, if one cell in a row needs 2" to accommodate the text or graphics, then all the cells in that particular row will be 2" high.

➡ **To adjust the height of a row, do this:**

1. Click anywhere in the row where you want to change its height.
2. Move the pointer to the vertical ruler at the left edge of the screen or to the top of the row. The pointer changes to an up-and-down arrow. Use it to drag the row to the desired height (See Figure 4.61).
3. Release the mouse button. Or

   Click Table Row Height scroll box, to change the height of row in the cell size group in the Table Tools contextual tab of Layout tab.

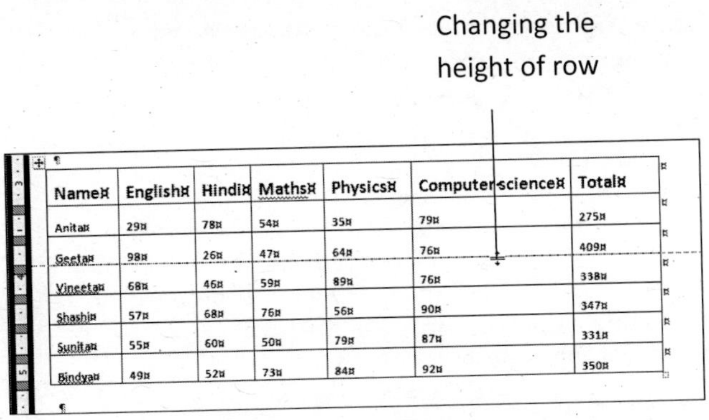

Figure 4.61 Changing table height

Changing Column Width

➡ **To change the width of column, using mouse do this:**

1. Point to a column boundary.

2. The pointer will change shape to a double arrow (See Figure 4.62). Drag the column width marker. Watch the dotted line as well as the ruler settings, then release the mouse button when it reaches the desired width. Or

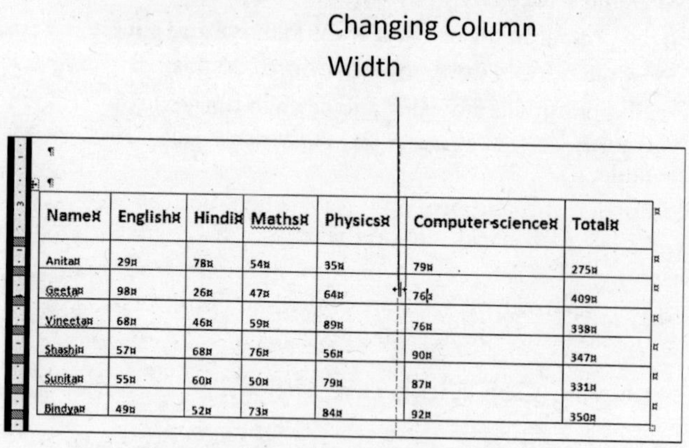

Figure 4.62 Adjusting column width

Click Table Column Width scroll box, to change the Table Column Width in the cell size group.

- If you hold down the Shift key while dragging, the column to the right does not changes size while the table's overall width increases.
- If you hold down Ctrl key while dragging mouse, all columns to the right changes size, but the table's overall width will not change. Thus, the width of the columns on the right will only change.

4.6.4 Delete/Insertion of Row and Column

Inserting Rows

To add a new row at the end of an existing table, position the insertion point anywhere in the last cell and press the Tab key. Word 2010 inserts a new row using the styles of the cells that are immediately above it.

➡ **To insert a single row in the middle of a table, do this:**

1. Position the insertion point below the row where you want the new row to be inserted.
2. Click the Layout contextual tab, click Insert Above or Below in the Rows   Columns group. The new row is inserted below or above the selected row.

   Alternatively, right click and select Insert, click the small triangle, a sub menu option appears as shown in Figure 4.63. Select the Insert Rows Above or Below option.
3. To add multiple rows, either repeat the Insert Rows command by clicking right mouse button or select as many existing rows as you want to insert. Word 2010 inserts as many rows as you have selected.

Inserting Columns

➡ **To insert a single column in the middle of a table, do this:**

1. Select the column to the right of which you wish the new column to appear.

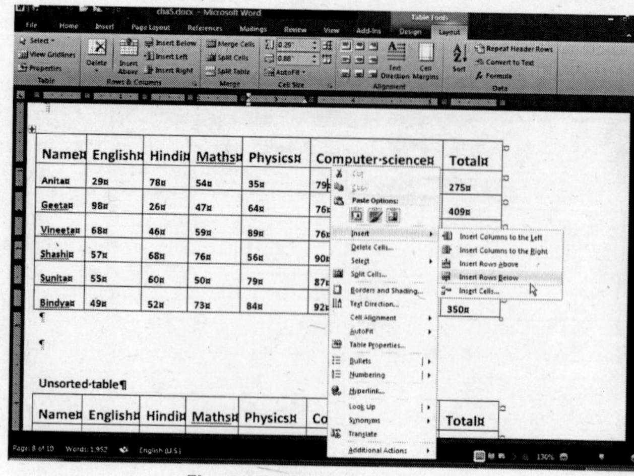

Figure 4.63 Inserting rows

2. Click the Layout contextual tab, click Insert Left or Right in the Rows   Columns group. The new column is inserted left or right to the selected column.

   Alternatively, right click and select Insert option. Click the small triangle. A sub menu appears. Select the Insert Columns to Left or Right option from the sub menu list.
3. Word 2010 will add a new column but it will not change the width of the earlier columns to accommodate this new inserted column. In order to make the enlarged table fit on your page, you will have to adjust margins, column widths or change page orientation.

☞ New column retains the format of the column, adjacent to which it is inserted but borders will not change.

To insert multiple columns, select as many existing columns as you want to insert new ones to the right of the desired location of the new columns. If you want to add three columns, select the three existing columns to the right of the desired insertion point, then click on the Insert columns to the Left button.

➡ **To insert a column at the right edge of a table, do this:**

1. Select an end-of-row marker (See Figure 4.64).
2. Right click and select Insert. A small triangle, a sub menu option appears. Select Insert Columns to Right option.

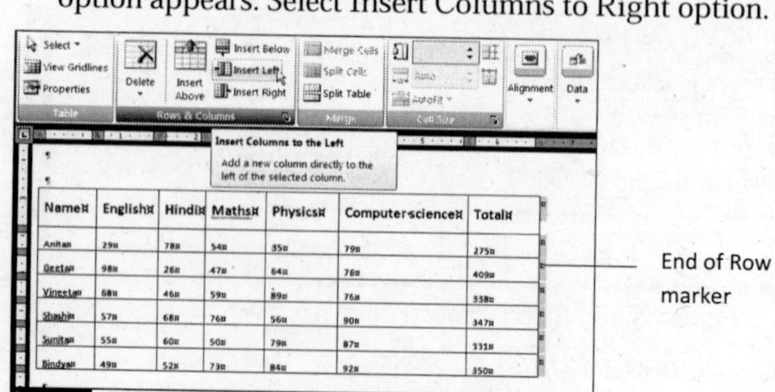

Figure 4.64 End of row marker

Deleting Rows

➡ **To delete a row or rows of cells, do this:**

1. Select the row(s) to be deleted.
2. Click the Layout contextual tab, click Rows Columns group. Click down arrow and choose Delete Rows. This will delete the rows and their contents.
3. To delete the contents of cells only, leave the cells intact, select text or graphic and press the Del key.

Deleting Columns

➡ **To delete columns, do this:**

1. Select the column or columns to be deleted.
2. Click the Layout contextual tab. Click Table down arrow and choose Delete Columns.
3. Click OK.

4.6.5 Alignment of Text in Cell

You can align text in a table cell in nine different ways: Top Left (the default alignment), Top center, Top Right, Centre Left, Centre Right, Bottom Left, Bottom Centre, and Bottom Right as shown in Figure 4.65.

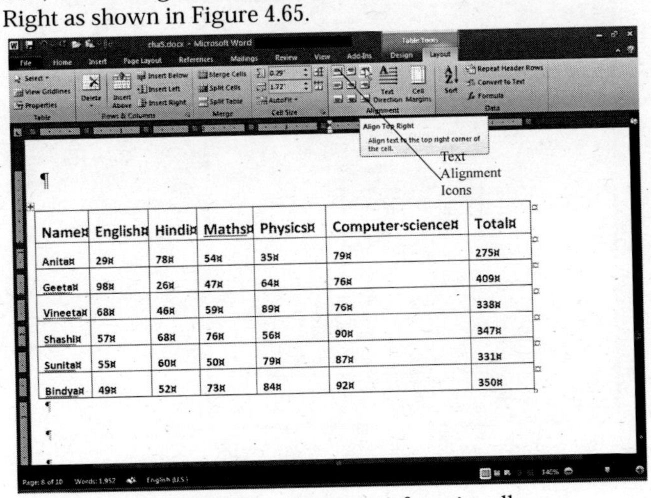

Figure 4.65 Alignment of text in cell

4.6.6 Border and Shading

A border may be a box around a paragraph (or paragraphs) from all sides. It could be a line that sets a paragraph off on one or more sides. A border can include shading, which fills a paragraph with a pattern. Boxes and lines can be solid black and shading can be gray or in colour.

If a group of paragraphs is formatted with a box around them and you press Enter key at the end of the last paragraph, your new paragraph falls within the box. However, if you want to create a new paragraph outside the border, then move the insertion point outside the border before you press Enter key.

Applying Borders

➡ **To apply borders to a paragraph, or group of paragraphs, do this:**

1. Position the insertion point anywhere in the paragraph to be enclosed in a border or select multiple paragraphs or select the text to be enclosed (See Figure 4.66).
2. In Paragraph group, click Borders and Shading. A drop-down menu appears. Choose the selected border you want to apply for paragraph as seen in Figure 4.66.

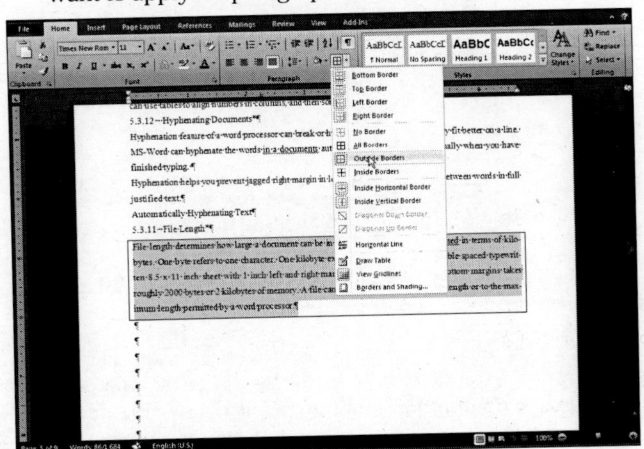

Figure 4.66 Paragraphs enclosed in border

3. In Paragraph group, select Borders and Shading... option. The Borders and Shading dialog box appears as in Figure 4.67.
4. Choose from the options given below:

Option	Effect
None	No box.
Box	A box with identical lines on all four sides, of the selected text or paragraphs.
Shadow	A box with a drop shadow on the bottom right corner.
3-D	A "Picture frame" box.
Custom	Custom design borders on one or more sides of the selected paragraph(s).

4. After selecting the setting, choose the Style: in the style scroll list. Style determines the type of line used for border.
5. In the Color: drop-down list, choose the colour you want the border to be in. If you choose Auto option, the default colour for text is used.
6. In the Width: drop-down list specify the width for the border.
7. The Preview box shows how the borders are applied to the selected text.
8. In Apply to: Choose width you want to apply border to a selected text or paragraph.
9. Click Options... to bring up dialog box as in Figure 4.67.

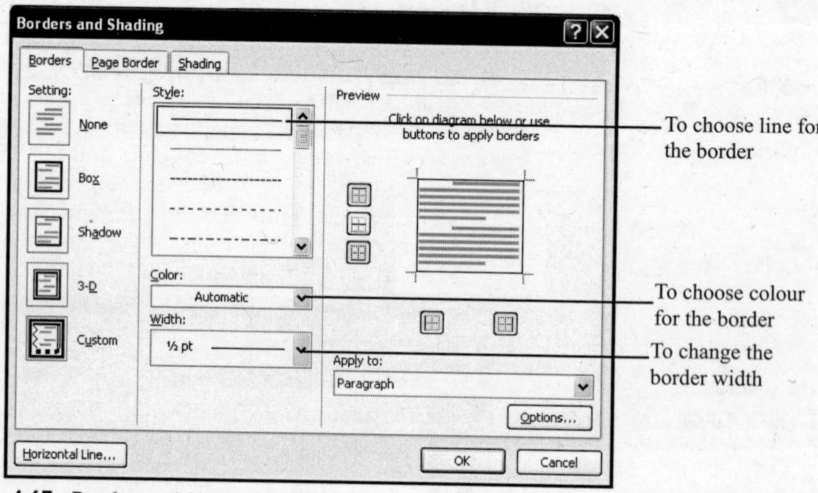

Figure 4.67 Border and Shading dialog box

In the dialog box specify the gap between the border and the text if need be.

10. Click OK or press Enter.

When paragraphs extend exactly to the margins of your page (as they always do if you do not indent the paragraphs), borders extend slightly outside the margins. If you want borders to fall within or exactly on the margins, you must indent the paragraph. To make borders fall on the margins, indent the paragraph by the width of the border.

➡ **To remove or change a box or line from the dialog box launcher command, do this:**

1. Select the paragraph or paragraphs for which you want to remove or change boxes or lines.
2. In Paragraph group, select Borders and Shading... click on option.
3. The Border and Shading Options dialog box appears as shown in Figure 4.68. Select the Borders tab. Click OK.
4. Select the None option in the Setting: group to remove all borders.
5. Select the line you want to change and choose a different option from the Style: box. You also can select a different line colour from the Color: list box.
6. Select Box, Shadow, 3-D, or Custom to Change the Setting border style.
7. Click OK.

➡ **To remove or change a line or box, do this:**

1. Select the paragraph(s) for which you want to remove or change boxes or lines.
2. Click the Borders and Shading option on the Home tab of Paragraph group. A list of options appears.
3. Select the No Border option to remove all borders.

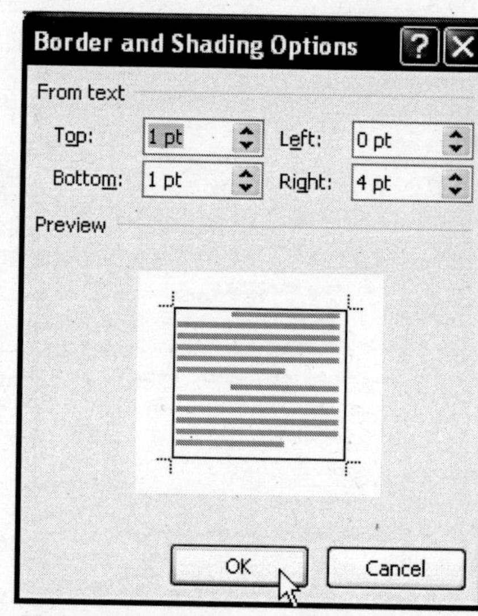

Figure 4.68 Border and Shading options

Applying Shading

Shading can be applied in different percentages of black or the selected colour, and in patterns (See Figure 4.69). Percentages of black appear as grays of various intensities. For each shade or pattern, you can select a foreground or background colour.

Colours are converted to shades of gray or patterns on a black-and-white printer.

➡ **To shade paragraph with the mouse, do this:**

1. Select the text or paragraph/paragraphs on which you want to apply shading.
2. In Paragraph group click Border down arrow and choose Borders and Shading.. . In the Borders and Shading dialog box click the Shading tab property sheet as seen in Figure 4.69 appears.

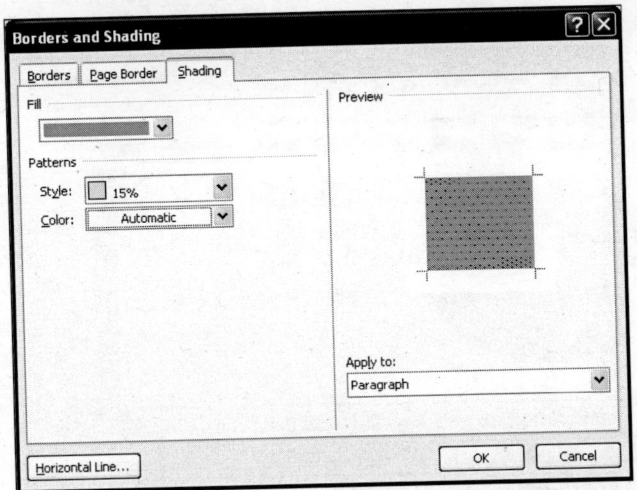

Figure 4.69 Shading tab of Borders and Shading dialog box

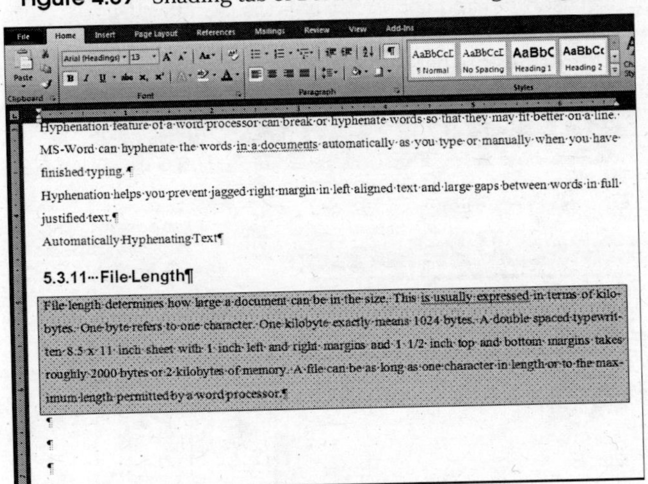

Figure 4.70 Paragraph with shading effects

3. Fill: In this box click the fill colour you want for the shading or click None to remove shading colour.
4. Style: In this drop-down list click the shading style you want to apply "over" this fill colour.
5. Color: In this drop-down list, click a colour for the line and dots in the selected shading pattern. The Color: box is not visible if you click colour in the style: box.
6. Select a colour from the Fill list to colour a percentage pattern or a pattern background. The effect of the selection option appear in the preview box.
7. Click OK.
8. The selected shading style option is applied in the paragraph as shown in Figure 4.70.

➡ **To remove shading using mouse, do this:**

1. Select the paragraph or paragraphs from which you want to remove shading.
2. In Borders and Shading dialog box, select the Shading tab.
3. Choose No fill from the Fill group and also clear Style from the patterns group.
4. Click OK.

Table Formula

When you want to perform calculations on numbers in Word 2010 table, you can create formula that uses a built-in mathematical function.

1. Position the insertion point in the cell in which you want to enter the formula.
2. Click Layout tab. Click Data group. Click Formula. The Formula dialog box appears.
3. In the Formula: box enter the formula or In the Paste function: drop down list select the function you want to use and specify the range of cells to be used for the calculation (See Figure 4.71). Or
   In the Number format: drop down list, select the number format.
4. Click OK.

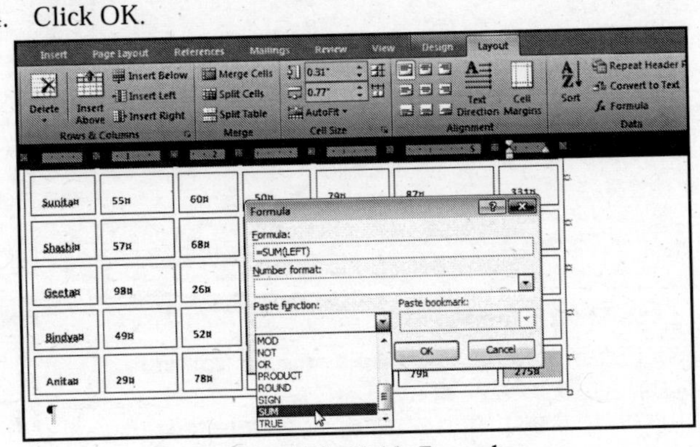

Figure 4.71 Table Formula

☞ You can define the range of the columns or row of table under the brackets in the formula. You can use ABOVE, LEFT, RIGHT to indicate the range of the cells in the formula, such as SUM (LEFT) or SUM (B2:E2).

4.6.7 Inserting Graphics Elements

Graphics can include a wide variety of images, including pictures and drawing objects. Pictures and graphics that have been created outside Word 2010 namely, a scanned photograph, Clip Art, that are created within Word, a shape, a diagram, a line, or WordArt text. You can use the buttons on the Insert tab to insert pictures and draw different kinds of objects. Word 2010 lets you to draw, place, resize, reposition and format all above type of graphics.

4.6.8 Insert Picture Command

You can insert scanned photographs or pictures created in any program into a Word 2010 document. Two buttons in the illustrations group on the Insert tab can be used to specify the source of the picture as follows:

- Picture: Click this button to insert a picture from a file. Or you an also insert a picture directly from the camera.
- Clip Art: Click this button to insert one of the hundreds of Clip Art images that come with Word 2010, such as photos and drawings of people, places and things, etc.

➡ **To insert a picture, do this:**

1. Open the document in which you want to insert the graphics.
2. Position the insertion point where you want the graphics to be appeared.
3. Click the Insert tab and choose Picture icon in the Illustration group. Insert Picture dialog box of Word 2010 appears as shown in Figure 4.72.

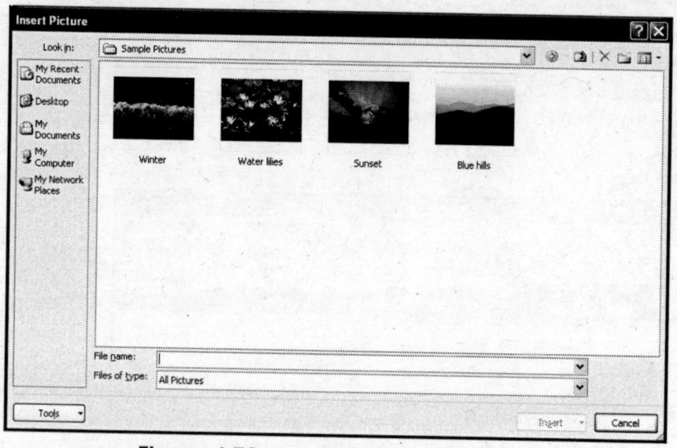

Figure 4.72 Insert Picture dialog box

4. In Insert Picture dialog box, displaying the contents of your Sample Pictures folder.
5. Select the desired picture you want to insert in the document.
6. On the Format contextual tab, in the Adjust group, choose the desired option you want to apply in the picture.

   Click Corrections down-arrow button. A list of brightness and contrast options appears. Select the desired type of brightness and Contrast under the Brightness and Contrast category from the list.

   Color: You can adjust the color intensity and color tone of a picture.

   Artistic Effects: You can apply artistic effects to a picture to make the picture look like a sketch, drawing and painting.
7. In the Picture Styles group, click the More button. The picture Styles gallery opens as shown in Figure 4.73.
8. In the gallery, point to each thumbnail in turn to see its effect. Then, click the desired style you want to apply.

➡ **To insert a Clip Art, do this:**

1. Open the document in which you want to insert the graphics.
2. Position the insertion point where you want the graphics to appear.

Figure 4.73 Picture styles gallery

3. Click the Insert tab and choose Clip Art icon in the Illustration group.
4. In the Clip Art task pane, select the graphics you want to insert in the document.

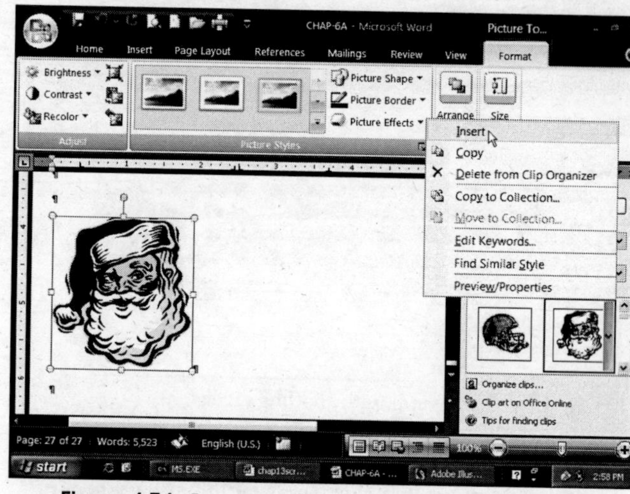

Figure 4.74 Insert graphics in the Clip Art task pane

5. Click the arrow present on the right side of the picture. A pop-up menu appears. Click Insert as shown in Figure 4.74.

4.6.9 Customizing Graphics

Resizing Graphics

➡ **To resize the graphics, do this:**

1. Click the graphics you want to resize. The picture is surrounded by a box containing eight handles (See Figure 4.74). You will find one in each corner and one on each side of the outline box.

   When you position the mouse pointer on a handle, it turns into a two-headed arrow.

2. To increase or decrease the size of the entire graphic proportionally (height and width increases proportionally), drag a corner handle diagonally, releasing it when the image is of proposed size.
3. To distort a dimension, use the handles on the edges of the graphics.

4.6.10 Using a WordArt

Office 2010 enables you to create special effect with text by using WordArt. You can use vibrant color, 3-D effects and outline effects.

➡ **To insert WordArt in a document, do this:**

1. Open the document in which you want to insert the WordArt.
2. Click the Insert tab, in the Text group.
3. Click WordArt drop-down arrow. A list of WordArt styles appears as shown in Figure 4.75.

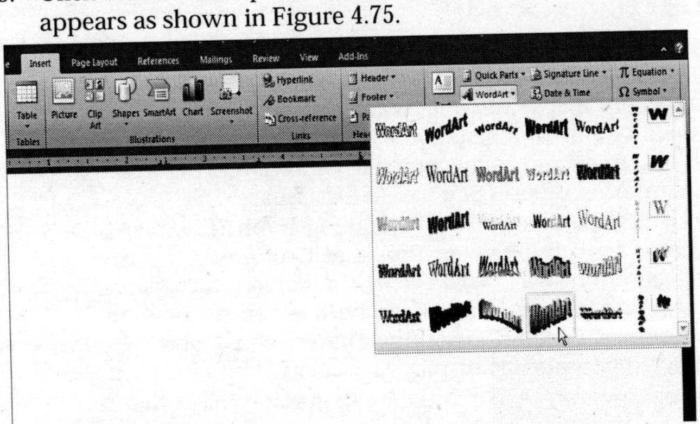

Figure 4.75 Selecting WordArt from the Insert tab

4. Select the desired style you want to apply.
5. A WordArt graphic displays an Edit WordArt Text dialog box that appears as shown in Figure 4.76.

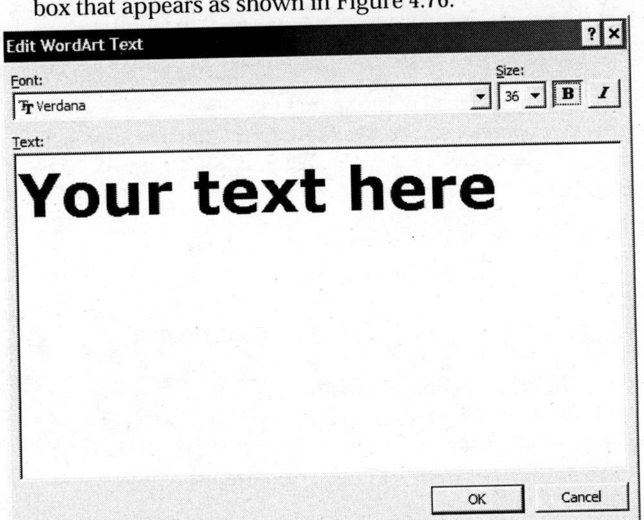

Figure 4.76 Edit WordArt Text dialog box

6. Type the text that you want to insert in the WordArt Text: box.
7. Click the Font: drop-down arrow and choose the desired font.
8. Click the Size: drop-down arrow and choose the desired font size.
9. Click a text style button if desired.
10. Click OK to return to the document window.
11. The WordArt graphic placeholder is inserted in the document as shown in Figure 4.77.

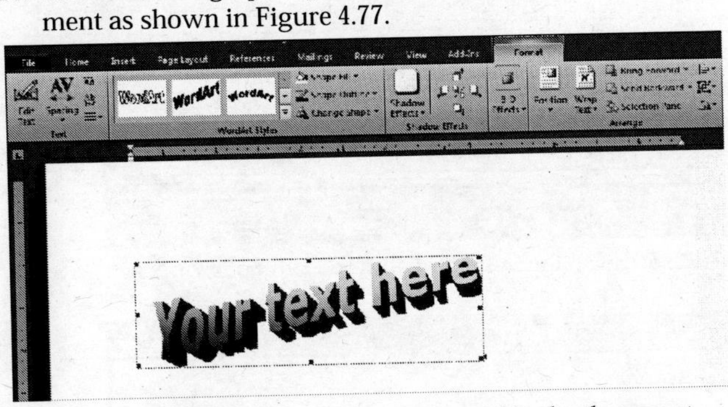

Figure 4.77 WordArt graphic is inserted in the document

4.6.11 Inserting Symbols and Special Characters

Some documents require characters which are not found on a standard keyboard. These characters might include the sign such as copyright © or registered (®) symbols, currency symbols (such as), Greek letters, or letters with accent marks. You might want to add arrow (such as ↑, ↓, →, ←,) or graphic icons. Word 2010 gives you access to an array of symbols that you can easily insert into any document.

➡ **To insert symbol in a document, do this:**

1. Mover the cursor where you want to insert a symbol in the document.
2. Click Insert tab of Symbols group, click the symbol icon in the Symbols group or click the pull-down menu as shown in Figure 4.78.
3. Click the symbol you want to insert. Word 2010 inserts your chosen symbol in the document.
4. If you want to see more options in the symbols, click the More Symbols... . A Symbol dialog box appears as shown in Figure 4.79.
5. In the Symbols tab, select the desired font in the Font: list, and you can see the selected font in the preview box.
6. Click Insert button and then click Close button.

Special Characters

Word refers to a specific set of characters as special characters. The special characters are listed on the Special Characters tab of the Symbol dialog box.

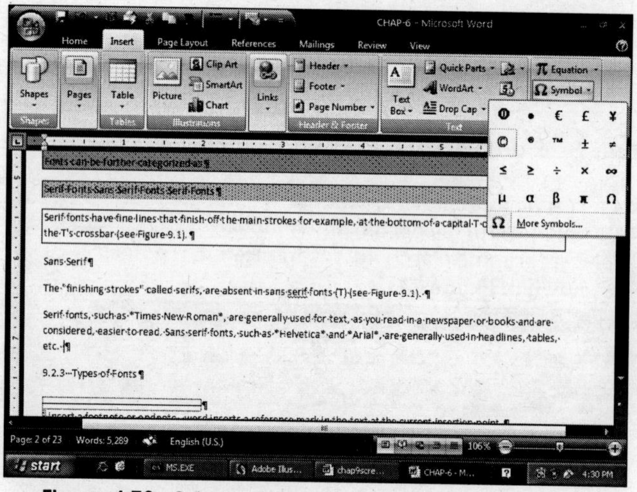

Figure 4.78 Selecting Symbols list in the Symbol group

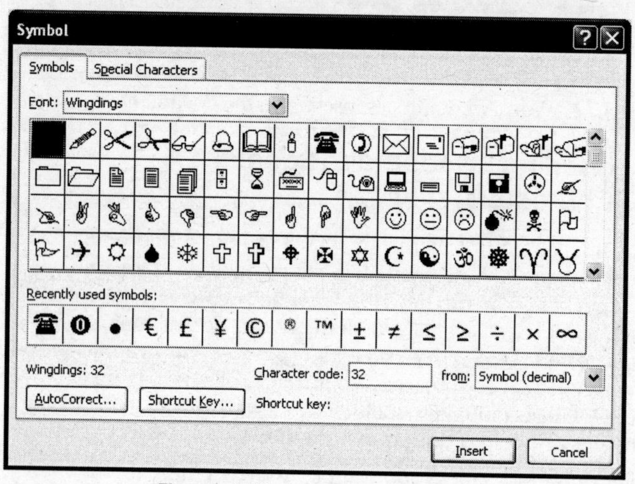

Figure 4.79 Symbol dialog box

➡ **To insert Special character in a document, do this:**

1. To open the Symbol dialog box, in the Symbols group on the Insert tab of the Ribbon, click Symbol, and then click More Symbols. After the Symbol dialog box opens, click the Special Characters tab.
2. The Symbol dialog box appears as shown in Figure 4.80. Click the Special Characters tab.
3. Double-click on any of the special characters listed to insert it into your document. Or select the desired character and click Insert button to insert in the document.

Special Characters options

Word's special characters include both special symbols and nonprinting characters that do something other than display a symbol or white space. The latter group of special characters includes the following special characters.

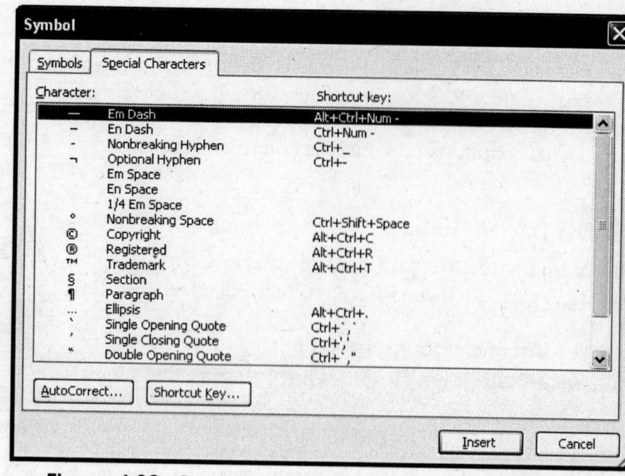

Figure 4.80 Special character tab in Symbol dialog box

- Nonbreaking space–A nonbreaking space, which is also called a hard space keeps the text before it and after it together on the same line while inserting a space in between. Nonbreaking spaces are often used to keep the parts of names and dates together. A nonbreaking space can be inserted by pressing Ctrl+Shift+Space.
- Nonbreaking hyphen–A nonbreaking hyphen, which is also call a hard hyphen, ensures that two words that are separated only by a hyphen remain together on the same line. A nonbreaking hyphen can be inserted by pressing Ctrl+Shift+_. When nonprinting characters are shown, a nonbreaking hyphen is displayed as a long hyphen.
- Optional hyphen–An optional hyphen is a hyphen that is displayed or printed only when the part of the word after it needs to be moved to the next line. An optional hyphen can be inserted by pressing Ctrl+-. When nonprinting characters are shown, an optional hyphen is displayed as a hooked hyphen.
- Em space–An em space is a space that is equal in length to the length of the em dash of the same font.
- En space–An en space is a space that is equal in length to the length of the en dash of the same font.

When a special character is not available in the current font, Word inserts the applicable character from another font that supports the character.

4.6.12 Adding a Watermark

You can also apply custom watermark to add it in the pages of the document.

➡ **To add custom watermark in the document, do this:**

1. Click the Page Layout tab of Page Background group. Click the Watermark drop-down arrow.
2. A list of different Watermark options appears. Select the desired option from the list. Or
3. Click Custom Watermark... option from the list as shown in Figure 4.81.

4. The Printed Watermark dialog box appears as shown in Figure 4.81, from where you can choose either to create and add a text water mark or a picture watermark.
5. Click the Picture Watermark radio button to insert a picture watermark.
6. The Select Picture... button get activate, click the Select Picture... button.
7. The Insert Picture dialog box appears as shown in Figure 4.82.
8. Select the Picture you want to add as a watermark in the document. For example, we have selected Water Lilies.jpg from the Sample Picture folder.
9. Click the Insert button.

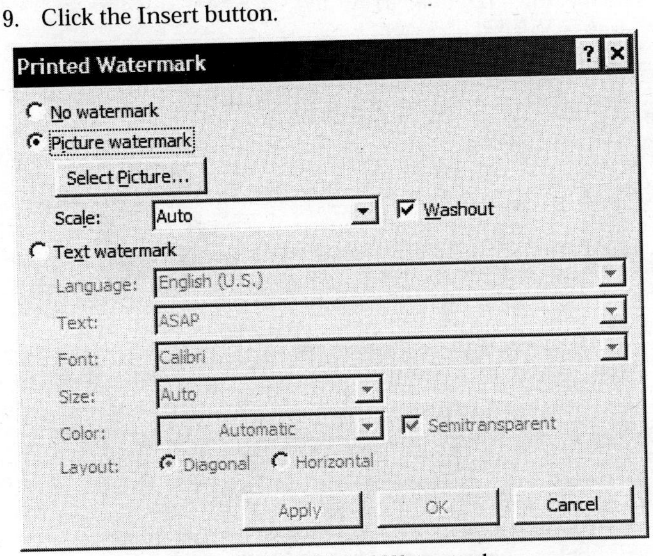

Figure 4.81 Printed Watermark

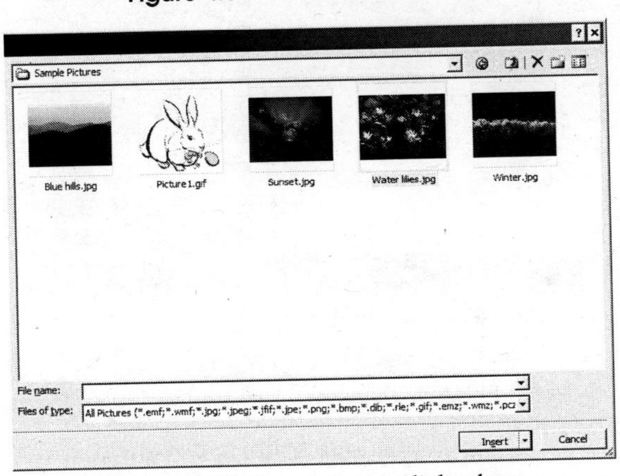

Figure 4.82 Insert picture dialog box

10. The Insert Picture dialog box closes and again you can see the Printed Watermark dialog box. You can specify how much the picture watermark is to be scale in the document.
11. Click the desired option from the Scale: drop-down list. For example, we have selected the 100% option from the list.
12. Click the Washout check box.
13. Click the Apply button in the Printed Watermark dialog box.
14. The selected Watermark picture appears in the document as shown in Figure 4.83.

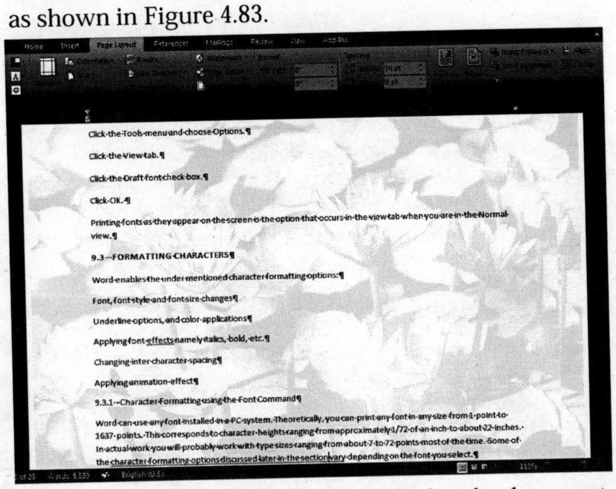

Figure 4.83 Watermark picture applied in the document

Adding a Drop Cap

A drop cap is a feature of Word in which the first letter of a paragraph is of a much bigger size than the rest that follow. The letter formatting is such that, the letter 'drops down' to cover the few lines following the first one. Drop caps have been extensively used, from the early days of printing to the advent of web publishing.

You can add a drop cap to your document by selecting the first character of the first word at the start of your text.

➡ To convert the first character of the first word of a paragraph, do this:

1. Click anywhere on the paragraph or block of text which you want to begin with the drop cap.
2. Click the Insert tab.

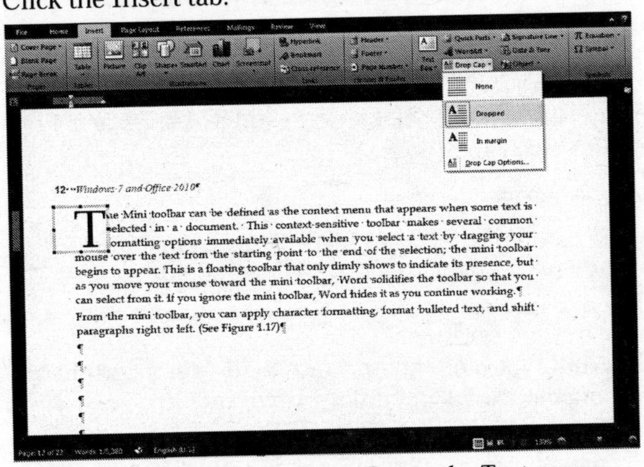

Figure 4.84 Selecting Drop Cap in the Text group

3. Click the Drop Cap button in the Text group from the Insert tab as shown in Figure 4.84.
4. A drop down list appears. Click the desired Dropped option from the drop-down list as shown in Figure 4.84.
5. The selected text is converted into drop cap as shown in Figure 4.84.

4.7 MAIL MERGE

Mail Merge is a mass-mailing facility that takes names, addresses and pertinent facts about the recipients and merges the information into the form of a letter. Mail Merge printing (merge printing in short) uses two files: a data file that contains a listing of data items (or fields) arranged in some specific order and a master file that contains the standard text as well as the data variables which are replaced with specific data items from the data file during the merge operation performed by Word 2010.

4.7.1 Creating a Mail Merge Letter

The best way to learn how to create and print a merged document is to consider a practical example. This is described in the following sections.

Creating a Document for Mail-Merge

For mail-merge, you need to do the following:

- Create a data source.
- Create main document.
- Insert fields into the main document.
- Check for design and data entry errors.
- Merge the data source document and the main document and finally, print merged documents.

Planning Data Source

Designing a data source document is one of the most important parts of mail merge feature. To begin with, you may want to create a data source document which has one field for the name of your friend; one field for the address and one field each for the city and pincode. It is always good if you read data into multiple fields. That is you should use two fields namely, Last name and First name for name field. Similarly, keep separate fields for house number, colony, city and pin. For example, if you want to deliver an invitation through a messenger, you may need to sort the addresses on the basis of colony field in the address, so that invitations belonging to one colony can be sent together through a messenger.

Starting Mail Merge

Word 2010 has a step-by-step Mail Merge Wizard that guides you through the steps for creating merged documents.

➡ **To use the mail merge helper, do this:**

1. First create a blank document.
2. Click the Mailings tab, choose Start Mail Merge group and click on the down pointing arrow, after that a list appears as seen in Figure 4.85 offering five options – Letters, E-Mail Messages, Envelopes, Labels and Directory.

The first step in the mail merge process is to Create the Main document, because the type of main document governs the subsequent choices you can make in the Mail Merge Helper. Note that Letters, E-Mail Messages, Envelopes, Labels, and Catalogues are various types of documents you can produce using Mail Merge Wizard. Hence, the Helper offers you different choices of data source.

Creating Main Document

Word 2010 has a step-by-step Mail Merge Wizard that guides you through the steps for creating merged documents.

➡ **To create main document, do this:**

1. Click the Mailings tab in the Start Mail Merge group and click on the down pointing arrow and select Step by Step Mail Merge Wizard... .

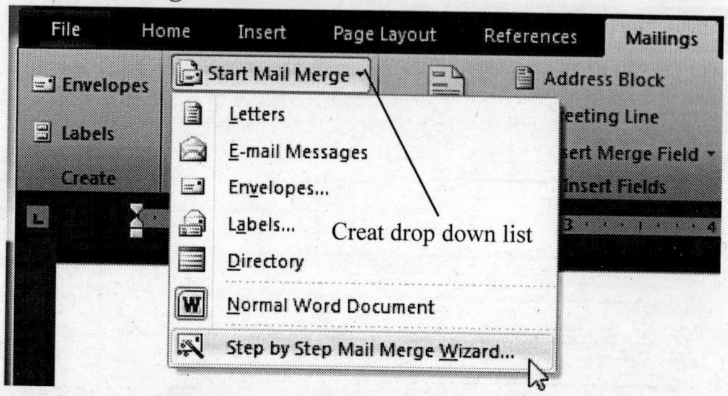

Figure 4.85 Select step-by-step Mail Merge Wizard

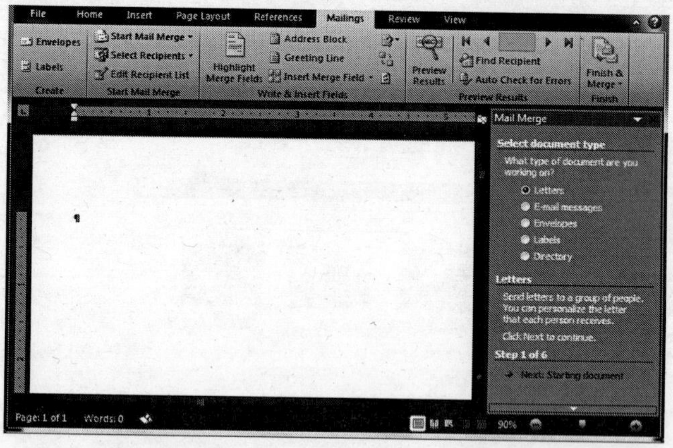

Figure 4.86 Step 1 of Mail Merge task pane

2. On the right hand side the Mail Merge task pane box appears as seen in Figure 4.86 showing Step 1 of the Wizard's six steps.
3. Under the Select document type, click Letters radio button.
4. Click Next: Starting document.
   - The wizard guides you through the rest of the mail process. The following are more details, listed in step-by-step order.

- There are three options under select starting document, click use the current document radio button, which specifies how do you want to set up your letters? (See Figure 4.87).

5. Click Next: Select recipients.
   - Under Select recipients, click Type a new list radio button (Figure 4.88).
   - Click Create... under Type a new list section.

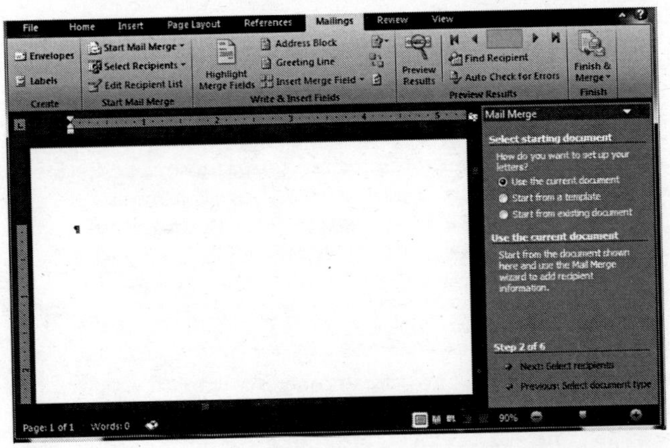

Figure 4.87 Step 2 of Mail Merge task pane

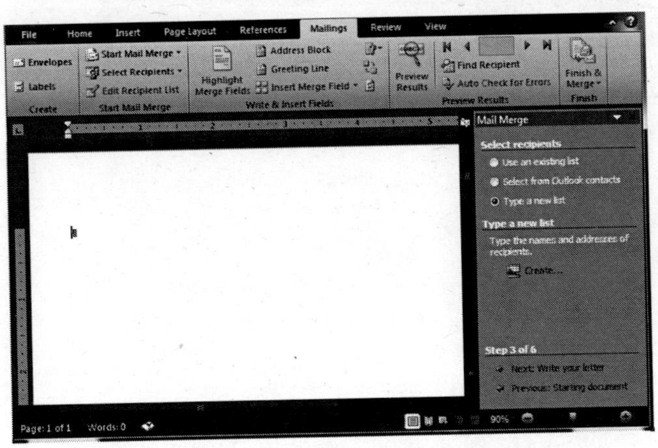

Figure 4.88 Step 3 of Mail Merge task pane

6. A New Address List dialog box appears as shown in Figure 4.89. Type the information you want to include for the data source.

Adding and Removing Field Names

As you may not require all the field names in the New Address List dialog box, so for each of the following field names, first select the field and then click the Customize Columns... button. The Customize Address list dialog box appears as shown in Figure 4.90.

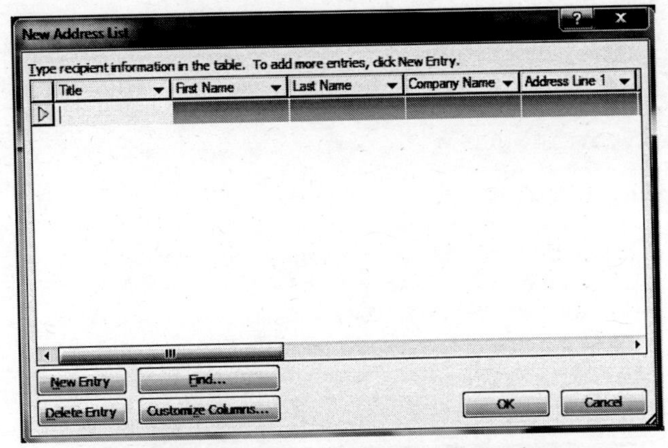

Figure 4.89 New Address List dialog box

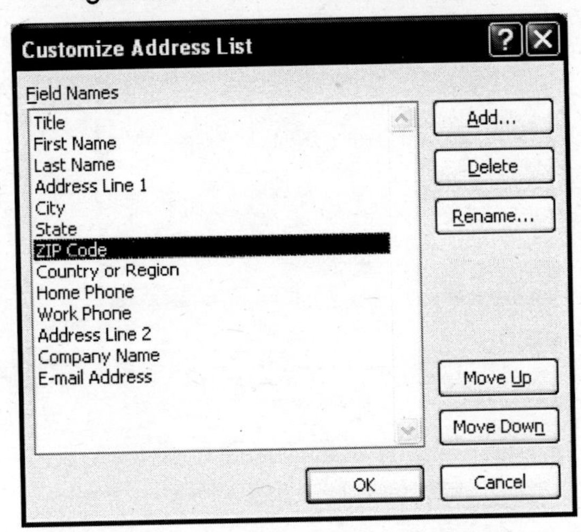

Figure 4.90 Customize Address list dialog box

7. Select the Field names order appears in the Customize Address list dialog box, If you don't want any field, select the field and then click delete button.
8. The Selected Field names are: Title, First Name, Last Name, Address Line 1, City, Zip Code.
9. Under Field names: type (use tab key to go next field)

```
Title: Mr.
First Name: Sanjay
Last Name: Sharma
Address Line 1: 120-A, Vikaspuri
City: New Delhi
Zip Code: 110 018
```

After completing the First entry, click New Entry to enter another data records as follows:

```
Title: Ms.
First Name: Uma
Last Name: Shankar
Address Line 1: A-3, Janakpuri
City: New Delhi
Zip Code: 110 049
```

Title: Ms.
First Name: Asha
Last Name: Arora
Address Line 1: B2/4, Model Town
City: New Delhi
Zip Code: 110 009

Saving Data Source

When you have finished adding, removing and arranging fields, click OK to save your data source.

10. The Save Address List dialog box appears as in Figure 4.91. Enter a name and location for your data source file, say, **Data.doc** and click Save button to save the file.

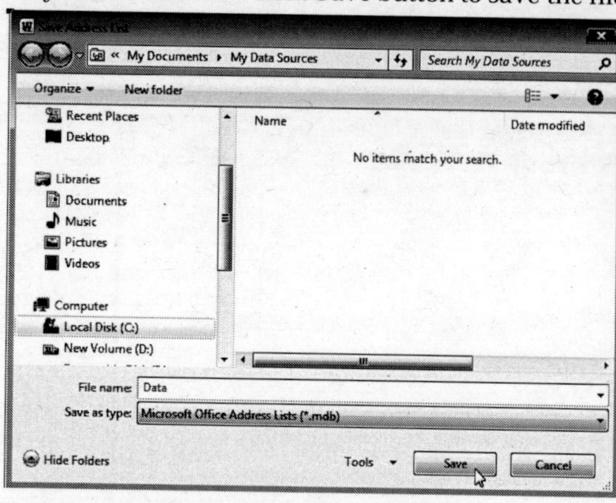

Figure 4.91 Save Address List dialog box

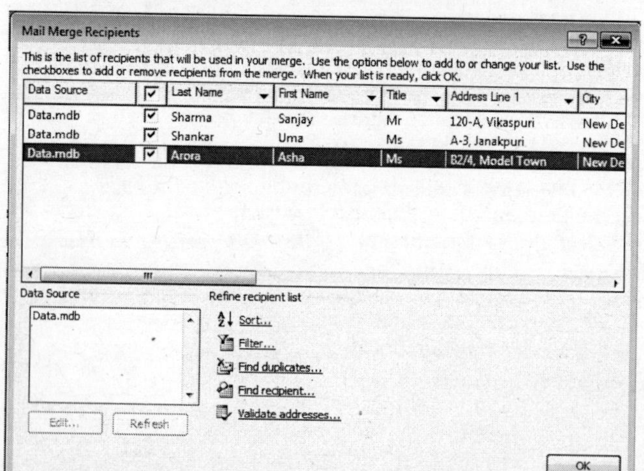

Figure 4.92 Mail Merge Recipients dialog box

11. The Mail Merge Recipients dialog box appears as in Figure 4.92. Select the recipients that will be used in your merge process.
12. Click OK.
13. Click Next: Write your letter.

Typing Letter

Now type the following letter.

Rohini
New Delhi-110 056
Ref.Rahul/Comm/20

Dated: 3rd January, 2017

To
<<Title>> <<First_Name>>
<<Last_Name>>
<<Address_Line_1>>
<<City>>-<<ZIP_Code>>

Dear <<Title>> <<Last_Name>>

I have to inform you that the meeting of the club committee will be held at the Club House, 36-N, Chanakyapuri, Vinay Marg on Wednesday 25th January, 2017 at 10.30 A.M. I hope you will make it convenient to attend the conference.

The agenda for the conference is as under:

1. Confirmation of the minutes of the last meeting (enclosed).
2. Accounts and Internal Auditors Report for the months of Feb and March 2017 (enclosed).
3. Election of new members.
4. List of outstanding.
5. Any other matter with the permission of the Chairman.

Yours faithfully,

P.K. Verma
(Secretary)

Inserting Fields Names in the Master Document

When you place the merge field names into a master document, you will see that Word 2010 encloses each field name in chevrons, i.e. the marks represented as << >>.

➡ **To insert a field, do this:**

1. In the Mailing tab, click Insert Merge Field in the Write Insert Fields group. Click the down pointing arrow and choose the field names that you can insert in your master document appears. You can also select the field names from this list (See Figure 4.93).
2. Click the Title from merge field name to insert it into the document.
3. Press the Spacebar key to insert a blank space between the Title and the FirstName.
4. Click the Insert Merge Field button to insert the next field name and select FirstName.
5. Press the Spacebar key to insert a blank space between the fields FirstName and LastName.

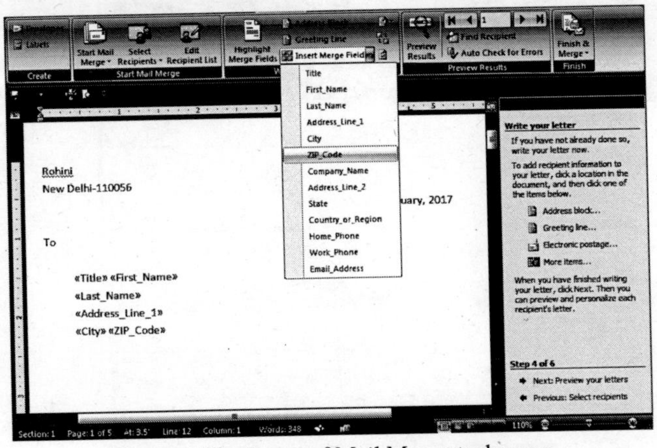

Figure 4.93 Step 4 of Mail Merge task pane

6. Click the Insert Merge Field button and select LastName.
7. Press the Enter key to move to the next line.
8. Place the cursor below the **`<<Title>>`**. Click the Insert Merge Field button. Select **`<<Address1>>`** and press the Enter key.
9. Again place the cursor below **`<<Address1>>`**. Click the Insert Merge Field button. Select **`<<City>>`** type a hyphen and select **`<<ZIP_Code>>`** from the merge field button and press Enter key.
10. Press the Enter key twice to leave a blank line.
11. Type Dear and press the Spacebar key.
12. Click the Insert Merge Field button and select **`<<Title>>`**.
13. Press the Spacebar to leave a space between the Title and the LastName.
14. Click the Insert Merge Field button and select **`<<LastName>>`**.
15. Type a comma, and then press the Enter key twice to leave a blank line.

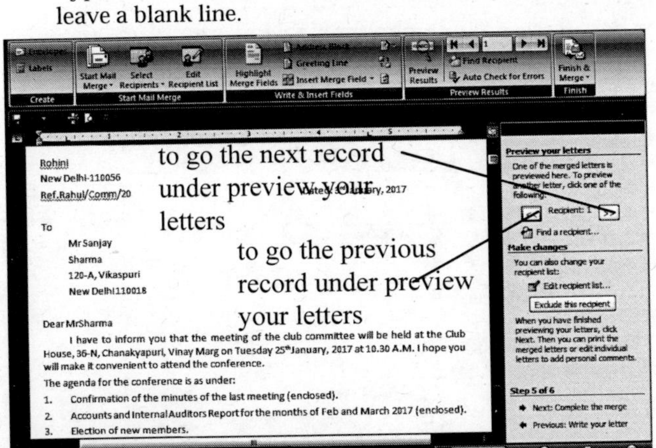

Figure 4.94 Step 5 of partially completed screen

16. After completing the above steps, your screen will be as shown in Figure 4.94.
17. Now type the remaining part of the letter.

Saving the Master Document

18. After you have completed the main document and inserted all of the merge fields, click Save As on the Office button.
19. Give the name of the document, and then Click Save button.
20. Click Next: Preview your letters.
21. In the Preview your letters, click arrow button, i.e., (<<) to show the first record, and to go the second record click (>>) arrow button (See Figure 4.94).
22. Click Next: Complete the merge (See Figure 4.95).

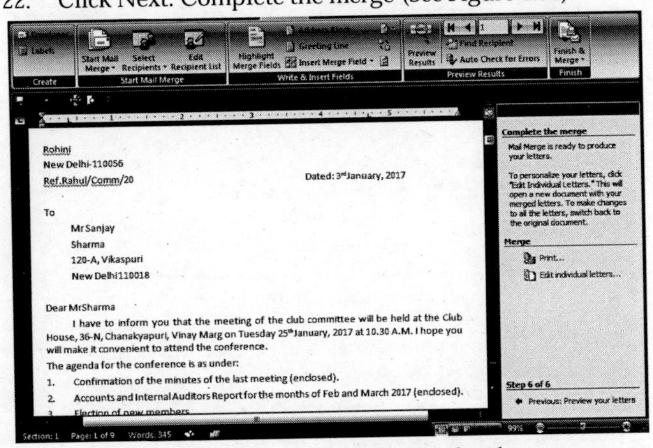

Figure 4.95 Step 6 of partially completed screen

23. To personalize individual documents, you actually complete the merge, and then edit the information you want in the resulting merged document.
24. Click Edit individual letters.... . under Merge section. The Merge to New Document dialog box appears as shown in Figure 4.96.
25. In the Merge records area, select the records you want to merge.
26. Click All radio button and then click OK.
    Word 2010 creates and opens a new merged documents. Your main document also remains open. You can switch back to it if you want to make a change to all the documents and then save all the merged documents. Click Office button and Save the file.

Printing the Merged Letters

If you want to print the letters, make sure that the printer is switched on and is in ready to print. Then click Finish Merge in Finish group. Click down pointing arrow and choose Print Documents... . The Merge to Printer dialog box appears. Select the records and click OK.

Merging for sending emails using outlook.

27. In the Finish group on the Mailings tab you will see a button called Finish Merge. Click on it, and then click Send E-mail Messages... as shown in Figure 4.97)

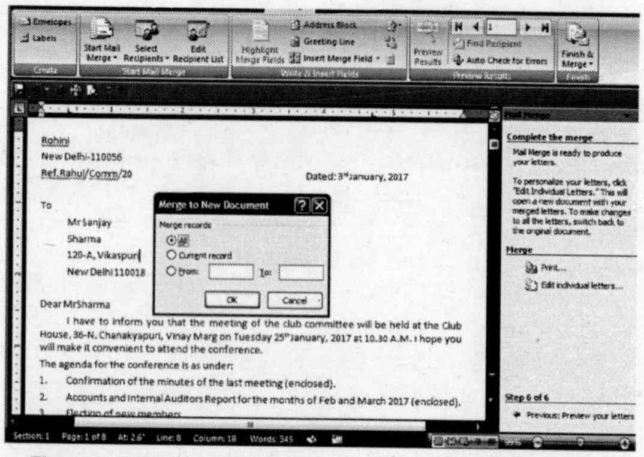

Figure 4.96 Merge to New Document dialog box

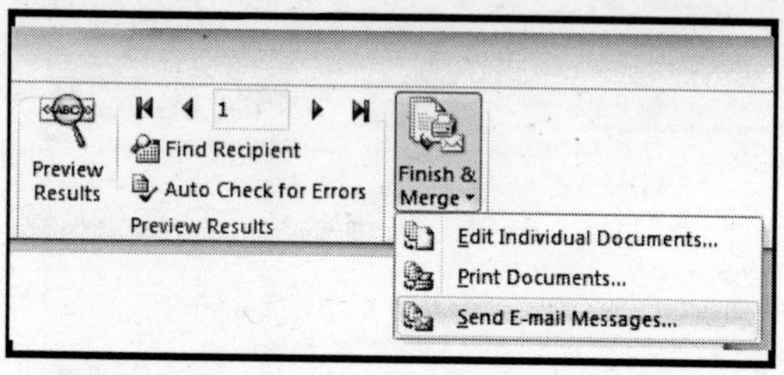

Figure 4.97 Selecting Send E-mail messages

28. Merge to E-mail dialog box appears as shown in Figure 4.98. You will be asked to give your message a Subject line: and then you can click on OK to send the messages.

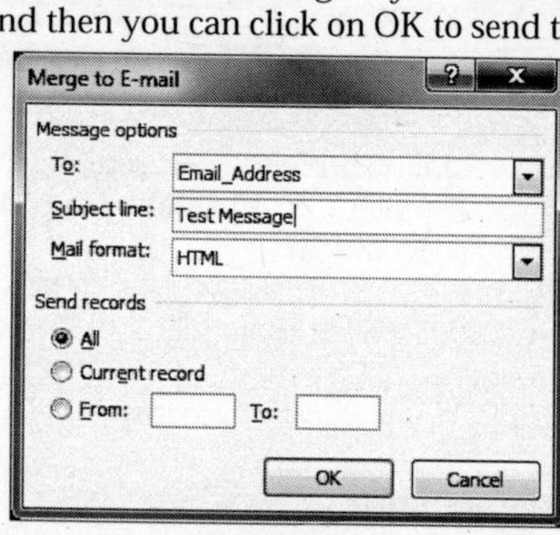

Figure 4.98

29. Now Word 2010 automatically generates all the individual emails, and sends them to your Outlook 2010 outbox (or your default email client). Your email merges will be recorded in your sent items folder.

☞ Attachments are not an option in an email merge. All data must be within the body of the email message.

4.7.2 Printing Mailing Labels

1. Open a document, which you want to use as a label.
2. Click the Mailings tab on the Ribbon.
3. Click the Labels button as seen in Figure 4.99.

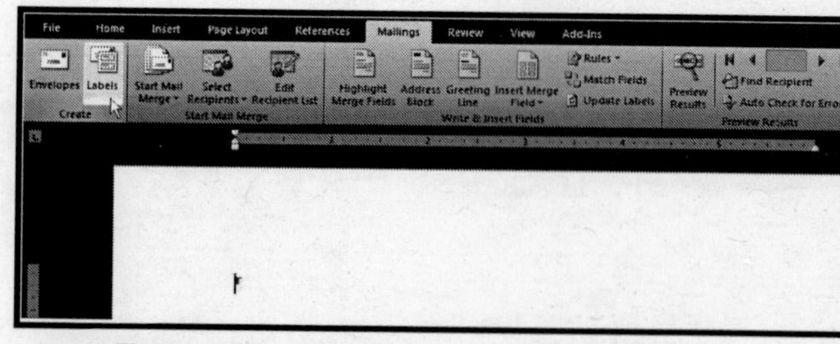

Figure 4.99 Selecting Labels in the Mailings tab

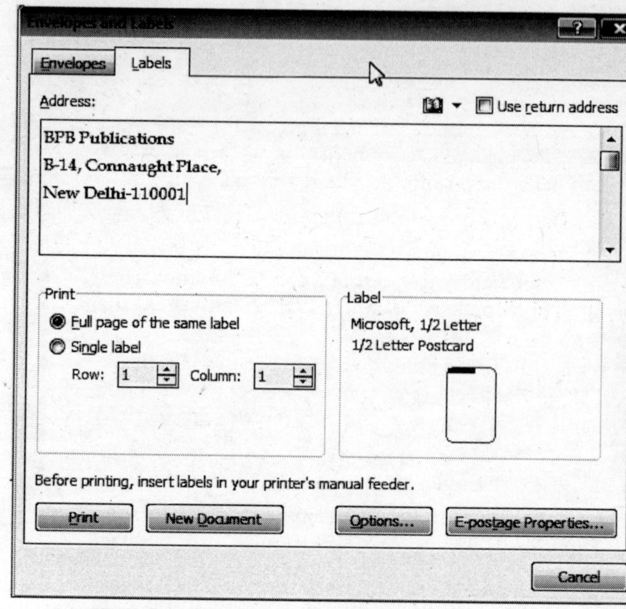

Figure 4.100 Envelopes and Labels dialog box

4. The Envelopes and Labels dialog box appears as seen in Figure 4.100.
5. Click the Labels tab. Type the Address in the Address: list box.
6. Click the Options... button in the Envelopes and Labels dialog box as seen in Figure 4.100.
7. The Labels Options dialog box appears as seen in Figure 4.101.

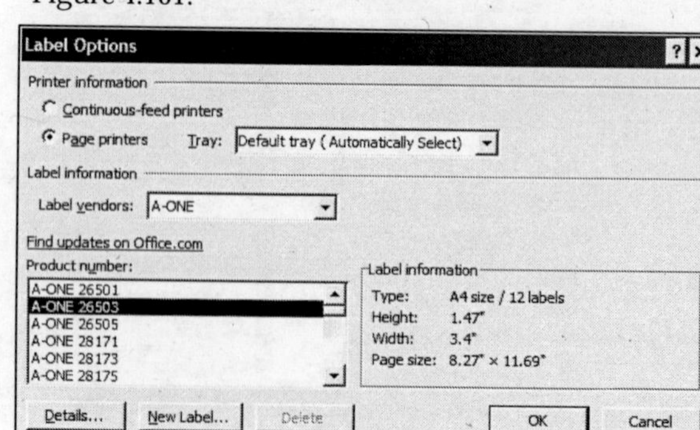

Figure 4.101 Label Options dialog box

8. Under the Label Information, click the Label Vendors drop-down list to select the maker of your labels. For example, we have selected A-ONE.
9. Click the Product number of your label in the Product number: list box. For example, we have selected A-ONE 26503.
10. Click the OK button. Again it appears Envelops and Labels dialog box.
11. Click the New Document button in the Envelopes and Labels dialog box as seen in Figure 4.102.

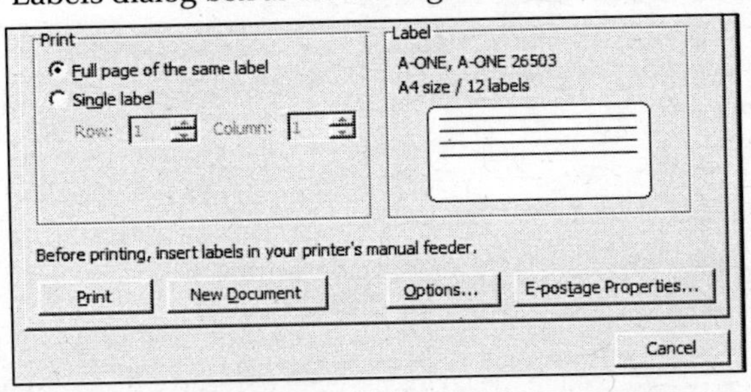

Figure 4.102 Select New Document button in the Envelopes and Labels dialog box

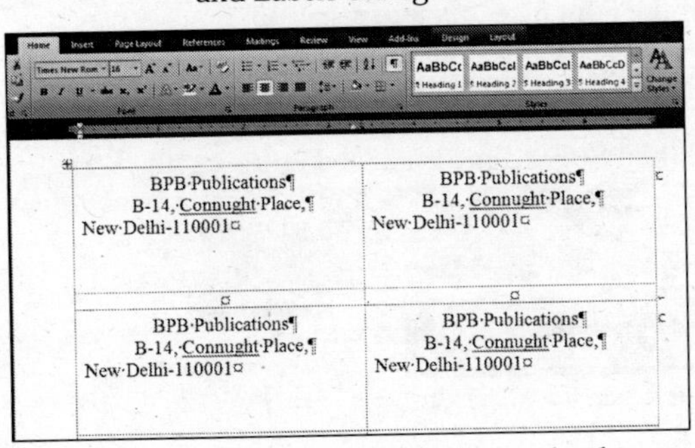

Figure 4.103 New document Label list in the document

12. Word 2010 displays a New document label list in the document as seen in Figure 4.103.

4.7.3 Use Local Language

If you want to work in a language other than the default one, follow the steps:

1. Launch an Office 2010 application (Word, Excel or any other).
2. Go to File menu and click Options to open settings box. In the left pane, click Language tab to see list of installed languages.
3. Click on the drop-down box that says "Add additional editing languages" to see a list of languages. Select the one you want from the list, then click the Add button (See Figure 4.104).
4. Select your new language and click Set as default button. You can also set your new language as the help language by clicking the Set as default button under Help language.

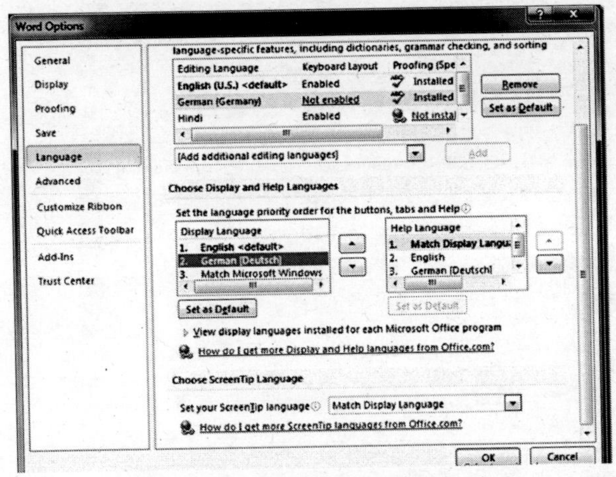

Figure 4.104 Word Options dialog box

5. Click OK button. You will be asked to restart the Office program, and will change your Office 2010 display language as shown in Figure 4.105.

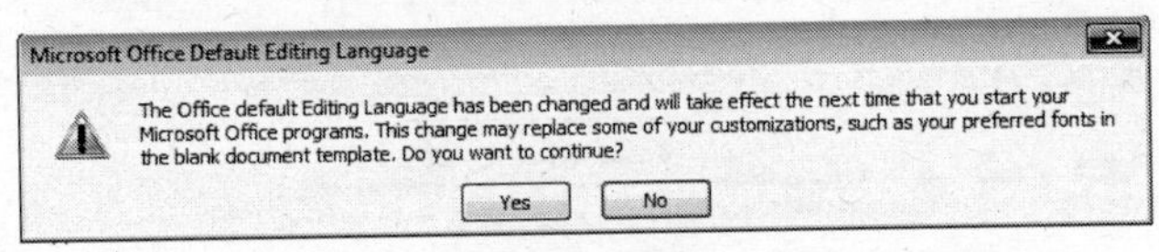

Figure 4.105

Before you have to change to default language you must installed Office 2010 language pack.

4.7.4 Macros

A macro is simply a recording of a repetitive task. Through Macros, you do not need to perform same action, i.e. change formatting, font style, size, and color over and over again in document. It actually records each and every click and keystroke you press while performing the task, so that you can play them back to perform same action over your documents.

➡ **To create a macro:**

1. Open a document to record a macro. We have highlight some text in your document, click the View tab, from Macros group, click Record Macro as shown in Figure 4.106.
2. Record Macro dialog box appears as shown in Figure 4.107.
3. Enter a Macro name: for example, we have typed formatting. Under Assign macro to options, click Keyboard button to assign a hotkey.
4. The Customize keybord dialog box appears as shown in Figure 4.108.

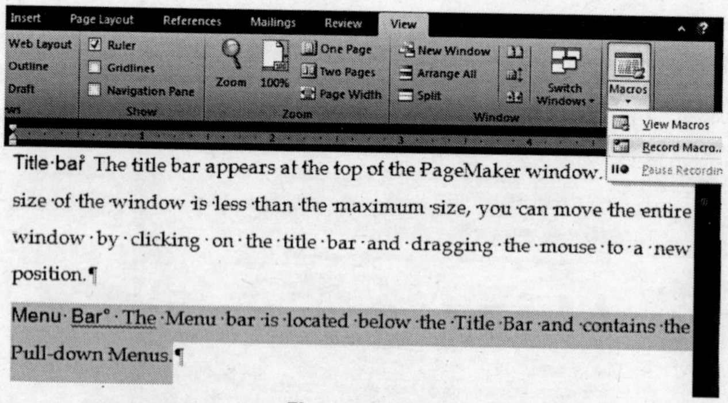

Figure 4.106

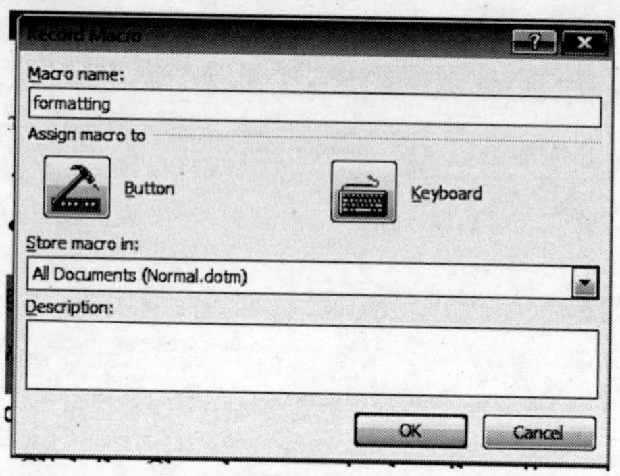

Figure 4.107 Record Macro dialog box

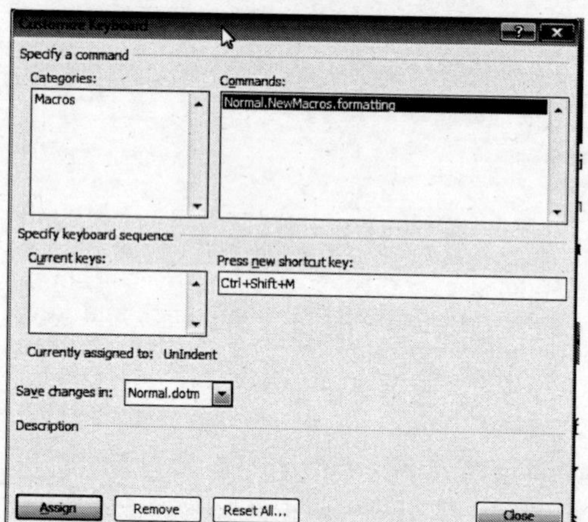

Figure 4.108 Customize keyboard dialog box

5. Now place insert cursor in Press new shortcut key: box, and assign a hotkey by pressing keys combination like Ctrl+Shift+M. Click Assign to assign hotkey to macro, and then click close button (See Figure 4.108).

☞ If you use more than one word in your macro name it must have an underscore between the two words or Word will reject it.

6. You will see recorder-like image with pointer, indicating that macro is being recorded. Here, we will do some formatting over the text such as (See Figure 4.109).

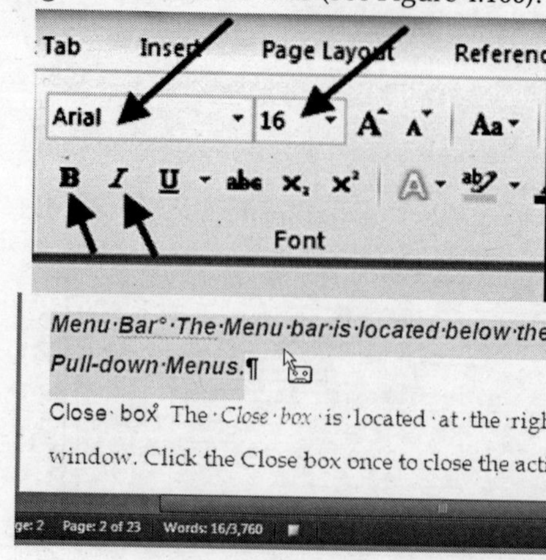

Figure 4.109 Selecting the style you want to record

- Click on the Current Font box and select Ariel.
- Click on the Font Size box and select 16.
- Click on the Bold and Italics icons.

7. After selecting above formatting options, to make it stop recording, again click on the View tab from Macros group, and then Stop recording (See Figure 4.110).

Figure 4.110 Selecting stop recording

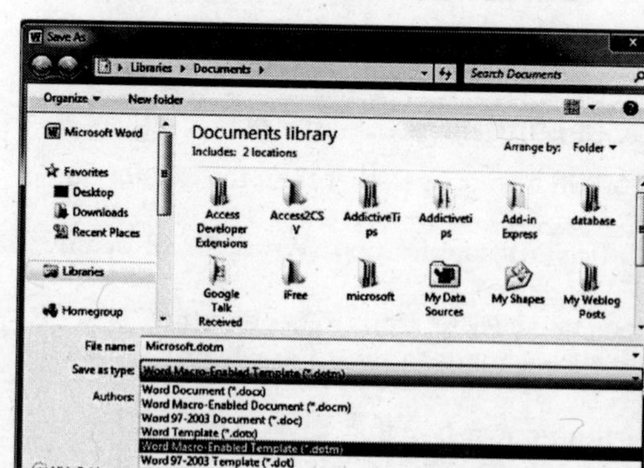

Figure 4.111 Save As dialog box

8. Run the macro by pressing the specified hotkey. In our case, it is Ctrl+Shift+M. It will immediately apply recorded formatting style to the new paragraph.

9. For saving a macro-enabled document, on File menu, click Save As from Save As dialog, under Save as type options, click Word Macro-Enabled Template (*dotm) (See Figure 4.111).
10. Enter an appropriate name of document and click save.

MODEL QUESTIONS AND ANSWERS

A. Multiple Choice

1.1 When Word gets loaded, the opening screen displays a document named:
a. Document1 b. Document
c. Doc1 d. No document name is displayed

1.2 You specify the save details of your file in the
a. Save As... dialog box
b. Save the File As... dialog box
c. File Save dialog box
d. None of the above

1.3 Word offers certain ways by which you can move around in a document
a. By scrolling b. By moving to a specific page
c. Both a and b above d. None of the above

1.4 The contents of the Clipboard remain the same until
a. You cut other text b. You shut down your computer
c. You copy other text d. All of the above

1.5 Word text can be made Italic by
a. Ctrl+I c. Ctrl+B
b. Ctrl+U d. None of the above

1.6 In Word you can align the selected paragraph to its right by pressing
a. Ctrl+E b. Ctrl+L
c. Ctrl+R d. None of the above

1.7 Word automatically places a default left aligned tab stop at every
a. 0.2" b. 0.4"
c. 0.3" d. 0.5"

1.8 What is the term used for the word processing programs that show you directly on the PC screen the appearance of your final document as you might expect when the document is printed on the paper.
a. Search & Replace b. Pagination
c. Soft Copy d. WYSIWYG

1.9 When you insert a table in a document
a. Word outlines each cell with continuous lines so that you see the cells when you work in a table.
b. Word outlines each cell with dotted gridlines so that you see the cells when you work in a table.
c. No line is drawn.
d. None of the above

1.10 After a table has been created, which of the following operations cannot be performed?
a. Insert rows in a table b. Delete and insert columns
c. Split the table into two tables d. None of the above

1.11 How many scroll bars can be visible on the text area if your document is over 200%?
a. Four b. Two
c. One d. Three

1.12 What Ribbon will you find where you can add a chart?
a. View b. Reference
c. Insert d. Page Layout

1.13 What Ribbon do you use to change margins?
a. Page Layout b. View
c. Insert d. Home

1.14 What can be shown on the status bar?
a. Name of document, insert button, spell check
b. Number of spellings errors, page number, document name
c. Size of Margins, word count, web layout
d. Number of pages in the document, word count, spelling/grammar check

1.15 Which Ribbon shows what fonts are available for use?
a. View b. Page Layout
c. Reference d. Home

1.16 What Ribbon do you need to be on to see the document views that are available?
a. Insert b. View
c. Page Layout d. Home

1.17 What page view can you use to see what it will look like when printed?
a. Outline view b. Draft view
c. Reading view d. Print view

1.18 What is NOT a new feature in Word 2010?
a. Ribbon b. Button
c. Charts d. Drop down menu

1.19 What is the name of the small toolbar at the top that can show the save disk?
a. My Documents b. Quick Access
c. Title bar d. Find Me

1.20 What is NOT on the insert Ribbon?
a. Shapes b. Clip Art
c. Page Numbers d. Thesaurus

1.21 How can you delete the record displayed in the New Address List dialog box?
a. Remove Entry b. Delete Entry
c. Remove/Delete Entry d. None of the above

1.22 You can refine the list of recipients by using the option such as ________, __________ and __________.
a. Filter, Find duplicates and Find recipient

b. Ascending and Descending
c. Sorting and Finding, Replacing
d. Find, Select and Replace

1.23 When you are in the Mailings tab, what is the next option that you click on?
a. Insert Merge Field b. Labels
c. Start Mail Merge d. Highlight Merge Fields

1.24 On the Mailings tab in the Finish menu, what is the option that you click on to finish off the mail merge?
a. Finish and Merge b. Edit Recipient list
c. Update Labels d. Finish button

1.25 Which button do you click to add or delete fields when creating a new Address List?
a. Add/Delete Fields b. New Entry
c. Customize columns d. Add Fields

B. State whether the following are True or False

2.1 To highlight the paragraph, double-click in the selection bar next to the paragraph.

2.2 To select an entire document, you will double click the mouse in the selection bar.

2.3 Right justification makes the ends of lines uneven.

2.4 Italic character are slanted than regular characters.

2.5 Margins are the distances between the text and the edges of the paper.

2.6 MS Word operating system was developed by MS to overcome the limitations of its own MS-DOS operating system.

2.7 In order to save a file, on the Standard toolbar, click on the Save button.

2.8 A blank line is also called as a paragraph. It is called as an empty paragraph.

2.9 You cannot undo certain operations like saving, printing, opening and creating documents.

2.10 Print button on the Quick Access toolbar will print the entire document using the default settings.

2.11 Using Home tab you can perform editing functions such as cut, copy, paste, find and replace etc.

2.12 Using Insert menu you can insert various objects such as page numbers, headers and footers, picture etc.

2.13 Using Review tab you can access to various utilities of word such as spell check, macros and mail merge etc.

2.14 In MS Word every command is available in Ribbon.

2.15 Formula bar is available in MS Word 2010.

Answers

A. 1.1 a 1.2 a 1.3 c 1.4 d 1.5 a
1.6 c 1.7 d 1.8 d 1.9 b 1.10 c
1.11 b 1.12 c 1.13 a 1.14 d 1.15 d
1.16 b 1.17 d 1.18 d 1.19 b 1.20 d
1.21 b 1.22 a 1.23 c 1.24 a 1.25 b

B. 2.1 T 2.2 F 2.3 T 2.4 T 2.5 T
2.6 T 2.7 T 2.8 T 2.9 T 2.10 T
2.11 T 2.12 T 2.13 F 2.14 T 2.15 F

CHAPTER 5

Spreadsheet

5.1 INTRODUCTION

Spreadsheet applications (sometimes referred to simply as spreadsheets) are computer programs that let you to create and manipulate spreadsheets electronically. In a spreadsheet application, each value sits in a cell. You can define what type of data is in each cell and how different cells depend on one another. The relationships between cells are called formulas, and the names of the cells are called labels.

A table of values are arranged in rows and columns. Each value can have a predefined relationship to the other values. If you change one value, therefore, you may need to change other values as well, or they will change automatically.

Once you have defined the cells and the formulas for linking them together, you can enter your data. You can then modify selected values to see how all the other values change accordingly. This enables you to study various what-if scenarios.

Excel 2010 is a popular spreadsheet program, where you design worksheets by using this software package. Excel 2010 uses a workbook-style presentation which is made up of several worksheets, like pages in a notebook.

5.2 ELEMENTS OF ELECTRONIC SPREADSHEET

When you are working with a spreadsheet package, such as MS Excel 2010 you have to know some spreadsheet terminologies. Some such terms are given in the following paragraphs.

Workbook

A workbook is a collection of many worksheets. In a single workbook, you can store information in an organized manner. By default, a workbook opens with three worksheets and it can contain a maximum of 255 worksheets.

Worksheet

A worksheet is a sheet which is made up of rows and columns. It is used for planning a project or financial documents of an organization. Worksheet refers to the actual document you create by using the spreadsheet program. A worksheet is always stored in a workbook.

☞ Excel is a popular spreadsheet program, where you design worksheets by using this program.

Chartsheet

Chartsheet is a separate sheet in a workbook that contain only graphs or charts. It is useful when you want to see a chart or tabular data separated from other type of data.

Row

A row is a horizontal block of cells that runs through the entire width of the worksheet. The rows are numbered from top to bottom along the left edge of the worksheet. The first row is numbered 1, the second 2, and so on. There can be a maximum of 1,048,576 rows and 16,384 columns in an Excel 2010 worksheet.

Column

A column is a vertical block of cells that runs through the entire worksheet. A worksheet contains 16,384 (A to XFD) columns. The first column is A, the second is B and so on until you reach Z. Then comes column AA through XFD. The last (or rightmost) column of the worksheet, XFD is the 16,384th column.

Cell

A cell is the intersection of a row and a column. For example, the uppermost cell is A1 (column A, row 1). Cell G9 is the intersection of column G, row 9. When you select a cell by clicking it with the mouse, or moving to it using the keyboard, it becomes an active cell.

Formula

Formulas are equations that perform calculations on values in your worksheet. It is an order of values, names, cell references, functions and operators in a cell that together give a new values. A formula always begins with = (equal) sign.

Function

Functions are the pre-defined formulas or programs that perform calculations in Excel on specific values, called arguments. Each function takes specific types of arguments such as numbers, references, text, or logical values.

Working with Spreadsheet

In Excel 2010, each workbook can contain many worksheets. These sheets may also contain charts, macros, etc. Sheets may contain different types of information but all the data or information is related to each other.

☞ Generally, spreadsheet is a software tool and worksheet is a work file created with spreadsheet software. But sometimes, worksheet is also called a spreadsheet.

Each worksheet contains 16,384 columns and 1,048,576 rows. The intersection of a row and a column forms a cell in which you can enter data or a formula. Column headings start at A and as they reach the letter Z column, headings restart with AA, AB, and so on till XFD. Row headings, down the left side of a sheet, go from 1 to 1,048,576. It is equally easy for formulas to refer to information in another worksheet of the same workbook as it is in the same worksheet.

Terminologies used in MS Excel

The following terminologies should be kept in mind, while using MS Excel.

Select	Highlight a cell or group of cells, dialog box option, or graphical object with the keyboard or mouse action.
Choose	Execute and complete a command.
Active	Bring an application or document window to the foreground.

Table 5.1 gives the details of the terminology for the mouse operations.

Table 5.1 Terminologies for Mouse Function

Action	Function
Position	Position the mouse pointer on an item.
Click	Point to an item and then quickly press and release the mouse left button.
Double click	Point to an item and quickly press and release the mouse left button two times.
Drag	Point to an item, press and hold the mouse left button as you move the mouse pointer to a new location, then release the mouse button.
Right click	Point to an item and click the right mouse button.

5.2.1 Opening of Spreadsheet (Excel 2010)

MS Excel 2010 needs Windows 7 as an operating system to run on an IBM PC. However, Excel 2010 can also be run on Windows XP operating system, if service pack 3 is installed on Windows XP.

➡ **To start Excel 2010 in Windows 7, do this:**

1. Click the Start button on the taskbar, highlight All Programs, click MS Office and then click MS Excel 2010 (See Figure 5.1).

➡ **To start Excel 2010 in Windows XP, do this:**

1. Click the Start button on the taskbar, highlight All Programs, click MS Office and then MS Excel 2010 (See Figure 5.2).

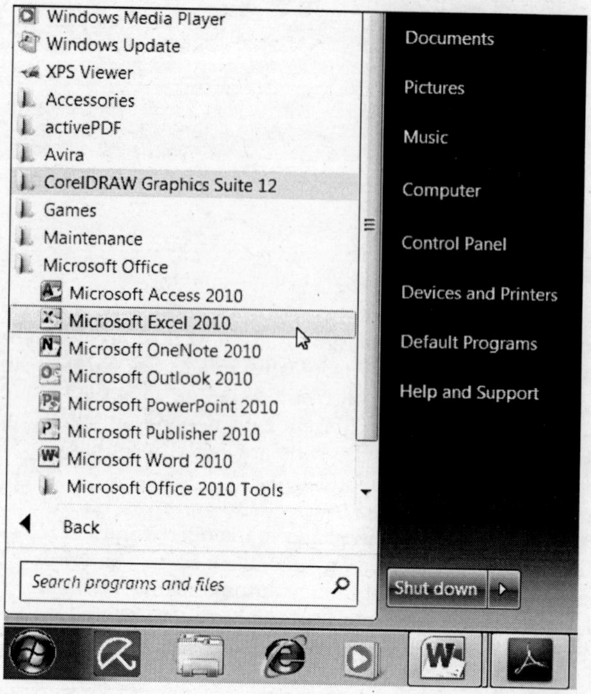

Figure 5.1 Starting Excel 2010 in Windows 7

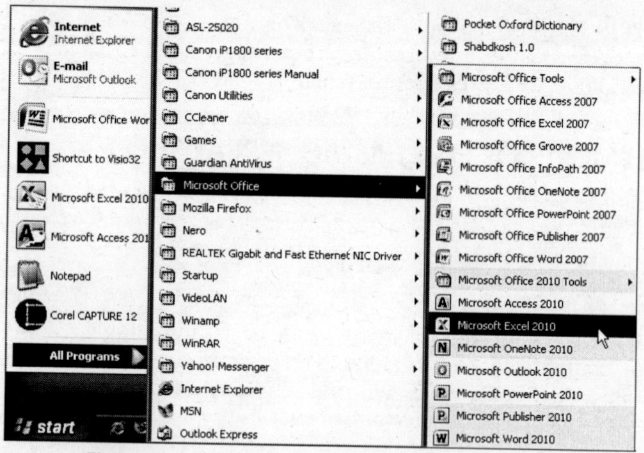

Figure 5.2 Starting Excel 2010 in Windows XP

Excel 2010 Interface

Excel 2010 includes the MS Office Fluent interface, which consists of a customizable visual system of tools and commands. Figure 5.3 shows the elements of Excel 2010 application window and an open Excel 2010 workbook in detail.

Title Bar

At the top of an Excel 2010 window, there is the title bar. The left edge of this bar has the Office button next to which the name of the open document is displayed. On the right edge of the title bar, the Minimize, Restore/Maximize and Close button are placed (See Figure 5.3).

Application Window

The window within which Excel 2010 runs.

Quick Access Toolbar

The Quick Access Toolbar is a customizable toolbar that

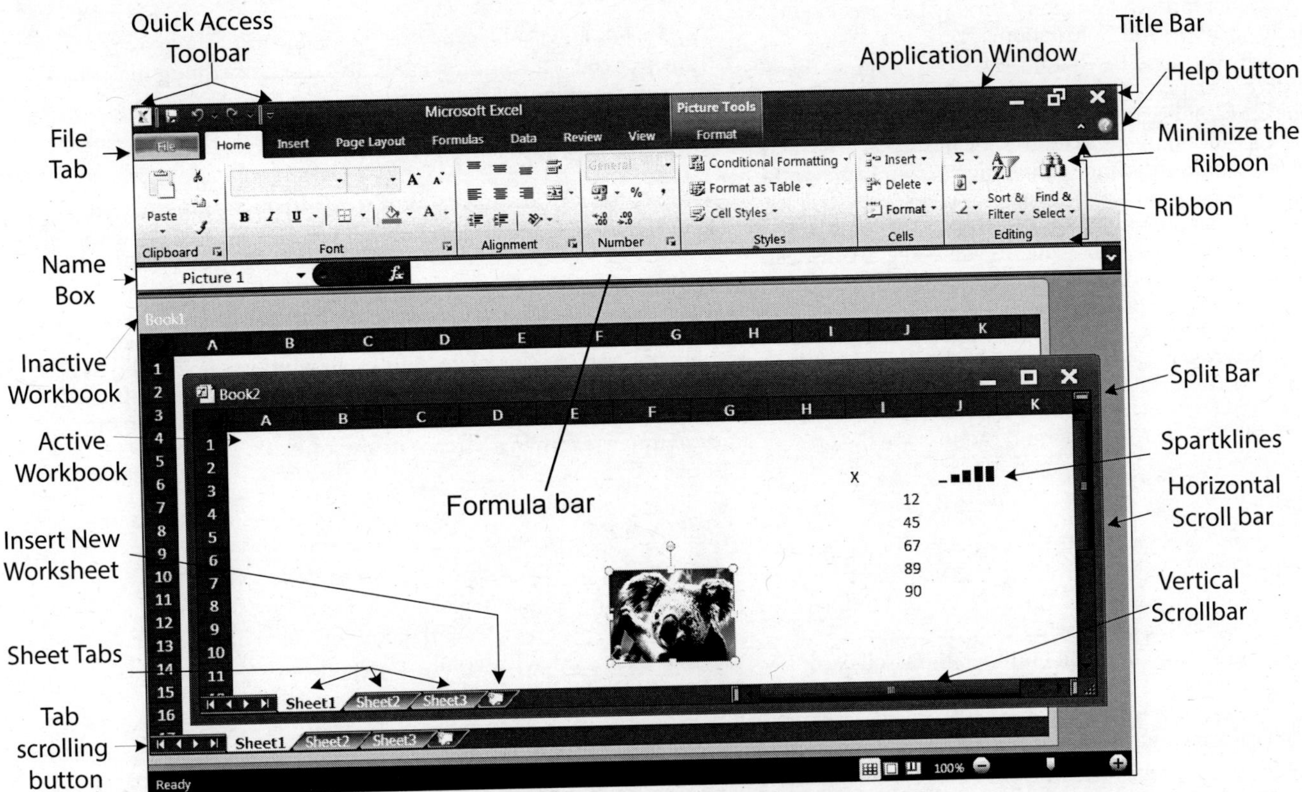

Figure 5.3 Elements of Excel 2010 window

contains a set of commands that are independent of the tab that is currently displayed. You can add buttons that represent commands to the Quick Access Toolbar. You can move the Quick Access Toolbar from one of the two possible locations. This toolbar is located by default at the top of Excel 2010 window. It provides tools that you use frequently, such as Save, Undo and Repeat buttons (See Figure 5.3). You can customize the Quick Access Toolbar by adding commands to it.

Workbook Window

A window within the Excel 2010 application window in which a worksheet, chart, or dialog box is shown.

File Tab

File tab is the coloured tab which is located in the upper-left corner of MS Office 2010 programs and below the Quick Access Toolbar (See Figure 5.3). When you click the File tab, you can see the Backstage view. File Tab replaces the Office button in Excel 2007. It contains commands like New, Open, Save, Save As, Print, etc.

Active Workbook

The Excel 2010 workbook window that accepts entries and commands.

Inactive Workbook

A window that contains Excel 2010 information. It is not affected by commands. Such a window has a gray title bar and is behind the active workbook window.

Ribbon

Ribbon is displayed just below the title bar (See Figure 5.3). In Ribbon, Commands are organized in logical groups, which are collected together under tabs. You can hide the Ribbon by double-clicking the active tab. Different types of Tabs described here under are available in the Ribbon of Excel 2010.

- Home Tab: When you open Excel 2010, Home Tab is active. It contains the buttons related to the worksheet contents, such as entering, editing, and formatting data. It is divided into seven groups, i.e., Clipboard, Font, Alignment, Number, Style, Cells and Editing.
- Insert Tab: Insert tab contains the button related to the items which you can insert in your worksheet. Groups of this tab are Tables, Illustrations (picture, clipart) Charts, Sparklines, Filter, Links, Text and Symbols.
- Page Layout Tab: It includes the buttons related to the appearance of the worksheet. This tab is divided into five groups, i.e., Themes, Page Setup, Scale to Fit, Sheet Options, and Arrange.

- Formulas Tab: It contains the button related to functions. Group of this tab are Function Library, Defined Names, Formula Auditing and Calculation.
- Data Tab: It contains the button related to data analysis. Get External Data, Connections, Sort & Filter, Data Tools, Outline and Analysis are the group of this tab.
- Review Tab: It contains the button related to security and accurate data. Proofing, Language Comments and Changes are the group of this Tab.
- View Tab: It contains the button related to the view of the worksheet, i.e., how you want to view the worksheet. Workbook view, Show/Hide, Zoom, Window are the group of this tab.
- Developer Tab: It contains the button related to create, run and edit macros. It also includes commands or buttons to import XML (eXtensible Markup Language) view of the worksheet, i.e., how you want to view the worksheet Code, Add-Ins Controls, XML and Modify are the groups of this tab.

Scroll Bar

The scroll bar appears at the left for vertical scrolling and at the bottom right for horizontal scrolling as seen in Figure 5.3.

- To scroll one cell at a time, click the scroll button with arrows at the corners of the scroll bars.
- To scroll more, drag the scroll button in the scroll bar.

Split Bar

The split bar is located at the top of the vertical scroll bar and to the right of the horizontal scroll bar (See Figure 5.3). Double click the split button on the vertical scroll bar. It splits the sheet horizontally.

Tab Scrolling Buttons

These are the arrow buttons to the left of the sheet tabs for scrolling the worksheet (See Figure 5.3).

- To scroll between sheet tabs, click an arrow for the direction you want to scroll.
- To scroll one sheet tab at a time in left or right direction, click the middle tab scrolling buttons.
- To scroll through a group of sheet tabs in left or right direction, click the tab scroll buttons at the left and right corner.
- To display a list of the sheets in the workbook right click a tab scrolling button to display the menu.

Sheet Tabs

A tab is near to the bottom of a work book window that displays the name of a sheet (See Figure 5.3). Click the sheet tab to move to the next sheet. To display the shortcut menu, right click the sheet tab. To scroll through the sheet tabs, use the tab scrolling button.

Name Box

The name box is at the left end of the formula bar (See Figure 5.3). It identifies the selected cell, chart item or drawing object.

Formula Bar

The formula bar displays the constant value or formula used in the active cell. The formula bar is also used for editing the cell contents (See Figure 5.3).

Shortcut Menus

Shortcut menus are meant to display frequently used commands related to the selected item or object.

ScreenTips

ScreenTips show the name of the command button shown in ribbon. ScreenTips are shown in small windows appearing as soon as you position the mouse pointer on the toolbar button. Enhanced ScreenTips are larger windows that display more descriptive text than a ScreenTip and can take a link to a Help topic.

Status Bar

Status bar appears at the bottom of the Excel 2010 window. It displays information regarding a selected command or an operation in progress. Note that the right side of the status bar shows zoom slider, different views tool, such as Normal, Page Layout and Page Break view.

Creating a New Workbook

➡ **To create a new workbook, do this:**

1. Click the File Tab as seen in Figure 5.4. Here, Select New. Under Available Templates, click Blank Workbook and then click Create button or alternatively, press Ctrl + N keys together.

☞ You can create a blank workbook or create new workbook based on an existing workbook, the default workbook template, or any other template.

5.2.2 Opening a Workbook

➡ **To Open a workbook, do this:**

1. Click the File Tab as seen in Figure 5.4. Here, choose Open or alternatively, press Ctrl + O keys together. The Open dialog box appears as shown in Figure 5.5.
2. In dialog box, choose the drive, folder name that contains the workbooks. After finding the required workbook, select it.
3. Then click OK.

➡ **To Open more than one workbook simultaneously, do this:**

1. Repeat step 1. and 2. of opening a single workbook.
2. Click the name of one file and then hold down Ctrl key and click another file name and then press Enter key.

Figure 5.4 File Tab

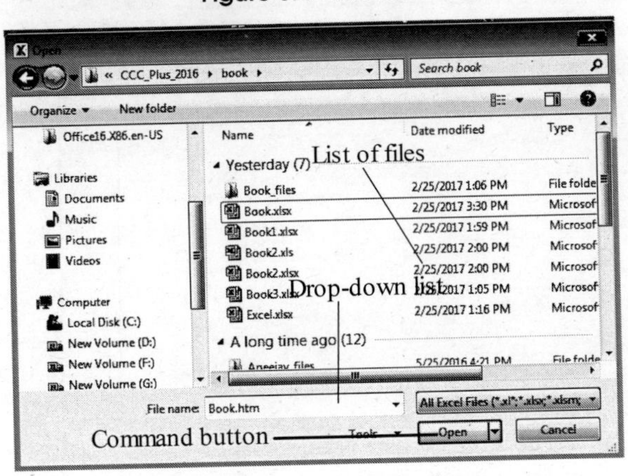

Figure 5.5 Open dialog box

5.2.3 Saving a Workbook

Excel has two commands for saving workbooks. Save command is use to save an existing workbook; Save As command is use to save the workbook when you save it for the first time or save the workbook under a new name.

➡ **To save the workbook for the first time, do this:**

1. Click on the File Tab as seen in Figure 5.4. Here, choose Save As. The Save As dialog box appears as in Figure 5.6. You can also specify the location where you want to save the file in the Save in: box
2. In the File name: box give the name of the file.
3. In the Save as type: box give the type of file.
4. Click Save button.

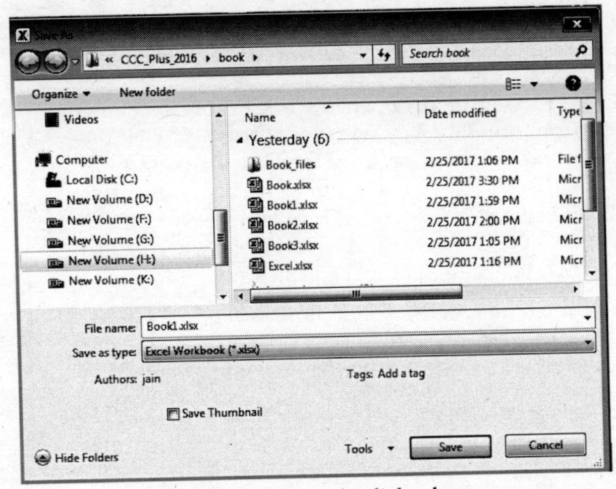

Figure 5.6 Save As dialog box

☞ Excel 2010 worksheet is saved with .xlsx extension indicating that it uses the XML-based file format.

Closing a Workbook Window

When you finish using worksheet or chart, you close its window. If you have made any changes since the last time you saved the workbook, Excel 2010 displays an alert dialog box, as seen in Figure 5.7, asking whether you want to save your work before closing.

Figure 5.7 Alert dialog box

➡ **To close a file in a workbook, do this:**

1. Click on the File Tab as seen in Figure 5.4. Here, choose Close. The window closes provided no change has been made to the workbook since it was saved last.
2. If you have made changes to the workbook since the last save, the Alert dialog box appears. In the dialog box, choose Don't Save if you do not want to save a changed version of the file, or choose Save if you do want to save changes (See Figure 5.7). Type a new file name and choose Save button.

Quitting Excel 2010 Program

➡ **To quit Excel 2010, do this:**

1. Click on the File Tab and then choose Exit. Alternatively, click the Close button (x) in the top-right corner or press Alt+F4 or double-click the Control icon at the left of the title bar.

2. When all workbooks are closed, Excel 2010 window closes, and the application is terminated.

5.2.4 Printing a Spreadsheet

The simplest way to print any opened worksheet is to choose Print option from the Backstage view or alternately, click the Print Preview and Print button from the Quick Access toolbar. In Excel 2010, you can print entire or partial worksheets and workbooks, one at a time, or several at once. And if the data that you want to print is in a MS Excel table, you can also print just the Excel table by setting the print area.

☞ You can also print a workbook to a file instead of to a printer. This is useful when you need to print the workbook on a different type of printer from the one that you originally used to print it.

➡ **To print a spreadsheet, do this:**

1. Open the worksheet that you want to print.
2. Click the File tab and then choose Print command (See Figure 5.8). or Alternatively, press Ctrl+Shift+F12 keys together.
3. The Print Backstage view appears. Here, click Print icon.
4. The Print Backstage view closes and in the status bar displays the process of the print job.

Backstage Print Options shown in Figure 5.9, are described in Table 5.2 below.

Table 5.2 Backstage print options

Option	**Function**
Print Section:	
Copies	Specify the number of copies to be printed.
Printer Section:	This section shows selected printer from a drop-down list, print queue status, type, printer port being used, and whether the printer is busy or idle is also shown below the print selection. Select the desired printer from the Printer drop-down list.
Print to File	Select this option to create a disk file for the selected printer.
Settings:	This section shows the Page Setup options such as page orientation, paper size, and page margins. These options are described below:
Print what option:	
Print Active Sheets	Prints only selected worksheet.
Print Entire Workbook	Prints currently open workbook
Print Selection	Prints selected cells.
Ignore Print Area	Select this option if you want to ignore the print area you have selected.
Page(s) From:/To:	Select this option to print pages you wish to print.
Collate	Select this option to collate multiple copies.

(Contd...)

Option	**Function**
Page Orientation	Allows you to change the page orientation, i.e., portrait (vertically) or landscape (horizontally).
Page Size	Allows you to select the paper size.
Margin	Allows you to set the margin of the pages.
Scaling	Allows you to adjust the size of the worksheet.

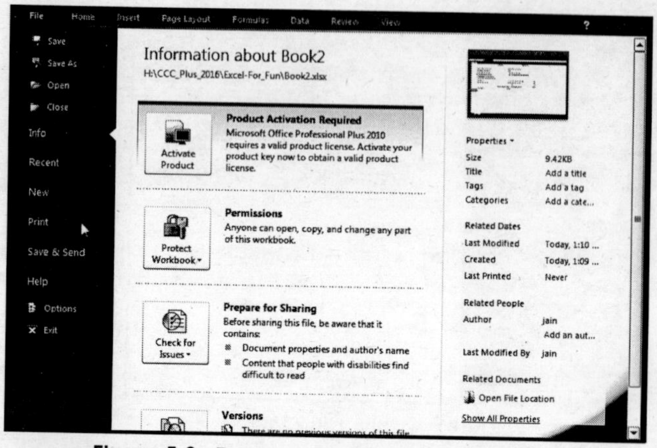

Figure 5.8 Print command in Backstage view

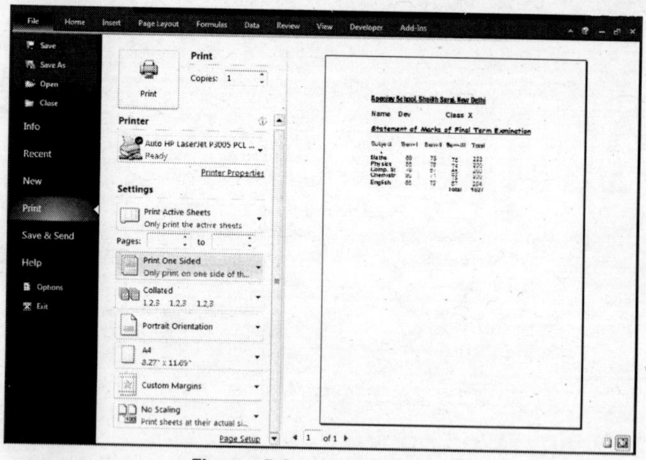

Figure 5.9 Print Options

Printing Sections of a Worksheet or Multiple Worksheets

Suppose you have a year's worth of data accumulated in a given worksheet, but you want to print just one month's worksheet data, then you use this method.

➡ **To print a section of a worksheet, do this:**

1. Select the range of cells to print.

2. In the Print Backstage window, under Setting section, in the Print what drop-down list, select Print Selection to print the selected cells (See Figure 5.9). Excel 2010 ignores any Print Area that has been set and prints the selected range.

➡ **To print several worksheets with one command, do this:**

1. Select all the sheets (the worksheets must be within the same workbook) you want to print.
2. In the Print Backstage window, under Setting section, in the Print what drop-down list, select Print Active Sheets.

5.2.5 Addressing of Cells

A spreadsheet consists of rows and columns which combine to form cells. A cell is a box where you can enter data. Columns form the vertical lines of cells while rows form the horizontal lines of cells. Cell is an intersection of rows and columns. To describe the location or address of a cell, we have to write the names of the column and the row whose intersection has created this cell. Figure 5.10, the intersection of the Column C and the Row 3 is C3. Here C3 is called as a cell and C3 is its address.

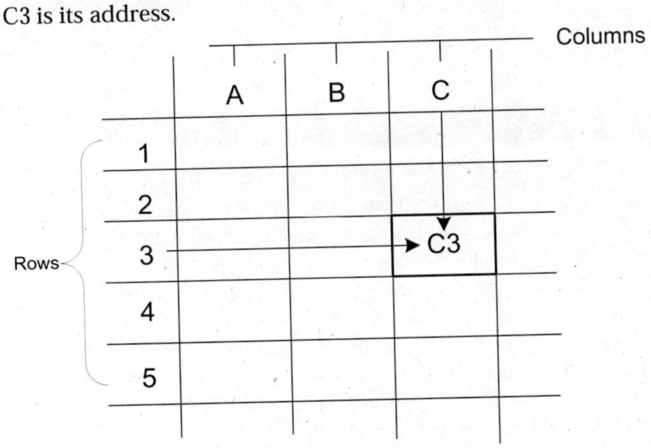

Figure 5.10 Addressing of cells

Cells can have two types of data in a worksheet.

Constant value: A constant value is data that you type directly into a cell. It can be a number, a date, time, currency, percentage, fraction or text. Constant values do not change unless we edit them.

Formula: A formula is a sequence of values, cell references, names, functions or operators that produce a new value from the existing values. Formulas always start with the equal sign (=). A value that is produced as the result of the formula changes automatically when other values involved in the formula in the worksheet to change.

MS Excel helps you to perform calculations on numerical data. For example, you need to find the sum of some data or calculate through a complex set of formulas and Excel can quickly provide the answer. By using formulas, you can efficiently keep track of your business or personal finances.

To find the sum of numbers from cell address A1 to A10 the formula would be as follows:

= +Al+A2+A3+A4+A5+A6+A7+A8+A9+A10

A function is a shortcut for a formula. For example, to calculate the sum of numbers from cell address Al to A10, the function used would be as follows:

= Sum(A1:A10)

Colon (:) Symbol indicates a group of cell addresses. It is easier to write a function as compared to a formula.

Formulas using Cell Addresses

A formula can also contain cell addresses instead of values or numbers. In that case, the formula is applied on the contents of cell address included in it. Cell addresses could be included in a formula by typing or highlighting them. In a formula, the cell addresses can be used along with numbers, mathematical operators and functions. For example, if the contents of cell address B20 have to be added to that of cell address D13, then type the following formula:

= B20+D13

If a formula contains various operators then Excel performs calculations in a preset order, i.e., multiplication is done before addition. For example, in the formula 2*3+4, it will multiply 2 and 3 first. And then, 4 will be added to their product. So, the result will be 10 and not 14.

5.3 MANIPULATION OF CELLS

The power of Excel lies in storing, manipulating, and displaying data items. Before you can manipulate and display data, you must enter it correctly. This chapter discusses the types of data you can enter in a cell of the Excel worksheet.

Types of Data Entered in a Cell

There are four distinct types of data that can reside in a cell (See Figure 5.11). These types of data are:

a. Text
b. Numerals
c. Logical values
d. Error

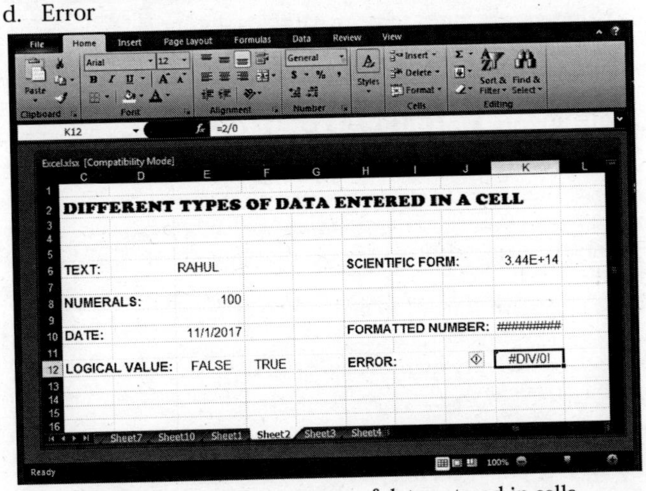

Figure 5.11 Different types of data entered in cells

Text

Text in a cell can include any combination of letters, numbers and keyboard symbols.

- A cell can contain up to 32,000 characters.
- If column width prevents a text string from fitting visually in a cell, the display extends over neighboring cells. However, if the neighboring cells are occupied, the display is truncated.

Numerals

Numerals contain all the decimal digits, such as 0 to 9 on which you can do addition, subtraction, multiplication, and other mathematical or statistical operations. Numeric calculations is the most common thing that is done with Excel 2010. Therefore, it is important to understand how Excel understands numerals.

- A number may be displayed by using commas, scientific notation, or one of many built-in numeric formats. The number's in Excel have two aspects displaying format and the underlying value. The display format is what you see in the cell and the underlying value is the calculated value (which you can see in the formula bar).
- Date and time are numbers, but with special formatting. If you try to enter 1-9 as a text string. Excel 2012 will interpret this as 9th January as a date and display it as 9-Jan.
- When an unformatted number does not fit in a cell, it is displayed in scientific notation (See Figure 5.11).
- When a formatted number does not fit in a cell, number signs like hash (####) are displayed.

Logical Values

You can enter the logical values namely, TRUE or FALSE into cells. Logical values are often used in writing conditional formulas. Also, there are many formulas that give the calculated result in terms of logical values. Thus, if you say 3 > 4, the result is FALSE because 3 is not greater than 4.

Error

An error value is a distinct type of data. For example, if a formula attempts to divide a number by zero, the result is the # DIV/0! Error value.

5.3.1 Entering Text, Numbers and Dates in a Worksheet

When you see the message Ready as shown in Figure 5.11 in the status bar then you can enter data items in a worksheet. Entering data in Excel 2010 worksheet actually consists of three steps:

1. Activate the cell in which you want to enter data.
2. Type the data you want to enter.
3. Finalize the data entry by pressing Enter key, Tab, or any one of the arrow keys.

Example 1

How do you enter data item in a cell?

Solution

1. Click on the desired cell where you want to enter data, just to make it active. The active cell appears with a dark border and its row and column headings appear to be raised to easily identify the cell address.
2. Type your data in the active cell. Two buttons appear in the formula bar: *nter* button and *ancel* button. The status bar shows Enter to indicate that you are in the process of entering data (See Figure 5.12).

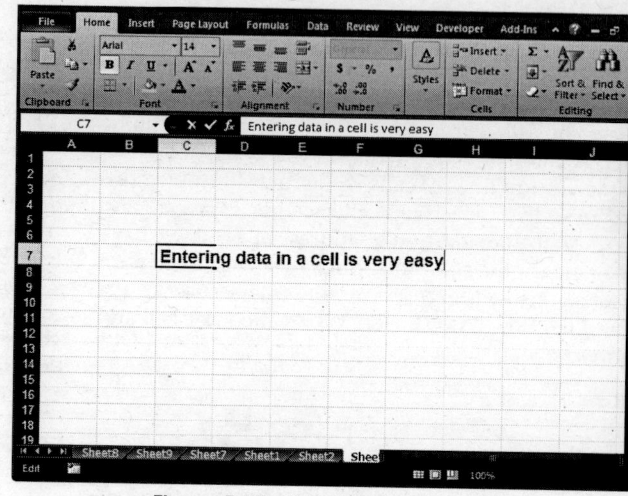

Figure 5.12 Entering data in a cell

3. Click the *nter* button to indicate that you have completed the data typing. You can also press Enter key, Tab key or any one of the arrow keys to complete the data entry.
4. If you make a mistake before finalizing your data entry, press the Backspace key to delete the character to the left of the insertion point. To erase every thing that you have typed, click the cancel button or press Esc key.
5. Repeat the above steps to complete the data entry.

Excel provides you with the following two option to enter and edit data:

- You can enter data in the formula bar.
- You can also enter and edit data directly in the cell.

To enter and edit data directly in the cell you need to turn on the in-cell editing option, if not done already.

☞ If the Edit directly in-cell feature is turned off, the entry you type appears in the cell but the cursor appears in the formula bar.

➡ **To turn on in-cell editing option, do this:**

1. Click the File Tab and then click Options. Excel Options dialog box appears. In this dialog box, click on Advanced button on the left side. Excel Options dialog box appears with Advanced properties as seen in Figure 5.13.
2. Click on the check box i.e. Allow editing directly in cells under the Editing options group as seen in Figure 5.13. The option is on when a check mark appears.
3. Click OK to accept the settings you change.

Entering Text

Text entries can include alphabetical characters, numbers and symbols.

➡ **To enter text in a cell, do this:**

1. Select the cell, type the text entry, and then enter the text by clicking the Enter button in the formula bar or by pressing Enter key.

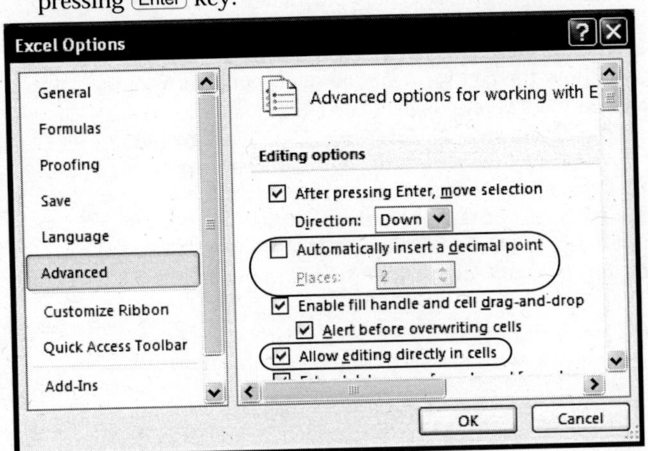

Figure 5.13 Excel Options with Advanced Properties

- To enter numbers as text, type an apostrophe (') followed by the number—for example, '45,000. Alternatively, place an equal sign in front of the numbers and enclose the number in quotation marks. For example, to enter the number 45,000 as text, type ="45,000".
- Notice that in a cell with the General format, numbers entered as text will align on the left like text. When you enter a number as text, you can still use the number if it is needed in a numeric formula.

Example 2

How do you quickly format a range of numbers as text in your worksheet by using the Text numeric format?

Solution

1. Select the range of cells containing the numbers.
2. Select the Text option from the drop down list of the Number group from the Home Tab (See Figure 5.14). Alternatively, press Ctrl+1 keys or click on the Home tab and then in the Number group, click the Dialog Box Launcher. In this dialog box, click on the Number tab, and select the Text from the Category list: and click OK.

Entering Numbers

Numbers are having constant values and contain the following characters given in Table 5.3.

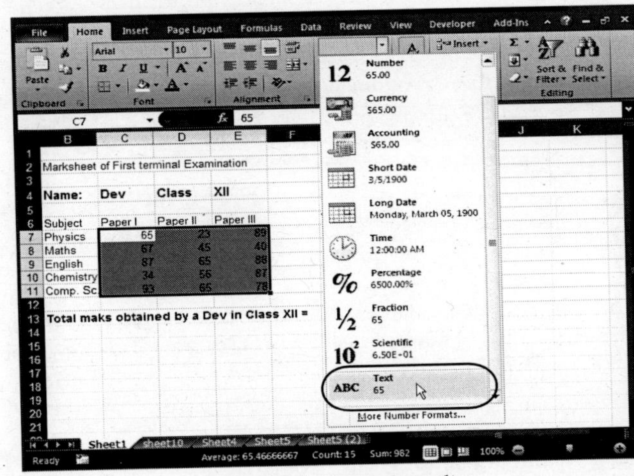

Figure 5.14 Drop-down list

Table 5.3 Special Characters for Numeric Entries

Character	Function
0 through 9	Any combination of numerals.
+	Indicates exponents when used in conjunction with E, such as 3E+3 means $3x10^3$.
–	Indicates negative number.
()	Indicates negative number.
, (comma)	Thousands marker.
/	Fraction indicator (when fraction is preceded by a space) or date separator.
$	Currency indicator.
%	Percentage indicator.
. (period)	Decimal indicator.
E	Exponent indicator.
e	Exponent indicator.
:	Time separator.
(single space)	Separators of compound fractions (e.g 4 1/2); and date time entries (e.g 1/2/94 5:00).

➡ **To enter a number, do this:**

1. Select the cell, type the number, and then press Enter key or click the Enter button in the Formula bar.
2. You can enter integers, such as 145; decimal fractions, such as 145.437; integer fractions, such as 1 1/2; or scientific notation, such as 1.45437E+2.

☞ Entering a number as text enables the number display to exceed the cell's width. If you enter a number in the normal way and the cell is not wide enough to display it, the cell fills with # signs or in some cases may display the number in scientific notation.

Excel 2010 stores the numbers typed into a cell as well as the format or appearance in which the numbers should be shown. When you enter a number into a cell, Excel tries to establish how the number should be formatted. For example, it accepts and displays the entries listed in Table 5.3 with the formats indicated. The entries of the Table 5.4 are displayed in Figure 5.15, as entry would appear in an Excel 2010 worksheet.

Table 5.4 Excel's Automatic Formats

Typed Entry	Chosen Format	Result
897	Number, General	897
7999 Mg Rd.	Text, left aligned	7999 Mg Rd
450.09	Number, dollar format	$450.09
54.6%	Number, percent format	5460.00%
(678)	Number, negative	-678
2 3/4	Number, fraction	2 3/4
45600	Number, comma format	45,600.00
-678	Number, negative, decimal	-678.00
1/5/16	Date, m/d/yyyy	01/05/2016
4/5	Date, m/d/yy (current year assumed)	05-Apr

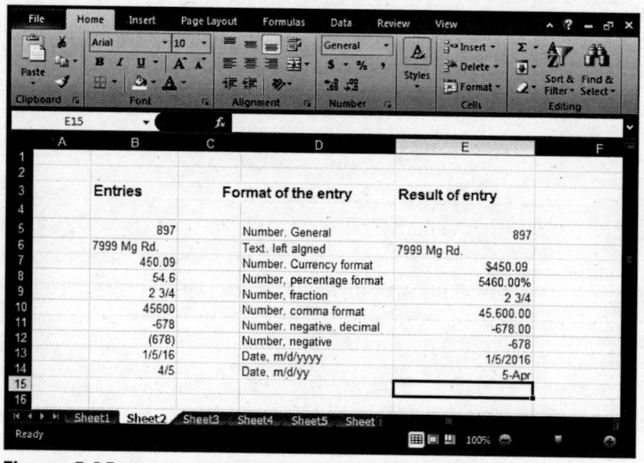

Figure 5.15 Automatic formats done for data given in Table 5.4

☞ Entering a number as text enables the number display to exceed the cell's width. If you enter a number in normal way and cell is not wide enough to display it, the cell gets fills with # signs or in some cases may display the number in scientific notation.

➡ **To control fixed decimal option, do this:**

1. Click the File Tab and then click Options. Excel Options dialog box appears. In this dialog box, click on Advanced button on the left side. Excel Options dialog box appears with Advanced properties as seen in Figure 5.13.
2. Click the Automatically insert decimal point: check box under the Editing options group so that the check mark does not appear (See Figure 5.13).
3. Click OK.

☞ Using fixed decimal representation feature of Excel 2010, you can automatically add decimals to every value entered in a worksheet.

Entering Date and Time in a Worksheet

Excel 2010 automatically understands date and time typed in most of the common ways. When you type a date or time, Excel converts your entry to a serial number. The serial number represents the number of days from the beginning of the century until the date you type. Time is recorded as a decimal fraction of a 24-hour day.

If your entry is recognized as a valid date or time format, you see the date or time on-screen. Correctly entered dates appear in the formula bar with the format `mm/dd/yyyy`, regardless of how the cell is formatted. Here, mm for month, dd for day and yyyy is for year.

For example, if you type `2 January 17` in a cell formatted to show numbers with a comma and two decimal places (#,##0.00), you will see that date as `42,737.00`.

If Excel 2010 does not recognize the entry as a valid date or time format and you type a text date, such as `Feb 5 17`, Excel treats the entry as text. It aligns it to the left in the cell.

Example 3

Explain the step to be followed to enter date in different formats.

Solution

1. Select the cell in which you want to enter the date.
2. Type the date into the cell with any of the following formats. For example to enter 7th January 2017 type:
   `1/7/16`
   `7-Jan-17`
   `7-Jan` (The year from the system date is used)
   `Jan-17` (Only the month and year are shown)
   `1/7/16 0:00`

You can also enter the dates as `1/7`, `01/07/17`, `Jan-17`, or `January 7, 2017` (See Figure 5.16). In any of these date formats, you can use either /, -, or space to separate different elements.

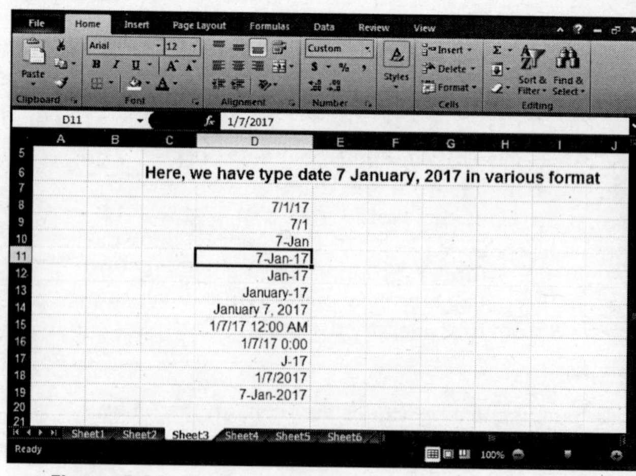

Figure 5.16 Various ways to enter date in a worksheet

Example 4

How do you enter time in an Excel 2010 worksheet?

Solution

1. Select the cell in which you want to enter the time.
2. Type the time in any of the following formats. For example to enter `1:32 PM`, type:

```
13:32
13:32:45
1:32 PM
1:32:45 PM
3/7/16 13:32
```

The first two examples are from a 24-hour clock. If you use a 12-hour clock, follow the time with a space and A, AM, P, or PM (in either upper or lowercase letters).

☞ Leave a space before the AM or PM. Do not mix a 24-hour clock time with an AM or PM. As the last format shows, you can combine the date or time during entry.

➡ **To enter the current date/time in a cell, do this:**

1. To enter the current date select the cell and press Ctrl+; keys together.
2. To enter the current time select the cell and press Ctrl+: keys together.

☞ To format a date in the default date format, press Ctrl+# keys together. To format a time in the default time format, press Ctrl+@ keys together.

5.3.2 Creating Text, Number and Data Series

Creating Text

To create text in a cell, position the cell-pointer at the desired cell address and then type the entry from the keyboard. For example, to enter text Entering text in cell address A1, do the following steps:

1. Move the mouse-pointer to cell address Al and click the left mouse-button just once. Instantly, the cell pointer changes like rectangle shape at cell address Al (See Figure 5.17).
2. Now type Entering text in a cell.
3. Then press the Enter key from the keyboard. Your workbook will look like as shown in Figure 5.17.
4. Text entries are normally used as row and column headings, for entering phone numbers, addresses, etc. All texts are left aligned. And a formula cannot be applied over text entries.

Each cell has a default width of 9-10 characters, i.e., each cell can hold up to 9-10 characters. In case, the entry of cell address is more than its default width, its display gets extended to the next cell. This does not mean that it has occupied the space of the next cell. It has just got displayed over it.

For example, entering text in a cell at cell address A1. You will observe that the type text gets extended to the next cell B1 (See Figure 5.17).

Although the label occupying two cell addresses (Al and B1) it is normally in cell address A1. To find out cell, in which the text is actually displayed, do this:

- Click the left mouse button over the cell address B1. You will see that the Formula bar does not display the text entry.
- Now, click the left mouse-button over the cell address A1. You will see that the Formula bar displays the text Entering text in a cell.

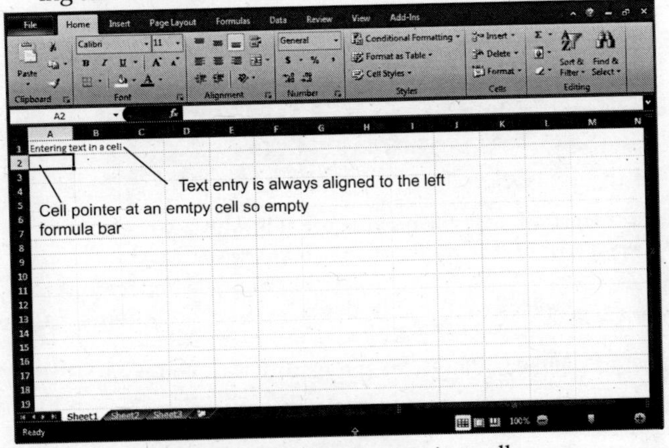

Figure 5.17 Creating text in a cell

Using Number and Date Series

Excel 2010 makes it very easy to enter a series of dates, number or text. For example, you can insert column heading like Jan, Feb, Mar, etc., or enter number at equal intervals, such as 2, 4, 6, 8, etc., very easily.

You can enter the above type of series in two ways:

1. Using the mouse to drag the fill handle.
2. Using a command that gives you the capability to create many types of series.

☞ Dragging the fill handle to the right and down fills the series in increasing order; dragging the fill handle up or left fills the series in decreasing order.

Creating a Linear Series

➡ **To create a linear series, do this:**

1. Enter the first two elements of data in the series in adjacent cells, namely 1 and 3 in cells D6 and E6 (See Figure 5.18). Excel uses these two data items to determine the amount of increment in each step and the starting number for the series.
2. Select these two cells and then drag the fill handle down or right to fill in increasing and drag the fill handle up or left to fill in decreasing order. The fill handle is the small square located at the lower right corner of a selection (See Figure 5.18).

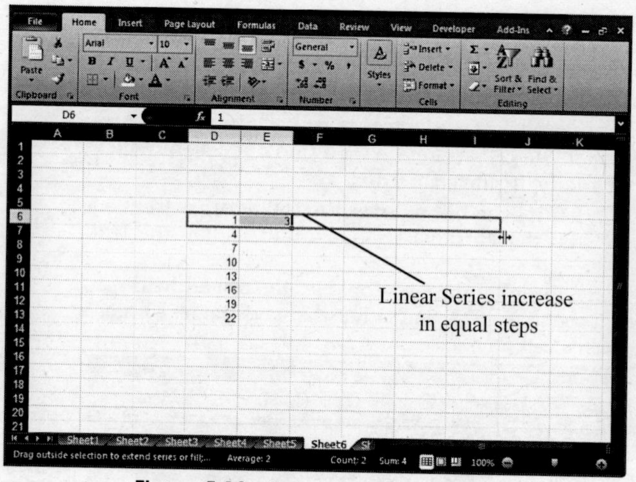

Figure 5.18 Creating a Linear series

3. Release the mouse button.

☞ The area enclosed with the gray border fills with a series of numbers determined by the first two cells you selected.

Example 5

Create a series of linear data with the help of AutoFill command.

Solution

1. In the first cell, enter the starting number, if you want the range to be filled with values that increment by one. If you want the range filled with values that increment differently, fill the first cell in the range with the initial value and the second cell in the range with the second value that increases or decreases as you want the series to increase or decrease.

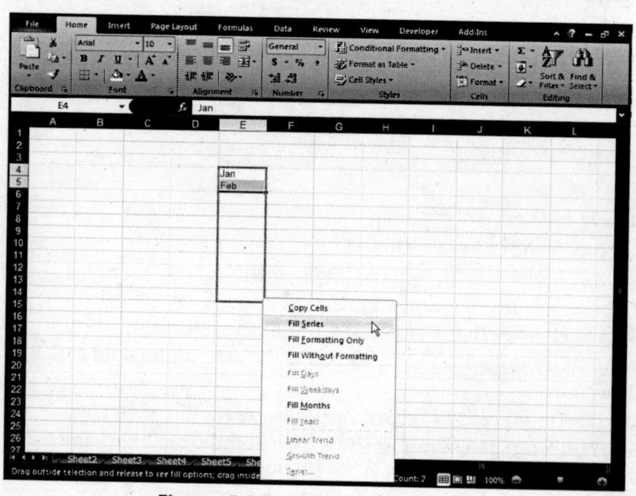

Figure 5.19 Shortcut Fill menu

2. Select the range of cells containing numbers used as starting values for the series. At the lower-right corner of the selection is the square fill handle.
3. Select the range to be filled by dragging the fill handle with the right mouse button. Release the right mouse button to display the shortcut fill menu as shown in Figure 5.19.

Some of the options of shortcut menu are as follows:

Command	Description
Fill Series	Fills the selection with values that is increased by one from the value in the first cell.
Fill Days	Fills the selection with days that is increased by one starting from the day in the first cell.
Fill Weekdays	Fills the selection with weekdays that is increased by one beginning with the day in the first cell.
Fill Months	Fills the selection with months that is increased by one beginning with the year in the first cell.
Linear Trend	Fills the blank cells in the selection with linear regression (best fit) values. Starting values are not overwritten. This command is only available when more than one cell is filled with a starting value.
Growth Trend	Fills the blank cells in the selection with values calculated from growth (exponential) regression. Starting values are not over written. This command is only available when more than one cell is filled with a starting value.
Series	Displays the Series dialog box.

4. Select the option as shown in the Table given above that you want.

Example 6

Create a number series with the help of Fill Series dialog box.

Solution

1. In the first cell, enter the first number or date.
2. Select the range of cells you want to be filled.

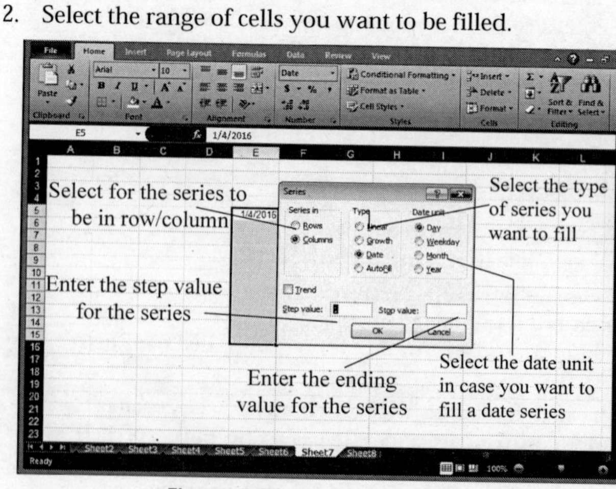

Figure 5.20 Series dialog box

3. Click on Home Tab and then in Editing group, click on the Fill drop down list and then choose Series... to display the Series dialog box (See Figure 5.20).
4. Click the Rows or Columns option that matches the type of range you want to fill. This is automatically selected to match the orientation of the cells you choose.
5. Select the Trend check box if you want selected values to be replaced by values for a linear or exponential best-fit. This selection limits Step 6 to Linear or Growth options.
6. Select one of the following Type options:

Option	Description
Linear	Adds the Step Value to the preceding number in the series.
Growth	Multiplies the Step Value by the preceding number in the series.
Date	Enables the Date Unit group so that the increment applies to a Day, Weekday, Month, or Year.
AutoFill	Creates automatic series that may include text dates and labels.

7. Depending on the kind of series you want to create, use one of the following sets of steps.

➡ **To create a Linear or Growth, do this:**

1. In the Step value: box enter the step value. This number is the constant amount by which the series changes from cell to cell. The Step Value may be positive or negative.
2. In the Stop value: box enter a value at which you want to stop the fill. This is required only if you think that you highlighted too many cells when you selected the range to fill.
3. Click OK.

➡ **To create Date Series, do this:**

1. Click the Date unit area of the Series dialog box (See Figure 5.20).
   Select either Day, Weekday, Month or Year to designate the date increment. Note that Weekday gives you dates without Saturdays and Sundays.
2. To specify the increment amount, enter the Step value in the Step value box. If the starting value is `12/1/2016`, and you choose Month as the Date Unit and 2 as the Step Value, the second date in the series becomes 2/1/2016.

☞ When the series reaches either the end of the selected range or the Stop Value, Excel stops filling the cell. If you use a negative Step Value, the Stop value must be less than the starting value.

3. To stop the series enter the Stop value in the Stop value: box (e.g. `12/1/2016`). The stop value indicates the last date in the series.
4. Click OK.

Creating Series of Text and Headings

Excel can extend series of headings which are not dates or numbers. For example, there may be a text headings that includes a number, such as Trend, Quarter, Task, etc. (See Figure 5.21).

The text series that Excel recognizes includes the text shown in Table 5.5.

Table 5.5 Text Series Recognized by Excel

Type	Example
Day	Tuesday, Wednesday, or Tue, Wed
Month	September, October, or Sep, Oct
Text	Project, Task
Text number	Task 1, Task 2, Paragraph 1.2, Paragraph 1.3
Quarterly	Quarter 1, Quarter 2, Qtr 2, Qtr 3, Q1, Q2

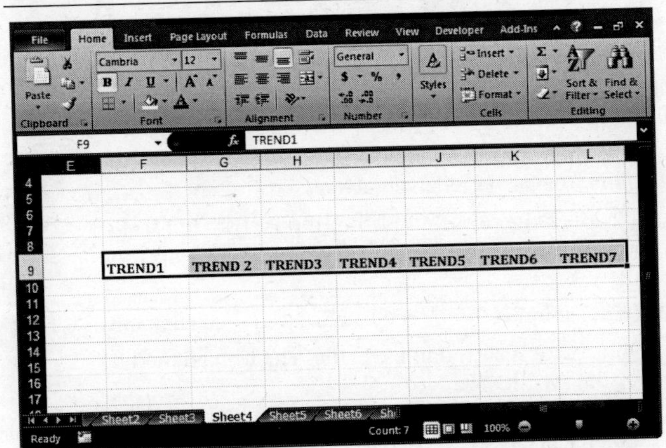

Figure 5.21 Headings that are not Dates or Numbers in a Series

The AutoFill feature in Excel recognizes key words, such as days of the week, month names, and Quarterly abbreviations. Excel extends a series to repeat correctly, namely, Qtr1 follows Qtr4 and then the series continues.

➡ **To type in a custom list for use with AutoFill, do this:**

1. Click the File Tab and then click Options. Excel Options dialog box appears. In this dialog box, Click on Advanced button on the left side. Excel Options dialog box appears with Advanced properties. In this dialog box, under the General group, click on the Edit Custom Lists... Custom Lists dialog box appears as seen in Figure 5.22.
2. Select NEW LIST in the Custom lists: box.
3. Select the List entries: list box, and type each item you want in the list. Press Enter to separate items.
4. To add the list to the Custom lists: list box, click Add. Your list appears in the Custom lists: list box.
6. Click OK if you have no more lists to enter. If you have additional lists to enter, select NEW LIST from the Custom Lists list box, and then begin typing your list in the List entries: list box.

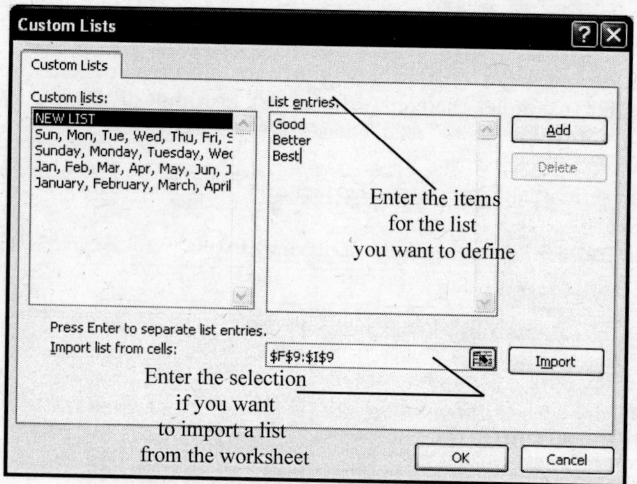

Figure 5.22 Custom Lists Dialog box

➡ **To add a list that is in a range of cells on the worksheet, do this:**

1. Select the cells that contain the list you want to create. Now follow the Step 1 as given above.
2. The selection range appears in the Import list from cells: box you can reselect the list by clicking the arrow on the right.
3. After the selection is final, click Import, and then click OK.

The list you create is stored in Excel file. The list can then be used in any other worksheet also.

5.3.3 Editing Worksheet Data

While editing a cell entry, you can edit the text either in the formula bar or in the cell itself.

Editing Cell Entry in the Formula Bar

➡ **To edit cell entry in the formula bar, do this:**

1. Select the cell containing the data you want to edit.
2. Move the insertion point into the text in the formula bar. Position the pointer in the text you want to edit, and then click. A flashing insertion point indicates where typing and editing take place.
3. Edit the cell entry or type new text.

Editing Directly in a Cell

➡ **To edit an entry directly in a cell, do this:**

1. Double-click the selected cell or press F2 key.
2. Press the arrow keys to move the I-beam that marks the insertion point to place where you want to edit.
3. Make the desired changes to the cell entry.
4. Press Enter key to change the text. Alternatively, press Esc key to leave the contents unchanged.

Using Paste Special Feature

Paste Special feature is very useful to copy and paste part of a cell's attributes, such as the format or value, but not both. With this command, you can reorient database layouts into worksheet layouts and vice versa. This command also enables you to combine the attributes of cells by pasting them together.

☞ *aste b tton of the lipboard gro p places the contents of the clipboard here the c rsor is he drop do n arro of the aste b tton called aste re ie sho n belo t describes ario s a s to paste data oint to an option for a description click to select it*

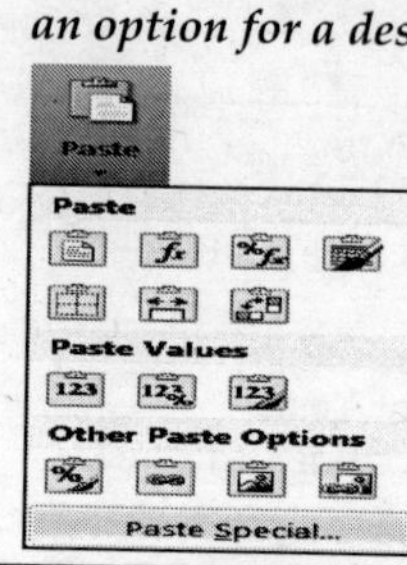

➡ **To use Paste Special Feature, do this:**

1. Select the cell or range of cells.
2. Click on the Home Tab and then click Copy button under the Clipboard group, or press Ctrl+C keys together.
3. Select the upper-left corner of the worksheet where you want to paste. When transporting (flipping) rows and columns, be sure to consider which cells are covered when the pasted area is rotated 90 degrees.
4. Click the arrow next to Paste button under the Clipboard group and then select Paste Special... to display Paste Special dialog box (See Figure 5.23).

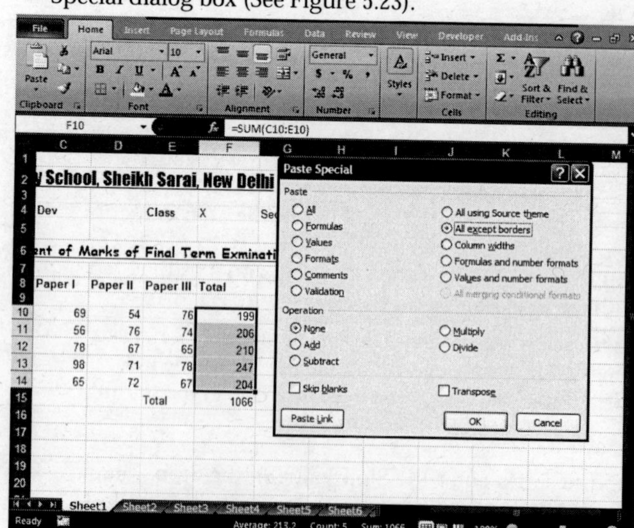

Figure 5.23 Paste Special dialog box

5. Select the characteristics you want to be transferred as explained in the following Table 5.6.

Table 5.6 Characteristics of Paste special options

Option	Function
All	Paste all the original contents and characteristics.
Formulas	Paste only the formulas.
Values	Paste only the values and formula results.
Formats	Paste only the cell formats.
Comments	Paste only note contents.
Validation	Paste data validation rules.
All using Source theme	Paste all cell contents and formatting using the theme.
All except border	Paste everything except any borders applied to the selected range.
Column widths	Paste the width of one column to another.
Formulas and number formats	Paste formulas but not values with their number format.
Values and number formats	Paste only values with their number format.

6. Select from the dialog box how you want to transferred characteristics or information combined with the cells being pastes into.

   Table 5.7 below gives the different options and their functions.

Table 5.7 Different options and their functions

Option	Function
None	Replaces the receiving cell.
Add	Adds to the receiving cell into which they are being pasted.
Subtract	Subtracts from the receiving cell into which they are being pasted.
Multiply	Multiplies by the receiving cell into which they are being pasted.
Divide	Divides into the receiving cell into which they are being pasted.

7. Select the Skip Blanks check box if you do not want to paste blank cells which you have selected when you copy a range.
8. Select the Transpose check box to change rows to columns or to change columns to rows.
9. Click OK.

5.3.4 Inserting and Deleting Rows, Columns

With Excel 2010, you can delete or insert entire rows or columns. You can also easily delete or insert cells, leaving the surrounding rows and columns unaffected. This technique enables you to add or remove cells without having to change entire rows or columns.

Inserting Cells, Rows, or Columns

Sometimes you may need to insert cells, rows, or columns to make room for new formulas or data. You can insert cells, rows, or columns as easily as you can delete them.

➡ **To insert cells, do this:**

1. Select a cell or range of cells where new cells are to be inserted. Or, select cells in the rows or columns where you want to insert new rows or columns.
2. Select Insert Cells... option from Insert drop down list of the Cells group of the Home Tab. Alternatively, press Ctrl + + (plus) keys or click the right mouse button and select Insert... . The Insert dialog box appears as in Figure 5.24.
3. To insert cells, select the direction you want selected cells to be inserted.

   The various options to insert cells are summarized in Table below.

Option	Function
Shift cells right	Selected cells move right.
Shift cells down	Selected cells move down.
Entire row	Insert a row at each selected cell.
Entire column	Insert a column at each selected cell.

4. Click OK.

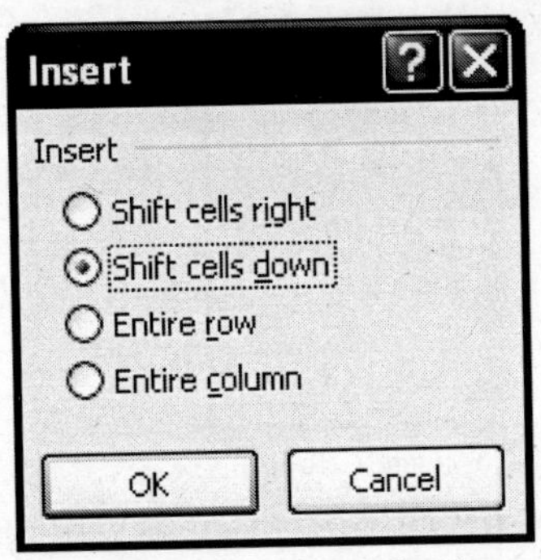

Figure 5.24 Insert dialog box

➡ **To insert *rows* or *columns*, do this:**

1. Select cells in the rows or columns where you want to insert new rows or columns.
2. Select Insert Sheet Rows from Insert drop-down list of the Cells group of the Home Tab to insert rows.
3. Select Insert Sheet Columns from Insert drop-down list of the Cells group of the Home Tab to insert columns.

Deleting Cells, Rows or Columns

The Delete command completely removes cells, rows, or columns from the worksheet. This is different from the Clear command in the Editing Group. The Clear command removes a cell's contents, format, or comments, but it leaves the cell intact.

➡ **To delete *cells*, *rows* or *columns*, do this:**

1. Select the cells or range of cells to be deleted, or select cells in the rows and columns to be deleted.

2. Click on the Home Tab and then click arrow next to Delete button under the Cells group and then select Delete Cells... as shown in Figure 5.25, or press Ctrl+- (minus) keys together, or click the right mouse button and select Delete... . The Delete dialog box appears (See Figure 5.26).

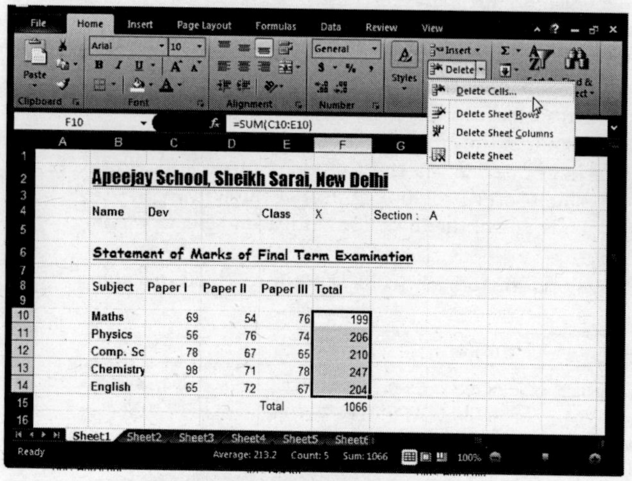

Figure 5.25 Selected group of cells

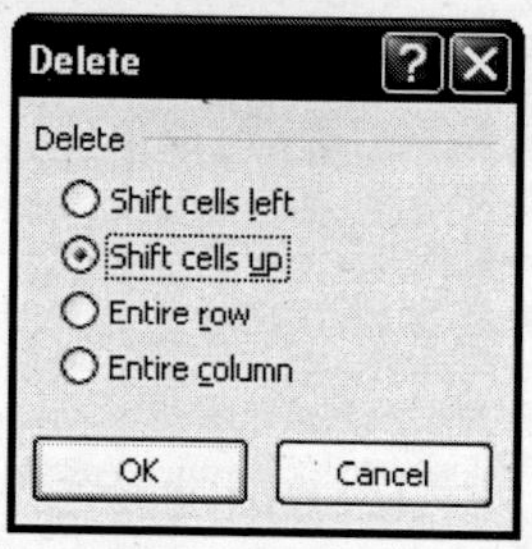

Figure 5.26 Delete dialog box

3. To delete cells, select the direction in which you want the remaining cells to move.
4. Click OK.

Option	Description
Shift cells left	Cells to right of the deleted cells move left.
Shift cells up	Cells below the deleted cells move up.
Entire row	Deletes entire row containing a selected cell.
Entire column	Deletes entire column containing a selected cell.

Clearing, Inserting or Deleting Cells in a Worksheet

After you have drafted and tested the worksheet, you may find that you need to reorganize or restructure the layout of the worksheet. When you restructure, you may need to insert or delete cells, rows or columns.

Shortcuts keys that are very helpful in reorganizing the worksheet layout are given in Table 5.8.

Table 5.8 Shortcut Keys for Changing the Worksheet Layout

key(s)	Action
Del	Clears selected formulas or contents; same as the Home, Tab, Editing Group and then Clear Contents.
Backspace	Clears the formulas bar; activates and clears the formula bar's contents.
Ctrl+C	Copies the selection so that it can be pasted; same as the Home Tab, Clipboard Group and then Copy Command.
Ctrl+X	Cuts the selection so it can be pasted; same as the Home Tab, Clipboard Group and then Cut Command.
Ctrl+V	Paste at the selected cell; same as the Home Tab, Clipboard Group and then Paste Command.
Ctrl+Z	Undoes last command.
Ctrl+ Backspace	Repositions the worksheet so that the active cell is in view.

5.3.5 Changing Cell Height and Width

In order to improve the appearance of a worksheet or table in it, you can adjust columns width and row height. Thus, you can fit more data on a page. If need be, you can even hide confidential data.

How to adjust Column Width?

You can adjust the width of one or more columns to get better look in a worksheet. If a column is not wide enough to display a number, date, or time, Excel 2010 displays it by using # characters in the cell. Therefore, you may need to adjust columns width to show complete information.

Example 7

Describe the ways by which you can adjust columns width.

Solution

Adjust column width with mouse

1. Select the columns of which you need to change the width.
2. Move the pointer onto the column separator to the right of the column heading (See Figure 5.27). Pointer changes to a two-headed, horizontal arrow.
3. Drag the column left or right until the column is of the required width. Then release the mouse button. The Width box that appears as you drag the column, displaying the numeric value for the column width.

Adjust column width using Ribbon

1. Select the columns of you want to change the width.
2. Under Home Tab, click Cells group and then click arrow next to Format. It pops up the menu (See Figure 5.28).
3. Use one of the following options to adjust column width (See Figure 5.28).

➡ **To copy a column width, do this:**

1. Select cells in the columns that you want to copy the column width.

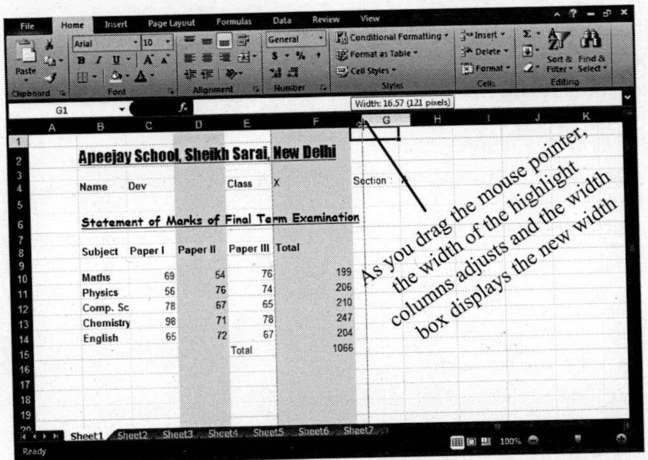

Figure 5.27 Changing Column Width with Mouse

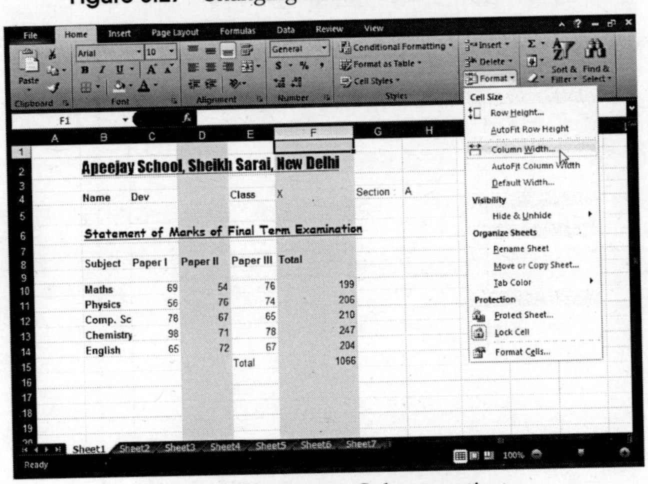

Figure 5.28 Format Column option

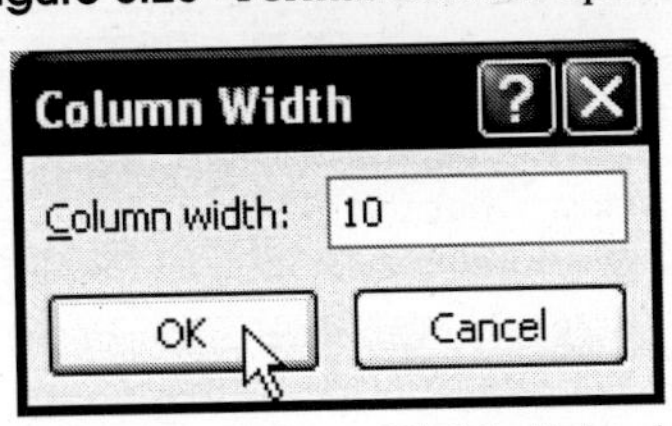

Figure 5.29 Column Width dialog box

Option	Description
Column Width...	The Column Width dialog box appears (See Figure 5.29). Type the width, and then click OK.
AutoFit Selection	This option adjusts the column width automatically.
Default Width...	This option would adjust to the default column width for all the selected columns.

2. Click Copy button on Clipboard group of the Home Tab.
3. Select the cells where you want to apply this width.
4. Under the Home Tab, click the arrow next to the Paste button in the Clipboard group and then click Keep Source Column Widths button as shown in Figure 5.30 or choose Paste Special... . Paste Special dialog box appears .
5. In this dialog box, choose Column widths from Paste group.
6. Click OK.

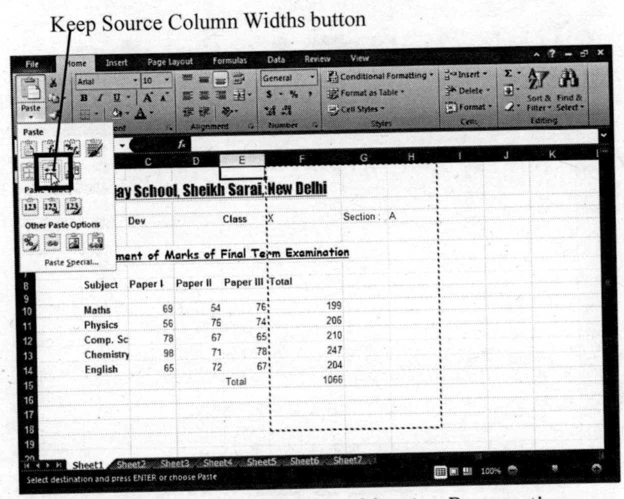

Figure 5.30 Copy column width using Paste options

How to adjust Row Height?

You can adjust row height in a worksheet to create enough space for titles, subtotals, grand totals, etc.

Example 8

How would you adjust row height?

(a) Using mouse

(b) Ribbon

Solution (a)

1. Select the rows of which you want to adjust the height.
2. Move the mouse pointer to the line directly under the header of the row you want to change. The mouse pointer changes to a two headed vertical arrow (See Figure 5.31).
3. Drag the two-headed arrow pointer up or down until the row is of the required height. Then release the mouse button. The screen tip displays the numeric value for the row height.

Solution (b)

1. Select a cell in each row you want to change.
2. Under Home Tab, click Cells group and then click arrow next to Format. It pops up menu (See Figure 5.28).

3. Click one of the following options.

Option	Description
Row Height...	To display the Row Height dialog box. Here, type the row height and click OK (See Figure 5.32).
AutoFit Row Height	Excel 2010 adjusts rows height automatically.

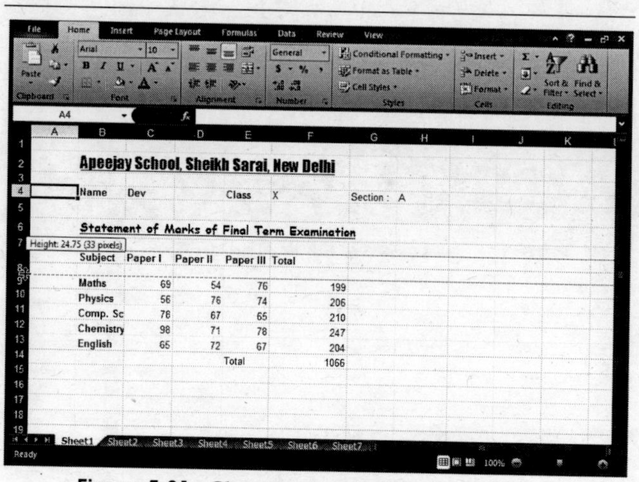

Figure 5.31 Changing row height with a mouse

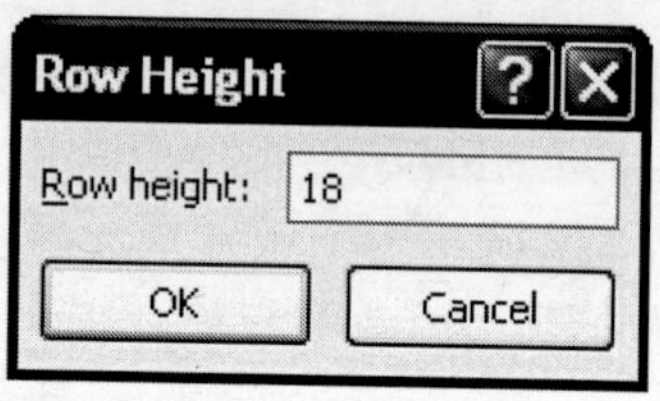

Figure 5.32 Row Height dialog box

5.4 FORMULAS AND FUNCTION

A formula in Excel is a mathematical equation that performs calculations based on constants, cell references or both. A formula always begins with = (equal) sign. For example, the formula =A1+A2 add the numbers contained in the cells A1 and A2 of the worksheet. Formulas include the use of operators which tell Excel what to do with the constants and cell references. For example, * (asterisk) represents the multiplication operator.

A function is built-in formula, which can save time when working with lot of numbers. While entering functions, the name of the function appears immediately after the = sign. The arguments to the function are contained in parentheses. Arguments are the constants or cell references that function uses to perform calculations. For example, instead of using the formula = A1+A2+A3+A4 to add up the numbers in the cell range, you can use the function =SUM(A1:A4).

5.4.1 Using Formulas

A formula is entered into a cell. It performs a calculation of some type and returns a result, which is displayed in the cell. Formulas in Excel always begin with an equal sign (=) and can include the following types of data items:

a. Numeric and text values (constants)
b. Arithmetic operator, comparison operators, text operators, functions, parentheses
c. Cell references, and names

☞ By combining these components, you can calculate the result you want by using the information in the worksheet.

Excel also gives you the option to display formulas on a worksheet, or the results of the formulas.

➡ **To control the display of formula result, do this:**

1. Click the File Tab and then click Options. Excel Options dialog box appears. In this dialog box, click on Advanced button on the left side. Excel Options dialog box appears with Advanced properties as seen in Figure 5.33.

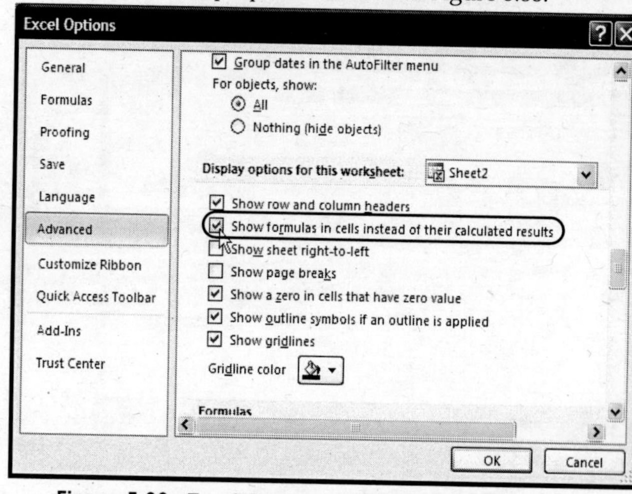

Figure 5.33 Excel Options with Advanced Properties

2. Click on the Show formulas in cells instead of their calculated results check box so that it appears under the Display options for this worksheet group.
3. Click OK.

☞ To switch between viewing formulas and the results of formulas, click Show Formulas button from the Formula Auditing group of Formulas Tab or alternatively, click Ctrl + ` keys pressed together (See Figure 5.34).

When you display formulas, Excel automatically doubles the width of all columns (See Figure 5.34). The column widths will return to their original settings when you return to displaying the formula results. Formulas automatically recalculate and produce current results after you update data used by the formulas.

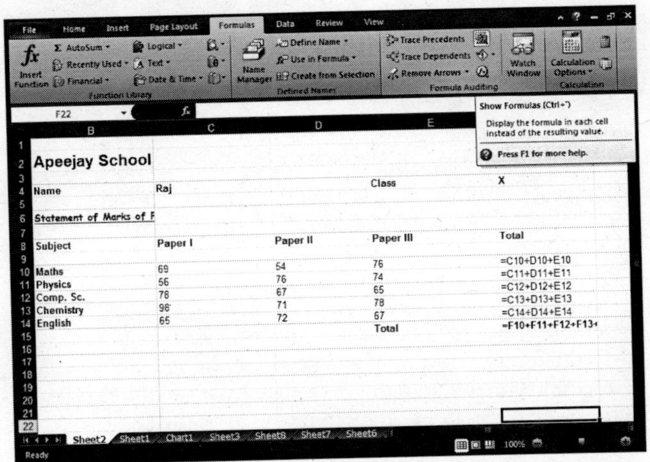

Figure 5.34 Formula displayed in cells

☞ Make sure that you start the formula with an equal sign (=). If you forget to put an equal sign, Excel 2010 does not interpret the entry as a formula. For example, if you enter B12*D15 (with no equal sign), the B12*D15 is actually entered into the cell as text.

How to Enter Formulas?

To enter a formula, start a formula with an equal sign (=) and then construct the formula using values, operators, cell references, functions, and names to calculate the required result.

You can enter formulas either in the formula bar or in the cell. You can enter a formula using the formula bar by simply typing in it and pressing Enter. You can also enter a formula directly in the cell and bypass the formula bar.

☞ Make sure you remember to start the formula with an equal sign (=). If you forget the equal sign, Excel 2010 does not interpret the entry as a formula. If you enter B12*D15 (no equal sign), then B12*D15 is actually entered into the cell as text.

➡ **To enter a formula in the formula bar, do this:**

1. Select the cell in which you want to enter the formula.
2. Then click on the Formula bar and type an equal sign (=).
3. Type a value, cell reference, function, or name.
4. If the formula is complete, press Enter or click the Enter box (a check mark) in the formula bar. If the formula is incomplete, go to Step 5.
5. Type an operator. There are many types of operators. The most common operators are math symbols, such as + (plus) and – (minus).
6. Return to Step 3.

➡ **To enter a formula in a cell, do this:**

1. Double-click the cell or select the cell and press F2 key in which you want to enter the formula and type an equal sign (=) (See Figure 5.35).
2. Type a value, cell reference, function, or name.
3. If the formula is complete, press Enter key. If the formula is incomplete, go to Step 4.
4. Type an operator.
5. Return to Step 2.

Always separate terms in a formula with an operators or parentheses.

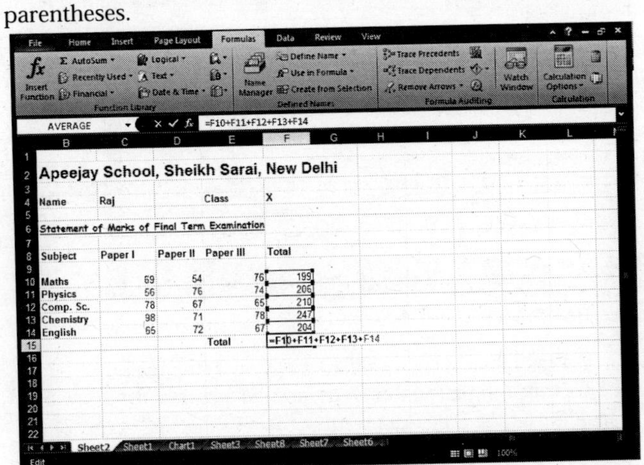

Figure 5.35 Entering a formula in Excel

Use the SUM function to Sum Several Ranges

To sum several ranges, simply refer to each of them, separated by a comma, using the SUM function.

➡ **To sum several ranges, do this:**

1. In cells A20:A26 enter prices from Re. 1 to Rs. 100.
2. Select cells B20:B26 and type the formula = A20*8% to calculate the tax amount.
3. Press Ctrl + Enter keys together.
4. In Cells C20:C26 type some discount values from -1 to -3.
5. In Cell C28, sum all three columns with the following functions (See Figure 5.36). =SUM(A20:A26, B20:B26,C20:C26) (Figure 5.36).
6. Press Enter key.

Moving or Copying Formula

When you move a formula from one cell to other, the cell references within the formula do not change. But when you copy a formula, then

- Absolute cell references do not change.
- Relative cell references will change when you copy a formula.

➡ **To move or copy a formula, do this:**

1. Select the cell that contains the formula you want to move or copy.
2. Point to the border of the selection.
3. To move the cell, drag the selection to the upper-left cell of the paste area. Excel 2010 replaces any existing data in the pasted area.
4. To copy the cell, hold down Ctrl key as you drag the mouse.

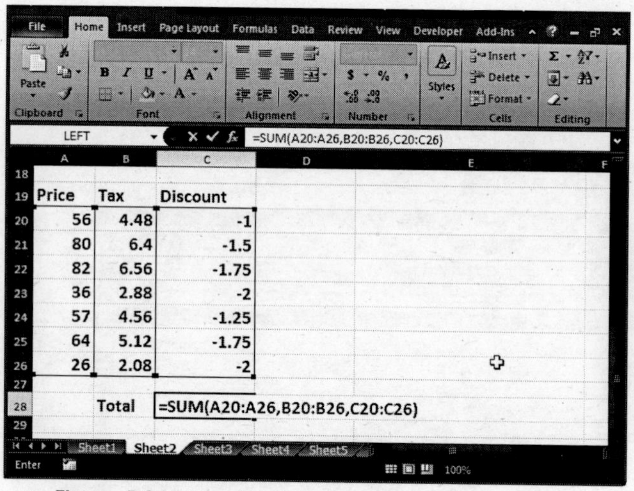

Figure 5.36 Entering Sum function to several ranges

☞ You can also copy formulas into adjacent cells by using the fill handle. Select the cell that contains the formula and then drag the fill handle over the range you want to fill.

Entering Cell References

Cell references allow you to use values from different parts of a worksheet and execute and enables you to do the desired calculation. You can use any cell or group of cells in a formula.

☞ The reference of the active cell is displayed in the name box at the left end of the formula bar.

Entering the Cell References by Pointing

The easiest method of entering cell references in a formula is by pointing to the cell you want to include in a formula. Although you can type an entire formula, you often can make a typing error or misread the row or column headings. Say for example, you may end up with D52 in a formula when it should be E52.

☞ When you point to a cell to include it in a formula, you actually move the pointer to the cell you want in the formula. It is found out only when you select the correct cells.

➡ **To enter a cell reference into a formula by pointing, do this:**

1. Select the cell for the formula.
2. Type an equal sign (=).
3. Point to the cell you want it in the formula and click, or press the arrow keys to move the dashed marquee to the cell you want in the formula. The address of the cell you point to appears at the cursor location in the formula bar.
4. Enter an operator, such as the + symbol.
5. Point to the next cell.
6. Repeat the steps from step 4 to continue the formula, or enter the formula by clicking the Enter box or pressing Enter key.

☞ The cell reference in a formula changes after you copy the formula to a new location or after you fill a range with a formula. You would usually want formulas to use relative cell references, only.

Using Cell References in Formulas

You refer to a cell's location with a relative reference or an absolute reference. Let us understand the difference in the two types of cell references.

Suppose that you are in your office, and you want someone to take a letter to the post office. Using a relative reference, you tell the person. "Go out the front door; turn left cross the road and move two building then turn right and go to the second building." These directions are relative to your office location at the time you give the instructions. If you move to a different location, these directions are no longer valid.

To make sure that the letter gets to the mailbox no matter where you are then you give different set of directions. You must say something like this. "Take this letter to the I.P. Estate post office." No matter where you are when you speak, the post office is at one absolute location: I.P ESTATE.

☞ Thus, the difference between relative and absolute reference is that in absolute reference, the cell is fixed once for all. In the relative reference it depends on the location where your pointer is.

Using Relative References

A relative cell reference in a formula, is based on the relative position of the cell that contains the formula and the cell the reference refers to. If the position of the cell that contains the formula changes, the reference is changed. If you copy or fill the formula across rows or down columns, the reference automatically adjusts.

Excel uses relative referencing for cell addresses when you enter a formula.

In Figure 5.37, the formula in cell F10 is =C10+D10+E10. All these references are relative. The formula, translated into English, would read as follows:

"In cell F10, add the number in the 10th column to the left (C10), second column to the left (D10) and the adjacent column on the left (E10)" in the same row.

Suppose you copy formula across Column G, the formulas adjust their cell references to their new positions. The copied formulas are as follows:

Cell Containing Formula	A1 Format
G10	= D10+E10+F10
G11	= D11+E11+F11
G12	= D12+E12+F12

You will notice that the formulas change to give the cell references with relative position from the cell that contains the formula.

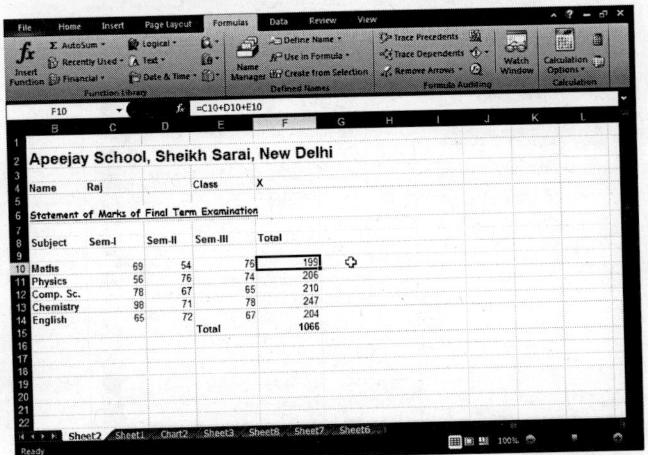

Figure 5.37 Formula entered with relative reference

Using Absolute References

You use absolute references only to keep the cell reference values from changing as and when you copy a formula to a new location in a worksheets.

➡ **To enter an absolute reference by using the F4 key, do this:**

1. Type an equal sign (=) and the cell reference you want to be absolute.
2. Press F4, the absolute reference key, until the correct combination of dollar signs appears.

☞ Indicate absolute references by putting a dollar sign ($) in front of the column letter or row number that you want to freeze or both (See Figure 5.38).

3. Type the next operator and continue to enter the formula, also.

You can use the F4 key when editing an existing formula.

Using Mixed References

In some cases, you may want either the row to stay fixed or the column to stay fixed when copying the cells from one place to other in a worksheet. In such cases, use a mixed reference. Such references contain both absolute and relative reference. For example, the reference $B5 prevents the column from changing, but the row changes relative to a new copied location. The dollar sign prevents the column from changing. In B$5, just the opposite occurs. The column adjusts to a new location but the row always stays fixed at 5 because the dollar sign prevents the row from changing.

☞ Each time you press F4, Excel 2010 cycles through all combinations of relative and absolute references. Press F4 four times, for example, and you cycle from B22 through $B$22, B$22, $B22, and B22.

You can create mixed references the same way as you can create absolute references. Type the dollar signs or specific row and column numbers without brackets or press F4 key. Each press of F4 cycles the cell reference to a new combination.

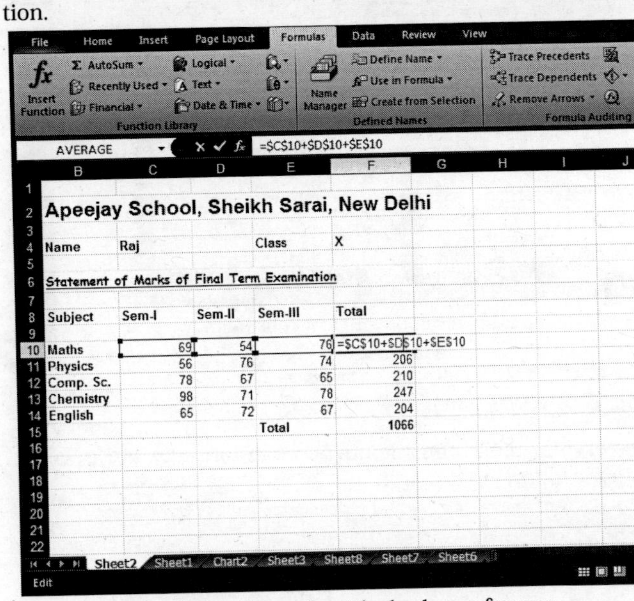

Figure 5.38 Formula with absolute reference

Referring to Other Sheets in a Workbook

You can also refer to other sheets in a workbook by including a sheet reference as well as a cell reference in a formula. For example, to refer to cell A1 on Sheet6, you would enter Sheet6!A1 in the formula.

You can use the mouse to enter a reference to a cell or range of cells on another worksheet in a workbook.

➡ **To refer to cell or range of cell in a different worksheet, do this:**

1. Start entering the formula in the cell where you want the result to appear.
2. Click the sheet tab for the worksheet you want to refer to.
3. Select the cell or range of cell that you want to refer to. The complete reference, including the sheet reference, appears in the formula bar (See Figure 5.39).
4. If the sheet name includes spaces, Excel surrounds the sheet reference with single quotation marks.
5. Finish the formula and press Enter key.

5.4.2 Using Operators in Formulas

Operators are used in formulas to execute operations on the values taken by formulas. Excel uses four types of operations. These are given below:

Operators	Signs
Arithmetic	+, –, *, /, %, ^
Text	&
Comparative	=, <, <=, >, >=, <>
Reference	Colon (:), comma(,), space ()

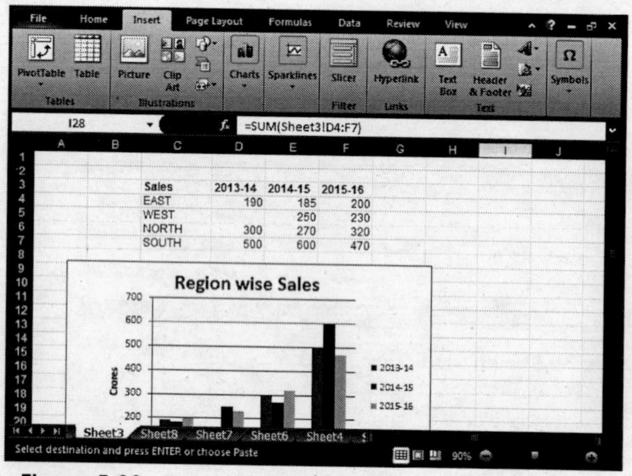

Figure 5.39 Referring a cell or range of cells in another worksheet

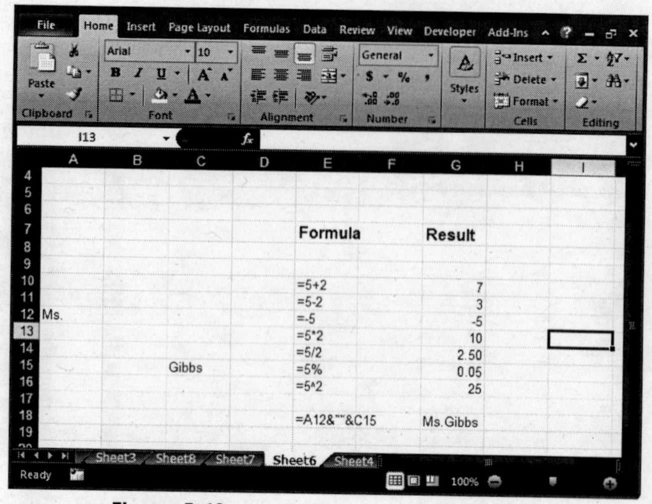

Figure 5.40 Arithmetic and text operators

Arithmetic Operator

How to use each of the arithmetic operators in formulas are explained in the following example.

Example 9

Figure 5.40 shows the result of the use of arithmetic operator used in the following Table 5.9.

Table 5.9 Arithmetic Operator

Operator	Formula	Result	Type of Operation
+	=5+2	7	Addition of 5 with 2
–	=5–2	3	Subtraction of 2 from 5
–	–5	–5	Negation (negative of the number)
*	=5*2	10	Multiplication of 5 with 2
/	=5/2	2.5	Division of 5 by 2
%	5%	.05	Percentage
^	=5^2	25	Exponentiation (to the power of)

Text Concatenation Operator

The ampersand (&) operator, joins text within quotation marks or text contained in referenced cells. Joining text is known as concatenation, as explained in the following example.

Example 10

Figure 5.40 shows the result of the concatenation operator used in the following table.

Operator	Formula	Result	Type of Operation
&	=A12&""&C15	Ms.Gibbs	Text in A12 and C15 is joined

Comparison Operators

To compare values, you can create formulas using comparison operators. These operators return a TRUE or FALSE result, depending on how the formula evaluate the condition. Subsequent Table formulates some Comparison operators and Figure 5.41 shows the use of such comparison operators.

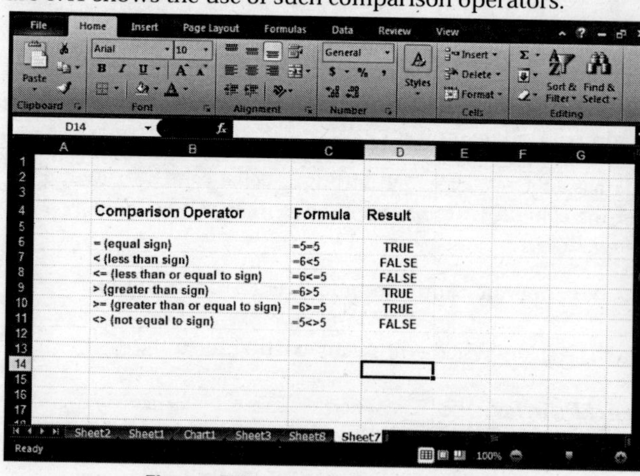

Figure 5.41 Comparison operators

Operator	Type
=	Equal to
<	Less than
<=	Less than or equal to
>	Greater than
>=	Greater than or equal to
<>	Not equal to

The following are examples of comparative operators in formulas:

Formula	Result
=A12<15	TRUE if the contents of cell A12 is less than 15; FALSE if the contents of cell A12 is 15 or more.
=B36>=15	TRUE if the contents of cell B36 is 15 or more; FALSE if the contents of cell B36 is less than 15.

Reference Operator

Reference operators make no changes to constants or cell contents as summarized in Table 5.10. Instead, they control how a formula groups the cells and ranges of cells when the formula is made to calculate. The examples of Reference operators are shown in Figure 5.42.

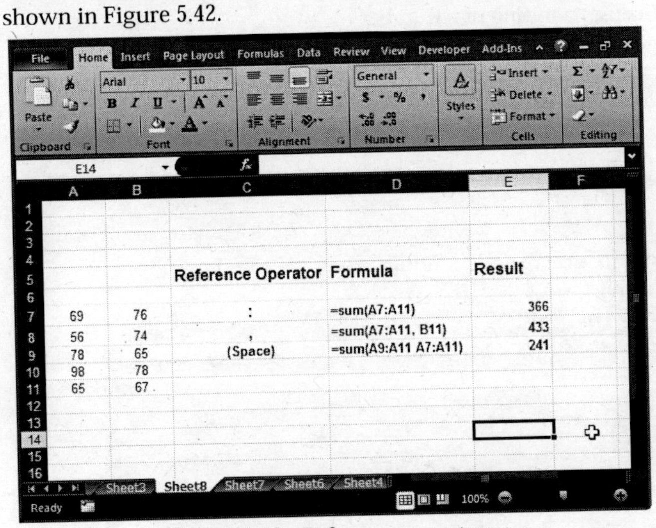

Figure 5.42 Reference operators

Table 5.10 Reference Operators

Operator	Example	Type	Result
:	SUM(A7:A11)	Range	Evaluates as a single reference the cells in the rectangular area between the two corners.
,	SUM (A7:A11,B11)	Union	Evaluates two references as a single reference.
space	SUM(A9:A11 A7:A11)	Intersect	Evaluates the cells common to both references (if no cells are common to both, then #NULL results).
space	=Yr99 Sales	Intersect	Cell contents at the intersect of the column named Yr99 and the row named Sales.

☞ Reference operators enable you to combine absolute and relative references and named ranges. Reference operators are valuable for joining cells (union) or referring to a common area shared between different ranges (intersect).

Range Operator

Use the range operator (:) to reduce your work in formulas. If you want a formula to refer to all cells in column B, type B:B. Similarly, the range that includes all cells in rows 5 through 12 is entered as 5:12.

Evaluation (Precedence) of Formulas

Excel 2010 follows a set of rules when applying operators in a formula. Working from the first calculation to the last, Excel 2010 evaluates operators in the order shown in Table 5.11.

Table 5.11 The Order in which Excel 2010 Evaluates Operators

Operator	Definition
()	Parentheses
:	Range
space	Intersect
,	Union
–	Negation
%	Percentage
^	Exponentiation
* and /	Multiplication and division
+ and –	Addition and subtraction
&	Text joining
=, <, and <= >, >=, and <>	Comparisons

If you want to change the order in which calculations are performed then enclose in parentheses the terms you want Excel 2010 to calculate first.

For example, you will notice the difference between the results of the following formulas:

Formula	Result
`=6+21/3`	`13`
`=(6+21)/3`	`9`

Entering Text, Date and Time in Formulas

You can use text, dates, and times in formulas by including the data in quotation marks. For example.

```
="The Total Budget is" &TOTAL_BUDGET
```

shows the Total Budget and the value in the cell named TOTAL_BUDGET.

If you want to perform date math on explicit dates, which are the dates that are not in cells, then:

```
="4/14/2017" – "4/14/2016"
```

or

```
="14April17" – "14April16"
```

These formulas produce the number of days between the two dates.

5.4.3 Functions

Functions are the predefined formulas that perform calculations on specific values, called arguments. Each function takes specific types of arguments, such as numbers, references, text, or logical values. You can enter the arguments, enclosing them in parentheses, i.e., ( ), after the function name. Functions use these arguments in the same way that algebraic equations use variables. For example, the SUM function adds values or range of values, and the PMT function calculates the loan payments based on an interest rate, the period of loan, and the principal amount of loan. Excel includes many functions that can be divided into the following categories:

5.4.4 Find the Right Function

Functions are basically a fast way to enter a complex formula. Excel 2010 has hundreds of functions you can use, and are grouped together into the following categories:

1. Math and trigonometry
2. Logical
3. Statistical
4. Date and time
5. Text
6. Financial
7. Database
8. Engineering
9. Information
10. Lookup and Reference
11. Add-ins and Automation
12. Cube
13. Compatibility

By using functions, you can save time and cuts down on typographical errors that are so easy to make when typing formulas.

5.4.5 Fixing Formula Errors

There are a number of error messages that may appear when you type a formula. Some are typing mistakes and some may be a result of a cell value. Other errors may appear in the formula result cell.

Following are a few common error messages.

- DIV/0 : This type of error occurs when a number is divided by either an empty cell (a cell that contains no value) or one with a value of zero (0). Make sure all cells in the division have a nonzero value.
- REF : This type of error occurs when the formula includes an invalid cell reference.
- N/A: This type of error occurs when the value is not available to a function or formula.
- VALUE : This type of error occurs when formula includes cells that contain different data types. This type of problem can be fixed by making minor changes to the formula.
- NAME?: This type of error occurs when Excel does not recognize text in a formula because of a range name or function name misspelling.
- NUM : This type of error occurs when a formula or function contains invalid numeric values.
- : This type of error occurs when a column is not wide enough to display all of its content, or that a negative date or time is used in a cell.

Now you are familiar with the basic concepts of functions, function syntax and the different types of error which generate when you use incorrect function. Let us now move on how to add functions in a worksheet.

Basic Mathematical Functions

Excel 2010 includes many math and trigonometry functions. Mathematical functions are used to perform, wide variety of simple or complex calculations, such as totaling the value for a range of cells, rounding of a number.

SUM( )

Adds all the numbers in a range of cells (See Figure 5.43).

Syntax

`SUM(number1,number2,...)`

Round( )

`Round()` function rounds a number to a specified number of digits (See Figure 5.43).

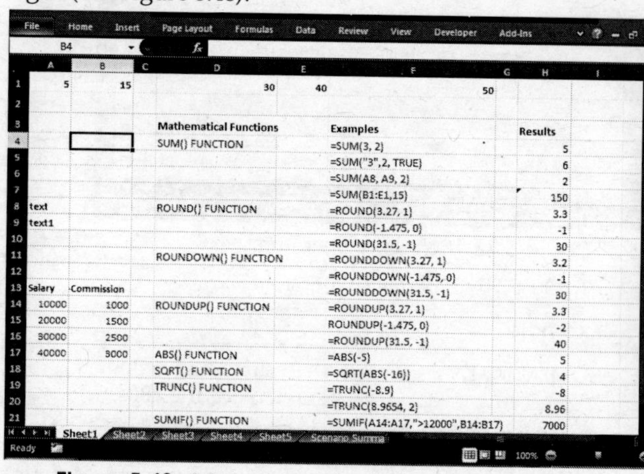

Figure 5.43 Mathematical functions and their results

Syntax

`ROUND(number,num_digits)`

Rounddown( )

`Rounddown()` function rounds a number down towards zero (See Figure 5.43).

Syntax

ROUNDDOWN(number, num_digits)

Roundup( )

`Roundup()` function rounds a number up away from 0 (zero) (See Figure 5.43).

Syntax

ROUNDUP(number,num_digits)

ABS( )

`ABS( )` function returns the absolute value of a number. The absolute value of a number is the number without any + or – sign.

Syntax

`ABS(num)`

Where `num` is the real number of which you want the absolute value.

SQRT( )

`SQRT( )` returns a positive square root of a number.

Syntax

`SQRT(num)`

TRUNC( )

`TRUNC( )` function truncates a number to an integer value by removing the fractional part of the number.

Syntax

`TRUNC(num,num_digits)`

Logical Functions

Logical functions are used when we want to check whether a given condition is true or false.

IF( )

`IF( )` function is used to determine whether a condition specified with in braces is true or false. It returns one value if a specified condition evaluates to TRUE and another value if it evaluates to FALSE (See Figure 5.44).

Syntax

`IF(logical_test,value_if_true,value_if_false)`

Where

`Logical_test` is a value or expression that can be evaluated to TRUE or FALSE. For example, A10 = 100 is a logical expression.

`Value_if_true` is the value that is returned if logical_test is TRUE. For example, if the value in cell A10 is equal to 100, the expression evaluates to TRUE.

`Value_if_false` is the value that is returned if logical_test is FALSE. For example, if the value in cell A10 is not equal to 100, the expression evaluates to FALSE.

☞ In Excel 2010, up to 64 IF() functions can be nested to construct more elaborate tests.

Example 11

On a Marksheet, cell A10 contains a formula to calculate the result. If the result of the formula in A10 is greater than 50, then the following function displays "Pass". Otherwise, the function displays "Fail" (See Figure 5.44).

`IF(A10>=50,"Pass","Fail")`

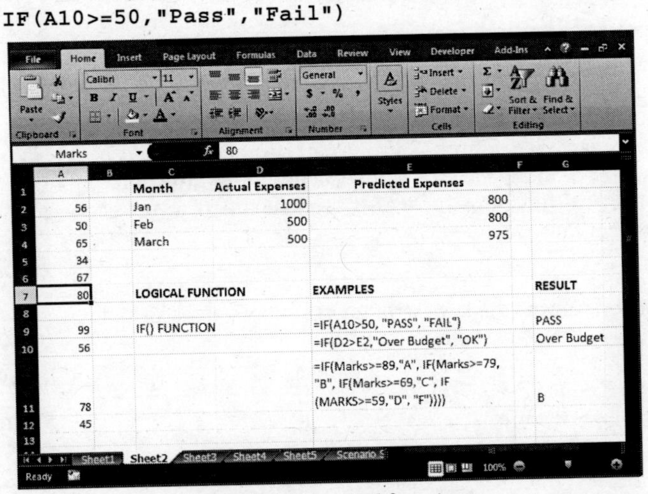

Figure 5.44 Logical functions

Suppose an expense worksheet in D2:D4 contains the following data for "Actual Expenses" for January, February, and March: 1000, 500, 500. E2:E4 contains the following data for "Predicted Expenses" for the same periods: 800, 800, 975.

You can write a formula to check whether you are over budget for a particular month, generating text for a message with the following formulas:

`IF(D2>E2,"Over Budget","OK")` equals "Over Budget"

`IF(D3>E3,"Over Budget","OK")` equals "OK"

We can also use nested IF function:

```
IF(Marks>89,"A",IF(Marks>79,"B",
IF(Marks>69,"C",IF(Marks>59,"D","F"))))
```

In the above example, `Marks` in the name of the cell A7 if the first logical_test (Marks>=89) is TRUE, "A" is returned (See Figure 5.44). If the first logical_test is FALSE, the second IF statement is evaluated, and so on.

☞ When averaging cells, keep in mind the difference between empty cells and those containing the value zero, especially if you have cleared the Zero values check box from the Advanced properties of the Excel Options. Empty cells are not counted, but zero values are counted and evaluated.

TRUE( )

`TRUE( )` returns the logical value TRUE and it takes no arguments.

Syntax

`TRUE( )`

FALSE( )

`FALSE( )` function is same as TRUE( ) but it returns the logical value FALSE.

Syntax

```
FALSE( )
```

Statistical Function

Statistical functions are used to perform statistical analysis on ranges of data. Excel 2010 includes simple as well as complex statistical functions, such as average, min, max, standard deviation, slopes etc (See Figure 5.45). Apart from this, it also includes a set of more accurate statistical and other functions. Certain existing functions have also been renamed to better describe what they do.

MAX( )

Max function returns the largest value in a set of values stored in a cells.

Syntax

```
MAX(number1,number2,...)
```

MIN( )

Min function returns the smallest number in a set of values.

Syntax

```
MIN(number1,number2, ...)
```

Average( )

The Average function returns the average (arithmetic mean) of the arguments which are passed in function as an argument (See Figure 5.45).

Syntax

```
AVERAGE(number1,number2,...)
```

Count( )

Count function counts the number of cells that contain numbers and numbers within the list of arguments. Use COUNT to get the number of entries in a number field in a range or array of numbers (See Figure 5.45).

Syntax

```
COUNT(value1,value2,...)
```

Date and Time Function

With date and time functions, you can analyze and work with date and time values in formulas (See Figure 5.46). For example, if you need to use the current date in a formula, you can use the TODAY () function, which returns the current date.

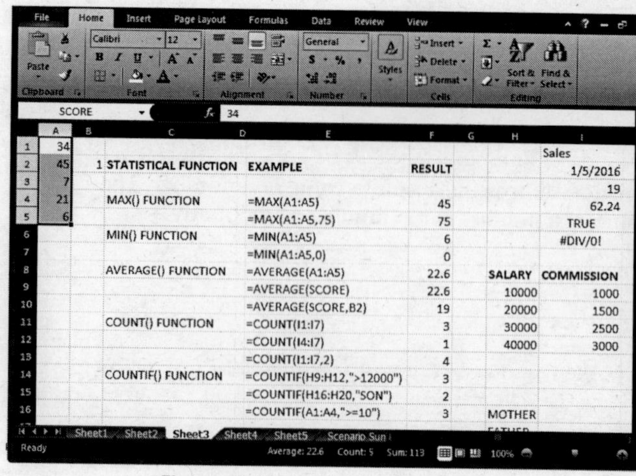

Figure 5.45 Statistical functions

Today ( )

It returns the current date of the system (See Figure 5.46).

Syntax

```
TODAY( )
```

Now()

Returns the current date and time (See Figure 5.46).

Syntax

```
NOW( )
```

Day()

It returns the day of a date passed as an argument. The day is given as an integer ranging from 1 to 31 (See Figure 5.46).

Syntax

```
DAY(serial_number)
```

Where `serial_number` is the date of the day you are trying to find. Dates may be entered as text strings within quotation marks.

Example 12

`DAY("01-Feb")` equals `1`
`DAY("02-Feb-2017")` equals `2`
`DAY("02/02/2017")` equals `2`
`DAY("2017/10/10")` equals `10`

Month()

It returns the month of a date which is passed as argument. The month is given as an integer, ranging from 1 (January) to 12 (December) (See Figure 5.46).

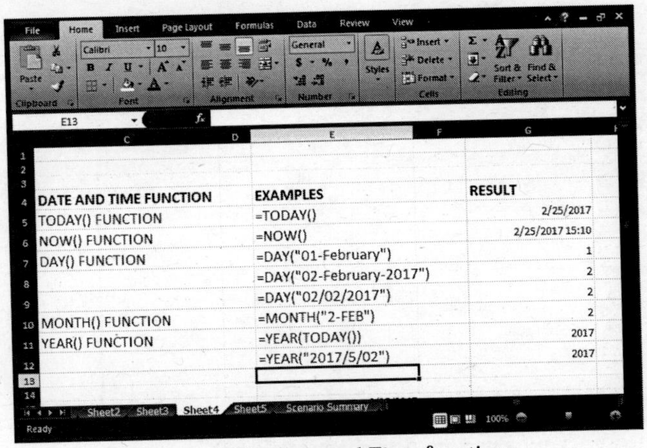

Figure 5.46 Date and Time functions

Syntax

`MONTH(serial_number)`

Where `serial_number` is the date of the month you are trying to find.

Example 13

`MONTH("23-Feb")` equals `2`

`MONTH("2017/02/01")` equals `1`

Year()

Returns the year corresponding year to a date (See Figure 5.46).

Syntax

`YEAR(serial_number)`

Where `serial_number` is the date of the year you want to find.

Text Function

With text functions, you can use text strings in formulas. You can also change the case of the string, find out the length of a text string or you can join two strings, etc (See Figure 5.47).

Concatenate( )

Joins two or more text strings into one text string (See Figure 5.47).

Syntax

`CONCATENATE (text1,text2,...)`

Where `text1, text2,...` are 2 to 255 text items to be joined into a single text item.

The `"&"` operator can also be used to join text items.

Example 14

`CONCATENATE("Total"," Value")` equals `"Total Value"`.

If you use '&' operator to join strings then `"Total"&" "&"Value"`

LEFT( )

LEFT returns the first character or characters in a text string, based on the number of characters specified as arguments (See Figure 5.47).

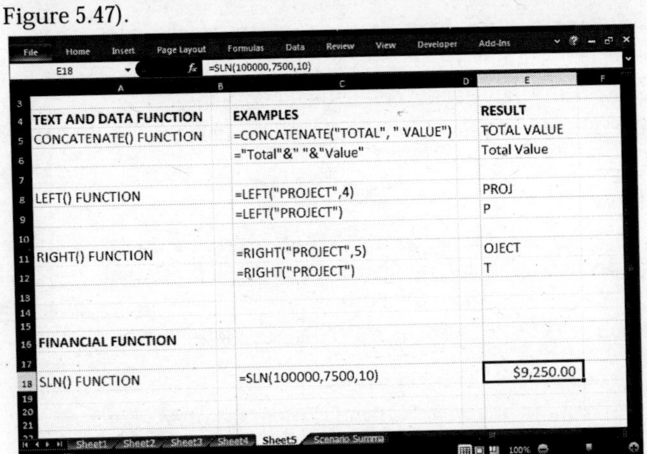

Figure 5.47 Text and Financial functions

Syntax

`LEFT(text,num_chars)`

Where `text` is the text string.

`num_chars` specifies the number of characters to be extracted. By default, it is assumed to be 1.

Example 15

`LEFT("PROJECT",4)` equals `"PROJ"` (See Figure 5.47)

If A1 contains "SUBJECT", then:

`LEFT(A1)` equals `"S"`

Because S is the left most character and by default it will be left most character value.

RIGHT( )

It is same as LEFT but it returns the last character or characters in a text string, based on the number of characters specified as a arguments (See Figure 5.47).

Syntax

`RIGHT(text,num_chars)`

Where `text` is the text string.

`num_chars` specifies the number of characters to be extracted.

Example 16

`RIGHT("PROJECT",5)` equals `"OJECT"` (See Figure 5.47)

`RIGHT("PROJECT")` equals `"T"`

Financial Function

Financial functions perform common business calculations For example, determination of the payment for a loan.

SLN( )

Returns the straight-line depreciation of an asset for one period (See Figure 5.47).

Syntax

`SLN(cost,Last_value,life)`

Where `Cost` is the initial cost of the asset.

`Last_value` is the value at the end of the depreciation.

`Life` is the number of year in which the asset is being depreciated (the useful life of the asset).

Example 17

Suppose you purchased a Car for `1,00,000` that has a useful life of 10 years and a salvage value of `7,500`. The depreciation allowance for each year is:

`SLN(100000, 7500, 10)` equals `9,250` (See Figure 5.47)

PMT( )

Suppose you want to buy a car and you want to calculate your monthly installment you can use the `PMT()` function built in Excel 2010.

Example 18

1. Activate a cell.
2. Under the Formulas tab, click on the Insert Function. Alternatively, click on the Insert Function button on the center of the formula bar, i.e., *f* or press Shift+F3 keys together. It will display the Insert Function Dialog box as seen in Figure 5.48.

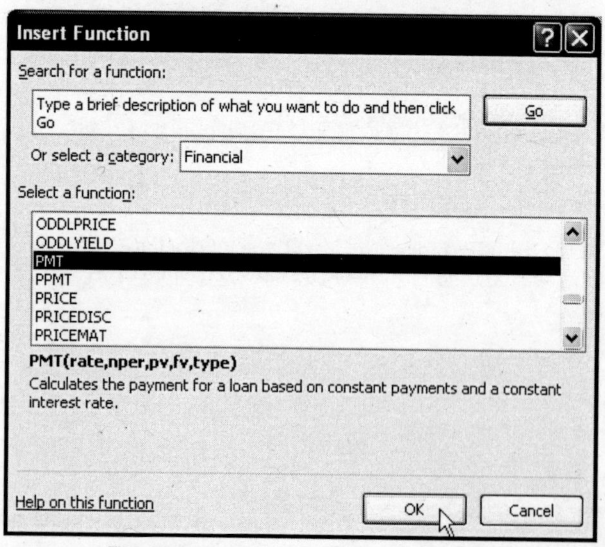

Figure 5.48 Insert Function dialog box

3. Select a Financial category from the select a category: drop-down list.
4. Click on PMT Function from the Select a function: list box.
5. Click OK. It will display a Function Arguments dialog box as seen in Figure 5.49.

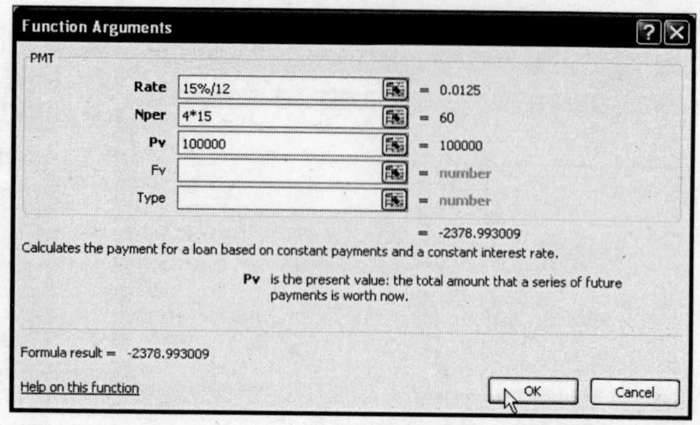

Figure 5.49 Function Arguments dialog box

The arguments required by the function are as follows:

Argument	Description
Rate	Is the interest rate for the loan.
Nper	Is the total number of payments for the loan.
Pv	Is the present value, or the total amount that a series of future payments is worth now; also known as the principal amount which is 100000 in our case.
Fv	Is the future value, or a cash balance you want to attain after the last payment is made. If Fv is omitted, it is assumed to be 0 (zero), that is, the future value of a loan is 0.
Type	Is the number 0 (zero) or 1 and indicated when payments are due.

Set type equal to	If payments are due
0 or omitted	At the end of the period
1	At the beginning of the period

Example 19

The following Figure 5.50 shown a simple Excel for Salary Calculation.

HRA = House Rent Allowance 40% = Basic * 40%

DA = Dearness Allowance 50% = Basic * 50%

Gross = Total of HRA + DA = Basic + HRA + DA

PF = Provident Fund (Employee PF contribution) = Basic + DA = 0.12%

ESI = Employ Salary Insurance = Basic * .0475%

Net Salary = Gross - PF - ESI

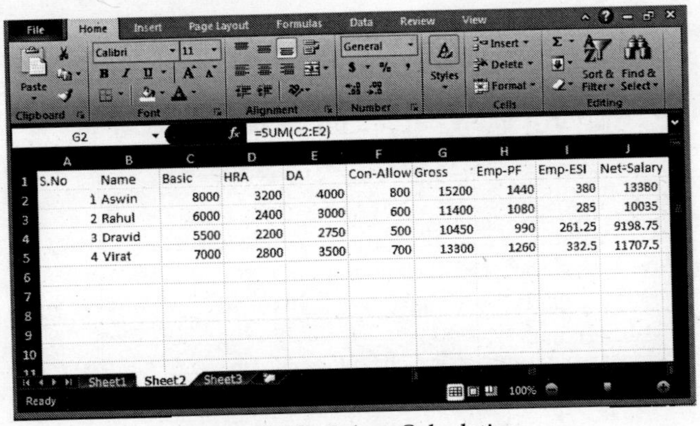

Figure 5.50 Salary Calculation

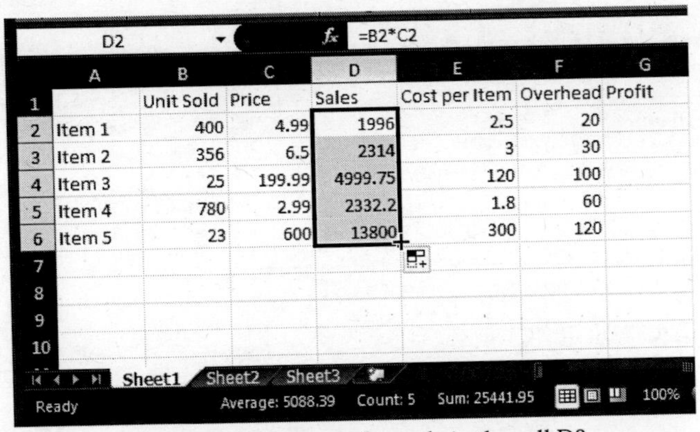

Figure 5.52 Entering formula in the cell D2

5.4.6 Using Formulas with multiple Cell References

In Excel one can use multiple pieces of data for each calculations. You will need to be able to reference multiple cells at the same time

The following table of data: (See Figure 5.51)

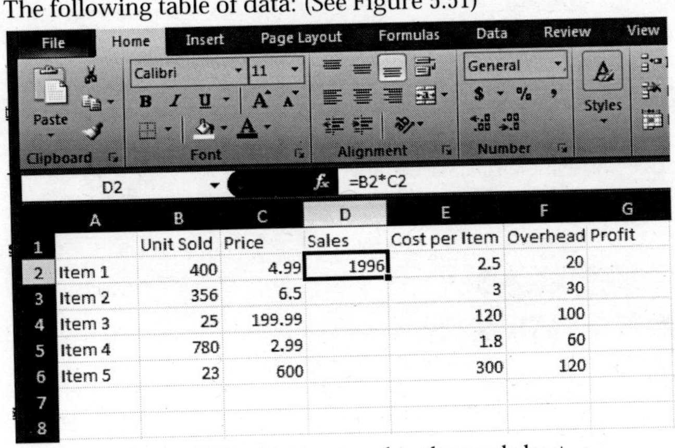

Figure 5.51 Data entered in the worksheet

In order to calculate profit for item, sales need to be calculated and then the cost of the items need to be subtracted from the sales.

To do this, first calculate the sales. Enter =B2*C2 in cell D2: (See Figure 5.52)

This calculation is easy to type because it only deals with two cells. However, if you need to create a formula based on many different fields, it can be very tedious to track down the correct cell reference. To make entering formulas easier, you can simply click the cells you need to use to automatically insert them.

Instead of entering the same formula as rest of the data you entered the above (units sold × price) (i.e. same formula), simply click and drag the cells as shown below: (See Figure 5.53).

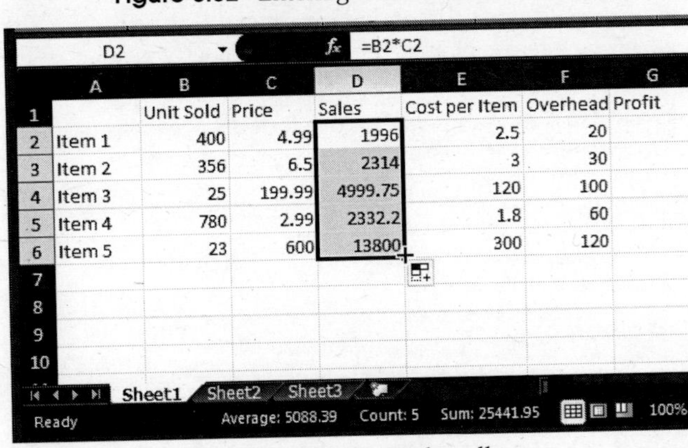

Figure 5.53 Drag the cells

Once all the sales values have been calculated, we can now calculate the profit. Profit is calculated by subtracting the expenses from the sales.

Sales - (Unit sold * cost per item + Overhead) = profit

In our example, this translates into the following formula. Note the color coding for each cell: (See Figure 5.54)

Once the correct formula has been entered in the cells in the Profit column, the worksheet is complete. For the rest of the data you need not to enter the same formula, simply click and drag the cells as shown in Figure 5.55.

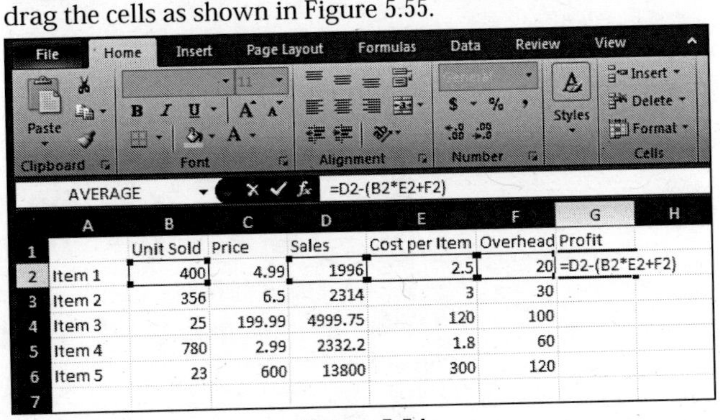

Figure 5.54

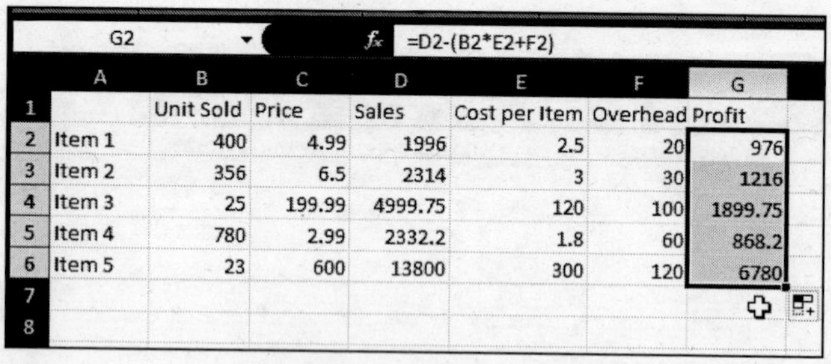

Figure 5.55 Drag the cells

5.4.7 Charts in Excel

You can create different types of charts using Excel 2010 that will help you to analyze data in a worksheet and give you a visual presentation of results. You can even customize the chart by adding text, arrows, titles, and legends, etc. If you print a chart on a laser printer or plotter, the quality of charts is as good as that of a chart created by a professional artist.

☞ With Excel 2010, you can instantly access formatting options by double-clicking a chart element.

How to Create a Chart?

You can create two types of charts namely, embedded charts and charts that appear in a chart sheet.

Embedded Chart

An embedded chart appears in a worksheet next to tables or text. Figure 5.56 shows an embedded chart.

☞ Embedded charts are required when you want a chart side-by-side with the data for the chart, such as in a report.

Chart in a Chart Sheet

A chart can be created by itself in its own chart sheet within a workbook (See Figure 5.57). Thus, you are able to work with the chart sheet separately from the worksheet containing data. If you insert a chart in a sheet, you add the chart to the active workbook and save it along with the workbook.

☞ If you need to print a chart on its own, creating the chart on a chart sheet is the best approach.

To quickly create a chart, select data and press F11 key then Excel 2010 insert a chart in a chart sheet, using the default chart type. But, when you press Alt + F1 keys together, the chart is displayed as an embedded chart (See Figure 5.56).

Chart Terminology

An Excel 2010 chart may contain objects that you may like to modify individually. Figure 5.56 showed some of these objects. Table 5.12 describes each object. Note that if you move mouse pointer over an object in a chart, a tip appears to give the description of the chart object.

Table 5.12 Parts of an Excel Chart

Object	Description
Axis (x-axis and y-axis)	The horizontal or x-axis along the bottom of most charts is also referred to as category axis. The vertical or y-axis against which data points are measured is also referred to as value axis. This axis contains the scale against which data is plotted.
Data point	A single piece of data.

(Contd...)

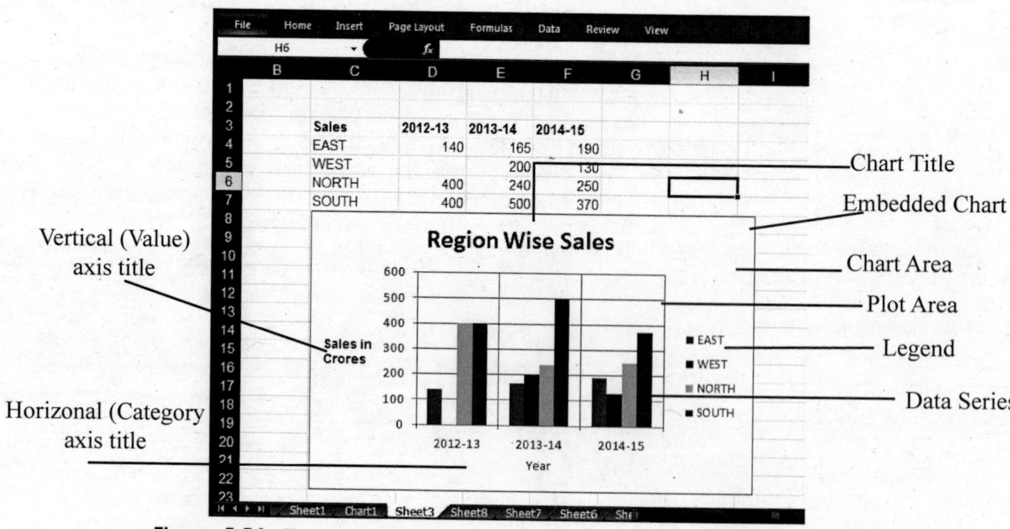

Figure 5.56 Embedded Chart with data Elements in the same worksheet

Data series	A collection of data points.
Legend	The name of each data series is used as a legend title.
Marker	An object that represents a data point in a chart such as bars, pie and symbols. Markers that belong to the same data series appear as the same shape, symbol and colour.
Plot area	The Rectangular area bounded by the two axes.
Text	Text associated with data points or free-floating text that can be moved easily. The box containing the text that can be resized.

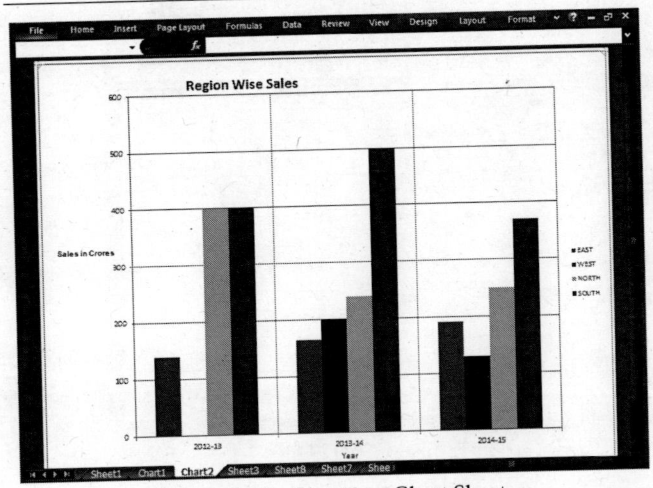

Figure 5.57 Chart in a Chart Sheet

Creating a Chart

➡ **To create a chart, do this:**

1. Select the data items you want to appear as chart.
2. Under the Insert tab, in Charts group, click arrow next to that chart which you want to insert and then select the chart from the chart subtype (Here, we select Column chart sub type) (See Figure 5.58).

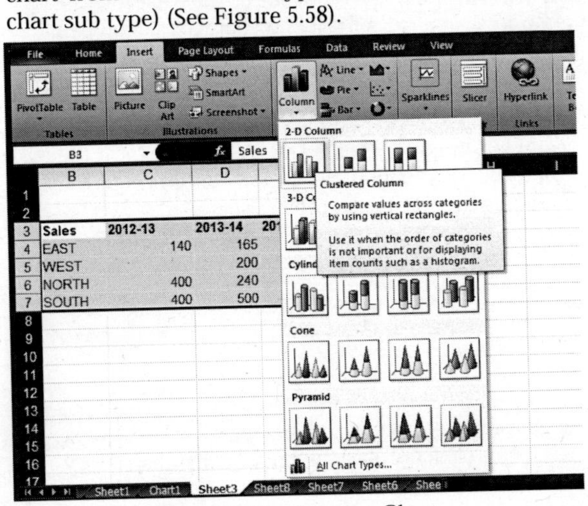

Figure 5.58 Creating Chart

☞ When you create a chart, chart tools become available and the Design, Layout and Format tabs are displayed as in Figure 5.57. You can use command on these tabs to modify the chart so that data is presented the way you want.

3. Chart will appear as seen in Figure 5.56.

Changing the Type of Chart

Excel 2010 offers you eleven different chart types and within each of these general types, you can select any sub-types. The easiest way to create chart is to select a chart type and sub-type you want. Thereafter, you may customize this chart according to your requirement.

☞ In Excel 2010, you can use the macro recorder to record formatting changes to charts and other objects.

Example 20

How will you change to a different type of chart?

Solution

1. Activate the chart you want to change by positioning the mouse pointer on the tab and clicking the tab for the chart sheet. In case, the chart is embedded, then click the chart itself.
2. Under the Design tab, in Type group, click Change Chart ype. A Change Chart Type dialog box showing different chart types appear as seen in Figure 5.59.
3. Select a chart type from the left side's list.
4. Select a sub-type from the right side's list.
5. Click OK to close the Change Chart Type dialog box.

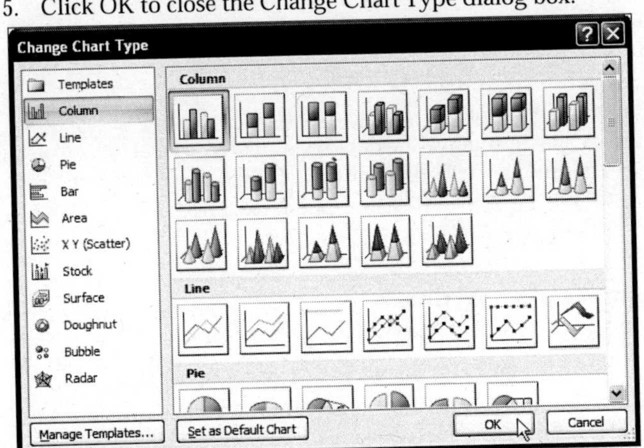

Figure 5.59 Change Chart Type dialog box

Changing Data Source

You can add data to an existing chart. You can even add new data series or data points to existing series or change the range of data used by a chart.

Example 21

How will you change the data source of a chart?

Solution

1. Activate the embedded chart or activate the chart sheet for the chart in which you want to add data.
2. Under the Design tab, in Data group, click Select Data. Select Data Source dialog box appears as seen in Figure 5.60.

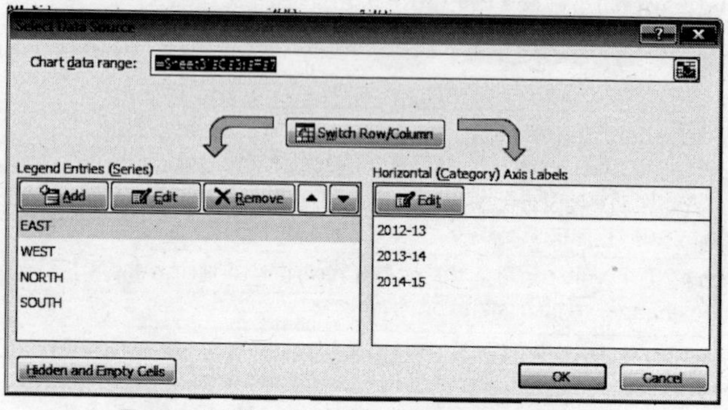

Figure 5.60 Select Data Source dialog box

3. In this dialog box, make the following changes according to your need.

   Chart data range: This box displays the range of data that is plotted in the chart. If you want to change the range, click on the collapse Dialog button at the right end of this box. It will temporarily minimizes. Now select the new range and click this button again after you select the range.

   Switch Row/Column: It switches the rows of worksheet from rows to the columns and vice versa.

   Legend Entries (Series): It displays an existing data series names.

   Add: Click to add a new data series to the chart.

   Edit: If you want to edit the existing range, click in this button to make changes to the data series

   Remove: Click to remove the data series that you select in the Legend Entries (Series) box from the chart.

   Horizontal (Category) Axis Labels: Lists existing horizontal (category) axis labels.

   Edit: Click to modify the horizontal (category) labels.
4. After making changes, click OK.

Inserting Text

When you create a chart, Excel 2010 automatically includes labels along the category and value axes. This happens only if you had selected data and included cells containing labels. There are two types of text you can add. These are as follows:

1. Text associated with specific objects in a chart, such as the title, axes, or data points. After you insert this type of text, you can select it and revise it whenever you want. You can also reposition it.
2. Text not associated with objects in the chart are known as floating text. Such unattached text appears in a box which can be resized and repositioned anywhere on the chart.

Example 22

Write down the procedure to
(a) Insert the title in a chart.
(b) Edit a title.

Solution (a)

1. Activate the Chart to which you want to add a title.
2. Under the Layout tab, in Labels group, click arrow next to Chart Title. Select the option whichever you want as seen in Figure 5.61.

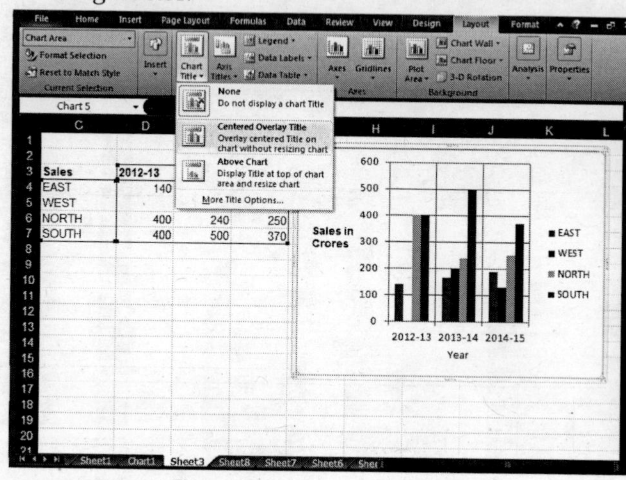

Figure 5.61 Insert Chart Title

3. In the Chart Title text box that appears in the chart, type the text that you want.

Solution (b)

1. Click the title to select it and then click inside the box that contains the text.
2. The insertion point appears where you click. You can then use the arrow keys to move around the text or the Backspace and Delete keys to delete characters. You can press letter keys on the keyboard to enter the new text.

Modifying the Axes

Excel 2010 creates a Category (X) axis and Value (Y) axis at the time of creating a chart. But you can modify any one of the axes using the Axes group of Layout tab.

Example 23

How will you remove an axis from the chart?

Solution

1. Activate the chart where you want to remove an axis.
2. Under the Layout tab, in the Axes group, click arrow next to Axes and then click Primary Vertical Axis or Primary Horizontal Axis and then click None (See Figure 5.62).

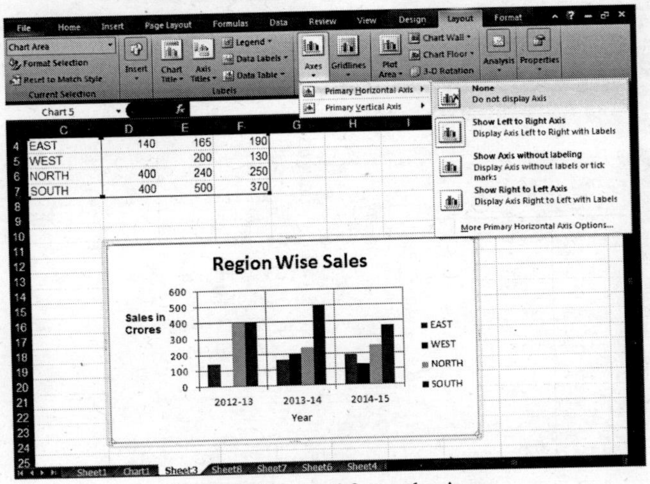

Figure 5.62 Modifying the Axes

Inserting Data Labels

You can insert a label that can either be the value for that data point, or the category axis label associated with the data point. You can also attach labels to many data points. This would help a viewer to interpret data in a chart easily.

Example 24

Write down the steps to insert data labels in a chart?

Solution

1. Activate the chart to which you want to add data labels.
2. Under the Layout tab, in the Labels group, click arrow next to Data Labels and then select the display option where you want to insert the data labels (See Figure 5.63).

☞ To add data label to an individual data series, right-click the data series and choose Add Data Labels.

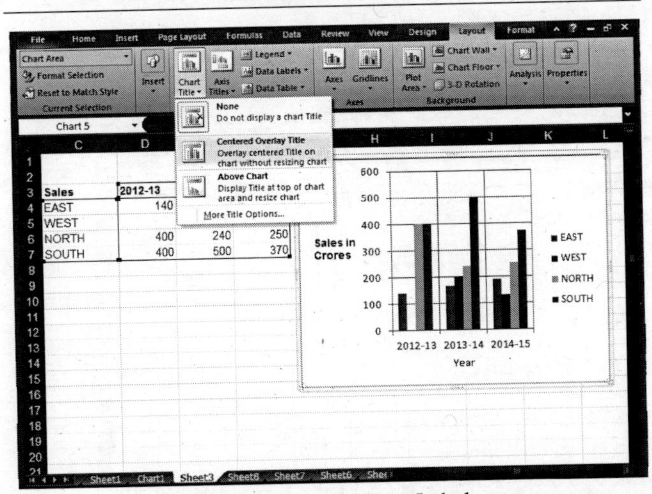

Figure 5.63 Add Data Labels

Inserting Legends

Legend describes the symbols used in a chart. Excel 2010 creates legends from the labels on the shorter side of the worksheet data series.

➡ **To insert a legend, do this:**

1. Activate the chart.
2. Under the Layout tab, in the Labels group, click arrow next to Legend and select the display option where you want to insert the legends (See Figure 5.64).

Inserting Gridlines

Gridlines help you to compare markers and in reading values accurately.

➡ **To add gridlines to a chart, do this:**

1. Activate the chart you want to add gridlines to.

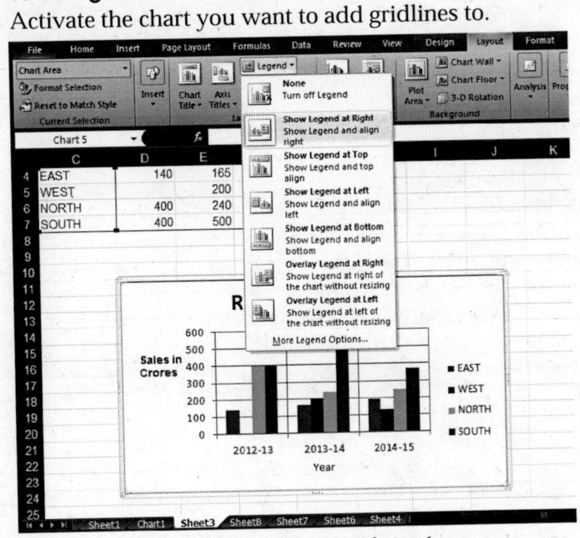

Figure 5.64 Add Legends in chart

2. Under the Layout tab, in the Axes group, click arrow next to Axes and then click Primary Vertical Gridlines or Primary Horizontal Gridlines and then click the option according to your requirement (See Figure 5.65).

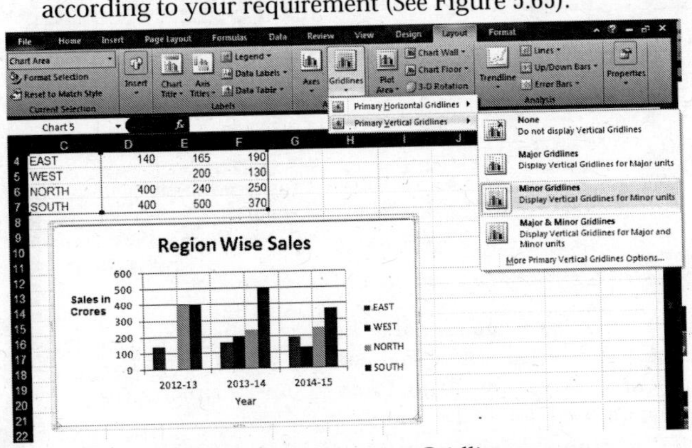

Figure 5.65 Inserting Gridlines

☞ Drawing gridlines in a chart helps you to compare values more easily.

5.4.8 Previewing Charts

After creating a chart and before printing, it is a good practice to see the full page view (preview) of the chart.

☞ In Excel 2010, you can preview and print your Excel files in one location–on the Print tab in the MS Office Backstage view. To go back to your workbook and make changes before you print it, click the File tab.

Example 25

How will you preview a chart if
(a) Chart is in a Chart sheet?
(b) Chart is Embedded on a worksheet?

Solution (a)

1. Activate the chart sheet.
2. Click on the File Tab. Menu appears. Here, click on Print Option.
3. In this view, the properties of the default printer automatically appears in the left section and the preview of the chart sheet automatically appears in the right section (See Figure 5.66).

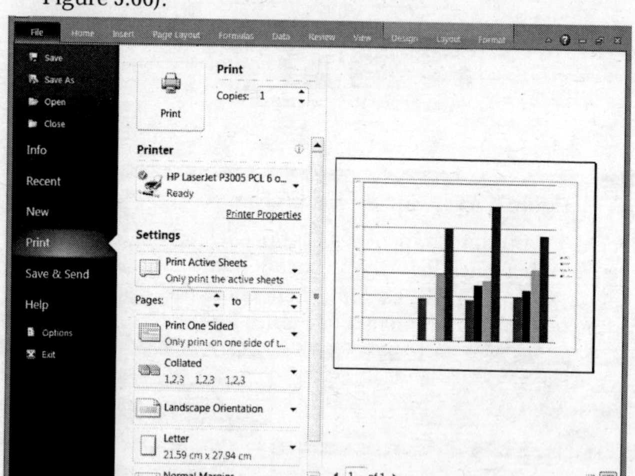

Figure 5.66 Preview of Chart sheet

Solution (b)

1. Activate the sheet containing the chart.
2. Click on the File Tab. Menu appears. Here, click on Print Option or click on the Print Preview and Print button from the Quick Launch Toolbar.
3. A window containing the preview of the chart along with data appears as seen in Figure 5.67.

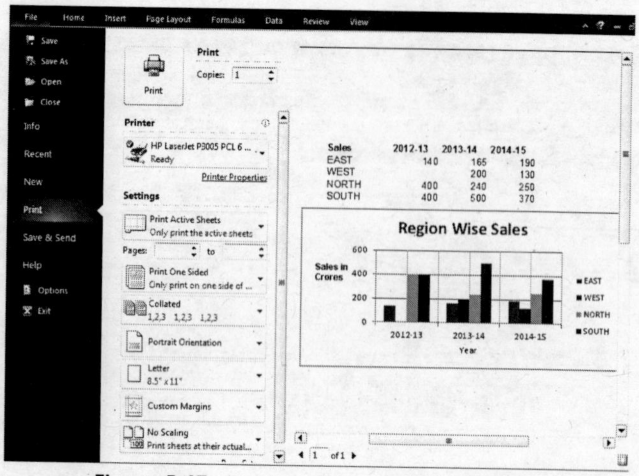

Figure 5.67 Preview of the Embedded chart

☞ Positioning a chart along with data items helps you to analyse data easily. By making changes in the data items, you can immediately preview the effects in the chart.

5.5 WORKING WITH GRAPHICS

Graphical Representations makes it easy to understand and interpret the data at a glance. Excel includes the SmartArt graphic feature. SmartArt graphics are predefined graphic objects that you can use to create graphical lists and diagrams in a worksheet.

5.5.1 SmartArt Graphic

A SmartArt graphic is a visual representation of information that you can quickly and easily create, choosing from many different layouts. Each type contains several different layouts. After you choose a layout, it is easy to change the layout for your SmartArt graphic.

➡ **To insert a SmartArt Graphics in a worksheet, do this:**

1. Under the Insert tab, in Illustrations group, click SmartArt (See Figure 5.68).

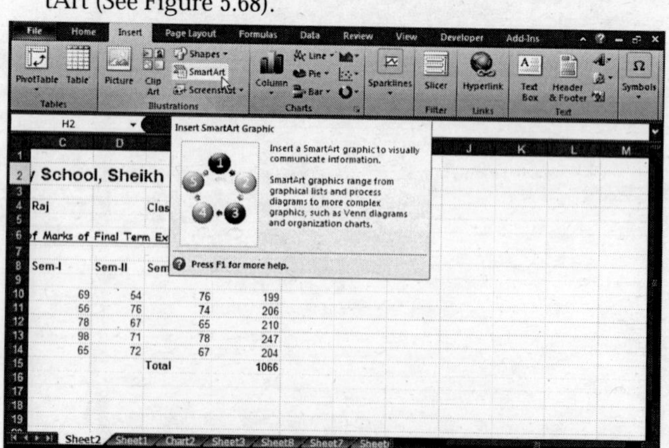

Figure 5.68 Inserting SmartArt Graphics

2. It will display Choose a SmartArt Graphic dialog box as shown in Figure 5.69. In this dialog box, click the type and layout that you want and then click OK.

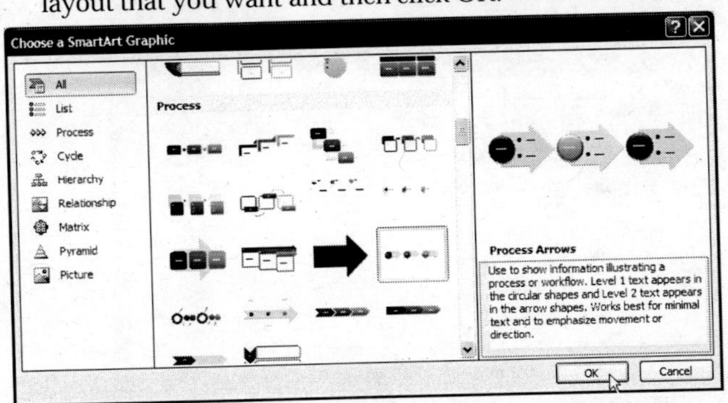

Figure 5.69 Choose a SmartArt Graphic dialog box

☞ When you create a SmartArt Graphic, SmartArt Tools become available and the Design and Format tabs are displayed as in Figures 4.71 and 4.72, respectively. You can use commands on these tabs to modify the SmartArt graphic as per your need.

3. Enter your text by doing one of the following:
   - Click in a shape in your SmartArt graphic, and then type the text.
   - Click [Text] in the Text pane, and then type your text.
   - Copy text from other program, click [Text], and then paste into the Text pane. You can also click on the Text Pane control to type the text as shown in Figure 5.70.

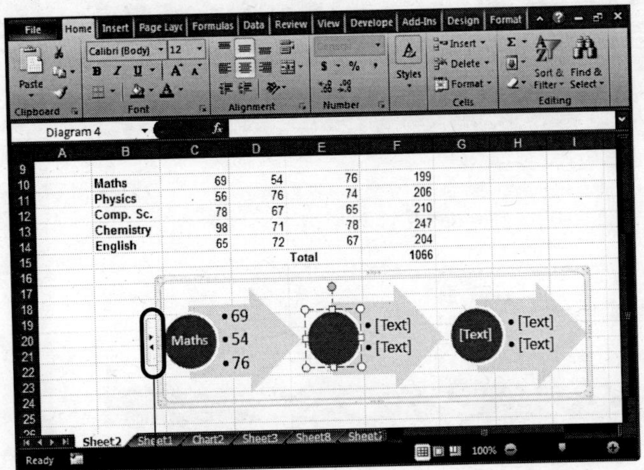

Text Pane Control

Figure 5.70 Adding text in the SmartArt graphic placeholder

➡ **To add or delete shapes in SmartArt graphic, do this:**

1. Click the SmartArt graphic's shape where you want to add new shape (See Figure 5.71).
2. Under the Design tab, in the Create Graphic group, click the arrow next to Add Shape.
3. Then click Add Shape After to insert a shape after the selected shape or click Add Shape Before to insert a shape before the selected shape (See Figure 5.73).

To delete a shape, click the shape and then press Del key.

More button

Figure 5.71 Design Tab of SmartArt Tools

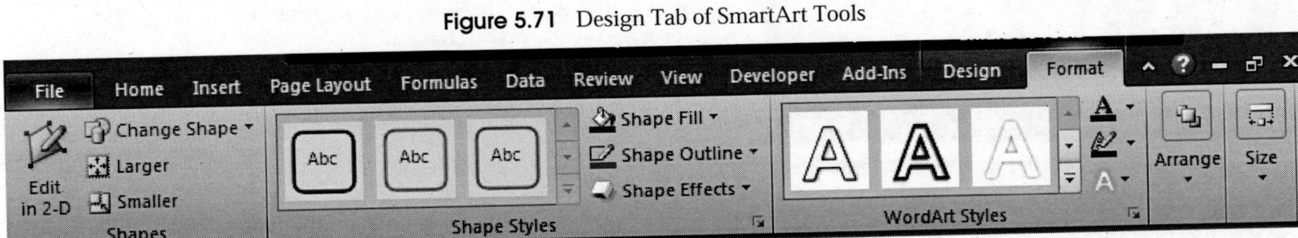

Figure 5.72 Format Tab of SmartArt Tools

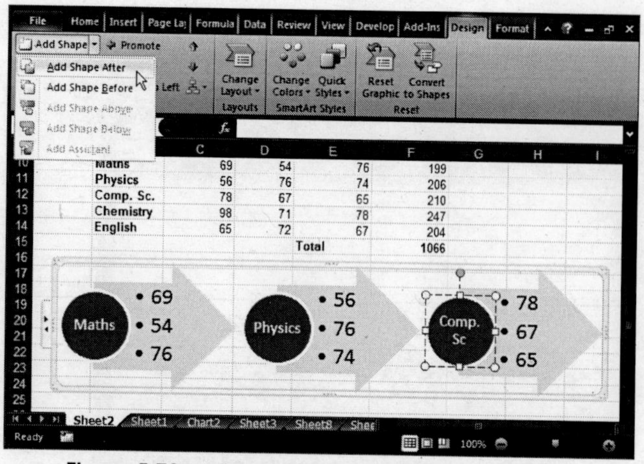

Figure 5.73 Adding shapes in a SmartArt Graphic

5.5.2 Apply a SmartArt Style to a SmartArt Graphic

A SmartArt Style is a combination of various effects, such as line style, bevel, or 3-D, that you can apply to the shapes in your SmartArt graphic to create a unique and professionally designed look.

➡ **To apply a SmartArt style to a SmartArt graphic, do this:**

1. Click your SmartArt graphic.
2. Under SmartArt Tools, on the Design tab, in the SmartArt Styles group, click the SmartArt Style that you want (See Figure 5.74).
3. To see more SmartArt Styles, click the More button (See Figure 5.71).
4. Select the desired styles you want to apply.

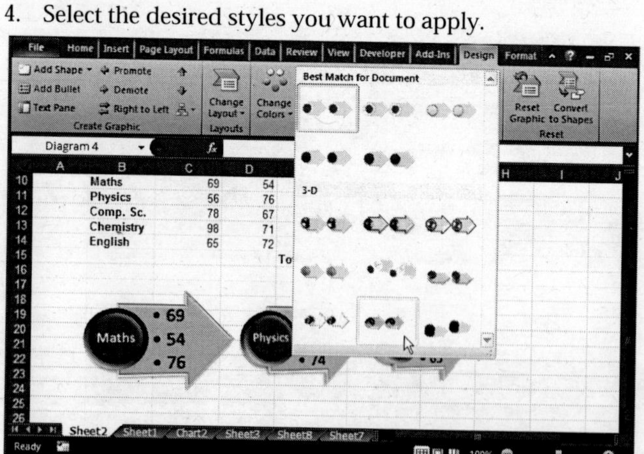

Figure 5.74 Selecting styles from the SmartArt Styles group

5.5.3 Change the Colours of an Entire SmartArt Graphic

You can apply colour variations that are derived from the theme colors to the shapes in your SmartArt graphic.

➡ **To change the colors of entire graphic, do this:**

1. Click your SmartArt graphic.
2. Under SmartArt Tools, on the Design tab, in the SmartArt Styles group, click Change Colors (See Figure 5.75).
3. Click the color variation that you want.

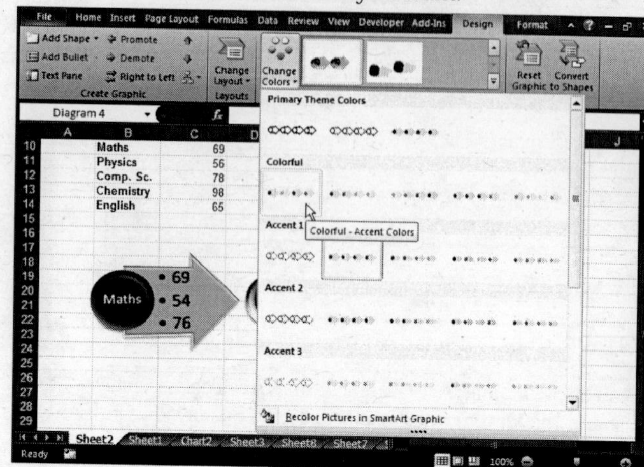

Figure 5.75 Change the colour of an entire SmartArt Graphic

5.5.4 Inserting Clip Art

Adding Clip Art to your documents can enhance their visual appeal and help to convey information more clearly.

➡ **To insert clip art in a worksheet, do this:**

1. On the Insert tab, click the Clip Art button in the Illustrations group.
   Excel 2010 displays the Clip Art task pane, where you search for the type of art you want to use.
2. Click in the Search for: text box and enter the keyword(s) for the type of clip art you want to find.
   When you enter keywords for finding particular types of clip art, try general, descriptive terms, such as trees, flowers, people, flying, and the like.
3. Click the Results should be: drop-down button and select the Illustrations check box, if it is not already selected.
   By default, Excel searches all the collections of clip art (including the Office.com collection on the Web). To limit your search to clip art only, select the Illustrations check box and remove check marks from the Photographs, Videos, and Audio check boxes.
4. Click the Go button to the right of the Search For text box to initiate the search (See Figure 5.76).
   Excel displays several images that match your search keywords.
5. Select the desired clip art image.
   Position the mouse pointer over the image you want to use to display its drop-down button. Click the drop-down button and choose Insert at the top of its drop-down menu. The clip art image appears in the worksheet (See Figure 5.76).
6. Move and resize the image as necessary.

Clip art graphics are normally a bit larger than you actually need them to be. Click and drag the circular resizing handles around the outer edge of the image to make it the right size, and then click and drag inside the image to position it where you want it.

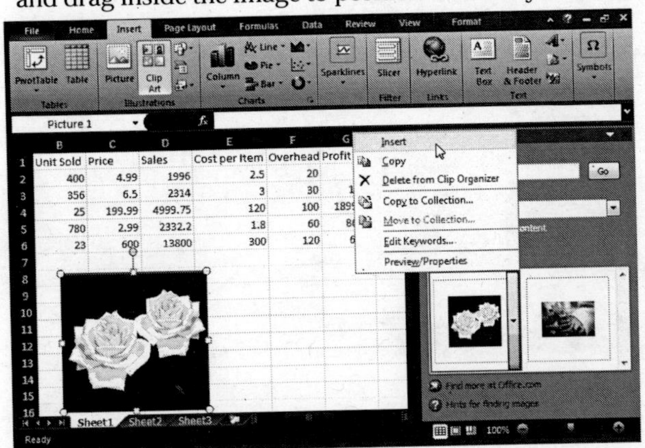

Figure 5.76 Change the colour of an entire SmartArt Graphic

5.6 PIVOTTABLE

A PivotTable is an interactive table that lets you analyze and view large size of data in a list or database form so that it can be easily understood and analysed. You can rotate its rows and columns to see different summaries, details and views of the source data as per your need. You can use PivotTable report when you want to do sorting, totaling or to compare related items. In Excel 2010, multithreading help speed up data retrieval, sorting, and filtering in PivotTables.

☞ In Excel 2010, it is possible to fill down labels in a PivotTable so that you can more easily use the PivotTable. You can also repeat labels in PivotTables to display item captions of nested fields in all rows and columns.

Example 26

(a) How will you create PivotTable report?

(b) How will you filter a PivotTable?

Solution (a)

1. Select the cells (including column labels) that you want to include in the PivotTable.
2. Under the Insert Tab and in the Tables group, click arrow next to PivotTable and then choose PivotTable (Figure 5.77). The Create PivotTable dialog box appears (Figure 5.78).
3. In this dialog box, Select a table or range: if you want to select the cells.

   Use an external data source: option when you want to select range from external source.

   New Worksheet: option puts the PivotTable on the new worksheet.

   Existing Worksheet: option puts the PivotTable on an existing worksheet.
4. Click OK

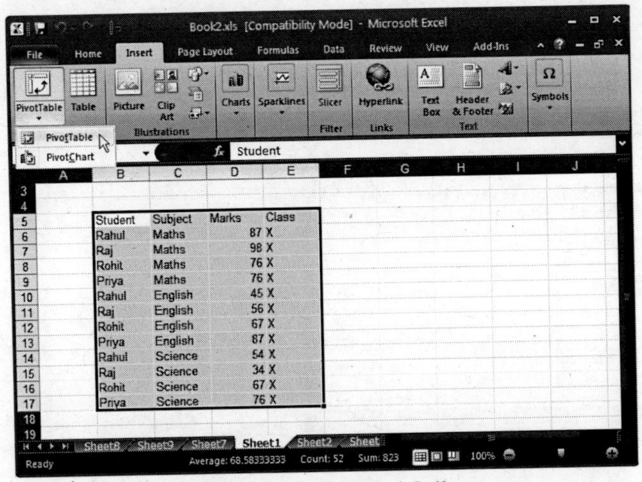

Figure 5.77 Selected Cells

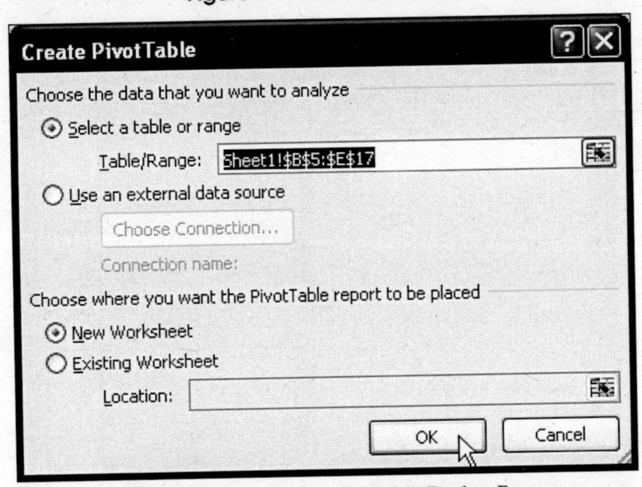

Figure 5.78 Create PivotTable Dialog Box

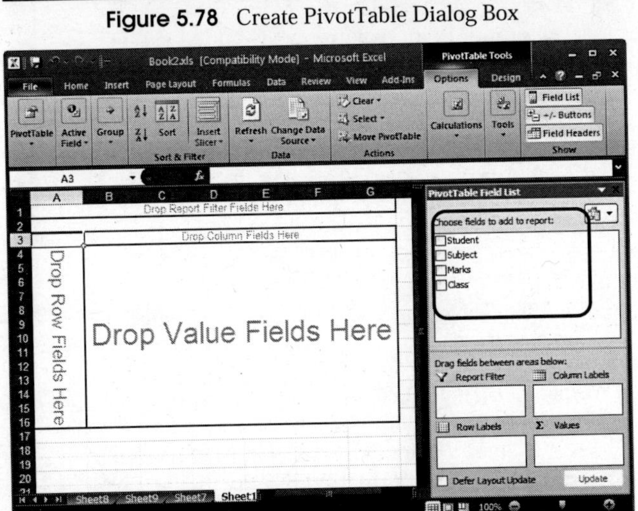

Figure 5.79 PivotTable field list pane to choose data

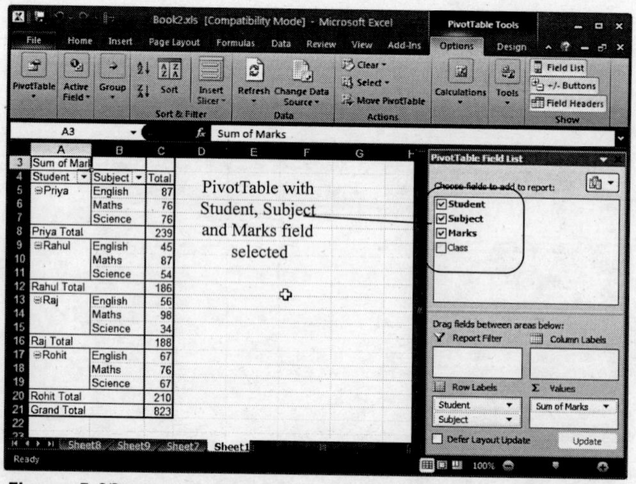

Figure 5.80 PivotTable with Student, Subject and Marks fields selected

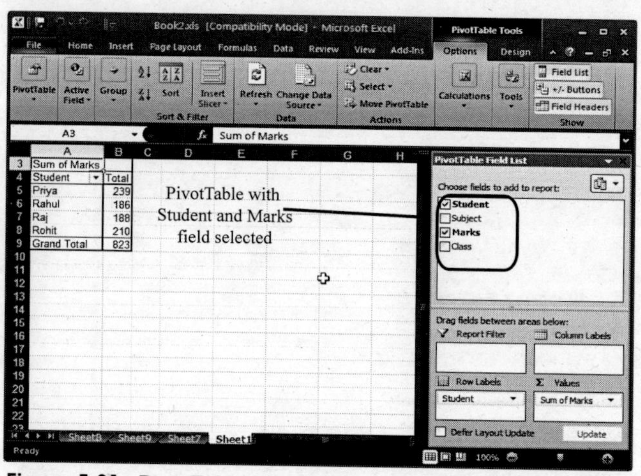

Figure 5.81 PivotTable with Student and Marks fields selected

5. After that, an empty PivotTable report is added (PivotTable Tools are also displayed with Options Tab as shown in Figure 5.79) to the location that you entered with the PivotTable field list so that you can start adding fields (Figure 5.79).
6. Mark one or more check boxes inside the PivotTable Field List pane. Each time you select another check box, Excel 2010 modifies how data appears in your PivotTable (Figures 5.80 and 5.81).

Solution (b)

1. Click on the PivotTable you want to filter. The PivotTable list pane appears as seen in Figure 5.80.

   Click a heading in the Row Labels or Column Labels group in the PivotTable field list pane. A pop up menu appears as seen in Figure 5.82.

   Select Move to Report Filter. Now Excel 2010 moves your chosen label into the Report Filter group in the Pivot Table Field List pane and displays a filter list box at the top of your PivotTable (Here, we have selected Subject from Row Label and moved it to the Report Filter) as seen in Figure 5.82. Now your report will show only Student, Marks and Class fields. Subject field is removed from the Report (Figure 5.83).

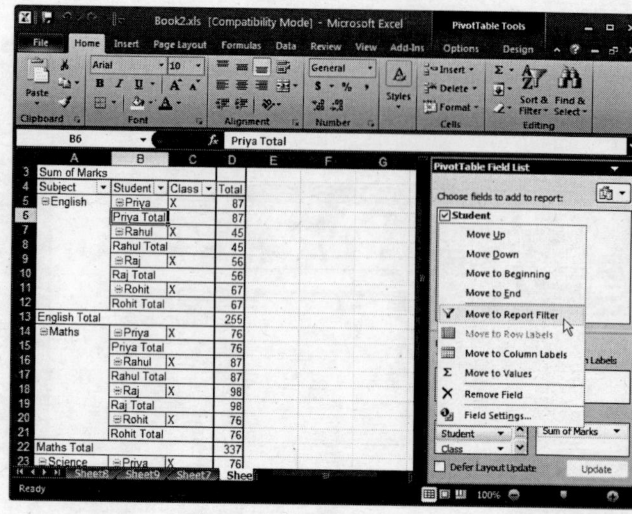

Figure 5.82 Pop-up menu

In Excel 2010, it is now easier to filter data directly in a PivotChart report and to reorganize the chart's layout by adding and removing fields. Similarly, with a single click, you can hide all field buttons on the PivotChart.

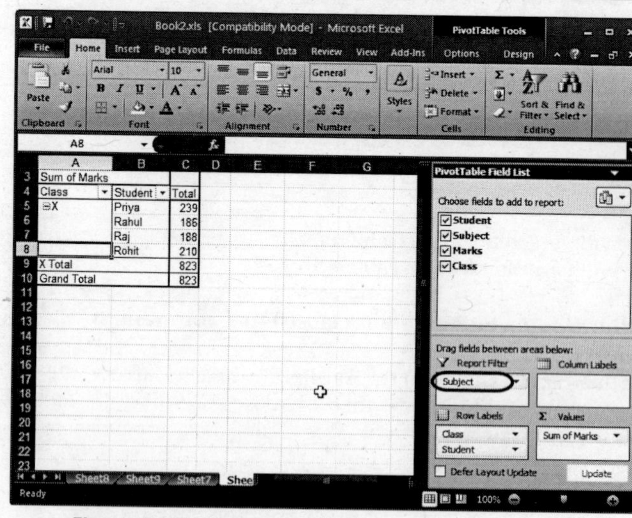

Figure 5.83 Subject field is moved in Report Filter

5.6.1 Pivot Charts

A pivot chart is a graphical representation of a data displayed in a pivot table. A pivot chart is always based on a pivot table.

Although Excel lets you create a pivot table and a pivot chart at the same time, you can not create a pivot chart without a pivot table.

➡ **To insert a pivot chart:**

1. Select the cell that contain data inside the pivot table.
2. On the Insert tab, click Column and select one of the sub-types. For example, Stacked Column as shown in Figure 5.84.
3. You can find the pivot chart as shown in Figure 5.85.

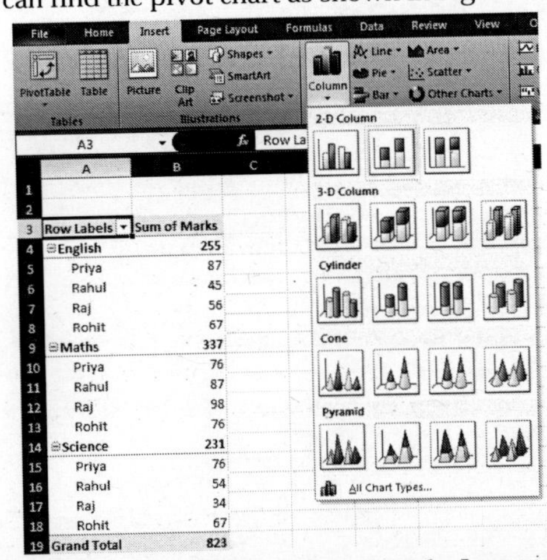

Figure 5.84 Select the chart type in the Insert tab

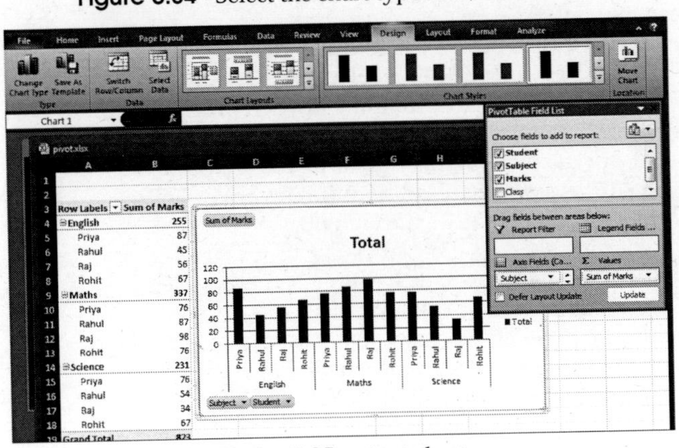

Figure 5.85 pivot chart

MODEL QUESTIONS AND ANSWERS

A. Multiple Choice

1.1 In Excel the intersection of a row and column is called

a. Square b. Cell

c. Cubicle d. Worksheet

1.2 By default, Excel sheet displays the following font style

a. Strikethorugh b. Italic

c. Bold d. None of the above

1.3 Extension of Excel file is

a. .TMT b. .XXL

c. .xls d. None of the above

1.4 The first electronic worksheet was known as

a. VisiCalc b. MS Excel

c. Lotus 1-2-3 d. None of the above

1.5 A worksheet can be opened by clicking on the

a. Start button c. Both a and b

b. Open button d. None of the above

1.6 The Formatting toolbar

a. Is placed just below the Standard toolbar

b. Is used to apply common formats to the worksheet text selection, like making it bold, italics, underlined or changing the font style and size

c. Both a and b above

d. None of the above

1.7 To change the cell reference B2:B9 to an absolute row and column reference, you would enter it as

a. B2:B9 b. $B$2:$B$9

c. B$2:B$9 d. none of the above

1.8 A function in Excel

a. Is a ready made formula b. Is a shortcut formula

c. Can be built using Function Wizard d. All of the above

1.9 Which of the following is not a financial function?

a. FV() c. SUM()

b. NPV() d. PMT()

1.10 Which of the following is not a text function

a. CHAR() c. VAR()

b. LEN() d. ABS()

1.11 The number of rows in a worksheet is

a. 36500 c. 64536

b. 1,048,576 d. 256

1.12 When a formatted number does not fit within a cell, it displays

a. ##### c. #DIV@

b. #DIV/0 d. None of these

1.13 What symbol is used to enter number as text?

a. = c. '

b. " d. +

1.14 Which of the following is concantenating operator?

a. Apostrophe (') c. Exclamation (!)

b. Ampersand (&) d. Hash (#)

1.15 To select multiple non-adjecent cells in a worksheet you will click and then hold

a. ALT key c. Ctrl+Shift key

b. Shift Key d. Ctrl key

1.16 What does the Now() function return?

a. It returns the serial number of the current date and time

b. It returns the serial number of the current date
c. It returns the serial number of the current time
d. None of the above

1.17 What is shortcut key to insert current date in a cell?
a. Ctrl + D
b. Ctrl + ;
c. Ctrl + T
d. Ctrl + /

1.18 Which Chart can be created in Excel?
a. Area
b. Pie
c. Line
d. All of the above

1.19 What will be the output if you format the cell containing 5436.8 as '#,##0.00'?
a. 5,430.00
b. 5,436.80
c. 5,436.8
d. 6.8

1.20 In the formula, which symbol specifies the fixed columns or rows?
a. $
b. *
c. %
d. @

1.21 What is the correct way to refer the cell A10 on sheet3 from sheet1?
a. sheet1!A10
b. sheet3.A10
c. sheet3!A10
d. A10

1.22 An Excel 2010 Workbook is a collection ________.
a. Workbooks
b. Worksheets
c. Charts
d. Worksheets and Charts

1.23 In Excel 2010, you can sum a large range of data by simply selecting a tool button called _______.
a. AutoFill
b. AutoCorrect
c. Auto Format
d. Auto sum

1.24 Which function is used to calculate depreciation, rates of return, future values and loan payment amounts?
a. Logical
b. Math & Trigonometry
c. Statistical
d. Financial

1.25 Getting data from a cell located in a different sheet is called
a. Accessing
b. Referencing
c. Updating
d. Functioning

1.26 Which command will you choose to convert a column of data into row?
a. Cut and Paste in the clipboard group.
b. Paste Special of Clipboard group.
c. Paste Special in the Font group
d. None of the above

1.27 You can enter which types of data into worksheet cells?
a. Lables, values and formulas
b. Labels, values but not formulas
c. Values and formulas but not labels
d. Formulas only

1.28 To drag a selected range of data to another worksheet in the same workbook, use the
a. Tab key
b. Alt key
c. Shift key
d. Ctrl key

1.29 In Excel, a Data Series is defined as what?
a. A type of chart
b. A cell reference
c. A collection of related data
d. A division of results

1.30 Excel uniquely identifies cells within a worksheet with a cell name
a. Cell names
b. Column numbers and row letters
c. Column letters and row numbers
d. Cell locator coordinates

B. State whether the following are True or False

2.1 To create a new worksheet, select worksheet from the file menu.
2.2 Cells are named by their positions either by rows or columns.
2.3 You can apply multiple conditional formatting criteria or rules to the same set of data.
2.4 Standard width of a column is 18.43.
2.5 To open a file quickly from the open dialog box, double click the file's icon.
2.6 You cannot move the active cell within a selected range.
2.7 You can simultaneously select an entire row and an entire column.
2.8 Sheet tab is displayed when you split a sheet.
2.9 Last column of the worksheet window is XFD.
2.10 You cannot split a single worksheet cell that has not been merged.
2.11 Receives the data the user enters is known as active cell.
2.12 A Workbook is a grid with labeled columns and rows.
2.13 Tabs that appear at the bottom of each workbook is called sheet tabs.
2.14 Deleting a cell is the same as clearing a cell's content.
2.15 Excel 2010 is a powerful communication S/W package.
2.16 B7:B9 it indicates cells B7 through B9.
2.17 A hyperlink enables you to navigate to a web page, another file, or to a specific location in another file.
2.18 A21 is an example of a cell address.
2.19 The box on the chart that contains the name of each individual record is called the axis.
2.20 Character type is not a valid data type in Excel.

Answers

A.

1.1 b	1.2 d	1.3 c	1.4 a	1.5 b
1.6 c	1.7 c	1.8 d	1.9 c	1.10 d
1.11 b	1.12 a	1.13 c	1.14 b	1.15 d
1.16 a	1.17 b	1.18 d	1.19 b	1.20 a
1.21 c	1.22 b	1.23 d	1.24 d	1.25 b
1.26 b	1.27 a	1.28 d	1.29 c	1.30 c

B.

2.1 F	2.2 F	2.3 T	2.4 F	2.5 T
2.6 F	2.7 F	2.8 T	2.9 T	2.10 T
2.11 T	2.12 F	2.13 T	2.14 F	2.15 F
2.16 T	2.17 T	2.18 T	2.19 F	2.20 T

CHAPTER 6

Presentation

6.1 INTRODUCTION

PowerPoint 2010 is a presentation program developed for the Windows and Mac OS computer operating systems. Being widely used by business people, educators, and trainers, it is among the most prevalent forms of persuasion technology. According to its vendor, MS Corporation, some 30 million presentations are made with PowerPoint every day.

In MS PowerPoint, as in most other presentation software, text, graphics, movies, and other objects are positioned on individual pages or "slides". The "slide" is a reference to the slide projector, a device which has become somewhat obsolete due to the use of PowerPoint and other presentation software. Slides can be printed, or displayed on-screen and navigated through at the command of the presenter. Transitions between slides can be animated in a variety of ways, as can the emergence of elements on a slide itself. The overall design of a presentation can be controlled with a master slide. The overall structure, extending to the text on each slide, can be edited using an outliner. Presentations can be saved and run in many types of file formats.

6.2 BASICS OF POWERPOINT

PowerPoint is the largest selling presentation graphics software package by MS Corporation of USA and since its introduction in 1987, PowerPoint has set new standards for the working of presentation graphics.

PowerPoint 2010 helps you in bringing ideas and information that you want to convey to your audience with no difficulty. With PowerPoint 2010, you can:

- Quickly create paper for Overhead Projector (OHP), 35mm slide, or on-screen presentations.
- Supplement your presentations with speaker's notes.
- Use material you have created in other application packages, such as Word 2010 and Excel 2010.

6.2.1 Using PowerPoint

Presentations

You can make presentation in the form of slides, handouts or speaker's notes.

Slides

Slides are individual "pages" of a presentation. It may contain text, graphs, clipart, etc. You can even print slides for overhead projector transparencies.

Handouts

Handouts consist of printed versions of your slides – either two, three, or six slides per page.

6.2.2 Opening PowerPoint 2010 for Presentation

➡ **To start PowerPoint 2010, do this:**

1. Click the Start button on the Taskbar.
2. Highlight All Programs menu item and click MS Office and choose MS Office PowerPoint 2010 (Figure 6.1).

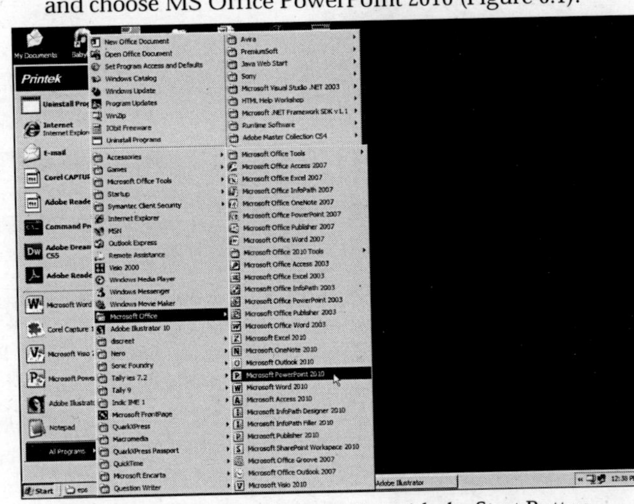

Figure 6.1 Starting Powerpoint with the Start Button

When you first start PowerPoint 2010, it displays a blank presentation with a single slide showing. The layout is simple, with a title at the top and a subtitle below (See Figure 6.2).

Understanding the Screen Elements

You will notice a close resemblance of the PowerPoint 2010 opening screen with the opening screens of Word 2007 and Excel 2007. The main elements of the PowerPoint window are as shown in Figure 6.2.

Title bar: The Title bar is at the top of the screen (See Figure 6.2). It shows the title PowerPoint and the name of presentation. If you have not yet saved any presentation then it displays the default name for the presentation which is Presentation1.

Ribbon: Ribbon is displayed just below the title bar. In Ribbon, Commands are organized in logical groups, which are collected together under tabs (Figure 6.2).

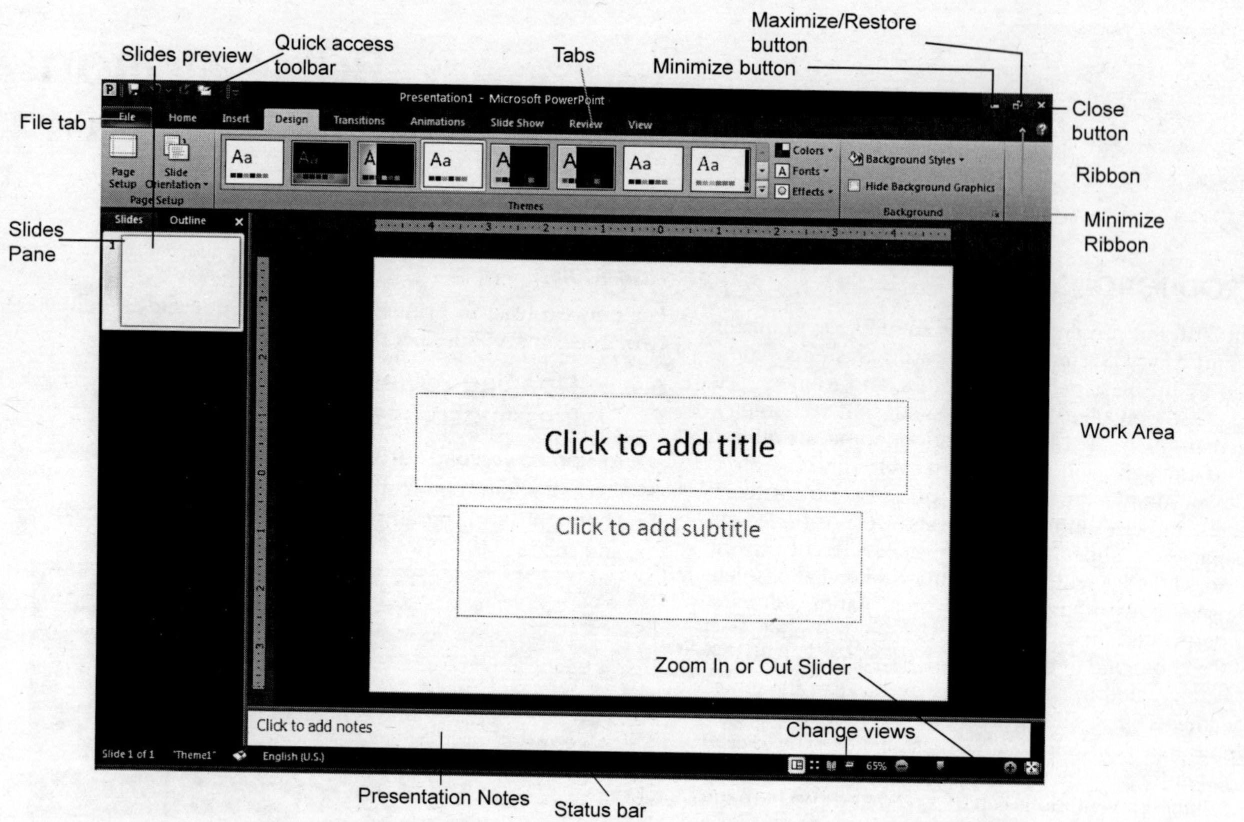

Figure 6.2 A blank presentation displayed by PowerPoint

Quick Access Toolbar: This toolbar is located by default at the top of PowerPoint 2010 window. By default, this toolbar displays the Save, Undo and Repeat buttons.

Minimize button: Shrinks the application window to a bar on the taskbar, you can click its button on the taskbar to reopen it.

Restore button: A double box at the right of a title bar that restores an application or document into a sizable window.

Close button: A box at the right of a title bar (X) that closes the window or dialog box.

Work area: Where active PowerPoint slide(s) appear. Figure 6.2 shows it in Normal view, but other views are available that make the work area appear differently.

Status bar: It gives the information about the presentation and provides shortcuts for changing the view and the zoom.

Exploring PowerPoint 2010 Interface

There is a new look for PowerPoint 2010. There is also a new user interface that replaces menus, toolbars, and most of the task panes from previous versions of PowerPoint. The new user interface is designed to help you to be more productive in PowerPoint; more easily find the right features for various tasks and also be more efficient.

The PowerPoint 2010 interface consists of various components, which are as follows:

Minimize/Maximize/Restore and Close buttons

The Minimize, Maximize and Close buttons are located on the top right corner of the MS PowerPoint window. The Minimize button is used to minimize the MS PowerPoint window over the Task bar whereas the Maximize button is helps to restore or maximize the MS PowerPoint window. The Close button is used to close the document (See Figure 6.2).

File Tab

File tab is the colored tab which is located in the upper-left corner of MS Office 2010 programs and below the Quick Access Toolbar. When you click the File tab, you can see the Backstage view. File tab replaces the office button in PowerPoint 2010. It contains commands like New, Open, Save, Save As, Print, etc.

Quick Access Toolbar

The Quick Access Toolbar is a customizable toolbar that contains a set of commands that are independent of the tab that is currently displayed. You can add buttons that represent commands to the Quick Access Toolbar. You can move the

Quick Access Toolbar from one of the two possible locations. This toolbar is located by default at the top of PowerPoint 2010 window. It provides tools that you use frequently, such as Save, Undo and Repeat buttons (See Figure 6.2). You can customize the Quick Access Toolbar by adding commands to it.

➡ **To add command to Quick Access Toolbar, do this:**

1. Right click the appropriate command that you want to add to the Quick Access Toolbar (See Figure 6.3).
2. Then click Add to Quick Access Toolbar from the context menu as shown in Figure 6.3.

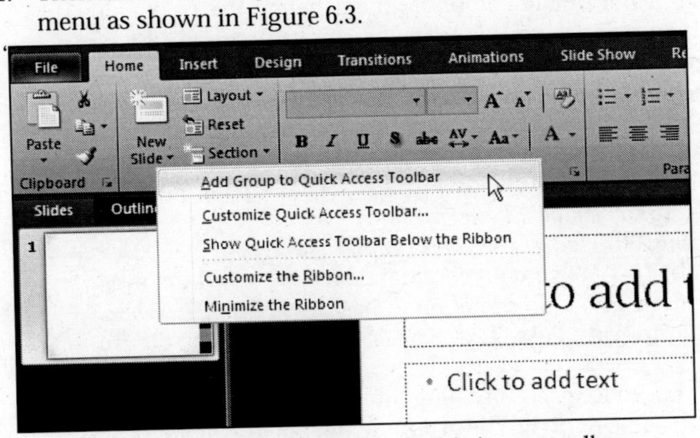

Figure 6.3 Add command to Quick Access toolbar

Dialog Box Launchers

The dialog box launchers are small icons that appear in some groups on the Ribbon. Clicking a Dialog Box Launcher opens a related dialog box or task pane, providing more options related to that group.

Ribbon

The primary replacement for menus and toolbars in PowerPoint 2010 is the Ribbon. Designed for easy browsing, the Ribbon consists of tabs that are organized around specific scenarios or objects. The controls on each tab are further organized into several groups. The Ribbon can host richer content than menus and toolbars can, including buttons, galleries, and dialog box contents (See Figure 6.4).

1. Tabs are designed to be task-oriented.

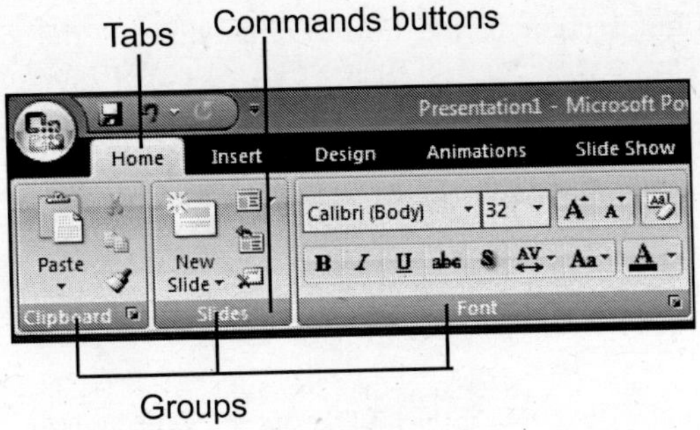

Figure 6.4

2. Groups within each tab break a task into subtasks.
3. Command buttons in each group carry out a command or display a menu of commands.

Contextual Tools

Contextual tools enable you to work with an object that you select on the page, such as table, picture, or drawing. When you click the object, the pertinent set of contextual tabs appear in colour next to the standard tabs (See Figure 6.5).

Scroll Bar

The Scroll bar appears at the right side of the PowerPoint. You can also scroll between different slides by using the up and down arrow buttons present in the scroll bar.

Work Area

Where active PowerPoint slide(s) appears. It shows it in Normal view, but other views are available that make the work area different.

Status Bar

It gives the information about the presentation and about the current slide, such as slide number, theme name. The slide number displays the currently selected slide with the total number of the slides present in the presentations; whereas, the theme name represents the name of the theme applied to the presentation.

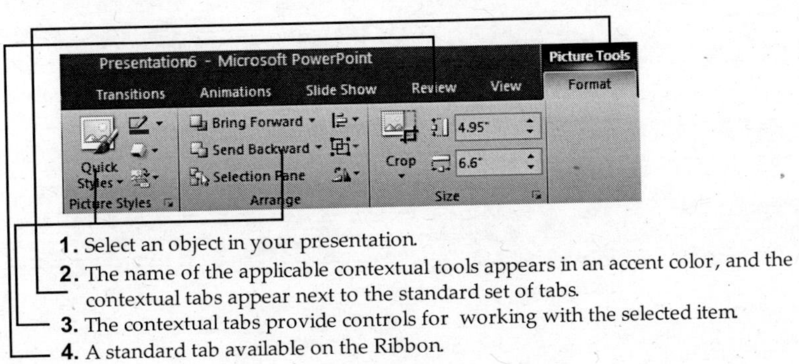

Figure 6.5 Contextual Tools

Slides Pane

In the upper-right section of the PowerPoint window, the Slide pane displays a large view of the current slide. With the current slide shown in this view, you can add text and insert pictures (picture: A file (such as a metafile) that you can ungroup and manipulate as two or more objects, or a file that stays as a single object (such as bitmaps).), tables, SmartArt graphics, charts, drawing objects, text boxes, movies, sounds, hyperlinks, and animations.

Notes Pane

In the Notes pane below the Slide pane, you can type notes that apply to the current slide. Later, you can print your notes and refer to them when you give your presentation. You can also print notes to hand out to your audience or include the notes in a presentation that you send to the audience or post on a Web page.

Zoom Control

You can use Zoom controls to get a larger or smaller view of your presentation by dragging the Zoom slider right to left. You can click the Zoom In (+ plus) button to get a larger view of the presentation and the Out (- minus) button to get a smaller view of the presentation.

Exploring the Tabs

Ribbon in PowerPoint 2010 is a group of tabs. This tab consists of two tasks, command tabs and contextual tabs. A command tab is a collection of commands of a specific category. Commands in a command tab are placed into different group. Each command set represents a subcategory of commands. Contextual tabs appear on the Ribbon when you add or select some object, such as image, a table, or a chart on a PowerPoint slide. An example of a contextual tab is the Format tab Some of the tabs are discuss in the following sections.

Home Tab: When you click it, this tab gets activated. Buttons related to working with document contents are organized in this tab. It has six groups: Clipboard, Slides, Font, Paragraph, Drawing and Editing. Only the button representing commands that can be performed on the currently selected document element are active (See Figure 6.6).

The groups for the Home Tab are:

(a) ***lipboard*** This contains the Cut, Copy, and Paste commands.

(b) ***lides*** This section allows you to insert new slides (clicking on the 'New Slide' button allows you to select the slide type you wish), as well as adjust the layout of your individual slides, reset slides to default, and delete slides.

(c) ***ont*** Select the font here. Adjust the font type and size. Make it bold, italic, or underline. Change the colour or highlighting. Using this tab, you can also change case of selected text to uppercase or lowercase.

(d) ***aragraph*** Bullets or numbered lists. It also changes the alignment of text and change the spacing between lines.

(e) ***ra ing*** Insert shapes. Arrange objects on a given slide. It also applies fill colour in the selected shape and add effect to the shapes.

(f) ***diting*** Find, edit, select, and replace text.

Insert Tab: This tab contain commands related to all the item you can insert into a presentation. It has seven groups: Tables, Images, Illustrations, links, Text, Symbols and Media (See Figure 6.7).

When you need to insert anything into your slide show, this is where you come to do it. The groups available to you are:

(a) ***ables*** Insert tables into the slide. These can be pre-made, or you can make them as you like.

(b) ***mages*** It allows you to insert pictures from a file as well as from the Clip Art in a slide. You can also create photo album and apply visual effects to pictures. Screenshot which allows you to take screenshot of all currently opened windows on the computer.

(c) ***ll strations*** It allows you to insert pre-defined shapes, Smart Arts and charts in the presentation.

(d) ***inks*** Add a hyperlink, to take you out of your slide-show to a Web resource. Add an action to cause something to happen in the slide show if you point to an object with the mouse.

Figure 6.6 Home tab

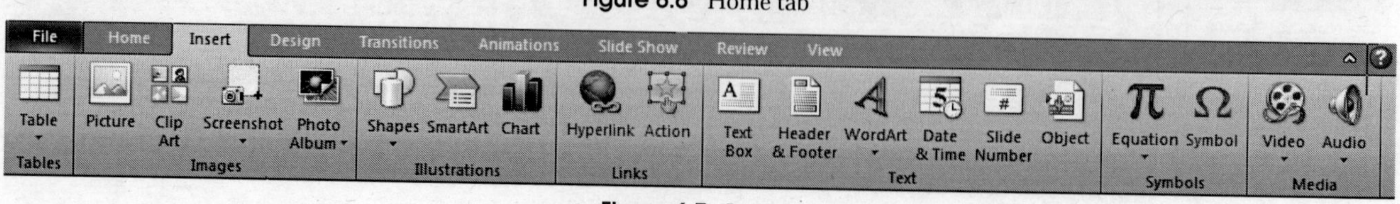

Figure 6.7 Insert

(e) *e t* It is not just about typing text into a slide: Insert text boxes, which allow you to play with the location and orientation of words. Insert headers and footers. Turn your text into " *ord rt*". Insert date, times, slide numbers and other embedded objects.

(f) *mbols* It allows you to insert and edit equations and insert symbols in the presentation.

(g) *edia* Insert video and sound into your slide, to create a truly vibrant presentation.

Design tab: This tab contain commands related to the appearance of a presentation to give design to your slides. It has three groups: Page Setup, Themes, Background (See Figure 6.8). Adjust the look of individual slides with the contents of the design tab. Change just one slide, or apply your changes to the whole presentation:

(a) *age et p* Adjust margins, page size, and orientation (portrait or landscape).

(b) *hemes* PowerPoint 2007 comes with 20 built-in themes (combinations of color, layout, and font). You can browse the Web for more themes, or create your own custom ones.

(c) *ackgro nd* It adjust the background look of your slides by changing the color, or adding special images like watermarks.

Transitions: The transitions tab lets you to preview the presentation after applying effects, add transitions to a slide, and set the timing for the slide show of the presentation. It has three groups: Preview, Transition to this slide, timing (See Figure 6.9).

(a) *re ie* It helps to view the slide after the transition effect is applied.

(b) *ransition to this slide* It allows you to apply transition to a slide and set the effect option specific to a transition.

(c) *iming* It allows you to add transition sound and set the time to move to the next slide.

Animations tab: This tab contain commands related to slide animation in your presentation. For example, you can animate individual objects on the slide. It has four groups: Preview, Animation, Advance Animation and Timing (See Figure 6.10).

(a) *re ie* To preview the animation applied in the slide, include transition effect and animation applied on objects and text.

(b) *nimation* It allows you to apply animation to a slide and the effect based on the animation type.

(c) *d anced nimation* It allows you to apply advanced features to the applied animation and apply trigger effect.

(d) *imings* To set the duration of the slides and delay between the slides. You can reorder the animation.

Slide Show: This tab contain commands related to displaying a presentation. You can view; take up the full computer screen, like an actual presentation. For example, you can see how your graphics animated effects will look during the presentation. It has three groups: Start slide show, Set Up and Monitors (See Figure 6.11).

(a) *tart lide ho* Run it from the beginning or from a selected slide. Or, create a second slide show using only those slides in the presentation you want to use.

(b) *et p* Record narration for your slide show.

(c) *onitors* It allows you to select a screen resolution or a presenter view.

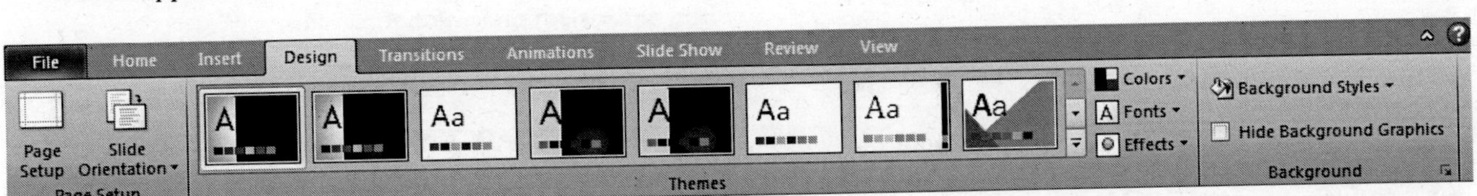

Figure 6.8 Design tab

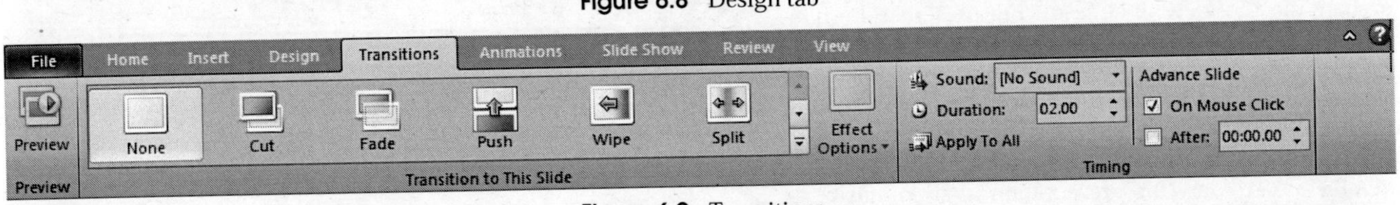

Figure 6.9 Transitions

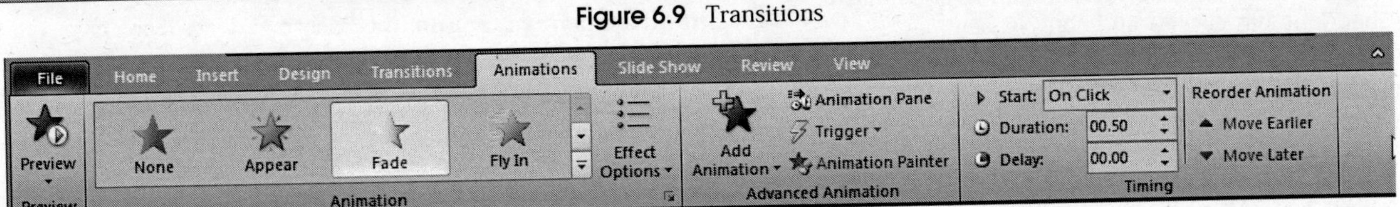

Figure 6.10 Animations tab

Figure 6.11 Slide Show

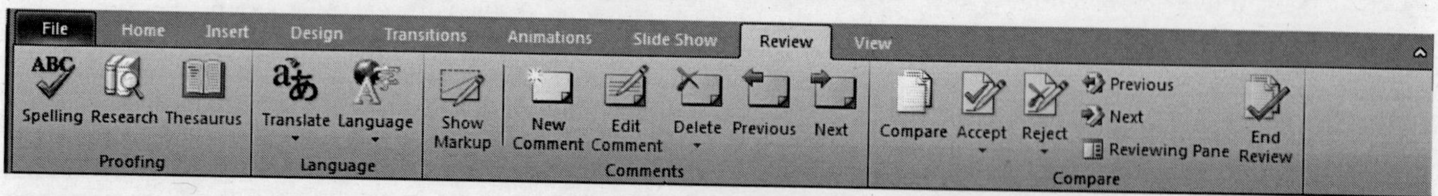

Figure 6.12 Review tab

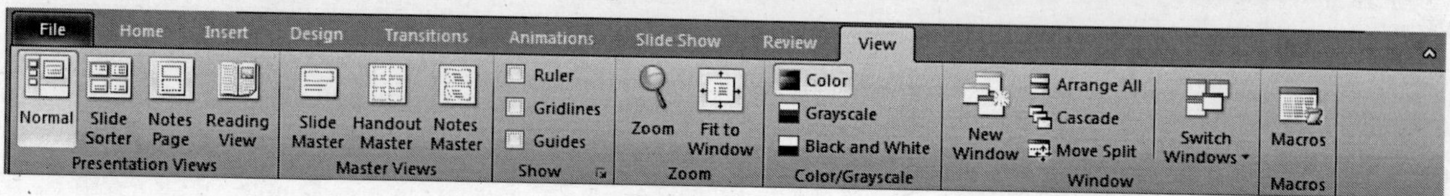

Figure 6.13 View tab

Review tab: Click this tab which will show buttons that are related to items. In this tab, you can view and add comments to your presentation and you might prefer to check spelling all at once when you finish your document. It has four groups: Proofing, Language, Comments and Compare (See Figure 6.12).

(a) *roofing* Check the spelling, open research task pane to references for more information; find synonyms so that you do not use the same word repeatedly, check the grammar etc.

(b) *ang age* It allows you to translate the text in other language.

(c) *omments* Add or edit comments about a given slide, or about a specific bit of content on a slide. Helpful when planning narration.

(d) *ompare* To compare different presentations, accept or reject the changes, and show the review pane.

View tab: Click this tab which will show buttons that are related to changing the view of slide during presentation. It has seven groups: Presentation views, Master Views, Show/Hide, Zoom, Color/Grayscale, Window and Macros (See Figure 6.13).

(a) *resentation ie* Choose from normal, slide sorter, notes view, handout view, and other options, either for on screen viewing, or printouts.

(b) *aster ie s* To view the presentation in slide master view, handout master view and notes master view.

(c) *ho ide* It display, gridlines, rulers and other tools to help you to place objects into the slides exactly where you want them.

(d) *oom* Zoom In or Out to change the size of the slide window.

(e) *olor ra scale* View the presentation in color, grayscale or even black and white.

(f) *indo* Arrange the windows in which you are working to help you to be more productive.

(g) *acros* Create and use custom macros to do complex tasks with just a click or two.

6.2.3 Opening an Existing Presentation

PowerPoint 2010 opens files in any of the several format, such as (.pptx, .pptm, .potx, .ppt, .pot, etc.)

➡ **To open an existing presentation, do this:**

1. Open the File tab on the Ribbon. The Backstage view appears. Alternatively, press Ctrl+O (See Figure 6.14).

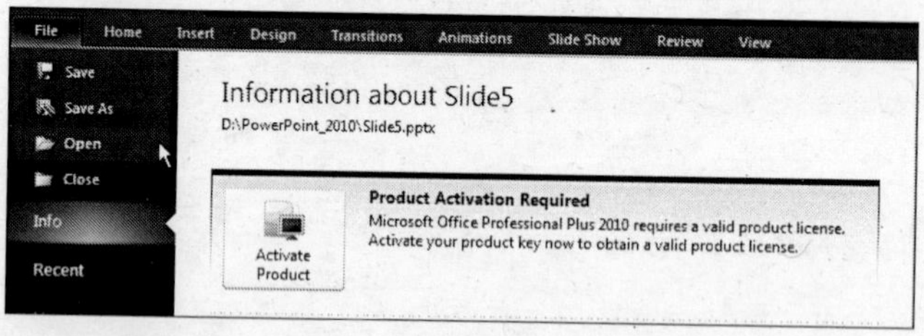

Figure 6.14 Selecting Open option from the File tab

2. Click the Open option from the Backstage view (See Figure 6.14).
3. The Open dialog box appears as shown in Figure 6.14.
4. Choose the files and folders in the Look in: drop-down list.
5. Select the name of the file you want to open from the list.
4. Click Open button to open the presentation.

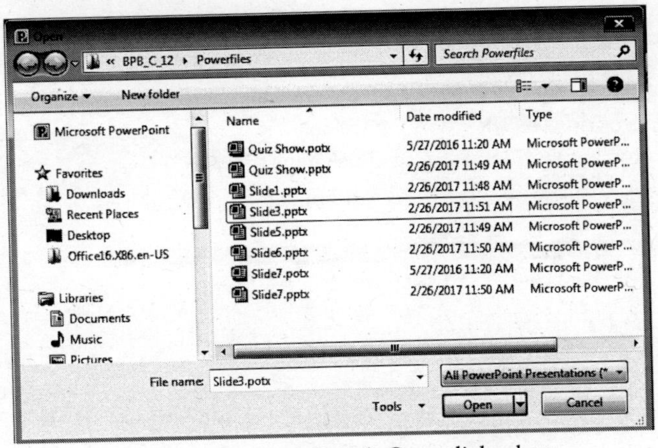

Figure 6.15 PowerPoint's Open dialog box

6.2.4 Saving the Presentation

When working on a presentation, it is very important that you save it at regular intervals so that in case of a system failure you do not loose much of your work.

PowerPoint has two commands to save your file – Save and Save As command.

- The Save command is used to save the presentation.
- The Save As command is used when you want to save an existing presentation under a new name or you are saving your presentation for the first time.

➡ **To save a presentation, do this:**

1. Click the File tab and on the Ribbon. The Backstage view will appear. Select the Save option from the File tab. Or click the Save button on the Quick Access toolbar or from the keyboard press Ctrl+S.
2. If you have already saved the file then PowerPoint updates the earlier saved file. If you have not saved the file before, the Save As dialog box as in Figure 6.16 appears.
3. In the Save As list box specify the location where you want to save the file in the Save in: drop-down list. (Choose PowerPoint Template). It adds the template to your list of available templates.
4. Type the desired file name which you want to save the presentation in the File Name: list box.
5. Click Save button.

➡ **To save a presentation using Save As command, do this:**

1. Click the File tab and choose Save As... . The Save As dialog box in Figure 6.16 appears. Now follow Step 1 through 5 in the save procedure.

6.3 CREATION OF PRESENTATION

PowerPoint is designed to give your slide presentations a consistent look. There are four ways that PowerPoint helps you to control the look of your slides – with design related elements, Visual elements, colour schemes, and layouts of slides.

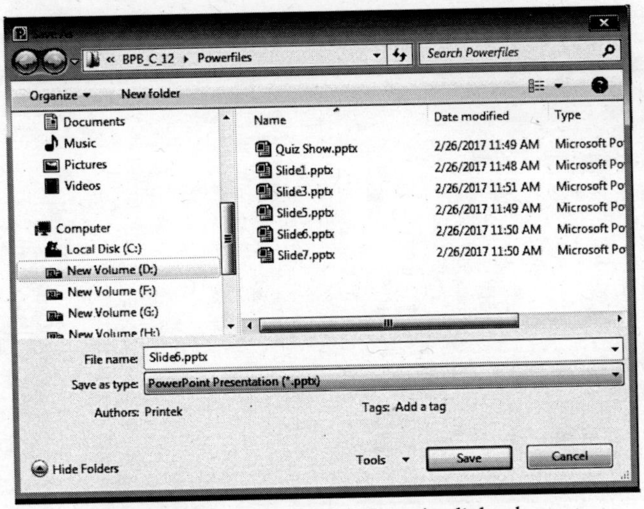

Figure 6.16 PowerPoint's Save As dialog box

6.3.1 Creating a Presentation using an Installed Template

A template is a file that contains many types of documents, including resumes, cover letters, business plans, business cards, etc. MS provided templates and presentations that come pre-installed with PowerPoint. These templates offer various layouts, visual elements, and other design-related elements to create presentations.

➡ **To create a presentation by using an installed template, do this:**

1. Click the File tab. The Backstage view appears as shown in Figure 6.17.

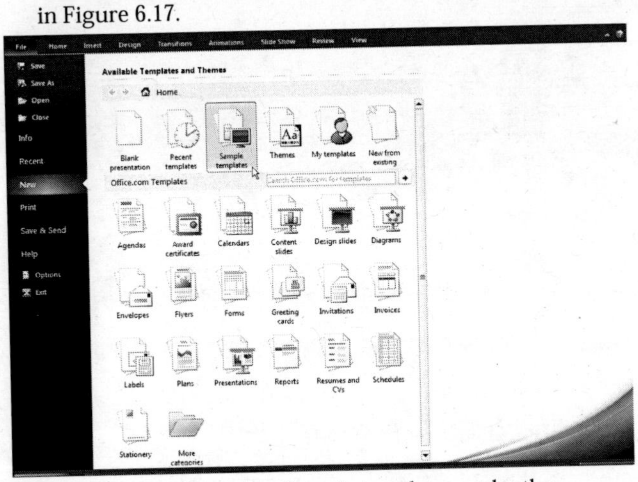

Figure 6.17 Select Sample templates under the available templates themes

2. Select the New option from the Backstage view. It displays the list of all available templates appears in the middle pane as shown in Figure 6.17.
3. Under the Available Templates and Themes category, select the Sample templates option.

4. In the Sample templates, you can see a different types of templates, with all formatting, such as background, themes colors, font, etc., (See Figure 6.18).

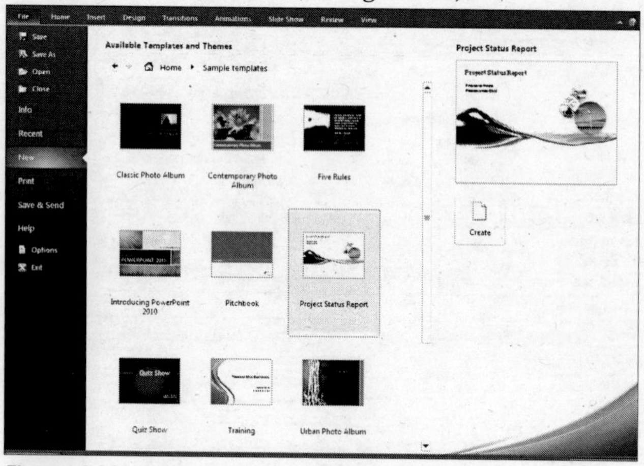

Figure 6.18 Select desired template from the sample templates

5. Select the desired template you want to apply. For example, we have selected, Project Status Report (See Figure 6.18).
6. In the preview box, you see a sample presentation for which the template is designed.
7. Click Create button.
8. You can see the selected template as default presentation title name (See Figure 6.19).

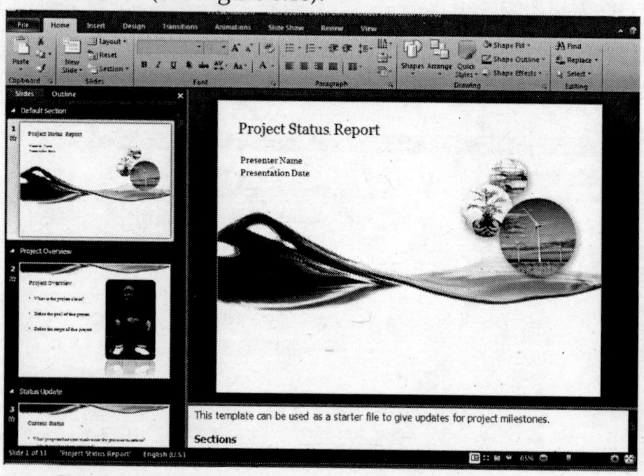

Figure 6.19 PowerPoint opens the selected template

6.3.2 Creating a Blank Presentation

When you start PowerPoint 2010, the program displays a blank title slide by default. You can begin to add text and pictures on that slide choose a different slide layout, apply a design, etc.

If you want to create a PowerPoint presentation on your own, you can use the blank template in PowerPoint 2010. The blank template offers only the basic visual elements of a presentation, such as placeholder to add a title to a slide.

➡ **To create a presentation by using the blank template, do this:**

1. Click the File tab. The Backstage view appears, displaying various options as shown in Figure 6.20.
2. Select the New option from the Backstage view.
3. The list of all available templates appears in the middle pane.

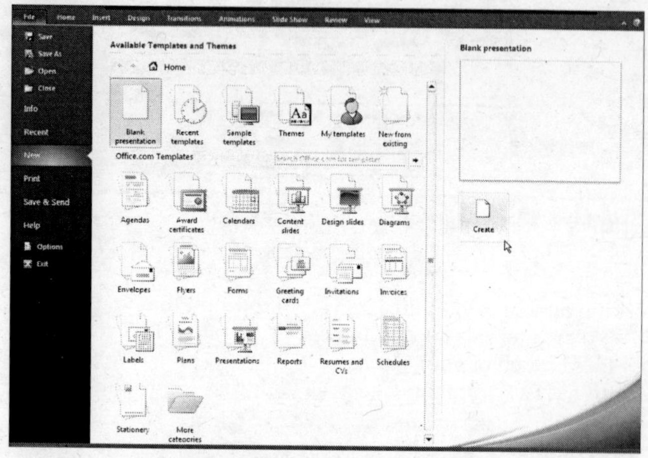

Figure 6.20 File Backstage view

4. Under the Available Templates and Themes category, select the Blank presentation option.
5. Click the Create button.
6. The new presentation is created with the name Presentation2 as shown in Figure 6.21.

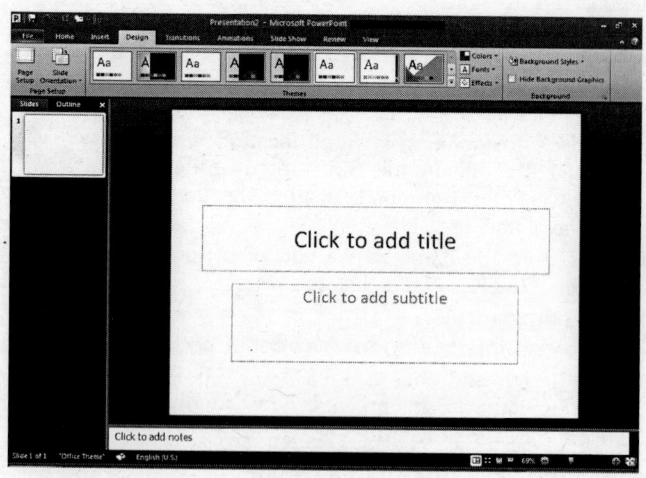

Figure 6.21 Blank presentation with the default name presentation2

You can see that a blank presentation contains a single slide

with text boxes (placeholders) to enter a title and a subtitle. You can also apply different styles and background to it.

Creating a New Template based on an Existing Presentation

You can create a template in almost the same way as you create a presentation. If you have a template that already has most of the features you want, you will save time by creating a new presentation based on that existing template.

1. Click the File tab on the ribbon. The Backstage view appears. A list of options appears as seen in Figure 6.20.
2. Click the New option from the list.
3. Under Available Template and Themes click New from existing icon (See Figure 6.17).
4. The New from Existing Presentation dialog box appears as shown in Figure 6.22.
5. Select the template that is similar to the one that you want to create.
6. Then click Create New. Make the changes you want to apply, such as themes colours, fonts and other formats.

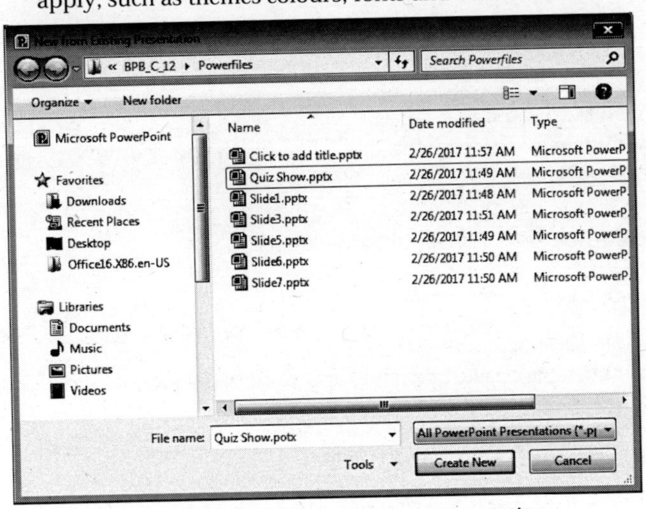

Figure 6.22 New from existing presentation

7. Click the Save As button to save the template.
8. The Save As dialog box appears. Give the new name to template file in the File name: drop-down list.
9. Select the PowerPoint template in the Save as type: drop-down list, and then click Save button (See Figure 6.16).

6.3.3 Entering and Editing Text

PowerPoint slide always contains text of some kind, even if it is just a title. Entering and editing text in PowerPoint is similar to entering and editing text in Word or Excel.

Entering Text to Slides

You can enter text in a presentation in two ways:

- Inserting a new slide with text place holder.
- Inserting text in an existing slide.

Adding Text in a Placeholder

PowerPoint 2010 comes with predefined layouts you want to use, or you can add a blank slide and create a custom layout. Many of these layouts contain text placeholders for title, body and bulleted list.

➡ **To insert a new slide with text, do this:**

1. Click the Home tab. In the Slides group click New slide down pointing arrow. A list of layout slides appears as shown in Figure 6.23.

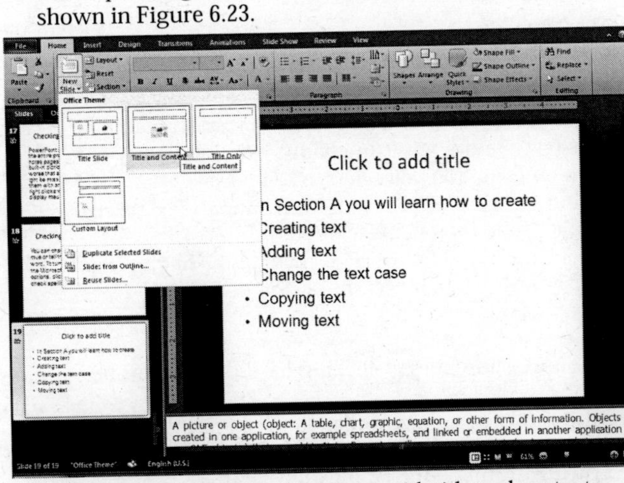

Figure 6.23 Selecting slide layout with title and contents

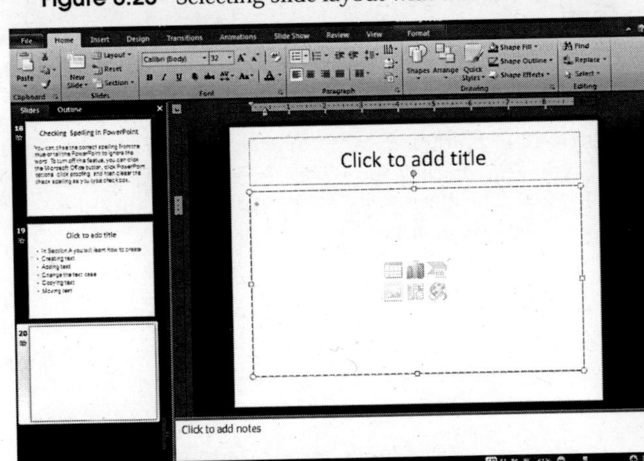

Figure 6.24 The Slide Layout with Placeholder

2. Click anywhere within a placeholder to select it. This border indicates that the current placeholder is selected (See Figure 6.24).
3. The sample text disappears and an insertion point appears inside the placeholder, indicating that you can enter text.
4. In a title or subtitle placeholder, the insertion point may be centered.

5. In a bulleted-list placeholder, the sample text disappears and the bullet remains, with the insertion point positioned where the text will begin.
6. Type the text for the slide inside the selected placeholder and press Enter key.
7. In the case of bullets, press Enter key when you want to begin a new bulleted item. If the bulleted text is too long to fit on one line, PowerPoint automatically wraps the text to the next line and aligns the text.
8. When you finish entering text, deselect the object by clicking a blank area of the slide of the gray border around the slide.

Editing Text on a Slide

You can make changes to the text in any text object simply by clicking the object. An insertion point appears, indicating that the text is ready for editing. Then you can start making changes to the text. Before you can change existing text, you have to select it by using the following techniques:

- Select an individual word by double-clicking it. The word and the space following it are selected.
- Alternatively, position the insertion point at the beginning of the text you want to select, hold down the Shift key, and either press an arrow key to select characters one at a time or click the end of the text you want to select.
- Select an entire slide title by clicking its slide icon on the Outline tab.
- Select all the text in a placeholder by clicking inside the placeholder and then clicking select and then Select All in the Editing group on the Home tab.

Copying Text

You can copy text that appears in one place to another place. Copying of text occurs with the assistance of the Windows Clipboard. The Clipboard is an area of your computer's memory that is used for holding data. As long as the data is on the Clipboard, you can place it anywhere in any Windows software application. The data stays on the Clipboard until you replace it with new data, or until you exit Windows.

➡ **To copy text using ribbon command, do this:**

1. Select the text you want to copy.
2. In the Home tab, click copy icon on the Clipboard group or (press Ctrl+C keys together).
3. Move to the place in your presentation where you want to insert this text.
4. Click Paste down pointing arrow and choose Paste command on the Clipboard group (or press Ctrl+V keys together.

Moving Text

The move operation is similar to the copy operation except that text is moved, i.e., it is deleted from the original location and copied to a new place.

➡ **To move the text using Ribbon command, do this:**

1. Click the text to put the text box in edit mode.
2. Select the text you want to move.

☞ Cut and Paste, moves the text between the slides. And by using select and cut the text, move to the appropriate slide, and paste it where you want it.

3. Right-click and choose Cut from the shortcut menu or click the Cut button on the Home tab (or press Ctrl+X keys together). Move to the new location, right-click, and choose Paste or click the Paste button on the Home tab (or press Ctrl+V keys together) .

Deleting Text

You can delete characters, words, or all the text in a text box. Using one of these methods:

- The Delete key erases the character to the right of the cursor.
- The Backspace key erases the character to the left of the cursor.

If you delete text accidentally, you can undo your action by clicking the Undo button on the Quick Access toolbar. (You can also press Ctrl+Z keys together).

6.3.4 Inserting and Deleting Slides in a Presentation

➡ **To insert slide, do this:**

1. In the slide view, display the slide after which you want to insert the slide.
2. In the Home tab click New Slide drop-down arrow and then choose New slide with layout. The New slide is inserted.

Deleting Slides

➡ **To delete slide, do this:**

1. In the Slides pane select the slide you want to delete.
2. Press Delete key. The selected slide gets deleted.

6.4 PREPARATION OF SLIDES

6.4.1 Inserting Word Table or an Excel Worksheet

To add some tabulated data, you can do it in many ways such as inserting table from word file or can choose layout options of Powerpoint. You can insert data from Excel worksheet as well.

You can also create a table in your presentation without using Word 2010.

➡ **To create a new slide with table, do this:**

1. Click the Insert tab. Click New Slide down pointing arrow in the Slides group. A list of slides appears.
2. Click the Title and Content Slide. A new slide appears as shown in Figure 6.25.
3. Click the insert table place holder. Insert Table dialog box appears as shown in Figure 6.26.

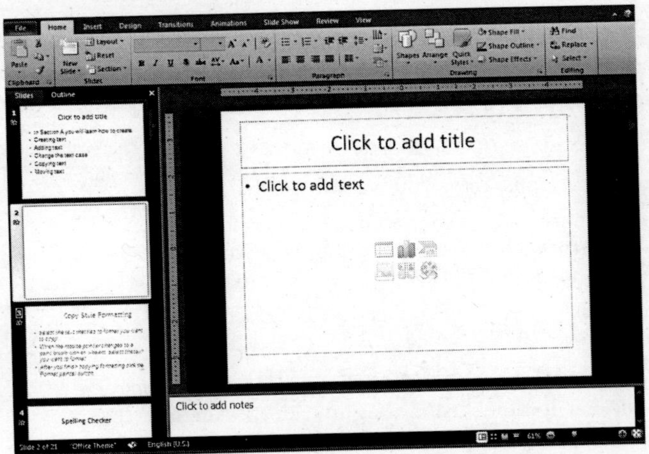

Figure 6.25 A new slide with table placeholder

4. In the Insert Table dialog box, enter the number of columns and the number of rows you want to insert in the table. You can type the number of rows and the number of columns or click the up or down arrow on the right of the edit boxes to specify these numbers.

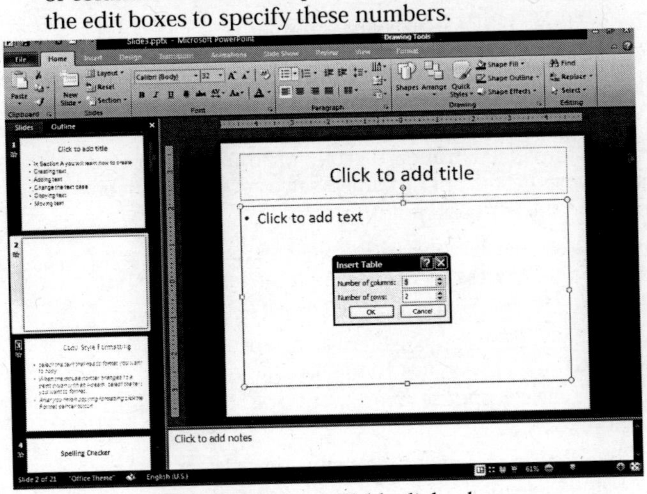

Figure 6.26 Insert Table dialog box

5. After you specify the number of rows and columns, click OK to create the table.
6. A table appears on the slide as shown in Figure 6.27.

Entering Text in a Table

When you create a new table, an empty table appears within a gray frame on the slide as seen in Figure 6.27. When you insert a table, the insertion point flashes in the first cell in the upper left corner of the table. The text you type appears at the insertion point. After entering the text in the table and to exit the editing mode, click anywhere outside the table.

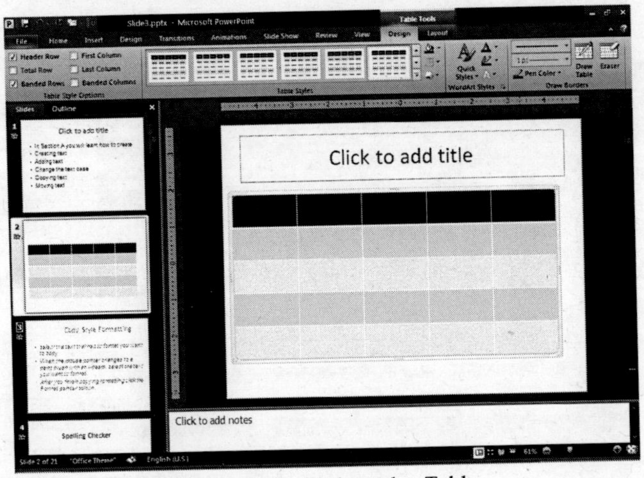

Figure 6.27 Slide with a Table

Editing a Table

Once you have created a table and entered text or numbers, you can modify its structure by adding, deleting, moving and copying cells, columns and rows. You can also change the width of columns, height of rows and merge or split cells to accommodate typed text in the cells.

Selecting Cells, Columns and Rows

➡ **To select cells, do this:**

1. For selecting a single cell, position the mouse pointer near the left inside edge of the cell. Once the pointer changes to a right arrow, click the cell.
2. To select adjacent cells in the same column, click any where in the first cell and drag the mouse pointer down the column.
3. To select adjacent cells in the same row, click anywhere in the first cell, and drag the mouse pointer across the row.
4. To select multiple cells click the first cell, press and hold down the Shift key, and click the other cell. Both the cells and any cell in between these two cells are selected.

➡ **To select a row of cells, do this:**

1. Position the mouse pointer near the left ledge of the table. Once the pointer changes to a right arrow, click the row as seen in Figure 6.28. Alternatively, in Table Tools contextual tab, click Layout tab. In Table group, click Select down pointing arrow and choose Select Row.

➡ **To select column or columns of cells, do this:**

1. Position the mouse pointer on the top border of the column or columns. The pointer changes to a down arrow. Click the left mouse button to select the entire column or columns (See Figure 6.29). Alternatively, in Table Tools contextual tab, click Layout tab. In Table group, click Select down pointing arrow and choose Select Column.

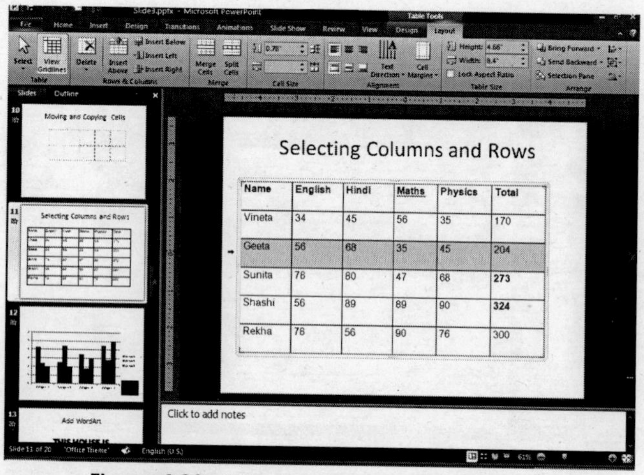

Figure 6.28 Selecting the entire row in a table

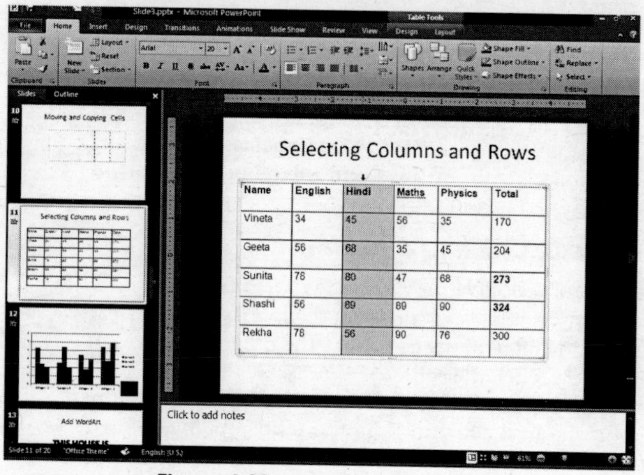

Figure 6.29 Selecting a Column

Adding Columns and Rows

➡ **To insert a column, do this:**

1. Click anywhere in the column next to where you want the new column to appear.
2. In Table Tools contextual tab, click Layout tab. In Rows Columns group choose Insert Columns to the Left or Right. A column is inserted to the left or right of the selected column. Or

   Right click the mouse, choose Insert, a sub menu appears, choose Insert Columns to the Left or Right.

➡ **To insert a row, do this:**

1. Click anywhere in the row next to where you want the new row to appear.
2. In Table Tools contextual tab, click Layout tab. In Rows Columns group choose Insert Rows to the Above or Below. A row is inserted to the above or below of the selected row. Or

   Right click the mouse, choose Insert Rows Above or Insert Rows Below. A row is inserted above or below of the selected row.

Deleting Columns and Rows

➡ **To delete columns/rows, do this:**

1. Select the columns/rows you want to delete.
2. In Table Tools contextual tab, click Layout tab. In Rows Columns group choose Delete Columns or Rows. Or right click the mouse, choose Delete Rows or Columns.

Copying and Moving Cells

Once you select the contents of a cell, you can copy or move these to another location using drag and drop. Alternatively, use the Cut, Copy and Paste commands from the Home tab or from the shortcut menu that appears when you select a cell and click the right mouse button.

➡ **To move or copy cell contents using *drag* and *drop*, do this:**

1. Select the text you want to move or copy.
2. From the Home tab of Clipboard group or from the shortcut menu, choose Cut (to move) or Copy.
3. Click in the table, to position the insertion point where you want to insert the cut or copied text.
4. From the Home tab Clipboard group or from the Shortcut menu, choose Paste. Cut or copied selected text is moved or copied at the insertion point.
5. To move the selected text – Position the mouse pointer over the selected text, press and hold down the left mouse button and drag the text to the destination cell.
6. To copy the selected text – Position the mouse pointer over the selected text, press and hold the Ctrl key, press and hold down the left mouse button and drag the text to the destination cell.

   A plus sign appears next to the pointer to indicate that you are copying instead of moving (See Figure 6.30).

Changing Column Width and Rows Height

You can change the size of rows of a table by adjusting the height of the rows. Similarly, you can also change the size of the columns by adjusting the width of the columns.

Changing Column Width

➡ **To change the width of a column in a table, do this:**

1. Position the pointer anywhere on the column's right border until the pointer changes to a double line and arrow (See Figure 6.31).

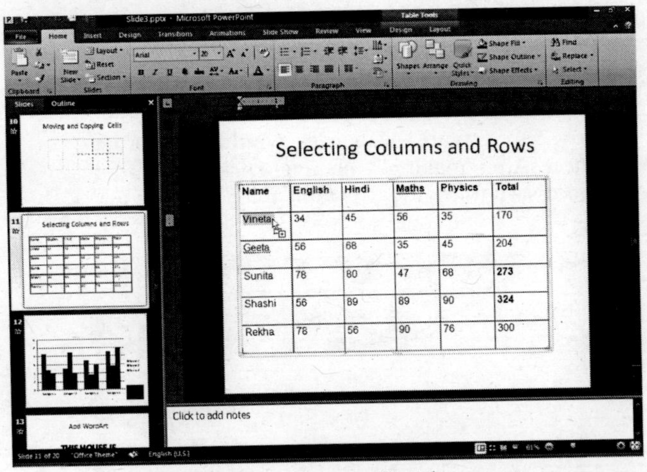

Figure 6.30 Copying a cell with contents

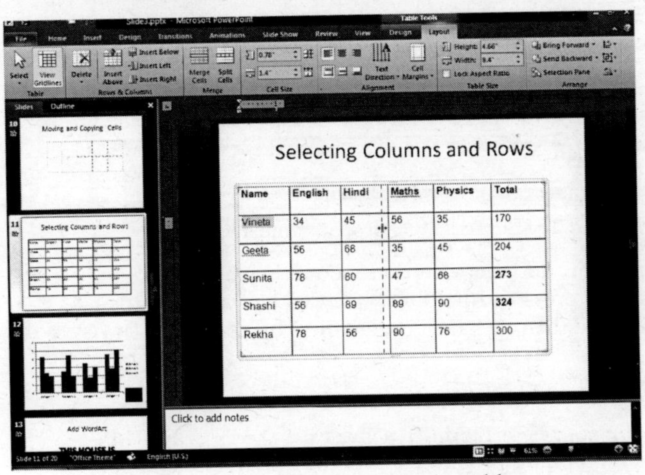

Figure 6.31 Changing column width

2. Drag the column border to the left or right to decrease or increase the column width. A dashed line indicates the target column width.
3. Release the mouse button. The column width is changed to the new size you specified by dragging.
4. In Table Tools contextual tab, click Layout tab. In the Cell Size group, click the Table Column Width up and down arrow, to set the width of the selected cells.

Changing Row Height

➡ **To change the height of a row in a table, do this:**

1. Position the pointer anywhere on the row's right border until the pointer changes to a double line and arrow.
2. Drag the row border up or down to decrease or increase the row height. A dashed line indicates the target row height (See Figure 6.32).
3. Release the mouse button. The row height is changed to the new size you specified by dragging.

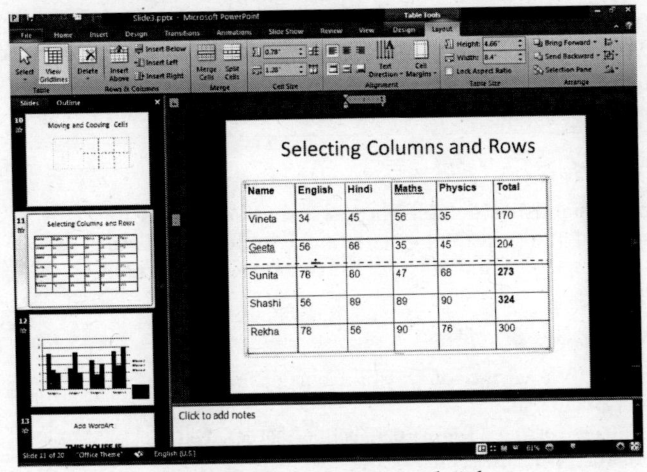

Figure 6.32 Changing row height

4. In Table Tools contextual tab, click Layout tab. In the Cell Size group, click the Row height up and down arrow, to set the height of the selected cells.

Merging and Splitting Cells

To create one cell that spans two or more cells, you can merge adjacent cells. In Figure 6.33, merging cells allows you to enter a column heading in one large cell that occupies the same width as several smaller cells below.

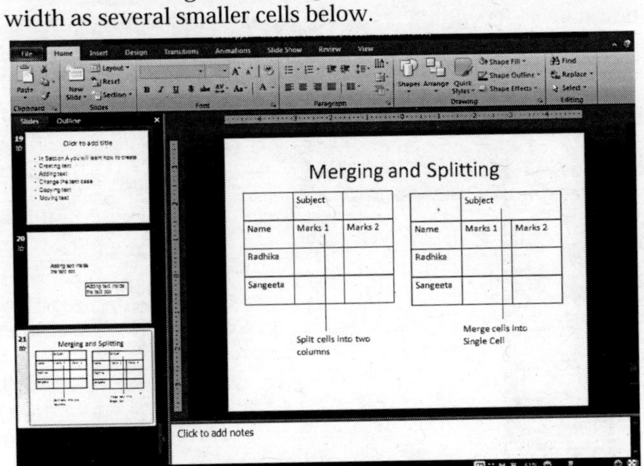

Figure 6.33 Merging cell in first row and split it in two cells in row 2

➡ **To merge two or more cells, do this:**

1. Select the cells you want to merge.
2. Click the Table Tools contextual tab, click the Layout tab. Click Merge cells in the Merge group.
   Or right click the mouse and choose Merge Cells.

➡ **To split a cell, do this:**

1. Select the cell that you want to split. You can only split one cell at a time.
2. Click the Table Tools contextual tab, click the Layout tab. Click Split cells in the Merge group.

3. The cell is split into two cells of equal width, with any text appearing in the cell on the left. Or right click the mouse and choose Split Cells... .

☞ After splitting a cell, you might want to adjust the cell width to make it look right in your current cell structure and layout.

Adding Borders and Fills

PowerPoint establishes default borders around cells and the table itself, on the current presentation template. You can change borders separating cells, columns and rows or around the entire table.

Changing Table Borders

You may specify a variety of ways for border formatting in a table. You can choose:

1. The border format (Top border, bottom border, Left border, Right border, All border, etc.)
2. The border style (solid line, dashed line, dotted line, etc.)
3. The border width (1/4 point to 6 points)
4. The border colour.

➡ **To select the table cells that you want to add or change the table border, do this:**

1. Select the entire table, or the cells, columns, or rows around which you want to specify the border.
2. Under Table Tools, on the Design tab, click Border down arrow in the Table Styles group. The actual name of this button changes depending on what was last selected. Borders option shows all the different border types (See Figure 6.34).

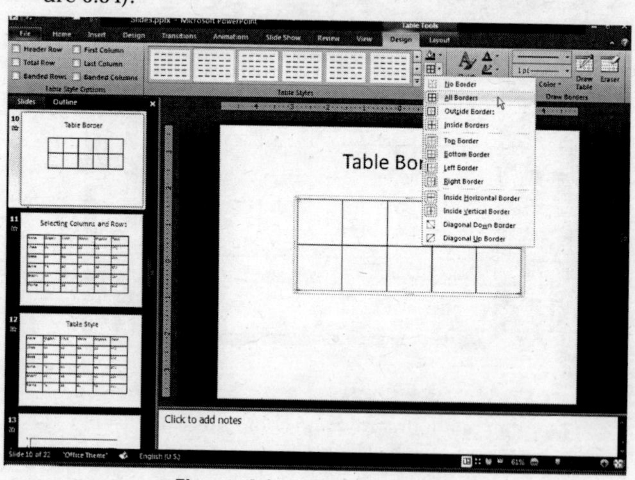

Figure 6.34 Borders palette

3. Click the border you want. The selected portion of the table changes to reflect the new border type.
4. If you want to change the border line style, click Draw borders down arrow, and choose Pen Style. Pen Style palette drop-down menu appears as in Figure 6.35.
5. Click the border style you want. The mouse pointer changes to pen style. Click the table row or column line. You can see the selected portion of your table get changes to the new border style.
6. If you want to change the border width or border colour, repeat steps 2 to 4 with the border width and border colour button. After making a change, click the Border button if necessary to redraw the table with the new formatting.

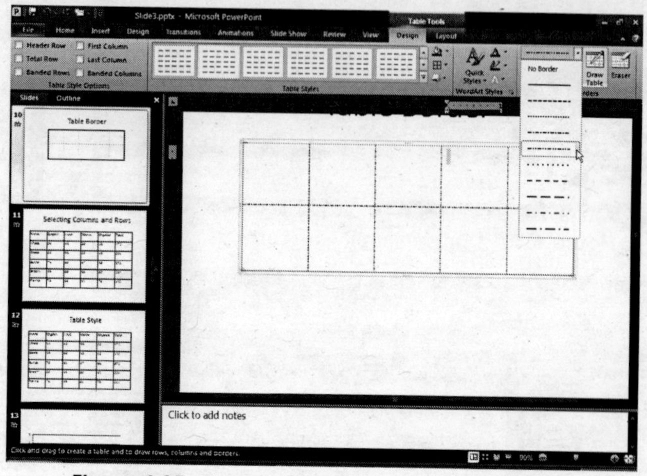

Figure 6.35 Borders Style drop down list appears

7. If you want to delete borders between table cells, click Eraser, or press and hold (Shift) key while the pointer is a pencil, and then click the borders that you want to delete.

Creating a Chart Slide

PowerPoint creates or modifies a chart using MS-Graph. MS-Graph is a graphing program shared by all components like Word, Excel, PowerPoint. So if you know how to create graphics in one of the components, you can use the same technique in other components also.

Charts that you create will be embedded in PowerPoint 2010, and the chart data is stored in an Excel 2010 worksheet that is incorporated in the PowerPoint file.

➡ **To create a chart slide, do this:**

1. Click the New slide in the Slides group. It display, the slides after which you want to add the chart slide. Or click the Insert tab, on the Illustrations group, click the Chart icon.
2. The new slide appears. In the center of the slide contains table, chart, Media clips, SmartArt, etc., as seen in Figure 6.36.
3. Click the Insert Chart in the new slide. The Insert Chart dialog box appears as seen in Figure 6.37.

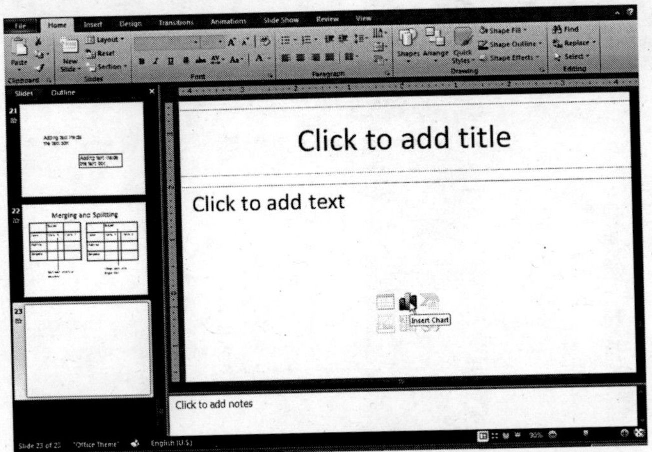

Figure 6.36 A new slide contains chart

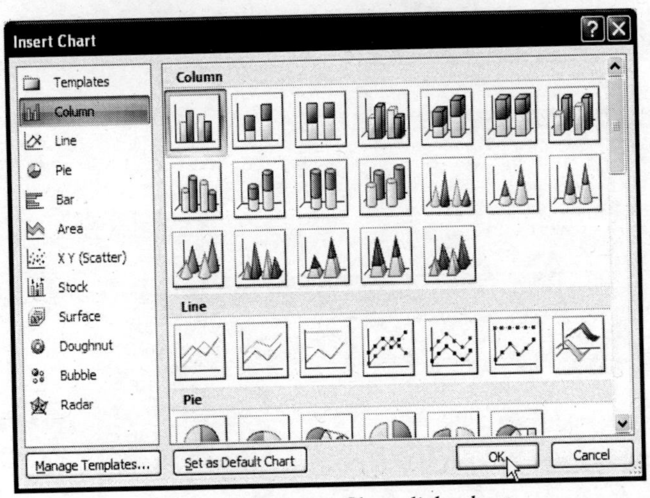

Figure 6.37 Insert Chart dialog box

4. Select the chart type under Templates. For example, if you click the Column chart type, there are different types of columns in the column section. Select the desired chart type. Click OK.
5. A sample chart appears in the Excel worksheet and the data sheet window containing the sample data for the chart overlays as seen in Figure 6.38.
6. In Excel to replace the sample data, click a cell on the worksheet, and then type the data that you want. When you enter data in Excel you can see the PowerPoint the data as well chart, simultaneously appearing in the PowerPoint (Figure 6.39).
7. In Excel, click the Office Button and then click Save As.

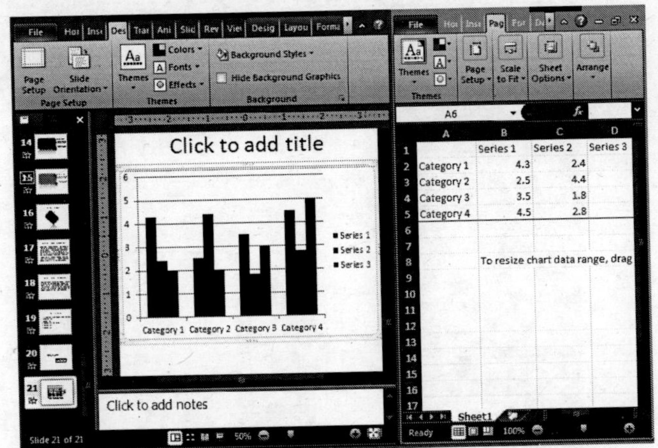

Figure 6.38 Sample Data graphically displayed

8. In the Save As dialog box in the save in: list, select the folder or drive in which you want to save the worksheet.
9. In the File name: box, type a new name for the file.
10. Click Save.
11. In Excel, Click the Office button and then click Close.

Entering Data in the Datasheet

Entering data in the Datasheet consists of two steps. These are:

- Entering the labels in the left most column and top most row.
- Entering the data to be graphed in the remaining cells.

➡ **To enter data in a datasheet, do this:**

1. Click the top cell in column A and enter the category labels across the top row. (The categories along the rows appear along the x-axis in the graph).
2. Enter the name of the data series along the column, starting from the first cell labeled. Each row represents the data series for each category.
3. Enter the values for each category in the cell (See Figure 6.40).

Now type the numbers for each cell along the column and press Enter. For practice, enter the numbers given below.

20.4	27.4	29.4
30.6	38.6	31.6
45.9	46.9	43.9
32.1	31.6	45

6.4.2 Adding Clip Art Pictures

Clip Art gallery is a collection of graphic files in PowerPoint that you can insert in presentations. It has in-built gallery of Clip Art images in the Clip Art gallery. But you also have your own collection of artwork available.

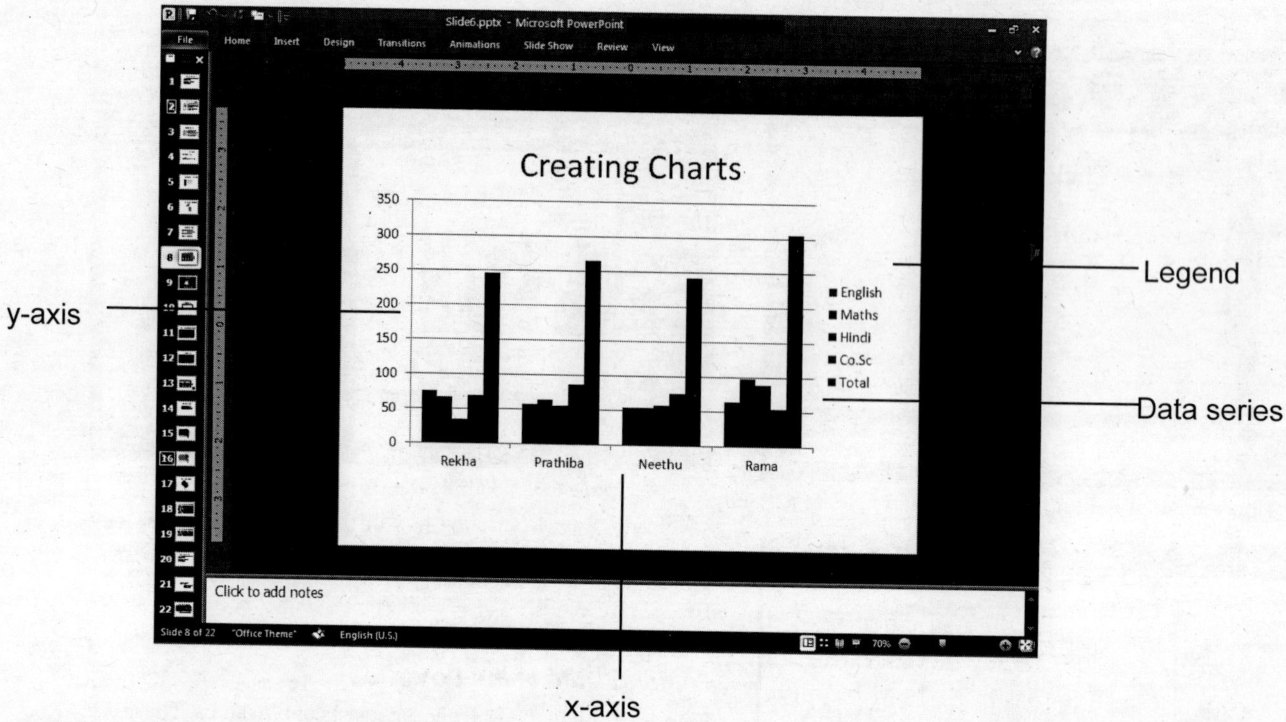

Figure 6.39 A Sample Chart appearing in PowerPoint

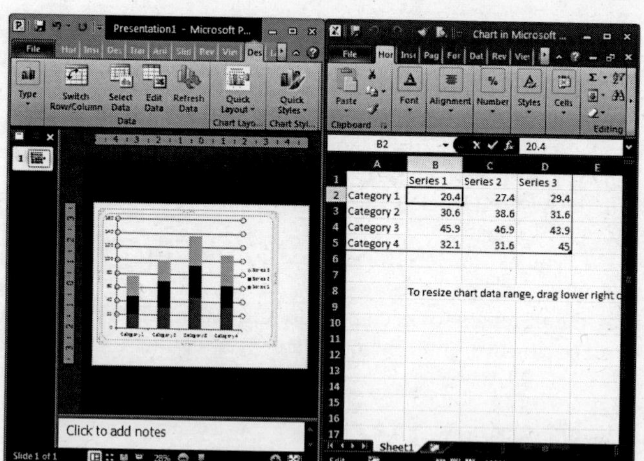

Figure 6.40 Entering Data in the cell B2 of the datasheet

Figure 6.41 Clip Art task pane

PowerPoint can help you to select an appropriate piece of art for your slides by looking at keywords in your presentation and trying to find pictures to match.

Inserting a picture from the Clip Art Gallery

1. Select the slide that contain a Clip Art slide.
2. Click the Clip Art icon in the slide. A Clip Art task pane appears (Figure 6.41).
3. Select the current entry in the Search for: box or click in the box if there is no entry, type animals, and then click Go. The task pane displays animals list.
4. Click the selected picture, once it appears at the center of the slide or select the picture, it appears a small arrow at the right of the side of the picture. Click the arrow and then Insert (See Figure 6.41).
5. When you are finished using the Clip Gallery, click the Close button on the Clip Gallery title bar.

6.4.3 Inserting Other Objects

You may want to add a particular graphic to a presentation but not maintain it in the Clip Gallery. You can insert picture from another application.

➡ **To insert a picture from a file, do this:**

1. Click where you want to insert the picture.
2. On the Insert tab, in the Images group, click Picture.
3. The Insert Picture dialog box appears as shown in Figure 6.42.

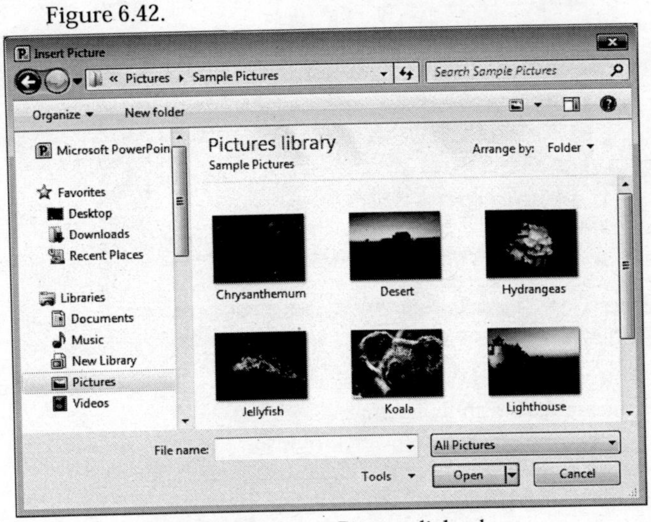

Figure 6.42 Insert Picture dialog box

3. Search a file in the Look in: drop-down list.
4. Click Insert button to place the graphic on the current slide.

6.4.4 Resizing and Scaling an Object

Resize an object

To resize or reshape an object, drag one of the object's handles in the direction you want. If you want to maintain the proportions of the object, hold down Shift key while drag a corner handle. If you want the object to grow out from its current center, hold down Ctrl while you drag a corner handle.

➡ **To resize an object, do this:**

1. Select the object you want to resize.
2. Drag a size handle until the object gets desired shape and size as you want (See Figure 6.43).

Scaling an object

Rather than dragging objects into position, you can set object placements and sizing on the size and position tabs of the Format Picture.

➡ **To scale an object, do this:**

1. Select the object you want to scale.
2. Click the Picture Tools contextual Format tab in the Size group.
4. Enter the percentage you want to change in the Height: and Width: boxes. Alternatively, click the Size and Position dialog box launcher dialog box.
5. The Format Picture dialog box appears as shown in Figure 6.44.

Figure 6.43 Object has to be resized

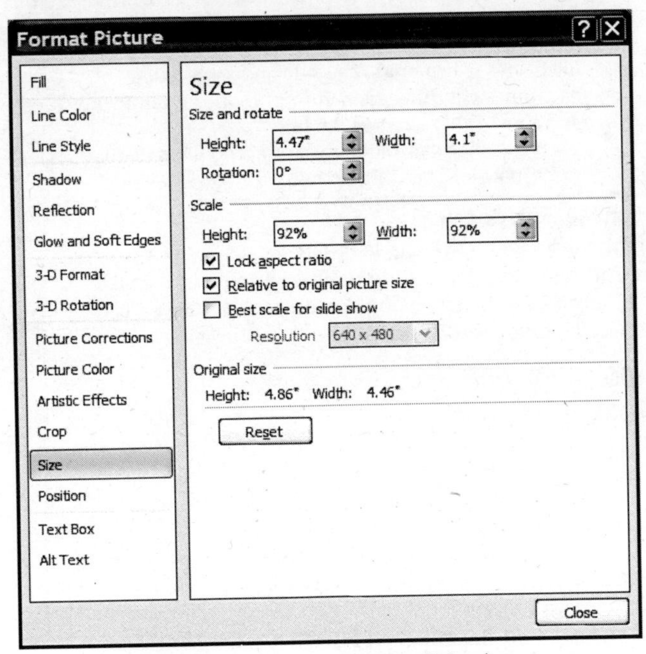

Figure 6.44 Format Picture dialog box

6. Click the Size tab, under the Scale, enter the percentage you want to change in the Height: and Width: box.

☞ To maintain the ratio between the object's height and width whenever to resize it, select the Lock aspect ratio check box on the size tab.

6.5 PROVIDING AESTHETICS

PowerPoint is designed to give your slide presentations a consistent look. There are four ways that PowerPoint helps you to control the look of your slides – with design templates, masters, colour schemes, and layouts of slides.

6.5.1 Enhancing Text Presentation

Enhancing the text presentation makes your presentation in a more presentable manner by formatting features, such as bold, italic, underline, alignment of text, font size, font style, colours, etc.

Aligning Text in a Slide

Alignment is the way in which the text is placed between the margins of a page or a text box on a slide. The alignment choices are summarized in Table 6.1.

Table 6.1 Aligning Text in a Slide

Alignment	Effect
Left Align	The left margin of each line is at the same place on the left, while the right edge of each line ends wherever appropriate (called a ragged right edge).
Right Align	The right margin of each line is at the same place on the right. The left edge of each line falls in a different place, depending on the contents of the line (called a ragged left edge).
Center	Each line is centered. The left and right edges of each line will differ, depending upon the number and size of characters in the line.
Justified	Each line starts at the left margin and ends at the right margin. There are no ragged edges.

➡ **To align the text, do this:**

1. Select the text, then click the Left, Center, or Right alignment button on the Formatting toolbar. Alternatively, click the Paragraph Launcher dialog box and select the desired option in the alignment section.

Changing Fonts

Fonts are also called typefaces in computer programs. There are groups of characters that share the same style or look.
Fonts are divided into two groups.

- On the basis of the way, characters are spaced – monospaced or proportionately spaced (See Figure 6.45). In monospaced font, all the characters have the same width. In proportionately spaced font the widths are different, i.e., w has more width than i.
- On the basis of the finishing strokes. That is Serif and Sans serif. In Sans Serif the finishing strokes are not there (See Figure 6.45). In Serif fonts the finishing strokes are there.

While choosing fonts for your presentation, keep in mind the following points:

- Using too many fonts on the same slide looks unprofessional. It is advisable to use one font for the headline and another for the rest of the text or a third font for bulleted items. But do not use too many fonts.
- Fancy fonts, do not work well on slides, especially for headlines.
- Sans - Serif fonts tend to have a more authoritative and bold look.
- Proportional fonts work extremely well in body text.

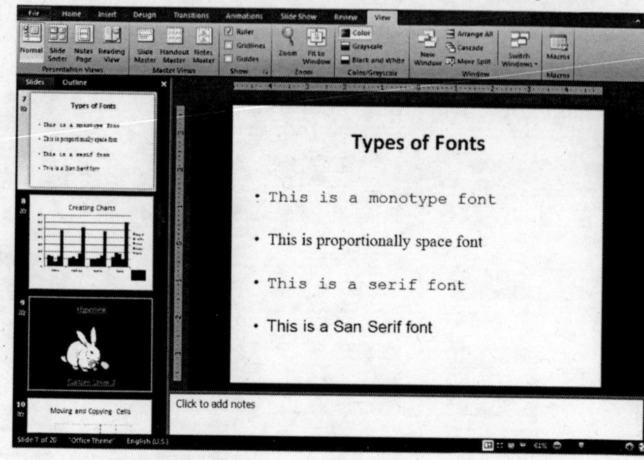

Figure 6.45 Display of various kind of fonts

➡ **To change the font of any text in a slide, do this:**

1. Select the text you want to change.
2. Click the Home tab and choose Font group. Or select the text, a mini toolbar appears. Select the font themes appears choose the desired font you want to apply. Or
3. Click the right mouse button and choose Font... from shortcut menu. The Font dialog box appears as in Figure 6.46. Click the Font drop-down list and select the required font. Alternatively, click the down arrow to the right of the Font box on the Ribbon command. A drop-down list of available fonts appears.

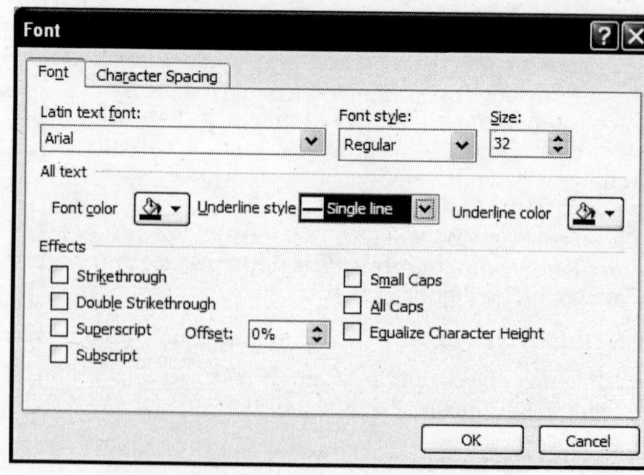

Figure 6.46 Selecting font using dialog box

☞ Right type and size of font creates good impression on your audience.

4. Click the font you want to use. The selected text changes to the selected font.

Changing the Text Size

Font size is measured in points, which is a height measurement, each point is 1/72 of an inch.

➡ **To change the size of text, do this:**

1. Select the text you want to change.
2. Click the Home tab and choose Font group. Or select the text. A mini toolbar appears. Choose the desired font size you want to apply. Or click the right mouse button and choose Font... . In the Font dialog box that appears, click the size drop-down list and choose the desired size or type the size. Alternatively, click the arrow to the right of the Font Size box on the Ribbon command to see the list of available sizes.
3. Select the new size. Or
4. Click the Increase and decrease font size on the Ribbon command.

Adding Special Effects to Text

One of the easiest ways to make text stands out is to add special formatting effects to characters, sentences, or paragraphs. PowerPoint makes these tasks very easy.

➡ **To add special effect, do this:**

1. Select text to which you want to apply special effect.
2. In the Font dialog box, Font style: box has the following options:
   - Regular—The text appears in regular way.
   - Bold—Text appears bold or highlighted.
   - Italic—Text appears italic.
   - Bold Italic—Text appears bold and italic.

   The All text has this option:
   - Font color— Specifies the colour of the selected text. In the box, select the color. You can see the colour under the bucket.
   - Underline style— Specifies whether selected text is in underlined. Click None to remove underlining.
   - Underline color— Specifies the color of the underlined text. This option remains unavailable until you apply an underline style.

   The Effect Areas has following options:
   - Strikethrough—Draws a line through selected text.
   - Superscript—Text appears raised like x^2y
   - Subscript—Text appears lowered like H_20
   - Small caps—Selected text appears reduce size. It does not affect on numbers, punctuation, non-alphabetic characters.
   - All caps—It converts lowercase to capitals.
   - Equalize Character Height—It reformats text effects to apply an even character height to text.

The font style and special effects of above explanation are shown in Figure 6.47.

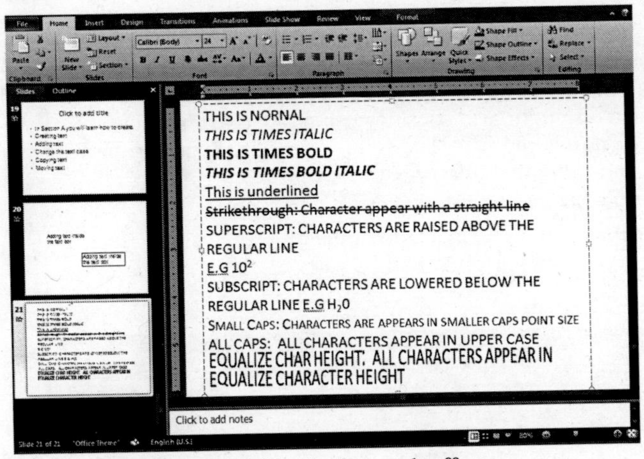

Figure 6.47 The font style effect

Changing Text Colour

➡ **To change the text colour, do this:**

1. Select the text you want to change.
2. In the Home tab, click the Font group. Click the font colour by pointing arrow. The font colors theme palette appears.
3. Move the mouse pointer over the colour, you can see the effect changes in the text. Choose the desired colour you want to apply to the text.

Applying Character Formatting using the Keyboard

Most of the character formatting can also be applied using the keyboard shortcut as discussed in the following sections.

➡ **To format using shortcut keys, do this:**

1. Select the text you want to format and use the shortcut key combinations for the desired formatting effects.

Format	Shortcut
Bold	Ctrl + B
Italic	Ctrl + I
Underline	Ctrl + U
Superscript	Ctrl + Shift + +
Subscript	Ctrl + =
Copy formatting	Ctrl + Shift + C
Paste formatting	Ctrl + Shift + V
Remove formatting	Ctrl + Spacebar
Change case of letters	Shift + F3
Change the font	Ctrl + Shift + F
Change the font size	Ctrl + Shift + P
Increase the font size	Ctrl + Shift + >
Decrease the font size	Ctrl + Shift + <

Bullets and Numbering

PowerPoint 2010 provides the ability to create bulleted, numbered lists. A bulleted list is a list with a graphic character, very small picture or bullet at the beginning of each paragraph in the list. You might also consider using SmartArt for many bulleted or numbered lists. The style of each list type can be changed and different bullets can be used.

➡ **To create a bulleted list, do this:**

1. Select the text you want to add bullet.
2. Click the down arrow of the bullets command icon, in the Paragraph group.

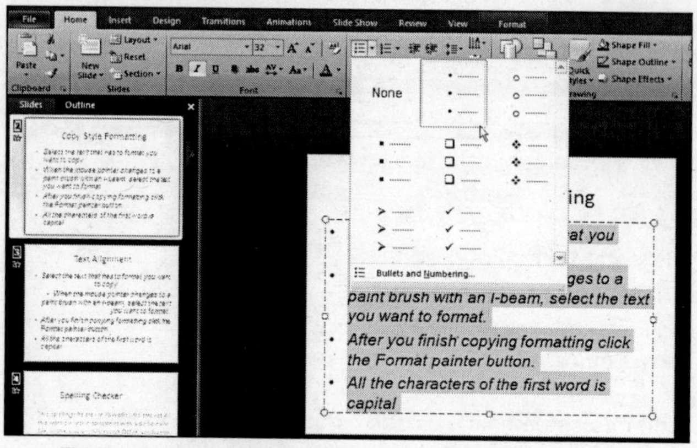

Figure 6.48 Selecting Bullets in the paragraph group

3. A drop-down list shows with the pre-defined bullet list.
4. Select the desired bullet type from the drop-down list. For example, we have selected the circled bulleted List (See Figure 6.48).
5. The selected bullet type is applied to the text as seen in Figure 6.49.

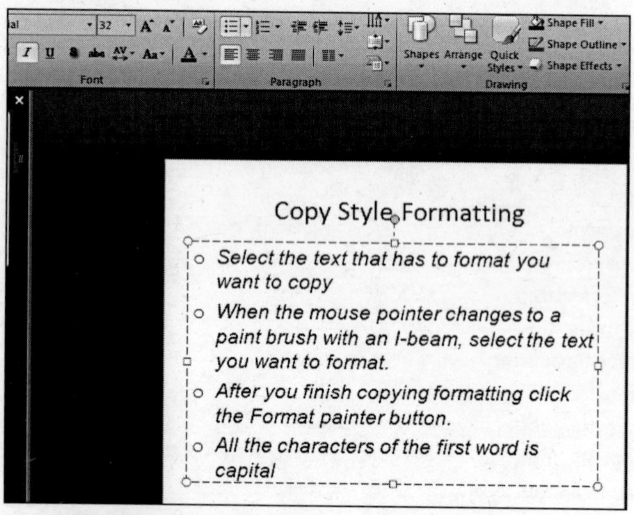

Figure 6.49 Bullet applied in selected paragraph

Adding Symbols

PowerPoint provides a full range of special symbol characters like the copyright or trademarks, registration symbol, etc.

➡ **To add symbol, do this:**

1. Click the Insert tab. In the Symbols group, click Symbol icon. The Symbol dialog box appears as shown in Figure 6.50.

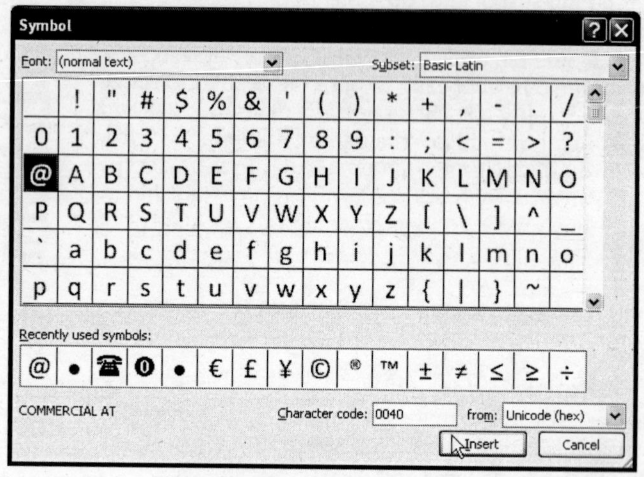

Figure 6.50 Symbol dialog Box

2. By default, the Font: box is set to Symbol. Click the down arrow to see the choices for fonts, each of which provides a different set of symbols.
3. Select the font with the symbols you want to use. Select the symbols to insert by clicking it once. Or click the Insert button to insert the symbol.
4. In the Subset: name box, specify a subset of special characters for the selected font, if available. A font subset can include an extended list of language characters, such as Greek or Russian (Cryillic), or a category of characters, such as Currency Symbols.
5. In Symbol list represents the full list of symbols that can be inserted from the selected Font and Subset.
6. In Recently used symbols: box, lists the most frequently used symbols that have been inserted.
7. Description: Provides a meaningful description of the selected symbol. For example, if the ® symbol is selected, the description will appear as Registered sign.
8. Character code: list box displays a unique code representing a symbol.
9. From: drop-down list, specifies the character set on which the character code is based on. ASCII is a character-encoding standard based on the English alphabet. Unicode is a character-encoding standard that enables almost all of the written languages in the world to be represented by using a single character set.
10. Click Close to leave the Symbol dialog box and return to your slide.

Removing Bullets and Numbering

➡ **To remove bullets and numbering, do this:**

1. Select the text or placeholders you want to remove bullets and number form.
2. In the Paragraph group of Home tab, choose the bulleted down pointing arrow, a bullet palette list appears, choose None. Or
   You can press Backspace to remove bullet or numbering from an item in a list. PowerPoint automatically adjusts the number sequence of a numbered list.
3. If you want to reorganize the elements of the list after removing bullets and numbering, use the promote and demote bullet on the Quick Access toolbar.

6.5.2 Working with Themes Color and Line Style

In earlier version colour and line styles and colour scheme is present. It provides the various parts of a presentation with a coordinated set of eight default colours. The most distinctive design element of the presentation is the background, so the first colour in colour scheme is background colour. Other seven colours effectively complement the background colour and are applied to text, charts, and other objects that appear against the background.

A layout determines where text, graphics, charts and other elements appear on an individual slide. A theme determines the look of an entire presentations' colours, fonts, and overall format. A layout is to a slide what a theme is to an entire presentation. Both specify the way a slide or overall presentation looks.

In Latest version of PowerPoint 2010, Themes refer a set of unified design element that provides a look for your document by using colors, fonts and graphics. You can use predefined themes that come with PowerPoint, or you can define your own.

➡ **To select a New slide and apply themes effect, do this:**

1. Click the Home tab, in the slides group. Click the New Slide down pointing arrow. PowerPoint opens a layout list from which you can select (See Figure 6.51).
2. When you click to select a layout, PowerPoint inserts a new slide at that location in your presentation with that layout.
3. Click the Design tab, in the Themes group. In the Themes group click the More button at the lower right corner. A list of themes appears as seen in Figure 6.52.
4. Select a desired style you want to apply to your presentation.
5. If you want to modify the theme, select from the Font, Colors, and Effect buttons to the right of the Themes group.
6. After you have modified a theme to your liking, click down arrow next to the Ribbon's themes and select Save Current Theme.
7. The Save Current Theme dialog box appears as seen in Figure 6.53.

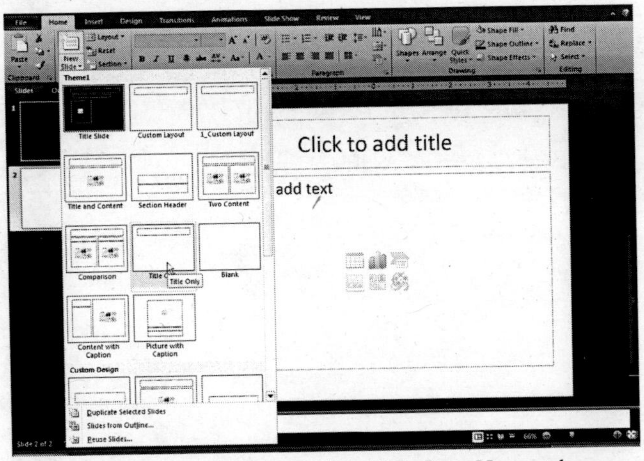

Figure 6.51 Selecting a New Slide from Home tab

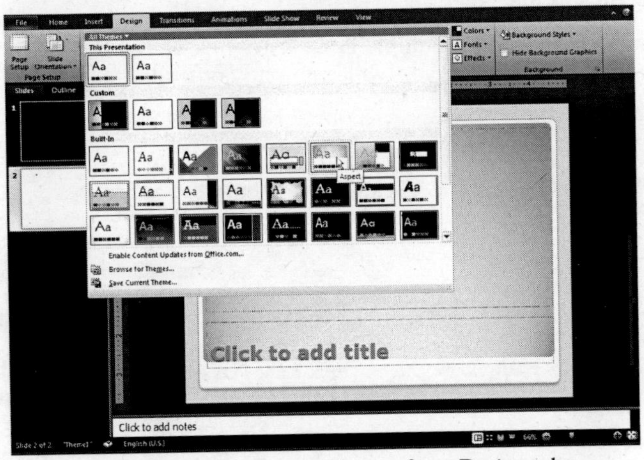

Figure 6.52 Selecting a Themes from Design tab

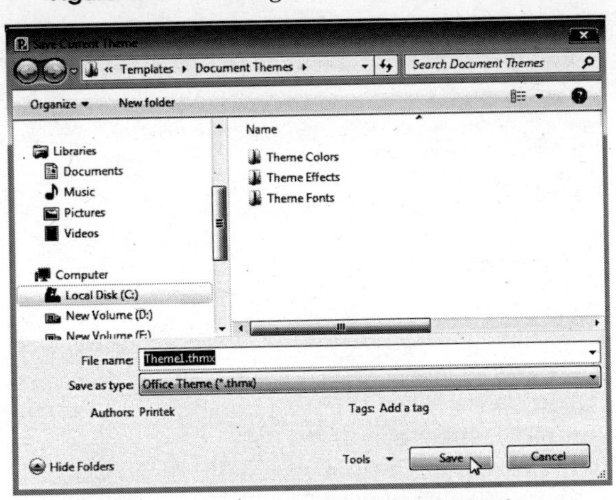

Figure 6.53 Save Current Theme dialog box

8. In the Save in: drop-down list contains a default folder (Document Themes).
9. Give the name in the File name: in the drop-down list.

10. Click the Save button.
11. After giving a name to the theme, PowerPoint makes that theme available in the Themes list.

Change the Color, Style and Weight of a Line

You can change the look of a line shape by changing its colour, line style, or weight.

- Add a Quick Style to a line
- Change the color of a line
- Make a line dashed
- Change the weight of a line

Add a Quick Style to a line

Quick Styles for lines include theme colours from the document theme, shadow, line styles and three-dimensional perspectives.

1. Select the line that you want to change.

   If you want to change multiple lines, select first line, and then press and hold Ctrl key while you select other lines.

2. Under Drawing Tools on the Format tab, in the Shape Styles group, click the Quick style that you want.

3. To see more Quick Styles, click the More button (See Figure 6.54).

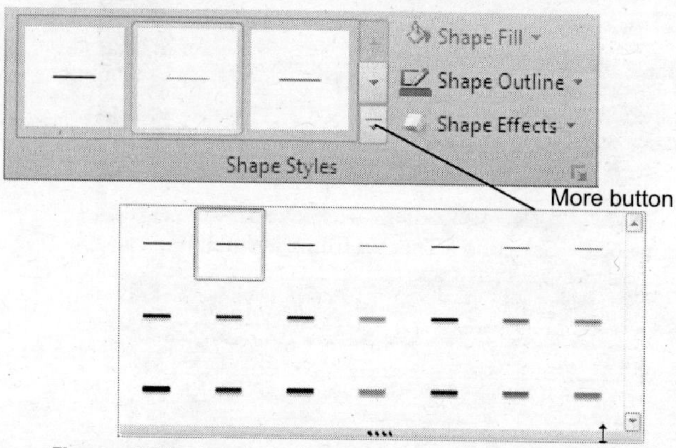

Figure 6.54 Select the line style from the More button

Change the Color of a Line

1. Select the line that you want to change.
2. Under the Drawing Tools, on the Format tab, in the Shape Styles group, click the arrow next to Shape Outline, and then click the colour you want (See Figure 6.55).
3. To change to a colour that is not in the theme colours, click More Outline Colors, and then either click the colour that you want on the Standard tab, or mix your own colour on the Custom tab. Custom colours and colours on the Standard tab are not updated if you later change the document theme.

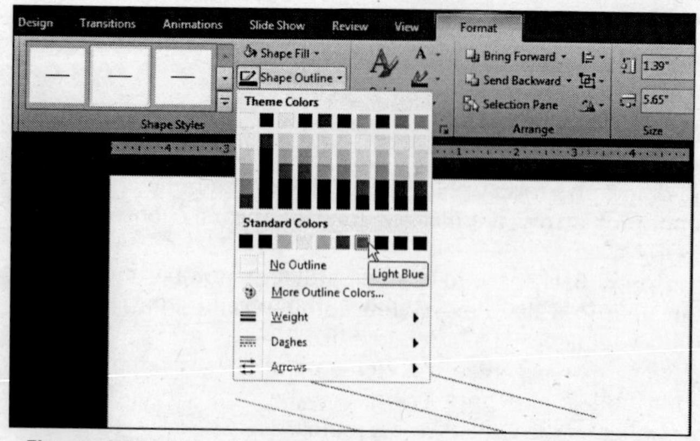

Figure 6.55 Select the color of a line from the Shape Outline drop-down list

Make a Line Dashed

You can change thickness, style and color. To format a line first select it by clicking it. For selecting multiple lines press and hold the Shift key while you click the lines. The selected lines appear dimmed and dashed.

1. Select the line that you want to change.
2. Under Drawing Tools, on the Format tab, in the Shape Styles group, click the arrow next to Shape Outline.
3. Point to Dashes, and then click the line style that you want (See Figure 6.56).

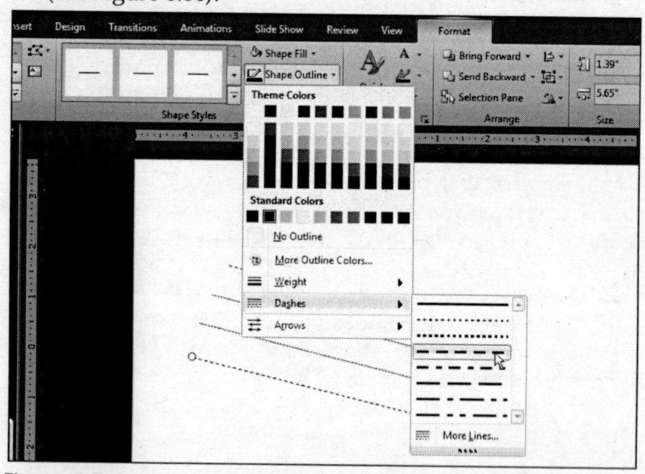

Figure 6.56 Select the line Dashes from the Shape Outline drop-down list

4. To create a custom style, click More Lines, and then choose the options that you want.

Change the weight of a line

1. Select the line that you want to change.
   If you want to change multiple lines, select the first line, and then press and hold Ctrl key while you select the other lines.
2. Under Drawing Tools, on the Format tab, in the Shape Styles group, click the arrow next to Shape Outline.

3. Point to Weight, and then click the line weight that you want (See Figure 6.57).

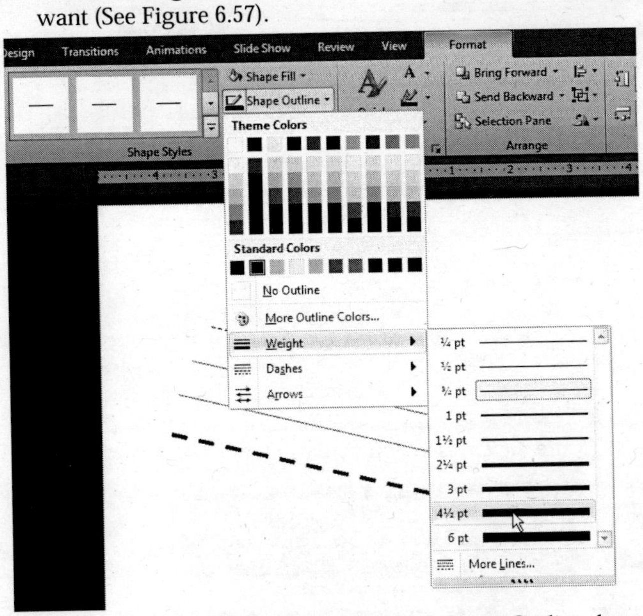

Figure 6.57 Select the line weight from the Shape Outline drop-down list

4. To create a custom style, click More Lines, and then choose the options that you want.

6.5.3 Adding Movie or (Video) and Sound

You can insert a music, sound, or video clip on a slide where you want it to play during a slide show. You can choose either to have the sound or video start automatically when you move to the slide, or to have the sound or video start only when you click its icon during a slide show.

One of the exciting new features in PowerPoint 2010 is that you now have the ability to edit and style the video clips you add to your slides. You can insert video files from your computer, download them from the Web, or insert video clips from MS Office Clip Art. This enables you to add life to your slides and share compelling stories in a way that is sure to hold your audience's attention.

PowerPoint supports videos in various formats, such as Audio Video Interchange (.avi), Motion Pictures Group (.mpg) and Movie (.mov).

➡ **To insert a video from a Clip Art video, do this:**

1. Insert the new slide or display the slide that will contain Media Clip Art.
2. Click the Insert tab.
3. Click Video button under the Media Group. A drop-down list appears as seen in Figure 6.58.
4. Select the Video from File option from the list.
5. The Insert Video dialog box appears as seen in Figure 6.59.

Figure 6.58 Selecting Video from file from the Insert tab

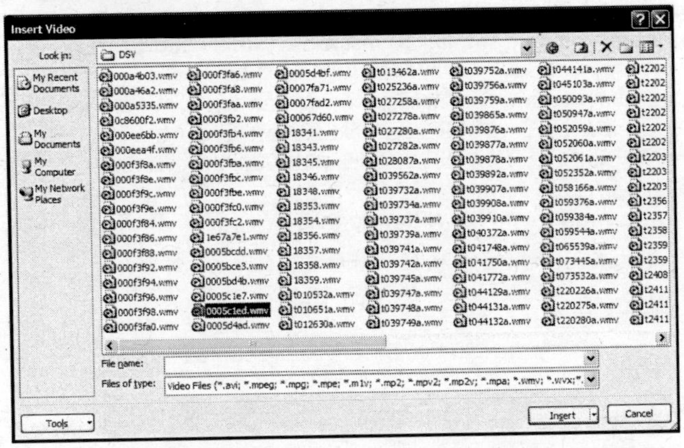

Figure 6.59 Insert video dialog box

6. Browse the location where the video is saved on your computer.
7. Select the desired video file. Then click Insert button.
8. The desired video is inserted in the slide as seen in Figure 6.60.

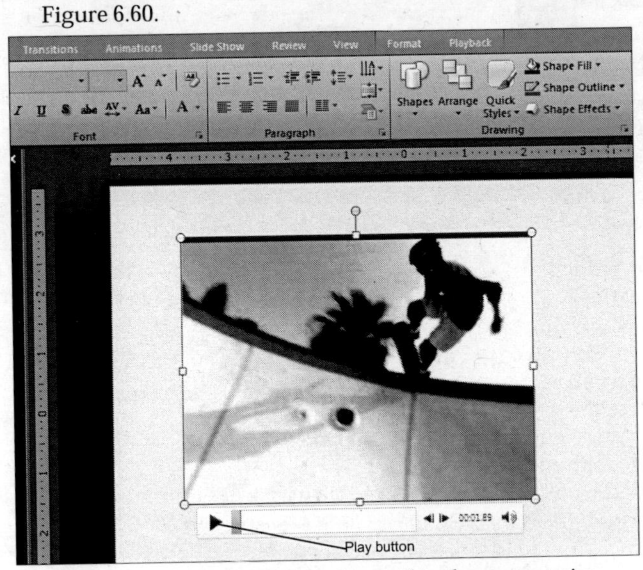

Figure 6.60 The video file is inserted in the presentation

9. Drag the sizing handles of the image to set the size of your video, and then drag it to the location you want.
10. Play the video by clicking the Play button.

Adding Sound file

In PowerPoint 2010, you can easily add sound effects, voice-overs and music to individual slides. You can add a sound-track and narration to the presentation as well. Sound effects, such as music and voice recordings, can add another level of professionalism to slide presentations. Music is an effective way to introduce or end a presentation and it gives your audience something to listen to as they enter and leave the presentation room. You could play a movie theme song as background music for several slides, or play a voice recording that contains advertising slogans to insert on a single slide, for example.

There are many sound file formats. Two common types are wave files (with the .wav filename extension) and Musical Instrument Digital Interface (MIDI) files (with the .mid, .midi, or .rmi filename extension).

➡ **To insert a sound, into the slide, do this:**

1. Select the slide in which you want to insert the desired sound.
2. Click the Insert tab.
3. Click the Audio button under the Media group as seen in Figure 6.61.

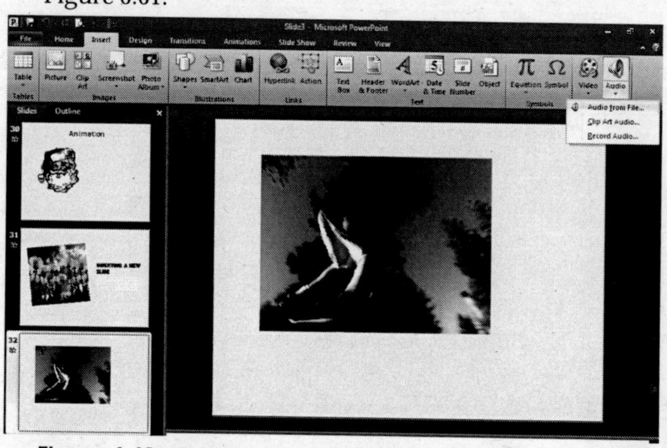

Figure 6.61 Selecting Audio from file from the insert tab

4. A drop-down list appears.
5. Select the Audio from file option from the drop-down list as seen in Figure 6.61.
6. The Insert Audio dialog box appears as seen in Figure 6.62.
7. Browse the location where the sound clip is saved on your computer. For example, we have selected the Sample Music folder as seen in Figure 6.62.
8. Select the desired sound clip and then click OK button.
9. The audio file is inserted in the slide as seen in Figure 6.63.

6.5.4 Adding Headers and Footers

You can add headers, footers and page numbers to each of the slide or the Note Pages.

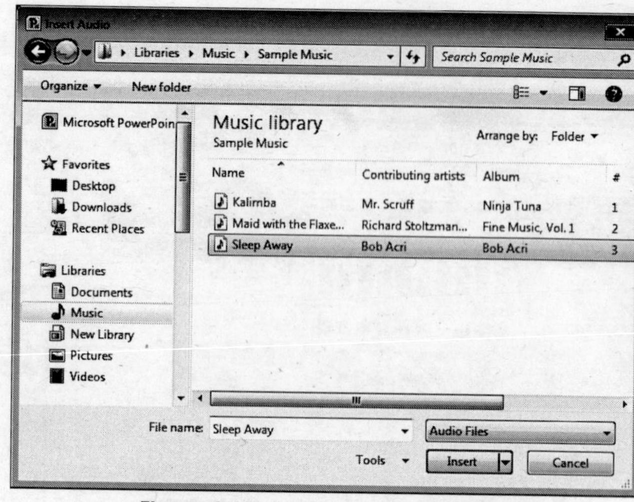

Figure 6.62 Insert Sound dialog box

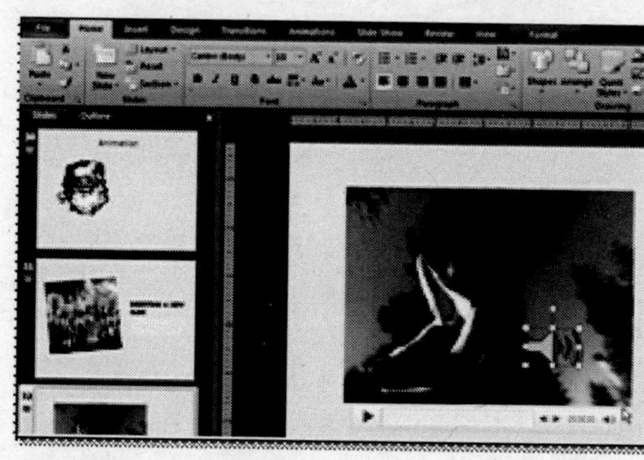

Figure 6.63 The audio file is inserted in the presentation

➡ **To insert header and footer to the slide, do this:**

1. In the Insert tab, click Header Footer in the Text group. Or In the Print Backstage view click Edit Header Footer link option.
2. The Header and Footer dialog box appears. Now click the Notes and Handouts tab property sheet as in Figure 6.64.

The Notes tab property sheet of Header and Footer dialog box offers the following options.

Date and time – If you select this option, the date and time appear in the upper-right corner of the page.

- Update automatically – select this option to print the actual date and time when printouts are made. Use the list box to select the format you would like the date and time to appear in.
- Fixed – Choose this option if you want to specify the specific date to be printed in text box.

Header – The header appears on the top left corner of the page. Enter the text for the header in the box below the option.

Page Number – The page numbers are shown as numerals only and appear in the lower-right corner of the page. Numbering is automatic increased once this option is on.

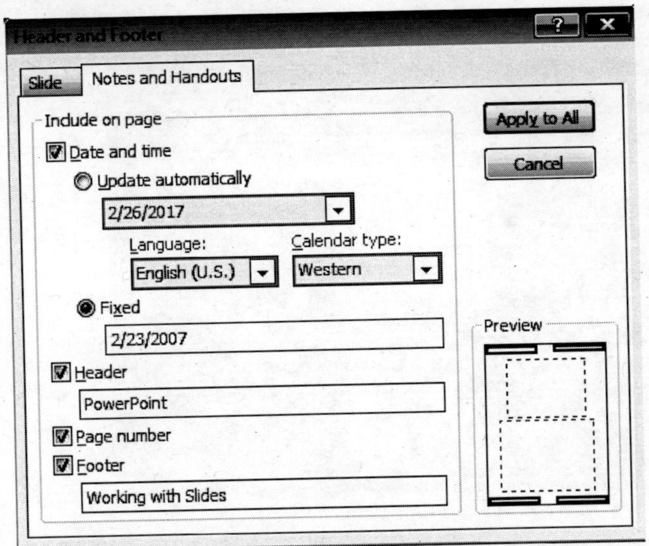

Figure 6.64 Header and Footer dialog box with Notes and Handouts Tab

Footer – The footer appears in the lower-left corner of the page. Enter the text for the footer in the box below the option.

3. Click Apply to All to use the selected settings.

6.6 PRESENTATION OF SLIDES

6.6.1 Viewing a Presentation

PowerPoint offers five ways (views) to look at your presentation. Each view enables you to work on a different aspect of the presentation. The changes made in one view are also reflected in all other views.

To understand the function of views, consider that you are looking at a house. Now assume you are standing in front of a house. You see one view. Now you move to one of the sides and you see a different view of the same house. PowerPoint views also allow you to see a presentation in various ways.

The buttons located at the lower left corner of the PowerPoint window just above the status bar as shown in Figure 6.65 help you to switch to different views.

In the following section, you will conceptually learn about the view.

Normal View

Normal view is the main editing view, where you write and design your presentation. The view has four working areas:

- Outline tab
- Slides tab
- Slide pane
- Notes pane

These panes let you to work on all the aspects of your presentation in one place. You can adjust the size of different panes by dragging the pane borders.

- Outline tab: Use the Outline tab to organize and develop the contents of your presentation. You can type all of the text of your presentation and rearrange bullet points, paragraphs and slides. The Outline tab shows your slide text in outline form.

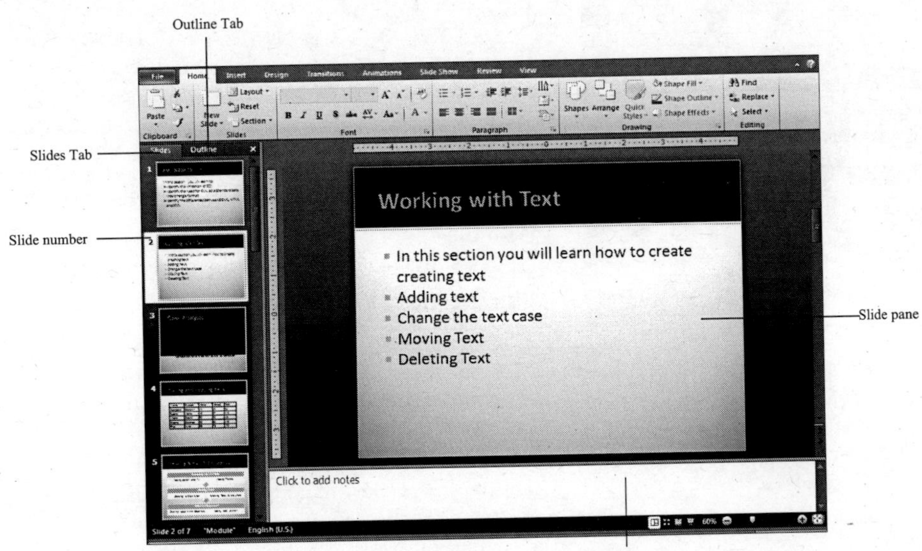

Figure 6.65 Viewing of a Presentation

- Slides tab: This is a great place to view the slides in your presentation as thumbnail-sized images while you edit. The thumbnails make it easy for you to navigate through your presentation and to see the effect of any design changes. You can also easily rearrange, add or delete slides.
- Slide pane: In the slide pane, you can see how your text looks on each slide. You can add SmartArt graphics, movies and sounds, create hyperlink and add animations to individual slides.
- Notes pane: The Notes pane lets you to add speaker notes or information you want to share with the audience. If you want to have graphic in your notes, you must add the notes in Notes page view.

These pane are also shown when you save a presentation as a Web page. The only difference is that the outline pane displays a table of contents so that you can navigate through the complete presentation.

Slide Sorter View

The slide sorter view is a view of your slides in thumbnail form (See Figure 6.66). Working in this view is like laying out the pages of your presentation or report on the table so that you can see them all at once. In this view, you can see the design consistency and the flow of your presentation. If need be, you can easily reorder the slides, copy or delete the slides.

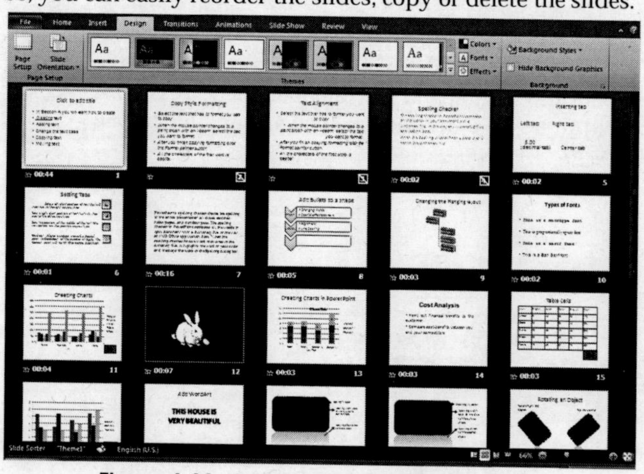

Figure 6.66 PowerPoint's Slide Sorter View

Notes Page View

This view helps you to prepare the speaker notes used while making the presentation to your audience. Notes pages view produces a smaller version of the slide on the top part of a page and leaves the lower part free for notes or keypoints (See Figure 6.67).

Slide Show View

This view of PowerPoint shows the progress of the presentation form slide to slide just like a real slide show. In this view, all menus, toolbars, rulers, status bar, scrollbars, and the Windows taskbar are removed from the screen (See Figure 6.68).

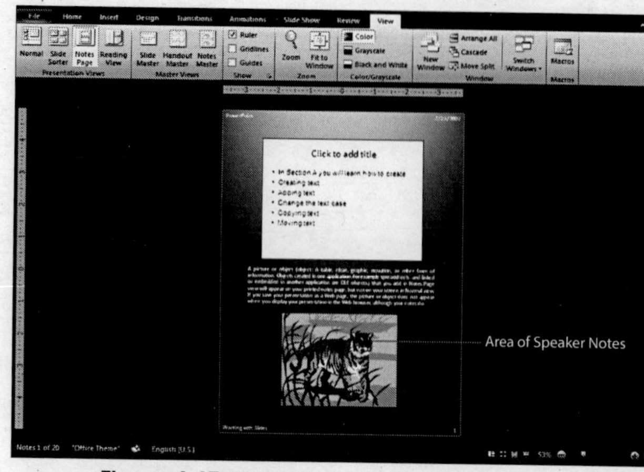

Figure 6.67 PowerPoint's Notes Pages View

Figure 6.68 Slide Show View

6.6.2 Choosing a Set Up for Presentation

With the options in the Set up dialog box, you can choose the type of show to run and how the show should proceed.

Starting the Slide Show

When you view a slide show, you have following options:

1. Click Slide Show tab in the Start Slide Show group, choose Slide Show from beginning or press Shift+F5 keys together.
2. In the Slide show, you go to next slide, press N or click the Backspace key to go to the previous slide.

➡ **To set a slide show option, do this:**

1. Click Slide Show tab in the Set Up group, choose Set Up Show icon. The Set Up Show dialog box appears as shown in Figure 6.69.

2. To Show all slides in your presentation, Click All in the Show slides section.
3. To show a specific group of slides from your presentation, enter a starting and ending slide in From: and To: edit boxes.
4. To start a custom slide presentation that derives from another presentation, click Custom Show: drop-down list and then click the presentation that you want to view as a custom show.

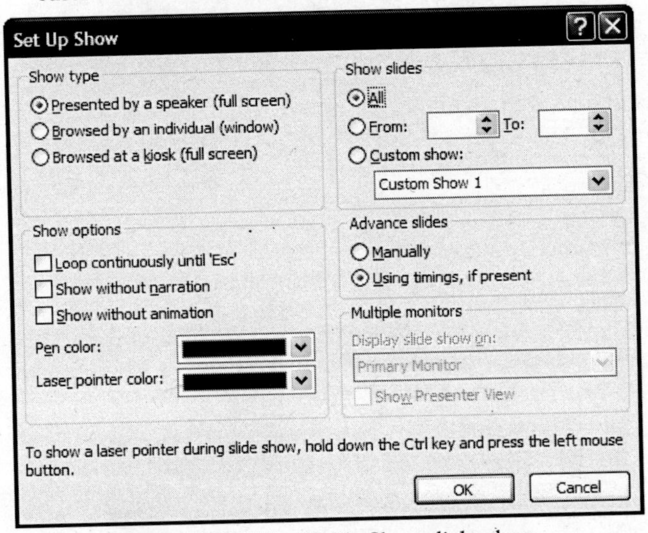

Figure 6.69 The Set Up Show dialog box

Giving Special Show

PowerPoint offers three special slide show types. These are available on the Set Up Show dialog box (See Figure 6.69).

1. Click Presented by a Speaker (full screen): Is the traditional, full-screen slide show.
2. Click Browsed by an Individual (window): Runs the slide show in a standard window.
3. Click Browsed at a Kiosk (full screen): It displays a full screen as a self running show which restarts after 5 minutes.

6.6.3 Printing Slides and Handouts

Handout lets you to include two, three, or six small images of the slides in your presentation. You can select the format when you print them.

Handouts can be created in the following two ways:

- Print the Handouts using the standard PowerPoint format, i.e., two, three or six slide on a page format.
- The Handout format can be customized to your requirement using the handout master.

If you make Handouts, PowerPoint shrinks the slides you have created and fits them on a page, according to the option you choose in the print Backstage view. To use standard Handout formats, you only have to select the number of slides you want to print on a page when you take the printouts for Handouts.

☞ The header, footers, page numbers and the date on each handout will be printed if you have selected any of these items on your Notes Pages. The same is automatically applied to your Handouts.

In case you want to use different headers, footers, page numbers or dates on your Handouts as compared to the Notes Pages then you are required to change these in the Headers and Footer dialog box.

☞ The golden rule in presentations is "Say more than you show and handout more than you say". Therefore the material that you hand out (either before or after your presentation) should be more than just pictures of your slides.

Printing Handouts

You can print your entire presentation – slides, outline, notes and audience handouts. You can also print specific slides, handouts, notes pages, or outline pages.

➡ **To print handouts, do this:**

1. Open the presentation you want to print.
2. Click the File tab, the Backstage view appears.
3. To click one or multiple slides per page in handout format, under Handouts, click the number of slides you want per page, and whether you want them to appear in order vertically or horizontally (See Figure 6.70).
4. After applying the desired option, click OK.

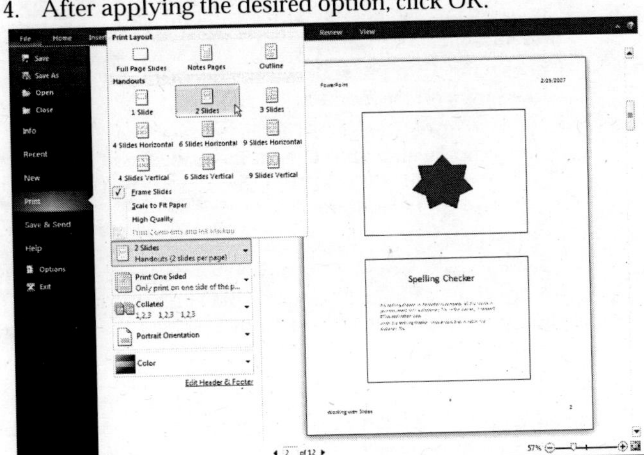

Figure 6.70 Selecting slides per page in handout format in the File tab

Printing Slides

In PowerPoint 2010, you can either print all the slides or the current slide of a presentation. In addition, you can decide how many slides you want to print on a single page.

➡ **To print a slides, do this:**

1. Open the presentation that you want to print.
2. Click the File tab on the ribbon, click Print tab. The Print Backstage view appears as shown in Figure 6.71.

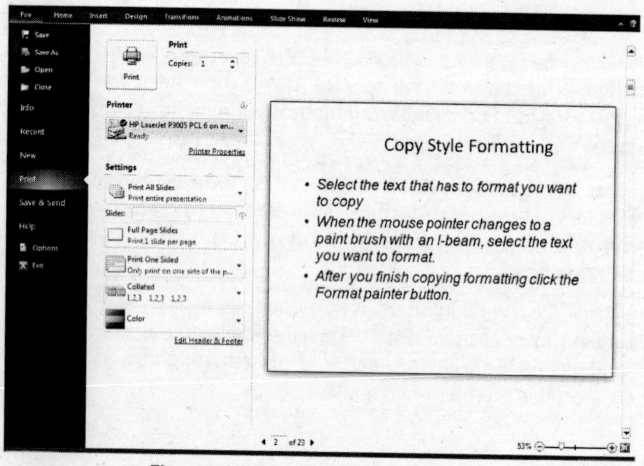

Figure 6.71 Print Backstage view

3. The name of the currently selected printer is shown at the under Printer drop-down arrow. To print the presentation on a different printer, select the desired printer from the Printer drop-down list.
4. Specify the number of copies you want to print, for each slide in the Copies: spinner box.
5. The Setting drop-down list has the option which allows you to select the pages you want to print.

Option	Description
Print All Slides	Choose Print All Slides option to print the entire presentation at one time.
Current slide	Choose the Current slide option to print the slide shown on the monitor.
Custom Range	Choose to print the selected slides, and enter the corresponding slide numbers in the Slides: edit box, e.g., to print slide 3 and 6 through 8, enter 3,6-8 in the Slides edit box.
Custom Show	Prints a certain custom show which has been set up. Each custom shows appears on the list.
Print Hidden Slides	If slides are hidden (do not display during a slide show), they can be printed by checking the Print Hidden Slides check box.

6. Collate: Specify if you want to arrange slides while printing multiple copies. When you choose collate option, each set is printed completely from first page to the last page. Then the next set is printed.
7. Click the Color button, and select the colour setting for the printouts:
   - Color–This is default. When you use this settings with a black-and-white printer, it results in slides with grayscale or black backgrounds.
   - Grayscale–To print in grayscale, select the grayscale check box.
   - Pure black white option–Converts all colours in the presentation to either black or white. Prefer this option if you need to print on a printer that cannot print gray shades.

6.7 SLIDE SHOW

6.7.1 Running a Slide Show

When you develop a slide show in Slide Sorter view, you can get a preview of transition effects for all slides. But to see the transitions full-screen and to see animated or bulleted text slides, you must select the presentation as a slide show.

Assigning Slide Transitions

Slides transitions are the animation-like effects that occur in the slide show view, when you move from one slide to the next. You can control the speed of each slide transition effect, and you can also add sound.

➡ **To assign the transitions, do this:**

1. Select the slide(s) you want to add a transition effect.
2. Click the Transitions tab. In the Transition to This slide group, click down arrow and then select the effect that will be applied during the slide show. For example here we select Flash under subtle (See Figure 6.72).

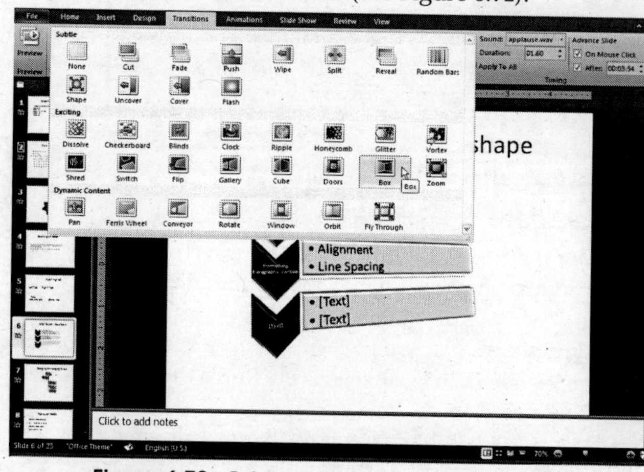

Figure 6.72 Selecting Transition effect to Slide

3. If you Apply to all slides, click Apply To All in the Timings group.
4. Select the Sound option to give sound transitions to your slide show from the Sound: drop-down list in the Timings group.
5. The Advance section has two options for transition:
   - On mouse click check box – if you want the transition to take place on clicking the mouse.
   - Automatically after – in this case the transition takes place automatically after the time you specify in the seconds box.

6. After apply all options, you can see the effect in the Slide show. Click the Slide Show tab, in the Start Slide Show group, click From Beginning icon. Click the next button (i.e. →) to go to the next slide.
7. Click preview command to preview the current transitions effect in the Preview group

Controlling the Slide Show with a Mouse

During a slide Show, you can use the pop-up menu button. A pop-up menu appears as shown in Figure 6.73. As mentioned earlier, the button appears in the lower left corner of the current slide as soon as you move the mouse pointer. You can then click the button to display slide show pop-up menu.

The Next and Previous commands on the pop-up menu lets you to move forward or backward through the slides in your slide show.

To move to a specific slide, click Go to Slide and then choose slide from the menu (See Figure 6.73).

To stop a slide show at any time during a presentation, simply choose End Show from the pop-up menu.

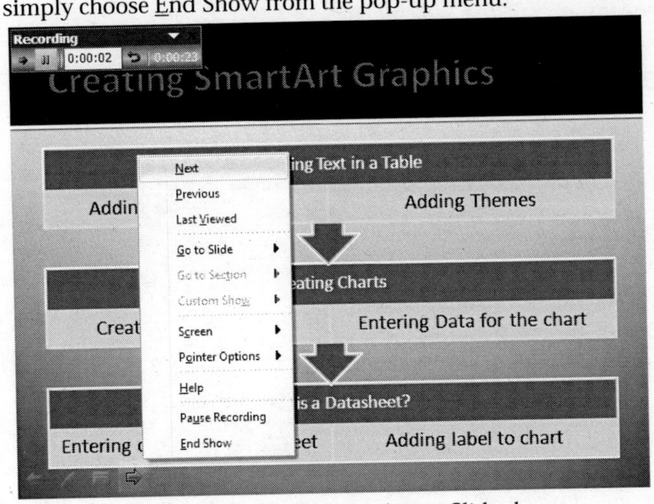

Figure 6.73 Pop-up menu during Slide show

Controlling the Slide Show with a Keyboard

In addition to the slide show pop-up menu, you can use the keys listed in Table 6.2 to control various aspects of the show.

Table 6.2 Slide Show keyboard controls

Press This	To Perform This Action
Spacebar, →, ↓, PgDn, N	Advance to next slide.
Backspace, ←, ↑, PgUp, or P	Return to previous slide
Slide number + Enter	Go to slide number
B or period	Blacks/Unblacks the screen
W or comma	Whites/Unwhite the screen
Ctrl+A	Show mouse pointer as arrow
Ctrl+P	Show mouse pointer as pen
S or + (numeric keypad)	Stop/Restart automatic show
H	Go to next slide if hidden.
T	Rehearse – use new time
O	Rehearse – use original time
Esc, Ctrl+break or (-)	End Show

(Contd...)

6.7.2 Transitions and Slide Timings

If you do not want to move through a slide show manually, there are two ways you can set the length of time a slide appears on the screen. One way is to set a time manually for each slide, and then run the slide show and view the timings you set. The other way is to use rehearsal feature, where you can record timings automatically as you rehearse. You can also ajdust the timings you have already set and then rehearse the new ones.

Setting Slide Show Timings Manually

1. On the Slide Show tab, in the Set Up group, click Rehearse Timings to start the show in rehearsal mode.
2. It starts a full-screen slide show in which you can rehearse your presentation.
3. The Rehearsal dialog box appears in the slide show as seen in Figure 6.74. It starts slide timings in the first slide.

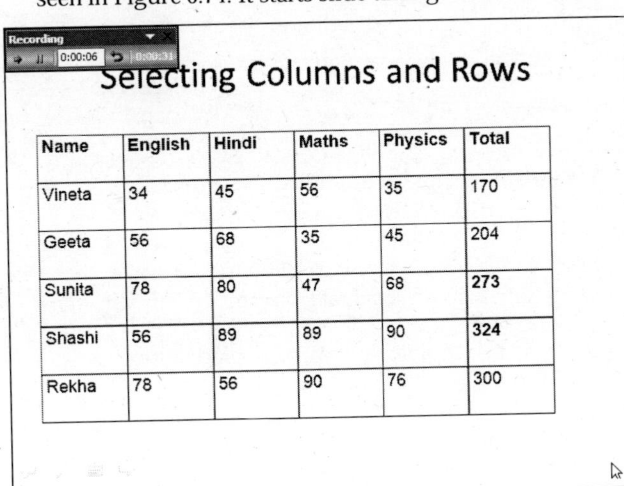

Figure 6.74 Rehearsal Timings dialog box appears in the slide show

4. Click Next button in the Rehearsal dialog box, and fix the time in the second slide.
5. When you reach the end of the slide show, the PowerPoint dialog appears. It asks The Total time for the slide show was 0:00:42. Do you want to keep the new slide timings to use when you view the slid show? Yes or No. Click Yes to accept the timings or No to try again.
6. The amount of time you spend on each slide is recorded and you can save those timings to run the show automatically in the future.

MODEL QUESTIONS AND ANSWERS

A. Multiple Choice

1.1 Which of the following views in not one of the PowerPoint views?
a. Slide Sorter view b. Slide view
c. Slide Show view d. Sorter view

1.2 The Save As dialog box can be used
a. for saving the file for the first time
b. to save file by some alternative name
c. to save file in a format other then Word
d. All of the above

1.3 In which tab to insert the video from file in PowerPoint 2010
a. Insert tab of media group
b. Insert tab of symbols group
c. Home tab of editing group
d. Insert tab of Images group

1.4 An electronic page in a presentation in called
a. Slide b. W-slide
c. E-page d. Page

1.5 Which of the following shortcuts is used to insert a New Slide.
a. Ctrl+M b. Ctrl+N
c. Ctrl+O d. None of the above

1.6 Which extension is given to PowerPoint document by default?
a. .EXT b. .COM
c. .PPT d. None

1.7 Which of the following menus has the Background?
a. Format b. View
c. Insert d. Slide Show

1.8 Which of the following is true in relation to Clip Art?
a. PowerPoint displays available pictures in the Clip Art Gallery
b. You can use a toolbar button or a placeholder to insert Clip Art
c. You can re-color Clip Art.
d. All of the above

1.9 In which view notes pane appears
a. Normal view c. Both (a) and (b)
b. Outline view d. None of the above

1.10 In Handout master footer area appears at
a. Top of the page c. Center of the page
b. Bottom of the page d. None of the above

1.11 You can show the shortcut menu during the slide show by
a. Clicking the shortcut button on the ribbon
b. Right clicking the current slide
c. Clicking an icon on the current slide
d. Both a and b

1.12 Which of the following allows you to select more than one slide in a presentation?
a. Alt + click each slide c. Shift + click each slide
b. Shift + drag each slide d. Ctrl + click each slide

1.13 The PowerPoint view that displays only text (title and bullets) is
a. Slide show c. Notes page view
b. Slide sorter view d. Outline view

1.14 To add a header or footer to your handout, you can use
a. Title master c. Handout master
b. Slide master d. All of the above

1.15 What is the easy way to apply varied animations to test on slides?
a. Apply effects in the custom animation text pane
b. Apply an animation scheme
c. Customize bullets with animated clipart
d. All of above

1.16 How can you create a uniform appearance by adding a background image to all slides?
a. Design tab of background group
b. Insert tab of Illustrations group
c. Design tab of Themes group
d. None of the above

1.17 Which of the following is the default page setup orientation of slide in PowerPoint?
a. Vertical c. Portrait
b. Landscape d. None of above

1.18 What is defined by the handout master?
a. Slide formatting
b. Layout of audience handout notes
c. Handout content formatting for Word export
d. All of the above

1.19 Which command brings you to the first slide in your presentation?
a. Next slide button
b. Page up
c. Ctrl + Home
d. Ctrl + End

B. State whether the following are True or False

2.1 You can view a presentation using one out of ten views provided by PowerPoint.

2.2 The Slide Sorter View button automatically sorts the slides alphabetically.

2.3 Outline view, Slide view, and Slide Show are just different ways of viewing the same set of slides.

2.4 Closing a presentation and exiting PowerPoint are the same thing.

2.5 You shut down PowerPoint 2010 by using the close button.

2.6 The first time you save a presentation you must name it.
2.7 A text box can be place any where on the slide.
2.8 Bullets and numbering appears in the standard toolbar.
2.9 A table can be inserted in PowerPoint slide only if the MS Word is installed.
2.10 Animation effects appears in the Design tab.
2.11 Both .wav and .mid files are the two kind of sound effects files that can be added to the presentation.
2.12 To edit a chart, you can click the chart object.
2.13 Rotate is the term used when a clip art image changes the direction of faces.
2.14 Inserting a new slide is used when you want to add a slide to an existing presentation.
2.15 Slide sorter view is the best view to use when setting transition effect for all slides in a presentation.

Answers

A. 1. a 2. d 3. a 4. a 5. a
6. c 7. a 8. d 9. c 10. b
11. b 12. c 13. d 14. c 15. b
16. a 17. b 18. b 19. c

B. 1. F 2. T 3. T 4. T 5. T
6. T 7. T 8. F 9. T 10. F
11. T 12. F 13. T 14. T 15. T

CHAPTER 7

Database Management Systems

7.1 INTRODUCTION

A Database is a collection of related information stored to provide the availability of information to many users for different purposes. The content of database is obtained by combining data from various sources in an organization. So that data are available to all users and redundant data can be minimized or elimi-nated. Database systems are designed to manage large bodies of information. The management of data involves both the definition of structure for storage of information.

The collection of data, usually referred to as the database, which contains information relevant to an enterprise. The primary goal of a DBMS is to provide a way to store and retrieve data-base information that is both convenient and efficient. For example, consider the names, telephone numbers, and addresses of the people you know. You may have recorded this data in an indexed address book, or you may have stored it on a diskette, using a personal computer and software such as DBASE IV or V, Microsoft ACCESS, or EXCEL.

7.2 CONCEPTS OF DATABASE MANAGEMENT SYSTEM (DBMS)?

A database management system (DBMS) is a software package designed to define, manipulate, retrieve and manage data in a database. DBMS generally manipulates the data itself, the data format, field names, record structure and file struc-ture. It also defines rules to validate and manipulate this data. A DBMS relieves users of framing programs for data maintenance. Fourth-generation query languages, such as SQL, are used along with the DBMS package to interact with a database.

DBMS also makes it possible for end users to create, read, update and delete data in a database. The interface between the data-base and end users or application programs, ensures that data is consistently organized and remains easily accessible.

The DBMS is perhaps most useful for providing a centralized view of data that can be accessed by multiple users, from multiple locations, in a controlled manner. A DBMS can limit what data the end user sees, as well as how that end user can view the data, providing many views of a single database schema. End users and software programs are free from having to understand where the data is physically located or on what type of storage media it resides because the DBMS handles all requests.

The DBMS can offer both logical and physical data independence. That means it can protect users and applications from needing to know where data is stored or having to be concerned about changes to the physical structure of data (storage and hardware). As long as programs use the application programming interface (API) for the database that is provided by the DBMS.

7.2.1 Need for DBMS

First, we need the ability to have multiple users insert, update and delete data to the same data file without "stepping on each other's toes". This means that different users will not cause the data to become inconsistent, and no data should be inadvertently lost through these operations.

We also need to have a standard interface for data access, tools for data backup, data restore and recovery, and a way to handle other challenges such as the capability to work with huge volumes of data and users.

7.2.2 What is Database?

A database is an organized collection of facts. In other words we can say that it is a collection of information arranged and presented to serve an assigned purpose.

An example of a database is a dictionary, where words are arranged alphabetically. Another example is a telephone directory, where subscriber names are listed in an alphabetic order. Similarly, when you think of a box of cards with names and addresses written as a mailing list, then the box and its contents form a mailing database. Figure 7.1 contains cards with mailing addresses. All these cards are placed in alphabetic order of names and the collection of these cards would be called a database.

☞ Thus, information stored in a database is arranged in a particular order.

In order to keep the database updated, we may need to perform operations like adding information, removing information, editing existing information, etc. Take the case of a telephone diary, in which you note down the names, addresses and phone numbers of your friends. This is also a type of database. If you make a new friend, you note the information about him/her in the diary which is equivalent to adding data to a database. If address of your friend changes then you note the new address in your diary which means editing a database. If you want to send a letter to your friend then you look into the diary to locate the address. This is called searching a database.

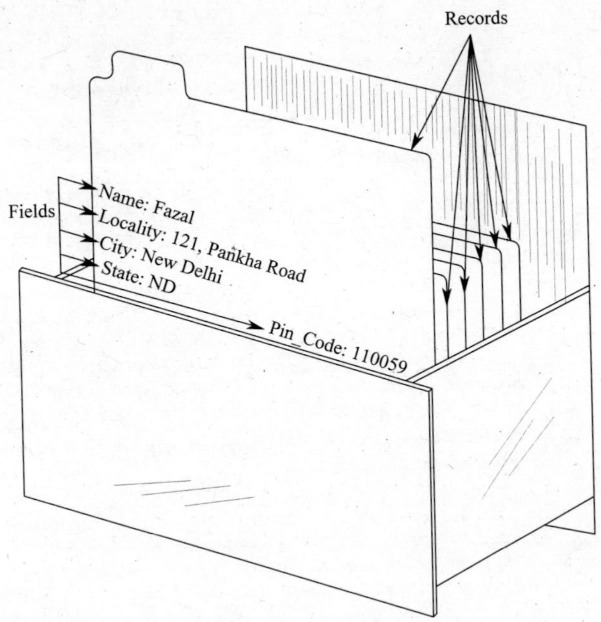

Figure 7.1 Each card represents a record in which information is organized into fields and records

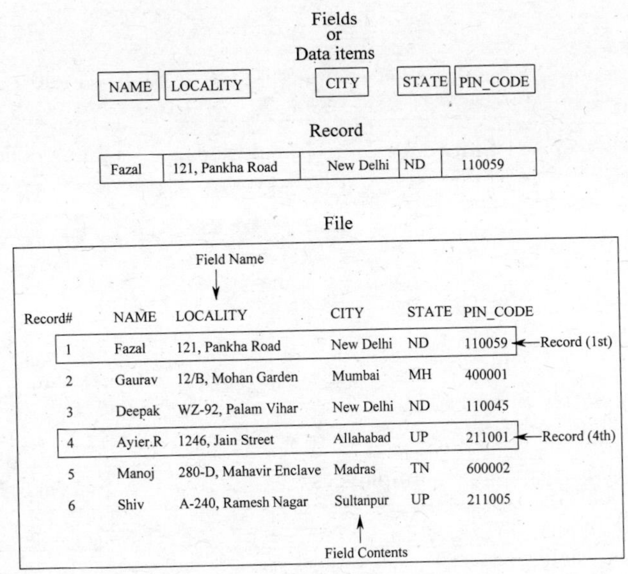

Figure 7.2 Data items in a file record

7.2.3 Characteristics of Data in Database

Computer uses database by adopting a set of well defined rules. You should note that just as a mailing box, in Figure 7.1, is filled with cards, so is a computer database filled with records Figure 7.2. And while each card in the box may contain several lines of written information, a record in a database contains several fields of data items. Thus, a mailing box contains cards, each of which has several lines of information on it. Similarly, a database contains records, each of which in turn has fields in it.

Assume that each card in the mailing box has five lines of data items, namely,

(a) Name;
(b) Locality;
(c) City;
(d) State; and
(e) Pin_code.

Then, all these fields combined to form a record. We shall now understand each part of a database one by one.

Field

The smallest piece of meaningful information in a file is called a data item or field. A data item is generally used for a group of alphanumeric characters. Figure 7.2 displays the data items (fields) in a record.

NAME, LOCALITY, CITY, STATE, PIN_CODE are all known as data items or fields.

Record

The collection of related fields is called a record. For example, Figure 7.2 contains six records and each record has five related fields namely; **NAME, LOCALITY, CITY, STATE and PIN_CODE.**

File

File is the collection of all related records. In Figure 7.2, the file contains the list of addresses of six friends.

Database

Database is a collection of related files. Figure 7.3 shows Employees database having related files containing records of employees.

Key Field

The keyfield in a record is a unique field which is used to identify the record for the purpose of searching and manipulating files. In Figure 7.3,

- File 1 contains employee records with fields **Emp_Code** and **Address**.
- File 2 contains employee records with fields **Emp_Code** and **Salary**.
- File 3 contains employee records with fields **Emp_Code** and **Name**.

All the three files have one common field namely, **Emp_Code**. Such a field is known as keyfield. A keyfield is unique and establishes an identifying factor for a record.

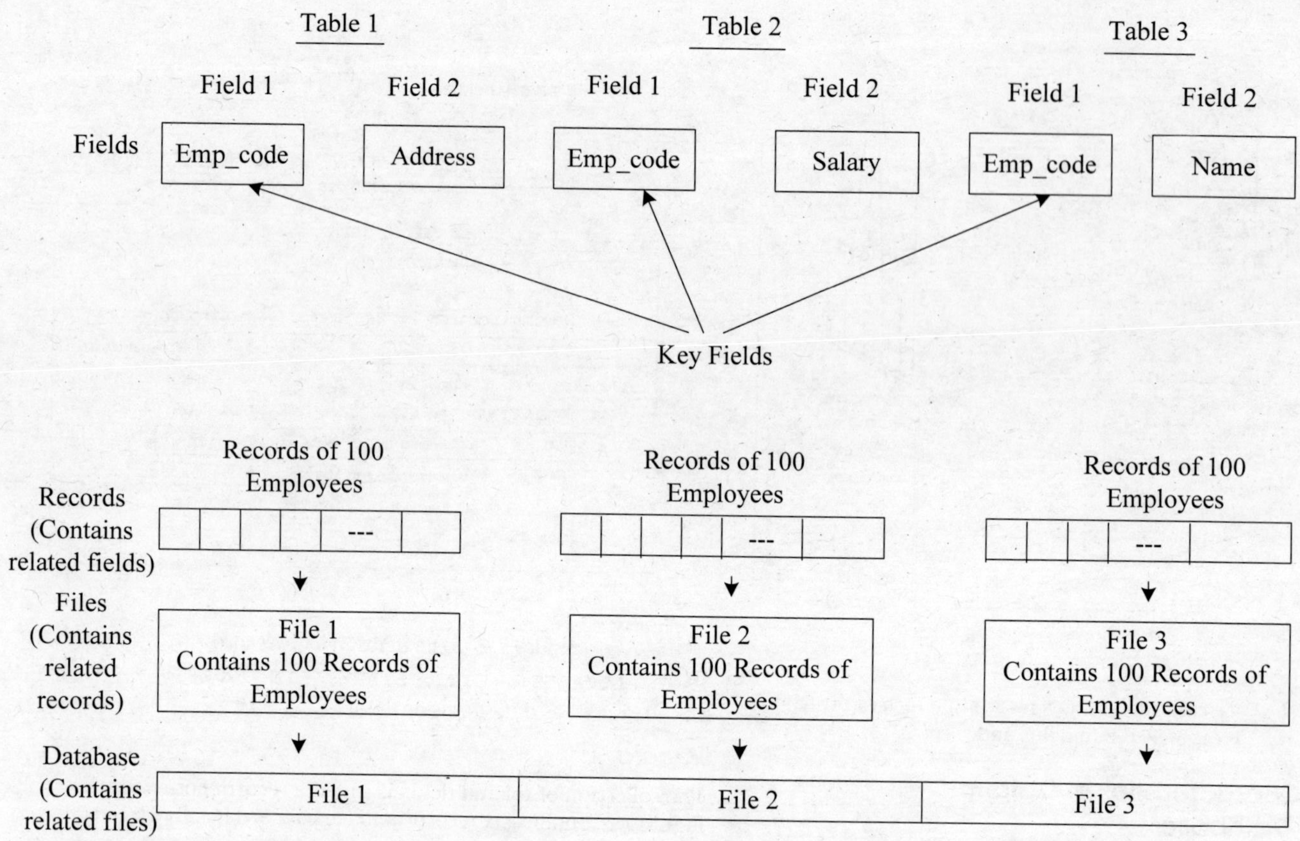

Figure 7.3 Concept of Database

Figure 7.3 illustrates the concepts of fields, records, files and database. For example, in business, we may have files, containing address of friends, relatives and business associates. All these different files put together constitute an address database.

Primary Key

The field or group of fields that is unique identifier for a Table is called the primary key. Primary key uniquely identifies each record in the table and it is never same for two records. Use a unique number for primary keys.

For example, see a Student's table given in Table 7.1.

Table 7.1 Student's Table

Roll No.	Name	Father s Name	Marks
101	Ramesh Chadha	Mr. S.C. Chadha	56
102	Ram Chandra	Mr. A. Chandra	78
103	Ahmed Khan	Mr. U. Khan	80
104	Gurmeet Singh	Mr. R. Singh	93
105	Ramesh Chadha	Mr. S. Chadha	23
106	David John	Mr A.K. John	56

In the Student table shown above, there can be more than one student called by the same name say Ramesh Chadha. Therefore if we say "Get the marks of Ramesh Chadha", more than one records will be accessed. As the computer cannot distinguish between their marks. But if we have a unique field (Roll Number) called Primary Key defined in the Student table, then it will be easy to access the required record by saying "Get the marks of Roll Number 105".

Composite Keys

There may be some cases where a record cannot be uniquely identified by a single field. In such cases, a composite key is used. A composite key is a group of fields that uniquely identify a record. A composite key is also a primary key for a Table.

For example, in Table 7.1, the Name and Father's Name make a composite key.

7.2.4 Relationships between Tables

A relationship is what a keyfield establishes between two or more tables. The values stored in key fields are duplicated in the related tables. For example in a department table, `dept_id` field is designated as the key field. In another table called employee table, the employee's department is identified by the field **dept_id**. Thus, the tables employee and department are related to each other through the key field **dept_id**.

7.2.5 Arranging Information in a Database

How do we lay down rules to arrange information in a database management package? First, we have to decide exactly what we want to store as database. To do so, we have to break down the information into meaningful units or small pieces of information called field. For example, one address card in a mailing box may hold the following:

1. name
2. locality
3. city
4. state
5. pin_code

A record in a database refers to one card in the cardbox, and each field in a record refers to one piece of information on the card. (See Figure 7.3). Thus, in a database we may like to keep each record containing the under mentioned fields:

NAME, LOCALITY, CITY, STATE, PIN_CODE

In this way, each field has meaningful as well as the smallest piece of information. Note that in the above example there are five fields in one record. You can also assign a unique field named as a keyfield.

7.2.6 Managing a Database

Once you have decided the number and the names of fields in a record, you can learn to manage records by giving precise instructions using a DBMS package, such as MS Access. Managing a database would involve the following jobs:

- Adding a new record to a database.
- Arranging records into some meaningful order.
- Searching a record in a database.
- Printing data from a database to compile a report.
- Editing or modifying a record in a database.
- Deleting a record from a database.

All these jobs can be done with the help of a PC using MS-Access package. The main advantage would be that we would be able to perform operations, such as searching on addresses or printing reports very fast.

7.2.7 Advantages of Database

The advantages of database are the following:

1. Databases reduce the data redundancy
2. Databases can control data inconsistency to a larger extent
3. Database facilitate sharing of data
4. Database enforce standards
5. Databases can ensure data security
6. Database maintain data integrity

7.3 INTRODUCTION TO ACCESS 2010

Access 2010 is a software package for database management. It comes as a component of the MS Office. Access 2010 is an easy to use, full-featured database development application.

MS Access allows you to manage all your information from a single database file. Database files in MS Access are stored with extension .MDB. Within the file, you can divide your data into separate storage containers called tables. You can add, view and update table data by using on-line forms. Using queries you can retrieve required data and then analyze or print data in a specific layout by using reports.

7.3.1 Components of Access Database

Access 2010 databases consist not only of the basic data items, but also of related items you use to work with them. Every database may contain six different types of objects. These objects are:

- Tables
- Queries
- Forms
- Reports
- Macros
- Modules

Tables: Containers for Information

In Access 2010 database, you store information in objects called Tables. Tables are rectangular arrangements of rows and columns, where each column represents a field and each row represents a record. (See Figure 7.4).

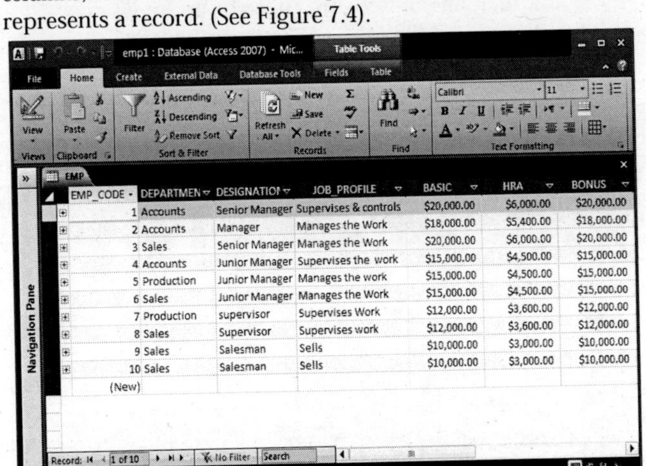

Figure 7.4 Access 2010 Table with Rows and columns

Queries: Asking Questions about Stored Data and Getting Results

Query is a statement that gives filtered data according to specified conditions. Access has powerful search capabilities. For example, if you have an employee database and you want to see the list of those employees who are getting Basic salary more than Rs. 12000. Such an enquiry can be easily put to Access database and it displays the answer immediately.

☞ Queries are questions you ask and the database replies after doing process on it (See Figure 7.5).

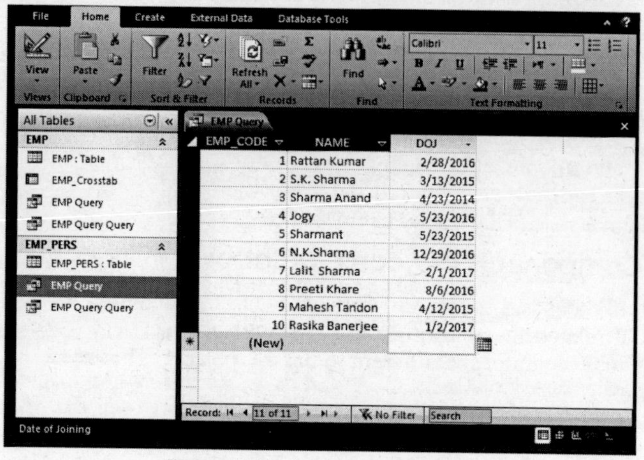

Figure 7.5 Access 2010 Query

Forms: Making Data Entry Correctly and Easily

Form is an interface in user specified layout that allows users to view, enter or change data directly in table. In order to make data entry easier, you can create objects called Forms. Forms provide you with a "template" that you fill in whenever you enter the information for record. Thus, form shows a blank box for each field in the table. Data entry becomes a simple matter of filling in the appropriate boxes (See Figure 7.6).

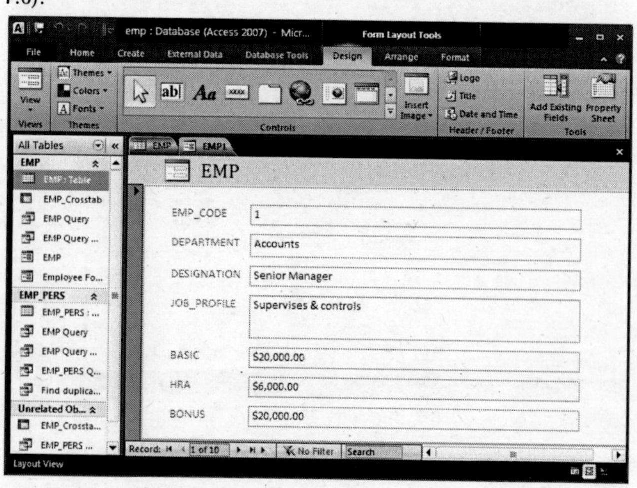

Figure 7.6 Access 2010 Form for filling data

Reports: Making Your Data easily Readable and Understandable

To make your data more easily readable and understandable, you create a report. Report is a presentable printed document that lists data in formatted manner. Reports let you to define how you want the data to be printed on paper or shown on the screen (See Figure 7.7).

You can moreover decide which fields to include in the report and where they should appear on the page or the screen. Further, you can add text and graphics, etc., in the report.

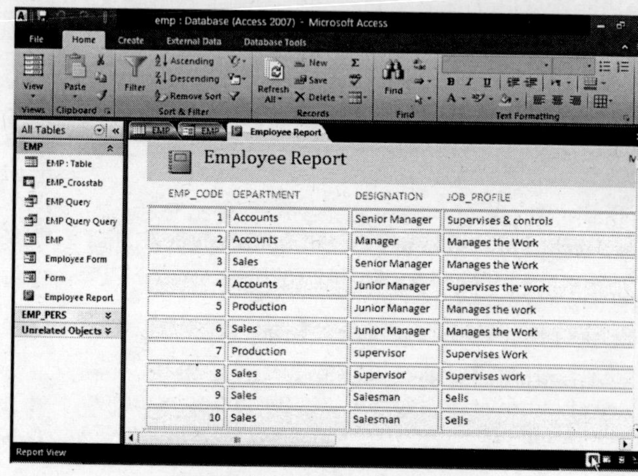

Figure 7.7 Access 2010 Report

Macros: For Automating Repetitive Tasks

Macros are small programs used to automate a repetitive task or set the database setup and exit code. Access has a feature that you can use to perform several actions with a single command. Such a feature, is called Macros which operate by running a series of actions that can do various jobs again and again by just typing single word command only.

Modules: For Designing and Developing MS Access Database Applications

Modules add functionality to a database. A module is similar to a macro which is a collection of actions that can be performed together. For example you can use macros to open report and print its first three pages automatically. For full-scale database applications, Access provides Visual Basic for Applications (VBA). With VBA, you can create programs for project development. It has facilities for table creation data entry, queries, forms and reports generations.

7.3.2 Starting Access 2010

➡ **To start Access, do this:**

1. Click the Start button on the taskbar, highlight All Programs, click Microsoft Office and then Microsoft Access 2010. (See Figure 7.8).

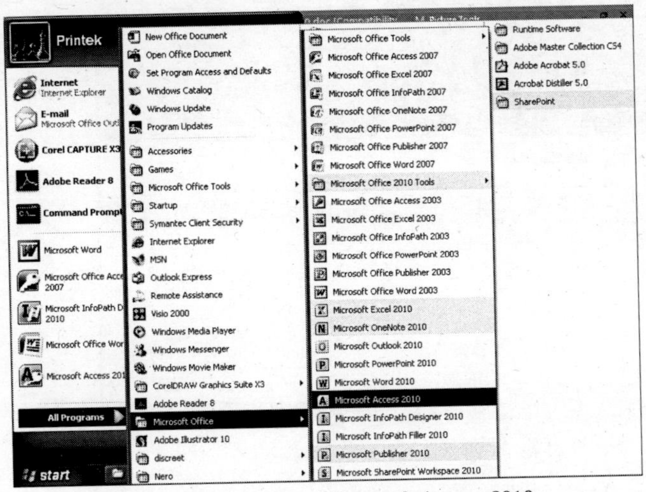

Figure 7.8 Starting Microsoft Access 2010

2. A starting page of Access is displayed as shown in Figure 7.9. The center of the screen is dominated by the Office.com templates. The right side of the screen contains a list of recently opened databases, while the left side of the screen contains a number of tabs for revealing other options for working with Access.

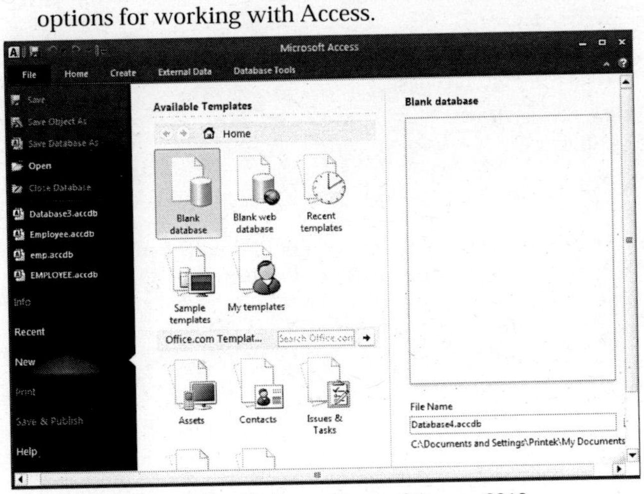

Figure 7.9 Welcome Page of Access 2010

7.4 CREATING NEW DATABASE

Access 2010 gives you three ways to create a new database. These are as follows:

- Creating a blank database: When you create a database using the Blank Database option, you start from scratch. This method is advisable for experienced users.
- Creating a database using template i.e. installed with Access: When you create a database using template, Access provides you ready-to-use database containing all the tables, queries, forms, and reports needed to perform a specific task. There are many variety of templates in Access that can help you to speed up the database creation process.
- Creating a database using template from Office.com: Access 2010 comes with many in-built templates, but if you want more templates as available templates did not fulfill your requirements then you can find many more templates on Office.com. You do not even have to open a browser, the templates are available in the New tab.

☞ Access 2010 also supports creating web databases. So that you can use a web database with a web browser. Access 2010 is not required unless you want to make design changes.

7.4.1 Creating a Blank Database

A blank database is a file that does not contain any objects or data. It is an empty shell that you can use to add new tables, queries, forms, and reports.

➡ **To create a blank database, do this:**

1. Click the File Tab as shown in Figure 7.9. Here, select New. Under Available Templates, click Blank database.
2. In the Blank database right pane, type a file name (say Database1.accdb) in the File Name: box. If you want to change the location of the file, click on the Browse.
3. Click Create.

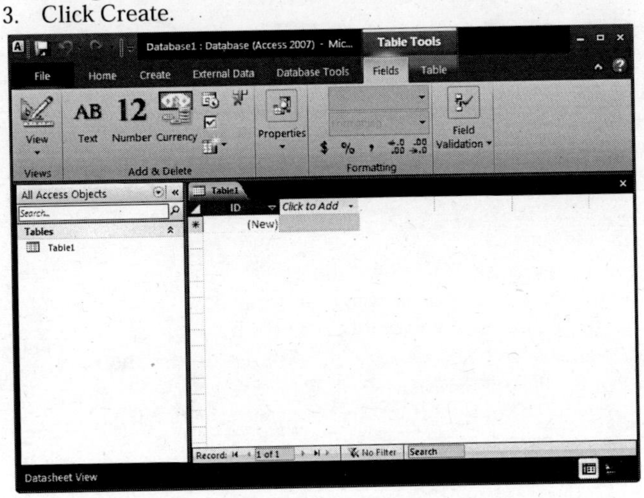

Figure 7.10 Table Created using the Blank Database

4. Access creates the database with an empty table named Table1 along with Table Tools (Fields and Table Tab), and then opens Table1 in Datasheet view. The cursor is placed in the first empty cell in the Click to Add column (See Figure 7.10). Begin typing to add data. If you do not want to enter information in Table1 at this time, click Close [X] button that appears to the right side of the window of Table1 tab.

☞ You can also press Ctrl+N to start a new database from anywhere in Access. After you give the database a name, Access closes the database that you were working on and opens a blank database window.

7.4.2 Creating a Database using Template

Access 2010 provides you with a suite of prebuilt tracking applications in the form of templates that you can use to speed up the database creation process and refine them to track information in your way. The Office.com Templates section contains popular templates from Microsoft Office online.

☞ A template is a ready-to-use database containing all the tables, queries, forms, and reports needed to perform a specific task.

➡ **To create a database using template, do this:**

1. Click the File Tab as shown in Figure 7.9. Here, Select New. Under under Available Templates, click Sample templates.

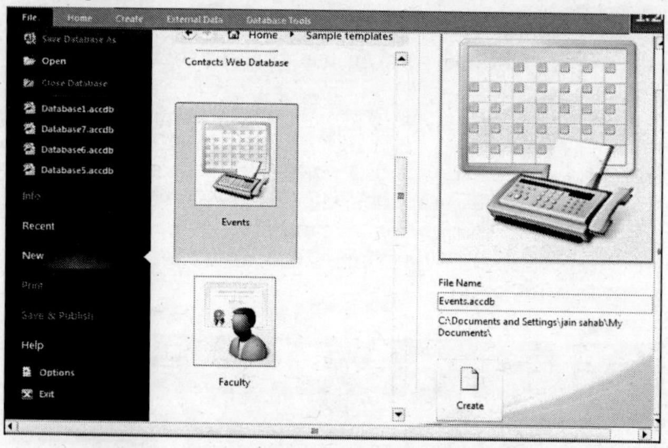

Figure 7.11 Database creation using template

2. Then, click on the template from the center of the window that you want to use. Here, we have selected Events template (See Figure 7.11).
3. Now, in the right side of the window, Access suggests a file name for your database in the File Name box. You can change the file name, if you want.
4. If you want to save the database in different folder then you have to click on the Browse.
5. After that click Create button. Access creates the database and then opens it. (See Figure 7.12)

This is how you can create database. Now in the following sections, you will learn how to create new tables, queries, forms and reports.

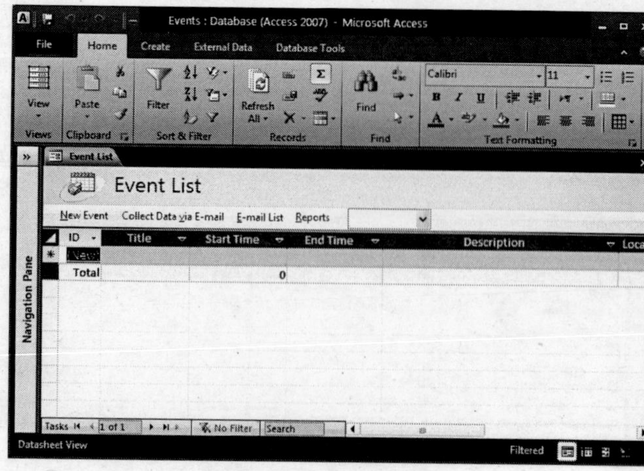

Figure 7.12 Access database

7.4.3 Working in Access 2010

In a database, you store information as an object which is called a Table in Access 2010.

Tables are rectangular arrangements of rows and columns, where each column represents a field and each row represents a record (a single entry in the table).

Each field in a table has a set of properties that you use to customize how a field's data is stored, handled or displayed. The field's data are of two types:

- Data type properties
- Field properties

7.4.4 Data Type Properties

The properties that are available for each field are determined by the data type you select for the field. For example, if data type property is set to Text, then the Field Size can be between 0 and 255 (the default setting is 50).

Table 7.2 gives a list of data types available in Access 2010 and their corresponding settings.

7.4.5 Field Properties

Field properties of each data types is as per the list given in Table 7.3.

Table 7.2 Data types available in Access 2010

Data Type	Type of Data Stored	Field Size
Text	Text or combinations of Text and Numbers, as well as Numbers that do not require calculations, such as phone numbers or postal codes. This is the default Data Type.	Up to 255 characters.
Memo	Lengthy texts or combination of Text and Numbers, such as notes, remarks or comments. You can now apply the rich text formatting to the data in the memo field.	Upto 1 GB of characters.
Number	Numeric data used in mathematical calculations except calculations involving money.	1, 2, 4, 8 or 16 bytes.

(Contd...)

Data Type	Type of Data Stored	Field Size
Date/Time	Date and Time values for the years 100 through 9999.	8 bytes.
Currency	Currency values and numeric data with one to four decimal places. Used in mathematical calculations involving money. You do not have to manually enter a currency symbol. Access 2010 applies the currency symbol specified in you Windows Regional settings.	8 bytes.
AutoNumber	Sequential (incremented by 1) or random unique numbers automatically inserted when a record is added. AutoNumber fields cannot be edited by us. Mainly used as data type for primary key fields.	4 bytes.
Yes/No	Fields that will contain only one of two values, such as Yes/No, True/False and On/Off. These are also called logical fields.	1-bit.
OLE Object	Objects created in some other programs that can be linked or embedded into an Access table.	Limited by disk space.
Hyperlink	Used for storing hyperlinks. A hyperlink address can have the following three parts: Text to display: the text that appears in a field. address: the path to another file or page. subaddress: a location within the file or page. For example if you type `c:\access.doc` in a hyperlink field, the Word file access.doc will get opened when this hyperlink is clicked.	Upto 64,000 characters.
Attachment	This field attachs data from other programs, but in this field you cannot type or enter text or numeric data.	Upto 1 GB
Calculated	This is the new feature in Access 2010. Calculate data (such as multiplying the price field by the quantity field) and store the calculation in the table which automatically updates when the underlying data changes. It brings up the Expression Builder automatically.	
Lookup Wizard	Creates a field that allows you to choose a value from another table or from a list of values using a combo box. Choosing Lookup Wizard in the data type list starts a wizard to define this for you.	Same size as the primary key field that is also the lookup field, typically 4 bytes.

Table 7.3 Field properties available for different data types

Field Property	Description
Field Size	The size and type of values for the field.
New Values	How new values should be generated for the field. Available only with the AutoNumber data type.
Format	Select predefined format for the field to customize when displayed or printed.
Caption	The label for the field when it is used on a form, reports and queries.
Indexed	Speed up access to data in this field by creating and using an index.
Input Mask	Allows you to specify the pattern of values entered in this field.
Default Value	Value which will be automatically entered in this field for new records.
Validation Rule	An expression that defines the values that can be entered into this field.
Validation Text	The error message that appears when a value which is not in accordance with the validation rule is entered into this field.
Required	Specifies whether data entry into this field is required or not.
Allow Zero Length	Determines whether the field can be left blank or not.
Decimal Places	The number of digits to the right of decimal dot. Found with Currency and Number data type.
Unicode Compression	Compress text stored in this field when a large amount of text is stored, i.e., text is > 4096 characters.
SmartTags	Attach a smart tag to this field.
AppendOnly	It allows versioning, i.e., history (by setting to Yes) of a Memo field.
TextFormat	Choose Rich Text to store text as HTML and allow rich text formatting.
TextAlign	Specify the default alignment of text within a control.
Show Date Picker	It shows date picker.

Access 2010 gives you two methods to create Tables. We already learnt about the methods for creating databases. Now we will create tables. The creation of tables are explained in the following Sections:

7.4.6 Create a Table in Blank Database

When you create a new blank database, a new empty table is automatically inserted for you. You can then enter data to start defining your fields.

7.4.7 Create a Table in an Existing Database

➡ **To create a new Table in an existing database, do this:**

1. Open the blank database named as `Database1.accdb` that we created earlier in Chapter.
2. Under the Create Tab, in the Tables group, click Table as shown in Figure 7.13.

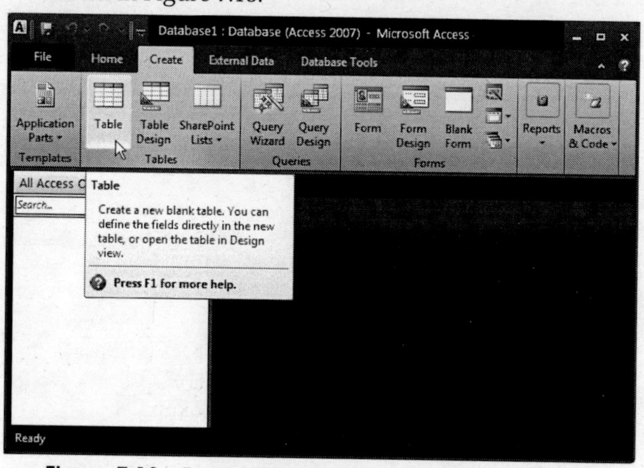

Figure 7.13 Creating new table in an existing database

3. A new table gets inserted in the database.
4. Double click on the Click to Add Column to add a field (such as Name, Address, E-mail address, etc.).
5. Now, type data in the cell below the Click to Add column header.

When you enter data in the new column, Access 2010 automatically recognizes the appropriate data type for the field.

☞ You can also paste data from Microsoft Excel tables into a new datasheet–Access 2010 creates all of the fields and recognizes the data types automatically.

7.4.8 Create a Table based on Template

➡ **To create a Table based on template, do this:**

1. Open the database in which you want to create table.
2. Under the Create Tab, in the Templates group, click Application Parts and then select any one template from Quick Start section (Here, we select Contacts) as shown in Figure 7.14.
3. A new table is inserted based on the table template (i.e. Contacts) you selected (See Figure 7.15).

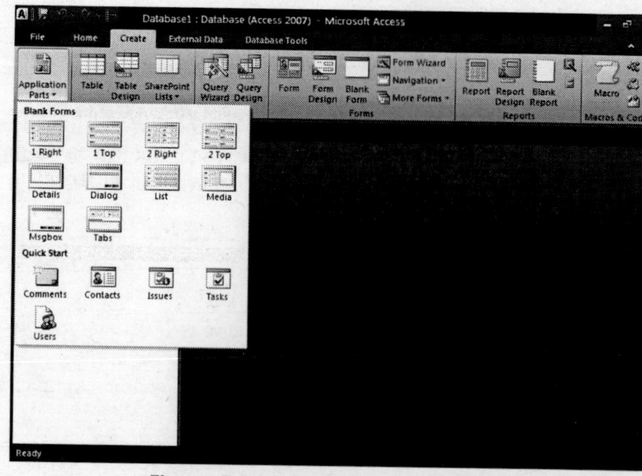

Figure 7.14 Choosing the template

Figure 7.15 Table created by using template, Contacts

7.4.9 Create a Table using Design View

Use any of the readymade sample databases that Access provides or create a new database. Here, we will create a Database named Employee with two tables EMP and EMP_PERS.

➡ **To create a Table using Design View, do this:**

1. Under Create Tab, in the Tables group, click Table Design. You will find Design tab and a grid that has only three columns across the top (See Figure 7.16). Also the complete screen is divided into two sections called panes. The top pane is used to enter information about the field and the lower pane is used to change the properties of the fields.
2. Under the Field Name column, type the name of the field which you want to insert into the Table.
3. Move to the Data Type column and select a data type for the newly entered field. Type a small description about the field in Description column. Data Type field specifies the format for the information that will be stored in that field. Text is the default data type field. You may leave it blank also (See Figure 7.17).

☞ In Access 2010, new data type (Calculated) lets you to create a field that is based on a calculation of other fields in the same table. When you select Calculated data type, an Expression builder opens up. Here, type the calculation you want to perform. In this example, we type Basic * 30/100 in Expression builder (See Figure 7.17).

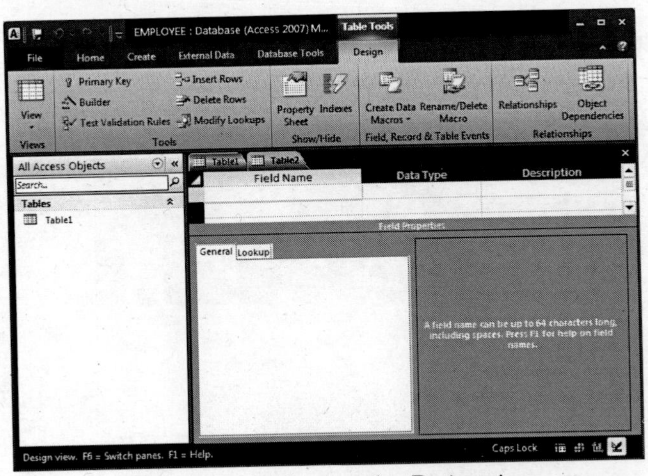

Figure 7.16 Table created in Design view

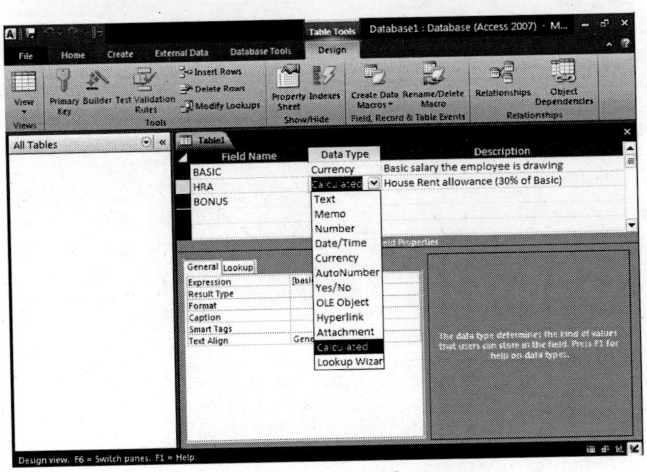

Figure 7.17 Selecting data types

Each data type you choose for a field is associated with field properties. These can be changed according to requirement.

4. Similarly, go on adding fields into the table as described in Table 7.4.
5. To set a field as the primary key of the table, click the field and under the Design Tab, in the Tools group, click Primary Key. This field will now be assigned as the primary key. It is advisable to assign **EMP_CODE** field of the table as Primary Key. (See Figure 7.18)

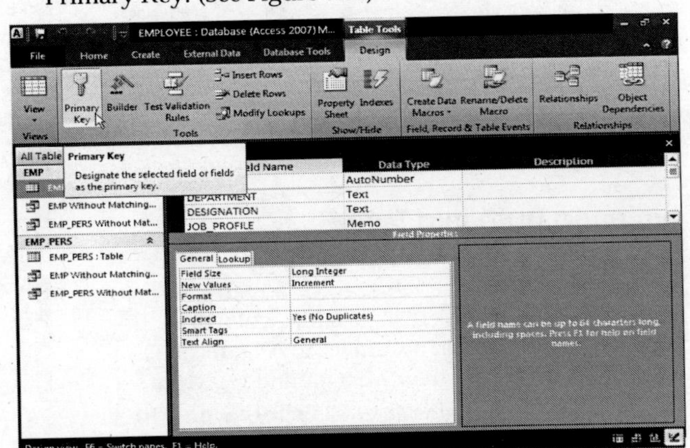

Figure 7.18 Selecting **EMP_CODE** as the Primary key in a table

6. Click on the File tab and then choose Save option and type a name **EMP** for this Table and click on OK button. (See Figure 7.19)

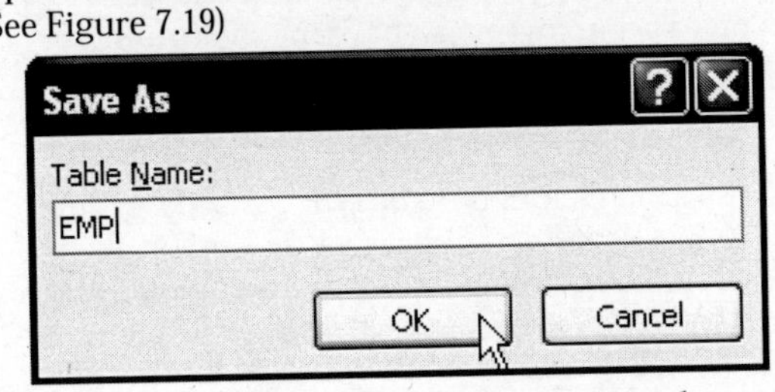

Figure 7.19 Save As dialog box with entered name

7. If you have not set a primary key for this table, Access will ask you to define the Primary Key. Primary key is needed to define the relationship between a table with other tables.

Table 7.4 Fields of EMP Table

Field Name	Data Type	Description
EMP_CODE	AutoNumber	Unique Code assigned to each employee as Primary key
DEPARTMENT	Text	Name of department
DESIGNATION	Text	Designation of employees
JOB_PROFILE	Memo	Type of work done by employee
BASIC	Currency	Basic Salary the employee is drawing
HRA	Currency	House Rent Allowance (30% of BASIC)
BONUS	Currency	Bonus the employee is getting

8. If Access asks you to create a primary key now? as shown in Figure 7.20 then do as in step 9.
9. Click Yes. Once you designated **EMP_CODE** as Primary key, notice an icon of a key against this field name. Then click Close button.
   Since we have already created primary key, the dialog box will not appear.

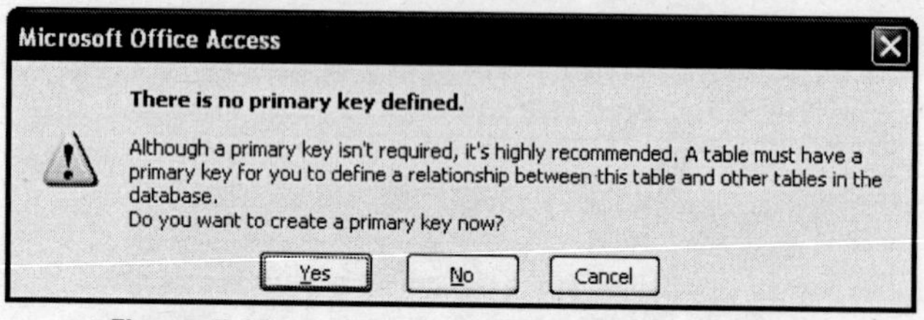

Figure 7.20 Setting Primary key in the Database

7.4.10 Entering Data in a Table

Notice that the first field in the table, ID, is already defined. The ID field is always included in a table when it is first created. It automatically assigns a number to each record as it is added to a table and is useful for maintaining record order. The second column header displays Click to Add and is used to add a new field in the table.

In Datasheet view, you can enter data for a record and create a new field at the same time. The first field of data you will enter is the employee number, which is assigned to each employee. Each new employee is given the next consecutive number, so that no two employees can have the same number. Each number is a maximum of five digits. When you enter data in a record, it should be entered accurately and consistently (See Figure 7.21).

The data you enter in a field should be typed exactly as you want it to appear. This is important because any printouts of the data will display the information exactly as entered. It is also important to enter data in a consistent form.

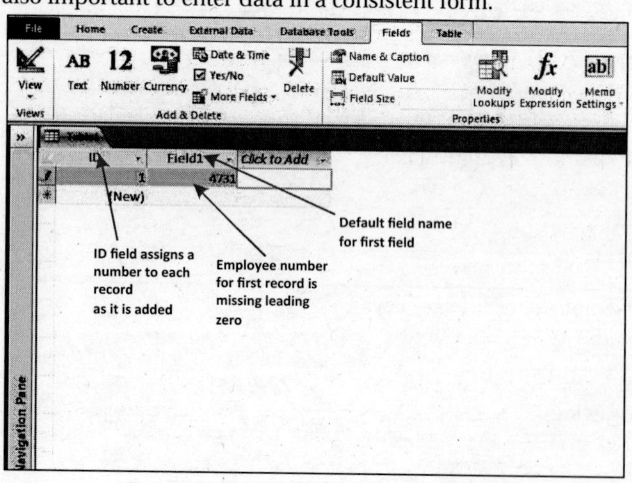

Figure 7.21 Entering data in the table

Changing Field Names

Before entering data, you want to replace the default field name with a more descriptive field name. A field name is used to identify the data stored in the field. A field name should describe the contents of the data to be entered in the field. It can be up to 64 characters long and can consist of letters, numbers, spaces, and special characters, except a period, an exclamation point, an accent grave (‘), or brackets ([]). You also cannot start a field name with a space. It is best to use field names to make the tables easier to manage. For example, here we type the ID field as Emp Code, Department, etc., as shown in Figure 7.22.

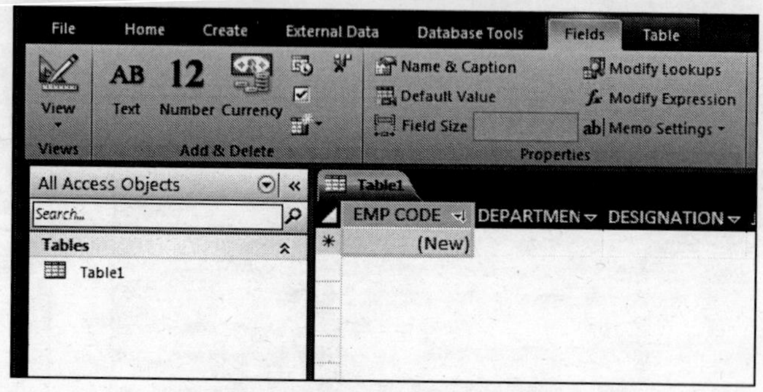

Figure 7.22 Changing Field names

7.5 PREVIEW AND PRINT A TABLE

7.5.1 Previewing the Table

The print preview feature in Access gives you the chance to modify your margins, paper orientation, and so on, before you send your table to the printer. To preview a table, open it (or select it in the navigation pane), choose File menu and choose Print, and then click the Print Preview button.

Previewing a table displays each page in a reduced size so you can see the layout. Then, if necessary, you can make changes to the layout before printing to save time and avoid wasting paper.

➡ **To Preview a Table, do this:**

1. Open the table.
2. Click the File tab highlight Print tab and choose Print privew (See Figure 7.23).
3. The Print Preview window displays how the table will appear when printed. The Print Preview contextual tab is open and includes commands that are used to modify the print settings.

7.5.2 Printing a table

The button in the Print group of the Print Preview tab is used to define the printer settings and print the document.

➡ **To Print a Table, do this:**

1. Click the Print tab in the Print Preview tab. The Print dialog box appears as shown in Figure 7.24.
2. If you need to change the selected printer to another printer, open the Name drop-down list box and select the appropriate printer.

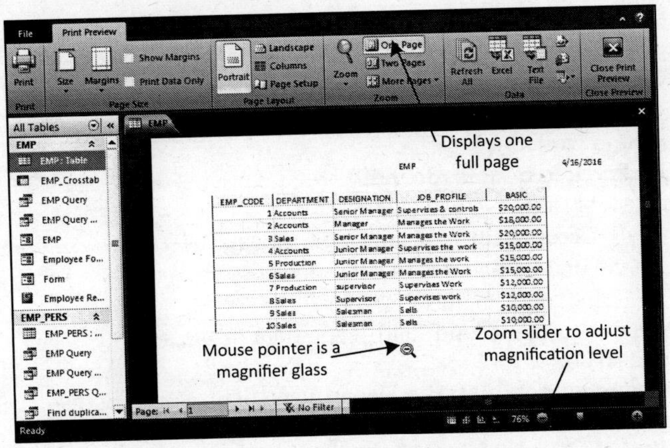

Figure 7.23 Previewing a table

3. The Print Range area of the Print dialog box is used to specify the amount of the document you want to print. The range options are described in the following table.

Option	Action
All	Prints the entire document.
Pages	Prints pages you specify by typing page numbers in the text box.
Selected Records	Prints selected records only.

4. After you select the desired settings click OK button.
5. A status message box is displayed briefly, informing you that the table is being printed.

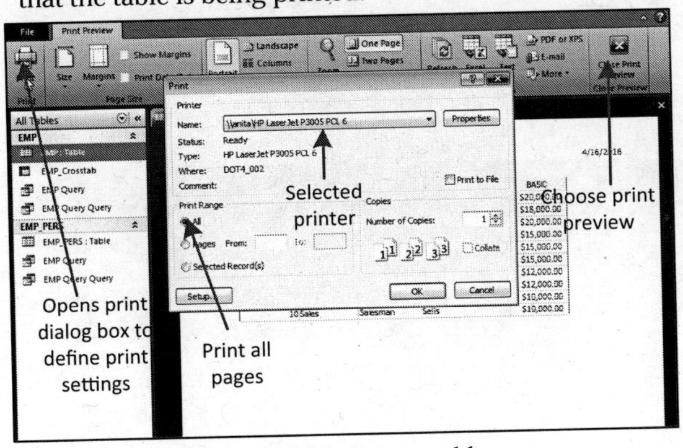

Figure 7.24 Print a table

How to set Lookup Wizard?

Lookup Wizard allows you to select a value out of a list of values by using a list box or combo box. This makes the data entry process easier in a table. Suppose for the EMP table, you wish to change the type of Department field to Lookup Wizard. Also suppose there are four departments namely, Accounts, Production, Sales and Human Resource. Then, while entering data, user has to just choose any one department from these four departments list by clicking on it. This will reduce the typing effort every time a department entry is to be made.

➡ **To set the Lookup Wizard data type, do this:**

1. In the Navigation Pane, right click the EMP table and then choose Design View.
2. In the Design view of the EMP table, click the data type column against Department. Select the Lookup Wizard... data type as shown in Figure 7.25.

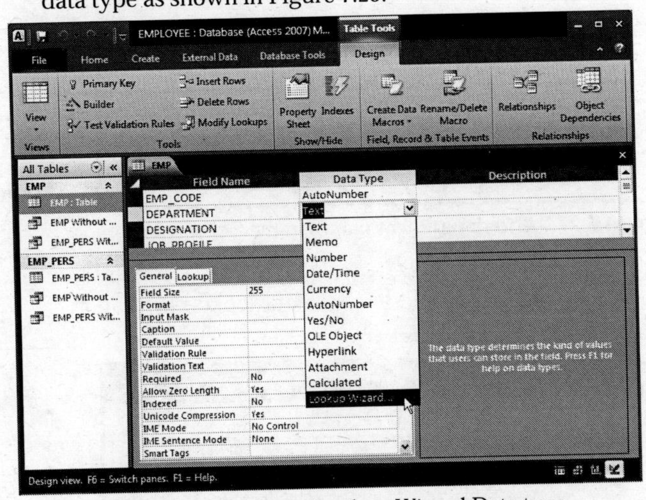

Figure 7.25 Selecting Lookup Wizard Data type

4. A Lookup Wizard screen as shown in Figure 7.26 appears. In this dialog box, click the radio button against the "I will type in the values that I want". Click the Next > button.

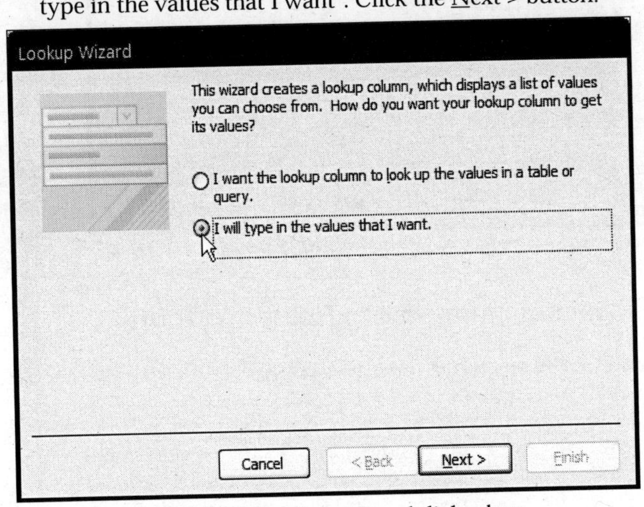

Figure 7.26 Lookup Wizard dialog box

5. A dialog box as shown in Figure 7.27 appears. In the Col1 area, first type Accounts.
6. Press Tab key and the type Sales.
7. Similarly type Production and Human Resource. Click Next > button.

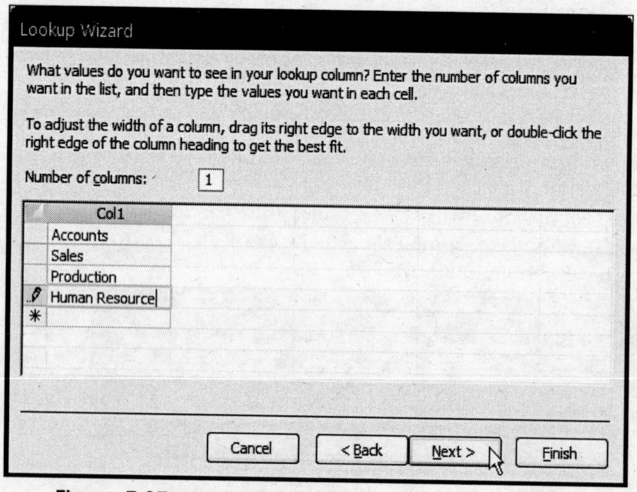

Figure 7.27 Add department names in the Col1 area

8. In the dialog box that appears as shown in Figure 7.28, type a label that you would like for your lookup column say Department and Click Finish.

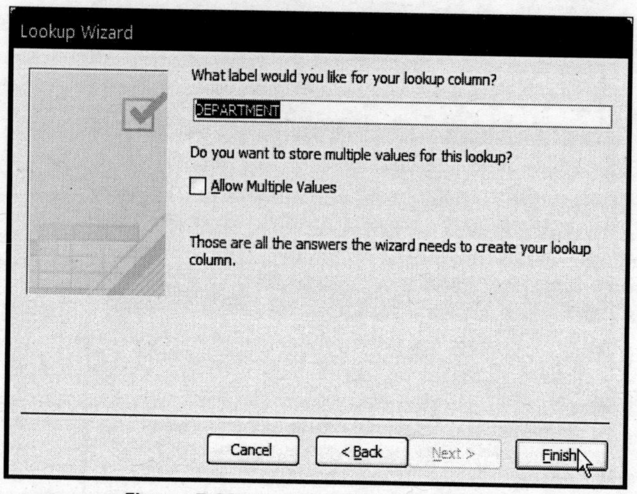

Figure 7.28 Type label for the column

7.5 3 Inserting or Removing Fields in a Table

The buttons for inserting or removing entire row are located on the Table Tools Design Tab. To insert a row click on the Insert Rows option in the Tools group. An empty row will be added. Now you can enter the desired field name, data type and description.

Similarly, to delete row click on Delete Rows option from Tools group.

☞ You can also insert or delete fields by clicking right mouse button and choosing Insert Rows or Delete Rows from the shortcut menu that appears.

7.5.4 Opening and Editing Table

In order to view data stored in a table or to add new data, you must open the table.

➡ **To open a table, do this:**

1. In the Navigation Pane, double click the name of the table you want to work on.

➡ **To add data into a table, do this:**

1. Open the table as explained above.
2. By default, Access 2010 opens the table in Datasheet view.
3. Click on the first field and then enter data.
4. After entering data in the first field, press Tab key to move cursor to the second field. Type data in the second field and so on.
5. While entering data into the Department field, you will find a list box. You can select the required department from the list.
6. Press Tab key after the last field in the record and start entering data into the new field.

☞ When data entry of records is complete, it would get saved automatically.

Add the data given in Table 7.5 into the EMP table.

➡ **To edit data in a Table, do this:**

1. Open the Table to be edited
2. Double click the field you want to edit.
3. Make changes in the field(s).
4. Click the Close [X] button. Changes you applied will automatically get saved.

➡ **To delete a record in a Table, do this:**

1. Open the Table.
2. Right click the record which is to be deleted.
3. Click Delete Record from the shortcut menu (See Figure 7.29). You will see a dialog box. Click Yes.
4. The record gets deleted.

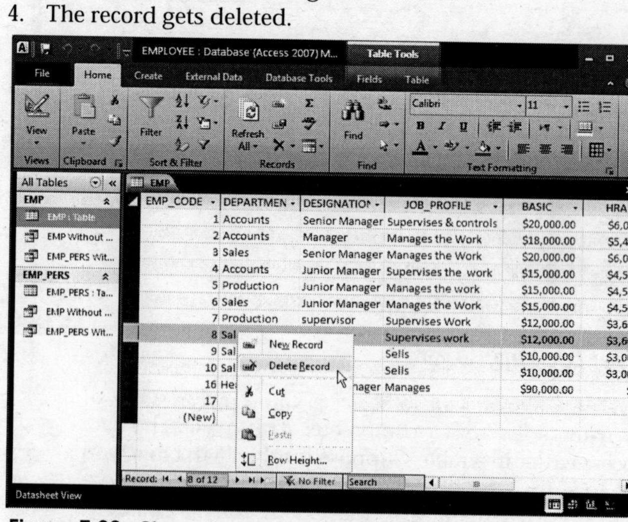

Figure 7.29 Shortcut menu with Delete Record option selected

Table 7.5 Sample data for EMP table

Emp_code	Department	Designation	Job_Profile	Basic	HRA	Bonus
1.	Accounts	Senior Manager	Supervises & controls	20000.00	6000.00	20000.00
2.	Accounts	Manager	Manages the work	18000.00	5400.00	18000.00
3.	Sales	Senior Manager	Manages the work	20000.00	6000.00	20000.00
4.	Accounts	Junior Manager	Supervises the work	15000.00	4500.00	15000.00
5.	Production	Junior Manager	Manages the work	15000.00	4500.00	15000.00
6.	Sales	Junior Manager	Manages the work	15000.00	4500.00	15000.00
7.	Production	Supervisor	Supervises work	12000.00	3600.00	12000.00
8.	Sales	Supervisor	Supervises work	12000.00	3600.00	12000.00
9.	Sales	Salesman	Sells	10000.00	3000.00	10000.00
10.	Sales	Salesman	Sells	10000.00	3000.00	10000.00

Table 7.6 Different Fields of EMP_PERS (Employee personal file) table

Field Name	Data Type	Description
EMP_CODE	AutoNumber	A unique code assigned to each employee
NAME	Text	Employee Name
ADDRESS	Text	Employee's Address
PHONE	Text	Employee's Phone Number
EMAIL	Text	Employee's Email ID
DOJ	Date/Time	Date of Joining

Table 7.7 Sample data for EMP_PERS table

Emp_Code	Name	Address	Phone	E-mail	Doj
1	Rattan Kumar	345, Vikaspuri	546 6789	rattan@hotmail.com	2/28/2016
2	S. K. Sharma	1142 Jain Street	340 2323	sharma_1973@netaddress.com	3/13/2015
3	Anand	222 Lakshmi Puri	120 1211	anand@vsnl.net.in	4/23/2014
4	Jogy	123 A, Sompuri	645 4555	jogy@sify.com	5/23/2015
5	Sharmant	461 Alipur	797 3421	taru_chhaya@yahoo.co.in	5/23/2016
6	N. K. Sharma	12- Janakpuri	5550012	sharma_2k1@yahoo.co.in	12/2/2017
7	Lalit Sharma	102 Keshavpur	2048921	-	1/2/2016
8	Preeti Khare	A-41, Vikas Nagar	6268554	pk23@yahoo.com	6/8/2016
9	Mahesh Tandon	225/B, Vasant Kunj	6965080	m_tandon@indiatimes.com	12/4/2015
10	Rasika Banerjee	B-115, Sector 16, Pitampura	5510154	rbanerjee@rediffmail.com	2/1/2017

Create another table using the methods described earlier. This table will contain fields as given in Table 7.6. We will be using these two tables in further study of Access 2010. Also add sample data given in Table 7.7, to the MS Access Table just created.

7.5.5 Changing Data Types

When you create a table, you also specify the data type for each field in the Table Design View. You can select data of the type Text, Number, Date/Time, Currency and logical (Yes/No). Note that Text fields can contain up to 255 characters, while Memo field can include text as large as 1 GB of characters.

OLE (Object Linking and Embedding) Objects enable you to insert graphics, sounds and other data types. Moreover, the Lookup data type will enable you to choose from a list of options. The Hyperlink data type enables you to launch an Access object (a table, form, query, etc.), in another file or in another application. The Attachment data type enables you to attach file from other program and the Calculated data type lets you to create a field that is based on a calculation of other fields in the same table. But, if you want to change the data type, then follow the mentioned steps:

➡ **To change the field's data type, do this:**

1. In the Navigation Pane, right click the table that you want to open and then choose Design View.
2. Move to the field and click the Data Type column, then choose the new data type you want.
3. Click Close button on the right side of the tab and choose Yes when prompted to save the changes.

7.6 SORTING OF TABLE

To sort records, you must specify the field that would be used as the reference. To do this, on the table or query, click a field under the column of your choice. To arrange the list in an alphabetical, incremental, chronological, or Boolean order, on the table or query, click the column header or a field under the column. Then, in the Sort & Filter section of the Home tab, click Ascending . You can also right-click to sort the list.

When you have finished sorting the records, it is sometimes important to reset the table before continuing unless you want to keep the list sorted. When you have sorted the values of a column, the down-pointing arrow button on the right side of the column header becomes equipped with an arrow.

7.6.1 Sorting Data in the Datasheet

One of the useful features of a database application is its capability to sort (arrange) data in particular order. The records displayed in the datasheet window can be sorted or arranged in any order on one or more columns merely by clicking the appropriate toolbar button. You can sort data in either ascending (first to last) or descending (last to first) order. To sort on more than one column, the columns must be adjacent to each other in the datasheet window. Access will sort the records starting with the leftmost column.

☞ To change the position of a column in datasheet view, click on its header and drag it to the desired location.

You can sort on any type of data type except OLE Objects and Attachment.

If you want to sort on multiple adjacent columns, simply select the columns by clicking in the column header for each column and then click the sort button or use the appropriate menu item. We shall now sort data in the EMP table.

➡ **To sort data in the Datasheet view, do this:**

1. Click on the desired column (here, we select the Name column).
2. Then click on the Home Tab.
3. In the Sort Filter group, click on the Ascending or Descending button whichever you want. After clicking the descending option, the result should look like the one given in Figure 7.30.

☞ To revert the data back to its original sort order, click under the Home Tab, in the Sort and Filter group and then click on the Clear All Sorts.

7.7 DATA VALIDATION

Validation is the process or rules which ensure that all data being added or edited in the records of a table meet specific conditions. A value entered in the specified field for a new record is compared against the expression in the validation rule field property.

7.7.1 Validation Rules and Validation Text

If the value being entered in a Table does not meet the validation rule, Access 2010 will display a message to the user. The message that is displayed is the entry that has been entered in

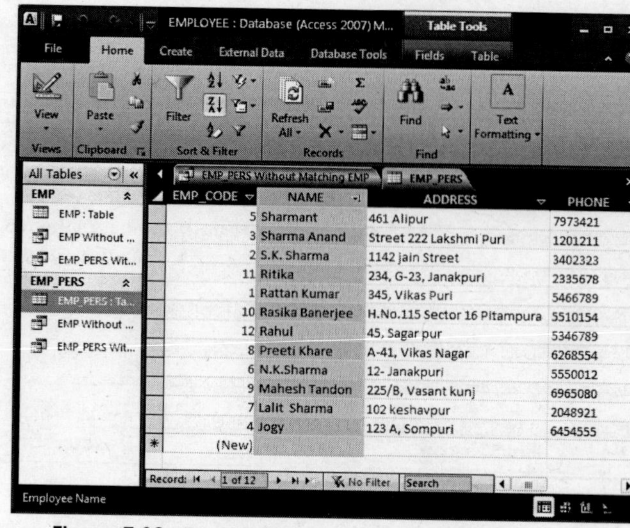

Figure 7.30 Result of the sorted data in the Name field

the Validation text field property. For example, if a company does not provide basic salary greater than Rs. 1,00,000, the validation rule <=1,00,000 could be created for the BASIC field. An entry similar to "Salary must be less than or equal to 1,00,000" and this could be used as the Validation text. The Validation rule can be entered at the time of creating a Table or while you modify the design of the Table.

➡ **To define Validation Rules in Table EMP, do this:**

1. Open the **EMPLOYEE** database.
2. In the Navigation Pane, right click the EMP table and then choose Design view (Figure 7.31).

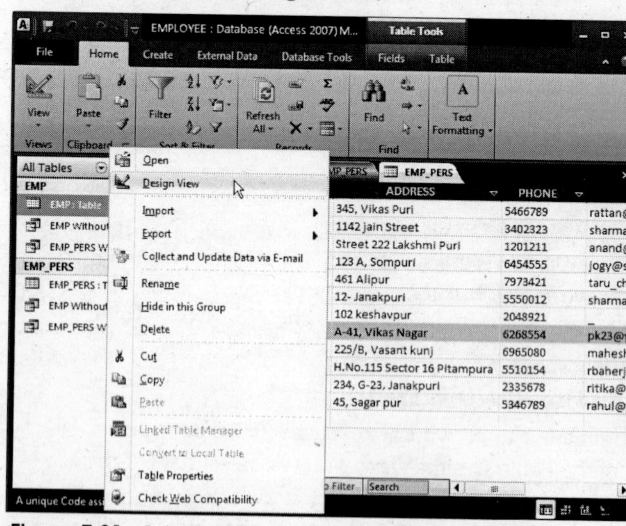

Figure 7.31 Selecting Design view by right clicking the mouse button

3. Define a validation rule that will only accept BASIC salary entry less than or equal to 1,00,000 by completing the following steps:

a. Place the insertion point anywhere within the field row named BASIC to display the Field Properties for the field.

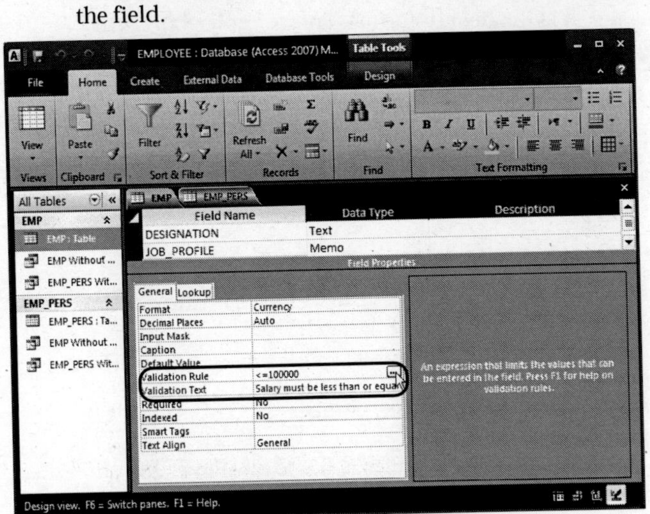

Figure 7.32 Validation Rule and Validation text box

b. Click on the Validation Rule text box in the Field Properties section (Figure 7.32).

c. Click the small button located at the right of this text box (See Figure 7.32). The Expression Builder dialog box appears (See Figure 7.33).

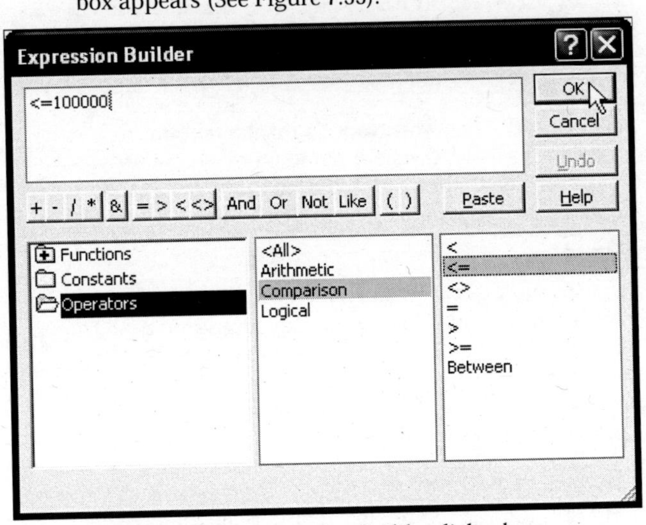

Figure 7.33 Expression Builder dialog box

d. Click Operators, then click Comparison and then double click the less than equal to sign (<=).

e. You will observe <= sign in the White area in the Expression builder. To the right of <= type 100000. Now click OK.

f. Type ***alar m st be less than or eq al to*** in the Validation Text box. (See Figure 7.33).

g. Click the Save button on the Table Design toolbar.

h. Click Yes at the prompt : "Data integrity rules have been changed; existing data may not be valid for the new rules. This process may take a long time. Do you want the existing data to be tested with the new rules?" (See Figure 7.34). Click Yes.

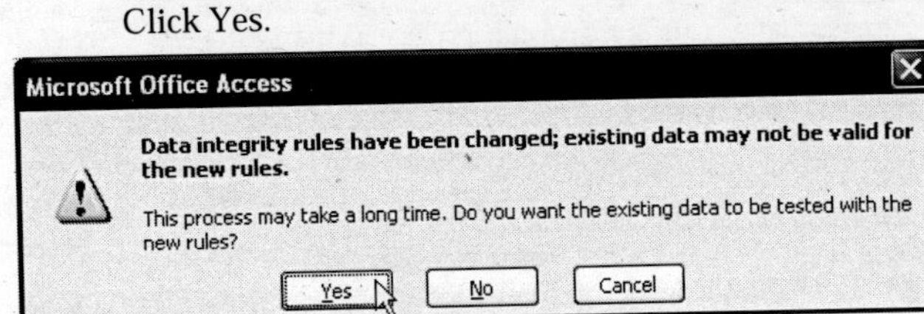

Figure 7.34 Defining Validation Rule for BASIC salary field of Employee Database

4. Test the validation rule by adding a new record to the table that violates the validation rule expression by doing the undermentioned steps.
   a. Open the **EMP** table by double clicking the Table.
   b. Click the last row to enter a New Record.
   c. Enter Production under **DEPARTMENT**, Chief Engineer under **DESIGNATION** and 110000 under **BASIC**.
   d. When you try to enter 110000 under the field BASIC, it displays a message ***alar m st be less than or eq al to*** as shown in Figure 7.35.
   e. Type the value 100000 for the Basic field and save the file.

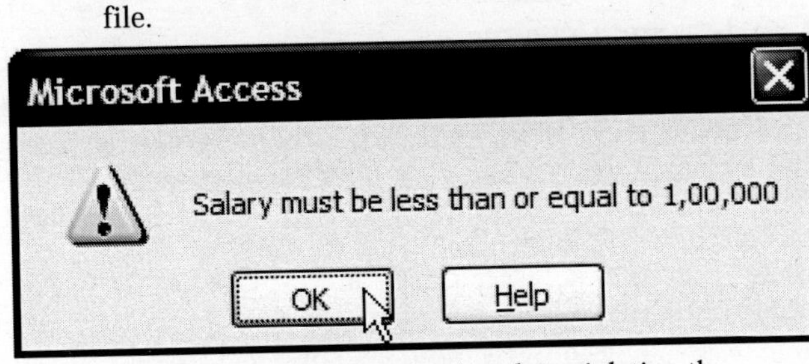

Figure 7.35 Message displayed on violating the Validation Rule for BASIC field

Field Size

Field size property is available for the Text and Number data types. For Text fields, the property specifies the maximum number of characters that can be stored in the fields for a single record. Access uses only enough disk space to store the data actually entered in the field–not the amount of space required to hold the number of characters specified by the Field Size property.

For Number fields, Field Size specifies the type of number that will be stored in the field. The available choices are:

- Byte (a number from 0 to 255, whole numbers only)
- Integer (–32,768 to 32,767, whole numbers only)
- Long Integer (–2,147,483,648 to 2,147,483,647, whole numbers only)
- Single (can store a very large number and fractional numbers)
- Double (stores numbers larger than Single)

- Replication ID
- Decimal

The choice made in this case does affect the amount available of disk space. The most common choices you will see are Integer, Long Integer and Double.

☞ Long Integer fields can store numbers larger than Integer. Double fields can store data with numbers to the right of the decimal point.

Field Properties: Format

Format property controls how the data is displayed. You can use predefined formats or customize your own. It allows you to display data in a format different from the way you actually stored data.

Text and Memo Formats

Access uses four user-defined format symbols in text and memo data types:

Format	Symbols
@	Required text character
$	Text character not required
<	Converts all characters to lowercase
>	Converts all characters to uppercase

Numeric and Currency Formats

You can choose from the following predefined formats and many other symbols for creating your own custom formats. The standard format property settings for numbers are shown below:

a) General Number: Displays numbers as entered. For example, you enter 2456.789, numbers are displayed as it is, i.e., 2456.789. General is the default format.
b) Currency: Uses thousand separator For example, 34,437 and displays negative numbers enclosed in parenthesis e.g. (32,015.25). The amounts are displayed to two decimal places.
c) Euro: Excel 2010 provides full support for entering the Euro sign and working with values in Euro currency.
d) Fixed: No rounding off is done. Generally its displays at least one digit with two decimal places. For example, 2456.79.
e) Standard: This property uses thousand separator with two decimal places. For example, 2,456.79.
f) Percent: This property multiplies the values by 100 and adds a percent sign. For example,, if you enter a value 6 in the field, it will show 600%. Similarly for the value entries 0.62, it will display 62%.
g) Scientific: This property uses standard scientific notation for displaying number.

Date/Time Format

You can define seven predefined options for Date/Time formats.

General Date: It is the default format. For example, 4/6/2016 11:50 AM.
Long Date: Thursday, Feb 5, 2017
Medium Date: 5-Feb-17
Short Date: 5/2/17
Long Time: 5:24:23 PM
Medium Time: 05:34 PM
Short Time: 17:34

Yes/No Format

Yes/No format is also known as logical format. The three predefined format settings for logical data type are:
Yes/No: It displays No, if the number is 0 and Yes for any other number.
True/False: It displays False if the number is 0 and displays True for any other number.
On/Off: Displays Off if the number is 0 and displays On for any other number.

Decimal Places

Decimal places are valid only for numeric and currency data. The decimal places number varies from 0 to 15 depending upon the field size. It specifies the number of decimal places to the right of the decimal.

☞ The decimal places property has no effect if the format property is set to general number.

Caption

Caption field is used when you want to display an alternate name for the field to make the field name more explanatory. For example, for field Emp_no caption can be set as Employee_No. It can contain up to 2,048 characters.

Default Value

The default value is used to specify the default value for a field or control, i.e., default value is displayed automatically for the field when you add a new record to the table. For example, for field country you might set default as 'India'. When users add records to the table, he/she can either accept this value or enter name of a different city.

Validation Rule or Validation Text

This property specifies an expression that defines data entry rules. Data validation enables you to limit values that can be accepted into a field. Validation may be automatic, such as invalid date (For example, 31st Feb) or you may define data validation rules that your field requires. For example, >= 5000 in the data validation rule box means that the value entered should be greater than or equal to 5000.

Validation text specifies the text of the message that appears if the field, control, or record does not satisfy the conditions listed in the validation rule setting. For example, in above case if you can write validation text as "Value must be greater than or equal to 5000". This message is displayed if the date entered violates the validation rule.

Data: Blanks, Nulls, and Zero-Length Strings

While entering information into table records, you can leave fields blank if it is not available. However, a blank field can mean more than one thing.

- It might signify that you do not know what the field's value is Or
- That a value for the field does not exist.

You can leave a field blank if you do not know what the value is (the value in this field is actually called a Null value). Access allows you to set the zero-length property, that is it decide whether a user can enter a zero length string or not. You can enter two quotes ("") side-by-side in the field to indicate there is no value.

Required Values

The Required Values Property specifies whether or not a value is required in a field. If the Required Values Property of a field is set to Yes, the user must enter a value in the field. Such a field cannot be left blank. If the Required Values Property is set to NO, the field can be left blank without entering any data into it. Figure 7.36 shows the message that appears when you leave a field, which has its Required Values Property set to Yes, blank.

☞ Required Value Property does not apply to AutoNumber field.

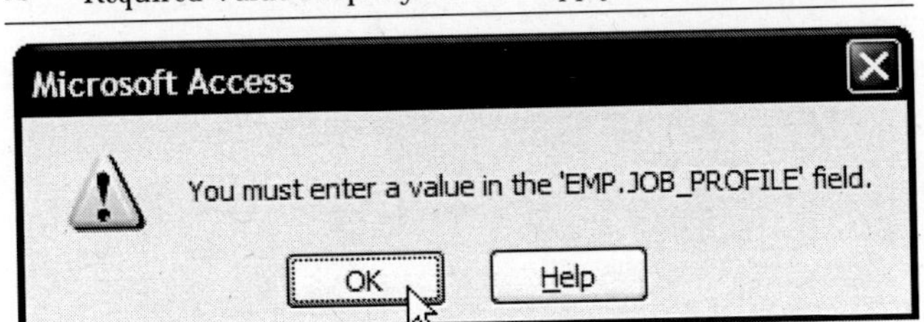

Figure 7.36 Error Message displayed on leaving a required field blank

Allow Zero Length

Allow Zero Length means that the user can enter a zero length string in a field. If the Allow Zero Length Property of a field is set to Yes, the user can enter zero length string, i.e., "". But if Allow Zero Length Property is set to No, the user cannot enter Allow Zero Length string. The field must then contain either some zero length string. The field must then contain either some value or NULL. Figure 7.37 shows the message that appears when a zero length string is added to the Department Field (Allow Zero Length Property of Department Field has been set to No).

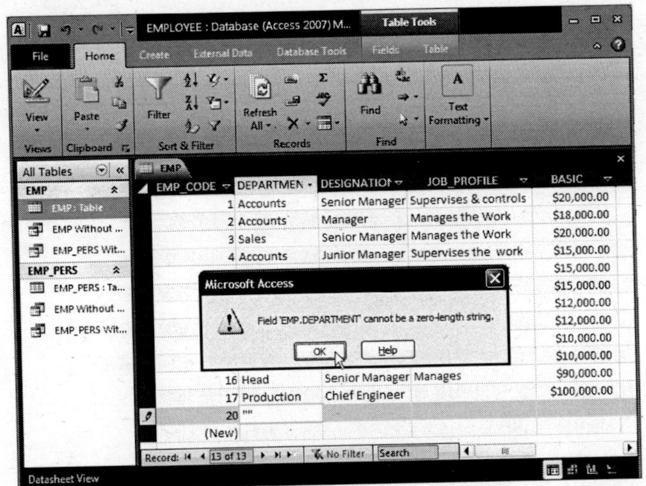

Figure 7.37 Error Message displayed on adding Zero Length string

☞ Allow Zero Length property applies to Text, Memo and Hyperlink fields only.

➡ **To set Allow Zero length/required values property, do this:**

1. Open the database **EMPLOYEE** you have created in the earlier Section.
2. In the Navigation Pane, right click the EMP table and then choose Design View.
3. Click the Department field. In the General tab at the bottom of the dialog box click Required: drop-down box and set the property to YES (See Figure 7.38).

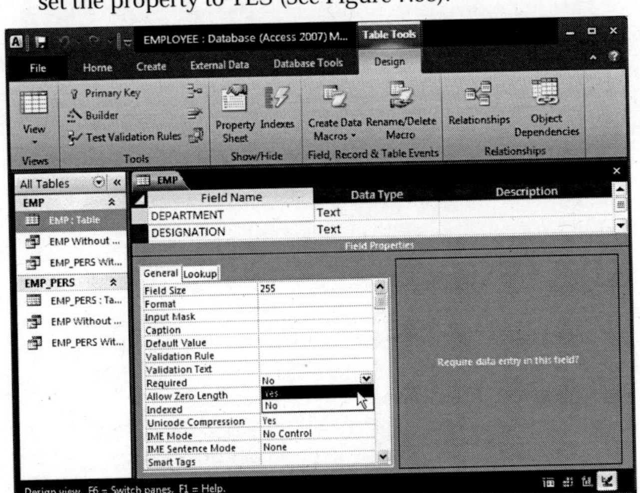

Figure 7.38 Set Required property of Department Field

Table 7.8 Results of setting Required Values and Allow Zero Length properties

Allow Zero Length	Required Values	Value Entered	Results
No	No	Press Enter	Null
		Enter ""	Not Allowed
Yes	No	Press Enter	Null
		Enter ""	Null
No	Yes	Press Enter	Not Allowed
		Enter ""	Not Allowed
Yes	Yes	Press Enter	Not Allowed
		Enter ""	Not Allowed

4. To set Allow zero length property, click the Designation field. In the General tab at the bottom of the dialog box click the Allow zero length: text box and Set the property to NO (Figure 7.39).

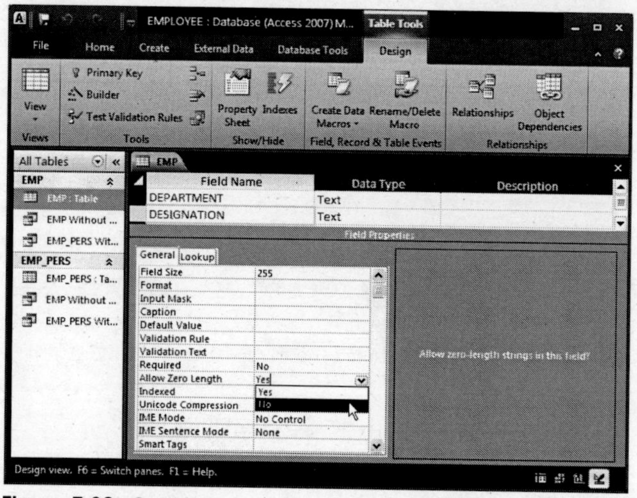

Figure 7.39 Set Allow zero length property of Designation field

The Table 7.8 shows the result of combining the settings of the Required Values and Allow Zero Length properties.

7.8 CREATING A TABLE USING DATASHEET VIEW

When you create a table through the Datasheet view, a spreadsheet like format appears. The data type and size of the fields are determined and table is created automatically. In Access, the rows of the table are called records and columns are called fields.

1. The Create tab on the Ribbon contains tools for adding new objects to your database. Each group on Create tab enables you to add a different types of objects to your database. The Table group offers three ways to create a table. Let's use the Table button, so that you can create the table in Datasheet view. When a table is selected, the Table Tools Fields and Table tabs become available on the ribbon. The Fields tab provides tools for commonly used commands when working in Datasheet view (See Figure 7.40).

Let's use Datasheet view to add a new table say emp_address.

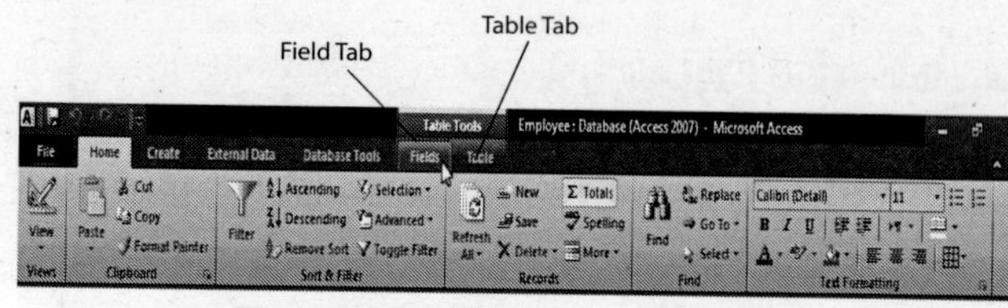

Figure 7.40 Field tab and Table tab

Clicking the Table button adds a new table to the Access environment (See Figure 7.41). The new table appears to Datasheet view in the area to the right of Navigation pane. Notice that the new table appears in Datasheet view with an ID column already inserted and a Click to Add column to the right of ID field. Click Create. Figure 7.42 shows an empty datasheet. The Click to Add column is intended to permit users to quickly add tables to an Access database. All that you do is start entering data in the new column. You can assign the fieldname by right clicking on the field's heading, selecting Rename Field option from the shortcut that appears. Now enter new name for the field. Or To change the field name, double click on the field name and enter the appropriate field label.

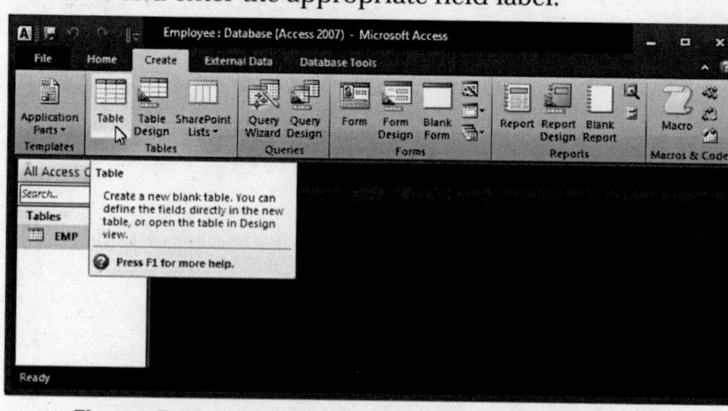

Figure 7.41 Creating New Table in Datasheet view

2. The width of the field can be increased or decreased by dragging the columns line to the right or to the left. To add new record in Datasheet view click the New Record button. Type in the values for all fields of the table, move between fields by pressing the Enter key or the Tab key.

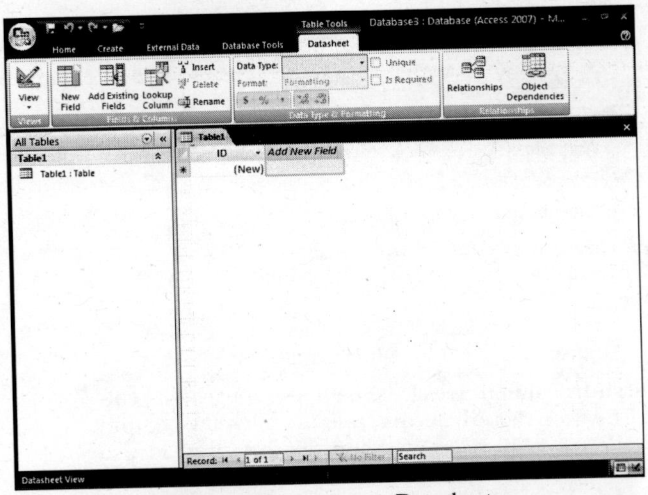

Figure 7.42 An empty Datasheet

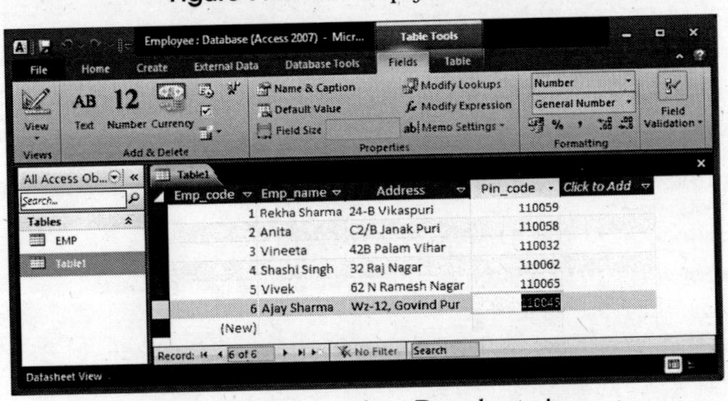

Figure 7.43 Records in Datasheet view

3. Enter the data records in the Datasheet as shown in Figure 7.43. To enter records simply click on the last row, which contains the asterisk(*). The asterisk turns into a pencil when you begin entering data, indicating that the record is being edited. A new row containing an asterisk appears below the one you are entering data into. The new record pointer always appears in the last row of the Datasheet.
If the record contains an AutoNumber field, Access shows the (New) in the field. You cannot enter a value in this type of field, rather simply press the Tab or Enter key to skip the field. Access automatically puts the number in when you begin entering data.
4. To save the table, choose either the close or the save option from the File menu. A Table Save As dialog box appears.
5. Enter the table name and click OK button (See Figure 7.44).

7.8.1 Add Records in Datasheet View

New records are always added after the last record in the table. To add new record you can click the New Record button in the navigation area. You can also click the new button in the Record group on the Home tab. There are a number of ways to add a record to the database.

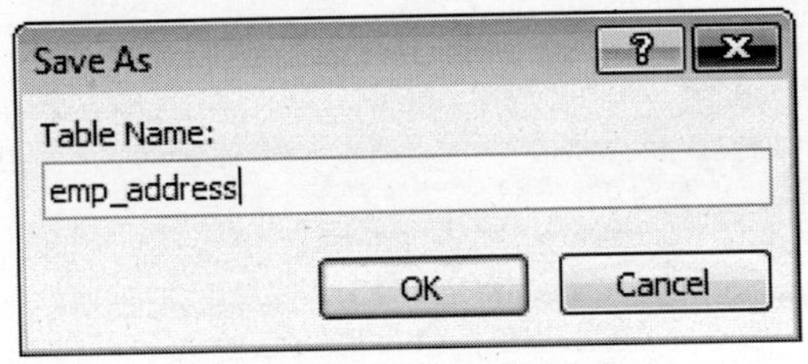

Figure 7.44 Save As dialog box

- Click on the datasheets last line, where the record pointer is an asterisk.
- Click the new record Navigation button (the furthest button on the right).
- Click the New command from the Ribbon's Records group.
- Click Goto New command from the Ribbon's Find group.
- Move to the last record and press the down arrow (↓) key.
- Press Ctrl++ (plus sign).

☞ The navigation area at the bottom of the window indicates the number of records in the table along with the number of currently selected record.

7.8.2 Editing Data in a Table

You can easily change the information in any field of any record. To edit data in a table, do the following:

1. Open the table in datasheet view, click any field in the table to position an insertion point in that field or you can double click on any word or number in a field to select it.
2. Make changes in data or type new data in a table. Once you have made changes in your record you need to save the record. To save the record, click on Save button in the Record group. When you make another record active, Access will automatically saves changes to the record you just changed.

7.8.3 Deleting record in a Table

1. Open the table in Datasheet view.
2. To delete records, select one or more records using the record selectors, then press the Delete command in the Ribbon's Record group. The Delete command's drop-down contains the Delete Record command, which deletes the current record, even if it's not selected. You can also delete record by right clicking on the records and choosing Delete Record from shortcut menu.

☞ You can select multiple rows or columns by pressing and holding the Shift key while clicking another row or column selector.

3. When you press Delete or choose the Ribbon command, a dialog box asks you to confirm the deletion (See Figure 7.45).
4. Click 'Yes' to permanently delete the record(s).

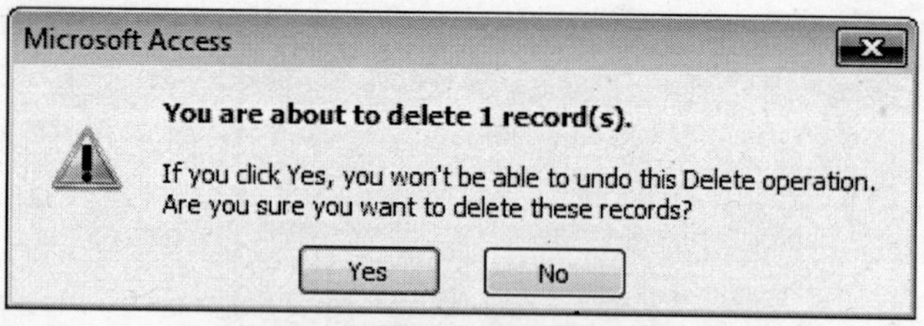

Figure 7.45 Delete dialog box

7.8.4 Hide a Column in a Datasheet View

You can temporarily hide a column so that you can view more columns in a larger datasheet.

To hide a column do the following:

1. Right click the column heading in Datasheet view to open the shortcut menu.
2. Click Hide Fields option from the shortcut menu.
3. Select the column heading in Datasheet view.
4. Click on More and choose Hide Fields option from the Records group.

You will see that the hidden columns are not displayed in Datasheet view (See Figure 7.46).

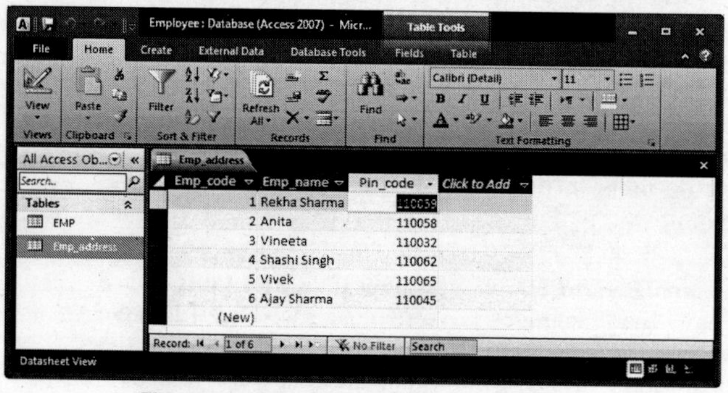

Figure 7.46 Address column is hidden

7.8.5 Unhide a Hidden column from Datasheet View

To unhide hidden columns, do the following:

1. Choose More Unhide columns option from Ribbon's Records group. The Unhide Fields dialog box appears as shown in Figure 7.47.
2. Select the check box next to each column that you wish to display.
3. Click on the Close button.

7.8.6 Freeze Columns

Freezing a field means that no matter how far you scroll in a datasheet, you will always see the frozen field, which become the leftmost column and are visible all the time. To freeze columns, do the following:

1. Open a table in Datasheet view.

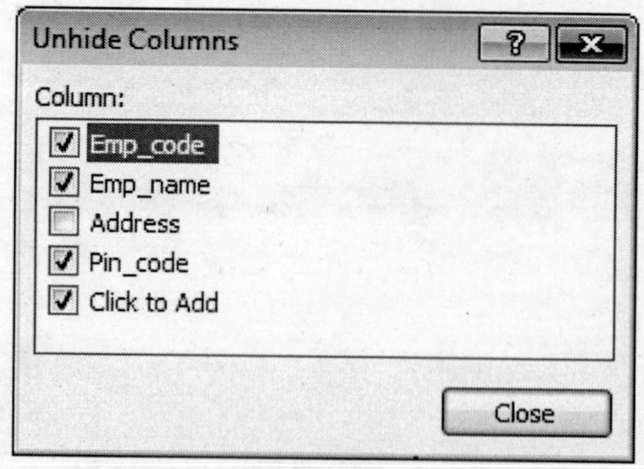

Figure 7.47 Unhide Columns dialog box

2. To select the column, select the field selector for that column. To select more than one column, click the column field selector and then, without releasing the mouse button, drag to extend the selection.
3. Click More Freeze Fields on the Ribbon's Records group. Or Right click to open shortcut menu and then select Freeze Fields option.

7.8.7 Unfreeze Columns

To unfreeze all columns, choose Unfreeze All Fields from More Unfreeze column option from Ribbon's Records group.

7.8.8 Insert a Field in Datasheet View

The steps to add a field to a table while you are working with in Datasheet view are as follows:

1. Right click the header (field name) of the field that will follow the new field.
2. Choose Insert Field from shortcut menu. Access will create a new field called Field1.
3. To rename the inserted field double click the field name. The field name will be highlighted and the cursor will appear to the left of the field name. Or you can right click the header of the new column (field) and choose Rename Field from the shortcut menu that appears.

7.8.9 Move a Field in Datasheet View

The steps to move a field are:

1. Click the column heading of the field you want to move to select it.
2. Drag the column heading of the selected column to the desired location.
3. When you drag the column heading, the mouse pointer changes to an arrow with a transparent rectangle under it.
4. This indicates that the selected column will be moved.

☞ The column will not move until you release the mouse button. As you drag the mouse a column border with a dark line appears down the border. This line indicates where the column will be placed when you release the mouse button.

7.8.10 Delete a Field in Datasheet View

1. Right click the header of the field you want to delete.
2. Choose Delete Column from the shortcut menu.
3. Choose 'Yes' to delete the field and all the data it contains from the table.

7.8.11 Insert a Lookup Field in Datasheet View

You can start the Lookup Wizard to create a drop-down field in the Datasheet View.

1. Right click the header of the field after the place you want to insert the lookup field (See Figure 7.48)

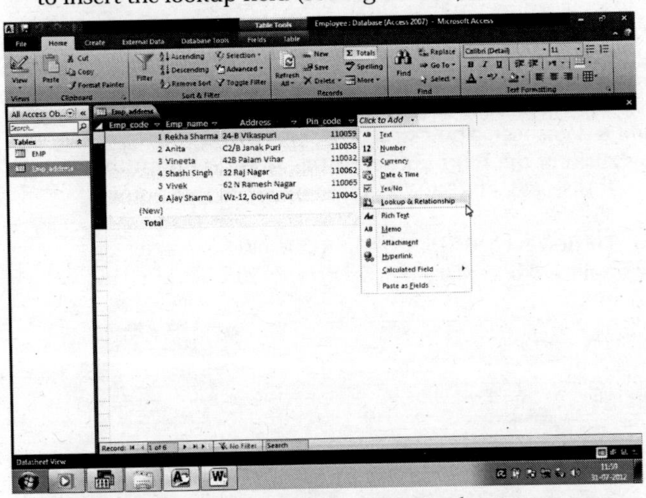

Figure 7.48 Look up column option in shortcut menu

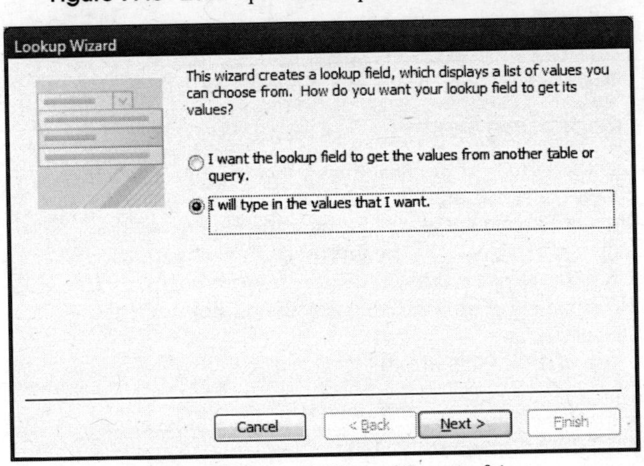

Figure 7.49 Look Wizard Step 1 of 4

2. Choose Lookup Relationship... from the shortcut menu.
3. The Lookup wizard screen will appear as shown in Figure 7.49.

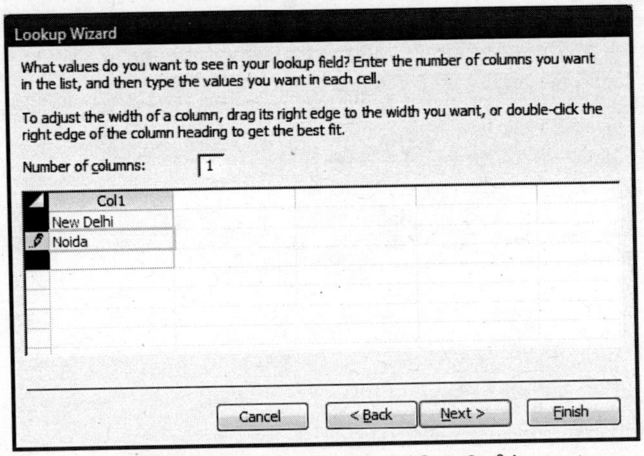

Figure 7.50 Lookup Wizard Step 2 of 4

4. Select 'I will type in the values that I want' and click Next > button. The next screen will appear as shown in Figure 7.50.
5. Enter the number of columns you want to see on the drop-down list in the columns shown in the dialog box. (See Figure 7.50).
6. In the Col1 area, first type New Delhi and then Noida. Click Next > button.
7. In the dialog box that appears (See Figure 7.51), type in a label that you would like for your lookup column.

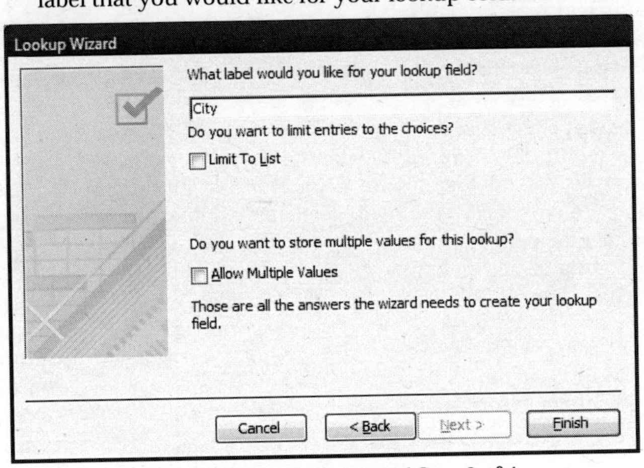

Figure 7.51 Lookup Wizard Step 3 of 4

8. Click Finish button.
9. Now Enter the following in the City field.

```
New Delhi
New Delhi
New Delhi
Noida
Noida
New Delhi
```

When you click on City field, a drop-down arrow will appear as shown in Figure 7.52. Click on it to display the list, click on the appropriate option to display the value.

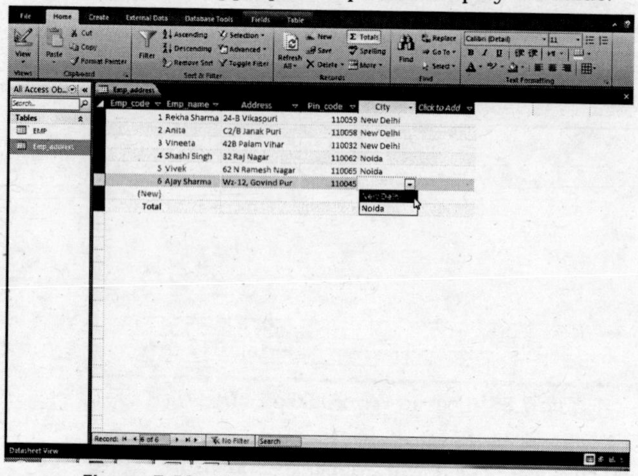

Figure 7.52 Choosing city from drop-down list

7.8.12 Adjust Datasheet Column width and Row Height

Open a table in Datasheet view.

Column Width

If you are unable to see all information in a column, you can increase the width of the field.

1. Right click the field column selector. A shortcut menu appears. Choose Field width command using the column width dialog box.
2. You can type any column width of the column. Choose to set the width of column to the standard width or choose the Best Fit button. (See Figure 7.53). The Best Fit button automatically determines the longest entry in the column and make the entire column width the length of the entry.

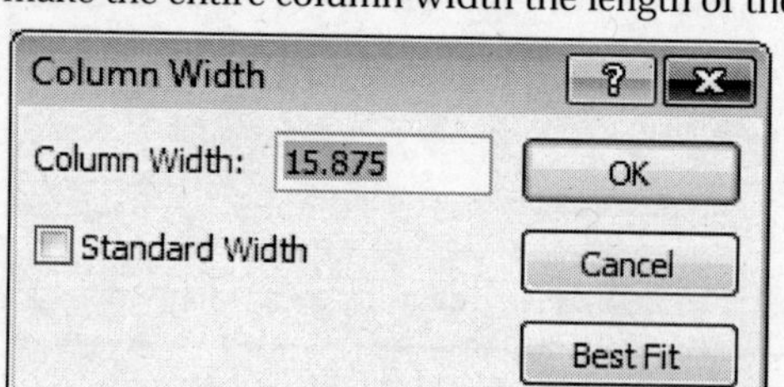

Figure 7.53 Column Width dialog box

Another way to resize a column to the width of its longest entry is to double click the right border of the fieldname in the column selector.

Row Height

1. Move the mouse pointer near the bottom border of a record selector.
2. When the pointer changes to an arrow head, click and drag the pointer up or down to resize the rows.

   or

   You can also increase row height by choosing More option from Record group . Choose Row Height from the short-cut menu that appears. It displays a dialog box as shown in Figure 7.54. Type new row height or click on Standard Height option. Now click on OK button.

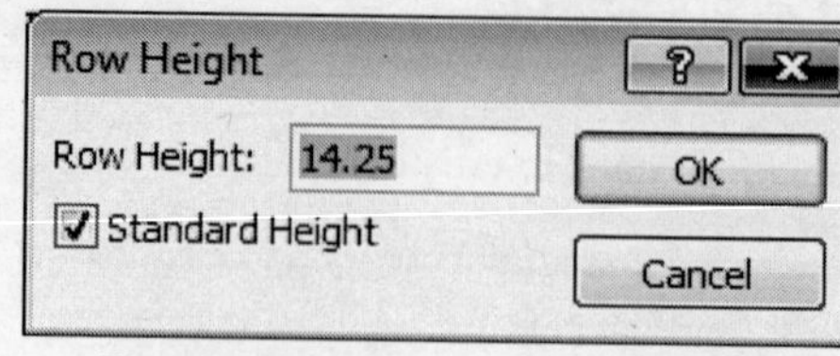

Figure 7.54 Row Height dialog box

7.8.13 Finding Text

Find feature is a powerful tool to search for specific information within a datasheet. You can search for specific records in a table by clicking the Find button in the Find group on the Home tab. It displays Find and Replace dialog box as shown in Figure 7.55.

Here you can find records that contains specific character or using the Replace tab, replace one occurrence of a set of character with another.

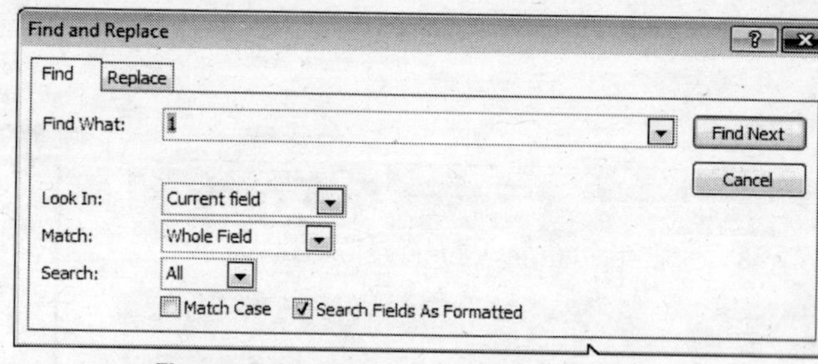

Figure 7.55 Find and Replace dialog box

7.8.14 Replacing Text

You can use the Find and Replace dialog box to simply locate a value. Instead of just finding it, you may want to replace the found value with an alternate. You can use the Replace section of the dialog box. To get it, in the Find section of the Ribbon, you can click the Replace button or you can press Ctrl + H. This would open the Find and Replace dialog box with the Replace tab selected:

1. In the Navigation Pane, double-click Emp_PERS: Table to open it
2. In the Find section of the Ribbon, click the Replace button. The Find and Replace dialog box appears as shown in Figure 7.56.
3. In the Find What: combo box, type Jogy
4. In the Replace With: combo box, type Joy.
5. In the Look In: combo box, select Current document.
6. In the Match: combo box, select Any Part of Field.

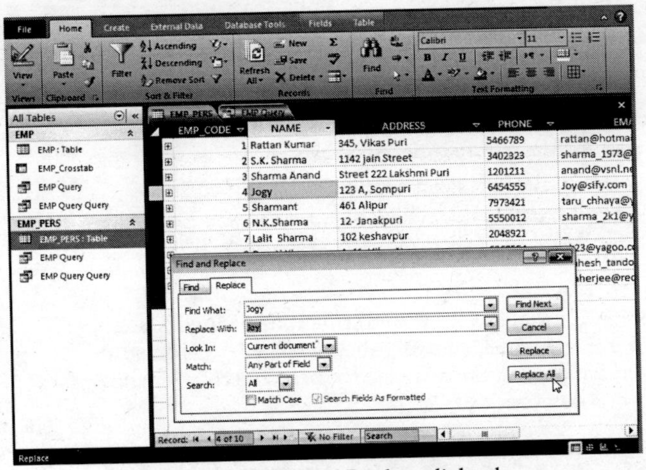

Figure 7.56 Find and Replace dialog box

7. Click Find Next
8. Once the value is found, click Replace or Relace All button.
9. Close the Find and Replace dialog box and close the Table.

7.8.15 Filtering Records

You can work with specific records in a table by filtering. Filtering allows you to display just the records that meet your criteria and hide the rest of the records temporarily. The filtering tools are located in the Sort and Filter group. The selection tool lets you to filter the table based on the value in the current field. For example, if you place the insertion in the first field of the Emp_address table that contains the City name 'New Delhi'. Clicking will display filtering option for the value "New Delhi" (See Figure 7.57).

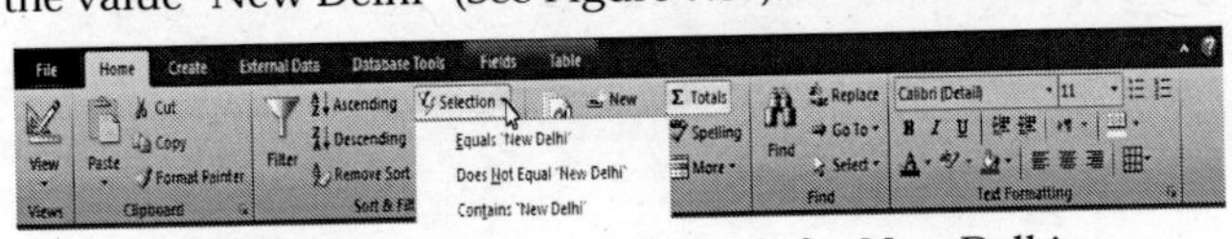

Figure 7.57 Selection of records for New Delhi

Now you can choose to display records where city fields contain only the word "New Delhi" by clicking on Equals "New Delhi". It will display only the records that contains New Delhi as the city name (See Figure 7.58).

To remove the filter and restore the display of all records click the Remove Filter button in the Sort & Filter group. See Figure 7.59.

7.8.16 View Table in Design View

To view the table structure, click on Design view from views group.

7.9 RELATIONSHIPS

Relationships are those attributes defined from one table to another in the same database.

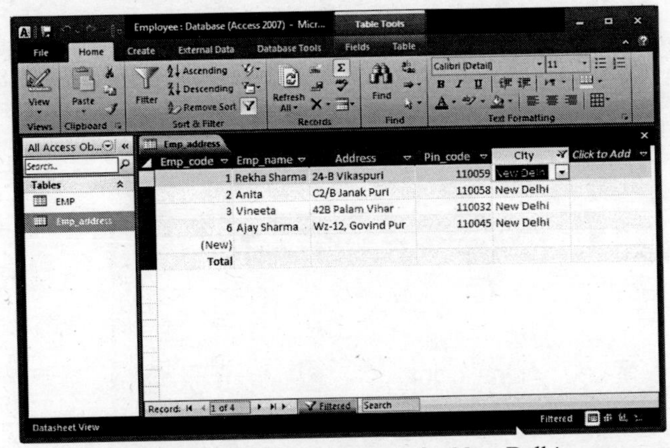

Figure 7.58 Filtered records for New Delhi

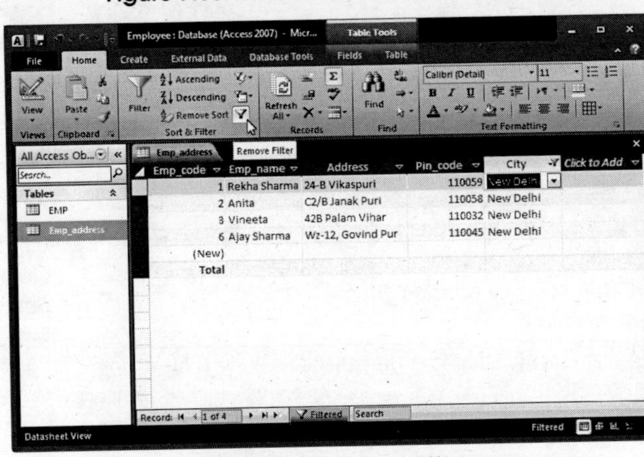

Figure 7.59 Remove Filter

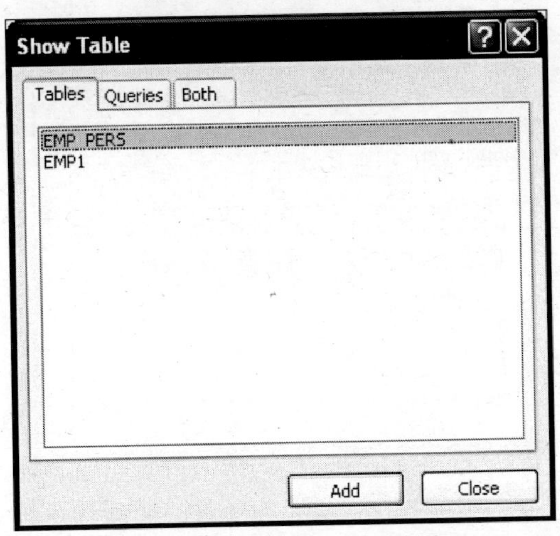

Figure 7.60 Show Table dialog box

➡ **To create relationships between Tables, do this:**

1. Open the EMPLOYEE database.
2. Under the Database Tools, in the Relationships group, click Relationships.

3. A Show Table dialog box appears as shown in Figure 7.60. In this dialog box, in Tables Tab, select one or more tables and Click Add button.
4. Then click Close button.
5. Now drag fields (primary key) from one table to the common field (foreign key) in the other table.
6. After that Edit Relationships dialog box appears as shown in Figure 7.61.

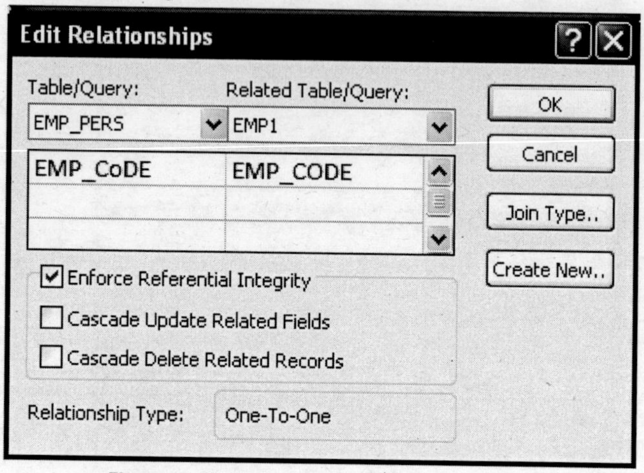

Figure 7.61 Edit Relationships dialog box

7. In this dialog box, verify the fields name shown that are common field for the relationship.
8. Then Click Create.

☞ If you create relationship first time then the Show Table dialog box automatically appears. If it does not appear, click under the Design tab, in the Relationships group, click Show Table.

Access 2010 makes a relationship between tables by lines (Figure 7.62).

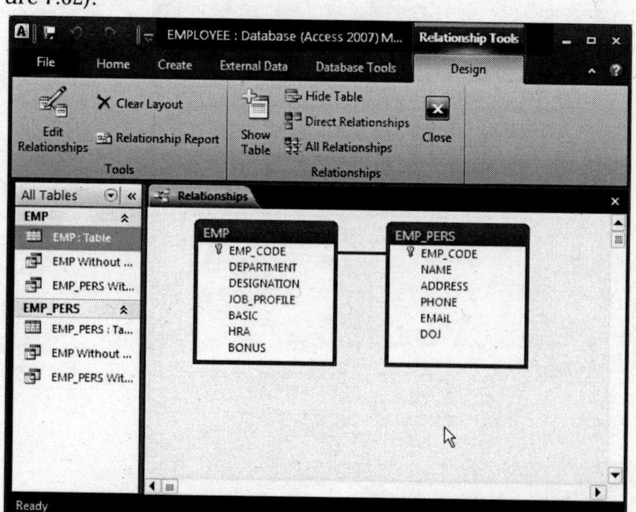

Figure 7.62 Relationship between Table

➡ **To delete relationships, do this:**

1. Open the EMPLOYEE database.
2. Under the Database Tools, in the Relationships group, click Relationships. A Relationships window appears as shown in Figure 7.62.
3. Click Under the Design Tab, in the Relationships group, then click All Relationships. All tables that have relationships are displayed, showing relationship lines.
4. Click the line of that relationship which you want to delete. When you select the line, the relationship line appears thicker.
5. Press Del key.
6. Access 2010 displays the confirmation dialog box as shown in Figure 7.63, showing the message "Are you sure you want to permanently delete the selected relationship from your database?"
7. Click Yes.

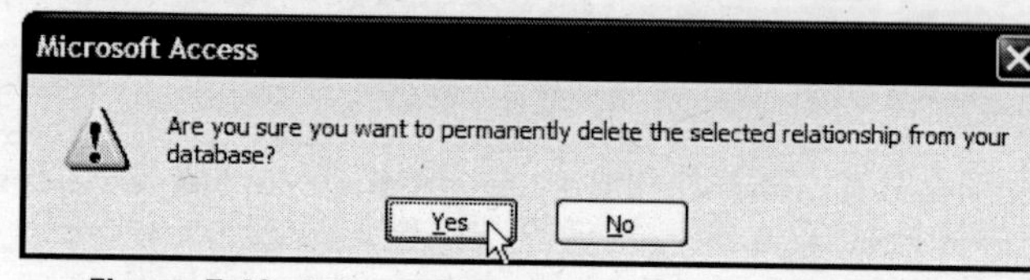

Figure 7.63 Microsoft Access Confirmation dialog box

7.10 WHAT ARE QUERIES?

Queries are questions you ask from database. Access 2010 has powerful search capabilities. For example, suppose from the **EMP_PERS** database you want to know how many Employees have surname Sharma? Such an enquiry can be easily put to Access and you will get the answer very fast. In the above example, you would ask Access to display a list of all the Employees with surname Sharma.

☞ Queries that are used to retrieve data from a table or to make calculations are called Select queries. Queries that add, change, or delete data are called Action queries.

Access lets you to create queries in two ways:

- Using the query wizard
- Using the design view

☞ You cannot undo the results of a delete query. Therefore, you should back up your database before deleting a query.

7.10.1 Creating Query using the Query Wizard

When you create a query using the query wizard, the wizard guides you through a series of dialog boxes where you make the selection for the query.

Simple Query

A simple query strips away fields so that you can see only the fields that you want to see.

➡ **To create a simple query using the Query Wizard, do this:**

1. Click under the Create tab, in the Queries group and then click Query Wizard (See Figure 7.64).

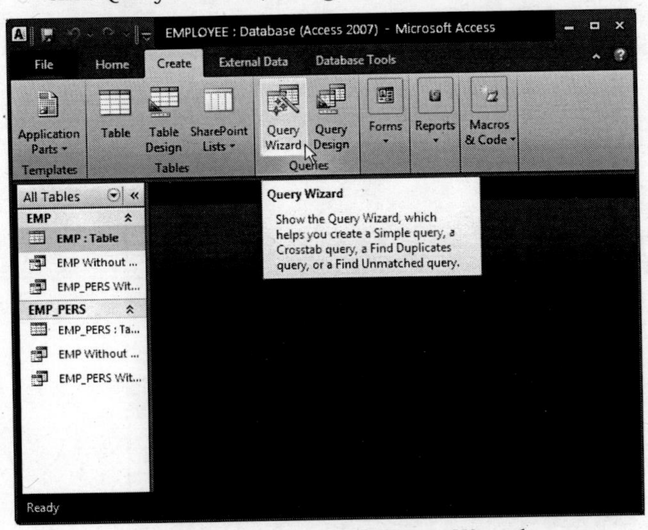

Figure 7.64 Query using Query Wizard

2. A New Query dialog box appears as shown in Figure 7.65. In this dialog box, click Simple Query Wizard and then click OK.

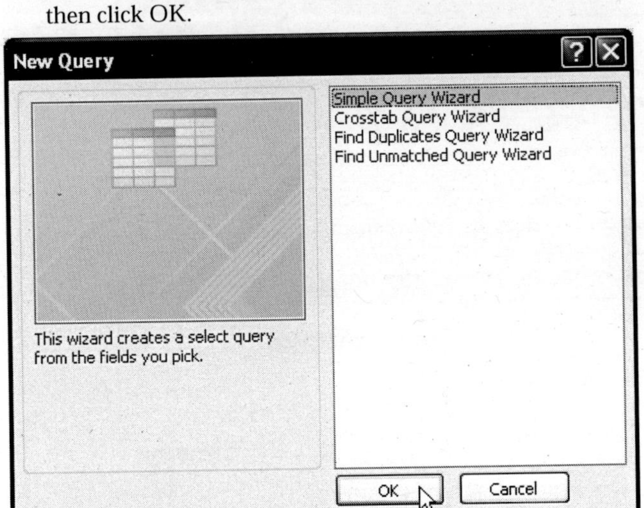

Figure 7.65 New Query Dialog Box

3. In the Simple Query Wizard dialog box (See Figure 7.66), from the Table/Queries: list box, select any previously, made query or table, on which you want to base your new query.
4. From the Available Fields: area select the fields which you want in your query, then click > button. The selected fields will move to Selected Fields: area. If you want to select all the fields present in the Available Fields: area click the >> button.

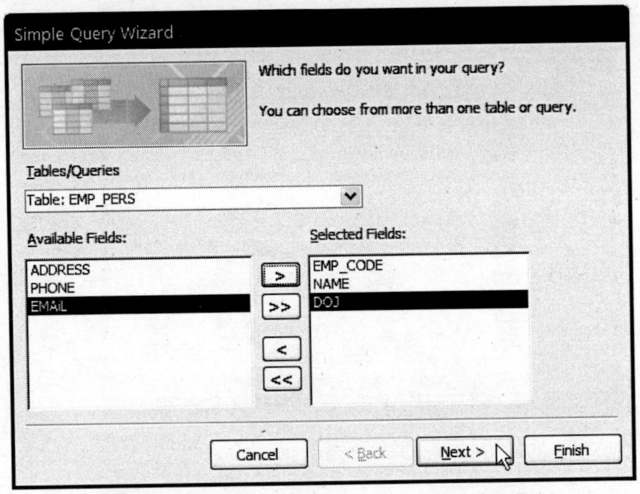

Figure 7.66 Simple Query Wizard Dialog Box

5. To remove a field from the Selected Fields: area click the < button. To remove all the fields, click the << button.
6. Click Next > button.
7. In the dialog box that appears as shown in Figure 7.67 type a title for your Query. Then click Finish.

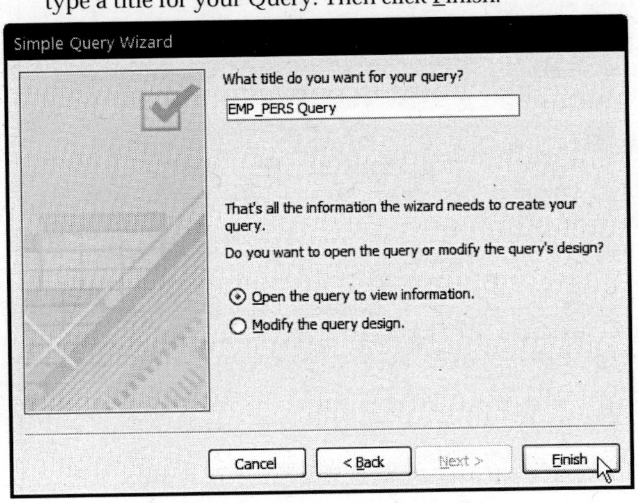

Figure 7.67 Provide a title for the Query

Access 2010 displays the result of the query in a Datasheet View as a separate tab as shown in Figure 7.68.

Crosstab Query

A crosstab query lets you to combine two or more fields to calculate and display a calculation based on a third field.

➡ **To create a crosstab query using the Query Wizard, do this:**

1. Click under the Create tab, in the Queries group and then click Query Wizard. (See Figure 7.64).
2. A New Query dialog box appears as shown in Figure 7.65. In this dialog box, click Crosstab Query Wizard and then click OK.

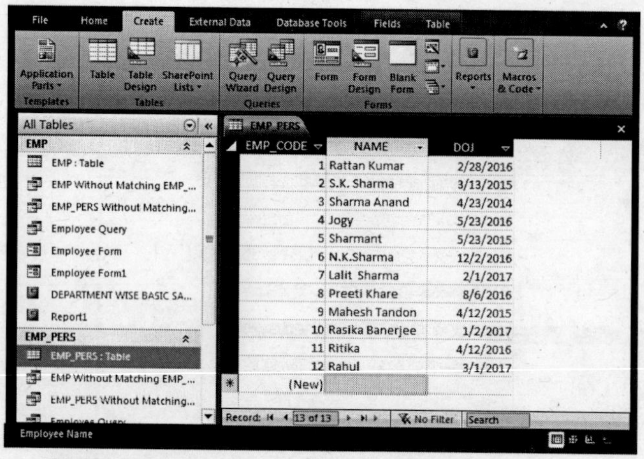

Figure 7.68 Simple Query Result in a Datasheet View

3. In the Crosstab Query Wizard dialog box (See Figure 7.69), click the table name and click Next >.

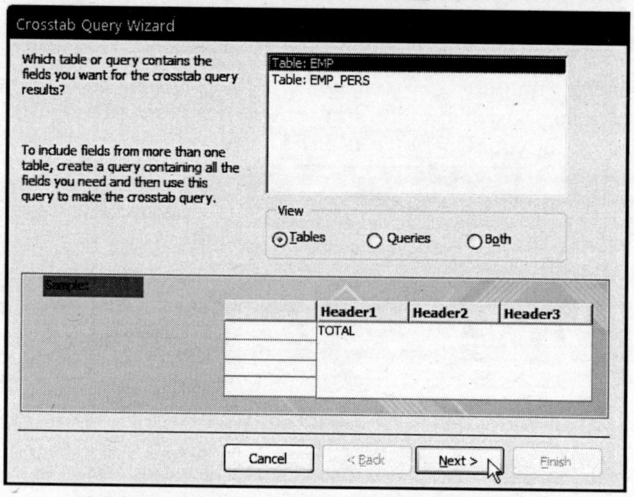

Figure 7.69 Crosstab Query Wizard Dialog Box

4. Another dialog box appears that asks for the fields (See Figure 7.70). From the Available Fields: area select the fields which you want in your query, then click > button. The selected fields will move to Selected Fields: area. If you want to select all the fields present in the Available Fields: area click the >> button.
5. To remove a field from the Selected Fields: area click the < button. To remove all the fields, click the << button and then Click Next >.
6. In the dialog box that appears (See Figure 7.71) asking for a single field to use to crosstabulate data with the field you choose from last dialog box as shown in Figure 7.70.
7. In this dialog box, selected field should consist text information that lists different data. But if you choose field that contains numerical data, your crosstab query will appear meaningless. Click the field and then click Next >.

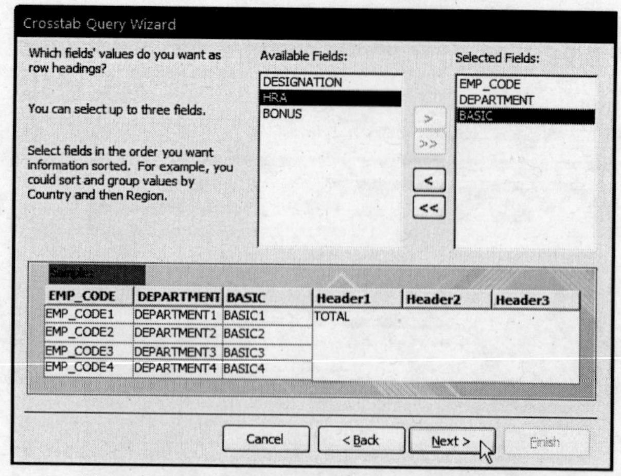

Figure 7.70 Selecting the Field for the query

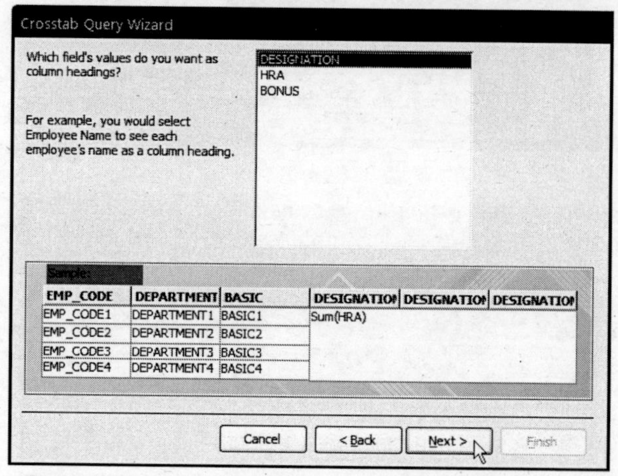

Figure 7.71 Select the Field containing text information

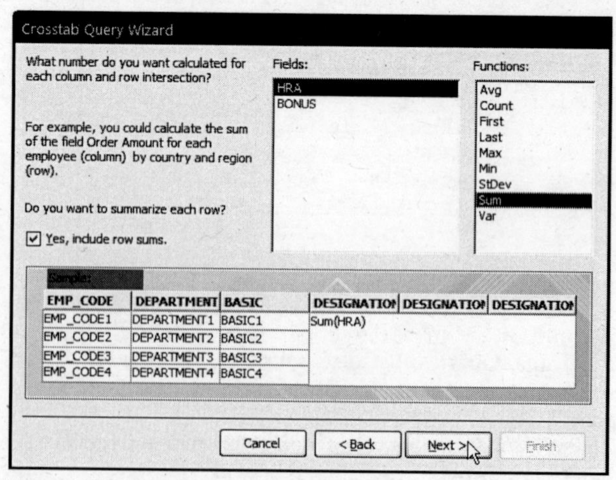

Figure 7.72 Select the Field containing numeric information

8. Another dialog box appears as shown in Figure 7.72. Click a field that contains numerical data and then click mathematical function that you want to Access to calculate sum, average or count and then click Next >.

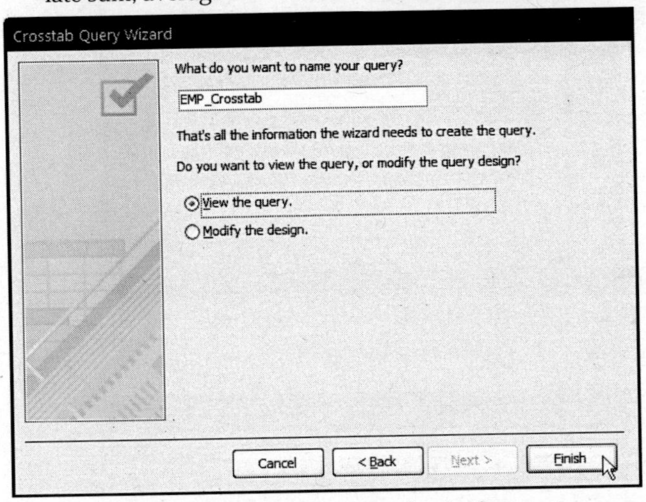

Figure 7.73 Provide a name for the Query

9. In the dialog box that appears as shown in Figure 7.73 type a name for the Query. Then click Finish.

Access 2010 displays the result of the query in a Datasheet View as a separate tab as shown in Figure 7.74.

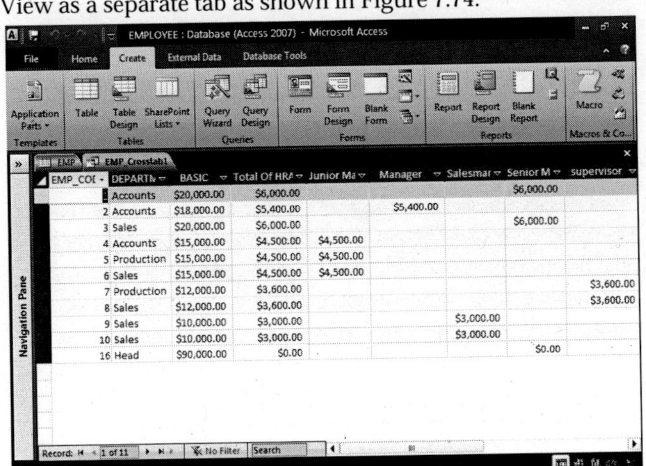

Figure 7.74 Result of the Crosstab Query in Datasheet View

Finding Duplicate Items

Suppose, on the same day several employees had joined the company. But how can you find on the particular day who had joined. For this you could search database manually. It is very time consuming. But, with the help of Access 2010, you can create a query that finds the duplicate data items in the database.

➡ **To create a query to find duplicate field data, do this:**

1. Click under the Create tab, in the Queries group and then click Query Wizard. (data with the field you choose from last dialog box as shown in Figure 7.72.

2. A New Query dialog box appears as shown in Figure 7.65. In this dialog box, click Find Duplicates Query Wizard and then click OK.

3. In the Find Duplicates Query Wizard dialog box (See Figure 7.75), click the table name that you want to search and click Next >.

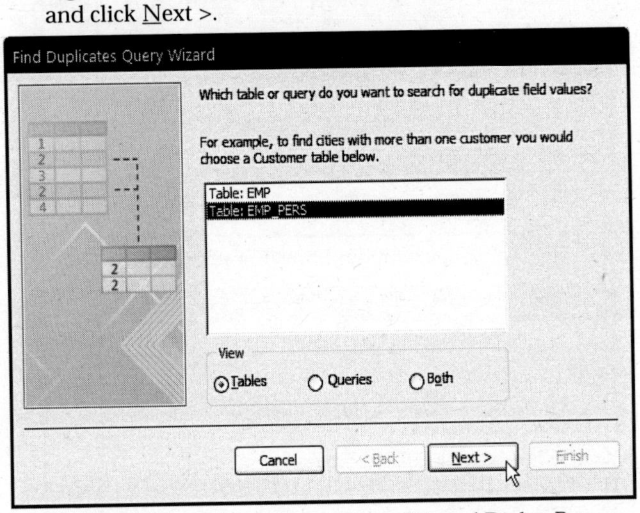

Figure 7.75 Find Duplicates Query Wizard Dialog Box

4. In the dialog box that appears (See Figure 7.76), asking you to choose the fields which contains duplicate information. Click a field name and then click > button and then click Next >.

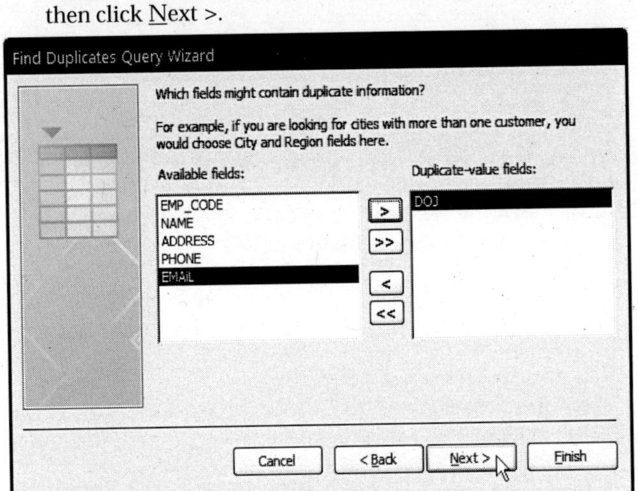

Figure 7.76 Dialog box to select fields which contain duplicate information

5. In the dialog box that appears (See Figure 7.77), asking whether you want to display any additional field. Click a field name and then click > button and then click Next >.

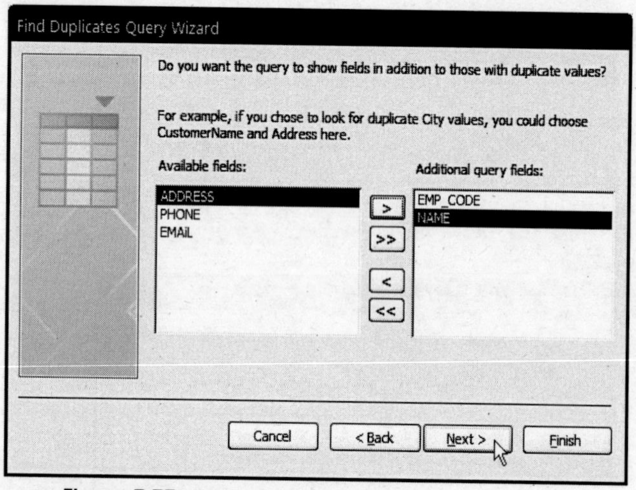

Figure 7.77 Dialog box with duplicate information

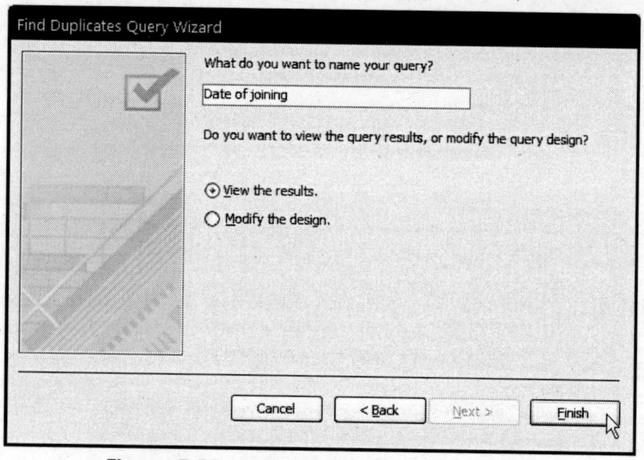

Figure 7.78 Provide a name for the Query

6. Another dialog box appears as shown in Figure 7.78. Here, you have to give the name for the query. After giving name, click Finish.

Access 2010 displays the result of the query in a Datasheet View as a separate tab as shown in Figure 7.79.

Find Unmatched Query

An unmatched query examines two (or more) tables to look for missing information.

➡ **To create an unmatched query, do this:**

1. Click under the Create tab, in the Queries group and then click Query Wizard (See Figure 7.64).
2. A New Query dialog box appears as shown in Figure 7.65. In this dialog box, click Find Unmatched Query Wizard and then click OK.
3. In the Find Unmatched Query Wizard dialog box (See Figure 7.80), click the table name that you want to search and click Next >.

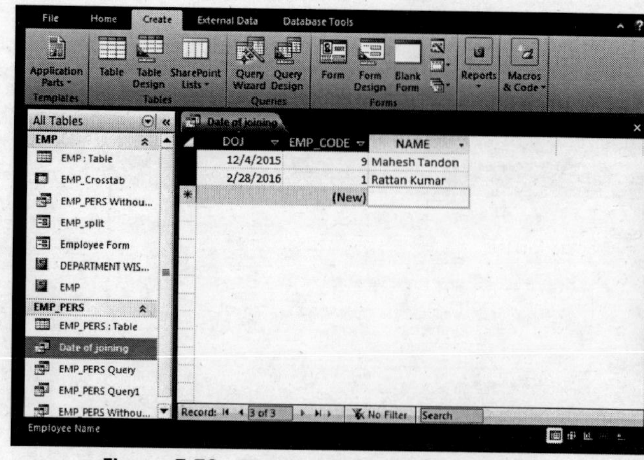

Figure 7.79 Result of Find Duplicates Query

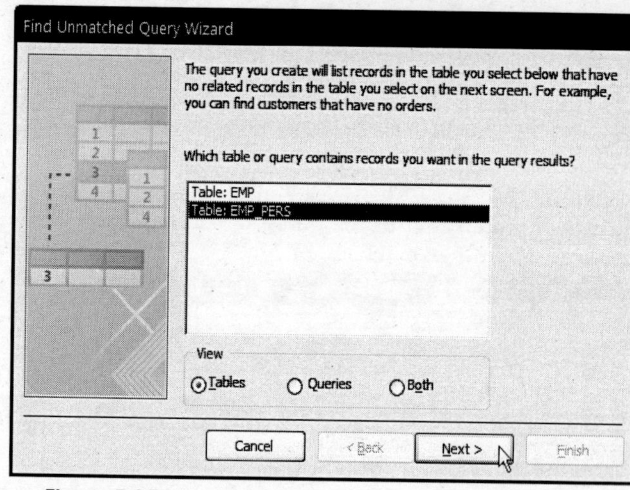

Figure 7.80 Find Unmatched Query Wizard Dialog Box

4. In the dialog box that appears (See Figure 7.81), asking you to choose a table that contains at least one field that also appears in the table you choose earlier. Click a second table and then click Next >.
5. In the dialog box that appears (Figure 7.82), asking you to identify the field that both database tables have in common. Click on the common field that both database tables share. (In our case, it is EMP_CODE).
6. Click on the gray <=> button that appears between the two fields and then click Next >.
7. Another dialog box appears (See Figure 7.83) that asks for the fields From the Available Fields: area select the fields which you want in your query, then click > button. The selected fields will move to Selected Fields: area. If you want to select all the fields present in the Available Fields: area, click the >> button and then Click Next >.

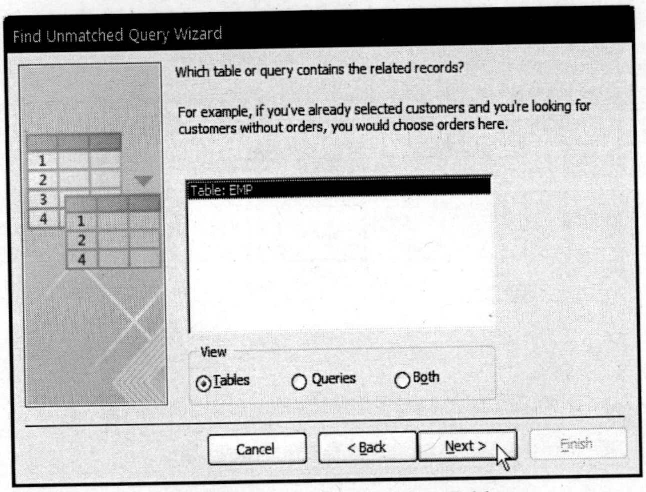

Figure 7.81 Choose Another Table

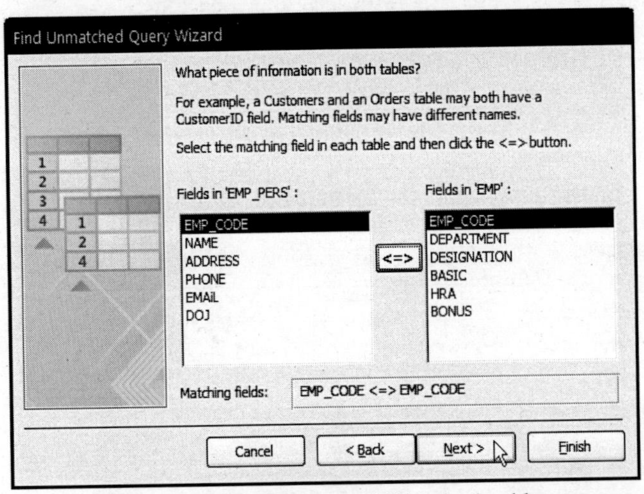

Figure 7.82 Identify same field in both tables

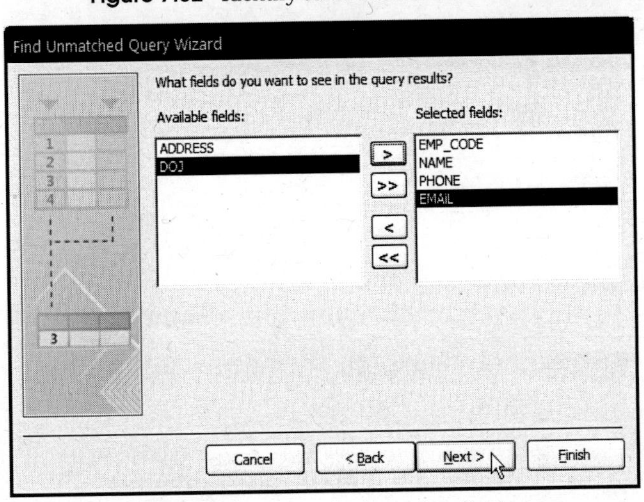

Figure 7.83 Dialog box to select fields

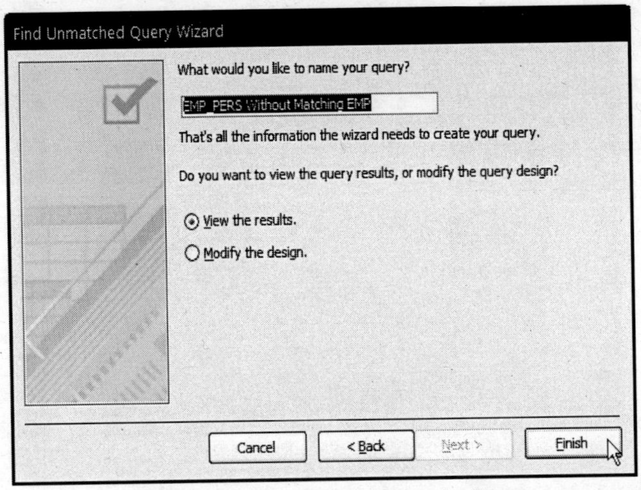

Figure 7.84 Provide a name for the Query

8. Another dialog box appears as shown in Figure 7.84. Here, you have to give the name for the query. After giving name, click Finish.
Access 2010 displays the result of the query in a Datasheet View as a separate tab as shown in Figure 7.85.

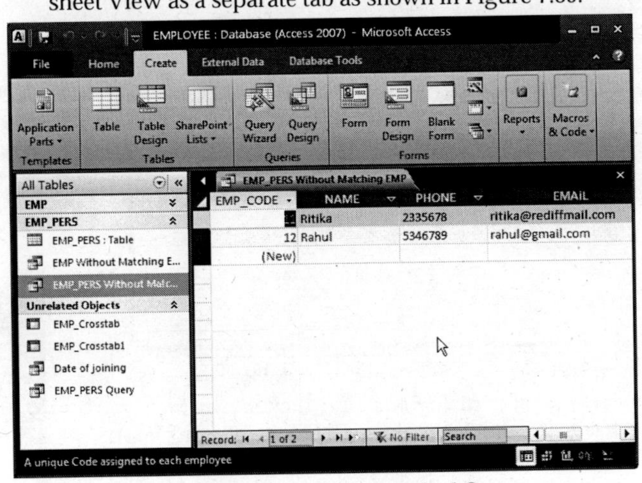

Figure 7.85 Result of Unmatched Query

7.10.2 Creating Query using the Design View

When you use the Design view, you have more control over the query and Access 2010 lets you to create complete queries in the Design view.

➡ **To create queries using the Design View, do this:**

1. Click under the Create tab, in the Queries group and then click Query Design (See Figure 7.86).
2. It will display Show Table dialog box as shown in Figure 7.87. In this dialog box, click Simple Query Wizard and then click OK.

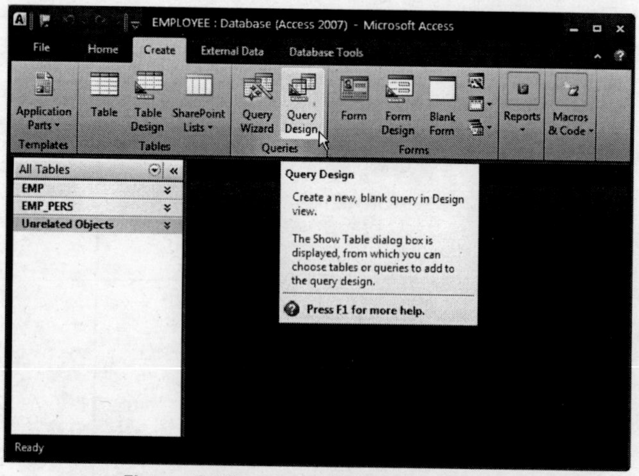

Figure 7.86 Query using Design View

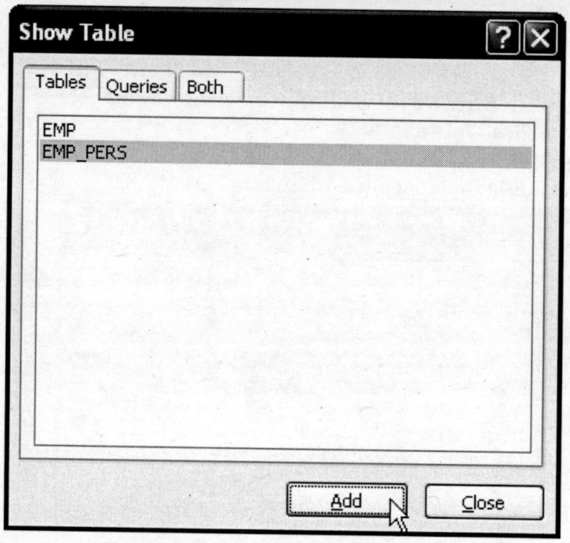

Figure 7.87 Show Table Dialog Box

3. In the Show Table dialog box, add the tables which you want in the query. Select the **EMP** and **EMP_PERS** tables and click Add button. After that click Close button.
4. Notice that the tables already have proper relations displayed. (See Figure 7.88). Because we have already created a relationship between these tables in the last Chapter.
5. Drag the fields you want in your query from the tables to the Field: row as shown in Figure 7.88.
6. The Table: row automatically gets filled up.
7. The sort order determines how the records are ordered when the query executes. Sort is specified in the drop-down list of Sort: row. From the drop-down list box choose Ascending, Descending or Not Sorted. The default is Not Sorted.
8. In the Criteria: row, add any criteria you want in the query.

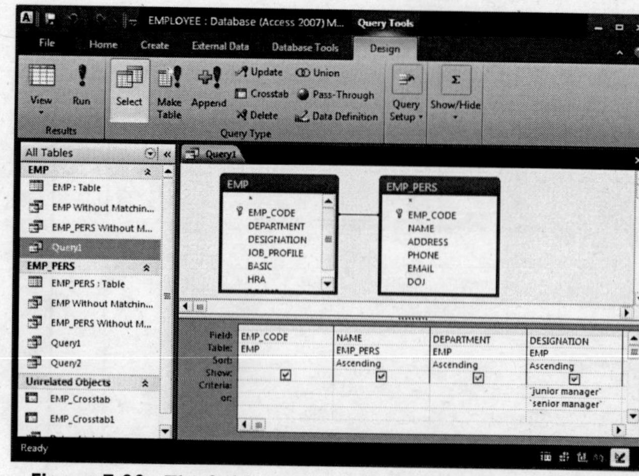

Figure 7.88 The fields are dragged from the Tables into the Field: row

9. In the Criteria: row and in the Column of DESIGNATION, type the expression "junior manager". This will lead to the display of details of only those employees who are junior managers.
10. Alternative conditions can be entered in the or: row, say "senior manager".
11. To view the query, click the Design Tab, in the Results group, click on the Run button. You will see all the employees with the information from the fields you selected in a Datasheet View as a separate tab as shown in Figure 7.89.
12. Click the Save button and enter a name for the Query. We have supplied the name "Employee Query".

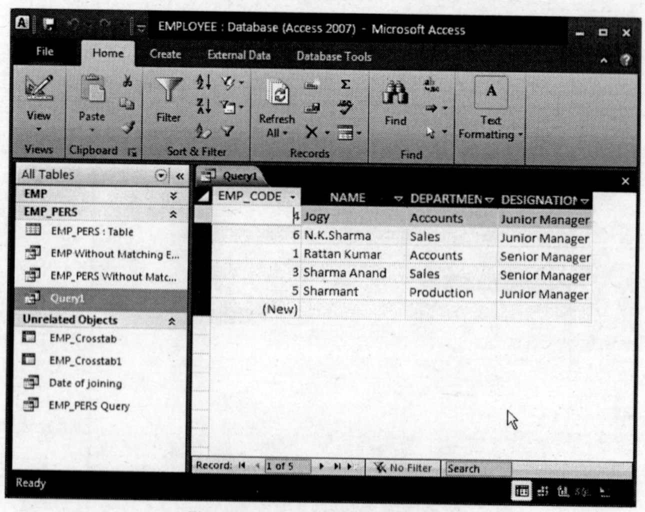

Figure 7.89 Query Result

Criterians are restrictions you place on a query or an advanced filter to identify the specific records you want to work with. For example, instead of viewing the details of all employees, you can choose to have a list of those employees who are drawing a basic salary greater than Rs 10,000. For this you have to enter an expression in the Criteria field. You can use expressions like ">10000", or "Between 1000 and 5000", etc.

➡ **To open/modify an existing query, do this:**

1. In the Navigation pane, from the list of queries that appear, right click the query which is to be modified and then click Design View option to modify the query as shown in Figure 7.90.
2. Click the Open option to run the query and see its preview.

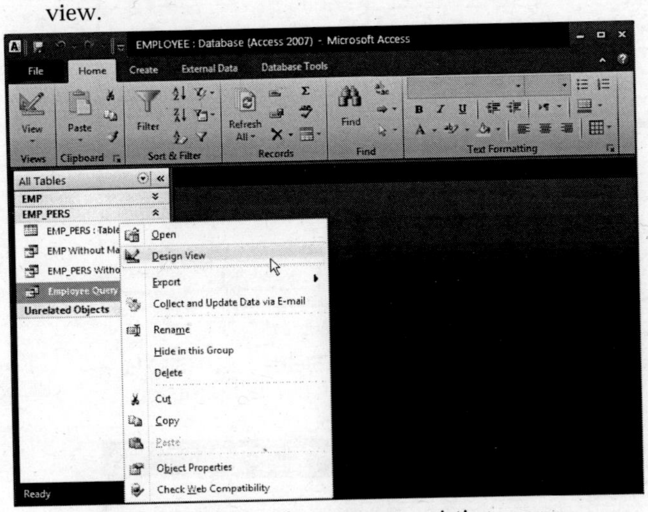

Figure 7.90 Modify or open an existing query

7.11 ADD CRITERIA TO THE QUERY

To restrict the records that are returned in the query results, you can specify one or more criteria.

You can think of a query criterion as a condition that you specify for a field. The criterion specifies a condition, based on field values, that expresses what you want to include in the query, such as "show only those records where the surname of Name field is Sharma".

☞ The LIKE operator is used to match the string pattern. Special characters '*' and '?' are used with LIKE operator to specify a pattern. * is for zero or more character but, ? is for single character.

➡ **To add a criteria to the query, do this:**

1. In the Navigation pane, from the list of queries that appear, right click the query which is to be modified and then click Design View option to open the query in Design view as shown in Figure 7.90.
2. In the Criteria: row of the Name field, type Like *Sharma as shown in Figure 7.91.
3. Switch to Datasheet view to see the results (Figure 7.92).

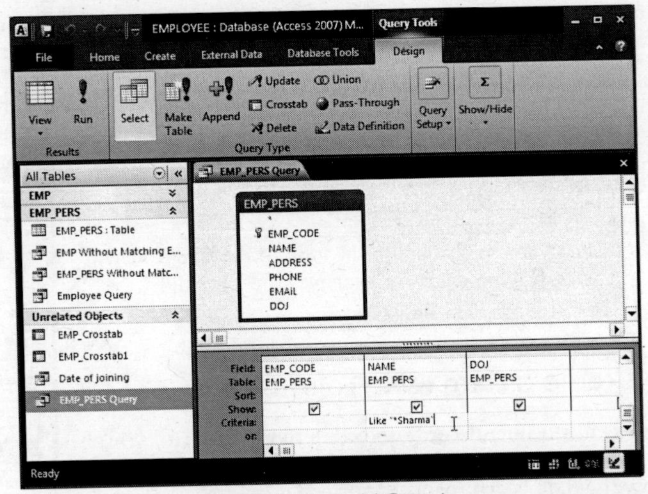

Figure 7.91 Add Criteria

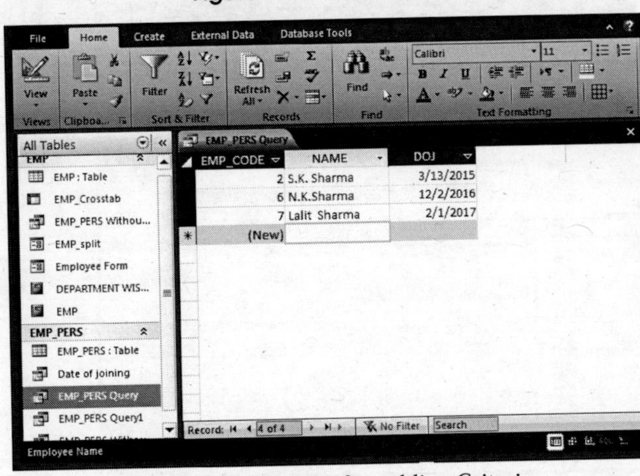

Figure 7.92 Result after adding Criteria

7.12 WHAT ARE FORMS?

Forms provide you a "template" that you fill in whenever you enter a record. The form displays a blank box for each field in the table. Data entry thus becomes a simple matter of filling in the appropriate boxes. All the information which a form shows is contained in controls. Controls are the objects that display data, perform certain actions and create special effects on the form. Text boxes, labels, list boxes, option buttons, push buttons and command buttons are examples of various controls.

In this Chapter, to create a form, we use the tables that are already created earlier in Chapter.

7.12.1 Create a Form using the Form Tool

You use Form tool in Access 2010 to create a form with a single mouse-click. When you use this tool, all the fields from the underlying data source are placed on the form. You begin using the new form or you can also modify form in Layout view or in Design view to suit your needs.

➡ **To create a form using form tool, do this:**

1. In the Navigation Pane, click the table or query of which you want to make a form.
2. Then under the Create tab, in the Forms group, click Form.
3. Access creates the form and displays it in Layout view along with the Form Layout Tools, i.e., Design, Arrange and Format Tabs in the Ribbon (See Figure 7.93).

☞ You can make design changes to the form in the layout view while it is displaying data. For example, you can adjust the size of the text boxes to fit the data.

7.12.2 Create a Form using Form Wizard

When you want to include only selective fields in form, you can use the Form Wizard instead of Form tools. You can also define how the data is grouped and sorted.

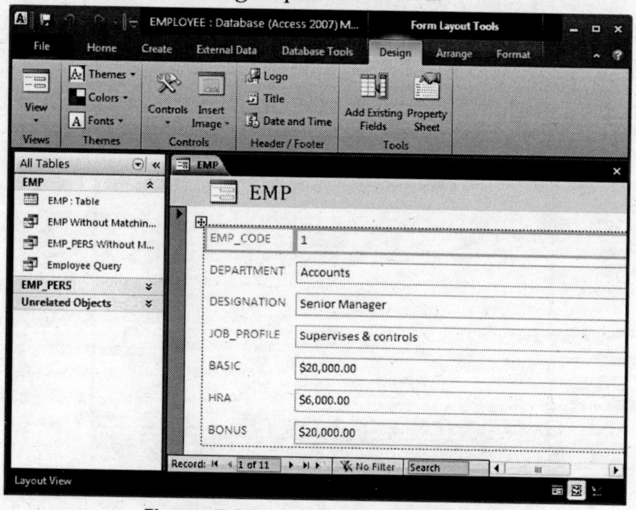

Figure 7.93 Form using Form tool

➡ **To create a form using Form Wizard, do this:**

1. Click under the Create tab, in the Forms group, click Form Wizard. (See Figure 7.94).

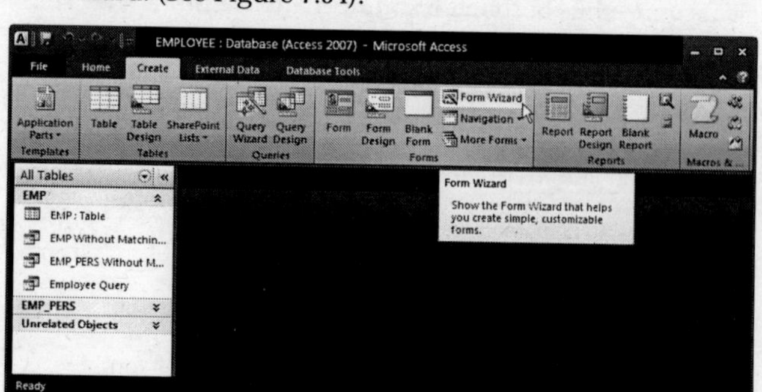

Figure 7.94 Form using Form Wizard

2. A Form Wizard dialog box appears as shown in Figure 7.95. In this dialog box, from the Available Fields: area, select the field which you want in your form. Then click > button. To add more fields, highlight the field and click > button. To select all the fields present in the Available Fields: area click the >> button.

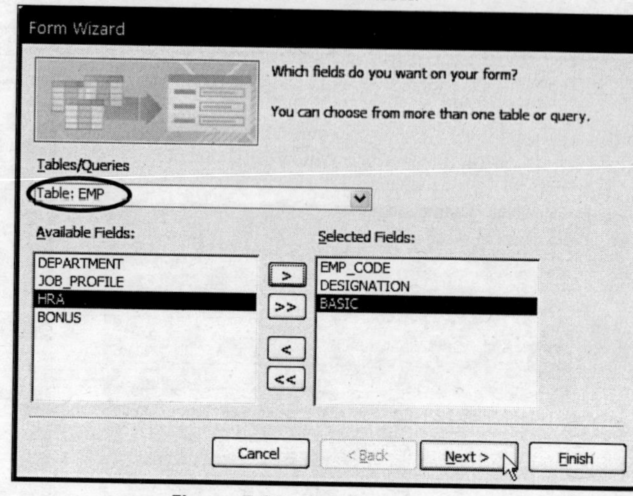

Figure 7.95 The Form Wizard

3. To remove a field from the Selected Fields: area click the < button. To remove all the fields, click the << button.
4. Click Next >.

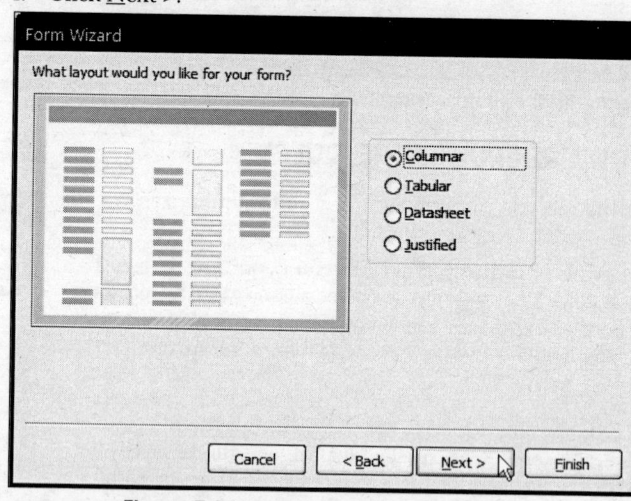

Figure 7.96 Select a layout for the form

5. In the dialog box that appears select a layout for the form (Figure 7.96). The various forms available are columnar, Tabular, Datasheet and Justified. We have selected the Columnar radio button. Click Next >.
6. In the dialog box that appears (See Figure 7.97) provide a title for the form.
7. Then click Finish.

The form will open in Form view as shown in Figure 7.98.

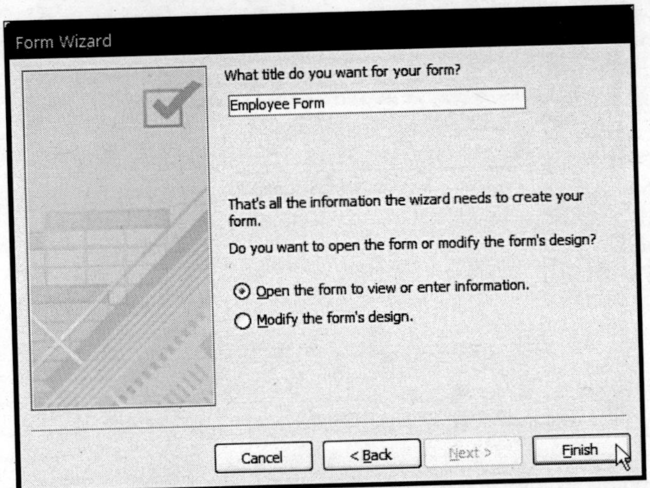

Figure 7.97 Provide a title for the form

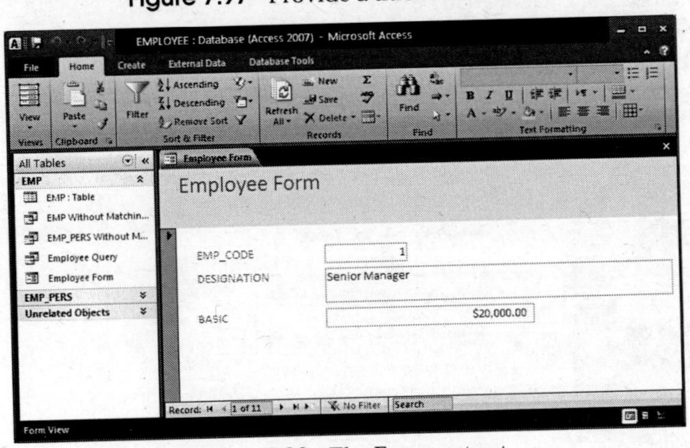

Figure 7.98 The Form output

Entering Data through Forms

Database performs many tasks, and storing data is one of them. After you have tables, you need a way to enter and modify data. The most efficient way to work with your data is through forms. Forms let you to determine what data is displayed and what types of changes you can make to it. You know how to create a form, let us learn how to use it to enter and modify data in the form.

➡ **To enter a data, do this:**

There are two ways to add a new record to a form:

1. In the Records group on the Home tab of the Ribbon, click the New command.

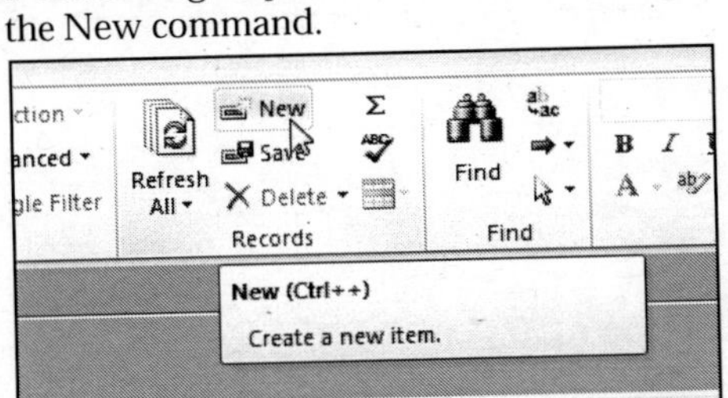

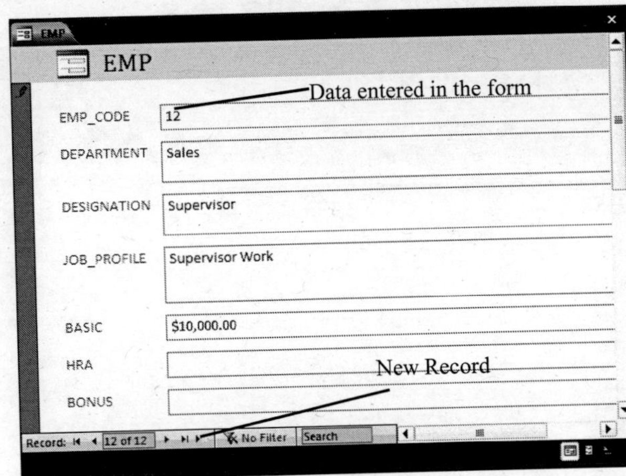

Figure 7.99 Select New Record button

2. On the Record Navigation bar at the bottom of the window, click the New Record button (See Figure 7.99).

   You can see the new recored added in the EMP Table list.

7.12.3 Formatting Forms

Access offers many options that let you make your forms look exactly the way you want. While some of these options –like command buttons–are unique to forms, others may be familiar to you.

Command buttons

If you want to create a way for users of your form to quickly perform specific actions and tasks, consider adding command buttons. When you create a command button, you specify an action for it to carry out when clicked. By including commands for common tasks right in your form, you are making the form easier to use.

Access offers many different types of command buttons, but they can be divided into a few main categories:

- Record Navigation command buttons, which easily allow users to move among the records in your database
- Record Operation command buttons, which let users do things like save and print records.
- Form Operation command buttons, which give users the ability to quickly open or close a form, print the current form, and complete other actions
- Report Operation command buttons, which offer users a quick way to do things like preview or mail a report from the current record

➡ **To add a command button to a form, do this:**

1. In Form Layout views, select the Form Layout Tools Design tab and locate the Controls group.
2. Select the Button command.
3. Your cursor will turn into a tiny crosshairs with a button icon. Place it in the spot where you want your command button to be, then click.

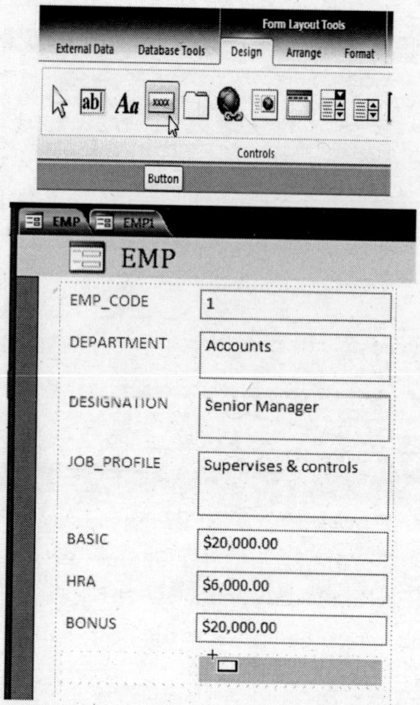

4. The Command Button Wizard will appear as shown in Figure 7.100. In the Categories pane, select the category of button you want to add. We want to find a way to move more quickly to specific records, so we will choose the Record Navigation category.

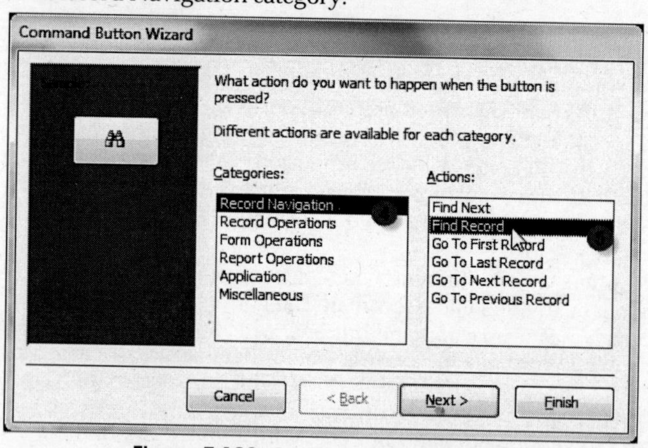

Figure 7.100 Common Button Wizard

5. The list in the Actions pane will update to reflect your chosen category. Select the action you want the button to perform, then click Next. For our example, we will choose Find Record (See Figure 7.101).
6. You can now decide whether you want your button to include text or a picture. A live preview of your button appears on the left.
   - To include text, select the Text option, then type the desired word or phrase into the text box (See Figure 7.101).

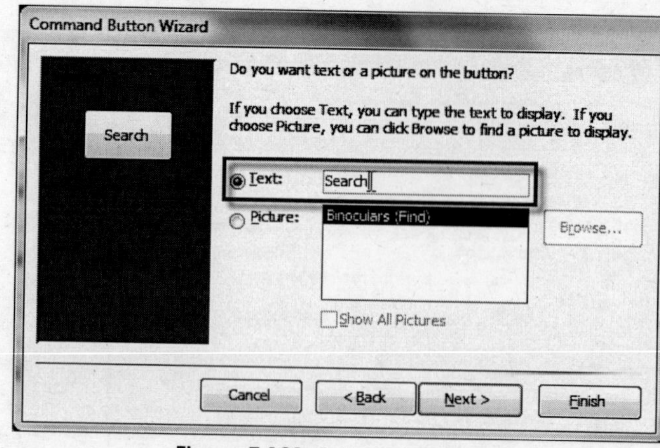

Figure 7.101 Select Find Record

7. When you are satisfied with the appearance of your command button, click Next.
8. Type a name for the button. This name would not appear on the button, but knowing the name will help you to quickly identify the button if you ever want to modify it with the Property Sheet. After typing the button name, click Finish (See Figure 7.102).

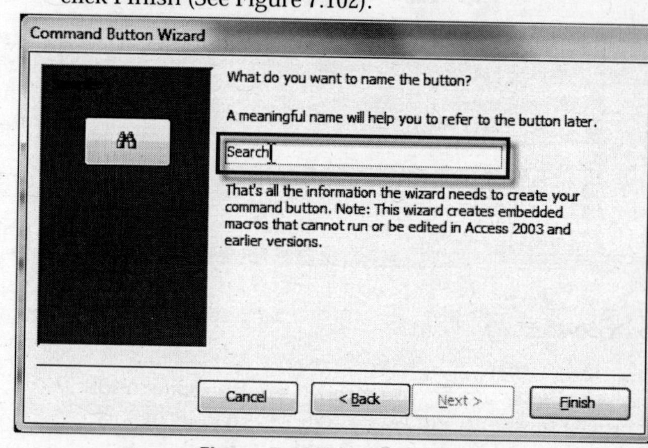

Figure 7.102 Finish button

9. Switch to Form view to test the new button. Our Find Record button opens the Find and Replace dialog box appears.

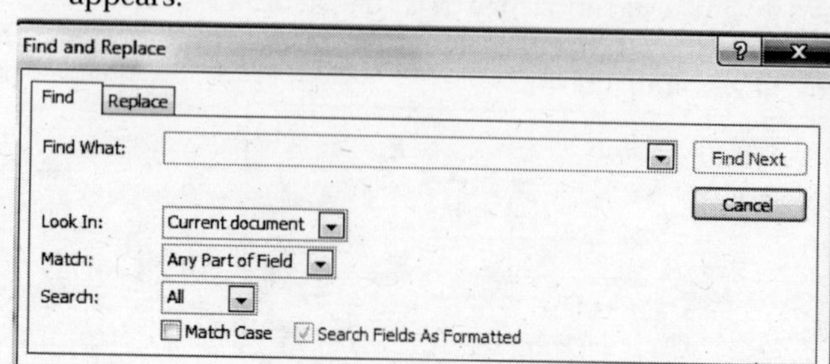

7.12.4 Create a Form using Blank Form Tool

If the wizard or the form tools do not fit according to your need then you can use Blank Form tool to build a form. This can be a very quick way to build a form, especially if you plan to put only a few fields on your form.

➡ **To create a form using blank form tool, do this:**

1. Click under the Create tab, in the Forms group, click Blank Form. Access opens a blank form in Layout view along with the Field List pane (See Figure 7.103).

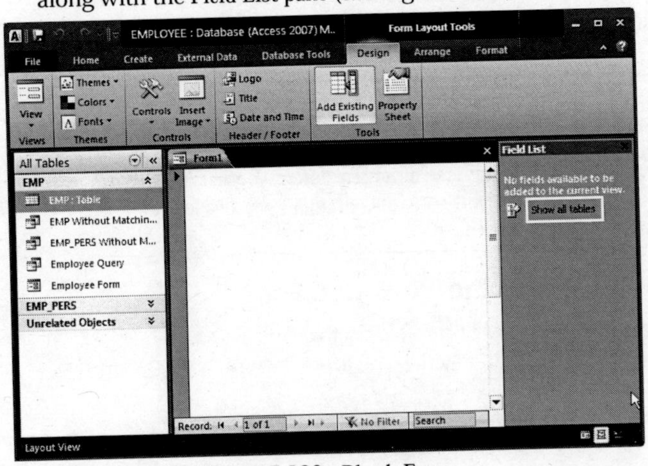

Figure 7.103 Blank Form

2. In the Field List pane, click Show all tables to view the tables in a database (See Figure 7.103).
3. Then, click the plus sign (+) next to the table that contains the fields that you want to include in the form (See Figure 7.104).
4. To add a field to the form, double-click it.
5. If you want to add tools in the form such as logo, title, page numbers, etc. click the tool you want under the Design Tab, in the Controls group.

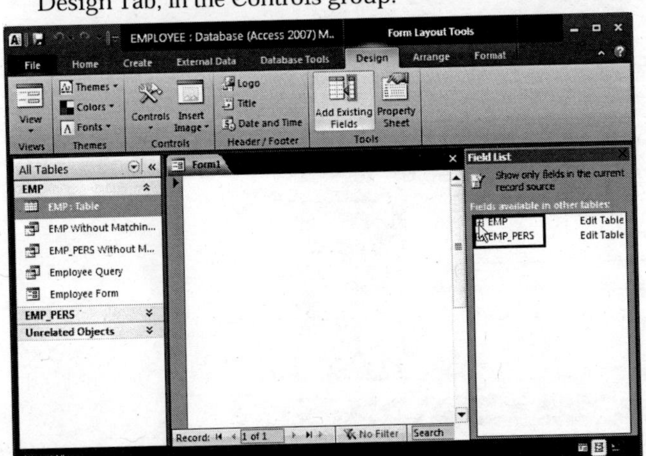

Figure 7.104 Selecting the Table

6. After adding tool such as title for the form from the Header/Footer group group, the form will look like as shown in Figure 7.105.

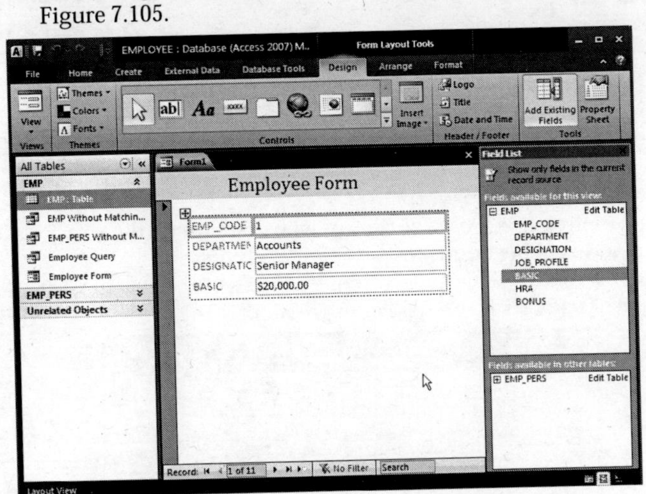

Figure 7.105 Form created using a Blank Form tool

7.12.5 Create a Split Form using the Split Form Tool

Split Form tool gives you two views of the data at the same time i.e., Form view and Datasheet view. The two views are connected to the same data source and are synchronized with each other at all times.

Split form feature gives you the benefits of both types of forms in a single form. For example, you can use the datasheet portion of the form to quickly locate a record and then use the form portion to view or edit the record.

➡ **To create a split form using split form tool, do this:**

1. In the Navigation Pane, click the table or query for which you want to make a form.

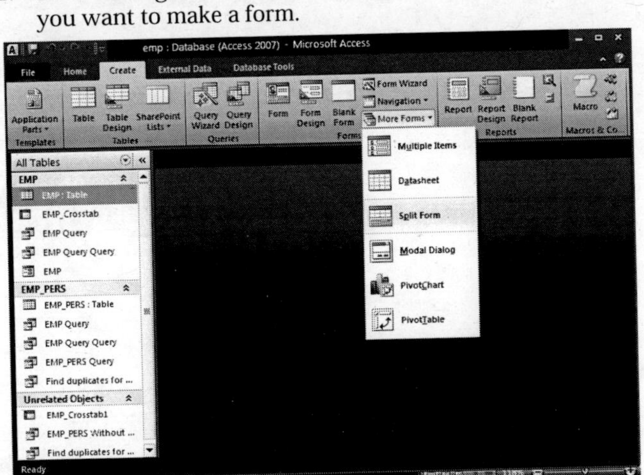

Figure 7.106 Form using Split Form tool

2. Under the Create tab, in the Forms group, click More Forms and then click Split Form (See Figure 7.106).
3. Access 2010 creates a form in Layout view (See Figure 7.107).

7.12.6 Adding Controls To The Form

Control is a graphical user interface object, such as a text box, check box, scroll bar, or command button, that allows users to control the program. Controls can be used to display data, perform an action, or make the user interface easier to read.

Controls can be of three types:

(a) Bound control: It is a type of control whose source of data is a field in a table or query.

(b) Unbound control: This type of control does not have a source of data, such as a field or expression.

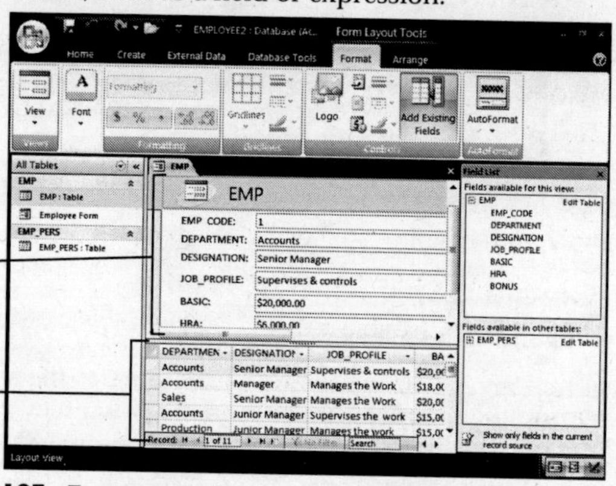

Figure 7.107 Form created using a Split form command

(c) Calculated control: The source of data of calculated control is an expression, rather than a field.

Some controls, such as the bound control is created when you add a field from the Field List pane to your form. But other controls can be created in Design view only.

➡ **To add control in a form, do this:**

1. In the Navigation Pane, right click the table that you want to open and then choose Design View.
2. Click under the Design tab then in the Controls group, click the tools for the type of control that you want to add (See Figure 7.108).
3. Click in the form design grid where you want to position the upper-left corner of the control. Click the tool and then drag the mouse pointer in the form design grid to create a control of the size that you want.
4. A form after adding controls appears as shown in Figure 7.108.

☞ The two most common views to work with forms are Form view, in which you view or enter data. Another is Design view, in which you add controls, change form properties, and change the form layout.

7.12.7 Changing the View of a Form

➡ **To change the view of a form, do this:**

1. In the Navigation Pane, click the form for which you want to change the view.
2. Now under the Home tab, in the Views group, click arrow next to View and choose the desired view. (See Figure 7.109).

If you choose the Form view, then form will look as shown in Figure 7.103.

If you choose the Layout view, then form will be look as shown in Figure 7.94.

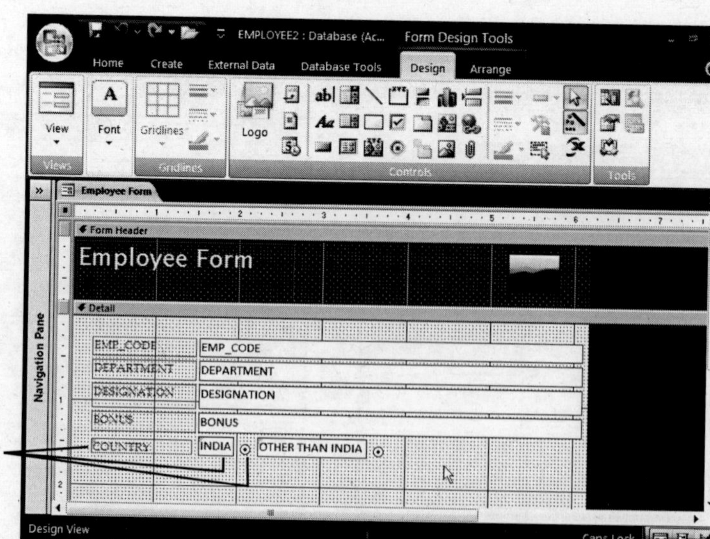

Figure 7.108 Form after adding controls

If you choose the Design view, then form will be look as shown in Figure 7.108.

7.12.8 Moving through Records

Initially form displays only one record at a time. But you can see all the records one by one through the navigation button. You will find navigation button at the bottom of your form view (See Figure 7.109). There are five navigation buttons. These are:

First Record: Displays the first record of the table.
Previous Record: Displays the previous record of the table.
Next Record: Displays the next record of the table.
Last Record: Displays the last record of the table.
New (blank) Record: Inserts new record at the end of the table.

7.13 WHAT ARE REPORTS?

To make your data more presentable for others to read and understand, you would need to create reports.

☞ Reports let you to define how you want your data to appear on the printed page.

You have to decide which fields to include in the report, where they appear on the page, and which typeface to be used. You can add your own text and graphics in the report.

☞ In Access 2010, you can export report to a .pdf or .xps file format that lets you to capture an information in an easy-to-distribute form that retains all your formatting characteristics, but does not require others to install Access 2010 on their computers to print or review your output.

7.13.1 Using Reports

Reports are the most powerful and flexible way to view and print the information in your database. The Quick Create feature automatically generates reports with professional looking designs along with headers and informative footers and totals. Report are very useful in the following cases:

- Controlling font styles and sizes.
- Performing calculations on the underlying data.
- Formatting data to fit forms such as purchase orders, invoices and mailing labels.
- Adding graphics, such as pictures, graphics and other elements.
- Grouping and organizing data to form reports to read them easily.

7.13.2 Report Creation by using the Report Tool

The Report tool in Access 2010 provides the fastest way for you to create a report, because it generates a report immediately without prompting you for information. The report displays all the fields from the underlying table or query. The Report tool may not create the final, polished product that you ultimately want. It is however, useful as a means to quickly look at the underlying data. You can then save the report and modify it in Layout view or Design view so that it better serves your purposes.

➡ **To create a report using report tool, do this:**

1. In the Navigation Pane, click the table or query for which you want to make a report.
2. Then click on Create tab, and again in the Reports group, click Report.

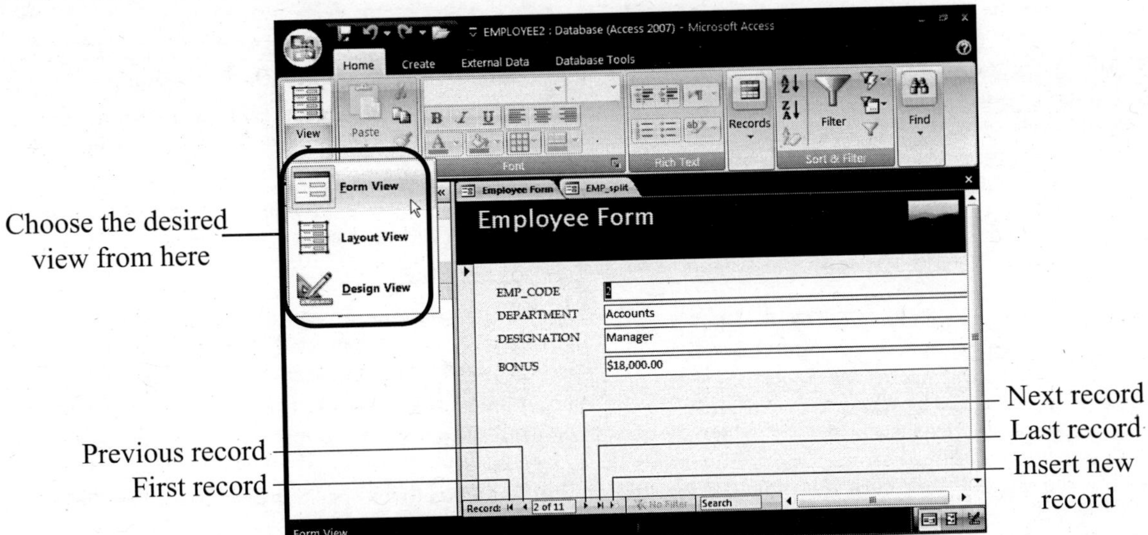

Figure 7.109 Choose desired view for the form

3. Access generates the report and displays it in Layout view along with the Report Layout Tools, i.e., Design, Arrange, Format and Page Setup Tabs in the ribbon (See Figure 7.110).

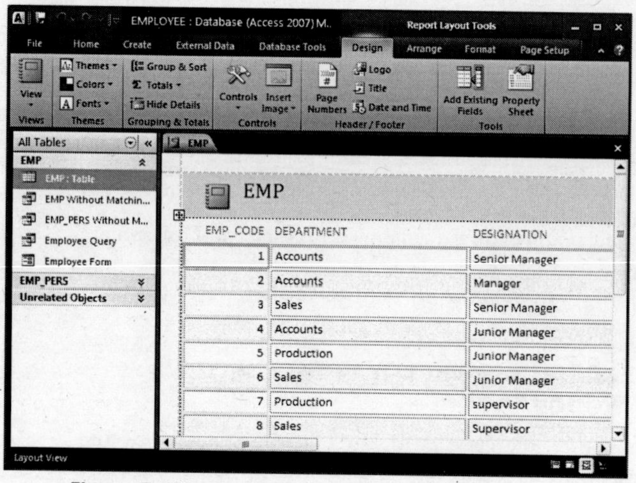

Figure 7.110 Report created by using Report tool

7.13.3 Report Creation using the Report Wizard

Report Wizard is a tool that guides you through the process of creating reports. You can also specify how the data is grouped and sorted, and you can use fields from more than one table or query, provided you have specified the relationships between the tables and queries beforehand.

☞ Creating report using Report Wizard is the easiest way because it guides you step-by-step through arranging and selecting which data you want to print on a report.

➡ **To create a report using Form Wizard, do this:**

1. Click Create tab, under the Reports group, click Report Wizard.
2. A Report Wizard dialog box appears as shown in Figure 7.111. In this dialog box, click in the Tables/Queries list box and choose the table or query that contains the data you want to print in a report and then from the Available Fields: area, select the fields which you want in your report, then click > button.
   To add more fields highlight the field and click > button. To select all the fields present in the Available Fields: area click the >> button.
3. To remove a field from the Selected Fields: area click the < button. To remove all the fields, click the << button.
4. Click Next >.
5. Another dialog box appears, asking whether you want to group your data by a specific field, such as EMP_CODE, DEPARTMENT as shown in Figure 7.112. Click a field name displayed in the box and then click > button. Click Next >.

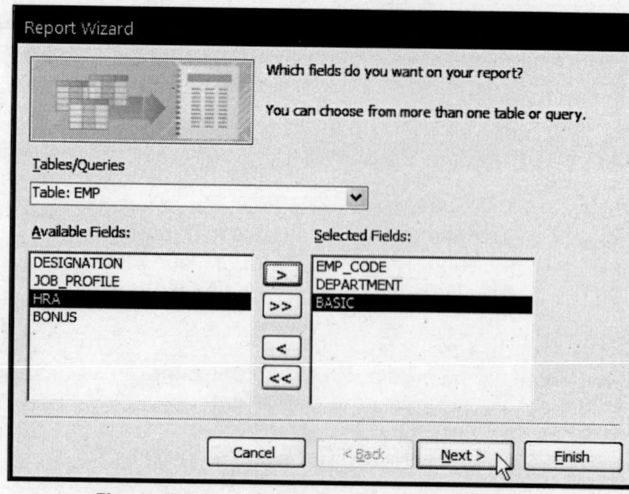

Figure 7.111 The Report Wizard Dialog Box

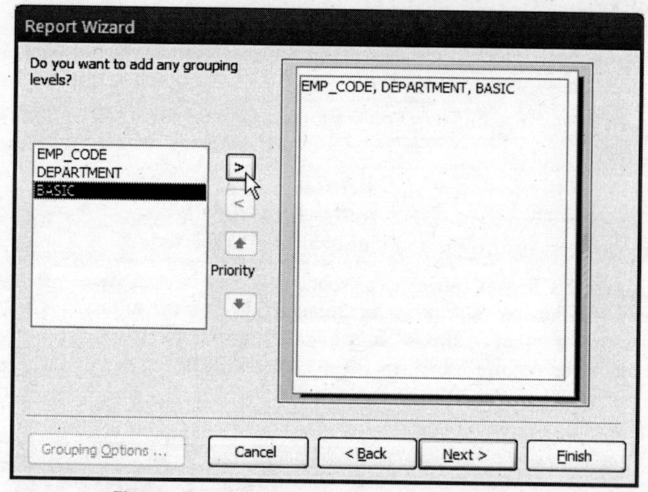

Figure 7.112 Select the field for the group

6. In the dialog box that appears, choose a field for sorting your data in report (See Figure 7.113). We have chosen BASIC field. Click Next >.

☞ By using Report view, you can browse an accurate rendering of your report without having to print or display it in Print Preview.

7. In the dialog box that appears (See Figure 7.114) select a layout for the report from the Layout group. The various layout available are Stepped, Block and Outline. We have selected the Stepped radio button. Select orientation of the page from Orientation group, i.e., Portrait or Landscape. Click Next >.
8. In the dialog box that appears provide a title for the report (See Figure 7.115).

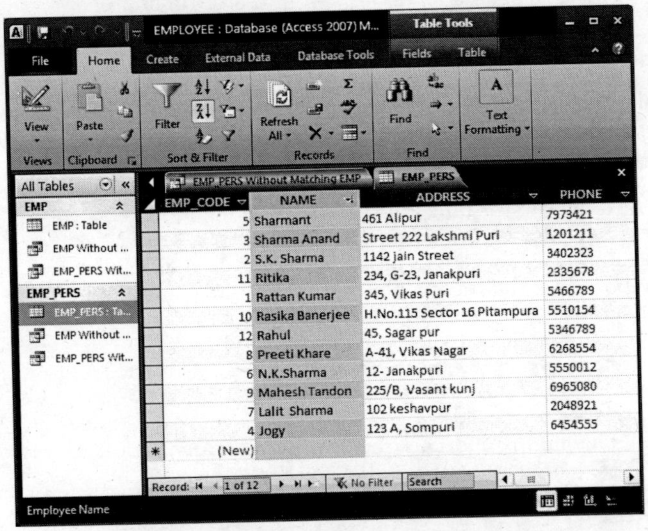

Figure 7.113 Choose a field for sorting

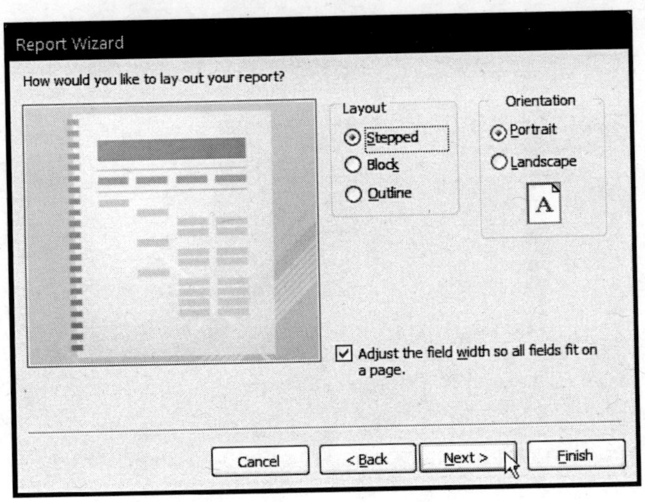

Figure 7.114 Select a layout for the report

9. Then click Finish.

The report will open in report view as shown in Figure 7.116.

7.13.4 Report Creation by using the Blank Report Tool

If you are not interested in using the Report tool or the Report Wizard, you can use the Blank Report tool to build a report from scratch. This is a very quick way to build a report, especially if you plan to put only a few fields on the report.

➡ **To create a report using Blank Report tool, do this:**

1. Under the Create tab, in the Reports group, click Blank Report. Access opens a blank form in Layout view along with the Field List pane (See Figure 7.117).

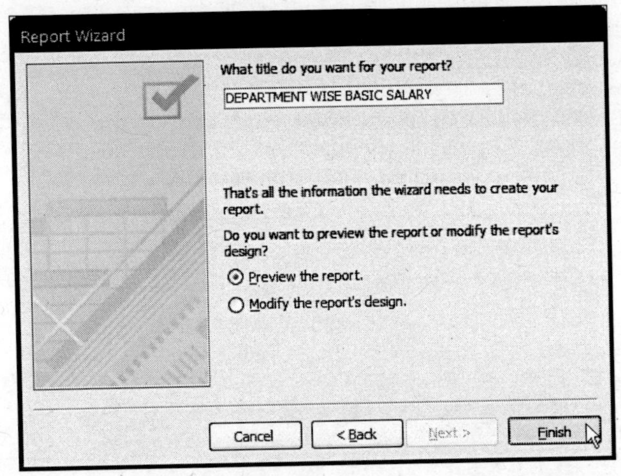

Figure 7.115 Provide a title for the report

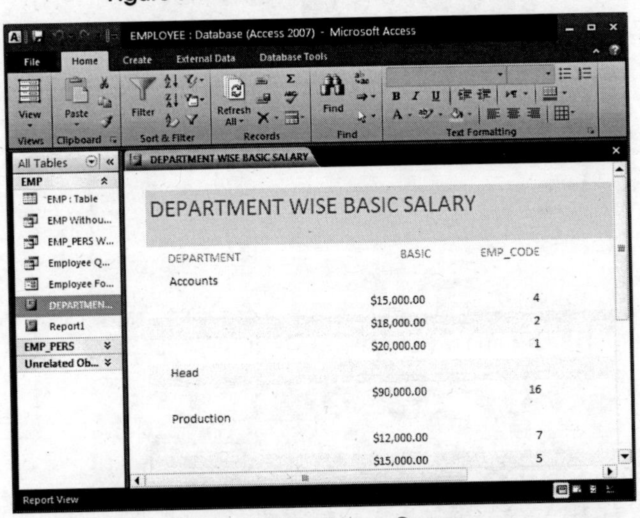

Figure 7.116 Report Output

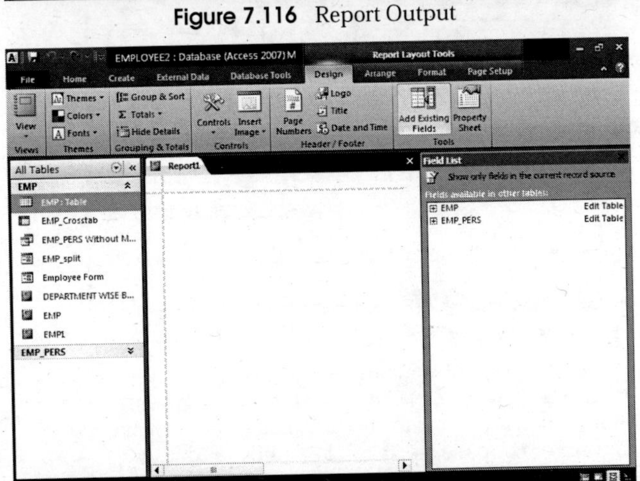

Figure 7.117 Blank Report

2. In the Field List pane, click the plus sign (+) next to the table that contains the fields that you want to include in the report.
3. To add a field to the report, double-click it.
4. If you want to add tools in the report, such as logo, title, page numbers, etc., click under the Design Tab and then click the desired tool from the appropriate group.
5. After adding tool, such as title for the report, the report will look as shown in Figure 7.118.

7.13.5 Sections of the Report

In Access 2010, the design of a report is divided into various sections. You can view a report in Design view to see its sections (Figure 7.119).

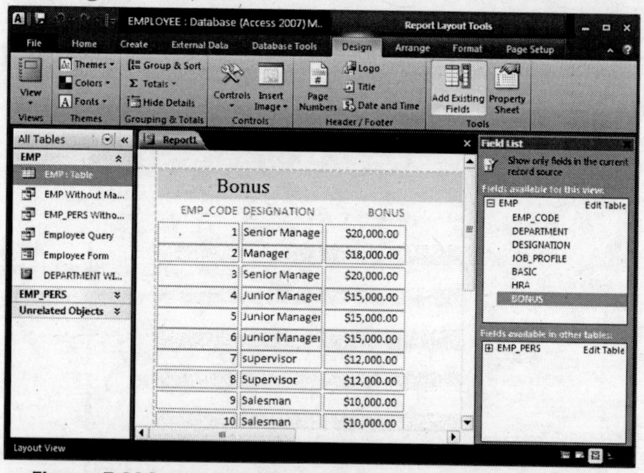

Figure 7.118 Report created by using a Blank Report tool

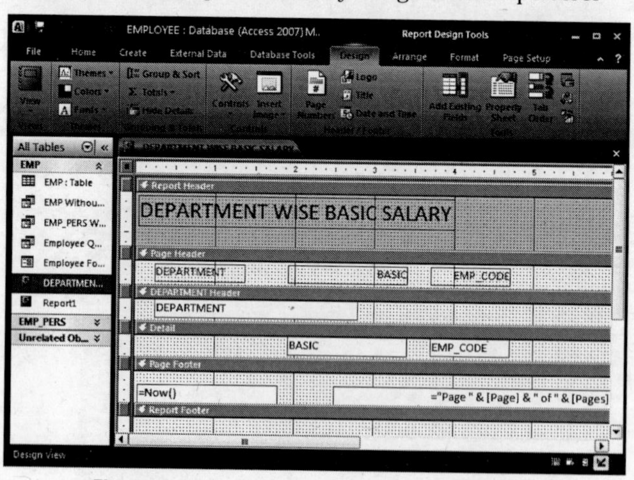

Figure 7.119 Different Sections of the report

Following are the different sections of the report:

- Report Header: This section is present at the beginning of the report. It contains information that might normally appear on a cover page, such as a logo, title, or date.
- Page Header: This section is printed at the top of every page. For example, fields of the table.
- Group Header: This section is printed at the beginning of each new group of records. For example, in a report that is grouped by Department, use the group header to print the Department name.
- Detail: This section is printed once for every row in the record source.
- Group Footer: This section is printed at the end of each group of records.
- Page Footer: This section is printed at the end of every page. Use a page footer to print page numbers.
- Report Footer: This section is printed just once, at the end of the report. Use the report footer to print report totals or other summary information for the entire report.

7.13.6 Viewing and Printing a Report

➡ **To view a report, do this:**

1. In the Navigation Pane, click the downward arrow. A pull down menu appears as shown in Figure 7.120.

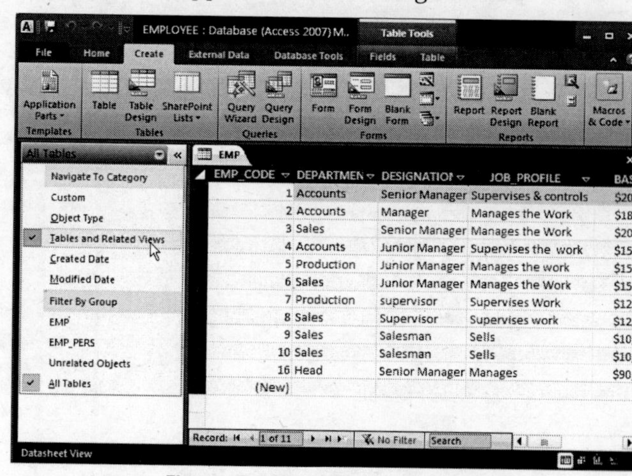

Figure 7.120 Viewing a Report

2. In this menu, click Tables and Related Views. Access displays a list of all previously saved reports in the navigation pane.
3. Double click a report name which you want to view. Now you can see a report using Design view, report view or print preview whichever you want.

➡ **To Print Preview a report, do this:**

1. Click on the File Tab. Then click on Print. Now click on Print Preview from the option of the print (See Figure 7.121).
2. Access 2010 switches to Print Preview mode (See Figure 7.122).

➡ **To print a report, do this:**

1. Click on the File Tab. Then click on Print. Now click on Print from the option of the print.
2. In Print dialog box, click OK button to print the report. Besure, the printer is ON and it is online.

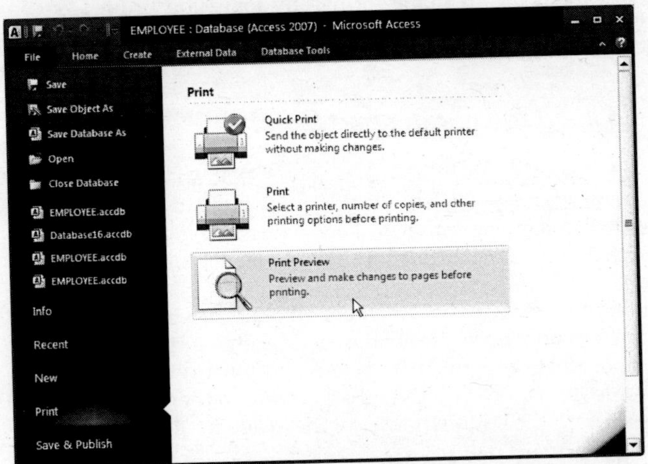

Figure 7.121 Print Preview Option of the Print Tab

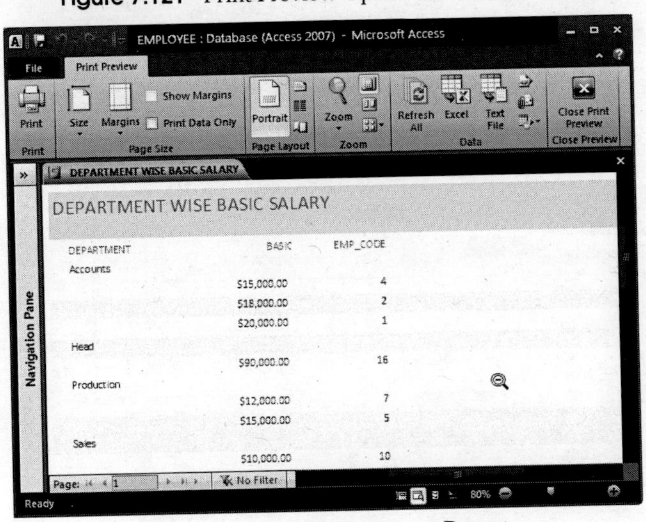

Figure 7.122 Print Preview a Report

7.14 MANIPULATING DATA IN A REPORT

After you create a report, you can manipulate the data displayed in that report, i.e., sorting data in ascending or descending order or apply filter to display the data that meet the criteria. To manipulate data in a report, first of all you have to switch in Layout view. To switch to the Layout view, click the Layout view button from the Status bar.

7.14.1 Sorting Data in a Field

Access 2010 can also sort data in each field in ascending or descending order. Sorting a field rearranges the data in report accordingly to your convenience.

➡ To sort data in a field, do this:

1. Open the report in Layout view.
2. Right click the column or field that you want to sort (Here, we have select DEPARTMENT column). Access displays pop-up menu almost similar to Figure 7.123.

Choose Sort A to Z if you want to sort in ascending order. Choose Sort Z to A if you want to sort in descending order.

3. Here, we have selected Sort Z to A. Access sorts data according to the option we have selected (See Figure 7.123).

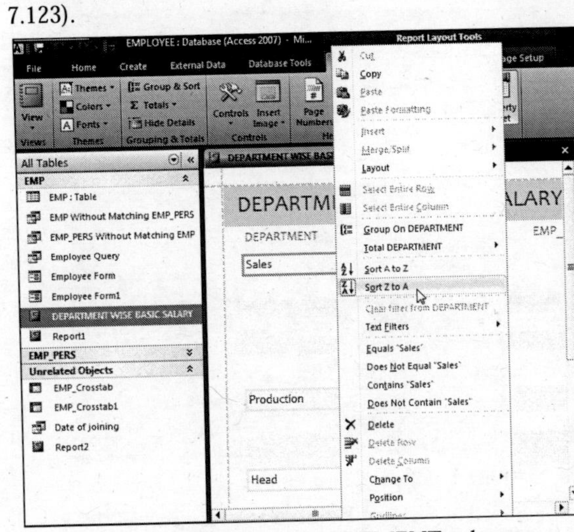

Figure 7.123 Sort DEPARTMENT column

7.14.2 Editing a Report

After creating a report, if you want to modify it, then you must switch to the Design view of the report. After you view the report in Design view, you can modify the report. At this point you can move, resize, add or delete fields in the report.

➡ **To resize a field, do this:**

1. Open the report in Design view.
2. Click the field you want to resize.
3. Move the mouse pointer over the left or right edge of the field until the mouse pointer turns into a two-way pointing arrow (See Figure 7.124).

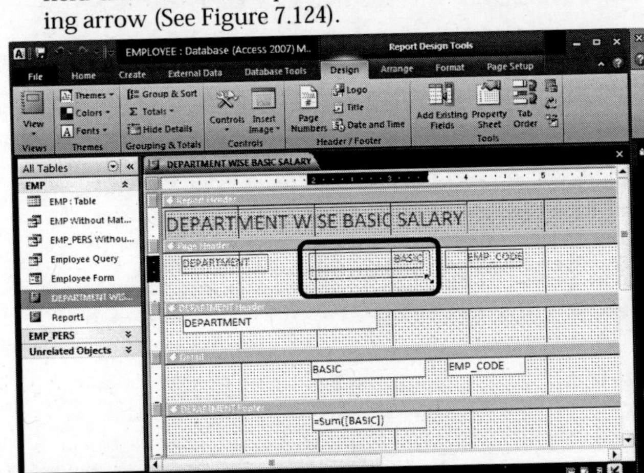

Figure 7.124 Resize a field in a Design view

4. Drag the mouse to resize and expand or shrink the field.

7.14.3 Deleting a Report

Eventually, you may find that you no longer need a report. So you want to delete it.

➡ **To delete a report, do this:**

1. In the Navigation Pane, click the downward arrow as shown in Figure 7.125.

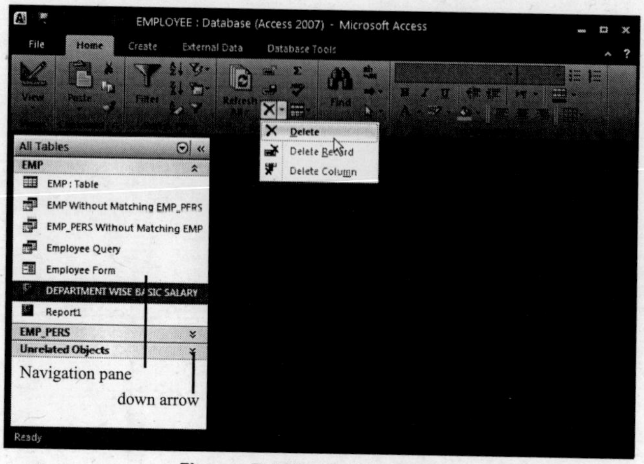

Figure 7.125 Delete Report

2. In this menu, click Tables and Related Views. Access displays a list of all previously saved reports in the navigation pane.
3. Click the report you want to delete.
4. Now, click under the Home tab, in the Records group. Click Delete. (See Figure 7.125).

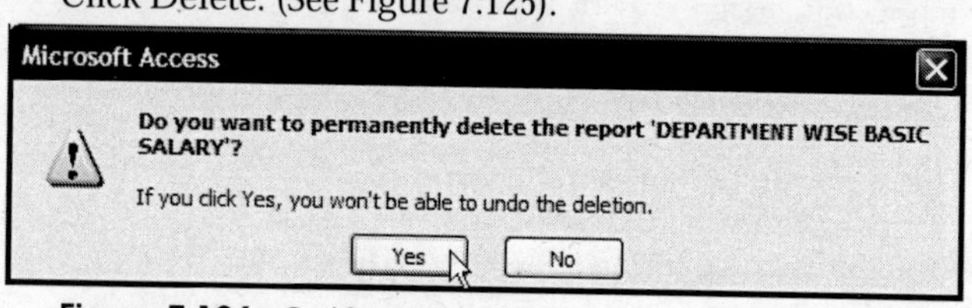

Figure 7.126 Confirmation dialog box to delete a report

5. A dialog box appears as shown in Figure 7.126, asking whether you want to delete report. Click Yes.

7.14.4 Formatting Reports

One of the strengths of reports is that you can modify their appearance to make them look how you want. You can add headers and footers to your report, apply new colors to the layout, and even add a logo. All of these things can help you to create visually appealing reports.

7.14.5 Modifying Report Text

The information in your report comes from the query or table you built it from, which means you can't edit it within the report. However, you can change, add, or delete label text, headers, and footers to make your report clearer and easier to read.

When working with text and text boxes in reports, you can use many of the text and shape formatting tools you use in other Office programs to modify color, font, and other settings.

Modifying the page header and footer

To view and modify the header and footer that appear on every page of your report, select the View command on the Ribbon and switch to Design view. The header and footer are located in the white space beneath the Page Header and Page Footer bars.

Depending on your report's design, sometimes you may find that there is no white space in the page header and footer, as in the image below. If this is the case, you must resize the header and footer before you can add anything to them. Simply click and drag the bottom border of the header or footer to make it larger.

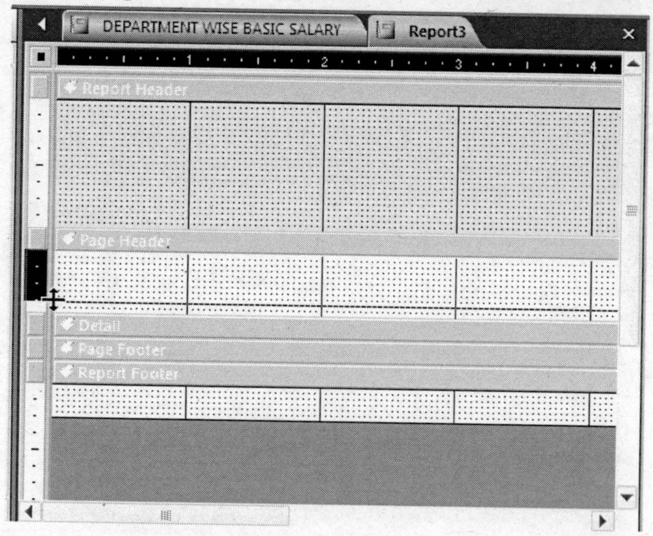

Applying Themes

A theme is a set of colors that applies to the entire database to give it a consistent, professional look. By default, databases use the Office theme. When you change the theme, all of the theme font and colors in your database to change the new theme. Designing and modifying reports using theme elements can help you keep the appearance of your reports consistent.

➡ **To change the theme, do this:**

1. Select the Design tab and locate the Themes group.
2. Click the Themes command (See Figure 7.127).
3. A drop-down menu will appear as shown in Figure 7.128. Hover the mouse over a theme to see a live preview of it.

Figure 7.127 Selecting Themes drop-down list

4. Select the desired theme. The theme will be applied to your entire database (See Figure 7.129).

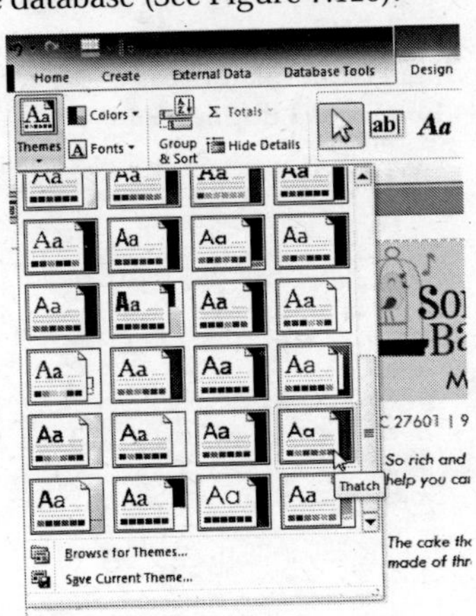

Figure 7.128 Theme options

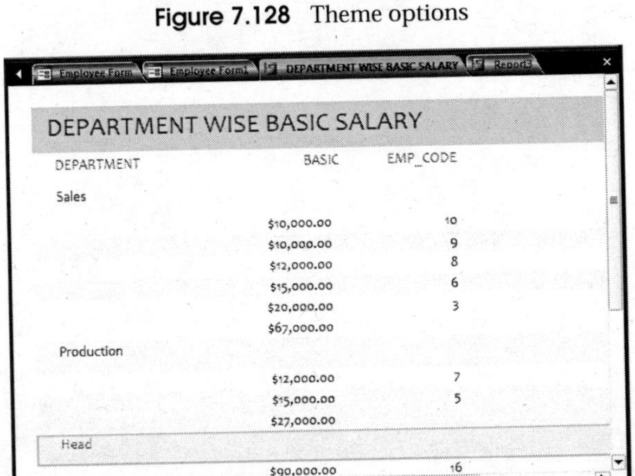

Figure 7.129 Theme applied in the form

MODEL QUESTIONS AND ANSWERS

A. Multiple Choice

1.1 Description of data stored in database is called

a. Schema b. Meta data
c. Information d. None of the above

1.2 The collection of related fields is called a

a. record b. file
c. field d. None of the above

1.3 The collection of related records is called a

a. field b. database
c. file d. None of the above

1.4 The collection of related files is called a

a. record b. database
c. fields d. None of the above

1.5 A unique data item which is used to identify a particular record is called a

a. Key b. Roll No
c. Unique number d. None of the above

1.6 How does the New Record button look like?

a. An arrow pointing to an asterisk
b. A folder with an arrow on it
c. A folder with an left triangle on it
d. An arrow pointing to a line

1.7 Named collection of fields which represents a complete unit of information is called

a. Field b. Record
c. Table d. None of these

1.8 A field that uniquely identifies records in the table is known as

a. Primary Key b. Special Key
c. Unique Key d. Candidate Key

1.9 When a picture or other graphic image is placed in the report header section it will appear __________.

a. Once in the beginning of the report
b. At the top of every page
c. Every after record break
d. On the 1st and last pages of the report

1.10 This data type allows alphanumeric characters and special symbols.

a. text b. memo
c. auto number d. None of the above

1.11 To create a new table, in which method you do not need to specify the field type and size?

a. Create table in Design View
b. Create Table using wizard
c. Create Table by Entering data
d. All of above

1.12 Which of the following is not a database object?

a. Tables b. Queries
c. Relationships d. Reports

1.13 The size of a field with Number data type can not be
a. 2 b. 4
c. 8 d. 16

1.14 The basic elements of a form or a report are called:
a. Controls b. Objects
c. Windows d. Properties

1.15 In table design view, the first column of buttons indicates:
a. Primary Key b. Current Row
c. Both (a) and (b) d. None of above

1.16 ________ allows you to resize controls, adjust column widths, move columns, and change labels while viewing the actual data in the report.
a. Design view b. Layout view
c. Print view d. Report view

1.17 Which is not a view for displaying a report object?
a. Datasheet view b. Design view
c. Print view d. Layout view

1.18 A ________ name must be unique within a database.
a. Table b. Field
c. Record d. Character

1.19 Query can be use to select data from
a. Single Table b. Multiple Tables
c. Both (A) and (B) d. None of the above

1.20 Which of the following is use to get data from user?
a. Query b. Pages
c. Form d. Report

B. State whether the following are True or False

2.1 You can edit records in Design view.

2.2 When you change the column width, you also change the field size.

2.3 You can add a record only at the end of a table.

2.4 The only way to delete a record is to use the Delete Record button.

2.5 You can undo record deletions.

2.6 A composite key is a group of fields that uniquely identify a record.

2.7 Computer can tell that 5424775 is not a name.

2.8 A unique data item which is used to identify a particular record is called a Key field.

2.9 There can be multiple primary keys in a table.

2.10 Memo is a valid data type in Access 2010.

2.11 A common field called foreign key relates two tables.

2.12 Columns in tables are called records rows in tables are called fields.

2.13 If an employee works in more than one department, then such a relation will be called many to many.

2.14 Named collection of fields which represent a complete unit of information is called table.

2.15 Datasheet can be sorted on more than one column.

2.16 IMS (Information management system) is a hierarchical database system.

2.17 IDMS is an example of network database system.

2.18 An hierarchical data model is partially ordered.

2.19 Hierarchical model is preferred over relational model by many organizations.

2.20 In an hierarchical database, modelling of many-to-many relations is achieved by record duplication.

Answers

A.	1.	b	2.	b	3.	c	4.	b	5.	a
	6.	a	7.	b	8.	a	9.	a	10.	a
	11.	c	12.	c	13.	d	14.	a	15.	c
	16.	b	17.	a	18.	a	19.	c	20.	c

B.	2.1	F	2.2	F	2.3	F	2.4	T	2.5	T
	2.6	T	2.7	F	2.8	T	2.9	F	2.10	T
	2.11	T	2.12	F	2.13	T	2.14	F	2.15	T
	2.16	T	2.17	T	2.18	F	2.19	F	2.20	T

CHAPTER 8

Cyber Security

8.1 INTRODUCTION

Cyber security, deals with the security of information technology. It also refers to protecting computers, networks, programs and data from unauthorized users.

The information stored in the cyber environment and user's assets are connected to computer devices, applications, services and telecommunications systems.

8.2 BASIC CONCEPTS OF THREATS

Threat in a computer security is a danger which exploit a vulnerability to breach security and cause possible harm. It can be "intentional" (i.e. hacking: an individual cracker) or "accidental" (computer malfunctioning).

8.2.1 Vulnerabilities

In computer security, vulnerability is a kind of weakness that allows an attacker to reduce the system's information assurance. It can be consider as an intersection of three elements:

1. A system flaw
2. Attacker access to the flaw
3. Attacker capability to exploit the present flaw.

If an attacker wants to exploit vulnerability, then he/she must have at least one applicable tool which will get connected to a system weakness.

8.2.2 Controls

Security controls are the countermeasures which are used to avoid, detect or minimize the security risks to any kind of information, computer systems, etc.

Controls mainly helps to:

- Reduce the risk of damage
- Reduce the loss by deterring it
- Slow down an attack against an asset.

8.2.3 Risk

Computer security risk is an event or action which cause a loss or damage to computer hardware, software, data, or information. Risk to computer security can either be accidental or planned. Any illegal act which involves in a computer is a computer crime.

Most common computer security risks include:

- Computer viruses
- Unauthorized access to computer
- Hardware theft
- Software theft
- Information theft
- System failure

8.2.4 Confidentiality

It means protecting an information from getting disclose to an unauthorized parties, Or it may be interpret as only an authorized person has the right to access the information.

As, we know an information has value, so one must keep it secret. Key component of protecting information is by encryption. Encryption ensures that only person who has key can read the information.

Confidentiality may include enforcing file permissions and access control list, so that an access to sensitive information can be given to only authorized user.

8.2.5 Integrity

It means protecting information from an unauthorized user so that information cannot be modified.

8.2.6 Availability

It means only an authorized user has the right to access the information when needed.

8.2.7 Security Policy

It defines the goals and elements of an organization's computer systems. Security policies are enforced by an organizational policies. It defines whether a computer system is secure or insecure. Security policy models are categorized into core security principles of: Confidentiality, Integrity and Availability.

8.2.8 Security Mechanism

Computer "security" is the conceptual idea, which is attained by using threat prevention, detection, and response.

These processes are based on various policies and system components, and it include:

- User account access controls and cryptography that protect the systems files and data.
- Firewalls, the most common prevention systems from a network security perspective which shield the access to internal network services, and block attacks through packet filtering.
- Intrusion Detection System (IDS) is use to detect network attacks which is in-progress and assist in post-attack forensics.
- "Response" is an assessed security requirements of an individual system which range from simple upgrade of protections to notification of legal authorities.

Today, computer security mainly consists of "preventive" measures, like firewalls which filters the network data among a host or a network and another network, such as the Internet.

8.3 DATA SECURITY AND PROTECTION

It means protecting data, either from destructive forces and unwanted actions of an unauthorized users.

Data protection is an attempts of ensuring the security of computer-processed data from an unauthorized access, any kind of destructive user actions, and from computer failure.

8.3.1 Concept

Data security technology includes:

- Disk encryption: It refers to encryption technology which encrypts data on a hard disk drive.
- Backups: It is done to ensure that the data which is lost can be recovered from another source.
- Data masking: It is the process of masking specific data within a database in order to ensure that the data security is maintained and the sensitive information is not exposed to unauthorized user.
- Data erasure: It is a software-based overwriting method which completely destroys all electronic data which resides on a hard drive, and ensure that no sensitive data is leaked.

With increasing use of computer-based information systems, a concern for the protection of computer-processed data is increasing day by day. Design of entry and display of data, sequence control, user guidance, and data transmission functions can affect the security of the data which is being processed.

Data protection mainly deal with two general problems.

1. Data must be protected from an unauthorized access, which is actually a problem of data security.
2. Data must be protected from errors by an authorized system users.

Design techniques which are needed to achieve data security and prevent user errors are different.

8.3.2 Creating Strong Password

Passwords gives the first line of protection against any unauthorized access to your computer. The stronger your password, the more protected your computer is from hackers and malicious software.

What makes a password strong (or weak)?

A strong password must:

- be eight characters long (characters: uppercase A-Z, lower case a-z, Numbers 0-9, Symbols which found on the keyboard and spaces ' ~ ! @ # $ % ^ & * ( ) _ - + = { } [ ] \ | : ; " ' < > , . ? /)
- not contain user, real or company name.
- not contain a complete word.
- be different from previous passwords.

Example of strong password: 12@a!08

8.3.3 How to stay safe when surfing on the Internet

Few things which one must remember while surfing on Internet, in order to stay safe, are:

- Avoid using same passwords: Hackers can easily find password of another account, if the password of the connected account is same. So, try to use different passwords or insert a bit variation in all the passwords.
- Download from secure websites: Sometimes when you download free software from unreliable websites, these software detect all the personal information of user as they are loaded with spywares. So, try to download software from free website only after reviews and checking the security certificate.
- Avoid clicking on unknown links: Clicking on unknown kinds of links may either spread virus on your computer and hack all your accounts and passwords.
- Anti-virus Software: Try to keep updating antivirus software and keep it 'ON'. Follows all the alerts sent by Anti-virus software companies.
- Online Shopping: It is very risky when it comes to security, as it may ask you to enter your address, account details and other personal details that can be easily hacked by others. So, try to do online shopping from reliable websites and never give your personal details.

8.3.4 Private Browsing

All browsers have privacy features for cookies, private browsing, and deleting browsing history which you can use to manage your privacy according to your needs.

Control Cookies

Many websites add small text files to your computer called !cookies. It help your computer to communicate with a web server, and are widely use to track your browsing activity. Tools which browser had are used for controlling, blocking, and deleting cookies from your computer.

Use Private Browsing

Most of the browsers have tool option which allows user to browse in private. Following information will not be saved by the browser, while browsing in private:

- Pages you visit will not be recorded to your history.
- Cookies will be deleted at the end of the session.
- The cache which stores temporary Internet files will be emptied at the end of the session.
- Forms, search bars, and text boxes will not save the data you have entered, including passwords.
- Downloads listed in your download window or folder will be deleted, although the download itself will remain on your computer.

Note: private browsing does not make you anonymous on the Web, as it can still track your visit and activity through your IP address.

8.3.5 Identify Secure Website

While visiting a website it may asks for sensitive information such as credit card numbers or your social security number, the first step you can take to secure your privacy is to create a strong password. Always try to verify that any information you enter on this site is transmitted and stored properly, as once information is entered online, is transmitted as plain text which can be to intercept by any one.

To avoid this, make sure that the website is encrypted over a secure connection.

- HTTPS: Secure website's URL begin with "https" rather than "http". "s" in this stands for secure and is using SSL (Secure Sockets Layer) connection. Information will be encrypted before being sent to a server.
- THE LOCK ICON: It is displayed somewhere in the window of your web browser and gives you detailed information on the security status of the website.

8.3.6 Clear Cookies

Follow the simple steps to delete Cookies in Internet Explorer

1. Press Start
2. Click on Control Panel
3. Double click on the Internet options
4. Under the General Tab, Click Delete
5. The Delete Browsing History dialog box will appear.
6. Click the 'cookies' checkbox.
7. Click the delete button present at the bottom of the dialog box.
8. You will be taken back to the Internet properties dialog box.
9. Click "OK".

How to Delete Cookies in Chrome

1. At the top right side of browser toolbar, click on the Chrome icon.
2. Click on Settings.
3. Scroll down to the bottom.
4. Click "Show advanced settings".
5. Under "Privacy", Click on "Content Settings", option.
6. Under "Cookies", Click on "All cookies and site data", option.
7. Full list of all your cookies appears.
8. Click REMOVE ALL to clear all your cookies or pick a particular website and clear your cookies from that site.

8.4 KNOW HOW TO IDENTIFY A SECURE WEB SITE

Nowadays people are using internet for online purchasing, online banking day to day activities. During this process we might transfer our personal, sensitive data to the web site. When web page asks sensitive information like your bank account details, credit card number, your password etc., you might be aware about the security status of the site. This is very important as online fraud cases have going arise now.

While you are viewing data in a web site the information transmit as plain text, which every body can read it as it passes through many computers.

People might misuse your sensitive data and do online transactions as you do and you might loss your money and some times you might have to face legal issues.

When you type your password or credit card number next time make sure to check that the site is secured. For secure transmission data must be encrypted i.e. while transmission the others can't read your data. So for this process Secure Socket Layer(SSL) was created.

8.5 HTTP (Hypertext Transfer Protocol)

It is an application-level protocol used is distributed, collaborative, hypermedia information systems.

HTTP is a TCP/IP based communication protocol, which is used to deliver data such as HTML file, image file, etc. on the World Wide Web. It provides a standardized way of communication with other computers.

HTTP specification specifies how clients' requested data is constructed and sent to the server, and how the servers respond to these requests.

An HTTP "client" is a program (Web browser) which establishes a connection to a server for the purpose of sending one or more HTTP request messages. An HTTP "server" is a program (web server) which accepts connections in order to serve HTTP requests by sending HTTP response messages.

8.5.1 Basic Features

- HTTP is connectionless: In this, HTTP client (browser) initiates HTTP request and after that, the client get disconnected from the server and waits for a response. The server then processes the request and re-establishes the connection with the client and send a response back.
- HTTP is media independent: In this any type of data can be sent by HTTP, only requirement is that the client must specify the content type by using appropriate MIME-type.
- HTTP is stateless: HTTP is connectionless protocol, in which the server and client are aware of each other during a request, and after the request is fulfilled both forget about each other. So, neither the client nor the browser can retain information about each other.

8.5.2 Basic Architecture

The diagram shown in Figure 8.1, shows a basic architecture of a web application and depicts HTTP.

How HTTP Works:

The HTTP protocol is a request/response protocol which is based on the client/server based architecture where the web browsers acts like a HTTP client, and Web server acts like a server.

- Client: The HTTP client, sends a request to the server in the form of a request method, followed by a MIME message which contains request modifiers, client information, and possible body content over a TCP/IP connection.
- Server: The HTTP server responds with a status line, including the message's protocol version and if request is fulfilled then a success message or if not then an error code, followed by a MIME-like message which contains server information, entity meta information, and possible entity-body content is sent.

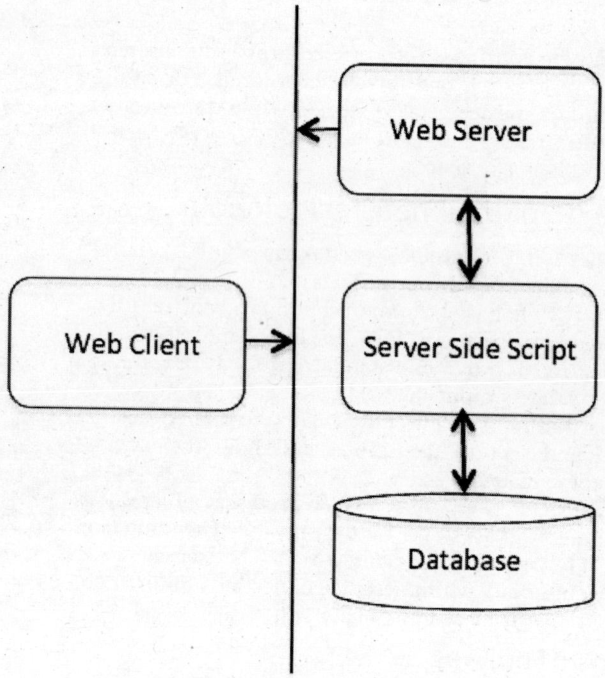

Figure 8.1 HTTP Basic Architecture

8.6 LOCK SYMBOL

Whenever a web page asks you for the sensitive information, before giving any sensitive information you need to identify if the page is secure or not; as online fraud cases have increased substantially.

Secure: Whenever you view a web site, an information is sent from your computer to the web server and from web server to your computer; this transmission takes place in "plain text" form, which anyone can read or view it.

To see if the web page is secured or not, there are two general indications of a secured web page:

Check the web page URL: When browsing the web, the URLs, which is the address of web page, begin with the letters "http". However, over a secure connection the address displayed should begin with "https".

Check for the Lock icon: Web browsers display a "lock" icon somewhere in the window of the browser, but not in the web page display area. For example, Microsoft Internet Explorer displays the lock icon in the lower-right of the browser window.

This lock icon, gives you a details of the site's security.

Consider an example of Google chrome:

One can easily get connected to any website which one wants through any web browser (Google chrome). Before establishing any connection, Chrome will alert you if it can't establish a secure connection with the site, for this:

1. Open a site in Google Chrome.
2. In the top left of address bar, click the lock icon or page icon.
3. Click the Connection tab.
4. Depending on the site, you'll see two or three sections of information and a summary at the top highlighting important issues.

Different icons, displayed on web page:

- Green lock icon ◘ : The site's certificate is valid and its identity has been verified by a trusted third party.
- Orange exclamation icon ◘ : The site has not provided the browser a valid certificate. This is normal for regular HTTP sites as certificates are usually provided if the site uses SSL.
- Lock icon with yellow warning triangle ◘ : Site has weak security setup, which mean that your connection might not be private.
- Red lock icon ◘ : There is some problems with the site's certificate, might be your confidential information get leaked out.

Connection Information

- Green lock icon ◘ : Google Chrome has established a secure connection with the site you are viewing.
- Orange exclamation icon ◘ : Your connection to the site is not encrypted.
- Lock icon with yellow warning triangle ◘ : Your connection to the site is encrypted, but Google Chrome has found something unwanted on the page, so it suggests you not to enter any private or personal information on this page.
- Red lock icon ◘ : Your connection to the site is encrypted, but Google Chrome has detected mixed scripting. Be careful if you're entering personal information on this page.

8.7 SECURITY CONSIDERATIONS

Threats to a computer system can come from many sources, including government, terrorist groups, malicious intruders, etc. To protect the computer system against these threats, it is mandatory to create a secure cyber-barrier around an Industrial Control System (ICS).

8.7.1 Computer Security

"Computer Security" refers to the security of one computer, but we require the overall security of each individual computer present in the network for network security. So, the term "network security" is used, for the security of the network which includes the issues, such as password security, network sniffing, intrusion detection, firewalls, network structure, etc.

Computer security is needed because computer can be damaged by hostile software or intruders, which results in destruction of:

- Computer system
- Internal data
- Sensitive information to external party

The methods used to accomplish these unscrupulous objectives are many and varied depending on the circumstances.

Today, many network security threats are spread over the Internet, most common one include:

- Viruses, worms and Trojan horses
- Spyware and Adware
- Zero-day attacks, also called zero-hour attacks
- Hacker attacks
- Denial of service attacks
- Data interception and theft
- Identify theft

In this section, we will be going to discuss about Virus, worm, Trojan horse, Spyware.

8.7.2 Virus

A computer virus is a kind of malware program which, when run, get replicated by inserting copies of itself into another computer programs, data files of the hard drive. When the replication process of virus get succeeds, the affected areas are called as "infected".

Computer viruses can be considered as small software programs which are designed to spread from one computer to another through an interface program.

Some type of harmful activity, performed by virus on infected hosts, are:

- stealing hard disk space
- stealing CPU time
- accessing information
- corrupt or delete data on your computer
- erase everything on your hard disk, etc.

So, one can say the viruses are self-replicating computer programs that install themselves without the user consent.

Computer virus can also execute instructions which cause harm, that is why computer viruses affect security.

Common Types of Viruses are:

- Resident Viruses: This type of virus is a permanent virus that dwells in the RAM memory and then interrupt all of the operations which are executed by the system. Examples: CMJ, Meve, etc.
- Multipartite Viruses: It is distributed through infected media and usually get hide in the memory.
- Direct Action Viruses: In this virus replicate and when a specific condition is met, the virus comes into an action and infect files present in the directory or folder which are specified in the AUTOEXEC.BAT file PATH.
- Overwrite Viruses: In this, virus deletes the information contained in the files. Examples: Way, Trj.Reboot.
- Boot Virus: It affects the boot sector of a floppy or hard disk.
- Macro Virus: It infect files which are created by using certain applications or programs which contain macros.
- Directory Virus: It change the paths which indicate the location of a file. So, when you are executing a program infected by a virus, you are actually running a virus program, as the original file and program have been previously moved by the virus.
- Polymorphic Virus: These kind of virus encrypt itself by using different algorithms and encryption keys every time they infect a system.
- File Infectors: In this virus infects the program or executable files and when the programs are run, the virus gets activated, thus produces the damaging effects.
- Network Virus: It spread through a Local Network Area (LAN), and sometimes throughout the internet.
- E-mail viruses: It travels as an attachment to e-mail messages, and replicates by mailing to dozens of people in the victim's e-mail address book.

Figure 8.2 Computer virus

There are three types of viruses

- Boot Sector Virus: It install itself on the beginning track of a hard drive.
- File infector: It attach themselves to a program file.
- Macro Virus: Infect data file.

Characteristics of Computer Virus

- It requires a host program as a carrier.
- It gets activated by an external action.
- It is able to replicate.

Computer viruses can spread through many ways, which are:

- Email
- Removable hardware
- Downloading
- By attaching itself to file or boot records, etc.

Damage Caused by Virus

- It gives you fake pop ups which tell you to buy non-existent antivirus software.
- Some can monitor what you are doing.
- Slow down your computers performance
- Steal files from your computer, passwords, bank account details.

Viruses are extremely dangerous - be aware of using the internet.

8.7.3 Computer Worm

It is a standalone malware computer program which replicates itself, so that it can spread to other computers, through computer network. Computer worm does not need to attach itself to an existing program, unlike virus; but it harms to network, by consuming the bandwidth.

Worms are mainly created or designed to spread, but not to change the systems through which they pass. Worms such, as the Morris worm and Mydoom are payload (It is an action done by a program apart from the act of spreading in itself and causes damage to the operating system or even to the BIOS), which cause major disruption by increasing the network traffic.

To minimize the threat of worms, try to keep computers' operating system, other software up-to-date, avoid opening of unrecognized or unexpected emails, install firewall and keep your antivirus software updated.

Worms can also install backdoors (a secret method, of bypassing normal authentication in a product, computer system, cryptosystem or algorithm etc. and is used for securing the unauthorized remote access to a computer) on computers.

Figure 8.3 Computer Worm

The characteristics of a worm are

- It is self-contained.
- It can replicate
- It is activated by creating Process

How worm spread

Worms are autonomous agents who are capable of propagating themselves without the use of other program or intervention or action by a user.

Damage cause by worm

- Disrupt services
- Create system management problems
- It can scan for passwords and send information back to attacker.

Different types of Computer Worm

- Email Worms: It spread through infected email messages as an attachment or a link.
- Instant Messaging Worms: It spread by sending links to the contact list of instant messaging applications.
- Internet Worms: It scan all available network resources by using local operating system services, it will connect and gain access to computer if it is found to be vulnerable.
- IRC Worms: It spread through IRC chat channels, which sends infected files or links to an infected websites.

8.7.4 Trojan Horse

A Trojan horse, is a malicious computer program which misrepresents itself to appear useful or interesting just to persuade a victim to install it. Typically, an individual e-mails use a Trojan in the form of a joke program, which appears to be useful but that actually does damage. So, in Trojan horse, code is hidden in a program such as game or spreadsheet which looks safe to run but has hidden side effect.

It can be employed by cyber-thieves and hackers to get the access to users' systems, by tricking some form of social engineering on systems. Once Trojans get activated, then it can enable cyber-criminals to spy and steal your sensitive data, gain backdoor access to your system. Trojans can not self-replicate themselves.

Trojan can:

- Delete the data
- Block the data
- Modify the data
- Copy the data

Types of Trojan

Trojans are classified according to the type of actions:

- Backdoor: It gives remote control to the malicious users of an infected computer.
- Exploit: These are the program which contain data or code and it takes an advantage of a vulnerability within application software which is running on your computer.
- Rootkit: These are designed to conceal certain objects or activities in your system. It prevents malicious programs to get detected.
- Trojan-Banker: It is designed to steal the account data for online banking systems, e-payment systems, and credit or debit cards.
- Trojan-DDoS: It conduct DoS (Denial of Service), which is done by sending multiple requests from your and several other infected computers, the attack then overwhelm the target address.
- Trojan-Downloader: It automatically download and install new versions of malicious programs onto your computer.
- Trojan-Dropper: It is used by hackers to install Trojans and / or viruses for preventing the detection of malicious programs.

How Torjan Horses Spread

They generally spread through e-mail.

Limitations

Since Trojan Horse malware is not technically viral, it cannot self-replicate and requires a user interaction to function.

Protection against Trojans

By installing anti-malware software, on either PCs, laptops, Macs, tablets, and smartphones; one can get protection against Trojans.

8.7.5 Spyware

It is a malware which is installed on a computer with the aim of collecting the owner's private information. Spyware gathers the information about internet interaction, keylogging, passwords, and other valuable data, without even knowing the user of computer.

Spyware is sometimes incorporated into adware (Adware is a kind of software which usually causes "pop-up" or banner advertisements to appear on the computer's screen when a user clicks on a link.), but performs the additional function of monitoring the details of computer usage and website activity, making this information available without the knowledge of the user.

Negative affect of spyware:

- It automatically installs an additional software, through web browser searches.
- Changes computer settings
- Reducing connection speeds
- Changing the homepage
- Disrupting the network connection ability.

Figure 8.4 Spyware

Spyware is installed when a user installs a piece of free software. On installation of the required software, the spyware will piggyback and start collecting data from the user's activities.

Spyware is classified into four types: system monitors, trojans, adware, and tracking cookies. It is mostly used for the purposes of tracking and storing Internet users' movements on the Web and serving up pop-up ads to Internet users.

Whenever spyware is used for malicious purposes, its presence is typically hidden from the user and can be difficult to detect. Some spyware, such as key loggers, may be installed by the owner of a shared, corporate, or public computer intentionally in order to monitor users.

8.7.6 Malware

It is a piece of software which is inserted into an information system to cause harm to that or some other systems. Malware can gain remote access to an information system, record and sent data to third party without the user permission or knowledge.

Different types of malware are commonly described as viruses, worms, Trojan horses, backdoors, keystroke loggers, root kits or spyware. These terms correspond to the functionality and behaviour of the malware (e.g., a virus is self-propagating while a worm is self-replicating).

8.8 INTERNET ETIQUETTES (Netiquette)

"Netiquette" stands for "Internet Etiquette", and are set of practices which are created over the years to make an Internet experience pleasant for everyone; it is primarily concerned with matters of courtesy in communications.

Netiquettes are the conventional rules for correct behaviour on the internet. Netiquette distinct the Internet from traditional forms of communications such as telephone conversion, face-to-face meetings, paper based letters. It helps you to avoid misunderstanding that may arise during communication accomplished via any Internet services especially E-mail, chat and mailing lists, etc.

Nature of Poor Netiquette

Poor Netiquette have following parts:

- poor grammar and spelling errors
- junk mails
- harsh language

Internet Etiquette Rules

1. Do not write in capitals, as the person who reads the message thinks like your screaming.
2. Use emotions to make your conversation interesting.
3. Make the conversation or message brief and clear.
4. Never reply a private message on "reply all."
5. If someone bullies you don't bully back, just block them or report abuse them.
6. Do not talk to strangers online.
7. Always greet people before start of the conversation.
8. Do not create the chains of message.
9. Do not shop in a site if you don't know it.
10. Be discrete, do not give fake information.
11. Do not give out your personal information like phone numbers and addresses.

8.9 DOS

DoS is the acronym for Denial of Service. It is an attack that is aimed at either cutting off access to a resource such as a web site/app/service etc or making it extremely slow. This type of attack is usually implemented by hitting the target resource such as a web server with too many requests at the same time. This results in the server failing to respond to all the requests. The effect of this can either be crashing the servers or slowing them down.

What Does an Attack Look Like?

Basically, an attack is composed of a few bytes of redundant data, which appear to be a simple request for acknowledgement, like a communicative handshake on a network. The problem occurs when these requests become so numerous that the processing server or servers concentrate on handling the bogus request to access an online game. You may not be able to see the attack happen, but you can recognize the effects.

There are two types of Dos attacks namley:

Dos–This type of attack is performed by a single host.

Distributed Dos–This type of attack is performed by a number of machines are affected the same victim. It floods the network with data packets.

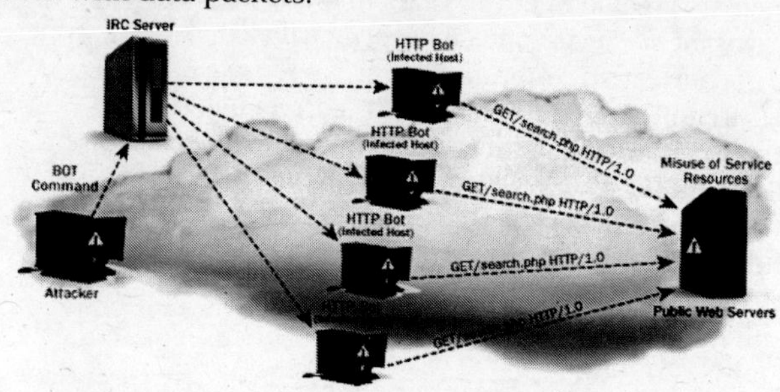

Dos attacks tools

The following are some of the tools that can be used to perform DoS attacks.

- Nemesy–This tool can be used to generate random packets. It works on windows. This tool can be downloaded from http://packetstormsecurity.com /files/25599 /nemesy13.zip.html . Due to the nature of the program, if you have an anti virus, it will most likely be detected as a virus.
- Land and LaTierra–This tool can be used for IP spoofing and opening TCP connections.
- Panther-This tool can be used to flood a victim s network with UDP packets.
- Botnets–These are multitudes of compromised computers on the internet that can be used to perform a distributed denial of service attack.

How to avoid DoS

An organization can adopt the following policy to protect itself against Denial of Service attacks.

- Attacks such as SYN flooding take advantage of bugs in the operating system. Installing security patches can help reduce the chances of such attacks.
- Intrusion detection systems can also be used to identify and even stop illegal activities.
- Firewalls can be used to stop simple DoS attacks by blocking all traffic coming from an attacker by identifying his IP.
- Routers can be configured via the Access Control List to limit access to the network and drop suspected illegal traffic.

8.10 DDOS

DDoS stands for Distributed Denial of Service. A Distributed Denial of Service Attack or DDOS, is an attempt to make a web service unavailable to its intended users. An attacker accomplishes this by flooding the target server with unnecessary network traffic in the form of web service requests. In this manner, the web service becomes overburdened responding to the requests and it slows down responses to valid requests from actual users.

DDoS attacks are designed to target any aspect of a business and its resources and can easily:

- disable a specific computer, service or an entire network.
- target alarms, printers, phones or laptops.
- hit system resources like bandwidth, disk space, processor time or routing information.
- execute malware that affects processors and triggers errors in computer microcode.
- exploit operating system vulnerabilities to drain system resources.
- crash the operating system.

But DDoS attacks are not all the same. On a very high level, a DDoS attack can be first divided into the following two categories:

- Connection-based: An attack that occurs once a connection between a server and a client has been established via certain standard protocols.

  Connectionless: An attack that does not require a session to be formally established before a sender (server) can send "data packets" – a basic unit of communication over a digital network - to a receiver (client).

Secondly, a DDoS attack have three broad categories, depending on the area of the network infrastructure on which the attack is:

Volumetric Attacks (connectionless)–Also known as "floods," the goal of this type of attack is to cause congestion and send so much traffic that it overwhelms the bandwidth of the site. Attacks are typically executed using botnets, an army of computers infected with malicious software and controlled as a group by the hacker.

TCP State-Exhaustion Attacks–This type of attack focuses on actual web servers, firewalls and load balancers to disrupt connections, resulting in exhausting their finite number of concurrent connections the device can support.

Application Layer Attacks (connection-based)–This type of attack, also known as "Layer 7 attacks", specifically targets weaknesses in an application or server with the goal of establishing a connection and exhausting it by monopolising processes and transactions.

8.10.1 Types of DDOS Attacks

Let us look at how DDoS attacks are performed and the techniques used. They are common types of attacks.

Ping of Death–
The ping command is usually used to test the availability of a network resource. It works by sending small data packets to the network resource. The ping of death takes advantage of this and sends data packets above the maximum limit (65,536 bytes) that TCP/IP allows. TCP/IP fragmentation breaks the packets into small chunks that are sent to the server. Since the sent data packages are larger than what the server can handle, the server can freeze, reboot, or crash.
Smurf–This type of attack uses large amounts of Internet Control Message Protocol (ICMP) ping traffic target at an Internet Broadcast Address. The reply IP address is spoofed to that of the intended victim. All the replies are sent to the victim instead of the IP used for the pings. Since a single Internet Broadcast Address can support a maximum of 255 hosts, a smurf attack amplifies a single ping 255 times. The effect of this is slowing down the network to a point where it is impossible to use it.
Buffer over flow–A buffer is a temporal storage location in RAM that is used to hold data so that the CPU can manipulate it before writing it back to the disc. Buffers have a size limit. This type of attack loads the buffer with more data that it can hold. This causes the buffer to overflow and corrupt the data it holds. An example of a buffer overflow is sending emails with file names that have 256 characters.
Teardrop–This type of attack uses larger data packets. TCP/IP breaks them into fragments that are assembled on the receiving host. The attacker manipulates the packets as they are sent so that they overlap each other. This can cause the intended victim to crash as it tries to re-assemble the packets.
SYN attack–SYN is short form for Synchronize. This type of attack takes advantage of the three-way handshake to establish communication using TCP. SYN attack works by flooding the victim with incomplete SYN messages. This causes the victim machine to allocate memory resources that are never used and deny access to legitimate users.
UDF Flood–In a UDP Flood, DDoS attackers send highly-spoofed UDP packets at a very high packet rate using a large source IP range. The victim's network (routers, firewalls, IPS/IDS, SLB, WAF and/or servers) is overwhelmed by the large number of incoming UDP packets. This attack normally consumes network resources and available bandwidth, exhausting the network until it goes offline.
NTP Amplification–In NTP Amplification attacks the perpetrator exploits publically-accessible Network Time Protocol (NTP) servers to overwhelm the targeted server with User Datagram Protocol (UDP) traffic. In an NTP amplification attack, the query-to-response ratio is anywhere between 1:20 and 1:200.
HTTP Flood–In HTTP flood DDoS attack the attacker exploits seemingly-legitimate HTTP GET or POST requests to attack a web server or application. HTTP floods do not use malformed packets, spoofing or reflection techniques, and require less bandwidth than other attacks to bring down the targeted site or server. The attack is most effective when it forces the server or application to allocate the maximum resources possible in response to each single request.
Zero-day DDoS Attacks–"Zero-day" are simply unknown or new attacks, exploiting vulnerabilities for which no patch has yet been released. The term is well-known amongst the members of the hacker community, where the practice of trading Zero-day vulnerabilities has become a popular activity.

8.11 NETIQUETTES, SECURITY CONSIDERATION

8.11.1 Be aware of the Possibility of Receiving Fraudulent and Unsolicited e-mail

A fraudulent (also called as phishing) is an email which pretends to be coming from a well-known company, is actually an attempt to get personal information from you. People who send phishing emails use your information (credit and debit card numbers) for doing identity theft.
To identify a fraud email:

- Many phishing emails begin with a general greeting, such as: "Dear HDFC member".
- Most phishing emails try to deceive you with the threat that your account is in jeopardy if you don't update it ASAP.
- The text in a link may attempt to look valid, but actually links are fake address.

Email send from an authorized person or an organisation will never ask for the following personal information:

- Credit and debit card numbers
- Bank account numbers
- Driver's Licence numbers
- Email addresses
- Passwords
- Your full name

Steps to take in order to prevent from fake email:

- Keep your security software updated.
- Check your account periodically to see any suspicious activity.
- Change your password often.
- Use a unique password.

8.12 PHISHING

It is an attempt of acquiring sensitive information such as usernames, passwords, and credit card details by hacker in an electronic communication.

Phishing is carried out either by email spoofing (creation of email messages with a forged sender address), instant messaging (online chat which offers real-time text transmission over the Internet) and it directs users to enter the details at a fake website whose looks are identical to the legitimate one.

8.12.1 Recognise Attempted Phishing

Few tips to identify the phishing are:

- Do not trust the display name
- Look the content of the email but do not click it.
- Check for spelling mistakes: Brands are serious about email and you do not find any major spelling mistakes or poor grammar.
- See the salutation: Legitimate businesses use a personal salutation with your first and last name.
- Do not give up personal information.
- Review the signature: Lack of details about the signer or company's contact number suggests a phish as Legitimate businesses always provide contact details.
- Do not click on attachments: It may contain viruses and malware which damages the files present on your computer.

8.13 SOFTWARE LICENCING

It is a legally binding agreement which specifies the terms of use of an application and defines the rights of both software producer and of end-user.

All of the software must be licensed legally before installation. Proof of the purchase of software must be maintained by an individuals or departments for all non-ITS provided software which is installed on a university owned computer.

8.14 OVERVIEW AND UNDERSTANDING OF IT ACT 2000

It is an Act of the Indian Parliament in India which deals with cybercrime and electronic commerce. It is based on the United Nations Model Law on Electronic Commerce which is recommended by the General Assembly of United Nations.

The original Act contained 94 sections, which is divided in 19 chapters and 4 schedules. This act provides a legal framework for electronic governance by giving recognition to electronic records and digital signatures.

The formations of Controller of Certifying Authorities was directed by the Act, to regulate the issuing of digital signatures.

8.14.1 Amendments

- A major amendment was made in 2008, when Section 66A which penalised the sending of "offensive messages".
- Section 69 was also introduced that gave authorities the power of "interception or monitoring or decryption of any information through any computer resource".
- It introduced penalties for child porn, cyber terrorism.

MODEL QUESTIONS AND ANSWERS

A. Multiple Choice

1.1 Http is:

a. Hypertext Transport Protocol
b. Hypertext Transfer Protocol
c. Hypertransfer Text Protocol
d. Hypertext Transfer Path

1.2 Green lock icon means:

a. The site's certificate is valid and its identity has been verified by a trusted third party.
b. The site hasn't provided the browser a valid certificate.
c. Site has weak security setup, which mean that your connection might not be private.
d. There are some problems with the site's certificate, might be your confidential information get leaked out.

1.3 ________ is a kind of malware program which, when run, get replicated by inserting copies of itself into another computer programs.

a. Worm
b. Virus
c. Trojan horse
d. Spyware

1.4 Which of the following requires a host program as a carrier?

a. Worm
b. Trojan horse
c. Virus
d. Spyware

1.5 ________ is a standalone malware computer program which replicates itself, so that it can spread to other computers, through computer network.

a. Worm
b. Trojan horse
c. Virus
d. Spyware

1.6 ________ is a kind of weakness that allows an attacker to reduce the system's information assurance.

a. Vulnerability
b. Risk
c. Virus
d. Worm

1.7 ________are the countermeasures which are used to avoid, detect or minimize the security risks.

a. Control
b. Security controls
c. Antivirus software
d. System control

1.8 ________ is an event or action which cause a loss or damage to computer hardware, software, data, or information.

a. Vulnerability
b. Risk
c. Virus
d. Worm

1.9 Protecting an information from being disclose to unauthorized parties is:

a. Confidentiality
b. Integrity
c. Availability
d. Software control

1.10 ________ means protecting information from an unauthorized user so that information cannot be modified.

a. Confidentiality
b. Integrity
c. Availability
d. Software control

1.11 A fraudulent is also called as:

a. Phishing
b. Phish
c. Mailing
d. Spam mail

1.12 ________ is an attempt of acquiring sensitive information such as usernames, passwords, and credit card details by hacker in an electronic communication.

a. Phisheng
b. Phishing

c. Pheshing d. Phesheng

1.13 Phishing is carried out either by:
a. Email spoofing b. Sending message
c. Sending attachment d. Sending salutation

1.14 ________ is a legally binding agreement which specifies the terms of use of an application and defines the rights of both software producer and of end-user.
a. Software binding b. Software licencing
c. Software act d. Licensed

1.15 All of the software must be ______ legally before installation.
a. Software binding b. Software licencing
c. Software act d. Licensed

1.16 Some specific and particularly popular and dangerous type of attacks
a. UDF Flood b. ICMP Flood
c. Slowloris d. All of the above

1.17 Name the tools that can be used to perform Dos attacks
a. Botnets b. Zero day DDos
c. Nuke d. None of the above

B. State whether the following are True or False

2.1 Backdoor gives remote control to the malicious users of an infected computer.

2.2 Torjan generally spread through e-mail and exchange of disk and information between computers.

2.3 Virus is a malware which is installed on a computer with the aim of collecting the owner's private information.

2.4 Malware is a piece of software which is inserted into an information system to cause harm to that or some other systems.

2.5 "Netiquette" stands for "Internet Etiquette".

2.6 Availability means only an unauthorized user has the right to access the information when needed.

2.7 Security policy defines the goals and elements of an organization's computer systems.

2.8 Data security means protecting data, either from destructive forces and unwanted actions of an unauthorized users.

2.9 Some of the browsers have privacy features for cookies, private browsing, and deleting browsing history.

2.10 The lock icon is displayed somewhere in the window of your web browser and gives you detailed information on the security status of the website.

2.11 IT act 2000 deals with cybercrime and electronic commerce.

2.12 Phishing emails begin with a general greeting, such as: "Dear HDFC member".

2.13 Email spoofing involves creation of email messages with a real sender address.

2.14 The original Act contained 94 sections, which is divided in 19 chapters and 4 schedules.

2.15 All of the software must be licensed legally before installation.

2.16 A distributed dos attack's intent is to deny legitimate users access to a resource such as a network, server etc.

2.17 Smurf attack uses large amounts of ICMP ping traffic target at an Internet Broadcast Address.

2.18 Firewalls can be used to stop simple DOS attacks by blocking all traffic coming from an attacker by identifying his IP.

Answers

A. 1. b 2. a 3. b 4. c 5. a
6. a 7. b 8. b 9. a 10. b
11. a 12. b 13. a 14. b 15. d
16. d 17. a

B. 2.1 T 2.2 T 2.3 F 2.4 T 2.5 T
2.6 F 2.7 T 2.8 T 2.9 T 2.10 T
2.11 T 2.12 T 2.13 F 2.14 T 2.15 T
2.16 F 2.17 T 2.18 T

CHAPTER 9

PC Maintenance, Security and Troubleshooting

9.1 OVERVIEW OF COMPUTER MAINTENANCE AND SECURITY

Maintenance is the actions associated with equipment repair when it does not work properly. The dictionary defines maintenance as "the work of keeping equipment in proper condition". This would imply that the maintenance should be the actions taken to prevent a device or component from failing. It is to repair normal equipment degradation experienced due to the operation of the device and to keep it in proper working order.

A computer system, like any mechanical or electrical system is likely to fail. There are many causes, including disk crash, power failure, software errors, a fire in the machine room, or even sabotage. Maintenance will to prevent all such occurrences.

9.1.1 Types of Maintenance

Maintenance is divided into two types:

(a) Preventive maintenance

(b) Breakdown maintenance

Preventive Maintenance

Preventive maintenance can be defined as: Actions performed on a time - or machine-run-based schedule that detect, preclude, or mitigate degradation of a component or system with the aim of sustaining or extending its useful life by controlling degradation to an acceptable level.

Preventive maintenance is a schedule of planned servicing action aimed at the prevention of breakdown and failures. The primary goal of preventive maintenance is to prevent the failure of equipment. It is designed to preserve and enhance equipment reliability by replacing worn out components before they actually fail.

The personal computer (PC) is a machine with electrical and electronic circuits as well as electromechanical assemblies. For reliable operation and long life, a PC should be handled carefully. Computer room should be cleaned and must be dust free. Preventive maintenance steps prescribed by the manufacturer should be done periodically before using appropriate materials.

A good preventative maintenance program incorporates a comprehensive backup plan, measures to secure the system against malicious exploits, periodic hardware and software maintenance and steps to maintain general system tidiness.

The goal of preventative maintenance is to reduce the likelihood of hardware failures, extend the useful life of the system, minimize system crashes caused by outdated driver and other software problems, secure the system against viruses and prevent data loss.

Breakdown Maintenance

Breakdown maintenance is the repair carried out once the PC stops working.

☞ Breakdown maintenance is also called corrective maintenance.

Breakdown maintenance is a repair service and can be categorized into three classes.

(a) Routine repairs when the breakdown is seen as an inconvenience but otherwise does not affect usual service.

(b) Urgent repairs where vital facilities and services are disrupted.

(c) Emergency repairs where failure of an item can present an immediate danger.

9.2 BASIC COMPUTER MAINTENANCE

1. Backup: Backing up your data just means saving your files in a separate location so that in the event of disaster, you can easily copy your files back onto your computer. Using an external hard drive (connected via USB) is usually the simplest method as it can be easily configured using the automatic backup software included in the operating system. There are also online backup systems like iCloud that provide space to store your backup files using the Internet. Dropbox is another free service that allows users to save copies of their files on online servers for backup purposes, or to be able to share files easily with other computers connected to the Internet.
2. Invest in an UPS (uninterruptible power source): A UPS is a device that works as a surge protector and a battery backup all in one. Not only does it keep your computer safe from electrical spikes that travels through the lines, it also gives you time to save your work, and properly power down your computer in event of a power failure. You do not lose your work, and your computer gets to be shut down properly.
3. Never turn the computer off with the power switch: The one exception to this rule is when your computer locks up

and your hard drive is not running (the hard drive light is not blinking). In this situation, you can turn the power off without harmful effects to the hard drive. As cutting the power can also result in lost data or Windows files.

Doing this can helps to prevent permanent hard drive damage caused by the hard drive heads contacting the surface of the drive disc. This can prevent a lots of Windows problems.

Whenever possible, recover from crashed by pressing the Ctrl + Alt + Del keys at the same time and going into your Task Manager. You can often find programs that are not responding here, and choose to close them from this utility. Press Ctrl + Alt + Del keys against to reboot your computer from this screen.

☞ Switch off the monitor, system unit and the printer before switching off the mains.

4. Scan disk and defrag it once in a month: These utilities help to keep your hard drive in optimal shape and error free.
5. Do not unplug peripheral devices while the power supply is on: Unplugging devices such as your mouse, keyboard, printer, etc. with the power on can short out the connector socket or even the motherboard itself.
6. Remove programs from your startup: Often when you install a program, it will ask you whether it should load up as soon as the Windows loads (or just decide to do so on its own). The more programs you are trying to start up at the same time, the slower your Computer will start. Also, all those programs running in the background while you working will slow your computer's response time.
7. Run virus checks and adware/spyware scans regularly (at least once a week): There are so many types and variations of viruses, spyware and adware floating around the Internet that at times it may seem daunting to even have Internet access on your computer. However, regular scans with virus scanner, and adware scanners, can ensure your computer to remains healthy.
8. Keep disks handy: If the worst thing happens, and you need to format your system for one reason or another, then it is good idea to have all your driver disks, operating system disks, backup disks, etc. in a readily available place.
9. Keep your software updated: Software developers are always writing and releasing patches that update the software you have already bought from them. A lot of these patches fix problems you may be experiencing yourself with a particular program.

   Other patches plug security leaks. Still other patches update reference files for your virus/spy/adware scanners to make sure you are scanning for as many variants as possible. So make sure you regularly update/patch your operating system, virus scanners, and various other applications.
10. Develop a schedule of maintenance practices: All this advice is meaningless if you keep forgetting to do it, or only remember after something has gone wrong. Write yourself a maintenance schedule, with a list of what tasks should be performed daily, weekly, and monthly.

☞ If you develop a routine and stick to it, then you should avoid the larger problems by always being on top of the smaller ones.

9.2.1 Why Proper Computer Maintenance is Important?

Proper computer maintenance is important because of the following reasons:

1. Because it will increases the speed of your PC.
2. Prevent errors, which will save money.
3. Secure your data and information.
4. Save time.

By maintaining your PC in good condition and operating it in dust free air condition environment you will notice that you will work for more number of hours without its failure. In this way you will save your data as well as damaged to the machine you will not require any hardware engineer for repair and spend money on the repair of the machine.

9.3 UNDERSTANDING SECURITY

Due to the wide spread use of PCs and developments in networks connecting PCs to company's computers, there has been an increase in the chances of feeding undesirable data deliberately by outsiders. A person with a PC at a remote place can use a phone line and illegally collect information without leaving any clues. Individual users can copy confidential data from a company's computer or other details from a remote station connected via communication network.

Security means preventing the network communication system falling in the hands of unauthorized people. The sender of data may wish to be assured that only the intended party actually receives designated data. The receiver must authenticate first that it is the one who is authorized to receive data and thereafter the sender exchanges data. A total approach to computer security involves both external and internal security. These are as under:

(a) External security: It deals with securing the computer system against external factors such as fires, floods, earthquakes, stolen disks/tapes, leaking out of stored information by a person who has access to the information and so on.

(b) Internal Security: It mainly deals with user authentication and access control. User authentication means once a user is allowed to physical access the computer facility, the user's identification must be checked by the system before the user can actually use the facility. A computer system contains many resources and several types of information. Obviously, not all resources and information are meant for all users. Therefore, even when a user passes the authentication phase and is allowed to use the the computer facility, a way is needed to prohibit the user from accessing those resources/information that he/she is not authorized to access. This requirement is taken care of by access control mechanism.

9.4 INBUILT PC SECURITY

Security in computer systems deals with protecting the various resources and information of a computer system against destruction and unauthorized access.

9.4.1 Tools

Before getting to the details of securing your PC, it will be very helpful to look at the inbuilt security and privacy tools available in Windows 7. These tools are as under:

(a) User Account Password
(b) User Account Control
(c) Parental Control
(d) Firewall
(e) Windows Defender programs
(f) Biometric Service
(g) Data encryption
(h) Internet Explorer's anti-phishing and anti-spam features

User Account Password

In Windows 7, we have to assign a password to each user account on the computer. This prevents unauthorised users from accessing the system and it enables you to lock your computer.

User Account Control

User Account Control is used to help you to stay in control of your PC. This tool asks you to confirm certain actions that could harm your system. If you have an administrator account, click Yes to continue; if you have a standard account, you must enter an administrator's user name and password to continue.

Parental Controls

Windows 7's Parental Controls provides tools to protect children from inadvertently running certain programs, playing unsuitable games, and using the computer at inappropriate times.

Windows Firewall

Windows 7 comes with the Windows Firewall feature turned on. This prevents intruders from accessing your computer while you are online.

Windows Defender

Windows Defender is an antispyware program. It continuously monitors system settings to prevent the installation of known spyware and to alert you the presence of spyware-like activity.

Biometric Service

Windows Biometric Service provides support for fingerprint biometric devices so that you can use a fingerprint reader to log on to your computer and to enter administrative credentials in response to UAC elevation prompts.

☞ Spyware is a software program that installs on your computer without your knowledge or consent. This program surreptitiously gathers data from your computer, steals your passwords, displays advertisements, and hijacks your Web browser.

Data encryption

BitLocker Drive Encryption encrypts entire hard drives and makes the data completely inaccessible to a thief. In Windows 7, BitLocker To Go can also be used to protect removable storage drives, such as portable hard drives and USB flash drives.

Internet Explorer's anti-phishing and anti-spam

Security improvements in Internet Explorer include restrictions on ActiveX controls, a SmartScreen phishing filter, and InPrivate Filtering and InPrivate Browsing to prevent information about your browsing habits from being tracked.

9.4.2 Checking Computer's Security

In Windows 7, security-related options about the current state of PC have been gathered in Action Center. In particular, Action Center warns you if your computer has any current security problems. For example, the Action Center tells you if your PC does not have virus protection installed, or if the Windows Defender spyware database is out of date or turned off. Action Center also warns you if User Account Control is turned off or if the Windows Firewall is deactivated.

To see action center messages, do this:

1. Click the Action Center icon in the taskbar's notification area.

Figure 9.1 Action Center messages

2. The current Action Center messages appear in the popup as seen in Figure 9.1.
3. To launch Action Center, click Open Action Center, the Action Center window will appear as shown in Figure 9.2.

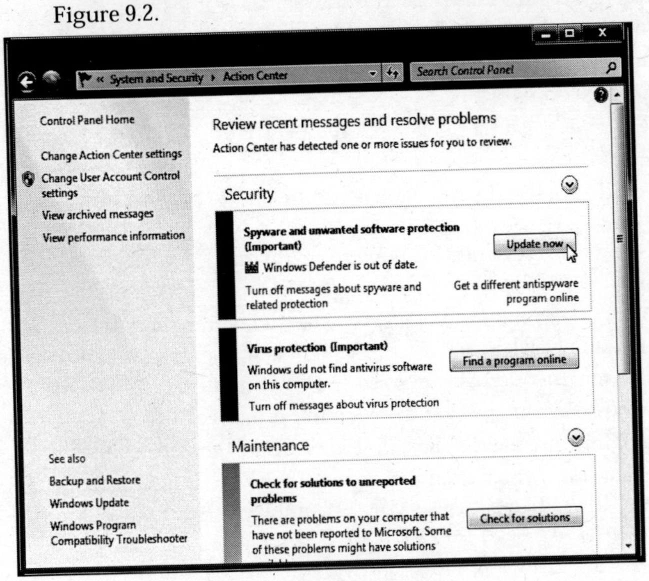

Figure 9.2 Action Center window

To check action center for security problems, do this:

1. Click the Start button and then choose Control Panel. The Control Panel window appears.
2. In Control Panel window, click Review your computer s status under the System and Security.
3. The Action Center window appears as seen in Figure 9.2.
4. Click a message button to resolve the security issue, such as clicking Update now if Windows Defender is out of date.

9.4.3 Securing Documents

In our lives we use different methods to protect the things that are important to us. We use banks to protect our money, insurance plans to protect our physical assets and various systems to protect ourselves. From unauthorized access and the associated risks. In our ever changing technology based world it is imperative to have control over all of your documents in order to maintain control of your organization and your future.

Challenges Securing Paper Documents

Paper documents are basically difficult to manage and particularly to secure. Other than locking file rooms or storage devices there simply aren't a lot of options when it comes to securing paper documents. Document Management systems provide some level of document security by requiring that paper files be checked out by reading a file ID barcode and identifying the user requesting the file. These systems, are carefully used to prevent an unauthorized user.

9.5 ANTIVIRUS

Before we concentrate on the antivirus, let us look at the brief description on the virus.

A computer virus is a small block of coded instruction that obtains control of a PC's Central Processing Unit (CPU) and directs it to perform unusual and often destructive actions. (See Figure 9.3)

☞ *ir s*, also called as perverse software is a program which knows how to copy itself and attaches itself to other programs which further spread the infection. Anti virus is the method to get rid of perverse software or the viruses.

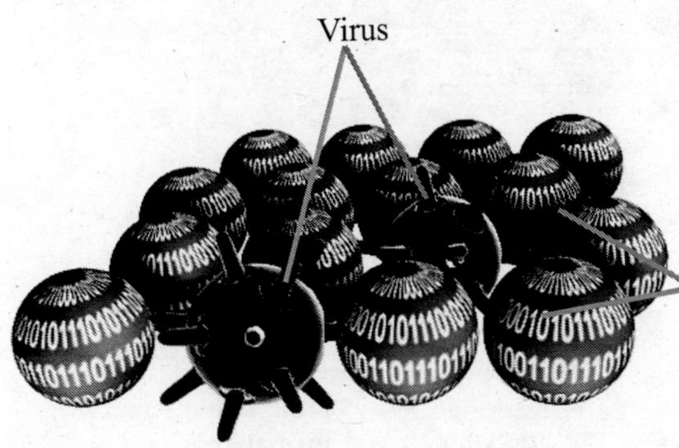

Figure 9.3 Computer Virus

Viruses spread through pen drives, e-mails, Internet downloads and other networks. They may remain dormant and strike when the infected programme or file is used. One can detect the presence of a virus by strange messages which may pop up on the screen. There may be unusual changes in the size of programs, strange file names in the contents, reduction on free space in the memory and prolonged disk activity or drives working on their own. If you do not identify these glitiches, viruses go undetected and get enough time to get activated and spread out.

Viruses can be disguised as attachments of funny images, greeting cards, or audio and video files. Computer viruses also spread through downloads on the Internet. They can be hidden in illicit software or other files or programs you might download.

☞ Virus scanners do help in detecting such viruses.

Viruses are of the following types:

(a) First type would infect .exe files, adding a foreign string to them so that when they are executed, the virus would run and do its dirty work.
(b) Second type of virus would travel from one PC to another via pen drive or disk or any other media, and when a PC is booted from such an infected media devices, the virus would copy itself to the boot sector of that PC.

Depending on the mode of infecting the computer systems, viruses can be broadly classified into the following types: (See Figure 9.4)

Figure 9.4 Virus Types

1. Trojan Horse: A Trojan Horse is a program that invades a computer system by secretly attaching itself to a valid program downloaded into the computer. It may be used to locate password information, or it may alter an existing program to make it easier to gain access to it.
2. Time and Logic Bombs: A time bomb as the name suggests, is triggered by an event. It can format the hard disk on a given date or slow down computer every Friday or make a ball bounce around the screen.

   A logic bomb may be brought into a PC by downloading a public-domain program that has been tampered with. Once executed, the logic bomb usually does its damage right away, whereas a software virus slowly invades a system and attaches itself to other programs too.
3. Melissa and SKA Virus: Melissa virus attacks MS Word documents and spreads very fast. This virus affects MS Word documents by installing itself to Normal.doc and disabling the macro protection message and infects all the Word files opened or created subsequently. The message generated by the virus says "Here is a document you asked for ...don't show anyone else".

   There is another virus called SKA which increases the size of the file and changes the extension of the files to .ska. These viruses delete the MS Document files or change their contents.
4. Worms and Viruses: A worm is a destructive program that is designed to adulterate database either all at once or over a period of time. It is very similar to the logic bomb.

   A virus is similar to a worm, which is also a destructive program. However, the virus always attaches itself to other programs, whereas the worm may not. Worms are less harmful than viruses as they do not require any carrier program and spread by duplicating themselves. They are merely found in the network environment.

9.5.1 Preventive Measures and Treatments

The saying "Prevention is better than cure" should be the guiding principle for an organisations to control virus spread. There are various things one can do to prevent viral infection in a computer system. These are as follows:

(a) Limit the sharing of software with Outsiders.
(b) Limit transitivity.
(c) Limit functionality.
(d) Use the virus scanner and virus remover more often.
(e) Using Vaccine Program weekly.
(f) If you do a folder listing, look carefully at the contents of the folder.
(g) Observe whether your PC is slowing down.
(h) Watch for files that disappear or get hidden.
(i) Keep a lookout for decrease in the main memory or reduction of disk space.
(j) Watch for unusually large sizes on program files.
(k) Watch for recent creation dates on old program files.
(l) Watch for unusual displays on the computer screen.
(m) Use caution when using any new software package. There have been cases, where commercial software packages have been sold with virus.
(n) If you are down loading software from the Internet, make sure your browser and virus-protection program will scan the data before it is saved to the local hard drive. It means, you use a firewall.
(o) Make sure that there is virus-protection software not only on the local host but on any application or file servers, you use.

Limit Sharing of Software with Outsiders

One can limit the sharing of software by limiting an information flow so as to form a post office kind of communicating information domains in a network system. In such a system, a virus will spread only to those domains which are in the transitive flow path from its initial source.

Limit Transitivity

In a system with unlimited information paths, limited transitivity may have an effect. If users do not use all available paths, but since there is always a direct path between any two users, there is always the possibility of software virus infection. As an example, in a system, with transitivity limited to a distance of 1 km, it is safe to share information with any user you trust without having to worry about whether the user has wrongly trusted another user.

Limit Functionality

Although isolationism and limited transitivity offer solutions to the virus infection problem they are not ideal solutions in the sense that widespread sharing and is generally considered a valuable tool in computing.

The third option for absolute prevention is limited function. Most real-world users do not exploit the general purpose capabilities provided to them, and it would be a substantial advantage for the defender if limited function could be applied. However, all modern software packages allow general purpose functions, including most application programs such as databases, spreadsheets, editors and mail systems etc.

Use Virus scanner and Virus Remover

You should install the latest anti-virus software and update it regularly. The anti-virus programme should ideally start by default when the computer is switched on. The system should also be equipped with the ability to self-repair the damage caused by virus attacks.

Virus scanners are the products designed to help in identifying viruses within files, boot sectors, master boot sectors, memory, and other hiding places, name them, and eventually remove them. The capability to detect and identify a virus is probably the most important feature of a scanner.

☞ A scanner is critical for providing a precise identification of a virus in your system. Without a precise identification, you cannot know the best course of action for removing it, and you cannot be sure that you have removed it completely.

A scanner is the only kind of anti-virus program that can spot a virus before the program runs. Thus, if you use a scanner to check new software before running it, you can prevent even one of your files from becoming infected. Scanners are always out-of-date. Most scanners are usually somewhat incomplete when they are released. No virus researcher has access to every virus on earth. So even if your program was absolutely a month ago, there may be some viruses that it cannot detect today. Although your odds of encountering a brand new virus are very remote, you must recognize that scanners will not catch everything.

If an organisation has a network then all pen drives must be disabled, except one or two, preferably in the IT support cell of the organisation. If any pen drive is sent to other organisation, it should be write-protected to prevent virus invasion.

☞ A virus also spreads through the Internet. Employees should properly scan the documents before downloading from the Internet. An e-mail from an unidentifiable source should be discarded.

One should always maintain a complete back-up of all important information and data, which should be updated regularly. The system software and other executable files should be backed up with originals. Even after an organisation is properly fire walled against any imminent attack, the viruses may still silently creep in. It should be ensured that the virus has been completely cleaned. This is because the virus is able to become dormant for some time and re-emerges if the system is not properly cured.

Using Vaccine Program Weekly

Vaccine program is a program that watches for typical things that viruses do, halts them and warns the computer operator about the computer security being threatened. These should be run frequently say every or more often.

Treatment Method

If your computer has a bootable hard disk, it is a prime target for boot virus attack. Depending on the kind of ROM BIOS on your computer, you might be able to alter the bootup sequence, so drive A: is not sought for a bootable and potentially infectious disk. For example, if your computer is equipped with an American Magatrends Inc. BIOS, change the bootup sequence to C:, A:; this prevents floppy disks infected with boot sector viruses from infecting your hard drive. It will allow drive A: to be used for booting a computer when drive C: is damaged, and does not affect the operation of drive A: in any other way.

9.5.2 Virus Detection by using Antivirus Programs

Anti-virus software can identify and block many viruses before they can infect your computer. However, it is important to keep it up-to-date after installing it. Anti-virus software scans files and your computer's memory for certain patterns that may indicate an infection. The patterns it looks for are based on the signatures, or definitions, of known viruses. Virus authors are continually releasing new and updated viruses, so it is important that you have the latest definitions installed on your computer. Many anti-virus packages include an option to automatically receive updated virus definitions. In this way, new information is added frequently to the program. It is a good idea to take advantage of this option.

☞ Once you have installed an anti-virus package, you should scan your entire computer periodically. You can configure your antivirus software to perform an automatic scan. In automatic scans, it automatically scans specific files or directories and prompts you at set intervals to perform complete scans.

It is a good idea to manually scan files you receive from an outside source before opening them. This includes the following:

(a) Saving and scanning e-mail attachments or web downloads rather than selecting the option to open them directly from the source.

(b) Scanning media, including CDs and DVDs, for viruses before opening any of their files.

Choosing Antivirus Software

There are many vendors who produce anti-virus software, and deciding which one to choose can be confusing. The following is a list of some anti-virus vendors.

1. Aladdin Knowledge Systems
2. AVG

3. Central Command, Inc.
4. Computer Associates International, Inc.
5. Frisk Software International
6. F-Secure Corporation
7. McAfee (a Network Associates company)
8. Network Associates, Inc.
9. Norman Data Defense Systems
10. Panda Software
11. Proland Software
12. Sophos
13. Symantec Corporation
14. Trend Micro, Inc.
15. Guardian Antivirus

☞ All anti-virus software packages perform the same functions, so your decision in use should be based on various factors such as recommendations, particular features, availability, and/or price.

Anti-Virus Software Installation

The overall installation process of antivirus software may be same for all vendors. However, there may be some variations. You should go through the installation manual before installing virus scanner. We shall explain the procedure to install Symantec Antivirus software on your Windows based machine.

To use Symantec Antivirus for Windows, you need the following:

(a) A PC running Windows XP, Windows 7 or higher versions.

(b) 1 GB maximum available hard disk space.

(c) An active Internet connection.

The following are the steps to be pursued for installing a Symantec Antivirus software on PC using Windows operating system:

1. Disable or uninstall all other anti-virus and firewall applications, because they might interfere with the installation process.
2. Close all open programs on your machine, so you will not lose any unsaved work when you restart the machine during installation.
3. Double-click on the installer. Double-click the Symantec Antivirus folder. Click Install to begin installation.
4. Click Next when the installer screen appears.
5. Read the license agreement screen, and if you agree to it, select I accept the terms of the license agreement checkbox.
6. Click Next to install all components using the default settings, or click Custom to specify components and installation path.
7. In the Network Setup Type window, select Unmanaged, and then click Next.

☞ The Managed option takes advantage of a companion server product that automatically installs program patches, virus definition updates, and protection policies. This means that you do not need to configure your software for automatic updates. However, you can select this option only if your department operates a management console Check with your department's network administrator to find out if you have this capability.

8. If you chose Managed, enter the management server's DNS name or IP address in the Select Server window.

☞ In the Install Options window, select Auto-Protect if you want Symantec Antivirus to automatically monitor your system as you work.

9. If you have an active Internet connection, select Run LiveUpdate to acquire the latest version of the software from the Internet and update your virus definition files during installation.
10. Click Next, and then click Install.
11. If you have selected Run LiveUpdate above, the installer will automatically launch the LiveUpdate program. Click Next to have LiveUpdate check with Symantec for the latest virus definitions. When the update is complete, click Finished.
12. In the Symantec AntiVirus - InstallShield Wizard window, click Finish to complete the installation process.

To open the program as in Figure 9.5, double-click the Symantec AntiVirus Corporate Edition icon in the Windows taskbar. You can check the date of the virus definition file update on this screen as marked in Figure 9.5. If it is showing an older date click on the LiveUpdate button for the latest virus definitions.

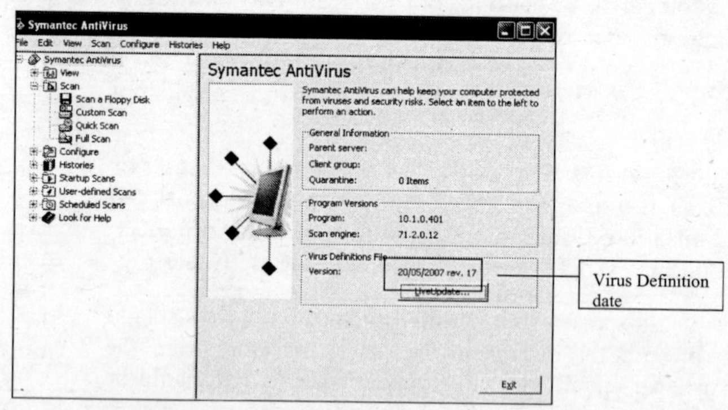

Figure 9.5 Symantec Anti Virus Main Screen

9.6 UPGRADING OPERATING SYSTEM AND APPLICATION SOFTWARE

9.6.1 Upgrading Operating System

Operating system upgrades are only supported when upgrading from one version of an OS to a newer version of the same OS to boost the performance of computer.

There are few steps you can take to make the upgrade process smoother:

Check Compatibility

1. Open Add/Remove Programs from the control panel and make a list of all the applications that appear there.
2. Open System from the Control Panel, go to the Hardware tab and open Device Manager, then make a list of the components in your PC.
3. Check whether version is supported by the new operating system.
4. Download updates and drives for new OS from the web site.

Back up Data

Back up all your important files before upgrade.

To update your Windows 7 to 8 operating system

1. Open Windows Update by clicking the Start button. In the search box, type Update, and then, in the list of results, click Windows Update.
2. Click Check for updates, and then wait while Windows looks for the latest updates for your computer.
3. If you see a message telling you that important updates are available, or telling you to review important updates, click the message to view and select the important updates to install.
4. In the list, click the important update for more information. Select the check box for any updates that you want to install, then click OK.
5. Click Install updates.

There are many benefits beyond security involved in upgrading your operating system. These are:

1. Increased productivity
2. Safety
3. Better features

9.6.2 Application Software

To find the need of upgrade software for various reasons. When new hardware is used in a system it needs to upgrade software to a supported version. Similarly, if you need to upgrade an application to utilize new software features to upgrade software, because components of their system (operating systems, hardware, software etc) become obsolete. When the components are upgraded, need a compatible software version. So in that situations a software upgrade is inevitable.

When it comes to upgrading software application there are:

1. New features might be added which were not available in the older version of the software. Upgrading might offer you new functions, and can increase productivity. For example, if there are more different features added, could be faster and more efficient.
2. Upgrading software can add additional security for your computer. It is always important to keep up computer safer and up to date with antivirus software. This will help to stop viruses from catching to the computer when you are downloading.
3. Support for more recent operating system.
4. Ease of future upgrades
5. Faster resolution of technical issues.

9.7 SECURITY

In the absence of proper internal controls, employees with doubtful integrity or newly recruited employees including outside agents can steal data and/or develop software packages and use them to meet their needs or sell them. They can add, delete, or change data for misappropriation purposes. They can do these things at the computer site or from a remote station connected via network.

☞ Thieves (called hackers) are interested in computerized records because the job of keeping an account of the assets of many organizations has now been entrusted to computer systems.

When paper money was introduced, thieves used printing presses to counterfeit the currency in the paper form. Now plastic money (credit cards) are used and hackers are using computers to divert the money from one account to another intentionally. Hence, measures must be taken to protect the system against the theft of assets.

Data security involves the following:

(a) Protection of data against accidental or malicious disclosure;

(b) Physical protection of hardware and software against damage or destruction.

Computer system's insecurity has increased due to the following two reasons:

(a) The information found in a relatively complete and up-to-date, so, data bank may be of sufficient value to tempt hackers to seek access to it.

(b) More and more people now have the skills needed to program, penetrate and manipulate data stored in computer systems.

9.8 CLEANING THE MONITOR, KEYBOARD AND CPU

Cleaning your computer, components, and peripherals helps to keep everything in good working condition and helps to prevent germs from spreading. While you cleaning with a Computer there is a risk of static electricity passing an electronic component inside of the computer or by cleaning accessories attached to the computer while they are still plugged into the computer, such as a Keyboard, Mouse or Monitor. Once the Power Cord is unplugged there is no Electricity running through the computer, there are some parts in the Power Supply that hold an Electrical charge. Before you touch anything inside the computer case touch the Metal Frame to discharge any static electricity supply.

Cleaning the Monitor

While cleaning monitors you must take some precautions. Normally, there is a special coating on monitor screens that will permanently streak if you use an ammonia-based cleaning product to bathe the screen. If you wipe the screen while it is on and warm, a static electricity is generated which is harmful to your system. The best way to clean your monitor's screen is, to dry-dust with a lint-free cloth or by spraying some window cleaner with a soft cloth.

☞ Never spray cleaning solution directly on the screen.

Precautions to take while cleaning the monitor:

- Do not use glass cleaner to clean a monitor. Many screens have anti-glare coatings that can be damaged by glass cleaner.
- Turn off the computer.
- Unplug the monitor from the power. If you are using a laptop, unplug the laptop.
- Use a soft clean cloth moistened with water to wipe the screen.
- Do not spray any liquids directly onto the screen. The liquid could leak into the monitor and damage the internal components.

Cleaning the Keyboard

Shutdown your PC and remove the main plug. Unplug the keyboard and hold it upside down to release any debris present in between the keys (pressing the key is a good way to clean it).

A dirty keyboard does not look nice and may not work properly. Dust, food, liquid, and other particles can get stuck underneath the keys, which can prevent them from working properly. The following steps are basic cleaning tips that can help to keep your keyboard clean.

- Unplug the keyboard from the USB or PS/2 port. If the keyboard is plugged into the PS/2 port, you will need to shut down the computer before unplugging it.
- Turn the keyboard upside down, and gently shake it to remove dirt and dust.
- Use a can of compressed air to clean between the keys.
- Moisten a cotton cloth or paper towel with rubbing alcohol, and use it to clean the tops of the keys. Do not pour alcohol or any other liquid directly onto the keys.
- Reconnect the keyboard to the computer once it is dry. If you are connecting it to a PS/2 port, you will need to connect it before turning on the computer.

Cleaning the CPU

Dust inside your computer can slow down your computer and cause some computer components to fail. The steps for cleaning the CPU from inside are:

1. Gather the tools: You need compressed air and a screwdriver (only needed if you use a screwdriver to open the computer case). A small vacuum might clean up the mess you make around the computer, but should never be used inside it. A dust mask is suggested because it can save you a bit of sneezing if you need to clean a computer quickly.
2. Shut down and unplug your computer.
3. Disconnect the LAN cable and all peripherals, such as monitors, scanners, printers, keyboards, mice and speakers.
4. Open your computer: Once you have a suitable work area, open your computer. Most machines have screws holding a side panel down. After removing these, you can then slip the side off your machine.

5. Prepare to Clean: After opening the computer cabinet, use compressed air to remove a dust mask. Never touch the inside of your computer unless it is necessary.
6. Begin dusting: Use compressed air to blow out the dust inside the machine. In this manner you can sweep out all the dust that settles on lower components. Keep your air source a moderate distance from the component you are working on.
   - Make sure to hold your can of compressed air upright. If inverted, it can let out liquid which can cause severe damage to your computer.
   - Compressed air is freezing cold when it leaves. Don't let frost to form on your chips.
   - A lot of dust can be raised; try not to breathe it. If the PC is very dusty, take it out of doors before using the compressed air.
7. Clean the CPU cooling fan and heatsink: The heatsink/fan area accumulates dust easily because the fan moves a lot of dust-laden air through the closely spaced

heatsink fans. As dust accumulates, it covers the blades of the heatsink, insulating them and thereby reducing their ability to radiate the heat produced by the processor. The CPU cooling fan spins faster (and makes more noise) as it tries to draw enough air through the heatsink to cool the processor. Eventually, the air channels in the heatsink become completely clogged and the heatsink loses its ability to cool the processor.

To avoid such problems, it is important to keep the CPU cooler clean. To begin cleaning the CPU cooler, use a brush or vacuum cleaner to remove the muck from the top of the cooling fan.

8. Look inside and outside the CPU for any dust you may have missed.
9. Clean up your work space: Depending on your workspace, you may need to get a small vacuum and clean the area around the computer.
10. Close your computer: Once the machine is tightly shut reattach the power cord and other cables. A clean computer will run significantly cooler and last much longer.

9.9 DELETING UNNECESSARY PROGRAMS AND FILES

Many things happen when you install program. First, they sit on your hard drive taking up space, and they have installed files on your "Registry" and some Dynamic Link Library files (these are little files needed for Windows to make the program run) in your PC.

These go in a Windows initializing file called "system.ini". INI for Initialization File. When Windows starts it looks at the "system.ini" to see what programs have to be available so they will start when you want to use them.

Windows also reads the Registry to see what programs are on your Computer and what it has to do to make them work. Also, Windows reads your Startup Folders to see what has to start automatically and hide in the background. Also the "msconfig" place all these programs in your "Startup". All this will slow down the operation of your PC.

To uninstall unnecessary programs and clean up your PC do the following:

1. Click on the Start button, then double click on Control Panel. Find the program you want to remove and select it then click on Add/Remove button. Follow the instructions.
2. You may get a message that Some files could not be removed. Click on a Details button that will give you the information about "Leftover Stuff". Write down the information and try to find them so that you can remove them manually.
3. After you have removed the "Old files" you should run "Scandisk" and then "defrag" your hard drive. Removing files and programs will leave holes or spaces all over on your drive thus slowing it down even more. You will be amazed at the performance change after you run "Scan disk".

9.9.1 Disk Cleanup

You can use Disk Cleanup to free up space on your hard disk by removing temporary Internet files, removing installed components and programs that you no longer use, and emptying the Recycle Bin.

☞ Disk Cleanup helps to free space on your hard disk drive. Disk Cleanup searches your drive, and then shows you temporary files, cache files, and unnecessary program files that you can safely delete. You can direct Disk Cleanup to delete some or all of those files.

To open Disk Cleanup, do this:

1. Click Start button, highlight All Programs, highlight Accessories, highlight System Tools and then choose Disk Cleanup.
2. Disk Cleanup: Drive Selection dialog box appears as seen in Figure 9.6.

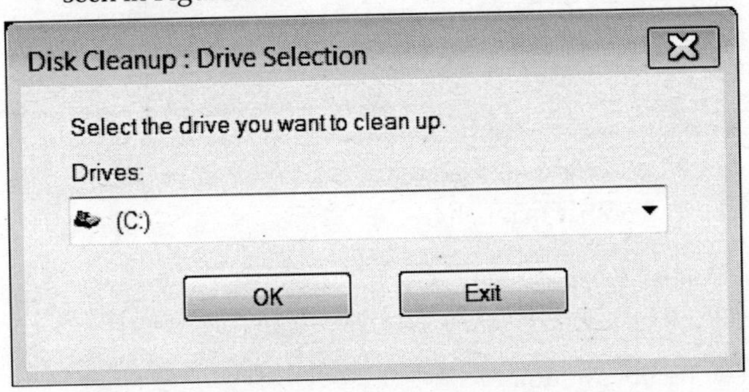

Figure 9.6 Disk Cleanup: Drive Selection dialog box

3. Choose the drive which you want to clean and then click OK.
4. The Disk Cleanup dialog box appears for the drive you have selected (Figure 9.7).
5. In Files to delete: list, click the check box for each file that you want to delete.
6. Then click OK.

9.9.2 Deleting Toolbars

Toolbars get automatically installed whenever you installed other programs. These toolbars can either hijack your homepage, search engines and leads to decrease in the browsing speed of the browser.

The removal tool is used to remove these unwanted search or toolbar. It is a complex process as toolbar components are installed in various locations.

Automated Removal of Toolbar

Automated removal is safe and efficient, as it helps to avoid the errors that can compromise the integrity of computer system.

Security software although removes all the malicious programs which it finds on your computer system and protects it against future malware infections.

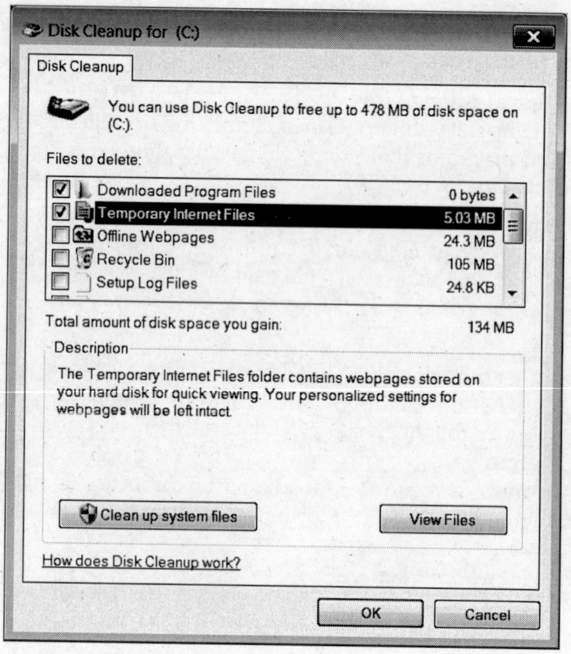

Figure 9.7 Disk Cleanup dialog box for a specific drive

To Remove Toolbar manually:

1. Click on Start button.
2. Open Control Panel.
3. Scroll through the list and right-click on the unwanted program.
4. Click on Remove button.
5. Click "Yes" button of the message box to confirm uninstallation process.
6. Close Control Panel window.

To Remove Toolbar or Search Extensions from the browser:

1. Start Chrome or any other browser.
2. Click on "Menu" icon which is present in the top right corner.
3. Select "Settings" in the drop-down list
4. Click on "Extensions" to open Chrome extensions
5. Find unwanted program.
6. Click "Trash Can" icon
7. Close and restart your web browser

To Remove Unwanted Search Engine from the browser:

1. Start Chrome or any other browser.
2. Click on "Menu" icon which is present in the top right corner.
3. Select "Settings" from the drop-down list.
4. Open "Search" item.
5. Click on "Manage search engines".
6. Select your preferred search provider.
7. Click "Make Default".
8. Remove unwanted web address.
9. Restart your browser.

9.9.3 Defrag Hard Drive

Fragmentation makes your hard disk to do extra work that can slow down your computer. Disk Defragmenter rearranges fragmented data so your disks and drives can work more efficiently.

Disk Defragmenter and disk clean up tool are available in Windows Operating System. This is a program which optimizes PC performance by rewriting the data on your hard drive to ensure that files are written together on the same part of the hard drive or are written in a manner to speed the boot up process.

Basic PC operation will create pockets of unused space all over the hard drive, that utilize those unused pockets to store data. In many cases, data from the same file or program will be written to these blank pockets all over the hard drive, often degrading the PC's performance. The operating system or an application program has to access a wide area of hard drive space to make a program run.

Removable storage devices such as USB flash drives can also become fragmented. Disk Defragmenter runs on a schedule, but you can also analyze and defragment your disks and drives manually.

To open Disk Defragmenter, do this:

1. Click Start button, highlight All Programs, highlight Accessories, highlight System Tools and then choose Disk Defragmenter.
2. The Disk Defragmenter window will open up as shown in Figure 9.8.

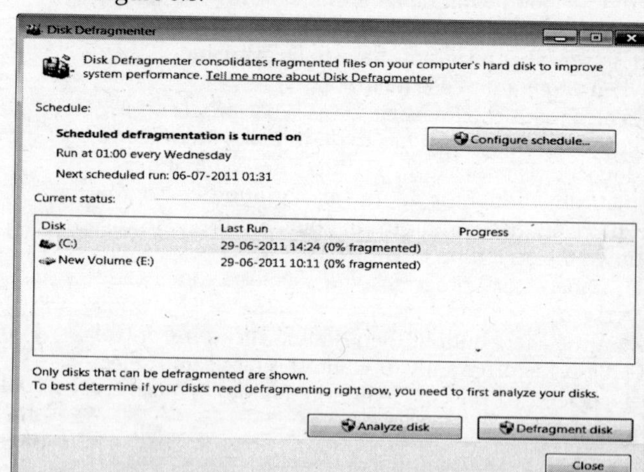

Figure 9.8 Disk Defragmenter window

3. To start defragmentation, under Current status, select the disk you want to defragment.
4. Click Defragment disk.
5. If you want to schedule disk defragment to run regularly, Click on Configure schedule... . It will display Disk Defragmenter Modify Schedule dialog box as shown in Figure 9.9.

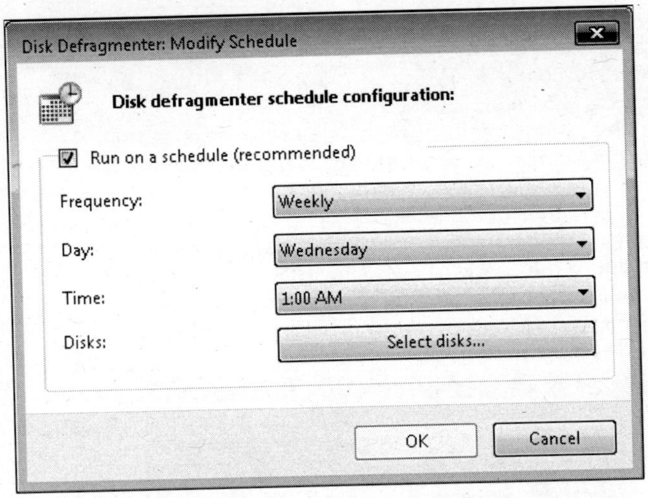

Figure 9.9 Disk Defragmenter Modify Schedule dialog box

6. In this dialog box, click Run on a schedule (recommended): check box to run disk defragmenter in scheduled time.
7. In Frequency: drop-down list, select the frequency with which you want to defragment i.e. Daily, Weekly, or Monthly.
8. In Day: drop-down list, enter the day of the week or the day of the month.
9. In Time: drop-down list, select the time of day to run the defragment.
10. Click OK button and then click Close button.

☞ If you use your computer every day, defragment hard drive weekly. If you use your computer only occasionally, defragment hard drive monthly.

9.10 COMPUTER MAINTENANCE PROGRAMS

Computer maintenance can be broken down into two main areas. Physical and Software.
Physical means to clean the various external components such as the monitor, printer, scanner, mouse and keyboard etc. Or the internal components of you computer case.

Software maintenance involves regular virus scanning, spyware/malware scanning, defragging and backing up of critical data.

Computer programs such as Ccleaner, myDefrag and Spinrite maintain your software programs properly and help you to prevent major problems. The software programs are discussed in the following sections:

9.10.1 Ccleaner

CCleaner is a small, effective utility. It is basically used for computers running MS Windows that cleans out the 'junk' that accumulates over time i.e., temporary files, broken shortcuts, and other problems. CCleaner cleans browsing history and temporary Internet files. It protects your privacy and allowing you to be a more confident Internet user and less susceptible to identity theft.

CCleaner can clean unneeded files from various programs saving you hard disk space, remove unneeded entries in the Windows Registry, help you to uninstall the software and select which programs start with Windows.

CCleaner will run on any PC running MS Windows XP, Windows 8, Windows 7, Windows Vista, Windows 2003 and 2008 Server (all editions), Mac 10.6 to 10.9 64-bit editions.

9.10.2 myDefrag

MyDefrag is a freeware disk defragmenting utility for Windows. It is formerly known as JkDefrag. MyDefrag has a GUI (graphical user interface) based, which can be used to load and monitor scripts. Scripts designed for use on system disks will use prefetch data present in Windows about the most commonly used files in order to optimize boot and program performance. A unique key feature of MyDefrag is wrap-around fragmentation, which, when enabled by default, will surround unmovable sectors with defragmented data. This is done to minimize the number of empty gaps between files and to load more data into the faster regions of hard disks.

9.10.3 Spinrite

SpinRite is a computer software program for scanning magnetic data storage devices such as hard disks, recovering data from them and refreshing their surfaces. SpinRite is run from a bootable medium like floppy disc, optical disc, bootable external storage device such as a USB stick on a PC-compatible computer. Spinrite uses its own operating system and ignores any boot loader or file system structure that may be on the drive being examined.

SpinRite tests the data surfaces of writeable magnetic disks, including IDE, SATA, and floppy disks. It analyzes their contents and can refresh the magnetic disk surfaces to allow them to operate more reliably.

SpinRite recovers data from hard disks with damaged portions that may not be readable via operating system. When the program encounters a sector with errors that cannot be corrected by the disk drive's error-correcting code, it tries to read the sector up to 2000 times, to verify the successive results. The data is then saved onto a new block on the same disk. In this respect, SpinRite differs from most data recovery software, which usually provides an option to save the recovered data onto another disk, or onto a separate partition on the same disk.

9.11 BASIC TROUBLESHOOTING

Troubleshooting is the process of diagnosing the source of a problem. It is used to fix problems with hardware and software.

9.11.1 Restart Computer

It is important to know how to properly shut down or restart your computer so that you do not lose data. Many users think computer can be shut down simply by pressing the power button. On some configurations, this will work as Windows will recognize that you press the power button and shut it down gracefully. On the other hand, if your computer is not configured to do this, when you press the power button the computer will turn off and any unsaved data in Windows will be lost. Shutting down a computer may could also cause data corruption on your hard drive or within Windows.

The steps on how to shut down or restart Windows XP/7.

1. To shut down or restart your computer in Windows 7, click on the Start button to open the Windows 7 start menu.

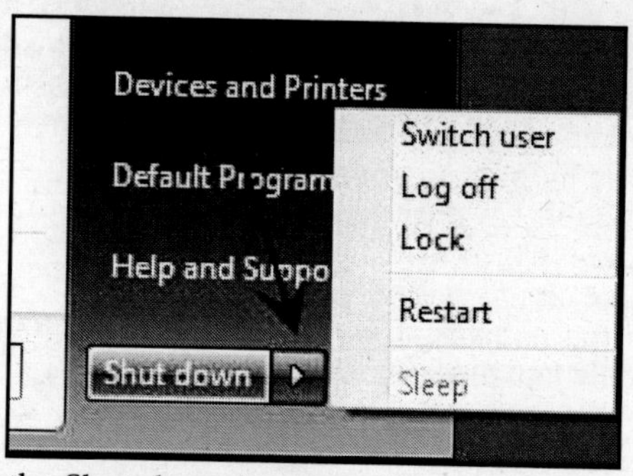

2. Click the Shut down button to shut down Windows and your computer. If you would like to restart computer, click on the arrow next to the shut down button. It is indicated by the arrow in the picture above.
3. Click the right triangle. A sub menu options appear, click on Restart to restart your computer and boot back into Windows.

9.11.2 Checking Cables

One of the most common causes of computer problems is that, a connector has comes loose. In order to troubleshoot, check all the cables on the outside of the computer. If you find all of those in place, you may want to check the cables on the inside of your computer.

To ensure that cables are properly attached, follow these steps:

1. Open the console.
2. Locate the spot where the cable attaches.
3. Give the cable a little tug.
4. If the cable is loose, it falls out. If it does, reattach it.
5. Gently press the cable so that it's snugly attached.
6. Cables have two ends. You need to check both the ends.

9.11.3 Uninstalling Software

Use Uninstall Program in the Control panel to uninstall the program. This is where you Remove Software from your Computer.

➡ **To add or remove Windows Component, do this:**

1. Click the Start button and then choose Control Panel. The Control Panel window opens.
2. Click Add/Remove Windows Programs dialog box appears as shown in Figure 9.10.
3. Click the Add/Remove Windows Components button. Windows searches your computer for installed Windows components and then displays the Windows Components Wizard as shown in Figure 9.11.
4. Select a component from the list of available components by enabling the check box next to it. Some components have subcomponents that you can choose from. If so, the Details button become active, and you can click it to see a list of subcomponents to choose from.

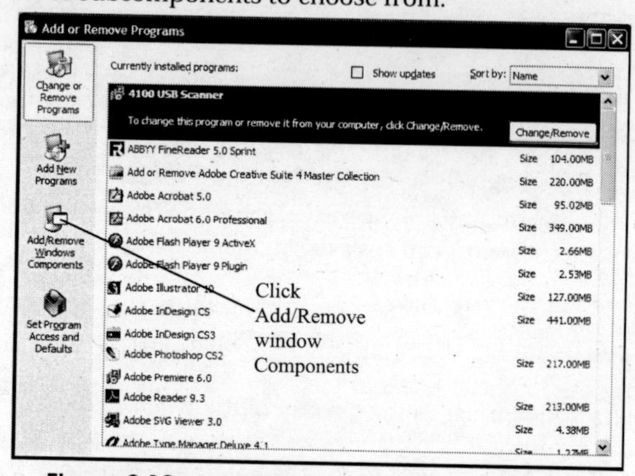

Figure 9.10 Add/Remove Programs dialog box

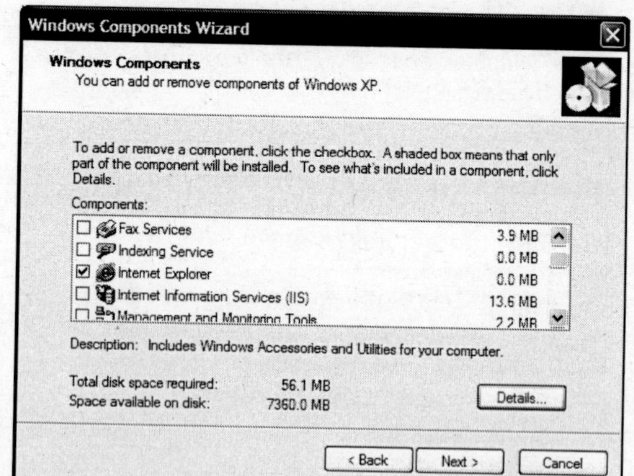

Figure 9.11 Windows Components Wizard dialog box

5. Once you select all the components that you want to install, click the Next button. Windows OS builds a list of files that must be installed and copies them to your drive. Windows might prompt you to insert your Windows CD-ROM during this process.

6. After Windows has installed the components, it lets you to know that the process has been completed successfully. Click the Finish button to finish. Depending on the components you added. Windows might restart your computer.

9.11.4 Start Windows in Safe Mode

Safe mode is an alternate boot method for Windows OS that makes it easier to diagnose the problems. It is used when the computer stalls, slows down, does not work right, improper, intermittent errors or new hardware/software installation causes problems. Safe Mode is used to start Windows with minimum device drivers and services. Software that automatically loads during startup is disabled in Safe Mode and users profiles are not loaded.

When the computer boots in safe mode, the mouse, keyboard, CD-ROM and VGA video device drivers are loaded. Safe Mode allows you to access configuration files and make necessary changes. Safe Mode with Command Prompt is used to start the system with the minimum files and drivers and a command prompt where you must use commands instead of a graphic interface. To Access Safe Mode by press F8 key during the boot process and select Safe Mode from the Windows Advanced Options menu.

The Windows Advanced Options menu contains used to troubleshoot Windows which are Enable Boot Logging, Enable VGA Mode, Directory Services Restore Mode and Debugging Mode. Enable Boot Logging is used to create a log file, NTBTLOG.TXT, that records drivers and services loaded during the boot process.

9.12 WINDOWS INSTALLATION AND UPGRADES

To ensure and complete installation of Windows 7, you need to some fundamental hardware requirements on your computer. Depending on the edition of Windows 7 that you want to install, the minimum system requirements for installing Windows 7 are shown in Table 9.1.

Table 9.1 Minimum System Requirements to install Windows 7

Requirements	Minimum System Requirements
Processor	1 GHz
Memory	For 32-bit system: 1 GB of RAM For 64-bit system: 2 GB of RAM
Hard Disk Drive	For 32-bit syst em: 16 GB of available hard disk space For 64-bit system: 29 GB of available hard disk space
Graphics	DirectX 9 graphics device with Display Driver Model (WDDM) 1.0 or higher and 128 MB graphics memory

Apart from the system requirements, you need a Compact Disc (CD) or DVD drive for installing Windows 7. Let us start the process of installing Windows 7.

New Installation

If you are installing Windows 7 for the first time on a computer and you do not have any existing version of Windows, you can start a fresh installation of Windows 7 on your computer. Therefore, Windows 7 becomes the only operating system on your computer.

➡ To install Windows 7:

1. First insert the Windows 7 Enterprise DVD in the DVD-ROM drive. It starts the setup and the Windows is loading files screen appears, as shown in Figure 9.12.

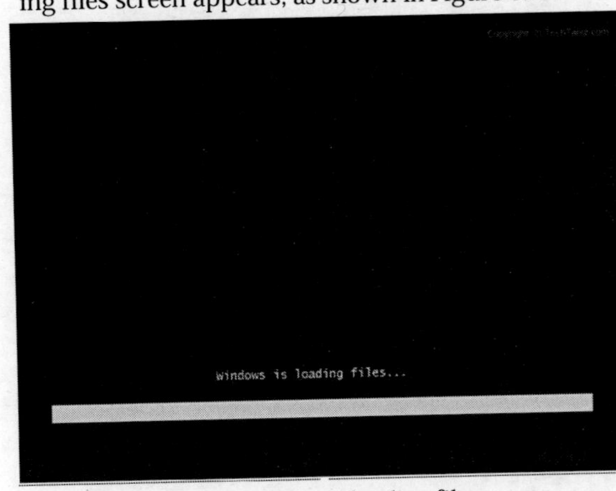

Figure 9.12 Windows loading files screen

☞ After you insert the Windows 7 DVD, you may see the Press any key to boot from CD/DVD message on your computer screen. In such case, you press any key on the keyboard to boot from CD/DVD.

2. After the Windows files are loaded, the Install Windows wizard appears as shown in Figure 9.13.

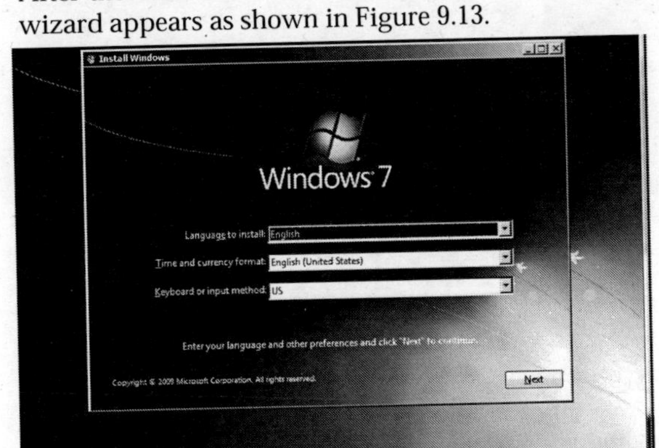

Figure 9.13 Installation of Windows 7 wizard dialog box

3. Select the appropriate installation language from the Language to install: drop-down list as shown in Figure 9.2. For example, we have to select the English language.
4. Select the desired format for Time and currency format: form the Time and currency from drop-down list. For example, we have selected English (United States).
5. Select the method for input from the Keyboard or input method: drop-down list.

Click the Next button, as shown in Figure 9.12. The Install Windows wizard displays the next page.

6. This screen is where the installation wizard begins. Click the Install now button in the Install Windows screen (See Figure 9.14).

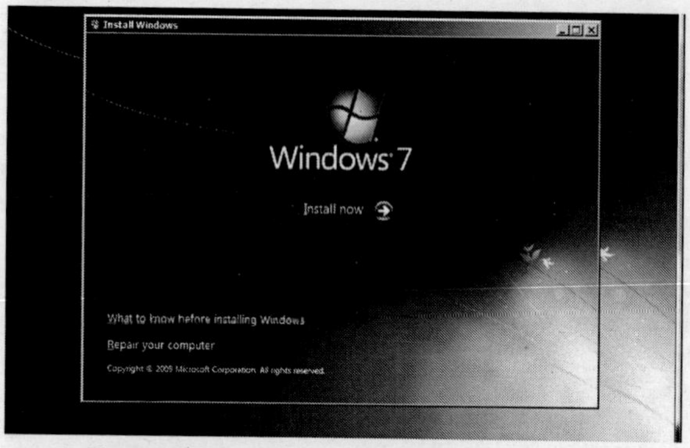

Figure 9.14 Windows 7 Install now screen

7. The Setup is starting screen appears for a while, and then Please read the license terms page appears as shown in Figure 9.15.

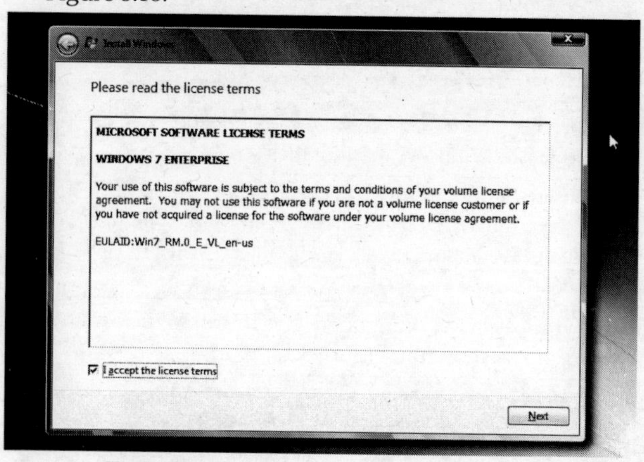

Figure 9.15 License terms window screen

This page you can find the User License Agreement specifying the terms and conditions for using Windows 7.

8. Click the I accept the license terms check box, and then click Next button to proceed the next page.
9. Click the Next button to go the next page wizard as shown in Figure 9.15.
10. Which type of installation do you want? page appears as shown in Figure 9.16. This screen provides two options, Upgrade and Custom (advanced). Choose one of the following options from the list.
    - The Upgrade option allows you to upgrade from a previous version of Window.
    - The Custom (advanced) option allows you to have a fresh or a side-by-side installation of Windows 7.
11. Click the Custom (advanced) option to have a fresh installation.

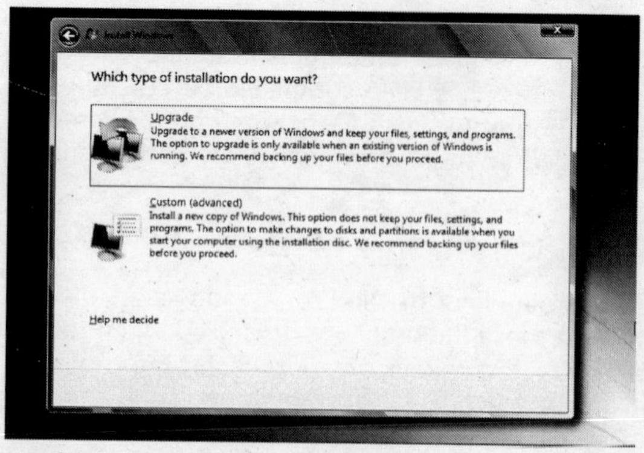

Figure 9.16 Selecting type of installation from the window screen

12. Where do you want to install Windows? page appears (See Figure 9.16). This page you need to select the hard disk (or a partition of the hard disk) where Windows 7 will be installed.
13. Select the appropriate location from the hard disk on which you want to install Windows 7. For example, we have selected the Disk 0 unallocated space hard disk as shown in Figure 9.17.
14.. Click the Next button.
15. The Installing Windows page appears, as shown in Figure 9.18.

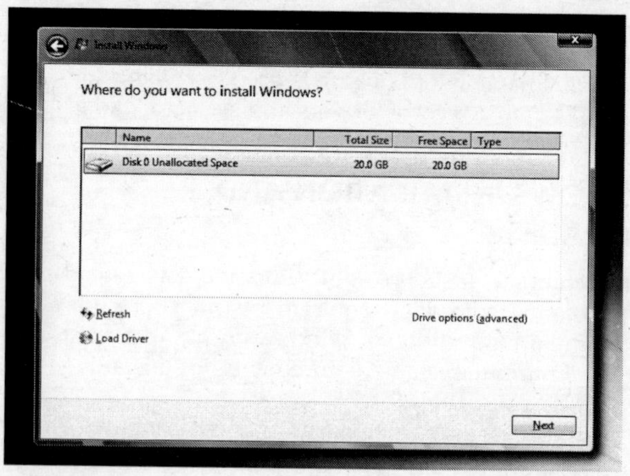

Figure 9.17 Selecting the location from the hard disk

This page, you see the various actions are perform to install Windows 7 that includes copying files, expanding files, installing features and installing updates. All these actions would take approximately half an hour. After these actions have been performed, you computer reboots and the Setup is updating registry setting screen appears.

After that, the Setup starting services screen appears as shown in Figure 9.19, and finally, the Installing Windows page of the Install Windows 7 wizard appears.

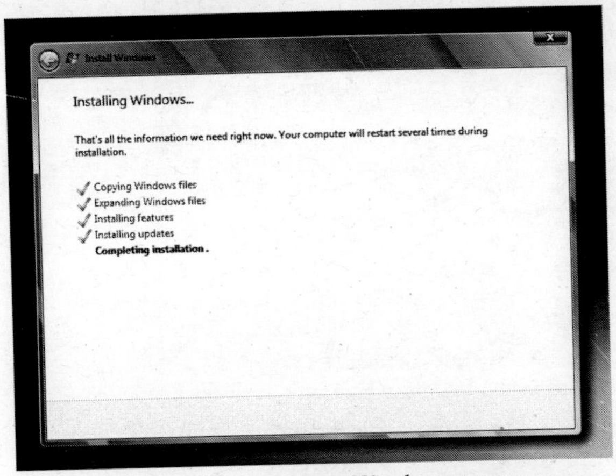

Figure 9.18 Installing Windows screen

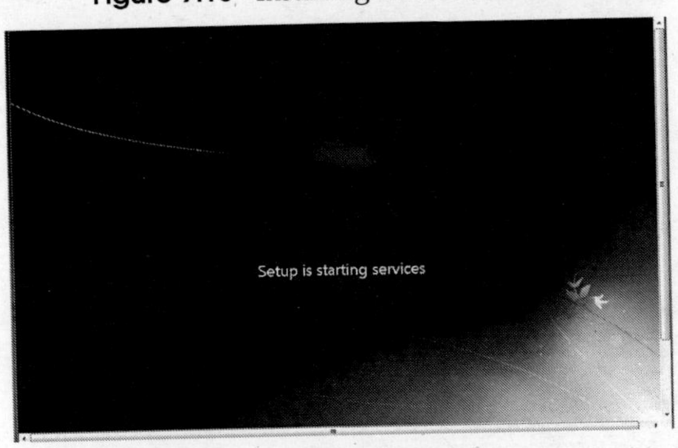

Figure 9.19 Setup starting services screen

16. The setup again restarts and the Setup is preparing your computer for first use screen appears.
    After the checking is complete, the Setup Windows wizard appears as shown in Figure 9.20. On this screen, you need to specify the user name to launch Windows 7.

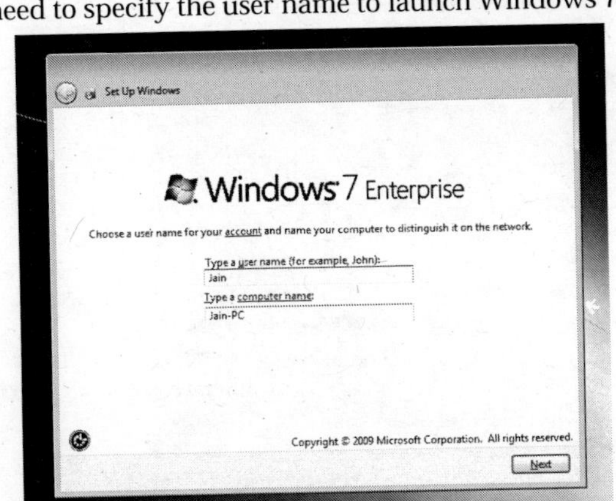

Figure 9.20 Installing Windows screen

17. Enter the user name in the Type a user name text box (See Figure 9.19).
    The Computer name is automatically displayed according to the user name.
18. Click the Next button (See Figure 9.19).
    Set a password for your account page appears as shown in Figure 9.20.
19. Type a password for the user account in the Type a password (recommended): text box (See Figure 9.21).

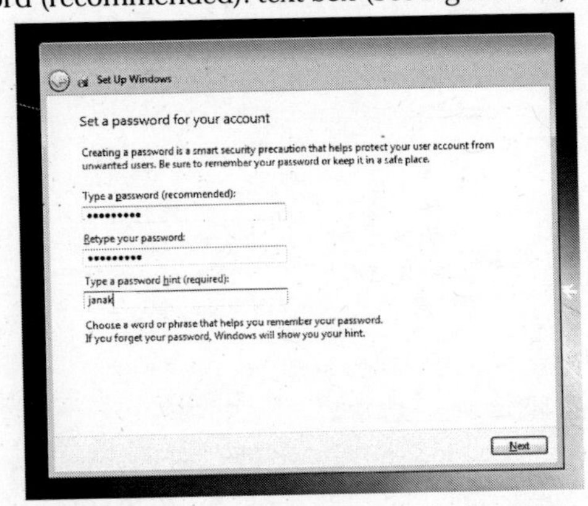

Figure 9.21 Setup starting services screen

20. Retype the password in the Retype your password: text box.
21. Type a hint for the password in the Type a password hint (required): text box.
22. Click the Next button.
23. In the Help protect your computer and improve Windows automatically page appears (See Figure 9.22). For this, you can choose any of the following options:
    - Use recommended settings: It allows you to install important as well as recommended updates that help in ensuring the security of your computer.
    - Install important updates only: It allows you to install the important updates.
    - Ask me later: It allows you to postpone the installation updates.

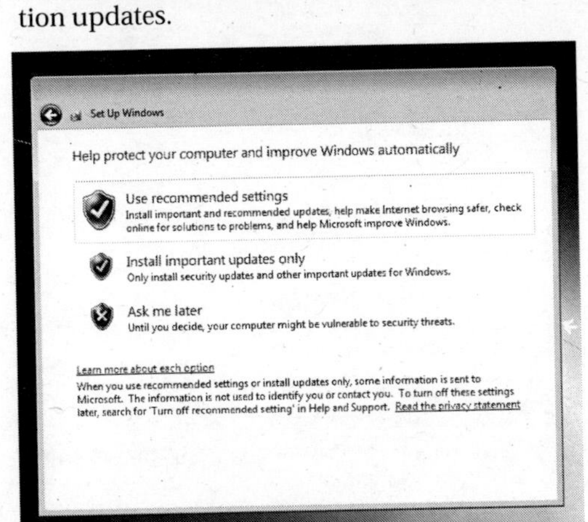

Figure 9.22 Set Up windows shows recommended settings

24. Click the Use recommended settings option to download and install the important and the recommended updates.

25. The Review your time and date settings page appears as shown in Figure 9.23. On this page, you need to select a time zone. You can also set the current date and time for your computer.

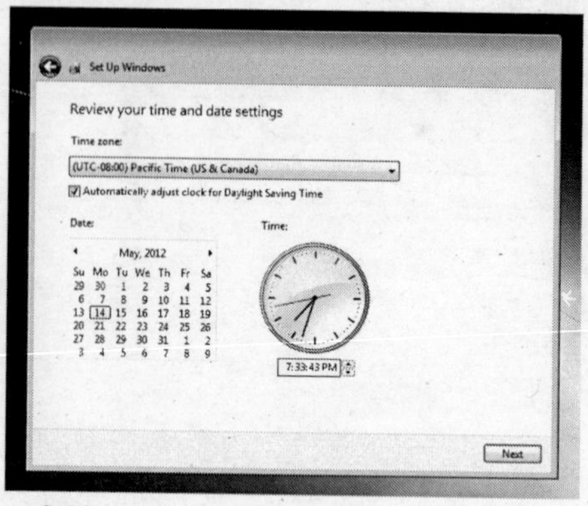

Figure 9.23 Review time and date settings dialog box

26. Select the desired time zone in the Time zone: drop-down list (See Figure 9.23).
27. Select the date from the calendar under the Date option (See Figure 9.23).
28. Enter the current time in the list box under the Time option (See Figure 9.23).
29. Click the Next button.
30. The Select your computer s current location page appears.
31. Select the current location of the computer on the page. For example, we have selected Work network.
32. After the system is successfully connected to the network, the Set Up Windows wizard appears that shows the progress of finalizing the settings (See Figure 9.24).

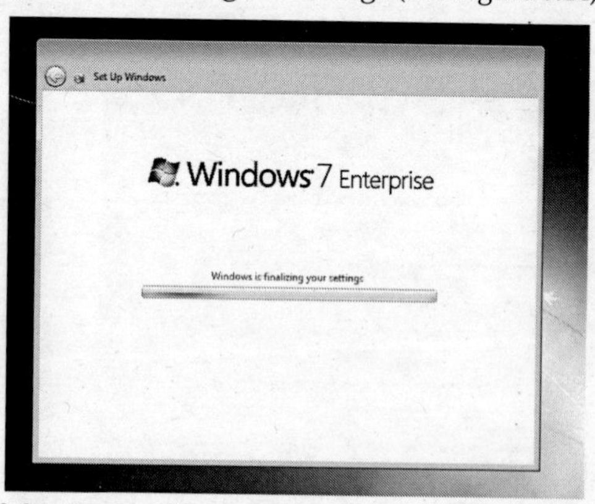

Figure 9.24 Set Up Windows page shows finalizing the settings window screen

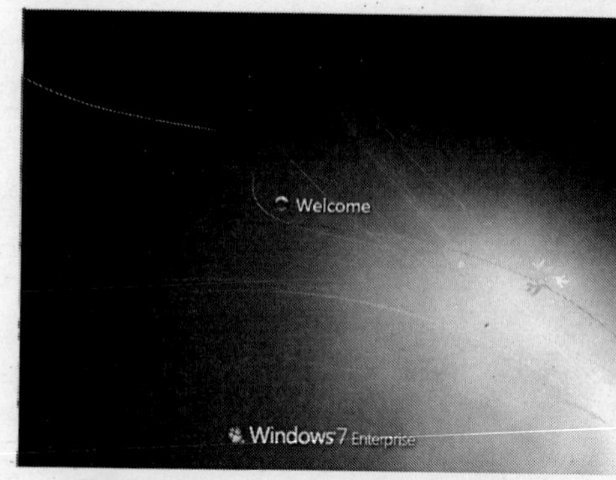

Figure 9.25 Window Welcome screen

33. After the Windows completes the process of finalizing the settings, the Welcome screen appears as shown in Figure 9.25.
34. Next, the Preparing your desktop message appears on the screen as shown in Figure 9.26.
35. After you have successfully completed the installation, the Desktop is prepared with all the default settings. The Desktop of Window 7 appears as shown in Figure 9.27.

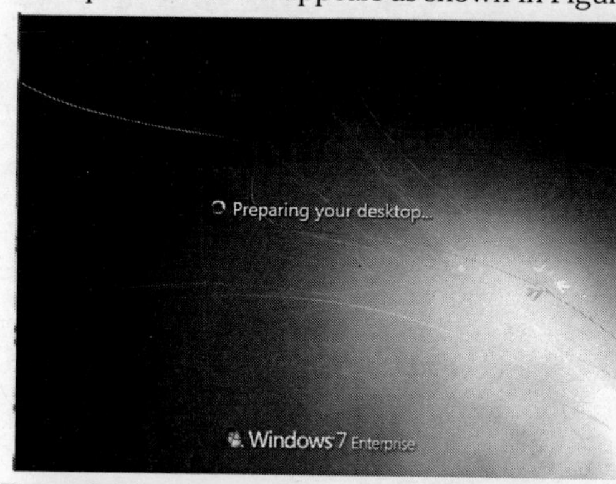

Figure 9.26 Preparing your desktop window screen

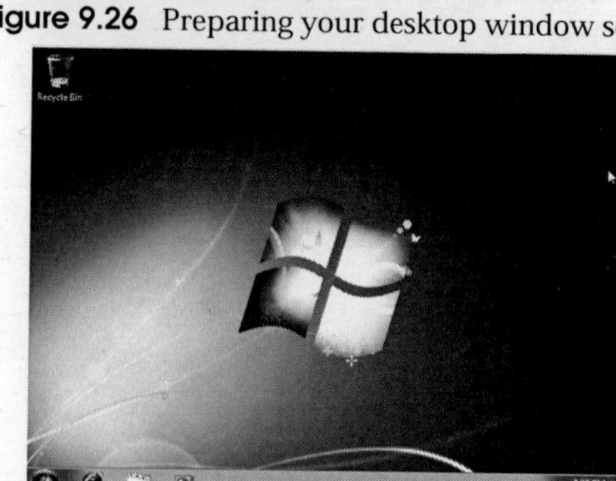

Figure 9.27 The Windows 7 screen appears with default settings

9.12.1 Windows 7 Upgrade Advisor

A upgrade installation allows you to keep intact the files, settings, and programs from your current version of Vista SP1 or SP2. This will show you how to do a upgrade installation with a Upgrade version of Windows 7 from Vista. XP users will now be able to upgrade to Windows 7, but will have to do a clean install or custom install of Windows 7 instead.

Windows 7 Upgrade Advisor will run on the following 32-bit and 64-bit operating systems:

- Windows 7
- Vista
- XP with SP2

.NET 2.0 Framework or higher is required to be installed with XP. Before installing Windows 7 Upgrade Advisor is an application that is used to check if the existing hardware and software support Windows 7.

You want to do a in place upgrade from either a 32-bit version of Windows Vista to a 32-bit version of Windows 7, or a 64-bit version of Windows Vista to a 64-bit version of Windows 7 do the following steps:

1. Download the setup file Windows 7 Upgrade Advisor from the Microsoft s site.
2. Double-click the setup file to start the process of Windows 7 Upgrade Advisor. The Open File Security Warning message box appears as shown in Figure 9.28.
3. Click the Run button in the Open File –Security Warning message box as shown in Figure 9.28.

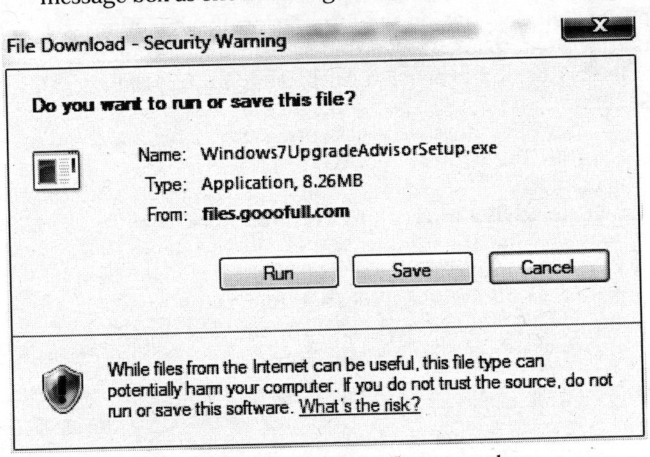

Figure 9.28 File Download message box

4. The Windows 7 Upgrade Advisor wizard appears with the Welcome to the Windows 7 Upgrade Advisor Setup Wizard window appears as shown in Figure 9.29.

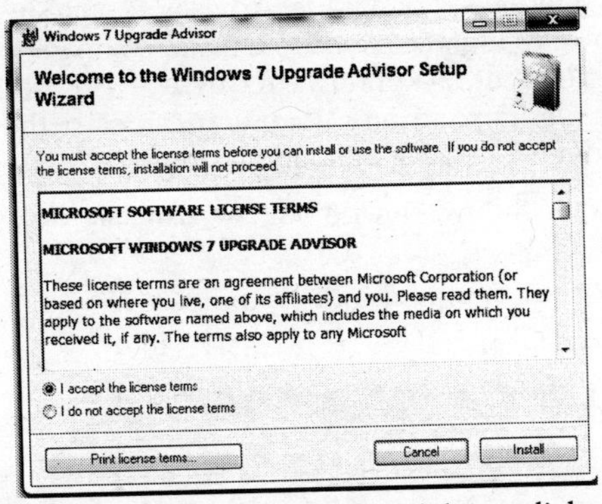

Figure 9.29 Windows 7 Upgrade Advisor dialog box

5. Select the I accept the license terms radio button on the page.
6. Click the Install button as shown in Figure 9.29.
7. The Installing Windows 7 Upgrade Advisor wizard page appears as shown in Figure 9.30.
8. After the installation is completed, the Installation complete page appears as shown in Figure 9.31.
9. Click the Close button on the Installation complete page as shown in Figure 9.31.

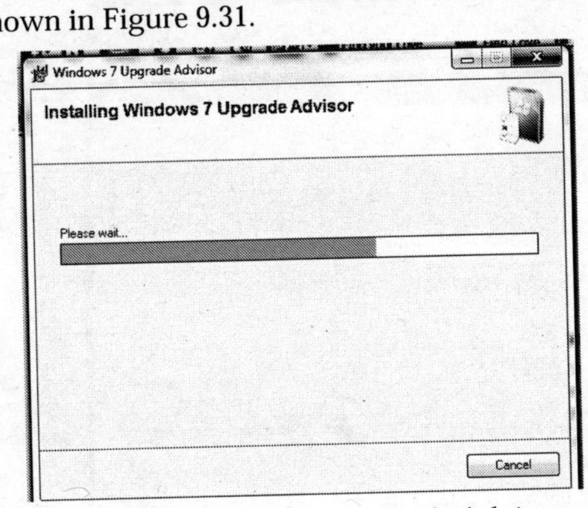

Figure 9.30 Installing Windows 7 Upgrade Advisor screen window

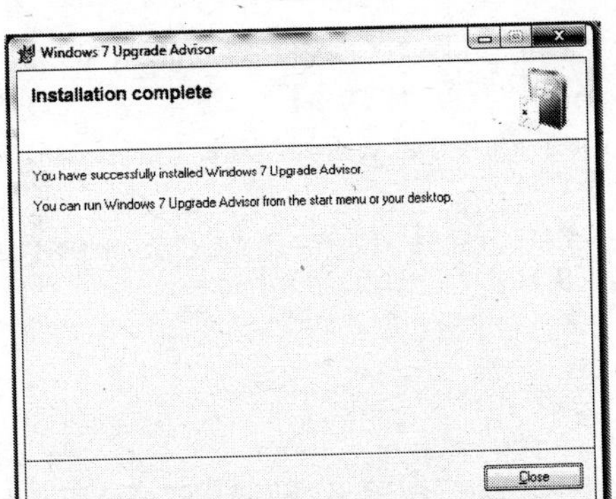

Figure 9.31 Installation Completed window screen

The setup of Windows 7 Upgrade Advisor screenThe setup of Windows 7 Upgrade Advisor in installed on your computer. The shortcut of Windows 7 Upgrade Advisor appears on the Desktop. At any time, you can start the application by double-clicking its shortcut icon.

10. Double-click the Windows 7 Upgrade Advisor shortcut icon from the desktop.
11. Click the Start check button in the Windows 7 screen as shown in Figure 9.32.

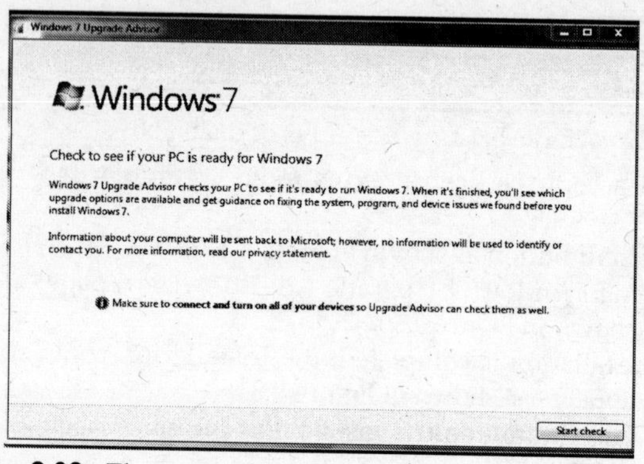

Figure 9.32 The setup of Windows 7 Upgrade Advisor screen

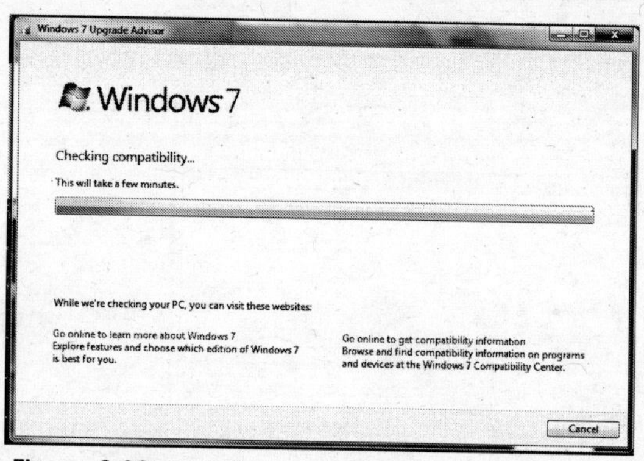

Figure 9.33 Installation Completed window screen

12. The Windows 7 Upgrade Advisor checks your system for compatibility, as shown in Figure 9.33.
13. After checks the compatibility, it displays the result as shown in Figure 9.34.
14. Click the Close button after the results are displayed as shown in Figure 9.34.

9.13 CPUs

CPU is considered as the brain of computer. It performs all types of data processing operations. It stores data, intermediate results and instruction (program). It controls the operation of all parts of computer. CPU itself has three components Memory or Storage unit, control unit and ALU.

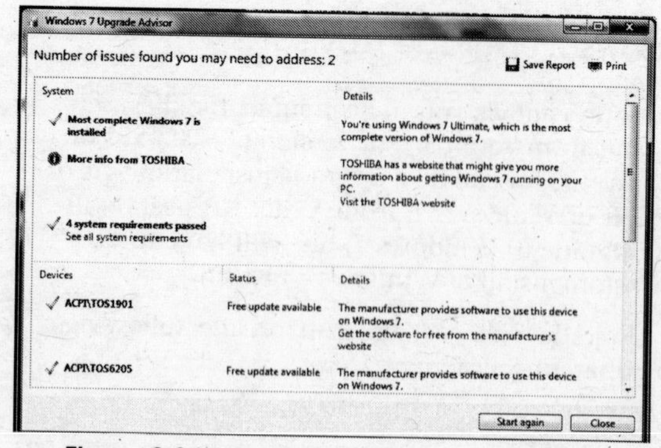

Figure 9.34 Windows 7 checks your system

Motherboard

The motherboard serves as a single platform to connect all of the parts of a computer together. A computer connects CPU, memory, hard drives, optical drives, video card, sound card, and other ports and expansion cards directly via cables. It can be considered as the backbone of a computer.

Memory Systems

A memory is just like a human brain. It is used to store data and instructions. Computer memory is the storage space in computer where data is to be processed and instructions required for processing are stored. The memory is divided into large number of small parts called cells. Each location or cell has a unique address which varies from zero to memory size minus one. For example if computer has 64k words, then this memory unit has 64 * 1024=65536 memory locations.

Expasion Cards

The purpose of an expansion card is to provide and expand extra functions to the computer system. The expansion card is found on the motherboard, in the expansion slot. The type of expansion card all depends on the form factor of the mother board and the case. Up to 19 expansion cards can be installed at once. However some expansion cards take you two slots. The most common types of expansion cards are video cards, sound cards, graphic cards and network cards. The main expansion slots are PCI express and AGP.

Data Storage Device

A data storage device is a device for recording (storing) information (data). The most common type of storage device is hard drive. The computer's primary hard drive stores the operating system, application and files and folders for users of the computer. Several other types are flash memory devices, such as USB drives are popular ways to store data.

Ports

A port is a physical point using which an external device can be connected to the computer.

The main ports like:

USB port–USB ports allows connection between the computer and a device such as a pen drive. USB was made to take over serial and parallel ports. However USB is not just to connect storage devices, you can also use it to connect a mouse, keyboards, printers, etc.

Serial port–Serial ports allow you to attach devices to the computer. For example this port will allow you to connect modems to it.

Parallel port–Parallel ports are mainly used to connect printers. However like the serial port, the USB ports are taking over and most printers now can be connected with a USB port. Parallel ports can also connect some scanners, CD burners and external hard drives.

Ethernet port–Modem connections allow connecting the computer to a modem by a wire.

Connectors

Connectors, normally called "input-output connectors" (or I/O for short), are interfaces for linking devices by using cables. They generally have a male end with pins protruding from it. This plug is meant to be inserted into a female part (also called a socket), which includes holes for accommodating the pins.

Cables

A cable is one or more wires covered in a plastic covering that connects a computer to a power source or other device. There are two main types of computer cables, a data cable and a power cable. A data cable is a cable that provides communication between devices. For example, the data cable that connects your monitor to your computer and allows your computer to display a picture on the monitor. Other examples of data cables include the CAT5, IDE/EIDE, SATA, and USB cables. A power cable is any cable that powers the device. For example, the power cord that connects to your computer and a cable inside the computer are both good examples of power cables.

Printers and Scanners

Printers

A single print device that serves several functions, including printing, faxing, scanning, and copying. Also called a multifunction printer (MFP).

printers also have basic input/output (I/O) features:

Input: Built with network drivers for different operating systems, page description languages, parallel connection/printing types, direct interpreters and USBs.

Output: Built with printing speed/technology, paper formats, dot-per-inch (DPI) resolution and duplex and direct printing.

Scanner

A scanner is an input device that scans documents and images, which can be imported into a computer. They are available in flatbed or sheet-fed versions and are usually connected via a high-speed USB port. OCR software can be used to recognize text documents imported from a scanner.

A scanner can be connected to a computer using many different interfaces although today is most commonly connected to a computer using a USB cable.

Display Devices

Display device that forms an image by converting electronic signals from the computer into points of colored light on the screen. The most-used output device on a computer. Most desktop display use a cathode ray tube. Laptops use liquid crystal display, light-emitting diode and gas plasma or other image projection technology. Monitors using LCD technologies are beginning to replace CRT.

Portable Computers and Devices

A portable computer is a computer that comes with a keyboard and display and one which can be easily moved. Portable computers generally take up less space than desktop systems. Compared to other mobile computing device or laptop, portable computer makes use of standard motherboards and also provide plug in slots for add in cards. Compared to a desktop computer, the power consumed is less in case of portable computer and can help in power and cost savings.

Networking

A network is a collection of interconnected independent computers. A network includes a group of computers connected in some fashion in order to share resources. This grouping provides greater storage capacity and processing power than that by stand-alone independent machines. In addition to computers, a network also consists of peripheral devices with carriers and data communication devices used for the purpose of exchanging data and information.

Network Security refers to any activity designed to protect the usability and integrity of your network and data. It includes both hardware and software technologies. Effective network security manages access to the network. It targets a variety of threats and stops them from entering or spreading on your network.

Security

Security is "freedom from risk or danger." In the context of computer science, security is the prevention of, or protection against, access to information by unauthorized recipients, and intentional but unauthorized destruction. This can be restated – Security is the ability of a system to protect information and system resources with respect to confidentiality and integrity.

Computer security, also known as cybersecurity or IT security, is the protection of computer systems from the theft or damage to the hardware, software or the information on them, as well as from disruption or misdirection of the services they provide.

It includes controlling physical access to the hardware, as well as protecting against harm that may come via network access, data due to malpractice by operators, whether intentional, accidental, or due to them being tricked into deviating from secure procedures.

Maintaining the PC environment

"Take good care of your PC, and it won't crash, lose your data, and cost you your job probably." Follow these steps to stop PC problems before they stop you.

Your PC's two mortal enemies are heat and moisture. Excess heat accelerates the deterioration of the delicate circuits in your system. The most common causes of overheating are dust and dirt: Clogged vents and CPU cooling fans can keep heat-dissipating air from moving through the case, and even a thin coating of dust or dirt can raise the temperature of your machine's components.

If your PC resides in a relatively clean, climate-controlled environment, an annual cleaning should be sufficient. But in most real-world locations, such as dusty offices or any dirt, but especially the residue of cigarette smoke, can corrode exposed metal contacts your system may need a cleaning every few months.

Tips of Longer Life PC

1. Keep your PC in a smoke-free environment–Tobacco smoke can damage delicate contacts and circuits.
2. Leave your PC running–Powering up from a cold state is one of the most stressful things you can do to your system's components. If you don't want to leave your PC running all the time, use Windows' Power Management settings to put your machine into hibernation rather than completely shutting down.
3. Don t leave your monitor running–The best way to extend your display's life is to shut it off when it's not in use.
4. Avoid jostling the PC–Whenever you move your system, even if it's just across the desktop, make sure the machine is shut down and unplugged.

The detailed explanation of CPUs and motherboards, Memory systems, Expansion cards, Data storage devices, ports, connectors and cables, portable computers and devices are discussed in Chapter 3 in section 3.4, 3.5, 3.7, 3.9, 3.10, 3.11, 3.12, 3.13 and 3.14.3.

MODEL QUESTIONS AND ANSWERS

A. Multiple Choice

1.1 Which type of maintenance deals with the problems arise during the use of the software?
a. Corrective b. Adaptive
c. Preventive d. None of these

1.2 The key tools to maintenance on your hard drive is:
a. Disk Defragmentation b. Disk Cleanup
c. myDefrag d. All of the above

1.3 By using the Disk Cleanup tool, you can delete
a. Temporary Internet files
b. Empty the Recycle Bin
c. Windows components that you are using
d. All of the above

1.4 Before storing data in a new disk, it has to be
a. Initialized b. Cleaned
c. Formatted d. Fragmented

1.5 Which of the following should be first choice to remove an application that you no longer need?
a. Delete the program files
b. Use the uninstall program that came with the application
c. Use the Add or Remove Programs applet
d. Use the Registry Editor to remove references to the application

1.6 Place where large amounts of data are stored outside central processing unit is called:
a. Backing store b. peripherals
c. Control unit d. ALU unit

1.7 Devices that are under the control of computer and are directly connected to it are said to be
a. off-line devices b. on-line devices
c. In gate devices d. IF gate devices

1.8 Actual equipment of computer system that can be touched are called
a. Hardware b. Software
c. Computer system d. Computer accessories

1.9 Booting up a PC, you see a message that says: keyboard error, it could very likely be:
a. The keyboard is not attached to the PC b. The keyboard has failed
c. Both (a) or (b) d. None of these

1.10 If you turn on PC and the system unit is clearly ON, but the monitor is dark, the problem could be that:
a. The monitor is not turned ON
b. The monitor is not plugged in
c. The monitor is not connected to the PC
d. All of the above

B. State whether the following are True or False

2.1 The Disk Cleanup program frees up space on computer hard disk.

2.2 Keeping a backup increases the availability of data.

2.3 Never repair your computer with the power supply on.

2.4 The disk defragmenter program groups the fragmented files together on the computer hard disk drive to improve PC performance.

2.5 System case is the box that holds the different components of computer.

2.6 Defrag utility is destructive process.

2.7 The physical part of the PC that keeps track of the hardware resources on the system is the ROM BIOS chip.

2.8 The proper way to shut down Windows is to press Ctrl+Alt+Del.

2.9 Anit virus software finds only known viruses.

2.10 The process of finding and consolidating fragmented files and folders is called disk cleanup.

Answers

A.	1.	a	2.	d	3.	d	4.	c	5.	b
	6.	a	7.	b	8.	a	9.	c	10.	d
B.	1.	T	2.	T	3.	T	4.	T	5.	T
	6.	F	7.	T	8.	F	9.	T	10.	F

CHAPTER 10

Networking & Troubleshooting

10.1 BASIC OF COMPUTER NETWORKS

A computer network, often simply referred to as a network. It is a collection of computers and devices connected by communications channels that facilities communciations to allows users to share resources with other users. Networking means connection computers so that they can share files, printers, applications and other computer-related rescources. Computer networking is the practice of interfacing two or more computing devices with each other for the purpose of sharing data. Computer networks are built with a combination of hardware and software components.

Computer network can be classified on the basis of following features:

- Local Area Network (LAN)
- Wide Area Network (WAN)

Computer networks can also be classified according to the hardware or software technology that is used to connect the individual devices in the network such as Optical fibre, Ethernet, Wireless LAN.

Purpose of Computer Networks

Purpose Computer networks can be used for several purposes:

- Facilitating communications–Using a network, people can communicate efficiently and easily via email, instant messaging, chat rooms, telephone, video telephone calls, and video conferencing.
- Sharing hardware–In a networked environment, each computer on a network may access and use hardware resources on the network, such as printing a document on a shared network printer.
- Sharing files, data, and information–In a network environment, authorized user may access data and information stored on other computers on the network. The capability of providing access to data and information on shared storage devices is an important feature of many networks.
- Sharing software–Users connected to a network may run application programs on remote computers.

10.1.1 Local Area Network (LAN)

Local Area Network (LAN) is a group of computers located in the same room, on the same floor, or in the same building that are connected to form a single computer network. Local area networks allow users to share storage devices, printers, applications, data and other network resources. They are limited to a specific geographical area, usually less than one kilometer in diameter.

Figure 10.1 illustrates the basic physical characteristics, information transfer and shared device concepts underlying LAN operation. The line printer and magnetic tape storage are "shared" resources, since any user attached to the network can access these devices through PCs acting as the resource manager, or server, as it is commonly called in LAN terminology. In some networks, the users can directly exchange data or files from Mainframe or mini computers.

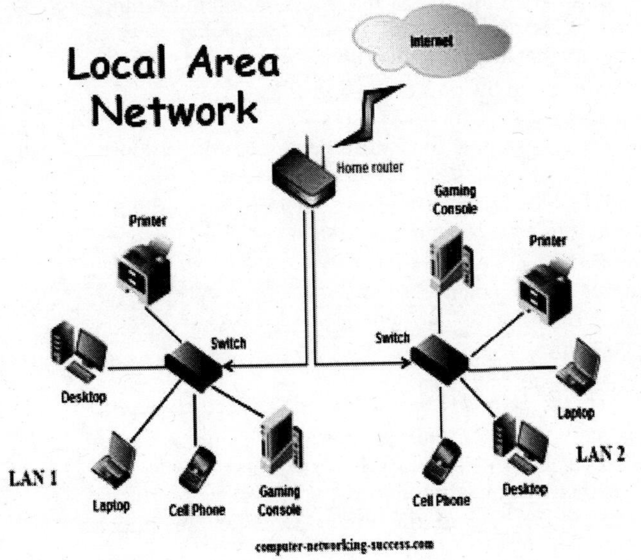

Figure 10.1 Typical LAN system in an organization

Advantages of LANs

(a) Local area networks allow sharing of expensive resources, such as coloured laser printers and high capacity, high-speed mass storage devices among a number of users.

(b) Local area networks allow for high-speed exchange of essential information between key people in an organization. If properly managed, this sharing will promote greater efficiency and productivity and will lead to more sophisticated applications, such as electronic mail and company's Web site.

(c) Local area network provides the catalyst to increase the range of potential applications for the IBM PCs (International Business Machines Personal Computers) where an application package can be used by users.

(d) LANs contribute to increased productivity. In the case of a business, a LAN contributes to increased profitability.

Disadvantages of LANs

(a) The financial cost of local area networking is still high. If one plans to use a network to share a laser printer, the user might find it cheaper to purchase another laser printer than to purchase networking hardware and software.

(b) Local area networking software requires memory space in each of the computers used on the network. For an IBM PC computer, with 256 megabyte of main memory, in an IBM Token-Ring Network that has a printer or a disk space shared with other users, almost 10 per cent of the computer's memory will be needed to manage the network interface. This reduces the memory space available for the user's programs.

(c) Local area networking adds another level of complexity to the computer operation. The installation and management of a LAN requires far more technical and administrative skills than installing and managing several computers that are not networked.

(d) Some control on the part of the user is lost. You may have to share a printer with other users. You may face a situation like, for example, the entire network suddenly locking up because one user has made a mistake.

(e) Some type of security system must be implemented if it is important to protect confidential data.

(f) Memory-intensive programs, such as RDBMS (Relational Database Management System) and expert systems, are particularly vulnerable to networking because of memory requirement.

Characteristics of LANs

Local area networks are a specialized form of communication systems. There are three primary characteristics of LANs that distinguish them from wide area networks, such as Telnet, Tymnet, CompuServe and the Public-Switched Telephone Network (PSTN). These are as follows.

(a) LANs work in a restricted geographical area.

(b) LANs operate at relatively high speed when compared to the typical wide area networks currently in use. LAN data transfer speeds may be as high as 80 million bits per second (80 Mbps), or slightly less than 10 million characters per second (10 Mcps).

(c) LANs are private networks, not subject to tariffs or other regulatory controls.

10.1.2 Wide Area Network (WAN)

WAN (Wide Area Network) is a digital communication system which interconnects different sites, computer installations and user terminals. It may also enable LANs to communicate with each other. This type of network may be developed to operate nationwide or worldwide. The transmission media used in WANs are normally public systems such as telephone lines, microwave link and satellite links.

☞ WAN is used to interconnect LANs which may be at opposite sides of a country or located around the earth's globe.

Wide area networks (WANs) combine the continuous error detection and correction techniques included in synchronous communications with robust network problem determination and data routing to form powerful backbones that ensure high-quality, reliable service for end users. These networks allow multiple users to access a variety of host computers simultaneously through the same physical medium, while separating each user's session so that no user is aware of another user on the network. Wide area networks also operate at speeds much higher than the 19,200-bps limit of normal voice-grade telephone lines.

Figure 10.2 shows a wide area network that a large company might use to connect regional computers. In this example, different centres, such as manufacturing, distribution and accounting are all connected to national headquarters and to each other for communication purposes. Most WANs are complex and serve many users and many functions as compared to LANs. WANs are typically created by using specially conditioned telephone lines, microwave communications or satellite data transmission.

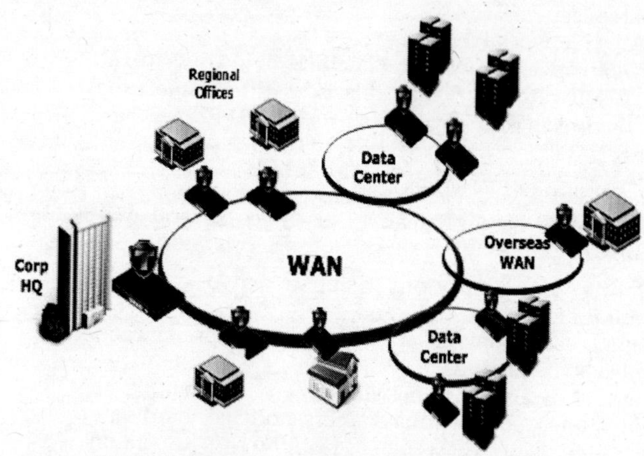

Figure 10.2 A wide area network connected to regional computers

Advantages of WAN

- Messages can be sent very quickly to anyone else on the network.
- Share informtion/files over a larger area.
- Shared by all the computers on the network without having to buy a different peripheral for each computer such as printer or phone lines to the internet.
- Large network cover

Disadvantages of WAN

- WAN is avery big and complex network
- It is slow in speed.
- Need a good firewall to restrict outsiders from entering and disrupting the network.

- WAN is not very much secured means not reliable.
- It is very expensive because we have to pay every time for transferring data.
- Very much dependency on the third party because it is public network.

Characterisitcs of WAN

- It connects devices the are separated by a wide geographical area than a LAN.
- Lower bandwidth compared to LANs.
- Typically interconnect multiple LANs
- Usually data communication equipment, is managed externally to organisations using the WAN.
- It use serial connection.

10.1.3 Bluetooth

Bluetooth is a wireless personal area network (WPAN) technology from the Bluetooth Special Interest Group founded in 1998 by Ericsson, IBM, Intel, Nokia and Toshiba. It is an open standard for short-range transmission of digital voice and data. It supports point-to-point and multipoint applications. Some Bluetooth applications have been developed for cellphones, providing a wireless connection to a headset and to an automobile's audio system for hands-free operation. It operates in the frequency band of 2.45 GHz. Data transfer rate of Bluetooh is 2.1 Mbps.

☞ Bluetooth is a global short-range wireless standard that allows a broad range of electronic devices to connect and communicate with each other. It is a cable replacement technology..

Advantages of Bluetooth

- Wireless: There are many advantages to using wireless devices that we don't required wire, sometime when traveling one place to another with our laptop or other devices we will no longer have to worry about the bring the cables with us.
- Bluetooth is inexpensive: The Bluetooth technology is very cheap for companies to implementation which can get in lower price.
- Bluetooth is automatic: The Bluetooth is automatic software which does not have to set up the connection when two or more than wireless devices enter a range of up to 10 meter of each others they will be automatically start to communicate each others.
- Low interference: Bluetooth is avoiding to interference to other wireless devices.
- Standard protocol: Bluetooth is the standardized wireless.
- Instant PAN (personal area network): We can connected seven Bluetooth device to each others within the range of 10 meter.

Disadvantages of Bluetooth

- Infrared can be up to 4 mbps which is very fast while Bluetooth only provide 1 mbps.
- When many mobile devices in the same room it is possible to attempting the same data or operation.
- Bluetooth has several security mechanisms that it could have to carry out in order to prevent eavesdropping in the future.

Characterisitcs of Bluetooth

Bluetooth is specifically designed to provide low-cost, efficient, high capacity, ad hoc voice and data networking with the following characteristics:

- Fast frequency hopping to avoid interference.
- Fast acknowledge, which allows low coding overhead for links.
- Short data packets to maximize capacity during interference.
- Adaptive output power to minimize interference.
- 1 MB/sec. transmission/reception rate that exploits maximum available channel bandwidth.
- Flexible packet types that supports a wide application range.
- Transmission/reception interface convert to minimize current consumption.
- CVSD (Continuous Variable Slope Delta Modulation) voice coding, which enables operation at high bit-error rates.

10.1.4 Wi-Fi (Wireless-Fidelity)

WiFi is a local area network that uses high frequency radio signals to transmit and receive data over distances of a few hundred feet, uses ethernet protocol. A WiFi enabled device such as a personal computer, video game console, mobile phone, MP3 player or personal digital assistant can connect to the Internet when within range of a wireless network connected to the Internet. The coverage of one or more interconnected access points are called a hotspot which comprises an area as small as a few rooms or as large as many square miles covered by group of access points with overlapping coverage. WiFi technology has been used in Wireless mesh networks. Earlier laptops can be Wi-Fi enabled by plugging in a Wi-Fi adapter via the USB port or PC Card. The term Wi-Fi was chosen as a play on the term "Hi-Fi", and is thought to be an abbreviation for wireless fidelity.

Advantages of Wi-Fi

- The main advantages of using Wi-Fi technology is the lack of wires. This is a wireless connection that can merge together multiple devices.
- Wi-Fi allows managing or communicating network. It can reduce the cost of Cables and laying charges.
- It is eady to setup Wi-Fi and configuration than cabling process. You can add any number of Wi-Fi clients and moving to other location.
- You can send and receive the any amount of data in the air; its completely safe and it will not interfere with any network.
- Wi-Fi networks are widely used to connect a variety of devices, not only between themselves but also to the

Internet. And almost all modern laptops, tablets, and some mobile phones have this feature. It is very convenient and allows you to connect to the internet almost anywhere, not just where the cables are laid.

Disadvantages of Wi-Fi

- Wi-Fi has a limited radius of action and it is suitable for home networking, which is more dependent on the environment. For example, a typical home router with Wi-Fi in the room has a range of up to 45 meters and up to 450 meters outside.
- At high density Wi-Fi-points operating in the same or adjacent channels, they can interfere with each other. This affects the quality of the connection. This problem is common in apartment buildings, where many residents are using this technology.
- Wi-Fi technology is not perfect and has many flaws that limit its use.
- Wi-Fi network implementation is more costly than wired network. There are some limit to transfer the data rate, it can't send the huge data compared to wired technology.
- Wi-Fi will generates some radiation which is effects on human health. Stop Wi-Fi devices or equipment when it is not in use to reduce the radiation.

Characterisitics of Wi-Fi

There are currently three WiFi transmission standards, IEEE 802.11a, b and g. IEEE 802.11n was recently approved. Top speeds are 11 or 54 Mbps, but with protocol overhead the effective speeds will be around half. If the signal is too weak to transmit reliably at top speed, the radios automatically slow down, increasing reliability.

In car radios and TV sets, broadcasts are on different channels to avoid interference. 802.11 b and g have only 3 non-overlapping channels. To avoid interference, the radio power, and therefore transmission distances are short. Much longer links can be achieved with specialized antennae and amplifiers. Note that the distance is lower for higher frequency transmission. The frequency ranges are referred to as 2.4ghz and 5ghz. IEEE 802.11n has been agreed upon and standard products are expected. Speeds will be around 300 Mbps (100 effective) and distances increased.

10.1.5 Broadband

The term commonly refers to an Internet access via cable and Digital Subscriber Line (DSL). Broadband is as much as 400 times faster than analog dial-up. The term has always referred to a higher-speed connection, but the threshold speed varies with the times.

Broadband is transmitting data by modulating a carrier wave in order to differentiate it from other signals in the air or in a single line.

10.2 CONCEPT OF INTERNET

Internet is an interconnection between several computers of different types belonging to various networks across the world. It is a network of networks. Millions of people use the Internet to search and share information and ideas, etc. It has grown into an important infrastructure supporting a widespread, multi-disciplinary community. This community now consists of students, scientists and researchers, large corporations, non-profit organizations, government agencies, and individual consumers.

The Internet is an immensely complex combination of thousands of technologies and dozens of services used by millions of people around the world each day. Figure 10.3 shows a Web of computers which is laid around the globe. The Internet links thousands of computer networks. Every network and every computer in these networks exchange information according to certain rules called protocols. These different computers and networks are united with the common thread of two protocols, i.e., Internet Protocol (IP) and Transmission Control Protocol (TCP).

10.2.1 Applications of Internet

With the help of Internet you can:

- Exchange messages using e-mail (Electronic mail).
- Transfer files as well as software.
- Browse through information on any topic on web.
- Communicate in real time (chat) with others connected to the Internet.
- Search databases of government, individuals and organizations.
- Read news available from leading news groups.
- Send or receive animation and picture files from distant places.
- Set up a site with information about your company's products and services.

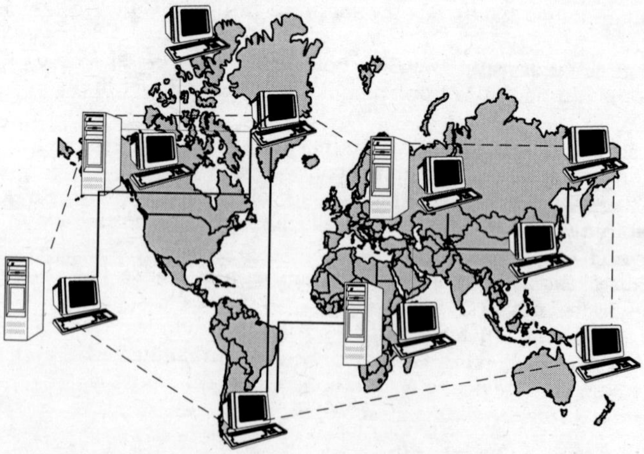

Figure 10.3 Internet as the network of computers connected with one another all over the world

10.2.2 Connecting to the Internet

To activate Internet services an Internet connection from a Internet Service Provider is required. To have a connection one needs to contact the Internet Service Providers. There are several Internet Service Providers (ISP) in each locality. There are some nominal charges that you need to pay to the ISP for the installation of the connection and for the rent (either monthly or annually). Depending on the requirement you can choose any one of the available options. If you need a high speed dedicated network then you can opt for a high bandwidth broadband or leased line connection.

If you need to have connection on a single PC then you choose a low bandwidth or dialup connection . For small services at your hand you can even have mobile phones connected to your Internet. There are many ways to get connected to the Internet.

You can get internet connection in any of the following ways:-

1. Through dial-up connection: User is supposed to get connected to the internet after dialing up the number used for connection. This is useful if your network is either confined to small group of computers or for a single PC.
2. Through leased lines: In this a dedicated line is laid specifically for connection. Typically, leased lines are used by businesses to connect geographically distant offices. Unlike normal dial-up connections, a leased line is always active. For example, a T-1 channel is a type of leased line that provides a maximum transmission speed of 1.544 Mbps.
3. Though broadband: In this you can get a broadband connection which provides a high bandwidth for the internet connection. This also provides high-speed internet, also commonly called broadband internet, is internet access of at least 200 Kilobits per second (Kbps).

Now a days even wireless connections are available. For this you need to have a Wi Fi card attached to your computer which can be useful if you do not have proper place to lay down the wires.

To connect to the Internet you need a PC (personal computer) with requisite software including a browser, a telephone connection or a leased line, and a modem, which allows the PC to communicate with other computers.

10.2.3 Troubleshooting

Troubleshooting Internet connection problems can be a challenge because there are so many possible causes. First, try these steps:

1. Reboot your computer–Rebooting your computer should be the first thing to do when finding yourself offline. This can be done by going to the start menu and selecting "Turn Off" or "Shutdown". Then once your PC has powered down, press the power button to power it back on. Then test your internet connection again.
2. Ping–One of the second things to try when your connection does not seem to be working properly is the ping

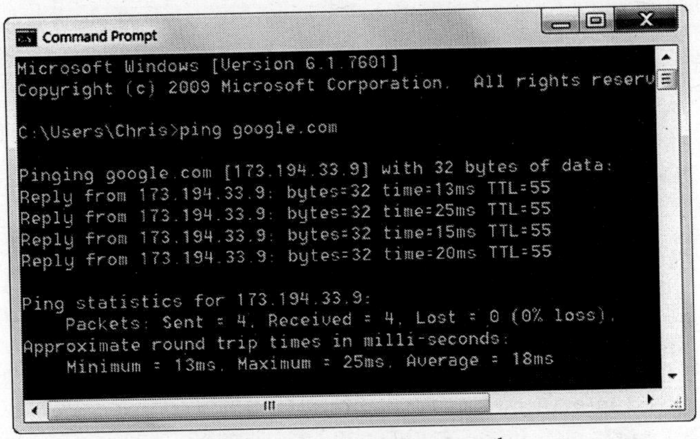

Figure 10.4 Ping command

command. Open a Command Prompt from your start menu and run a command for example, ping.google.com (See Figure 10.4).

This command sends several packets to the address you specify. The web server responds to each packet it receives. In the command see Figure 10.4, we can see that everything is working fine, then there are 0% packet loss and the time each packet takes is fairly low.

If you see packet loss (in other words, if the web server did not respond to one or more of the packets you sent), this can indicate a network problem. If the web server takes a much longer amount of time to respond to some of your other packets, this can also indicate a network problem. This problem can be with the website itself (unlikely if the same problem occurs on multiple websites), with your Internet service provider, or on your network (for example, a problem with your router).

3. Modem Router Issues–They may be caused by your modem or router. The modem is the device that communicates with your Internet service provider, while the router shares the connection among all the computers and other networked devices.
   - Please ensure that the power light on the router is on. If it is not lit then please locate the power plug for the device. To locate the plug, follow the power cord from the back of the device down to where it ends, it should be plugged into an outlet. If it is not, please plug it in at this time. Then wait 2 minutes and try your internet connection again (See Figure 10.5).

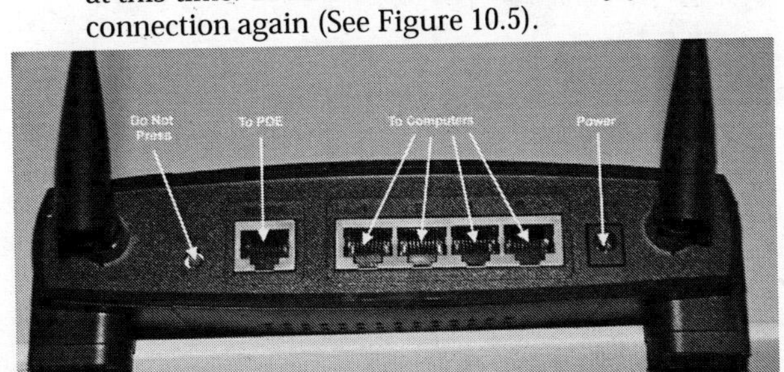

Figure 10.5 Router

- Now unplug the power from the power port on the back of your router. Wait at least for 30 seconds, then plug it back. Then wait for additional two minutes for the router to power up and connect, then try your internet connection again.
- Next locate the POE Adapter for your radio. This can be located by following the cable plugged into the POE/internet port on the back of your router, or the internet cable plugged directly into the back of your computer. This cable will look like a phone line, only a little bit wider.
- Once you have located the POE Adapter (See Figure 10.6) at the other end of the cable. Ensure that all cables are firmly connected. Then Follow the power cord on the POE to the plug at the other end and ensure it is plugged into an outlet. If it is not plugged in, do so now. Then wait for 2 minutes, and try your internet connection again.
- Now unplug the power cable from the POE device, wait at least 30 seconds, and plug it back in. Then wait for 2 minutes (wait time varies by radio device) and try your internet connection again.
- Next go back to your router and unplug the power cable from the power port, wait for at least 30 seconds and plug it back in again. Then wait for 2 minutes and try your internet connection again.
- Check for spyware, viruses and malware. These programs are easily downloaded and installed, while you are surfing the Web. They can run undetected and have a significant impact on your web speed and overall system performance.

10.2.4 World Wide Web (WWW)

The World Wide Web, or simply "the Web" is a global information system that is the fastest-growing area of the Internet. In other words World Wide Web is a series of servers that are interconnected through hypertext. Hypertext is a method of presenting information in which certain text are highlighted, that, when selected, displays more information on that particular topic (See Figure 10.6).

The Web, like all Internet services, is based on the interaction and transfer of data between special server computers (Web servers) and your PC (using Web browser software such as Internet Explorer from Microsoft).

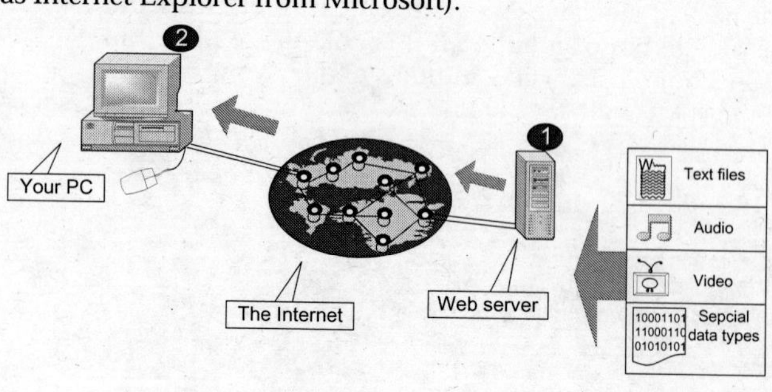

Figure 10.6 Some data types available on the Web

☞ Different browsers may format and display the same file differently, depending on the capabilities of the hardware and the default layout options for the browser itself.

How it Works?

1. The World Wide Web is the fastest growing and most innovative part of the Internet. When you browse the Web, you view multimedia pages composed of text, graphics, sound and video. The Web used hyptertext links that allow you to jump from one place to another on the Web. The language that allows you to use hypertext links and to view Web pages is called Hypertext Markup Language, more commonly knows as HTML.
2. The Web works on client/server model in which client software–known as Web browser–runs on a local computer. The server software runs on a Web host. To use the Web, you first make an Internet connection, and then launch your Web browser.
3. In a Web browser, you type the Uniform Resource Locator (URL) for a location you want to visit or click on a link that will send you to the desired location. The names for Web locations are URLs. Your Web browser sends the URL request using HTTP (Hyper text Transfer Protocol), which defines the way the Web browser and the Web server communicate with one another.
4. URLs contain several parts. The first part–the http://–details which Internet protocol to use. The second part–the part that usually has a www in it–Sometimes tells what kind of Internet resource is being contacted. The third part –such as satishibm.com, can vary in length and identifies the Web server to be contacted. The final part identifies a specific directory on the server and a home page, document or other Internet object.
5. The request is sent to the Internet. Internet routers examine the request to determine which server to send the request to. The information just to the right of the http://in the URL tells the Internet on which Web server the requested information can be found. Routers send the request to that Web server.
6. The Web server receives the request using the HTTP protocol. It is told which specific document is being requested.
7. When the server find the requested home page, document, or object, it sends that home page, document, or object back to the Web browser client. The information is then displayed on the computer screen in the Web browser.

10.2.5 TCP/IP

TCP/IP is a routable protocol that is suitable for connecting dissimilar systems (such as Microsoft Windows and UNIX) in heterogeneous networks. It is the protocol of the worldwide network known as the Internet. TCP/IP is a two-layer program. It is higher fourth transport layer protocol. TCP manages the assembling of a message or file into smaller packets that are transmitted over the Internet and received by a TCP layer that reassembles the packets into the original message. The lower layer, Internet Protocol, handles the address part of each packet so that it gets to the right destination. Each gateway computer on the network checks this address to see where to forward the message. Even though some packets from the same message are routed differently than others, they will be reassembled at the destination.

TCP/IP uses the client/server model of communication in which a computer user (a client) requests and is provided a service (such as sending a Web page) by another computer (a server) in the network. TCP/IP communication is primarily point-to-point, meaning each communication is from one point (or host computer) in the network to another point or host computer.

Many Internet users are familiar with the even higher layer application protocols that use TCP/IP to get to the Internet connection. These include the World Wide Web's Hypertext Transfer Protocol (HTTP), the File Transfer Protocol (FTP), Telnet (Telnet) which lets you to logon to remote computers, and the Simple Mail Transfer Protocol (SMTP). These and other protocols are often packaged together with TCP/IP as a "suite."

Personal computer users with an analog phone modem connection to the Internet usually get to the Internet through the Serial Line Internet Protocol (SLIP) or the Point-to-Point Protocol (PPP). These protocols encapsulate the IP packets so that they can be sent over the dial-up phone connection to an access provider's modem.

10.2.6 DNS

Sun Microsystems developed the Domain Name System (DNS) in the early 1980s as an easier way to keep track of Internet addresses. The Internet Protocol (IP) uses Internet address information to deliver mail and other data from computer to computer. Every IP address on the Internet is actually a series of four numbers separated by periods called dots, such as 163.52.128.72. But it will be difficult to remember numeric addresses to communicate with someone using electronic mail. The DNS establishes a hierarchy of domains, which are groups of computers on the Internet.

The purpose of DNS is to translate domain names into IP addresses. Whenever we use a domain name, a service is used for translating domain names into IP addresses and is known as DNS. DNS implements a distributed database to store this name and address information for all public hosts on the Internet. DNS assumes IP addresses do not change (are statically assigned rather than dynamically assigned). For example, the domain name www.computer-games.com might translate to 192.111.221.2. So what DNS basically do, is that it translated the domain name "computer-games" into corresponding IP address.

If one DNS server does not know how to translate the particular domain name, it asks another DNS server and this process continues until the correct IP address is returned. As in the above example, if one domain server does not know how to translate www.computer-games.com, it will move to another DNS until the corresponding IP address 192.111.221.2 is returned. DNS scheme uses alphabets and it is easier to remember, but actually each domain name has an address and DNS scheme which is used to convert this domain name into its corresponding address.

10.2.7 Search Engine

A Web search engine is used to search for information on the Internet. The search results are generally presented in a list and are often called hits. The information may consist of Web pages, images, and other types of files.

A search engine is a program which looks through its database for information that matches your request. Information in the database are about websites and their contents. Examples of search engines are, Alta Vista, Yahoo, Hot Java Excite, Infoseek, HotBot, Google etc. Some Indian search engines are Jadoo, Khoj, I love India, 123 India etc.

10.2.8 Web Browser Features

Browsers are the software that allows you to access the World Wide Web. The most popular browsers are Microsoft's Internet Explorer and Mozill Firefox.

Internet Explorer was made by Microsoft Corporation and bundled together into Windows operating system. The latest operating system, Windows comes with Microsoft's latest web browser named Internet Explorer 8. If you purchase a genuine copy of Windows you will get Internet Explorer 8 for free otherwise it is free for downloading from Microsoft's Web site (http://www.microsoft.com/ie/).

➡ **To open Internet Explorer, do this:**

1. Click on the Start button.
2. Type Internet in the Search box.

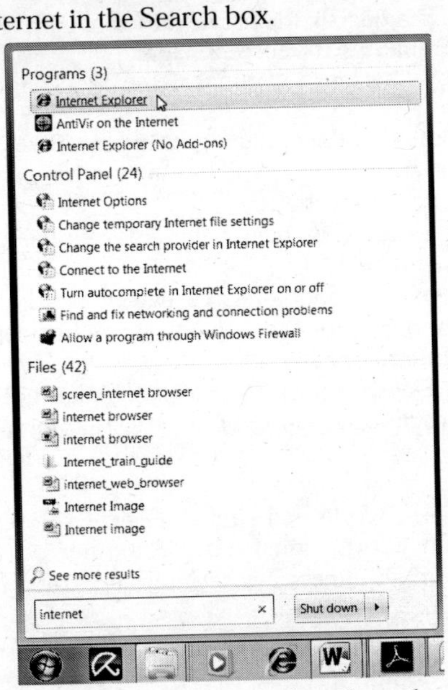

Figure 10.7 Selecting Internet Explorer from the start menu

3. Select Internet Explorer from the list of results (See Figure 10.7).
4. Finally, press Enter key.

Browser Features

Most browsers contain the following features. Some of these may be presented as button (or icons) in a toolbar.
The part of browser features are explained below:

Title Bar—On the left the title bar displays the name of the Web page currently open and on the right side the maximize/minimize, restore and close buttons (See Figure 10.8).

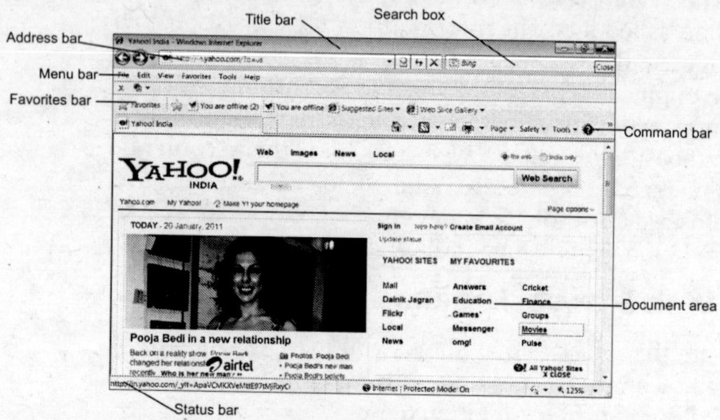

Figure 10.8 Different components marked as seen on Internet Explorer Window

Address bar—It displays the address of the page you are currently viewing. You can also use the Address bar for navigation. Type the address of a page you want to go to in the Address bar and press Enter key. Address Bar contains the following buttons:

- Back: Displays a page in the list of previously viewed pages.
- Forward: Displays a page in the list next to viewed pages.
- Stop: Stops downloading the current page.
- Refresh: Displays the latest version of the Web page is displayed.

Search box—It is located in the upper-right corner next to the Address bar. To search any topic, type in the search box and then press Enter or click on the button .

Menu bar—This is located just below the Address bar and has the pull-down menu.

Command bar—The Command bar is located at the upper-right side of the Internet Explorer window and offers easy access to setting in Internet Explorer.

Favorites bar—The Favorites bar replaces the Links toolbar that appeared in previous versions of Internet Explorer. It provides one-click access to your favorite Web sites, as well as feeds and Web Slices.

Explorer animation—It is indicated when Internet Explorer is waiting to receive an information from a computer on the Internet. The flag icon shimmers incase Internet Explorer is waiting.

Status bar—It gives you information about what Internet Explorer is currently doing.

Document area—It displays the Web page you are currently viewing.

10.2.9 Switches

A switch is a network device that selects a path or circuit for sending a data unit to its next destination. In smaller networks, switch is not required. It is required in large internetworks, where there can be many possible ways of transmitting a message from a sender to destination. The purpose of the switch is to select the best possible path.

Switches are the linkage points of an Ethernet network. Just as in hub, devices in switches are connected to them through twisted pair cabling. But the difference shows both the devices hub and a switch treat the data they receive. Hub works by sending the data to all the ports on the device whereas a switch transfers it only to that port which is connected to the destination device. Switches operate in full-duplex mode where devices can send and receive data from the switch at the simultaneously in half-duplex mode. The transmission speed in switches is double than in Ethernet hub transferring a 20Mbs connection into 30Mbps and a 200Mbps connection to become 300Mbps.

10.2.10 Routers

Routers are devices (computers) containing software that help in determining the best path out of the available paths, for a particular transmission (See Figure 10.9). They consist of a combination of hardware and software. The hardware includes the physical interfaces to the various networks in the internetwork. The two main pieces of software in a router are the operating system and the routing protocol.

A gateway can receive e-mail messages in one format and convert them into another format. You can connect systems with different communications protocol, languages and architecture using a gateway. While considering use of a gateway, it should be kept in mind that they can be slow because they need to perform intensive conversion, and that they can be very expensive.

10.2.11 Gateways

To connect totally dissimilar networks, a device called a gateway is used. Gateways perform protocol conversion for all seven layers of the OSI (Open Systems Interconnection) model. A common use for a gateway is to connect a LAN and an SNA Mainframe computer, changing protocols and transmitting packets between two entirely different systems.

Gateways handle messages, addresses and protocol conversions necessary to deliver a message from one network to another. Gateways offer greatest flexibility in internetworking communications. This flexibility is at the cost of higher price, more complex design, implementation, maintenance and operation of a gateway (See Figure 10.10).

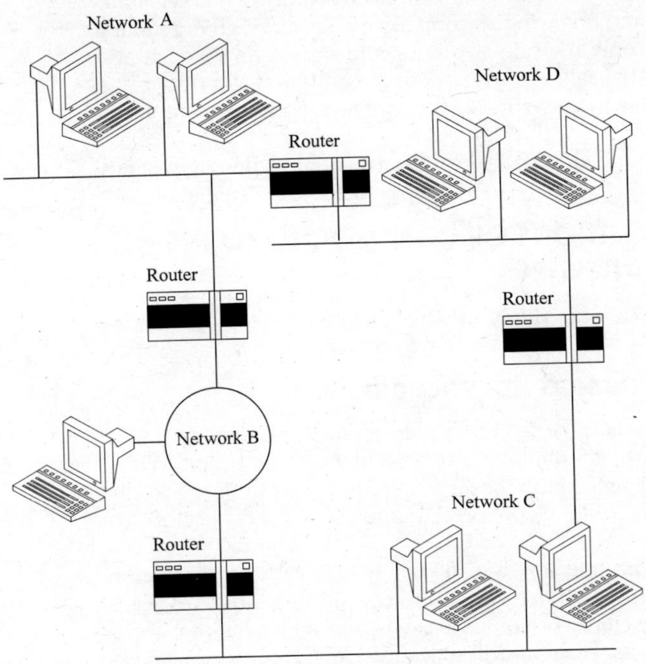

Figure 10.9 Networks connected by routers

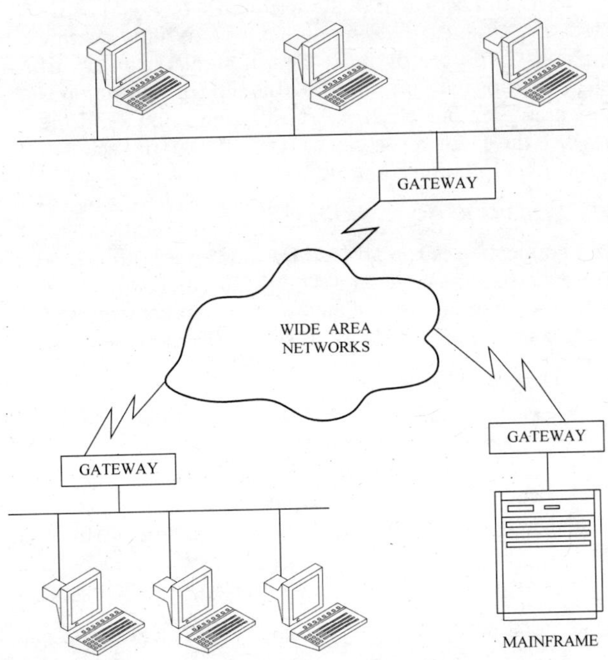

Figure 10.10 Pictorial representation of gateway functions

10.3 VARIOUS APPLICATIONS OF INTERNET

The Internet has many important applications. Of the various services available via the Internet, the three most important are e-mail, information gathering and retailing etc. E-mail, also known as electronic mail, is the most widely used and successful Internet applications.

10.3.1 E-mail

E-mail is the electronic equivalent of sending a letter through the mail. The primary component of the electronic mail system is a "post office," an area on the shared hard disk that is reserved for mail. This post office serves as the central message holder and has both "in" and "out" baskets for each user.

E-mail is a service which allows us to send the message in electronic mode over the internet. It offers an efficient, inexpensive and real time mean of distributing information among people.

E-Mail Address

Each user of email is assigned a unique name for his email account. This name is known as E-mail address. Different users can send and receive messages according to the e-mail address.

E-mail is generally of the form username@domainname. For example, abc@tutorials.com is an e-mail address where abc is username and tutorials.com is domain name.

- The username and the domain name are separated by @ (at) symbol.
- E-mail addresses are not case sensitive.
- Spaces are not allowed in e-mail address.

The volume of e-mail also continues to increase because there are more users, and because users now have the ability to attach documents of various types to e-mail messages. The formulation of Multipurpose Internet Mail Extensions (MIME) and its adoption by software developers has made it much easier to send and receive attachments, including word-processed documents, spreadsheets, and graphics. The result is that the volume of traffic generated by e-mail, is measured in terms of the number of data packets moving across the network, has increased dramatically in recent years, contributing significantly to network congestion.

10.3.2 Information Gathering

Information Gathering is a key part of feasibility analysis. Information Gathering is therefore is the process of gathering information about the present system. We must know what information to gather, where to find it, how to collect it, and ultimately how to process the collected information.

Information gathering is both an art and a science. It is an art because the person who collects the information needs to be sensitive, and must have an understanding of what to collect and what to focus on, the channels where the source of information can be gathered. It is a science because it requires proper methodology and the use of specific tools in order to be effective. However, there is always a chance that one can find oneself drowned in an ocean of information, not knowing which specific information to collect, where to collect it and how to collect it.

The following are categories of information that can be broadly classified:

Organizational Information

The kind of information that one could collect depending upon the need are:

- Policies of the Organization–Policies are guidelines that defines the code of business. Policies are then translated into rules and procedures for achieving goals.
- Goals of the organization–Goals describe the managements commitment to the objectives. Objectives are milestones of accomplishments toward achieving goals.
- Organization Structure–Organization structure helps to understand the hierarchy level in an organization and the mode of communication.

User Information

User information relates to the individuals who are using the present system. When collecting user information one should focus on job function, information requirements and interpersonal relationships within the organization.

Work Information

Work information relates to the work itself. When collecting Work information one should focus on work flows, data flows between various systems, work schedules and methods and procedures.

10.3.3 Retailing

Retailing is a convenient, convincing and comfortable method of selling goods and services. Retailing is one area of the broader term, e-commerce. Retailing is buying and selling of both goods and consumers services.

Retailing is defined as a conclusive set of activities or steps used to sell a product or a service to consumers for their personal or family use. It is responsible for matching individual demands of the consumer with supplies of all the manufacturers. The word 'retail' is derived from the French work retailer, meaning 'to cut a piece off' or 'to break bulk'. In simple terms, it implies a first-hand transaction with the customer.

A retailer is a person, agent, agency, company, or organization which is instrumental in reaching the goods, merchandise, or services to the ultimate consumer. Retailers perform specific activities such as anticipating customer's wants, developing assortments of products, acquiring market information, and financing. A common assumption is that retailing involves only the sale of products in stores. However, it also includes the sale of services like those offered at a restaurant, parlour, or by car rental agencies. The selling need not necessarily take place through a store. Retailing encompasses selling through the mail, the Internet, door-to-door visits–any channel that could be used to approach the consumer.

10.4 METHODS OF CONNECTING TO THE INTERNET

There are a lot of different ways of connecting to the Internet today.

10.4.1 Dial-up Connections

There are many different ways to connect to the Internet. One of the most common ways is via a dial-up connection. With a dial-up connection, the Internet user can connect to the Internet via his telephone line and an Internet service provider.

Dial-up connection is also known as Level Two connection. This provides connection to Internet through a dial-up terminal connection. The computer, which provides Internet access is known as 'Host' and the computer that receives the access, is known as 'Client'. The client computer uses modem to access a "host" and acts as if it is a terminal which is directly connected to that host. 56K modem access is now widely available and supported by most ISPs. It allows user to surf the Web at 56 Kbps with graphics. So this type of connection is also known as "Remote Modem Access" connection. And the host to which the client gets connected is actually connected to the Internet by a full time connection.

Dial-up Types and Bandwidth

A dial-up connection is categorized by the bandwidth it provides and whether it is analog or digital. Dial-up connectivity has evolved substantially in only a few years. Six categories of dial-up connectivity are available, as seen in Table 10.1 (top to bottom, slowest to fastest).

Table 10.1 Five Categories of Dial-up Internet Connectivity

Bandwidth	Common Reference	Comments
14.4 Kbps	"fourteen-four"	The slowest analog dial-up connection in common use.
28.8 Kbps	"twenty-eight-eight"	The previous industry standard; now the second most common type of analog Internet connection.
33.6 Kbps	"thirty-three-six"	The most common type of analog Internet connection (27% of all connections)
56.6 Kbps	"fifty-six-K"	The fastest analog dial-up connection available; actually never faster than 53.3 Kbps
Integrated Services Digital Network	ISDN	A digital (not analog) dial-up connection type that is also available as a direct connection.
Digital Subscriber Line	DSL [in the forms of ADSL (the most common), HDSL, IDSL, SDSL, and VHDSL]	A digital connection that operates over common copper phone lines. DSL is the fastest dial-up connection type available. Few metropolitan cities in India currently offer DSL; very small installed base (25,000)

Your ISP or online service must support the type of modem you are using. If your ISP has installed 33.6 Kbps modems and you are using a 56.6 Kbps modem, your connection speed will only be 33.6 Kbps (because modems are bandwidth backward compatible).

10.4.2 ISDN Connections

ISDN stands for "Integrated Services Digital Network". ISDN is a data transfer technology, created in 1984, that can transfer data significantly faster than a dial-up modem. ISDN enables wide-bandwidth digital transmission over the public telephone network, which means more data can be sent at one time. It support transfer rates of 64K or 128K of data per second. While these speeds are faster than what you can get with a dial-up modem. The newer DSL technology can support even faster transfer rates and is less costly to set up and maintain.

The characteristics of ISDN are as follow:

- Both your PC and your ISP must employ special digital ISDN modems.
- A digital ISDN phone line from a local telephone provider is required.
- ISDN is unique among dial-up connectivity types because it is available in both dial-up and direct connection types.
- ISDN connections are defined in terms of channels; two channels can be combined to form a single data path. Thus, a "dual-channel" ISDN connection has a bandwidth of 128 Kpbs (2 x 64 Kbps), as shown in Table 10.2.

Table 10.2 ISDN Types and Speeds

ISDN Type	Bandwidth
Single-channel ISDN	64 Kbps
Dual-channel ISDN	128 Kbps

Advantages of ISDN

1. Constant data rate at 64 kbit/s for each DS0 channel.
2. Two way broadband symmetric data transmission.
3. One of the data channels can be used for phone conversation without disturbing the data transmission through the other data channel. When a phone call is ended, the bearer channel can immediately dial and re-connect itself to the data call.
4. Call setup is very quick.
5. Low latency.
6. ISDN Voice clarity is unmatched by other phone services.
7. Caller ID is almost always available for no additional fee.
8. Maximum distance from the central office is much greater than it is for DSL.
9. When using ISDN-BRI, there is the possibility of using the low-bandwidth 16 kbit/s "D" channel for packet data.

Disadvantages of ISDN

1. ISDN offerings are dwindling in the marketplace due to the widespread use of faster and cheaper alternatives.
2. ISDN routers, terminal adapters ("modems"), and telephones are more expensive than ordinary Plain Old Telephone Service (POTS) equipment, like dial-up modems.
3. ISDN provisioning can be complicated due to the great number of options available.
4. ISDN users must dial in to a provider that offers ISDN Internet service, which means that the call could be disconnected.
5. ISDN is billed as a phone line, to which is added the bill for Internet ISDN access.
6. "Always on" data connections are not available in all locations.
7. Some telephone companies charge unusual fees for ISDN, including call setup fees, per minute fees, and higher rates than normal for other services.

10.4.3 Broadband Connections

A high speed Internet connection is termed as a Broadband connection. A channel may be broadband if it sends a signal without modulation on a carrier. The signal covers the whole range of frequency that medium can carry. It services at a high-speed internet transmission (usually 256 Kpbs) a permanent connection.

A customer's basically use land line phone for getting this service. He can use his telephone for a normal telephone call even while he is browsing Internet. There is no separate telephone charges for the connection to the Internet. The access to the Internet will be around 8 times faster than a normal dial up access. The advantage are

(i) Low (ii) High (iii) No setup time (iv) Always On

Dial-up uses regular phone lines to connect, whereas broadband uses a variety of other means. There are different types of Broadband service. These are as follows:

DSL Broadband

Digital Subscriber Line (DSL) is a technology that delivers broadband over your phone line to be used in home or office. With DSL technology, large volumes of information are sent over a copper cable at rapid speed. DSL allows you to download web pages, text, graphics, music and video in real time.

Cable Broadband

Cable is another broadband connection option, where the cable operator provides the internet connection. It requires a special modem which is connected to the cable TV box. Majority of the cable companies provide packages which have telephone and TV channels as well as a broadband internet connection.

Satellite Broadband

Satellite is the ultimate option for people living in remote areas and who can not receive any other form of broadband internet. It requires the installation of a special satellite dish. There are mainly two types of connections: one-way connections and two-way connections. In the one-way connection, you will be able to receive data, but for sending data, you will need a dial-up modem through a telephone line or IDSN line. In the two-way connection, data is both sent and received through the satellite dish, though it is more expensive. Satellite transmission may be affected by weather conditions. The cost of installing and running satellite broadband can be quite expensive as compared with other types of broadband.

10.5 INTRODUCTION TO INTERNET ADDRESSING

The Internet has more than a million computers attached to it. In order to communicate, every computer connected to the Internet has a unique address whose format is defined by the IP addressing system. An IP address is a number that represents a single unique computer on the Internet. IP addresses are similar to telephone numbers in which each computer (or telephone) must have its own unique IP address (telephone number). Like telephones, there is a directory system called the Domain Name System or DNS that can convert a name such as "www.microsoft.com." Into a corresponding numeric IP address.

Each computer on the network is called a host, and has a name and a number that identifies it. The IP addressing system uses:

a. Letter addressing system
b. Number addressing system

Letter Addressing System

Few examples of letter addressing are:

1. cbseindia.org
2. Gmail.com

The last three letters of the address are important because they provide information about the kind of organization to which the address belongs. Some of the abbreviations used are listed here:

.edu Educational institutions
.com Commercial organizations
.org Nonprofit organizations
.gov Government departments
.net Networking organizations
.mil Military
.co Company

The letter addressing system also uses country codes comprising of two letters. Examples of country codes are:

ca for Canada
jp for Japan
in for India
uk for United Kingdom

http://www.microsoft.co.in here the last in suggests that it is based in India (.in)

The letter addressing system is called the DNS.

Number Addressing System

A numeric address called IP address is made up of four numbers, each less than 256, joined together by periods, such as 192. 12. 248. 73 or 131. 58. 97. 254

☞ IP address is the identifier for a particular machine (computer) on a specified network.

10.6 INTERNET PROTOCOLS

The internet Protocol (IP) is the primary network protocol used on the Internet, developed in the 1970s. On the Internet and many other networks, IP is often used together with the Transport Control Protocol (TCP) and referred to interchangeably as TCP/IP. IP supports unique addressing for computers on a network. Most networks use the Internet Protocol version 4 (IPv4) standard that features IP addresses four bytes (32 bits) in length. The newer Internet Protocol version 6 (IPv6) standard features addresses 16 bytes (128 bits) in length.

The Internet Protocol (IP) is a network-layer (Layer 3) protocol that contains addressing information and some control information that enables packets to be routed. IP is documented in RFC 791 and is the primary network-layer protocol in the Internet protocol suite. Along with the Transmission Control Protocol (TCP), IP represents the heart of the Internet protocols.

10.6.1 TCP/IP

TCP is a set of rule (protocol) used along with the Internet Protocol (IP) to send data in the form of message units between computers over the Internet. While IP takes care of handling the actual delivery of the data, TCP takes care of keeping track of the individual units of data (called packets) that a message is divided into packets for efficient routing through the Internet.

For example, when an HTML file is sent to you from a Web server, the Transmission Control Protocol (TCP) program layer in that server divides the file into one or more packets, numbers the packets, and then forwards them individually to the IP program layer. Although each packet has the same destination IP address, it may get routed differently through the network.

TCP is a connection-oriented protocol, which means that a connection is established and maintain until the message or messages to be exchanged by the application program at each end have been exchanged. TCP is responsible for ensuring that a message is divided into the packets that IP manages and for reassembling the packets back into the complete message at the other end. In the Open Systems Interconnection (OSI) communication model, TCP is present in layer 4, the Transport layer.

10.6.2 FTP

The File Transfer Protocol (FTP) service allows an Internet user to move a file from one computer to another on the Internet. A file may contain any type of digital information such as text document, image, artwork, movie, sound, software, etc. Hence, anything that can be stored on a computer can be moved with FTP service. Moving a file from a remote computer to individual (ones own) computer is known as downloading the file and moving a file from ones own computer to a remote computer is known as uploading the file.

☞ FTP is an *interacti e* system. The FTP client that comes with Windows NT or 2000 is a character-based client.

Numerous FTP servers present all over the world allow users anywhere on the Internet to log in and download the files which are placed on them. The main competitor for FTP is HTTP (Hyper Text Transfer Protocol) and the day is not very far when sites would run HTTP servers instead of the FTP servers. It is so because HTTP servers can do whatever FTP server can do and do it more efficiently.

One problem with downloading files over the Internet is that some files are so large that it can take a tremendous amount of time to download them. As a way to speed up file transfers and save space on the FTP server, files are commonly compressed. Many different methods are used to compress files. After the files have been downloaded, you will need to run the decompression software such as PKUNZIP to decompress the files to use them.

☞ FTP executes on top of TCP/IP stack and uses the Open System Interconnection (OSI) protocols to enable users and applications to transfer files among networked stations.

10.6.3 HTTP

The Hypertext Transfer Protocol (HTTP) is a set of rules for exchanging files (text, graphics, images, sound, video and other multimedia files) on the WWW. It is an access method to access web pages used on the Internet. The HTTP generally works in combination with WWW.

☞ The http is responsible for accessing hypertext documents on WWW.

Your web browser is an HTTP client, sending requests to server machines. When the user enters a file request in the browser program by either opening a web file (typing in a URL) or clicking on a hypertext link, the browser builds an HTTP request and sends it to an HTTP program in the destination server machine, which receives the request and after any necessary processing returns the requested file.

☞ HTTP is a protocol used by WWW to create, display and link hypertext files.

10.7 DEFINE AND UNDERSTAND THE TERMS

10.7.1 Internet Service Provider

Internet service provider is a company that provides access to the internet. An Internet Service Provider, or ISP is one gateway to the Internet. In most cases, you connect to an ISP by using a PC modem to dial into your ISP's modems over a standard telephone line. Your modem connects to a single modem among a bank of modems at your ISP. This is called a dial-up connection. Users within corporations and large organizations typically connect to an ISP via a high-speed link (typically over fiber optic cabling but not phone lines) called a direct connection.

10.7.2 Uniform Resource Locator (URL)

URL or Uniform Resource Locator refers to address on the Internet. Billions of documents and multimedia files can be accessed on the Internet through their URLs. The URL contains the following information:

- The Internet name of the site containing the resource (document data).
- The type of service the resource is served by (HTTP, FTP, etc.).
- The Internet port number of the service (if this is omitted, the browser assumes a commonly accepted default value).
- The location of the resource in the directory structure of the server.

The syntax for specifying a URL is given in Figure 10.11. URLs contain information about both the access method to use and also about the resource itself. They are used by Web browsers to connect you directly to a specific document or page on the WWW. You do not have to know where that resource is located physically. A sample URL might look like the following:

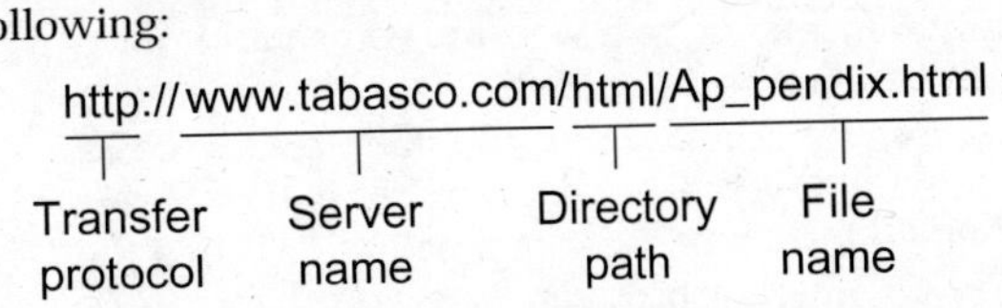

Figure 10.11 Syntax used in specifying a Uniform Resource Locator (URL)

First part of the URL before the colon specifies the access method. On the Web this is usually http (Hypertext Transfer Protocol). But ftp or gopher also may be specified. The second part of the URL after the colon, specifies the resource. The text after the two slashes (//) indicates a server name, and the text after the single slash defines the directory or individual file you will be connected to. If you are linking to a document, it will usually have the file name extension `.html`, the abbreviation for Hypertext Markup Language.

Every page on the Web has a unique address, called a Uniform Resource Locator (URL). The example of absoulte URLs is:

`http://www.entertainment.satyam-online.com/contents/horoscope.asp`

A fully qualified URL that specifies the location of a resource that resides on the Internet is called an absolute URL. Table 10.3 shows the components that make up a URL.

Table 10.3 Components that make up a URL

Example	Explanation	Description
`http://`	Protocol	HTTP is the protocol used to transmit Web pages for this URL.
`www.entertainment.satyamonline.com`	Domain name	The server where the page is located. Every domain name is unique. Here Internet Service Provider (ISP) is Satyam online.
`contents/`	Directory path	The directory where the page is located.
`horoscope.asp`	Filename	The filename of the Web page.

10.7.3 Hyperlinks

Hyperlinks, or links are Web navigation elements that allow you to move, or navigate, between Web pages. They also allow you to download audio, video, and other types of multimedia files. Web pages accessed via link may reside at the same Web site as the source link or at another site anywhere on the Web.

There are three types of hyperlinks.

- text hyperlinks
- image hyperlinks
- image maps (containing multiple hyperlinks)

Functionally, all the three categories of hyperlinks are identical. Text hyperlinks are generally denoted in blue colour and underlined, while image hyperlinks and maps are indicated by a blue coloured border. In all the three cases, the mouse pointer will change from an arrow to a pointing hand when it passes over a hyperlink.

10.7.4 Know how to Identify a secure Web site

Before giving any information to a website, you should make sure it is secure. There are some quick tips that you can use to tell if a site is secure.

HTTPS–If you are on a web page that requires entry of your personal or private information, check to see if the URL in the address bar of your internet browser starts with "https://". The letter S is very important, since it signifies that the website is using Hypertext Transfer Protocol Secure (HTTPS), a communications protocol for secure communication. Do not enter any information if the page is not secured by HTTPS.

Lock Icon–Most internet browsers have built-in encryption detection. You can check if a website is secure by clicking on the lock icon in the address bar of your browser (usually located to the left of the URL). A pop-up will appear, showing you website permissions, security certificate information and other related details.

Security Considerations

Before the great explosion of interest in the World Wide Web, it was common practice to run utilities or programs on the Internet. The Internet was virtually wide open, operating with a high level of trust and a low level of security. Now, because there are millions of users, security has become a huge concern. Companies are securing their networks to prevent uncontrolled or unsolicited access to their private networks from the outside.

User Authentication–Authentication is the process of verifying that a user who logs into a network or database has permission to log in. Examples of authentication include the use of a user name and password when logging into a local-area network (LAN) and the use of digital certificates when sending or receiving secure e-mail over the Internet.

Server Authentication–With server authentication, a client machine verifies that a server is who it claims to be. For example, when a client sends confidential data to a server, the client can verify that the server is secure and is the correct recipient of the client's confidential data.

Authorization–Authorization is the process of giving authenticated users access to the network. It also prevents them from accessing resources they do not need or do not have permission to use. For example, a manager may be authorized to access tables that contain employee payroll information, but a stock clerk would not be authorized to access this information. The methods used to enforce network and database resource authorization vary depending on the level of security desired and the type of network or database being protected.

Secure Transmission (Encryption)–When information is transmitted over lines of communication, whether they be coaxial cable, telephone lines, fiber optics, or satellite, there is the risk that the communication can be intercepted by third parties. Often, the information can be intercepted without the sender or receiver ever knowing the data was compromised. The most common method of securing transmission is to encrypt the data. When encryption is used, the sender and receiver of the data have a "key" that can encode and decode the information.

Firewall–A firewall is usually a combination of hardware and software that filters the types of data that can be received by your network. For example, a firewall can be configured to allow only HTTP traffic through to the protected network.

Virtual Private Network (VPN)–A Virtual Private Network (VPN) is an authenticated connection between two networks or between a network and a remote user where communication is considered completely private.

Viruses

Viruses consist of malicious code that infects a device after you install a software. Typically this infection happens through USB drives, Internet downloads, or email attachments. The infection happens once the program runs for the first time, whether through Autorun, a manual install, or an executable file that the user opens. A computer Virus is more dangerous than a computer worm as it makes changes or deletes your files while worms only replicates itself with out making changes to your files/data.

Worms

Worms are malicious programs that make copies of themselves again and again on the local drive, network shares, etc. The only purpose of the worm is to reproduce itself again and again. It does not harm any data/file on the computer. Unlike a virus, it does not need to attach itself to an existing program. Worms spread by exploiting vulnerabilities in operating systems.

Worms are the most damaging types of computer threat especially for computers connected in a network. They usually make use of security loopholes in a network to sneak inside every computer in the network without user intervention. They can (potentially) destroy all the computers in the network within a few minutes.

Trojan Horses

A Trojan horses is a malicious computer program hidden inside another program that masks its purpose and appears to be legitimate. Trojan horses rely on users to install them or can be installed by intruders. It can be sent as an attachment to an email message or can be placed on a website for an intruder to entice victims. A Trojan horse may be in the form of a Java applet, JavaScript, ActiveX control, or any other form of executable file.

Spyware

Spyware is any software that collects information about computer usage and/or the computer user. It is installed on one computer and send information to another computer. Symptoms of spyware infection includes:

- very slow system performance while browsing the Internet.
- Your homepage changing mysteriously on its own.
- Excessive apperance of pop-ups, on sites like Google, Yahoo and MSN, which do not use them.

10.7.5 Using Favorites Folder

Internet Explorer provides a series of Favorites commands and a Favorite Explorer bar for surfing the Web pages you like most. Using Favorites commands, you can create a list of favorite pages and organize them into folders. Then, to go to a favourite page, you simply select the page you want from the Favorites menu.

To display your saved favorites in the Favorites Center, click on the Favorites icon from the Favorites bar.

Adding an Item to Favorites

Internet Explorer makes it easy to add the currently displayed webpage or an entire group of tabs to your Favorites. The Add To Favorites command allows you to create a favorite-page listing for the page you are currently viewing.

➡ **To add the Web page to your Favorites list, do this:**

1. Click Command bar.
2. Click on Add To Favorites button (star button) from the Favorites Center.

OR

3. Open the Favorites Center, then drag the icon to the left of the URL in the address bar and drop it into the Favorites bar. A Move button in the Figure 10.12 indicates where the page will be added.

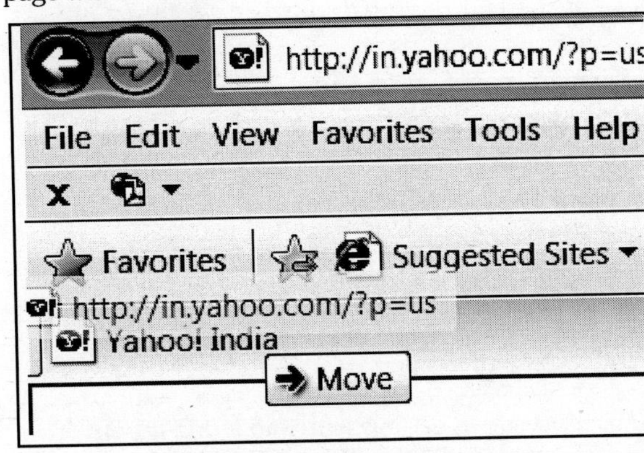

Figure 10.12 Favorites center

☞ If the Favorites bar is not displayed just to the left of your browser tabs, press Ctrl + Shift + I or Alt + C key together to open the Favorites Center.

Organize Favorites

This command permits you to view, organize, and return to your favorite pages. The Organize Favorites dialog box's buttons are used to add subfolders to your Favorites tree, move items between folders, rename folders and shortcuts, and delete folders.

➡ **To open Organize Favorites dialog box, do this:**

1. In the Favorites Center, click the down arrow next to Add to Favorites.

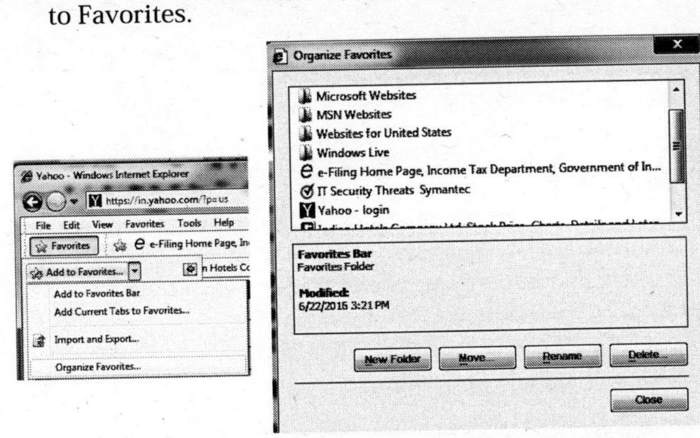

Figure 10.13 Organize Favorites dialog box

3. Choose Organize Favorites... option.
4. It will display Organize Favorites dialog box as shown in Figure 10.13.
5. The dialog box's button provide a quick way to create new folders, rename items, and organize things as you like.

Bookmark a Web page

➡ **To access your Bookmarks:**

1. Open the Google Chrome Internet browser.
2. Click Customize and control Google chrome (icon) in the upper right-hand corner of the browser window. Or click the star icon at the end of the address bar as shown in Figure
3. Select Bookmark this page or ctrl + D.

➡ **To delete a Bookmark:**

1. Highlight the bookmark or folder that you want to delete.
2. Press the delete key on your keyboard to remove the bookmark or folder. Or

   You can also right-click a bookmark, or folder, then select Delete from the menu.

Setting the Home Page/Start Page

While browsing, it is easy to get puzzled wandering around the Web. Therefore, you should designate one page or multiple pages as your home page. Home page is the first page which appears after opening a Web browser. It is also known as by different name like 'front page' 'start page' or 'Web page'.

➡ To set the home page, do this:

1. Open a site which you want to set as your home page.
2. Click on the arrow next to Home button of the command bar as shown in Figure 10.14.
3. Then choose Add or Change Home Page as shown in Figure 10.14.
4. The Add or Change Home Page dialog box appears as shown in Figure 10.15.
5. In this dialog box, select an option according to your need.
6. Then click Yes button.

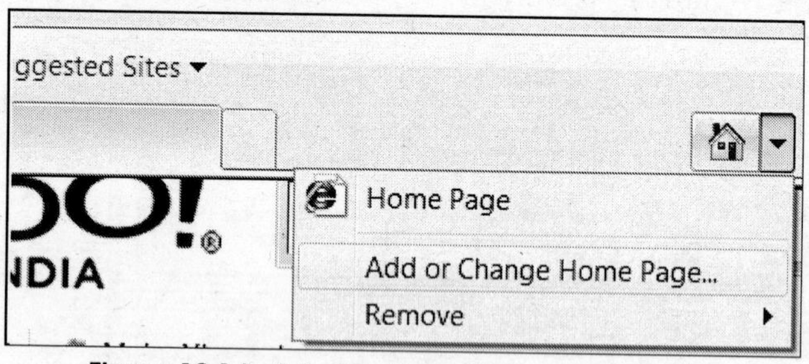

Figure 10.14 Selecting home in the command bar

10.7.6 Publishing on the Web

Web publishing is the process of publishing content on the Internet. It includes creating and uploading websites, updating webpages, and posting blogs online. The published content may include text, images, videos, and other types of media.

In order to publish content on the web, you need three things: 1) web development software, 2) an Internet connection, and 3) a web server. The software may be a professional web design program like Dreamweaver or a simple web-based interface like WordPress. The Internet connection serves as the medium for uploading the content to the web server.

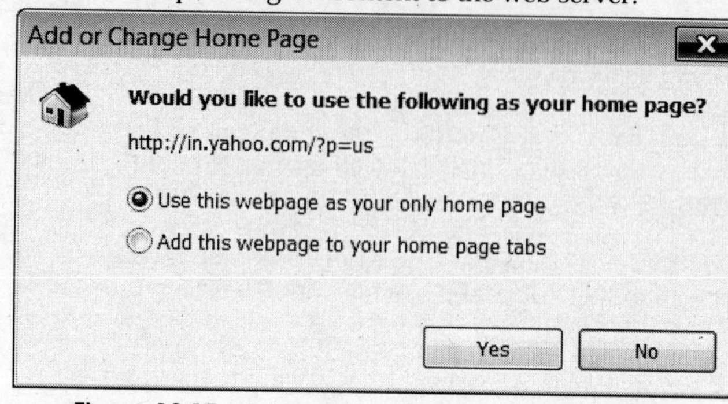

Figure 10.15 Add or Change Home Page dialog box

How to upload (download) files to (from) the server?

First, you need a FTP Client. E.g. FileZilla - The free FTP solution. You can download this software here - Client Download. Download it and install it on your computer.

Installation

- Run FileZilla Client installation file, e.g.: FileZilla_3.0.4.1_win32-setup.exe (Windows)

Follow the installation instructions step-by-setp.

- Run FileZilla Client.
- First, you must add your website information: Go to File - Site Manager as shown in Figure 10.16.

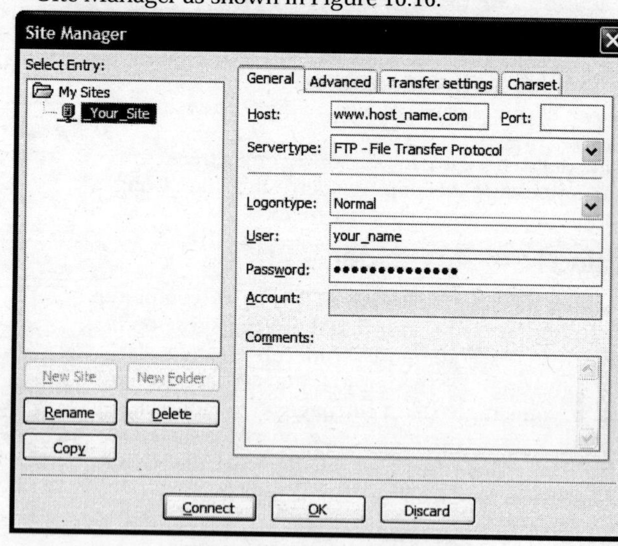

Figure 10.16 Site Manager

- Click on New Site button and add required information in General folder:
- Host - hostname of your website
- Servertype - mostly FTP - File Transfer Protocol
- Logontype - Normal
- User - your username
- Password - your password.

- Click on OK button to save the changes
- Now information about your site are stored.
- You can connect your website (server) now.
- Click on File - Site Manager, Select your site and click on Connect button.

Uploading or downloading files:

- You are now connected to your server as shown in Figure 10.17 On the left side of client, there are files which are saved on your personal computer. On the right side of client, there are files which are saved on the webserver.
- Click the right mouse button on file(s) on the left side of client and select Upload. Your file(s) will be uploaded to the server.
- Click the right mouse button on file(s) on the right side of client and select Download. Your file(s) will be downloaded to your computer.

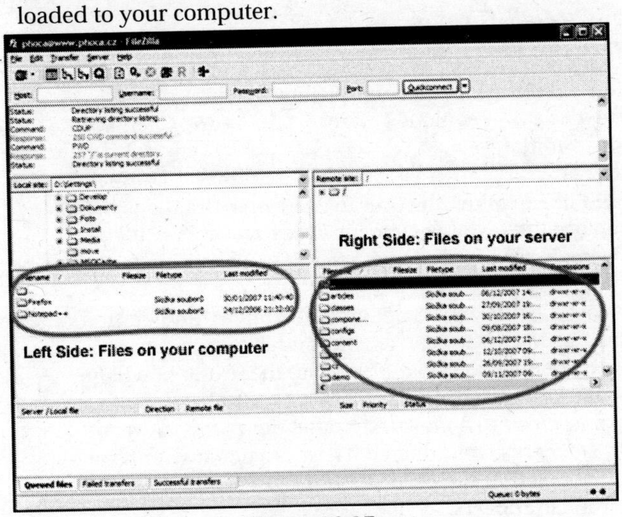

Figure 10.17

10.7.7 Complete a Web-based Form

Forms are such HTML tools which allow readers to communicate with one another via the Web. It is a collections of markup tags that work with Web servers to produce a means of obtaining whatever information we need from visitors of our Web site.

A FORM tag is used in an HTML document just like any other element. It has a start tag, **<FORM>** and an end tag **</FORM>**, The form itself contains regular text, other HTML elements such as tables and form elements such as check boxes, pull-down menus and text fields. Forms can not be nested i.e. you cannot put one into another. Forms can include other elements, such as list or <PRE>. FORM attributes are mentioned in the following paragraphs. For example,

```
<FORM ACTION = "HTTP://WWW.GOOGLE.COM\HTML\
FORMS.HTML"METHOD = "POST">
```

Different attributes of the forms are as follows:

(a) Action attribute
(b) Method attribute
(c) Enctype attribute

Action Attribute

It specifies the Uniform Resource Locator (URL) of the program or script that accepts the contents of the form for processing. If this attribute is absent, the base URL (URL where the form is located on the server) of the form is automatically used.

Method Attribute

Method attribute specifies which method type will be used to submit the form data. Which method we use depends on how our particular server works. The possible values are:

(a) get
(b) post

These are the HTTP methods that a browser uses to talk to a server.

GET

This is the default method for browsers to submit information. HTML pages are generally retrieved by requesting a single URL from a Web server using the GET method. For example, when we write

```
HTTP://WWW.GOOGLE.COM\HTML\FORMS.HTML
```

The above URL is translated into a valid HTTP GET request like the following:

```
GET HTML/FORMS.HTML
```

The GET method is not very secure, since that data input appears in the URL. Furthermore, It is impossible to append a large amount of data with the GET method. Another problem is that it is not suitable for foreign languages other than English.

POST

In situations in which a large amount of information must be passed, the POST method is more appropriate than GET method. This transmits all form input information immediately after the requested URL. Or we can say, once the server has received a request from a form using POST, it knows to continue listening for the rest of the information.

Enctype Attribute

ENCTYPE specifies the encoding for the fill-out form contents. It only applies if METHOD is set to POST. It identifies the media type. This media type is used for encoding the name/value pairs of the form's data.

Form Controls

There are a number of HTML elements that represent user interface controls or widgets in a form. These controls allow the user to enter information that will be sent to a web server. These controls buttons are radio buttons, check boxes, dropdown menus, list boxes, text boxes and text areas. These control are show in Figure 10.18.

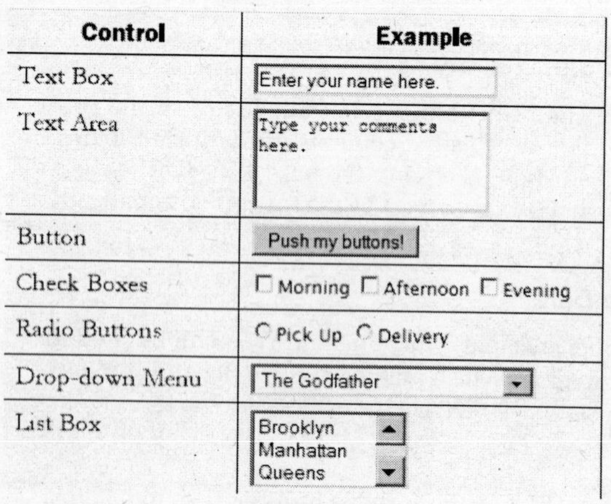

Figure 10.18

Text Boxes (Single-line)

Element–Input
Description–Box for entering a single line of text
Syntax–<input type= text name= name attributes />

The simple kind of form input is a text box that lets the user enter text input such as ZIP code or name. HTML has two types of text entry boxes: A single-line text box and a multi-line text area.

A text box is created using the input element. Though it is not required, the tag's type attribute should be set to text to indicate a text box. So we will give the tag a name attribute attribute with a unique value.

A text box can specify additional attributes in its input tag. The Value attribute specifies any initial text you want in the box. The Size attribute indicate how long the characters text box should appear on the screen. The maxlength attribute constrains the maximum number of characters the user can enter into the text box. Table 10.4 lists these attributes of text boxes. Example 1 shows two text boxes and the output as shown below the code.

Table 10.4 Attributes for text boxes

Attribute	Value(s)	Defintion and Usage
value	text	Initial text to appear in text box
size	integer	visible length of text box in characters
maxlength	integer	maxmimum number of characters that may be typed into text box

Example 1

```
<!DOCTYPE html>
<html>
<head>
<title>Text Input Control</title>
</head>
<body>
<form>
First name: <input type="text"
name="first_name" />
<br>
<br>
Last name: <input type="text" name="last_name"
value="Enter your name here" />
</form>
</body>
</html>
```

The above code output as shown below.

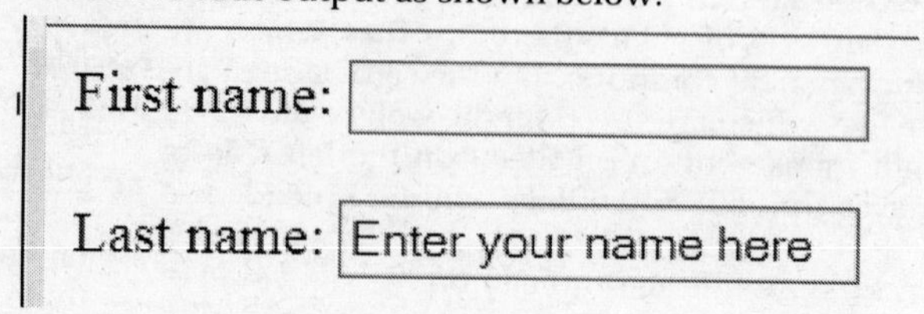

Text Areas (Multi-Line)

Element–textarea
Description–Box for entering multiple line of text
Syntax–<textarea name= name rows= height cols= width >initial text </textarea>

If you would like to allow the user to enter more than one line of text, then use the textarea element. A textarea is considered an inline element and must be enclosed in a proper block element.

Any text placed between the opening <textarea> and closing </textarea> tags will appear as the initial text in the area when the page loads. If no text is written, the text area will be initially blank.

The rows and clos attributes designate how many rows and columns the text area should have. These are not any limits on the amount of text that can occupy the text area; if more text is typed, a scrollbar appears.

Example 2 shows a text area. Notice that the closing </textarea> tag is not indented. This is because if you do indent it, that whitespace becomes part of the initial text inside the text area. If you do not wnat this, you must not indent the closing tag and the Table 10.5 lists these attributes of textarea.

Table 10.5 Attributes for textarea

Attribute	Defintion and Usage
name	Used to give a name to the control which is sent to the server to be recognized and get the value.
rows	Indicates the number of rows of the textarea box
cols	Indicates the number of columns of the textarea box

Example 2

```
<!DOCTYPE html>
<htm l>
<head>
<title>Multiple-Line Input Control</title>
</head>
<body>
<form >
```

```
Description : <br/>
<textarea  rows="5"  cols="50"  name="descrip-
tion">
Enter description here...
</textarea>
</form>
</body>
</html>
```

The above code output as shown below.

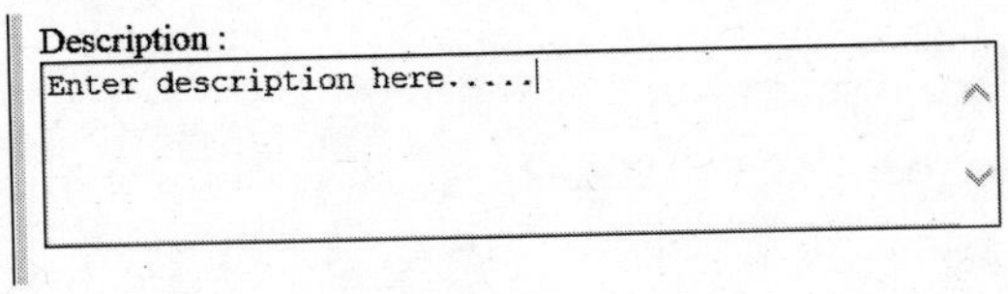

Checkbox

Element–Input

Description–Checkbox (inline)

Syntax–<input type= checkbox name= name />text

Checkbox are used when more than one option is required to be selected. They are also created using HTML <input> tag but type attribute is set to checkbox. Example 3 demonstrates the use of check boxes and the Table 10.6 lists these attributes of checkbox.

Table 10.6 Attributes for checkbox

Attribute	Defintion and Usage
type	It indicates the type of input control and for checkbox input control it will be set to checkbox.
name	Used to give a name to the control and get the value.
value	The value that will be used if the checkbox is selected.
checked	Set to checked if you want to select it by default.

Example 3

```
<!DOCTYPE html>
<html>
<head>
<title>Checkbox Control</title>
</head>
<body>
<form>
Font options:
<input type="checkbox" name="bold" value="on">
Bold
<input type="checkbox" name="italics"> Italics
</form>
</body>
</html>
```

The above code output as shown below.

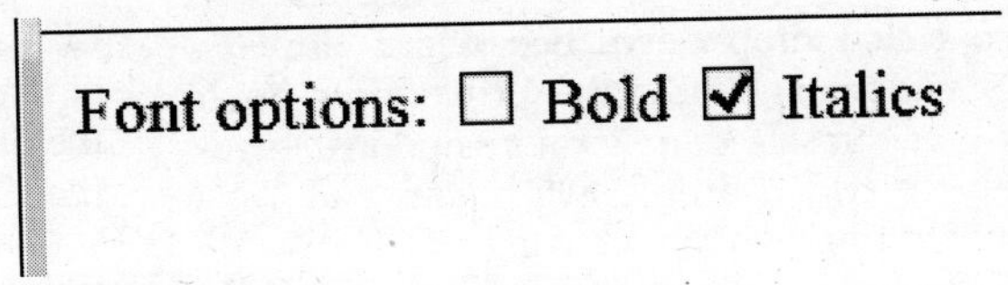

Radio Buttons

Element–input

Description–Radio button

Syntax–<input type="radio" name="group" value="param" /> text

Radio button allow the user to choose one of a set of options. This button is represented as input tag with a type of radio. The name attribute desinages a group of buttons. Normally every control should have a unique name, but if you give several radio buttons the same name, the browser will ensure that only one radio button can be checked at a given time. Example 4 demonstrates the use of radio button and Table 10.7 shows list of attributes for radio button.

Table 10.7 Attributes for radio button

Attribute	Defintion and Usage
type	It display the type of input control and for checkbox input control it will be set to radio.
name	It is used to give a name to the control which is sent to the server to be recognized and get the value.
value	The value that will be used if the radio box is selected.
checked	Set to checked if you want to select it by default.

Example 4

```
<!DOCTYPE htm l>
<htm l>
<head>
<title>Radio Box Control</title>
</head>
<body>
<form >
<input  type="radio"  name="card"  value="Visa
card">Visa card
<input type="radio" name="card" value="Master
card">Master card
<input type="radio" name="card" value="Credit
card">Credit card
</form>
</body>
</html>
```

The above code output as shown below.

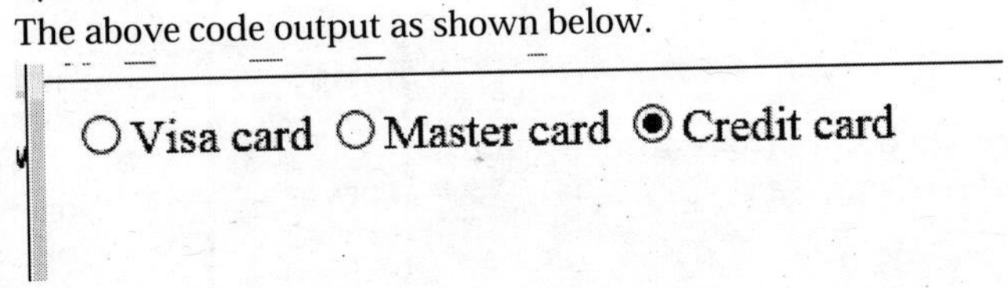

Drop-down Menus

A select box, also called drop down box which provides option to list down various options in the form of drop down list, from where a user can select one or more options. Example 5 demonstrates the use of drop-down menus and Table 10.8 shows the list of attributes of <select> tag.

Table 10.8 Attributes for drop-down menus

Attribute	Description
Name	Used to give a name to the control which is sent to the server to be recognized and get the value.
Size	This can be used to present a scrolling list box.
Multiple	If set to multiple then allows a user to select multiple items from the menu

The Select command sets the form for a field of information. The Option commands create the list within the field. The <option> tag defines the single items in the menu. The list of attributes of <option> tag:

Attribute	Description
Value	The value that will be used if an option in the select box is selected
Selected	Specifies that this option should be the initially selected value when the page loads
Label	An alternative way of labelling options

Example 5

```
<!DOCTYPE html>
<html>
<head>
<title>Select Box Control</title>
</head>
<body>
<form>
Choose the option from drop-down list:
<select name="continent">
   <option value="Europe">Europe</option>
   <option value="America">America</option>
   <option value="Mexico">Mexico</option>
   <option value="Italy">Italy</option>
   <option value="Canada">Canada</option>
   <option value="Other">Other</option>
</select>
</form >
</body>
</html>
```

The above code output as shown below.

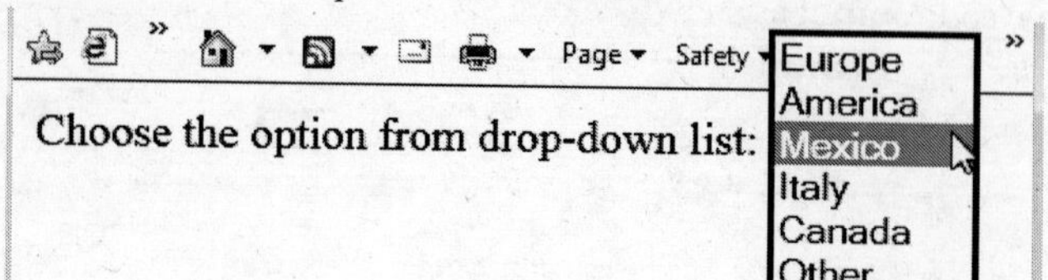

List boxes

LIST BOX is similar to a text box. It shows a declared number of text rows and gives the visitor a list of choices. Similar to the drop list, the list box length is determined by the length of the longest OPTION.

The only difference you will see from the code of a drop list is the first line. The size property is now added. The rest of the code is the same as the drop list. Example 6 demonstrates the use list boxes.

Example 6

```
<!DOCTYPE html>
<html>
<head>
<title>Select Box Control</title>
</head>
<body>
<form>
Choose an software packages:
<select size="3" name="dropdown">
<option value="Word processing">MS Word
2010</option>
<option value="Spreadsheet">MS Excel
2010</option>
<option value="Presentation">MS PowerPoint
2010</option>
<option value="Database">MS Access 2010</op-
tion>
<option value="Photoshop">Photoshop
CS6</option>
</select>
</form>
</body>
</html>
```

The above code output as shown below.

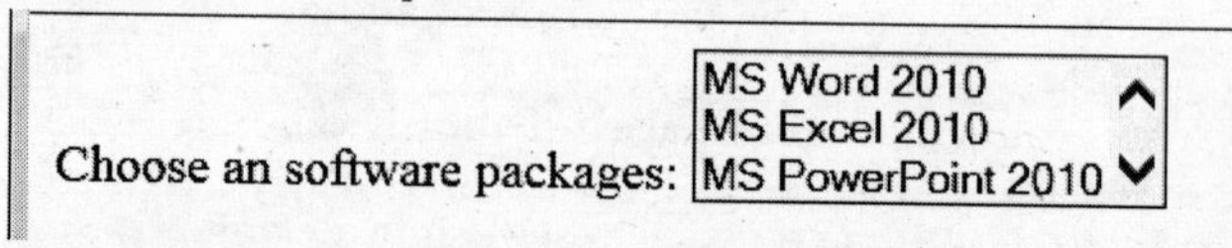

Size creates the number of text lines the box is going to show going down. If the list is longer than the declared size, scroll bars will appear to view the OPTIONS further down the list. In the above example, there are 5 options, but only 3 of them are in view at one time.

10.7.8 Downloading Web Pages

Uploading is the transmission of a file from one computer system to another, usually larger computer system. From a network user's point-of-view, to upload a file is to send it to another computer that is set up to receive it. People who share images with others on Bulletin Board Services (BBS) upload files to the BBS.

Transmission in the other direction is downloading -- from one, usually larger computer to another, usually smaller computer. From an Internet user's point-of-view, downloading is receiving a file from another computer.

The FTP is the Internet facility for downloading and uploading files. (If you are uploading a file to another site, you must usually have permission in advance to access the site and the directory where the file is to be placed).

When you send or receive an attached file with an e-mail note, this is just an attachment, not a download or an upload. However, in practice, many people use "upload" to mean "send" and "download" to mean receive.

In short, from the ordinary workstation or small computer user's point-of-view, to upload is to send a file and to download is to receive a file.

The Web is one of the most popular components parts of the Internet. The Web is made up of hypertext documents stored on many servers around the world.

☞ *perte t doc ments* contain links you can click on to move to another section of the page, to different documents, or to another type of Internet resource, such as electronic mail (e-mail) or newsgroups.

Web pages include text, graphics, animation, sound, and sometimes movies also. The rich content, along with the ability to jump from one page to other page using links, has contributed to the explosive growth of the Web.

For example, you have found a file that you want to save. As a example, let us imagine you are researching an art course paper and want to save an entire page.

➡ **To download a web page, do this:**

1. Click the File menu and choose Save Web page dialog box appears as shown in Figure 10.19.
2. Notice that there is a default value in the File name: text box. Either accept this name or change it to something appropriate.
3. Choose the Location you want to save the file in the Save in: list box.
4. Then click Save button to save the file.

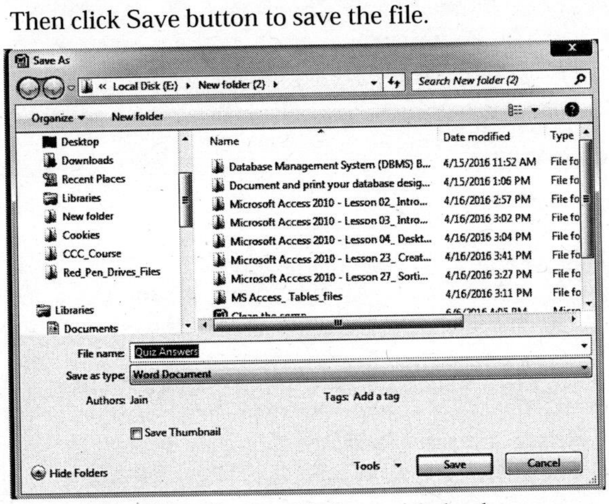

Figure 10.19 Save Web page dialog box

10.7.9 Printing Web Pages

As you browse, you may come across pages containing information that you want to keep as hard copy. Internet Explorer (IE) 8.0 provides many print options. These are:

- Printing all documents linked to the current page
- Printing a list of links contained on the current page
- Printing selected portions of a page that has been constructed using frames. This option is available only if the current page has frames.

➡ **To print a Web page using the Print dialog box, do this:**

1. Click on the File menu and choose Print. Or
2. Click on the arrow next to Print button on the Command bar.
3. Then choose Print Option.
4. A Print dialog box appears as seen in Figure 10.20. In this dialog box, select the printer, pages, and number of copies you want.

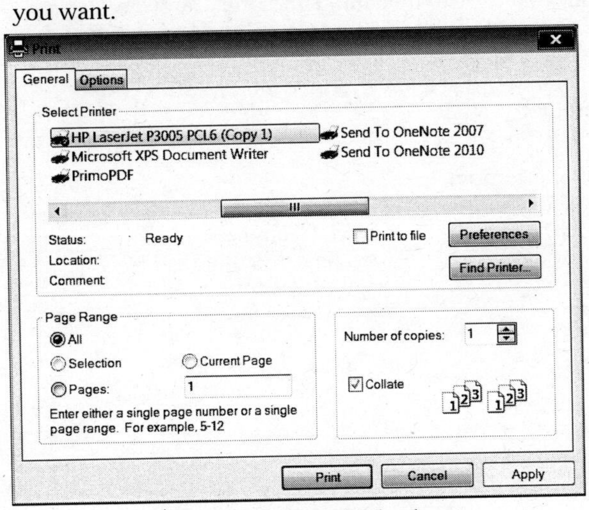

Figure 10.20 Print Dialog box

10.7.10 Understanding URL

Every page on the Web has a unique address, called a Uniform Resource Locator (URL). The URL contains the following information.

- The Internet name of the site containing the resource (document data).
- The type of service the resource is served by (HTTP, FTP etc).
- The Internet port number of the service. (If this is omitted, the browser assumes a commonly accepted default value).
- The location of the resource in the directory structure of the server.

Table 10.9 shows the components that make up a URL. The URL used as the example in the Table 10.9 is

`http://www.entertainment.satyam-online.com/contents/horoscope.asp`

Table 10.9 Components that make up a

Example	Explanation	Description
`http://`	Protocol	HTTP is the protocol used to transmit Web pages for this URL.
`www.entertainment.satyamonline.com`	Domain name	The server where the page is located. Every domain name is unique. Here Internet Service Provider (ISP) is Satyam online.
`contents/`	Directory path	The directory where the page is located.
`horoscope.asp`	Filename	The filename of the Web page.

Domain Names

Most organizations use domain names that are easy to remember. Each domain name ends with an identifier that tells you what type of Web site it is. Table 10.10 shows the identifiers commonly used today, and identifiers proposed for use in the future.

Table 10.10 Current and Proposed Domain Name Identifiers

Current Domain Identifiers	
`.com`	Commercial business
`.edu`	Educational institutions
`.gov`	Government entities
`.net`	Internet service providers
`.mil`	Military sites
`.org`	Organizations that do not fit any other category

Proposed Domain Identifiers	
`.arts`	Cultural and entertainment-related organizations
`.firm`	Businesses
`.info`	Information services
`.nom`	Web sites of individuals
`.rec`	Recreation-related organizations
`.store`	Stores and shops
`.web`	World Wide Web-related organizations

☞ To know the full URL of a Web page is not always necessary to locate the page. If you know the domain name, you can start at the home page of the site and click links until you find the Web page you want.

10.7.11 Understanding Benefits of Search Engines

Search search engine provide ways of finding information on the Internet. There is a wide variety of search engines and features.

Variety–An Internet search can generate a variety of sources of information. The variety allows anyone searching for information to choose the types of souces they would like to use, or to use a variety of sources to gain a greater understanding of a subject.

Precision–The ability to provide refined or more precision results. Putting quotations marks around a set of words will bring up results with the exact same words, excluding others. Some search engine, such as Google or Yahoo, enable you to specify the type of web sources to be searched.

Organization–Internet search engines help to organize the Internet and individual websites. Search engines aid in organizing the vast mount of informtion that can be scattered in various places on the same web page into an organized list that can be used more easily.

Popular Search Engines

There are many search engines available on the Web. Most of the search engines provide Web site reviews and homepage services, in addition to keyword searches. Some of the popular search engines are:

Google

Google is an interesting search engine having many unique features. For example, you want search company information. It is useful for company searches because of the unusual way it ranks Web sites. Type `http://www.google.com` in the Address bar and press Enter to go to the Google homepage. When you are there, type the company name in the search box and click the Google Search button. Google is so good at finding the best matching Web sites in a search, it offers a feature to automatically look for the best possible match and load it. To use this feature, type a company's name in the search box and click the I'm Feeling Lucky button. It gives the related company information.

AltaVista

This has been created by the research facility of Digital Electronic Corporation (DEC) of USA. This search engine has a spider called scooter that traverses the Web and Usenet newsgroups.

Indexing is based on the full text of a document and the first few lines are used as an abstract. AltaVista search supports full Boolean, phrase and case—sensitive searches. The engine has two modes of search types namely, simple and advanced search.

In simple search, AltaVista will attempt to find pages that include as many of your search words as possible, and rank those pages highest to lowest in the result. In advanced search, the page uses the same syntax rules as the basic search, but it adds Boolean operators to make searches much more flexible. The operators include &(AND), | (OR), and !(NOT).

The advanced search ranks results on the basis of giving a higher score to documents that contain the query terms in the first few words or the documents in which the query terms are found close to each other.

Excite

It uses a spider and indexer for the full text search of documents. The spider retrieves only Web and Usenet newsgroup documents. Users can submit URLs for indexing. The indexer generates index terms and a short document summary. The Excite index consists of about 50 million URLs.

This engine is a full-featured search engine. It offers services like searches that are case—sensitive. The Boolean operators used by Excite are AND, NOT and OR.

10.7.12 Commerce on Internet

The term covering all commercial activity on the Internet, including auctioning, placing orders, making payments, transferring funds and collaborating with trading partners, Internet commerce is not a synonym for electronic commerce (e-commerce) but one of its subsets.

Internet Commerce is the use of the Internet for creating and completing business transactions. It also includes:

- The sales and marketing cycle–For example, by analysing online feedback to ascertain customer's needs.
- Identifying new markets–Through exposure to a global audience through the World Wide Web.
- Developing Customer Relationships–Achieving loyalty through ongoing email interaction.
- Assisting potential customers with their purchasing decision–For example, by guiding them through product choices in an intelligent way.
- Providing round-the-clock points of sale–Making it easy for buyers to order online, irrespective of location.
- Supply chain management–Supporting those in the supply chain, such as dealers and distributors, through online interaction.

Internet Commerce also provides business a growing, dynamic channel for efficient delivery of goods and services to consumers: business-to-consumer. In business-to-consumer, goods to consumers online in a more personalized, dynamic environment. Businesses-to-consumer will increasingly include the delivery of digital goods–software, electronic media, and information. Consumers will also look more frequently to the Internet for the delivery of serices, including ticketing, reservations, and financial services. In short, Internet commerce–business-to-business and business-to-consumer-will dramatically impact the way goods and services are managed, bought and sold form manufacturer to consumer.

10.7.13 Impact of Internet on Society

The Internet has caused a great revolution in the society, allowing people from all over the world to communicate their ideas and feelings. The Internet has also changed the way society treats people. It has allowed minor groups much more power than they had in real life. There are many changes to society because of the Internet; whether such changes enhance or ruin our life is up to us.

Now a days Internet availability is not limited to computers and laptops. Evern mobile phone woth internet facility at affordable process helping indirectly the Internet to reach maximum number of users.

Some of the changes on the society are given in the following sections:

Unlimited Knowledge–We increasingly use the World Wide Web as a universal reference library. Type any keyword into a search engine you will find a host of sites with information on that topic.

Virtual relationships–One major impact that the Internet has had on society is in transforming the field of personal relationships. The new breed of online dating sites allow people to meet at a distance, chat in real time or by e-mail, exchange photographs, even talk to each other with voicemails.

Chat rooms are another popular way for meeting people from all round the world online.

Remote Intervention–The Internet and multimedia have the potential to transform healthcare by removing the need for doctor and patient to be in the same room.

E-mail–The impact on e-mail is the most important method for communicating and developing relationships.

10.7.14 Use of Search Engines

Search engines are programs that search documents for specified keywords and returns a list of the documents where the keywords were found. A search engine is really a general class of programs, however, the term is often used to specifically describe systems like Google, Bing and Yahoo! Search that enable users to search for documents on the World Wide Web.

There are some uses of search engines. These are:

- Full Text Search Engine: Full Text Search Engine retrieves information from internet, establish database and retrieve the records according to user's query. It can be divided into two parts: first one has its own crawler. Another one is to hire other search engine's database.
- Directory Search Engine: We cannot call it a true search engine. It retrieves all the entries of directory listing.
- META Search Engine: It provides search results from multiple search engines simultaneously according to user's query.
- Vertical Search Engine: Vertical Search Engine focuses on specific search field.

10.7.15 E-mail Messages

An email message is a text, typically brief and informal, that is sent or received over a computer network. While email messages are usually simple text messages, attachments (such as image files and spreadsheets). An email message can be sent to multiple recipients at the same time.

Uses of E-mail

Email allows individuals and groups to communicate with one another. Email is useful for communication, marketing, promotion, and mobility. Email is a tool that delivers messages instantaneously and is accessible from nearly anywhere around the world. Email consists of text, images, documents, links and other attachments useful for communication. Correspondence with friends and internal business communication are both daily uses for email.

It is also used for:

- Group discussion by making groups in hotmail, yahoo, etc.
- Stay in touch with users attached in the group.
- Transmitting documents through attachments.
- Convenient way of sending job application.
- Easy method of advertisement.
- Service subscription.

10.8 INSTANT MESSAGING AND COLLABORATION

Instant Messaging (IM) is a form of real-time direct text-based communication between two or more people using personal computers or other devices, along with shared clients. The user's text is conveyed over a network, such as the Internet. More advanced instant messaging software clients also allow enhanced modes of communication, such as live voice or video calling.

Instant messaging allows effective and efficient communication, allowing immediate receipt of acknowledgment or reply. In many cases, instant messaging includes added features which can make it even more popular. For example, users may see each other via Webcams, or talk directly for free over the Internet using a microphone and headphones or loudspeakers. Many client programs allow file transfers, although they are usually limited in the permissible file-size.

Many instant messaging services offer video calling features, Voice Over Internet Protocol (VoIP) and Web conferencing services. Web conferencing services can integrate both video calling and instant messaging abilities.

☞ Some instant messaging companies are also offering desktop sharing, IP radio, and IPTV to the voice and video features.

10.8.1 Using Instant Messaging

Instant Messaging (IM) is a form of electronic communication enabling ad hoc collaboration through sending and receiving messages across a network connection. Some of the popular and widely used instant messenger programs available today. Steps given below will make you to understand exactly what happens with an instant-messaging service:

1. You go to download page i.e http://www.google.com/talk/ or http://www.skype.com and get a free software client for your computer.
2. You install the software and open the client.
3. The client tries to connect to the server. It uses a proprietary protocol for communication.
4. Once the client is connected to the server, you can enter your name and password to log in to the server. If this is your first time on, you can sign up for an account and immediately begin using it. When server verifies your name and password, you are logged in.
5. The client sends connection information (IP address and number of the port assigned to the client) to server of the computer you are using. It also provides user with names of everyone in your contacts list.
6. The server creates a temporary file that has the connection information for you and the list of your contacts. It then checks to see if any of the users in your contact list are currently logged in.
7. If the server finds any of your contacts logged in, it sends a message back to the client on your computer with the connection information for that user. The server also sends your connection information to the people in your contact list that are signed on.
8. When your client gets the connection information for a person in your contact list, it changes the status of that person to "online." You click on the name of a person in your contact list who is online, and a window opens in which you can enter text into. You enter a message and click "send" or hit return to communicate with that person.
9. Because your client has the IP address and port number for computer of the person that you sent the message to, your message is sent directly to the client on that person's computer. In other words, the server is not involved at this point. All communication is directly take place between the two clients.
10. The other person gets your instant message and responds. The window that each of you sees on your respective computers expands to include a scrolling dialog of the conversation. Each person's instant messages appears in this window on both computers.
11. When conversation is complete, you close the message window. Eventually, you go offline and exit. When this happens, your client sends a message to the server to terminate the session. The server sends a message to the client of each person on your contact list who is currently online to indicate that you have logged off. Finally, the server deletes the temporary file that contains the connection information for your client.

Some of the popular Instant Messenger are Yahoo Messanger, MSN Messenger, Rediff Bol, Google Talk and Skype.

Using the Skype Instant Messengers

Skype is is one of the well known Instant Messengers. It allows the users to explore the facilities of instant messaging provided by it. Apart from instant messaging, the other feature of Skype are file transfer, video conferencing, etc. Skype also provides the users with short message service. It is Niklas Zennstrom and Janus Friis who have created the Skype software program.

You have to download a Skype program, install it, register as a Skype user, and make use of the Skype applications.

Once installed, the program itself has the feel and look of any chat program. You can add contacts, block them, see if they are online, and communicate with them.

10.8.2 Instant Messaging Providers

The first instant messaging service was introduced in 1996 by an Israeli based ICQ. ICQ is an instant messaging computer program, owned by Time Warner's AOL subsidiary. ICQ was first developed by the Israeli company Mirabilis. The first version of the program was released in November 1996. After that it was later acquired by America Online. The major Instant Messaging Providers are AOL's Instant Messenger (AIM), ICQ, Yahoo! Messenger, Rediff Bol, Google Talk, Jabber and Microsoft's incarnations: Microsoft Network or MSN Messenger, Windows Messenger and Windows Live Messenger.

Instant messaging providers may also provide services like video phoning, file sharing, PC-to-PC voice calling and PC-to-regular-phone calling. Instant messaging has promoted IP telephony because the IM software makes it easy to switch from "text chat" to "voice chat," provided the user has a headset or microphone and speakers. The instant message providers give the option to the users to set up a buddy list. You also have to add the user names of the people you want to message with to your "buddy list" which is also called friend list or contact list. When they log on to the Internet with their Instant message software, and provided they have not configured themselves as "invisible," you are instantly alerted. When they log off, you are also notified. Each system has its own method for blocking incoming and outgoing messages.

Many of us e-mail instead of writing letters or even calling people on the phone. People around the world send out billions of e-mail messages every day. One should remember that sometimes even e-mail is not that fast enough. You might not know if a person you want to e-mail is online at that moment. Also, if you are e-mailing back and forth with someone, you usually have to click through a few steps. This is why instant messaging (IM) has become so popular. Most of the Instant Messaging Providers give you the following facilities:

- Instant messages - Send notes back and forth with a friend who is online.
- Chat - Create a chat room with friends or co-workers.
- Web links - Share links to your favorite Web sites.
- Video - Send and view videos, and chat face to face with friends.
- Images - Look at an image stored on your friend's computer.
- Sounds - Play sounds for your friends.
- Files - Share files by sending them directly to your friends.
- Talk - Use the Internet instead of a phone to actually talk with friends.
- Streaming content - Real-time or near-real-time stock quotes and news.
- Mobile capabilities - Send instant messages from your cell phone.

10.8.3 Use of Social Networking Sites

A social networking service is an online service, platform, or site that focuses on building and reflecting of social networks or social relations among people, e.g., who share interests and/or activities. A social network service essentially consists of a representation of each user (often a profile), his/her social links, and a variety of additional services. Most social network services are Web based and provide means for users to interact over the Internet, such as e-mail and instant messaging, video calling, chat, file sharing, discussion groups, voice chats, e-mails, blogging and so on. Online community services are sometimes considered as a social network service. Social networking sites allow users to share ideas, activities, events, and interests within their individual networks.

Social networking is all about communication. People with common interests are able to share information with each other via a huge variety of social networking sites. Sites created specifically to make sharing, communicating, and creating information as simple and efficient as possible. Examples of social networking sites:

(a) Twitter

(b) Facebook

(c) LinkedIn

The top social network, MySpace, has over two-hundred and fifty million subscribers, with actors, authors, musicians and comedians counted among them. For example, Newegg.com, a computer hardware reseller, has a profile highlighting computer deals offered at their Web Site.

Twitter

Twitter is a free social networking and micro-blogging service that has changed the way so that many people communicate with each other. It is a message service that allows people to send and receive short messages (called tweets) within your Twitter community. Twitter community consists of:

1. *eople o ollo* You define your community by following other Twitter users. You see the tweets created by everyone you follow. Following someone means that you subscribe to their tweets.
2. *eople ho ollo o* Other people read your tweets and decide to follow you. Your followers see the tweets you send out.

Twitter was created by a software development team to solve their own communication challenges. They took features from other communication tools like e-mail, chat, and instant messaging and mashed them together to create Twitter.

Facebook

Facebook is a social networking Web Site intended to connect friends, family, and business associates. It is the largest networking site. People have been 'facebooking' each other for about 6 years now, making Facebook the most used social network all over the world.

LinkedIn

LinkedIn is a social network within the larger world of social media that is geared toward business. LinkedIn is very popular with those who are seeking work and trying to build their network of contacts so they can reach out to employers. LinkedIn is also popular as a way of marketing a business, because business owners can interact with those who are interested in their services by answering questions, participating in discussions and more.

10.8.4 Concepts of IPv4 and IPv6 Networks

IPv4

IPv4 was the first version of Internet Protocol to be widely used, and accounts for most of today s Internet traffic. There are just over 4 billion IPv4 addresses. While that is a lot of IP addresses, it is not enough to last forever.

IPv4 is defined and specified in IETF publication RCF 791. It is used in the packet-switched link layer in the OSI model. IPv4 uses 32-bit addresses for Ethernet communication in five classes, named A, B, C, D and E. Classes A, B and C have a different bit length for addressing the network host. Class D addresses are reserved for multicasting, while class E addresses are reserved for future use.

IPv6

IPv6 is a newer numbering system that provides a much larger address pool than IPv4. Internet Protocol Version 6 (IPv6) is an Internet Protocol (IP) used for carrying data in packets from a source to a destination over various networks. IPv6 is the enhanced version of IPv4 and can support very large numbers of nodes as compared to IPv4. It allows for 2128 possible node, or address, combinations. IPv6 is also known as Internet Protocol Next Generation (IPng).

What is the major difference?

The major difference between IPv4 and IPv6 is the number of IP addresses. There are 4,294,967,296 IPv4 addresses. In contrast, there are 340,282,366,920,938, 463,463,374, 607,431,768,211,456 IPv6 addresses.

The technical functioning of the Internet remains the same with both versions and it is likely that both versions will continue to operate simultaneously on networks well into the future. To date, most networks that use IPv6 support both IPv4 and IPv6 addresses in their networks. Table 10.11 shows the difference between IPv4 and IPv6.

Table 10.11 Difference between IPv4 and IPv6

	Internet Protocol version 4 (IPv4)	Internet Protocol version 6 (IPv6)
Deployed	1981	1999
Address Size	32-bit number	128-bit number
Address Format	Dotted Decimal Notation: 192.149.252.76	Hexadecimal Notation: 3FFE:F200:0234:AB00: 0123:4567:8901:ABCD
Prefix Notation	192.149.0.0/24	3FFE:F200:0234::/48
Number of Addresses	2^{32} = ~4,294,967,296	2^{128} = ~340,282,366, 920,938,463,463,374,607, 431,786,211,456

Networking Troubleshooting

Troubleshooting is the process of identifying, planning and resolving a problem, error or fault within a software or computer system. It enables the repair and restoration of a computer or software when it becomes faulty.

Network troubleshooting is primarily done by network engineers or administrators to repair or optimize a network. It is generally done to recover and establish network or Internet connections on end nodes/devices.

Finding and resolving problems and establishing Internet/network connection of a computer/device/node:

- Configuring a router, switch or any network management device.
- Installing cables or Wi-Fi devices.
- Updating firmware devices on router switch.
- Removing viruses.
- Adding, configuring and reinstalling a network printer.

Network troubleshooting can be a manual or automated task. When using automated tools, network management can be done using network diagnostic software.

MODEL QUESTIONS AND ANSWERS

A. Multiple Choice

1.1 Which protocol is used for browsing website:

a. TCP b. HTTP
c. FTP d. TFTP

1.2 The ________ is the physical path over which a message travels

a. Path b. Medium
c. Protocol d. Route

1.3 A set of rules that governs data communication

a. Protocols b. Standards
c. RFCs d. None of the above

1.4 What is Internet?

a. a single network
b. A vast collection of different networks
c. Interconnection of local area networks

d. None of the above

1.5 To join the Internet, the computer has to be connected to a

a. Internet architecture board
b. Internet society
c. Internet service provider
d. None of the above

1.6 Internet access by transmitting digital data over the wires of a local telephone network is provided by

a. Leased line
b. Digital subscriber line
c. Digital signal line
d. None of the above

1.7 ISP exchanges internet traffic between their networks by

a. Internet exchange point
b. subscriber end point
c. ISP end point
d. None of the above

1.8 Which one of the following protocol is not used in Internet?

a. HTTP
b. DHCP
c. DNS
d. None of the above

1.9 IPv6 addressed have a size of

a. 32 bits
b. 64 bits
c. 128 bits
d. 265 bits

1.10 Internet works on

a. packet switching
b. circuit switching
c. both (a) and (b)
d. none of the mentioned

1.11 Which is not the search engine:

a. Altavista.com
b. Google.com
c. Yahoo.com
d. Facebook.com

1.12 Which protocol assigns IP address to the client connected in the internet?

a. DHCP
b. IP
c. RPC
d. None of the above

1.13 In the network HTTP resources are located by

a. Uniform resource identifier
b. Unique resource locator
c. Unique resource identifier
d. None of the above

1.14 In FTP protocol, client contacts server using ____ as the transport protocol.

a. Transmission control protocol
b. User datagram protocol
c. Datagram congestion control protocol
d. Stream control transmission protocol

1.15 The file transfer protocol is built on

a. Data centric architecture
b. Service oriented architecture
c. Client server architecture
d. None of the mentioned

1.16 A piece of icon or image on a web page associated with another webpage is called

a. URL
b. Hyperlink
c. Plugin
d. None of the above

1.17 What is a web browser?

a. A program that can display a web page
b. A program used to view html documents
c. It enables user to access the resources of Internet
d. All of the above

1.18 URL stands for

a. Unique reference label
b. Uniform reference label
c. Uniform resource locator
d. Unique resource locator

1.19 How long is an IPv6 address?

a. 32 bits
b. 128 bytes
c. 64 bits
d. 128 bits

1.20 A modem is connected in between a telephone line and a

a. Network
b. Computer
c. Communication adapter
d. serial port

1.21 Which of the following device is used to connect two systems, especially if the systems use different protocols?

a. Hub
b. Bridge
c. Gateway
d. Repeater

1.22 Which of the following TCP/IP protocol is used for transferring electronic mail messages from one machine to another?

a. FTP
b. SNMP
c. SMTP
d. RPC

1.23 How many hosts are attached to each of the local area networks at your site?

a. 128
b. 254
c. 256
d. 64

1.24 Which of the following is used for modulation and demodulation?

a. Modem
b. Protocols
c. Gateway
d. Multiplexer

1.25 Google Chrome, Mozilla Firefox, Internet Explorer, Netscape Navigator are examples of

a. Web server
b. Web browser
c. Internet
d. World Wide Web

1.26 An ISP is a company that allows you to connect to internet via its servers. ISP stands for

a. Internal Service Provider
b. International Service Provider
c. Internet Service Provider
d. Internat Service Provider

B. State whether the following are True or False

2.1 The World Wide Web is a collection of electronic documents called web pages.

2.2 Web server is an electronic document that links to another place in the same document or to an entirely different document.

2.3 Electronic Mail is a paperless method of sending messages.

2.4 File Transfer Procedure is a commonly used protocol for exchanging files over any network.

2.5 FTP is used to promote sharing of files.
2.6 WAN is based on Ethernet.
2.7 Virtual hypertext network is called WWW.
2.8 The Internet is a collection of files.
2.9 TCP/IP is a layered set of cables.
2.10 A set of rules is known as protocol.
2.11 Every computer system on the Internet has both a domain name and domain address.
2.12 Domain name edu describe educational institutions site.
2.13 A web page may contain text, graphics, sound, hypertext links, video, etc.
2.14 Web browser is a program, which enables you to display the Web pages on the Internet.
2.15 Internet is not a commercial information service.

Answers

Multiple Choice

A.

1. b	2. b	3. a	4. b	5. c
6. b	7. a	8. d	9. c	10. a
11. d	12. a	13. a	14. a	15. c
16. b	17. d	18. c	19. d	20. c
21. c	22. c	23. b	24. a	25. b
26. c				

True or False

B.

1. T	2. F	3. T	4. F	5. T
6. F	7. T	8. F	9. F	10. T
11. F	12. T	13. T	14. T	15. T

CHAPTER 11

Latest Trends in IECT & e-Governance

11.1 APPLICATIONS OF INFORMATION ELECTRONICS

IECT or Information, Electronics and Commuicatin Technology is used in various sectors. Electronic governance or e-governance is the application of information electronics and communication technology (ICT) for delivering government services to common people directly. IECT is common and used by most of people now a days like Internet, Cell Phones, radios, television and satellite etc. are medium of communication and all it works electronically. The term communication is used to make contact or sending and receiving messages from other people, institution or government.

11.2 E-GOVERNANCE

E-Governance is the application of modern information and Communication Technologies such as Internet, Local area networks, mobiles etc. which is provided by Government to improve the effectiveness, efficiency, service delivery.

It is also use to enhance the access to and delivery of government services to benefit citizens, business partners and employees.

11.2.1 Why e-Governance?

E-Governance can transform citizen service, provide access to information to empower citizens, enable their participation in government and enhance citizen economic and social opportunities, so that they can make better lives, for themselves and for the next generation.

Difference between E-government and E-governance

While E-Government has traditionally been understood as being centered around the operations of government whereas, E-Governance is understood to extend the scope by including citizen engagement and participation in governance.

Activities of e-Government using e-Governance

The primary delivery models of e-Government can be divided into:

- Government-to-Citizen or Government-to-Consumer (G2C)
- Government-to-Business (G2B)
- Government-to-Government (G2G)
- Government-to-Employees (G2E)

Within each of these interaction domains, four kinds of activities take place.

- Pushing information over the Internet, e.g., regulatory services, general holidays, public hearing schedules, issue briefs, notifications, etc.
- Two-way communications between the agency and the citizen, a business, or another government agency. In this model, users can engage in dialogue with agencies and post problems, comments, or requests to the agency.
- Conducting transactions, e.g., lodging tax returns, applying for services and grants.
- Governance, e.g., online polling, voting, and campaigning.

11.2.2 Risks and Benefits of e-Governance

Risks–There are many considerations and potential implications of implementing and designing e-government, including disintermediation of the government and its citizens, impacts on economic, social, and political factors, vulnerability to cyber-attacks, and disturbances to the status quo in these areas.

Hyper-surveillance: Increased contact between government and its citizens goes both ways. Once e-government begins to develop and become more sophisticated, citizens will be forced to interact electronically with the government on a larger scale. This could potentially lead to a lack of privacy for civilians as their government obtains more and more information on them. In a worst case scenario, with so much information being passed electronically between government and civilians. When the government has easy access to countless information on its citizens, personal privacy is lost.

Cost: Although "a large amount of money has been spent" on the development and implementation of e-government, some say it has yielded only a second-rate product. The outcomes and effects of trial internet-based governments are often difficult to gauge or unsatisfactory.

Inaccessibility: An e-government site which provides web access and support often does not offer the "potential to reach many users including those who live in remote areas, are homebound, have low literacy levels, exist on poverty line incomes, suffer from chronic illness, are single parents or older adults.

Benefits: It is convenient and cost-effective for businesses, and the public benefits by getting easy access to the most current information available without having to spend time, energy and money to get it.

E-government helps simplify processes and makes access to government information more easily accessible for public sector agencies and citizens.

The benefits of e-government include:

- efficiency
- improved services
- better accessibility of public services

- transparency and accountability.

Democratization: One goal of e-government will be greater citizen participation. Through the internet, people from all over the country can interact with politicians or public servants and make their voices heard. Blogging and interactive surveys will allow politicians or public servants to see the views of the people they represent on any given issue. Chat rooms can place citizens in real-time contact with elected officials, their offices or provide them with the means to replace them by interacting directly with public servants, allowing voters to have a direct impact and influence in their government. These technologies can create a more transparent government. This helps voters to decide who to vote for in the future or how to help the public servants become more productive. A government could theoretically move more towards a true democracy with the proper application of e-government. Government transparency will give insight to the public on how decisions are made and hold elected officials or public servants accountable for their actions. The public could become a direct and prominent influence in government legislature to some degree.

Environmental bonuses: Proponents of e-government argue that online government services would lessen the need for hard copy forms. Due to recent pressures from environmentalist groups, the media, and the public, some governments and organizations have turned to the Internet to reduce this paper use.

Speed, efficiency, and convenience: E-government allows citizens to interact with computers to achieve objectives at any time and any location, and eliminates the necessity for physical travel to government agents sitting behind desks and windows. Improved accounting and record keeping can be noted through computerization, and information and forms can be easily accessed, equaling quicker processing time.

Public approval: Recent trials of e-government have been met with acceptance and eagerness from the public. Citizens participate in online discussions of political issues with increasing frequency, and young people, who traditionally display minimal interest in government affairs, are drawn to e-voting procedures.

11.3 MULTIMEDIA AND ENTERTAINMENT

Multimedia and Entertainment are almost interlinked terms in today's increasingly evolving and technological world. Multimedia and Entertainment is one of the most happening things in the world of computers. The Multimedia and Entertainment that come along with a computer is almost an absolutely necessary feature of possessing one's PC. It is quite unthinkable to possess a Personal Computer that does not have any kind of Multimedia and Entertainment related to it.

11.3.1 Multimedia

'Media' is something, which can be used for presentation of information. There are two basic ways to present information.

- Unimedia presentation, in this a single media is used to present information. For example, a stereo system is a unimedia device because it presents information by using only sound media.
- Multimedia presentation, in this more than one media is used to present information. For example, a TV system is a multimedia device because it presents information by sound and video media.

Multimedia presentations can be non-linear (interactive) or linear (passive) Multimedia, is a combination of media - used for creating audio, video, text, graphics and animation as shown in Figure 11.1.

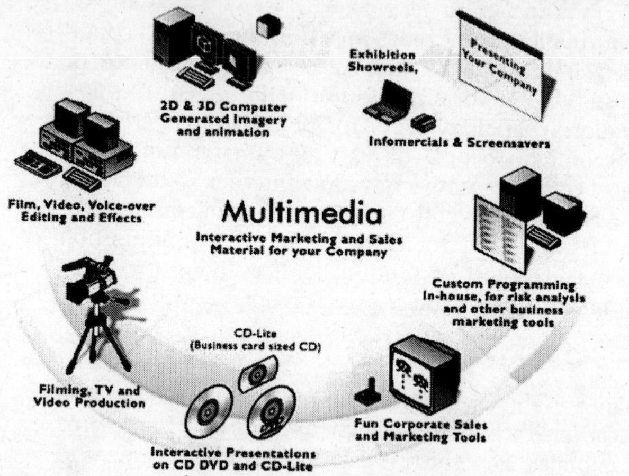

Figure 11.1 Multimedia is a combination of various media

Let us imagine a lion hunting its prey. A picture of a lion with a prey under its paws will reflect the mood a lot better than a hundred words. A 30-seconds sound clip of the same lion killing its prey will impact a lot better than many pictures. Again a 10-seconds full motion video of the lion chasing its prey before overpowering, will give much better perception than many minutes of pure sound of the spectacle. However, when you put together all the above elements in one burst, it is a good example of multimedia.

Multimedia technology facilitates an integration of text, image, graphics, audio and video animation in digital form in computers. It provides new ways to enhance the delivery of information and its impact on the user.

11.3.2 Advantages of Multimedia

The use of multimedia offers many advantages

- Enhancement of text only messages: Multimedia enhances text only presentations by adding interesting sounds and compelling visuals.
- Improves over Traditional Audio-Video Presentations: Audiences are more attentive to multimedia messages than traditional presentations done with slides or overhead transparencies.
- Gains and Holds attention: People are more interested in multimedia messages which combine the elements of text, audio, graphics and video because it offers greater understanding and retention of information.

- Multimedia is entertaining as well as educational.

11.3.3 Multimedia Presentation and its Characteristics

Multimedia presentation is a digital show whose contents are expressed through various media type like text, image/graphic, audio, video and animation.
Some characteristics of multimedia presentation are:

- Use of multiple media
- Interactive
- Digital representation
- Non-linear
- Integrity

11.3.4 Entertainment

Media and Entertainment industry are a major benefactors of multimedia technology. Images, animation and sound are widely used for making animation movies. Capability of computer is widely used by musicians to record, edit and mix sounds. Entertainment CDs, games, comics and stories for children are used for education and training.

Video editing, mixing, 3D animation and morphing are some of the techniques widely used for creating video films for various purpose.
Electronic Encyclopedia: Electronics books, Dictionaries, Encyclopedia and Magazines extend the printed word into digital domain. They offer not only text illustrations, and photos but add sound, video, and animation providing access and understanding which are not available with printed books. They offer greater storability, interactivity and irretrievability.
Entertainment Software: Entertainment software allow computer system to be used as an entertainment tool. A few examples of such applications are:

- Video Games: Thousands of video game applications are available on computer systems. Special audio and visual effects are used in these applications to make the games thrilling and exciting the users.
- Interactive Television: These applications allow users to either use their computer systems as an interactive television or to convert their conventional televisions into an interactive television. An interactive TV allows users to select TV programs of their interest from a massive video archive, view at the time they wish, and interact with the programs via VCR-like functions, such as fast-forward and rewind.

11.4 INTRODUCTION TO PROJECT MANAGEMENT

Every project is unique in terms of the problems which arise, the priorities and resources assigned to it, the environment in which it operates, project manager's attitude and style which is used to guide and control the project activities. So, the organizational structure for the project must be designed in order to fit within that project's operating constraints.

The organizational structure which is implemented may not be the same structure which is used throughout the life cycle of the project as priorities, available resource, project personnel, laws, changes over time.

Irrespective of the project management structure chosen, management must realize that the dynamic state of equilibrium among limited personnel or financial resources and the objectives of the project will be necessary to achieve, if personnel want the project to get successful in the organization.

11.4.1 Projects

Each activity within an organization can be labelled as a project which possess a unique characteristics and levels of importance to the organization. A project can be defined as a planned undertaking of related activities to achieve an objective that has a beginning and an end.
Characteristics of a project are:

1. Objective: Each has a specific goal to reach.
2. Schedule: Time in which stage of project to be executed.
3. Complexity: Does the technology exist to achieve the project objectives?
4. Size and Nature of Task: Step-by-step plan of action.
5. Resources: Labour, personnel, equipment, materials, facilities, etc.
6. Organizational Structure: The 'meshing' of project requirements into the existing organization.
7. Information and Control Systems: These must be structured to handle problems through the typical lines of authority.

11.4.2 Project Management

Project management is the act of initiating, planning, executing, controlling the work of a team in order to achieve a specific defined goals and to get success. A project is designed to produce a unique product, service that have a defined beginning and ending, just to meet unique goals and objectives, typically to bring about beneficial change or added value.
Challenge of project management: To achieve all the project goals and constraints (scope, time, quality and budget).
Phases of Project Management
The process of directing and controlling a project from start to finish is divided into five basic phases:

1. Project Conception and Initiation: Initially a project before its start is carefully examined to know is it going to benefits the organization in future or not. During this phase, a decision making team will identify if the project can realistically be completed.
   Project Initiation Phase Include:
   I. Establishing the project initiation team: In this organizing team members is assisted in carrying out the project initiation activities.
   II. Establishing a relationship with the customer.

III. Establishing the Project Initiation Plan: In this the activities required to organize the team is define, working to define the goals and scope of the project is define.

IV. Establishing Management Procedures: It is concerned with developing team communication and reporting procedures, job assignments and roles, project change procedure, and how project funding and billing will be handled.

V. Establishing the project management environment and workbook: It focuses on the collection and organization of the tools which is to be use while managing the project.

2. Project definition and planning: A project plan put in writing, which outlines the work to be performed. During this phase, a team prioritize the project, calculate a budget and schedule, and determine the resources which are needed.

   This phase includes:

   I. Describing project scope, alternatives, and feasibility.
      a. Some relevant questions that should be answered include:
         - Does the project address the problem/opportunity?
         - What results are to be achieved?
         - What needs to be done?
         - How will the success be measured?
         - How will we know that the project is finished?

   II. Divide the project into tasks.

   III. Estimating resources and creating a resource plan.

   IV. Developing a preliminary schedule, in which time estimates to each activity is defined, from which the target start and end dates for the project is determined.

   V. Developing a communication plan between management, team members, and the customer.

   VI. Determining project standards and procedures, to know how various deliverables are produced and tested by the project team.

   VII. Identifying and assessing risk.

   VIII. Creating a preliminary budget, which summarize the planned expenses and revenues related to the project.

   IX. Developing a list of work to be done and the expected outcome of the project.

   X. Setting a baseline project plan, in which estimate of the project's tasks and resource requirements are defined.

3. Project launch or execution: Resources' tasks are distributed and responsibilities are assigned to teams.

4. Project performance and control: In this, project managers compare the project status and progress of the ongoing project with the actual plan. During this phase, project managers may adjust schedules or do what is necessary to keep the project on track.

5. Project close: After project tasks are completed and the client has approved the outcome, then evaluation is done to know the project success.

   Note: Projects and project management processes may vary from industry to industry; but the explained stages, are traditional elements of a project.

   The techniques listed above enable a project team to:
   - Link project goals
   - Focus on customer needs
   - Build high-performance project teams.
   - Work across functional boundaries.
   - Develop work breakdown structures.
   - Estimate project costs and schedules.
   - Meet time constraints.
   - Calculate risks.

11.5 PROJECT MANAGEMENT TOOLS

Project management is a challenging task as it has many complex responsibilities, and there are many tools available to assist with accomplishing the tasks and executing the responsibilities. For this, some require a computer with supporting software, while others can do it manually.

Project managers must choose a project management tool which best suits their management style. Program Evaluation Review Technique (PERT) and Gantt Charts are the two most commonly used project management tools, that can either be produced manually or with commercially available project management software.

11.5.1 PERT

It is a planning and control tool which is used for defining and controlling the tasks required to complete a project. PERT charts and Critical Path Method (CPM) charts are often used interchangeably; the only difference is how task times are computed. Both charts display the total project with all scheduled tasks in sequence. The displayed tasks show which of the task are in parallel, and can be performed at the same time.

A graphic representation of PERT is called a "Project Network" or "CPM Diagram" which portray the interrelationships of the elements of a project graphically and show the order in which the activities are performed (See Figure 11.2).

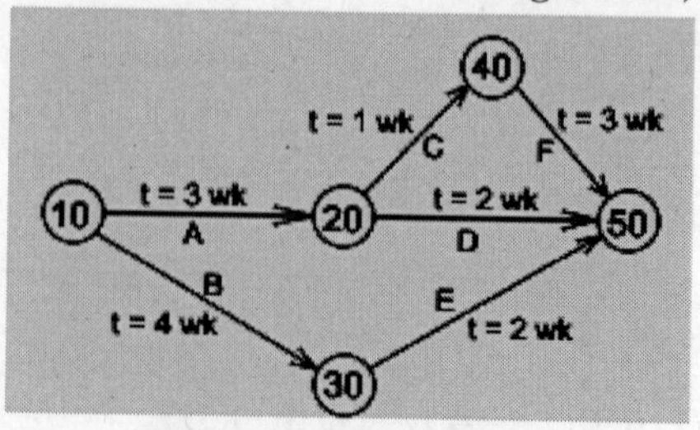

Figure 11.2 PERT Chart

PERT planning involves the following steps:

1. Identify the specific activities and milestones: The activities and milestones are the tasks and events of the project respectively, which mark the beginning and the end of one or more activities.
2. Determine the proper sequence of activities.
3. Construct a network diagram: By using the activity sequence information, a network diagram can be drawn which shows the sequence of the successive and parallel activities. The arrowed lines represent the activities and circles represent milestones.
4. Estimate the time required for each activity: Weeks are a commonly used unit to represent the time for activity completion. For each activity, the model usually includes three time estimates:
   - Optimistic time: the shortest time in which the activity can be completed.
   - Most likely time: the completion time having the highest probability.
   - Pessimistic time: the longest time that an activity may take.
5. Determine the critical path: The critical path is determined by adding the times for the activities in each sequence and determining the longest path in the project. It determines the total time required by the project for completion.
6. Update the PERT chart as the project progresses: As the project proceed, the estimated times can be replaced with actual times. In cases where there are delays or additional resources needed then PERT chart may be modified to reflect the new situation.

Benefits of using a PERT chart or the Critical Path Method:

- Improved planning and scheduling of activities.
- Easy identification of repetitive planning patterns that can be followed in other projects, thus it simplifies the planning process.
- Ability to see and reschedule activities to reflect interproject dependencies.
- It also provides expected project completion time.

11.5.2 Gantt Charts

It is used to show calendar time task assignments in days, weeks or months, by using graphic representations one can show start time, elapsed time, and completion times of each task within a project (See Figure 11.3).

Gantt charts are mainly used for tracking the progress, by calculating the number of days actually required to complete a task as compared with the estimated number. The actual workdays, from actual start to actual finish, are plotted below the scheduled days, which determines the failure points.

To draw up a Gantt chart, follow these steps:

- List all activities in the plan.
- Head up graph paper with the days or weeks through completion.
- Plot tasks onto graph paper.
- Schedule activities in such a way that sequential actions are carried out in the required sequence.

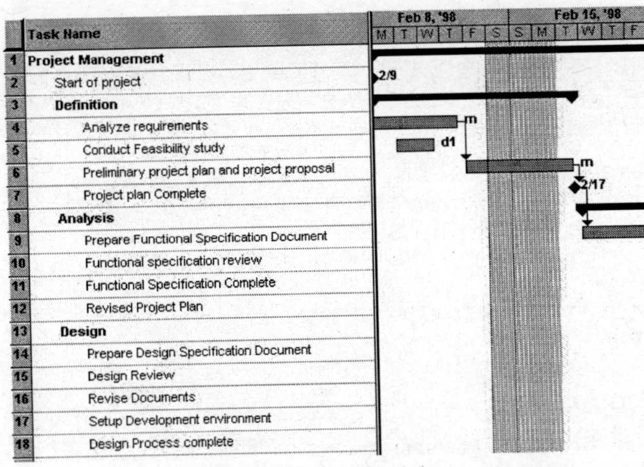

Figure 11.3 Gantt chart

- Presenting the analysis: In this combine your draft analysis with your scheduling and analysis of resources. This chart will show when you anticipate when the jobs should start and finish.

  Benefits of using a Gantt chart:
- Gives a visual display of the scheduled time of a task or activity.
- Makes it easy to develop "what if" scenarios.
- Shows the actual progress against the planned schedule.
- Can report results at appropriate levels.
- Allows comparison of multiple projects to determine resource allocation.

11.6 CLOUD COMPUTING

Cloud computing or on-demand computing is an Internet-based computing service which involves the use of the network of remote servers rather than local server or personal computer, which host on the Internet for storing, managing, and processing the data (See Figure 11.4).

In cloud computing, Cloud is a large group of interconnected computers, which may be personal or public.

Consider an example: If you have a Gmail or Yahoo account, then you are already using Cloud Computing. As you donot

Figure 11.4 Cloud Computing

know where exactly your e-mail and contacts are stored, and you can access your account via Internet.

Cloud computing allows

- Companies to focus on only projects which differentiate their businesses instead of on infrastructure and to avoid upfront infrastructure costs.
- Enterprises to get their applications up and run faster, with less maintenance.
- To rapidly adjust the resources, to meet fluctuating and unpredictable business demand.

Cloud computing is highly demanded service or utility because of its:

- High computing power and performance
- Cheap cost of services
- Scalability, accessibility and availability.

11.6.1 Properties

The key properties of Cloud computing are:

- User-centric: Once the user gets connected to cloud, any data which is present there, such as images, videos, applications, becomes his/her property.
- Task Centric: In this, documents are given more priority than applications from which they are created.
- Powerful: Due to its computing power and mass data storage capability.
- Self-Healing: Backups of every document is created automatically in the cloud.
- Multi-tenancy Intelligence: Multi-tenancy means sharing of data among a large number of users, by using data mining and analysis for accessing information in an intelligent manner.
- Programmable: Programming is associated with cloud computing, as processes such as backing up of data is done automatically, which requires programming.
- Flexible: It matches with the needs of user.

11.6.2 Characteristics

Key characteristics of cloud computing are:

- Agility: It improves with users' ability to re-provision technological infrastructure resources.
- Cost reductions claimed by cloud providers: The capital investment in the data centre is assumed by the cloud provider and operation costs are passed onto the cloud data centre user.
- Device and location independence: It enables the users to access systems through web browser irrespective of their location or the device they are using.
- Maintenance: cloud computing applications maintenance is easier, as it does not need to be installed on each user's computer and can be accessed from many places, provided that there must be an internet connection.
- Multitenancy: It enables the sharing of resources and costs across a large number of users.
- Productivity: It is increased as multiple users work on the same data simultaneously than waiting for it to be saved and emailed.
- Time: Time is saved as information does not need to be re-entered again and again when fields are matched, nor the users need to install an application software upgrades to their computer.
- Reliability: It enables the use of multiple redundant sites, which makes well-designed cloud computing suitable for business continuity.
- Security: It is improved due to centralization of data, security-focused resources, etc.

11.7 SERVICE MODEL

Service-oriented architecture advocates "everything as a service", whereas, on the other hand, cloud-computing providers offer their "services" according to different models. The three generally accepted modes of type of service offered are:

11.7 1 IaaS - Infrastructure as a Service (Servers and storage)

It provides physical hardware and software required by companies on the Internet. In other terms, IaaS refers to an online service which abstract the user from the detail of infrastructure (Infrastructure includes physical computing resources, location, data partitioning, scaling, security, backup etc.)

In this basic requirement for the consumer is to send a provisioning request for the number of server with data storage requirement. The server is provisioned and the access to the server is granted by the service provider.

IaaS provides a cloud-based platform for servers, storage, memory, bandwidth and computing power on demand. User needs a platform substantial customization of IaaS services. Vendors such as Rack space and Amazon's EC2 provides server and storage on demand. What applications to be use and how to configure the data storage are left to the client. Sub- class of IaaS is Communications as service .

11.7.2 PaaS - Platform as a Service (Development)

It provides a development environment or a real-time in cloud environment. The provider mainly develops toolkit and standards for the development and channels for distribution and payment. Generally, developer use PaaS (who develop and run their software solutions on a cloud platform without the cost and complexity of buying and managing the underlying hardware and software layers) and consumer user SaaS.

In this, cloud providers deliver a computing platform (which includes operating system, programming-language execution environment, database, and web server), on which an application developer can develop and run their software solutions without spending much cost.

Example, web-hosting platform or a collaboration program which provides access to document sharing or video archival and retrieval.

11.7.3 SaaS- Software as a Service (Application)

It provides software applications over the Internet, Cloud based software services such as customer resource management or enterprise resource management and user gain access to application software and database.

Example: Microsoft Live, which duplicates the Microsoft office suite for free on the Internet.

SaaS is sometimes referred to as "on-demand software" as in this cloud providers manage the platform and infrastructure, on which the applications are run. It is priced on a pay-per-use basis or using a subscription fee.

11.7.4 DaaS- Desktop as a Service

Desktop as a service, also known as a virtual desktop or hosted desktop services, is a cloud computing solution in which virtual desktop infrastructure is outsourced to a third-party provider.

Its functionality relies on the virtual desktop which transforms on-demand cloud services for users and organizations around the world. This is an efficient model in which the service provider manages the back-end responsibilities that would normally be provided by application software.

It builds on the concept that the product can be provided to the user on demand irrespective of the geographic or organizational separation of provider and consumer. Additionally, when service-oriented architecture (SOA) emerged, it rendered the actual platform on which the data resides irrelevant and this leads to the emergence of the relatively new concept of DaaS.

11.8 DEPLOYMENT MODELS

Cloud hosting deployment models represent the type of cloud environment which is mainly distinguished by the proprietorship, size and access. It tells about the purpose and the nature of the cloud. Organisations implement cloud to reduces the capital expenditure and controls the operating cost.

Some of the deployment models are:

1. Public cloud
   It is also called as multi-tenancy, which features client from more than one organisation sharing the same infrastructure and may provide free service.
   A cloud is called a "public cloud" when the services are rendered over a network which is open for public use.
   Example: Amazon AWS, Microsoft, Google.
2. Private cloud
   This is developed to give only one organisation or entity the control over the infrastructure and on the shared resource solely for the benefit of organisation exerting that control, that may be managed internally or by third party and hosted either internally or externally.
   Example: Private wiki sites, which allows access to the site only by members of the same corporation.
3. Community clouds
   It is a group united by a common cause or purpose, which shares an infrastructure between several organisations from a specific community with a common concern (such as security) that may be manages internally or by third-party either hosted internally or externally.
   Example: public-private partnership site which host collaborative efforts to help airlines to improve maintenance practices. Membership is limited to industry and government, but the overall portal is hosted by an industry trade group.
   Cost savings potential of cloud computing are realized by using community cloud as, the costs are spread over fewer users than a public cloud but is more than a private cloud.
4. Hybrid cloud
   It is a combination of two or more than two clouds (private, community or public) which remain distinct but are bounded together, thus providing the benefits of multiple deployment models.
   Example: Gartner, Inc., which is a hybrid cloud service (combination of private, public and community cloud services) from different service providers.

11.9 MOBILE COMPUTING

Mobile Computing is a technology which allows the transmission of data, voice and video through computer or wireless enabled device without connected to a fixed physical link.

Mobile computing involves:

1. Mobile communication: It refers to the infrastructure that put in place to ensure, seamless and reliable communication. Devices which are included in mobile communication are protocols, services, bandwidth, and portals which support the services. In this stage data format is defined (See Figure 11.5).

Figure 11.5 Mobile communication

2. Mobile Hardware: It includes mobile devices which receive or access the service of mobility. It ranges from portable laptops, smartphones, tablet Pc's, Personal Digital Assistants (See Figure 11.6).

Hardware devices have a receptor medium which is capable of sending and receiving signals, and devices are configured to operate in full- duplex mode (in this data can be transmitted in both directions (sender <--> receiver) on a signal carrier at the same time), so, they don't have to wait until one device has finished communicating for the other device to initiate communications.

Figure 11.6 Mobile hardware

3. Mobile software: It is the program which runs on the mobile hardware, deals with the characteristics and the requirements of mobile applications and act as an engine of the mobile device. So, one can say that it is the operating system of the appliance and an essential component which operates the mobile device.

11.9.1 Mobile Computing Classification

Today, there are various gadgets available in the market which are built on a platform to support mobile computing. Devices which supports mobile computing are:

Personal Digital Assistant (PDA)

It functions as an electronic organizer or day planner which is portable, easy to use and capable of sharing information with your computer systems.

It is an extension of the PC, which are capable of sharing information (either by using infrared or Bluetooth) with a computer system through a process known as synchronization. It has a stylus and a touch sensitive screen used for input and output purposes (See Figure 11.7).

This device enables, a user to browse the internet, listen and watch audio - video clips, edit and modify office documents, etc.

Smartphones

In this the features of a PDA are combined with that of a mobile phone or camera phone. These have the capability to run multiple programs concurrently and include high-resolution touch screens, web browsers which can access and display standard web pages rather than mobile-optimized sites.

Figure 11.7 Personal Digital Assistant (PDA)

Figure 11.8 Smartphones

Most common mobile Operating Systems (OS) used by modern smartphones are Google's Android, Apple's iOS, Nokia's Symbian, RIM's BlackBerry OS, Microsoft's Windows Phone. Such operating systems can be installed on different phone models, and each device receive multiple OS software updates over its lifetime. (See Figure 11.8)

Tablet PC and iPads

These mobile devices are larger as compared to mobile phone or PDA and integrate with a touch screen which is operated by touch sensitive motions on the screen. They are often controlled by a pen or by the touch of a finger (See Figure 11.9). Examples: ipads, Galaxy Tabs, Blackberry Playbooks etc.

11.9.2 Advantages of Mobile Computing

Mobile computing has changed the complete landscape of our day-to-day life. Some of the major advantages of Mobile Computing are:

- Location Flexibility: It enabled users to work from anywhere if an internet connection is established.

Figure 11.9 Tables PC and iPads

- Saves Time: One can now access all the important documents and files over a secure channel or portal and work as if they were on their computer while travelling.
- Enhanced Productivity: Users can work efficiently and effectively from any location they find comfortable.
- Ease of Research: It has made it easier for field officers and researchers to collect and feed data from wherever they are without making unnecessary trips to and from the office to the field.
- Entertainment: One is able to watch news, movies, and documentaries among other entertainment offers over the internet.

11.9.3 Components of Mobile Computing

The following components comprise of a complete end-to-end solution for mobile computing applications:

Hardware

- Mobile computing device (notebook, hand-held computer, PDA, smart phone with Wireless Internet connectivity etc).
- Wireline or wireless WAN modem
- Wireless LAN adapter
- Flash card
- Web Server with wireless support
- WAP gateway
- Communication Server
- An application or database server.

Software

- Mobile client OS-type software which resides in the mobile device.
- Mobile application user interface with application logic in a handheld PDA, smartphone, Palm or a Wintel notebook.
- Application server and/or database server software.
- Application middleware (IBM's WebSphere, BEA's WebLogic or Oracle's 9i).
- Wireless middleware which links multiple wireless networks to application servers.
- Data synchronization software which synchronizes data in the mobile device with the network server or the back-end server.
- Mobile Device management software.
- End user application like messaging, public query, data collection, etc.

Network

- A wireless network, which may be either a private network or a public shared network which is provided by network providers.
- Wireless network provides mobility.

11.9.4 Characteristics of Mobile Computing

- Portability: One can move a device within a learning environment or to different environments with ease.
- Social Interactivity: One can share data and collaboration among users.
- Context Sensitivity: The ability to gather and respond to real or simulated data unique to a current location, environment, or time.
- Connectivity: The ability to connect device for the purpose of communication of data in any environment.
- Individual: The ability to use the technology to provide scaffolding on difficult activities and lesson customization for individual learners.

11.10 DIGITAL SIGNATURE

Digital signature is use to make recipient to believe that the message was created by a known sender, and the sender cannot deny that he/she had sent the message and that the sent message was not altered in transit process.

Digital signature scheme typically consists of three algorithms:

- A key generation algorithm: It selects a private key uniformly at random from a set of possible private keys. The algorithm outputs the private key and a corresponding public key.
- A signing algorithm: It gives a message and a private key, thus produces a signature.
- A signature verifying algorithm: It gives the message, public key and signature, either accepts or rejects the message's claim to authenticity.

11.10.1 Digital Signature as Per IT Act 2000

According to IT Act 2000, (IT-act-notification-no-735) "digital signature" means authentication of any electronic record by a subscriber by means of an electronic method or procedure in accordance with the provisions of section 3 of the Act.

Section 3 of the ITA 2000:

Authentication of electronic records are:

- Subject to the provisions of this section, any subscriber authenticates an electronic record by affixing his digital signature.
- The authentication of the electronic record shall be effected by the use and hash function that envelop and transform the initial electronic record into another electronic record.

- Any person by the use of a public key of the subscriber can verify the electronic record.
- The private key and the public key are unique to the subscriber and forms a functioning key pair.

11.10.2 How Digital Signature Work

Encrypting a Document

To use a digital signature, user must have a digital id / digital certificate. Digital id/digital certificate is used for:

- Email encryption or encrypt files so that it can be read by the person they are intended for.
- "sign" or place a digital signature on a document, and it guarantee that it arrives in the same state as it was originally sent i.e, no one has added or changed the message.

It consists of a public key (key which is shared with everyone) and private key (key which is kept private). These keys are the text documents which consist of random numbers and letters, but with the proper algorithm, and the text document have a very unique property. Like, if you take a document and run it through an algorithm by using your public key, you can get an encrypted document or an encrypted email.

Once the document is encrypted, then the public key cannot be used to decrypt the document. This process is one way so other people who have the public key, can't read the document. To decrypt the document, user must use its private key to get back the original document (See Figure 11.10).

Figure 11.10 Decrypting a message

So, far we have studied that an encrypted document does two things.

- It guarantees that the document was not modified in transit.
- It guarantees that no one else can read the document.

To ensure that, each recipient got guaranteed that the document came from an original sender and that was not modify in transit, for that user usually put digital signature on it, in order to guarantees who sent it and it was not modified. People can verify your digital signature without getting a digital ID or digital certificate for themselves.

How it operates:

Checksums

It is a simple way of sending an extra piece of information with some data to make sure that the data which is sent and received is the same. Computers would send an 8-bit byte in which the last bit was a checksum. E.g. 01101010.

The first 7 bits contained the data: 0110101, and the last bit is the checksum which tells the even or odd numbers of ones present in the data. In the above example, we are using a 0 to say that there are an even number of ones. In case, if the computer received byte, the number of even bits and the checksum bit disagreed, then it would demand to send the data again.

It reduces accidental errors, but it does not prevent someone from intentionally changing the data.

Hashes for Digital Signatures

It is an algorithm through which you can run a piece of and get out a number that represents the original. You can not recreate the original from the number, but you can use that number to represent the input.

Example:

To construct a simple hash of the following text: "The quick brown fox jumped over the lazy hound."

Hash is created by multiplying the number of letters (38 in this example) by the number of words (9 in this example).

38 x 9 = 342

So to send a message, user include the number 342 and you can do the math on the message you receive and get an idea if the message is the same as what was sent.

This algorithm, will only protect against unintentional changes in the data, but in case if someone changes the email in route, they can simply change the number "342" to match the hash of their modified message. To avoid this, send the hash value through a different channel. Also, one can encrypt the hash number by using public key, and the only person who has that public key will only be able to decrypt the hash number.

To encrypt the hash number by using the private key.

Now the value 342 is encrypted in such a way that it can be opened by anyone having a sender's public key and it guarantees that the sender was the one who originally encrypted the number 342.

If someone changes the message and the hash value, they can only be able to encrypt it with sender's private key.

So, whenever you send a messages signed with a digital signature, the hash value guarantees that the message has not been changed.

RSA signature keys

To create RSA signature keys (first practical public-key crypto systems which is widely used for secure data transmission), generate an RSA key pair which contains a modulus, N, which is the product of two large primes, along with integers, e and d.

Such that e,d ≡ 1 (mod φ(N)), where φ is the Euler phi-function (arithmetic function which counts the positive integers less than or equal to n that are relatively prime to n).

The signer's public key consists of N and e, and the signer's secret key contains d.

To sign a message, m, the signer calculates σ ≡ md (mod N). To verify, the receiver checks that σe ≡ m (mod N).

This is a basic scheme, which is not very secure. To prevent attacks, first apply a cryptographic hash function to the message, m, and then apply the RSA algorithm to the result. This is the secured approach and is called random oracle model.

Example:

Using M and N, in this example, we explain how a digital signature is applied and verified. The signing operation by seeing seems to be as simple as a click of a button. But it involves certain things with that one click, which are explained in the steps given below:

1. In order to digitally sign a document, M needs to obtain a private and public key, it is a one-time process.
2. Depending on the software used, M needs to initiate the signing process by clicking a "Sign" button present on the software's toolbar.
3. Then, a unique digital fingerprint of the document is created by using a mathematical algorithm (such as RSA).
4. Append the signature to the document.
5. The hash result and the user's digital certificate including user's public key, are combined into a digital signature. The resulting signature is unique to both the document and the user.
6. Digital signature is appended to the document.
7. M sends the signed document to N.
8. N uses M's public key, which is included in the digital certificate in order to authenticate M's signature.
9. It ensures that no changes were made to the document after it was signed.
10. Depending on the software used, N needs to initiate the validation process.
11. Validation is done by clicking on a "Validate Signature" button present in the menu option button on the software's toolbar.
12. Decrypt the digital signature by using M's public key, N decrypts M's digital signature and receives the original document.
13. Now the Comparison of the document fingerprint is done with M calculated one, now N's software calculates the document hash of the received document and then compares it with the original document hash.
14. If the result of the comparison comes out to be the same, it means the signed document has not been altered.

11.10.3 Role of Certifying Authority

Certificate Authority (CA) is a trusted entity which issues a Digital Certificates and public-private key pairs. It guarantees that an individual granted a unique certificate to who he or she is claims to be.

It also verifies that the owner of the certificate is one, who he/she says he/she is. It can either be an external/public (such as verisign) or an internal/private which is configured inside our network.

Certificate Authority (CA) performs the following functions.

- Verifies the identity: It validate the identity of the person or an entity who requested a digital certificate before issuing it.
- Issues digital certificates: Once the validation process is over, CA issues a digital certificate to the entity who requested it.
- Maintains Certificate Revocation List (CRL): It is a list of digital certificates which are no longer valid and one should not depend on it.

11.11 DIGITAL CERTIFICATE

It is an electronic document which is used to prove the ownership of a public key. The certificate includes the information about the key, owner's identity, and digital signature of an entity which has verified that the certificate's contents are correct.

It can be considered as an attachment to an electronic message which is used for security purposes, and is used to verify that an actual user is sending a message, who is claims to be a sender of the message.

If the signature is valid, and the person examining the certificate trusts the signer, then that key can be used to communicate with its owner.

In this, the signer is a certificate authority (CA), which can also be a company that charges from customers to issue certificates for them.

Contents of a digital certificate:

- Serial Number: To identify the certificate uniquely.
- Subject: The person.
- Signature Algorithm: It is used to create the signature.
- Signature: Actual signature to verify that it came from the issuer.
- Issuer: The entity which verified the information and then issued the certificate.
- Valid-From: The date from which the certificate is valid from.
- Valid-To: expiration date.
- Public Key
- Thumbprint Algorithm: It is used to hash the public key certificate.
- Thumbprint: The hash itself, used as an abbreviated form of the public key certificate.

11.11.1 Uses of Digital Certificate

Digital certificate adopts the Public Key Infrastructure (PKI) framework which enables the deployment of the three major functional uses, which are:

- Public Key Encryption: It ensure the confidentiality of message, which involves encryption of data with a pair of asymmetric keys but matching keys, which are private key and a public key. Private key is kept secretly and securely by the owner of the digital certificate and the public key is published at an online repository by certification authority (CA) and is publicly available to others for use.
- Digital Signature: It is created by digital certificate to ensure the data integrity (It alert the reader if anything has been changed, in the signed document), user authenticity (It provides many ways to identify a signer so that persons cannot later say they did not sign the document.) and non-repudiation of transaction (User requires to follow certain steps to sign a document and tracks all of those steps, so the possibility of a signer of committing a mistake got eliminated).
- Electronic Authentication: It is the process of confirming user identity which is presented electronically to an information system for accessing the data or conducting the transactions.

11.11.2 Certifying Authority Regulation in India

Certification Authority issues a digital signature certificate for electronic authentication of users and stands responsible for them. It signs the issued certificates, thus enables the users to know which CA created which certificate. The signature also ensures that a third party has not altered the certificate at any point of time.

In India, the Indian IT Act authorises the Controller of Certifying Authorities (CCA) to licence and regulate the working of CAs.

Some organisations who acts as a licenced CAs are the National Informatics Centre, Customs and Central Excise, Institute for Development & Research in Banking Technology, Tata Consultancy Services, MTNL, etc.

11.11.3 Obtaining a Trial Version of Digital Certificate

Organizations which require an ability to digitally sign a documents, authenticate to users, computers, VPN need a digital certificate.

One such organisation, Entrust Managed Services PKI; which enables your organizations to easily issue a digital certificate to customers.

To experience the benefits of Entrust's hosted PKI service, one need to sign up and after that follow the steps to create an administrator digital ID. Once the step got completed, user can create user accounts and begin issuing certificates within the 60-day trial.

Follow the simple steps which are described below, to experience the Entrust Managed Services PKI:

1. Register for the Managed Services PKI Trial
2. Create your administrator digital ID
3. Log in
4. Create end-user accounts
5. Verify end-user identities
6. Begin issuing and managing of the certificates

☞ It requires browser such as Microsoft Internet Explorer 6.0 or Mozilla Firefox 2.0 or later.

During the duration of the free trial, user have to access to a certification authority (CA) which is hosted by Entrust, or through a simple Web application which lets you to generate a certificates. A single Entrust certificate can be shared by multiple applications and for multiple purposes.

One can use test certificates to:

- Sign the digitally documents
- Secure email
- Authenticate users

To enroll for the free trial:

1. Click "Sign Up Now".
2. Enter your email address when asked to enter.
3. You will receive an email along with an instruction to continue your registration.
4. Once you are registered successfully, you have access to the Web application.
5. Start creating an accounts and issuing certificates.

Time Limits

This trial is valid for 60 days.

☞ Digital certificates issued via the Entrust Managed PKI Services for trial purpose only and it can not be used for production purposes.

11.11.4 Legal aspects Covering Digital Signature in India

Section 3 of the Information Technology Act 2000 provides for authentication of electronic records by using digital signatures. It states the technology requirements for digital signatures, and also describe the use of an asymmetric crypto system and hash function for the authentication of electronic records.

Authentication of an electronic document is done by using asymmetric system and hash function and it ensures that the message has not been tampered and the sender of the message cannot deny its creation. It converts the electronic message into an unreadable form for preventing the tampering of electronic record.

11.11.5 How to use Digital Signature on Electronic Document?

In this section, we will be going to learn how to sign the electronic documents in Adobe Acrobat:

Obtain a digital ID: In case, if you donot have a digital ID, create a self-signed digital ID in Acrobat. Digital ID includes an encrypted private key for signing or decrypting the documents and a public key in a certificate used to validate signatures and encrypt the documents

1. To create a self-signed digital ID:
    - Choose Tools from the right hand side of the menu bar.
    - Select Sign & Certify.

- Select More Sign & Certify.
- Choose Security Settings.
- Select Digital IDs from the menu present on the left side of the pop-up panel.
- Choose Add ID button in the toolbar.
- Select A New Digital ID- Want to Create Now.
- Continue through the wizard.
- Type the personal information (name) for your digital ID.
- When you certify or sign a document, the name appears in the Signatures panel and in the signature field.
- Name your digital ID.
- Create a password for it, which contains at least six characters, punctuation marks or special characters are not allowed in this.
- Click Finish.

☞ Take a backup copy of your digital ID file.

2. Enter the information for the digital ID
   - Review the document carefully.
   - Before you sign any document, make sure to read exactly what you are signing and where the signature fields are.
3. View documents in preview document mode to ensure there are no hidden features in the document before signing.
4. Sign the PDF document.
   - Click the signature field.
   - Choose Sign & Certify in the Tools pane.
   - Sign Document and draw a signature field on the page.
5. Sign the document.
   - In the Sign Document dialog box, add any information if prompted.
   - Enter a password.
   - Click Sign.
   - Give the document a new name so that you can change the original PDF file without invalidating the signature.
   - Click Save
   - Now, whenever you apply a digital signature, Acrobat embeds an encrypted message digest in the PDF file, with the details from your certificate and a version of the document at the time it was signed.
6. Distribute your certificate.
   - Choose Tools
   - Select Sign & Certify
   - Choose more Sign & Certify
   - Click on security Settings
   - Select Digital IDs which is present on the left.
   - Select the digital ID you want to share.
   - Click Export.
   - Follow the on-screen instructions to email your certificate
7. Share your certificate with anyone who needs to verify your digital signature.

11.12 E-GOVERNANCE

Electronic governance OR e-governance is the application of information and communication technology (ICT) that can be used for:

- delivering government services,
- exchange of information communication transactions,
- services among government-to-customer (G2C), government-to-business (G2B), government-to-government (G2G) within the entire government framework.

11.12.1 Pillars of e-governance

In this, the government makes the best possible use of internet technology in order to communicate and provide the information to common peoples and businessman.

There are four pillars of E-Governance, which are:

- Connectivity: It is required to connect the people to the services of the government. Its aim is to provide user a seamless facility.
- Knowledge: Government should employ skill full engineers to handle any kind of fault which occurs during working in an efficient way.
- Data content: There should be a database which contains the data content related to government service through which any kind of knowledge or information can be shared over the Internet.
- Capital: It is the money which is used by government to provide the services.

11.12.2 Infrastructure for e-governance

The Government has approved the Scheme of establishing State Wide Area Networks (SWANs) throughout the country. Under this Scheme, technical and financial assistance are provided to the States/UTs in order to establish SWANs for connecting all State/UT Headquarters up to the Block level via District/ sub-Divisional.

SWAN infrastructure

It is considered as the converged backbone network for data, voice and video communications throughout a State/UT.

Salient features:

- One PoP to be present at each State / District / Block Headquarter (See Figure 11.11.
- Each PoP must have a Configurable Aggregation Equipment which enable vertical & horizontal connectivity.
- State/ NIC should receive discounted price for BSNL BW cost.

Implementation

Two Options are there for SWAN implementation:

- Option I:
  Public Private Partnership (PPP) Model which identifies the suitable PPP model such as BOO, BOOT and after that it selects an appropriate agency by a suitable competitive process for the establishment, operation and the maintenance of the Network.
- Option II:

NIC Model which state designates National Informatics Centre as the prime implementation agency for SWAN for establishment, operation and the maintenance of the Network.

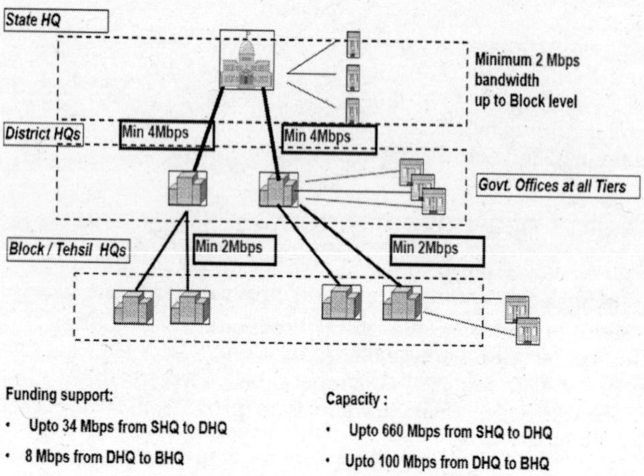

Figure 11.11 SWAN infrastructure

Present status

It has been made operational in 34 States which are Andhra Pradesh, Kerala, Chandigarh, Chhattisgarh, Delhi, Gujarat, Goa, Haryana, Himachal Pradesh, Jharkhand, Karnataka, Maharashtra, Puducherry, Sikkim, Tamil Nadu, Tripura, Uttar Pradesh, West Bengal, Punjab, Assam, Bihar, Madhya Pradesh, Uttarakhand, Manipur, Lakshadweep, Arunachal Pradesh, Mizoram, Orissa, Nagaland, Meghalaya Rajasthan Dadar & Nagar Haveli and Daman & Diu.

11.12.3 Mission Mode Project (MMPs)

It is an individual project within the National e-Governance Plan (NeGP) which focuses on only one aspect of electronic governance. In total there are 31 MMPs, provided by National e-Governance Plan and are further classified as state, central or integrated projects.

In this section we will going to discuss about the five mission mode projects out of 31.

1. Banking Technology
   In India, it had brought the accessibility of anytime and anywhere banking to the Indian customers, that provides an efficiency and reduce the time in handling and settling the transactions, thus it improves customer service and facilitating regulatory compliance.
2. Agriculture
   It has been included in NeGP in order to associate various learnings from the past, and integrate all the diverse and disparate efforts currently underway, and upscale them to cover the entire country.
   Aim of such service is to provide, information to farmers on:
   - Seeds, fertilizers, pesticides
   - Soil recommendations
   - Crop management
3. Central Excise Customs
   Central Board for Excise and Customs (CBEC) gives a view to facilitate trade and industry by streamlining and simplifying the customs and excise processes, and is widely used to create a climate for voluntary compliance.
   Services that are covered in this are:
   - Simplification of registration, returns, revenue reconciliation and exports procedures
   - e-Registration for excise and service tax
   - e-Filing of returns and refunds
   - Improved dispute resolution mechanism
4. Income tax
   The Income Tax Department of India is implementing a plan of setting a service which enables the citizens to transact all businesses with the Department on an anywhere, anytime basis.
   Some of the services under this are:
   - Tax accounting
   - Processing of tax return
   - Processing of tax-deducted-at-source (TDS) return, etc.
5. Insurance
   It provides user a facility of customer service through education, information, speedy processing of claims and online issuance of policies on web.

11.13 CHANGE MANAGEMENT

It can be considered as a processes or tools that can be used for encouraging individuals to make successful personal changes. Departments introduce change, and those newly introduced changes impact the way by which an individuals do their work, and also on the degree to which individuals adopt the changes to their work.

11.14 PROCESSING ENGINEERING

It involves the design, operation, control, and optimization of either chemical, physical, and biological processes. It also involves the changing of needs of the customer into production facilities where the "raw materials" are converted into value-added goods and after that the goods are transported to the next stage of the supply chain, called "packaging engineering".

11.14.1 Government Processing Engineering and Governance

According to Ministry of Information Technology, Government of India, e-Governance can be considered as an application of Information Technology which is used to processes the government functioning in order to bring a Simple, Accountable and Transparent governance.

The traditional approach to e-Governance can be consider as one of IT enablement of existing processes, without any change to the underlying processes.

So, IT enablement initiatives included:

- Automation of existing processes
- Making services of the department available online

Table 10.1 E-Governance project life cycle

E-governance Strategy Development	Current State Assessment	Future State Definition	Implementation approach sourcing	Develop Implement IT system	Operate systain
Needs Assessment	Assessment of current processes and pain area	Process reengineering and to be process	Implementation approach and phasing plan (Functional and geographic)	Functional and technical requirements	System operations and maintenance
Vision	Best practices in similar environments	Identity IT enablement opportunities	Funding and business model	System design	Software change management
Prioritize		Changes to the regulatory environment	Vendor evaluation criteria	Acceptance testing	Rollout services and system (functionality and geography)
Domestic and Global learnings	Regulatory framework	People change and capacity building plan	KPIs and SLAs for services and systems	Training and capacity building	Objectives and benefits evaluation and reinforcement
Institutional structures & capacities for implementation	ICT systems		RFP bid evaluation and vendor selection	Change management	Sustained change, capacity building and communications
Funding requirements	Capacities and their preparedness for e-governance	Project awareness and communication requirements		Project documents and Project go-live	

In Processing engineering, the process is same, but now it is being carried out electronically.

Advantage

- Easier implementation with minimal legal changes.
- Easier status updates

11.14.2 E-Governance Project Life Cycle

A project has its start and end date. Project has its distinct life cycle phases and decision points, which includes starting, organising, preparing, carrying out and closing the project.

Well documented project life cycle model enables the user to apply system to create, plan, schedule and manage the project through all of its phases and finally to evaluate the success and the value and the result of the project. E-Governance project life cycle is shown in Table 10.1.

Phase 1: E-Governance strategy development

In this phase:

- Need to develop the project, its vision, objectives, its priority is define.
- Way through which the services, delivery channel will be receiving is define.
- When does the plan is implemented is decided?
- Who will identify the institutional structure is decided?
- Performance is check at various stage.

Phase 2: Current State Assessment

Key activities and its deliverables which are included in this phase are:

Key Activities	Deliverables
Current approach for performing the business functions and service delivery	Process maps
The key challenges and to identify improvement areas	Identifying pain points and Initial improvement areas
Stakeholder needs and expectations	Stakeholder needs
Good practices and learnings from similar implementations in similar domains	Scope and functionality, Strengths and gaps, the change barriers.
Current systems (IT) implemented	IT Systems & IT infrastructure
Organization structures and people capacities etc	Organizational structures, Roles and responsibilities, Capacities and skill sets

Phase 3: To define the future state.

Key activities and deliverables which are included in this phase are:

Key Activities	Deliverables
Define how the identified business functions and services shall be performed going forward	• To-be business processes • New process KPIs/metrices • Changes to legal and policy environment
Define the new business processes	• Functional Architecture • Requirements specifications

(Contd...)

Key Activities	Deliverables
Define IT solutions and services for automation of new business	• Enterprise Architecture (Application, data, network, security, data center) • Data digitization and migration strategy • SLAs
Define people change management, capacity building and communication requirements for project implementaton	• Institutional structure for project implementation • Training and capacity building plan • Change Management Plan • Communication Management Plan

Phase 4: Implementation approach and sourcing
Key activities and deliverables which are included in this phase are:

Key Activities	Deliverables
Development of Implementation Approach and Plan	• Implementation Approach and Plan • Implementation timelines • Identification of key stakeholders and their roles and responsibilities • Monitoring and Evaluation (M & E) Plan
Development of Business Model	• Project investments and costs • Revenue Opportunities • Business/Implementation model • Payment terms • SLAs • Procurement approach
RFP Development	• Request for Proposals (RFP) • Contract Documents/Agreements • Pre-bid minutes and clarifications
Vendor Evaluation and Selection	• Vendor evaluation reports • Vendor(S) identification • Signed contract documents

Phase 5: Develop and implement IT system
Key activities and deliverables which are included in this phase are:

Key Activities	Deliverables
Application Software Development	• e-Governance Solution/-Software
IT Infrastructure Creation	• IT infrastructure
Third Party Acceptance Testing	
Training and Capacity Building	

Phase 6: Operate and sustain
Key activities and deliverables which are included in this phase are:

Key Activities	Deliverables
IT Systems Operations and Annual Maintenance Contract Maintenance	
Monitoring and Evaluation	• SLA Monitoring & Compliance • Release of Payments to Vendor on AMC

11.15 ELECTRONICALLY DELIVERY OF SERVICE

E-Service, represents a prominent application of utilizing the information and communication technologies (ICTs) in various areas. According to Rowley, e-services can be consider as a deeds, efforts or performances whose delivery is mediated by information technology.

Consider an example, as concerned to public e-service, public agencies are the service provider and citizens, businesses are the service receiver and the Internet is the channel of e-service delivery.

Messaging system

In E-Governance, there are generally four basic models:

1. government-to-citizen (customer)
2. government-to-employees
3. government-to-government
4. government-to-business

The goal of Government to Customer (G2C) is to offer various ICT services to citizens in an efficient and economical manner, and to strengthen the relationship among the government and citizens using technology.

There are various methods of Government to Customer e-Governance. One such method is Two-way communication which allow citizens to message instantly to any public administrators, and also citizen can cast remote electronic votes.

Transactions facilities, such as payment of services, can be done online by using Internet or over the phone.

11.16 CASE STUDY

Filing RTI Online

In order to make RTI (Right to information) accessible to the citizens, the department of personnel and Training (DOPT) launched an online application of RTI application, which address all the queries related to central ministries.

Here in this section we will learn about a step-by-step guide of filling RTI online:

1. Go to the web portal, https://rtionline.gov.in.
2. Now, you can either register yourself first before submitting your request or you can submit your request directly. In both the cases, you have to provide your email id.
3. Click on "submit request", and fill the required details on the page that will appear.

i. All the fields which are marked * are mandatory to fill while the others one are optional.
ii. Text can only be typed in the space provided for the prescribed column.
iii. Maximum limit for the text to be typed in the space is 3,000 characters and in case if the text of the application exceeds the given limit, then text can be uploaded as an attachment, by using "supportive document".

4. After filing the first page, click on "make payment" for paying the prescribed fee. Fee can either be paid by Internet banking through SBI, by debit/credit card of Master/ Visa.
Note:
The fee for making an application is as per the rules prescribed under RTI Rules, 2012. In case if the applicant is below poverty line, then no RTI fee will be charged and applicant have to attach a copy of the certificate which is issued by the appropriate government, along with their application.
5. Once, the payment has made, the application can be submitted.
6. Now, a unique registration number will be issued, which can be use in the future in case of query.
7. The application filled online will reach the concerned nodal officer, who will transmit it electronically to the concerned information officer.

☞ In case if an additional fee is required for providing an information, applicant will be informed through the web portal. This information can be seen in the status report or applicant can get it through an email alert.

MODEL QUESTIONS AND ANSWERS

A. Multiple Choice

1.1 ________ is the application of modern information and Communication Technologies such as Internet, Local area networks, mobiles etc. provided by Government to improve the effectiveness, efficiency, service delivery.
a. E-Governance b. E-Government
c. E-application d. E-service

1.2 ________ has traditionally been understood as being centered around the operations of government.
a. E-Governance b. E-Government
c. E-application d. E-service

1.3 The primary delivery models of e-Government can be divided into how many modes?
a. One b. Two
c. Three d. Four

1.4 Increased contact between government and its citizens goes both ways is called:
a. Cost b. Hyper-surveillance
c. E-governance d. E-Government

1.5 Goal of e-government is to make ______ citizen participation.
a. Greater b. Lesser
c. Maximum d. Minimum

1.6 ______ can be defined as a planned undertaking of related activities to achieve an objective that has a beginning and an end.
a. Activity b. Project
c. Task d. Work

1.7 Time in which stage of project to be executed is called as:
a. Objective b. Schedule
c. Task d. Resources

1.8 Act of initiating, planning, executing, controlling the work of a team in order to achieve a specific defined goals and to get success is:
a. Project management b. Project
c. Task d. Work

1.9 ________is a challenging task as it has many complex responsibilities, and there are many tools available to assist with accomplishing the tasks and executing the responsibilities.
a. Project management b. Project
c. Task d. Work

1.10 Pert is:
a. Project Evaluation Review Technique
b. Program Evaluate Review Technique
c. Program Evaluation Revise Technique
d. Program Evaluation Review Technique

1.11 In ______ documents are given more priority than applications from which they are created.
a. Task Centric b. Powerful
c. Self-Healing d. Multi-tenancy & Intelligence

1.12 ________ enables the users to access systems through web browser irrespective of their location or the device they are using.
a. Maintenance b. Multitenancy
c. Device and location independence d. Productivity

1.13 Which of the following, provides physical hardware and software required by companies on the Internet?
a. IaaS b. SaaS
c. PaaS d. DaaS

1.14 ______ provides a development environment or a real-time in cloud environment.
a. IaaS b. PaaS
c. DaaS d. SaaS

1.15 ______ provides software applications over the Internet, Cloud based software services
a. IaaS b. SaaS

c. PaaS d. DaaS

1.16 Mobile Computing is a technology which allows:
a. transmission of data b. transmission of hardware
c. transmission of software d. transmission of data, voice and video

1.17 ________ refers to the infrastructure that put in place to ensure, seamless and reliable communication.
a. Mobile communication b. Mobile software
c. Mobile hardware d. Mobile data

1.18 ________ includes mobile devices which receive or access the service of mobility.
a. Mobile communication b. Mobile software
c. Mobile hardware d. Mobile data

1.19 ________ is the program which runs on the mobile hardware, deals with the characteristics and the requirements of mobile applications and act as an engine of the mobile device.
a. Mobile communication b. Mobile software
c. Mobile hardware d. Mobile data

1.20 PDA is:
a. Personal Digital Assistance b. Person Digital Assistant
c. Personal Digital Assistant d. Personal Data Assistant

1.21 ________ selects a private key uniformly at random from a set of possible private keys.
a. A key generation algorithm
b. A key generation algorithm
c. A signature verifying algorithm
d. Digital certificate

1.22 ________ means authentication of any electronic record by a subscriber by means of an electronic method
a. Digital certificate b. Digital Signature
c. A key generation algorithm d. A signing algorithm

1.23 CA is:
a. Certificate Authority b. Certification Authority
c. Certificate Aim d. Certifying Authority

1.24 ________ validate the identity of the person or an entity who requested a digital certificate before issuing it.
a. Verifies the identity b. Issues digital certificates
c. Certificate Revocation List d. Revocation List

1.25 CRL is:
a. Certificate Registration List
b. Certificate Revocation List
c. Certifying Revocation List
d. Certificate Rotatory List

1.26 There are _____ pillars of E-Governance.
a. One b. Two
c. Three d. Four

1.27 SWAN Is:
a. State Wide Area Networks b. Slate Wide Area Networks
c. State Wide And Networks d. State Wire Area Networks

1.28 PPP Is:
a. Private Public Partnership b. Public Private Partnership
c. Public Private Partner d. Public Public Partnership

1.29 NIC Is:
a. National Informatics Centre b. National Information Centre
c. Nation Informatics Centre d. National Informatics Centres

1.30 MMPs Is:
a. Mode Mission project b. Mission mode project
c. Mission modes project d. Mission mode program

B. State whether the following are True or False

2.1 Multimedia and Entertainment are almost interlinked terms in today's technological world.

2.2 'Media' is something, which can be used for presentation of information.

2.3 Electronics books, Dictionaries extend the printed word into printing domain.

2.4 Entertainment software allow computer system to be used as an entertainment tool.

2.5 Interactive Television allow users to use their computer systems as an interactive television.

2.6 PERT charts and Critical Path Method (CPM) charts are often used interchangeably.

2.7 Optimistic time is the time in which the activity can be completed.

2.8 Most likely time is the longest time that an activity may take.

2.9 Gantt charts are used for tracking the progress.

2.10 Gantt charts does not give a visual display of the scheduled time of a task or activity.

2.11 Public cloud is also called as multi-tenancy.

2.12 A cloud is called a "Private cloud" when the services are rendered over a network which is open for public use.

2.13 Private cloud is developed to give more than one organisation or entity the control over the infrastructure.

2.14 Hybrid cloud is a combination of two or more than two clouds which remain distinct.

2.15 Multicloud uses multiple cloud computing services in a single heterogeneous architecture.

2.16 Location Flexibility enables users to work from anywhere if there is an internet connection.

2.17 Data synchronization software synchronizes data in the mobile device with the network server or the backend server.

2.18 Portablility means one cannot move a device within a learning environment or to different environments with ease.

2.19 In Social Interactivity one cannot share data and collaboration among users.

2.20 Context Sensitivity is ability to gather and respond to real or simulated data unique to a current location, environment, or time.

2.21 Digital certificate is an electronic document which is used to prove the ownership of a public key.

2.22 Public Key Encryption ensure the confidentiality of message.

2.23 Certification Authority issues a digital signature certificate for electronic authentication of users and stands responsible for them.

2.24 Organizations need a digital certificate to digitally sign a documents.

2.25 Section 3 of the Information Technology Act 2000 provides for authentication of electronic records by using digital signatures.

2.26 Processing engineering is a processes that can be used for encouraging individuals to make successful personal changes.

2.27 Change management involves the design, operation, control, and optimization of either chemical, physical, and biological processes.

2.28 A project has its start and end date.

2.29 E-Service, represents a prominent application of utilizing the information and communication technologies (ICTs) in various areas.

2.30 The goal of Government to Customer (G2C) is to offer various ICT services to citizens in an efficient and economical manner.

Answers

A.

1.1 a	1.2 b	1.3 d	1.4 b	1.5 a
1.6 b	1.7 b	1.8 a	1.9 a	1.10 d
1.11 a	1.12 b	1.13 a	1.14 d	1.15 c
1.16 d	1.17 a	1.18 c	1.19 b	1.20 c
1.21 a	1.22 b	1.23 a	1.24 a	1.25 b
1.26 d	1.27 a	1.28 b	1.29 a	1.30 b

B.

2.1 T	2.2 T	2.3 F	2.4 T	2.5 T
2.6 T	2.7 T	2.8 F	2.9 T	2.10 F
2.11 T	2.12 F	2.13 F	2.14 T	2.15 T
2.16 T	2.17 T	2.18 F	2.19 F	2.20 T
2.21 T	2.22 T	2.23 T	2.24 T	2.25 T
2.26 F	2.27 F	2.28 T	2.29 T	2.30 T

CHAPTER 12

Application of Digital Financial Services

12.1 INTRODUCTION

Digital financial services, expands the delivery of basic financial services to the people through new technologies like the Internet, mobile phones and transfer of money through new digital channels. These channels have significantly drive down the costs for customers and service providers, thus opening the doors to provide 24 hours' service for 365 days. (Figure 12.1)

Figure 12.1 Digital Financial Service

12.2 WHY SAVINGS ARE NEEDED?

We need to save money for future needs, emergencies and for large expenses.

12.2.1 Emergencies

Saving must be top most priority for everyone, which allows you to easily meet any unexpected emergencies, such as:

- The emergency fund not only provides you with the money to pay for expenses, but gives you a "peace of mind".
- To meet unexpected expenses like Illness, accident, death of earning members, fire, flood, etc.
- Job layoff and sudden loss of income.
- It allows you to avoid borrowing money from others.

Figure 12.2 Savings

12.2.2 Future Needs

We save, because we cannot predict the future. With savings, in the future you can buy what you cannot buy today. There are few reasons why we need saving (See Figure 12.2):

- To buy something which we cannot afford from our regular income.
- To meet needs at old age when not able to earn.
- The costs for education is rising every year, and to provide better educational facilities to your family member.
- Starting of new business, purchasing own house.
- To meet regular expenses for life after retirement.
- In future, when the income is less and expenses are more.

12.2.3 Large Expense

Large expenses sometimes surprise us by popping up at the most inappropriate times.

Large expense includes:

- Plan for higher education of family members in India or abroad.
- Plan for marriage.
- Buying home.
- Starting of new business

12.3 DRAWBACKS OF KEEPING CASH AT HOME

Money can either get stolen by anybody if it is kept at home. In this section we will discuss few drawbacks of keeping cash at home.

12.3.1 Unsafe

Money kept at home can be stolen or lost. It can also be lost due to calamities (such as fire). While in the bank money is safer.

12.3.2 Loss of Growth Opportunity

Loss of Interest Income. By keeping your money in bank, you can earn extra income as an interest from the bank.

12.3.3 No Credit Eligibility

Deposits in Bank creates Credit Eligibility.

- You are not eligible to get a credit card/loan as no credit history is available to your bank.
- Bank can also give loans for future needs.

12.4 WHY BANK IS NEEDED?

A bank is a financial institution, which acts as an intermediary in transactions, and offer services like safekeeping and lending of money. It can be considered as an establishment, which is authorized by government to accept – Cash Deposits, pay interest and to provide following financial services which people requires.

Bank is majora needed to (Figure 12.3):

1. Safety of money
2. Inculcate habit of saving
3. Earn interest
4. Remittances using Cheque/Demand Draft
5. Loans-Home/Business/Vehicle
6. Avoid risk of chit funds, sahukars
7. Online banking
8. Bank lockers
9. Credit/Debit cards

Figure 12.3 Why bank is needed

12.4.1 Secure Money, Earn cash, Get loan

- Saving money in a bank account, offers you the opportunity to earn interest on deposits.
- Rates of interest of savings account also depends on how much you saved, i.e., more money you keep in the bank for longer duration, the higher the interest will be.
- Once you established good relationship with bank, you can apply for loans (vehicle, house, education or business loans) as deposited in bank creates credit eligibility.
- If you do not want carry cash with you because of safety issues, you can carry debit card or credit card provided by bank.
- Your money is secure as money can be stolen/lost otherwise.

12.4.2 Inculcate Habit of Saving

Person, whether doing a job, business, student, kids or housewives must have the habit of saving money, which can be used for future needs.

12.4.3 Remittances using Cheque /Demand Draft

Banks acts as a medium for the transfer of money (both domestic and foreign) from one place to another and from person to person safely, speedily and efficiently.

12.4.4 Avoid Risk of Chit Funds and Sahukars

Chit funds

Chit implies a transaction under which a person goes into an agreement with a predefined number of persons. Each one of them will subscribe to a certain amount of money by method for periodical instalments over a definite period of time.

Such subscriber shall, in his turn, as dictated by a lot or by auction or by tender or in such other way as might be determined in the chit agreement, be entitled to the prize sum.

Chit fund frauds have become a major issue and many people have been cheated in the past. The fund manager may disappear with the corpus amount. A member could default in an instalment payment or disappear after winning the first bid. The discount rate might be rigged and a desperate member might end up paying a higher discount. Due to this, it is not advisable to invest in chit funds.

Sahukars

They are Moneylenders,!who offers loans!at high!rates of interest and normally people go there when bank refuses to give them the loan.

Unfair Practices of Sahukars

Sahukars deceive in many ways such as:

- They manipulate the amount given to debtors (like, they may enter large amount than they actually lent.
- They give no receipt for repayments and sometimes they deny such repayments.
- They charge very high rate of interest.

☞ Facts: The rate of interest on Bank loans is very low as compared to money lenders. So, if a money lender mentions 3% per month interest rate, it means 36% per year whereas a Bank might only give maximum interest rate of 12% per year for long term deposits.

12.5 BANKING PRODUCTS

Banks not only give a safe place to keep your money and valuable jewellary in lockers. However, they additionally offer accounts and products that permit you to pay your bills and, in the meantime, earn interest and help your money to grow and also offers the following types of Accounts and Deposits.

12.5.1 Types of Accounts and Deposit

Accounts: (See Figure 12.4)

a. Saving Accounts: It is meant for saving purposes. The benefit of having savings account is that Banks pay interest on the money present in the account.
Features:
- Flexibility in deposits and withdrawal of funds from the account.
- Passbook, Cheque Book, Automated Teller Machine (ATM), Debit Card are issued to customers.
- Interest is earned on the amount deposited.

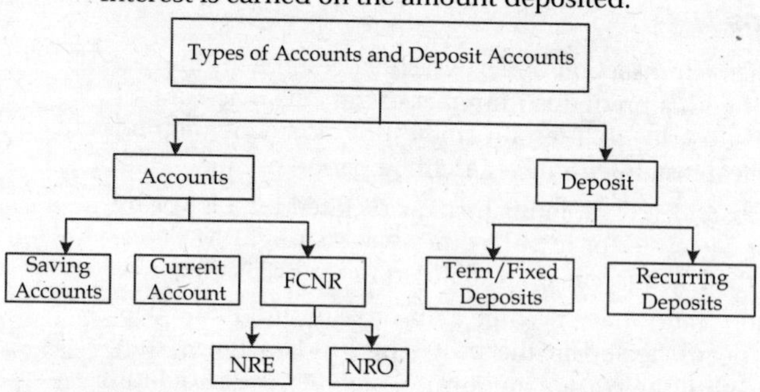

Figure 12.4 Types of Accounts and Deposits Accounts

b. Current Account: It is mainly used by business persons, firms, companies, public enterprises, etc.
Features:
- Current accounts are opened in the names of firm/company.
- No limits for number of transactions.
- No interest is paid by Banks on these accounts.

c. NRO/NRE/FCNR Accounts
   i. Foreign Currency Non-Resident Account (FCNR): Account is opened by the NRIs in designated currencies, such as US Dollar (USD), Great Britain Pound (GBP), Euro (EUR), Japanese Yen (JPY), Canadian Dollar (CAD) and Australian Dollar (AUD), etc.
   ii. Non-Resident Ordinary Accounts (NRO): Resident outside India can open this account. When a resident becomes a non-resident, his domestic rupee account gets converted to the NRO account, and he cannot take his money out of India.
   c. Non-Resident (External) Rupee Account NR(E)RA: It is a Rupee account, and the NRI (Non-Resident Indian) can remit money to India from the abroad and can also take money out of India.

Deposits (See Figure 12.4):

a. Term/Fixed deposits: In this a particular amount of money is deposited in a bank for a given period of time mainly from 7 days to 10 years.
Features:
- Term deposits are for fixed tenure from 7 days to 10 years.
- Banks pay higher interest rates on Term deposits.
- Interest can be withdrawn at monthly/quarterly intervals or cumulated.

b. Recurring deposits: It is used to save a certain amount of money regularly for a particular period and earn a higher interest rate on recurring deposits.
Features:
- Periodic deposit of money for a fixed period.
- Interest paid on Recurring deposit accounts is higher than saving A/c.
- Withdrawal is permitted on maturity or pre-mature closure of account.

c. Small Accounts
- 'Small Account' can be opened by submitting recent photograph and putting signature or thumb impression in the presence of the Bank official.
- Valid for 12 Months.
- Balance in accounts at any point of time should not exceed Rs.50,000/-

d. Basic Savings Bank Deposit Account
- There is no requirement of minimum balance.
- Facility of Debit card.
- Any individual above the age of 10 years can open Basic Savings Bank Deposit (BSBD) Account.

*Interest Rate may vary from bank to bank and time to time.

12.5.2 Types of Loan and Overdrafts

Banks provide loans for purchase of home, car household goods, business, education, etc. Loans are also provided for economic activities like agriculture, business, industry and service sector. Loans are not provided for unlawful activities like gambling. The rate of interest on bank loans is very low as compared to money lenders.

- Home Loan: This type of Loan is taken by people for a variety of home-related purposes, such as construction, renovation, extension of home or buying of property. Home loans comprise of an adjustable or fixed interest rate and payment terms.

- Personal Loan: This includes loan for paying debt, marriage expenses or vacation expenditure, and is given to individuals after accessing their credentials based on their profession or business.
- Education Loan: Provided to students who want to pursue higher education / vocational studies in India for Rs. 10 Lakhs or abroad for 20 Lakhs or more.

☞ Do you Know?
Students can also register on GOI Vidya Laxmi Portal for Educational Loan application and tracking.

- Business Loan: This type of loan is provided to either existing businesses or those getting into new business, on the basis of individual's credentials. For existing businesses, loan is provided in the following ways:
  - Term loans: Amount provided for a fixed tenure at the applicable interest rate, like 3 years for short term loan and 10-15 years for long term loans. You pay part of interest and part of loan in equal installments to bank every month.
  - Bank overdraft limits: Ability to withdraw more money than what is deposited.
  - Bill Discounting: Short-term borrowing used to improve a company's working capital and cash flow against bills/invoices raised by the company.
  - Letter of credit for international business: Bank guaranteeing a buyer's payment to a seller for a specified period against letter of credit.
  - Hypothecation: The established practice of a borrower pledging an asset as!collateral!for a loan, while bank retains the ownership of the assets till the amount is paid back.
- Vehicle Loan: This is provided to you for the purchase of old/new vehicle. The interest rates may vary from bank to bank and repayment process involves monthly EMIs (Equated Monthly Instalments) and early repayment options.
- Loan against PPF (Public Provident Fund) /insurance policy/bonds/shares/
Gold/Vehicle Loan are kept as a security by the bank to provide loan.
- Gold Loan: Gold loan is given on providing gold as security to a bank.

Overdrafts

It is a kind of Loan!arrangement!under which bank!extends the credit up to a maximum!amount!(overdraft limit) against a!current!account. Consider an example, suppose you have Current Account, and its balance is Rs.10,000/-, Suddenly you need Rs.15000/- but you may be allowed to overdraw from your account under some terms and conditions as agreed by you and the bank on the basis of your eligibility.

12.5.3 Filling up of Cheques, Demand Draft

How to Fill Cheques?

In order to fill a cheque, person needs to mention the date, name of the person/ company (Payee), amount to be paid in words and in Figures as shown in Figure 12.5.
To fill the cheque do the following:

- Put your sign above your name to approve the transaction.
- Do not sign on the MICR (Magnetic Ink Character Recognition) Band.
- Do not forget to put the date.
- Do not overwrite/mark cut on the cheque.
- Keep the records of your cheques, by notifying it on a front page. Figure 12.6 shows the overwrite/cutting on the Cheque.

How to fill Demand Draft (DD)?

Suppose you want to make a demand draft of Rs. 50,000/-. Bank will give you a form, you have to fill it, which contains the details like, amount or if you are giving a cheque you have to write cheque number on it, in whose favor the DD (Demand Draft) is to be made, your bank account number, the place (branch of bank) where your DD (Demand Draft) has to be issued and your signature, etc. Fill up the form, hand over the cash/cheque and the form to the designated bank employee. He will give you a receipt for it. Bank will take

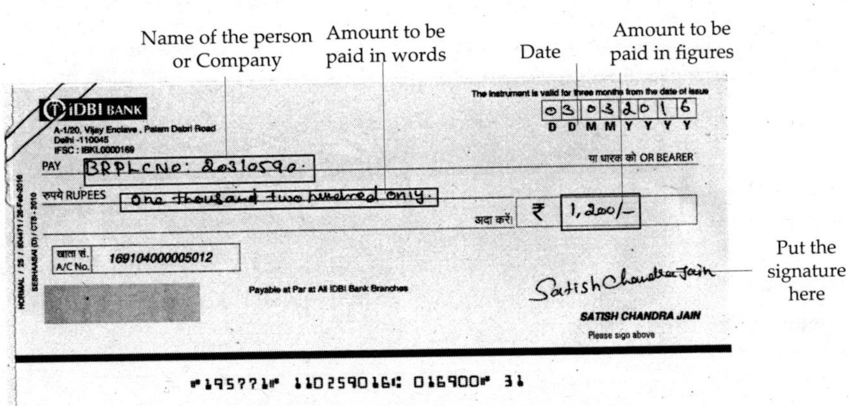

Figure 12.5 Cheque and its various fields

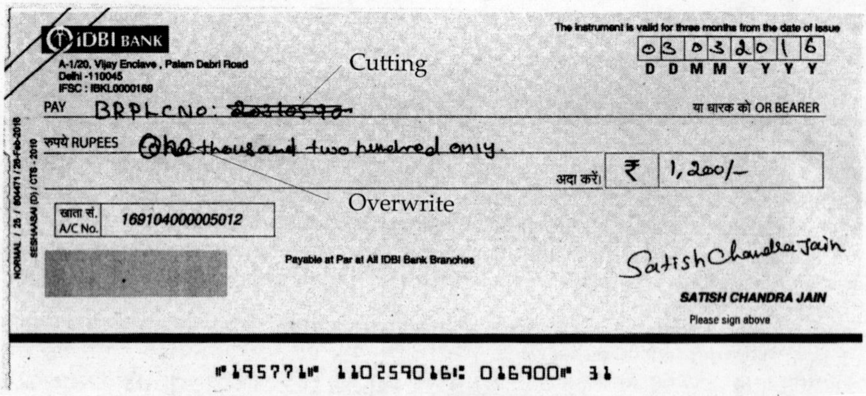

Figure 12.6 Overwrite/Cutting on the Cheque

some commission/charges to make the draft for you and will deduct that money from your account. Figure 12.7 shows a sample Demand Draft.

Figure 12.7 Sample Demand Draft

12.6 DOCUMENTS FOR OPENING ACCOUNTS

Presenting a copy of any one of the following documents can open a standard account:

- Idendity card or ID Card with person's picture issued by Central/State Ministry, Statutory/Regulatory Authorities, Public Sector Undertakings, Scheduled Commercial Banks, and Public Financial Institutions; Or
- A letter issued by a Gazetted officer, with a duly attested photograph of the person.

12.6.1 Know Your Customer (KYC)

It is a process by which banks acquire data about the identity and address of the clients. This procedure guarantees that banks' administrations are not abused. The KYC strategy is to be finished by the banks while opening accounts and also occasionally update the same from time to time.

☞ Fresh KYC Documents to be submitted on attaining majority, i.e. 18 years in case of minor accounts.

12.6.2 Photo ID Proof, Address Proof

Documents which are used for identity proof and are official valid are: (See Figure 12.8)

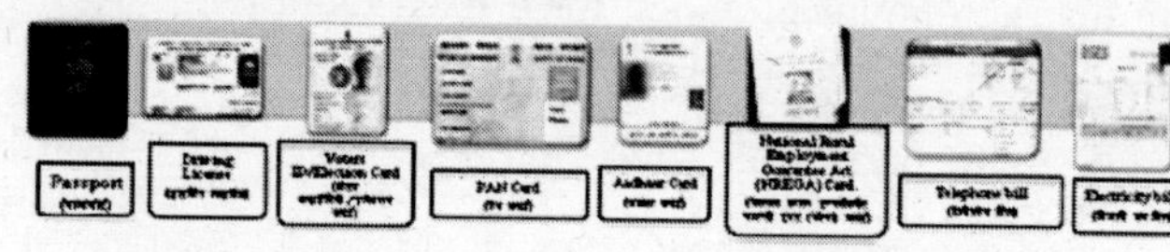

Figure 12.8 Eight Valid Documents for Identity Proof

- Passport
- Driving License
- Voter ID Card
- PAN Card
- Aadhar Card
- National Rural Employment Guarantee Card
- Electricity Bill
- Telephone Bill

You need to submit any one of these documents as proof of identity. If these documents also contain your address details, then it would be accepted as "proof of address". If the document submitted by you for evidence of identity does not include address details, then you will have to submit another officially valid document, which provides address details. These documents must contain the address details, then it would be also accepted as the proof of address.

12.6.3 Indian Currency

It is the official currency of the Republic of India, issued by Reserve Bank of India (RBI) and guaranteed by the Central government (See Figure 12.9).

Figure 12.9 Indian Currency and Symbol of Rupees

☞ Do you Know?
Two Rupees and above Note is signed by the Governer or RBI, while One Rupee Note is signed by the Finance Secretary, Ministry of Finance and the Coin is issued by the Government of India Mint.

12.7 BANKING SERVICE DELIVERY CHANNEL–I

In the Banking Sector, Delivery Channels are the channels and methods which are used for providing banking services directly to the customers. By using this, customers can perform banking transactions through ATM, contact the bank's call centre for any inquiry, access the digital Interactive Voice Response (IVR), perform transactions through Internet Banking, and on smartphones through mobile banking, etc. These channels have enabled banks to reach a wide consumer-base across geographies.

Delivery channels ensure the smooth flow of regular transactions and provide banks with higher profit with lower operational expenses and transaction cost.

12.7.1 Bank Branch, ATM

Bank branch: It is a retail location where a bank offers a wide range of face-to-face and automated services to its customers. A bank has its branches at various location across the city or state so that customer can go there and avail its services.

ATM: (Automatic Transaction Machine or Automatic Teller Machine) enables the customers of a bank to perform financial transactions (cash withdrawal/deposit) without going to the bank.

In this machine, customer is identified by inserting a debit/credit card, which is provided with a magnetic stripe or a plastic smart card having a!chip which contains information like some unique card number, expiration date (Card Verification Value - CVV). Customer need to insert a Personal Identification Number (PIN), for authentication purpose before using an ATM. Using an ATM, customers can withdraw cash, check balances and deposit money. One can use ATM service 24 hours per day throughout the year.

12.7.2 Bank Mitra with Micro-ATM

Bank Mitra: Bank Mitra are those individuals, who act as an agent of bank at those places where it is not possible to open a branch of bank. They provide all kind of assistance required in opening an account.

Micro-ATMs: Biometric authentication system enabled hand-held device. To make ATMs viable at rural/semi-urban centers, low cost Micro-ATMs are deployed at each Bank Mitra location, thus enables a person to instantly Deposit-Withdraw cash, Fund transfer and Balance enquiry. This devices work on a mobile phone connection.

12.7.3 Point of Sale

Point of sale is a stage at which a customer makes a payment to the merchant in exchange of goods or service. In this, the merchant prepares an!invoice!for the customer, calculate the amount owed by the customer and after that provide options to customer for making payment (either by Credit or Debit card).

12.8 BANKING SERVICE DELIVERY CHANNEL-II

In today's regulated and competitive market, banks need to stand with the customer expectations. Bank needs to offer a non-stop interactivity with customer, for building up loyalty with them. To achieve this, banks need to increase their business agility by anticipating customer needs and offer an engaging user experience. In this section we will learn about various banking services offered by bank.

12.8.1 Internet Banking

Internet banking is an electronic system which enables the customers to conduct transactions on bank's Website and perform activities, such as maintaining his account, transferring money, paying bills, etc. It is safe, secure but only thing required is that the customer must have the Internet connection, computer or mobile.

To access Internet banking:

- Open the bank secure website.
- Login to the Internet banking facility by using the Customer ID and other Password as shown in Figure 12.10.

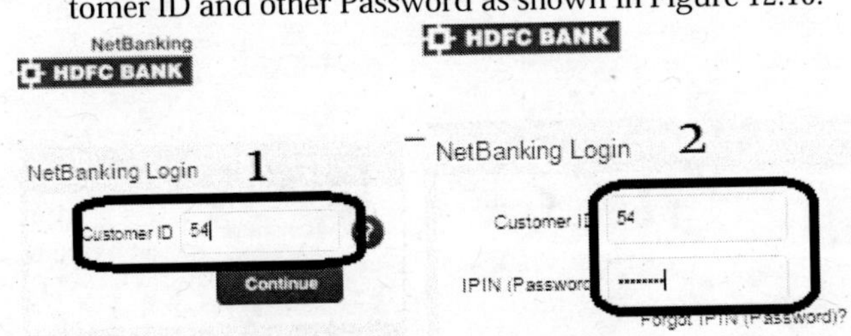

Figure 12.10 Login Form

After successful authentication you will enter the customer area of the online banking (see Figure 12.11).

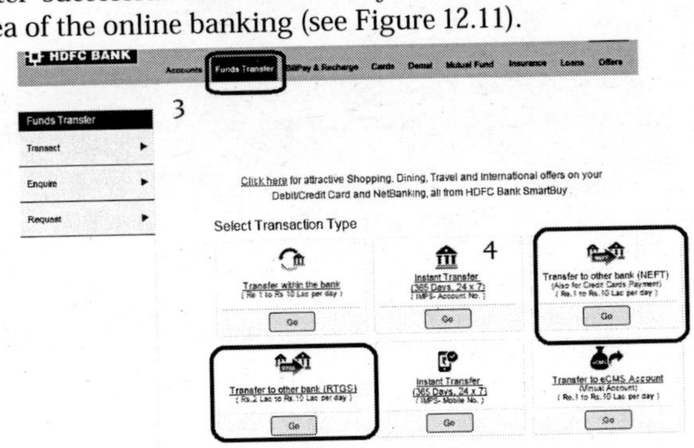

Figure 12.11 Customer Area

Features:

By using Internet banking, user can:

- View account balances, statement history, recent transactions and can transfer the fund!between the customer's linked accounts.
- Pay credit card bills.
- View the records of paid cheques, order and cheque books.
- Pay income tax, online tax remittance and other tax.

- Apply online for loan and top up for existing loan.
- Invest in mutual funds, buy insurance.
- Pay utility bills (Electricity, telephone, gas, mobile).
- Get the Demand Draft in favour of anybody.

Note: Donot/Don't give password to anybody else, under any circumstances.

12.8.2 National Electronic Fund Transfer (NEFT), Real Time Gross Settlement (RTGS)

National Electronic Funds Transfer, is the most prominent inter-bank electronic funds transfer systems of India, which provides a facility to bank customers to transfer the funds easily and securely on a one-to-one basis, which saves the time and is done via electronic messages. It is a "net" transfer facility, executed in hourly batches Figure 12.12 show the working of NEFT.

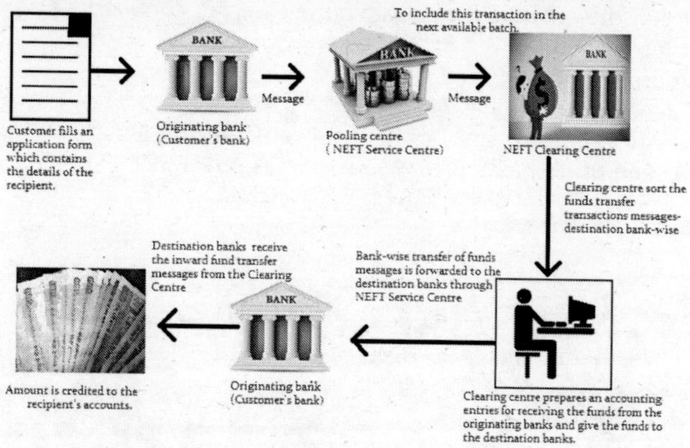

Figure 12.12 Process of NEFT

Real time gross settlement (RTGS), inter-bank transfer systems, which transfers money, from one bank to another on a "real time" and on "gross" basis. RTGS systems is used for high-value transactions which require an immediate clearing and is used to transfer of Rs.2 Lakhs and above.

How this works?

In this example consider customer as a person who transfers the money and the recipient as a person who will get the money.

1. Customer fills an application form, in which the details (name, bank, bank branch name, IFSC code, type of account, account number and the amount to be deposited) of the recipient is filled.
2. After filling all the details, the Customer authorizes his/her bank branch to debit his account and pay the specified amount to the recipient.
3. Next, the originating bank (Customer's bank) branch prepares a message for the pooling center, called as NEFT Service Centre.
4. NEFT Service Centre, then forwards the received message to the NEFT Clearing Centre, operated by National Clearing Cell, Reserve Bank of India, Mumbai, for including this transaction in the next available batch.
5. NEFT Clearing Centre, then sort the funds transfer transactions messages; destination bank-wise and prepares an accounting entries for receiving the funds from the originating banks (to debit the amount from customer's account) and give the funds to the destination banks (to credit the amount in Recipient's accounts).
6. After that, bank-wise transfer of funds message is forwarded to the destination banks (originating bank or Customer's bank) through NEFT Service Centre.
7. Finally, the destination banks (originating bank or Customer's bank) receive the inward fund transfer messages from the Clearing Center and then pass the credited amount to the recipient's accounts. See Figure 12.12 for its working.

Note: Once the payment is processed, it is final and is irrevocable.

Table 12.1 Difference between NEFT and RTGS

Factors	NEFT	RTGS
Full form	National Electronic Fund Transfer	Real Time Gross Settlement
Speed	Slow	Fast
Time to credit the amount	Transactions are completed in batches at specific times.	Transaction is completed on a one-to-one basis
Used for Minimum amount to be transfer*	Small money transfer Rs. 10,000/- to Rs. 2 lakh	Large money transfer above Rs. 2 lakh
Maximum amount to be transfer*	Rs. 2 lakh	No limit

12.9 INSURANCE

An agreement in which a person makes regular payments to a company and the company promises to pay money, up to the insured amount if the person is injured or dies, or to pay money equal to the value of something (such as a house or car) if it is damaged, lost, or stolen.

12.9.1 Necessity of Insurance

As insurance protects the interest of people or party from loss and the Insurer buys for the loses of insured.

Insurance is necessary as it:

- Provide financial safety and security to family members in case of untimely death.
- Provides medical support for managing risk in health by providing money in case of medical emergency.

12.9.2 Life Insurance and Non- Life Insurance

Life Insurance

Life insurance is a kind of contract among an insurance policy holder and an insurer, where the insurer promises to pay a sum of money in exchange for a premium, upon the death of an insured person. (See Figure 12.13)

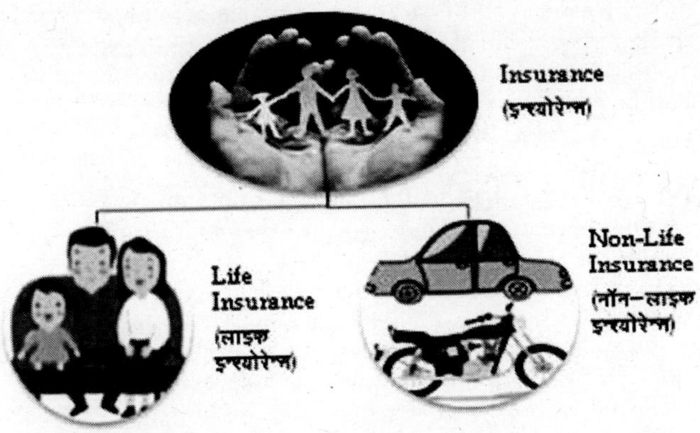

Figure 12.13 Types of Insurance

In this, a policy holder pays a premium, either on a regular basis or as one lump sum amount.

According to Bunion "A contract of life insurance is that in which one party agrees to pay a given sum on the happening of a particular event contingent upon the duration of human life, in consideration of the immediate payment of a smaller sum or certain equivalent periodical payments by another."

Goal of life insurance is to provide financial security. The main risks that are covered by life insurance are:

1. Premature death
2. Income during retirement
3. Illness

Non-Life Insurance

It is basically an insurance policy that protects you against losses and damages other than those covered by life insurance. For more comprehensive coverage, it is vital for you to know about the risks covered to ensure that you and your family are protected from unforeseen losses.

The coverage period for most general insurance policies and plans is usually one year, whereby premiums are normally paid on a one-time basis.

The risks that are covered by general insurance are:

1. Property loss, for example, stolen car or burnt house
2. Liability arising from damage caused by yourself to a third party
3. Accidental death or injury

12.10 VARIOUS SCHEMES

The ministry of the Government of India have come up with numerous schemes from time to time with an aim to support its poor citizens. These schemes can be Central specific, state specific or may be joint collaboration among the Centre and the state. Some scheme has been detailed in this section.

12.10.1 Pradhan Mantri Jan-Dhan Yojana

Pradhan Mantri Jan Dhan Yojana (PMJDY) is a nationwide scheme launched by Hon'ble Prime Minister on August 28, 2014. In this scheme financial inclusion of every individual who does not have a bank account is to be achieved in rural and urban areas.

The scheme will ensure financial access to everyone who was not able to get benefits of many other finance related government schemes.

These financial services include Banking/ Savings & Deposit Accounts, Remittance, Credit, Insurance, Pension which will be made available to all the citizens in easy and affordable mode.

1. Under the Jan Dhan Yojna anyone who is an Indian citizen and above the age of 10 years and does not have a bank account, can open the account with zero balance.
2. Account can be opened in any bank branch or Business Correspondent (Bank Mitra) outlet, specially designed for the purpose of opening the accounts under this scheme.
3. The scheme also provides facility of accidental insurance cover up to rupees one lac without any charge for the account holder.
4. The account holders under the jan dhan yojana will be given a RuPay debit card which can be used at all ATMs for cash withdrawal and at most of the retail outlets for making transaction for purchases.

Special Benefits under PMJDY Scheme

- Interest on deposit
- Ru-Pay debit card provides in-built Accidental insurance cover of Rs. 1 lakh.
- No minimum balance required.
- Overdraft facility up to Rs. 5000/-
- Life insurance cover of Rs. 30,000/-
- Easy transfer of money across India.
- Access to pension, insurance products.

12.10.2 Social Security Schemes

According to the Article 22 given in Universal Declaration of Human Rights, social security states: "Everyone, as a member of society, has the right to social security and is entitled to realization, through national effort and international co-operation and in accordance with the organization and resources of each State, of the!economic, social and cultural rights!indispensable for his!dignity!and the free development of his personality."

In simple terms, it means that a society in which a person lives should help him or her to develop, make the most of all the features provided to them which may be of culture, work, social welfare.

Social security refers to the following terms:

- Social insurance, in this people receive benefits in recognition of their contributions to an insurance program. These plans include retirement pensions, disability insurance etc.
- Services, which are provided by government for social security provision. It includes facilities such as medical care, financial support during unemployment.
- Basic security, which is an insurance programs where eligibility may otherwise be an issue.

Some of the social security schemes have been discussed in the following sections.

Pradhan Mantra Suraksha Bima Yojna (PMSBY)

This scheme has been started by the government because poor people were not given insurance by the companies and they are not covered or death and disability.

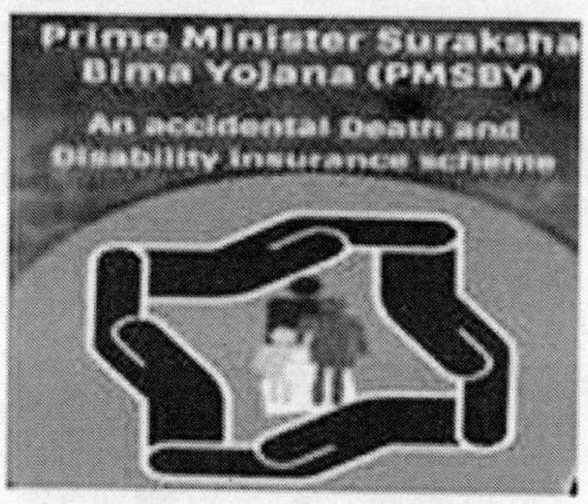

Pradhan Mantri Suraksha Bima Yojana is available to people between 18 and 70 years of age with bank accounts. It has an annual premium of Rs.12 excluding service tax, which is about 14% of the premium. The amount will be automatically debited from the account. In case of accidental death or full disability, the payment given to the nominee will be Rs.2 lakhs and in case of partial disability, payment of Rs.1 lakh, will be given. This scheme will be linked to the bank accounts opened under the Pradhan Mantri Jan Dhan Yojana scheme. Most of these account had zero balance initially. The scheme is valid for a year and it can be renewed every year.

Eligibility: Any person of the age group 18 to 70, with a savings bank account and with an Aadhaar Card can join this scheme.

To avail this service:

- Person will have to fill a simple form, mentioning the name of the nominee and Aadhaar Card number, and submit this form each year before 1st June to continue the scheme.
- By doing this, the account can be easily activated.
- Entire premium due will get auto-debited from the bank account.

Who will implement the PMSBY: All the government-sponsored insurance companies will offer this scheme. Other insurance companies have to sign-up with banks to offer this service.

Pradhan Mantri Jeevan Jyoti Bima Yojna (PMJJBY)

Pradhan Mantri Jeevan Jyoti Bima Yojana is available to people between 18 and 50 years of age with bank accounts. It has an annual premium of Rs.330/- excluding service tax, which is above 14% of the premium. The amount will be automatically debited from the account. In case of death due to any cause, the payment to the nominee will be Rs.2 lakhs.

This scheme will be linked to the bank accounts opened under the Pradhan Mantri Jan Dhan Yojana scheme. Most of these account had zero balance initially.

Eligibility: This scheme is available to the people of age group between 18 and 50 years and has a bank accounts from which the amount will get automatically debited.

Premium: Rs.330/- per annum per member, which will be deducted from the account holder's savings bank automatically.

Atal Pension Yojna (APY)

Atal Pension Yojana!is a government-backed pension scheme launched in India to target the unorganised sector. This scheme was formally launched by Prime Minister Narendra Modi.

In this scheme, for every contribution made to the pension fund, The Central Government would also co-contribute 50% of the total contribution, whichever is lower, to each eligible subscriber account, for a period of 5 years.

The minimum and maximum age to join this scheme is 18 years to 40 years, respectively.

Aadhaar is the primary, necessary document required for the identification. The subscribers are required to opt for a monthly pension from Rs. 1000/- to Rs. 5000/- and they have to pay a stipulated monthly contribution regularly, which is deducted automatically from the bank account.

Pradhan Mantri Mudra Yojna (PMMY)

Micro Units Development and Refinance Agency Ltd. (MUDRA), a new institution which is set up by Government of India for providing funds to the non-corporate, non-farm sector, shopkeepers, fruits/ vegetable vendors, truck operators, food-service units, repair shops, machine operators, below Rs.10 Lakh.

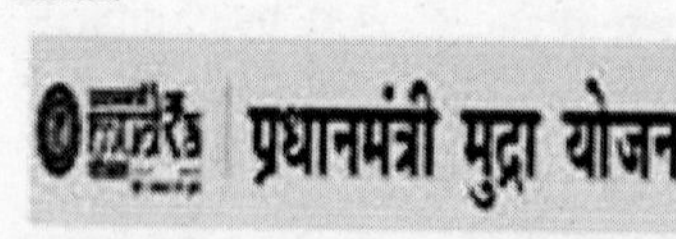

In this scheme, MUDRA has created three products as a stage of growth, which covers a loan amounts:

- Shishu: Covering loans up to Rs. 50,000/-
- Kishore: Covering loans above Rs. 50,000/- and up to Rs. 5 Lakhs.
- Tarun: Covering loans above Rs. 5,00,000/- and up to Rs 10 Lakh.

Bank branches gives loans facility under Mudra scheme as per customer requirements and the loans given under this scheme are collateral free loans.

Mudra Loans could be either availed for Vehicle loan (two wheelers, four wheeler), Business Instalment Loan (for working capital requirement) and Business Loans Group Loans (working capital loan).

12.10.3 National Pension Scheme (NPS)

It is a defined-contribution pension system, which is operated by Government of India. This scheme offers a range of investment options to employees which enables them to make their own decisions regarding where to invest their pension fund, to permit the withdrawal amount prior to retirement and reduces the total pension liabilities of the Government of India.
This scheme consists of two tiers

- In tier 1: Basic retirement pension account is available to all citizens and person cannot withdrawal its funds before retirement.
- In tier-2: Prospective payment system (PPS) account is there, which permits some withdrawal of pension amount prior to retirement.

The pension scheme is administered by the Pension Fund Regulatory and Development Authority (PFRDA), on the behalf of government.
Eligibility: All the citizens of India between the ages of 18 and 60 can avail this scheme.

12.10.4 Public Provident Fund (PPF) Scheme

It is a savings-cum-tax-saving instrument, which mobilizes small savings by offering an investment with reasonable returns and provides income tax benefits. It is established by centre government.

Individuals who are residents of India are eligible to open their account under the Public Provident Fund. Person need to deposit a minimum of Rs 500/- for opening and maintain the account and can deposit maximum amount to Rs 1.5 lakh. The current interest rate for PPF is 8.1 per annum. Original duration is of 15 years, which can be extended for 5 years.
Pension: A plan for setting aside money to be spent after retirement On the maturity of PPF, person can:

- Either Completely withdraw all the money.
- Extend the PPF account with no contribution (does not pay any money) for 15 years.
- Extend the PPF account with contribution, in which person can put money in PPF account after extension.

12.11 BANK ON YOUR MOBILE

Bank on mobile means you can access bank from anywhere, anytime from your mobile and it has become simple to see your account, transfer funds, pay bills. It provides a convenient way to get connected with the bank.

12.11.1 Mobile Banking

It is a service provided by a bank, due to which customers can conduct transactions remotely by using a mobile device. By using this, you can access your account on your mobile. (See figure 12.14)

Figure 12.14 Mobile Banking

12.11.2 Mobile Wallet

It is a payment services which are operated under financial regulation and performed via a!mobile device. Consumer can pay for a wide range of services and digital or hard goods. It can be considered as a digital versions of traditional wallets, which holds digital information about credit and debit cards for making payments, store coupons and loyalty programs.

Working of Mobile Wallet

A customer can utilize all its stored information by opening an app on their phone, entering a PIN, password and then selecting the information they need to access. The app then does the transactions required and utilizes information transfer technology such as Near-Field Communications!(NFC) to interact with a mobile wallet ready payment terminals.

	Check List for Students	Tick the Appropriate	
1.	Have you ever visited a Bank Branch/Bank Mitra?	YES	NO
2.	Do you have a Bank Account?	YES	NO
3.	Have you ever used an ATM?	YES	NO
4.	Do you have a Debit Card?	YES	NO
5.	Have you received PIN?	YES	NO
6.	Do you have a Life Insurance?	YES	NO
7.	Do you have a insurance for your vehicle?	YES	NO
8.	Have you ever taken any loan?	YES	NO

MODEL QUESTIONS AND ANSWERS

A. Multiple Choice

1.1 We should keep our savings with banks because

a. It is safe
b. Earns interest
c. Can be withdrawn anytime

d. All of above

1.2 ATM password to be shared only with
a. Spouse b. Obedient son
c. Obedient daughter d. None of above

1.3 KYC means
a. Know your customer
b. Know your character
c. Both (a) and (b)
d. None of above

1.4 Loans from money lenders involves:
a. High rate of interest
b. No proper accounting
c. No transparency
d. All of above

1.5 Life insurance means
a. Insurance of human
b. Insurance of life of Cattle
c. Insurance of Machines
d. Insurance of house

1.6 Non-life Insurance relates to insurance against
a. Fire b. Theft
c. Burglary d. All of above

1.7 Bank provides loans for
a. Home b. Car
c. Education d. All of above

1.8 Two Rupee note is signed by:
a. Finance Secretary b. Governor of RBI
c. Government of India Mint d. Ministry of Finance

1.9 The safest place for keeping money
a. A pit dug in the ground b. An iron box
c. Bank d. Money lender

1.10 Gold and silver ornaments should be kept in bank lockers as:
a. It is safe b. No risk of theft
c. Both (a) & (b) d. None of above

1.11 POS is:
a. Point of Sale b. Position of Sale
c. Point of Saling d. Position of Saling

1.12 Banks pays interest on
a. Deposits b. Loans
c. Withdrawal d. Transaction

1.13 Bank charges interest on
a. Deposits b. Loans
c. Withdrawal d. Transaction

1.14 Internet banking refers to
a. Operation of account through internet
b. Opening of account through ATM
c. Opening bank through Internet
d. All of the above

1.15 In Recurring Deposits,
a. A fixed sum is deposited every month
b. Period of deposit is a fixed tenure
c. Interest is paid at FDR rate
d. No interest is paid

1.16 ATM can be used for
a. Cash withdrawal b. Account enquiry
c. Statement of account d. All of above

1.17 What is RuPay Debit Card?
a. Domestic debit card
b. Introduced by National Payments Corporation of India
c. Accepted at all ATMs & PoS machines
d. All of above

1.18 Aadhaar is
a. 12 digit number card
b. Identity proof issued by UIDAI
c. A saving account
d. Both (a) and (b)

1.19 PAN means
a. A kind of utensil b. Primary Account Number
c. Permanent Account Number d. Position Account Number

1.20 Currency notes are issued by
a. RBI b. NABARD
c. Public sector banks d. Central Government

1.21 Coins are issued by
a. Government of India b. NABARD
c. Public sector banks d. State Bank of India

1.22 Education Loans
a. Cover tuition fee & expenses
b. Are repayable after completion of course
c. Granted for studies in India & abroad
d. All of above

1.23 Who can open bank account
a. Indian citizen b. Non Resident Indian
c. Illiterate d. All of above

1.24 What is meant by Aadhaar seeding?
a. Linking of Aadhaar with Bank account
b. Issue of Aadhaar card
c. Transfer of Aadhaar
d. 12- digit number card

1.25 What are the benefits attached to PMJDY?
a. Accident insurance cover of Rs.1 lac
b. Life insurance cover of Rs.30,000/-
c. Overdraft facility up to Rs.5,000/-
d. All of above

1.26 Who can open an account under PMJDY?
a. Minor above the age of 10 years
b. Only lady of the house
c. Only head of the family
d. All of above

1.27 Who is Bank Mitra?
a. Banking Correspondents engaged by Banks
b. Valuable customer of Bank
c. Security guard in a branch

d. Bank accountant

1.28 What is Atal Pension Yojana (APY)?
a. Provides social security to the unorganized sector
b. Encourages workers to voluntarily save for their retirement
c. Fixed pension is paid on attaining age of 60 years
d. Provide social security to organized sector

1.29 What is Pradhan Mantri Suraksha Bima Yojana (PMSBY)?
a. Accidental insurance cover
b. Life insurance cover
c. Overdraft up to Rs.5,000/-
d. Overdraft of Rs. 5000/-

1.30 What is Pradhan Mantri Jivan Jyoti Bima Yojana (PMJJBY)?
a. Covers life insurance up to Rs.2 lac
b. Accident insurance cover
c. Life Insurance up to 1 lac
d. Accidental Insurance up to l lac

1.31 Which type of deposits earns higher interest rate?
a. Current account b. Savings Account
c. Fixed Deposits d. Recurring deposit

1.32 Under PMSBY, accidental death claim is available for:
a. Rs.1 lac b. Rs.2 lac
c. Rs.3 lac d. Rs.4 lac

1.33 Can illiterate person be issued Debit card?
a. No
b. Yes
c. Only with joint account
d. Only for head of family

1.34 NEFT stands for
a. National Electric Fund Transfer
b. National Electronic Fund Transfer
c. National Electrical Fund Transfer
d. National Electronic Fund Transferring

1.35 RTFG stands for
a. Real Time Gross Settlement
b. Ready Time Gross Settlement
c. Ready Time Grocery Settlement
d. Real Time Grocery Settle

B. State whether the following are True or False

2.1 Digital financial services, does not expands the delivery of basic financial services to the people through new technologies like Internet.

2.2 Saving must be at the top of priority for everyone.

2.3 It is unsafe to keep cash at home.

2.4 Banks acts as a medium for the transfer of money.

2.5 Saving account is an account, which share a wealth of privileges and tailor-made solutions with your family.

2.6 Bank Mitra are branch of bank, who act as an agent to transfer the money.

2.7 Internet banking is used to pay utility bills.

2.8 Pradhan Mantri Suraksha Bima Yojna (PMSBY),is an accidental death and a disability insurance scheme.

2.9 MUDRA is Micro Units Development and Refinance Agency Ltd.

2.10 Kishore covers a loans above Rs 50,00 and up to Rs 5 Lakh.

Answers

A.	1.	d	2.	d	3.	a	4.	d	5.	a
	6.	d	7.	d	8.	b	9.	c	10.	c
	11.	a	12.	a	13.	b	14.	d	15.	c
	16.	d	17.	d	18.	d	19.	c	20.	a
	21.	a	22.	d	23.	d	24.	a	25.	d
	26.	d	27.	a	28.	d	29.	a	30.	a
	31.	c	32.	b	33.	b	34.	b	35.	a
B.	1.	F	2.	T	3.	T	4.	F	5.	F
	6.	F	7.	T	8.	T	9.	T	10.	F

CHAPTER 13

Electronic Mail - A Detailed View

13.1 BASICS OF E-Mail

E-mail is a method of sending messages, voice, video and graphics over digital communication link, such as the Internet any where in the world at very cost-effective rate. Technically, e-mail is a type of client/server application that provides a routed, stored message service between any two e-mail accounts. Because all modern computers can be connected to the Internet, users can send e-mail over the Internet to any location that has telephone or wireless digital service.

☞ The backbone of an electronic mail system is a communication network that connects remote terminals to a central system or a local area network that interconnects personal computers. Users can send mail to a single recipient or they can broadcast it to any number of selected users on the system.

13.1.1 What is an Electronic Mail (E-mail)

E-mail is the electronic equivalent of sending a letter through the mail. The primary component of the electronic mail system is a "post office," an area on the shared hard disk that is reserved for mail. This post office serves as the central message holder and has both "in" and "out" baskets for each user (See Figure 13.1). To send a message, a link is established between the sender's "out" basket and the addressee's "in" basket.

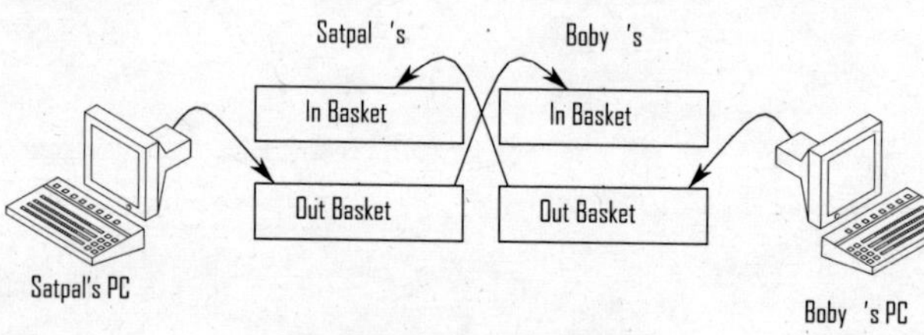

Figure 13.1 Sending mail

The method for receiving mail depends on the sophistication of the system. When multitasking personal computers and workstations are used, mail can be delivered to users while they are working on something else. Otherwise, users have to interrogate their mailboxes (diskspace) in a central system, or file server.

☞ Electronic mail programs often come with local area network software or as add-on options. Or, they may be independent programs designed to work with a particular network environment.

How does E-Mail Work?

The person you communicate with could be any other user on the Internet, some one using the same computer system as you, or someone on a computer system thousands of miles away. The e-mail is transmitted between computer system, which exchange messages or pass them onto other sites according to certain Internet protocols or rules for exchanging e-mail. You do not need to be concerned with many of the details, that is the computer's job. But you should know a little bit about the way e-mail works. Sending e-mail is similar to sending something by a postal service.

Steps for sending a mail through posted service are:

- Write the letter or make up the package.
- Put an address on it.
- Put on the proper postage or pay the charge to send it.
- Drop it in the post box so it can be sent on its way and eventually delivered.

You do not have to worry about the methods that are used to deliver it or what route it takes. You prepare what you want to send, address it, and hand it to the postal office.

The steps for sending an e-mail are:

1. Start an e-mail program.
2. Give the address of where to send the e-mail.
3. Compose a message using that e-mail program.
4. Give a command to send the message.

You have probably noticed that we have left out the part about adding postage and paying charges. Individual users do not pay a per message fee for e-mail in many organizations, such as schools, companies – that have Internet access.

You use an e-mail program to address, compose, and send the message. E-mail programs are called mail user agents, because they act on the user's behalf. User agent lets you prepare and send messages and also work with the mail you have received. E-mail program acts as a go-between with you and computer systems, and the computer systems handle the details of delivering and receiving mail. Once again, you do not have anything to do with how mail is delivered.

Messages are sent from one site to another on the Internet in this way. When you compose your message it is all in one piece, but when it is sent out to the Interent, it is divided into several pieces called packets. The number of packets depends on the size of the message. Each of the packets contains, among other things:

- The e-mail address of the person who sent the mail, the sender.
- The e-mail address of the person to receive the mail, the recipient.

- Between 1 and 1500 characters of the message.

The packets are sent to the destination, passing through several Internet sites. Thousands of networks and millions of computers make up the Internet, and packets are passed from system to system. Each site accepts the packets addressed to it, but passes on the messages destined for another address. The packets can travel or arrive at their destination in any order and they do not all have to take the same path. When you communicate with a remote site, you may think you have direct connection, but that is usually not the case. At the destination the packets are collected and put in order, so the e-mail appears to be in the same form it was sent. If there are errors in the packets or if some are lost, the destination sends a request back to the source, asking for the message to be resent. All of this takes place according to Simple Mail Transfer Protocol (SMTP) the protocol the Internet uses to transport message between computer systems. SMTP uses Transmission Control Protocol (TCP) which provides a reliable means of communication.

When you read your e-mail, once again you use a program (a mail user agent) that helps you work with the messages you have been waiting for you. On many systems you are told if you have e-mail when you log in, access the system you use to contact the Internet, or start your system. The e-mail message can arrive at any time. They are added to a file that is part of a directory that holds all the e-mail for the system. The packets making up an e-mail message arrive at the system, they are assembled, and then added to the file for each user. That file is often called a system mailbox. It holds all the messages on the system addressed to you and only you can read your mail. If for some reason your mailbox gets scrambled, corrupted, or is changed so you can not read your mail, allocated for the directory that holds e-mail. Usually there is enough space to hold a lot of messages, but it is important that you delete old e-mail messages and messages you have read so there is space to hold everybody's e-mail.

Advantages and Disadvantages of E-Mail

Advantages

E-mail has a number of advantages over some other forms of communication. It is quick, convenient, and non-intrusive.

- Easy to Use: You can communicate quickly with anyone on the Internet. E-mail usually reaches its destination in a matter
  of minutes or seconds. An e-mail service helps manage our contacts, allows us to send mails quickly, helps maintain our mailing history and provides sufficient storage space. An email can be sent from any terminal (computer) in the world with Internet access.
- Environment Friendly: Mails sent by postal service make use of paper. Thus, electronic mail prevents a large number of trees from getting axed. Using the electronic mailing service also saves the fuel that is consumed in the process of transporting letters.
- Speed: An e-mail can be delivered instantly and almost anywhere across the globe. No other mailing service matches the e-mail in terms of speed. You can send a message/mail simultaneously to multiple users; thus, e-mail service saves a lot of time.
- Informal and Conversational: Generally, the language used in emails is simple. It makes the process of communication informal. The process of sending and receiving emails does not require much time. Therefore, it can be used as a tool for conversing, just like chatting.
- Data Storage: The e-mail service providers with enough space for storage of data. Also, the process of sorting and arranging mails, as per the subject or other criteria (date, sender, etc.), is made easier for users.
- Provision of Attachments: The feature of attachment allows users to send huge chunks of data in a single mail.
- Easier for Reference: When a person has to reply to an email, he/she can use the provision of attaching previously sent/received mails. Such mails can be used for the purpose of reference in the communication process. It helps the recipient understand what he/she is reading.
- Reliable and Secure: Constant efforts are taken to improve the security needed for using an electronic mailing service. Today, electronic mailing service is considered as one of the most secure ways of communicating online.
- Use of Graphics: Users can send colorful greeting cards and interesting pictures through emails. This provision adds great value to the email service.
- Advantages of Technological Development: Development in computer technology has enabled users to send emails not only from their desktop computers, but also smartphones and other such devices. Thus, a user can send and receive emails even while he/she is travelling.

Disadvantages

The email service, although has many benefits to offer, it also has certain limitations. Disadvantages of the email service are listed below.

- Spam: Emails when used to send unsolicited messages and unwanted advertisements create nuisance and are termed as spam. The activity of checking and deleting unwanted mails may consume a lot of user's time. Therefore, it has become necessary to block or filter unwanted emails through spam filters. Email spoofing is another practice which is commonly used for spamming. The act of spoofing involves deceiving a recipient by altering email headers or addresses from which a mail is sent.
- Hacking: The act of breaking into computer security is termed as hacking. In this form of security breach, e-mails are intercepted by hackers.
- Not Suited for Business: Many a time, business documents go unnoticed amidst large number of mails which get accumulated in the inbox. Thus, urgent transactions and especially those which require signatures cannot be easily managed through emails.

- Viruses: Viruses are computer programs which have the potential to harm computer systems. Viruses are known to copy themselves and further infect the computer system.

  Recipients are required to scan their mails because, viruses can be transmitted through them.
- Crowded Inbox: The email inbox tends to get crowded with mails after a certain period of time. Thus, it becomes difficult for users to manage huge chunks of emails.
- Misinterpretation: One has to be careful while posting content through an email. If typed in a hurry, the matter can be misinterpreted by readers.
- Checking the Inbox Regularly: In order to stay updated, one has to check his/her email account regularly. If a person, due to his/her busy daily routine, does not check the inbox, he/she can miss out on some of the important and urgent messages.

Every new technology which enters the social world has its share of advantages and limitations. Different people interpret and utilize technology in different ways. In order to make the most of the available technology, users should try to understand both, the positive and negative aspects of the tools they use.

Structure of E-Mail Message

An e-mail message is made up of binary data, usually in the American Standard Code for Information Interchange (ASCII) text format. ASCII is a standard that enables any computer, regardless of its system or hardware, to read the text. ASCII code describes the characters you see on your computer screen.

Figure 13.2 shows the similarity of an e-mail message with the postal mail message. In the To line, you type in the e-mail address of the person to whom you are sending a message. The address must be typed according to a set of very strict rules. If you type a single letter or the syntax is wrong, your message will not get to the intended recipient. Your e-mail address will appear on the From line. Using this address, the recipient of your message will be able to respond to you.

On the subject line, you may type in the subject of your message or a very brief summary. At the bottom of the message is a "signature" area that can contain personalized information about you. Some mail programs will automatically append this signature to the bottom of every message you send. Signature areas are not required and are used at the discretion of the person who creates the e-mail message. Signature portion should not exceed five lines.

There are five sections of an e-mail message:

- E-mail address
- Header
- Body
- Signature (optional)
- Attachment(s) (optional)

Figure 13.2 shows the major sections of an e-mail message. Note that signatures and attachments are optional. Many messages do not show them, and some e-mail applications do not support them.

<table>
<tr><td>Mr. Ram Singh
18, Gandhi Lane
Ramesh Nagar,
New Delhi - 110051</td><td>To: bpb@vsnl.com</td></tr>
<tr><td></td><td></td></tr>
<tr><td>United Diamonds
180, Main Street,
Connaught Place
New Delhi - 110051

June 2, 2016

Subject:Interview for Programmers

Dear Mr. Singh
You will be pleased to know that the company has selected you for the post of Senior programmer. Please send your confirmation of the acceptance of our offer.

Yours Truly
(S. Jain)
M.D.</td><td>From: "Sales@bpbonline.com

Subject: Interview for Programmers

Date: Thu, 2 Jun 2016 11.47:10+0530

Dear Mr.Singh,
You will be pleased to know that the company has selected you for the post of Senior programmer. Please send your confirmation of the acceptance of our offer.

Yours Truly
(S. Jain)
M.D.</td></tr>
<tr><td>(a)</td><td>(b)</td></tr>
</table>

Figure 13.2 (a) Postal mail format (b) e-mail format

13.1.2 E-Mail Addressing

An e-mail address is composed of two separate parts.

- The domain name of the mail server computer on which you have an e-mail account.
- Your personal identity or account name (user name) on that mail server.

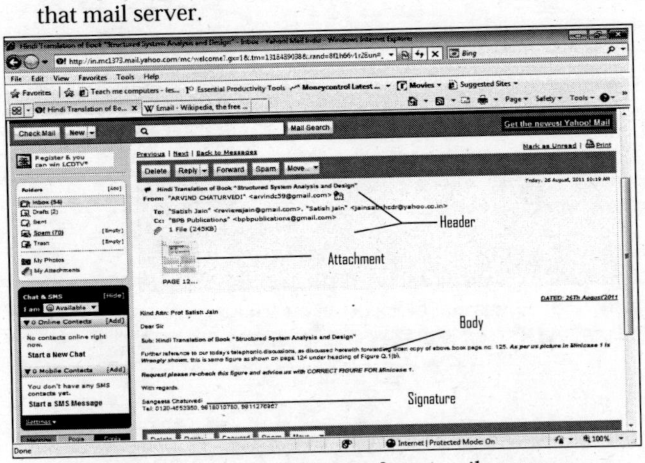

Figure 13.3 Major sections of an e-mail message

For example, 100 people have e-mail accounts with the same Internet Service Provider (ISP) or organizations. All 100 users will share the same domain name (say **`hotmail.com`**), but each person will possess a unique user name, such as "rakesh" or "aparna." The user name and domain name are separated by an @ ("at") symbol. Together, they form a complete e-mail address.

The components of a typical e-mail address are shown in Figure 13.4. Users with multiple e-mail accounts – perhaps with different ISPs or organizations – will have a different e-mail address for each account.

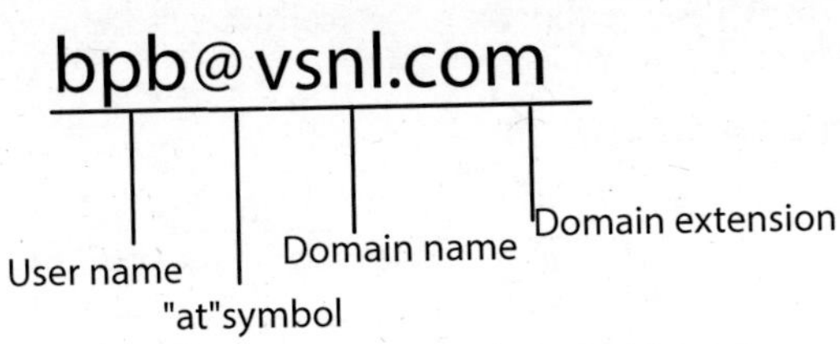

Figure 13.4 Syntax for E-mail address

Header

The header of e-mail message is the upper-most section. It displays information regarding the status of the messages. A header records message information and provides it to the recipient(s) of the message. Headers are present in both outgoing (sent) and incoming (received) messages.

The principal header fields related to message transported are listed in Table 13.1. These are mandatory to be used by all the people using e-mail facilities on the Internet.

Table 13.1 Header Fields in an E-mail

Name	Function
To:	E-mail address/addresses of primary recipient (s).
Cc:	E-mail address/addresses of secondary recipient (s) to whom copy needs to be sent.
Bcc:	E-mail address/addresses of secondary recipient (s) to whom copy needs to be sent but the primary recipient should not know about the dispatch of mail to these addressees.
From:	The originator or the creater of the e-mail.
Sender:	E-mail address of the actual sender.
Received:	Line added by each transfer agent along the route containing the agent's identity, the date and time the message was received.
Return Path:	May be used to identify the path back of the sender.

☞ Note that there are no spaces in the above address; e-mail software and server computers will not accept spaces in an address. Messages will not reach their destination if spaces are included.

In addition to the header fields given in Table 13.2, there are additional headers which are not mandatory but may be used if required.

Table 13.2 Additional Header Fields in a E-mail

Name	Function
Date:	Date and time the message was sent.
Reply-to:	E-mail address to which replies should be sent.
In-Reply-to:	Message-identification number of the message to which this is a reply.
Message-ID:	A unique number identifying the message and may be used to refer to the message.
References:	Other relevant message identification numbers.
Keywords:	Keywords selected by the user.
Subject:	A summary of the message for the one-line display.

The header shows information, such as:

- Time and date of a message,
- Subject of a message (as typed by the sender),
- Whether carbon copies were sent,
- Whether files are attached to the message, and
- The e-mail address of the sender.

Body

The body of e-mail message is the primary focus because it contains the actual message. Although there is no limit to the size (number of characters) of an e-mail message, but many ISPs do limit the size of an e-mail message.

Attachments

E-mail has become all the more attractive to businesses because now it allows users to attach a file to any e-mail message. Any file format – such as word processing documents, spreadsheets, images, or video files – can be attached to an e-mail message. E-mail allows complex data as attachments but not in the body.

☞ E-mail messages cannot contain viruses, but they can still be sent through attachments. Therefore, you should scan all e-mail attachments with a virus detection and eradication software program, such as McAfee VirusScan or Norton Anti Virus before opening, or forwarding them.

Most e-mail applications alert you if an incoming message contains an attachment. Such e-mail applications show an icon within the body of the messages to represent an attached file. The icon indicates the type of file that is attached and allows the recipient to double-click the icon to automatically launch the attachment on their computer.

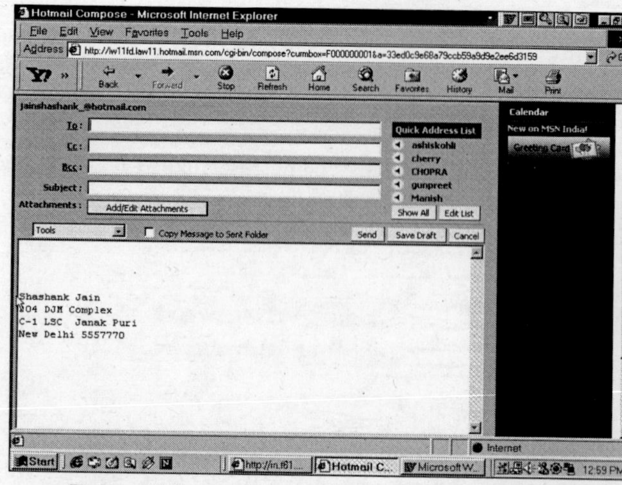

Figure 13.5 Signature block on an e-mail message

Signature

The signature for an e-mail message is the personal information which automatically appears at the bottom of the outgoing message. Use of a signature is optional. You can provide any signature information you wish.

☞ The purpose of a signature (also called a signature block, signature file) is to provide a message recipient with personal contact information.

Information in a signature block may include the following:

- Full name
- Job title/position
- Organization name and division
- Phone and fax numbers
- Physical (snail mail) address
- E-mail address
- Web site address Uniform Resource Locator (URL)

☞ A signature allows information in this part to be included with each outgoing message in an automated and time-saving manner for the message sender.

Under Blind Carbon Copy (Bcc) option, the recipient of your mail does not know the other recipients of the same mail.

By utilizing the signature feature of the e-mail software, you can avoid typing information for each outgoing message. Figure 13.5 shows a typical e-mail signature.

Carbon copy (Cc)

This feature lets you send a copy, i.e., carbon copy of the mail to another recipient. In this case the main recipient is informed about the other people who receive the same message (See Figure 13.6).

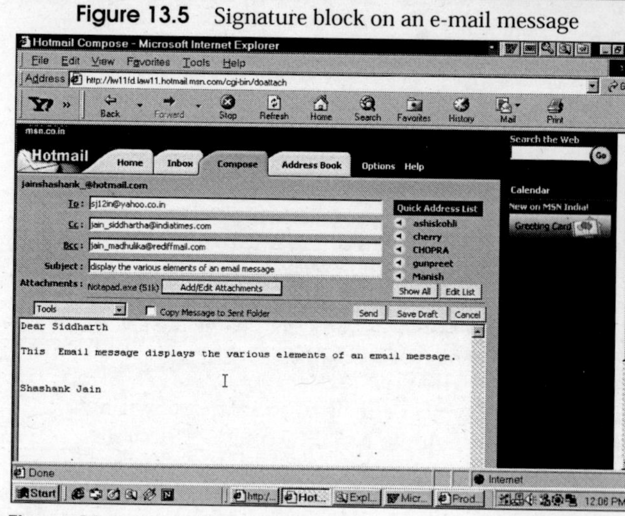

Figure 13.6 E-mail message with the carbon copy and Bcc, and attachments

Blind Carbon Copy (Bcc)

In this option the recipient of the first e-mail copy does not come to know the name of the other recipients, who receive the carbon copies of the same message.

Bounced Mail

Bounced mail is an e-mail message that has failed to reach its destination and therefore such e-mail messages are returned to the sender. The message "bounces" back to its sender from the mail server after the server fails to locate the message recipient address (or the recipient's Internet Service Provider).

Bounced mail messages typically feature a text clip near the top of the message and/or in the subject field, such as "Returned Mail" or "Mail Undeliverable". A bounced message alerts you that your e-mail has gone undelivered and that you must again send the message with correct address in order to ensure that your message reaches its recipient.

Configuring E-mail Client

When an e-mail software is run, the user may ask for a summary of his e-mail. The mailbox may contain a number of messages. In a simple e-mail message system, the choice of fields displayed is built into the program which may be one of the following types.

Sl. No.	Flags	Size in bytes	Sender	Address	Subject

In the above format, the first field is the message number. The second field is the Flags, which can contain various words, such as the new message, etc. The third field gives how long the message is and the next field indicates the sender and its address. The final column indicates the subject of the e-mail message. Once the messages are listed by the e-mail package, the user can process his e-mail box and can lay priority to the different messages received from various senders. E-mail has come a long way from the earlier days when it was just file transfer to very sophisticated software, such as Lotus Notes and Microsoft Outlook Express. The user agents make it possible to manage a large volume of e-mail.

☞ The RFC 822 gives the format of the e-mail messages and multimedia extensions.

Outlook 2010

Outlook 2010 is the Microsoft's e-mail program that is included with Windows and with Internet Explorer 8.0 onwards. Outlook 2010 puts the world of online communication on your computer's desktop. If you want to exchange e-mail with colleagues and friends or join newsgroups to trade ideas and information, then you have to use the different tools of Outlook 2010. You can perform the following functions with the help of Outlook 2010.

Manage Multiple Mail If you have several mail or news accounts, you can use them all from one window with the help of Outlook 2010. You can also create multiple users, or identities, for the same computer.

Browse Messages quickly Using the message list, you can view a list of messages and read individual messages at the same time. The Folders list contains mail folders, news servers, and newsgroups, and you can easily switch among them.

Keep Mail on a Server If your ISP uses an IMAP mail server for incoming mail, you can place your messages in folders on the server without downloading the messages to your computer so that you can view messages from any computers.

Address Book You can save names and addresses in your Address Book automatically by simply replying to a message or by importing them from other programs.

Send and Receive Secure Messages You can digitally sign and encrypt messages by using digital IDs. So that you can send and receive secure messages.

Download Newsgroup Messages for Offline Reading You can also use Outlook 2010 to use your online time efficiently by downloading messages or entire newsgroups, so that you can read newsgroup messages for offline reading.

Web based E-Mail

Each e-mail service – whether it is an online service, commercial e-mail service, has its own way to handle mail. Most of the E-mail services use the Internet as their gateway (describe the path how messages are passed from one service to another service). Internet connects the computers around the world so that people could share information with each other. When we send the message from e-mail service to someone's system, the message will travel across the Internet to reach its destination. We have given only the addressing of the message properly so that the Internet knows where to deliver the message. Here is some Web based free E-mail account, such as HotMail and rediffmail.com, that offer Web based e-mail access.

13.2 USING E-MAIL

E-mail or electronic mail can be sent over the Internet to anybody who has an e-mail address. To use e-mail, you need both an e-mail address and a program to handle it. To create a free e-mail account by Internet or Outlook Express.

13.2.1 Opening E-Mail Account/Client

Before you actually settle down to send a mail, you will first need to create an e-mail account. There are various sites in the Internet by which you can create free e-mail account. Some of the sites are given below:

(a) www.yahoo.com (b) www.rediffmail.com
(c) www.msn.com (d) www.hotmail.com

Here, you create an e-mail account with the Gmail.com.

➡ **To open an e-mail account, do this:**

1. Log on to site www.gmail.com. Type the www.gmail.com in the address bar as shown in Figure 13.7.

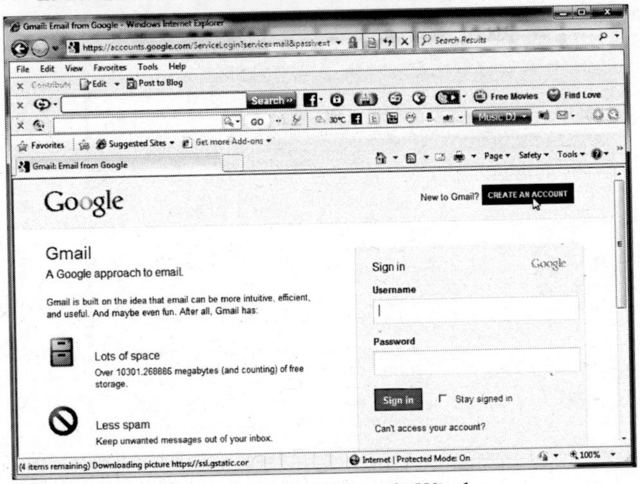

Figure 13.7 Gmail Google Window

2. Click the Create an account button in the Gmail from Google window as shown in Figure 13.7.
3. The Gmail Accounts window appears as shown in Figure 13.7.
4. Type the first and last name in the Name box as shown in Figure 13.8.
5. Type a desired login id which you want to create in the Choose your username text box.
6. Type the password in the Create a password text box (See Figure 13.8).

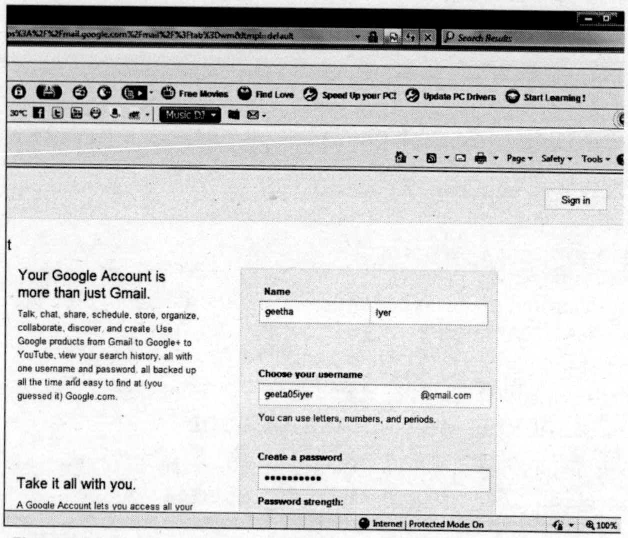

Figure 13.8 Type the information in the Google account text box

7. Again, type the password in the Confirm your password textbox as shown in Figure 13.9.
8. Type the Date of Birth in the Birthday text box as shown in Figure 13.9.
9. Select the Type of Gender in the Gender drop-down list (See Figure 13.10).

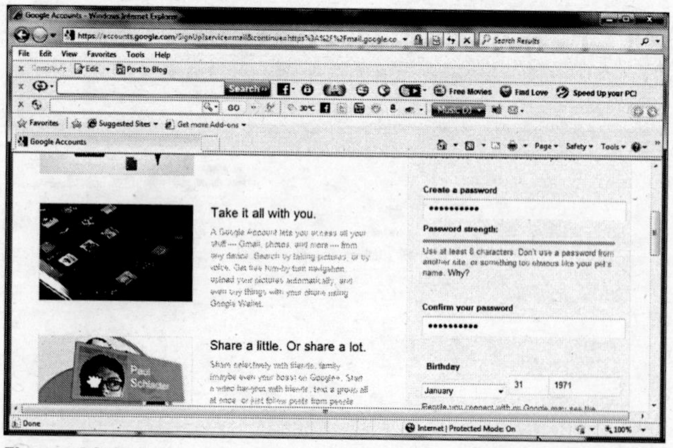

Figure 13.9 Type the password in confirm your password text-box

10. Type the mobile number in the Mobile phone text box (See Figure 13.10).
11. Type an e-mail address in the Your current e-mail address text box to keeping your account secure.
12. Type the character you see in the picture in the text box below Type the two pieces of text: box (See Figure 13.11).
13. Select the place in the Location drop-down list.
14. Click the Next Step to continue to next page.

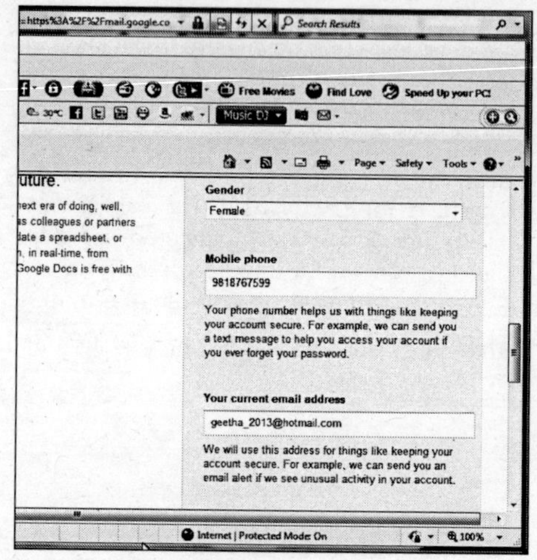

Figure 13.10 Type Mobile number in the Mobile Phone textbox

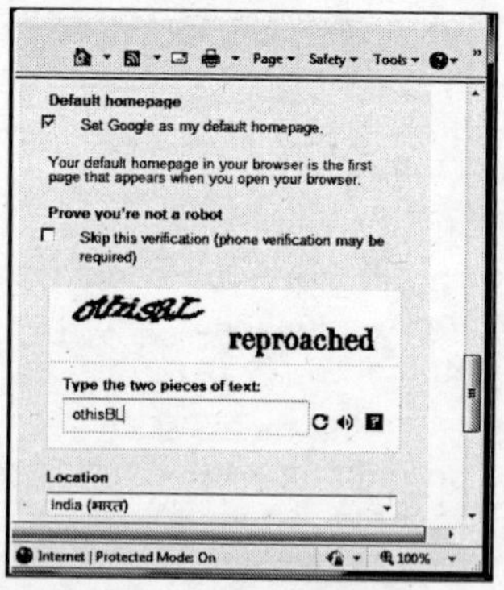

Figure 13.11 Character

15. The verify your account page appears as shown in Figure 13.12.
16. Select the desired option from verify your account page i.e., how should we send your codes? by Text message (SMS) or Voice call. For instance, if you select the Text message (SMS), you will receive a verification code form the Google to your mobile number, then you have entered in the Verify your account page.
17. Click Continue button (See Figure 13.12).

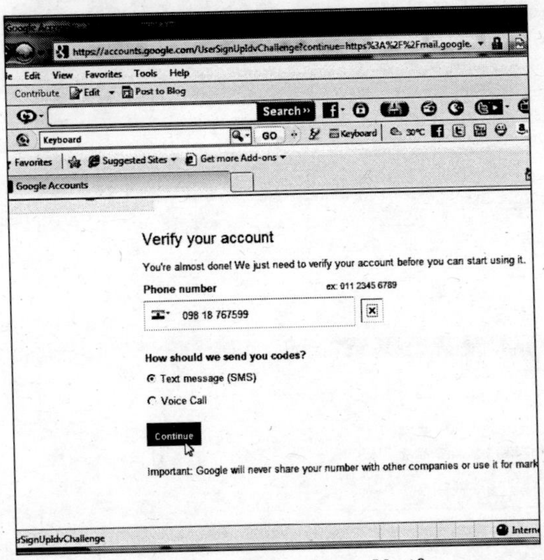

Figure 13.12 Google Accounts shows Verify your account

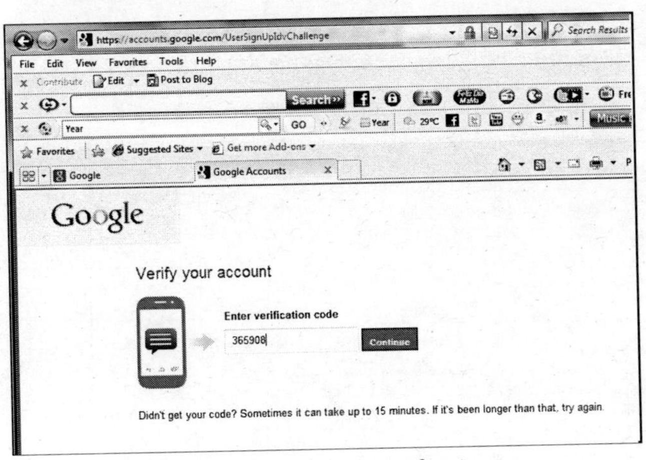

Figure 13.13 Mobile verification

18. Type the code that you have received in your mobile number in the Enter verification code text box in the Verify your account page (See Figure 13.13).
19. Click Continue button.
20. The Google Welcome! page shows, which you have created a new e-mail address. Click Continue to Gmail button which is ready to use (See Figure 13.14). The Gmail inbox shows the e-mail messages that you have entered. You can click the e-mail to view the message (See Figure 13.15).
21. Click the e-mail that you have received from the Gmail Team, as shown in Figure 13.15. You will see the e-mail message on the Gmail window as shown in Figure 13.15.
22. To write an e-mail message click the Compose mail button at the left side of the Gmail window. The Compose Mail window appears as shown in Figure 13.16.

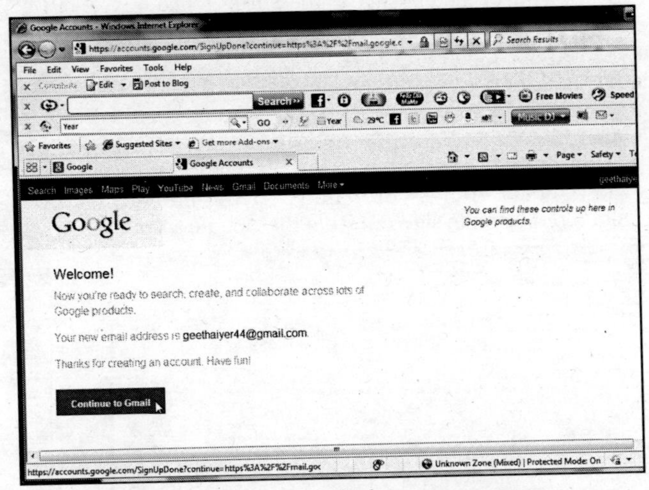

Figure 13.14 Google Welcome page screen

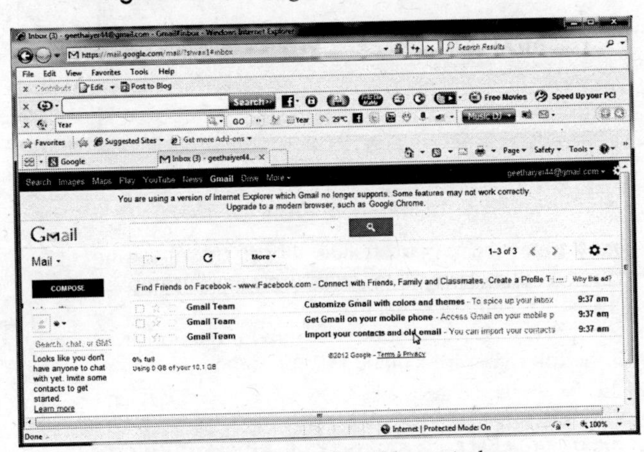

Figure 13.15 Gmail mail box window

Figure 13.16 Selecting Compose mail

23. In the Compose Message window, you will see various fields, which are to be used for the following things (See Figure 13.17).
    (a) Type the e-mail address in the To: text box, which you want to send the Mail-id address of recipient.

(b) Type the Title of the message in the Subject: text box.
(c) Type the body of the e-mail message in the message area as shown in Figure 13.17.

24. Click the Send button to send the message on the address of the recipient's Inbox.
The Gmail inbox window appears showing the message that your message has been sent.
25. Click your e-mail address drop-down arrow and then select Sign out button to sign out from the Google account.

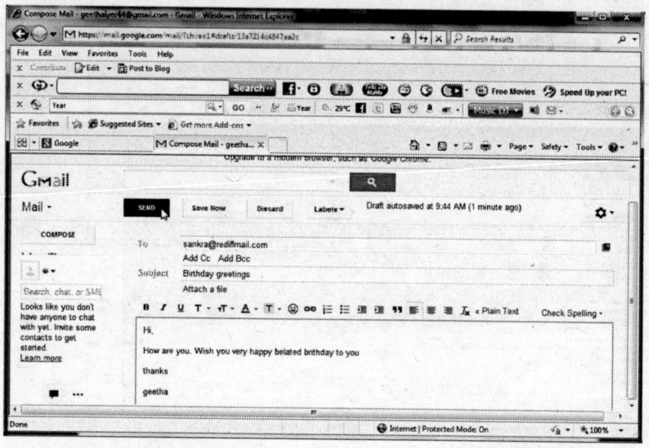

Figure 13.17 Showing various fields of compose mail window

Adding an E-mail Account in MS Outlook 2010

The Internet Connection Wizard makes short work of setting up your online mailbox by walking you through each step for every e-mail account you have set up.

Before you get going, make sure you know e-mail address along with the following information. [You may need to contact your ISP, to get it.

First, information about the e-mail servers:

(a) The type of e-mail server you use: POP3 (post office protocol 3), Hyptertext Transfer Protocol (HTTP) (such as Hotmail), or IMAP
(b) The name of the incoming e-mail server

For POP3 and IMAP servers, the name of the outgoing e-mail server (generally Simple Mail Transfer Protocol (SMTP).

Second, information about your account:

(a) Your account name and password.
(b) Find out if your ISP requires you to use Secure Password Authentication (SPA) to access your e-mail account.

Let us look at the steps which we need to follow for setting up an e-mail account in Outlook 2010.

➡ **To set up an e-mail account in Outlook 2010, do this:**

1. Click the File Tab and then choose Info Tab.
2. Under Account Information, click Add Account or Account Settings drop-down arrow (See Figure 13.18).
3. The Account Settings dialog box appears as shown in Figure 13.19. In this dialog box, click the New... button. It will display Add New Account dialog box as shown in Figure 13.20.

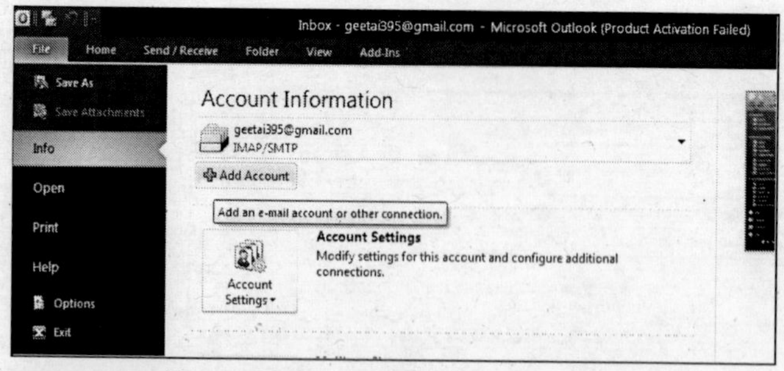

Figure 13.18 Setting E-mail Account

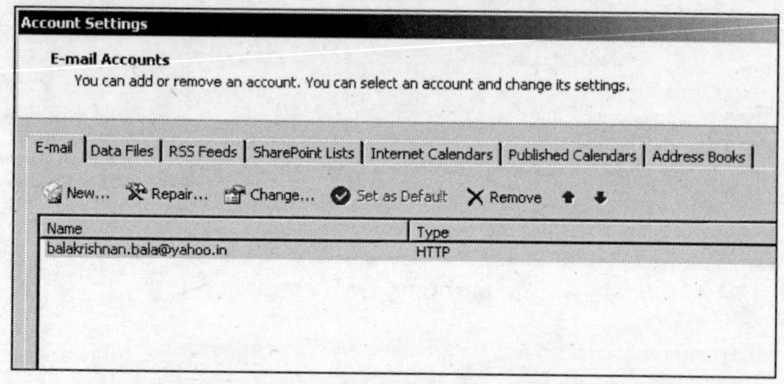

Figure 13.19 Account Settings dialog box

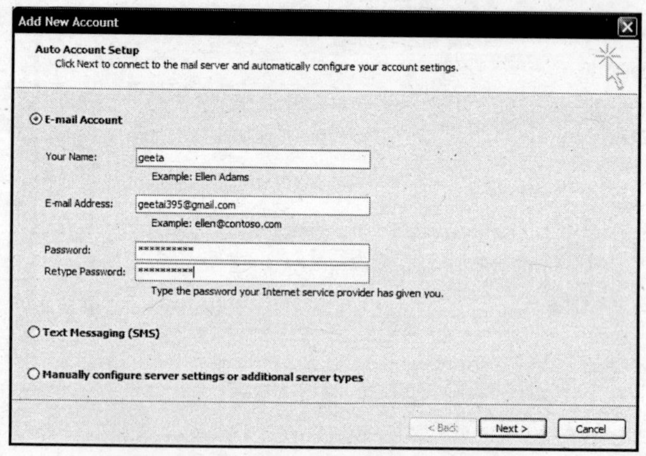

Figure 13.20 Add New Account dialog box

4. In this dialog box, type the name in the Your Name: text box and type e-mail address in the E-mail Address: text box. After that Type password in the Password: text box and in the Retype Password: text box confirm the password. Then click Next > button.
5. Another dialog box appears to the choose the service (See Figure 13.21). In this dialog box, click the Internet E-mail radio button and then click Next > button.
6. As soon as you click the Next> button, it will display another dialog box showing the progress indicator as your account is being configured. It may take several minutes (See Figure 13.22).

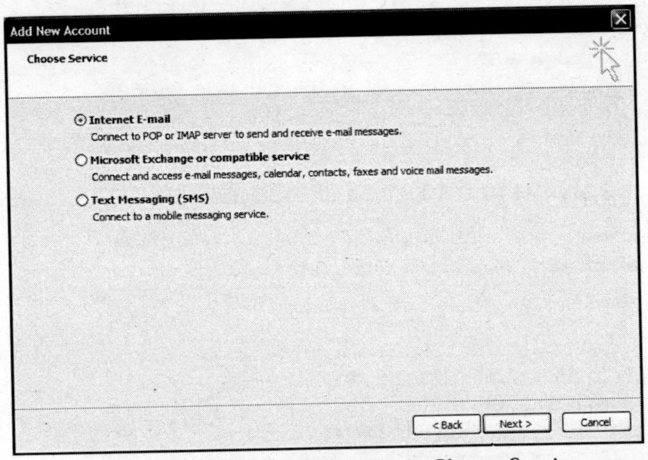

Figure 13.21 Add New Account to Choose Service

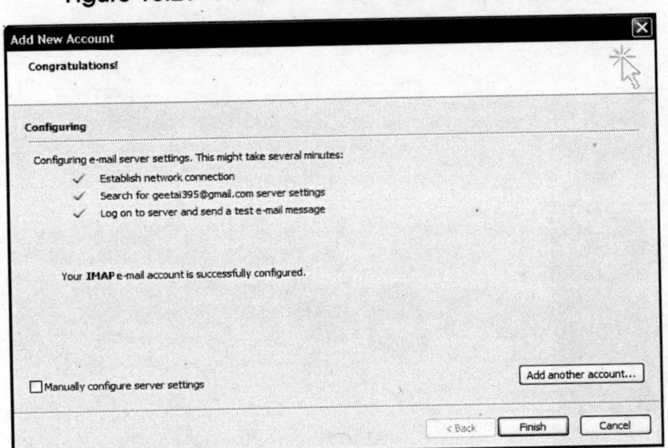

Figure 13.22 Add New Account showing configuring e-mail server settings

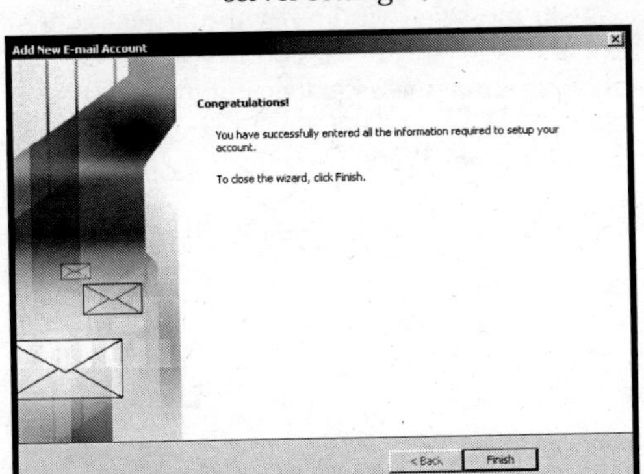

Figure 13.23 Add New E-mail Account dialog box

7. After the account is successfully added, you can add more accounts by clicking Add another account... button.
8. To exit the Add New Account dialog box, click Finish button to configure your e-mail account ready to use as seen in Figure 13.23.

> ☞ If Outlook 2010 fails to set up the e-mail account automatically, there is one more thing you can try, if you get this message: An encrypted connection to your server is not available. Click Next to attempt using an unencrypted connection.

13.2.2 Mailbox: Inbox and Outbox

To receive electronic mail, a user must have a mailbox, a storage area, that holds incoming e-mail messages until the user has time to read them. When a messages arrives, e-mail software automatically stores it in the user's mailbox.

Inbox

In Outlook 2010 Inbox, messages are sorted by the date and time received in descending order, which means the most recent message is at the top of the Inbox and the oldest at the bottom. You can click on any of the Field headers (From, Subject, Received, etc.) to sort the message list by that field. Clicking a second time alternates the list between ascending and descending order.

Outbox

The New Message window closes and your message is now in the Outbox. It has not actually been sent yet. You are still offline. You can write messages to several people and store them in the Outbox. When you are ready, you can send them all at once. This uses only a few seconds of online time and saves on the phone bill. You can look at the contents of the Outbox and edit a message before you send it.

➡ **To edit a message in the Outbox do this:**

1. Click Outbox in the Folders pane to select it.
2. Double-click the message header in the Message List pane.
3. An Edit window appears and you can edit the message.
4. Click Send to put it back in the Outbox.
5. If prompted to Connect, click Cancel.

Sending a message from the Outbox

6. Click the Send/Receive tab. Select the message you want to edit.

   If you are offline, you will be prompted to go online. Click Yes, then Connect at the next prompt.
7. After click the Connect button the message will be sent to the recipient address.
8. Edit the message and then click the Send button.

13.2.3 Creating and Sending a New E-mail

One of the most common task for Outlook users is sending and receiving e-mail. The mail message window, like other item windows in Outlook 2010, features the new Ribbon in place of menus and toolbars.

☞ To send and receive e-mail, you need to be connected to a mail server. You can think of the mail server as the post office. It is the computer with the network connection that receives your messages and directs your outgoing messages to other computers on a network. The computer is used to create your messages and read the messages you have received. This is known as the mail client.

➡ **To create a new e-mail message and type the e-mail address, do this:**

1. In the Home Tab, under the New group, click New E-mail as shown in Figure 13.24.

☞ Shortcut key to open New mail message is Ctrl + N or Ctrl + Shift + M keys pressed together.

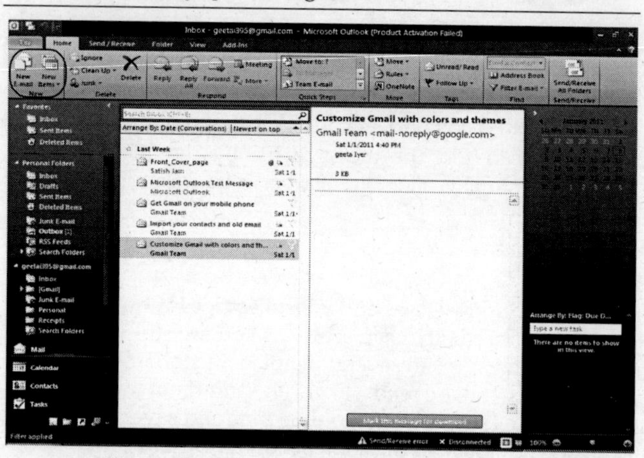

Figure 13.24 Creating new e-mail message

2. Outlook 2010 opens an Untitled Message window.
3. In this window, enter the recipient addresses in the To... text box (See Figure 13.25). If you want to enter multiple recipient addresses, you can separate it by a semicolon and one space.

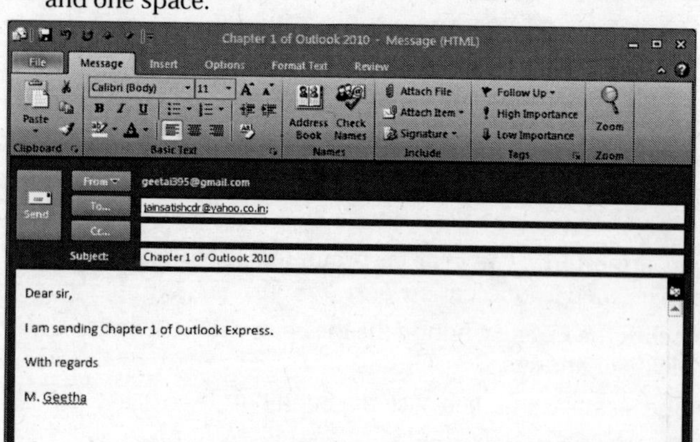

Figure 13.25 Message Window

4. If you want to send a copy of the message to someone besides the recipient, enter the address in the Cc... text box.
5. The new message window's title bar appears. It displays Untitled - Message (Plain Text) until you enter text on the Subject line. The subject line then appears in the title bar of the message window.
6. Type the body of the message in the message window below the subject line.
7. Then click Send icon to send the message.

13.2.4 Replying to an E-mail Message

Replying to an e-mail is like answering a letter – it acknowledges your receipt of the message and allows you to respond.

☞ The Shortcut key to Reply a message is Ctrl + R keys pressed together.

➡ **To reply to an e-mail message, do this:**

1. In the Home Tab, under the Respond group, click Reply or Reply All icon as shown in Figure 13.26.

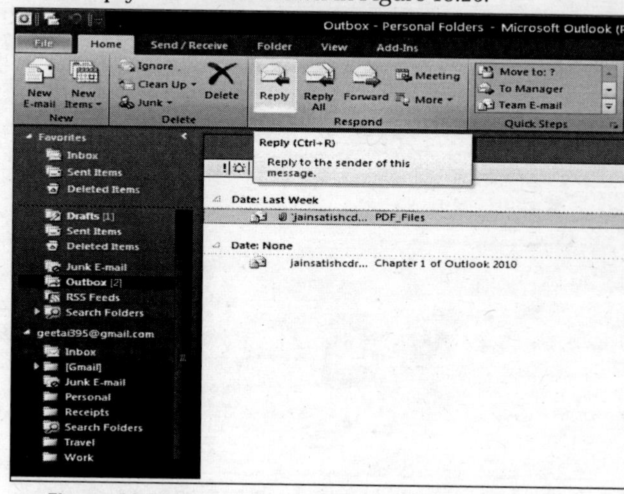

Figure 13.26 Select Reply button in the Respond group

2. Outlook displays a message window with the recipient's e-mail address and subject line already typed in along with a copy of the original message (See Figure 13.27).
3. To add a recipient, click in the To, Cc or Bcc box. Compose the message and then click the Send icon.

13.2.5 Forwarding an E-mail Message

Sometimes you may receive a message, but rather than reply to it, you want to send it (forward it) to someone else. Forwarding a message essentially copies a message and sends it to someone else whom the original sender may not even know.

☞ The Shortcut key to forward a message is Ctrl + F keys pressed together.

➡ **To forward an e-mail message, do this:**

1. In the Home Tab, under the Respond group, click Forward icon or double-click the message that you want to forward.

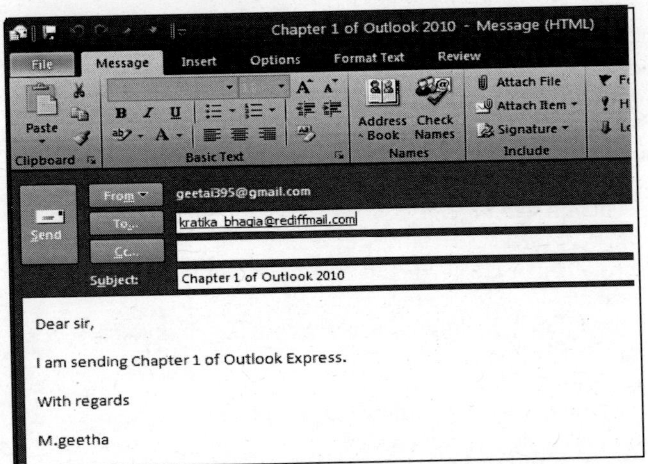

Figure 13.27 Message window with the recipient's e-mail address

2. A message window appears that contains your chosen message.
3. Click in the To: text box and type an e-mail address.
4. Click in the message window and type any additional text you want to send along with the forwarded message.
5. Click the Send button.

☞ You can forward only one message at a time. If you want to forward two or more messages, select the first message, hold Ctrl key and then select each additional message. Each message will be forwarded as attachments in a new message.

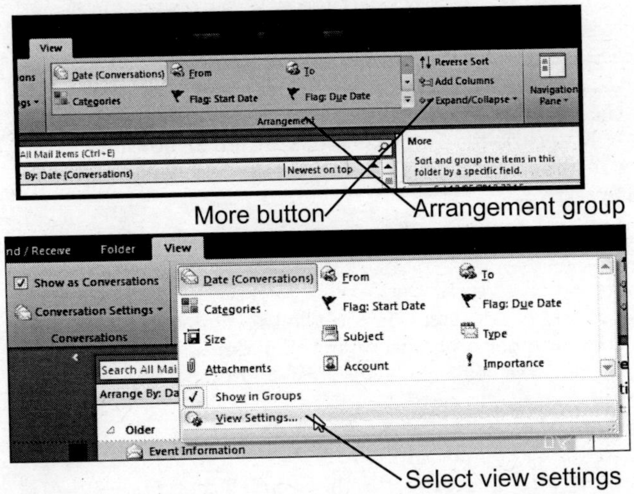

Figure 13.28 Selecting View Settings in the Arrangement group

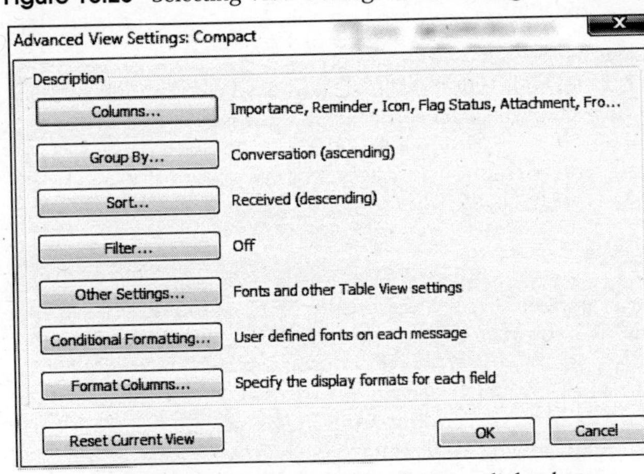

Figure 13.29 Advanced View Settings dialog box

13.2.6 Sorting and Searching E-mails

Sorting E-mail

Outlook 2010 lets you sort by single column or multiple columns. For example, if you select the column heading that is the exclamation mark (!) icon (located below the folder banner), all your important messages will be listed at the top of the Message list. Or if you click the From button, the messages will be sorted in alphabetical order by first name of the person who sent you the message. To sort by more than one column, select the column headings in reverse order.

In addition, to sorting your e-mail using the column headings, you can sort e-mail using the Sort dialog box.

➡ **To sort e-mail using the Sort command, do this:**

1. Click the View tab on the Ribbon. In the Arrangement group click the More drop-down arrow as shown in Figure 13.28. Select View Settings....
2. The Advanced View Settings dialog box appears as shown in Figure 13.29.
3. In the Advanced View Settings dialog box, click the Sort... button. The Sort dialog box appears as shown in Figure 13.30.

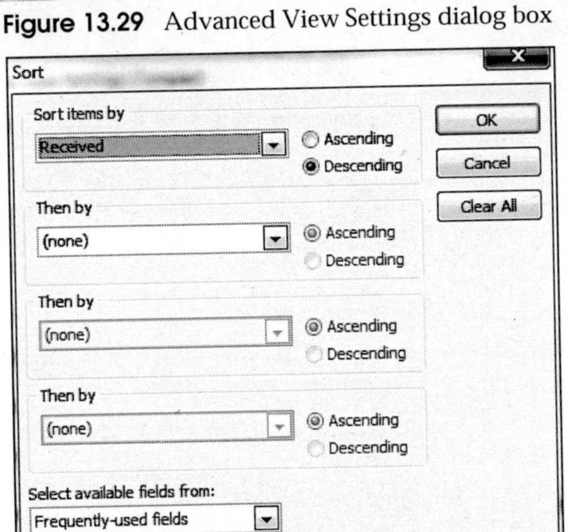

Figure 13.30 Sort dialog box

4. In the Select available fields from: drop-down list at the bottom of the dialog box, select the field set containing the fields that you want to use for sorting.
5. In the Sort Items by drop-down list, select an item from the list, such as Subject, Received, Sent and Size and then choose either the Ascending or Descending option.
6. Click OK to close the Sort dialog box, again OK to close the Advanced View Settings dialog box and see your changes.

Searching E-mail

Several sites on the World Wide Web (WWW) offer huge directories of e-mail addresses. If you want to contact a person, company, or other organization but don't know the contact's e-mail address, you can use Outlook 2010 to search through each of these directories.

➡ **To search someone's e-mail address do this:**

1. To look for the e-mail address of a person in Outlook 2010, type word to search for in the Search box and press Enter. You can see the highlighted yellow items in the middle of the window.

Search Address Book

2. To search through your personal address book in Outlook 2010, choose Address Book in the Find group of Home tab. The Address Book dialog box appears. Type the name you are looking for in Search box – Name, E-mail Address, Display Name. Click the Go button to start the search.

Send a Message

3. The search item display the result of the Find items. Double click the mail message address. The mail message window appears. Click the Move group in the Message group. Click Actions drop-down arrow and choose Resend this Message... option from the list and then click the Send button in the e-mail message window.

Sending document by E-mail

Send a document directly from Word as e-mail.

➡ **To send a document directly from Word as e-mail, do this:**

1. If you are using MS Word, select File tab highlight Save Send. The Save Send options appears, then click Send as Attachment to send the document as the body of the message.
2. The mail Message window appears.
3. Type the e-mail name of the recipient in the To: line or select the e-mail name from your Address Book.
3. Leave the Cc: box blank. This is used if you want to send a copy of the message to someone.
4. Type a subject for the e-mail on the Subject line.
5. Click the Send button to send the document as an attachment.

Sending Softcopy as Attachment

Any file that is stored on computer can be sent through e-mail. Before the file can be opened by the recipient, it must be downloaded–transferred from the mail server to the recipient's computer. The amount of time take depends on the Internet connection speed and the file's size.

➡ **To send a softcopy as attachment, do this:**

1. You send any type of file by attaching it to e-mail messages you are sending out.

Starting MS Word

2. In Word, open or create the file that you want to send as attachment.
3. Click the File tab highlight Save Send. A sub options appears. Select Send Using Email and then choose Send as Attachment.
4. The Outlook Message window appears as shown in Figure 13.31.

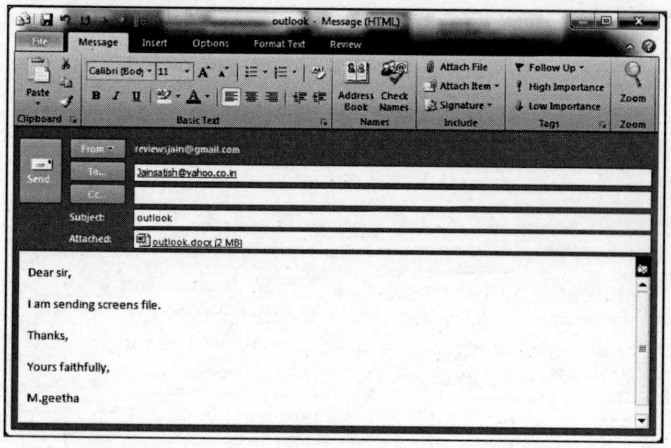

Figure 13.31 Word Attached the file in the outlook message window

5. Select the From address in From: drop-down list.
6. Type the e-mail name of the recipient in the To: line or select the e-mail name from your Address Book.
7. Leave the Cc: box blank. This is used if you want to send a copy of the message to someone.
8. Type a subject for the e-mail on the Subject line.

Attach a File

9. Word attached the file in the Attached: list box as shown in Figure 13.31.
10. Click the Send button to deliver the message and its attached file. The file is uploaded to mail server, so the time it takes to send the message depends on the speed of Internet connection and the size of the file.

Opening and Saving Attachments

Attachments are files that can be included with an e-mail message. Messages that have attachments are identified by a paper clip icon in the message list. Depending on the format of the message that you receive, attachments appear in one of two locations in the message.

- If the message format is Hypertext Markup Language (HTML) or plain text, attachments will appear in the attachment box under the Subject line.
- If the message format is the less-common Rich Text Format (RTF), attachments will appear in the body of the message. Even though the file appears in the message body, it actually remains a separate attachment.

➡ **To open/save a mail containing an attachment, do this:**

1. Select any e-mail message in the Inbox folder containing an attachment of a Portable Document Format (PDF) document. After selecting the e-mail message, read the message boy in the Reading pane.
2. In the Reading pane, you can see a pdf document attached along with the e-mail message.
3. The following commands are listed in the context menu, which is displayed when you right click a pdf document:
   - Preview: It enables a preview of the attached file in the reading pane.
   - Open: It opens the attached document.
   - Quick Print: It sends the currently selected attachment to the default printer for printing.
   - Save As: It Opens the Save Attachment dialog box, where you can specify the appropriate location and file name to save the attached item.
   - Save All Attachments: It saves all the attachments included with an e-mail message on your computer system.
   - Remove Attachment: It removes the currently selected attachment from an e-mail message.
   - Copy: It copies the currently selected attachment. You can place the copy of the attachment at a desired location on your system using the Paste command.
   - Select All: Selects all the attachments included in an e-mail message.
4. Select the Save As option from the context menu to save the pdf document.
5. The Save Attachment dialog box appears.
6. Click the Save button to save the file.

Deleting E-mail Messages

To delete an e-mail message from the message window or from the Inbox do the following options:

1. Click the e-mail in the Inbox folder you want to delete.
2. On the Home tab in the Delete group, click Delete icon.
3. Your message is deleted and send to the Deleted Items folder.

13.3 DOCUMENT COLLABORATION

Document collaboration enables organizations to share project-specific information across departments without time and space constraints. By logging into just one common virtual platform employees can instantly collaborate with one another. Routine work and time critical functions can be managed and reviewed. Business persons can communicate with employees, share documents, schedule work and effectively monitor performance . Employees can gain timely clarifications from company experts and information can be shared globally.

☞ Document collaboration refers to share data in a consistent manner, so it can be retrieved, reviewed, approved and audited by authorized individuals.

Your success in using document collaboration depends on selecting tools that provide a secure way to upload, find, and review documents and then involving others in the review process.

Let us take a look at some of the risks associated with sending documents over e-mail compared to more secure methods.

Document Review Risks

The risk associated with document collaboration can improve the business processes. Here some examples of how we get started.

1. Guidelines–We work with organizations to develop a set of guidelines for reviewing the documents so each contributor understands what is expected of them during the review process. What may be obvious to you, especially if you are more proficient with Web technologies, may be more challenging for other individuals.
2. Ownership–Each document must have a Document Owner. Thus, person is responsible for driving the document through the review cycle and ensuring that it is approved on time.
3. Security–Sharing documents by e-mail creates different security risks, especially for confidential documents.
4. Progress Reports–While we all enjoy the convenience of e-mail, there is no way to tell if others have started reviewing the document or if they have even opened it.
5. Scheduling–One of the limitations of e-mail is that while you can remind others to complete the document review by a specific date, they may ignore this or simply do not see it in e-mail.
6. Workflow–The true measure of success with Document Collaboration lies in improvements to the current processes, reduction in costs, and satisfied clients. You do not want a scenario where highly-paid team members spend hours in cutting and pasting between documents.

13.4 INSTANT MESSAGING AND COLLABORATION

Instant Messaging (IM) is a form of real-time direct text-based communication between two or more people using personal computers or other devices, along with shared clients. The user's text is conveyed over a network, such as the Internet. More advanced instant messaging software clients also allow enhanced modes of communication, such as live voice or video calling.

Instant messaging allows effective and efficient communication, allowing immediate receipt of acknowledgment or reply. In many cases, instant messaging includes added features which can make it even more popular. For example, users may see each other via Webcams, or talk directly for free over the Internet using a microphone and headphones or loudspeakers. Many client programs allow file transfers, although they are usually limited in the permissible file-size.

Many instant messaging services offer video calling features, Voice Over Internet Protocol (VoIP) and Web conferencing services. Web conferencing services can integrate both video calling and instant messaging abilities.

☞ Some instant messaging companies are also offering desktop sharing, IP radio, and IPTV to the voice and video features.

13.4.1 Using Instant Messaging

Instant Messaging (IM) is a form of electronic communication enabling ad hoc collaboration through sending and receiving messages across a network connection. Some of the popular and widely used instant messenger programs available today. Steps given below will make you to understand exactly what happens with an instant-messaging service:

1. You go to download page i.e http://www.google.com/talk/ or http://www.skype.com and get a free software client for your computer.
2. You install the software and open the client.
3. The client tries to connect to the server. It uses a proprietary protocol for communication.
4. Once the client is connected to the server, you can enter your name and password to log in to the server. If this is your first time on, you can sign up for an account and immediately begin using it. When server verifies your name and password, you are logged in.
5. The client sends connection information (IP address and number of the port assigned to the client) to server of the computer you are using. It also provides user with names of everyone in your contacts list.
6. The server creates a temporary file that has the connection information for you and the list of your contacts. It then checks to see if any of the users in your contact list are currently logged in.
7. If the server finds any of your contacts logged in, it sends a message back to the client on your computer with the connection information for that user. The server also sends your connection information to the people in your contact list that are signed on.
8. When your client gets the connection information for a person in your contact list, it changes the status of that person to "online." You click on the name of a person in your contact list who is online, and a window opens in which you can enter text into. You enter a message and click "send" or hit return to communicate with that person.
9. Because your client has the IP address and port number for computer of the person that you sent the message to, your message is sent directly to the client on that person's computer. In other words, the server is not involved at this point. All communication is directly take place between the two clients.
10. The other person gets your instant message and responds. The window that each of you sees on your respective computers expands to include a scrolling dialog of the conversation. Each person's instant messages appears in this window on both computers.
11. When conversation is complete, you close the message window. Eventually, you go offline and exit. When this happens, your client sends a message to the server to terminate the session. The server sends a message to the client of each person on your contact list who is currently online to indicate that you have logged off. Finally, the server deletes the temporary file that contains the connection information for your client.

Some of the popular Instant Messenger are Yahoo Messanger, MSN Messenger, Rediff Bol, Google Talk and Skype.

Using the Skype Instant Messengers

Skype is one of the well known Instant Messengers. It allows the users to explore the facilities of instant messaging provided by it. Apart from instant messaging, the other feature of Skype are file transfer, video conferencing, etc. Skype also provides the users with short message service. It is Niklas Zennstrom and Janus Friis who have created the Skype software program.

You have to download a Skype program, install it, register as a Skype user, and make use of the Skype applications.

Once installed, the program itself has the feel and look of any chat program. You can add contacts, block them, see if they are online, and communicate with them.

13.4.2 Instant Messaging Providers

The first instant messaging service was introduced in 1996 by an Israeli based ICQ. ICQ is an instant messaging computer program, owned by Time Warner's AOL subsidiary. ICQ was first developed by the Israeli company Mirabilis. The first version of the program was released in November 1996. After that it was later acquired by America Online. The major Instant Messaging Providers are AOL's Instant Messenger (AIM), ICQ, Yahoo! Messenger, Rediff Bol, Google Talk, Jabber and Microsoft's incarnations: Microsoft Network or MSN Messenger, Windows Messenger and Windows Live Messenger.

Instant messaging providers may also provide services like video phoning, file sharing, PC-to-PC voice calling and PC-to-regular-phone calling. Instant messaging has promoted IP telephony because the IM software makes it easy to switch from "text chat" to "voice chat," provided the user has a headset or microphone and speakers. The instant message providers give the option to the users to set up a buddy list. You also have to add the user names of the people you want to message with to your "buddy list" which is also called friend list or contact list. When they log on to the Internet with their Instant message software, and provided they have not configured themselves as "invisible," you are instantly alerted. When they log off, you are also notified. Each system has its own method for blocking incoming and outgoing messages.

Many of us e-mail instead of writing letters or even calling people on the phone. People around the world send out billions of e-mail messages every day. One should remember that sometimes even e-mail is not that fast enough. You might not know if a person you want to e-mail is online at that moment. Also, if you are e-mailing back and forth with someone, you usually have to click through a few steps. This is why instant messaging (IM) has become so popular. Most of the Instant Messaging Providers give you the following facilities:

- Instant messages - Send notes back and forth with a friend who is online.
- Chat - Create a chat room with friends or co-workers.
- Web links - Share links to your favorite Web sites.
- Video - Send and view videos, and chat face to face with friends.
- Images - Look at an image stored on your friend's computer.
- Sounds - Play sounds for your friends.
- Files - Share files by sending them directly to your friends.
- Talk - Use the Internet instead of a phone to actually talk with friends.
- Streaming content - Real-time or near-real-time stock quotes and news.
- Mobile capabilities - Send instant messages from your cell phone.

13.4.3 Netiquette

Netiquettes are the rules for correct behaviour on the Internet. Netiquettes distinct the Internet from traditional forms of communications, such as telephone conversion, face-to-face meetings, paper based letters. It helps you to avoid misunderstanding that may arise during communication accomplished via any Internet services especially e-mail, chat and mailing lists, etc.

Nature of Poor Netiquette

Poor Netiquette have following parts:

- Poor grammar and spelling errors
- Junk mails
- Harsh language

Rules for Internet Etiquettes

- Be concise, Use appropriate language
- No Spam and Include a subject line

Characteristics of Good Netiquette

Communications that do not waste the users' time are considered as good netiquette.

13.4.4 Configuring Mail on Mobile

You can always use Web-Based Email to send and receive email messages. But you also can view your email with an email client. To access your email on your mobile phone, add an account with the settings outlined below.

Internet Message Access Protocol (IMAP) lets you access email stored on a mail server from multiple computers and devices without transferring them between computers. Post Office Protocol (POP) lets you retrieve email from a remote server through your third-party email client.

➡ To configure mail on mobile:

1. Click on Email icon in the main menu.
2. Click on the POP3 account or the IMAP account depending on the account type you want to use.
   - POP3 is the standard protocol for receiving email from a mail server and it allows you to download all of your emails to one location.
   - IMAP is best if you access your email from multiple locations, clients and devices as it does not require downloading of your email content. Using IMAP settings on Windows Live because if anything were to happen to your computer or mobile device, you would still be able to access your emails.
3. Incoming Mail Server: pop.example.com if you are using POP settings. If you are using IMAP settings for example imap.example.com and then substitute your domain name.
4. Incoming Port: 110 for POP, 143 for IMAP
5. Outgoing Mail Server: smtp.example.com and then substitute your domain name.
   Outgoing Port (SMTP): 25 or 587
6. Username: full e-mail address (i.e. abc.xyz@example.com)
7. Password: [password for e-mail account]

☞ The username and password must be used for both the incoming and outgoing mail servers.

SMTP Authentication: This option must be enabled. If prompted, select "password" as the authentication type. Use the username and password above.

Creating Groups

It is common for a group of people who's want to share data or contact each other. Several standard methods using a mobile computing device are available. Communications applications using technologies such as Bluetooth, allow group members to exchange data related to the particular purpose of the group.

Data transferred among group members may include text, graphics, streaming media, and the like. But these methods of group formation need a lot of manual interaction and input to the applications in the mobile computing device. After the group is formed, data sharing has to follow the group-sharing conventions of those applications. Other methods of group formation include NFC or other short range communications to exchange contacts or electronic mails (emails).

The data sharing is done via emails or short message service (SMS). However, these methods do not involve formation of a group but only send person to person communication. Thus, the user needs to follow a step-by-step process for creating a group and sharing the data to the group members. This disclosure provides an easy way for forming a group and sharing data with a group of members using mobile computing devices.

Message Formations

Using e-mail, a message is an individual piece of mail. In computer system in general, a message is an information unit that the system sends back to the user with information. Using some telecommunication or data access methods, a message can be unit of information or data that is transmitted from one program to another.

Do's & Don't using Mobile

Consider the following while using mobile phone

Do s

- Note down your IMEI number.
- Security pin code should be used to avoid misuse of your mobile phones.
- MMSs/SMSs received should be checked for their source before opening.
- Delete all pornographic text, images, SMS/MMS from your mobile phones which you might have received or stored.
- Anti-virus software should be loaded in the mobile phone.
- Mobile phone keypad should be locked after every use.
- Use your mobile phone only when necessary.
- Hold it at the bottom.

Don t

- Don't talk too long.
- Do not use a mobile phone when driving a car. Stop at a safe place and talk.
- Do not use your mobile phone in places where there is a lot of electrical equipment, such as hospitals and aircraft.
- Do not send pornographic text, images using SMS.
- Do not handover your mobile phone to unauthorized service centers, to avoid cloning.

Attachment

An Attachment is a file attached to an email message. An attachment can be a picture, a word document, a movie, a sound file or any other supported file types. When your recipients open your messages, they can double-click on the attached file to open it with the program. Also note that some email providers place limits on the size of the files that can be attached to email messages, while others block certain types of attachments such as executable to prevent viruses. A paper clip image is the standard image for an attachment in an email client.

Difference Between Bcc & Cc

When referring to email, "cc" means carbon copy and "bbc" means "blind carbon copy". Both "cc" and "bcc" are additional fields you can enter when sending an email. Every recipient email address you enter into the "To" and "cc" fields to see each other. The email addresses you add to the "bcc" field will not be visible to the "to" and "cc" recipients or the other "bcc" recipients.

When you send an email, you have three field choices: "to", "cc", and "bcc". Here is how to use each field:

- To: Mail-id address of recipient
- Cc: Mail-ids address of recipients to whom copy needs to be sent.
  CC stands for carbon copy. This field allows you to send the same mail message to multiple recipients at the same time.
- Bcc: Mail-ids address of recipients of Blind Carbon Copy.
  BCC stands for blind carbon copy. This field allows the sender to send same mail message to multiple recipients without letting them know that some other person also have received the same message.

13.5 EMAIL PROTOCOLS

13.5.1 SMTP

SMTP Simple Mail Transfer Protocol is a protocol used to send and receive email. SMTP (Simple Mail Transfer Protocol) is a TCP/IP protocol used in sending and receiving e-mail. However, since it is limited in its ability to queue messages at the receiving end, it is usually used with one of two other protocols, POP3 or IMAP, that let the user save messages in a server mailbox and download them periodically from the server. In other words, users typically use a program that uses SMTP for sending e-mail and either POP3 or IMAP for receiving e-mail.

13.5.2 POP3

POP3 is a protocol that is used for downloading email from an ISP to the recipient mail program. POP3 allows mail retrieval by a workstation for receiving mail which is held by the server.

Post Office Protocol Version 3 (POP3) is a standard internet protocol, which was developed as the standard client-server protocol for retrieving Internet mail by using an email client ie: Outlook Express, Netscape Communicator, Eudora, etc. to communicate with the mail server (Protocol, a method of sending and receiving data).

Post Office Protocol Version 3 rfc 1939 are used for delivering messages to (client) mail readers (fetch mails from a remote mail server and store it locally). The client sends a login (UserID) and a password to authenticate the session. If it is accepted--the client sends commands to retrieve messages. The server transfers the messages and deletes them from the permanent mailbox.

13.5.3 IMAP4

Is a standard protocol for accessing e-mail from your local server. IMAP is a client/server protocol in which e-mail is received and held for you by your Internet server. As this requires only a small data transfer this works well even over a slow connection such as a modem. Only if you request to read a specific email message will it be downloaded from the server. You can also create and manipulate folders or mailboxes on the server, delete messages etc.

13.5.4 MIME5

Multipurpose Internet Mail Extensions stands for (MIME). It is widely used Internet standard for encoding binary files to send them as e-mail attachments over the Internet. MIME allows an E-mail message to contain a non-ASCII file such as a video image or a sound and it provides a mechanism to transfer a non text characters to text characters.

Traditional e-mail sent over the Internet using Simple Mail Transfer Protocol (SMTP) as specified by Request for Comments messages as consisting of a header and a body part, both of which are encoded using 7-bit ASCII text encoding. The header of an SMTP message consists of a series of field-/value pairs that are structured so that the message can be delivered to its intended recipient. The body is unstructured text and contains the actual message.

Multipurpose Internet Mail Extensions (MIME) defines five additional extensions to SMTP message headers, supports multipart messages with more than two parts, and allows the encoding of 8-bit binary data such as image files so that they can be sent using SMTP. The encoding method for translating binary information used by MIME, Base64 Encoding, essentially provides a mechanism for translating nontext information into text characters.

The MIME extensions are implemented as fields within the e-mail message header. These fields define the following:

a. MIME version number
b. Content type Header
c. Content transfer encoding method
d. Content-ID Header
e. Content-Description Header

13.5.5 Email Clients

Both webmail and email clients are applications for sending and receiving email. Email clients are programs that are installed on local machines (i.e. your computer, or the computers in your office) to interact with remote email servers to download and send email to whomever you want to.

The advantage of using an email client is that the emails are stored on your computer and are accessible faster than using a web based email interface. Also, with an email client you can read the messages you already received without being connected to the internet. You can also compose email while offline. Once connected again to the Internet, the emails can be sent.

There are various email client programs available. Some of the more common email clients are Outlook Express, Outlook and Thunderbird.

13.5.6 Netscape mail Clients

The Netscape Navigator is a free open source mail and news client developed by Netscape. It is also known as Netscape Messanger, it is a cross platform desktop email client available for Windows.

Netscape is a complete internet suit and used for multiple purposes as shown below:

Netscape Mail Newsgroups: The application is used for messaging purposes. B using Netscape email client you can configure and mange multiple email accounts. You can also subsribe newsgroups.

Netscape Browser: By using Netscape as a web browser you can simply surf internet.

Protocols used by Netscape email client

Netscape Mail and Newsgroups supports all email protocols such as POP3, IMAP and SMTP.

13.5.7 Outlook Express

Outlook Express is an email service that allows users to store their email data to thier own hard disk. The easiest way to access your Outlook Express email is to et up a web-based email account and link your Outlook Express mailbox to it.

➡ To access a web-based email:

1. Go to a web-based email account website such as Hotmail.com and create an account.
2. Set up the account to allow you to use Outlook Exprss by selecting your email server type as HTTP in your Outlook Express user settings. Create a username and password.
3. Log into the web-based email website.
4. Open Outlook Express email inbox from your web-based email account.

13.5.8 Web-based E-mail

With Web mail you can read and send mail through browser and the web mail interface. Many sites offer free Web-based email. Some examples of Web mail are

- Yahoo! Mail
- Gmail
- Hotmail

When you access a web mail account you use your browser.

1. You will be given a web address to access your web mail. For example, we use Yahoo! mail as an example. The web address to access Yahoo! mail is: https://login.yahoo.com/config/login_verify2? .src=ym.

2. Next, you will need to login. This requires your user name and password. Enter your Yahoo! id and password, then click, Sign in.
3. Once logged in, you can now read the emails sent to your web based email acount and send emails from this email address.

13.5.9 Email Encryption

Email encryption hides the email content by encrypting it into an unreadable form. Emails can be encrypted and decrypted by means of a digital signature mechanism that uses public and private keys. The publick key is shared with everyone while the private key is kept private.
There are different methods for email encryption. These are PGP (Pretty Good Privacy) and S/MIME (secure Multi-Purpose Internet Mail Extension).

MODEL QUESTIONS AND ANSWERS

A. Multiple Choice

1.1 SMTP is a simple
a. TCP protocol b. IP Protocol
c. TCP/IP protocol d. None of the above

1.2 A simple protocol used for fetching e-mail from a mailbox is
a. POP3 c. IMAP
b. POP2 d. None of the above

1.3 A popular application of computer networking is the World Wide Web of newsgroup called
a. News c. Netnews
b. Gateways d. Both (a) and (b)

1.4 E-mail address is made up of
a. Single part c. Three parts
b. Two parts d. None of the above

1.5 The program supplied by VSNL when you ask for Internet connection for the e-mail access is
a. ISP c. Pine
b. HotDog d. None of the above

1.6 SMTP stands for
a. Server Mail Transfer Protocol
b. Simple Mail Transfer Protocol
c. Small Mail Transmission Protocol
d. Short Mail Transmission Protocol

1.7 The steps for sending an e-mail are:
a. Start an e-mail program
b. Give the address of where to send
c. Compose a message to send the message
d. All of the above

1.8 Messenger Mailbox is present in
a. Internet Explorer c. Both a and b
b. Netscape Communicator d. None of the above

1.9 The convenient place to store contact information for quick retrieval is
a. Message box c. Address book
b. Address box d. None of the above

1.10 Which one of the following statements is not correct for Digital signature?
a. It is a mechanism for authentication
b. It is the scanned image of one's signature
c. It is created by encrypting information
d. It cannot be duplicated

B. State whether the following are True or False

2.1 To specify multiple recipients of carbon copy of same mail message, Cc: field is used.
2.2 In SMTP, the message can be of any length.
2.3 A protocol used for fetching e-mail from a mailbox is POP1.
2.4 All incoming e-mail messages are to be stored in the Outbox folder.
2.5 The e-mail component of Internet Explorer is called "Outlook Express"
2.6 When sending an e-mail, the subject line describes the contents of the message.
2.7 Recipient's log-in name must form a part of his e-mail address.
2.8 Unsolicited e-mail advertising is known as spam.
2.9 E-mail is limited to text based messages.
2.10 The two parts of e-mail address is separated by @ symbol.

Answers

A. 1.1 a 1.2 a 1.3 c 1.4 b 1.5 c
1.6 b 1.7 d 1.8 b 1.9 c 1.10 b

B. 2.1 T 2.2 F 2.3 F 2.4 F 2.5 T
2.6 T 2.7 F 2.8 T 2.9 F 2.10 T

CHAPTER 14

Introduction to Multimedia

14.1 INTRODUCTION

"Multimedia" comes from the word "multi" and "media". "Multi" means various. "Media" refers to any hardware or software used for communicating. Multimedia meand that computer information can be represented through audio, video, and animation.

In multimedia presentation more than one media is used to present information. For example, a TV system is a multimedia device because it presents information by sound and video media.

Multimedia technology facilitates an intergration of text, image, graphics, audio and video animation in digital form in computers. It provides new ways to enhance the delivery of information and its impact on the user.

Multimedia information is displayed in picture/sound form and it does not include plain text exclusively. Thus, it includes pictures (graphics), sound (audio) and movies (video). Multimedia requires additional hardware which can handle sound, video etc. The additional pieces of hardware are sound card, video capture card, etc. Apart from this, multimedia machines must have large size of main memory. Multimedia information such as pictures, sounds and video are captured and digitized by input devices to get the information ready for manipulation by the computer. For example, to get a picture into the computer, we can scan it and then enter it in the computer.

Computer stores multimedia information in a variety of standard file formats. We can display or play multimedia information on output devices. For example, to play a sound file, we need speakers or headphones. In some cases, computer needs special hardware to connect to the output device. For example, to connect a speaker to a PC, we need a sound card (which comes as a standard with most new computers).

14.1.1 Hardware Requirement for Multimedia Computer

Multimedia hardware requirements consists of the following items, namely Processing unit, memory and storage devices, USB Device, Monitor, CD Drives, Graphics Card, Speaker and Headphones and Network Interface card.

Processing unit

Central Processing Unit (CPU) is an essential part in any computer. It is considered as the brain of computer, where processing and synchronization of all activities takes place. The efficiency of a computer is the speed of the CPU in processing of data. The CPU is also known as a processor. or microprocessor. For a multimedia computer a Intel Corei3 is preferred because of higher efficiency.

Memory and storage devices

RAM also called primary memory locates the operating system, application programs, and data in current use so that the computer's processor reaches them quickly. Most modern computers use DDR 2 RAM. A minimum of 1024MB (1GB) of RAM is recommended for general purpose PCs. 2048MB (2GB) of RAM is recommended for PCs running multimedia applications, i.e., those on which digital music, digital video or high-end graphics are being created/edited.

Storage devices (Hard Drive)

The hard drive is the computer's primary storage area. It stores the applications and programs that run on the PC, as well as any work created by users. A hard drive capacity of at least 80GB is recommended for general purpose PCs. A hard drive capacity of 200GB or more is recommended if working with multimedia applications where large graphics and digital audio/video files are being created and stored.

USB Device

It allows you to connect the computer devices such as digital camera, thumb drive, and printer using a socket. We just simply need to plug these devices into our PC USB port.

Monitor

The older CRTs have been largely replaced by TFT flat-screens. A 15" TFT has the same viewing area as the older 17" CRT. Average PCs usually come with a 15" flat-screen and this is for most general purpose applications. Larger 17" flat-screens are appropriate for video editing and advanced graphics work is being carried out.

CD Drives

A compact disk (CD) is a small medium that can store data pertaining to audio, video, text, and other information in digital form. (Compact Disc, read-onlymemory) can store computer data in the form of text, graphics and sound. To record data into a CD, you need a CD recorder. Normally this type of CD is either CD-Recordable (CD-R) or CD-Rewritable (CD-RW).

Graphics Card and Graphical Processing Unit (GPU) and Sound Card

The function of a graphics card is to generate better output images on a monitor. This card is normally a separate card that we plug into an expansion slot in our computer motherboard. These cards is responsible for determining the quality of the audio and visuals (graphics and video) output by the computer. They hold their own memory (in MB), which is add to a computer's capability. A integrated graphics card with

256MB of memory is recommended for general purpose PCs. Computers running high-end applications generally require a separate PCI 128MB graphics card.

Besides the graphics card, another processor that is Graphics Processing Unit or GPU, this is a special processor for graphics rendering that we can find in PCs. The GPU is important to enable the best computer graphics output display such as 3D image rendering. Current GPUs even support almost-real video-related functions. We can obtain better gaming experience if we have a GPU fixed at our computer. Among the GPU manufacturers are AMD, NVIDIA, Matrox, and XGI.

Sound Card

A sound card (also known as an audio card) is an internal expansion card that provides input and output of audio signals to and from a computer under control of computer programs. It also applied to external audio interfaces used for professional audio applicatons. It also providing the audio component for multimedia applications such as music composition, editing video or audio, presentation, education and entertainment (game) and video projection.

Speakers and Headphones

Output device such as speaker or headphones, for audio output to be recorded. The D/A converter of the sound board takes care of converting the sound from its digital to analog form.

Network Interface Card (NIC)

A network card allows a computer to be connected to a network. A 10/100/1000 Mbps (Mega bits per second) card is the standard network card.

14.1.2 Textual Information

World Wide Web (WWW) is making of vital importance the problem of effective retrieval of Web documents for users. The complexity of Web documents is rapidly increasing with the wide use of multimedia components, such as images, audio and video, associated to the traditional textual content. This requires extended capabilities of the Web search engines in order to access documents according to their multimedia content.

A large number of search engines support indexing and content-based retrieval of Web documents only the textual information is taken into account. Initial experimental systems providing support to the retrieval of Web documents based on their multimedia content are limited to the use of features extracted from multimedia data.

The approach tries to overcome the limits of existing systems making use of the information about the "context" in which a multimedia object (e.g., an image) appears: this contextual information includes the information contained in the same Web document where the multimedia object is contained, the information carried by other Web documents. pointing to it, the (possible) internal structuring of the multimedia object (i.e., components of an image).

This approach permits one to combine, during query processing, the result of efficient information retrieval techniques, working on text components, with less precise results of generalised feature based images search techniques, exploiting the inter/intra-relationships in WWW documents.

We have implemented a prototype system that gathers documents from the Web. After an analysis of its structure identifies the different types of data (e.g. text, images, audio, video) and "classifies" them. Textual information is used to extract the terms to be used for text retrieval purposes; images are analysed in order to compute the values of the physical visual features and to derive the presence of one of the pre-defined concepts.

14.2 COMPONENTS OF MULTIMEDIA

Components of multimedia like text can be used for adding emphasis. Graphics can be used for giving visual impact, and animation can be used for attracting attention. Multimedia software is used for the creation, conversion, editing, and manipulation of either (digitized) analog data or pure digital data, which is ultimately used for conveying information.

14.2.1 Text

Text contains alphanumeric characters used to present information. Text delivers information that can have some meaning. Text is the simplest data type that requires the least amount of storage. Designing texts for multimedia involves the correct choice of font style, font colour and font size. Content design involves both quantitative and qualitative aspects of multimedia text. Many text editing software tools are available for content development, title development and font design.

Hardware requirement for text

Text processing using computer requires the following hardware devices.

1. Keyboard is one of the most important input device for entering text data in a computer.
2. Optical Character Recognition (OCR) is another input device used to input a wide variety of document including pictures, graphics, typed text or handwritten text.
3. Monitor is an output device used to display information on the computer screen.
4. Printer is also an output device used to take out hard copy in the printed form.

Software requirement for text

Text processing capabilities are highly desirable in a multimedia computer system for better presentation and use of text information.

Text editing

Text editors and word processing packages are used to generate, edit and layout a text document

Text style

The major attributes of text include paragraph styling, character styling (such as bold, italics, etc), font families and sizes, and relative location in a document. For example, newspapers use a good combination of all these styles to better highlight more important news than less important ones.

Text Searching

Usage of text information can be greatly enhanced by text searching feature of a word processor. This feature allows the user to enter a word or phrase and quickly finds and displays that part of the text where the word or phrase appears in the text information with the word or phrase highlighted. Almost all word processing packages have this feature. Several software having this feature are also available on the Internet that help in searching the desired information.

Hypertext

Hypertext is an application of indexing text to provide a rapid search of specific text strings in one or more documents. This feature provides great flexibility of structuring and accessing computer based text information. User can get the required information just by clicking on an anchor (a hotword). This means that if the user wants more information about a particular hotword, he/she can select that hotword just by clicking on it and it will open a window with additional text explaining the word or phrase.

☞ Hypertext is a document that are prepared by using special linking facility for easier electronic access and manipulation.

Text importing and exporting

The task of creating a text document can often be greatly simplified if the document preparation software has text importing feature. This is because some of the text you want to incorporate in your document may already exist as a file created by a word processor or a database file. The file can be simply imported into the new document at the desired location instead of retyping the entire text again. Similarly, text exporting feature is very useful in allowing other packages to use an existing document.

14.2.2 Pictures/Graphics

Computer graphics deal with the generation, representation, manipulation and display of pictures with the help of a computer. Graphics is an important component of multimedia by which we can illustrate information in video form. For example, to educate children with the help of multimedia, we can make illustration more descriptive with the help of pictures. Because for small children, it is difficult to explain new concepts with text. In a multimedia application meant for educating small children, displaying the photograph of a horse along with its text description makes the illustration much more effective. Without the photograph, it will be very difficult to explain using only text how a horse looks like.

☞ Pictures, photographic image and other artwork is called graphics.

Graphics Types

There are two types of computer graphics. These are:
(a) Line Drawing
(b) Images

Line Drawing

These are drawings and illustrations in the form of 2D (two dimensions) and 3D (three dimensions) pictures from mathematical representation of simple objects like lines, circles, arcs, etc. Simple object types are used to create complex objects. For example, the picture of a chair can be drawn using lines and arcs.

The area of computer graphics that deals with this type of pictures is known as generative graphics. Generative graphics is extensively used in creating illustrative diagrams. Another very important application of generative graphics is CAD (Computer Aided Design) and CAM (Computer Aided Manufacturing). Now a days, CAD packages are extensively used in designing models for aircraft, ship and building structures. The greatest advantages of using CAD and CAM packages for such applications is that design changes may be quickly modified and also creating accurate assembly drawings and associated parts and subassembly list.

Images

Images are defined as visual representation of the information. These are graphics and photographs composed of a collection of pixels, which are arranged in two-dimensional matrix. The area of computer graphics that deals with this type of pictures is called cognitive graphics. Cognitive graphics along with image processing techniques is extensively used in applications that deal with recognition and classification of pictures. For example, an image database containing images of people's fingerprints is commonly used now a days in criminal investigation and identification.

Hardware for Pictures/Graphics

Following are the hardware components needed for graphics:

(a) A locating device such as mouse, joystick or a stylus to draw pictures on computer screen.

(b) A flatbed scanner or rectangular coordinate digitizer which is used as an input device for generative graphics applications for inputting existing line drawings to a computer.

(c) Scanners for capturing photographs and drawings as digital images.

(d) Computer screen for display graphics.

(e) Laser printers or plotters for output graphics in hard copy.

Software for Pictures/Graphics

In addition to the above listed devices, software packages given below will improve the presentation of graphics:

(a) Software for painting or drawing: Such packages allow the user to create graphics by using a mouse and modify and enhance graphic images produced using a scanner or screen capture software for better understanding. All these features make this software very useful in a multimedia application.

(b) Screen capture software: Screen capture software packages are used to capture the computer screen as a graphic image. These packages allow the users to save the graphic images in a variety of graphic formats and are also useful in converting a graphic image from one storage format to another because a multimedia software might have been designed to accept image only in a particular format.

(c) Clip art: Clip art is a library of commonly used graphic images such as personal computer, printer, telephone, building etc. These images can be directly imported from the library and used in a multimedia application. This saves enormous amount of time and effort that might otherwise be required to create or search and capture a similar image object.

(d) Software for high resolution: In a multimedia application, we use very high quality images. Therefore, we need such software packages to enhance images for high resolution.

14.2.3 Audio

Computer audio deals with developing, recording and playback of audio with the help of a computer. Audio is very important component of multimedia because in many cases sound can be very useful for better understanding the information than in other ways. In some cases, sound may be the only way to provide the desired information. For example, the sound created by a dog called barking of a dog.

☞ Speeches, music and other types of sounds are called audio. Audio element is generally used to enhance the usual multimedia environment.

Computer Hardware for Audio

Audio needs the following computer hardware devices:

(a) A sound card.

(b) Input device such as microphone, for audio input to record voice or music or any other type of sound in a computer. The A/D converter of the sound board takes care of digitizing the input sound, which is in the analog form.

(c) Output device such as speaker or headphones, for audio output to be recorded. The D/A converter of the sound board takes care of converting the sound from its digital to analog form.

(d) Sound editors to cut and paste sound clipping and to add special effects.

Software for Audio

In addition to the above listed tools and devices, the following capabilities are highly desirable in a multimedia computer system with audio facility.

(a) Audio clips: With the help of audio clips (pre-made sound effects, music and narration) one can select and directly import and use audio in a multimedia applications. This saves time and effort that might otherwise be required to create a similar audio clip.

(b) Software for high quality sound: Multimedia application needs very high quality audio to reproduce the sound effectively. It is important to use not only the necessary hardware but also software support for both recording and playback of high quality audio.

(c) Recording and playback capabilities: A multimedia system with audio capability should allow the user to control the recording and playback of an audio sequence. For example, it should provide the user with options to "pause" and "replay" the sound sequence.

(d) Voice recognition software: This is used to identify the speaker of a given voice by matching the voice with a set of voices stored in a database along with details of the speaker of each voice.

14.2.4 Video

Computer video deals with the recording and display of sequence of images. Each individual image in sequence is called a frame. For a jerk-free full motion video, 25 to 30 frames have to be displayed per second. It is an important component of multimedia because it is very useful for illustrating concepts that involve movement.

Computer Hardware for Video

(a) Video camera for capturing video data.

(b) Video monitor for displaying video data.

(c) A video board, (video card) equipped with A/D and D/A converters. In addition to performing the basic function of A/D and D/A conversion of video signals, a video board also has connectors for video camera and video monitor.

(d) Video editors to cut and paste video sequences, to add special effects, and to create new video sequences from existing video sequences.

Software for Video

(a) Video clips: This is a library of video clips from which one can select and directly import a video clip and use it in a multimedia application. This saves time and effort that might otherwise be required to create a similar video clip.

(b) Recording and playback capabilities: A multimedia system with video capability should allow the user to control the recording and display the video sequence.

14.3.5 Animation

The term "animation" refers to any visual movement effect created automatically i.e. without manual user interaction. Animation is one of the most dynamic form of multimedia. Unlike graphics, animations can provide dynamic movements to the objects. For example, to show a bird flying in the air, all that graphics can provide is a digital photograph of the same. However, with animations, we could actualy view the bird flying in the monitor of the PC. Computer animation deals with the generation, sequencing and display (at a specified rate) of a set of images (called frames) to create an effect of visual change or motion, similar to a movie film (video). Animation is an important component of multimedia because just as a picture is a powerful way to illustrate information, a small animation clip is even more powerful and is very useful for illustrating concepts that involve movement.

Hardware requirements for animation

1. Image generation tool and devices such as scanners, digital camera, and video capture board interfaced to some standard video source like video camera or video cassette recorder (VCR) are used to generate images to be used in animation.
2. Computer monitors with image displaying capability is the minimum requirement for displaying animation. In addition, multimedia computer systems capable of handling animation also require a graphics accelerator board that not only controls the resolution and number of colours of display, but also speeds up the refresh rate.

Software Requirements for Animation

1. Animation creation software: This software allows the user to create animation sequences from scratch by using a mouse and various simple objects such as lines, circles and polygons with various supporting colours.
2. Screen capture software: Screen capture software packages are used to capture the displays of a computer screen as graphic images, which can be used in animation.
3. Animation clips: This is a library of animation clips from which one can select and directly import an animation clip and use it in a multimedia application. This saves enormous time and effort that might otherwise be required to create a similar animation clip.
4. Software support for high resolution: If the animation sequences of a multimedia application are made up of very high quality images, it is important to have not only the necessary hardware but also software support for displaying high resolution images having many colours to maintain high quality of animation display.
5. Recording and playback capabilities: A multimedia system with animation capability should allow the user to control the recording and display of an animation sequence. For example, it should provide the user with option to 'pause' or 'replay' the animation sequence.
6. Transition effects: Transition effect uses to describe the way that slide arrives on the screen. In cartoon film when one scene ends and another scene begins, there is a transitions between them. For example, the picture can fade out and then fade in to the new scene or the first scene slides off the screen as the second scene slides onto the screen. Animation can be more interesting if it is enhanced with transition effects such as fade-in, and fade-out, layering, zooming and rotation of objects.

14.3.6 Images and their Types

There are many standards for image or graphic files. But they are all incompatible with each other. Most of the multimedia programs can, however, load or save a wide variety of graphic formats.

Graphics files

TIFF

TIFF stands for Tagged Image File Format. TIFF images create very large file sizes. TIFF images are uncompressed and thus contain a lot of detailed image data. It also extremely flexible in terms of color (they can be grayscale, or CMYK for print, or RGB for web) and content (layers, image tags). TIFF is the most common file type used in photo software (such as Photoshop), as well as page layout software (such as Quark and InDesign), again because a TIFF contains a lot of image data.

TIFF is widely used for transferring bitmap images between application programs. TIFF images have .tiff or .tif extension. It is used in desktop publishing, faxing, 3-D applications and medical imaging applications. It is a file format designed by Microsoft Corporation of USA.

JPEG (also known as JPG)

JPEG stands for Joint Photographic Experts Group, which created this standard for this type of image formatting. JPEG files are images that have been compressed to store a lot of information in a small-size file. Most digital cameras store photos in JPEG format, because then you can take more photos on one camera card than you can with other formats.

A JPEG is compressed in a way that loses some of the image detail during the compression in order to make the file small (and thus called "lossy" compression). JPEG files are usually used for photographs on the web, because they create a small file that is easily loaded on a web page and also looks good.

GIF

GIF stands for Graphics Interchange Format. It is another format that is widely used for picture displayed on the World Wide Web. GIF file format is commonly used to display indexed color graphics and images in Hypertext Markup Language (HTML) documents over the World Wide Web. GIF files have .gif extension.

GIFs also have an extremely limited color range suitable for the web but not for printing. This format is never used for photography, because of the limited number of colors. GIFs can also be used for animations.

BMP (Bitmap)

A bitmap is a type of image file format used to store digital images. The BMP format is a commonly use raster graphic format for saving image files. The BMP format stores color data for each pixel in the image without any compression. For example, a 10x10 pixel BMP image will include color data for 100 pixels. This method of storing image information allows for high-quality graphics, but also produces large file sizes.

PNG

PNG stands for Portable Network Graphics. It was created as an open format to replace GIF, because the patent for GIF. It also allows for a full range of color and better compression. It is used almost exclusively for web images, never for print images. For photographs, PNG is not as good as JPEG, because it creates a larger file.

PNG supports a large set of technical features; including superior lossless compression feature. Compression in PNG is called the ZIP (Zone Information Protocol) method. PNG comes in two formats, PNG-8 and PNG-24.

Raw Image Files

Raw image files contain data from a digital camera (usually). The files are called raw because they haven t been processed and therefore can t be edited or printed yet. There are a lot of different raw formats each camera company often has its own proprietary format.

Raw files usually contain a vast amount of data that is uncompressed. Because of this, the size of a raw file is extremely large. Usually they are converted to TIFF before editing and color-correcting.

Audio File Format

A sound file's format is simply a recognized methodology for organizing the digitized sound's data bits and bytes into a data file. The structure of the file must be known before data can be saved or later loaded into a computer to be edited or played as sound.

There are various types of sound files to support different types of playback requirements. Different types of software are used to playback different kinds of sound files. Types of sound files are discussed in following sections.

AIFF

AIFF (Audio Interchange File Format) is a proprietary Audio Format developed by Apple. This format can store monaural or multichannel sampled sounds in a range of sample rates and sample resolutions. The extension for this file type is .aif and .ief when it is used on a PC. An AIFF file contains the raw audio data, channel information (monophoic or stereophonic), bit depth, sample rate and application-specific data areas. The application-specific data areas let different applications add information to the file header that remains there even if the file is opened and processed by another application. For example, a file could retain information about selected regions of the audio data used for recalling zoom level not used by other applications.

MIDI

MIDI refers to Musical Instrument Digital Interface. In computer science, it is a serial interface standard that allows for the connection of music synthesizers, musical instruments and computers.

Synthesizers are electronic instruments which allow us to generate digital samples of sound of various instruments synthetically, i.e., without the actual instrument being present. The sound samples can be modulated through appropriate hardware to change their loudness, pitch, etc.

MIDI sound file stores a list of events that describe a specific step, which is used by a play back device or sound card to generate the sound specified by the events in the MIDI file. The playback device or the sound cards have predefined tasks of generating sound for each step in the events of the MIDI sound file. MIDI sound files are smaller than digital audio files.

WAV

A Wav (Wave Form) file is an audio file format. WAV sound files end with a .wav extension. It has became a standard PC audio file format that can be played by nearly all Windows applications that support sound. WAV files store actual sounds, much as music CDs and tapes do. WAV files can be large and may require compression. In addition, to the uncompressed raw audio data, the WAV file format stores information about the file's number of traces (mono or stereo), sample rate and bit depth.

The sound is sampled at regular intervals and each sample of the sound is stored as digital information in bit and bytes. The frequency at which the sound is sampled is called sampling rate, and is usually in the range 11 kHz-44 kHz. The amount of information stored at each sample point is the sample size, which is called resolution.

MP3

MP3 (Moving Pictures Expert Group Layer–3) is a file format for storing compressed digital audio on computers. By using compression, MP3 files take up only one-tenth of the space of uncompressed high-quality audio. MP3 files generally end with extension .mp3. These files can be download from a number of Websites. Winamp (PC) MacAmp (Mac) and mpg123 (UNIX) are popular MP3 players.

WMA

WMA stands for Windows Media Audio. WMA, an audio format owned by Microsoft, is a part of Microsoft's Windows Media technology, which includes Microsoft's Digital Rights Management tools, Windows Media Video encoding technology and Windows Media Audio encoding technology.

AVI

AVI (Audio Video Interleaved) is a multimedia file format that can be used for storing sound and moving pictures in Resource Interchange File Format (RIFF) developed by Microsoft. As AVI combines audio and video into a single frame or track, it saves valuable disk space and keeps audio in synchronization with the corresponding video. AVI files are widely supported by media player and video production programs.

Video File Format

File Format, in computer science, is the structure of a file that defines the way through which it is stored on the hard disk and laid out on the screen or taken as printout print. The format can be fairly simple and common (files stored as plain ASCII (American Standard Code for Information Interchange) text or it can be quite complex and may include various types of control instructions and codes used by programs and by printers and other devices. Examples include RTF (Rich Text Format), DCA (Document Content Architecture), PICT, DIF (Data Interchange Format), DXF (Drawing Exchange Format), TIFF (Tagged Image File Format), and EPSF (Encapsulated PostScript Format).

As with audio, in the early days of the Web, adding movie/video to a Web page meant using one of the currently available movie/video formats (such as QuickTime or AVI) and linking it to a page for download.

Some of the movie/video file formats are as follows:

(a) `.avi`: The standard movie/video format for Windows.

(b) `.mpg/mpeg`: A standard movie format for saving movies on the Internet, using the MPEG (Motion Picture Expert Group) compression scheme.

(c) `.mov`: The common format for QuickTime movies, the Macintosh native movie platform.

AVI File Format

Audio Video Interleave (AVI) format is the standard Windows format for audio/video data. This format exports a movie as a Windows video, but discards any interactivity. Because, AVI is a bitmap-based format, movies that contains long or high-resolution animations can quickly become very large in a file size.

AVI is a raster-based video format that will transfer nicely into a video editing application.

MPEG File Format

MPEG is the acronym for Moving Pictures Experts Group, a committee that developed the MPEG standard. It is a set of specifications for compressing and playing back full-motion video, including movies and video clips. Viewing a MPEG video on a microcomputer requires a MPEG decoder, which can be hardware, software, or a combination of the two.

MPEG achieves high compression rate by storing only the changes from one frame to another, instead of each entire frame. Although MPEG is a lossy compression method, the loss of video data is generally imperceptible to human eye. For this reason, MPEG generally produces better-quality video than competing formats, such as AVI and QuickTime. For example MPEG-1, MPEG-2, MPEG-4 and MPEG-7 and MPEG-21. MPEG is a family of popular multimedia file formats and associated compression schemes defined by the Moving Pictures Expert Group. MPEG-1 video was designed for use on CD-ROMs and provides picture quality somewhat comparable to VHS. MPEG-2 video was designed for use on DVD (Digital Versatile/Video Disk), and can provide high quality full screen video with smaller file sizes.

SWF File Format

Macromedia Flash (SWF or Shock Wave File) is a file format of the Macromedia Flash Player for creating and displaying Interactive vector-based images and animated Web graphics. Macromedia Flash files are very compact and of high quality, making them ideal for use on the Web. The SWF file format was designed as a very efficient delivery format and not as a format for exchanging graphics between graphics editors. It was designed to meet the following goals:

(a) On-screen Display: The format is primarily intended for on-screen display. Therefore, it supports anti-aliasing, fast rendering to a bitmap of any color format, animation and interactive buttons.

(c) Network Delivery: The files can be delivered over a network with limited and unpredictable bandwidth. The files are compressed to be small and support incremental rendering through streaming.

(d) Simplicity: The format is so simple that the user has to depend upon only a very limited set of operating system functionalities.

(e) File Independence: Files can be displayed without any dependence on external resources, such as fonts.

(f) Scalability: Different computers have different monitor resolutions and bit depths. Files work well on limited hardware, while taking advantage of more expensive hardware when it is available.

(g) Speed: The files are designed to be rendered very quickly with high quality of graphics.

The SWF format for images on the Internet has several valuable advantages over other format types. Some of these advantages include:

(a) Since it has good compression, the Web pages can be loaded extremely fast.

(b) It can also support embedded forms, script, user interface components and XML (eXtensible Markup Language) feeds.

(c) It allows vibrant animations and sounds in its presentation.

MOV File Format

The QuickTime (MOV or Movie) file format is used for video and animation. QuickTime files run on all Macintosh computers and on Windows based computers that have a QuickTime driver installed.

QuickTime is a file format for storing and playing back movies with sound. QuickTime files usually appear with the `.MOV` extension in Windows. With its high compression, Quick Time 4.0 was the first version to fully support streaming audio and video. The QuickTime 5 also plays MP3s, MIDIs and WAV files. Because it can handle multiple audio, video and graphic file formats, QuickTime is popular for multimedia development.

DAT File Format

DAT file format is not a video file format, rather video data given an alternative extension. DAT Files containing generic input or output. For example, if you open up a VCD (Video Compact Disk) and take a look at its contents, you will notice there are several folders is there and not one single `.mpg` file. The files have either a VCD or DAT extension. The actual videos you burned are not the VCD files but the DAT files. With a VCD, the video files are converted to DAT files named sequentially in the following format - AVSEQ01.DAT, AVSEQ02.DAT, AVSEQ03.DAT, etc. You will find these DAT files in the folder MPEGAV on the CD. Thus, DAT file can be played from your hard drive, just like regular video files, except that you will have to choose Open With to associate the DAT file with Windows Media Player 7 and up, which will recognize it as a valid video file.

MPEG

MPEG standards have been developed by the moving picture experts group convened by the International Standard Organization (ISO) and the International Electro technical commission to create standards for digital representation of moving pictures and associated audio and other data.

MPEG–1

MPEG–1 specification was released in 1992. In this you can deliver 1.2 Mbps of video and 250 kbps of two channel stereo audio using CD-ROM technology.

The MPEG-1 standard was developed in response to industry needs for an efficient way of storing and retrieving video information on digital storage media. One such inexpensive medium is the CD-ROM (Compact Disk Read Only Memory), other storage and transmission media can include DAT, Winchester disk, optical disk, ISDN (Integrated Services Digital Network) and LAN (Local Area Network). In fact, the data rate is variable and all decoders must be able to decode at rates up to 1.856 mb/s. The video is strictly progressive (i.e., non interlaced) and picture quality is equivalent to VHS (Video Home System).

MPEG–2

MPEG–2 specifications was released in 1994. It is completely different system from MPEG–1, requires higher data rates (3 to 15 mbps) but delivers higher image resolution, picture quality, interlaced video formats and interlaced video formats and interlaced video formats. MPEG-2 is the video compression standard required for Digital Television (DTV) and making DVDs.

The MPEG-2 standard was developed to provide the capability of compressing, coding, and transmitting high quality, multichannel, multimedia signals over broad-band networks. Since MPEG-2 was designed mainly as a transmission standard, it supports a variety of packet format and provide error correction capability that is suitable for transmission over cable and satellite links.

MPEG–4

MPEG–4 specification was released in 1998 and 1999. It provides a content based method for assimilating multimedia element. It offers not only indexing, hyperlinking, querying, browsing uploading, downloading, and deleting functions but also "hybrid natural and synthetic data coding". With MPEG–4, multiple views, layers, and multiple sound tracks of a scene, as well as stereoscopic and 3D views are available, making virtual reality workable.

Recently, the focus of video coding has shifted to object based coding at bit rates of 8 Kb/s or lower and 1 Mb/s or higher. Key aspects of this newly proposed MPEG-4 standard include independent coding of objects in a picture frame, the ability to interactively composite these objects into a scene at the display; the ability to combine graphics, animated objects in the scene, and the ability to transmit scenes in higher dimensionality formats (e.g. 3D). Also, inherent in the MPEG-4 standard is the concept of video scalability, both in the temporal and spatial domains, in order to effectively control the video bit rate at the transmitter, in the network, and at the receiver so as to match the available transmission and processing resources.

MPEG–21

MPEG–21 is an audio/video specification providing an Intellectual Property Management and Production (IPMP) system. The idea here is that when you get what is called a digital item, e.g. an image on the Web appears where you right-click to download that the file will let you know where to go to find who holds the rights to it.

RealVideo (.rm)

RealVideo is usually paired with RealAudio and packaged in a RealMedia (.rm) container. RealMedia is suitable for use as a streaming media format, that is one which is viewed while it is being sent over the network. Streaming video can be used to watch live television, since it does not require downloading the entire video in advance. Player for RealVideo is RealNetworks RealPlayer SP and is available for various platforms including Windows, Macintosh, and Linux.

14.3.7 Animation

Animation is the process of displaying still images to create the illusion of movement. These images can be hand drawn, computer generated or pictures or 3D objects.

Types

There are three main types of animation: traditional, stop motion and computer generated. Each can be used to make 2D or 3D images.

Traditional–Traditional animation involves every frame of a film by hand. After all the drawings are completed and colored, they can be photographed or scanned into a computer and then combined with sound on film.
Stop motion–In this process animators manipulate and photograph objects one motion and frame at a time.
Computer Generated–Animators can also use comptuer software to create films and models, which is generally faster than the traditional method. The characters and objects they make can be either two-dimensional or three-dimensional.

14.3.8 Digital Audio

Digital sound or audio is the technology, by which sound signals are represented as a series of binary digital data, i.e., zero and ones, which the computers can understand and comprehend.

Advantages of Digital Audio

Digital audio is the technology, by which sound signals are represented as a series of binary digital data, i.e., zero's and one's which computers can understand and comprehend. Once digitized, the sound can be processed like any other binary files, using the relevant editing and playback software. Digital audio has its own advantages over it predecessor analog audio.

1. Digital audio is less susceptible to degradation or distortion, because the entire transmission and all other transaction processes take place as electronic signals, avoiding the intervention of air or any other medium. Thus, the quality of the parent signal is maintained throughout.
2. Editing audio with computers makes cutting, pasting and manipulating of parent signals, very easy. Also a lot of special effects like the 'Echo' can be artificially added, without the need of any other hardware. On the other hand audio demanded very expensive hardware and a host of equipments to accomplish the same.
3. Digital audio is of superior quality during reproduction, because of non-intervention of air and other loss incurring mediums.
4. Digital audio can be stored as digital data, in reliable mediums like the CD-ROM (Compact Disk Read Only Memory). Thus extending their life of more than fifty years on an average without losses.

Digital Sampling
An audio signal is represented in digital memory with a binary code that stores a massive amount of numbers that are used to represent a signal. An ADC (Analog to Digital Converter) is a computer chip that is used to convert an analog signal into digital information. This process is called sampling.
Sample rates
Sample rates are measured in hertz (Hz), or cycles per second. This value is the number of samples captured per second to represent the waveform. Higher sample rates allow higher audio frequencies to be represented. The sample rate is more than double the highest audio frequency present, the waveform can be reconstructed exactly from the digital samples. Frequencies that are more than half the sample rate cannot be correctly represented in digital samples, and, if present in the original audio, must be removed before converting to digital. "Half the sample rate" therefore represents an upper limit called the Nyquit frequency, and the analog waveform must be entirely below this limit to be correctly represented digitally. Analog frequencies at this limit or above cannot be correctly represented by the digital samples and would cause a kind of distortion called aliasing.
As per audio specifications, CD sampling rate is of the orer of 44.1 kHz, or 44,100 samples per second. Therefore, the CS sampling rate of 44.1 kHz will capture frequencies up to 22 kHz.
Sample formats
The measure of audio quality is the sample format (or bit depth), which is usually measured by the number of computer bits used to represent each sample. The more bits that are used, the more precise the representation of each sample. Increasing the number of bits also increases the maximum dynamic range of the audio recording, in other words the difference in volume between the loudest and softest possible sounds that can be represented.
Dynamic range is measured in decibels (dB). To record digital audio with a dynamic range of far more than 90 dB, so that sounds that are too soft can be amplified for maximum fidelity.
Sample Resolution
The size of digital samples determiens how accurately a signal can be sampled. 8-bit sampling is poor because only 2^8 (256) discreate levels of a waveform can be representd. 16-bit resoultion can represent 65,536 different values so it is much better than 8-bit.
Digital Data Transmission
A digital signal can be transmitted in two ways; paralle and serial. In parallel transmission each bit is transmitted along its own path. In serial transmission each bit is transmitted one after another along a single path. Parallel transmission is faster but also more expensive and provided multiple lines for each bit whereas, serial transmission is less expensive but also slower as it requires a fixed transmission speed and word size.

14.3.9 Digital Video Software For Multimedia

Video editing is the process of manipulating video images. Video editing software can be used to record video, but is used more often in post-production design and editing raw footage in digital file formats.
Video Editing Software Features

Video editing software consists of software for the post-production of video editing. The source material is collected by digital video cameras, and this is imported into the software for editing. However, today video editing software is now available for personal computers and workstations. Typical video editing software includes tools to convert file formats, cut segments (trimming), join clips, re-sequence clips, adjust brightness/contrast, rotate or crop footage, add sound or add transitions and other special effects.

Cloud-Based Video Editing

Video editing applications are typically desktop programs, however there are several cloud-based options that allow you to upload a video and edit the file online. Cloud video editing applications typically allow you to connect to various social and online accounts to share your movie.

Free Video Editing Software

Many people use digital cameras or smartphones to record video, then use video editing software to add sound, trim clips and so on.

14.3.10 Introduction to MS-Publisher

MS-Publisher is a desktop publishing program that allows users to create professional-quality publications. It offers many options for design and fonts, and it can be used to create magazines, newsletters, pamphlets etc.
It includes templates for many types of common business needs, such a business cards, brochures, address labels and calendars. It offers the options to directly mail the file, export it as another file type or upload it to the cloud and publish online.

14.3.11 Photodraw

PhotoDraw is a business graphics program designed for Office users as it makes easy to create a professional graphics for printed documents. The product comes out with an extensive collection of ready-made design elements, which includes special effects for business users to customize content.

14.3.12 Developing Simple Application and Presentation using MS-Publisher

Here, we create a simple poster using MS-Publisher.

1. Click Start button then All Programs, and choose MS Publisher.
2. You will shown with the File tab, then select New from the side bar. The New page which offers a range of templates and designs to work.
4. Click on the More blank Page sizes icon in the Home page section as shown in Figure 14.1.

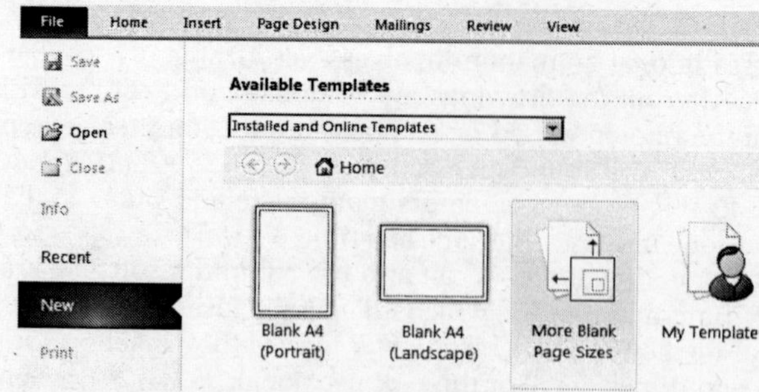

Figure 14.1 Select More blank page sizes

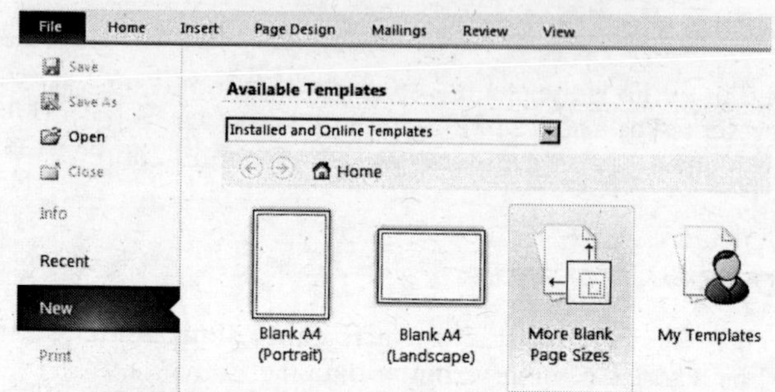

Figure 14.2 Select Create new page size

Click on the Create new page size icon in the Custom section as shown in Figure 14.2.

5. Create New Page size dialog box appers as shown in Figure 14.3.

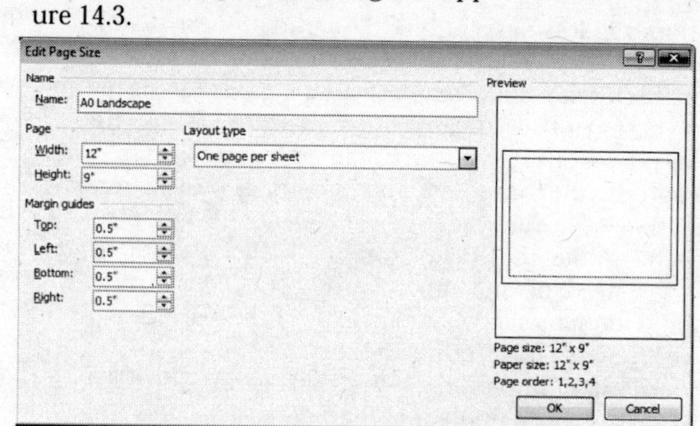

Figure 14.3 Select Create new page size

6. Enter "A0 Poster Landscape" in the name box.
7. Enter "12" inch for the widht and "9" inch for the height.
8. Enter "0.5" inch in each of the boxes under the margin guides (left,right,top, bottom)
   This will set the page size to that of an A0 Landscape poster with a 0.5 inch margin.
9. Press OK.
10. Under the Custom Page Sizes - you will see that you have two new A0 Poster sizes available as shown in Figure 14.4.
    Select the style you want to use:
    Landscape: for wide/short
    Portrait for tall/thin

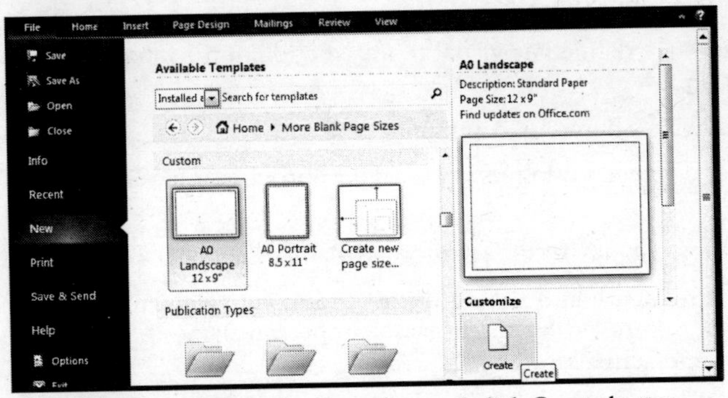

Figure 14.4 Select the Page size and click Create button

11. Click on the Create button. The application opens with the selected size document.

12. To apply the background color, click the Page Design tab, then select the desired background color in the Page Background group.

12. Here, to create a simple posert. Draw Text box in the Text group of Insert tab. Type BPB BOOK STORE, Available all Comptuer Books and CD/DVD Drive.

15. Click Insert tab, to insert Picture icon in the Illustrations group. The Insert Picture dialog box appears, select the picture file that you want to use and click Insert button as shown in Figure 14.5.

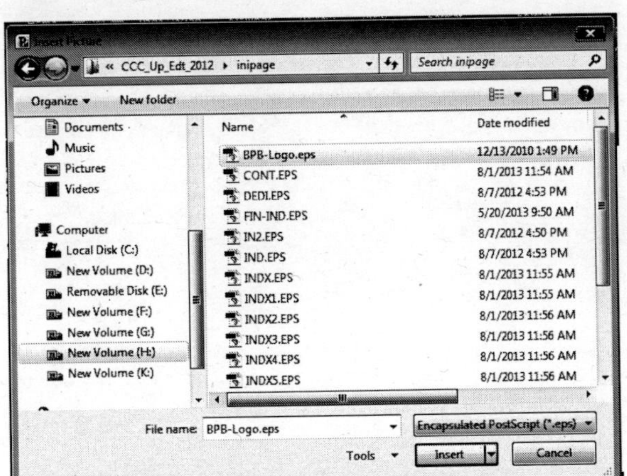

Figure 14.5 Insert picture dialog box

16. Select the object you want to group. Select the Drawing Tools, click Format tab and from the Arrange group, choose Group. The objects become single object as shown in Figure 14.6.

17. Click the Save As button to the save the poster. The Save As dialog box appears as shown in Figure 14.7.

18. Type the name of the file in the File name: list box and click Save button.

Figure 14.6

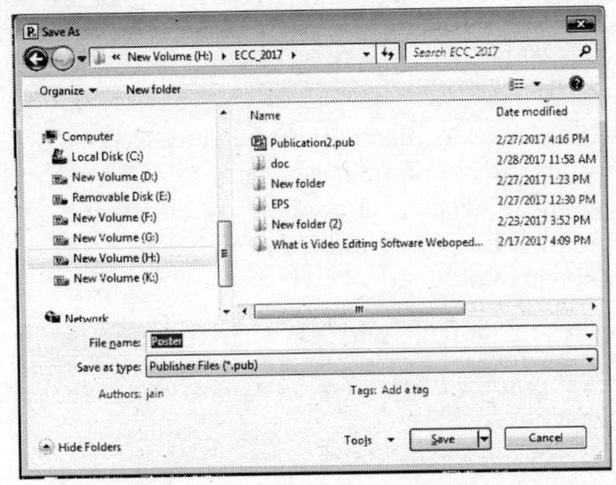

Figure 14.7 Save As dialog box

MODEL QUESTIONS AND ANSWERS

A. Multiple Choice

1.1 Multimedia is combination of:

a. Text b. Audio and Video
c. Graphics d. All of the above

1.2 To make a good multimedia communication, you need:

a. Hardware and software b. Good ideas
c. Talent and skill d. All of the above

1.3 Multimedia hardware requires:

a. Sound card b. Video capture card
c. Large size of main memory d. All of the above

1.4 Which one of the following is not an input device?

a. Microphone b. Mouse
c. Scanner d. None of the above

1.5 Which one of the following is not an output device?

a. Monitor b. Printer
c. Plotter d. Digitizer

1.6 Which one is not a multimedia device?

a. TV System b. A book having only text (no diagram)

c. A modern personal computer d. None of the above

1.7 Which of the following is an example of hypermedia application?
a. World Wide Web b. PowerPoint
c. Adobe Acrobat d. All of the above

1.8 The elements of multimedia are:
a. Video, animation, interactivity
b. Sound, video, animation, interactivity
c. Graphics, sound, video, animation, interactivity
d. Text, graphics, sound, video, animation, interactivity

1.9 Historically, the term "hypertext" was used when textured information was linked in ____ ways.
a. Sequential b. Real time
c. Non-sequential d. Linear

1.10 Multimedia is used in which three main areas?
a. Television, Movies and Newspapers
b. Education, Television and Radio
c. Education, Information and Entertainment
d. All of the above

B. State whether the following are True or False

2.1 Pictures, photographic image and other artwork is called graphics or pictures.

2.2 Multimedia requires additional hardware which can handle sound, video, etc.

2.3 Images are defined as visual representation of the information.

2.4 Clip Art is a library of commonly used text.

2.5 Laser printers or plotters are used for output graphics in hardcopy.

2.6 Multimedia may include text-based elements.

2.7 If the sequence and timing of the multimedia elements can be controlled by the user, then one can name it as Non-Interactive Multimedia.

2.8 Touch screen is basically a monitor that allows user to interact with computer by touching the display screen.

2.9 A scanner's resolution is measured in megapixels.

2.10 Animation is used to create movements on the screen.

Answers

A.	1.1	d	1.2	d	1.3	d	1.4	d	1.5	d
	1.6	b	1.7	a	1.8	d	1.9	c	1.10	d
B.	2.1	T	2.2	T	2.3	T	2.4	F	2.5	T
	2.6	T	2.7	F	2.8	T	2.9	F	2.10	T

CHAPTER 15

HTML Programming Basics

15.1 INTRODUCTION

Hypertext Markup Language (HTML) is a language understood by your web browser like Internet Explorer or Netscape Navigator. All the documents available on the World Wide Web are written in HTML, that run on any type of computer having a Web browser. It has a collection of styles (indicated by tags) that define the various components of a World Wide Web document. An HTML document can be opened in any operating system or any hardware such as PC, Macintosh or Unix operated machine.

15.2 FRONTPAGE/INTERDEV

Microsoft FrontPage is a full featured HTML editor. A Web site is a group of HTML pages and graphics that are interconnected with hyperlinks. A FrontPage Web site is a site created in FrontPage. It contains Web pages graphics, documents, multimedia.

FrontPage includes the FrontPage Explorer, where you can create, design and manage your Web site and the FrontPage Editor, where you create and edit Web pages without HTML. It includes many features that make Web-site creation eady for any user.

You use the FrontPage Editor to create, design, and edit World Wide Web pages. As you add text, images, tables, form fields, and other elemetns to your page, the FrontPage Editor displays them as they would appear in a Web browser. If you want to edit HTML code directly, you can using the FrontPage Editor's HTML view. In this view, you can enter text, edit HTML tags or script code, and use standard word-processing commands such as cutting, pasting, finding and replacing.

Visual InterDev was a Microsoft IDE used to build dynamic websites using Active Server Pages (ASP). The Visual InterDev interface is very similar to the Visual Basic environment and was included as part Visual Studio.

Visual InterDev is a comprehensive development tool that allows you to build Web sites and Web applications. You can use Visual InterDev to build individual HTML pages. Active Server Pages, as well as large scale Web applications that involve hundreds of pages designed to be used by thousands of people. In addition, the tool has features allowing you to do complete site design and to debug the pages within your site.

15.3 CONCEPTS OF HTML PAGE STRUCTURE

An HTML page consists of the following tags:

<HTML> : This tag specifies the document as an HTML document.

<HEAD> : This tag contains information about the document, including its title, scripts used, style definitions and document descriptions.

<TITLE> : This tag contains the document title. The title specified inside <Title> tag appears on the browser's title bar. You should be very careful while choosing the title because a title is also used to identify a web page for search engines.

<BODY> : This forms the largest part of the HTML document. The <Body> tag encloses all the tags, attributes and information to be displayed in the web page. The information written within the body tag is displayed in the browser window.

The following Example 1 shows the tags that make up the standard skeletal structure of an HTML document:

Example 1

```
<HTML>
<HEAD>
<TITLE>Document Title</TITLE>
</HEAD>
<BODY>
Contents of Document
</BODY>
</HTML>
```

Above tags are explained in detail in following section.

15.3.1 Different HTML Tags

HTML Element <Html>

The HTML element tells the web browser that the file contains HTML-coded information. The file extension **.html** also indicates that this is an HTML document. An HTML document must contain this extension.

HEAD Element <Head>

Head element identifies the first part of the HTML-coded document containing the title. The title is shown as part of the browser's window.

Information placed in the Head is essential to the inner working of the document and has nothing to do with the content of the document. With the exception of information contained within the **<TITLE> </TITLE>** tags, all information placed within the **<HEAD> </HEAD>** tags is not displayed by the browser. HTML tags that are used to show the start and end of the head section are:

```
<HEAD>
   <TITLE> </TITLE>
</HEAD>
```

TITLE Element <Title>

Title element contains the document's title and identifies its contents in a global context. The title is displayed somewhere in the browser window (usually at the top), but not within the text area.

☞ You should choose title head somewhat descriptive, unique and relatively short.

For example, you might include a shortened title of a book along with the chapter contents: WINDOWS 7 Guide: Installation. This tells the software name, the platform, and the chapter contents, which is more useful than simply calling the document Installation. Generally, you should keep the title limited to 64 characters or less.

ADDRESS Element <ADDRESS>

Just as the title can be placed in the title bar of the browser window, certain information is commonly placed at the foot of the web page. For example, Copyright information and contact details of a company, etc.

The HTML tags used for this purpose are:

<ADDRESS> **</ADDRESS>**

The **<ADDRESS>** tag should be placed immediately after the last line of the textual material of the web page. However, it could also be placed anywhere in the body of the document. The text typed within these **<ADDRESS>** tags appears in Italics.

BODY <BODY>

The second and largest part of HTML document is the body, which contains the contents of the document (displayed within the text area of a browser window). The tags explained below are used within the body of the HTML document.

The tags used to indicate the start and the end of the main body of textual information are:

<BODY>

</BODY>

The default characteristics of a page, such as background colour, text colour, font size and font width, etc., can be specified as attributes of the **<BODY>** tag. The attributes for the **<BODY>** tag are as follows:

(a) BACKGROUND
(b) BGCOLOR
(c) TEXT
(d) LINK, ALINK AND VLINK
(d) LEFT MARGIN
(e) TOP MARGIN

BACKGROUND

This attribute is used to specify a URL, which is pointing to an image. It specifies the name of the GIF file (image) that will be used as the background of the document. The GIF tiles up across the page to give a background.

Syntax:

```
<Body background="filename.gif">
```

Example 2

```
<html>
  <head>
  <TITLE>Simple Background Image</TITLE>
  </head>
  <body background="Mountain.jpg">
  <H1>HTML is very EASY to Learn </H1>
  <P>Welcome to the world of HTML.</P>
  </body>
  </html>
```

The output of the above example as shown in Figure 15.1.

Figure 15.1 Display of the HTML document shown in Example 2 as shown by the Internet Explorer

BGCOLOR

`BGCOLOR` changes the default background colour as per the specified colour. The program in Figure 15.2 gives the background as Gray but text displayed in Yellow. This is possible by giving the body attribute BGCOLOR = GREY and TEXT = YELLOW.

The COLOR attribute is used to specify the colour of the text to be shown on the screen. A six-digit number and letter combinations represent colors by giving their RGB (red, green, blue) values. The six digits are actually three two-digit numbers in sequence, representing the amount of red, green, or blue as a hexadecimal value in the range 00-FF. For example, 000000 is black (no color at all), FF0000 is bright red, 0000FF is bright blue, and FFFFFF is white (fully saturated with all three colors). Table 15.1 gives the RGB values of some common colors.

Table 15.1 Colors and their RGB values

Color name	Hexadecimal Value	RGB
Aqua	# 00FFFF	
Black	# 000000	

(Contd...)

Color name	Hexadecimal Value	RGB
Blue	# 0000FF	
Fuchsia	# FF00FF	
Grey	# 808080	
Green	# 008000	
Lime	# 00FF00	
Maroon	# 800000	
Olive	# 808000	
Purple	# 800080	
Red	# FF0000	
Silver	# C0C0C0	
White	# FFFFFF	
Yellow	# FFFF00	

Example 3

```
<html>
<head>
<TITLE>A Simple HTML Example</TITLE>
</head>
<body bgcolor = Grey Text=Yellow>
<H1>HTML is very EASY to Learn </H1>
<P>Welcome to the World of HTML.</P>
</body>
</html>
```

The output of the above example 3 is shown in Figure 15.2.

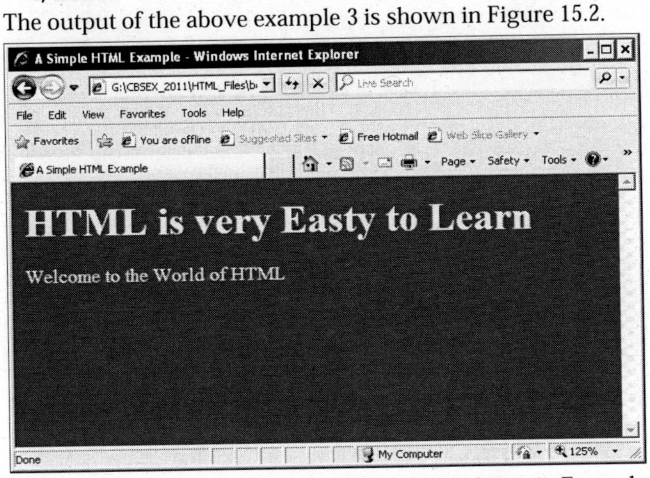

Figure 15.2 Display of the HTML document shown in Example 3 as read by the Internet Explorer

TEXT

This command changes the body text colour from its default value to the colour specified with this attribute. A sample HTML document containing **<BODY>** attributes is shown in Figure 15.3. This HTML document contains various elements described so far.

Example 4

```
<html>
<head>
<TITLE> A Simple HTML Example</TITLE>
</head>
<body TEXT = BLUE>
<H1>HTML is very EASY to Learn </H1>
<P>Welcome to the world of HTML.</P>
</body>
</html>
```

The output of the above example 4 as shown in Figure 15.3.

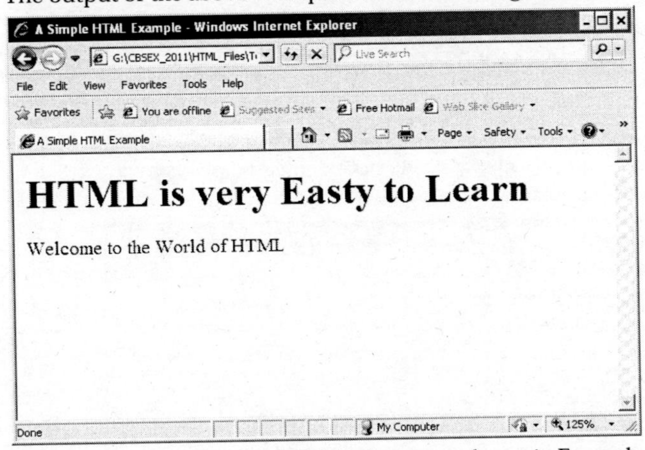

Figure 15.3 Display of the HTML document shown in Example 4 as read by the Internet Explorer

LINK, ALINK and VLINK

To change the background colour and the text, it also possible to define the colours of links by setting the <BODY> element attributes: LINK, ALINK and VLINK.

LINK–Sets the colour of unvisited links in a document. The default colour of Link attribute is Red.

ALINK–It defines the colour of the link as it is being clicked. The default colour of Link attribute is Blue.

VLINK–It defines the colour of a link after it has been visited. The default colour of VLINK attribute is purple.

Example 5

```
<html>
<head>
<TITLE>A Simple HTML Example</TITLE>
</head>
<Body    bgcolor="#808000"    text="#00FFFF"
link="#FF0000"                vlink="#0000FF"
alink="#8000080">
<H1>HTML is very EASY to Learn </H1>
<P>Welcome to the world of HTML.</P>
</body>
</html>
```

The above example 5 will create a Navy page with Aqua text, red links, blue visited links and purple active links.

LEFT MARGIN

The LEFTMARGIN attribute of <Body> tag is used to specify the distance between the left side of the document and the left edge of the browser window.

Syntax:

<Body leftmargin=value> </body>

Example 6

```
<html>
<head>
<TITLE>LEFT MARGIN ATTRIBUTE</TITLE>
</head>
<Body Leftmargin="90" TEXT="RED">
<H1>This is Left Margin</H1>
</body>
</html>
```

The output of the example 6 is shown in Figure 15.4. The text between the <Body> element will be indented 90 pixels away from the left-hand side of the page.

Figure 15.4 Display of HTML document shown in Example 6 as read by the Internet Explorer

TOP MARGIN

The TOPMARGIN attribute of <Body> tag is used to specify the distance between the Top of the document and the Top of the browser window.

Example 7

```
<html>
<head>
<TITLE>TOP MARGIN ATTRIBUTE</TITLE>
</head>
<Body Leftmargin="80" Topmargin="160"
TEXT="RED">
<H1>HTML is very EASY to Learn </H1>
<P>Welcome to the world of HTML.</P>
</body>
</html>
```

The output of example 7 as shown in Figure 15.5. The text between the <Body> element will be indented 80 pixels away from the left-side and then 160 pixels away from the Top of the page.

Font Element

The font element **<FONT> </FONT>** is used to format the size, type face and colour of the enclosed text. This element will change the appearance of the text of the body for visual markup of the contents.

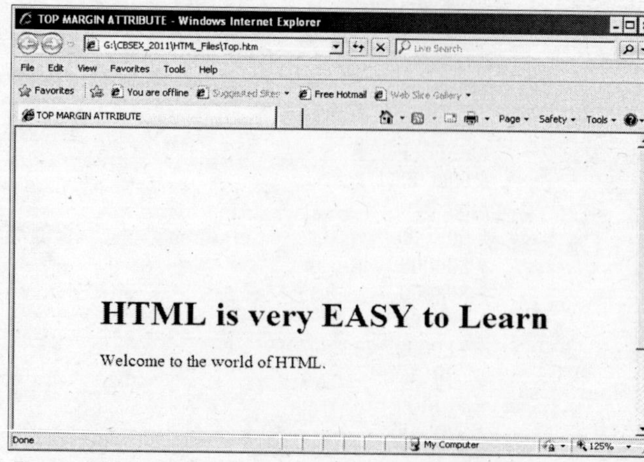

Figure 15.5 Display of the HTML document given in Example 7 as read by the Internet Explorer

The **<FONT>** tag has three attributes namely SIZE, FACE and COLOR. All text specified within the tags **<FONT> </FONT>** will appear in the font, size and colour as specified by the attributes of the tag **<FONT>**.

Font Size

To set the relative size of the text by setting the SIZE attribute at the <FONT> element. The SIZE attribute is represented as <FONT SIZE = Value>

The SIZE attribute can be specified in absolute or relative vlues ranging from 1(smallest) to 7 (largest). Using a relative font size (putting a plus or a minus sign before the number) will change the font size relative to the BASEFONT tag or the default font size. For example, **<FONT SIZE = "+12">**.

Example 8

```
<html>
<head>
<TITLE>A Simple HTML Example</TITLE>
</head>
<Body Bgcolor="Aqua" TEXT="Black">
<Font size="7">
<p>This font is largest size</P> <BR>
<Font Size="3">
This font is Smallest size.
<font size="+12">This font size is larger than
font size 7.
</body>
</html>
```

The above example will display the text in the largest and smallest font size. The output of example 8 is shown in Figure 15.6.

Font Face

The FACE attributes specifies a typeface that you would like to use for the text enclosed by the font element. You can use a single typeface (such as Arial, Courier and Verdana) or you can give a list of typefaces sepearated by commas. The FACE attribute is represented as:

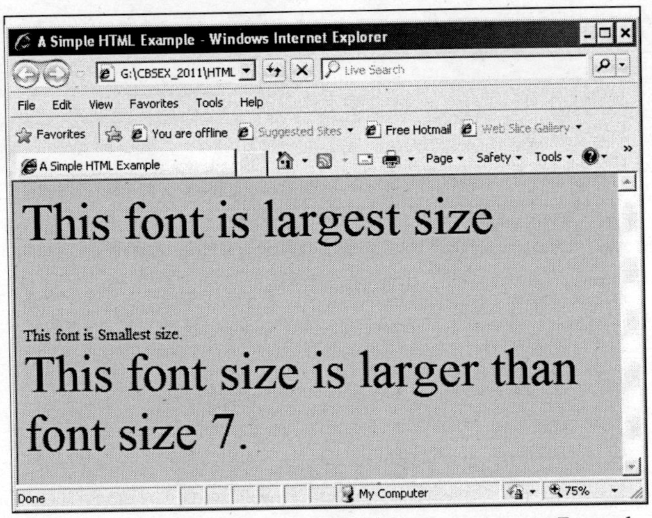

Figure 15.6 Display of the HTML document given in Example 8 as read by the Internet Explorer

```
<FONT FACE = "Font Name">
```

Example 9

```
<html>
<head>
<TITLE>A Simple HTML Example</TITLE>
</head>
<Body Bgcolor="Aqua" TEXT="Black">
<p><Font face="Arial" font size = "5">This
text is dispalyed in Arial</p> <BR>
<p><Font face="Courier, Verdana">This text is
displayed in either Courier or Verdana</p>
</body>
</html>
```

The above example will display the text in different faces as shown in Figure 15.7.

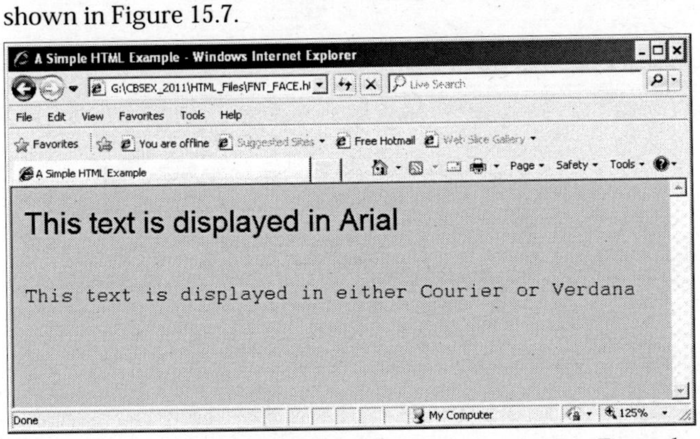

Figure 15.7 Display of the HTML document given in Example 9 as read by the Internet Explorer

Font Color

The COLOR attribute is used to specify the colour of the text to be shown on the screen. The colour can be set by giving the name of the colour supported by the browsrer or by giving the value as #RRGGBB, the hexadecimal colour value.

The FACE of attribute is represented as:

```
<FONT COLOR = "Aqua">
```

Example 10

```
<html>
<head>
<TITLE>A Simple HTML Example</TITLE>
</head>
<Body Bgcolor="Aqua">
<p><Font color="Red" font size = "5">This text
is dispalyed in colour red and size is
5</p></font> <BR>
<p><Font color="#808000" Font face = "Calibri"
font size="8">This text is displayed in color
Maroon and font face is Calibri</p>
</body>
</html>
```

The above example will display the text in different faces as shown in Figure 15.8.

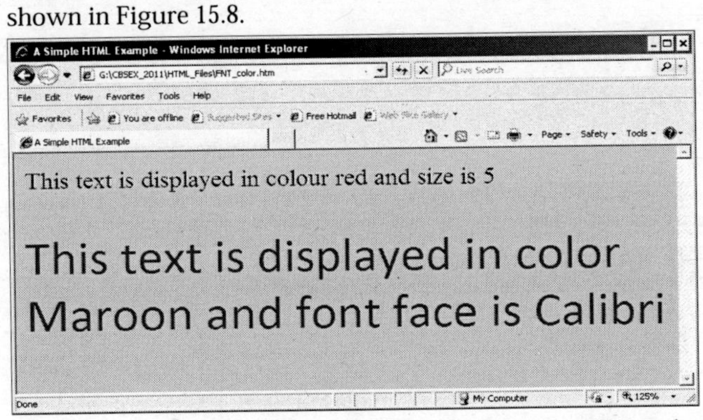

Figure 15.8 Display of the HTML document given in Example 10 as read by the Internet Explorer

15.3.2 HTML Images

An image can be inserted into a Web page using the tag `<IMG> </IMG>`. This tag takes the name of the image file (filename.gif) as an attribute. In addition, HTML also allows control of the height, width, border, etc., of every image placed on Web page. The attributes are associated with <IMG> tag.

The IMG element is empty, meaning there is no closing `</IMG>`. It has several attributes:

```
SRC = "image_url"
```

SRC gives the URL of the image document. The URL points the location where the image is stored.

Aligning Image in Web Page

ALIGN tells the browser how to align the image with the text. There are different types of alignments these are:

Top align: It aligns the Top of the image with the top margin of the item in the line Align="TOP".

Bottom align: It aligns the Bottom of the image with the baseline of the text Align="BOTTOM".

Middle align: It aligns the Middle of the image with the baseline of the text Align="MIDDLE".

Left and Right align: It supports left and right-aligned images. The image floats to the left or right margins, with the text following the image element flowing around the image, for example, Align="Left" and Align="Right".

Border: Specifies the size of the border to place around the image.

Width: Specifies the width of the image in pixels.

Height: Specifies the height of the image in pixels.

HSPACE: Indicates the amount of space to the left and right of the image.

VSPACE: Indicates the amount of space to the top and bottom of the image.

ALT: Indicates the text to be displayed in case the browser unable to display the image specified in the SRC attribute.

Example 11

```
<html>
<head>
<TITLE>Image at the Top of the Image</TITLE>
</head>
<Body Bgcolor="Aqua" Text="Black">
<H2 ALIGN="CENTER">Inserting Images with IMG
Element</H2>
<p> <IMG SRC="sea.jpg" Align = "Top">
The IMG tag is used for inserting images in
HTML pages. The image may be located on the
same server as the page which it is inserted
into, but it may also be located on a differ-
ent server, if the full URL is specified.
</body>
</html>
```

The output of the above Example 11 is shown in Figure 15.9.

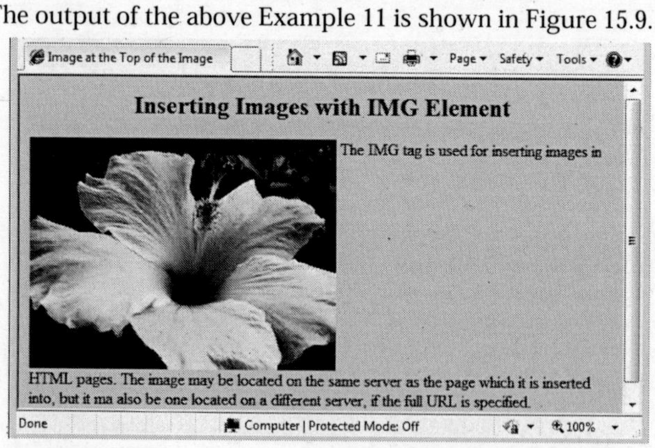

Figure 15.9 Viewing the image which is the result of Example 11

Using Alternate Text

Alternative text indicated by the attribute ALT = describes an image that you have inserted. You include alternative text for the following reasons:

- Some of your visitors may be using text-only browsers.
- A visitor may have turned off images for faster loading of files on the Internet.
- Sometimes, some browsers do not display images correctly.
- Sometimes, images do not display when the links do not work properly.
- Sometimes, browsers display alternative text while images load.

To add alternative text to your images, simply add the ALT = attribute to the <IMG> tag:

```
<IMG SRC = "Mount.jpg" ALT = "Beautiful Gar-
den">
```

Example 12

```
<html>
<head>
<TITLE>Image message with ALT attrib-
ute</TITLE>
</head>
<Body Bgcolor="Aqua" Text="Black">
<H2 ALIGN="CENTER">Inserting Images with IMG
Element and also insert ALT attribute</H2>
<p> <Center> <IMG SRC="Nature.jpg" Alt =
"Beautiful Garden"></center>
The IMG tag is used for inserting images in
HTML pages. The image may be located on the
same server as the page which it is inserted
into, but it may also be one located on a
different server, if the full URL is speci-
fied.
</body>
</html>
```

The output of the above example 12 as shown in Figure 15.10.

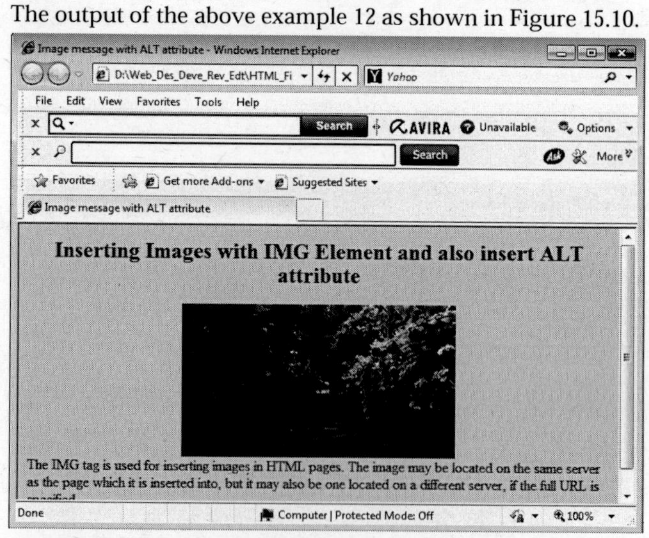

Figure 15.10 Viewing the image which is the result of Example 12

Setting an Image Border

You can set an image border around an image with the BORDER=attribute. In most browsers, by default, the border is visible only on images that are used as links. To turn the border off for all images, add the BORDER="0" attribute to the <IMG> tag. For example,

```
<IMG SRC = "Mount" ALT = "Beautiful Flower"
HEIGHT="180" WIDTH="250" BORDER="0">
```

Likewise, you can increase the border width around an image by increasing the value in the BORDER=attribute as in the following example:

```
<IMG SRC = "Mount" ALT = "Beautiful Flower"
HEIGHT="180" WIDTH="250" BORDER="8"
ALIGN=LEFT>
```

Example 13

```
<html>
<head>
<TITLE>Setting an Image Border</TITLE>
</head>
<Body Bgcolor="Aqua" Text="Black">
<H2 ALIGN="CENTER">Giving the border around an
Image</H2>
<p> <IMG SRC="Flower.jpg" Alt = "Beautiful
Flower" Border="8" Height="180" Width="250"
Align=LEFT>
The IMG tag is used for inserting images in
HTML pages. The image may be located on the
same server as the page which it is inserted
into, but it may also be one located on a
different server, if the full URL is speci-
fied.</p>
</body>
</html>
```

The output of the above example 13 is shown in Figure 15.11.

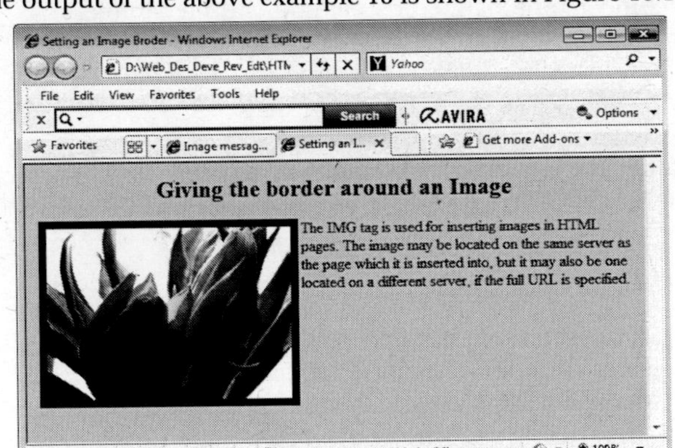

Figure 15.11 Viewing the image which is the result of Example 13

Resizing an Image

Images can be loaded faster by specifying the height and width of an image. As
the browser loads the page, it notes the height and width attributes and leaves that much space for the image.

To specify image height and width, add the HEIGHT= and WIDTH= attributes in the <IMG> tag as shown below:

```
<img scr="Mount.jpg" width="100" height="50">
```

Example 14

```
<html>
<head>
<TITLE>Resizing an Image</TITLE>
</head>
<Body Bgcolor="Aqua" Text="Black">
<H2 ALIGN="CENTER">Using the Height and Width
attributes</H2>
<IMG SRC="Mount.jpg" Align = "Left" Alt =
"Beautiful Mountain"
Height="180" Width="250">
<p>
The IMG tag is used for inserting images in
HTML pages. The image may be located on the
same server as the page which it is inserted
into, but it may also be one located on a
different server, if the full URL is speci-
fied.</p>
</body>
</html>
```

The output of the Example 14 is shown in Figure 15.12.

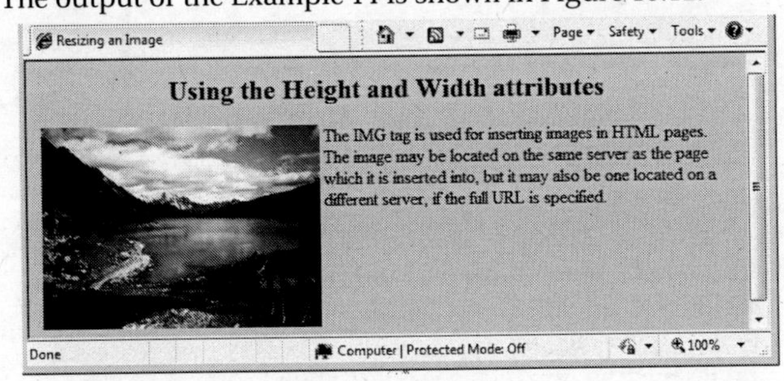

Figure 15.12 Viewing the image which is the result of Example 14

15.3.3 Creating Image Links

To add an image as a link, start by adding an image tag. The following steps need to be followed to add an image as a link in the HTML file program.

(a) Add an image tag and an SRC=attribute to the document as shown below:

```
<IMG SRC="Roses.jpg">
```

Note that Roses.jpg is the file which will be used for linking.

(b) Include an alternative text using the ALT=attribute as shown below:

```
<IMG SRC = "Roses.jpgf" ALT = "About
Roses">
```

(c) Add the remaining attributes you want to include, such as the HEIGHT= and WIDTH = and BORDER = attributes as follows:

```
<IMG SRC="Roses.jpg" WIDTH="300"
HEIGHT="80" BORDER="2" ALT="About Roses">
```

(d) Add the link anchor tag, <A> before and after the image as shown below:

```
<A><IMG     SRC="Roses.jpg"      WIDTH="300"
HEIGHT="80"   BORDER="2"    ALT    ="About
Roses"></A>
```

Example 15

```
<!DOCTYPE html>
<html>
<body>
<p>The image is a link. You can click on
it.</p>
<a href="Rose Flowers.html">
<img src="Nature.jpg" alt="HTML tutorial"
     style="width:42px;height:42px;border:1">
</a>
</body>
</html>
```

The output of the Example 15 is shown in Figure 15.13.

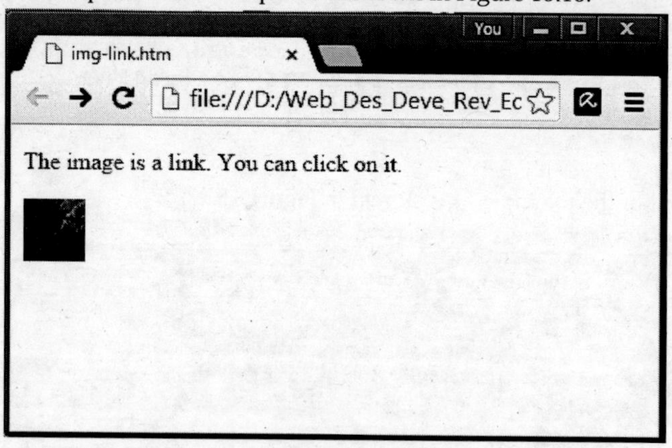

Figure 15.13 Viewing the image which is the result of Example 15

If you click the image, the link of the image opened.

Hyperlinks

Hyperlinks are created with an "href" tag (hyperlink!reference). The tag looks like this:

```
<a href="page1.html">Go To Page 1</a>
```

In this example, the text "Go To Page 1" becomes a hyperlink to a page called "page1.html". The link looks like this: Go To Page 1.

There are two distinct types of hyperlink: "absolute" and "relative". Absolute links are quite simple, but relative links are actually divided into two further categories: "document-relative" and "site-root-relative".

Absolute Links

An absolute link (or "absolute URL link") contains a complete internet address, just the same as if you typed the address into your browser's address bar. It doesn't matter where the source page is in relation to the destination page, the link will always work as long as the destination page exists. Most absolute links begin with "http://" and follow this simple format:

```
<a href="http://www.mywebsite.com/index.html"
>Go To My Site</a>
```

Document-Relative Links

Document-relative links use directions from the source page to the destination page.

There are three ways to do this - the method you use will depend on the location of the source and destination pages in relation to each other. To create hyperlinks from the page called!sourcepage.html to other pages in the site.

1. If the destination page is in the same directory as the source page All you need to specify is the source file name:
   <a href= page1.html >Go To Page 1</a>
2. If the destination page is in a folder inside the source page's folder Specify the folder name and then the file name:
   <a href= directory2/page2.html >Go To Page 2</a>
3. If the destination page is in a folder outside the source page's folder
   Use the special instruction!../!which signifies "one directory higher".
4. The following link means "Go up one directory level, then go to a folder called!directory3, then to a file called!page3.html":
   ```
   <a  href="../directory3/page3.html">Go  To
   Page 3</a>
   ```

Site-Root-Relative Links

Site-root-relative links use a single forward-slash!/!to signify the instruction: "Start at the document root of the site and go down the directory path from there." The format is:

```
<a href="/main-directory/directory4/page4.htm
l">Go To Page 4</a>
```

Despite the cumbersome name, this method is quite simple. The link begins at the same level as your domain and works down from there. The link above is the same as:

```
<a  href="http://www.mysite.com/main-directory
/directory4/page4.html">Go To Page 4</a>
```

This method has the significant advantage of staying intact if you move the source page. The exact same link will work from any page anywhere in the site.

15.3.4 HTML Text Links

A webpage can contain various links that take you directly to other pages and even specific parts of a given page. These links are known as hyperlinks.

A link is specified using HTML tag <a>. This tag is called anchor tag and anything between the opening <a> tag and the closing </a> tag becomes part of the link and a user can click that part to reach to the linked document.

```
<a    href="Document    URL"...    attributes-
list>Link Text</a>
```

Example 16

```
<!DOCTYPE html>
<html>
<head>
<title>Hyperlink Example</title>
```

```
</head>
<body>
<p>Click following link</p>
<a href=" http: //www.bpbonline.com" tar-
get="_self">Books Stores</a>
</body>
</html>
```

This will produce following result, where you can click on the link generated bpbonline to reach to the home page of BPB Publications.

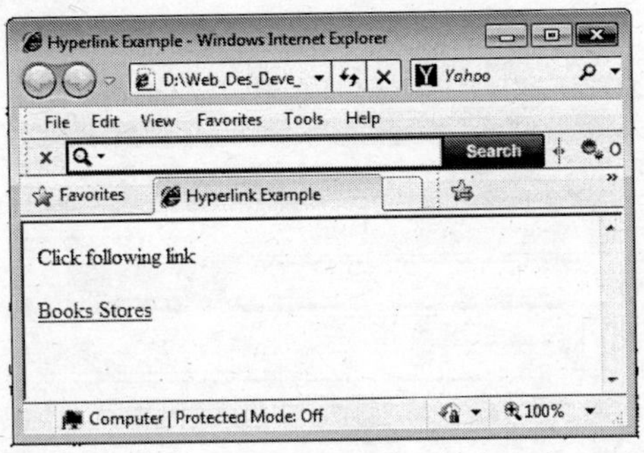

Figure 15.14 Viewing the image which is the result of Example 16

The Target Attribute

The!target!attribute specifies where to open the linked document. This attribute is used to specify the location where linked document is opened.
This example will open the linked document in a new browser window or in a new tab. The target window options are:

Options	Description
_blank	Opens the linked document in a new window or tab
_self	Opens the linked document in the same frame
_parent	Opens the linked document in the parent frame
_top	Opens the linked document in the full body of the window
targetframe	Opens the linked document in a named targetframe.

In example to understand basic difference in few options given for target attribute

```
Example 17
<!DOCTYPE html>
<html>
<head>
<title>Hyperlink Example</title>
</head>
<body>
<p>Click any of the following links</p>
<a href="Rose Flowers.html" target=" _blank"
>Opens in New</a>
<a href="Rose Flowers.html" target=" _self"
>Opens in Self</a>
<a href="Rose Flowers.html" target=" _parent"
>Opens in Parent</a>
<a href="Rose Flowers.html" target=" _top"
>Opens in Body</a>
</body>
</html>
```

The output of the Example 17 is shown in Figure 15.15.

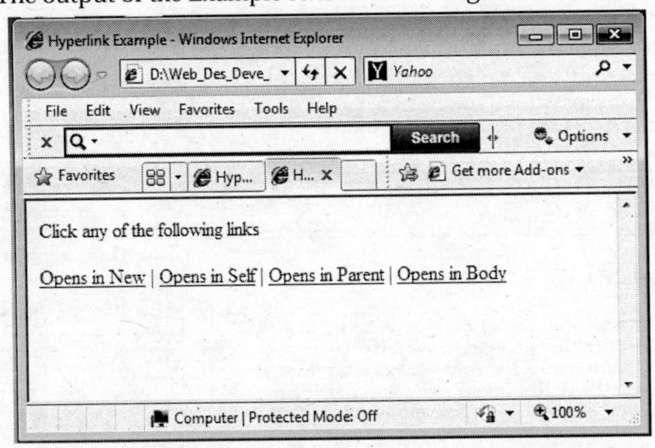

Figure 15.15 Viewing the image which is the result of Example 17

Internal Hyperlink

You can create a link to a particular section of a given webpage by using name attribute. An internal hyperlink is a link which points to a particular part of a page. This can be useful in long pages with lots of sub-sections. For example, the links at the top of this page are internal links pointing to each subheading.
Internal hyperlinks require an anchor tag with the "name" attribute like so:

```
<a name="top"> </a>
```

Create an anchor like this at the place in the page you want to link to. It doesn't matter if there is anything between the open and close tags.
Then create a hyperlink which refers to this anchor with a hash (#) like so:

```
<a href="#top">Go To Top of Page</a>
```

This assumes that the name anchor is on the same page as the hyperlink. To link to an anchor on a separate destination page, simply create a normal link with the anchor name appended to the file name like so:

```
<a href="page1.html#part2">Go To Page 1, Part
2</a>
```

Example 18

```
<! DOCTYPE html>
<html>
<head>
<title>Internal Link</title>
</head>
<body>
<H1>Anchors Tags</H1>
<p>To link to a specific spot on a web page,
```

```
you need to use a pair of anchors. One where
you are linking from, and one where you would
like to link to. The first one, is where you
are linking from. It is very similar to the
normal link tag. </P
<a name="top"></a>
<a href="#top">Go To Top of Page</a>
</body>
</html>
```

The output of the Example 18 is shown in Figure 15.16.

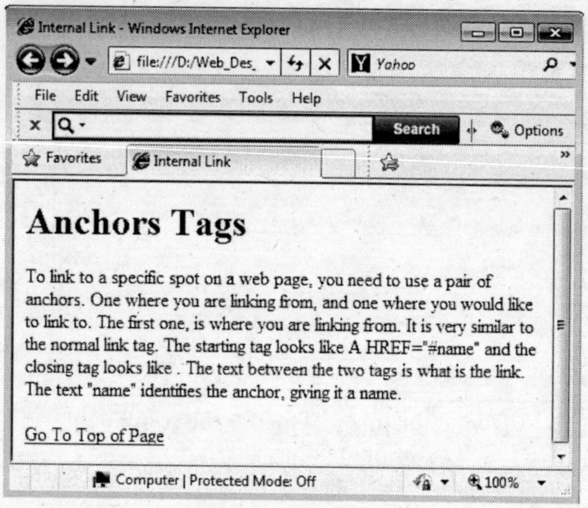

Figure 15.16 Viewing the image which is the result of Example 18

Setting Link Colors

You can set colors of your links, active links and visited links using link, alink and vlink attributes of <body> tag.

To see how link, alink and vlink attributes work in Example 19.

Example 19

```
<!DOCTYPE html>
<html>
<head>
<style>
a:link {
    color: green;
    background-color: transparent;
    text-decoration: none;
}
a:visited {
    color: pink;
    background-color: transparent;
    text-decoration: none;
}
a:hover {
    color: red;
    background-color: transparent;
    text-decoration: underline;
}
a:active {
    color: yellow;
    background-color: transparent;
    text-decoration: underline;
}
</style>
</head>
<body>
<p>You can change the default colors of
links</p>
<a href="rose.jpg" target="_blank">HTML Ima-
ges</a>
</body>
</html>
```

The output of the Example 19 is shown in Figure 15.17.

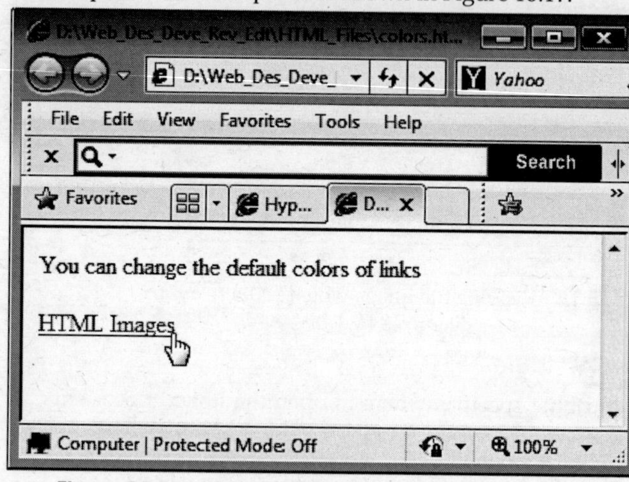

Figure 15.17 Viewing the image which is the result of Example 19

15.3.5 Using Tables

HTML Tables are contained within a TABLE element. The TABLE element denotes the range of the table, and uses attribute to define properties of it. For example, the BORDER attribute indicates the size of the border to draw around the table and between each of the table's cells. In the tables, each box within the table is called a cell. There are several other attributes besides BORDER.

15.3.6 HTML Document Tables

The table element in HTML is <Table> </Table>. Everything within a table is enclosed between these two "tag" which are both required.

```
<Table>
.......
.......
</Table>
```

There are a number of optional attributes we can specify in the `<TABLE>` tag, but these are discussed after the creation of as simple table.

After the `<TABLE>`, the next thing we need is the `<TR>` tag. `<TR>` creates a table row, which contains one or more cells of information. To create these individual cells, we use the `<TD>`

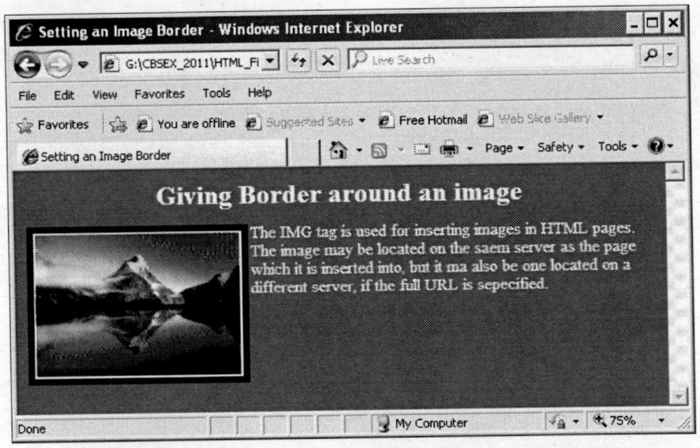

Figure 15.18 View the file in the Internet Explorer

tag. `<TD>` stands for table data. We place the table information within the `<TD>` and `</TD>` tags. Within the table element, we use `<TH>` for table headers and the CAPTION element for the table's caption.

Creating a Table

To create the simple Table in the HTML document

Example 20

```
<HTML>
<HEAD>
<Title>An Example of Table Format</Title>
</head>
<body>
<table>
<caption>This is the caption of Table</cap-
tion>
<TR>
<TH> </TH>
<TH>Column 1</TH>
<TH>Column 2</TH>
<TH>Column 3</TH>
</TR>
<TR>
<TH>ROW 1</TH>
<TD>row1 column1</TD>
<TD>row1 column2</TD>
<TD>row1 column3</TD>
</TR>
<TR>
<TH>ROW 2</TH>
<TD>row2 column1</TD>
<TD>row2 column2</TD>
<TD>row2 column3</TD>
</TR>
<TR>
<TH>ROW 3</TH>
<TD>row 1 column1</TD>
<TD>row 2 column2</TD>
<TD>row 3 column3</TD>
</TR>
</TABLE>
</Body>
</HTML>
```

The output of the above Example 20 as shown in Figure 15.19.

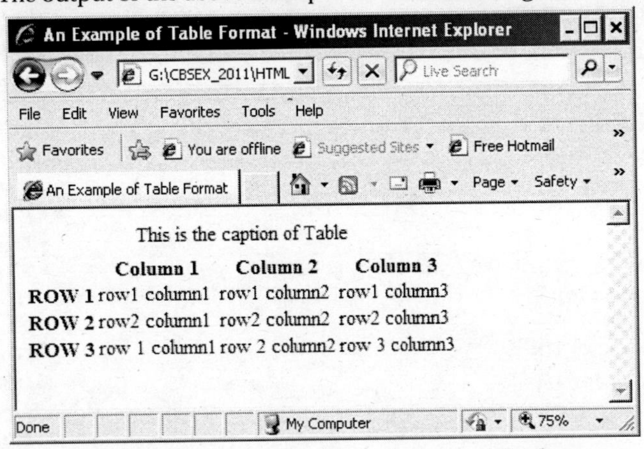

Figure 15.19 View of the file in the Internet Explorer

Table Attributes

Align

To align table, ALIGN attribute of <TABLE> tag may be used. This can have values left, right and center indicating that the table should be placed.

Left align

Aligned at the left window border.

Right align

Left-align table

Center align

Center-align table

Right align

Right-align table

Example 21

```
<Html>
<Head>
<Title>Table Alignment</Title>
</head>
<body>
<p> This is Left Alignment</p>
<Table Border="4" Align = "left">
<TR>
<TD>Data 1</TD>
<TD>Data 2</TD>
</TR>
<TR>
<TD>Data 1</TD>
<TD>Data 2</TD>
</TR>
```

```
</table>
<HR>
<p Align="Center">This is Center Alignment</p>
<Table Border="4" Align = "center">
<TR>
<TD>Data 1</TD>
<TD>Data 2</TD>
</TR>
<TR>
<TD>Data 1</TD>
<TD>Data 2</TD>
</TR>
</table>
<HR>
<p>This is Right Alignment</p>
<Table Border="4" Align = "right">
<TR>
<TD>Data 1</TD>
<TD>Data 2</TD>
</TR>
<TR>
<TD>Data 1</TD>
<TD>Data 2</TD>
</TR>
</table>
</Body>
</Html>
```

The output of Example 21 is shown in Figure 15.20.

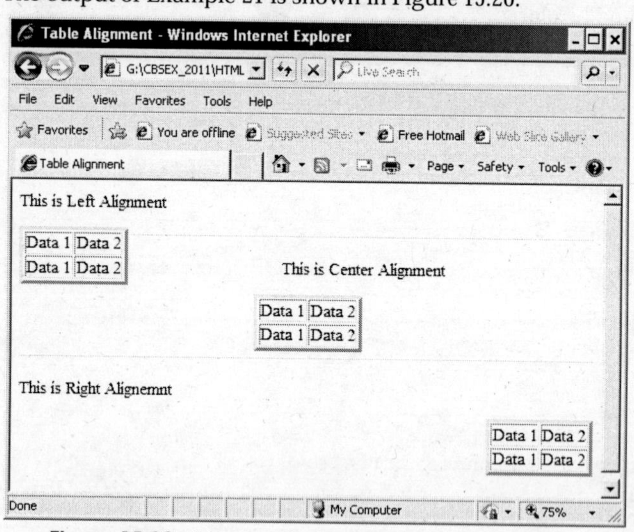

Figure 15.20 Viewing the file in the Internet Explorer

Table Background

A Table background specified with BACKGROUND attribute of <TABLE> tag. With BACKGROUND, you need to specify URL of the desired image file you want to make as background. The attribute of Background is BACKGROUND="file name".

Example 22

```
<Html>
<Head>
<Title>Add Background to the table</Title>
</head>
<body>
<table Border="4" Background = "Flower3.jpg">
<TR>
<TD>Data 1</TD>
<TD>Data 2</TD>
<TD>Data 3</TD>
<TD>Data 4</TD>
</TR>
<TR>
<TD>Data 1</TD>
<TD>Data 2</TD>
<TD>Data 3</TD>
<TD>Data 4</TD>
</TR>
<TR>
<TD>Data 1</TD>
<TD>Data 2</TD>
<TD>Data 3</TD>
<TD>Data 4</TD>
</TR>
<TR>
<TD>Data 1</TD>
<TD>Data 2</TD>
<TD>Data 3</TD>
<TD>Data 4</TD>
</TR>
<TR>
<TD>Data 1</TD>
<TD>Data 2</TD>
<TD>Data 3</TD>
<TD>Data 4</TD>
</TR>
<TR>
<TD>Data 1</TD>
<TD>Data 2</TD>
<TD>Data 3</TD>
<TD>Data 4</TD>
</TR>
</table>
</Body>
</Html>
```

The output of Example 22 is shown in Figure 15.21.

Table Background Colour

A Table's background colour specified with BGCOLOR attribute of <TABLE> tag. To specify the desired background colour. The attribute of Background colour is BGCOLOR="Gray".

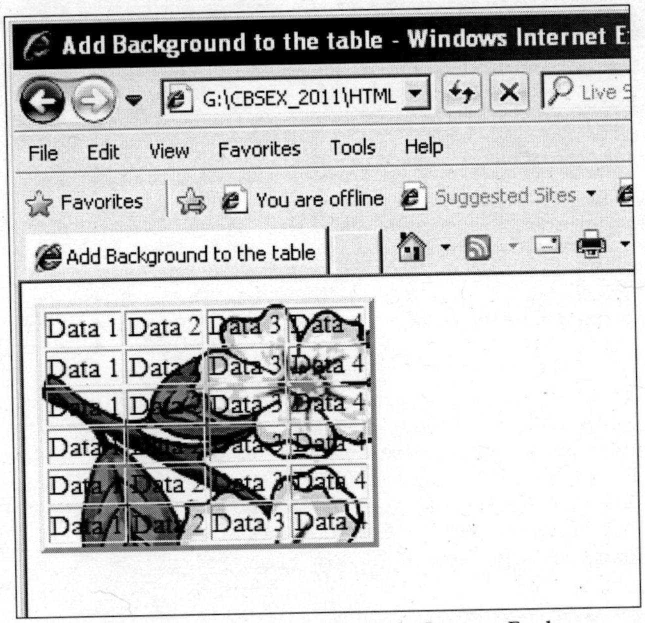

Figure 15.21 Viewing the file in the Internet Explorer

Example 23

```
<Html>
<Head>
<Title>Add Background to the table</Title>
</head>
<body>
<table BORDER="4" BGCOLOR = "Grey">
<TR>
<TD>Data 1</TD>
<TD>Data 2</TD>
<TD>Data 3</TD>
<TD>Data 4</TD>
</TR>
<TR>
<TD>Data 1</TD>
<TD>Data 2</TD>
<TD>Data 3</TD>
<TD>Data 4</TD>
</TR>
<TR>
<TD>Data 1</TD>
<TD>Data 2</TD>
<TD>Data 3</TD>
<TD>Data 4</TD>
</TR>
</table>
</body>
</Html>
```

The output of Example 23 is shown in Figure 15.22.

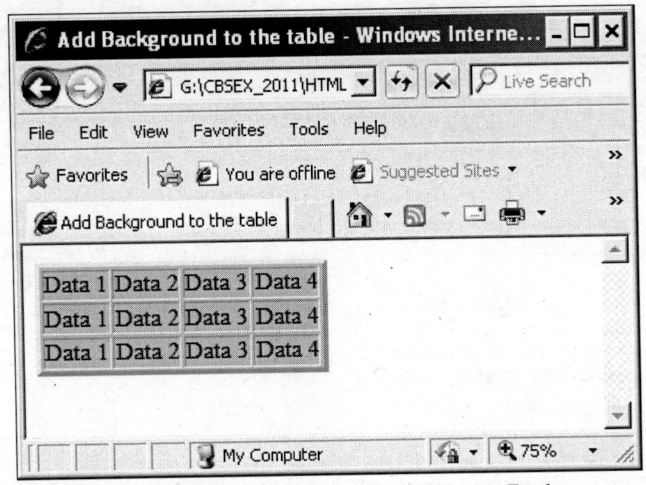

Figure 15.22 Viewing the file in the Internet Explorer

Table Border

BORDER is an attribute of the table element which specifies how wide a table border shall be. BORDER="0" specifies no border at all. The default value for the BORDER attribute is 1, If you do not specify the value, the border will be one pixel wide. The attribute of BORDER="value".

Example 24

```
<Html>
<Head>
<Title>Add Border to the table</Title>
</head>
<body>
<table BORDER="4">
<TR>
<TD>Data 1</TD>
<TD>Data 2</TD>
<TD>Data 3</TD>
<TD>Data 4</TD>
</TR>
<TR>
<TD>Data 1</TD>
<TD>Data 2</TD>
<TD>Data 3</TD>
<TD>Data 4</TD>
</TR>
</table>
</body>
</Html>
```

The output of Example 24 is shown in Figure 15.23.

Table's Border Colour

BORDERCOLOR attribute is used to specify the color of table's border. The attribute of BORDERCOLOR is BORDERCOLOR="colorname".

Figure 15.23 Viewing the file in the Internet Explorer

Example 25

```
<Html>
<Head>
<Title>Add Border and Border color to the
table</Title>
</head>
<body>
<table BORDER="3" BORDERCOLOR="Brown">
<TR>
<TD>Data 1</TD>
<TD>Data 2</TD>
<TD>Data 3</TD>
<TD>Data 4</TD>
</TR>
<TR>
<TD>Data 1</TD>
<TD>Data 2</TD>
<TD>Data 3</TD>
<TD>Data 4</TD>
</TR>
</table>
</body>
</Html>
```

The output of Example 25 is shown in Figure 15.24.

Cellspacing and Cellpadding

To control the spacing in cells, use CELLSPACING AND CELLPADDING attributes. Cellpadding refers, to the inner margins of free space that each cell of a table has as its "padded" border. On the other hand , Cellspacing refers, to how space is left between each cell wall in a table.

Example 26

```
<Html>
<Head>
<Title>Table using border and cellpa-
ding</Title>
```

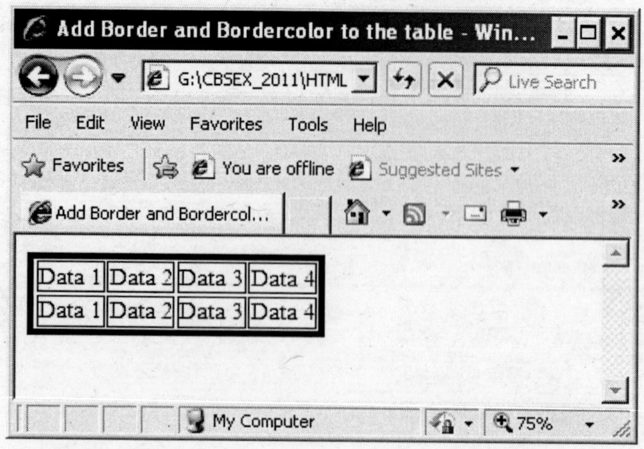

Figure 15.24 Viewing the file in the Internet Explorer

```
</head>
<body>
<table BORDER="3" Cellpadding="20">
<caption>Good Food Timings</caption>
<TR>
<TH>Break Fast</TH>
<TH>Lunch </TH>
<TH>Dinner</TH>
</TR>
<TR>
<TD>8.00 AM</TD>
<TD>1.00 PM</TD>
<TD>8.00 PM</TD>
</TR>
</table>
</body>
</Html>
```

The output of the Example 26 is shown in Figure 15.25.

Example 27

```
<Html>
<Head>
<Title>Table using border and cellpa-
ding</Title>
</head>
<body>
<table BORDER="3" Cellpadding="20" Cellspa-
cing="20">
<caption>Good Food Timings</caption>
<TR>
<TH>Break Fast</TH>
<TH>Lunch </TH>
<TH>Dinner</TH>
</TR>
<TR>
<TD>8.00 AM</TD>
<TD>1.00 PM</TD>
<TD>8.00 PM</TD>
</TR>
```

```
</table>
</body>
</Html>
```

The output of the Example 27 is shown in Figure 15.26.

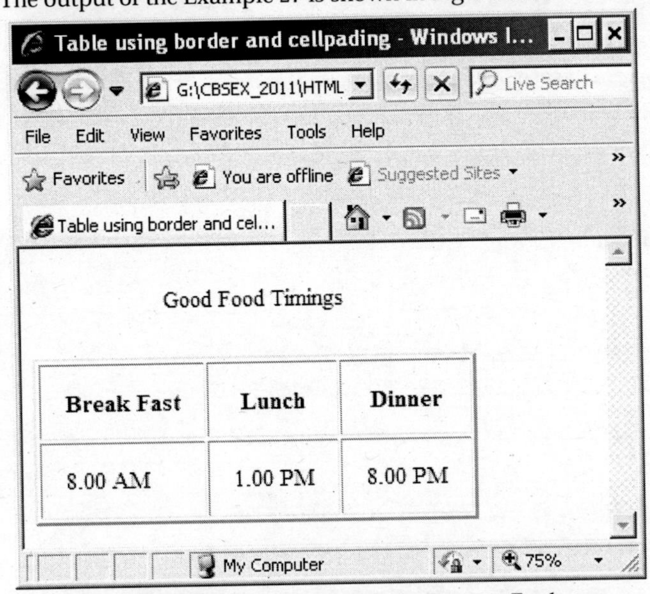

Figure 15.25 Viewing the file in the Internet Explorer

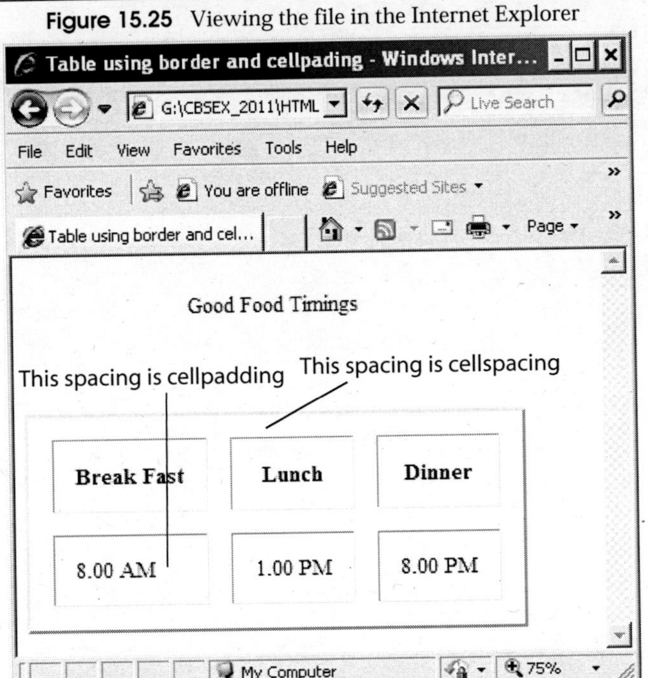

Figure 15.26 Viewing the file in the Internet Explorer

Table Height and Width

You can also set the table's height and width in terms of pixels and percentage of browser window. For instance, to set the width to 50% and height to 40% of the margins:

Example 28

```
<Html>
<Head>
<Title>To set the height and width of a tab-
le</Title>
</head>
<body>
<Table BORDER="3" Height=120, Width=150>
<TR>
<TD>Data 1</TD>
<TD>Data 2</TD>
</TR>
<TR>
<TD>Data 1</TD>
<TD>Data 2</TD>
</TR>
</Table>
<Table BORDER="3" Height=50%, Width=50%>
<TR>
<TD>Data 1</TD>
<TD>Data 2</TD>
</TR>
<TR>
<TD>Data 1</TD>
<TD>Data 2</TD>
</TR>
</table>
</body>
</Html>
```

The output of the Example 28 is shown in Figure 15.27.

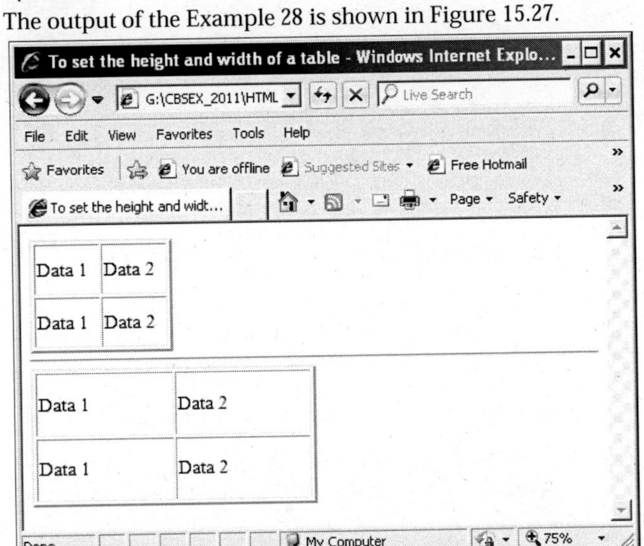

Figure 15.27 Viewing the file in the Internet Explorer

Vertical Alignment of cell Contents

VALIGN-"Top"|"Center"|"Bottom"

It positions the data in each cell of a row at a specific location vertically within the cell. The syntax of <td valign="value">

Top Align: Top-align content

Center Align: Center-align center

Bottom Align: Bottom-align center

Example 29

```
<Html>
<Head>
<Title>To set the VALIGN of a table</Title>
</head>
<body>
<Table BORDER="3" height="100%">
<TR>
<TH>Heading 1</TH>
<TH>Heading 2</TH>
<TH>Heading 3</TH>
</TR>
<TR>
<TD Valign="top">Data 1</TD>
<TD Valign="bottom">Data 2</TD>
<TD Valign="center">Data 3</TD>
</TR>
<TR>
<TD Valign="center">Data 1</TD>
<TD>Data 2</TD>
<TD>Data 3</TD>
</TR>
<TR>
<TD Valign="bottom">Data 1</TD>
<TD valign="bottom">Data 2</TD>
<TD valign="bottom">Data 3</TD>
</TR>
</table>
</body>
</Html>
```

The output of the Example 29 is shown in Figure 15.28.

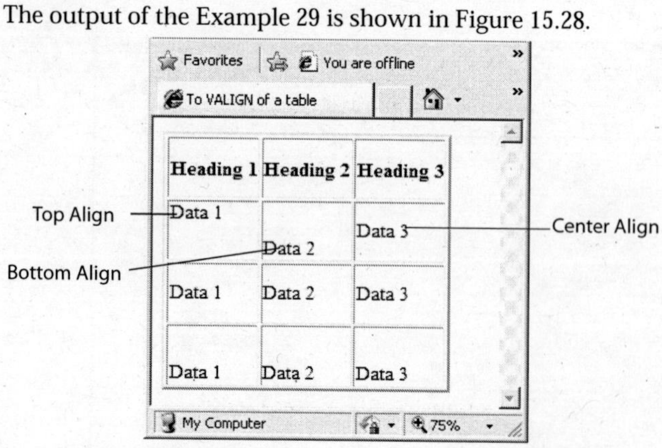

Figure 15.28 Viewing the file in the Internet Explorer

TD and TH Attributes

Align

Align is used to align the data within the cell horizontally, according values of left, right and center.

Left

Align content to the left of the cell.

Center

Align content to the center of the cell.

Right

Align content to the Right of the cell.

Example 30

```
<Html>
<Head>
<Title>Table Data Alignment</Title>
</head>
<body>
<table  BORDER="3"  cellspacing="3"  cellpad-
ding="3">
<TR>
<TH>Heading 1</TH>
<TH>Heading 2</TH>
<TH>Heading 3</TH>
</TR>
<TR>
<TD Align="center">Data 1</TD>
<TD Align="right">Data 2</TD>
<TD>Data 3</TD>
</TR>
<TR>
<TD Align="center">Data 1</TD>
<TD Align="right">Data 2</TD>
<TD>Data 3</TD>
</TR>
</table>
</body>
</Html>
```

The output of Example 30 is shown in Figure 15.29.

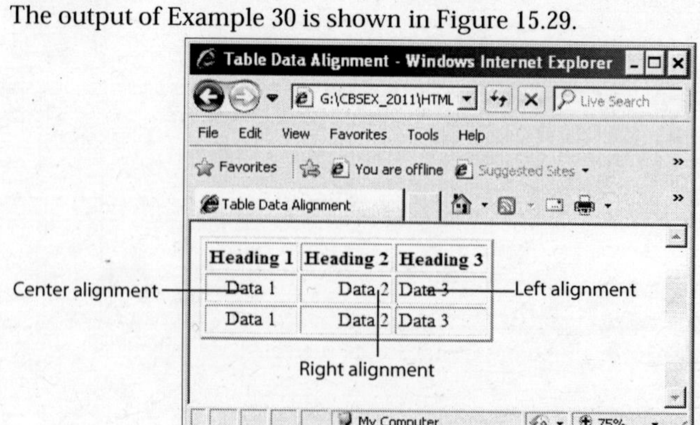

Figure 15.29 Viewing the file in the Internet Explorer

Setting the Cell Width

The Width attribute of <TD> is used to define the width of a cell either in pixels or percentage value of table width. The WIDTH attribute of <TABLE> gives table-width and WIDTH attribute of <TD> specifies individual cell width.

Example 31

```
<Html>
<Head>
<Title>Table Data Alignment</Title>
</head>
<body>
<table BORDER="3" cellspacing="4" cellpad-
ding="4">
<TR>
<TH>Heading 1</TH>
<TH>Heading 2</TH>
<TH>Heading 3</TH>
</TR>
<TR>
<TD Align="center">Data 1</TD>
<TD Align="right">Data 2</TD>
<TD>Data 3</TD>
</TR>
<TR>
<TD Align="center">Data 1</TD>
<TD Align="right">Data 2</TD>
<TD>Data 3</TD>
</TR>
</table>
</body>
</Html>
```

The output of Example 31 is shown in Figure 15.30.

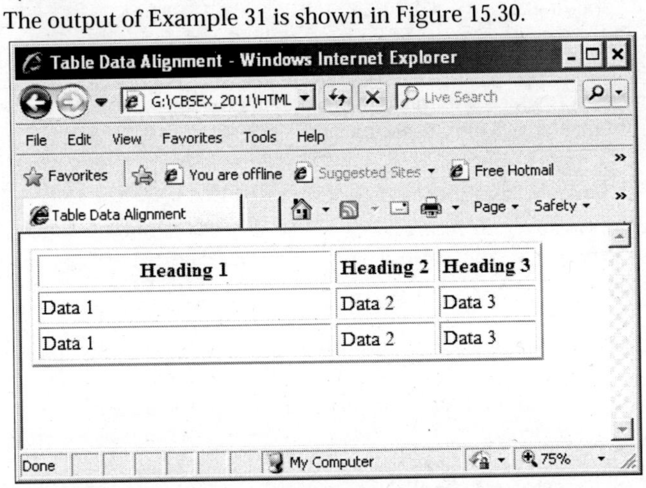

Figure 15.30 Viewing the file in the Internet Explorer

Setting the Cell's Background and Background Colour

The BACKGROUND and BGCOLOR attributes are used in the <TD> and you used them in <TABLE> element. The only difference is that with <TABLE> tag, these attributes affect the entire table and with <TD> tag these attributes affect a single cell. The following example displays background image and background colour for individual cells in table.

Example 32

```
<Html>
<Head>
<Title>Setting Cell's Background and Back-
ground colour</Title>
</head>
<body>
<table BORDER="3" cellspacing="4" cellpad-
ding="4">
<TR>
<TH>Heading 1</TH>
<TH>Heading 2</TH>
<TH>Heading 3</TH>
</TR>
<TR>
<TD Background=jokfalls.jpg">Data 1</TD>
<TD>Data 2</TD>
<TD>Data 3</TD>
</TR>
<TR>
<TD>Data 1</TD>
<TD>Data 2</TD>
<TD bgcolor="Yellow">Data 3</TD>
</TR>
</table>
</body>
</Html>
```

The output of Example 32 is shown in Figure 15.31.

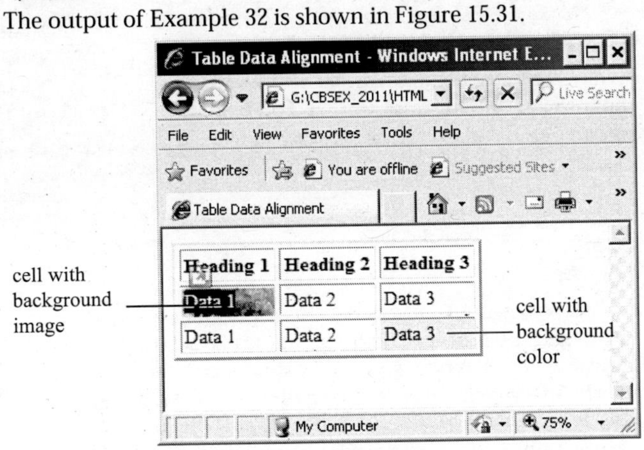

Figure 15.31 Viewing the file in the Internet Explorer

15.3.7 HTML FRAMES

One of the most significant developments that Netscape and Internet Explorer have contributed the introduction of frames. In olden days, we could see only one page at a time. Frames overcome this limitation. With the help of frames, we can divide the reader's browser window into multiple panes of information that can be viewed and changed independently.

We can also display different HTML documents in each of the window. We can also control the display of one frame from another.

☞ A *frame* is a rectangular region within the browser window that displays a Web page, alongside other pages in other frames. Or, it is basically a way of arranging and presenting several Web pages at a time.

The main advantage of using frames becomes apparent when a user clicks on one of the links of any frame, the other frames on the same Web page do not change at all, but a new page is loaded and displayed in the same frame.

There are three ways to specify the dimensions of the frame. These are as follows:

a. As a percentage of the area allotted to the parent frame set.
b. As a 'relative size'.
c. As an absolute (specific) number of screen pixels (e.g., 250).

The first two types are further elaborated in the successive paragraphs.

Percentage Dimension to Parent Frameset

We can specify the size of the ROWS or COLS as percentages of the total size of the browser window. For example, for three rows, the first and the last being smaller than the center row, we can give the following statement:

```
<FRAMESET rows = "20%, 60%, 20%">
```

Take another example, to clear the concept. For three rows, the first and the last being fixed height, with the remaining space assigned to the middle row, we will give the following statement:

```
<FRAMESET rows = "100, *, 100">
```

Relative Dimension to Parent Frameset

A relative dimensions is specified with an asterisk, e.g., '1*', '2*', '3*' ('1*' can also be written simply as '*'). For example:

```
<FRAMESET rows = "30%, 400, *, 2*">
  <FRAME ... >
  <FRAME ... >
  <FRAME ... >
  <FRAME ... >
</FRAMESET>
```

Suppose the browser window is currently 1000 pixels high. The first frame gets 30% of the total height, that is, 300 pixels; the second frame gets 400 pixels, since an absolute dimension was specified. This leaves 300 pixels to be divided between the other two frames. The fourth frame's height is specified as '2*', so it is twice as high as the third frame, whose height is only '*' (1*). Therefore, the third frame is 100 pixels high and the fourth is 200 pixels high.

A single '*' character is a "relative-sized" frame and is interpreted as a request to give the frame all remaining space. If multiple relative-sized frames are specified, the remaining space is divided evenly among them. If there is a value in front of the '*', the frame gets that much more relative space. "2*, *" would give 2/3 of the space to the first frame and 1/3 to the second.

☞ Use ***relati e*** and ***percentage*** sizes whenever possible. If you use an absolute size for one of your frames, be sure to use relative sizes for the others.

<FRAMESET> TAG

To create a frame definition document, we use the `<FRAMESET>` tag. When we use `<FRAMESET>` tag in an HTML document, it is replacement for the `<BODY>` tag, as shown below:

```
<HTML>
<HEAD>
</HEAD>
<FRAMESET rows = "33%, 33%, 33%">
  <FRAMESET cols = "50%, 50%">
      <FRAME name = "frame1">
      <FRAME name = "frame2">
  </FRAMESET>
  <FRAME name = "frame3">
  <FRAME name = "frame4">
</FRAMESET>
<BODY>
..contents to display in non-frame-capable
user agent..
</BODY>
</HTML>
```

If we include a `<FRAMESET>` tag in an HTML document, we cannot include a `<BODY>` tag. Basically, the two tags are mutually exclusive. In addition, no other formatting tags, hyperlinks, or document text should be included in a frame definition document, except in one special case – the `<NOFRAME>` tag. `<FRAMESET>` tags contain only the definitions for the frames in this document.

☞ A frameset is the set of frames defined by the *<FRAMESET>* tags in the frame definition document.

Creating Two or More Columns (<FRAMESET COLS>)

When we define a `<FRAMESET>` tag, we must include one of the two attributes as part of the tag definition. The first of these attributes is the COLS attribute. The syntax of the COLS attribute is as follows:

```
<FRAMESET COLS = "column width, column
width, ...">
```

The COLS attribute informs the browser to split the screen into a number of vertical frames whose widths are defined by column width values separated by commas. We define the width of each frame in three different ways:

a. Pixels,
b. Percentage of the total width of the <FRAMESET>,
c. An asterisk (*).

When we use *, the browser uses as much space as possible for the specified frame. The following `<FRAMESET>` tag creates a screen with three vertical frames. The first frame is 100 pixels wide, the second is 50 percent of the width of the screen, and the third uses all the remaining space.

```
<FRAMESET COLS = "100, 50%, *">
```

The COLS attribute defines the number of vertical frames or columns in a frameset.

☞ To define a frameset with three equal-width columns, use COLS="*, *, *".

Creating Two or More Rows (<FRAMESET ROWS>)

The ROWS attribute works in a similar way as the COLS attribute, except that it splits the screen into horizontal frames rather than vertical ones. For example, to split the screen into two equal-height frames, we write either of the following:

```
<FRAMESET ROWS = "50%, 50%">  or
<FRAMESET ROWS = "*, *">
```

The ROWS attribute defines the number of horizontal frames or rows in a frameset.

<FRAME> TAG

Within the `<FRAMESET>` and `</FRAMESET>` tags, we should have a `<FRAME>` tag indicating which HTML document to display in each frame. If we have fewer `<FRAME>` tags than the number of frames defined in the `<FRAMESET>` tag, any remaining frames will be left blank. We do not need to specify a closing `</FRAME>` tag.

<FRAME SRC> Attribute

The `<FRAME SRC>` attribute in each `<FRAME>` tag specifies the address of the document to be displayed in the frame. When omitted, the frame is displayed as a blank space. The syntax of the SRC attribute is shown below:

```
<FRAME SRC="document URL">
```

For each frame defined in the `<FRAMESET>` tag, we must include a corresponding `<FRAME>` tag, as shown in Figure 15.32.

```
<HTML>
<FRAMESET rows = "40%, 60%">
<FRAME src =
         "http://www.rediffmail.com/">
<FRAMESET cols = "50%, 50%">
<FRAME src = "http://www.google.com/">
<FRAME src =
         "http://www.epfindia.com/">
</FRAMESET>
</FRAMESET>
</HTML>
```

Figure 15.32 Code of <FRAME> tag to define the contents of each frame

Figure 15.33 Output of the program given in Figure 15.32

The coding shown in Figure 15.33 causes three frames to be displayed. The first (outer) FRAMESET element divides the browser window into two horizontal regions. The upper region contains a single frame displaying the document http://www.rediffmail.com/, and the lower region displays the frames defined in the second (inner) FRAMESET element. This FRAMESET divides the lower part of the window into two vertical frames, displaying the documents http://www.google.com/ and http://www.epfindia.com/ (See Figure 15.33).

<FRAME NAME> Attribute

The NAME attribute is used to assign a name to a frame so that it can be targeted by links in other documents. The NAME attribute is optional. By default, all windows are unnamed. Names must begin with an alphabetic character.

```
<FRAME SRC="main.htm" NAME="main">
```

This displays the main.htm page in that frame when the page loads, and names the frame "main." (The frame name need not match the name of its contents. It is given so in this example).

<FRAME MARGINHEIGHT> Attribute

To adjust the margin that appears above and below a document within a frame, set the MARGINHEIGHT to a number indicated by pixels. The general form of MARGINHEIGHT attribute is as follows:

```
MARGINHEIGHT="VALUE"
```

<FRAME MARGINWIDTH> Attribute

The MARGINWIDTH attribute enables you to adjust the margin on the left and right side of a frame to the number indicated by pixels. Margins cannot be less than one. This ensures that frame objects will not touch frame edges, and cannot be specified in a way that leaves no space for the document contents. MARGINWIDTH attribute is optional. The general form of MARGINWIDTH attribute is as follows:

MARGINWIDTH="VALUE"

<FRAME SCROLLING> Attribute

The <FRAME SCROLLING> attribute allows you to control scrollbar as and when the scrollbars appear in the frame. Normally, scrollbars are added only if there is not enough room to display all the contents in a frame. The general form of SCROLLING attribute is given below:

SCROLLING="YES|NO|AUTO"

The SCROLLING attribute is optional. The default value is "auto". Different parts of the SCROLLING attribute are as follows:

a. AUTO (default): By default, if the contents of a frame take up more space than the area available, the browser automatically adds scrollbars to either the side or the bottom of the frame so that the user can scroll through the document.

b. NO: Setting the value of SCROLLING to NO disables the use of scrollbars for the current frame. If we set SCROLLING = NO but there is more text in the document than can fit inside the frame, we will not be able to scroll the additional text into the frame view.

c. YES: If we set SCROLLING to YES, the scrollbars are included in the frame regardless of whether they are required or not.

<NORESIZE> Attribute

By default, users can move the position of borders around each frame on the current screen by grabbing the border and moving it with their mouse. To lock the borders of a frame and prevent them from being moved, we use the NORESIZE attribute. The NORESIZE attribute does not require a value. It can simply be used as a flag to indicate that the frame is not resizable by the user. The NORESIZE attribute is optional. However, all frames are resizable by default.

<NOFRAMES> Tag

If we load a frame definition document into a Web browser that does not support frames, we get only a blank page. To get around this problem, the **<NOFRAMES>** tag enables us to include body text as part of the document. Frame-capable browsers ignore all tags and data contained in a NOFRAME element.

In the code shown in Figure 15.34, the **<NOFRAMES>** element is used to include in a document a table of contents, which is otherwise displayed in a separate frame. The output is shown in Figure 15.35.

```
<BODY>
<H1>The Different Fish Species</H1>
<NOFRAMES> <!-- TOC for no frames display -->
  <UL>
   <LI><a href=#sec1>The fresh and sea water
     species</a>
    <LI><a href=#sec2>A subjective compari-
son</a>
  </UL>
</NOFRAMES>
<H1><a name=sec1>The fresh and sea water
species</a></H1>
Fishes can be classified into several cate-
gories starting by the type of water in which
they live.
...
<H1><a   name=sec2>A   subjective   compari-
son</a></H1>
This section is clearly not objective. I much
prefer sea water fishes which are generally
speaking more colorful and therefore more
beautiful.
...
</BODY>
```

Figure 15.34 Use of <NOFRAME> tag

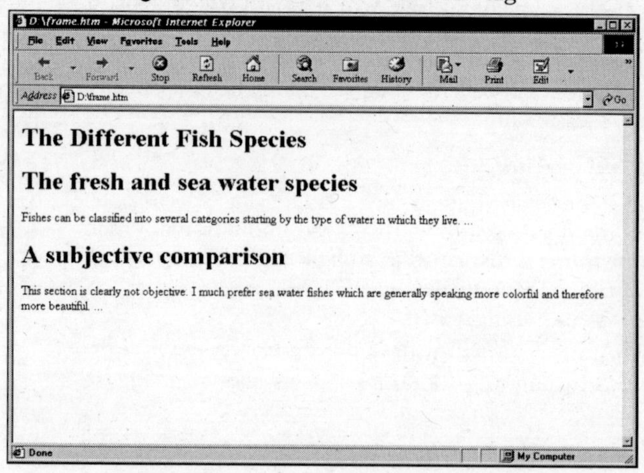

Figure 15.35 Output of the program given in Figure 15.34

☞ Using both frames' content and tags inside <NOFRAME>, we can create pages that work well with browsers.

15.3.8 Using Cascading Style Sheet (CSS)

CSS is an abbreviation for Cascading Style Sheets. CSS works with HTML and other Markup Languages (such as XHTML and XML) to control the way the content is presented. Cascading Style Sheets is a means to separate the appearance of a webpage from the content of a webpage. CSS is a recommendation of the World Wide Web Consortium (the W3C).

The concept of style sheet is very simple. First the designer creates a standard Web page, using standard HTML tags. It is designed so that it can be displayed properly in browsers that do not support style sheets. But now suppose designer wants the heading (H1) should be displayed in red color and the paragraph (P) should be displayed in blue and Helvetica font. To accomplish this, the author creates style rules that format the content on the Web page in the manner that he or she chooses.

Style sheets would thus combine HTML tags (H1) with properties (such as color: red) to format each HTML tag. In the case of style sheets, an HTML tag is used as a selector. The property and value of the selector are combined into what is called a declaration. Following are some examples of style rules:

```
H1 {COLOUR: RED}
P {FONT-FAMILY: HELVETICA; COLOUR: BLUE}
```

In the above stylesheet tag H1 and P is used as selector and their properties such as colour and font-family is used as a declaration part.

The Web designer designs the page content and the style rules that define its appearance. The designer also attaches the style rules to the standard HTML document using methods through the use of external style sheet, an embeddedstyle sheet or an inlinestyle sheet.

Different Ways to Add Styles in Document

There are three ways to adding style to a document. These are as follows:

1. External style sheet can be linked to one or more pages, applying the same style rules to all.
2. Embed a document-wide style sheet in the <HEAD> element of the document. or
3. Use Inline style exactly where the styles need to be applied.

Each of these style sheet linking are explained in further sections.

Linking External Style Sheet

External style sheets keep the style rules in a separate file, apart from the HTML Web documents. The advantage of using external style sheets is that you can apply the same style rules to more than one document in you Web site. This enables you to create pages that have a consistent appearance. External style sheets also provide the advantage of enabling you to quickly change the appearance of your Web page in the future. By defining your styles in a single document and linking them to multiple pages, you only need to edit the style sheet to change the presentation style to all pages linked to it.

External style sheet consists set of rules in 4 part:

1. External Source link
2. Selector (element, class, id)
3. Property and
4. Value

How to write External Stylesheet

External style sheet linked to a webpage. Selector is normally HTML element (or class, id) to assign CSS properties and set suitable values.

External Style Sheet Source Link

```
<head>
<link rel="stylesheet" type="text/css" href="style.css" />
</head>
```

Property value

```
Body {
        font: 12pt; font-family: serif;
        color: black; background: white
     }
```

Although a Web page is saved with an .htm or .html extension, an external style sheet is saved with a .css extension. It defines all the common style rules that are shared in your Web documents. Then, using the <LINK> tag, you link the external style sheet to each HTML Web page.

Now suppose we link a file STYLE.CSS to the HTML document. For this, first of all we have to create a .css file for style sheet. Following is the style for text you have to write in your notepad file and then save it as STYLE.CSS.

```
Body {font: 12pt; font-family: serif; color:
    black; background: white}
H3 {font: 24pt; font-family: comic sans ms; color: black}
H4 {font: 16pt; font-family: sans-serif; color: black}
P {text-indent: 0.5 in}
A:link {color: yellow; text-decoration: none}
A:visited: {color: red; text-decoration: 'u'}
A:active: {color: blue; text-decoration: none}
```

After that we link this .css file to the HTML tags as shown in Example 2, using the <LINK> tag.

Various attributes are explained here with: REL attribute controls the persistent style, default styles and alternate styles. Here, we set

```
Rel = "stylesheet"
```

It forces the use of persistent styles and applies the styles in our style sheet, regardless the users' local selection.

HREF attributes is used to indicate the URL of the style sheet to use. In this example, the style sheets resides in the same directory in which HTML file is saved.

MEDIA attribute is used to provide an indication of which media the style sheet should apply to. This attribute enables the page designer to define one style for computer screens and another for printer.

TYPE attribute when set

```
TYPE = "TEXT/CSS"
```

It indicates that the linked style sheet is a cascading style sheet, but another form of style sheet certainly could be linked.

The output as seen on Internet Explorer of the coding in Example 33 as shown in Figure 15.36.

Example 33

```
<html>
<head>
<title>cascading style sheets</title>
<link rel="stylesheet" href="style.css"
media = "screen" type = "text/css">
<head>
<body>
<h3>chapter content</h3>
<h4><a href="#dsl" >digital subscriber
line</a></h4>
<h4><a href="#www" >world wide web</a></h4>
<h4><a href="#inet" >Internet</a></h4>
<h4><a href="#lan" >local area net-
work</a></h4>
<h4><a href="#wan" >wide area network</a></h4>
<h4><a href="#hlink">hyperlink</a></h4>
<h4><a name="dsl">digital subscriber
line</a></h4>
<p> here we have to write the details of
digital subscriber line </p>
<h4><a name="#www" >world wide web</a></h4>
<p> here we have to write the details of world
wide web</p>
<h4><a name="#inet" >internet</a></h4>
<p> here we have to write the details of
internet </p>
<h4><a name="#lan" >local area net-
work</a></h4>
<p> here we have to write the details of local
area
network </p>
<h4><a name="#wan" >wide area network</a></h4>
<p> here we have to write the details of wide
area network.</p>
<h4><a name="#hlink">hyperlink</a></h4>
<p>here we have to write the details of
hyperlink.</p>
</body>
</html>
```

Embedding Style Sheets

Another way to include an external style sheet is to embed it. When we embed a style sheet, we write the style rules directly within the HTML document. You have to enclose the style rules within the <STYLE> and </STYLE> tag pairs and place this pair within the head section of the HTML document. Because multiple forms of style sheet may be included (beyond the standard css format), therefore, you should still include the TYPE attribute to indicate which format of style sheet you are using. This is regardless of the browser? support for other style sheet technologies.

One concern when including style sheets within an HTML document is that not all browsers understand style information. To avoid problem, comment out the style information by

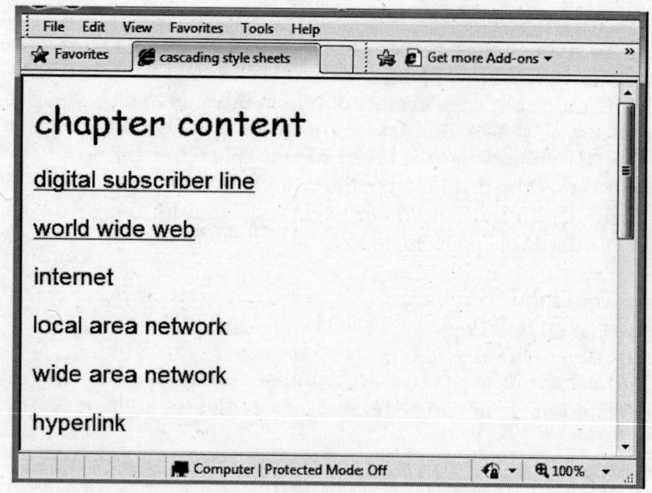

Figure 15.36 Output of the program given in Example 33

using an HTML comment tag <!---> so that the comments are not displayed onscreen by older browsers. A complete example of Embedded style sheet is given in Example 34.

Example 34

```
<html>
<head>
<title>cascading style sheets</title>
<style type = "text/css">
body {font: 12pt; font-family: serif; color: black;
    background: white}
H3 {font: 24pt; font-family: comic sans ms; color: black}
h4 {font: 16pt; font-family: sans-serif; color: black}
p {text-indent: 0.5in}
a:link {color: yellow; text-decoration: none}
a:visited: {color: red; text-decoration: ?u?}
a:active: {color: blue; text-decoration: none}
</style>
</head>
<body>
<h3>chapter content</h3>
<h4><a href="#dsl" >digital subscriber line</a></h4>
<h4><a href="#www" >world wide web</a></h4>
<h4><a href="#inet" >internet</a></h4>
<h4><a href="#lan" >local area network</a></h4>
<h4><a href="#wan" >wide area network</a></h4>
<h4><a href="#hlink">hyperlink</a></h4>
<h4><a name="dsl">digital subscriber line</a></h4>
<p> here we have to write the details of digital subscriber line
</p>
<h4><a name="#www" >world wide web</a></h4>
<p> here we have to write the details of world wide web
</p>
<h4><a name="#inet" >internet</a></h4>
<p> here we have to write the details of internet </p>
<h4><a name="#lan" >local area network</a></h4>
<p> here we have to write the details of local area
network </p>
```

```
<h4><a name="#wan" >wide area network</a></h4>
<p> here we have to write the details of wide area
network.</p>
<h4><a name="#hlink">hyperlink</a></h4>
<p>here we have to write the details of hyperlink.</p>
</body>
</html>
```

Inline Style Sheets

External and Embedded style sheets create a style for the whole document. However, you can add style information right down to the single element. The simplest way to add style information, but not necessarily the best is to add style rules to the particular HTML element.

Suppose you want to set one particular <H1> tag to render in 22 pt, red, comic sans ms font. You could apply that style to all <H1> elements, or to a class of them by applying a embedded style. On the other hand, you could apply the style to only the tag in question. This is done with the STYLE attribute, which can be used within HTML element.

```
<P STYLE = "FONT-SIZE: 12PT; FONT-FAMILY:
COMIC SANS MS; COLOR: RED">Get whatever you
love otherwise you will be forced to love
whatever you get.</p>
```

This sort of style information need not be hidden from a browser that may not be style-sheet-aware. This is so, because browsers ignore any attributes that they do not understand. By using inline style, you can easily apply a style to a certain section or division of a document by using the <DIV> element. The tag <DIV> works well to surround block elements, such as paragraph. Setting a two paragraph portion of a document to have a yellow background with red text is shown below:

```
<DIV STYLE = "FONT-SIZE: 12PT; FONT-FAMILY:
COMIC SANS MS; COLOR: RED; FONT-WEIGHT=:
BOLD">
<P>Get whatever you love otherwise you will be
forced to love whatever you get. This is the
rule of the nature, we can't help this.</P>
<p>This is another paragraph describing the
philosophy of spending happy life.</P>
```

MODEL QUESTIONS AND ANSWERS

A. Multiple Choice

1.1 A frame definition file __________.

a. Contains the layout of the frames on the Web page

b. Specifies the Web pages contents of the frames on the Web page

c. Includes the HTML for all of the Web pages to be contained in the frames on the Web page

d. Both b and c

1.2 The __________ attribute indicates that there are two rows and they will display in 30% and 70% of the screen, respectively.

a. cols="30%, 70%" b. rows="30,70"
c. rows="30%, 70%" d. row="30%, 70%"

1.3 On all Web pages that use image maps for navigation, you should also include:

a. Links referring visitors to the home page
b. A list of elements in the image maps
c. Captions for the images in the image maps
d. Text links to the URLs reflected in the image maps

1.4 Is it possible to insert a table within another table?

a. Yes, but there must be exactly 2 rows and 2 columns in first table
b. Yes, table can be inserted into cell of another table
c. Yes, but there must be no border in second table
d. No, it is not possible

1.5 Choose the correct HTML tag to left align the content of a cell:

a. <tdleft> b. <td leftalign>
c. <td valign="left"> d. <td align="left">

1.6 Which of the following is correct HTML for inserting an image?

a. <image source="www.pictures.com/ganesh.jpg"alt="This is me"/>
b. <img src="www.pictures.com/ganesh.jpg"alt="This is me" />
c. <img source="www.pictures.com/ganesh.jpg"alt="This is me" />
d. <img alt="This is me">www.pictures.com/ganesh.jpg</img>

1.7 Which is true to change the text color to red?

a. <BODY BGCOLOR=RED>
b. <BODY TEXT=RED>
c. <BODY COLOR=RED>
d. None of the above

1.8 How to set a picture as a background Web page?

a. <body background="peacock.gif">
b. <body backgroundimage="peacock.gif">
c. <background="peacock.gif">
d. <background image="peacock.gif">

1.9 Which of the following is an attribute of <Table> tag?

a. Src b. Link
c. Cellpadding d. Bold

1.10 <TD>...</TD> tag is used for __________.

a. Table heading b. Table Records
c. Table row d. None of the above

B. State whether the following are True or False

2.1 The two main file formats for images on the Web are GIF and TIF.

2.2 You cannot designate an inline image as a hypertext link.

2.3 To define target in new page in HTML <a href = "http://www.interview.com/" target = "_blank">Click Here</a>.

2.4 The <ADDRESS> tag is similar to italics or emphasis.

2.5 Elements allowed within the <HTML> tag are the <HEAD> and <TITLE> elements.

2.6 ROWSPAN attribute with <TABLE> tag is used to merge more than one cell row wise.

2.7 BORDER is an attribute of <A> tag.

2.8 To set the color for table borders, use bgcolor=#003300.

2.9 By default, the text in ALIGN attribute is align to left.

2.10 Most of the time, the <LINK> tag does not create a clickable hyperlink.

Answers

A.	1.1	b	1.2	c	1.3	c	1.4	b	1.5	d
	1.6	b	1.7	b	1.8	a	1.9	c	1.10	b
B.	2.1	T	2.2	F	2.3	T	2.4	T	2.5	T
	2.6	T	2.7	F	2.8	F	2.9	F	2.10	T

CHAPTER 16

Soft Skills

16.1 INTRODUCTION

Soft skills have more to do with who we are than what we know. It decides how well one interacts with others, and are usually a definite part of one's personality. It is the ability required and expected from person for finding a suitable job and to grow in life. It is a term probably associated with a person's "EQ" (Emotional Intelligence Quotient), the group of character qualities, social graces, communication, language, individual habits, interpersonal skills, managing people, management, etc. That symbolize relationships with different people.

These skills are very important:

- To handle interpersonal relations
- To take appropriate decisions
- To communicate effectively
- To have good impression

Other words that are customarily used for these varieties of skills include: "people skills", "interpersonal skills", "social skills" or "transferable skills". Ironically, for a lot of individuals these skills are almost always one of the crucial hardest skills to develop. It is difficult to judge which soft skills are fundamental.

16.2 EFFECTIVE COMMUNICATION

It is a two way information sharing process which involves one party sending a message that is easily understood by the receiving party. Effective communication is the glue that helps you deepen your connections with others and enhance teamwork, decision-making, and problem-solving. It allows for you to communicate even negative or complicated messages without creating conflict or destroying trust.

16.2.1 Features of Effective Communication

Effective communication is an essential piece for any success which comes with others. (See Figure 16.1)

Simple language: The language used in the communication should be simple and understandable by the other person.

Clearness: The communicator should be clear in his mind about the objective and there should not be any doubt in communication.

Adequacy of information: It should contain adequate information and should be complete in all respect; otherwise it will not serve the purpose and the other person will not be able to understand it.

Figure 16.1 Effective communication

Proper medium of communication: The communicator should select the proper media of communication by considering factors such as the nature, urgency, distance between communicator and recipient of communication etc.

Accurate: An effective communication should be accurate. False and misleading statement will seriously undermine the reputation of the business. It may also lead to expensive actions.

Courtesy: Politeness is, of course, one of the most important attributes and a polite language should be used in communication. It helps in improving relations.

16.3 COMMUNICATION SKILLS & CALL HANDLING SKILLS

"We all use language to communicate, to express ourselves, to get our ideas across, and to connect with the person to whom we are speaking. When a relationship is working, the act of communicating seems to flow relatively effortlessly. When a relationship is deteriorating, the act of communicating can be as frustrating as climbing a hill of sand."

– Chip Rose, attorney and mediator

The way you speak to a person, in terms of the language used, tone of voice and clarity are also important and often referred to as the 'soft skills'. Being in a position to communicate comfortably is the most important of all life skills. Communication is simply the act of transferring information from one location to a different, whether that is vocally (utilizing voice), written (using printed or digital media similar to books, magazines, websites or e-mails), visually (making use of logos, maps, charts or graphs) or non-verbally (using body language, gestures and the tone and pitch of voice).

Bad Practice in Call Handling

- Inconsistency
- Stationery or documentation not to hand for taking notes
- Not taking complaints seriously
- Putting calls on hold (long periods)
- Wasting time during pauses
- Using jargon

16.4 LISTENING SKILLS

It is one of the most important skills one can have. How well you listen has a major impact on effectiveness, and on the quality of relationships with others. The way to improve listening skills is to practice "active listening." This is where one has to make a conscious effort to hear not only the words that another person is saying but, more importantly, try to understand the complete message being sent. 'Active listening' implies, as its name recommends, actively listening. That is completely focusing on what is being said as opposed to purely passively "listening to" the message of the speaker (See Figure 16.2). These are five keys of becoming an Active Listener. They all help to hear the other person, and that the other person knows you are hearing what they say.

Pay Attention: Give the speaker your undivided attention, and acknowledge the message. Recognize that non-verbal communication also "speaks" loudly.

- Look at the speaker directly.
- Put aside distracting thoughts.
- Don't mentally prepare a reply.
- Avoid being distracted by other factors.

Figure 16.2 Active Listening

Show That You re Listening: Use your own body language and gestures to convey your attention.

- Smile and use other facial expressions.
- Note your posture and make sure it is open and inviting.
- Encourage the speaker to continue with small verbal comments like yes, and uh huh.

Provide Feedback: Our personal filters, assumptions, judgments, and beliefs can distort what we hear. As a listener, your role is to understand what is being said. This may require you to reflect what is being said and ask questions.

- Ask questions to clarify certain points. "What do you mean when you say." "Is this what you mean?"
- Summarize the speaker's comments periodically.

Defer Judgment: Interrupting is a waste of time. It frustrates the speaker and limits full understanding of the message.

- Allow the speaker to finish each point before asking questions.

- Don't interrupt with counter arguments.

Respond Appropriately: Active listening is a model for respect and understanding. You are gaining information and perspective and therefore add nothing by asking irrelevent questions to the speaker or otherwise putting him or her down.

- Be candid, open, and honest in your response.
- Assert your opinions respectfully.
- Treat the other person in a way that you think he or she would want to be treated.

16.4.1 Types of Listening

Here are six types of listening, starting with basic discrimination of sounds and ending in deep communication.

Discriminative listening

It is the most major type of listening, whereby the difference between sounds is recognized. If you cannot listen to differences, then you cannot make sense of the meaning that is expressed by such discrepancies.

For example: different reactions to a ringing alarm in the morning to get up on working days and on Sundays/Holidays (See Figure 16.3).

Figure 16.3 Discriminative listening

Comprehension listening

The next step beyond dividing between distinctive sound and sights is to understand them. In communication, some words are more important and some less so, and grasp often benefits from an extraction of essential facts and items from a long speech. This is also known as content listening, informative listening and full listening (See Figure 16.4).

Figure 16.4 Comprehension listening

For example: while listening to a lecture you cannot remember the whole lecture so you just extract the essence from the lecture.

Critical listening

It is the listening to evaluate and judge, forming an opinion about what is being said. The judgment incorporates assessing qualities and shortcomings, understanding and endorsement (See Figure 16.5).

Figure 16.5 Critical listening

For example: your friend said that this movie is not worth watching and you make a perception not to watch it.

Biased listening

One-sided listening happens when the individual hears just what they need to hear, typically misinterpreting what the other individual says based on the stereotypes and other biases that they have. Such biased listening is often very evaluative in nature (See Figure 16.6).

Figure 16.6 Biased listening

For example: while listening to a cricket commentary you make up your mind for India wining the match.

Evaluative listening

This kind of listening is also known as critical listening, we make judgments about what the other individual is saying. We look to survey reality of what is being said. We seek to assess the truth of what is being said. We also judge what they say against our values, assessing them as good or bad, worthy or unworthy. Evaluative listening is also called critical, judgmental or interpretive listening (See Figure 16.7).

Figure 16.7 Evaluative listening

For example: you tell your friend a movie review & he responds, "I know what you want to say, you donot need to continue, I can tell you the answer right here."

Appreciative listening

In this kind of listening, we seek certain information which will appreciate. We use appreciative listening when we are listening to good music, poetry or maybe even the inspiring words of a great leader (See Figure 16.8).

Figure 16.8 Appreciative listening

For example: your friend narrating a poetry and you cheer for him and appreciate his effort.

Sympathetic listening

It is a listening in which we think about the other individual and demonstrate this worry in the way we give careful consideration and express our distress for their ills and satisfaction at their delights (See Figure 16.9).

Figure 16.9 Sympathetic listening

For example: your friend scored less marks in exam and you encourage him to do well next time.

Empathetic listening

When we are genuinely concerned, we feel what they are feeling. Keeping in mind the end result to motivate others to uncover there difficult parts to us, we additionally need to exhibit our sympathy in our disposition towards them, asking delicately and in a way that supports self-exposure (See Figure 16.10).

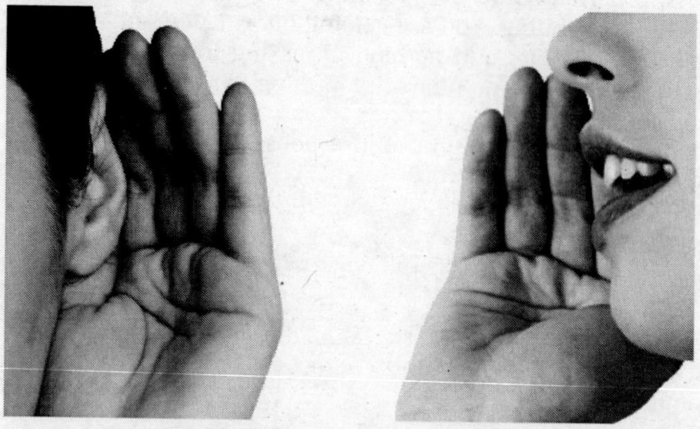

Figure 16.10 Empathetic listening

For example: you tell your friend that your dog got hit by a car in morning and he asks "was it hurt, I can see this has upset you".

Therapeutic listening

The receiver has a reason for relating to the speaker as well as to utilize this intense association with a particular end result to offer the speaker some assistance with understanding, change or create somehow. This likewise happens in work circumstances, where directors, HR individuals, mentors, and instructors try to offer representatives some assistance with learning and create (See Figure 16.11).

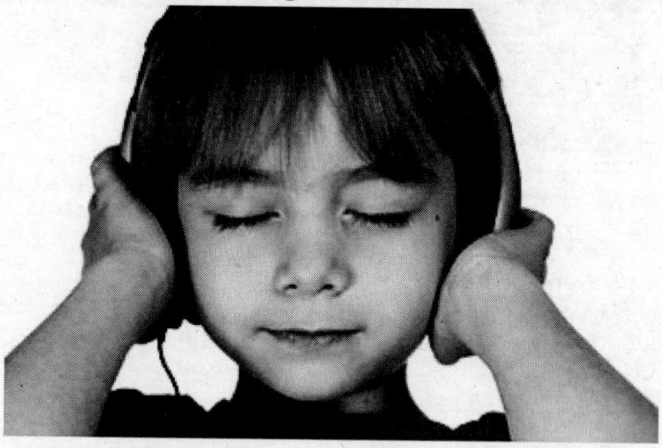

Figure 16.11 Therapeutic listening

For example: listening to a motivational speech from a motivational speaker.

Dialogic listening

"Dialog" comes from the Greek words 'dia', signifying "through" and "logos" meaning 'words'. In this way, It means learning through discussion and connected with the trade of thoughts and data in which we effectively look to take in more about the individual and how they think. It is known as 'relational listening' (See Figure 16.12).

Figure 16.12 Dialogic listening

For example: Role-plays or classroom drama activities.

Relationship listening

Some time, the most vital element in listening is to create or maintain a relationship. This is the reason partners talk for a considerable length of time and go to nearly to what one another needs to say when the same words from another person would appear to be somewhat exhausting (See Figure 16.13).

Figure 16.13 Relationship listening

For example: conversation between parent and kid/between family members.

16.4.2 Tips for Effective Listening

- Keep quiet while listening.
- Focus on what the speaker says rather than on his/her looks.
- Control and screen out the distractions.
- Show interest in the speaker.
- Be friendly and patient towards the speaker.
- Listen first and take notes afterwards.
- Look for the main theme and main ideas.
- Let the speaker finish whatever he/she has to say without interrupting him/her.
- Find an area of interest in the speech; look interested in the speech and act interested in listening.
- Try to repeat the key-ideas during the slow and long speeches.
- Avoid evaluating on a single point.
- Keep your mind open to every subject and speaker.
- Choose a quiet place to listen, if possible.
- Arrive early at the place of a seminar, lecture and meeting.
- Empathize with the speaker and try to understand his/her opinions, views and values.
- Try to explore the emotions and feelings of the speaker.
- Observe the non-verbal signals, the body movements, facial expressions and gestures.
- Try to look into the eyes of the speaker.
- Try to relate the speaker's message with your personal experience.
- Try to evaluate the speaker's message objectively.
- Keep on asking questions. This shows that how well you understand the speaker's ideas and also that you are listening.
- Communicate feedback to the speaker it may encourage the speaker.
- "Step into the shoes of others," i.e., put yourself in the position of the speaker and observe things from his /her viewpoint.

16.4.3 Academic listening (lecturing)

Lecturing is not simply a matter of standing in front of a class and reciting what you know. The classroom lecture is a special form of communication in which voice, gesture, movement, facial expression, and eye contact can either complement or detract from the content. No matter what your topic, your delivery and manner of speaking immeasurably influence your student's attentiveness and learning. Academic listening probably includes trying to follow a lecture or discussion and writing notes on it. When you attend lectures, you need to apply the highest level of listening skills you have.

Figure 16.14 Academic listening

Lecturing Basics

- Grab student's attention with your opening
- Incorporate anecdotes and stories in your lecture.
- Maintain eye contact with the class.
- Keep track of time.
- Pause occasionally.

- Budget time for questions.

You need to be doing the following:

- Evaluate Information: While listening, you need to be able to identify which parts are important to note down.
- Organize Information: Even as you write, you need to capture the relationships between the ideas/concepts that are being presented.
- Predict Information: Being able to anticipate how the information that comes up connects with what has been presented so far enhances your ability to understand the lecture.

Useful Tips:

- Read ahead of your lecture and keep up with assigned reading. This will enable you to be familiar with key vocabulary and develop an awareness of concepts.
- Do not attempt to take note of everything. Just note the main points.
- Improve your listening ability.

16.4.4 Listening to Talks and Presentation

People talk to you everyday-sometimes effectively, often not. If you want others to hear really what you have to say, you have to recognize how to say it in the most efficient manner possible. In any given situation a person's primary motive is, "What's in it for me?" That suggests whatever you say has to be fitted towards answering that very question for your listener.

"When you listen, you have power. When you talk, you give it away." How can we increase our power or influence by making sure we listen more than we talk?

Here are some ideas on encouraging the other person to talk so you will listen:

- Begin by asking the person s name: Not only will this make you a listener first, but it will also set up a pattern for listening more and talking less. When people give you their names, often you will get information, such as where they are from or what they do.
- Make sure you get the name: Ask the person to repeat the name if you are unclear about it, or make some comment about the name that allows you to repeat it to keep it firmly in mind.
- Follow any short comment you make after getting the name by asking an open question: Usually these questions begin with "What," "How," or "Why." If you are uncertain about what question to ask, you can connect the question to why both of you are at the same gathering. You could say, "What programs have you found most useful at the conference?" or "How do you like the convention /hotel /town/ movie/ performance?" Make a short comment when he or she finishes answering the question to avoid sounding like you are conducting an interrogation.
- Another way to encourage the other person to talk is to make an assertion and then pause: This will encourage the person to comment on your statement. You might say, "The meeting gave me new ideas about our program." Often, he or she will then add a comment to yours.
- You can encourage the other person to talk by your nonverbal reaction: Nod your head, smile, keep an open posture, and look as though you anticipate that the other person will add more information. When you make a comment such as "Oh," or "I see," say the words with an upward inflection to sound encouraging and positive, rather than a downward inflection, which would imply finality.
- Keep your own spoken contributions short when possible: Avoid telling a five-minute story or giving a three-minute opinion. Talk in 30-second segments, not three minutes. When it seems natural, end your comment by asking a question. Thus the other person will stay engaged and continue to provide you with information.

16.4.5 Listening to Announcements

It is a written or spoken statement that tells people about something : public or formal words that announce something It is a public statement that's usually format and has a specific purpose. There are many kinds of announcements, but they're all public and meant to inform (See Figure 16.15).

Figure 16.15 Listening to announcements

In school, the announcements might say whose birthday it is and where we are meeting after school. In a store, an announcement might mention a sale or a lost kid who's looking for her parents. So basically, if it is announcing something, it is an announcement. When someone declares something, it signifies that the information to be shared could be fundamental. Announcements can be joyous occasions, as when my Facebook friends proclaim their love for each different, and that they will be married or engaged. Social media instruments are excellent for announcing a grand opening and celebrations; giving suggestions and testimonials.

Rachel is meeting her friend Frank at the station. He is catching the 10.30 train from Glasgow.

At the station, Rachel finds out from the information desk exactly when the train is due to arrive and on what platform.

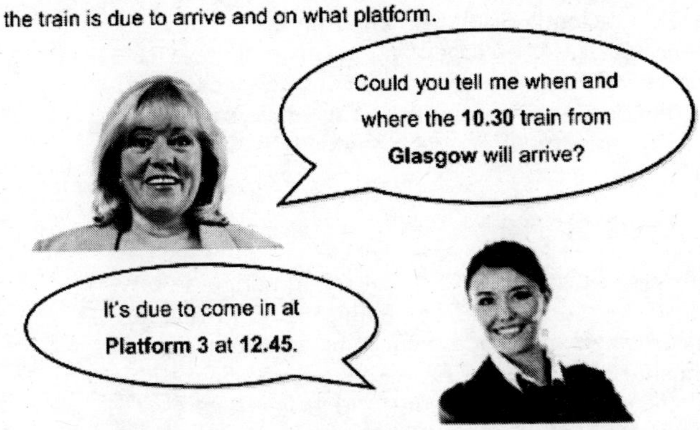

As she is waiting for Frank, announcements give Rachel new information about the train. It is late and she must get to a different platform.

16.5 CORPORATE CULTURE

It refers to the beliefs and behaviors that determine how a company's employees and management interact and handle outside business transactions. A company's culture will be reflected in its dress code, business hours, office setup, employee benefits, turnover, hiring decisions, treatment of clients, client satisfaction and every other aspect of operations (See Figure 16.16).

Figure 16.16

In a strong culture, employees view themselves as part of a workforce and acquire satisfaction from serving to the worldwide organization be successful. When employees insight that they are adding to a successful group effort, their degree of dedication and productivity, and thus the quality of the company's products or offerings, are prone to improve (See Figure 16.16).

16.6 CRM CONCEPTS

Customer Relationship management is the most efficient approach in maintaining and creating relationships with customers. Customer relationship management is not only pure business but also strong personal bonding within people. Development of this type of bonding drives the business to new levels of success.

Once this personal and emotional linkage is built, it is very easy for any organization to identify the actual needs of customer and help them to serve them in a better way. It is a belief that more the sophisticated strategies involved in implementing the customer relationship management, the more strong and fruitful is the business. Most of the organizations have dedicated world class tools for maintaining CRM systems into their workplace.

A CRM system allows you to manage all your customers, partners and prospects information all in one place.

For example, it helps:

- sales teams close deals faster
- marketing manage campaigns and track lead generation

Looking at some broader perspectives given as below we can easily determine why a CRM System is always important for an organization.

1. A CRM system consists of a historical view and analysis of all the acquired or to be acquired customers. This helps in reduced searching and correlating customers and to foresee customer needs effectively and increase business.
2. CRM contains each and every bit of details of a customer, hence it is very easy for track a customer accordingly and can be used to determine which customer can be profitable and which not.
3. In CRM system, customers are grouped according to different aspects according to the type of business they do or according to physical location and are allocated to different customer managers often called as account managers. This helps in focusing and concentrating on each and every customer separately.
4. A CRM system is not only used to deal with the existing customers but also useful in acquiring new customers. The process first starts with identifying a customer and maintaining all the corresponding details into the CRM system which is also called an "Opportunity of Business". The Sales and Field representatives then try getting business by sophistically following up with them and converting them into a winning deal. All this is very easily and efficiently done by an integrated CRM system.

5. The strongest aspect of Customer Relationship Management is that it is very cost-effective. The advantage of decently implemented CRM system is that there is very less need of paper and manual work which requires lesser staff to manage and lesser resources to deal with. The technologies used in implementing a CRM system are also very cheap and smooth as compared to the traditional way of business.
6. All the details in CRM system is kept centralized which is available anytime on fingertips. This reduces the process time and increases productivity.
7. Efficiently dealing with all the customers and providing them what they actually need increases the customer satisfaction. This increases the chance of getting more business which ultimately enhances turnover and profit.
8. If the customer is satisfied they will always be loyal to you and will remain in business forever resulting in increasing customer base and ultimately enhancing net growth of business.

Installing a CRM system can definitely improve the situation and help in challenging the new ways of marketing and business in an efficient manner. Hence in the era of business every organization should be recommended to have a full-fledged CRM system to cope up with all the business needs.

16.6.1 Features of CRM

CRM is a strategy which is customized by an organization to manage and administrate its customers and vendors in an efficient manner for achieving quality in business. It is specifically involve with following features.

1. Customers Needs–An organization can never assume what actually a customer needs. Hence it is extremely important to interview a customer about all the likes and dislikes so that the actual needs can be ascertained and prioritized.
2. Customers Response–Customer response is the reaction by the organization to the queries and activities of the customer. Dealing with these queries intelligently is very important as small misunderstandings could convey unalike perceptions. Success totally depends on the understanding and interpreting these queries and then working out to provide the best solution.
3. Customer Satisfaction–In today's competitive business marketplace, customer satisfaction is an important performance exponent and basic differentiator of business strategies. Hence, the more is customer satisfaction; more is the business and the bonding with customer.
4. Customer Loyalty–To continue the customer loyalty the most important aspect an organization should focus on is customer satisfaction. Hence, customer loyalty is an influencing aspect of CRM and is always crucial for business success.
5. Customer Retention–Customer retention is a strategic process to keep or retain the existing customers and not letting them to diverge or defect to other suppliers or organization for business.
6. Customer Complaints–Normally raising a complaint indicates the act of dissatisfaction of the customer. There can be several reasons for a customer to launch a complaint. A genuine reason can also exist due to which the customer is dissatisfied. Handling these complaints to ultimate satisfaction of the customer is substantial for any organization and hence it is essential for them to have predefined set of process in CRM to deal with these complaints and efficiently resolve it in no time.
7. Customer Service–In an organization Customer Service is the process of delivering information and services regarding all the products and brands. Customer satisfaction depends on quality of service provided to him by the supplier.

16.7 SELLING SKILLS

Selling skills are critical in method that rely on ongoing buying from customers or clients. The ability to build relationships with customers, persuade them to make purchases and generate business is at the heart of selling. Sales is a component of a company's marketing and promotions.

There are specific selling techniques that have been proven over time to be effective. As you become more skilled and advanced in selling, you will learn how to:

- Determine clients' needs, wants, and buying motives.
- Open and close sales
- Question clients
- Handle customer objections
- Suggest additional or substitute items
- Demonstrate products
- Follow up on sales

Selling is a service. You should be on the customer and what s/he wants. What can you offer the customer? How can you help him/her? You are not there to make a quick buck or "strong-arm" a customer into buying something s/he doesn't really need. Your job is to assist customers by giving them the accurate product information they need to make intelligent buying decisions. Think of yourself as the go-between for your business and your customers. By meeting the needs of your customers, you will be helping your company grow and prosper.

Good communication skills are handy in every industry, but they are especially important in sales careers. You must be able to express yourself clearly and simply so that clients understand how your products will benefit them and meet their needs. Sometimes, you may need to use technical terms and be prepared to explain them in a way the client can understand.

Personal appearance to make good impression. Customers judge you by the way you dress and groom yourself. If you present yourself as disheveled and sloppy, customers will assume your company does business in the same manner.

Some key points to make professional Selling Skills developed

- Enhance your success in developing customer relationships.

- Develop your own professional selling skills methodology.
- Heighten prospect interest in your product or service.
- Turn objections into benefits
- Learn to recognize conflicting, non-verbal behaviors.
- Learn successful sales techniques for group and committee presentations.
- Professionalize your proposals
- Discover new team sales skills and consultative selling approaches.
- Raise the profitability of each sales hour and the effectiveness of all sales techniques.

16.8 BEHAVIORAL SKILLS

It is a way in which one acts or conducts oneself, especially towards others. It is the skills you use to successfully interact with others. For example, telling a joke is a skill; laughing at a joke is a behavior. It is a set of training to develop specified behavioral skill in people, such as the right way to attend to calls/complaints, front office/reception and so on. It is the skills you utilize to interact successfully with others in the workplace and in your everyday life.

Here is a list of behavioral skills.

- Accurate Listening
- Answering a Complaint
- Asking for Help
- Asking Questions
- Commitment
- Concentration
- Creative Thinking
- Diplomacy
- Directing
- Expressing Feeling
- Flexibility
- Gestures
- Improvisation
- Integrity
- Listening
- Motivation
- Nonverbal Communication
- Planning
- Respect
- Speaking
- Strategic Planning
- Time Management
- Verbal Communication
- Analytical Thinking
- Apologizing
- Asking Permission
- Being a Good Sport
- Communication
- Convincing
- Dealing with Emotions
- Decision Making
- Expressing Affection
- Eye Contact
- Following Instruction
- Honesty
- Initiative
- Leadership
- Making Decisions
- Negotiation
- Patience
- Problem Solving
- Self Improvement
- Strategic Management
- Teamwork
- Training
- Written Communication

16.9 VOCABULARY DEVELOPMENT

It is the body of words used in a particular language and a process through which people collect words. As babies grow and produce their first words around the age of one year. By the age of 18 months, toddlers can ordinarily produce about 50 words and begin to make word combos. Many participants with finding out variations, problems and disabilities have vulnerable language skills, which immediately impact their vocabulary progress. A restricted vocabulary, in general, equals a restrained schooling and a confined profession. Most of us take vocabulary without any consideration because we study words and they are which means as we grow.

The reasons why individuals have weak vocabularies, here are a few of the common reasons for weak vocabularies.

The person

- lives in an environment where higher level vocabularies are not used,
- has a lower education level because the person either did not complete school or the education was of poor quality,
- attended special education classes in which lower level vocabulary was used in class and in textbooks,
- does not read much or has a reading problem,
- does not pay attention to words,
- has an auditory perception problem which makes it difficult to hear the subtle differences in words,
- does not have a good understanding of the structure of language including parts of speech and word parts, prefixes, suffixes and word roots.

16.10 PRONUNCIATION

It is the way in which a word is pronounced or a language is spoken, or the way in which any individual utters a word. If one is claimed to have "correct pronunciation", then it refers to each inside a certain language. A word can be spoken in different ways by various individuals or groups, depending on many factors, such as: the duration of the cultural exposure of their childhood, the location of their current residence, speech or voice disorders, their ethnic group, their social class, or their education.

16.11 READING

It is the action or practice of a person who reads. It is the process of looking at a series of written symbols and getting meaning from them. When we read, we use our eyes to receive written symbols (letters, punctuation marks and spaces) and we use our brain to convert them into words, sentences and paragraphs that communicate something to us. It can be silent (in our head) or aloud (so that other people can hear).

16.12 LISTENING AND SPEAKING

Hearing refers to the sounds that you hear, whereas listening requires more than that: it requires focus. Listening means paying attention not only to the story, but how it is told, the use of language and voice, and how the other person uses his or her body.

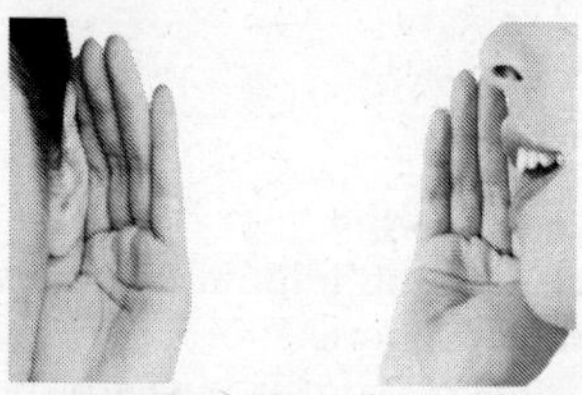

It is a process to give attention with ears and Speaking is the act, utterance, or discourse of a person who speaks. It is the capacity to acquire efficiently and interpret messages within the communication process. Listening is so essential that many top employers provide listening skills training for their employees.

16.13 WRITING

It is the act or process of producing and recording words in a form that can be read and understood. It is a medium of human communication that represents language and emotion via the inscription or recording of signs and symbols. In most languages, writing is a complement to speech or spoken language.

How to Make Your Writing Communicate

Effective writing allows the reader to thoroughly understand everything you are saying. This is not always easy to do. Here are a few tips that will help you:

1. Know your objective and state it clearly: Do you want the reader to do something for you or are you merely passing along information? Do you want a response from the reader or do you want him to take action? Your purpose needs to be stated in the communication. Avoid information that is not relevant. Clarity is key.
2. Tone can help your writing be more effective: Certain forms of communication, like memorandums and proposals need a formal tone. Writing to someone you know well would need a more informal tone. The kind of tone depends on the receiver and purpose of the writing.
3. Explain in clear terms what you want the reader to do: They cannot oblige if they do not understand. Also, they may not even want to try to help if the communication is vague and sloppily written. It is good to include why it is beneficial to them to do what you ask or to help you.
4. Language needs to be simple: Do not overuse clich s, jargon, and expressions or try to impress with big words. Keep sentences and paragraphs short and concise.
5. Less is more when it comes to length: Leave out words that do not contribute to the main focus of the communication. This can make the reader work harder to know why you wrote.
6. Using an active voice will strengthen your writing: Sentences that are written in the active voice will flow better and are easier to understand. Long, complicated sentences will slow the reader down, even more so if they are written in the passive voice. An active example is "I caught the ball" and a passive example is "The ball was caught by me." Active voice will engage the reader and keep his attention.
7. Good grammar and punctuation are very important: It is a good idea to have someone else proofread your writing before you send it. If you cannot do that, then try reading it out loud.

16.14 INTEGRATED SKILLS

The integrated of skills can be defined as the combination of two or more skills within a communication task.

Now, we can integrate the four languge skills. These are:

1. Why should we integrate the four skills?
2. How can we integrate the four skills?
3. What are the implications for teaching?
4. Whar are the limitations of integrating the four skills?

Why should we integrate the four skills?

There are many situations in which we use more than one language skill. For this reason alone, it is valuable to integrate the language skills, but there are other reasons why integration can enhance the students' communicative competence.

Also, integrating the kills allows you to build in more variety into the lesson because the range of activities will be wider. Instead of just having listening, the students can have speaking, reading and writing practice. This can raise their motivation to learn English.

Above all, integrating the skills means that you are working at the level of realistic communication, not just at the level of vocabulary and sentence patterns. Realistic communication is the aim of the communicative approach and many researchers believe that handling realistic communication is an integral part of essential conditions for language learning:

Conditions for Language Learning

Essential and desirable conditions for language learning

Integrating the four skills emphasizes the focus on realistic language and can therefore lead to the students' all-round development of communicative competence.

How can we integrate the four skills?

The essential form of integration is within the same medium (either oral or written), from receptive to productive skills.

	Receptive Skill		Productive Skill
Oral Medium	Listening	→	Speaking
Written Medium	reading	→	writing

In other words, we would use a listening text as a model for the students' speaking, and a reading text as a model for the students' writing. This is common practice among teachers, and we will call it simple integration. The information that the students get from the reading is useful in the oral activity, while the writing activity is based on information from the oral activity.

The fill-in-blanks activity that the students are asked to carry out in completing the dialogue is actually a form of reading comprehension. As the comprehension questions take the form of a realistic dialogue, the students can then practice their oral skills as well as their reading skills. The dialogue can then be used as a basis for the students' own conversations.

What are the implications for teaching?

As we noted earlier, integration of the four skills is concerned with realistic communication. This means that we are teaching at the discourse level not just at the level of sentences or individual words and phrases. Discourse is a whole unit of communicative text, either spoken or written.

Focus on discourse: The main implication for teaching is that we need to be aware of the discourse features of a text and to be able to make students aware of them. This helps the integration of skills because it makes clear the teaching points and, for simple integration, the discourse features are the main language aspects that we transfer from one skill to the other. Discourse features include aspects such as:

- the way that the text is organized
- its layout (for written text)
- the style of the language (formal or informal)
- the register (the vocabulary that is commonly found in such discourses).

As teachers, to use our professional judgment, based on our knowledge of the students, to decide how much detail we should include in our lesson. It is important to keep a balance. Too much information may confuse them. Too little information may mean that they are not clear about the features of a particular type of discourse.

Adjusting the textbook contents: Another aspect of our teaching that requires attention if we adopt an integrated approach is the use of the textbook. Although many modern textbooks have some integration of the four skills, we may still need to make some changes to the contents.

This could involve altering the order of the contents. If the discourse of the writing activity is closely related to the reading passage, but is placed in a different part of the unit in the textbook, we could focus on the writing straight after we finish the reading passage.

For simple integration, we can design a listening or reading comprehension activity that becomes a plan for speaking or writing. For complex integration, it could mean making changes to the activities in the textbook.

Adjusting timetable: There also are practical implications for integrating the four skills. One is related to timetabling. In some schools, a whole lesson reading given to teaching one skill. For example, there is a "listening" lesson one day, a "reading" lesson another day, and so on. Sometimes this is encouraged by the arrangement of materials in the textbook. We have to make the timetable arrangements more flexible so that we can integrate the skills better.

What are the limitations of integrating the four skills?

It is necessary for teachers to maintain an appropriate balance between integration and separation. Integrating the four language skills can be demanding of the teacher. We need to have a good understanding of discourse, and to be able to use textbooks flexibly. This can also be time-consuming, requiring a lot of preparation. Sometimes teachers are so busy that they cannot spare much time for extra preparatory work.

Another limitation is the problem of designing suitable materials that take account of students' different skill levels. The four skills tend to develop at a different pace: receptive skills are stronger then productive skills, for example. This means that teachers have to be skilful or designing integrated activities for their students.

16.15 NON-VERBAL COMMUNICATION

The term nonverbal communication was introduced in 1956 by psychiatrist Jurgen Ruesch. Non-verbal communication can be communicated through gestures and touch (Haptic communication), by body language or posture, by facial expression and eye contact. Speech contains nonverbal elements known as paralanguage, including quality, emotion and speaking style, as well as prosodic features such as rhythm, intonation and stress. It also referred to as the encoding or sending of information as well s the interpretation the decoding or receiving of information.

16.15.1 Types of Non-Verbal Communication

There are many different types of non-verbal communication. Theye include:

1. Body language is a type of nonverbal communication that relies on body movements (such as gestures, posture, and facial expressions) to convey messages.
   This study applies traditional linguistic principles to the body as a whole or to specific parts, particularly the face, hands and arms. It also deals with posture in standing and sitting, as well as with eye and facial expressions, such as the arching of eyebrows or rolling of the eyes.
2. Occulesics is closely related to kinesics. Occulesics deals with eye behavior as an element of communication.

3. Proxemics involves the social use of space in a communication situation. One aspect of this is the closeness between and among people when they speak. Distance is generally described on a continuum from intimate space (0-18 inches) to personal space or informal distance (18 inches to 4 feet) to social space or formal distance (4-12 feet), and public space or distance (beyond 12 feet).
4. Haptics focuses on touching as an element of communication, indicating both the type of touch as well as its frequency and intensity.
5. Vocalics (also called paralanguage) deals with vocal cues, more accurately referred to as the nonphonemic qualities of language. These include accent, loudness, tempo, pitch, cadence, rate of speech, nasality and tone, insofar as these convey meaning. Vocalics is sometimes subdivided into several categories.
6. Appearance deals with the communication role played by a person's look or physical appearance (as compared with physical gestures associated with kinesics). It deals with physical aspects of body shape, hair color and skin tone, as well as grooming, dress (both clothing and jewelry) and use of appearance enhancements such as body piercings, brandings and tattoos.
7. Olfactics is an aspect of nonverbal communication dealing with smells.

Uses of Nonverbal Communication

Nonverbal communication provides individuals and groups with many options for presenting their messages. Here are some of the uses of nonverbal communication.

- To create impressions beyond the verbal element of communication.
- To repeat and reinforce what is said verbally.
- To manage and regulate the interaction among participants in the communication exchange.
- To express emotion beyond the verbal element.
- To convey relational messages of affection, power, dominance, respect, and so on.
- To promote honest communication by detecting deception or conveying suspicion.
- To provide group or social leadership by sending messages of power and faith.

MODEL QUESTIONS AND ANSWERS

A. Multiple Choice

1.1 Soft skills is a term often associated with a person's ________.

a. Emotional Intelligence Quotient
b. Emotional Intellectual Quotient
c. Emerging Intelligence Quotient
d. Emotional Intelligence Quest

1.2 Soft skills contrast to______, which are generally easily quantifiable and measurable.

a. Personal skills b. Professional skills
c. Communication skills d. Hard skills

1.3 The phrase _______ is often used to describe the skills which characterize relationships with other people, or which are about how you approach life and work.

a. Hard skills b. Soft skills
c. Communication skills d. Presentation skills

1.4 ___________, by contrast, is a phrase usually used to describe job-specific skills.

a. Hard skills b. People skills
c. Interpersonal skills d. Social skills

1.5 Communication is about more than just exchanging_________.

a. Information b. Products
c. Services d. Money

1.6 __________ is about understanding the emotion and intentions behind the information.

a. Soft Skill b. Hard Skill
c. Communication d. Interpersonal Skills

1.7 _________is the glue that helps you deepen your connections to others and improve teamwork, decision-making, and problem solving.

a. Effective Communication b. Efficient Communication
c. Effective Coordination d. Efficient Combination

1.8 A _________that is read rarely has the same impact as a speech that is delivered (or appears to be delivered) spontaneously.

a. Skill b. Paragraph
c. Sentence d. Speech

1.9 In _________Compelling business communication utilizes brief and clear dialect that gets the point crosswise over totally and in a way that energizes productive activity.

a. Clear b. Communication
c. Concise d. None of the above

1.10 ___________ is completely focusing on what is being said as opposed to merely passively "listening to" the message of the speaker.

a. Active listening b. Distractive listening
c. Appropriate listening d. Organized listening

1.11 ________listening is the most major type of listening, whereby the difference between sounds is recognized.

a. Active b. Comprehensive
c. Discriminative d. Concise

1.12 Listening is a visual and additionally sound-related act, as we impart much through __________ communication.

a. Verbal b. Written
c. Formal d. Non-verbal

1.13 ___________listening is also known as content listening, informative listening and full listening.
a. Comprehension b. Active
c. Discriminative d. Concise

1.14 _________listening is listening in order to evaluate and judge, forming opinion about what is being said.
a. Comprehensive b. Discriminative
c. Critical d. Active

1.15 The judgment incorporates evaluating qualities and shortcomings, _________ and endorsement.
a. Understanding b. Listening
c. Interacting d. Communicating

1.16 ________ listening happens when the individual hears just what they need to hear, commonly confounding what the other individual says in light of the generalizations and different predispositions that they have.
a. Biased b. Comprehensive
c. Discriminative d. Active

1.17 ___________listening or necessary tuning in, we make judgments about what the other individual is stating.
a. Biased b. Evaluative
c. Comprehensive d. Discriminative

1.18 _________ listening, we look for certain data that will acknowledge, for instance, what addresses our issues and objectives.
a. Appreciative b. Biased
c. Comprehensive d. Discriminative

1.19 _________ listening, we think about the other individual and demonstrate this worry in the way we give careful consideration and express our distress for their ills and satisfaction at their delights.
a. Biased b. Comprehensive
c. Discriminative d. Sympathetic

1.20 ___________refers to the shared values, attitudes, standards, and beliefs that characterize members of an organization and define its nature.
a. National culture b. School culture
c. Corporate culture d. Home culture

1.21 Non-verbal communication does not include:
a. Silence b. gestures
c. Space d. Words

1.22 Postive gestures are body signals that make you look:
a. Relaxed b. arrogant
c. hurtful d. nervous

B. State whether the following are True or False

2.1 Behavioral skills are the skills you use to successfully interact with others in the workplace.
2.2 Vocabulary development is a process by which people acquire words.
2.3 A limited vocabulary often equals a growth in education and a growth in career.
2.4 Pronunciation is the way a word or a language is spoken, or the manner in which someone utters a word.
2.5 Academic reading should not be seen as an active activity, but a passive process that leads to the development of learning.
2.6 Listening is the ability to accurately receive and interpret messages in the communication process.
2.7 Listening is not so important that many top employers provide listening skills training for their employees.
2.8 Writing is a medium of human communication that represents language and emotion through the inscription or recording of signs and symbols.
2.9 Writing is a language not a form of technology that developed as tools developed with human society.
2.10 An employee with a high level of emotional intelligence has good communication skills.
2.11 Paralanguage is a kind of action language that refers to the tone of voice or speed of speech.
2.12 Grooming is a form of non-verbal communication that is conscious.

Answers

A. 1.1 a 1.2 d 1.3 b 1.4 a 1.5 a
1.6 c 1.7 a 1.8 d 1.9 c 1.10 a
1.11 c 1.12 d 1.13 a 1.14 c 1.15 a
1.16 a 1.17 b 1.18 a 1.19 d 1.20. c
1.21 d 1.22 a

B. 2.1 T 2.2 T 2.3 F 2.4 T 2.5 F
2.6 T 2.7 F 2.8 T 2.9 F 2.10 T
2.11 T 2.12 T

SOLVED SAMPLE PAPER

Total Time : 90 Minutes

Total Marks: 100

PART – ONE

(Answer all questions; each question carries one mark)

1. Multiple choice

1.1 The connection between the computers and peripherals is called a
a. Port c. Bus
b. I/O device d. None of the above

1.2 DBMS is a collection of __________ that enables user to create and maintain a database
a. Keys c. Program
b. Translators d. Language Activity

1.3 Which of the following can be used as a primary memory?
a. Cartridge tape c. Optical disk
b. Hard disk d. None of these

1.4 Which one of the following is not an output device?
a. Printer c. Keyboard
b. Monitor d. Mouse

1.5 The file in DBMS is called as ________ in RDBMS.
a. Console c. Table
b. Schema d. Object

1.6 A right click on the Windows desktop will:
a. Open the display Properties dialog box
b. Show a context-sensitive menu
c. Open the Control panel
d. Minimize all the open applications

1.7 Which of the following is the largest community in classification of e-commerce?
a. Business to Business (B2B)
b. Business to Consumer (B2C)
c. Business to Government (B2G)
d. Governmet to Government (G2G)

1.8 The resolution of a printer is measured in
a. Megabits c. Dots per inch (DPI)
b. Hz d. Inches (diagonal)

1.9 The utility used to increase the speed of programs is called
a. Disk Fragmenter c. Disk Formatter
b. Disk Cleanup d. None of the above

1.10 Internet access for transmitting digital data over the wires of a local telephone network is provided by
a. Leased line c. Digital Signal line
b. Digital Subscriber line d. None of the above

1.11 The printers that produce the output by pressing a print element and an inked ribbon against the face of a continuous paper form is called
a. Impact printer c. Non-impact printer
b. Scanning printers d. None of the above

1.12 The best products to sell in B2C e-commerce are:
a. Small products c. Specialty products
b. Digital products d. Fresh products

1.13 Virtual Memory is
a. Part of main memory only used for swapping.
b. A technique to allow a program, of size more than size of the main memory to run.
c. Part of secondary storage used in program execution.
d. None of the above

1.14 ________listening is listening in order to evaluate and judge, forming opinion about what is being said.
a. Comprehensive c. Critical
b. Discriminative d. Active

1.15 In the e-mail address BPBonline@gmail.com is?
a. Password c. User name
b. Server name d. Client computer

1.16 To insert Clip Art, pictures from disk into a Word Document, which of the following method is used?
a. Insert Picture command c. Add Picture command
b. Insert Object command d. Insert File command

1.17 The judgment incorporates evaluating qualities and shortcomings, ________ and endorsement.
a. Understanding c. Interacting
b. Listening d. Communicating

1.18 Green lock icon means:
a. The site's certificate is valid and its identity has been verified by a trusted third party.
b. The site hasn't provided the browser a valid certificate.
c. Site has weak security setup, which mean that your connection might not be private.
d. There are some problems with the site's certificate, might be your confidential information get leaked out.

1.19 Which file extensions indicate only graphics files?
a. BMP and DOC c. TXT and STK
b. JPEG and TXT d. BMP and GIF

1.20 A typical MS-Excel worksheet has __________ columns.
a. 128 c. 512
b. 256 d. 1024

1.21 Which of the following is not an example of an Application Software?
a. MS Word c. Operating system
b. Screen saver program d. Antivirus program

1.22 Hard disk is coated in both side by
a. Magnetic metallic oxide c. Carbon layer
b. Optical metallic oxide d. All of the above

1.23 A fraudulent is also called as:
a. Phishing c. Mailing
b. Phish d. Spam mail

1.24 CD-ROM stands for
a. Compactable Read only memory c. Compactable disk Read only memory
b. Compact Data Read only memory d. Compact disk Read only memory

1.25 Software in computer
a. Enhances the capabilities of the hardware machine
b. Increases the speed of central processing unit
c. Both (a) and (b)
d. None of the above

1.26 Which of the following devices can be used to directly image printed text?
a. OCR c. MICR
b. OMR d. All of the above

1.27 'Bluetooth' technology allows-
a. Landline phone to mobile phone communication
b. Signal transmission to mobile phone only
c. Wireless communication between equipments
d. Satellite television communication

1.28 Who designed the first electronics computer-ENIAC?
a. Van-Neumann
b. Joseph M.Jacquard
c. J.Presper Eckert and John W Mauchly
d. All of the above

1.29 ________ memory has the shortest access time:
a. Cache c. ROM
b. RAM d. Magnetic core

1.30 IP address number varies from
a. 1-255 c. 0-254
b. 2-255 d. 1-254

1.31 A computer program that translates one program instructions at a time into a machine language is called a/an
a. Interpreter c. Compiler
b. CPU d. None of the above

1.32 A computer consists of
a. A central processing unit c. Input and output unit
b. A memory d. All of the above

1.33 Options which Paster Special dialog box of Excel contains:
a. Characteristics c. Values
b. Formats and Formulas d. All of the above

1.34 The instructions for starting the computer are stored in
a. Random access memory c. Read only memory chip
b. CD-ROM d. All of the above

1.35 By using MS Word's Find and Replace feature one can:
a. Replace formatting of a document
b. Replace text of a document
c. Replace both the text and the formatting of a document
d. Replace the name of the document with a new name

1.36 How can you disable extended selection mode?
a. Press F8 again to disable c. Press Esc to disable
b. Press Del to disable d. Press Enter to disable

1.37 What is the shortcut key you can press to create a copyright symbol?
a. Alt + Ctrl + C c. Ctrl + C
b. Alt + C d. Ctrl + Shift + C

1.38 SpinRite will do a destructive/reconstructive low-level information (which does not destroy your data) on the following kinds of drivers.
a. All hard disks
b. MFM and RLL drives
c. MFM, RLL, and IDE drives
d. ESDI and SCSI drives

1.39 Which of the following is graphics solutions for word processors?
a. Clip Art c. Drop Cap
b. WordArt d. All of the above

1.40 The keystrokes Ctrl + I is used to
a. Increase font size
b. Insert a line break
c. Indicate the text should be bold
d. Applies italic format to selected text

1.41 Digital financial services, expands the delivery of basic financial services to the people through new technologies like
a. Internet
b. Mobile phones
c. Transfer of money through new digital channels
d. All of the above

1.42 What does CRM stands for?
a. Customer Relationship Management
b. Consumer Relations Management
c. Customer Relationship Marketing
d. Consumer Returns Management

1.43 The following is (are) non-verbal communication.
a. Facial expression
b. Appearance
c. Posture
d. All of the above

1.44 The 2-D representation of an image is known as:
a. Image routing c. Image reasoning
b. Image resolution d. 2-D Computer graphics

1.45 ________ means authentication of any electronic record by a subscriber by means of an electronic method
a. Digital certificate c. A key generation algorithm
b. Digital Signature d. A signing algorithm

1.46 Listening is a visual and additionally sound-related act, as we impart much through ________ communication.
a. Verbal c. Formal
b. Written d. Non-verbal

1.47 Any communication that conveys a message consisting of words is called:
a. verbal communication.
b. oral communication.
c. written communication.
d. non verbal communication.

1.48 Currency notes are issued by:
a. RBI c. Public sector bank
b. NABARD d. Central Government

1.49 A bank is a ________ institution.
a. Financial c. Joint
b. Commercial d. Sole

1.50 Who helps to Secure money, earn interest and get loans
a. Bank c. Home
b. Government d. None of these

PART – TWO

2. Select TRUE or FALSE in statements

2.1 A kilobyte is approximately 1,000 bytes.
2.2 Some of the browsers have privacy features for cookies, private browsing, and deleting browsing history.
2.3 When you connect to the internet your computer is communicating with a server at your ISP.
2.4 The most common type of memory that the computer uses to process data is ROM.
2.5 A Web browser is a special device that is installed in your computer that allows it to communicate with other devices on the network.
2.6 Being computer fluent means that you should be able to build a computer yourself.
2.7 The CPU and memory are located on a special circuit board in the system unit called the motherboard.
2.8 Hard disk drives and CD drives are examples of storage devices.
2.9 A cloud is called a "Private cloud" when the services are rendered over a network which is open for public use.
2.10 Main memory is a software component.
2.11 A computer's CD-ROM drive can read data disks, but it cannot play audio CDs.
2.12 Pronunciation is the way a word or a language is spoken, or the manner in which someone utters a word.
2.13 The original Act contained 94 sections, which is divided in 19 chapters and 4 schedules.
2.14 IT act 2000 deals with cybercrime and electronic commerce.
2.15 The laser printer uses a technology called thermal process.
2.16 You can protect scenario so other users cannot change or modify it.
2.17 E-Service, represents a prominent application of utilizing the information and communication technologies (ICTs) in various areas.
2.18 Folders organize files on a disk.
2.19 In Linux, error messages are placed in a standard byte stream called the standard error.
2.20 Right click press and release the right mouse button once, typically done to open a dialog box.
2.21 Digital certificate is an electronic document which is used to prove the ownership of a public key.
2.22 A unique data item which is used to identify a particular record is called a Key field.
2.23 If the text entered in a cell does not fit, Excel will display ##### to indicate that the text is too long.
2.24 A mouse is a pointing device.
2.25 A printer is an example of an input device.
2.26 Virtual hypertext network is called WWW.
2.27 When you download files you send files from your computer to the Internet.
2.28 A bit is bigger than a byte.
2.29 You can add dates to worksheets, but spreadsheets cannot use dates in calculations.
2.30 In a spreadsheet, ordinary text is called a "label".
2.31 TCP/IP is a layered set of cables.
2.32 A storage device is a hardware component that writes data to and reads data from a storage medium.
2.33 In a binary representation, we use digits 1 and 2.
2.34 ROM, which stands for read-only memory and is also known as firmware, cannot be written on or erased by the computer user.
2.35 High-end laser printers offer resolutions as high as 300 dpi.
2.36 One of the operating system's functions is to manage the way an information is stored on and retrieved from disks.
2.37 If an employee works in more than one department, then such a relation will be called many to many.
2.38 In order to create columnar data in Word you need to Set tabs or use the Table menu.
2.39 The primary function of I/O peripheral is to facilitate computer-to-computer data transmission.
2.40 Public Key Encryption ensure the confidentiality of message.
2.41 Saving is income spent.
2.42 Email spoofing involves creation of email messages with a real sender address.
2.43 In economics more broadly, Saving refers to any income which is not used for immediate consumption.
2.44 Change management involves the design, operation, control, and optimization of either chemical, physical, and biological processes.
2.45 In a deposit account, versus investment, wherein risk is low
2.46 Processing engineering is a processes that can be used for encouraging individuals to make successful personal changes.
2.47 IDMS is an example of network database system.
2.48 Writing is a medium of human communication that represents language and emotion through the inscription or recording of signs and symbols.
2.49 Listening is not so important that many top employers provide listening skills training for their employees.
2.50 Saving money in a bank account, offers you the opportunity to earn interest on deposits.

Answers

1.	1.1	a	1.2	c	1.3	d	1.4	c	1.5	c
	1.6	b	1.7	a	1.8	c	1.9	a	1.10	b
	1.11	a	1.12	b	1.13	a	1.14	c	1.15	c
	1.16	d	1.17	a	1.18	a	1.19	d	1.20	d
	1.21	c	1.22	a	1.23	a	1.24	d	1.25	a
	1.26	a	1.27	c	1.28	c	1.29	a	1.30	b
	1.31	a	1.32	d	1.33	d	1.34	c	1.35	c
	1.36	a	1.37	a	1.38	b	1.39	a	1.40	d
	1.41	a	1.42	a	1.43	d	1.44	d	1.45	b
	1.46	d	1.47	a	1.48	a	1.49	a	1.50	a
2.	2.1	T	2.2	T	2.3	T	2.4	F	2.5	F
	2.6	F	2.7	T	2.8	T	2.9	F	2.10	F
	2.11	F	2.12	T	2.13	T	2.14	T	2.15	F
	2.16	T	2.17	T	2.18	T	2.19	T	2.20	F
	2.21	T	2.22	T	2.23	T	2.24	T	2.25	F
	2.26	T	2.27	F	2.28	F	2.29	F	2.30	T
	2.31	F	2.32	T	2.33	F	2.34	T	2.35	F
	2.36	T	2.37	T	2.38	T	2.39	F	2.40	T
	2.41	F	2.42	F	2.43	T	2.44	F	2.45	F
	2.46	F	2.47	T	2.48	T	2.49	F	2.50	T

UNSOLVED SAMPLE PAPER

Total Time : 90 Minutes

Total Marks: 100

PART – ONE

(Answer all questions; each question carries one mark)

1. Multiple choice

1.1 Which of the following are the two main components of the CPU?
a. Control Unit and Registers
b. Registers and Main Memory
c. Control unit and ALU
d. ALU

1.2 A _________ is a unit of information in a _________.
a. Record, field
b. field, record
c. data source, field
d. record, data source

1.3 DSL is an example of a(n) connection?
a. Network
b. Wireless
c. Slow
d. broadband

1.4 In a datasheet, what does each column represent?
a. Record
b. Field
c. Database
d. Table

1.5 Benefits of Internet
a. Education
b. Careers
c. Advertisement
d. All of the above

1.6 Which of the following should you use if you want all the slides in the presentation to have the same "look"?
a. The slide layout option
b. Add a slide option
c. Outline view
d. A presentation design template

1.7 Alignment command available in the _________ group of ____ tab.
a. Click the home tab of paragraph group.
b. Click the home tab of Font group.
c. Click the insert tab of Ilustration group.
d. None of the above

1.8 Who is the father of the Internet?
a. Vinton G.Cerf
b. George W.Bush
c. Bill Clinton
d. George H.W

1.9 In order to edit a chart, you can
a. Triple click the chart object
b. Click and drag the chart object
c. Double click the chart object
d. Click the chart object

1.10 Which object is used to create a form?
a. Tables and Queries
b. Tables only
c. Tables and Reports
d. Queries and Reports

1.11 To preview a motion path effect using the custom animation task pane, you should
a. Click the play button
b. Click the show effect button
c. Double click the motion path
d. All of above

1.12 Which of the following is not one of the Internet protocols?
a. HTTP
b. SMTP
c. PPP
d. NetBIOS

1.13 An electronic page in a presentation is called
a. Slide
b. e-slide
c. e-page
d. page

1.14 The basic elements of a form or a report are called:
a. Controls
b. Objects
c. Windows
d. Properties

1.15 Which of the following should be your first choice to remove an application that you no longer need?
a. Delete the program files.
b. Use the uninstall program that came with the application
c. Use the Add or Remove applet
d. Use the Registry Editor to remove references to the application.

1.16 Which of the following Ribbon command provide different options in various presentations views?
a. View tab in the presentations views
b. Review tab in the comments group
c. Transitions tab in the timings group
d. Animations tab in the Preview view

1.17 SWAN Is:
a. State Wide Area Networks
b. Slate Wide Area Networks
c. State Wide And Networks
d. State Wire Area Networks

1.18 How do you create speaker note pages that show the slides, related notes, and your company logo on each page?
a. Edit the notes master and add your company logy.
b. Edit the slide master and insert your company logo and notes pane.
c. Edit the handout master to include your company logo and one slide per page with additional note space.
d. All of the above

1.19 Tab scroll buttons are placed on Excel screen
a. Towards the bottom right corner
b. Towards the bottom left corner
c. Towards the top right corner
d. Towards the top left corner

1.20 Which tool will you use to join some cells and place the content at the middle of joined cell?
a. From Format Cells dialog box click on Merge Cells check box.

b. From Format Cells dialog box select the Centered alignment.
c. Click Merged center in the alignment group of home tab.
d. Click on Merge and Center option in the home tab of alignment group.

1.21 The Name box on to the left of formula bar
a. Shows the name of workbook currently working on.
b. Shows the name of worksheet currently working on.
c. Shows the name of cell or range currently working on.
d. None of above

1.22 Each excel file is a workbook that contains different sheets. Which of the following cannot be a sheet in workbook?
a. Work sheet c. Module sheet
b. Chart sheet d. Data sheet

1.23 There are _____ pillars of E-Governance.
a. One c. Three
b. Two d. Four

1.24 Which of the following is concantenating operator?
a. Apostrophe (')
b. Ampersand (&)
c. Exclamation (!)
d. Hash (#)

1.25 ________ is the program which runs on the mobile hardware, deals with the characteristics and the requirements of mobile applications and act as an engine of the mobile device.
a. Mobile communication
b. Mobile software
c. Mobile hardware
d. Mobile data

1.26 What happens when you press Ctrl + X after selecting some cells in Excel?
a. The cell content of selected cells disappear from cell and gets stored in clipboard.
b. The cells selected are marked for cutting.
c. The selected cells are deleted and the cells are shifted left.
d. The selected cells are deleted and cells are shifted up.

1.27 PDA is:
a. Personal Digital Assistance c. Personal Digital Assistant
b. Person Digital Assistant d. Personal Data Assistant

1.28 Which of the following is not a financial function?
a. FV() c. SUM()
b. NPV() d. PMT()

1.29 The key F12 opens a
a. Save As dialog box c. Save dialog box
b. Open dialog box d. Close dialog box

1.30 ________ provides software applications over the Internet, Cloud based software services
a. IaaS c. PaaS
b. SaaS d. DaaS

1.31 A feature of MS Word that saves the document automatically after certain interval is available under
a. Save tab on Word Options dialog box
b. Save As dialog box
c. Both (a) and (b)
d. None of above

1.32 Which of the following, provides physical hardware and software required by companies on the Internet?
a. IaaS c. PaaS
b. SaaS d. DaaS

1.33 Which of the following is not available on the ruler of MS Word screen?
a. Tab stop box c. Right Indent
b. Left Indent d. Center Indent

1.34 Pert is:
a. Project Evaluation Review Technique
b. Program Evaluate Review Technique
c. Program Evaluation Revise Technique
d. Program Evaluation Review Technique

1.35 By how many ways you can save a document?
a. 3 c. 5
b. 4 d. 6

1.36 Background color or effects applied on a document is not visible in
a. Web layout view c. Reading View
b. Print Layout view d. Outline view

1.37 What is a portion of a document in which you set certain page formatting options?
a. Page c. Section
b. Document d. Page Setup

1.38 ____________ refers to the shared values, attitudes, standards, and beliefs that characterize members of an organization and define its nature.
a. National culture c. Corporate culture
b. School culture d. Home culture

1.39 Which of the following is not a type of page margin?
a. Left c. Center
b. Right d. Top

1.40 ______ key is use of spell check.
a. F3 c. F7
b. F5 d. F9

1.41 What is the full form of FCNR?
a. Foreign Contract Non-Resident
b. Forward Currency Non-Reliable
c. Foreign Currency Non- Resident
d. None of these

1.42 What is the full form of NRO?
a. Non-Reliable Ordinary Accounts
b. Non-Resident Original Accounts
c. Non-Resident Ordinary Accounts
d. No-Resident Ordinary Accounts

1.43 A ________ that is read rarely has the same impact as a speech that is delivered (or appears to be delivered) spontaneously.
a. Skill b. Paragraph

c. Sentence d. Speech

1.44 What is Pradhan Mantri Jivan Jyoti Bima Yojana (PMJJBY)?
a. Covers life insurance up to Rs. 2 lac
b. Accident insurance cover
c. Both (a) and (b)
d. None of above

1.45 __________, by contrast, is a phrase usually used to describe job-specific skills.
a. Hard skills b. People skills
c. Interpersonal skills d. Social skills

1.46 Who can open bank account?
a. Indian Citizen c. Iliterate
b. Non Resident Indian d. All of the above

1.47 __________ includes loan for paying debt, marriage expenses or vacation expenditure, and is given to individuals after accessing their credentials based on their profession or business.
a. Home Loan c. Business Loan
b. Education Loan d. Personal Loan

1.48 __________is a type of loan provided to either existing businesses or those getting into new business, on the basis of individual's credentials.
a. Business Loan c. Education Loan
b. Personal Loan d. Home Loan

1.49 Soft skills is a term often associated with a person's __________.
a. Emotional Intelligence Quotient
b. Emotional Intellectual Quotient
c. Emerging Intelligence Quotient
d. Emotional Intelligence Quest

1.50 Amount provided for a fixed tenure at the applicable interest rate is known as__________.
a. Home loan c. Term Loan
b. Personal Loan d. None of these

PART – TWO

2. Select TRUE or FALSE in Statements

2.1 Micro computer is called micro because it consists of micro processor.
2.2 Personal Computer is a micro computer.
2.3 Computer aided design packages are restricted to engineering workstation systems.
2.4 Header is not displayed by WORD in the Outline view.
2.5 A cell entry can be edited either in the cell or in the formula bar.
2.6 Character size is measured in points.
2.7 Different cells in a column can have different widths.
2.8 You cannot open two different workbooks in Excel simultaneously.
2.9 You cannot see Page Breaks in Excel Worksheet.
2.10 The primary function of I/O peripherals is to facilitate computer-to-computer data transmission.
2.11 Internet banking, refers to operating an account through Internet.
2.12 Dot-matrix printer technology is available in serial and line printers.
2.13 To start a new line within the same paragraph press Shift + Enter.
2.14 The formula bar displays the constant value or formula used in the active cell.
2.15 MICR stands for Magnetic Ink Course Reader.
2.16 The first time you save a presentation, you must name it.
2.17 Keyboard is a device which is used as the standard pointing device in Graphical User Environment.
2.18 An advantage of using the formula palette is that you can see the result of the formula as you create it.
2.19 All of the software must be licensed legally before installation.
2.20 Insertion point shows where the typed text will appear.
2.21 Backdoor gives remote control to the malicious users of an infected computer.
2.22 Ruler is displayed in the view tab of show group.
2.23 When you use the Merge and Center button to center a heading, the heading text remains in cell A1.
2.24 Virus is a malware which is installed on a computer with the aim of collecting the owner's private information.
2.25 To make a cell address absolute, you must type a dollar sign before each row and column reference in the formula.
2.26 In Word, the search is case sensitive by default.
2.27 Laser technology is used in compact disks?
2.28 Pure black and white is not available in the print options.
2.29 Malware is a piece of software which is inserted into an information system to cause harm to that or some other systems.
2.30 Information is retrieved from CD-ROM by using a laser beam.
2.31 You can draw objects in a presentation by using the Design toolbar.
2.32 In Word, you can set page numbers to appear in the header or footer region on the page.
2.33 A composite key is a group of fields that uniquely identify a record.
2.34 Ctrl + S shortcut is used to select text in MS Word.
2.35 You can change the character spacing in the home tab of paragraph group.

2.36 Columns in tables are called records and rows in tables are called fields.
2.37 Strikethrough is displayed in the Home tab of Font group.
2.38 There can be multiple primary keys in a table.
2.39 A chart can only be placed on the worksheet with the data.
2.40 More than one window can be opened on the screen at one time. However, we can work in only one window at a time.
2.41 Behavioral skills are the skills you use to successfully interact with others in the workplace.
2.42 FCNR account is opened by the NRIs in designated currencies.
2.43 NRO Resident outside India can not open this account.
2.44 Academic reading should not be seen as an active activity, but a passive process that leads to the development of learning.
2.45 NR(E)RA is a Rupee account, and the NRI (Non-Resident Indian) can remit money to India from the abroad and can also take the money out of India.
2.46 Interest Rate may vary from bank to bank and time to time.
2.47 Listening is the ability to accurately receive and interpret messages in the communication process.
2.48 Personal Loan includes loan provided to either existing businesses or those getting into new business, on the basis of individual's credentials.
2.49 You can edit records in Design view.
2.50 You can add a record only at the end of a table.

Specimen Answer sheet for Writing Answers to Objective Questions

PAPER CODE | | DATE |

PART ONE : Multiple Choice										PART TWO: True/False					
[Put mark (✓) to your Choice]										*[Put mark (✓) to your answer]*					
Ques.	A	B	C	D	Ques.	A	B	C	D	Ques.	T	F	Ques.	T	F
1					26					1			26		
2					27					2			27		
3					28					3			28		
4					29					4			29		
5					30					5			30		
6					31					6			31		
7					32					7			32		
8					33					8			33		
9					34					9			34		
10					35					10			35		
11					36					11			36		
12					37					12			37		
13					38					13			38		
14					39					14			39		
15					40					15			40		
16					41					16			41		
17					42					17			42		
18					43					18			43		
19					44					19			44		
20					45					20			45		
21					46					21			46		
22					47					22			47		
23					48					23			48		
24					49					24			49		
25					50					25			50		